# Western Civilizations

*Their History & Their Culture*

Joshua Cole

Carol Symes

# Western Civilizations

*Their History & Their Culture*

**NINETEENTH EDITION**

**VOLUME 1**

W. W. NORTON & COMPANY ▪ NEW YORK ▪ LONDON

W. W. Norton & Company has been independent since its founding in 1923, when William Warder Norton and Mary D. Herter Norton first published lectures delivered at the People's Institute, the adult education division of New York City's Cooper Union. The firm soon expanded its program beyond the Institute, publishing books by celebrated academics from America and abroad. By midcentury, the two major pillars of Norton's publishing program—trade books and college texts—were firmly established. In the 1950s, the Norton family transferred control of the company to its employees, and today—with a staff of four hundred and a comparable number of trade, college, and professional titles published each year—W. W. Norton & Company stands as the largest and oldest publishing house owned wholly by its employees.

*Editor:* Jon Durbin
*Associate Editor:* Scott Sugarman
*Editorial Assistant:* Kelly Rafey
*Managing Editor, College:* Marian Johnson
*Project Editor:* Sujin Hong
*Managing Editor, College Digital Media:* Kim Yi
*Media Project Editor:* Rachel Mayer
*Media Editor:* Laura Wilk
*Associate Media Editor:* Michelle Smith
*Assistant Media Editor:* Chris Hillyer
*Marketing Manager, History:* Sarah England
*Production Manager:* Andy Ensor
*Design Director:* Rubina Yeh
*Photo Editor:* Catherine Abelman
*Permissions Associate:* Elizabeth Trammell
*Composition:* Cenveo
*Cartographers:* Mapping Specialists
*Manufacturing:* Quad Graphics—Versailles

Permission to use copyrighted material is included in the Credits section of this book.

ISBN: 978-0-393-61597-5

W. W. Norton & Company, Inc., 500 Fifth Avenue, New York, NY 10110
wwnorton.com

W. W. Norton & Company Ltd., 15 Carlisle Street, London W1D 3BS

1 2 3 4 5 6 7 8 9 0

To our families:

Kate Tremel, Lucas, and Ruby Cole
Tom, Erin, and Connor Wilson

with love and gratitude for their support.
And to all our students, who have also been
our teachers.

**JOSHUA COLE** (PhD, University of California, Berkeley) is Professor of History at the University of Michigan, Ann Arbor. He has published work on gender and the history of population sciences, colonial violence, and the politics of memory in nineteenth- and twentieth-century France, Germany, and Algeria. His first book was *The Power of Large Numbers: Population, Politics, and Gender in Nineteenth-Century France* (Ithaca, NY: Cornell University Press, 2000).

**CAROL SYMES** (PhD, Harvard University) is Associate Professor of History at the University of Illinois, Urbana-Champaign, where she has served as Director of Undergraduate Studies in History and has won numerous teaching awards. Her main areas of study include the history of medieval Europe, cultural history, and the history of media and communication technologies. Her first book, *A Common Stage: Theater and Public Life in Medieval Arras* (Ithaca, NY: Cornell University Press, 2007), won four national awards. In 2014, she founded a new academic journal, *The Medieval Globe*.

# Brief Contents

MAPS                                                        xvii

PRIMARY SOURCES                                             xix

PREFACE                                                     xxi

MEDIA RESOURCES FOR INSTRUCTORS AND STUDENTS               xxvi

ACKNOWLEDGMENTS                                            xxviii


CHAPTER 1     Early Civilizations                            3

CHAPTER 2     Peoples, Gods, and Empires: 1700–500 B.C.E.   39

CHAPTER 3     The Civilization of Greece, 1000–400 B.C.E.   75

CHAPTER 4     The Greek World Expands, 400–150 B.C.E.      111

CHAPTER 5     The Civilization of Ancient Rome             147

CHAPTER 6     The Transformation of Rome                   181

CHAPTER 7     Rome's Three Heirs, 500–950                  213

CHAPTER 8     The Expansion of Europe, 950–1100            249

CHAPTER 9     The Consolidation of Europe, 1100–1250       285

CHAPTER 10    The Medieval World, 1250–1350                325

CHAPTER 11    Rebirth and Unrest, 1350–1453                359

CHAPTER 12    Innovation and Exploration, 1453–1533        391

CHAPTER 13    The Age of Dissent and Division, 1500–1564   425

CHAPTER 14    Europe in the Atlantic World, 1550–1660      455

CHAPTER 15    European Monarchies and Absolutism, 1660–1725 493

CHAPTER 16    The New Science of the Seventeenth Century   523

APPENDIX: RULERS OF PRINCIPAL STATES    A1

FURTHER READINGS    A6

GLOSSARY    A20

TEXT CREDITS    A47

PHOTO CREDITS    A49

INDEX    A52

MAPS    xvii

PRIMARY SOURCES    xix

PREFACE    xxi

MEDIA RESOURCES FOR INSTRUCTORS AND STUDENTS    xxvi

ACKNOWLEDGMENTS    xxviii


## Chapter 1 ▪ EARLY CIVILIZATIONS    3

Before Civilization    4

The Building Blocks of Civilization    5

Urban Development in Mesopotamia    8

The Culture of Sumer    11

The First Empires?    16

The Development of Civilization in Egypt    22

**Past and Present: Engineering Nature    24**

**Interpreting Visual Evidence: The Narmer Palette    26**

Egyptian Culture and Society    29

Conclusion    35


## Chapter 2 ▪ PEOPLES, GODS, AND EMPIRES: 1700–500 B.C.E.    39

Indo-European Languages and Peoples    41

The New Kingdom of Egypt    42

**Interpreting Visual Evidence: Remembering Hatshepsut    44**

Transnational Networks of the Late Bronze Age    47

Aegean Civilization: Minoan Crete, Mycenaean Greece    48

The States of the Early Iron Age    54

**Past and Present: The Fragility of Global Networks    57**

The Revival of the Assyrian Empire    59

The Rise of the Persians    64

The Development of Hebrew Monotheism    67

Conclusion    73

Chapter 3 ■ THE CIVILIZATION OF GREECE, 1000–400 B.C.E. 75

From Chaos to Polis    76

The Culture of Archaic Greece, 800–500 B.C.E.    80

**Interpreting Visual Evidence: The Ideal of Male Beauty    82**

Portraits of Three Poleis    87

The Challenge of the Persian Wars    92

**Past and Present: Political Satire    94**

The Golden Age of Classical Greece    96

"The Greatest War in History" and Its Consequences    101

The Failure of Athenian Democracy    102

Conclusion    107


Chapter 4 ■ THE GREEK WORLD EXPANDS, 400–150 B.C.E.    111

The Downfall of the Greek Polis    112

Reimagining the Polis: The Artistic and Intellectual Response    115

**Interpreting Visual Evidence: Reconstructing an Ideal
    of Female Beauty    118**

The Rise of Macedonia    121

The Conquests of Alexander (336–323 B.C.E.)    122

The Hellenistic Kingdoms    126

From Polis to Cosmopolis    130

**Past and Present: Mass Migration and the Challenges
    of Assimilation    131**

Hellenistic Worldviews    133

The Scientific Revolution of Antiquity    136

Conclusion    143


Chapter 5 ■ THE CIVILIZATION OF ANCIENT ROME    147

The Time of the Kings    148

The Triumph of the Early Republic    150

The Essence of Roman Identity    153

From Republic to Empire    156

The Consequences of Imperialism    159

**Past and Present: Spectator Sports    160**

"Restoring the Republic": The Struggle for Power    162

The Principate and the Pax Romana, 27 B.C.E.–180 C.E.    165

Making the World Roman    169

**Interpreting Visual Evidence: Roman Urban Planning    176**

Conclusion    178


## Chapter 6 ▪ THE TRANSFORMATION OF ROME    181

The Challenge of Christianity    182

The Challenge of Imperial Expansion    189

The Conversion of Christianity    194

**Interpreting Visual Evidence: The Power of the Invincible Sun    196**

**Past and Present: Resisting Imperialism    199**

Shifting Centers and Moving Frontiers    200

The Shaping of a New Worldview    205

Classical Learning and the Christian Life    207

Conclusion    211


## Chapter 7 ▪ ROME'S THREE HEIRS, 500–950    213

Justinian's Imperial Ambitions    214

The Roman Empire of Byzantium    217

Muhammad and the Teachings of Islam    223

The Widening Islamic World    225

**Past and Present: The Meanings of Medievalism    230**

The Conversion of Northwestern Europe    230

**Interpreting Visual Evidence: The Ship Burial of Sutton Hoo    232**

The Empire of Charlemagne    237

Disputed Legacies and New Alliances    243

Conclusion    246


## Chapter 8 ▪ THE EXPANSION OF EUROPE, 950–1100    249

A Tour of Europe around the Year 1000    250

The Agricultural Revolution of the Medieval Warm Period    255

The Growth of Towns and Trade    257

Violence, Lordship, and Monarchy    261

**Interpreting Visual Evidence: The Graphic History of the Bayeux Tapestry    264**

Religious Reform and Papal Power    266

Crusading Causes and Outcomes    270

**Past and Present: Ideas of Crusade    274**

The Culture of the Muslim West    278

Conclusion    283

Chapter 9 ▪ THE CONSOLIDATION OF EUROPE,
                     1100–1250    285

The Making of Medieval Monarchies    286

Continuing the Crusades    294

**Interpreting Visual Evidence: Picturing Legal Transactions    295**

**Past and Present: Medieval Plots and Modern Movies    299**

Unity and Dissent in the Western Church    300

An Intellectual Revolution    309

Courts, Cities, and Cathedrals    315

Conclusion    321

Chapter 10 ▪ THE MEDIEVAL WORLD,
                       1250–1350    325

The Mongol Empire and the Reorientation of the West    326

The Extension of European Commerce and Settlement    334

Ways of Knowing and Describing the World    336

**Interpreting Visual Evidence: Seals: Signs of Identity
    and Authority    340**

Papal Power and Popular Piety    342

Struggles for Sovereignty    345

From the Great Famine to the Black Death    350

**Past and Present: Global Pandemics    351**

Conclusion    357

Chapter 11 ▪ REBIRTH AND UNREST, 1350–1453    359

Life after the Black Death    360

The Beginnings of the Renaissance in Italy    366

**Interpreting Visual Evidence: Realizing Devotion    368**

The End of the Eastern Roman Empire    371

Warfare and Nation Building    374

The Challenges of the Roman Church    381

**Past and Present: Replacing "Retired" Popes    383**

Conclusion    388


## Chapter 12 ▪ INNOVATION AND EXPLORATION, 1453–1533    391

Renaissance Ideals—and Realities    392

The Renaissance North of the Alps    404

**Past and Present: The Reputation of Richard III    406**

The Politics of Christian Europe    409

New Targets and Technologies of Conquest    412

Europeans in a New World    417

**Interpreting Visual Evidence: America as an Object of Desire    418**

Conclusion    423


## Chapter 13 ▪ THE AGE OF DISSENT AND DIVISION, 1500–1564    425

Martin Luther and the Reformation in Germany    426

**Interpreting Visual Evidence: Decoding Printed Propaganda    430**

The Many Forms of Protestantism    435

The Domestication of Reform    439

The Reformation in England    442

The Rebirth of the Roman Catholic Church    446

**Past and Present: Controlling Consumption    447**

Conclusion    451


## Chapter 14 ▪ EUROPE IN THE ATLANTIC WORLD, 1550–1660    455

The Emergence of the Atlantic World    456

Conflict and Competition in Europe and the Atlantic World    463

The Thirty Years' War and Its Outcomes    470

The Crisis of Kingship in England    477

**Interpreting Visual Evidence: The Execution of a King    482**

An Age of Doubt and the Art of Being Human    483

**Past and Present: Shakespeare's Popular Appeal    486**

Conclusion    491

## Chapter 15 ▪ EUROPEAN MONARCHIES AND ABSOLUTISM, 1660–1725   493

The Appeal and Justification of Absolutism   495

The Absolutism of Louis XIV   495

**Interpreting Visual Evidence: The Performance and Display of Absolute Power at the Court of Louis XIV   496**

**Past and Present: The Persistence of Monarchies in a Democratic Age   500**

Alternatives to Absolutism   502

War and the Balance of Power, 1661–1715   508

The Remaking of Central and Eastern Europe   509

Autocracy in Russia   514

Conclusion   519

## Chapter 16 ▪ THE NEW SCIENCE OF THE SEVENTEENTH CENTURY   523

The Intellectual Origins of the Scientific Revolution   524

**Past and Present: Has Science Replaced Religion?   526**

The Copernican Revolution   526

Tycho's Observations and Kepler's Laws   528

New Heavens, New Earth, and Worldly Politics: Galileo   529

**Interpreting Visual Evidence: Astronomical Observations and the Mapping of the Heavens   530**

Dating the Age of the Earth: The Origins of Geology and the Environmental Sciences   534

Methods for a New Philosophy: Bacon and Descartes   536

"And All Was Light": Isaac Newton   544

Conclusion   549

APPENDIX: RULERS OF PRINCIPAL STATES   A1

FURTHER READINGS   A6

GLOSSARY   A20

TEXT CREDITS   A47

PHOTO CREDITS   A49

INDEX   A52

# Maps

The Growth of Agriculture   6
The Fertile Crescent   11
Ancient Egypt and the Eastern Mediterranean   23
Civilizations of the Bronze Age, 2000–1400 B.C.E.   40
Egypt and Its Neighbors, c. 1400 B.C.E.   48
Mycenaean Greece   52
Phoenician Colonization   55
The Hebrew Kingdoms, c. 900 B.C.E.   59
The Neo-Assyrian Empire, c. 700 B.C.E.   62
The Persian Empire under Darius I, 521–486 B.C.E.   67
The Attic Peninsula   79
Greek Colonization, c. 550 B.C.E.   81
The Peloponnesus   90
Ionia, Lydia, and the Persian Empire   91
The Persian Wars with Greece   95
The Peloponnesian War   103
The Inland Expedition of the Ten Thousand   113
The Campaigns of Alexander   125
The Hellenistic World   128
Roman Expansion in Italy, 485–218 B.C.E.   151
The Further Expansion of Rome, 264–44 B.C.E.   158
The Roman Empire at Its Greatest Extent, 97–117 C.E.   169
Judea and Galilee in the Time of Jesus   182
Paul's Missionary Journeys   185
Diocletian's Division of the Empire, c. 304 C.E.   194
The Migrations of Rome's Frontier Peoples   202
The Mediterranean World under Justinian, 527–565   214
The Expansion of Islam to 750   226
The Empire of Charlemagne in 814   238
Patterns of Viking Activity and Settlement,
     c. 800–1100   244

Europe, c. 1000   253
Medieval Trade Routes   259
The Byzantine Empire, c. 1025   271
The Routes of the Crusaders, 1096–1204   276
Henry II's Empire and the Kingdom of France,
     1180–1223   288
The Holy Roman Empire and Central and Eastern Europe,
     c. 1200   291
The "Reconquest" of Spain, 900–1250   293
The Crusader States   296
The Spread of Universities   313
The States of the Mongol Empire   327
The Medieval World System, c. 1300   330
European Outbreaks of the Black Death, 1347–1350   353
The Growth of the Ottoman Empire   374
The Phases of the Hundred Years' War   376
The Great Schism, 1378–1417   382
The Spread of Printing   393
The States of Italy, c. 1494   396
The Expansion of Muscovite Territory to 1505   410
Overseas Exploration in the Fifteenth and
     Sixteenth Centuries   415
The European Empire of Charles V, c. 1526   433
Confessional Differences, c. 1560   435
The Atlantic World and the Triangular Trade   460
Population Density, c. 1600   464
The Netherlands after 1609   468
Europe at the End of the Thirty Years' War   472
Europe after the Treaty of Utrecht (1713)   510
The Growth of the Russian Empire   518

# Primary Sources

Competing Viewpoints: The Flood: Two Accounts   12

Analyzing Primary Sources: The Code of Hammurabi   20

Analyzing Primary Sources: The Instruction of
Ptah-Hotep   31

Analyzing Primary Sources: The Prophecies of Neferty   35

Analyzing Primary Sources: The Diplomacy of the
Mycenaeans and the Hittites   53

Competing Viewpoints: Two Accounts of Saul's
Anointing   60

Competing Viewpoints: Two Perspectives on
Imperial Rule   68

Analyzing Primary Sources: Greek Guest Friendship
and Heroic Ideals   78

Analyzing Primary Sources: "The Beautiful and
The Good"   85

Analyzing Primary Sources: Songs of Sappho   86

Competing Viewpoints: Two Views of Socrates   104

Analyzing Primary Sources: Xenophon Describes
an Ideal Leader   114

Analyzing Primary Sources: Aristotle's Justification
of Slavery   120

Analyzing Primary Sources: Alexander Puts Down
a Mutiny   127

Analyzing Primary Sources: A Jewish Response to
Hellenization   135

Competing Viewpoints: Debating the Education
and Role of Women   138

Analyzing Primary Sources: Polybius Describes the
Romans' Worship of Their Ancestors   155

Analyzing Primary Sources: Antony and Cleopatra   167

Competing Viewpoints: Two Views of Augustus's
Rule   170

Analyzing Primary Sources: The Architecture of
Roman Water Management   174

Analyzing Primary Sources: The Prosecution of a
Roman Citizen   188

Competing Viewpoints: The Development of an
Imperial Policy toward Christians   190

Analyzing Primary Sources: A Senator Defends the
Traditional Religion of Rome   201

Analyzing Primary Sources: Roman or Barbarian?   208

Competing Viewpoints: Debating the Power of Icons   220

Analyzing Primary Sources: A Sura from the Qur'an   224

Analyzing Primary Sources: From Anglo-Saxon
Slave Girl to Frankish Queen   234

Analyzing Primary Sources: The Capitularies of
Charlemagne   240

Analyzing Primary Sources: A Miraculous Reliquary   268

Competing Viewpoints: Preaching the First Crusade:
Two Accounts   272

Analyzing Primary Sources: An Arab Aristocrat
Encounters the Crusaders   277

Analyzing Primary Sources: A Hebrew Poem from
Muslim Spain   281

Analyzing Primary Sources: The Canons of the
Fourth Lateran Council   302

Competing Viewpoints: Two Conversion Experiences   306

Analyzing Primary Sources: Peter Abelard Critiques
Theological Contradictions   311

Analyzing Primary Sources: Illicit Love and the
Code of Chivalry   319

Competing Viewpoints: Two Travel Accounts   332

Analyzing Primary Sources: Vikings Encounter the
Natives of North America   338

Analyzing Primary Sources: A Declaration of
Scottish Independence   348

Analyzing Primary Sources: The Code of Chivalry:
Putting Honor before Plunder   352

Competing Viewpoints: Responses to the
Black Death   354

Analyzing Primary Sources: Why a Woman Can
Write about Warfare   365

Analyzing Primary Sources: A Renaissance Attitude
toward Women   370

Analyzing Primary Sources: The Condemnation of
Joan of Arc by the University of Paris, 1431   378

**Competing Viewpoints: Council or Pope?** 384

**Competing Viewpoints: Printing, Patriotism, and the Past** 394

Analyzing Primary Sources: Leonardo da Vinci Applies for a Job 402

Analyzing Primary Sources: The Ottomans' Army of Slaves 416

Analyzing Primary Sources: A Spanish Critique of New World Conquest 421

**Competing Viewpoints: Marriage and Celibacy: Two Views** 440

Analyzing Primary Sources: The Six Articles of the English Church 444

Analyzing Primary Sources: The Demands of Obedience 449

Analyzing Primary Sources: Enslaved Native Laborers at Potosí 461

Analyzing Primary Sources: The Devastation of the Thirty Years' War 471

Analyzing Primary Sources: Cardinal Richelieu on the Common People of France 476

**Competing Viewpoints: Debating the English Civil War** 480

Analyzing Primary Sources: Montaigne on Cannibals 485

**Competing Viewpoints: Absolutism and Patriarchy** 498

Analyzing Primary Sources: The Siege of Vienna (1683) 512

Analyzing Primary Sources: The Revolt of the Streltsy and Peter the Great 516

Analyzing Primary Sources: Galileo on Nature, Scripture, and Truth 533

**Competing Viewpoints: The New Science and the Foundations of Certainty** 538

Analyzing Primary Sources: Gassendi on the Science of Observation and the Human Soul 542

Analyzing Primary Sources: Newton on the Purposes of Experimental Philosophy 546

This revised edition of *Western Civilizations* further hones the set of tools we have developed to empower students—our own and yours— to engage effectively with the themes, sources, and challenges of history. It presents a clear and concise narrative of events that unfolded over many thousands of years, supplemented by a compelling selection of primary sources and striking images. At the same time, it features a unified program of pedagogical elements that guide students toward a more thorough understanding of historical sources and of the ways that historians reconstruct the past on the basis of those sources. This framework helps students to analyze and interpret historical evidence on their own, encouraging them to become active participants in the learning process and helping them to think historically.

The wide chronological and geographical scope of this book offers an unusual opportunity to trace historical trends across several interrelated regions—western Asia, the Middle East, North Africa, and Europe—whose cultural diversity has been constantly reinvigorated and renewed. Our increasing awareness that no region's history can be isolated from global processes and connections has merely heightened the need for a richly contextualized and broad-based history such as that represented in *Western Civilizations*. In this edition, we have accordingly supplemented our treatment of human interactions with a new focus on humans and their environments. Environmental history has emerged as one of the most vital and important fields of study in recent years, and today's students are deeply interested and invested in the effects of globalization and climate change. It is important that they be able to put recent developments in historical context and to see their own concerns and aspirations reflected in the historical curriculum. And as in previous editions, we have continued to balance the coverage of political, social, economic, and cultural phenomena with extensive treatment of gender, race, sexuality, daily life, material culture, art, science, and popular culture.

Our history is also attentive to the latest developments in historical scholarship. As the title of this book asserts, few historians today would uphold a monolithic vision of a single and enduring "Western civilization" whose inevitable march to domination can be traced chapter by chapter through time. This older paradigm, strongly associated with the curriculum of early twentieth-century American colleges and universities, no longer conforms to what we know about the human past. It was also overly reliant on the nationalist histories of only a few countries, notably England, France, and Germany. In this edition, we therefore pay much closer attention to central and eastern Europe, as well as to Europeans' near neighbors in Asia, Africa, and the Atlantic world, with a particular focus on European and Muslim relations throughout the Mediterranean and Middle East. No narrative of Western civilizations can be coherent if it leaves out the intense conflicts, extraordinary ruptures, and dynamic changes that took place within and across all of these territories. Indeed, smoothing out the rough edges of the past does students no favors. Even an introductory text such as this one should present the past as it appears to the historians who study it: as a complex panorama of human effort, filled with possibility and achievement but also fraught with discord, uncertainty, accident, and tragedy.

# New and Revised Pedagogical Features

In our continuing effort to engage students in the active study of history, this book is designed to reinforce your course objectives by helping your students to master core content while challenging them to think critically about the past. In previous editions, we augmented the traditional strengths of *Western Civilizations* by introducing several exciting new features. These have since been refined in accordance with feedback from student readers and teachers of the book. The most important and revolutionary feature is the pedagogical structure that supports each chapter. As we know from long experience, many students in introductory survey courses find the sheer quantity of information overwhelming, and so we have provided guidance to help them navigate through the material and to read in meaningful ways.

At the outset of each chapter, the **Before You Read This Chapter** feature offers three preliminary windows onto the material to be covered: *Story Lines*, *Chronology*, and *Core Objectives*. Following the *Story Lines* allows the student to become familiar with the primary narrative threads that tie the chapter's elements together, while the *Chronology* grounds these *Story Lines* in the period under study. The *Core Objectives* alert the student to the primary teaching points in the chapter. The student is then reminded of these teaching points on completing the chapter, in the **After You Read This Chapter** section, which revisits the material in three ways. The first, *Reviewing the Objectives*, asks the reader to reconsider the core objectives by answering a pointed question about each one. The second, *People, Ideas, and Events in Context*, summarizes some of the particulars that students should retain from their reading, through questions that allow them to relate individual terms to the major objectives and story lines. Finally, *Thinking about Connections* allows for more open-ended reflection on the significance of the chapter's main themes, drawing students' attention to issues that connect it to previous chapters and to their own historical present. Together, these pedagogical features serve to enhance the student's learning experience by breaking down the process of reading and analysis into manageable tasks.

A second package of pedagogical features is designed to capture students' interest and to compel them to think about what is at stake in the construction and use of historical narratives. Each chapter opens with a vignette that showcases a particular person or event representative of the era as a whole. Within each chapter, an expanded program of illustrations and maps has been enhanced by the addition of **Questions for Analysis** that urge the reader to explore the historical contexts and significance of these images in a more analytical way. The historical value of visual artifacts is further emphasized in another feature we have introduced: **Interpreting Visual Evidence**. This section provides a provocative departure point for analytical discussions about the key issues raised by visual sources, which students often find more approachable than texts. Once this conversation has begun, students can further develop their skills by **Analyzing Primary Sources**, through close readings of primary texts accompanied by thought-provoking interpretive questions. The diversity of

Western civilizations is also illuminated through a look at **Competing Viewpoints** in each chapter, in which specific debates are presented through paired primary-source texts. The bibliographical **Further Readings**, located at the end of the book, has also been brought up to date.

In addition to these features, the previous edition of this book introduced an entirely new **Past and Present** comparison. Designed to help students connect events unfolding in the past with the breaking news of our own time, it pairs one episode from each chapter with a phenomenon that resonates more immediately with our students. To bring this new feature to life for students, we have also created a new series of **Past and Present Videos,** in which we analyze and elaborate on these connections. There are a number of illuminating discussions, including "Mass Migration and the Challenges of Assimilation," which discusses the Greek diaspora and Jewish diasporas of antiquity with reference to the Syrian refugee crisis; "Spectator Sports," which compares the Roman gladiatorial games with NFL football; "The Reputation of Richard III," which shows how modern forensics were recently used to identify the remains of this medieval English king; "The Persistence of Monarchies in a Democratic Age," which explains the origins and evolution of our ongoing fascination with royals such as Louis XIV and Princess Diana; and "The Internet and the Enlightenment Public Sphere," which compares the kinds of public networks that helped spread Enlightenment ideas to the way the Internet spreads political ideas to support movements such as the Arab Spring and Occupy Wall Street. For the current edition, there is a particularly timely **Past and Present** feature for Chapter 24 that relates the restructuring of the Middle East after the First World War to the present crisis in the region. Through this feature, we want to encourage students to recognize the continuing relevance of seemingly distant historical moments, but we also want to encourage historically minded habits that will be useful for a lifetime. If students learn to see the connections between their world and the past, they will be better able to place unfolding developments and debates in a more informed and complex historical context.

# A Tour of New Chapters and Revisions

Our previous edition of *Western Civilizations* updated and reorganized the late medieval and early modern chapters in order to place them in a larger global context. The highlight of this reorganization was a brand new chapter, entitled "Europe in the Atlantic World, 1550–1660," which situated the newly integrated frontier of the Atlantic at the center of the story. Another significant result of this reorganization was a clearer chronological framework for the entire narrative, enabling students to see how seemingly isolated events and trends fit into their historical contexts.

In Chapter 1, the challenges of locating and interpreting historical evidence drawn from nontextual sources (archaeological, anthropological, mythic) is a special focus. In keeping with our new emphasis on the environment, this chapter now features expanded consideration of the Neolithic Revolution as an early example of large-scale human impact on the natural world. It also reflects recent scholarship on the earliest "empires" of Mesopotamia, whose alleged strength may have been more the result of propaganda than of real power. Chapter 2 further underscores the degree to which recent archaeological discoveries and new historical methods have revolutionized our understanding of ancient history. It includes coverage of very recent excavations (2015) of the tomb of the "Griffin Warrior" at Pylos. In Chapter 3, alongside a revised discussion of early democracy in Athens, new sections deal with "Harnessing the Power of the Horse" and with chariot racing at the Olympic Games. Chapter 4's exploration of the Hellenistic world includes an unusually wide-ranging discussion of the scientific revolution powered by this first cosmopolitan civilization. Chapter 5's emphasis on the unique values and institutions of the Roman Republic, and their transformation through imperial expansion under the Principate, now includes a new section on "Imperial Infrastructure and the Environment" and a new source: the chapter on water engineering and management from the architectural textbook of Vitruvius.

The story of Rome's transformative encounter with early Christianity in Chapter 6 has been revised to account for the many varieties of Christian communities throughout the empire; for example, in Pannonia (modern Hungary), where an early basilica and tomb complex are preserved in the ancient city of Sopianae (Pécs). Chapter 7, which examines Rome's three distinctive successor civilizations, now offers expanded coverage of the Jewish diaspora and the emergence of Rabbinic Judaism, as well as extended coverage and analysis of early Islam and the Arab conquests. It includes an image from the newly discovered "Birmingham Qur'an," which has been recognized as the oldest extant manuscript of the Muslim holy book. Chapter 8 contains new sections on the early medieval kingdoms of eastern and central Europe—Hungary, Bohemia, and Poland—as well as thoroughly revised maps of the region and the neighboring territories of western Europe, the Baltic, and Rus'. Chapter 9 continues to focus more attention on "The States of Eastern and Central Europe" and the establishment of the Novgorod Republic in Rus'. It also includes a section on "The Aristocratic Landscape and Its Environmental Effects," which describes how the elite mania for hunting led to the introduction of invasive foreign plant and animal species into northern Europe (fallow deer, rabbits) and shows how maintaining the fragile habitats of prey caused significant hardships for indigenous human and animal populations.

Chapter 10's treatment of the medieval world between 1250 and 1350 has been further enriched by revised treatment of the relationship between Muscovy and the Mongol Khanate; and by a new section on urban growth in central Europe, where Poland became a refuge for Jewish communities expelled from many other kingdoms (especially England and France). It also reflects cutting-edge scholarship on the origins and extent of the Black Death, which has been hugely advanced by the sequencing of the *Yersinia pestis* genome, ancient DNA analysis of victims' remains, and archaeological evidence of violence against Jews. Chapter 11 continues to incorporate this new scholarship in its treatment of the abiding effects of the plague, which became endemic in many remote or mountainous regions of Eurasia. This chapter also includes a major new section on the young female King Jadwiga of Poland, her marriage alliance with the Lithuanian Grand Duke Jagiello of Lithuania, the formation of a massive unified kingdom, and the foundation of a university in the royal capital of Kraków. Chapters 12 and 13 feature many new and revised maps, with closer attention to the complexity of confessional differences in east-central Europe, especially in frontier regions such as Transylvania (in modern Romania). Chapter 14, the hinge between the book's first and second halves, illuminates the changing nature of Europe as it became fully integrated into the larger Atlantic world, the transatlantic slave trade, and the Columbian exchange. It also includes new sections on the early modern empire of Sweden and the destructive Swedish invasion of Poland-Lithuania.

The new emphasis on the emergence of the Atlantic world is carried over to Chapter 15, which covers the emergence of powerful absolutist regimes on the Continent and the evolution of wealthy European trading empires in the Americas, Africa, and Asia. The new edition also contains a new section on the Polish-Lithuanian Commonwealth whose tradition of representative institutions provides an instructive counterexample to the rise of absolutism in France. This material on central and eastern Europe is reinforced by a new image of the Polish parliament and a primary source document about the siege of Vienna in 1683. We have retained the emphasis on intellectual and cultural history in Chapter 16, on the scientific revolution, and in Chapter 17, on the Enlightenment. In Chapter 16 we have connected the history of science to our new environmental history theme with a new section on the history of geology and debates about the age of the earth. In Chapter 17, meanwhile, we have continued to present the Enlightenment more clearly in its social and political context, connecting it more explicitly not only to the theme of European expansion into the Americas and the Pacific but also to the growth of absolutist power in Prussia and Russia. We have added to our coverage of women in the Enlightenment with a new document by Émilie du Châtelet on the education of women.

Chapters 18 and 19 cover the political and economic revolutions of the late eighteenth and early nineteenth centuries. Chapter 18 covers the French Revolution and the Napoleonic Empire in depth while also drawing attention to the way that these central episodes were rooted in a larger pattern of revolutionary political change that engulfed the Atlantic world. A new primary source from Etta Palm d'Aelders adds to our coverage of women in the French Revolution. Chapter 19 emphasizes both the economic growth and the technological innovations that were a part of the Industrial Revolution while also exploring the social and cultural consequences of industrialization for men and women in Europe's new industrial societies. Here we have significantly revised our coverage of the demographic transition during the nineteenth century and added a new section on industry and environmental change. The *Interpreting Visual Evidence* feature in Chapter 19 allows students to explore the ways that industrialization created new perceptions of the global economy in Europe, changing the way people thought of their place in the world.

Chapters 20 and 21 explore the successive struggles between conservative reaction and radicals in Europe, as the dynamic forces of nationalism unleashed by the French Revolution redrew the map of Europe and threatened the dynastic regimes that had ruled for centuries. In Chapter 20, we have incorporated much new material on Russia and Poland after the end of the Napoleonic wars, balancing the traditional focus on western European nationalisms. A new primary source on the Decembrists in Russia supplements this attention to eastern Europe. Chapter 21 contains significant new material on the question of nationalism in the Habsburg and Russian Empires, including a new primary source document on Hungarian nationalism from Lajos Kossuth and coverage of the Polish insurrection in 1863. At the same time, we have retained our treatment of the important cultural movements of the nineteenth century, especially Romanticism.

Chapter 22 takes on the history of nineteenth-century colonialism, exploring both its political and economic origins and its consequences for the peoples of Africa and Asia. This chapter emphasizes the significance of colonial conquest for European culture as colonial power became increasingly associated with national greatness, both in conservative monarchies and in more democratic regimes. A new primary source document from Jamal ad-Din al-Afghani offers a Muslim perspective on the history of empire that is accompanied by a new section on the way that imperialism changed the relationship between Europe and the Muslim world. This chapter also contains a new section on imperialism, population movements, and global environmental change, continuing the story begun earlier with the story of the Columbian exchange. Chapter 23 brings the narrative back to the heart of Europe, covering the long-term consequences of industrialization and the consolidation of a conservative form of nationalism in many European nations even as the electorate was being expanded. This chapter emphasizes the variety of the new forms of political dissent, from the feminists who claimed the right to vote to the newly organized socialist movements that proved so enduring in many European countries. For the new edition we have expanded our coverage of European culture with a special section on the nineteenth-century novel.

Chapters 24 and 25 bring new vividness to the history of the First World War and the intense conflicts of the interwar period, while Chapter 26 uses the history of the Second World War as a hinge for understanding European and global developments in the second half of the twentieth century. The *Interpreting Visual Evidence* feature in Chapter 24 allows for a special focus on the role of propaganda among the belligerent nations in 1914–1918, and the chapter's section on the diplomatic crisis that preceded the First World War has been expanded in order to better illuminate the role of the Ottoman Empire and the politics of nationalism in the east. Our coverage of the Armenian genocide has also been expanded, and our strong coverage of the Western Front has now been balanced with more thorough coverage of the key turning points in eastern and central Europe. In Chapter 25 the *Interpreting Visual Evidence* feature continues to explore the theme touched on in earlier chapters, political representations of "the people," this time in the context of the fascist spectacles in Germany and Italy in the 1930s. These visual sources help students to understand the vulnerability of Europe's democratic regimes during these years as they faced the dual assault from fascists on the right and Bolsheviks on the left. For the current edition we have revised our accounts of Stalin's Great Terror to reflect current scholarship, added a new primary source document from Benito Mussolini, and created an entirely new section that compares human-made environmental change in the American Dust Bowl and in the Aral Sea region of Soviet Central Asia. In Chapter 26, on the Second World War, we have revised our account of the Nazi-Soviet pact to better foreground its consequences for Poland, and added a new primary source document from Occupied France by Jean Guéhenno.

Chapters 27 through 29 bring both volumes to a close in a thorough exploration of the Cold War, decolonization, the collapse of the Soviet Union and the Eastern Bloc in 1989–1991, and the roots of the multifaceted global conflicts that beset the world in the first decade of the twenty-first century. Chapter 27 juxtaposes the Cold War with decolonization, showing how this combination sharply diminished the ability of European nations to control events in the international arena, even as they succeeded in rebuilding their economies at home. Chapter 28 explores the vibrancy of European culture in the crucial period from the 1960s to the early 1990s, incorporat-ing new material from central and eastern Europe on the significance of 1989 and the collapse of the Soviet Union in 1991. Finally, extensive revisions to Chapter 29 add to the issues covered in our treatment of Europe's place in the contemporary globalized world. This chapter now includes a new section on efforts to deal with climate change, as well as expanded discussion of the impact of global terror-ism and recent developments in the Arab-Israeli conflict. The discussion of the financial crisis of 2008 and the presi-dency of Barack Obama has been brought up to date, and new sections have been added that explore the European debt crisis, the Arab Spring, the Syrian civil war, the rise of the Islamic State, and the current refugee crisis in Europe. Each of these very contemporary events is placed within the context of Europe's broader history, allowing students to connect what they have learned from the past to their contemporary lives.

# Media Resources for Instructors and Students

History becomes an immersive experience for students using Norton's digital resources with *Western Civilizations.* The comprehensive ancillary package includes tools for teaching and learning that reinforce the Core Objectives from the narrative while building on the history skills introduced in the pedagogy throughout the book. This nineteenth edition features a groundbreaking new formative adaptive system as well as innovative interactive resources, including the History Skills Tutorial, to help students master the core objectives in each chapter and continue to strengthen the skills they need to do the work of historians. Norton is unique in partnering exclusively with subject matter experts who teach the course to author these resources. As a result, instructors have all of the course materials they need to successfully manage their Western Civilization course, whether they are teaching face to face, online, or in a hybrid setting.

## STUDENT RESOURCES

- **New! Norton InQuizitive for History** . This groundbreaking formative, adaptive learning tool improves student understanding of the core objectives in each chapter. Students receive personalized quiz questions on the topics with which they need the most help. Questions range from vocabulary and concepts to interactive maps and primary sources that challenge students to begin developing the skills necessary to do the work of a historian. Engaging, gamelike elements motivate students as they learn. As a result, students come to class better prepared to participate in discussions and activities.
- **New! History Skills Tutorials** combine video and interactive assessments to teach students how to analyze sources. The series consists of three modules—maps, images, and documents—that provide a framework and practice for students developing the

skills of the history discipline. Each module opens with a video of the authors modeling the analysis process. Students then apply what they have learned in a series of interactive assessments that challenge them to analyze sources and identify what they reveal about the past. The History Skills Tutorials prepare students for primary source analysis work in class or chapter assignments, such as our Primary Source Exercises, available in our Coursepacks.

- **NEW! Student Site.** The Norton Student Site includes additional resources and tools to ensure students come to class prepared and ready to actively participate in discussions and activities: Office Hour Videos, iMaps, and Online Reader.

## INSTRUCTOR RESOURCES

- **NEW! Interactive Instructor's Guide** is the ultimate teaching guide for the Western Civilizations course. The Interactive Instructor's Guide features a series of videos created by the authors, where they discuss best practices for teaching the most challenging concepts in each chapter. The Guide also includes the robust Instructor's Manual, which is designed to help instructors prepare lectures and exams. It contains detailed chapter outlines, general discussion questions, document discussion questions, lecture objectives, interdisciplinary discussion topics, and recommended reading and film lists.
- **Learning Management System Coursepacks.** Our Coursepacks provide easy-to-implement course materials that integrate directly into your existing learning management system (LMS), making creating assignments and tracking grades easy. The Coursepacks contain a wealth of resources:

  - **NEW! Primary Source Exercises:** Students are presented with two to three sources that emphasize key themes from the book. An accompanying quiz guides students through the analysis process, providing valuable practice identifying what documents and images reveal about the past.

- **Author Office Hour Videos:** These segments feature the authors speaking for 90 seconds on the Core Objectives of each chapter, providing a library of more than 175 videos for students.
- **Past and Present Author Interview Videos:** These videos connect topics across time and place and show why history is relevant to understanding our world today. Examples include "Spectator Sports," "Medieval Plots and Modern Movies," "Global Pandemics," and "The Atlantic Revolutions and Human Rights."
- **Guided Reading Exercises:** These exercises help students learn how to read a textbook and, more important, comprehend what they are reading. The reading exercises instill a three-step Note-Summarize-Assess pedagogy. Exercises are based on actual passages from the textbook, and sample feedback is provided to model responses.
- **StoryMaps:** These presentations break complex maps into a sequence of four or five annotated screens that focus on the story behind the geography. The ten StoryMaps include such topics as the Silk Road, the spread of the Black Death, and nineteenth-century imperialism.

- **Interactive iMaps:** These interactive tools challenge students to better understand the nature of change over time by allowing them to explore the different layers of the maps from the book. Follow-up map worksheets help build geography skills by allowing students to test their knowledge by labeling.
- **Review Quizzes:** Multiple-choice, true/false, and chronological sequence questions allow students to test their knowledge of the chapter content and identify where they need to focus their attention to better understand difficult concepts.
- **Online Reader:** Over 400 additional primary source documents and images are aligned with each of the chapters to provide additional material for assignments, research, and study.

- **Test Bank.** The Test Bank contains over 2,000 multiple-choice, true/false, and essay questions. This edition of the Test Bank has been completely revised for content and accuracy. All test questions are now aligned with Bloom's Taxonomy for greater ease of assessment.
- **Lecture PowerPoint Slides.** These ready-made presentations provide comprehensive outlines of each chapter, as well as discussion prompts to encourage student comprehension and engagement. They can easily be customized to meet your presentation needs.

# Acknowledgments

Our first edition as members of the *Western Civilizations* authorial team was a challenging and rewarding one. In our second edition, we were able to implement a number of useful and engaging changes to the content and structure of the book to make it even more compelling and student-friendly. In the third edition, we continue to be very grateful for the expert assistance and support of the Norton team, especially that of our editor, Jon Durbin. Sujin Hong, our fabulous senior project editor, has driven the book beautifully through the manuscript process. Travis Carr has provided valuable critiques of the illustrations and the new *Past and Present* features, in addition to handling all other parts of the project so skillfully. His successor, Kelly Rafey, has a great eye for detail and has already made numerous suggestions for improving the new maps and images. Meanwhile, Cat Abelman and Dena Betz did an excellent job of finding many of the exact images we specified. Andy Ensor has efficiently marched us through the production process. The wonderful Laura Wilk has been tirelessly developing the book's fantastic e-media, particularly the new Norton InQuizitive for history and the History Skills Tutorials. Michelle Smith and Chris Hillyer have ably worked on the print ancillaries. Barbara Curialle and Greg Lauzon were terrific in skillfully guiding the manuscript through the copyediting and proofreading stages. We are also grateful to Jay Kreider for creating the index. Finally, we want to thank Sarah England for spearheading the marketing campaign for the new edition.

We are also indebted to the numerous expert readers who commented on various chapters, thereby strengthening the book as a whole. We are thankful to our families for their patience and advice, and to our students, whose questions and comments over the years have been essential to the framing of this book. And we extend a special thanks to, and hope to hear from, all the teachers and students we might never meet: their engagement with this book will frame new understandings of our shared past and its bearing on our future.

## REVIEWERS

### Seventeenth Edition Consultants

Paul Freedman, Yale University
Sheryl Kroen, University of Florida
Michael Kulikowski, Pennsylvania State University
Harry Liebersohn, University of Illinois, Urbana-Champaign
Helmut Smith, Vanderbilt University

### Seventeenth Edition Reviewers

Donna Allen, Glendale Community College
Ken Bartlett, University of Toronto
Volker Benkert, Arizona State University
Dean Bennett, Schenectady County Community College
Patrick Brennan, Gulf Coast State College
Neil Brooks, Community College of Baltimore County, Essex
James Brophy, University of Delaware
Kevin Caldwell, Blue Ridge Community College
Keith Chu, Bergen Community College
Alex D'Erizans, Borough of Manhattan Community College, CUNY
Hilary Earl, Nipissing University
Kirk Ford, Mississippi College
Michael Gattis, Gulf Coast State College
David M. Gallo, College of Mount Saint Vincent
Jamie Gruring, Arizona State University
Tim Hack, Salem Community College
Bernard Hagerty, University of Pittsburgh
Paul T. Hietter, Mesa Community College
Paul Hughes, Sussex County Community College
Kyle Irvin, Jefferson State Community College
Ilana Krug, York College of Pennsylvania
Guy Lalande, St. Francis Xavier University
Chris Laney, Berkshire Community College
Charles Levine, Mesa Community College
Michael McKeown, Daytona State College

Dan Puckett, Troy State University
Dan Robinson, Troy State University
Craig Saucier, Southeastern Louisiana University
Aletia Seaborn, Southern Union State Community
    College
Victoria Thompson, Arizona State University
Donna Trembinski, St. Francis Xavier University
Pamela West, Jefferson State Community College
Julianna Wilson, Pima Community College

**Eighteenth Edition Reviewers**
Matthew Barlow, John Abbott College
Ken Bartlett, University of Toronto
Bob Brennan, Cape Fear Community College
Jim Brophy, University of Delaware
Keith Chu, Bergen Community College
Geoffrey Clark, SUNY Potsdam
Bill Donovan, Loyola University Maryland
Jeff Ewen, Sussex County Community College
Peter Goddard, University of Guelph
Paul Hughes, Sussex County Community College
Michael Kulikowski, Penn State University
Chris Laney, Berkshire Community College
James Martin, Campbell University
Derrick McKisick, Fairfield University
Dan Puckett, Troy University
Major Ben Richards, US Military Academy
Bo Riley, Columbus State Community College
Kimlisa Salazar, Pima Community College
Sara Scalenghe, Loyola University Maryland
Suzanne Smith, Cape Fear Community College
Bobbi Sutherland, Dordt College
David Tengwall, Anne Arundel Community College
Pam West, Jefferson State Community College

Julianna Wilson, Pima Community College
Margarita Youngo, Pima Community College

**Nineteenth Edition Consultants**
Dawn L. Gilley, Northwest Missouri State
    University
Andrzej S. Kamiński, Georgetown University
Adam Kożuchowski, University of Warsaw
Peter Kracht, University of Pittsburgh Press
Eulalia Łazarska, Łazarski University
Krzysztof Łazarski, Łazarski University
John Merriman, Yale University
Daria Nałęcz, Łazarski University
Andrzej Novak, Jagiellonian University
Nicoletta Pellegrino, Regis College
Endre Sashalmi, University of Pécs
Robert Schneider, Indiana University

**Nineteenth Edition Reviewers**
Ken Bartlett, University of Toronto
Keith Chu, Bergen Community College
Bruce Delfini, SUNY Rockland Community College
Paul Fessler, Dordt College
Peter Goddard, University of Guelph
Bonnie Harris, San Diego State University
Anthony Heideman, Front Range Community College
Justin Horton, Thomas Nelson Community College
Catherine Humes, John Abbott College
Leslie Johnson, Hudson Valley Community College
Megan Myers, Howard Community College
Craig W. Pilant, County College of Morris
Christopher Thomas, J. Sargeant Reynolds
    Community College
Rebecca Woodham, Wallace Community College

ARCTIC
OCEAN

ARCTIC

GREENLAND

NORTH
PACIFIC
OCEAN

NORTH
AMERICA

NORTH
ATLANTIC
OCEAN

Hudson
Bay

Gulf of
Mexico

CENTRAL
AMERICA

TROPIC OF CANCER

Hawaii

EQUATOR

Amazon
Basin

SOUTH
AMERICA

SOUTH
PACIFIC
OCEAN

TROPIC OF CAPRICORN

SOUTH

ATLAN

OCEA

Falkland Islands

Cape Horn

Drake Passage

ANTARCTIC
PENINSULA

WEDDELL
SEA

ANTARCTIC CIRCLE

Marie Byrd Land

ANTA

### GLOBAL SATELLITE MOSAIC

The beauty and complexity of Earth's landscapes—above and below the oceans—is revealed with the Global Satellite Mosaic. The mosaic was produced for the National Geographic Society by NASA's Jet Propulsion Laboratory, using more than 500 satellite images from the National Oceanic and Atmospheric Administration. The cloud-free images show Earth in its natural colors as it would be seen from space. One can easily identify the world's major glaciers, deserts, mountain ranges, and rain forests. For example, follow the green ribbon of lush vegetation along the Nile into the stark, dry Sahara. The mountain ranges seem to rise off the map thanks to digital elevation databases from the Department of Defense. The deepest areas of the ocean realm are colored dark blue in contrast to the light blue areas highlighting continental shelves, submarine ridges, and underwater mountains.

### BIOSPHERE

Thousands of satellite images were combined to show a picture of biospheric productivity. In the oceans, red, yellow, and green indicate waters rich in phytoplankton. On land green areas show high potential plant productivity; tan areas suffer from productivity limitations due to aridity and temperature.

## THE
SATE

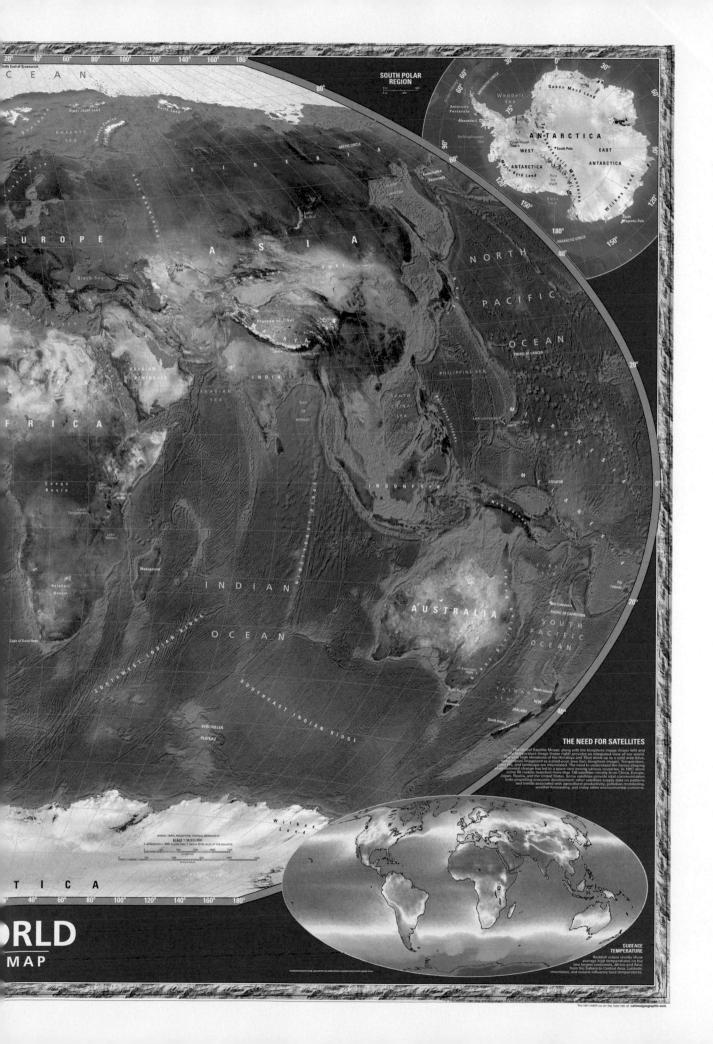

SOUTH POLAR
REGION

Weddell
Sea

ANTARCTICA

WEST          EAST
ANTARCTICA    ANTARCTICA

NORTH

PACIFIC

OCEAN

TROPIC OF CANCER

EUROPE

ASIA

SIBERIA

URAL MOUNTAINS

Aral
Sea

Black Sea

Lake Baikal

Plateau of Tibet

HIMALAYA

ARABIAN
PENINSULA

INDIA

ARABIAN
SEA

BAY
OF
BENGAL

PHILIPPINE
SEA

SOUTH
CHINA
SEA

MICRONESIA

AFRICA

Congo
Basin

Lake
Tanganyika

Lake
Malawi

Madagascar

INDONESIA

EQUATOR

MELANESIA

INDIAN

OCEAN

AUSTRALIA

SOUTH
PACIFIC
OCEAN

TROPIC OF CAPRICORN

New Caledonia

Fiji
Islands

SOUTHWEST INDIAN RIDGE

Cape of Good Hope

Kalahari
Desert

SOUTHEAST INDIAN RIDGE

TASMAN
SEA

North Island

NEW
ZEALAND

Kerguelen
Plateau

South Island

Wilkes
Land

SCALE 1:38,931,000

### THE NEED FOR SATELLITES

The Global Satellite Mosaic, along with the biosphere image (lower left) and the temperature image (lower right) provides an integrated view of our world. The very high elevations of the Himalaya and Tibet show up as a cool area there, rather than imagined as a plant-poor area than biosphere image. Temperature, plant life, and landscape are interrelated. The need to understand the forces shaping environmental change has led to a space race among various countries. In 1997 alone some 85 rockets launched more than 140 satellites—mostly from China, Europe, Japan, Russia, and the United States. Some satellites provide vital communication links propelling economic development; other satellites supply data on patterns and trends associated with agricultural productivity, pollution monitoring, weather forecasting, and many other environmental concerns.

TICA

## ORLD
MAP

### SURFACE
TEMPERATURE
Reddish colors vividly show average high temperatures on the two largest continents, Africa and Asia, from the Sahara to Central Asia. Latitude, mountains, and oceans influence land temperatures.

You can reach us on the Internet at nationalgeographic.com.

# Western Civilizations

*Their History & Their Culture*

## STORY LINES

- Historians gather and interpret evidence from a diverse array of sources, many of them environmental, visual, and archaeological.

- All civilizations emerge as the result of complex historical processes specific to a time and place, yet all share certain defining features.

- Prominent individuals can achieve power through the use of force, but maintaining power requires legitimacy.

- Those individuals wielding power in ancient Mesopotamia and Egypt responded in different ways to the challenge of establishing legitimacy.

## CHRONOLOGY

| | |
|---|---|
| 11,000 B.C.E. | Neolithic Revolution begins |
| 7500–5700 B.C.E. | Çatalhöyük flourishes |
| 6800–3000 B.C.E. | Jericho flourishes |
| 4300–2900 B.C.E. | The rise of Uruk in Sumer |
| c. 3200 B.C.E. | Development of writing |
| c. 3100 B.C.E. | King Narmer unites Upper and Lower Egypt |
| 2900–2500 B.C.E. | Early Dynastic Period in Sumer |
| c. 2700 B.C.E. | Reign of Gilgamesh |
| c. 2686–2160 B.C.E. | Old Kingdom of Egypt |
| c. 2650 B.C.E. | Imhotep engineers the Step Pyramid for King Djoser |
| c. 2350 B.C.E. | Sargon of Akkad consolidates power in Sumer |
| 2160–2055 B.C.E. | First Intermediate Period in Egypt |
| 2100–2000 B.C.E. | Ziggurat of Ur constructed |
| 2055–c. 1650 B.C.E. | Middle Kingdom of Egypt |
| c. 1792–1750 B.C.E. | Reign of Hammurabi |

Before
You
Read
This
Chapter

# Early Civilizations

## CORE OBJECTIVES

- **UNDERSTAND** the challenges involved in studying the distant past and the crucial importance of interdisciplinary methods and unconventional sources.

- **DEFINE** the key characteristics of civilization.

- **IDENTIFY** the factors that shaped the earliest cities.

- **EXPLAIN** Hammurabi's tools for governing the cities of his empire.

- **DESCRIBE** the main differences between the Mesopotamian and Egyptian civilizations.

There was a time, the story goes, when all the peoples of the earth shared a common language and could accomplish great things. They developed new technologies and aspired to build a city with a tower reaching to the sky. But their god was troubled by this, so he destroyed their civilization by making it impossible for them to understand each other's speech.

We know this story as the legend of the Tower of Babel. It probably circulated among peoples of the ancient world for thousands of years before it became part of the Hebrew book we call by its Greek name, Genesis: "the beginning." This story lets us glimpse some of the conditions in which the first civilizations arose, and it also reminds us of the ruptures that make studying them hard. We no longer speak the same languages as those ancient peoples, just as we no longer have direct access to their experiences or beliefs.

Such foundational stories are usually called *myths*, but they are really an early form of history. For the people who told them, the stories helped to make sense of the present by explaining the past. The story of the Tower of Babel conveyed a crucial message: human beings are powerful when they share a common goal,

3

and what enables human interaction is civilization. To the peoples of the ancient world, the characteristic benefits of civilization—stability and safety, government, art, literature, science—were always products of city life. The very word *civilization* derives from the Latin word *civis*, "city." Cities, however, became possible only as a result of innovations that began around the end of the last Ice Age, about 13,000 years ago, and that came to fruition some 8,000 years later. The history of civilization is therefore a short one. Within the study of humanity, which reaches back to the genus *Homo* in Africa, some 1.7 million years ago, it is merely a blip on the radar screen. Even within the history of *Homo sapiens*, the subspecies to which we all belong and which evolved about 40,000 years ago, civilization is a very recent development.

The study of the earliest civilizations is both fascinating and challenging. Historians still do not understand why the first known cities should have developed in the region between the Tigris and the Euphrates Rivers, in what is now Iraq. Once developed, however, the basic patterns of urban life quickly spread to other parts of western Asia—a region once called the Near East—both by imitation and by conquest. A network of trading connections linked these early cities, but intense competition for resources often made alliances fragile. Then, around the middle of the second millennium B.C.E. (that is, "Before the Common Era," equivalent to the Christian dating system B.C., "Before Christ"), rulers of these independent cities started to make broader claims to power over their citizens and other states. How this happened—and how we know that it happened—is the subject of Chapter 1.

# BEFORE CIVILIZATION

More than 9,000 years ago, a town began to develop at Çatalhöyük (*CHUH-tal-hih-yik*) in Anatolia, in what is now south central Turkey. Over the next 2,000 years, it grew to cover an area of thirty-three acres, within which some 8,000 inhabitants lived in more than 2,000 separate houses. If this seems small, consider that Çatalhöyük's population density was actually twice that of today's most populous city: Mumbai, India. It was so tightly packed that there were hardly any streets. Instead, each house was built immediately next to its neighbor and generally on top of a previous house. People entered their houses by walking across their neighbors' rooftops and climbing down ladders into their own living spaces.

The people of Çatalhöyük developed a highly organized and advanced society. They wove wool cloth; they made kiln-fired pottery; they painted elaborate hunting scenes on the plaster-covered walls of their houses; they made weapons and tools from razor-sharp obsidian imported from the nearby Cappadocian mountains. They honored their ancestors with religious rites and buried their dead beneath the floors of their houses. As settled agriculturalists, they grew grains, peas, and lentils and tended herds of domesticated sheep and goats. But they also hunted and gathered fruits and nuts, like their nomadic ancestors, and their society was egalitarian, another feature common to nomadic societies: both men and women did the same kinds of work. But despite their relatively diverse food supply, their life spans were very short. Men died, on average, at the age of thirty-four. Women, who bore the additional risks of childbirth, died around age thirty.

The basic features of life in Çatalhöyük are common to all early civilizations. But how, when, and why did such settlements emerge? And how do we have access to information about this remote past? The era before the appearance of written records, which begin to proliferate around 3100 B.C.E., is of far greater duration than the subsequent eras we are able to document—and no less important. But it requires special ingenuity to identify, collect, and interpret the evidence of the very distant past. In fact, historians have only just begun to explore the ways that climatology, neuroscience, and evolutionary biology can further illuminate this period, augmenting the older findings of paleontology, archaeology, and historical anthropology. The following summary of our knowledge may need to be radically revised in the next few years.

## Societies of the Stone Age

Primates with human characteristics originated in Africa 4 to 5 million years ago, and toolmaking hominids—species belonging to the genus *Homo*, our distant ancestors—evolved approximately 2 million years ago. Because these early hominins made most of their tools out of stone, all human cultures flourishing before the fourth millennium B.C.E. (that is, the thousand years ending in 3000 B.C.E.) are designated as belonging to the Stone Age. This vast expanse of time is divided into the Paleolithic ("Old Stone") and the Neolithic ("New Stone") Eras, with the break between them falling around 11,000 B.C.E.

Long before modern humans made their appearance, then, recognizable human traits had already begun to leave traces on the landscape. Early humans in Africa were kindling and controlling fire 164,000 years ago, and using it to make tools. The Neanderthals, a hominid species that flourished even earlier, about 200,000 years ago, made jewelry, painted on the walls of caves, and buried their dead in distinctive graves with meaningful objects such

**CAVE PAINTINGS FROM LASCAUX.** These paintings, which date to between 10,000 and 15,000 B.C.E., show several of the different species of animals that were hunted by people of the Ice Age. The largest animal depicted here, a species of long-horned cattle known as the *aurochs*, is now extinct.

as horns (blown to make music) and, in one case, flowers. Scientists have recently discovered that Neanderthals were capable of speech and that they began interbreeding with *Homo sapiens* around 60,000 years ago. How and why Neanderthals became extinct, around 40,000 years ago, is still a matter of intense debate.

Archaeology has shown that, about this time, in the last phase of the Paleolithic Era, the pace of human development began to accelerate dramatically. Around 40,000 B.C.E., human populations in Africa expanded, suggesting that people were better nourished, perhaps as a result of new technologies. In Europe, the subspecies *Homo sapiens sapiens* began to produce finely crafted and more effective tools such as fishhooks, arrowheads, and sewing needles made from wood, antler, and bone. The most astonishing evidence of this change was produced by these new tools: cave paintings like those at Lascaux and Chauvet (France)—those at Chauvet were discovered only in 1994—some of which may be 30,000 years old. These amazing scenes were purposefully painted in recesses where acoustic resonance is greatest, and probably were intended to be experienced as part of multimedia musical ceremonies. (Flutes made from bone and ivory, dating to around 33,000 B.C.E., were found in a cave in southern Germany in 2008.) This is further evidence for the development of language, as well.

Despite these extraordinary changes, the basic patterns of human life altered very little during this era. Virtually all human societies consisted of hunter-gatherers, bands of a few dozen people who moved incessantly in search of food. As a result of this constant movement, these groups have left no continuous archaeological record. Yet we can discern some of the social, economic, and political structures that make these subsistence societies different from those that can be called "civilizations." Early humans had no

domestic animals to transport goods, so they could have no significant material possessions aside from basic tools. And because they could not accumulate goods over time, the distinctions of rank and status created by disparities in wealth could not develop. Hierarchical structures were therefore uncommon. When conflicts arose among members of a group or resources became scarce, the solution probably was to divide and separate.

Although it was once assumed that men did the hunting and women the gathering, such gendered presumptions do not reflect the complex realities of modern hunter-gatherer societies, and they are probably not applicable to the Paleolithic Period, either. It is more likely that all members of a band (except for the very young and very old) engaged in the basic activity of acquiring food.

## THE BUILDING BLOCKS OF CIVILIZATION

What changes allowed some hunter-gatherer societies to settle and build civilizations? Around 11,000 B.C.E., very evident developments brought about by changes in the climate led to the growth of managed food production, which in turn fostered settlements that could trade with each other, both locally and over long distances. For the first time, it became possible for individuals and communities to accumulate and store wealth on a large scale. The results were far reaching. Communities became more stable and human interactions more complex. Specialization developed, along with distinctions of status and rank. Both the rapidity and the radical implications of these changes have given this era its name: the Neolithic Revolution.

## The Neolithic Revolution: The Beginnings of Human Impact on the Environment

The artists who executed the cave paintings at Lascaux and Chauvet were conditioned to survive in harsh climatic conditions. Between 40,000 and 11,000 B.C.E., daytime temperatures in the Mediterranean basin averaged about 60° F (16° C) in the summer and about 30° F (–1° C) in the winter. These are very low compared with today's temperatures in the city of Marseilles, not far from Lascaux, which average about 86° F (30° C) in summer and 52° F (11° C) in winter. Cold-loving reindeer, elk, wild boar, bison, and mountain goats abounded in regions now famous for their beaches and vineyards. But as the glaciers receded northward with the warming climate, these species retreated with them, all the way to Scandinavia. Some humans moved north with the game, but others stayed behind to create a very different world.

Within a few thousand years after the end of the Ice Age, the peoples living in the eastern Mediterranean accomplished the most momentous transformation in human history: a switch from food gathering for subsistence to food

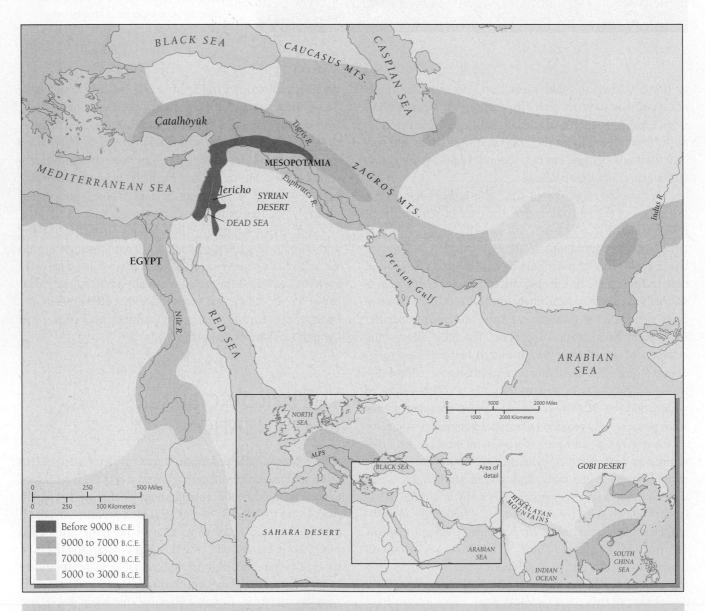

**THE GROWTH OF AGRICULTURE.** Examine the chronology of agriculture's development in this region. ▪ *What areas began cultivating crops first, and why?* ▪ *In what period did agriculture spread the most rapidly, and why?* ▪ *How might rivers have played a crucial role in the spread of farming technologies?*

production. The warmer, wetter climate allowed wild grains to flourish, geometrically increasing the food supply and making settlements possible. People then began to domesticate animals and cultivate plants. Stable settlements grew into cities. This process took several thousand years, but it still deserves to be called "revolutionary." In a relatively short time, people living in this area fundamentally altered patterns of existence that were millions of years old.

Humans also began to alter the environment, so much so that some scholars have argued that this was the beginning of a new epoch in the history of our planet: the Anthropocene (from the Greek word for "human," *anthropos*). During this epoch—our epoch—slow-moving geological and natural climatological fluctuations have been overtaken by intensive, large-scale human efforts to alter the Earth's ecosystems. We will be paying close attention to this process and its intensification throughout the following chapters.

The revolutionary changes of this period produced new surpluses of food, but they also produced new challenges and inequalities. For example, well-nourished women in sedentary communities can bear more children than women in hunter-gatherer groups, and so the women of this new epoch became increasingly sequestered from their male counterparts, who in turn gave up an equal role in child care. The rapid increase in population was also countered by the rapid spread of infectious diseases, and dependence on carbohydrates resulted in earlier deaths than were typical among hunter-gatherers.

Eventually, increased fertility and birthrates outweighed these limiting factors, and by about 8000 B.C.E. human populations were beginning to exceed the wild food supply. They therefore had to increase the food-growing capacity of the land and to devise ways of preserving and storing grain between harvests. Some peoples had learned how to preserve wild grain in storage pits as early as 11,500 B.C.E., and eventually they discovered that they could use this seed to produce even more grain the following year. Once humans began deliberate cultivation, they could support larger populations and also compensate for disasters (such as flooding) that might inhibit natural reseeding.

Even more important, intensified seeding and storage provided humans with the stable and predictable surpluses needed to support domestic animals. This brought a host of additional benefits, not only guaranteeing a more reliable supply of meat, milk, leather, wool, bone, and horn but also providing animal power to pull carts and plows and to power mills. But it also resulted in a pattern of environmental engineering that had devastating and unsustainable effects. In 2015, for example, a team of environmental scientists calculated that the number of trees on earth has diminished by over 50 percent since the Neolithic Revolution began. The planet we inhabit now has been fundamentally altered by human efforts.

## The Emergence of Towns and Villages

The accelerating changes of this epoch are exemplified by towns such as Çatalhöyük and by the simultaneous rise of trade and warfare: signs of increased specialization and competition among human societies. Thousands of new settlements grew up between 7500 and 3500 B.C.E. Some can be classified as cities: centers of administration and commerce with a relatively large population, often protected by walls. One of these was Jericho, in the territory lying between modern Israel and Jordan. Jericho first emerged as a seasonal, grain-producing settlement, but by

**EARLY POTTERY.** This ceramic cup, with its elegant abstract and animal designs, was fashioned sometime between 5000 and 4000 B.C.E. Although it cannot be dated precisely, distinctive design features such as these make it possible to track the shipment of commodities throughout the ancient world.

6800 B.C.E. its inhabitants were undertaking a spectacular building program to protect their stored surplus of food. Many new dwellings were placed on stone foundations, and a massive dressed stone wall was constructed around the western edge of the settlement. It included a circular tower whose excavated remains still reach to a height of thirty feet, a powerful expression of its builders' wealth, technical prowess, and political ambitions.

This wall and its tower served a growing and now permanent population: Jericho eventually covered at least eight acres and supported 3,000 people, so it was even more densely settled than Çatalhöyük. It was sustained by the intensive cultivation of recently domesticated strains of wheat and barley grown by farmers who were also irrigation engineers. Jericho's inhabitants also produced some of the earliest known pottery, which enabled them to store grain, wine, and oils more effectively. Pottery revolutionized cooking. For the first time, it was possible to produce nourishing stews and porridges, as well as fermented beverages such as beer. Pottery production was not only vital to ancient civilizations, it is vital to those who study them: as the techniques for making pottery spread throughout Eurasia, identifiable regional styles also developed. By studying the different varieties, archaeologists can construct a reasonably accurate chronology and can also trace the movements of goods and people.

Jericho and Çatalhöyük illustrate the impact that stored agricultural surpluses have on human relations. In these settled societies, significant differences began to arise in the amount of wealth individuals could stockpile for themselves and their heirs. Dependence on agriculture also made it more difficult for individuals to split off from the community when disputes and inequities arose. The result was the emergence of a much more stratified society, with more opportunities for a few powerful people to become dominant.

The new reliance on agriculture also meant a new dependence on the land, the seasons, and the weather, which led to new speculations about the supernatural. Different life forces were believed to require special services and gifts, and the regular practice of ritual and sacrifice ultimately produced a priestly caste of individuals or families who seemed able to communicate with these forces. Such spiritual leadership was allied to more worldly forms of power, including the capacity to lead war bands, to exact tribute from other settlements, to construct defenses, and to resolve disputes. Through their command of the community's religious, military, economic, and political structures, certain clans could establish themselves as a ruling class.

Trade was another important element in the development of early settlements. Local trading networks were already established around 9000 B.C.E., and by 5000 long-distance routes linked settlements throughout the region.

Exotic goods and luxury items were the most frequent objects of exchange, including marine shells and semiprecious stones such as turquoise and lapis lazuli. Long-distance trade also accelerated the exchange of ideas and information. And it further increased social stratification: because status was enhanced by access to high-prestige goods, local elites sought to monopolize trade by organizing and controlling the production of commodities within their own communities and by regulating their export. Certain people could now devote at least a portion of their labor to pursuits other than agriculture: making pottery or cloth, manufacturing weapons or tools, building houses and fortifications, or facilitating trade. The elites who fostered and exploited the labor of others eventually became specialized themselves, as full-time speculators and organizers, with the leisure and resources to engage in intellectual, artistic, and political pursuits. The building blocks of civilization had been laid.

# URBAN DEVELOPMENT IN MESOPOTAMIA

The Greeks called it Mesopotamia, the "Land between Rivers." This land received only about eight inches (20 cm) of rainfall per year. Its soils are sandy, and summer temperatures exceed 110° F (44° C). The two rivers supplying water—the Tigris and the Euphrates—are noted for their violence and unpredictability. Both are prone to flooding, and the Tigris was likely to jump its banks and change its course from year to year. It was in this challenging environment that the first urban society, the civilization of Sumer, flourished.

## The Ubaid Culture

The earliest cities of Mesopotamia were founded by the Ubaid peoples, so called because of their settlement at al-Ubaid (now in Iraq), which dates from around 5900 B.C.E. During this era, the headwaters of the Persian Gulf extended at least 100 miles farther inland than they do today, so some Ubaid settlements bordered on fertile marshlands, which enabled them to develop irrigation systems. Although these began as relatively simple channels and collection pools, Ubaid farmers quickly learned to build more sophisticated canals and to line some pools with stone. They also constructed dikes and levees to control the seasonal flooding of the rivers and to direct the excess water into irrigation canals. Despite the hostile environment, Ubaid communities were soon producing surpluses sufficient to support specialists

**THE WHITE TEMPLE AT URUK, c. 3400 B.C.E.** This temple may have been dedicated to the sky god, An, or designed to provide all the region's gods with a mountaintop home in a part of the world known for its level plains.

in construction, weaving, pottery making, metalwork, and trade: the typical occupations of Neolithic village life.

Yet there is also evidence of something quite new in Ubaid culture: central structures that served religious, economic, and administrative functions, something not found in Çatalhöyük. Starting out as shrines, these structures soon became impressive temples built of dried mud brick, like the bricks described in the story of the Tower of Babel—and unlike the plentiful stone used at Jericho; the scarcity of stone meant that builders in this region had to be more resourceful. Each large settlement had such a temple, from which a priestly class acted as managers of the community's stored wealth and of the complex irrigation systems that would make the civilization of Sumer possible.

## Urbanism in Uruk, 4300–2900 B.C.E.

After about 4300 B.C.E., these Ubaid settlements developed into larger, more prosperous, and more organized communities. The most famous of these sites, Uruk, is considered the first Sumerian city-state. Its sophistication and scale is exemplified by the White Temple at Uruk, built between 3500 and 3300 B.C.E. This massive, sloping platform looms nearly forty feet above the surrounding flatlands, and its four corners are oriented toward the cardinal points of the compass. Atop the platform stands the temple proper, dressed in brick and originally painted a brilliant white.

Such temples were eventually constructed in every Sumerian city, reflecting the central role that worship played in civic life. Uruk in particular seems to have owed its rapid urban growth to its importance as a religious center. By 3100 B.C.E. it encompassed some 6 square kilometers (2.3 square miles), enclosing a population of 40,000 people within its massive brick walls. The villages and towns of Sumer, although a mere fraction of the size, also grew rapidly, their teeming economic activity attracting immigrants just as the great cities did. Grain and cloth production grew tenfold. Trade routes expanded dramatically, binding the peoples of Mesopotamia to the Mediterranean and bringing foods from as far away as Scandinavia and China. To manage this increasingly complex economy, the Sumerians invented the technology on which most historians rely: writing.

# The Development of Writing

In 4000 B.C.E., the peoples of Mesopotamia were already using clay tokens to keep inventories. Within a few centuries, they developed the practice of placing tokens inside hollow clay balls and inscribing, on the outside of each ball, the shapes of all the tokens it contained. By 3300 B.C.E., priests (or their scribes) had replaced these balls with flat clay tablets on which they inscribed symbols representing the tokens. These tablets made keeping the tokens themselves unnecessary, and they could also be archived for future reference or sent to other settlements as receipts or requests for goods.

Writing thus evolved as a practical recording technology to support economic pursuits. And because it existed to represent real things, its system of symbols—called pictograms—was also realistic: each pictogram resembled the thing it represented. Over time, however, a pictogram might be used not only to symbolize a physical object but also to evoke an idea associated with that object. For example, the symbol for a bowl of food, a *ninda*, might be used to express something more abstract, such as "nourishment" or "sustenance." Pictograms also came to be associated with particular spoken sounds, or *phonemes*. Thus when a Sumerian scribe needed to employ the sound *ninda*, even as part of another word or a name, he would use the symbol for a bowl of food to represent that phoneme. Later, special marks were added to the symbol so that a reader could tell whether the writer meant it to represent the object itself, or an abstract concept, or a sound used in a context that might have nothing to do with food.

By 3100 B.C.E., Sumerian scribes also developed a specialized tool suited to the task of writing, a durable stylus made of reed. Because this stylus leaves an impression shaped like a wedge (in Latin, *cuneus*), this script is called *cuneiform* (*kyoo-NAY-i-form*). With it, cuneiform symbols could be impressed more quickly into clay. But because the new stylus was not suited to drawing pictograms that accurately represented things, the symbols became even more abstract; eventually they barely resembled the original pictograms at all. Meanwhile, symbols were invented for every possible phonetic combination in the Sumerian language, reducing the number of necessary pictograms from about 1,200 to 600. Whereas the earliest pictograms could have been written and read by anyone, writing and reading now became specialized, powerful skills accessible only to a small and influential minority taught in designated scribal schools.

Despite the complicated nature of the script, cuneiform proved remarkably durable. For over 2,000 years it remained the principal writing system of antiquity, even in societies that did not speak the Sumerian language. Documents using the script were still being produced as late as the first century C.E. ("Common Era," equivalent to the traditional Christian practice of designating dates by A.D., for *Anno Domini*, "in the year of the Lord"). By about 2500 B.C.E., Sumerians were using writing for a wide variety of economic, religious, political, and artistic purposes. Tens of thousands of clay tablets still survive, which makes it possible for us to know a great deal more about the Sumerians than we do about any other human society before this time. We can better understand the social structures that shaped their lives, their attitudes toward their gods, and their changing political circumstances.

**CUNEIFORM WRITING.** The image on the left shows a Sumerian clay tablet from about 3000 B.C.E. Here, standardized pictures are beginning to represent concepts as well as things: notice the symbol *ninda* ("food") at the top. On the right, carvings on limestone from about 2600 B.C.E. reveal the evolution of cuneiform into more abstract forms. ▪ *Why would such abstract pictograms have been easier to reproduce quickly than the earlier, more realistic images?*

# THE CULTURE OF SUMER

The great centers of Sumerian civilization—the cities of Uruk, Ur, Lagash, Eridu, and Kish—shared a common culture and a common language. But they also competed for natural resources and sources of labor, rivalries that could lead to warfare and the raiding of smaller settlements. Water rights and access to arable land and trade routes were frequently at stake.

Much of the economic production of each city passed through great temple warehouses, where priests redistributed the city's produce. During the third millennium, these great temples also began to control the production of textiles, employing thousands of servile women and children. Temple elites began to play a key role in long-distance trade as both buyers and sellers of goods. Each Sumerian city therefore had its own gods and its aristocracy from which priests were drawn. As much as half of the remaining population may have consisted of farming families who held only enough land to sustain themselves. The rest were dependents of the temple who worked as artisans or as agricultural laborers; many were slaves. Most were prisoners of war from other Sumerian city-states whose bondage was limited to three years, after which time a slave had to be released. But foreigners could be held indefinitely and were the property of their owners. They could be beaten, branded, bought, and sold like any other form of merchandise. Perhaps the only positive thing to say about slavery in antiquity is that it was egalitarian: anyone could become a slave. It was not until the beginning of the modern era that slavery became closely linked to new ideas about race (see Chapter 14).

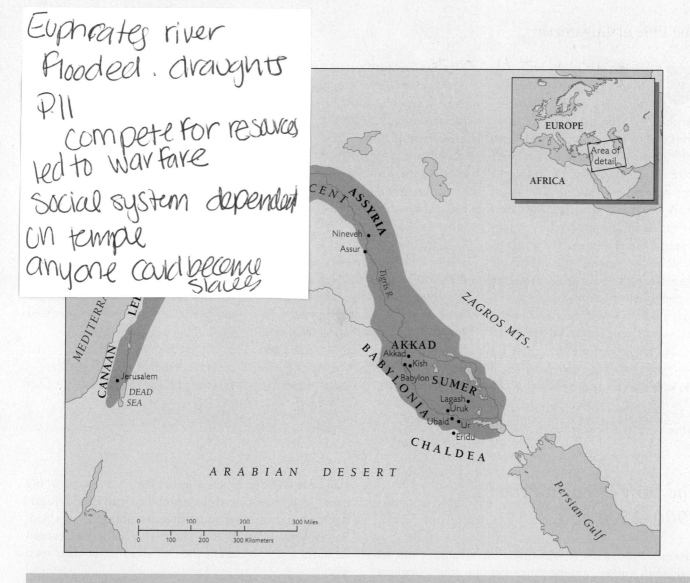

**THE FERTILE CRESCENT.** Notice the proximity of Sumerian cities to rivers; consider the vital role played by the Tigris and the Euphrates in shaping the Mesopotamian civilizations. ▪ *How many Sumerian cities can you identify on the map?* ▪ *Why might Sumerian cities have been clustered so closely together?* ▪ *What challenges and opportunities did this present?*

## The Flood: Two Accounts

> One of the oldest stories in the world tells of a great flood that devastated the lands and peoples of the earth, an event that can be traced to the warming of the earth's climate at the end of the last Ice Age. Many ancient cultures told versions of this story; two of these are excerpted below. The first, included in the Epic of Gilgamesh, was written down during the first half of the third millennium B.C.E., making it at least 1,500 years older than the similar account in the Hebrew Bible. But both are probably the products of much older storytelling traditions. The hero of the Sumerian story is Utnapishtim; the hero of the Hebrew story is Noah.

### The Epic of Gilgamesh

Utnapishtim spoke to Gilgamesh, saying: "I will reveal to you, Gilgamesh . . . a secret of the gods. . . . The hearts of the Great Gods moved them to inflict the Flood. Their Father Anu uttered the oath (of secrecy). . . . [But the god] Ea . . . repeated their talk [to me, saying]: 'O man of Shuruppak, son of Ubartutu: Tear down the house and build a boat! . . . Spurn possessions and keep alive living beings! Make all living beings go up into the boat. The boat which you are to build, its dimensions must measure equal to each other: its length must correspond to its width. Roof it over like the Apsu.' I understood and spoke to my lord, Ea: 'My lord, thus is the command which you have uttered. I will heed and will do it.' . . . On the fifth day I laid out her exterior. It was a field in area, its walls were each 10 times 12 cubits in height. . . . I provided it with six decks, thus dividing it into seven (levels). . . . Whatever I had I loaded on it. . . . All the living beings that I had I loaded on it. I had all my kith and kin go up into the boat, all the beasts and animals of the field and the draftsmen I had go up.

I watched the appearance of the weather—the weather was frightful to behold! I went into the boat and sealed the entry. . . . All day long the South Wind blew . . . , submerging the mountain in water, overwhelming the people like an attack. . . . Six days and seven nights came the wind and flood, the storm flattening the land. When the seventh day arrived . . . [t]he sea calmed, fell still, the whirlwind and flood stopped up. . . . When a seventh day arrived, I sent forth a dove and released it. The dove went off, but came back to me, no perch was visible so it circled back to me. I sent forth a swallow and released it. The swallow went off, but came back to me, no perch was visible so it circled back to me. I sent forth a raven and released it. The raven went off, and saw the waters slither back. It eats, it scratches, it bobs, but does not circle back to me. Then I sent out everything in all directions and sacrificed (a sheep). I offered incense in front of the mountain-ziggurat. . . .

The gods smelled the savor . . . and collected like flies over a sacrifice. . . . Just then Enlil arrived. He saw the boat

---

## The Early Dynastic Period, 2900–2500 B.C.E.

Around 2900 B.C.E., competition for resources intensified, and warfare among cities became more frequent. As a result, a new type of military leadership began to emerge. Historians therefore call this era the Early Dynastic Period because it was dominated by powerful dynastic clans, each headed by a war leader known as a *lugal*, a "big man." Unlike the priestly rulers of the Uruk Period, lugals did not see themselves as humble servants of a city's god. Rather, they believed that success in battle had earned them the right to exploit the city's wealth for their own glory.

The most striking expression of this development is the Epic of Gilgamesh, a series of stories recited over many generations and eventually written down on cuneiform

and became furious. . . . 'Where did a living being escape? No man was to survive the annihilation!' Ea spoke to Valiant Enlil, saying . . . 'How, how could you bring about a Flood without consideration? Charge the violation to the violator, charge the offense to the offender, but be compassionate lest (mankind) be cut off, be patient lest they be killed.' Enlil went up inside the boat and, grasping my hand, made me go up. He had my wife go up and kneel by my side. He touched our forehead and, standing between us, he blessed us. . . ."

Source: Maureen Gallery Kovacs, trans., *The Epic of Gilgamesh*, Tablet XI (Stanford, CA: 1985, 1989), pp. 97–103.

## The Book of Genesis

The Lord saw that the wickedness of humankind was great in the earth and . . . said, "I will blot out from the earth the human beings I have created . . . for I am sorry I have made them." But Noah found favor in the sight of the Lord. . . . God saw that the earth was corrupt and . . . said to Noah, "I have determined to make an end to all flesh. . . . Make yourself an ark of cypress wood, make rooms in the ark, and cover it inside and out with pitch. . . . Make a roof for the ark, and put the door of the ark in its side. . . . For my part I am going to bring a flood on the earth, to destroy from under heaven all flesh. . . . But I will establish a covenant with you, and you shall come into the ark, you, your sons, your wife, and your sons' wives with you. And of every living thing you shall bring two of every kind into the ark, to keep them alive with you. . . . Also take with you every kind of food that is eaten." . . . All the fountains of the great deep burst forth, and the windows of the heavens were opened. . . . The waters gradually receded from the earth. . . . At the end of forty days, Noah opened a window of the ark . . . and sent out the raven, and it went to and fro until the waters were dried up from the earth. Then he sent out the dove from him, to see if the waters had subsided from the face of the ground, but the dove found no place to set its foot, and it returned. . . . He waited another seven days, and again sent out the dove [which] came back to him . . . and there in its beak was a freshly plucked olive leaf, so Noah knew the waters had subsided from the earth. Then he . . . sent out the dove, and it did not return to him anymore. . . . Noah built an altar to the Lord . . . and offered burnt offerings. And when the Lord smelled the pleasing odor, the Lord said in his heart, "I will never again curse the ground because of humankind . . . nor will I ever again destroy every living creature as I have done." . . . God blessed Noah and his sons.

Source: Genesis 6:5–9:1, *The New Oxford Annotated Bible* (Oxford: 1994).

### Questions for Analysis

1. What are the similarities and differences between these two accounts?

2. What do these differences or similarities reveal about the two societies that told these stories? Does one seem to derive from the other? Why or why not?

3. How did the geography and climate of Mesopotamia affect the Sumerian version of the story?

tablets: the first literary monument in world history. It recounts the exploits of a lugal named Gilgamesh, who probably lived in Uruk sometime around 2700 B.C.E. Gilgamesh earns his legendary reputation through military conquest and personal heroism, particularly in campaigns against uncivilized—that is, nonurban, non-Sumerian—tribes. But he becomes so powerful that he ignores his own society's code of conduct. We hear at the start of the epic that his people complain about him because he keeps their sons away at war and shows no respect for the nobles, carousing with their wives and compromising their daughters; he also disrespects the priesthood and commits acts of sacrilege. So the people of Uruk pray to the gods for retribution, and the gods fashion a wild man named Enkidu to challenge Gilgamesh.

The confrontation between Gilgamesh and Enkidu reveals the core values of Sumerian society. Gilgamesh is a creature of the city; Enkidu is his uncivilized Other, like the hunter-gatherers who still subsisted in unclaimed wilderness lands between and around cities. But then Enkidu has a sexual encounter with a beguiling woman: his urban initiation civilizes him, and this allows him to befriend the lord of Uruk. Together they have many adventures. But Enkidu is eventually killed by the goddess Inanna, who punishes the friends for mocking her powers. Gilgamesh, distraught with grief, searches for a magical medicinal plant that will revive his friend. He finds it at the bottom of a deep pool, only to have it stolen from him by a water snake. In the end, he is forced to confront the futility of all human effort. He becomes "The One Who Looked into the Depths," the name by which his story was known to Sumerians. The larger message seems to be that not even civilization can shield humans from the forces of nature and the inevitability of death.

## Sumerian Religion

During the Uruk Period, the Sumerians identified their gods with the capricious forces of the natural world. During the Early Dynastic Period, however, many came to imagine their gods as resembling the lugals who now lorded over their cities. From either perspective, humans exist merely to work for their gods, to provide them with food, clothing, and luxuries. This was, indeed, why the gods had created people in the first place. There was thus a reciprocal relationship between humanity and divinity. The gods depended on their human servants to honor and sustain them; and in return, the gods occasionally bestowed gifts and favors on humans.

Some lugals claimed to be the gods' representative on earth, reigning as kings with special responsibilities and special privileges. They were thus set apart from all other men, including priests. But kings were also obliged to honor the gods through offerings, sacrifices, festivals, and massive building projects. Kings who neglected these duties, or who exalted themselves at the expense of the gods, were likely to bring disaster on themselves and their people. And even kings could not evade death, when the human body returned to clay and the soul crossed into the underworld, a place of silent darkness.

## Sumerian Science, Technology, and Trade

The Sumerians' worldview was colored by their adversarial relationship with their capricious surroundings. Because neither their gods nor their environment were trustworthy, Sumerians cultivated a high degree of self-reliance and ingenuity. These qualities made them the most technologically innovative people of the ancient world.

For example, despite the fact that their land had no mineral deposits, the Sumerians became skilled metallurgists. By 6000 B.C.E., a number of cultures throughout Eurasia had learned how to produce weapons and tools from copper. Mesopotamia itself has no copper, but by the Uruk Period (4300–2900 B.C.E.), trade routes were bringing raw copper ore into Sumer, where it was processed into weapons and tools. Shortly before 3000 B.C.E., perhaps starting in eastern Anatolia (now Turkey), people also discovered that copper could be alloyed with arsenic (or later, tin) to

**SUMERIAN WAR CHARIOTS.** The earliest known representation of the wheel, dating from about 2600 B.C.E., shows how wheels were fashioned from slabs of wood. (For a later Mesopotamian wheel with spokes, see the illustration on page 41.)

*neither gods nor environment trustworthy + self reliance*

*tech savy*

produce bronze. Bronze is almost as malleable as copper, and it pours more easily into molds; when cooled, it also maintains its rigidity and shape better than copper. For almost 2,000 years, until about 1200 B.C.E. and the development of techniques for smelting iron (see Chapter 2), bronze was the strongest metal known—the most useful and, in war, the most deadly. Following the ancient Greeks, we call this period the Bronze Age.

Along with writing and the making of bronze, the invention of the wheel was a fundamental technological achievement of this era. The Sumerians were using potter's wheels by the middle of the fourth millennium B.C.E. and could produce high-quality clay vessels in greater quantity than ever before. By around 3200 B.C.E., the Sumerians were also using two- and four-wheeled chariots and carts drawn by donkeys. (Horses were unknown in Mesopotamia until sometime between 2000 and 1700 B.C.E.) Chariots were another new and deadly military technology, giving warriors a tremendous advantage over armies on foot: the earliest depiction of their use, dating from 2600 B.C.E., shows one trampling an enemy. At the same time, wheeled carts dramatically increased the productivity of the Sumerian workforce.

The use of the wheel in pottery making may have suggested its use for vehicles, but such a connection is not inevitable. The ancient Egyptians, too, were using the potter's wheel by at least 2700 B.C.E., but they did not use the wheel for transport until a millennium later, when they learned the technique from Mesopotamia. In the Western Hemisphere, wheeled vehicles were unknown until the sixteenth century C.E., although the Incas had a sophisticated system of roads and probably used iron rollers to move huge blocks of stone for use in building projects. These two points of comparison help to explain why the wheel was probably invented by nomadic peoples living on the steppes of what is now Russia. By contrast, sedentary civilizations that can rely on the manpower of thousands, or that can transport heavy cargo by water, do not feel the same necessity for invention.

The Sumerians can also be credited with innovations that made the most of their scarce resources. An example is the seed drill, in use for two millennia before it was depicted on a stone tablet of the seventh century B.C.E. It is striking that this technology was unknown to any other Western civilization until the sixteenth century C.E., when Europeans adopted it from China; it would not be in general use until the nineteenth century of our era. Other impressive Sumerian inventions derived from the study of mathematics. In order to construct their elaborate irrigation systems, the Sumerians had developed sophisticated measuring and surveying techniques as well as the art of

mapmaking. Agricultural needs may also lie behind the lunar calendar they invented, which consisted of twelve months, six lasting 30 days and six lasting 29 days. Since this produced a year of only 354 days, the Sumerians eventually began to add a month to their calendars every few years in order to predict the recurrence of the seasons with sufficient accuracy.

The Sumerian practice of dividing time has lasted to the present day, not only in our notions of the 30-day month (which corresponds approximately with the phases of the moon) but also in our division of the hour into sixty minutes, each comprising sixty seconds. Mathematics also contributed to Sumerian architecture, enabling them to build domes and arches thousands of years before the Romans would adopt and spread these architectural forms throughout the West.

Sumerian technology depended not only on ingenuity but also on the spread of information and raw materials

**A SUMERIAN PLOW WITH A SEED DRILL.** Seed drills control the distribution of seed and ensure that it falls directly into the furrow made by the plow. By contrast, the method of sowing seed practiced elsewhere in the world—and as late as the nineteenth century in Europe and the Americas—was to broadcast the seed by throwing it out in handfuls. Sumerian-style plows were developed during the third millennium B.C.E. and were still being used in the seventh century B.C.E., when this black stone tablet was engraved. ■ *Think about what you have learned about the Sumerians and their environment. Why would they have developed this technology?*

through trade. Because their homeland was almost completely devoid of many natural resources, Sumerian pioneers traced routes up and down the rivers and into the hinterlands of Mesopotamia, following the tributaries of the Tigris and the Euphrates. They blazed trails across the deserts toward the west, where they interacted with and influenced the Egyptians. By sea, they traded with the peoples of the Persian Gulf and, directly or indirectly, with the civilizations of the Indus Valley (modern Pakistan and India). And, along with merchandise, they carried ideas: stories, art, the use of writing, and the whole cultural complex that arose from their way of life. The elements of civilization, which had fused in their urban crucible, would thus come together in many other places throughout the world.

## THE FIRST EMPIRES?

Sumerian inscriptions and other writings suggest that competition among Sumerian cities reached a new level around 2500 B.C.E., as ambitious lugals vied to magnify themselves and their kingdoms. But much of this written evidence is misleading, telling us more about these rulers' mastery of rhetoric than their actual control over their own citizen populations. Still, archaeological evidence from Ur showcases the extraordinary wealth of the city's ruling families during this period, so they certainly had a degree of real economic and political power. The dazzling armor and jewelry

uncovered by many other excavations also reveal a shift in Sumerian ideas about the afterlife, since they presuppose a belief that one could enjoy such goods in perpetuity.

Yet no Sumerian lugal was likely to be able to impose centralized rule on his city, much less to control the settlements that he conquered. As a result, Sumer remained a collection of interdependent but mutually suspicious and vulnerable states whose rulers were unable to forge any lasting structures of authority. This would ultimately make the people of Sumer vulnerable to a new style of rulership imposed on them from the north, in the person of Sargon the Akkadian.

## Sargon and the Akkadian Realm, 2350–2160 B.C.E.

The Akkadians were the predominant people of central Mesopotamia. Their Sumerian neighbors to the south had greatly influenced them, and they had adopted cuneiform script along with many other elements of Sumerian culture. Yet the Akkadians preserved their own Semitic language, part of the linguistic family that includes Hebrew, Arabic, Aramaic, Ethiopic, and Assyrian. Sumerians tended to regard the Akkadians as uncivilized, but they feared the ruler whom the Akkadians called "great king": Sargon. Indeed, Sargon's inscriptions suggest that he was ambitious to subject the cities of Sumer to his authority.

**OBJECTS FROM THE ROYAL TOMBS AT UR.** On the left is a helmet made from an alloy of gold and silver. Its cloth lining would have been attached through the holes visible around the edges of the helmet. On the right is a queen's headdress made of gold leaf, lapis lazuli, and carnelian.

The success of his efforts could not have matched these claims, but Sargon appears to have consolidated certain powers at his capital city, Akkad, by around 2350 B.C.E. He also appears to have installed Akkadian-speaking governors in the cities under his control, where they would collect tribute and work to impose his will. Sargon was thus attempting to knit the independent cities of Mesopotamia into a larger political unit: an empire, a word derived from the Latin *imperium*, "command." This would have enabled him to manage and exploit the network of trade routes crisscrossing the region and thus to extend his influence from Ethiopia to India.

Although Sargon's imperialism was probably aspirational rather than actual, it does seem to have had an effect on Sumerian religion and culture. Sargon attempted to merge the Akkadian and Sumerian divinities, so that, for example, the Akkadian fertility goddess Ishtar became identified with the Sumerian goddess Inanna. He also tried to lessen the rivalry of Sumerian cities by appointing a single Akkadian high priest or priestess, often a member of his own family, to preside over several temples. His own daughter Enheduanna (*en-he-doo-AH-nah*) was high priestess of both Uruk and Ur, and her hymns in honor of Ishtar/Inanna are the earliest surviving works by a named author in world history. The precedent she and her father established would continue even after the Sargonid dynasty finally fell: for several centuries thereafter, the kings of Sumer continued to appoint their daughters as high priestesses of Ur and Uruk. And by about 2200 B.C.E., most people in central and southern Mesopotamia would have been able to converse in the language of either the Sumerians or the Akkadians. Indeed, the two civilizations became virtually indistinguishable except for these different languages.

## The Dynasty of Ur and the Amorites, 2100–1800 B.C.E.

After the death of Sargon's son and heir, Naram-Sin, Akkadian rule in the region dissolved. Around 2100 B.C.E., however, a new dynasty came to power in Ur under a king called Ur-Nammu and his son Shulgi. Ur-Nammu was responsible for the construction of the great ziggurat at Ur, which originally rose 70 feet (over 21 m) above the surrounding plain, and for many other architectural marvels. Shulgi continued his father's work, raiding the lands up to the Zagros Mountains northeast of Ur and demanding massive tribute payments from them; one collection site accounted for 350,000 sheep per year. Shulgi then built state-run textile-production facilities to process the wool. He also promulgated a code of law, calling for fair weights and measures,

**THE ZIGGURAT OF UR.** Built around 2100 B.C.E., this great temple is the best-preserved structure of its kind. It is located at Nasiriyah, in what is now Iraq. Archaeological investigations (see diagram) reveal that its central shrine, the most sacred part of the temple, was reached by climbing four sets of stairs and passing through a massive portal.

the protection of widows and orphans, and limitations on the death penalty for crimes.

While there was no mechanism for actually enforcing this code, Shulgi's commercial expansion of his realm and his patronage of art and literature established a pattern that influenced other rulers in the region for centuries to come. It also influenced newcomers known as the Amorites, a Semitic people (like the Akkadians) who (unlike the Akkadians) had largely been nomads and warriors. But now, some Amorite leaders began to gain control of the ancient cities of Mesopotamia.

## The Empire of Hammurabi

In 1792 B.C.E., a young Amorite chieftain named Hammurabi (*hah-muh-RAH-bee*) became the ruler of Babylon, an insignificant city in central Mesopotamia. While Babylon was precariously wedged among a number of more powerful cities, its site on the Tigris and Euphrates had great potential. Hammurabi turned this situation to his advantage, recognizing that military intelligence, diplomacy, and strategic planning might accomplish what his small army could not. A rich archive of tablets found at the city of Mari (which eventually fell under his rule) testifies to his talents for the clever manipulation of his more powerful adversaries: for Hammurabi used writing itself as a weapon. He did not try to confront his mightier neighbors head on. Rather, through letters and embassies, double-dealing and cunning, he induced his stronger counterparts to fight each other. While other rulers exhausted their resources in costly wars, Hammurabi fanned their mutual hatred and skillfully portrayed himself as a friend and ally to all sides. Meanwhile, he quietly strengthened his kingdom, built up his army, and, when the time was right, fell on his depleted neighbors. By such policies, he transformed his small state into what historians call the Old Babylonian Empire.

Under Hammurabi's rule, Mesopotamia achieved a new degree of political integration that reached from the Persian Gulf into Assyria. The southern half of the region, formerly Sumer and Akkad, would henceforth be known as Babylonia. To help unify these territories, Hammurabi introduced another innovation, promoting the worship of the little-known patron god of Babylon, Marduk, and making him the ruler-god of his entire empire. Although he also paid homage to the ancient gods of Sumer and Akkad, Hammurabi made it clear that all his subjects now owed allegiance to Marduk.

The idea that political power derives from divine approval was nothing new, but Hammurabi's genius was to use Marduk's supremacy over all other gods to legitimate his own claim to rule, in Marduk's name, because he was king of Marduk's home city. Hammurabi thus became the first known ruler to launch wars of aggression justified in the name of his primary god. This set a precedent for colonial expansion that would become a characteristic feature of Western civilizations and that lies behind nearly all imperial ventures down to the present day.

Yet Hammurabi did not rely solely on religion to forge a kind of empire. Building on the precedents of past rulers, he also issued a collection of laws, copies of which were inscribed on stone and set up in public places throughout his realm. The example that survives is an eight-foot-tall *stele* (*STEH-leh*) made of gleaming black basalt, erected in the central marketplace of Babylon. The upper portion shows Hammurabi consulting with Shamash, the god of justice. The phallic form on which the laws were inscribed would have been immediately recognizable as a potent symbol of Hammurabi's authority, obvious even to those who could not read the laws themselves. (It still makes a strong impression on visitors to the Louvre museum in Paris.)

Hammurabi's decision to represent himself as a lawgiver was symbolically important—even if, like previous rulers, he had no effective mechanism for policing his state or enforcing these laws. By collecting and codifying legal precedents, Hammurabi declared himself to be (as he stated in the code's preamble) "the shepherd of the people, the capable king"—not a lugal ruling through fear and caprice. This was setting a new standard of kingship and expressing a new vision of empire as a union of peoples subject to the same laws.

## Law and Society in Hammurabi's Code

The Code of Hammurabi reveals a great deal about the structure and values of Babylonian society. The organization of its 282 pronouncements offers insight into the kinds of litigation that Hammurabi and his officials regularly handled and also suggests the relative importance of these cases. It begins with legislation against false testimony (fraud or lying under oath) and theft, followed by laws regulating business deals; laws regulating the use of public resources, especially water; laws relating to taverns and brothels, most of which appear to have been run by women; laws relating to debt and slavery; many laws dealing with marriage, inheritance, divorce, and widows' rights; and, finally, laws punishing murder, violent assault, and even medical malpractice. What emerges is a fascinating picture of a complex urban society that required more formal legislation than the accumulated customs of previous generations.

**WOMEN AND TEXTILES.** Women were the predominant producers of textiles throughout the ancient world. Even upper-class women were almost continuously engaged in spinning thread and weaving cloth for their households. Here, a servant fans an elegant lady at work with her spindle.

Most of these laws appear to be aimed at free commoners, who made up the bulk of the population. Above them was an aristocratic class, tied to the king's court and active in its bureaucracy, that controlled a great deal of the community's wealth: these were the palace officials, temple priests, high-ranking military officers, and rich merchants. Indeed, even legally free individuals were probably dependents of the palace or the temple in some way, or leased land from the estates of the powerful. They included laborers and artisans, small-scale merchants and farmers, and the minor political and religious officials. At the bottom of Babylonian society were the slaves, who were far more numerous than they had been in the older civilizations of Sumer or Akkad. Many, indeed, had become slaves not because of war but through trade: either sold as payment for debts or to the profit of a family with too many children, or because they had been forced to sell themselves on the open market. Others had been enslaved in punishment for certain offenses. Slaves in the Old Babylonian Empire were treated much more harshly than in previous civilizations and were more readily identifiable as a separate group: whereas free men in Babylonia wore long hair and beards, male slaves were shaved and branded.

The division among classes in this society was marked. As Hammurabi's code indicates, an offense committed against a nobleman carried a far more severe penalty than did the same crime committed against a social equal or against a dependent or slave; nobles were also punished more severely than were commoners for crimes they committed against other nobles. Marriage arrangements also reflected class differences, with bride-prices and dowries depending on the status of the parties involved. That said, Hammurabi's code also provides evidence as to the status of women in Babylonian society and shows that they enjoyed certain important protections under the law, including the right to divorce abusive or indigent husbands. If a husband divorced a wife "without cause," he was obliged to provide financial support for her and their children. However, a wife who went around the city defaming her spouse was subject to severe punishment. A woman would risk death, as would her lover, if she were caught in adultery. The sexual promiscuity of husbands, by contrast, was protected under the law.

## Hammurabi's Legacy

Hammurabi died around 1750 B.C.E. Although the imperial powers he had wielded were not sustainable, he had created a durable state. For another two centuries, Babylon continued to play a significant role in Mesopotamia until invaders from the north sacked the capital and occupied it. But even then, for another thousand years thereafter, Babylon remained the region's most famous city.

# The Code of Hammurabi

*The laws of Hammurabi, published on the authority of this powerful king and set up in central places throughout the Old Babylonian Empire, were influenced both by the needs of an urban society and by older ideas of justice and punishment common among Semitic peoples. In its entirety, the code comprises 282 laws, beginning and ending with statements of Hammurabi's devotion to the gods, his peacekeeping mission, and his sense of his duties as king. The following excerpts are numbered so as to show the order in which these provisions appear on the stele that publicizes them.*

 hen the god Marduk commanded me to provide just ways for the people of the land in order to attain appropriate behavior, I established truth and justice as the declaration of the land. I enhanced the well-being of the people.

\* \* \*

1. If a man accuses another man and charges him with homicide but cannot bring proof against him, his accuser shall be killed.

2. If a man charges another man with practicing witchcraft but cannot bring proof against him, he who is charged with witchcraft shall go to the divine River Ordeal, he shall indeed submit to the divine River Ordeal; if the divine River Ordeal should overwhelm him, his accuser shall take full legal possession of his estate; if the divine River Ordeal should clear that man and should he survive, he who made the charge of witchcraft against him shall be killed; he who submitted to the divine River Ordeal shall take full legal possession of his accuser's estate.

   If a man comes forward to give false testimony in a case but cannot bring evidence for his accusation, if that case involves a capital offense, that man shall be killed.

\* \* \*

6. If a man steals valuables belonging to the god or to the palace, that man shall be killed, and also he who received the stolen goods from him shall be killed.

7. If a man should purchase silver, gold, a slave, a slave woman, an ox, a sheep, a donkey, or anything else whatsoever, from a son of a man or from a slave of a man without witnesses or a contract—or if he accepts the goods for safekeeping—that man is a thief, he shall be killed.

8. If a man steals an ox, a sheep, a donkey, a pig, or a boat—if it belongs either to the god or to the palace, he shall give thirtyfold; if it belongs to a commoner, he shall replace it tenfold; if the thief does not have anything to give, he shall be killed.

\* \* \*

15. If a man should enable a palace slave, a palace slave woman, a commoner's slave, or a commoner's slave woman to leave through the main city-gate, he shall be killed.

\* \* \*

53. If a man neglects to reinforce the embankment of the irrigation canal of his field and then a breach opens and allows the water to carry away the common irrigated area, the man in whose embankment the breach opened shall replace the grain whose loss he caused.

\* \* \*

104. If a merchant gives a trading agent grain, wool, oil, or any other commodity for local transactions, the trading agent shall collect a sealed receipt for each payment in silver that he gives to the merchant.

\* \* \*

128. If a man marries a wife but does not draw up a formal contract for her, she is not a wife.

129. If a man's wife should be seized lying with another male, they shall bind them and throw them into the water; if the wife's master allows his wife to live, then the king shall allow his subject (i.e., the other male) to live.

\* \* \*

142. If a woman repudiates her husband, and declares, "You will not have marital relations with me"—her circumstances shall be investigated by the authorities of her city quarter, and if she is circumspect and without fault, but her husband is wayward and disparages her greatly, that woman will not be subject to any penalty; she shall take her dowry and she shall depart for her father's house.

Source: Martha T. Roth, ed., *Law Collections from Ancient Mesopotamia and Asia Minor* (Atlanta: 1995), pp. 76–135 (excerpted).

## Questions for Analysis

1. On the basis of these excerpts, what conclusions can you draw about the values of Old Babylonian society? For example, what types of crimes are punishable by death, and why?

2. In what ways does the Code of Hammurabi exhibit the influences of the urban civilization for which these laws were issued? What are some characteristics and consequences of urbanization? What, for example, do we learn about economic developments?

3. Examine the photographs of the stele preserving the code. What is the significance of the image that accompanies the laws, Hammurabi's conference with the enthroned god Shamash? What is the significance of the stele itself as the medium that conveyed these laws to the people?

---

Hammurabi's legacy also extended well beyond Babylonia, because he had shaped a new conception of kingship. After Hammurabi, unifying state religions became an increasingly important technique that kings used to annex and subjugate diverse territories and peoples. Hammurabi had also demonstrated the effectiveness of writing as a political tool. Diplomacy and the keeping of archives would be essential to all subsequent empires. So too would the claim that rulers should be the protectors of the weak and the arbiters of justice.

# THE DEVELOPMENT OF CIVILIZATION IN EGYPT

At about the same time that Sumerian civilization was transforming Mesopotamia, another civilization was taking shape in a different part of the world and in very different ways. Unlike the Sumerians, the Egyptians did not have to wrest survival from a hostile and unpredictable environment. Instead, their land was renewed every year by the flooding of the Nile River. The fertile black soil that was left behind every summer made theirs the richest agricultural region in the entire Mediterranean world.

The distinctiveness of Egyptian civilization rests on this fundamental ecological fact. It also explains why ancient Egypt was a narrow, elongated kingdom, running along the Nile north from the First Cataract (a series of rocks and rapids near the ancient city of Elephantine) toward the Mediterranean Sea for a distance of more than 600 miles (1,100 km). Outside this narrow band of territory—which ranged from a few hundred yards to 14 miles (23 km) at the widest—lay uninhabitable desert. This contrast between the fertile Black Land along the Nile and the dessicated Red Land beyond deeply influenced the Egyptian worldview, in which the Nile itself was the center of the cosmos and the lands beyond were hostile and beyond the pale of habitation.

In many respects, ancient Egyptian civilization enjoyed a remarkable continuity. Its roots date back to 5000 B.C.E. at least, and Egypt continued to thrive as an independent and distinctive entity even after it was conquered by Alexander the Great in 331 B.C.E. (see Chapter 4), until its assimilation into the Roman Empire after 30 B.C.E. (see Chapter 5). From about 3000 B.C.E., the defining element of this civilization would be the pervasive influence of a powerful, centralized, bureaucratic state headed by pharaohs (FARE-ohs) who were regarded as living gods. No other civilization in world history has ever been governed so steadily, for so long, as ancient Egypt.

For convenience, historians have traditionally divided ancient Egyptian history into distinctive "kingdoms" and "periods." Following ancient Egyptian chroniclers, modern historians have also tended to portray these Old, Middle, and New Kingdoms as characterized by unity and prosperity, punctuated by chaotic interludes, the so-called Intermediate Periods, when central authority broke down. Like all attempts at periodization, these divisions do not capture the complexities of human experience or even the real pace of historical development. In essence, this periodization still reflects the conservative perspective of the ancient Egyptian state, which prized continuity and feared change. As we will see, though, the First Intermediate Period in particular looks like a positive development if viewed from the perspective of individual communities and commoners, rather than from the viewpoint of the pharaoh's court.

## Predynastic Egypt, c. 10,000–3100 B.C.E.

The term *Predynastic Egypt* refers to the period before the emergence of the pharaohs and their royal dynasties, an era for which archaeological evidence is difficult to find and interpret. Many predynastic settlements were destroyed long ago by the waters of the Nile and are now buried under innumerable layers of silt. Furthermore, the very abundance of naturally occurring foodstuffs in the Nile Valley made the need for settlement and cultivation less pressing than in the Fertile Crescent, where (as we have seen) Mesopotamian peoples were already living together in villages during the eighth millennium B.C.E. In Egypt, by contrast, a growing population was able to sustain itself by hunting and gathering until the fifth millennium B.C.E.

The first known permanent settlement in Egypt, situated at the southwestern edge of the Nile Delta (near the modern town of Merimde Beni Salama), dates to approximately 4750 B.C.E. It was a farming community that may have numbered as many as 16,000 residents, and this number (based on burial remains) suggests that some Egyptian communities were much larger than those of a comparable period in Mesopotamia. Thereafter, evidence shows that the Egyptian economy rapidly became more diversified: by around 3500 B.C.E. the residents of Ma'adi, three miles away from Merimde Beni Salama (see map on page 23), had extensive commercial contacts with the Sinai Peninsula, the eastern Mediterranean, and the upper reaches of the Nile some several hundred miles to the south. Copper was a particularly vital import, since it enabled residents to replace stone tools with metal ones.

Many other Neolithic farming centers have also been discovered in or near the Nile Delta, where a degree of cultural cohesiveness was already developing, fostered by shared interests and trade. In later centuries, this northern area would be known as Lower Egypt, so called because it was downstream. Comparable developments were also occurring upstream. By the end of this Predynastic Period, Egyptian culture was more or less uniform from the southern edge of the delta to the First Cataract, a vast length of the Nile known as Upper Egypt.

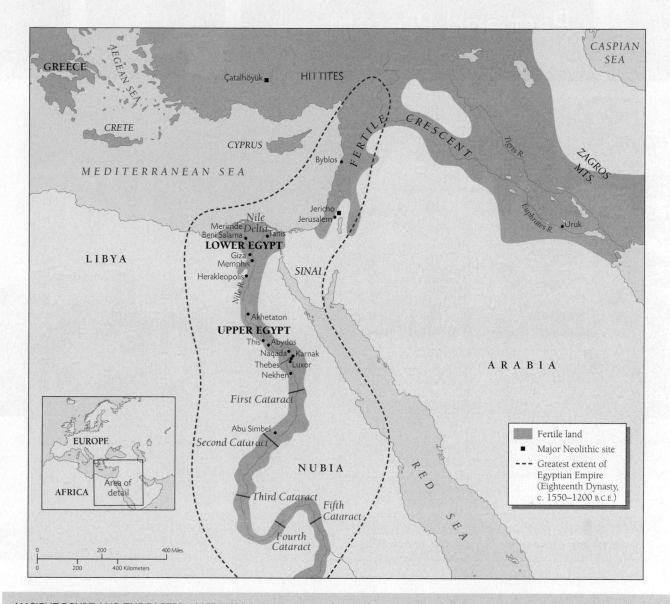

**ANCIENT EGYPT AND THE EASTERN MEDITERRANEAN.** Notice the peculiar geography of ancient Egypt and the role played by the Nile River. Identify the Nile on the map. ▪ *In what direction does the Nile flow?* ▪ *How did the lands on either side help to isolate Egyptian culture from outside influences?* ▪ *Consider how the Nile helped forge Egypt into a unitary state under a powerful centralized government. Yet how might Egypt's relationship to the Nile be potentially hazardous as well as beneficial?*

Although towns in Lower Egypt were more numerous, it was in Upper Egypt that the first Egyptian cities developed. By 3200 B.C.E.—when the Sumerian city of Uruk had been thriving for a thousand years—important communities such as Nekhen, Naqada, This, and Abydos had all developed high degrees of occupational and social specialization. They had encircled themselves with sophisticated fortifications and had begun to build elaborate shrines to honor their gods. Indeed, the establishment of permanent sites of public worship may be key to explaining the growth

of these towns into cities. As in Mesopotamia, a city's role as the center of a prominent religious cult attracted travelers and encouraged the growth of industries. And travel in Upper Egypt was relatively easy compared with travel in Mesopotamia. The Nile bound cities together, and the lack of competition for resources fostered peace.

It was due to the Nile, therefore, that the region south of the delta was able to forge a cultural and eventually a political unity, despite its enormous length. The Nile fed Egypt and was a conduit for people, goods, and ideas.

*The Development of Civilization in Egypt* | 23

## Engineering Nature

Humans have been manipulating our planet's environment since the Neolithic Revolution. The image on the left shows the irrigation canals that enabled ancient Egyptians to channel the Nile's life-giving waters into the desert. The image on the right shows a storm-surge barrier in the Netherlands, which protects reclaimed land from rising sea levels produced by the cumulative results of human-caused climate change.

 **Watch related author interview on the Student Site**

Centralizing rulers could project their power quickly and effectively up and down its course. Within a remarkably short time, just a century or two after the first cities' appearance in Upper Egypt, they had banded together in a confederacy under the leadership of the city of This. The pressure exerted by this confederacy in turn forced the towns of Lower Egypt to adopt their own form of political organization. By 3100 B.C.E., the rivalry between these competing regions had given rise to the two nascent kingdoms of Upper and Lower Egypt.

## The Power of the Pharaoh, c. 3100–c. 2686 B.C.E.

With the rise of powerful rulers in these two kingdoms, Egyptian history enters a new phase, one that can be

chronicled with unusual precision. The system for numbering the ruling dynasties that emerged in this era—known as the Archaic Period—was actually devised nearly 3,000 years later by an historian named Manetho (*mahn-EH-thoh*), who wrote in the third century B.C.E. By and large, Manetho's work has withstood the scrutiny of modern historians and archaeologists, although recent research has added a "Zero Dynasty" of early kings who were instrumental in bringing about the initial unification of Egypt.

Manetho did not record these rulers because he didn't know about them; we know them almost exclusively from archaeological evidence. Among them was an Upper Egyptian warlord known to us as King Scorpion, because the image of a scorpion accompanies engravings that assert his authority over most of Egypt. Another warlord, King Narmer, appears to have ruled both Upper and Lower Egypt. His exploits, too, come down to us in powerful pictures (see *Interpreting Visual Evidence* on page 26). Both of these kings probably came from Abydos in Upper Egypt, where they were later buried. Their administrative capital, however, was at Memphis, the capital city of Lower Egypt and an important center for trade with the Sinai Peninsula and the wider region.

Following the political unification of Upper and Lower Egypt, the basic features of Egypt's distinctive centralized kingship took shape along lines that would persist for the next 3,000 years, down to Manetho's own day. The title used to describe this kingship was *pharaoh*, a word that actually means "great household" and thus refers not only to an individual king but to the whole apparatus that sustained his rule. This fact, in turn, helps to explain the extraordinary stability and longevity of Egyptian civilization, which survived even a dynastic takeover by Macedonian Greeks in the century before Manetho wrote his chronicle. Indeed, it is comparable to some modern forms of government—none of which has yet lasted nearly so long. As we have seen, kingship in Mesopotamia tended to be a form of personal rule, dependent on the charisma of a particular individual; the empires of Sargon and Ur-Nammu scarcely survived another generation or two after their deaths. But in Egypt, the office of the pharaoh was durable enough to survive the deaths of many individual successors, facilitating the peaceful transition of power to new rulers and withstanding the incompetence of many.

This was accomplished, as we shall see, by the efficiency of palace bureaucracy, but it was also a function of the pharaoh's close identification with the divine forces credited with renewing Egypt every year. Like the seasons, the pharaoh died only to be born again, renewed and empowered. Egyptian rulers thus laid claim to a sacred nature quite different—and much more benign—than that governing Sumeria. And they were more powerful than any Sumerian lugal, who was never more than a mortal who enjoyed (all too temporary) divine favor.

How the earliest kings of Egypt came to be distinguished as pharaohs and to establish their claims to divinity is still not well understood. We do know, however, that legitimating their rule over Egypt was difficult. Local civic and religious loyalties remained strong, and for centuries Lower Egyptians continued to see themselves as distinct in some respects from their neighbors to the south. Efforts to create a united Egyptian state began very early, however, as the Narmer Palette may indicate. Indeed, it seems probable that the centralization of government in the person of the pharaoh, and his association with divinity, were related approaches to solving the problem of political unity. Together, they had astonishing success. By the end of the Second Dynasty, which coincides with the end of the Archaic or Early Dynastic Period (2686 B.C.E.), the pharaoh was not just the ruler of Egypt, he *was* Egypt: a personification of the land, the people, and their gods.

## The Old Kingdom, c. 2686–2160 B.C.E.

Because so few written documents of the Old Kingdom survive, historians have to rely on surviving funerary texts from the tombs of the elite in order to reconstruct the achievements of particular individuals. These sources are hardly representative, and they have tended to convey the impression that Egyptians were obsessed with death; they also tell us little about the lives of ordinary people. Further complicating the historian's task is the early Egyptians' own belief in the unchanging, cyclical nature of the universe. During this early period, there appears to have been little interest in maintaining a record of key events arranged in chronological order. This makes it difficult for us to reconstruct ancient Egyptian history in detail.

However, the surviving inscriptions, papyri, and art of the Third Dynasty (c. 2686–2613 B.C.E.) do tell us a great deal about the workings of the "great household" that undergirded individual rulers' power. This power was vast because the pharaoh, as the embodiment of Egypt, was considered to be the intermediary among the land, its people, and their gods. Hence, all the resources of Egypt belonged to him. Long-distance trade was entirely controlled by the pharaoh, as were systems for imposing taxation and conscripting labor. To administer these, the pharaohs installed provincial governors, known to the Greeks as *nomarchs*, many of whom were members of the pharaoh's own family.

Old Kingdom pharaohs kept tight control over the nomarchs and their armies of lesser officials, in order to prevent them from establishing local roots in the territories they administered. Writing was therefore critical to internal communication and the management and exploitation of Egypt's vast wealth. This gave rise to a whole class of scribal administrators who enjoyed the power, influence, and status that went along with literacy, a skill few people could command—especially in Egypt, since few could master the intricate writing system (see below). Even a child just beginning his scribal education was considered worthy of great respect because the training was so difficult. But it carried great rewards. Indeed, the scribal author of a document from the Middle Kingdom called "The Satire of the Trades" exhorted the beginning student to persevere by reminding him how much better off he would be than everyone else.

## The Narmer Palette

T he Narmer Palette (c. 3100 B.C.E.) is a double-sided carving made of green siltstone. Palettes were used to grind pigments for the making of cosmetics, but the large size (63 cm; over 2 feet) of this one is unusual. It was discovered in 1897 by archaeologists excavating a temple dedicated to the god Horus at Nekhen, the capital of Upper Egypt. Found nearby were other artifacts, including the so-called Narmer Macehead, thought to depict the marriage of Narmer, king of Upper Egypt, to a princess of Lower Egypt.

On the left, dominating the central panel, Narmer wears the White Crown of Upper Egypt (image A). He wields a mace and seizes the hair of a captive kneeling at his feet. Above the captive's head is a cluster of lotus leaves (a symbol of Lower Egypt) and a falcon representing the god Horus, who may be drawing the captive's life force (*ka*) from his body. The figure behind Narmer is carrying the king's sandals; he is depicted as smaller because he is an inferior. The two men in the lower panel are either running or sprawling on the ground, and the symbols above them indicate the name of a defeated town. On the right, the other side of the palette shows Narmer as the chief figure in a procession (image B). He now wears the Red

A. Narmer wearing the White Crown of Egypt.

B. Narmer wearing the Red Crown of Egypt.

Crown of Lower Egypt and holds a mace and a flail, symbols of conquest. Behind him is the same servant carrying his sandals, and in front of him are a man with long hair and four standard-bearers. There are also ten headless corpses. Below, the entwined necks of two mythical creatures (serpopards, leopards with serpents' heads) are tethered to leashes held by two men. In the lowest section, a bull tramples the body of a man whose city Narmer is destroying.

### Questions for Analysis

**1.** This artifact has been called "the first historical document in the world," but

scholars are still debating its meanings. For example, does it represent something that actually happened? Or is it political propaganda? In your view, is this proof that Narmer has united the two kingdoms? Why or why not?

**2.** Do the two sides of the palette tell a coherent story? If so, on which side does that story begin?

**3.** What might be significant about the site where the palette was found? Should the palette be interpreted as belonging with the mace, found nearby? If so, how might that change your interpretation of the palette's significance?

## The Power of Writing

Among the many facets of Egyptian culture that have fascinated generations of scholars is the Egyptian system of pictographic writing. Called *hieroglyphs* (*HI-eroh-glifs*) or "sacred carvings" by the Greeks, these strange and elaborate symbols remained completely impenetrable and mysterious to modern scholars until the nineteenth century, when a Frenchman named Jean François Champollion deciphered them with the help of history's most famous decoding device, the Rosetta Stone. This stele preserves three versions of the same decree issued by one of the Ptolemaic rulers of Egypt in 196 B.C.E. (see Chapter 3), written in ancient Greek, demotic (a later Egyptian script), and hieroglyphics—still in use after more than 3,000 years. Because he could read the text in Greek, Champollion was eventually able to translate the demotic and hieroglyphic texts as well. From this beginning, generations of scholars have added to and refined our knowledge of the ancient Egyptian language.

The development of hieroglyphic writing in Egypt dates to around 3200 B.C.E., about the time when pictograms began to appear in Mesopotamia. But the two scripts are so different that they probably developed independently, and the uses of writing for government and administration certainly developed far more quickly in Egypt than in Sumer. But unlike Sumerian cuneiform, Egyptian hieroglyphics never evolved into a system of phonograms. Instead, the Egyptians developed a faster, cursive script for representing hieroglyphics, called *hieratic*, which they employed for the everyday business of government and commerce. They also developed a shorthand version of hieratic that scribes could use for rapid note taking. Little of this hieratic script remains, however, owing to the perishable nature of the medium on which it was usually written: papyrus. Produced by hammering, drying, and processing river reeds, papyrus was much lighter, easier to write on, and more transportable than the clay tablets the Sumerians used. When sewn together into scrolls, papyrus also made it possible to record and store large quantities of information in very small packages. Production of this versatile writing material remained one of Egypt's most important industries and exports throughout antiquity and into the Middle Ages. Yet even in the arid environment of Egypt, which has preserved so many ancient artifacts that would have perished in wetter, colder climates, papyrus is fragile and subject to decay. Compared with the huge volume of papryrus documents that would have been produced, therefore, the quantity that survives is small, and this significantly limits our understanding of Old Kingdom Egypt.

The origins of the ancient Egyptian language in which these texts were written has long been a matter of debate. It can be plausibly linked to both the Semitic languages

**THE ROSETTA STONE.** This famous stone, carved in 196 B.C.E., preserves three translations of a single decree in three different forms of writing: hieroglyphs (top), demotic Egyptian (middle), and classical Greek (bottom). ■ *Why would scholars be able to use the classical Greek text to decipher the hieroglyphic and demotic scripts?*

**EGYPTIAN WRITING.** Egyptian scribes used a variety of scripts: hieroglyphics for inscriptions and religious texts (top row), a cursive hieratic script for administrative documents (middle row), and a more informal shorthand for note taking (bottom row). ■ *What are the relationships among these three forms of writing?*

of western Asia and a number of African language groups. Some historical linguists have postulated that early Egyptian might represent the survival of a root language from which the other languages of the Afro-Asiatic group evolved. The movements of people through the Nile Valley makes this theory a distinct possibility. Whatever its origins, the Egyptian language has enjoyed a long history. Eventually, it became the tongue known as Coptic, which is still used today in the liturgy of the Coptic Christian church, in Ethiopia.

## Imhotep and the Step Pyramid

One of the greatest administrative officials in the history of Egypt exemplifies both the skills and the possibilities for advancement that the consummate scribe could command. Imhotep (*im-HO-tep*) rose through the ranks of the pharaoh's administration to become a sort of prime minister, the right-hand man to Djoser (*ZOH-ser*), a pharaoh of the Third Dynasty (c. 2686–2613 B.C.E.). Imhotep's expertise embraced medicine, astronomy, theology, and mathematics; but above all, he was an architect. Earlier pharaohs had already devoted enormous resources to their burial arrangements at Abydos. It was Imhotep, however, who designed the Step Pyramid, the first extant building in history constructed entirely of dressed stone. It was not only to be the final resting place of Djoser but an expression of his transcendent power as pharaoh.

Built west of the administrative capital at Memphis, the Step Pyramid towers over the desert to a height of 200 feet (61 m). Its design was based on an older form of burial monument, the *mastaba*, a low rectangular structure built entirely of brick with a flat top and sloping sides. Imhotep probably began with the mastaba pattern in mind, but he radically altered it by stacking one smaller mastaba on top of another and constructing each entirely of limestone. Surrounding this structure was a huge temple and mortuary complex, perhaps modeled after Djoser's palace. These buildings served two purposes. First and foremost, they would provide Djoser's *ka*, his spirit or life force, with a habitation and sustenance in the afterlife. Second, the design of the buildings, with their immovable doors and labyrinthine passageways, would (it was hoped) thwart tomb robbers, a chronic problem as pharaonic burials became more elaborate and more tempting to thieves.

Imhotep set a precedent to which all other Old Kingdom pharaohs would aspire. The pyramids on the plain of Giza, built during the Fourth Dynasty (2613–2494 B.C.E.), are a case in point. The Great Pyramid itself, built for the

**STEP PYRAMID OF PHARAOH DJOSER.** This monument to the pharaoh's power and divinity was designed by the palace official Imhotep around 2650 B.C.E.

pharaoh Khufu (*KOO-foo*; called Cheops by the Greeks), was originally 481 feet high and 756 feet along each side of its base (147 by 235 meters), constructed from more than 2.3 million limestone blocks and enclosing a volume of about 91 million cubic feet (28 million cubic meters). In ancient times, the entire pyramid was encased in gleaming white limestone and topped by a gilded capstone, as were the two massive but slightly smaller pyramids built for Khufu's successors. During the Middle Ages, the Muslim rulers of nearby Cairo had their builders strip off the pyramid's casing stones and used them to construct and fortify their new city. (The gold capstones had probably disappeared already.) But in antiquity these pyramids would have glistened brilliantly by day and glowed by night, making them visible for miles in all directions. The Greek historian Herodotus (*heh-RAH-duh-tuhs*), who toured Egypt more than 2,000 years after the pyramids were built, estimated that it must have taken 100,000 laborers twenty years to build the Great Pyramid. This is probably an exaggeration, but it is a measure of the impression these monuments made.

Once thought to have been the work of slaves, the pyramids were in fact raised by tens of thousands of peasant workers, who labored most intensively on the pyramids while their fields were under water during the Nile's annual flood. Some workers may have been conscripts, but most probably participated willingly, since these projects glorified the living god who served as their link to the cosmic order. Still, the investment of human and material resources required to build the great pyramids put strains on Egyptian society. Control over the lives of individual Egyptians increased, and the number of administrative officials employed by the state grew ever larger. So too did the contrast between the lifestyle of the pharaoh's splendid

**PYRAMIDS AT GIZA.** The Great Pyramid of Khufu (Cheops), in the center, was completed c. 2560 B.C.E.

court at Memphis and that of Egyptian society as a whole. At the same time, a gap was opening between the pretensions of the pharaohs and the continuing loyalties of Egyptians to their local gods and local leaders.

## The End of the Old Kingdom

For reasons that are not entirely clear, the Fifth and Sixth Dynasties of the Old Kingdom (2494–2181 B.C.E.) witnessed the slow erosion of pharaonic power. Although pyramid construction continued, the monuments of this period are less impressive in design, craftsmanship, and size, perhaps mirroring the diminishing prestige of the pharaohs who ordered them built. Instead, the priesthood of Ra at Nekhen, which was the center of worship for the god Horus and the place where Narmer's unification of Egypt was memorialized, began to assert its own authority over that of the pharaoh. Ultimately, it declared that the pharaoh was not an incarnation of Horus or Ra, but merely the god's earthly son. This was a blow to the heart of the pharaoh's political theology. A more practical threat was the growing power of the pharaoh's nomarchs, whose increased authority in the provinces allowed them to become a hereditary local nobility: precisely what the vigorous kings of earlier dynasties had refused to permit. These nobles became so influential that one Sixth Dynasty pharaoh, Pepy I, even married into their ranks.

Scholars are uncertain as to how certain priests and local officials were able to take power away from the pharaonic center. It may be that the extraordinarily costly building efforts of the Fourth Dynasty had overtaxed the economy while the continued channeling of resources to the royal capital at Memphis increased shortages and resentments in the provinces. Other evidence points to changing climatic conditions that may have disrupted the regular inundations of the Nile, leading to famine in the countryside. Meanwhile, small states were beginning to form to the south in Nubia, perhaps in response to Egyptian aggression. With better organization and equipment, the Nubians may have restricted Egyptian access to precious-metal deposits in and around the First Cataract, further crippling the Egyptian economy.

As a result of these developments, the pharaoh's power diminished. Local governors and religious authorities began to emerge as the only effective guarantors of stability and order. By 2160 B.C.E., which marks the beginning of what historians call the First Intermediate Period, Egypt had effectively ceased to exist as a unified entity. The central authority of the pharaoh in Memphis collapsed, and a more ancient distribution of power reemerged: a northern center of influence based at Herakleopolis was opposed by a southern regime headquartered at Thebes, with families from each region claiming to be the legitimate pharaohs of all Egypt.

Compared with the centralized authority of the Old Kingdom, this looks like chaos. But redistribution of power always leads to the opening of new opportunities in any society. In Egypt, wealth became much more widely and evenly distributed than it had been, as did access to education, means for the creation of art, and possibilities for personal advancement. Resources that the pharaoh's court at Memphis had once monopolized now remained in the provinces, enabling local elites to emerge as both protectors of society and as patrons of local artisans. The result was a much wider and more rapid dispersal of cultural forms and goods throughout Egyptian society than had been possible under the old regime. Many of these arts and luxuries—including elaborate rites for the dead—had been developed originally at the pharaoh's court and limited to it. Now, however, they became available to Egyptian society at large.

## EGYPTIAN CULTURE AND SOCIETY

As we noted above, the unique environment of Egypt and the special benefits it conferred on its inhabitants were construed as divine gifts, renewed each year through the mediation of the pharaoh. From what we can discern, this meant that Egyptians saw themselves as superior to all other civilizations. A person was either an Egyptian or a foreigner, and the lines between the two were absolute. For

Egyptians, it was simply self-evident that their country—nurtured by the Nile and guarded by the deserts and seas that surrounded it—was the center of the universe.

## Religion and Worldview

Although the Egyptians told a variety of stories that dealt with the creation of their world, these were not greatly concerned with how humanity came to exist. Rather, what mattered was the means by which all life was created and re-created in an endless cycle of renewal. Unlike the peoples of Mesopotamia, who were constantly faced with new and terrible challenges, both environmental and political, the Egyptians experienced existence as predictably repetitive, and this was mirrored in their perception of the cosmos. At the heart of Egyptian religion lay the myth of the gods Osiris and Isis, not only brother and sister but husband and wife, two of the gods most fundamental to Egyptian belief. Osiris was, in a sense, the first pharaoh: the first god to hold kingship on earth.

His brother Seth, however, wanted the throne for himself. So Seth betrayed and killed Osiris, sealing his body in a coffin. But their loyal sister Isis retrieved the corpse and managed to revive it long enough to conceive her brother's child, the god Horus. Enraged by this, Seth seized Osiris's body and hacked it to pieces, spreading the remains all over Egypt. (All of Egypt could therefore claim to be part of Osiris, a belief witnessed by shrines dedicated to him throughout the land.) Still undeterred, Isis sought the help of Anubis, the god of the afterlife. Together, they found, reassembled, and preserved the scattered portions of Osiris's body, thus inventing the practice of mummification. Then Horus, with the help of his mother, managed to defeat Seth. Osiris was avenged and revived as god of the underworld. Like Egypt itself, he could not be killed, and the cycle of his death, dismemberment, and resurrection was reflected in the yearly renewal of life along the Nile.

## Life and Death in Ancient Egypt

In addition to embodying Egypt's continual regeneration, Osiris exemplified the Egyptian attitude toward death, which was very different from the Sumerians' rather bleak view. For the Egyptians, death was a rite of passage, a journey to be endured on the way to an afterlife that was more or less like one's earthly existence, only much better. To be sure, the journey was full of dangers. After death, the individual body's ka had to roam the Duat, the underworld, searching for the House of Judgment. There, Osiris and

**PHARAOH MENKAURE AND HIS QUEEN, KHAMERERNEBTY II.** A sculpture from the Fourth Dynasty, c. 2500 b.c.e., shows this queen as her husband's royal partner.

forty-two other judges would decide the ka's fate. Demons and evil spirits might try to frustrate the ka's quest to reach the House of Judgment, and the journey might take some time. But if successful and judged worthy, the deceased would enjoy immortality as an aspect of Osiris.

Egyptian funerary rites aimed to emulate the example set by Isis and Anubis, who had carefully preserved the parts of Osiris's body and enabled his afterlife. This is why the Egyptians developed their sophisticated techniques of embalming, whereby many of the body's vital organs were removed and then treated with chemicals—except for the heart, which played a key role in the ka's final judgment. A portrait mask was then placed on the mummy before burial, so that the deceased would be recognizable despite being wrapped in hundreds of yards of linen. To sustain the ka on his or her journey, food, clothing, utensils, weapons, and other items of vital importance would be placed in the grave along with the body.

## The Instruction of Ptah-Hotep

*Egyptian literature often took the form of "instructions" to or from important personages, offering advice to those in public life. This document declares itself to be the advice of a high-ranking official of the Old Kingdom to his son and successor, perhaps composed around 2450 B.C.E. However, the earliest surviving text dates from the Middle Kingdom period.*

Be not arrogant because of your knowledge, and be not puffed up because you are a learned man. Take counsel with the ignorant as with the learned, for the limits of art cannot be reached, and no artist is perfect in his skills. Good speech is more hidden than the precious greenstone, and yet it is found among slave girls at the millstones.

. . . If you are a leader commanding the conduct of many seek out every good aim, so that your policy may be without error. A great thing is *ma'at*, enduring and surviving; it has not been upset since the time of Osiris. He who departs from its laws is punished. It is the right path for him who knows nothing. Wrongdoing has never brought its venture safe to port. Evil may win riches, but it is the strength of *ma'at* that endures long, and a man can say, "I learned it from my father." . . . If you wish to prolong friendship in a house which you enter as master, brother, or friend, or anyplace that you enter, beware of approaching the women. No place in which that is done prospers. There is no wisdom in it.

A thousand men are turned aside from their own good because of a little moment, like a dream, by tasting which death is reached. . . . He who lusts after women, no plan of his will succeed. . . . If you are a worthy man sitting in the council of his lord, confine your attention to excellence. Silence is more valuable than chatter. Speak only when you know you can resolve difficulties. He who gives good counsel is an artist, for speech is more difficult than any craft.

Source: Nels M. Bailkey, ed., *Readings in Ancient History: Thought and Experience from Gilgamesh to St. Augustine*, 5th ed. (Boston: 1995), pp. 39–42.

### Questions for Analysis

1. According to Ptah-Hotep, what are the most important attributes of a man engaged in public life? What are the most dangerous pitfalls and temptations he will encounter?

2. Why does Ptah-Hotep emphasize the importance of acting in accordance with *ma'at*? How does this idea of *ma'at* compare with that in the "Prophecies of Neferty" (see page 35)?

3. Recall what you have learned about the changes in Egyptian politics and society. What might indicate that Ptah-Hotep lived during the prosperous Fifth Dynasty of the Old Kingdom? How might these instructions have resonated differently with later readers of the Middle Kingdom?

---

"Coffin texts," or books of the dead, also accompanied the body and were designed to speed the ka's journey. They contained special instructions, including magic spells and ritual incantations, that would help the ka travel through the underworld and prepare it for the final test. They also described the "negative confession" the ka would make before the court of Osiris, a formal denial of offenses committed in life. The god Anubis would then weigh the deceased's heart against the principle of *ma'at*: truth, order, justice. Because *ma'at* was often envisioned as a goddess wearing a plumed headdress, a feather from this headdress would be placed in the scales, along with the heart, at the time of judgment; only if the heart was light (empty of wrongdoing) and in perfect balance with the feather would the ka achieve immortality.

Throughout the era of the Old Kingdom, the privilege of undergoing these preparations (and thus of ensuring immortality) was reserved for the royal family alone. By the time of the Middle Kingdom, however, it was becoming possible for many Egyptians to ensure that their bodies would participate in these rituals, too.

As noted above, this careful manner of confronting death has often led to the erroneous assumption that ancient Egyptians were pessimistic, but in actuality their practices and beliefs were inherently life-affirming, bolstered by confidence in the resilience of nature and the

**FUNERARY PAPYRUS.** This scene, inscribed on a papyrus scroll dating from the Thirtieth Dynasty (380–343 B.C.), shows the heart of the princess for whom this book was prepared being weighed in a balance (left) before the god Osiris. On the other side of the balance (right) are the symbols for life (the *ankh*) and the feather of the goddess Ma'at.

renewal of creation. Binding together this endless cycle was *ma'at*, the serene order of the universe with which the individual must remain in harmony, and against which each person's ka would be weighed after death. And embodying *ma'at* on earth was the pharaoh, the earthly manifestation of all gods. For most of the third millennium, thanks to a long period of successful harvests and peace guaranteed by Egypt's geographic isolation from the outside world, the Egyptians were able to maintain their belief in this perfectly ordered paradise and the pharaoh that ensured it. But when that order broke down, so too did their confidence in the pharaoh's power.

## Egyptian Science

Given the powerful impression conveyed by their monumental architecture, it may seem surprising that the ancient Egyptians lagged far behind the Sumerians and Akkadians in science and mathematics, as well as in the application of new technologies. Only in the calculation of time did the Egyptians make notable advances, because their close observation of the sun for religious and agricultural reasons led them to develop a solar calendar that was far more accurate than the Mesopotamian lunar calendar. Whereas the Sumerians have bequeathed to us their means of dividing and measuring the day, the Egyptian calendar is the direct ancestor of the Julian calendar adopted for Rome by Julius Caesar in 45 B.C.E. (see Chapter 5) and later corrected by Pope Gregory XIII in 1582 C.E.: this is the calendar we use today. The Egyptians also devised some effective irrigation and water-control systems, but they did not adopt such labor-saving devices as the wheel until much later than the Sumerians, perhaps because the available pool of peasant manpower was virtually inexhaustible, so that the necessity for such innovations was not pressing.

## The Social Pyramid

The social pyramid of Old Kingdom Egypt was extremely steep. At its apex stood the pharaoh and his extended family, whose prestige and power set them entirely apart from all other Egyptians. Below them was a class of nobles, whose primary role was to serve as priests and officials of the pharaoh's government; scribes were usually recruited and trained from among the sons of these families. All of these Egyptian elites lived in considerable luxury. They owned extensive estates, exotic possessions, and fine furniture. They kept dogs and cats and monkeys as pets, and hunted and fished for sport.

Beneath this tiny minority was everyone else. Most Egyptians lived in crowded conditions in simple mud-brick dwellings. During a period of prosperity, master craftsmen—jewelers, goldsmiths, and the like—could improve their own conditions and those of their families by fulfilling the needs of the wealthy, but they did not constitute anything like a middle class. Other skilled professionals— potters, weavers, masons, bricklayers, brewers, merchants, and schoolteachers—also enjoyed some measure of respect as well as a higher standard of living. The vast majority of Egyptians, however, were peasants who provided the labor for agriculture and construction. Beneath them were slaves, typically captives from foreign wars rather than native Egyptians.

Yet despite the enormous demands the pharaohs placed on Egypt's wealth, this Egyptian social hierarchy does not appear to have been particularly oppressive. Commoners' belief in the pharaoh's divinity made them willing subjects, as did the material benefits of living in a stable, well-governed society. Even slaves had certain legal rights, including the ability to own, sell, and bequeath personal property.

Unfortunately, though, the written laws and other documentary practices produced by the lugals of Mesopotamia do not have any Old Kingdom parallels. The Egyptians of this era apparently had no need for written laws beyond what was customary in their communities or what was proclaimed as law by their pharaoh. This makes it difficult for historians to reconstruct their lives in any detail.

## The Status of Women

Despite the absence of formal law codes, there is evidence that Egyptian women enjoyed unusual freedoms by the standards of the ancient world. Female commoners were recognized as persons in their own right and were allowed to initiate lawsuits (including suits for divorce), to defend themselves and act as witnesses, to possess property of their own, and to dispose of it: all without the sanction of a male guardian or representative, as was typically required in other ancient societies—and in most modern ones until the twentieth century. Women were not allowed to undergo formal scribal training, but surviving personal notes exchanged between high-born ladies suggest that some could read and even write.

Normally, women were barred from holding high office, apart from that of priestess and also, more important, queen. Indeed, queens are often represented as the partners of their royal husbands and were certainly instrumental in ruling alongside them: note the proud, confident bearing of Queen Khamerernebty II (*kah-mehr-en-EB-tee*; see image on page 30). And occasionally, a woman from the royal family might assume pharaonic authority for a time, as did Queen Khasekhemwy (*kah-sehk-KEM-wee*; d. 2686 B.C.E.) on behalf of her son Djoser before he came of age. Some women may even have ruled in their own right; this was certainly the case during the New Kingdom (see Chapter 2).

**FOOD FOR THE JOURNEY OF THE KA.** These wooden models show peasants plowing, grinding grain, baking bread, brewing beer, and slaughtering a steer. Bread and beer were the staple foods of ancient Egypt; beef was too expensive for ordinary consumption, but cattle were frequently sacrificed as funeral offerings. Such models were placed in Middle Kingdom tombs to provide food for the afterlife.

Among the peasantry, gender divisions were less clearly defined. Peasant women often worked in the fields during the harvest alongside men and carried out a number of vital tasks in the community. The limitations of our sources, however, mean that we can only glimpse the lives of these people through the eyes of their social superiors. Whatever their status, it seems that women did not enjoy sexual equality. Although most Egyptians practiced monogamy, wealthy men could and did keep a number of lesser wives, concubines, and female slaves; and any Egyptian man, married or not, enjoyed freedoms that were denied to women, who were subject to severe punishments under the law if they were viewed as guilty of any misconduct.

## The Widening Horizons of the Middle Kingdom, 2055–c. 1650 B.C.E.

After the disruption of Old Kingdom authority around 2160 B.C.E., warfare between two competing pharaonic dynasties would continue for over a century. Then, in 2055 B.C.E., the Theban king Mentuhotep (*men-too-HO-tep*) II conquered the northerners and declared himself the ruler of a reunited Egypt. His reign marks the beginning of Egypt's Middle Kingdom and the reestablishment of a central government—but this time based in Thebes rather than Memphis. The head of this new government was Mentuhotep's chief supporter, Amenemhet (*ah-meh-NEHM-het*), who actually seized power after the king's death and established himself and his descendants as Egypt's Twelfth Dynasty.

This succession of remarkable pharaohs remained in power for nearly 200 years, and under them the Egyptians began to exploit more thoroughly the potential for trade. They secured their border with Nubia and began to send mounted expeditions to the land they called Punt, probably the coast of Somalia. By the middle of the nineteenth century B.C.E., Nubia was firmly under Egypt's control. Meanwhile, diplomatic relations with the smaller states and principalities of Palestine and Syria led to decisive Egyptian political and economic influence in this region. Yet these lands were not incorporated into Egypt; instead, Amenemhet constructed the Walls of the Prince in Sinai, to guard against incursions by foreigners.

The huge fortifications built along Egypt's new frontier demonstrate the great resourcefulness of the Twelfth Dynasty and its very different ways of allocating resources and expressing ambition. As such, the fortifications also display a marked shift in the Egyptian outlook on the world. The placid serenity epitomized by *ma'at* and the shared devotion to the pharaoh that had built the pyramids had

**SESOSTRIS III (1870–1831 B.C.E.).** This powerful Twelfth Dynasty pharaoh led military campaigns into Nubia; constructed massive, garrisoned fortresses along the Nile; and dug new waterways near Aswan. More than a hundred portrait busts of Sesostris survive, all with similar features. His overhanging brow, deep-set eyes, and drawn-down mouth are intended to communicate the enormous burden of responsibility the pharaoh bore as the ruler of all Egypt.

been challenged. Egyptians could no longer be dismissive of outsiders or disregard the world beyond their borders. Unlike their Old Kingdom ancestors, the Egyptians of the Middle Kingdom were not turned inward. Their attitude toward the pharaoh also seems to have changed. Although he continued to enjoy a special position as a divine representative, his authority did not derive solely from this source. Rather, the pharaohs of the Middle Kingdom represented themselves in a new light, as good shepherds, tenders of their flock. Only by diligently protecting Egypt from a hostile outside world could a pharaoh provide the peace, prosperity, and security desired by his subjects; his alignment with *ma'at* was now clearly conditional, and it had to be earned.

Portraits of the great pharaohs of the Twelfth Dynasty mirror this anxious outlook on the world. The literature of the Middle Kingdom also expresses the general change in attitude. Among the most popular of the new literary forms were manuals ostensibly written by or for kings, detailing the duties and perils of high office and offering advice for dealing with difficult situations. These include the *Instruction of Amenemhet*, which purports to be life lessons handed

## The Prophecies of Neferty

*This text presents itself as a prophecy foretelling the disasters that would strike Egypt during the First Intermediate Period. In fact, it was composed during the Middle Kingdom, shortly after the death of the pharaoh Amenemhet I, the founder of the Twelfth Dynasty. By contrasting the disorders that preceded Amenemhet's reign with the peace that he established, the document seeks to justify Amenemhet's usurpation of the throne and perhaps to legitimize his son's succession.*

Arise, oh my heart! Weep for this land wherein you were born! Falsehood is as the flood, and behold, evil is spoken with impunity. . . . The land perishes, and there is no one who cares for it. There is no one who speaks out, no one who makes lament. . . . Perished and gone are those joyful places, the fish ponds where dwell fish-eating birds, ponds alive with fish and fowl. All joy has been driven out, and the land is plunged into anguish by those voracious Asiatics who rove throughout the land. Foes have appeared in the east, Asiatics have entered Egypt. We have no (border) fortress, for foreigners now hold it, and there is no one to heed who the plunderers are. One may expect attack by night, the fortress will be breached and sleep driven from all eyes. . . . The land is destitute, although its rulers are numerous, it is ruined, but its taxes are immense. Sparse is the grain, but great is the measure, for it is distributed as if it were abundant.

But then there shall come a king from the south. His name will be Ameny, justified. He will be the son of a woman of Ta-Sety [Nubia], an offspring of the royal house of Nekhen. He shall receive the White Crown, he shall wear the Red Crown, he shall unite the Two Powers. . . . The people of his time will rejoice, for this son of a man will establish his name for ever and eternity. . . . The Asiatics will fall before his sword, the Libyans will fall before his fire, rebels will fall before his wrath, and enemies will fall through awe of him. . . .

Then Ma'at will return to her throne, and Chaos will be driven off. Joyful will he be who will see (these things), he who will serve the king.

Source: William Kelly Simpson, ed., *The Literature of Ancient Egypt: An Anthology of Stories, Instruction, Stelae, Autobiography, and Poetry*, 3rd ed. (New Haven, CT: 2003), pp. 214–20.

### Questions for Analysis

1. In what ways does the "Prophecies of Neferty" highlight the anxieties of Middle Kingdom Egyptians? What caused these anxieties?

2. Why would the author of this document choose to present it as a prophecy about the future, rather than as a description of current events?

---

down by this pharaoh to his son from beyond the grave, and *The Instruction of Ptah-Hotep* (see **Analyzing Primary Sources** above), an example of Egyptian "wisdom literature" attributed to a court official of the Old Kingdom, which achieved a wider readership in this new era—much as Machiavelli's *The Prince* (see Chapter 12) has become a "self-help" book for business executives and politicians in our own time. Ptah-Hotep's teaching is upbeat and practical; by contrast, the examples of this genre produced under the Middle Kingdom are bleakly pragmatic. A pharaoh must trust no one: not a brother, not a friend, not intimate companions. He must crush the ambitions of local nobles with ruthless ferocity. He must always be on the lookout for potential trouble. In return for his exertions on behalf of his people, he should expect neither gratitude nor reward; he should expect only that each year will bring new dangers and more pressing challenges. Reading between the lines, we discern that Egyptians' sense of their own superiority—a product of their former isolation and their comparatively benign environment—had been shattered. They saw themselves being drawn into a much wider world, and in the course of the next millennium they would become more fully a part of it.

## CONCLUSION

Whereas the story of the Tower of Babel records the legendary loss of a shared language, this chapter shows that people of the distant past can still communicate with us.

The marks they have left on the landscape, the remains of their daily lives, their written records, and their very bodies make it possible for historians to piece together evidence and to make sense of it. And every year new sources come to light, meaning that we have to be ready to revise—constantly—our understanding of what happened in the past.

Although this chapter has emphasized the differences between the early civilizations of Mesopotamia and Egypt, it is worth noting some significant similarities. Both developed the fundamental technologies of writing at about the same time, and this facilitated political alliances, long-distance trade, and the transmission of vital information to posterity. During the third millennium, both underwent a

# After You Read This Chapter

Go to **INQUIZITIVE** to see what you've learned—and learn what you've missed—with personalized feedback along the way.

## REVIEWING THE OBJECTIVES

- The study of the distant past is challenging because written sources are rare. What other sources of information do historians use?
- All civilizations require the same basic conditions for survival and share certain characteristics. What are they?
- The cities of Mesopotamia remained largely independent from one another yet shared a common culture. Why was this the case?
- Hammurabi's efforts created a new precedent for governance in Mesopotamia. How did he achieve this?
- The civilizations of ancient Mesopotamia and Egypt differ in profound ways. What were the major causes of their differences?

process of political consolidation, an elaboration of religious ritual, and a melding of spiritual and political leadership. Both engaged in massive building and irrigation projects, and both commanded material and human resources on an enormous scale. At the same time, each of these civilizations cultivated an inward focus. Although they had some contact with each other, and some transfers of information and technology probably took place, they had few significant political or cultural interactions. For the most part, they inhabited separate worlds. This relative isolation was about to change, however. The next millennium would see the emergence of large-scale, land-based empires that would transform life in Mesopotamia, Egypt, and the lands that lay between them. These are the developments we examine in Chapter 2.

## PEOPLE, IDEAS, AND EVENTS IN CONTEXT

- What fundamental changes associated with the **NEOLITHIC REVOLUTION** made early civilizations possible? Why is this considered to be the beginning of a new epoch, the **ANTHROPOCENE**?

- What new technologies allowed the **SUMERIANS** to master the environment of **MESOPOTAMIA**? How did these technologies contribute to the development of a new, urbanized society?

- By contrast, why did the Nile River foster a very different civilization and enable the centralized authority of the **PHARAOH**?

- How do the differences between **CUNEIFORM** and **HIEROGLYPHS** reflect the different circumstances in which they were invented and the different uses to which they were put?

- In what ways are the **EPIC OF GILGAMESH** and the **CODE OF HAMMURABI** rich sources of information about the civilizations of Sumer and **BABYLON**?

- How do the **ZIGGURATS** of Mesopotamia and the pyramids of Egypt exemplify different forms of power, different ideas about the gods, and different beliefs about the afterlife?

- Why was the worldview of ancient Egyptians, which was strongly reflected in the concept of *MA'AT* during the **OLD KINGDOM**, altered in significant ways by the time of the **MIDDLE KINGDOM**?

## THINKING ABOUT CONNECTIONS

- How do the surviving sources of any period limit the kinds of questions that we can ask and answer about the distant past? In your view, have sources for this early era been undervalued? For example, if writing had not been developed in Mesopotamia and Egypt, what would we still be able to know about the civilizations of these two regions?

- What features of ancient civilizations do modern civilizations share? What might be the implications of these shared ideas, social structures, and technologies?

- In particular, what lessons can we draw from humans' tendency to manipulate their environment? How should knowledge of the distant past influence current debates over sustainability and climate change?

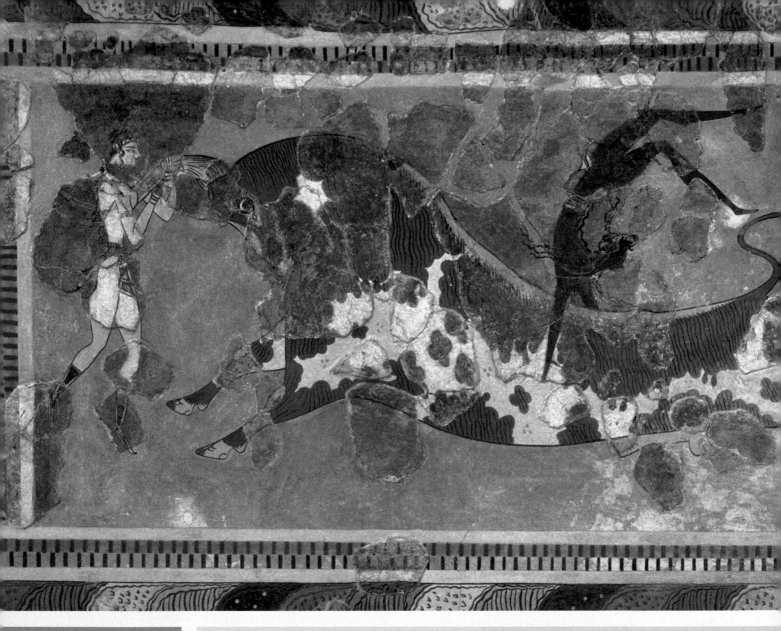

## STORY LINES

- During the second millennium B.C.E., new peoples settled in Eurasia, around the eastern Mediterranean, spreading a related set of Indo-European languages that are the ancestors of several modern language groups.

- In Egypt, the rise of the Eighteenth Dynasty fostered imperial expansion beyond the Nile Valley for the first time.

- During the late Bronze Age, an interconnected network of alliances bound peoples together in new ways. But this civilization was eventually destroyed by the raids of mysterious Sea Peoples.

- In the wake of these invasions, both oppressive new empires and smaller-scale states emerged.

- In the Iron Age, the worship of Yahweh among the Hebrews and of Ahura-Mazda among the Persians fostered a new view of the world: one in which a single creator god ruled over all peoples.

## CHRONOLOGY

| | |
|---|---|
| 1900–1500 B.C.E. | Minoan civilization flourishes |
| 1800–1400 B.C.E. | Formation of the Hittite Empire |
| 1792 B.C.E. | Rise of Babylon under Hammurabi |
| 1650–1550 B.C.E. | Hyksos invasion of Egypt and Second Intermediate Period |
| 1600–1200 B.C.E. | Mycenaean civilization flourishes |
| 1550–1075 B.C.E. | New Kingdom of Egypt established |
| c. 1200 B.C.E. | Invasions of the Sea Peoples begin |
| 1100–1000 B.C.E. | Philistine dominance in Palestine |
| 1000–973 B.C.E. | Hebrew kingdom consolidated |
| 924 B.C.E. | Israel and Judah divided |
| 883–859 B.C.E. | Neo-Assyrian Empire founded |
| 722 B.C.E. | Kingdom of Israel destroyed |
| 612–605 B.C.E. | Fall of the Neo-Assyrian Empire |
| 586 B.C.E. | Fall of the kingdom of Judah |
| 539–486 B.C.E. | Persian Empire consolidated |

Before You Read This Chapter

# Peoples, Gods, and Empires: 1700–500 B.C.E.

## CORE OBJECTIVES

- **DESCRIBE** the impact of new migrations and settlements on ancient civilizations.

- **DEFINE** the differences between Egypt's New Kingdom and the previous Old and Middle Kingdoms.

- **EXPLAIN** the workings of transnational networks during the late Bronze Age.

- **IDENTIFY** the new empires and kingdoms that emerged during the Iron Age.

- **UNDERSTAND** the historical importance of monotheism.

According to Hesiod, a Greek poet who flourished during the eighth century B.C.E., all of human history falls into five ages. The dawn of time was a golden age, when men lived like gods. Everything was good then, food was plentiful, and work was easy. The next age was silver, when men took gods for granted, killed one another, and lived in dishonor. So the gods destroyed them, sending a mighty flood that spared only the family of Deucalion, the son of wily Prometheus, who built an ark. Then came the age of bronze, when everything was made of bronze—houses and armor and weapons and tools. Giants fought incessantly from huge strongholds, causing destruction so great that no man's name survives. The time following was short but bright, a heroic age, the time of men who ventured with Theseus and fought with Achilles and sailed with Odysseus, men whose names will live forever. But Hesiod's own age was iron—a dull age, a time of tedium and strife and bickering and petty feuds.

Hesiod's periodization captures an understanding of history that had evolved with humanity itself and that reflects actual developments. The stories he knew told of a time before cities and the need for agriculture. They recalled a time when the harmony between gods and men broke down, and the human race was saved by one man's ingenuity: the Sumerian Utnapishtim, the Hebrew Noah, or the Greek Deucalion. These stories chronicled the wars of the age we still call Bronze, when the enormous, abandoned palaces still visible in Hesiod's day were built. And they remembered the race of heroes whose glory was measured by their abiding fame, and who bequeathed to us a further round of stories. Thanks to new archaeological finds, new linguistic discoveries, and new efforts at decoding the historical record, we can both confirm and correct Hesiod's perspective on the past.

In the second millennium B.C.E., the ancient world was transformed by the arrival of new peoples and by the emergence of extensive land-based empires built up through systematic military conquest. These migrations and conquests caused upheaval, but they also led to cultural contact and economic integration that not only encompassed the Mediterranean but even extended from Scandinavia to China. The last few centuries of the Bronze Age (1500–1200 B.C.E.)

were a period of intense diplomacy, trade, and exchange. By the thirteenth century B.C.E., peoples from the southern Balkans to the western fringes of Iran had been drawn into a wide-ranging web of relationships.

Yet this extraordinary system proved more fragile than its participants could have imagined. Around 1200 B.C.E., a wave of mysterious invasions led to the destruction of nearly every established Mediterranean civilization. As a result, around the turn of the first millennium B.C.E., we enter a world organized along profoundly different lines. In this Iron Age, iron would slowly replace bronze as the primary component of tools and weapons. New and more brutal empires would come to power, while new ideas about the divine and its relationship to humanity would emerge. Two of the Western world's most enduring religious traditions—Judaism and Zoroastrianism (*zoh-roh-AHS-tree-an-ism*)—were born, fundamentally altering conceptions of ethics, politics, and the natural world. This age would prove a fateful historical crossroads, as elements both old and new combined to reconfigure the ancient world.

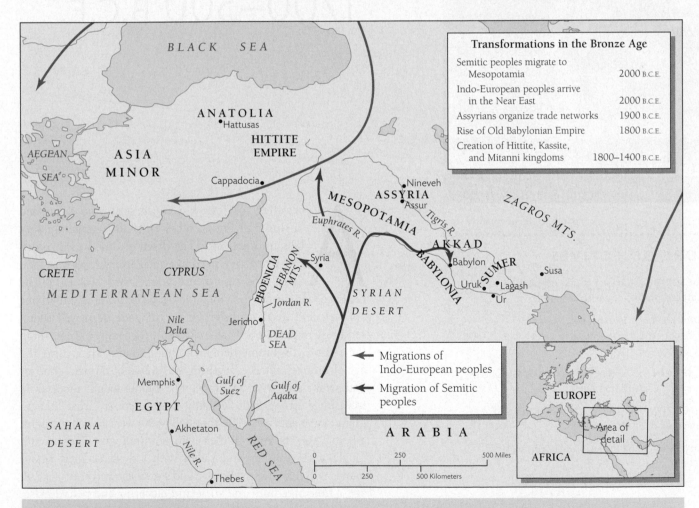

**CIVILIZATIONS OF THE BRONZE AGE, 2000–1400 B.C.E.** Notice the geographical relationships among the older centers of Mesopotamia and Egypt, and among newer civilizations such as Babylonia, Assyria, Phoenicia, and the Hittite Empire. ▪ *Which of these emerging cultures was most likely to come into contact with Egypt, and why?* ▪ *Where did the Indo-European peoples come from?* ▪ *What was the impact of Indo-European settlements?*

# INDO-EUROPEAN LANGUAGES AND PEOPLES

In 1786, a British judge serving in India made a discovery that transformed the prevailing understanding of history. Turning his spare time to the study of Sanskrit, the ancient language of South Asia, Sir William Jones discovered that it shares its grammar and vocabulary with ancient Greek and Latin, to an extent inexplicable by sheer coincidence. His interest piqued, he then examined the early Germanic and Celtic languages of Europe and the Old Persian language of Mesopotamia and found that they also exhibit marked similarities. He concluded that all of these languages must have evolved from a common source. Within another generation, the ancient language whose existence Jones had hypothesized, and the later languages derived from it, would be labeled Indo-European, reflecting a wide distribution from India to Ireland. The biblical story of mankind's shared language, the story of the Tower of Babel, turns out to be partly true.

Since then, scholars have greatly enlarged our understanding of Indo-European languages and their speakers. Yet much remains controversial. Was the original form of the Indo-European language spoken by a single population at some point in time? If so, when and where? How did it spread? Can the diffusion of its speakers be determined archaeologically, by tracing characteristic pottery types and burial rites? Or are such practices distinct from language? At the moment, we have no clear answers to any such questions. It is certain, however, that Indo-European linguistic forms began to appear in western Asia and the eastern Mediterranean shortly after 2000 B.C.E. Around this same time, a group of Indo-European speakers also moved into the Aegean basin, where the resulting language became an early form of Greek. Other Indo-European speakers went east; some may have reached western China.

These were not the only new peoples on the move. As we noted in Chapter 1, Semitic-speaking peoples were also making their mark, beginning with the Akkadians and the Amorites, from whose ranks Hammurabi came. The Assyrians, the Phoenicians, and the Canaanites would also become prominent. These newcomers did not wipe out existing cultures; rather, they built on established patterns of urban life and organization. But their collective impact was enormous.

## New Settlers in Anatolia

By 1900 B.C.E., the nomadic Assyrians had become caravan merchants whose extensive trade networks stretched across Anatolia and Mesopotamia. They did not seek military dominance over the region; instead, they relied on the protection of local rulers and, in turn, made these rulers rich. They also served as advisers and officials and married into important urban families. In the process, they carried Mesopotamian civilization and its trappings into far-flung regions of the world.

In the wake of Assyrian-assisted urbanization, new population groups were attracted to Anatolia, northern Syria, and Mesopotamia. The most formidable of these were the Hittites, an Indo-European-speaking people who arrived around 2000 B.C.E. In contrast to the Assyrians, the Hittites were military conquerors and colonists who imposed themselves and their language on the peoples they vanquished. By 1700 B.C.E., they had integrated many Hittite-dominated

**AN ANCIENT WAR CHARIOT.** A light, spoke-wheeled chariot, developed for warfare, is here being used for lion hunting by the Assyrian king Assurnasirpal II (883–859 B.C.E.), whose reign is discussed on page 59.

city-states into a larger kingdom. About fifty years later, they captured a strategic mountain stronghold, Hattusas, from which their king took a new name, Hattusilis.

Under Hattusilis and his successors, the Hittites' warrior aristocracy fielded the most fearsome army of the Bronze Age. They were quick to adopt the latest technologies, including the horse-drawn chariot; for up to this point, the horse—as a mount or an engine of war—had been unknown outside the steppes of central Asia. The Hittites' light, horse-drawn chariots became terrifying death machines, transporting archers rapidly around the battlefield. But the Hittites also adopted the more peaceful practices of those they conquered, using cuneiform to record their own language and laws. They also sought to control trade routes, particularly the overland trade in copper and arsenic, the raw materials for making bronze. By 1595 B.C.E., they had moved southeastward into Mesopotamia, capturing and sacking Babylon.

A century later, the Kassites, another new people, moved into the devastated city and took control of it. For the next 500 years, they presided over a largely peaceful and prosperous Babylonian realm. The Hittites, however, continued to dominate the region, until they were checked by the arrival of a people known as the Mitanni, who moved into Syria around 1550 B.C.E. The Mitanni extended their influence along the eastern Mediterranean coastline, forging an alliance with the Egyptians around 1400 B.C.E. Although Mitanni power was short-lived, it served to increase the links between the peoples of western Asia and the kingdom of the pharaohs.

# THE NEW KINGDOM OF EGYPT

As we have seen, Egypt's Middle Kingdom had been reshaped by the many internal changes of the First Intermediate Period, chiefly the redistribution of wealth and power. Now it was further transformed by external forces, through the dynamic movement of new peoples from western Asia and Nubia. Some of these came to Egypt as immigrants; others were hired as mercenaries. And for a while, a strategy of accommodation preserved Egypt from large-scale armed attack and fostered commercial exchange with neighboring regions. But around 1700 B.C.E., Egypt was invaded for the first time since the unification of the Upper and Lower Kingdoms. The invaders' origins and identity remain mysterious; the Egyptians called them simply Hyksos (*HIHK-sohs*), "rulers of foreign lands." From their power base in the eastern delta of the Nile, the Hyksos began to project their authority over most of Lower Egypt.

With this conquest, the central authority of the pharaoh once again dissolved, and Egypt entered what historians call the Second Intermediate Period (c. 1650–1550 B.C.E.). Significantly, however, the Hyksos did not destroy the machinery of pharaonic government in Lower Egypt but took steps to legitimize their rule in accordance with Egyptian precedents. Some Hyksos rulers even incorporated the name of the sun god Ra into their own names. In Upper Egypt, by contrast, Hyksos power was weak. Here, a native pharaonic regime maintained a tenuous independence at the traditional capital of Thebes, although it sometimes had to acknowledge the suzerainty (overlordship) of the foreigners to the north.

This relatively short period of Hyksos domination was regarded by later Egyptians as the greatest shame of their history. Although the Hyksos established Lower Egypt as a significant power, filling the temporary power vacuum left by the Hittites, their conquest also weakened the dominion of Upper Egypt over the Nubians, who eventually founded an independent kingdom called Kush. This Nubian kingdom posed a much greater threat to the native dynasty at Thebes than to the Hyksos in Lower Egypt—but it also provided an additional incentive to southern pharaohs determined to oust the Hyksos usurpers and reunify Egypt. Ultimately, they succeeded. By the end of the sixteenth century B.C.E., the pharaoh Ahmose had driven out the Hyksos, establishing the Eighteenth Dynasty and the New Kingdom of Egypt.

## The Pharaohs of the Eighteenth Dynasty

Under the Eighteenth Dynasty, Egyptian civilization reached the height of its magnificence and power, which it now exercised more widely than ever before. Although many Egyptian traditions were renewed and strengthened, the dynamism of the New Kingdom—particularly its new focus on imperial expansion—changed the very fabric of Egyptian life, which had never looked far beyond the narrow world of the fertile Nile Valley.

The Eighteenth Dynasty ruled Egypt for more than two and a half centuries, and striking developments took place during this period. Most important was the rise of an aristocracy whose wealth was acquired through warfare and the winning of lands (with slaves to work them), which they received from the pharaoh as rewards for service. The Eighteenth Dynasty itself was forged in battle, something that had not been true of a ruling family since the time of King Narmer, over a millennium and a half earlier (see Chapter 1). Ahmose, the man who expelled the Hyksos, had been reared by the warrior queen Ahhotep, who had ruled Upper Egypt in her own right. His eventual successor, Thutmose I (c. 1504–1492 B.C.E.), was the son of an unknown warrior who married Ahmose's daughter.

Under Thutmose's leadership, the Egyptians subdued the Nubians to the south, seizing control of their gold mines and securing the wealth needed to finance expanded commerce. They also penetrated beyond their northeastern frontier, driving deep into Palestine and Syria. By the time of his death, Thutmose could claim to rule the land from beyond the Nile's Fourth Cataract in the south to the banks of the Euphrates in the north. Never had Egypt held sway over so much territory or so clearly declared its imperial ambitions. Nor was this success fleeting. The Egyptians would sustain a strong military presence in the wider region for the next 400 years, using the new horse-powered battle chariots to devastating effect against their enemies.

## The Legacy of Hatshepsut

The early death of Thutmose's son and successor could have resulted in a crisis for the Eighteenth Dynasty. Instead, it led to one of the most remarkable reigns in Egypt's history, for Thutmose II (1492–1479 B.C.E.) passed the power of pharaoh to his sister, wife, and co-ruler Hatshepsut (HAIIT-shep-soot; 1479–1458 B.C.E.). Such brother-sister unions were common in the Egyptian royal family, although they do not appear to have been the routine way to produce royal children: pharaohs customarily kept a harem of subsidiary wives and concubines for this purpose. However, Thutmose II and Hatshepsut did conceive at least one child together, Neferure (neh-feh-RUH-reh); in fact, she may have been their designated heir. For twenty-one years, Hatshepsut ruled as pharaoh in her own right, while her daughter took on the usual duties of queen.

Like her great-grandmother Ahhotep, Hatshepsut was a warrior. Moreover, she was routinely portrayed on monuments and in statuary with the masculine figure and ceremonial beard characteristic of pharaohs. She did not pretend to be a man; inscriptions almost always indicate her gender, and she claimed to be the most beautiful woman in the world. But it was important to Egyptians that she use the conventional iconography of power to locate herself firmly within a long history of dynastic rule.

Hatshepsut's statecraft proved crucial to the continuing success of Egypt. With her stepson/nephew Thutmose III

**THE MORTUARY TEMPLE OF HATSHEPSUT.** Unlike the pharaohs of the Old Kingdom, those of the Eighteenth Dynasty chose to be buried in specially built temples rather than in separate pyramids. The innovative architecture of Hatshepsut's temple, which was built into a hillside and set off by rows of columns, was widely imitated by her successors.

# Interpreting Visual Evidence

## Remembering Hatshepsut

The pharaohs of Egypt's New Kingdom were obsessed with self-representation and carefully controlled their public images. The visual language they used was highly symbolic, an iconography (vocabulary of images) intended to make each successive pharaoh look as much like his royal predecessors as possible: godlike, steadfast, virile, authoritative—even when the pharaoh was a woman, Hatshepsut (1479–1458 B.C.E.). So many statues and portraits of her survive that nearly every major museum in the world has at least one. (The Metropolitan Museum of Art in New York has a whole room set aside for them.) But many of these images show signs of having been defaced (images A and B) during the reign of her successor, Thutmose III, who was also her nephew and stepson. Until very recently, scholars assumed that Hatshepsut must have usurped his powers and that this was his revenge. Yet the evidence clearly shows that Hatshepsut was Egypt's legitimate ruler. Why, then, would Thutmose III or his heirs have tried to efface her memory?

These two unblemished steles (images C and D) depict Hatshepsut and Thutmose III. In the stele on the left (image C), they sit back to back on matching thrones, under the protection of the gods. In the stele on the right (image D), Thutmose III wears a warrior's crown, while Hatshepsut wears the double crown of Upper and Lower Egypt and wields a mace.

A. Defaced head of Hatshepsut.

B. Undefaced statue of Hatshepsut.

(the son of one of her brother's lesser wives), she launched several successful military campaigns and extended trade and diplomacy. The arts also flourished, setting standards that would be emulated for a thousand years. Indeed, Hatshepsut was one of the most ambitious builders in Egyptian history, which is saying something. Her own mortuary temple, which housed the remains of her father and herself, was probably the first tomb constructed in the Valley of the Kings, the New Kingdom's answer to the pyramids.

Yet after Hatshepsut's death in 1458 B.C.E., her legacy was called into question. At some point late in her nephew's reign, attempts were made to remove her name from inscriptions and to destroy her images (see **Interpreting Visual Evidence** above). Scholars used to assume that Thutmose himself was responsible, because he resented his step-mother/aunt's power over him. But more recent research has suggested that the culprit was his son, Amenhotep II (1427–1400 B.C.E.), who was thereby blocking the claims of royal rivals, possibly the descendants of Hatshepsut or her daughter Neferure. In either case, the near erasure of Hatshepsut's legacy caused her to be neglected by historians until the late twentieth century.

**1.** Bear in mind that few Egyptians could read the hieroglyphs accompanying these images. How might they have "read" the relationship between these two royal relatives? Does this visual evidence support the hypothesis that Thutmose was slighted by Hatshepsut? Why or why not?

**2.** What can these images tell us about gender roles? What else would we need to know before making a judgment about masculine and feminine characteristics in ancient Egypt?

**3.** Given that Hatshepsut was Egypt's legitimate pharaoh, what might have motivated either Thutmose III or his son Amenhotep II to deface her image many years after her death?

C. Stele of Hatshepsut and Thutmose.

D. Stele of Thutmose and Hatshepsut from the Red Chapel at Karnak.

# Religious Change and Political Challenge

The great conquests of the Eighteenth Dynasty brought mind-boggling riches to Egypt. Much of this wealth went to the glorification of the pharaohs in the form of grand temples, tombs, and other monuments, including the thousands of steles that provide us with so much information about this era. Another significant portion of the plunder went to the military aristocracy that made such conquests possible. But the lion's share went to the gods as offerings of thanks for Egypt's success. As the temples became wealthy and powerful, so too did their priests. But no temple complex was so well endowed as that of Amon at Thebes.

Thebes was not only the capital of New Kingdom Egypt but was also the capital of the Eighteenth Dynasty and the place most sacred to Amon (or Amun), the god of creation. He therefore played an important role in the dynasty's self-image, and he is evoked in the dynastic name Amenhotep ("Amon Is Pleased"). But Amon was more than a local god. He had come into prominence when the political center of gravity shifted to Thebes during the Middle Kingdom, and his cult had steadily increased in status and popularity. By 1550 B.C.E., he had become identified as another manifestation of the sun god Ra, and as Amon-Ra he was believed to be the divine force behind the Eighteenth Dynasty's triumph over the Hyksos. This accounts for the favor shown to his priests at Thebes, who became a formidable political and economic force. Eventually, the priesthood of Amon surpassed even the military aristocracy in importance and influence. And because the dynasty's prestige was intertwined with that of Amon, the priests had seemingly gained the controlling voice in Egypt.

## The Reign of Akhenaten (1352–1336 B.C.E.)

All of these factors are important when we consider the reign of Amenhotep IV, who inherited the vast, well-governed kingdom assembled by his predecessors. This young pharaoh showed an early inclination toward the worship of the sun—but not as an aspect of Amon. Instead, Amenhotep exalted Ra as a discrete divinity and laid aside the traditional iconography of this god as a falcon (or a falcon-headed man), replacing it with the symbol *Aten*, the hieroglyph representing the sun's rays. He then went further, changing his own name to Akhenaten (*AH-ken-AH-ten*), "He Who Is Profitable to the Aten," and building a new capital to honor the god. Located halfway between Memphis in the north and Thebes in the south, it was called Akhetaten ("The Horizon of the Aten").

Although the priesthood of Amon exalted Amon-Ra, it had continued to recognize all the other gods of the Egyptian pantheon. Akhenaten's theology, by contrast, was closer to monotheism: unlike traditional Egyptian deities, the Aten could not be imagined as taking on human or animal form. As if this were not controversial enough, Akhenaten also celebrated his new religion by representing himself in a very unconventional way. In a complete departure from the divine virility of his ancestors—which even his ancestor Hatshepsut had emulated—Akhenaten had himself pictured as a normal human being with distinctive features and as a family man enjoying the company of his wife, Nefertiti, and their children. This emphasis on his own humanity might have been an extension of his theology, which honored the life force within every being. But it was very dangerous to the ideology of royal power. The pharaoh was not supposed to be approachable and affable, a man with quirky personality. He was supposed to be a god on earth.

Akhenaten's spiritual revolution therefore had enormous political implications. Indeed, some scholars have suggested

**AKHENATEN, HIS WIFE NEFERTITI, AND THEIR CHILDREN.** The Aten is depicted here as a sun disk, raining down power on the royal family. ▪ *What messages might this image have conveyed to contemporary Egyptians?* ▪ *How does this depiction of the pharaoh differ from earlier precedents?*

**THRONE OF TUTANKHAMUN.** Dating from about 1330 B.C.E., this relief in gold and silver is part of the back of the young pharaoh's throne. Although the reign of the boy king marked the rejection of Akhenaten's theology, the informal artistic style favored by his father is still detectable here in the relaxed, lounging position of the pharaoh and the intimate, confiding gesture of his queen, Ankhesenamen.

that it was part of a cunning attempt to undermine the influence of Amon's priests, to the pharaoh's benefit. Whatever the motives behind it, Akhenaten did not succeed in converting many Egyptians to his new religion. It is not surprising that the priesthood of Amon also put up strenuous resistance. To make matters worse, Akhenaten did not balance his theological enthusiasm with attention to Egypt's security or interests abroad. This cost him the support of his nobility and may even have led to his deposition.

He was ultimately succeeded by one of his younger sons, Tutankhaten ("Living Image of Aten"), a child of nine whose name was quickly changed to reflect his advisers' rejection of Akhenaten's beliefs and the restoration of the god Amon and his priesthood to a position of power. He thus became Tutankhamun (1333–1324 B.C.E.), the famous boy king whose sumptuous tomb was discovered in 1922. After his early death, he was succeeded by a general called Horemheb, a man unrelated to the royal family who nonetheless reigned as the last pharaoh of the Eighteenth Dynasty and managed to maintain stability for nearly three decades. When he died, he passed his office to another general. This was Ramses, the founder of the Nineteenth Dynasty, who would restore Egypt to glory.

# TRANSNATIONAL NETWORKS OF THE LATE BRONZE AGE

After 1500 B.C.E., Bronze Age history must be understood within the context of what we might call international relations. Yet it is more accurate to call the political and economic networks of this period *transnational*, because this web of alliances and relationships transcended any idea of national identity or national boundaries.

This Late Bronze Age was an age of superpowers. The great pharaohs of the Eighteenth Dynasty had transformed Egypt into a conquering state, and the Hittites had created an empire out of the disparate city-states and kingdoms of Anatolia. The Assyrians controlled trade, and the Kassite kingdom of Babylonia remained a significant force in economic and military relationships. In addition to these imperial entities, numerous smaller states also flourished and extended their influence westward into the Mediterranean. Holding it all together was a network of trade routes that created an interdependent Afro-Eurasian world.

## Transnational Diplomacy

Although warfare remained the fundamental mode of interaction in the Late Bronze Age, a balance of power among the larger empires gradually helped to stabilize the region and encourage trade. The archives discovered by archaeologists at Akhenaten's abandoned capital of Akhetaten (modern el-Amarna) provide us with a clear picture of this process. By the fourteenth century B.C.E., a wide-ranging correspondence was forging alliances and promoting a set of mutual goals and understandings among rulers and elites. This is reflected in the letters' vocabulary: the most powerful rulers address one another as "brother," whereas lesser princes and chieftains show their deference to the pharaoh, the Hittite king, and other sovereigns by using the term "father." Breach of this protocol could cause great offense. When a thirteenth-century Assyrian king presumed to address the Hittite ruler as "brother," he received a stern rebuke: "What is this you keep saying about 'brotherhood'? Were you and I born of the same mother? Far from it! Just as my father and grandfather were not in the habit of writing about 'brotherhood' to the king of Assyria, so should you stop writing to me about 'brotherhood'!"

Rulers of this period also exchanged lavish gifts and entered into marriage contracts with each other. Professional envoys journeyed back and forth among the centers of power, conveying gifts and handling politically sensitive missions. Some of these emissaries were also merchants, sent to explore the possibility of trading opportunities as well as to cement alliances.

## Transnational Trade

Indeed, it was trade that allowed smaller communities to become integral parts of this transnational network. Seaside centers became powerful merchant city-states and centers for the exchange of dazzling commodities. A single vessel's cargo might contain scores of distinct items originating anywhere from the interior of Africa to the Baltic Sea, as demonstrated by the contents of a merchant ship discovered at Uluburun off the Turkish coast in 1982. At the same time, the region was supplied with goods brought in over land, via contacts reaching into India and the Far East.

Long-distance trade was not only the basis for a new economy but also the conduit for art, ideas, and technology. In the past, such influences had spread slowly and unevenly; now, though, the societies of the Late Bronze Age could keep abreast of all the latest developments. Egyptians delighted in Canaanite glass, Greeks prized Egyptian amulets, and the merchants of Canaan admired Greek pottery and wool. Examples of avid desire for the products of other cultures can be endlessly enumerated.

This trend was particularly marked in large coastal towns. At Ugarit, on the coast of modern-day Syria, the swirl of

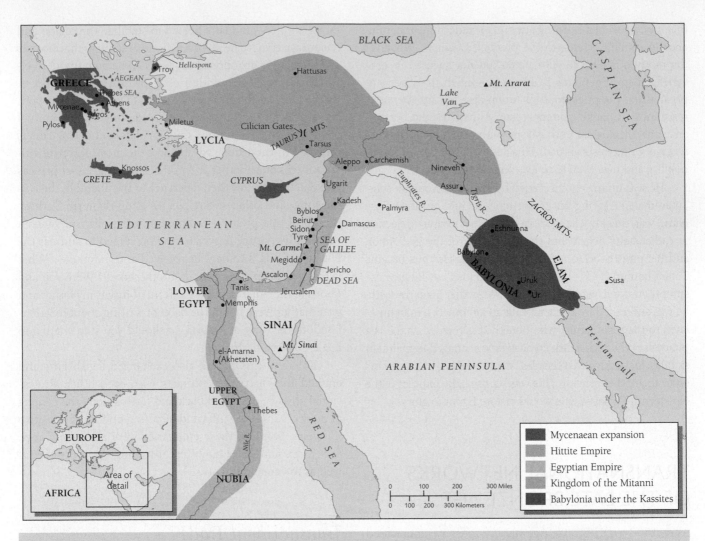

MAP LABELS (clockwise/geographic):
BLACK SEA · CASPIAN SEA · Hellespont · Troy · AEGEAN SEA · GREECE · Thebes · Athens · Mycenae · Argos · Pylos · Miletus · LYCIA · Hattusas · Mt. Ararat · Lake Van · Cilician Gates · TAURUS MTS. · Tarsus · Aleppo · Carchemish · Nineveh · Assur · ZAGROS MTS. · CYPRUS · Ugarit · Kadesh · Palmyra · Euphrates R. · Tigris R. · Knossos · CRETE · MEDITERRANEAN SEA · Byblos · Beirut · Sidon · Tyre · Damascus · Eshnunna · Mt. Carmel · SEA OF GALILEE · Megiddo · Jericho · DEAD SEA · Babylon · BABYLONIA · ELAM · Uruk · Ur · Susa · Ascalon · Jerusalem · LOWER EGYPT · Tanis · Memphis · SINAI · Mt. Sinai · ARABIAN PENINSULA · Persian Gulf · el-Amarna (Akhetaten) · UPPER EGYPT · Thebes · Nile R. · RED SEA · NUBIA · EUROPE · Area of detail · AFRICA

Legend:
- Mycenaean expansion
- Hittite Empire
- Egyptian Empire
- Kingdom of the Mitanni
- Babylonia under the Kassites

0   100   200   300 Miles
0  100  200  300 Kilometers

**EGYPT AND ITS NEIGHBORS, C. 1400 B.C.E.** ▪ *What is the major change on this map compared with the previous map of Bronze Age civilizations (page 40)?* ▪ *What factors appear to shape patterns of conquest and settlement in the eastern Mediterranean?* ▪ *What developments would have enabled trade to flourish during this period?*

commerce and the multiplicity of languages spoken by traders even propelled the development of a simpler form of written communication than the cuneiform still current throughout most of the region. The Ugaritic alphabet consisted of about thirty symbols representing the sounds of consonants (vowels had to be inferred). This system was far more easily mastered and more flexible than cuneiform, and it became the model for the development of all modern alphabets.

The search for markets, resources, and trade routes also promoted greater understanding among cultures. After a great battle between Egyptians and Hittites near Kadesh (c. 1275 B.C.E.), the pharaoh Ramses II realized that more was to be gained through peaceful relations with his northern neighbors than through warfare. The treaty he established with the Hittites fostered geopolitical stability in the region and allowed further economic exchanges to flourish. But greater integration also meant greater mutual

dependence. If one economy suffered, the effects of that decline were sure to be felt elsewhere. And the farther this transnational system spread, the more fragile it became. Many of the new markets depended on emerging societies in regions far less stable, where civilization was new.

## AEGEAN CIVILIZATION: MINOAN CRETE, MYCENAEAN GREECE

Like Hesiod, many ancient Greek poets described a heroic age when great men mingled with gods and powerful kingdoms contended for wealth and glory. For a long time, modern scholars dismissed these stories as fables. Tales of Theseus and the Minotaur, the Trojan War, and the wanderings of Odysseus were not regarded as reflecting any historical reality. Greek history was assumed to begin in 776 B.C.E., when the first recorded Olympic Games occurred. Greece in the Bronze Age was considered a primitive backwater that played no significant role in the Mediterranean world or in the later, glorious history of classical Greece.

But in the late nineteenth century, an amateur archaeologist named Heinrich Schliemann became convinced that these legends were really historical accounts. Using the epic poems of Homer as his guide, he found the site of Ilium (Troy) near the coast of northwest Anatolia. He also identified a number of once-powerful citadels on the Greek mainland, including the home of the legendary king Agamemnon at Mycenae (*MY-seh-nee*). Soon afterward, the British archaeologist Sir Arthur Evans took credit for discovering the remains of a great palace at Knossos (*kuh-NOHS-ohs*) on the island of Crete, a vast complex that predated any of the major citadels on the Greek mainland. He dubbed its magnificent culture (which no modern person had known to exist) "Minoan," after King Minos, the powerful ruler whom the ancient Greeks had described as dominating the Aegean and the man for whom the legendary engineer Daedalus had designed the Labyrinth. Although some of their conclusions have proven false, the discoveries of Schliemann and Evans forced scholars to revise, entirely, the early history of Western civilizations. It is now clear that

**MYCENAEAN DEATH MASK, C. 1550–1500 B.C.E.** When the archaeologist Heinrich Schliemann discovered this gold funeral mask in a burial shaft at Mycenae, he immediately declared it to be that of Agamemnon. Although it is certainly royal, this mask is too old to have been made for that legendary king, who lived several centuries later.

Bronze Age Greece—or, as it is often termed, Mycenaean Greece—was an important player in this integrated Mediterranean world during the second millennium B.C.E.

## The Minoan Thalassocracy

In the fifth century B.C.E., the Athenian historian Thucydides wrote that King Minos of Crete had ruled a *thalassocracy*, an empire of the sea. We now know that Thucydides was correct and that a very wealthy civilization began to flourish on the island of Crete around 2500 B.C.E. Thereafter, for about a millennium, the Minoans controlled shipping around the central Mediterranean and the Aegean and may have exacted tribute from many smaller islands. At its height between 1900 and 1500 B.C.E., Minoan civilization was the contemporary of Egypt's Middle Kingdom and the Hittite Old Kingdom. And unlike them, it was virtually unassailable by outside forces, protected by the surrounding sea. It is astonishing that neither the great palace at Knossos nor the other palaces on the island were fortified, so secure were they from attack.

Thanks to its strategic position, Crete was not only a safe haven but also a nexus of vibrant economic exchange. In this it resembled its counterparts on the mainland, because it acted as a magnet for the collection of resources which were then redistributed by its rulers and their emissaries. Knossos was also a production center for textiles, pottery, and metalwork. Minoan merchants traded these with Egypt, southwest Anatolia, and Cyprus for a range of exotic goods. Through Cyprus, the Minoans had further contacts with the Levantine coast of modern-day Lebanon and Syria. Artistic influences also traveled along these routes; among much else, Minoan-style fresco paintings from this period appear regularly in the Nile Delta and the Levant.

Traces of the bright colors and graceful lines of these paintings are still evident on the ruined walls of the palace at Knossos. Endowed with indoor plumbing, among other luxuries, it covered several acres and comprised hundreds of rooms joined by an intricate network of winding hallways that surely inspired the famous story of the Labyrinth, at the center of which lurked the terrible Minotaur. These legends, too, reflect historical evidence: the Minoans probably worshiped a god in the form of a bull or bull-man, and they appear to have devised an elaborate ritual sport known as bull-leaping, similar to bullfighting but involving an element of athletic dance. There is also some evidence that they practiced human sacrifice (possibly facilitated by the dangers of bull-dancing) as a religious rite.

Despite all these fascinating remains, Minoan culture remains mysterious because its language has yet to be decoded. Its script is called Linear A, to distinguish it

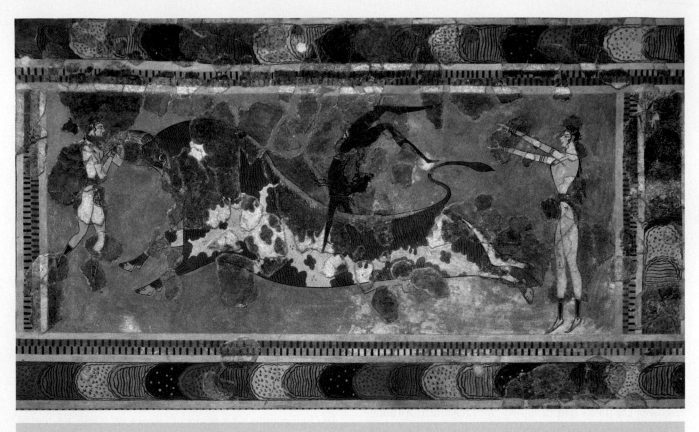

**MINOAN FRESCO, C. 1500 B.C.E.** A stylized representation of bull-leaping, painted into the plaster of a wall at Knossos. ▪ *Is this fresco likely to represent real practices?* ▪ *Why or why not?*

from Linear B, used in Mycenaean Greece—a script that *has* been deciphered. Although Linear A and Linear B represent different languages, the formal relationship between them reflects the close ties between Minoan Crete and the mainland of Greece. Yet the nature of that relationship is still debated. The Minoans were clearly much more sophisticated and originally may have dominated their Greek neighbors. One story told of the Greek hero Theseus describes how the young Athenian was sent to Crete as a hostage, intending to free Athens from the heavy tribute imposed by King Minos. Given what we have already learned about the close relationship between myth and history, it is probable that this story preserves ancient memory, just as the story of Daedalus, the brilliant inventor and engineer, is an attempt to explain the technological marvels of the palace at Knossos.

## Mycenaean Greece

In the early 1950s, the Englishmen Michael Ventris and John Chadwick joined their linguistic skills to expertise gained during the Second World War, when many classically trained scholars were employed in cracking enemy codes. Their efforts resulted in the decoding of Linear B, which proved that the history of ancient Greece stretched well back into the Bronze Age. Since then, new research shows that the Indo-Europeans whose language became Greek entered the region in several waves after the turn of the second millennium, dominating and displacing the indigenous inhabitants. By 1500 B.C.E., their huge citadels dotted the Greek landscape, ruled by warriors whose epitaphs boast of their martial prowess and who were buried with their weapons.

In 2015, American archaeologists excavating near one of these citadels—at Pylos in southwestern Greece, the same place where the first Linear B tablets on the Greek mainland were found—discovered an extraordinarily rich grave with all of its contents intact. Known as the tomb of the Griffin Warrior (from the decorative motifs of this mythical beast carved on an ivory plaque), it contained the body of a man in his early thirties who was buried with his sword and dagger, as well as combs, a mirror, jewelry, and other items; all made of ivory, silver, gold, and bronze; and all beautifully fashioned. Many of these of items came from Minoan Crete, and because the tomb was dug *before* the building of the great palace citadel, it allows us to glimpse

**LINEAR B TABLET FROM KNOSSOS.** Unlike cuneiform, whose characters are formed using the wedge-shaped tip of a reed, Linear B was inscribed with a sharp stylus that incised fine lines in clay or soft stone.

the process of cultural transfer that was shaping a new civilization on the Greek mainland. Analysis of ancient DNA (aDNA) extracted from the warrior's teeth and bones may soon yield even more information about him, while radiocarbon analysis of any surviving plant material or the bones themselves could assist in dating the burial.

This grave, and the close relationship between the writing systems of Crete and the mainland, reveal that Mycenaean society was decisively influenced by Minoan cultural, religious, and political models. The citadels, copying the great palaces of Crete, were both centers of government and warehouses for the storage and redistribution of goods and agricultural surpluses, of which they kept careful records. (Thousands of Linear B tablets testify to this.) By the thirteenth century B.C.E., some rulers had carved out territorial kingdoms with as many as 100,000 inhabitants, dwarfing the city-states of the later classical age; Hesiod imagined their citadels to have been built by giants. Indeed, their massive size was not ideally suited to the Greek landscape; nor were the war chariots that the Mycenaean elites adopted from their contemporaries on the plains of Anatolia, despite the fact that they were highly impractical on the rocky Greek terrain.

Gradually, the Mycenaean Greeks came to play a central role in Bronze Age networks. By about 1400 B.C.E., they had subjugated Crete, taking over Knossos and remaking it as a Mycenaean center. When the pharaoh Amenhotep III mentions a place called "Keftiu" in his correspondence, he is probably negotiating with Crete's Mycenaean conquerors. In western Anatolia, not far from fabled Troy, at least one Mycenaean king exercised enough influence for a Hittite ruler to address him as "my brother." This evidence suggests that the Mycenaeans earned prestige as warriors and mercenaries, just as the Greeks' heroic poems attest.

The basic political and commercial unit of the Mycenaean world—a powerful king and war leader, a warrior aristocracy, a palace bureaucracy, a complex economy, large territorial kingdoms—differs markedly from the tiny, self-contained Greek city-states of the later classical age (see Chapter 3). However, we can trace some features of this later civilization back to the Mycenaeans, including the Greek language. Linear B tablets speak of a social group with considerable economic and political rights, the *damos*; this may be the precursor of the *demos*, the urban population that sought political empowerment (*democracy*) in many Greek cities. The tablets also introduce the names of several gods familiar from the later period, such as Zeus, Poseidon, and Dionysus. Indeed, the later Greeks believed themselves to be descended from these legendary forebears, whom they credited with superhuman achievements. Although later Greeks such as Hesiod knew little about these Mycenaean ancestors in fact, the impact of what they imagined about them was considerable.

## The Sea Peoples and the End of the Bronze Age

The civilization of Mycenaean Greece seems to have collapsed around the end of the thirteenth century B.C.E. What triggered this cannot be determined with any certainty: drought, famine, disease, and social unrest have all been posited. But the consequences of the collapse are clear.

**THE GRAVE OF THE GRIFFIN WARRIOR AT PYLOS.** The contents of this Mycenaean tomb, discovered in 2015, reveal the extent of the connections between Mycenaean Greece and Minoan Crete. This photograph shows a bronze mirror in its original location.

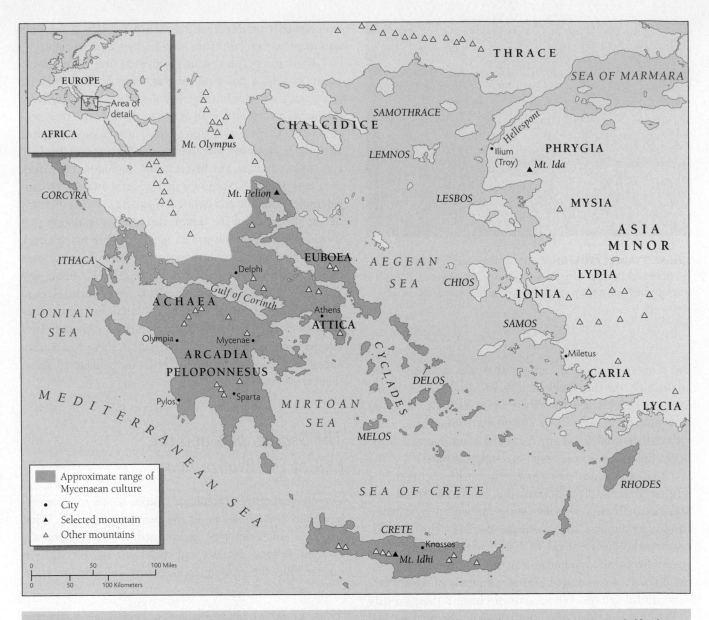

**MYCENAEAN GREECE.** ▪ *What stands out about the geography of Greece?* ▪ *How might this dry, mountainous country surrounded by the sea determine the nature of Greek civilization and economic interests?* ▪ *How might geography have allowed Mycenaean culture to spread so widely?*

Because Mycenaean Greece was an integrated part of a transnational network, the effects of its demise were felt throughout the region. Thereafter, a wave of devastation swept from north to south, caused by a group of people so thoroughly destructive that they obliterated everything in their path.

We might know nothing at all about them were it not for a narrow victory by the pharaoh Ramses III around 1176 B.C.E. In the stele set up to commemorate his triumph, near the modern city of Luxor on Egypt's West Bank, Ramses III referred to these invaders as the "Sea Peoples" and named several groups as parts of a coalition. Some were familiar to the Egyptians,

who had employed them as mercenaries. From Ramses' description of their battle gear, it seems that many were from the Aegean. Most notable were the Philistines who, after their defeat, withdrew to populate the coast of the region named after them: Palestine.

Because the Sea Peoples' arc of annihilation started in the north, it may have been one of the factors contributing to the collapse of Mycenaean Greece. Disruption of northern commercial networks would have devastated the Mycenaean kingdoms, which could not support their enormous populations without trade. Suddenly faced with an apocalyptic combination of overpopulation, famine, and

# Analyzing Primary Sources

## The Diplomacy of the Mycenaeans and the Hittites

*Around 1260 B.C.E., the powerful Hittite king Hattusilis III sent the following letter to a "King of Ahhiyawa," identifiable as a leader of the Mycenaean Greeks, who often called themselves Akhaiwoi, Achaeans. This fascinating document exemplifies the tangle of close ties that bound powerful men together within the transnational system of the Late Bronze Age, as well as the problems and misunderstandings that could arise from the misbehavior of the men under their command. The events referenced here all occurred in western Anatolia (Turkey), a region controlled partly by the Hittites and partly by the Greeks, the same region in which Troy (Ilium) was located. (See the map on page 52.)*

have to complain of the insolent and treacherous conduct of one Tawagalawas. We came into contact in the land of Lycia, and he offered to become a vassal of the Hittite Empire. I agreed, and sent an officer of most exalted rank to conduct him to my presence. He had the audacity to complain that the officer's rank was not exalted enough; he insulted my ambassador in public, and demanded that he be declared vassal-king there and then, without the formality of an interview. Very well: I order him, if he desires to become a vassal of mine, to make sure that no troops of his are found in Iyalanda when I arrive there. And what do I find when I arrive in Iyalanda?—the troops of Tawagalawas, fighting on the side of my enemies. I defeat them, take many prisoners ... scrupulously leaving the fortress of Atriya intact out of respect for my treaty with you. Now a Hittite subject, Piyamaradus by name, steals my 7,000 prisoners, and makes off to your city of Miletus. I command him to return to me: he disobeys. I write to you: you send a surly message unaccompanied by gift or greeting, to say that you have ordered your representative in Miletus, a certain Atpas, to deliver up Piyamaradus. Nothing happens, so I go fetch him. I enter your city of Miletus, for I have something to say to Piyamaradus, and it would be well that your subjects there should hear me say it. But my visit is not a success. I ask for Tawagalawas: he is not at home. I should like to see Piyamaradus: he has gone to sea. You refer me to your representative Atpas: I find that both he and his brother are married to daughters of Piyamaradus; they are not likely to give me satisfaction or to give you an unbiased account of these transactions. . . . Are you aware, and is it with your blessing, that Piyamaradus is going round saying that he intends to leave his wife and family, and incidentally my 7,000 prisoners, under your protection while he makes continual inroads on my dominion? . . . Do not let him use Achaea [in Greece] as a base for operations against me. You and I are friends. There has been no quarrel between us since we came to terms in the matter of Ilios [the territory of Troy]: the trouble there was my fault, and I promise it will not happen again. As for my military occupation of Miletus, please regard it as a friendly visit. . . . [As for the problems between us], I suggest that the fault may not lie with ourselves but with our messengers; let us bring them to trial, cut off their heads, mutilate their bodies, and live henceforth in perfect friendship.

Source: Adapted from Denys Page, *History and the Homeric Iliad* (Berkeley: 1959), pp. 11–12.

### Questions for Analysis

**1.** Reconstruct the relationship between Hattusilis III and the Achaean king, on the basis of the references to people and places in this letter. What picture emerges of their interactions and of the connections between the Hittite Empire and Mycenaean Greece?

**2.** Why is Hattusilis so concerned about the disrespect that the Achaeans have shown to him? Reading between the lines, what do you think he wanted to accomplish by sending this letter?

**3.** On the basis of this letter, what can you deduce about the standards of behavior expected of civilized participants in the transnational system of the Late Bronze Age? Within this code of conduct, what sanctions or penalties could be imposed on individuals or their nations?

violence, bands of desperate refugees would have fled the Aegean basin. Meanwhile, the damage to commerce had a domino effect and devastated the economy of the Hittites, whose ancient kingdom rapidly disintegrated. Along the Mediterranean coast we find other clues. The king of Ugarit wrote a letter to a "brother" king on the island of Cyprus, begging for immediate aid because he had sent all his own warriors to help the Hittites. It is poignant, however, that we have his letter only because the clay tablet on which it was written baked hard in the fire that destroyed his palace. The letter was never sent.

In the end, the Sea Peoples destroyed the Western civilizations that had flourished for over two thousand years. The devastation was not total; not all the cities disappeared, and trade did not cease entirely. But the Hittite Empire was eradicated, leaving behind it many weak, short-lived principalities. The great cosmopolitan cities of the eastern Mediterranean lay in ruins, and new groups—sometimes contingents of Sea Peoples like the Philistines—populated the coast. The citadels of Mycenaean Greece were depopulated by as much as 90 percent over the next century, and Greece entered into a period of cultural and economic isolation that would last for 250 years.

The victorious Egyptians survived; but with their major trading partners diminished or dead, their civilization suffered. The Assyrians, the original architects of the networks that had undergirded the transnational system, had to fight for their very existence. In Babylon, the peaceful and prosperous rule of the Kassites withered. In the vacuum left behind, new political configurations took shape, and a new metallurgical technology began to supplant the use of bronze. Out of the ashes arose the phoenix of the Iron Age.

## THE STATES OF THE EARLY IRON AGE

With the destruction of transnational networks, the geopolitical map of the ancient world changed significantly. In Anatolia, a patchwork of small kingdoms grew up within the territories once controlled by the Hittites. Similar developments took place in the Levant, the eastern Mediterranean coastline that today comprises Israel, Lebanon, and parts of Syria. For centuries, this region had been controlled either by the Egyptians or the Hittites. With the collapse of these empires, new states began to emerge there, too. They were small, but they had a huge impact on the history of Western civilizations.

## The Phoenicians

One of the most influential peoples of this period are usually called by their Greek name: the Phoenicians. They are also known as Canaanites, and were speakers of a Semitic language closely related to Hebrew, Amorite, and Ugaritic. Each Phoenician city on the coast of the Levant had its own hereditary royal government, and every Phoenician's first loyalty was to his or her own city. In the Phoenicians' overseas colonies, however, a new type of political system emerged in which power was shared among a handful of elite families. This aristocratic form of government would become a model for many other Western societies, including those of classical Greece and Rome (see Chapters 3 and 5).

During the Late Bronze Age, most Phoenician cities had been controlled by Egypt. But the erosion of Egyptian imperial power after 1200 B.C.E. gave these cities the opportunity to forge a new independence and to capitalize on their commercial advantages. One Phoenician city, Gubla, was a clearinghouse for papyrus, the highly prized Egyptian writing material. This explains why the Greek name for this city, Byblos, became the basis for the Greek word *biblion*, meaning "book." (The Bible is so called from the plural *biblia*, "the books.") Another valuable commodity that came to be associated with the Phoenicians, and that gave them their name, was a rare purple dye derived from the shells of snails culled from the seabed off the Levantine coast. As far as the Greeks were concerned, those who supplied this rich dye were *phoinikeoi*, "purple people." Phoenician textiles commanded a high price everywhere; so did timber from the Levant, especially cedar, and Canaanite glass. The Phoenicians also became expert metalworkers, ivory carvers, and shipbuilders.

## Phoenician Colonies and Cultural Influence

The Phoenicians became famous as merchants and seafarers, but they were also aggressive colonists. By the end of the tenth century B.C.E., they had planted settlements from one end of the Mediterranean to the other, and their merchants had begun to venture out into the Atlantic Ocean. We have good evidence that they traveled as far as Cornwall (southwest Britain) during this period. The Greek historian Herodotus later claimed that Phoenician merchant-explorers even circumnavigated Africa. At the end of the ninth century B.C.E., Phoenicians from the city of Tyre established Carthage in modern-day Tunisia (North Africa).

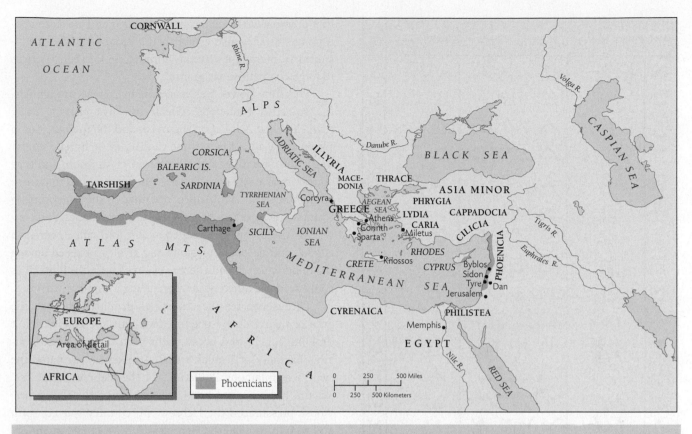

**PHOENICIAN COLONIZATION.** Compare this map with the more detailed one of the Hebrew kingdoms on page 59. ▪ *What part of the Mediterranean was the homeland for the Phoenician city-states?* ▪ *Where did Phoenicians establish colonies?* ▪ *Why would overseas colonization be of such crucial importance to Phoenician city-states?* ▪ *What does their westward colonization imply about the Phoenicians' aims and about the different opportunities available in the western Mediterranean?*

Carthage would ultimately become the preeminent power in the western Mediterranean; centuries later, this brought it into conflict with Rome (see Chapter 5).

The widespread colonial and mercantile efforts of the Phoenicians meant that they influenced cultures across the Mediterranean. Among their early overseas trading partners were the Greeks, and the Phoenicians may have played an important role in reintroducing urban life to Greece after the collapse of the Mycenaean citadels. They also brought with them a number of artistic and literary influences. Without question, however, the most important contribution of the Phoenicians was their alphabet.

As we noted earlier, a thirty-character alphabet had evolved at Ugarit by the end of the Bronze Age. Around 1100 B.C.E., the Phoenicians refined this writing system to twenty-two characters. This simpler system further facilitated communication and accounting, and the Phoenicians may have wanted to encourage similar practices among their trading partners, to safeguard their own interests. The Greeks certainly remained aware of their debt to the Phoenicians: their legends ascribe the invention of the alphabet to Cadmus, a Phoenician who settled in Greece. Their debt is also clear in the close relationship between the names of letters in Greek (alpha, beta, gamma, delta . . .) and Phoenician letter names (aleph, bayt, gimel, dalet . . .), and from the obvious similarities in letter shapes.

## The Philistines

Southward along the Levantine coast from Phoenicia lay the land of the Philistines, descendants of the Sea Peoples defeated by Ramses III (see the map on page 59). Their reputation is the result of their dominance over their pastoral neighbors, the herdsmen known as the Hebrews, who used writing as an effective weapon: the Philistines thus became the great villains of the Hebrew scriptures, and accordingly the word *philistine* has come to mean a boorish, uncultured person. Unfortunately, the Philistines do not appear to have made use of the same powerful technology to record their own outlook on the world, and almost everything we know about them comes from the work of archaeologists or has to be sifted through the bad press of their detractors.

| HEBREW | PHŒNICIAN | ANCIENT GREEK | LATER GREEK | ENGLISH |
|---|---|---|---|---|
| א | | | | A |
| ב | | | B | B |
| ג | | | Γ | G |
| ד | | | Δ | D |
| ה | | | E | E |
| ו | | | | F |
| ז | | | Z | Z |
| ח | | | | H |
| ט | | | Θ | Th |
| י | | | I | I |
| כ | | | K | K |
| ל | | | Λ | L |
| מ | | | M | M |
| נ | | | N | N |
| | | | Ξ | X |
| ס | | | O | O |
| | | | Π | P |
| | | | Q | Q |
| | | | P | R |
| ר | | | Σ C | S |
| ת | | | T | T |
| | | OMITTED NOT BEING IN GREEK | | |

**THE EVOLUTION OF THE ALPHABET.** This table shows how the shapes of letters changed as the Phoenician alphabet was adapted by the Hebrews, the Greeks, and eventually the Romans (from whom our modern alphabet derives).

that dominated the region in the twelfth and eleventh centuries B.C.E. They also established a monopoly over metalsmithing, making it virtually impossible for their enemies to forge competitive weaponry.

Philistine power was based in five great strongholds, the so-called Pentapolis (Greek for "five cities"): Gaza, Ashkelon, and Ashdod on the coast, and the inland cities of Ekron and Gath. (Again, these citadels are strikingly similar to the fortified palaces of Mycenaean civilization, and they appear to have had many of the same functions.) From these strongholds, the Philistines dominated the surrounding countryside by organizing agricultural production and controlling trade routes. An independent lord ruled over each citadel, and no doubt tensions and rivalries existed among them. But much like the heroes of Greek epic, the Philistines could set aside differences when facing a common enemy.

Because we see the Philistines primarily through the eyes of their Hebrew enemies, we must be careful about drawing conclusions about them from the stories of Goliath's brutality or Delilah's sexual treachery, to name the two most infamous Philistines of the Hebrew scriptures. Yet the Hebrews had good reason to fear the Philistines, whose pressure on the Hebrew hill country was constant and who threatened the Hebrews' holy sanctuary at Shiloh, where the sacred Ark of the Covenant—said to contain the original tablets of the law given to Moses on Mount Sinai—was kept. In Hebrew tradition, the tribes of Israel had once carried the ark before them into battle against the Philistines, only to lose it in the fray and to witness thereafter the destruction of Shiloh. The Philistines then established garrisons throughout the land of the Hebrews and exacted tribute, denied them access to weapons, and engaged in the typical abuses of an occupying people.

## The Hebrews and Their Scriptures

The central feature of Hebrew culture, their conception of and relationship to their god, will be discussed at greater length toward the end of this chapter. In this section, we focus our attention on the historical development of Hebrew society in the Iron Age Levant. In reconstructing this early history, we are indebted to an unusual textual source already mentioned: a series of scriptures (literally, "writings") that comprise mythology, laws and ritual practices, genealogical records, books of prophecy, proverbs, poetry, and royal chronicles. These are collectively known as the Hebrew Bible or (among Christians) the Old Testament. These multiple books were composed at different times for different purposes and were only gradually assembled over many centuries, mostly by unknown authors, copyists, and

The Philistines occupied a unique position in the Levant and retained a separate identity for several generations; each new archaeological discovery roots this identity more firmly in their Aegean past. We know little about their language, but their material culture, behavior, and organization all exhibit close affinities with Mycenaean Greece. For example, the Philistines introduced grapevines and olive trees to the Levant from the Aegean basin. With the profits from these industries, they created powerful armies

# Past and Present

## The Fragility of Global Networks

During the Late Bronze Age, the destruction of transnational commercial networks had a domino effect on the interlocking civilizations of the West, plunging many into a "dark age" of isolation and impoverishment. The global economic crisis of our own day was caused by a similar phenomenon: the collapse of mutually dependent financial systems that proved more fragile than anyone had anticipated.

 **Watch related author interview on the Student Site**

editors. Some are clearly derived from ancient oral traditions; others respond to immediate challenges. Like other historical sources, then, they have to be placed in their specific individual contexts and analyzed carefully. At the same time, of course, they can be read collectively as the story of a people's unification and religious awakening.

The first five books of the Hebrew Bible are traditionally attributed to the Hebrew leader Moses. But many of the materials in these books were borrowed from other cultures, including the stories of the creation and the flood, which parallel those of Sumer (as we saw in Chapter 1). The story of Moses's childhood draws on a legend told about the Akkadian king Sargon the Great. The laws and rituals of the patriarchs can be found in other traditions, too. Meanwhile, the story of the exodus from Egypt is fraught with contradictions. Although the later Book of Joshua claims that the Hebrews who returned from Egypt conquered and expelled the native Canaanites, archaeological and linguistic evidence suggests that the Hebrews were essentially Canaanites themselves.

They may have merged with scattered refugees from Egypt in the aftermath of the Sea Peoples' invasions, but for the most part they had been continuously resident in Canaan for centuries. In sum, the first five books of the Bible constitute a retrospective history whose purpose was to justify Hebrew traditions and claims to territory.

Among the other writings included in the Hebrew Bible are a group of texts that record events of the more recent past, the period we are considering now. These "historical books" are more straightforwardly verifiable, even if many details are difficult to confirm. According to the Book of Judges, the Hebrews were herdsmen who had just begun to establish permanent settlements around the time of the Philistines' arrival in the Levant. They had organized themselves into twelve tribes: extended clan units whose families owed each other mutual aid and protection in times of war, but who frequently fought over cattle and grazing rights. Each tribe was ruled by a patriarch known as a judge, who exercised the typical functions of authority in a clan-based society: war leadership, high priesthood, and dispute settlement. By the middle of the twelfth century B.C.E., these tribes occupied two major territories, with those settled in the south calling themselves the tribes of Judah, and those in the north the tribes of Israel.

## The Struggle for Hebrew Unity

The Hebrew tribes of this period had few occasions to work together as a group and little experience of organized activity. This made them highly vulnerable, especially when the Philistines conquered the Levantine coast, around 1050 B.C.E. Faced with the threat of extinction, the Hebrews appear to have put up desperate resistance from their bases in the hilly interior. To counter the Philistine threat effectively, however, they needed a leader. Accordingly, around 1025 B.C.E., an influential tribal judge called Samuel selected a king to lead the tribes of Israel against the Philistines. His name was Saul. However, Saul proved to be an ineffective war leader. Although he blocked Philistine penetration into the hill country, he could not oust the Philistines from the valleys or coastal plains. So Samuel withdrew his support from Saul and threw it behind a young man in Saul's entourage, Saul's son-in-law David, a warrior from Judah. Waging his own independent military campaigns, David achieved one triumph after another over the Philistines. By contrast, the armies of Saul met frequent reversals—that is, according to the chroniclers responsible for the historical books of the Bible, who wrote their accounts under David's patronage.

These same books reveal that David was not initially motivated by patriotism. He was a man on the make; when Saul finally drove him from his court, he became an outlaw on the fringes of Hebrew society and a mercenary in Philistine service. It was as a Philistine mercenary, in fact, that David fought against Saul in the climactic battle in which Saul was killed. Soon thereafter, David himself became king, first over the tribes of Judah, his home territory, and later over Saul's territory of Israel as well.

## The Consolidation of a Hebrew Kingdom

After David's victory around 1000 B.C.E., he strove to strengthen his authority within and beyond his kingdom. He took advantage of the opportunity afforded by Egypt's decline to expand his territory southward, eventually confining the Philistines to an inconsequential strip of coastal land. David also defeated the neighboring Moabites and Ammonites, extending his control to the Dead Sea. By the time of his death in 973 B.C.E., his kingdom stretched from the middle Euphrates in the north to the Gulf of Aqaba in the south, and from the Mediterranean coast eastward into the Syrian deserts. Israel was now a force to be reckoned with, although it partly owed that status to the temporary weakness of its imperial neighbors, Egypt and Assyria.

As David's power and prestige grew, he was able to impose on his subjects a highly unpopular system of taxation and forced labor. His goal was to build a glorious capital at Jerusalem, a Canaanite settlement that he designated as the central city of his realm. It was a shrewd choice. As a newly conquered city, Jerusalem had no previous affiliation with any of Israel's twelve tribes and so stood outside the ancient rivalries that divided them. Jerusalem was also a geographically strategic choice, lying between the southern tribes of Judah (David's people) and the northern tribes of Israel. David took steps to exalt the city as a religious center by making Jerusalem the resting place of the sacred Ark of the Covenant and elevating the priesthood of the Hebrew god, Yahweh. By these measures, he sought to forge a new collective identity centered on his own family and its connections to Yahweh. To this end, he also encouraged the writing of histories and prophecies that would affirm this identity and his central role in forging it.

## The Reign of King Solomon (973–937 B.C.E.)

Continuing his father's policies, but on a much grander scale, David's son Solomon built a great temple complex at Jerusalem to house the ark. Such visible support of Yahweh's cult was approved by the chroniclers whose works are included in the Bible, and who portray Solomon's reign as a golden age. Despite his proverbial wisdom, however, Solomon could be a ruthless and often brutal ruler whose promotion of Yahweh coincided with a program of despotism. According to his own histories, Solomon kept an enormous harem of some 300 wives and 700 concubines, many of them drawn from subject or allied peoples. His palace complex—of which the Temple was a part—allowed him to rule in the grand style of ancient Mesopotamian potentates. To finance his expensive tastes and programs, Solomon instituted oppressive taxation and imposed customs duties on the lucrative caravan trade that passed through his country. With the help of the Phoenician king of Tyre, Solomon constructed a commercial fleet whose ships plied the waters of the Red Sea and beyond, trading—among other commodities—the gold and copper mined by Solomon's slaves.

**THE HEBREW KINGDOMS, C. 900 B.C.E.** Notice the scale of the map and consider the comparatively small size of the Hebrews' world. ▪ *What advantages did the Philistines and Phoenicians possess, geographical and otherwise?* ▪ *Why did they present such a challenge to the Hebrews?* ▪ *What political and religious consequences might have resulted from the division of the kingdom after the death of King Solomon, given the location of Jerusalem?*

Israel's new wealth was bought at a high price. Solomon maintained a large standing army of unwilling conscripts from his own people, equipped with chariot and cavalry squadrons and powered by horses purchased abroad. To undertake his ambitious building projects, Solomon also required many of his subjects to perform forced labor four months out of every year. This level of oppression was too much for many Israelites, and the northern tribes seethed with rebellion against the royal capital. Within a decade or so of Solomon's death the fragile monarchy split in two. The dynasty descended from David continued to rule the southern kingdom of Judah with its capital at Jerusalem, but the ten northern tribes banded together as the kingdom of Israel, with their capital at Shechem. Archaeology, combined with accounts in the Bible, reveal that the cult of Yahweh was not yet dominant in either the north or the south, so major religious differences made reunification

even more difficult. In the meantime, the changing political situation of the larger region made the Hebrew kingdoms increasingly vulnerable.

## THE REVIVAL OF THE ASSYRIAN EMPIRE

As we have already seen, the Assyrians had long played an important role in spreading trade and promoting urban settlements. But like the other great powers of ancient world, their civilization had been devastated by the Sea Peoples. For several centuries afterward they struggled for survival. Then, in the ninth century B.C.E., a brilliant but brutal ruler laid the foundations of what historians call the Neo-Assyrian Empire. Under the leadership of Assurnasirpal II (*ah-sur-NAH-sur-PAHL;* 883–859 B.C.E.), the Assyrians began to conduct aggressive military campaigns against their neighbors on an annual basis. Those whom they defeated either had to pay tribute or face the full onslaught of the Assyrian war machine, which acquired a deserved reputation for savagery under Assurnasirpal.

Despite their military successes, Assurnasirpal and his son, Shalmeneser III (*SHAHL-meh-NEE-zehr;* 853–827 B.C.E.), inspired stiff resistance. The northern kingdom of Israel formed an alliance with other small states to halt Assyrian expansion. This coalition ultimately forced Shalmeneser III to settle for smaller victories against the Armenians to his northwest and the Medes to his northeast, until a great revolt within Assyria itself ended his reign. Thereafter, a usurper named Tiglath-Pileser III seized the Assyrian throne in 744 B.C.E. and immediately demanded tribute from various kingdoms that had not paid up for generations. Those who refused fell victim to his armies.

When Tiglath-Pileser III died in 727 B.C.E., many of these recently conquered states rebelled, but Tiglath-Pileser's son, Shalmeneser V, energetically crushed them. When he died in battle, he was quickly replaced by one of his military commanders, who took the name Sargon II (722–705 B.C.E.). Sargon claimed to be the direct successor of Sargon of Akkad, the great king of Sumer and the first great king in Mesopotamian history, nearly 1,500 years earlier (see Chapter 1). Like the Hebrews, Sargon and his successors skillfully deployed history as a political tool. Eventually, they extended the frontiers of the Assyrian Empire from western Iran to the shores of the Mediterranean; briefly, they even subjugated parts of Egypt. Sargon himself put an end to the kingdom of Israel in 722 B.C.E., enslaving and deporting most of the population, and he terrified the southern kingdom of Judah into remaining a

# Competing Viewpoints

## Two Accounts of Saul's Anointing

*When the charismatic judge Samuel chose Saul as the first king of the Hebrews, he opened a new chapter in the political history of Israel. But Saul's kingship was not a success, and Samuel ultimately turned against him, supporting Saul's rival (and son-in-law), David. These two quite different accounts of Samuel's anointing of Saul reflect the tensions that later arose between them—and probably were written down during the later kingship of David, Saul's successor. The first account also suggests the ambivalence some Hebrews felt about having a human king at all, doubts that Saul himself may have shared.*

### 1 Samuel 8:4–22, 10:20–25

All the elders of Israel gathered together and [said to Samuel]: "You are old and your sons do not follow in your ways; appoint for us, then, a king to govern us, like other nations." But the thing displeased Samuel [who] prayed to the Lord, and the Lord said to Samuel, "Listen to the voice of the people in all that they say to you; for they have not rejected you, but they have rejected me from being king over them. Just as they have done to me, from the day I brought them up out of Egypt to this day, forsaking me and serving other gods, so they are also doing to you. Now then, listen to their voice; only—you shall solemnly warn them, and show them the ways of the king who shall reign over them." So Samuel reported all the words of the Lord to the people who were asking for a king. "These will be the ways of the king who will reign over you: he will take sons and appoint them to his chariots . . . he will take your daughters to be perfumers and cooks and bakers . . . he will take one-tenth of your grain and your vineyards and give it to his officers and courtiers . . . and one-tenth of your flocks, and you shall be his slaves." But the people refused to listen, and Samuel said to the people, "Each of you return to his home."

Then Samuel brought all the tribes of Israel near, and the tribe of Benjamin was chosen by lot. He brought the tribe of Benjamin near, [organized] by its families . . . and Saul the son of Kish was chosen by lot. But when they sought him, he could not be found. So they inquired again of the Lord . . . and the Lord said, "See, he has hidden himself among the baggage." Then they ran and brought him from there. When he took his stand among the people, he was head and shoulders taller than any of them. Samuel said, "You see the one whom the Lord has chosen? There is no one like him among the people." And the people all shouted, "Long live the king!" Samuel told the people the rights and duties of the kingship; and he wrote them in a book and laid it up before the Lord.

loyal and quiet vassal. The ancient kingdom of Elam on the Iranian plateau—a civilization almost as old as Sumer—also fell during this period. By the seventh century B.C.E., Assyria was the unrivaled power of the ancient region.

## Neo-Assyrian Government and Administration

The Neo-Assyrian Empire was a military dictatorship, built on the ability of its army to spread terror and oppress both enemies and subjects alike. At its head was a hereditary monarch regarded as the earthly representative of the Assyrians' patron god, Assur. When his army was not in the field, the king's time was taken up with elaborate sacrifices and rituals to appease the "great god." Divination and the consultation of oracles were central features of this religion, because the Neo-Assyrian king—as chief priest—had to be able to discern the will of Assur through the portents of nature.

Supporting the empire's centralized authority was an extensive bureaucracy of governors, high priests, and military commanders—professions by no means

## 1 Samuel 9:1–10:1

There was a man of Benjamin whose name was Kish . . . [who] had a son whose name was Saul, a handsome young man . . . he stood head and shoulders above everyone else. Now the donkeys of Kish had strayed. So Kish said to his son Saul, "Take one of the boys with you; go and look for the donkeys." . . . As they were entering [a] town, they saw Samuel coming out toward them on his way up to the shrine. Now the day before Saul came, the Lord revealed to Samuel, "Tomorrow about this time I will send you a man from the land of Benjamin, and you shall anoint him to be ruler over my people Israel. He shall save my people from the hand of the Philistines; for I have seen the suffering of my people, because their outcry has come to me." . . . Saul approached Samuel inside the gate and said, "Tell me please, where is the house of the seer?" Samuel answered Saul, "I am the seer, go up before me to the shrine. . . . As for your donkeys that were lost three days ago, give no further thought to them, for they have been found. And on whom is all Israel's desire fixed, if not on you and your ancestral house?" Saul answered, "I am only a Benjaminite, from the least of the tribes of Israel, and my family is the humblest of all the families of the tribe of Benjamin. Why then have you spoken of me this way?" . . . As they were going down to the outskirts of town, Samuel said to Saul, "Tell the boy to go on before us . . . that I may make known to you the word of God." Samuel took a vial of oil and poured it on [Saul's] head and kissed him; he said: "The Lord has anointed you ruler over his people Israel. You shall reign over the people of the Lord and you will save them from the hand of their enemies all around."

*Source: The New Oxford Annotated Bible (Oxford: 1994) (slightly adapted, source for both documents).*

### Questions for Analysis

*1.* Do these two accounts fit together? How do they differ? Why were both preserved in the Book of Samuel?

*2.* What view of kingship emerges in the first account? What are the attributes of a king? What is the relationship among the king, his god, and the priest anointing him? What is the role of the people in his selection?

*3.* The writers of Jewish scripture judged kings by their observance of the law, their zeal in fighting against competing religious cults, and their support of centralized worship at the Temple in Jerusalem. How did this form of theocracy in ancient Israel compare with that in Egypt and Mesopotamia?

---

mutually exclusive. These administrators formed the highest class in Neo-Assyrian society and exercised local authority on behalf of the king. They maintained lines of transport and communication, which were the engines of imperial hegemony, and supervised the construction of an extensive network of roads that served these needs for centuries. The Neo-Assyrian state also deployed a system of spies and messengers to report to the royal court on the activities of subjects and provincial governors.

These provincial governors collected tribute, recruited for the army, and administered the king's law. It is not surprising that the Assyrians, so mindful of historical precedent, modeled their laws on the Code of Hammurabi, though many of their penalties were much more severe. The harshest punishments were reserved for practices deemed detrimental to human reproduction; the penalties for same-sex relations and abortion were particularly severe. Neo-Assyrian law was also rigidly patriarchal, which entailed substantial revision of Hammurabi's code: now only husbands had the power of divorce, and they were legally permitted to inflict a variety of penalties on their wives, ranging from corporal punishment to mutilation and death.

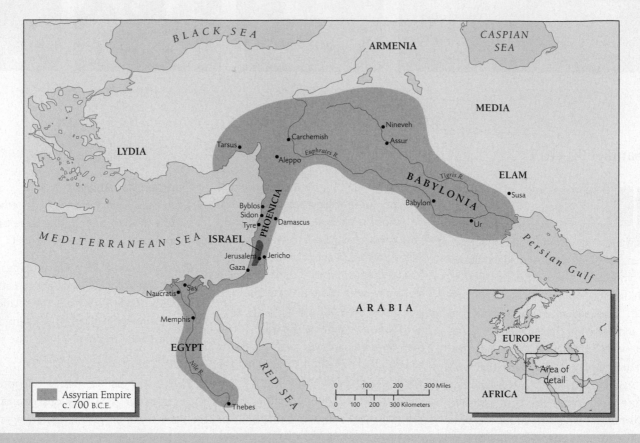

**THE NEO-ASSYRIAN EMPIRE, C. 700 B.C.E.** ▪ *What were the territorial boundaries of the Neo-Assyrian Empire?* ▪ *Why would the Assyrians concentrate their efforts in the river valleys and along the coast, neglecting the Syrian interior?* ▪ *Notice the location of the Neo-Assyrian capitals of Nineveh and Assur; how was their situation in Mesopotamia likely to affect the Assyrians' sense of their own historical identity?* ▪ *Consider the position of Egypt. Why might the Assyrians find it difficult to subjugate Egypt permanently?*

## The Assyrian Military-Religious Ethos

The Assyrians' new religious, political, and military ideology had taken shape during the long centuries when they fought for survival, and it then became the foundational ethos for their empire's relentless conquests. Its two fundamental tenets were the waging of holy war and the exaction of tribute through terror.

The Neo-Assyrians were convinced that their god demanded the constant expansion of his worship through military conquest. Essentially, their army belonged to Assur, and all who did not accept Assur's supremacy were, by that fact alone, enemies of Assur's people. Ritual humiliation of a defeated city's gods was therefore a regular feature of conquest. Statues of conquered gods would be carried off to the Neo-Assyrian capital, where they would remain as hostages at the court of Assur. Meanwhile, an image of Assur himself—usually represented as a sun disk with the head and shoulders of an archer—would be installed in the defeated city, and the conquered people would be

required to worship him. Although conquered peoples did not have to abandon their previous gods altogether, they were made to feel their gods' inferiority. The Assyrians were therefore strict henotheists, meaning that they acknowledged the existence of other gods but believed that one god should be the supreme deity of all peoples.

For the Neo-Assyrians, "receiving tribute" meant the taking of plunder. Rather than defeating their foes once and imposing formal obligations, the Assyrians raided even their vanquished foes each year. This strategy kept the Neo-Assyrian military machine primed for battle, but it did little to inspire loyalty among subject peoples, who often felt that they had nothing to lose through rebellion. Moreover, annual invasions toughened the forces of the Neo-Assyrians' subjects. To counter them, imperial battle tactics became notoriously savage—even by the standards of ancient warfare, which regarded the mutilation of prisoners, systematic rape, and mass deportations as commonplace. Neo-Assyrian artwork and inscriptions often celebrate the butchering and torture of their enemies. Smiling archers are shown shooting fleeing enemies in the back while remorseless soldiers impale captives on stakes.

The Neo-Assyrian army was not a seasonal army of part-time warriors or peasant conscripts, but rather a massive standing force of more than 100,000 soldiers. Because the Assyrians had mastered iron-smelting techniques on a large scale, they could equip their fighting men with high-quality steel weapons that overwhelmed opponents still reliant on bronze. The organization of this army also contributed to its success. At its core were heavily armed and armored shock troops, equipped with a variety of thrusting weapons and bearing tall shields for protection. They were the main force for crushing enemy infantry in the field and for routing the inhabitants of an enemy city once inside. To harass enemy infantry and break up their formations, the Assyrians deployed light skirmishers with slings and javelins, and they combined archery and chariotry as never before. They also developed the first true cavalry force in the West, with individual warriors mounted on armored steeds, wielding bows and arrows or heavy lances. They

**NEO-ASSYRIAN ATROCITIES.** Judean captives whose city has fallen to the Neo-Assyrian king Sennacherib (704–681 B.C.E.) are shown being impaled on stakes. This triumphal carving comes from the walls of Sennacherib's palace at Nineveh. ■ *What was the purpose of advertising these captives' fates?*

even trained a highly skilled corps of combat engineers to undermine city walls and to build catapults, siege engines, battering rams, and battle towers.

## The Legacy of Neo-Assyrian Power

The successors of Sargon II continued these military policies while devoting great energy to promoting an Assyrian cultural legacy. Sargon's immediate successor, Sennacherib (*sen-AH-sher-ib*; 704–681 B.C.E.), rebuilt the ancient Assyrian city of Nineveh, fortifying it with a double wall for a circuit of nine miles. He constructed an enormous palace there, raised on a giant platform decorated with marble, ivory, and exotic woods; and he ordered the construction of a massive irrigation system, including an aqueduct that carried fresh water to the city from thirty miles away. His son rebuilt the conquered city of Babylon along similar lines and was also a patron of the arts and sciences. His grandson Assurbanipal (*ah-sur-BAHN-ih-pahl*; r. 669–627 B.C.E.) was perhaps the greatest of all the Neo-Assyrian kings. For a time, he ruled the entire delta region of northern Egypt and also enacted a series of internal reforms, seeking ways to govern his empire more peacefully.

By Neo-Assyrian standards, Assurbanipal was an enlightened ruler, and one to whom we owe a tremendous debt. Like Sargon II before him, he had a strong sense of the rich traditions of Mesopotamian history and laid claim to it. But he did this much more systematically: he ordered the construction of a magnificent library at the great capital of Nineveh, where all the cultural monuments of Mesopotamian literature were to be copied and preserved. This library also was an archive for the correspondence and official acts of the king. Fortunately, this trove of documentation has survived. Our knowledge of history, not to mention all modern editions of the *Epic of Gilgamesh*, ultimately derive from the library at Nineveh.

When Assurbanipal died in 627 B.C.E., the Neo-Assyrian Empire appeared to be at its zenith. Its borders were secure, the realm was largely at peace with its neighbors, its kings had adorned their capitals with magnificent artwork, and the hanging gardens of Babylon were already famous: these were artificial slopes whose cascading flowers and trees were fed by irrigation systems that pumped water uphill, an amazing marriage of engineering and horticulture. The collapse of this empire is therefore all the more dramatic for its suddenness. Within fifteen years of Assurbanipal's reign, Nineveh lay in ruins. An alliance had formed between the Indo-European Medes of Iran and the Chaldeans, a Semitic people who controlled the southern half of Babylonia. By 605 B.C.E., the Chaldeans had occupied Babylon and destroyed the last

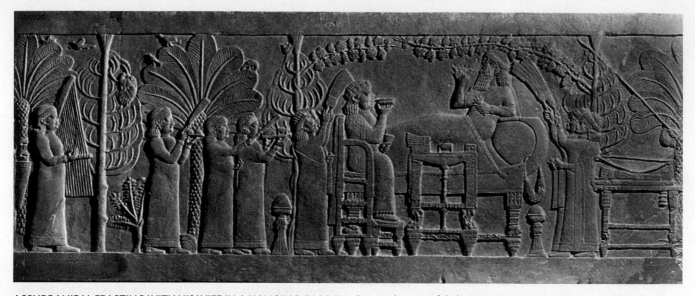

**ASSURBANIPAL FEASTING WITH HIS WIFE IN A HANGING GARDEN.** Even in this peaceful, domestic scene, the severed head of the king's recently defeated enemy, the king of Elam, can be seen hanging from the pine tree on the left.

remnants of Neo-Assyrian power on the upper Euphrates, becoming the predominant imperial power in Mesopotamia and the Levant. In 586 B.C.E., they captured Jerusalem, destroyed the Temple, and deported the population of Judah to Babylon. Meanwhile, the Medes retired to the Iranian Plateau to extend their suzerainty there.

## THE RISE OF THE PERSIANS

In the sixth century B.C.E., the Persian Empire emerged as the successor state to the Neo-Assyrian kings. This was after the region had been ruled for a few decades by the Chaldean Empire (612–539 B.C.E.) and the Lydian kingdom. Once the Persians had thrown off the Chaldeans' dominance, they in turn would construct the largest empire known to the world until that time.

### The Persian Empire of Cyrus the Great

The Persians came to power relatively suddenly, under an extraordinary prince named Cyrus, who succeeded to the rule of a single Persian tribe in 559 B.C.E. Shortly thereafter, Cyrus made himself ruler of all the Persians and then, around 549 B.C.E., challenged the lordship of the Medes and began to claim dominion over lands stretching from the Persian Gulf to eastern Anatolia.

This brought the Persians into close contact with the kingdom of Lydia. The Lydians had attained great prosperity as producers of gold and silver specie (money) and as intermediaries for overland commerce between Mesopotamia and the Aegean. Most important, they were the first people in antiquity to use precious-metal coinage as a medium of exchange for goods and services. When Cyrus came to power, the Lydians' king was Croesus (*CREE-suhs*), a man whose reputation as the possessor of untold riches survives in the expression "rich as Croesus." Distrusting his new neighbor, Croesus decided to launch a preventive strike against the Persians to preserve his own kingdom from conquest. According to the Greek historian Herodotus, he took the precaution of asking the oracle of Apollo at Delphi whether this strategy was a good one and was told that if he attacked the Persians he would destroy a great nation. The oracle's pronouncement was both ambiguous and true: the nation Croesus destroyed was his own. Cyrus defeated his forces in 546 B.C.E.

Cyrus then invaded Mesopotamia in 539 B.C.E., striking so quickly that he took Babylon without a fight. Once he was in Babylon, the entire Chaldean Empire was his for the taking, though his own imperial policies proved very different from those of his predecessors in that region. Cyrus freed the Hebrews who had been held captive in Babylon since 586 B.C.E. and sent them back to Jerusalem, helping them to rebuild their temple and allowing them to set up a semi-independent vassal state. Cyrus also allowed other conquered peoples considerable self-determination, especially with respect to cultural and religious practices—a marked reversal of Neo-Assyrian and Chaldean policies. When Cyrus died in battle in 530 B.C.E., Persian expansion continued and his son even conquered Egypt in 525 B.C.E. Two hundred years

**AN EARLY LYDIAN COIN.** Probably struck during the reign of Croesus, this coin was one of many that facilitated long-distance trade by making wealth portable.

later, a young Macedonian king, Alexander, would emulate many of Cyrus's policies and build an empire sustained by many of the same strategies (see Chapter 4).

## The Consolidation of Persian Rule

Cyrus's son Cambyses II was a warrior king like his father, but after his death he left the Persian Empire a cumbersome and poorly organized collection of rapid conquests. After a short period of civil war, the aristocratic inner circle that had served both him and his father settled on a collateral member of the royal family as the new king. This was Darius, whose long reign of thirty-five years (521–486 B.C.E.) consolidated his predecessors' military gains by improving the administration of the Persian state. Darius divided the empire into provinces, each of which was administered by an official called a *satrap*. Although satraps enjoyed extensive powers and considerable political latitude, they owed fixed tributes and absolute loyalty to the central government, as did vassal states such as the technically autonomous Hebrew kingdom.

Adhering to the tolerant policy of Cyrus, Darius allowed the various peoples of the empire to retain most of their local institutions while enforcing a standardized central currency and a system of weights and measures. Beyond this, he had little interest in imposing onerous taxes, martial law, or the Persians' own religious practices on subject peoples. After centuries of Neo-Assyrian and Chaldean tyranny, the light hand of Persian rule was welcomed throughout the empire's far-reaching lands.

Darius was also a great builder. He erected a new royal residence and ceremonial capital that the Greeks called Persepolis ("Persia City"). He ordered a canal dug from the Nile to the Red Sea to facilitate trade with the Egyptian interior, and installed irrigation systems on the Persian plateau and on the fringe of the Syrian desert to increase agricultural production. Darius also expanded the existing Assyrian road system to enhance trade and communications throughout his huge realm. The most famous artery was the Royal Road, stretching 1,600 miles from Susa, near the Persian Gulf, to Sardis (the former Lydian capital) near the Aegean. Government couriers along this road constituted the first postal system, carrying messages and goods in relay stages from one post to another. Each post was a day's horseback ride from the next, where a fresh horse and rider would be ready to carry the dispatches brought by the postman before him. An extensive imperial spy network also used this postal system and was famed throughout Persia as the "eyes and ears of the king."

Darius was an extraordinarily gifted administrator, but as a military strategist he made an enormous mistake when he attempted to extend Persian hegemony into Greece. Cyrus's conquest of Lydia had made Persia the ruler of some long-established Greek-speaking cities on the western coast of Anatolia, a region called Ionia. But these cities resisted even the easy terms of Persian rule, desiring instead to model themselves on the self-governing city-states that had come into being across the Aegean. Consequently, between 499 and 494 B.C.E., the Greeks of Asia waged a war for independence and briefly gained the support of troops from Athens, who joined the Greeks of Ionia in burning the Persian administrative center at Sardis. Darius quelled this uprising and then decided to send a force to punish Athens and serve notice of Persian dominion over all Greek states. But at the battle of Marathon in 490 B.C.E., the Athenians dealt Darius the only major setback of his reign. And when his son and successor, Xerxes (*ZEHRK-zees*), attempted to avenge this humiliation in 480 B.C.E., a resistance led by both Athens and Sparta forced him to retreat and abandon his plans a year later. (We will discuss these events at greater length in Chapter 3.)

The Persians were thus compelled to recognize that they had reached the westward limits of their expansion. Thereafter, they concentrated on their Asian possessions and used money and diplomacy to keep the Greeks in check. This was not difficult, because the Greeks' hasty union in the face of Persian hegemony was short lived, and they were too embroiled in wars with one another to pose any threat to Persia.

**A CYLINDRICAL SEAL OF DARIUS THE GREAT (522–486 B.C.E.).** Seals were used in place of signatures to authenticate documents and correspondence. The cylindrical matrix (right) was rolled in soft wax to create an impression. This finely wrought example shows the king in a chariot, hunting lions with a bow. A winged representation of the god Ahura-Mazda rises above the scene.

The richness of their culture and the general tolerance they exhibited served the Persians well in maintaining their enormous empire. Unlike the Neo-Assyrian or Chaldean rulers, the Persians could count on the loyalty and even the affection of their subjects. In fact, their imperial model—the accommodation of local institutions and practices, consistent administration through a trained bureaucracy, and rapid communications between center and periphery—would be adopted by the great and lasting empires of all subsequent Western civilizations.

## The Legacy of Zoroastrianism

The Persians' political and cultural achievements were paralleled by a spiritual one: Zoroastrianism. Along with Buddhism and Judaism, this important religion was one of the three major universal faiths before Christianity and Islam. Its founder was Zarathustra, known to the Greeks as Zoroaster, a Persian who probably lived shortly before 600 B.C.E. Zarathustra sought to reform the traditional customs of the Persian tribes by eradicating polytheism, animal sacrifice, and magic. That is, he wanted to redefine religion as an ethical practice common to all people, rather than a set of rituals and superstitions that caused divisions among them.

Zoroastrianism teaches that there is one supreme god in the universe, whom Zarathustra called Ahura-Mazda,

"Wise Lord." Ahura-Mazda is the essence of light, truth, and righteousness; there is nothing wrathful or wicked about him, and his goodness extends to everyone, not just to one people or tribe. How, then, can there be evil and suffering in the world? Because, Zarathustra posited, there is a counter-deity, Ahriman, treacherous and malignant, who rules the forces of darkness. Yet Zarathustra also posited that Ahura-Mazda must be vastly stronger than Ahriman. Later teachers and priests of Zoroastrianism, the magi (*MA-jeye*), placed greater emphasis on the dualism of these divine forces: they insisted that Ahura-Mazda and Ahriman are evenly matched, engaged in a desperate and eternal struggle for supremacy. According to them, light will not triumph over darkness until the Last Day, when the forces of Ahura-Mazda vanquish those of Ahriman forever. This vision of the universe proved enormously influential, informing the developing theologies of Christianity and Islam—not to mention the plots of much modern science fiction, fantasy literature, and film.

The devotion of the Persian imperial dynasty to Zarathustra's teachings made Zoroastrianism important to the conduct of Persian government and helps to explain the tolerance of Persian rule. Unlike the Neo-Assyrians, the Chaldeans, or even the Egyptians, the Persian kings saw themselves as presiding over an assemblage of different nations whose customs and beliefs they were prepared to tolerate. Whereas Mesopotamian potentates characteristically called themselves "true king," Persian rulers took the title "king of kings" or "great king," implying that they

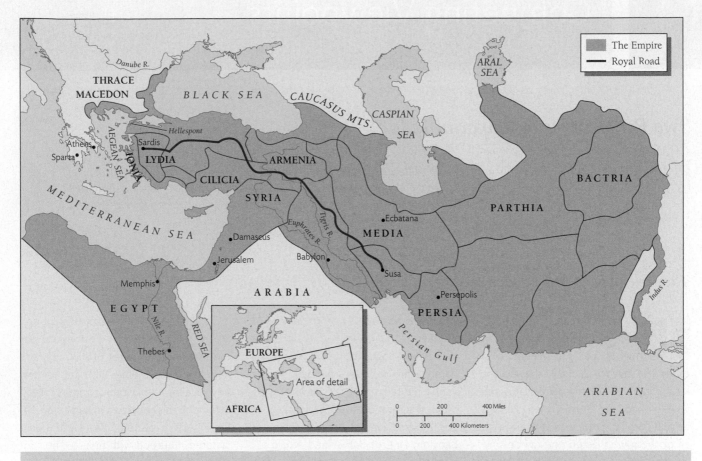

**THE PERSIAN EMPIRE UNDER DARIUS I, 521–486 B.C.E.** Consider the location of the Persian heartland and the four administrative centers of Persepolis, Susa, Ecbatana, and Sardis. ▪ *What older kingdoms and empires did the Persian Empire contain?* ▪ *Why is the Royal Road especially noted on this map?* ▪ *How did Darius I successfully rule such a large and complex empire?*

recognized the legitimacy of other kings who ruled under their canopy. This same spirit is reflected in Persian architecture, which drew freely and creatively on Sumerian, Babylonian, Assyrian, Egyptian, and Greek influences yet nonetheless created a distinctively Persian style.

Unlike other ancient religions, then, Zoroastrianism did not exalt the power of a godlike king or support any particular political regime. It was a personal religion, making private, spiritual demands as opposed to public, ritual ones. Its Wise Lord supports neither tribes nor states but only individuals who serve the cause of truth and justice. These individuals possess free will and can choose to sin or not to sin; they are not compelled by an array of conflicting gods to act in particular ways. Zoroastrianism thus urges its adherents to choose good over evil, to be truthful, to love and help one another to the best of their powers, to aid the poor, and to practice generous hospitality. Those who do so will be rewarded in an afterlife, when the dead are resurrected on Judgment Day and consigned either to a realm of joy or to the flames of despair. In the scriptures of the Zoroastrian faith, known as the Avesta (compiled, like the Bible, over the course of many centuries), the rewards for righteousness are great but not immediate. They are spiritual, not material.

## THE DEVELOPMENT OF HEBREW MONOTHEISM

Of all the important developments that we have traced in our study of the Iron Age, perhaps none is of greater significance than monotheism: the belief in a single god, the creator and ruler of all things. This development is traditionally associated with the Hebrews, but even the Hebrews were not always monotheists. Those who argued for the exclusive worship of Yahweh were a minority within Hebrew society, albeit a vocal and assertive one. How the Hebrews came to regard Yahweh as the only divine being in the universe, and to root their identity in such an exclusive religious outlook, is a phenomenon that can only be understood within its historical context.

# Competing Viewpoints

## Two Perspectives on Imperial Rule

> *These two inscriptions exemplify two very different attitudes toward imperial power and two very different methods of achieving it. The first glorifies the victories of the Assyrian king Esarhaddon in Syria and is one of the most important records of his reign (681–669 B.C.E.). The second commemorates the taking of Babylon by the Persian king Cyrus the Great (c. 559–530 B.C.E.), whose empire came to encompass and surpass that of the Assyrians.*

### The Stele of King Esarhaddon at Senjirli, c. 680 B.C.E.

To Assur, father of the gods, lover of my priesthood, Anu mighty and preeminent, who called me by name, Ba'al, the exalted lord, establisher of my dynasty, Ea, the wise, all-knowing . . . Ishtar, lady of battle and combat, who goes at my side . . . all of them who determine my destiny, who grant to the king, their favorite, power and might . . . the king, the offering of whose sacrifices the great gods love . . . their unsparing weapons they have presented him as a royal gift . . . [he] who has brought all the lands in submission at his feet, who has imposed tribute and tax upon them; conqueror of his foes, destroyer of his enemies, the king,

who as to his walk is a storm, and as to his deeds, a raging wolf; . . . the onset of his battle is powerful, he is a consuming flame, a fire that does not sink: son of Sennacherib, king of the universe, king of Assyria, grandson of Sargon, king of the universe, king of Assyria, viceroy of Babylon, king of Sumer and Akkad. . . . I am powerful, I am all-powerful, I am a hero, I am gigantic, I am colossal, I am honored, I am magnified, I am without an equal among all kings, the chosen one of Assur . . . the great lord [who], in order to show to the peoples the immensity of my mighty deeds, made powerful my kingship over the four regions of the world and made my name great.

. . . Of Tirhakah, king of Egypt and Kush, the accursed . . . without cessation I slew multitudes of his men, and him I smote five times with the point of my javelin, with wounds, no recovery. Memphis, his royal city, in half a day . . . I besieged, I captured, I destroyed, I devastated, I burned with fire. . . . The root of Kush I tore up out of Egypt and not one therein escaped to submit to me.

Source: Daniel David Luckenbill, ed., *Ancient Records of Assyria and Babylonia*, vol. 2 (Chicago: 1926–27), pp. 224–27.

### Inscription Honoring Cyrus, c. 539

He [the god Marduk] scanned and looked (through) all the countries, searching for a righteous ruler who would lead him. (Then) he pronounced the name of Cyrus, king of Anshan [Persia], declared him to be the leader of the world. . . . And he (Cyrus) did always endeavor to treat according to justice the black-headed [people] whom he (Marduk) made him conquer. Marduk, the great lord,

a protector of his people/worshipers, beheld with pleasure his good deeds and his upright mind, (and therefore) ordered him to march against his city Babylon. He made him set out on the road to Babylon, going at his side like a real friend. His widespread troops—their number, like the water of a river, could not be established—strolled along, their weapons packed away. Without any battle, he made them enter his town Babylon,

sparing Babylon any calamity. He delivered into his hands Nabonidus, the king who did not worship him. All the inhabitants of Babylon as well as of the entire country of Sumer and Akkad, princes and governors (included), bowed to him and kissed his feet, jubilant that he (had received) the kingship, and with shining faces. Happily they greeted him as a master through whose help they had come (again) to life from death (and)

had all been spared damage and disaster, and they worshiped his name.

I am Cyrus, king of the world, great king, legitimate king, king of Babylon, king of Sumer and Akkad, king of the four rims (of the earth), son of Cambyses, great king, king of Anshan, grandson of Cyrus, great king, king of Anshan, descendent of Teipes, great king, king of Anshan, of a family (which) always (exercised) kingship; whose rule Bel and Nebo love, whom they want as king to please their hearts.

When I entered Babylon as a friend and (when) I established the seat of the government in the palace of the ruler under jubilation and rejoicing. . . . My numerous troops walked around Babylon in peace, I did not allow anybody to terrorize (any place) of the (country of Sumer) and Akkad. I strove for peace in Babylon and in all his (other) sacred cities. . . . I abolished the . . . [yoke] which was against their (social) standing, I brought relief to their dilapidated housing, putting (thus) an end to their (main) complaints. . . . All the kings of the entire world from the Upper to the Lower Sea, those who are seated in throne rooms, (those who) live in other (types of buildings as well as) all the kings of the West living in tents, brought their heavy tributes and kissed my feet in Babylon.

Source: Excerpted from James B. Pritchard, ed., *Ancient Near Eastern Texts Relating to the Old Testament*, 3rd ed. (Princeton, NJ: 1969), pp. 315–16.

## Questions for Analysis

1. Both of these inscriptions constitute propaganda, but of different kinds. How do they differ? What audience(s) are they addressing? What function(s) does each inscription serve?

2. Each of these rulers claims to have a close relationship with the divine. How do those relationships differ? What do those differences reveal about their attitudes to kingship and its sources of power?

3. Both of these kings boast of their royal lineage and their connections to past rulers. How different or similar are these perspectives? What do they reveal about these kings' awareness of history?

## From Monolatry to Monotheism

For those who later advocated the exclusive worship of Yahweh, the early history of the Hebrews was full of embarrassments. Even the Hebrew scriptures reveal their propensity to worship many gods. Yahweh himself, in commanding that his people "have no other gods before me," clearly acknowledged the existence of other gods. The older, polytheistic Hebrew religion honored nature spirits such as Azazel and the Canaanite deity El, whose name is an important element in many Hebrew place-names (e.g., Bethel) and soon became a synonym for "god." The temple built by Solomon at Jerusalem had even included altars dedicated to Ba'al and his wife Asherah, a fertility goddess. Later Hebrew kings continued such practices, overriding the protests of religious purists devoted to Yahweh.

By the beginning of the first millennium, however, the Hebrews living under the rule of David began to promote monolatry, meaning that they exalted one god without denying the existence of others. Although the legendary prophet Moses is often credited as the first promoter of Yahweh's cult sometime around the middle of the second millennium B.C.E., the ascendancy of Yahweh really took place much later, under the influence of the Levites, a tribe who claimed unique priestly authority over Yahweh's worship and sought to enhance their own power and prestige by discrediting other gods.

The success of their campaign rested on the Levites' access to writing. As we have frequently noted, the written word was especially potent in the ancient world because the skills necessary for its mastery were rare. In an age of constant threats to Hebrew religious and political sovereignty, the literacy of the Levites thus helped to preserve and promote Yahweh's worship. So did the political supremacy of David's dynasty, which bolstered its own legitimacy by allying itself with the Levites. The result was a centralized cult situated in the new royal capital of Jerusalem, which attempted to link the political and the religious identity of the Hebrews with the acknowledgment of Yahweh as the supreme god.

Nevertheless, the worship of other Hebrew gods actually increased during the eighth and seventh centuries B.C.E., perhaps in reaction to the austere morality demanded and imposed by the Yahwists. One of these, Jeremiah (c. 637–587 B.C.E.), railed against "foreign" cults and warned of the disastrous consequences that would arise if Yahweh's people did not remain faithful to him. The Yahweh of this era was still imagined as a conventional god, possessing a physical body and portrayed as capricious and irascible. Further, he was not omnipotent; his power was largely confined to the territory occupied by the Hebrews.

Still, some of the Hebrews' most important contributions to subsequent Western religions crystallized during this period. One was a theology of Yahweh's transcendence: the teaching that God is not part of nature but exists outside of it. God can therefore be understood, in purely intellectual or abstract terms, as entirely separate from the operations of the natural world. Complementing this principle was the belief that Yahweh had appointed humans to be the rulers of nature by divine mandate. In the book of Genesis, when Yahweh orders Adam and Eve to "replenish the earth and subdue it, and have dominion over . . . every living thing," his injunction stands in striking contrast to other accounts of creation in which humans are made to serve the gods. Finally, Hebrew religious thought was moving during this period toward the articulation of universal ethics—a universal theory of justice and righteousness. According to the Babylonian flood story, for example, a particularly petulant god destroys humanity because their noise deprives him of sleep. In Genesis, by contrast, Yahweh sends a flood in punishment for human wickedness but saves Noah and his family because "Noah was a just man."

The Hebrews honored Yahweh during this era by subscribing to certain moral precepts and taboos. The Ten Commandments as they now appear in Exodus 20:3–17 may not yet have existed in that exact form, but they certainly reflect earlier ethical injunctions against murder, adultery, lying, and greed. In addition, the Hebrews observed an array of ritual practices unusual in the ancient world, such as infant circumcision, adherence to strict dietary laws, and refraining from labor on the seventh day of the week.

Yet the moral standards imposed by Yahweh on the Hebrew community were not binding when the Hebrews dealt with outsiders. Lending at interest, for example, was not acceptable among Hebrews but was quite acceptable between a Hebrew and a non-Hebrew. Such distinctions applied also to more serious issues, such as the killing of civilians in battle. When the Hebrews conquered territories in Canaan, they took "all the spoil of the cities, and every man they smote with the sword . . . until they had destroyed them." Far from having any doubts about such a brutal policy, the Hebrews believed that Yahweh had inspired the Canaanites to resist so that the Hebrews could slaughter them: "For it was the Lord's doing to harden their hearts that they should come against Israel in battle, in order that they should be utterly destroyed, and should receive no mercy but be exterminated" (Joshua 11:20).

With the political fragmentation of the fragile Hebrew kingdom after Solomon's death, important regional distinctions arose within Yahweh's cult. The rulers of the northern kingdom of Israel discouraged their citizens from participating in ritual activities at Jerusalem—at least according to the Jerusalem-based Yahwists, who shaped the biblical tradition and who wanted to represent their own Judah as the favored kingdom. The erosion of a cohesive Hebrew identity was further accelerated by the Neo-Assyrians, who under Sargon II absorbed the northern kingdom as a province and enslaved nearly 28,000 Hebrews. The southern kingdom of Judah survived, but political collaboration with the Neo-Assyrians also meant acceptance of the god Assur.

**THE GODDESS ASHERAH.** The Canaanite fertility goddess, Asherah, was the wife of the god Ba'al (or his father, El), but she also figures in some inscriptions as the wife of the Hebrew god Yahweh. One Hebrew king placed an image of her in the Temple of Yahweh at Jerusalem. ▪ *Why might this be viewed as controversial—then or now?*

This Neo-Assyrian threat was the whetstone on which the Yahwist prophets sharpened their demands for an exclusive monotheism that went beyond monolatry. Hebrew prophets were practical political leaders as well as religious figures, and most of them understood that military resistance to the Neo-Assyrians was futile. So if the Hebrews were to survive as a people, they had to emphasize the one thing that separated them from everyone else in the known world: the worship of Yahweh and the denial of all other gods. The prophets' insistence that Yahweh alone should be exalted was thus an aggressive reaction to the equally aggressive promotion of Assur by the Neo-Assyrians.

The foremost Hebrew prophets of this era were Amos and Hosea, who preached in the kingdom of Israel before it fell to the Neo-Assyrians in 722 B.C.E.; Isaiah and Jeremiah, who preached in Judah before its fall in 586 B.C.E.; and Ezekiel and the "second Isaiah" (the Book of Isaiah had at least two different authors), who continued to preach "by the waters of Babylon" during the Hebrews' exile there. Despite some differences in emphasis, these prophets' messages consistently emphasize three core doctrines:

1. Yahweh is the ruler of the universe. He even makes use of peoples other than the Hebrews to accomplish his purposes. The gods of other nations are false gods. There has never been and never will be more than this one god.
2. Yahweh is exclusively a god of righteousness. He wills only the good, and evil in the world comes from humanity, not from him.
3. Because Yahweh is righteous, he demands ethical behavior from his people. Over and above ritual and sacrifice, he requires that his followers "seek justice, relieve the oppressed, protect the fatherless, and plead for the widow."

The prophet Amos summarized these teachings when he expressed Yahweh's resounding warning in the eighth century B.C.E.:

I hate, I despise your feasts, and I take no delight in your solemn assemblies. Even though you offer

**RECONSTRUCTION OF THE ISHTAR GATE.** This is a reconstruction of one of the fifty-foot-high entrance gates built into the walls of Babylon by King Nebuchadnezzar around 575 B.C.E. About half of this reconstruction, in the Pergamon Museum of Berlin, is original.

me your burnt offerings and cereal offerings, I will not accept them, and the peace offerings of your fatted beasts I will not look upon. Take away from me the noise of your songs; to the melody of your harps I will not listen. But let justice roll down like waters, and righteousness like an ever-flowing stream. (Amos 5:21–24)

## Judaism Takes Shape

The Yahwists made it possible for the Hebrews to survive under Neo-Assyrian domination through their insistence on monotheism as the cornerstone of Hebrew identity, and they enjoyed political and religious triumph as this threat receded in the late seventh century B.C.E. Josiah (621–609 B.C.E.), the king of Judah during the waning years of the Neo-Assyrian Empire, was a committed monotheist whose court employed prominent prophets, including Jeremiah. With his own power increasing, Josiah found himself in a position to pursue significant reforms. He presided over the redrafting and revision of the "Law of Moses" to bring it into line with current policies, and it was during his reign that the Book of Deuteronomy was "discovered" and hailed as Moses's "Second Law." Deuteronomy is the most stridently monotheistic book of the Hebrew Bible, and it lent weight to this new political program.

But within a generation of King Josiah's death, the Chaldeans under Nebuchadnezzar conquered Jerusalem, destroyed the Temple, and carried thousands of Hebrews off to Babylon in 587/586 B.C.E. This Babylonian Captivity brought many challenges, paramount among them the maintenance of the Hebrews' hard-won religious identity. The leading voices in defining that identity continued to be the patriotic Yahwists, the same people who would later spearhead the return to Jerusalem two generations later, after Cyrus captured Babylon and liberated the Hebrews. Among the Yahwists, the prophet Ezekiel stressed that salvation could be found only through religious purity, which meant ignoring all foreign gods and acknowledging only Yahweh. Kingdoms and states and empires came to nothing in the long run, Ezekiel said. What mattered for those living in exile was the creature God had made in his image—man—and the relationship between God and his creation.

This period of captivity and exile was therefore decisive in forging a universal religion that transcended politics. Just as Yahweh existed outside creation, so the people who worshiped him could exist outside a Hebrew kingdom. In Babylon, the worship of Yahweh therefore became something different; it became Judaism, a religion that was not tied to any particular political system or territory, for there was neither a Hebrew ruling class nor a Hebrew state after 586 B.C.E. Outside of Judah, Judaism flourished and became the crucial factor in the emergence of a new Jewish identity. This was an unparalleled development in the ancient world: the survival of a religion that had no political power to back it and no holy place to ground it.

After 538 B.C.E., when Cyrus conquered Babylon, he allowed the Hebrews to return to their lands in a new Persian-governed province of Judea. Jerusalem became once again the central holy place of their religious life—although many Hebrews remained and flourished in Persia, while others had long since settled in Egypt. The Judaism that had emerged during the Hebrews' residence in Babylon would be promulgated by a new generation of Jews, particularly the prophet Ezra, who is credited with bringing the strict interpretation and application of the Torah from Persia to Jerusalem, and Nehemiah, the Persian-appointed governor of Judea who began the process of rebuilding the Temple. Eventually, the monotheistic religion that emerged from these historical processes would become common to the worldview of all Western civilizations.

## After You Read This Chapter

🐰 Go to **INQUIZITIVE** to see what you've learned—and learn what you've missed—with personalized feedback along the way.

### REVIEWING THE OBJECTIVES

- The settlement of Indo-European peoples in the Near East had marked effects on the older civilizations there. What were some major consequences?
- Egypt's New Kingdom differed profoundly from the Old and Middle Kingdoms that preceded it. Why was this the case?
- The civilizations of the Late Bronze Age were bound together by transnational networks. What were the strengths and fragilities of these relationships?
- What kingdoms and empires emerged in the ancient world after the devastation caused by the Sea Peoples?
- Monotheism was a significant historical development of the first millennium B.C.E. Why is it so important?

# CONCLUSION

The centuries between 1700 and 500 B.C.E. were an epoch of empires. Although the two great powers of the second millennium were New Kingdom Egypt and the Hittite Empire in Anatolia, a host of lesser empires also coalesced during this period, including Minoan Crete, Mycenaean Greece, and the trading empire of the Assyrians. All were sustained by a sophisticated network of trade and diplomacy. But between 1200 and 1000 B.C.E. the devastation wrought by the Sea Peoples destroyed this integrated civilization. These invasions cleared the way for the emergence of many new, small states, including those of the Phoenicians, the Philistines, the Hebrews, and the Lydians. Many crucial cultural and economic developments were fostered by these small states, including alphabetic writing, coinage, mercantile colonization, and monotheism. But the dominant states of the Iron Age continued to be great land empires centered in western Asia: first that of the Neo-Assyrians, then briefly the Chaldeans, and finally the Persians.

Yet the empires of the early Iron Age were quite different from those that had dominated the ancient world a thousand years before. These new powers were much more highly unified. They had capital cities, centrally managed systems of communication, sophisticated administrative structures, and ideologies that justified their aggressive imperialism. They commanded armies of unprecedented size, and they demanded from their subjects a degree of obedience impossible for any Bronze Age emperor to imagine or enforce. Their rulers declared themselves the chosen instruments of their god's divine will.

At the same time, we can trace the emergence of more personalized religions. Zoroastrian dualism and Hebrew monotheism added an important new emphasis on ethical conduct, and both pioneered the development of authoritative written scriptures that advanced religious teachings. Zoroastrianism, despite its radical reimagining of the cosmos, proved fully compatible with imperialism and became the driving spiritual force behind the Persian Empire. Judaism, by contrast, was forged in the struggle to resist the imperialism of the Neo-Assyrians and Chaldeans. Both systems of belief would exercise enormous influence on future civilizations. In particular, they provided the models on which Christianity and Islam would ultimately erect their own traditions, just as models of imperial governance forged in this period would become the template for future empires. In Chapter 3, we will look at the ways in which the city-states of ancient Greece both built on and departed from these models.

## PEOPLE, IDEAS, AND EVENTS IN CONTEXT

- How did the Hittite Empire integrate the cultures of **INDO-EUROPEANS** with the older civilizations of this region?
- What do the reigns of **HATSHEPSUT** and **AKHENATEN** tell us about the continuities and limitations of pharaonic power?
- What factors produced the transnational networks of the Late **BRONZE AGE**?
- How did the civilizations of **MINOAN CRETE** and **MYCENAEAN GREECE** differ from one another and from neighboring civilizations?
- In what ways do the **PHOENICIANS**, the **PHILISTINES**, and the **HEBREWS** exemplify three different approaches to state building at the beginning of the first millennium B.C.E.?
- What was new about the **NEO-ASSYRIAN EMPIRE**? How do its methods of conquest and its military-religious ethos compare with those of the **PERSIAN EMPIRE** that followed it?
- How and why did monotheism develop in the Hebrew kingdoms? In what ways might **JUDAISM** have been influenced by **ZOROASTRIANISM**?

## THINKING ABOUT CONNECTIONS

- In the religions of Akhenaten, the Persians, and the Hebrews, we see a rejection of polytheism. What cultural factors may have contributed to this? What would you consider to be the long-term effects of monotheism as a motivating force in history?
- What patterns of success or failure appear to be emerging when we consider the empires that flourished in the Iron Age, particularly those of the Assyrians and the Persians? Are similar patterns visible in other periods of history, including our own?

## STORY LINES

- The emergence of democracy in the ancient Greek world was dependent on specific historical circumstances, which included reliance on slavery and the exclusion of women from public life. It therefore differs markedly from the political system(s) described as democratic today.

- Although the different Greek *poleis* did not share a common political structure, they shared a strong sense of identity and were united by their language and culture.

- The Athenians' empire and their leadership in the Persian Wars enabled them to dominate the Mediterranean and also, through the use of writing, to influence our understanding of their role in history.

- The cultural achievements of the fifth century B.C.E. glorified the individual male and his role in the community.

## CHRONOLOGY

| | |
|---|---|
| 800–400 B.C.E. | Rise of the *polis* |
| c. 750 B.C.E. | Homeric epics transcribed |
| 725–650 B.C.E. | Hoplite tactics become standard |
| c. 600 B.C.E | Militarization of Sparta |
| 600–500 B.C.E. | Emergence of the Milesian School (pre-Socratic philosophy) |
| 594 B.C.E. | Solon's reforms in Athens |
| 546 B.C.E. | Cyrus of Persia conquers Lydia and controls the Greek cities of Ionia |
| 510 B.C.E. | Overthrow of the Peisistratid tyranny in Athens |
| 499–494 B.C.E. | Ionian Revolt |
| 490 B.C.E. | Battle of Marathon |
| 480 B.C.E. | Battles of Thermopylae and Salamis |
| 479 B.C.E. | Battle of Plataea |
| 478 B.C.E. | Formation of the Delian League |
| 431 B.C.E. | Peloponnesian War begins |
| 404 B.C.E. | Defeat of Athens by Sparta |
| 399 B.C.E. | Death of Socrates |

Before
You
Read
This
Chapter

# The Civilization of Greece, 1000–400 B.C.E.

## CORE OBJECTIVES

- **DESCRIBE** the factors that led to the emergence of the Greek polis.

- **EXPLAIN** the importance of hoplite warfare and its effects on democracy and military tactics.

- **DEFINE** the key differences among the poleis of Athens, Sparta, and Miletus.

- **IDENTIFY** the ways in which Athenian culture, philosophy, and art reflect democratic ideals.

- **UNDERSTAND** the impact of the Persian and Peloponnesian Wars on Greek civilization.

In the fifth century B.C.E., a Greek-speaking subject of the Persian Empire began to write a book. He had been to Egypt and along the African coast, to the Greek colonies of Italy, the cities of Persia, the wilds of Thrace and Macedonia, and all over the Aegean. He had collected stories about peoples and places even farther afield: Ethiopia, India, the Black Sea. We have already met this intrepid traveler, Herodotus (c. 484–c. 425 B.C.E.), who marveled at the pyramids of Giza (see Chapter 1) and who told how the king of Lydia lost his power to the Persians (see Chapter 2). His reason for compiling this information was timely: he wanted to write a history of recent events. As he put it, "Herodotus of Halicarnassus here sets forth the results of his research, with the aim of preserving the remembrance of what men have done, and of preventing the great and wonderful deeds of both Greeks and barbarians from losing their glory; and in particular to examine the causes that made them fight one another."

Herodotus's fascination with the Persians, Phoenicians, and Egyptians underscores the extent to which all Greek-speakers regarded themselves as different from other ancient peoples. While they struggled to cooperate politically, they

**THE ACROPOLIS OF ATHENS AND THE PARTHENON.** Many Greek cities were built upon mountain strongholds, but the most famous of these is the acropolis of Athens. First settled in the Neolithic Period, it was a fortified palace during the Bronze Age—allegedly that of the hero Theseus—and then a precinct sacred to the goddess Athena, for whom the city was named. The Parthenon, its most important surviving structure, was built on the site of an older temple after the Athenian victory over the Persians at Marathon in 490 B.C.E. It was then rebuilt after the Persians sacked Athens ten years later. Most of the damage it sustained thereafter occurred during modern wars. ▪ *Why was this site the focal point of so much activity?* ▪ *What does its longevity tell us about the relationship between place and identity in Greece?*

were able to forge a common language and culture, and they cherished values that were distinct from those of the people they called *barbarians:* peoples whose speech, to Greek ears, sounded like gibberish ("bar-bar-bar"). They celebrated individual liberty, participatory government, artistic innovation, scientific investigation, and confidence in the powers of the human mind. Although the practical implementation of these ideals would prove problematic—and continues to be so—our own civilization would be unimaginable without the political experiments and cultural achievements of ancient Greece.

## FROM CHAOS TO POLIS

By the end of the twelfth century B.C.E., Mycenaean civilization had vanished. Except at Athens, the great citadels that had crowned the heights of the mainland kingdoms had been destroyed. But even at Athens the population steadily declined, with severe effects on the economy and on social organization. Settlements shrank in size and moved inland, away from vulnerable coastlines, thus cutting themselves off from trade and communication. Indeed, the use of writing declined to such an extent that the knowledge of the system known as Linear B disappeared (see Chapter 2). Archaeological evidence suggests a world in stasis, isolated from the centers of civilization that were reemerging in western Asia.

The material realities of life in this era profoundly shaped one of the new civilizations that emerged from it. This civilization would emphasize male political equality and modest display, the importance of domestic economy, and self-sufficiency: these were the principles that formed the basis of early democracies. At the same time, this new historical reality had similar long-term effects on religion and philosophy, because the hardships of daily life contrasted sharply with the stories of a heroic and opulent past.

Although worship of the gods continued to be central to Greek culture and civic life, the power of individual human beings was celebrated, too. However, excessive pride in one's own accomplishments could be dangerous, because such *hubris* attracted the adverse attention of the gods. The gods favored those who showed initiative and daring, but they would punish the hubris of those who failed to acknowledge their own limitations.

## Homer and the Heroic Tradition

By the year 1000 B.C.E., the disruption of the transnational Bronze Age networks that had contributed to the isolation of Greece was alleviated by a period of relative peace. The standard of living improved and increased contact among individual settlements fostered trade. New techniques made Greek pottery, in particular, a sophisticated and sought-after commodity that Greek merchants could exchange for luxury goods from abroad.

As trade became an increasingly important feature of the new economy, the personal fortunes of those who engaged in commerce increased accordingly, leading to a new form of social status based on wealth, rather than on warfare or noble birth—as had been the case in the distant past. Members of this new economic class justified their preeminence as a reflection of their own superior qualities as *aristoi* ("best men"). Yet wealth in itself was not sufficient as a claim to aristocracy, the "rule of the best." Those who aspired to this status were also expected to emulate, as far as possible, the heroes of old, whose stories lived in the prodigious memories and agile voices of the singers of tales.

These singers, the guardians of a rich oral history that had never been written down, were part poets in their own right and part *rhapsodes* ("weavers of songs"). The most famous is Homer, a legendary poet credited with having woven together the mesh of stories that we know as the *Iliad* and the *Odyssey*. They appear to have crystallized around 800 B.C.E., at about the same time that Hesiod was working on shorter lyrics capturing a more practical perspective on life (see Chapter 2). The epics ascribed to Homer are vast encyclopedias of lore set at the end of the Bronze Age, the time Hesiod called the "Age of Heroes." These were the days when Agamemnon ruled in Mycenae and launched a vast expedition to conquer Troy, where the prince Paris had taken Helen, the ravishing wife of Agamemnon's brother, Menelaus; it was the age of Achilles and his Trojan rival, Hector; it was the age of Odysseus.

Like the much older Epic of Gilgamesh (see Chapter 1), these Greek epics preserve long-standing traditions. But over centuries of retelling, the social and political relationships portrayed in the poems changed to reflect the assumptions and agendas of later ages. As a result, the Homeric epics are of tremendous value to historians. They also offer significant analytical challenges. Although the events and many of the material objects described in them date from the late Bronze Age, the society they reflect is that of Homer's contemporaries, half a millennium later. Treating these epics as historical sources, therefore, requires the historian to work like an archaeologist, carefully peeling back layers of meaning and accumulated sediment.

For example, Homer depicts a world in which competition and status are of paramount importance to the warrior elite, just as they were of vital concern to the aristocrats of his own day. Through the exchange of expensive gifts and hospitality, men aspiring to positions of power sought to create strong ties of guest friendship (*xenia*, *zeh-NEE-ah*) with one another, and thus to construct networks of influence that would support their economic, social, and political ambitions. Indeed, it is almost impossible to overestimate the importance of guest friendship as a sacred institution, something that is well illustrated by the encounter between the Trojan warrior Glaucus and the Greek Diomedes in the *Iliad* (see page 78). It shows that aristocrats in the Greek world conceived themselves as having more in common with each other than they did with the local societies they dominated, something that is also reflected in the essential similarity of Trojans and Greeks in the *Iliad*, and the lack of perceived differences among various Greek tribes.

However, the practice of guest friendship and the shared sense of a common culture among aristocratic households did not lessen the competition that frequently led to violence. (The Trojan War, after all, is supposed to have begun when Paris violated the holy ties of hospitality by seducing the wife of the Spartan king, while he was a guest in the king's home.) It also led to competition over the epic past, as fledgling aristocratic clans vied to claim descent from one or another legendary hero. A hero cult might begin when an important family claimed an impressive Mycenaean tomb as that of their own famous ancestor, someone named in the *Iliad* and said to come from that place. They would then develop a pious tradition of practicing dutiful sacrifices and other observances at the tomb. This devotion would extend to their followers and dependents; eventually, an entire community might come to identify itself with the famous local hero. The heroic ideal thus became a deeply ingrained feature of Greek society, as did the stories that the epics preserved and propagated.

## Greek Guest Friendship and Heroic Ideals

*Before the emergence of the Greek poleis, relations among communities depended largely on the personal connections made among leading families of different settlements. Often founded on the exchange of gifts or hospitality, the resulting bonds of guest friendship imposed serious obligations on those involved in such relationships—and on their heirs. Honoring these ties was an important part of the heroic ideal, even among those fighting on opposing sides. In this episode from the* Iliad *(Book VI), the fierce Greek warrior Diomedes encounters Glaucus of Lykia, fighting for Troy, on the field of battle.*

hen Glaucus, son of
   Hippolochus,
Met Diomedes in
   no-man's-land.
Both were eager to
fight, but first Tydeus' son
Made his voice heard above the battle
   noise:
"And which mortal hero are you? I've
   never seen you
Out here before on the fields of glory,
And now you're here ahead of
   everyone,
Ready to face my spear. Pretty bold.
I feel sorry for your parents . . ."
And Glaucus, Hippolochus' son:
"Great son of Tydaeus, why ask me
   about my lineage? . . .
But if you really want to hear my
   story,
You're welcome to listen. Many men
   know it.
Ephyra, in the heart of Argive horse
   country,
Was home to Sisyphus, the shrewdest
   man alive,
Sisyphus son of Aeolus. He had a son,
   Glaucus,
Who was the father of faultless
   Bellerophon,
A man of grace and courage by the gift
   of the gods. . . .
*[Here, Glaucus relates the adventures of his grandfather, Bellerophon, and how he came to Lykia and fought many battles for its king.]*
When the king realized that Bellero-
   phon had divine blood,

He kept him there and gave him his
   daughter,
And half his royal honor. . . .
His wife, the princess, bore him three
   children,
Isander, Hippolochus, and
   Laodameia. . . .
His son Isander was slain by Ares,
As he fought against the glorious
   Solymi,
And his daughter was killed by Artemis
Of the golden reins. But Hippolochus
Bore me, and I am proud he is my
   father.
He sent me to Troy with strict
   instructions
To be the best ever, better than all the
   rest,
And not to bring shame on the race of
   my fathers. . . .
This, I am proud to say, is my lineage."
Diomedes grinned when he heard all
   this.
He planted his spear in the bounteous
   earth
And spoke gently to the Lykian prince:
"We have old ties of hospitality!
My grandfather Oeneus long ago
Entertained Bellerophon in his halls
For twenty days, and they gave each
   other
Gifts of friendship. Oeneus gave
A belt bright with scarlet, and
   Bellerophon
A golden cup, which I left at home.
I don't remember my father Tydeus,
Since I was very small when he left for
   Thebes

In that great war that killed so many
   Achaeans.
But that makes me your friend and you
   my guest
If ever you come to Argos, as you are
   my friend
And I your guest whenever I travel to
   Lykia.
So we can't cross spears with each
   other. . . .
And let's exchange armor, so everyone
   will know
That we are friends from our fathers'
   days."
With this, they vaulted from their
   chariots,
Clasped hands, and pledged their
   friendship.

Source: Excerpted from the *Iliad* of Homer, trans. Stanley Lombardo (Indianapolis: 1997), pp. 115–18 (vv. 120–241).

### Questions for Analysis

**1.** Why would Glaucus and Diomedes place such emphasis on lineage and on the stories of their ancestors?

**2.** What are the attributes of heroism, as described in this passage? Why is respect for the sacred ties of hospitality so important?

**3.** Why do these two men exchange armor? What might be the symbolic significance of this action? What might be its consequences on the battlefield?

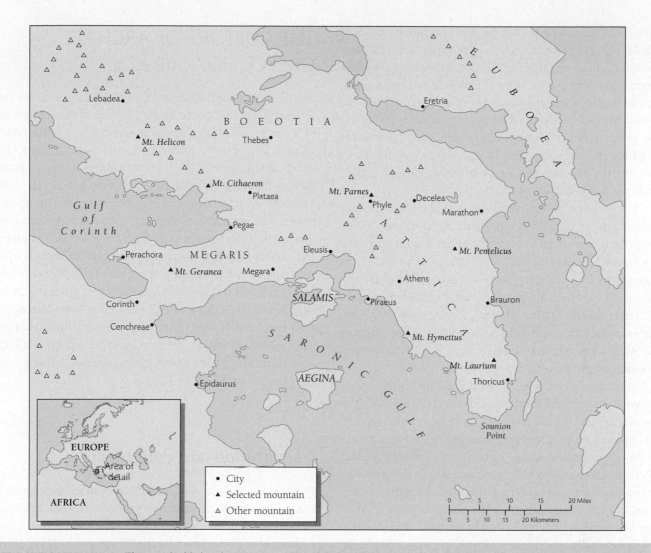

**THE ATTIC PENINSULA.** This map highlights the numerous poleis that dotted the Attic peninsula. It also shows the surrounding territories of Euboea, Boeotia, and Megaris. Consider the scale of the map and the geography of the peninsula. ▪ *Where is Athens located?* ▪ *How do natural boundaries appear to affect patterns of settlement?* ▪ *Why would citizens of the other Attic poleis be regarded as citizens of Athens also, even though they did not live in the city itself?*

## The Rise of the Polis

The ninth century B.C.E. saw dramatic changes throughout the Aegean basin. Contacts between Greeks and Phoenicians intensified. Moreover, the Greeks adopted the Phoenician alphabet, which replaced the Linear B of the Mycenaeans (Chapter 2) to such an extent that the older writing system became obsolete. They also incorporated into their culture many artistic and literary traditions from elsewhere in the ancient world, reshaping them to suit their own purposes.

The example of the Phoenicians also pointed the way to the revival of a lost art among the Greeks: seafaring. After the devastation of the late Bronze Age, Greek vessels no longer ventured out into the Mediterranean but hugged the shoreline and traveled only short distances. By the tenth century, however, Greeks were copying Phoenician designs for merchant vessels, which enabled them to launch trading enterprises of their own. As commercial activity increased, significant numbers of Greeks began to move back to the shores of the mainland, to outlying islands, and to the western coast of Anatolia, across the Aegean, which they called Ionia.

These developments were accompanied by a marked expansion of the Greek population. Around Athens, the population may have quadrupled during the ninth and early eighth centuries. Such rapid growth, however, placed heavy demands on the environmental resources of a mountainous country with limited agricultural land. As smaller villages grew into towns, inhabitants of rival communities came into more frequent contact with each other. Soon, some degree of economic, political, and social cooperation among the inhabitants became necessary. But the habits that had developed during centuries of isolation did not make such cooperation easy. Each local community treasured its autonomy and independence, celebrated its own rituals, and honored its own heroes. On what basis could such communities unite?

The solution to this challenge was the *polis*, the root from which we derive the word *politics*. Yet to the Greeks, the polis was a social collectivity rather than a state. For this reason, our sources speak of groups of people—"the Athenians," "the Spartans," or "the Thebans"—rather than the places in which these *poleis* (the plural of *polis*) were centered (Athens, Sparta, Thebes). Membership in the collective of the polis came to be so essential to Greek identity that Aristotle would later define man as "a political animal," someone whose identity depends on the polis.

Most poleis combined formal legal institutions with informal customs that could differ widely according to the size of the population and its material and historical circumstances. They were usually organized around a social center known as the *agora* ("central marketplace"), where meetings were held and business was conducted in the open air. Surrounding this was the urban settlement, the *asty*, and beyond this was the *khora*, "land." The khora of a large polis might support several other towns or smaller poleis, as well as numerous villages; for example, all the residents of the entire territory of Attica were considered to be citizens of Athens. Thus the vast majority of Athenian citizens were farmers who might come to the asty only at certain times of the year to participate in the affairs of their polis or to exchange goods in the agora.

The Greeks described this early process of urbanization as the "bringing together of dwellings" (*synoikismos,* synoecism). Polis formation could also come about through the conquest of one settlement by another and/or through the gradual alliance of neighboring communities. Some poleis took shape around fortified hilltops, such as the Athenian acropolis (literally, "the high city"). Other communities organized the urban center around a temple precinct. In other poleis, the main temple was not located within the city or its walls; at Argos, for example, the massive temple to Hera was located several miles away from any sizable settlement. In many Greek cities, indeed, temple building may have been a *consequence* of polis formation rather than a cause, as elites competed with one another to exalt their poleis and glorify themselves.

# THE CULTURE OF ARCHAIC GREECE, 800–500 B.C.E.

Scholars associate the Archaic ("early") Period of Greek history with the emergence of the polis and the renewed use of writing, which the Greeks would put to a wide variety of practical, artistic, intellectual, and political uses. The Athenians, in particular, used writing as a way of establishing their cultural dominance over other Greek poleis by controlling the inscription of the Homeric canon, promoting the work of contemporary poets, and fostering the writing of prose histories in which they themselves played the central role. It is therefore important to bear in mind that much of what we know about this early period derives from the work of later authors who wrote from this Athenian perspective: these include the Ionian-born Herodotus, who spent much of his later life in Athens; the historians Thucydides (c. 460–c. 395 B.C.E.) and Xenophon (430–354 B.C.E.); and the philosophers Plato (c. 428–348 B.C.E.) and his pupil, Aristotle (384–322 B.C.E.).

## Colonization and Panhellenism

During the eighth and seventh centuries B.C.E., small-scale Greek trading ventures and settlements gradually developed into full-fledged mercantile enterprises which followed the example set by the Phoenicians. Many larger poleis competed to establish colonies that functioned as trading posts, with Athens and Corinth being particularly successful. Although each new colony was technically an independent entity, it sustained familial and emotional ties to its mother polis; so even if it had no formal obligations to that city, it was often called on to support the polis and could become entangled in the political and military affairs of the mainland. At the same time, these scattered Greek colonies were united by their shared language and heritage, which was being exported to far-flung reaches of the known world, eventually creating a Panhellenic ("all-Greek") culture that stretched from the Black Sea (parts of modern Romania, Ukraine, and Russia) to the southern coastlines of modern France and Spain.

This process of Greek colonization permanently altered the cultural geography of the Mediterranean world. The western shores of Anatolia (modern Turkey) would remain a stronghold of Greek culture for the next 2,000 years. So many Greeks settled in southern Italy that later Romans called the region Magna Graecia, "Greater Greece";

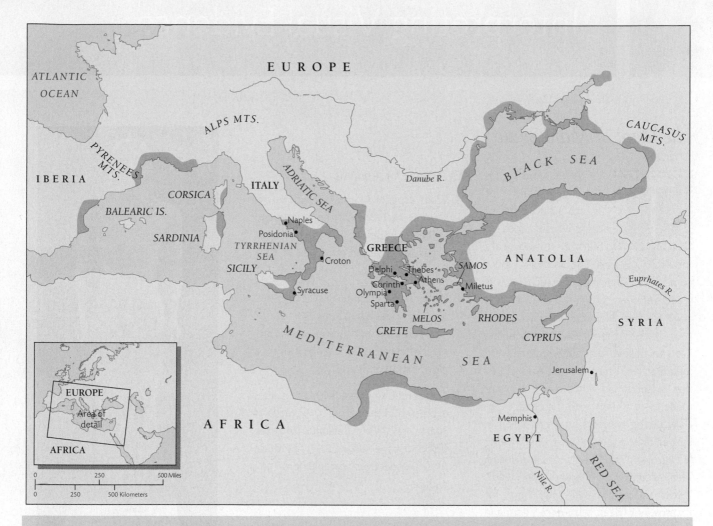

**GREEK COLONIZATION, C. 550 B.C.E.** Compare this map with that on page 55. ▪ *How do you account for the differences in Greek and Phoenician patterns of colonization?* ▪ *Were Greek colonies likely to compete with Phoenician colonies?* ▪ *Where were such conflicts most likely to erupt?*

Greek-speaking enclaves would survive there into the twentieth century. By the fourth century B.C.E., more Greeks lived in Magna Graecia than in Greece itself.

Motives for colonization varied. A polis such as Corinth was blessed by its strategic location on the land bridge between Attica and the Peloponnesus (*pel-oh-poh-NEE-suhs*), the large peninsula of mainland Greece, but cursed by the poverty of its land. Trade therefore became the lifeblood of this polis and of the ruling aristocracy, which bankrolled the ambitious planting of colonies up the coast of the Adriatic and into Sicily during the eighth century B.C.E. Other poleis, confronted by the pressures of growing populations and political unrest, sponsored new colonies as outlets for undesirable elements or unwanted multitudes. These colonial projects parallel, in many ways, those of modern nation-states.

Colonial expansion intensified Greek contacts with other cultures. Phoenician pottery brought new artistic motifs and mythological figures into Greece, while Egyptian artists profoundly influenced early Greek sculptural representations of the human form (see **Interpreting Visual Evidence** on page 82). However, intensified contact with other cultures also sharpened Greeks' awareness of their own identity as Hellenes: the Greeks' name for themselves. Such self-conscious Hellenism did not necessarily lead to greater political cooperation, but it did encourage the establishment of Panhellenic festivals, such as the Olympic Games, and shared holy sites. The most important of these was the temple of Apollo at Delphi, home to the oracle of the sun god and situated on the slope of the sacred Mount Parnassus. People from all over the Greek world (and beyond) came to seek advice from

# Interpreting Visual Evidence

## The Ideal of Male Beauty

The Greek word *kouros* ("young man" or "youth") is now applied to a whole series of life-size statues from the Archaic Period. The one shown here comes from Anavyssos in Attica and was made between 540 and 515 B.C.E. (It is now in the National Archaeological Museum of Athens.) Although scholars used to believe that such statues were meant to represent the god Apollo, further research has shown that most were made to commemorate the dead, especially young warriors who had fallen in battle. This one appears to be walking forward, smiling, but his eyes are closed. The accompanying inscription reads: "Stop and show your pity here for Kroisos, now dead, who once fighting in the foremost ranks of battle was destroyed by raging Ares."

### Questions for Analysis

1. What aspects of the body does the kouros emphasize? If this is intended to be a model of Greek manhood, what values would it convey to contemporary youths?

2. Is this a representation of the young man as he was when living or in death? How do your conclusions about the ideal of male beauty change if this is a glorification of death?

3. Compare this image with the values expressed in the verses by Tyrtaeus of Sparta on "The Beautiful and the Good" (page 85). How do these two perspectives complement one another?

---

the prophetic spirit embodied in Apollo's priestess, who lived in a state of trance induced by fumes rising from a fissure in the earth and enhanced by the chewing of eucalyptus leaves. Suppliants who sought to have their questions answered by the oracle would offer gifts to the shrine and then wait while the god spoke through the priestess, whose mysterious answers would be translated by an attending priest into enigmatic Greek verse. The resulting advice was essentially a riddle that called for further interpretation on the part of the recipient—who often misconstrued it—as we noted in Chapter 2, Croesus of Lydia thought that he was following the advice of the oracle when he attacked the Persians, but the great nation he destroyed turned out to be his own.

At the Olympic Games, Greeks honored the king of the gods, Zeus, near the giant temple dedicated to him at Olympia. The Greeks took great pride in these athletic competitions, and Greek historians dated events by olympiads, the four-year periods between games, traditionally believed to have begun in 776 B.C.E. Only Hellenes were permitted to participate in these sacred contests, and all wars among Greeks ceased while they took place. A victory in the games brought great prestige to the victor, who could be catapulted to a position of social and political power within his polis. These games did little to alleviate rivalry among the poleis; in fact, they often increased it. Yet they further strengthened the Greeks' awareness of their common culture, an awareness that they could call on when they faced a common threat.

## Harnessing the Power of the Horse

Horses are now common on all continents except Antarctica, but in antiquity they were found only on the steppes of eastern Europe and Central Asia. From this relatively circumscribed area, wild horse populations were gradually domesticated and interbred to yield the modern horse (*Equus caballus*). This animal's global spread testifies to its extraordinarily close relationship with the humans who tamed it, and who in turn became utterly dependent on its strength, intelligence, beauty, and utility: as a source of milk and meat and hides, as a draft animal, as the swift engine that powered the terrifying chariots of the Bronze Age (Chapter 2), and finally as a mount. Horses were first harnessed for riding on the plains of western Asia, and (as we will see) they became crucial components in the armies of the Persian Empire.

They also became essential markers of the new Greek aristocracy in the course of the eighth century. Whereas Homeric heroes had ridden into battle on chariots, dismounting to fight hand to hand only after they had thrown their javelins, their later aristocratic imitators were literally *hippeis* ("horsemen"), constituting the first cavalries of the ancient world. Chariots, which were virtually useless on the rocky, mountainous terrain of Greece, were however beautifully adapted to become the engine of a new type of sporting event. The first four-horse chariot race is attested at Olympia in 680 B.C.E., and chariot-racing would become

wildly popular in the Roman Empire, too. And since breeding, raising, feeding, training, and arming horses was extraordinarily expensive, owning a horse—or a team of horses, broken to pull a racing chariot—was the ultimate sign of wealth and status.

## Hoplite Warfare: A Military and Political Revolution

Commoners fighting on foot had long played a very minor role in ancient warfare. But, ironically, just as small cavalry contingents were being formed by the aristocracy, a revolution in military tactics was making their dominance obsolete. The effective defense of a polis increasingly required a standing militia, not just an ad hoc band of elite warriors. Accordingly, able-bodied citizens began to equip themselves for battle and train alongside each other. These citizen-soldiers became known as *hoplites*, from the large round shield (*hoplon*) each one carried. The shield was the chief element in a *panoply* (complete hoplite outfit) weighing as much as seventy pounds and consisting of a spear, short sword, breastplate, helmet, and sometimes leather greaves and wrist-guards.

In battle, hoplites stood shoulder to shoulder in a close formation called a *phalanx,* several columns across and several rows deep, with each hoplite carrying his shield on the left arm to protect the unshielded right side of the man standing next to him. In his right hand, each hoplite carried a thrusting weapon—spear or sword—so that an approaching phalanx presented a nearly impenetrable wall of armor and weaponry to its opponents. If a man in the front rank fell, the one behind him stepped up to take his place; indeed, the weight of the entire phalanx was literally behind the front line, with each soldier aiding the assault by leaning with his shield into the man in front of him.

This tight formation relied on a shared skill: the ability to stay together. As long as the phalanx remained intact, it was nearly unbeatable. But like the polis itself, it could fall apart if its men were not committed to a common goal. The "hoplite revolution" was therefore bound up with a parallel revolution in politics. As a polis came increasingly to draw on the resources of more and more citizens, it was forced to offer them a larger share in political power. Since every polis needed a hoplite force to protect its independence, any citizen who could afford the requisite panoply became a man with political and social standing. Together, these citizen-soldiers formed a new hoplite class, which demanded a share in decision making. Sometimes, though,

**A CHARIOTEER AND HIS TEAM RACING AT THE OLYMPIC GAMES.** Chariot racing was the most prestigious and expensive event at the Olympics, since only the very wealthy could afford to maintain and transport a racing team. All the glory of a win accordingly went to the owner, not the charioteer or trainer. Since women were forbidden to compete at the Olympics, sponsoring a team was the only way that a woman could claim an Olympic victory.

**HOPLITE INFANTRY ADVANCING INTO COMBAT.** This Corinthian vase, dating from around 650 B.C.E., displays the earliest known depiction of hoplites fighting in a phalanx formation.

they could be co-opted by an aristocratic faction or persuaded to throw their support behind an aspiring tyrant.

## Aristocracy, Tyranny, and Democracy

For the better part of the seventh and sixth centuries B.C.E., the aristocratic classes continued to control most Greek poleis. Struggles for influence among competing families were therefore commonplace, and factions often attempted to checkmate rivals by passing new laws that favored their interests or by sponsoring building projects or colonial expeditions. These rivalries affected polis government at every level, not least because aristocrats were the only members of society who could afford to hold unpaid and time-consuming political offices.

The aristocrats not only pursued wealth and power, they also cultivated a distinctive lifestyle. Participating in politics and holding elected office was part of this lifestyle. So too was the *symposium*, literally a "drinking party," an intimate gathering at which elite men would enjoy wine, poetic competition, performances by trained dancers and acrobats, and the company of *hetaeras* (courtesans) who provided witty conversation, music, and the promise of sex. Respectable women were excluded from such meetings as they were from most other aspects of social and political life (see below). So too were nonaristocratic men. The symposium was thus an arena for the display of aristocratic masculinity.

The glorification of male sexuality was another important aspect of this homosocial aristocratic culture. Typically, a man in his late twenties to late thirties, who had just begun to make his career in political life, would take as his lover and protégé an aristocratic youth in his early to mid-teens. The two would form an intimate bond that included sexual intercourse. This personal and social intimacy benefited both partners and their families and allowed the younger partner to learn the workings of politics while making valuable connections and alliances. Many later philosophers, including Plato, argued that true love could exist only between two such men, because only within this relationship could a man find an equal partner worthy of his affection. Other types of sexual relationships were considered illicit, including those between men of unequal social status.

A complex system of values, ideas, practices, and assumptions thus shaped aristocratic identity in this era. As a result, it was difficult for those outside this elite world to participate fully in the public life of the polis. Eventually, in many poleis, the circle of the aristocratic elite tightened further, as smaller and smaller groups came to dominate higher offices. This meant that even many aristocrats were left on the outside of their own culture, looking in. For these men, one remedy lay close at hand: they could form an alliance with the rising class of hoplites, who resented their exclusion from political power. And occasionally, a single aristocrat with the backing of the hoplites would succeed in setting up an alternative form of government, a *tyranny*.

## "The Beautiful and The Good"

*The poet known as Tyrtaeus of Sparta flourished during the middle of the sixth century B.C.E. He originally may have come from Athens, but whatever his origins, he expressed ideas of honor, beauty, and virtue that were universal among the hoplite warriors of the new poleis. The key terms he uses in the following verses cannot be adequately translated into English, since these short Greek adjectives are freighted with ancient meanings:* kalos *(beautiful, honorable),* agathos *(good, brave, manly). They stand in opposition to the term* aischros *(shameful, ugly, mean).*

*K*alos it is for an *agathos* warrior to die, fallen among the foremost fighters, in battle for his native land; but to leave his polis and rich fields and beg—that is most painful of all, as he wanders with his dear mother and aged father, his small children and his wedded wife. Detested he will be in the eyes of all those to whom he comes, constrained by need and hateful poverty. He shames his birth and belies his glorious appearance; dishonor and misery are his companions. If no account is taken of a warrior who is a wanderer, if there is no respect for him or his family in the future, then let us fight with all our hearts for this land and die for our children, no longer hesitating to risk our lives. Young men, stand firm beside each other and fight. Do not begin shameful flight or fear. Rather,

create a mighty, valorous spirit in your breasts, and show no love for your lives when you are fighting. Do not flee, abandoning the older men, whose knees are no longer nimble. For *aischros* it is for an older warrior to fall among the foremost fighters and lie out ahead of the young men—a man whose hair is already white and his beard grey—as he breathes out his valorous spirit in the dust, holding his bloody guts in his own hands, his body laid bare. *Aischros* is this to the eyes, and a cause of resentment to look upon. But to the young men all is seemly, while the glorious flower of lovely youth is theirs. To men the young man is admirable to look upon, and to women lovable while he lives and *kalos* when he lies among the foremost fighters. So let a man take a firm stance and stand fast, with both feet planted upon the ground, biting his lip with his teeth.

Source: Excerpted and modified from *The Greek Polis*, eds. W. H. Adkins and Peter White (Chicago: 1986), pp. 23–24.

### Questions for Analysis

**1.** How does Tyrtaeus characterize defeat? How does he describe the values and tactics of hoplite warfare?

**2.** Why is so much emphasis placed on physical beauty and youth? What other qualities are associated with the word *kalos*? Why is old age potentially *aischros*?

**3.** How does this ideal of male beauty compare with that made visible in the kouros of Anavyssos (page 82)? How does it compare with the heroic ideal expressed in the exchange between Diomedes and Glaucus (page 78)?

A tyrant in Archaic Greece was not necessarily an abusive ruler. Indeed, tyranny often led the way to wider political enfranchisement. A tyrant who had sought the support of the hoplite class would have to appease that class by extending it further rights of political participation while all the time striving to keep the reins of power in his own hands. This was an inherently unstable state of affairs, because after the original tyrant had fulfilled the wishes of the hoplites, the continuance of tyranny became an obstacle to even greater power for this segment of the population, which would work to overthrow it. For this reason,

tyrannies rarely lasted for more than two generations and could drive a transition from aristocracy to a more broadly participatory form of government: democracy.

It is important to stress that our notion of democracy is quite different from that of the Greeks. In fact, the philosopher Aristotle denigrated this form of government as "mob rule," because it gave too much power to the *demos*, a word meaning "neighborhood" or "affinity group." He saw it as a system too easily controlled by a particular faction. Our ideal of democracy is closer to what Aristotle would have called a polity, governance by the polis as a whole.

# Analyzing Primary Sources

## Songs of Sappho

*Although Sappho of Lesbos (c. 620–550 B.C.E.) was a prolific poet and skilled musician, we know very little about her life and only a few examples of her extraordinary verse survive. Of the nine books collected in the third century B.C.E., we now have just one complete lyric and a series of fragments, some consisting of only two or three words, often preserved because they were quoted admiringly by other authors. In an astonishing discovery, though, a papyrus scroll containing a previously unknown part of a poem was identified as recently as 2004 (see below). Another papyrus fragment, discovered in 2014, contains parts of two more lyrics: one on unrequited love, addressed to Aphrodite, and another that mentions Sappho's two brothers.*

### Fragment 16

Some say thronging cavalry, some say
    foot soldiers,
others call a fleet the most beautiful of
sights the dark earth offers, but I say it's
    whatever you love best.
And it's easy to make this understood by
everyone, for she who surpassed all
    human
kind in beauty, Helen, abandoning her
    husband—that best of
men—went sailing off to the shores of
    Troy and
never spent a thought on her child or
    loving
parents: when the goddess seduced her
    wits and left her to wander,
she forgot them all, she could not
    remember
anything but longing, and lightly straying
aside, lost her way. But that reminds me
    now: Anactória,
she's not here, and I'd rather see her lovely

step, her sparkling glance and her face
    than gaze on
all the troops in Lydia in their chariots
    and glittering armor.

Source: Translated by Jim Powell, *The Poetry of Sappho* (New York: 2007), pp. 6–7.

### A Newer Fragment (2004)

Live for the gifts the fragrant-breasted
    Muses
send, for the clear, the singing, lyre, my
    children.
Old age freezes my body, once so lithe,
rinses the darkness from my hair, now
    white.
My heart's heavy, my knees no longer
    keep me
up through the dance they used to
    prance like fawns in.
Oh, I grumble about it, but for what?
Nothing can stop a person's growing
    old.

They say that Tithonus was swept away
in Dawn's passionate, rose-flushed arms
    to live
forever, but he lost his looks, his youth,
failing husband of an immortal bride.

Source: Translated by Lachlan Mackinnon, *Times Literary Supplement*, July 15, 2005.

### Questions for Analysis

1. How does Sappho use stories from the older tradition she has inherited to address her own concerns? How does the perspective of this female poet transform masculine ideas about heroism, beauty, warfare, aging?

2. What are the challenges of working with such fragmentary sources as these? If these were the only pieces of evidence to survive from Archaic Greece, what conclusions could you draw about this society and its values?

## The Power of Poetry

Although aristocrats were deeply invested in the heroic ideals of an earlier age, they also expressed their unique culture in newer poetic forms. The most characteristic of these is the lyric, a series of rhythmic verses sung to the music of the lyre. Because these songs were composed orally, or even improvised, few of them survive. Those that do are valuable historical sources, because they concentrate on themes of immediate interest to their audiences: beauty, love, sorrow, ambition, or important life events. And because they were the focus of entertainment at gatherings, lyrics are often politically charged, sexually explicit, or daringly subversive of accepted norms. For example, the poet Archilochus of Paros (c. 680–640 B.C.E.) flouts the conventions of epic poetry by mocking his own failures on the battlefield:

"Some barbarian hefts my shield, since I had to abandon it / . . . but I escaped, so it scarcely matters / . . . I can get another just as good." So much for the heroic ideal of returning either with one's shield or on it! In another lyric, Archilochus castigates his faithless (female) lover and his even more faithless (male) lover, with whom she has an affair.

Given the male domination of Greek culture, it is surprising that the most famous poet of this age was not a man. Rather, it was Sappho (*SAF-foh*; c. 620–550 B.C.E.), who lived in the polis of Mytilene on the island of Lesbos. Sappho composed songs for a wide array of occasions and moods: songs of courtship and marriage, longing and desire, loss and old age. Sometimes her lyrics seem to be addressed to men, but more often they are passionately dedicated to women: both the women whom Sappho loved and the historical women who occupy the margins of masculine epic. In one song, Sappho compares herself with Agamemnon, who was able to return from Troy only after he prayed to Hera, a goddess worshiped at Lesbos; Sappho now prays that her beloved will arrive safely with the goddess's help. In another, she imagines a scene not included in the *Iliad*, the joyous wedding of the Trojan Hector and his bride, Andromache. Like later tragedies, the poignancy of this bridal song (such as those Sappho herself would have sung at the marriage feasts of friends) derives from the listeners' foreknowledge of the legendary couple's terrible fate: Hector's death at the hands of Achilles, Andromache's enslavement at the hands of the victorious Greeks, and the murder of their infant son. The intimacy of lyric reveals something that few other sources from antiquity are able to convey: the distinctive feelings and desires of individuals who were often at odds with the dominant culture of their time.

## PORTRAITS OF THREE POLEIS

The poleis of Greece developed in very different ways. To illustrate this diversity, we examine three particularly interesting examples: Athens and Sparta, both on the Greek mainland; and Miletus, on the Ionian coast of Anatolia. None of these cities can be considered typical: there were some one thousand poleis, and about most of them we know almost nothing. But at least we can survey some of the features that, with variations, made each polis unique—and yet comparable, in some ways, to its neighbors.

### Athens

In Greek, the name of this city is the same as that of its patron goddess Athena, the warlike and wise daughter of

**OSTRACISM.** This political practice takes its name from the pot shards (in Greek, *ostraka*) on which the names of candidates for political exile were scratched. Many of the ballots have survived. Here we see the names of Aristeides, Kimon, and Themistocles: prominent citizens of the fifth century B.C.E. who had fallen out of favor.

Zeus. When the Athenians first came together to form a polis, theirs was a distinctly agricultural economy. Whatever profits aristocrats acquired through trade, they reinvested in land on the Attic Peninsula. Indeed, the Athenian elites regarded commerce as a disreputable means of earning a living, a mentality that persisted even when the city's excellent harbors and orientation toward the Aegean made Athens famous as a mercantile center.

In the early centuries of its history, aristocratic dominance over the Athenian polis rested on monopolization of elected offices and control of the city's council, the Areopagus (*ah-ree-OP-ah-guhs*). It took its name from the rocky outcrop where the council met, just below the acropolis that rose above it. By the early seventh century B.C.E., the aristocrats who came to wield executive authority in Athens were called *archons* ("first men"). Ultimately, nine archons presided over the entire governance of the polis, including its military, judicial, and religious affairs. Although each served for only one year, all became lifetime members of the Areopagus. And because the Areopagus appointed the archons, it could therefore ensure that power remained in the hands of its own future membership. It also served as a kind of high court in judicial cases.

As this small group consolidated power, deep economic and social divisions developed. A significant proportion of the Athenian population fell into slavery through debt, while struggles among aristocratic families destabilized society and fomented cycles of revenge killings. This situation eventually inspired Athenians' first attempt to promulgate a set

**THE ATHENIAN PNYX, WITH A VIEW OF THE ACROPOLIS.** The Athenian assembly, the *ekklesia*, met on the sloping hill of the Pnyx. A speaker standing on the *bema* ("stepping-stone"; to the right) would have to make himself heard by all the citizens gathered in front of this platform, and all proceedings would have been plainly visible to noncitizens and foreigners in the agora at the foot of the hill (to the left). Overlooking it all was the temple of the city's patron goddess, Athena, on the crest of the Acropolis. ▪ *How is the relative openness and accessibility of Athenian democracy symbolized by this chosen site?*

of written laws. In 621 B.C.E., an aristocrat named Drakon sought to regulate civic violence through harsh punishments: hence our term *draconian* to describe any severe penalty or regime. The negative effects of this policy ultimately led both aristocrats and hoplites to an agreement. In 594 B.C.E., they agreed to support the election of the poet Solon as the sole archon for one year, and they gave him broad legislative powers. Solon was an aristocrat, but he had made his fortune as a merchant, so he was not allied with any one interest. Indeed, he does not appear to have cared about cultivating public opinion, and after his laws were enacted, he went into self-imposed exile for a decade.

Solon's reforms, though hardly democratic in their making, laid the foundations for the later development of Athenian democracy. He forbade the practice of debt slavery and set up a fund to buy back citizens who had been sold abroad. He encouraged the cultivation of olives and

grapes, thus spurring cash-crop farming and urban industries such as oil and wine production, and the manufacture of pottery storage jars and decorative drinking cups. He also broadened rights of political participation and set up courts in which a range of citizens served as jurors and to which any Athenian might appeal. He based eligibility for political office on property qualifications, thus making it possible for someone not born into the aristocracy to gain access to power. Moreover, he convened an Athenian assembly, the *ekklesia* (*eh-KLAY-see-a*) and gave it the right to elect archons. Now all free-born Athenian men over the age of eighteen could participate in government. Even those who were not eligible for citizenship were able to see the workings of government for themselves, since the assembled citizens met on the slopes of the Pnyx (*pNIX*), a hill visible from the central marketplace and overlooked by the sacred precincts of the acropolis.

Solon's reforms initially met with resistance. The aristocracy thought them too radical; the people of the demos, not radical enough. In the resulting decades of controversy, an aristocrat named Peisistratos (*pi-SIS-trah-tohs*) succeeded in establishing a tyranny in 546 B.C.E. In a somewhat ironic move, Peisistratos then proceeded to institute Solon's reforms. He also launched a massive campaign of public-works projects, including the collection and codification of Homer's epics. But the apparent mildness of his rule was undergirded by the quiet, persistent intimidation of Athenian citizens by foreign mercenaries and the ruthlessness with which Peisistratos crushed any dissent. Still, by enforcing Solon's laws, he strengthened the political role of the demos and remained a popular ruler until his death. His sons, however, were less able to control the various factions that threatened their rule. One was assassinated, and the other was ousted with the help of the Spartans in 510 B.C.E.

The following period of Spartan-sponsored oligarchy ("rule of the few") was brief. Two generations of increasing access to power had left the Athenian demos with a taste for self-government. For the first time in recorded history, a group of commoners can be credited with the overthrow of a regime: they rallied behind Cleisthenes (*CLIE-sthen-ees*), an aristocrat who championed the cause of the demos. Although he did not hold the elected office of archon at the time, Cleisthenes was able to build a coalition within the ekklesia and, by these democratic means, was able to check the power of the oligarchs in 508/7 B.C.E. Then, by reorganizing the Athenian population into ten voting districts, Cleisthenes suppressed traditional loyalties that had tied each demos to certain aristocratic families. He further strengthened the powers of the Athenian assembly and extended the machinery of democratic government to the local level throughout Attica. He also introduced the practice of ostracism, whereby Athenians could decide each year whether they wanted to banish someone for a decade and, if so, whom. This, Cleisthenes hoped, would prevent the return of a tyranny.

The result of these political struggles made the governance of Athens far more populist than that of any other Greek polis (at least, that we know of). In the meantime, Athens had become the principal exporter of olive oil, wine, and pottery in the Greek world. It was poised to assume the role it would claim for itself during the fifth century B.C.E.

## Sparta

Located in the southern part of the Peloponnesus, the polis of the Spartans took shape when four villages (and ultimately a fifth) combined to form a single entity. Perhaps as a relic of the unification process, Sparta retained a dual monarchy throughout its history, with two royal families and two lines of succession. Although seniority or ability usually determined which of the two ruling kings had more influence, neither was technically superior to the other, a situation that often led to competition among their respective supporters.

According to our only written accounts—all authored by Athenians—Spartan control over the surrounding region of Laconia began with the conquest of Messenia, one of Greece's few agriculturally rich territories. Around 720 B.C.E., the Spartans subjugated and enslaved the indigenous people there, the *helots*, who now became an unfree population forced to work under Spartan lordship. Around 650 B.C.E., however, the helots revolted, gaining support from several neighboring poleis and briefly threatening Spartan hegemony. Eventually, Sparta triumphed, but the shock of this rebellion brought about a permanent transformation.

Determined to prevent another uprising and to protect its superior position, Sparta became the most militarized polis in Greece. Within a few generations, everything was oriented to the maintenance of its hoplite army—a force so superior that the Spartans confidently left their city unfortified. At a time when Athenian society was becoming more democratic and citizens spent more time legislating than fighting, Spartan society was becoming increasingly devoted to an older aristocratic ideal of perpetual warfare, with personal freedom mattering less than the collective honor and security of the polis.

The Spartan system made every male citizen a professional soldier of the phalanx. At birth, every Spartiate child was examined by officials who determined whether it was healthy enough to raise; if not, the infant was abandoned in the mountains. This was a custom observed elsewhere in the ancient world, but only in Sparta was it institutionalized by the state. If deemed worthy of upbringing, the child was placed at age seven in the polis-run educational system. Boys and girls trained together until age twelve, participating in exercise, gymnastics, and other physical drills and competitions. Boys then went to live in barracks, where their military training would commence in earnest. Girls continued their training until they became the mates of eligible Spartiate males, usually when the girls were around the age of eighteen and the men often much older. But for most of their married lives, couples lived apart, so their domestic interests would not compete with the objectives of the polis.

Barracks life was rigorous, designed to accustom youths to physical hardship. At age eighteen, the young man who survived this training would try for membership in a brotherhood whose sworn comrades lived, ate, and fought together. Failure to gain acceptance would mean that the young man could not become a full Spartiate and would lose his rights as a citizen. If accepted, however, he remained with his

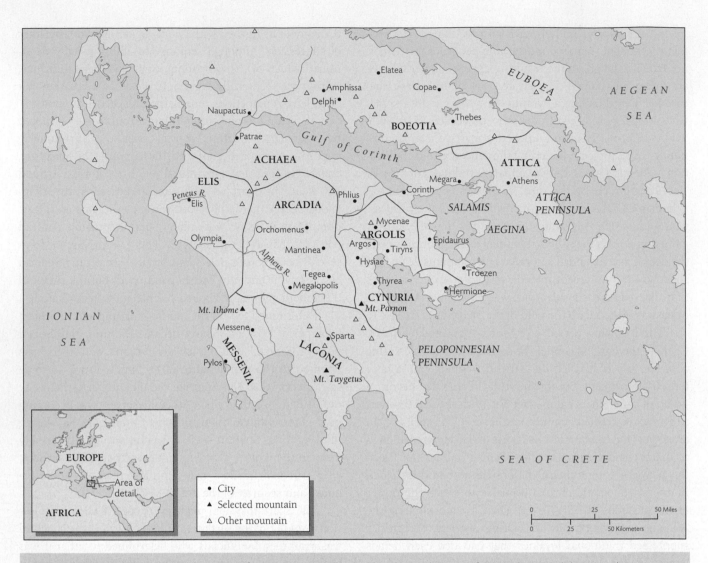

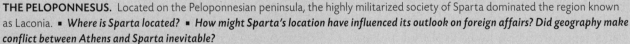

**THE PELOPONNESUS.** Located on the Peloponnesian peninsula, the highly militarized society of Sparta dominated the region known as Laconia. ■ *Where is Sparta located?* ■ *How might Sparta's location have influenced its outlook on foreign affairs? Did geography make conflict between Athens and Sparta inevitable?*

brotherhood until he was thirty years of age. Between the ages of twenty and thirty he was also expected to mate with a Spartiate woman—but occasions for this were few, a fact that partially accounts for the low birthrate among Spartan citizens. After age thirty, a Spartiate male could opt to live with his family, but he was still required to remain on active military duty until he was sixty.

All Spartiate males over the age of thirty were members of the citizens' assembly, the *apella*, which voted on matters proposed to it by a council, the *gerousia* (gher-oo-SEE-ah; "assembly of elders"), consisting of twenty-eight elders and the two kings. This gerousia was the main policy-making body of the polis and also its primary court. Its members were elected for life but had to be over the age of sixty before they could stand for office. Meanwhile, five *ephors* (over-seers), elected annually, supervised the educational system

and acted as the guardians of Spartan tradition. In the latter role, ephors could even remove an ineffectual king from command of the army while on campaign. The ephors also supervised the Spartan "secret service," the *krypteia*, recruiting agents from among the most promising young Spartiates. Agents spied on citizens, but their main job was to infiltrate the helot population and identify potential troublemakers.

This Spartan polity hinged on the precarious relationship with the helots, who outnumbered the Spartiates ten to one. Messenia routinely seethed with revolt. In wartime, helots accompanied the Spartans on campaign as shield bearers, spear carriers, and baggage handlers. At home, however, the helots were a constant security concern. Every year the Spartans ritually declared war on them as a reminder that they would not tolerate dissent. Moreover, the constant threat of unrest at home meant that the polis was notoriously

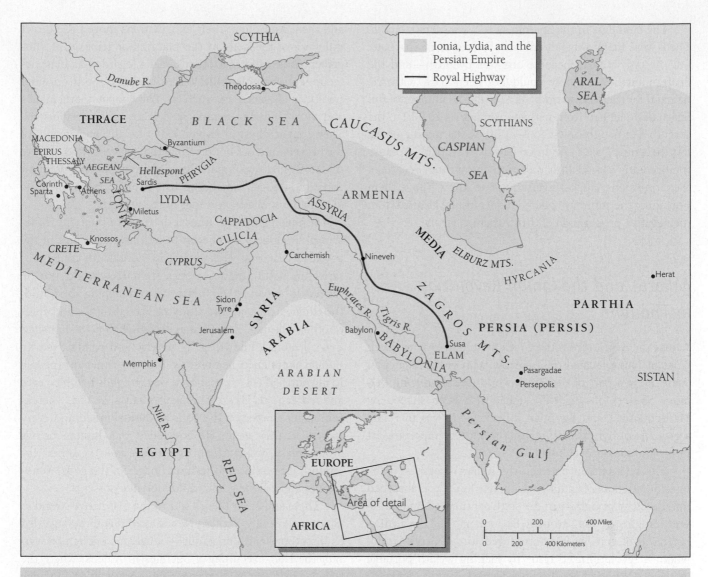

**IONIA, LYDIA, AND THE PERSIAN EMPIRE.** During the seventh and sixth centuries B.C.E., the Greek cities of the Ionian coast were the cultural and commercial leaders of Greece. But during the fifth century B.C.E., after the Persians conquered Lydia, they lost this position to Athens. ▪ *Where are Ionia, Lydia, and Miletus on this map?* ▪ *How does Ionia's geographical position help to explain the change in its fortunes?* ▪ *How might this change have influenced Ionian attitudes toward the Persian Empire?*

reluctant to commit its army abroad. So helot slavery made the Spartan system possible, but Sparta's reliance on a hostile population of slaves was also a serious limitation.

This system also limited the Spartans' contact with the outside world. Spartiates were forbidden to engage in commerce because wealth might distract them from the pursuit of martial glory. Nor did Spartiates farm their own lands, as many Athenians did. Economic activity in the Spartan state fell either to the helots or the free residents of other Peloponnesian cities who were known as *perioikoi* (*per-ee-OY-koi*; "those dwelling around"). The perioikoi enjoyed certain rights and protections within Spartan society, and some grew rich handling its business concerns. But unlike the residents of Attica, in the hinterland of

Athens, the perioikoi exercised no political rights within the Spartan polis. Spartiates who lost their rights as citizens also became perioikoi.

The Spartans rejected innovation. They styled themselves as the protectors of the "traditional customs" of Greece, by which they meant aristocratic dominance and a strict observance of older heroic ideals. In this role, Sparta tried to prevent the establishment of tyrannies in neighboring states and moved to overthrow them when they arose: hence their willing intervention in the affairs of Athens under the Peisistratids. Indeed, Sparta's stern defense of tradition made it an object of admiration throughout the Greek world, even though few Greeks had any desire to live as the Spartans did.

The fatal flaw in the Spartan system was demographic. There were many ways to fall from the status of Spartiate, but the only way to become one was by birth—and the Spartan birthrate simply could not keep pace with the demand for trained warriors. As a result, the number of full Spartiates declined from perhaps as many as 10,000 in the seventh century to only about 1,000 by the middle of the fourth century B.C.E. Another flaw is historical: because the Spartans placed little value on the written record of their traditions, almost everything we know about them (including the summary offered here) must be gleaned from the negative propaganda of their Athenian rivals.

## Miletus and the Ionian Revolution in Thought

Across the Aegean from the Greek mainland lay the Greek cities of Ionia, located on a narrow strip of the Anatolian coast. Long a part of the Greek world (see **Analyzing Primary Sources** on page 53), it had also been shaped by Mesopotamian and Egyptian influences. It was therefore a crucible of hybrid cultures that produced important art forms and modes of thought.

The relationship between the Ionian Greeks and the interior kingdom of Lydia—which, like Ionia, was absorbed into the Persian Empire in the sixth century (Chapter 2)—was fraught. It was through the Ionians that the Lydian invention of coinage was introduced to the Greek world, where it revolutionized trade by making wealth portable while also introducing a host of new philosophical and ethical problems. The Ionians, in turn, played a crucial role in Hellenizing western Asia while insisting on their independence. Ultimately, the major poleis of Ionia banded together to form the Ionian League, a political and cultural confederation. This was the first such organization known in the Greek world, and its aim was to insulate Ionian Greeks from the growing power of the Persians.

The Milesians founded many colonies, especially in and around the Black Sea. They were also active in Egypt, where the main Greek trading outposts were Milesian foundations. These colonial efforts, combined with its advantageous position for trade with the rest of Asia, brought Miletus extraordinary wealth. At the same time, it also became a center for speculative thinking, what the Greeks called *philosophia* ("love of wisdom"). Beginning in the sixth century B.C.E., a series of intellectuals now known as the pre-Socratics—because they came before the great philosopher Socrates—raised new and vital questions about the relationship between the natural world (the *kosmos*), the gods,

and men. And often, their explanations moved the direct influence of the gods to the margins or removed it altogether, something that other Greeks regarded as blasphemous. For example, Milesian philosophers built on older traditions of learning, such as Babylonian mathematics and astronomy, but complicated many older conclusions. They sought physical explanations for the movements of the heavens and did not presume that heavenly bodies were divine. By making human observation the starting point for their knowledge, they began to formulate more scientific explanations for the workings of the universe.

Stimulated by the cultural diversity of their city, Milesian philosophers also began to rethink their place in the cosmos. Hecataeus (*heck-ah-TAY-us*) derided his contemporaries' unquestioning acceptance of a narrow worldview; he set out to expand their horizons by mapping the world, traveling extensively and studying the customs and beliefs of other cultures. Xenophanes (*zee-NOFF-uh-nees*) posited that all human knowledge is relative and conditioned by human experience: he observed that the Thracians (people living north of Greece) believed that the gods had blue eyes and red hair, just as the Thracians themselves did, whereas Ethiopians portrayed the gods as dark skinned and curly haired, as they were. He concluded that human beings always make gods in their own image, not the other way around. If horses could fashion images of the gods, Xenophanes argued, the gods would look like horses.

These and other theories formed a distinctive strand in Greek philosophy, yet they would continue to be regarded as disturbing and dangerous—dangerous enough to warrant the later execution of Socrates in Athens, where the struggle between religion and philosophy would ultimately be fought more than a hundred years after Xenophanes' bold proclamation. By that time, the Persian conquest of Lydia had made Miletus and its sister cities subject to that great empire. Indeed, Ionian resistance to Persian rule triggered the greatest clash the Greek world had yet known.

## THE CHALLENGE OF THE PERSIAN WARS

The two major wars fought between the uneasily unified Greeks and the vast empire of the Persians were construed as defining events by those who witnessed and looked back on them. From the first, the contest was unequal. Persia was the largest and most efficient state the world had ever seen, capable of mustering over a million armed men. The Greeks, by contrast, remained a collection of disparate

**A MODERN REPLICA OF AN ATHENIAN TRIREME.** These versatile warships were much more powerful than the old 50-oared pentakonters that had been in use for centuries. As the name suggests, a trireme had three banks of oars on each side, 170 oars in total. These were manned by citizen rowers seated on benches at three different levels in the vessel's hold. In battle, rowers could help power a ship forward, turn it, and keep it on course in a chase, even when sailing into the wind. In favorable winds, the sails were hoisted for added speed. ▪ *How did this new military technology build on some of the same strategies as hoplite warfare?*

communities, fiercely competitive and suspicious of one another. An exceptionally large polis, such as Athens or Sparta, might put 10,000 hoplites in the field; but the vast majority of Greek states could only provide a few hundred each. So the threat of Persian conquest loomed large on the Greek horizon, and the experience of international warfare changed the Greek world immeasurably.

## The Ionian Revolt (499–494 B.C.E.)

For the first time in the history of Western civilizations, we can follow the unfolding of events through the narrative of a contemporary historian: Herodotus, the first person who self-consciously set out to write an account of his own times in careful, unambiguous prose—rather than in the form of heroic poetry or the boastful language of victorious inscriptions. And lucky for us, Herodotus was uniquely qualified to probe the long-term and more immediate causes of the Persian Wars. Raised in the Ionian polis of Halicarnassus, he was a product of the hybrid culture dis-

cussed above. He was also a keen observer of human nature and human diversity. He regarded both the Greeks and the Persians as great peoples. Yet as a Greek himself—albeit one born within the Persian dominion—he was not impartial. Indeed, his surviving account reflects many of the intellectual currents of mid-fifth-century Athens, where he spent the better part of his career, as well as many Athenian prejudices. This is something that must be borne in mind when reading his work.

Herodotus wanted to show that the war between the Persians and Greeks had ancient roots and could be traced back to long-standing cultural differences, but his narrative also shows that the catalyst was a political conflict in Miletus. In 501 B.C.E., the city was governed by Aristagoras (*EHR-is-STAG-or-uhs*), a tyrant who owed his power to the backing of the Persian emperor, Darius (Chapter 2). But Aristagoras apparently came to believe that his days as the emperor's favorite were numbered. So he turned abruptly from puppet to patriot, rousing the Milesians and the rest of Ionia to revolt against Persian rule. As a safeguard, he also sought military support from the sympathetic poleis

# Past and Present

## Political Satire

In the fifth century B.C.E., the playwright Aristophanes took an older form of comedy, the satyr play, and turned it into a vehicle for what we still call satire. Instead of gently mocking the gods, he lampooned the politics, popular culture, and current events of his own day—and so made his fellow citizens take a fresh look at themselves. If he were alive today, he might be writing for *The Daily Show*.

Ⓢ **Watch related author interview on the Student Site**

on the Greek mainland. The Spartans refused to send their army abroad, but Athens and Eretria (*er-eh-TREE-uh*), on the island of Euboea (*you-BOY-ah*), agreed to send twenty-five ships and crews. This small force managed to capture the old Lydian capital of Sardis (by then a Persian administrative center) and burn it to the ground. Then the Athenians and Eretrians went home, leaving the Ionians to their own devices. In 494 B.C.E., the rebellious poleis were finally overwhelmed by the vastly superior might of Persia.

Darius realized, however, that so long as his Greek subjects in Ionia could cast a hopeful eye to their neighbors across the Aegean, they would forge alliances with them. He therefore decided to launch a preemptive strike against Athens and Eretria, to teach these upstart poleis a lesson. In the summer of 490 B.C.E., a punitive expedition of 20,000 soldiers, under two of Persia's finest generals, crossed the Aegean and landed on the coast of Euboea. Their forces sacked and burned Eretria to the ground, sending its population into captivity in Persia. They then crossed the narrow strait to Attica, landing on the plain of Marathon, approximately twenty-six miles from Athens.

## Marathon and Its Aftermath

When the Persians landed in Attica, the Athenians quickly called on the only polis that could conceivably help them: Sparta. But the Spartans responded that they were unable to assist—they were celebrating a religious festival. Only the small, nearby polis of Plataea offered the Athenians aid. The Athenian and Plataean hoplites would have to engage the mighty Persians on their own.

Heavily outnumbered and without effective cavalry to counter that of the Persians, the Athenian phalanx took a position between two hills blocking the main road to the polis. After a standoff of several days, the Athenian general Miltiades (*mil-TIE-uh-dees*) received word that the Persians were watering their horses and that the Persian infantry was vulnerable to attack. So Miltiades led a charge that smashed the Persian force, resulting in crippling losses. In an almost unbelievable victory, the Athenians had defeated the world's major imperial power, and they had done it without Spartan help. It was a vindication of hoplite tactics and a tremendous boost to Athenian confidence.

Yet the Athenian politician Themistocles (*the-MIS-toh-klees*) warned that the Persians would not suffer such humiliation quietly and would retaliate with an even larger force. So when the Athenians discovered a rich vein of silver ore in the Attic countryside a few years later, Themistocles persuaded them not to divide the windfall among themselves (the customary practice) but to finance a fleet of 200 triremes,

state-of-the-art warships. Athens thereby transformed itself into the preeminent naval power of the Greek world, just in time to confront a new Persian onslaught.

## Xerxes' Invasion

Darius the Great died in 486 B.C.E. and was succeeded by his son Xerxes, who almost immediately began preparing a massive overland invasion of Greece designed to conquer the entire territory, thus eradicating any future threats to Persian imperial expansion while avenging his father's shame. Supported by a fleet of 600 ships, this grand army

**THE PERSIAN WARS WITH GREECE.** Imagine that you are the Persian emperor Xerxes, planning the conquest of Greece in 480 B.C.E.
▪ *What are the two possible routes that you could take to attack Greece?* ▪ *What geographical considerations would dictate your military strategy?* ▪ *Bearing in mind that Xerxes' attempt failed, what would you do differently?*

**GREEK FORCES DEFEAT PERSIANS.** This detail from a bowl commemorating the defeat of Xerxes' army depicts an Athenian hoplite poised to strike a deathblow to his Persian opponent. The artist has carefully delineated the differences between the enemies' dress and weaponry. To the Greeks, the Persian preference for trousers over short tunics seemed particularly barbaric and effeminate.

Salamis. From there, the Athenians watched the Persians torch their city. Time, however, was on their side. Xerxes' massive army depended on his damaged fleet for supplies, and the Persians' military tactics—which included a heavy reliance on cavalry and chariots—were not adapted for the rocky terrain of Greece. Bad weather also made sailing the Aegean in autumn a risky business; the Persians were now desperate to force a decisive battle and return home before the season turned against them.

In late September, the numerically superior Persian fleet sailed into the straits of Salamis, believing that the Athenians were preparing to flee the island. The report turned out to be false, but so confident was Xerxes that he had a throne placed on the headland above the bay, where he would have a good view of his victory. Instead, he watched as the battle-ready Athenian triremes demolished the Persian fleet. This was the turning point of the war. Xerxes retreated with the majority of his army to Persia, while an elite force stayed behind. But when the allied Greek army met the Persians on favorable terrain the next spring—an open plain near Plataea, which had been razed the year before—the Greeks prevailed. Against all odds, the small, fractious poleis had defeated the mightiest army of the known world.

## THE GOLDEN AGE OF CLASSICAL GREECE

During the half century after the Persian Wars, Athens enjoyed a meteoric rise in power and prestige, becoming the premier naval power of the eastern Mediterranean and the military rival of Sparta. Athens also emerged as leader of the Delian League, a group of poleis whose representatives met on the sacred island of Delos and pledged to continue the war against Persia, which was now being fought in the Aegean. As the league's leader, Athens controlled its funds and resources. This era simultaneously witnessed the greatest achievements in Athenian culture and politics. These were complicated, however, by the increasingly awkward relationship of Athens with its allies, which began to feel more like Athenian subjects than free poleis.

### Periclean Athens

In the decades before the Persian Wars, political reforms in Athens had continued to encourage experiments in democracy, including the practice of selecting major officeholders by lot. Only one key position was now filled by traditional

(which numbered at least 150,000 men and may have been as large as 300,000) set out from Sardis in 480 B.C.E., crossing the Hellespont (literally "bridge to Greece"), the narrow strait separating Europe from Asia. Unlike his father, who had dispatched talented generals against Athens, Xerxes led this campaign himself.

Many Greek poleis capitulated immediately. But Athens, Sparta, Corinth, and some thirty others refused to surrender. Instead, they hastily formed the Hellenic League, an unprecedented alliance in the face of an unprecedented external threat. In August of 480 B.C.E., a major Persian offensive was held at bay when the outnumbered Greek allies, under the military leadership of Sparta, confronted Xerxes at the mountain pass of Thermopylae (ther-MO-puh-lie). For three days, they valiantly held off the Persian multitude, whose way through the narrow pass was effectively blocked. Meanwhile, a Greek fleet led by Athens and guided by Themistocles engaged a Persian flotilla off the Attic coast. The Spartans' defense of Thermopylae ultimately failed, but their sacrifice allowed the new Athenian warships to inflict heavy losses on the Persians.

However, these engagements left Athens without any men to defend the city. Themistocles therefore persuaded the entire population to abandon Athens for the island of voting: the office of *strategos*, or general. And because a man could be elected strategos year after year, this office became the career goal of Athens' most ambitious figures. Themistocles had been strategos, as was Cimon (*KEY-mohn*), who led the Delian League to victories over Persia during the 470s and 460s B.C.E. But Cimon also used the league to punish poleis that tried to opt out of membership, even suppressing revolts in these cities by force of arms and so turning the league into an instrument of Athenian policy.

By then, the political mood in Athens was changing. New voices were demanding a greater role in government; most prominent were the *thetes* (*THAY-tees*), the lowest class of free men and the class that provided the triremes' rowers: the backbone of the all-important Athenian fleet. Like the hoplites of the Archaic Period, who had achieved citizenship because they were indispensable to the defense of the poleis, the thetes wanted higher status and equal representation. The man who emerged to champion their cause was Pericles (*PEHR-eh-klees*), an aristocrat from one of Athens' most prestigious families.

Pericles made the enfranchisement of the thetes the main plank of his political platform and also advocated a foreign policy that was oriented away from cooperation with Sparta. In 462–461 B.C.E. he was elected strategos and immediately used his position to secure the ostracism of his rival, Cimon. He then pushed through reforms that gave every Athenian citizen the right to propose and amend legislation, not just to vote yes or no in the citizen assembly. And by paying an average day's wage for attendance, he made it easier for poorer citizens to participate in the assembly and in courts of justice. Through such measures, the thetes and other free men of modest means became a dominant force in politics—and loyal to the man who had made that dominance possible.

In keeping with the ambitions of Pericles, this populist program glorified Athens through an ambitious scheme of public building and lavish festivals honoring the gods, especially Athena. Also, Pericles himself was a generous patron of the arts and sciences, attracting the greatest minds and talents of the day to Athens. His popularity, combined with his charisma and his promotion of the Athenians' sense of superiority, ensured his reelection as strategos for the next three decades. During these years Athens flourished, but it also alienated much of the Greek world by its arrogance and aggression.

## Athenian Literature and Theater

Athens was not the only city to produce great works of art during this period, but our knowledge of classical Greek culture is dominated by the dramas produced at its great religious festivals. The most important of these was the Dionysia, a great spring feast devoted to the god Dionysus, which became a celebration of Athenian exceptionalism and democratic ideals. From the beginning, therefore, drama was closely connected to the political and religious life of the state that sponsored it. Indeed, the very format of classical tragedy replicates the tensions of democracy, with its complex cast of characters and its conflict among opposing perspectives. This format was perfected under the great tragedian Aeschylus (*AY-skihl-uhs*; 525–456 B.C.E.) and his younger contemporary, Sophocles (496–406 B.C.E.). Their dramas made use of two or (eventually) three professional actors, each of whom could play numerous roles, and a chorus of Athenian citizens that represented collective opinion and could comment on the action.

Although Aristotle would later declare that the purpose of tragedy was to inspire pity and fear and so to purge these emotions through a process called *katharsis* ("purification"), this definition does not capture either the variety or impact of Athenian tragedy. Tragedies were almost always set in the distant or mythical past, but they were intended to address the cutting-edge issues of their day. Indeed, the very earliest of all surviving tragedies, Aeschylus' *Persians*, dramatizes events of the playwright's own lifetime; we know for certain that he fought at Marathon, because he had this fact proudly recorded on his tomb. Performed for the first time in 472 B.C.E., this contemporary tragedy tells the story of the great Athenian victory at Salamis—but through the eyes of the defeated Xerxes, who thus becomes its tragic hero.

Even when the subject matter was derived from the epics of Homer, the fundamental themes of tragedy—justice, the conflicting demands of personal desire and public duty, the unforeseen consequences of human actions, the brutalizing effects of power—addressed problems of immediate concern to Athenians. For example, Aeschylus' trilogy the *Oresteia* (458 B.C.E.) is ostensibly about the legendary family of the Mycenaean king Agamemnon and traces the long-term consequences of the king's sacrifice of his daughter Iphigenia; his subsequent murder at the hands of his grieving wife, Clytemnestra; and the vengeance the couple's son, Orestes, takes by killing his own mother. But the court of law that eventually tries Orestes is actually that of Periclean Athens, and the plays' debates over the rational application of law resonated with Aeschylus' contemporaries. O
at Colonus, one of Sophocles' later tragedies, used
of the mythical king of Thebes to comment bit
ens' disastrous war with Sparta (see below)
*Trojan Women* of Euripides (485–406 p
415 B.C.E., marks the tragic turning p
march toward defeat in this war
capture, rape, and enslavemen.

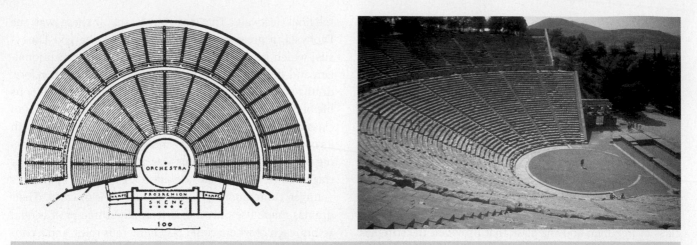

**THE THEATER AT EPIDAUROS.** Greek dramas were invariably presented in the open air, usually at dawn. Since these were civic spectacles, theaters had to be large enough to accommodate all citizens. Most, like this one at Epidauros (right), took advantage of the natural slope of a hill. The plan for the theater is shown above (left). The acting area would have been backed by a high wall, the *skene*, which housed stage machinery and enhanced the acoustics. A trained actor standing in the *orchestra* would have been plainly audible even to those seated in the top tier. ▪ *How would the size and setting of such a theater enhance the political character of the plays performed within it?*

Athenians were forced to look at the dreadful consequences of their own imperial policies.

Comedy was even more obviously a genre of political commentary and social satire and could deal openly with the absurdities and atrocities of current events. Not only was it unconstrained by any formal poetic framework, but comedy—then as now—could be effectively and safely deployed to deal with issues that were too hot to handle in any other medium: sexual scandals, political corruption, moral hypocrisy, intellectual pretension, popular fads. Aristophanes (*EHR-ih-STOFF-ah-nees*; c. 446–386 B.C.E.), the greatest of the Athenian comic playwrights, lampooned everything from the philosophy of Socrates to the tragedies of his contemporary Euripides and was an especially outspoken critic of Athenian warmongers and their imperialist aims. He regularly savaged the powerful figures whom he saw as leading Athens to its doom, and he was repeatedly dragged into court to defend himself against the demagogues he attacked. But the power and popularity of comic theater was such that politicians never dared to shut it down for long. It was too much an expression, and outcome, of Athenian ideals.

Periclean Athens was also fertile ground for the development of new literary forms. Even though the Greeks of this age were becoming more dependent on writing for legal and commercial transactions, they valued highly the arts of memory and oral debate; and intellectuals had long been [use]d to expressing themselves through poetry, which was [alway]s intended to be sung and enjoyed in performance, not [r]ead. (The Milesian philosophers had conveyed their ideas in verse, and Solon had used poetry in justifying his political reforms.) In the course of this century, though, the rise of functional literacy in Athens encouraged the emergence of prose as a distinct literary form. Herodotus found a ready market for his histories in Athens. His younger contemporary Thucydides (*thoo-SID-ih-dees*) followed suit, using his time in exile to write a masterful—and scathingly critical—history of the war between his polis and Sparta, in which he himself had unsuccessfully fought.

Between them, these two historians developed a new approach to the study of the past, emphasizing the need to collect and interpret multiple sources and focusing on human agency as the driving force of history (rather than divine intervention or divine will). Although in different ways, both conceived the historian's role as distinct from that of a storyteller. The word *historia* would continue to mean both "story" and "history," but for Herodotus and Thucydides the historian's task was to investigate and critically reflect on the events of his own time, as well as to illuminate those of the past. These methods and goals would increasingly come to inform other prose genres, including the philosophical writings of Plato and Aristotle (see Chapter 4).

## Art and Architecture

The visual artists of classical Greece revealed the same range of talents in the visual arts as poets did in their

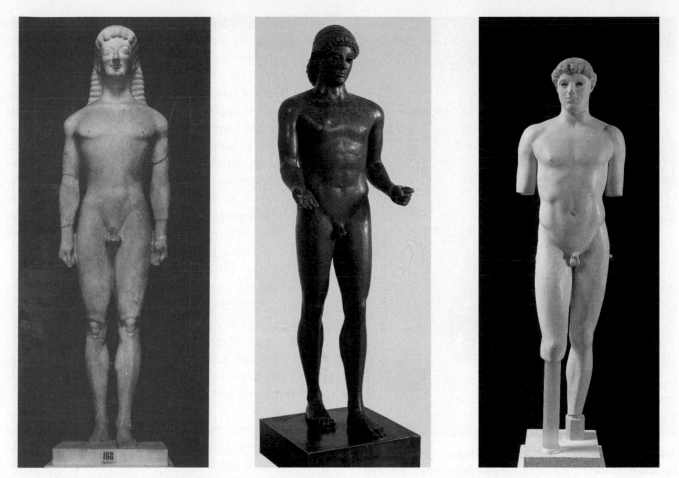

**APOLLO OF TENEA, APOLLO OF PIOMBINO, AND THE CRITIAN BOY.** These three statues, dating from about 560, 500, and 480 B.C.E., respectively, illustrate the development of Greek statuary art. The first rather stiff and symmetrical statue (left) is imitative of Egyptian sculpture. Roughly a half century later, the second representation (middle) of Apollo begins to display motion, not unlike the kouros on page 82. The last figure (right), showing a boy standing in a relaxed posture with his weight resting on one leg, displays even greater naturalism.

dramas. Their comic gift is exhibited in vessels made for festive use at symposia, which often depict the delights of sensuality, sexual encounters, and scenes from bawdy tales. By contrast, the heroic but humane mode of tragedy corresponds to the marble statues and sculptured reliefs made for temples and public places. Athenian sculptors in particular were drawn to the challenges of representing the human form accurately while celebrating an ideal of physical beauty.

Perhaps the most striking development in fifth-century Greek sculpture was the new attention paid to the crafting of naturalistic figures, both clothed and nude. This happened first in Athens. Nothing like it had ever been seen before, although it is a trend already discernible in the figure of the kouros examined on page 82 and in the successive refinements of the sculptor's art made in the previous century. What hastened the acceptance of naturalism in art is a matter of intense debate, but scholars have long wanted to link this innovation to the victories over the Persians

in those key decades. Greeks tended to regard the Persian male's modesty of dress, preference for trousers, fondness for jewelry, and luxurious long hair as proofs of effeminacy (see the bowl on page 96). Greek men took pride in sculpting their physiques, exercising, and participating in athletic contests in the nude. A Greek might have said that only barbarians bowed down to their rulers like slaves and covered their shameful bodies in constricting clothes; free men celebrate their individuality not only in politics but in the care of the body and its representation.

The Athenians also made exceptional contributions to architecture in this period. All Greek temples sought to create an impression of harmony, but the Parthenon of Athens, built between 447 and 438 B.C.E., is generally considered the finest example. Construction of this stunning, expensive, and structurally ambitious building was urged on the Athenians by Pericles as a tribute to their patron goddess, Athena Parthenos ("Athena the Virgin"), and as a symbol of their own power, confidence, and genius.

**THE SHRINE OF ATHENA IN THE PARTHENON.** This is a replica of the statue of Athena that once stood inside the Parthenon dedicated to her (see also the image on page 76). Made of gold and ivory and designed by the great sculptor Phidias, who was updating a more archaic style, the statue stood forty feet high and was visible to viewers outside the temple and some distance away. The statue was reflected in a shallow pool of water located in front of it.

## The Daily Life of Athens: Men, Women, and Slaves

Toward the end of his famous funeral oration, which Thucydides quotes in his history, Pericles addresses only a few brief remarks to the women of Athens who mourn their fallen fathers, husbands, and sons at the end of the first year of the disastrous war with Sparta. He urges them to do three things: rear more children for the support of Athens and its wars, show no more weakness than is "natural to their sex," and attract no attention to themselves. For as he says, the greatest glory of a woman is not to be spoken about at all, whether for good or ill. His remarks reveal widely held attitudes toward women in classical Greece, although they may not reflect complex historical realities.

The growth of democracy did not lead to greater equality between the sexes; in fact, it had the opposite result. In the Bronze Age of Mycenaean Greece, women were viewed as possessing extraordinary funds of courage and wisdom, as well as beauty and virtue. They were prized for their shrewd advice on political and military matters, and they played an active role in the world. Sometimes, elite women ruled kingdoms in their own right. Indeed, this was still the case in the northern territories of Macedonia and Epirus, as we will see (Chapter 4), as well as in some Ionian poleis.

But as aristocratic ideals gave way to more democratic ones, Greek women increasingly spent their lives in the confinement of the home. On the one hand, the importance of the hoplite infantry and its spirit of shared purpose encouraged men to train together and to develop close relationships, something that was also sanctioned by the political system. On the other hand, that spirit of equality discouraged the political agency of women. Instead, the production of children to supply the infantry became the female imperative. Public spaces were largely restricted to male activities, whereas domestic spaces were reserved for female endeavors, such as child care and weaving. Respectable women lived largely in the seclusion of a house's inner courtyard, rarely venturing forth from their homes.

In Athens, girls could be legally married at age fourteen to husbands more than twice their age. (Younger men were supposed to devote themselves to war.) A girl's father arranged her marriage and provided a dowry that her husband could use for her support. Shortly after a wife entered her new home, a regular schedule of childbirth would begin. Typically, the interval between births was two to four years, meaning that the average young wife would bear between four and six children before she died, usually around the age of thirty-five. Her place might then be taken by another, younger woman.

Because women seldom went out of doors or ventured beyond their immediate neighborhood—it was thought immodest for them to be seen by men other than those in their families—slaves did whatever shopping or marketing the household required. Even at home, women were expected to withdraw into private rooms if visitors arrived. But they were not supposed to sit around idly, and their main occupation—this was true of all women, from royalty to slaves—was the spinning and weaving of cloth. And since women's work was basically menial, men looked down on them for it, even though their own livelihoods and comfort depended on it. Some evidence even suggests that husbands were not encouraged to form emotional attachments to their wives, although many certainly did. In a revealing passage, Herodotus talks of a certain Lydian king who "fell in love with his own wife, a fancy that had strange consequences." By contrast, an Athenian orator remarked that "we have prostitutes for pleasure, concubines for daily

**WOMEN AND WEAVING.** Wool working and weaving were gender-specific activities throughout the ancient world, in which women of all social ranks were expected to participate. On this red-figure vase, dating from 460–450 B.C.E., we see the woman on the left carding wool, and the two women on the right preparing fibers for spinning into threads, which could then be woven into cloth.

physical needs, and wives to bear us legitimate children and be our faithful housekeepers." But these perspectives are offset by a range of archaeological and material evidence that testify to women's valued social roles, the affection of their husbands and children, and even their wider economic and legal powers.

In addition to depending on the labor and fertility of women, Athenians were as reliant on slaves as Spartans were on helots. Without slavery, none of the Athenian accomplishments in politics, thought, or art would have been possible. The Athenian ideal of dividing and rotating governmental duties among all free men depended on slaves who worked in fields, businesses, and homes while free men engaged in politics. In fact, the Athenian democratic system began to function fully only with the expansion of Athenian mining and commerce around 500 B.C.E., which enabled the Athenians to buy slaves in larger numbers. Freedom and slavery were thus an inescapable contradiction of this democracy—much as they would be many centuries later in the United States.

Although widespread, Athenian slavery was modest in scale. Slaves did not ordinarily work in teams or in factories; the only exceptions were the state-owned silver mines, where large numbers of slaves toiled in miserable conditions. Most slaves were owned in small numbers by a wide range of Athenian families, including the relatively poor. As domestic servants and farm laborers, slaves might even be considered trusted members of the household, although their masters were legally empowered to beat them or abuse them; concubines and sex workers (of both genders) were often drawn from among this class of slaves. Yet slaves

could never be entirely dehumanized as they were in modern slaveholding societies: the misfortune of becoming a slave through debt was a reality of Athens' recent past, and the real possibility of being enslaved in war became a widespread consequence of Athens' overreaching ambitions.

## "THE GREATEST WAR IN HISTORY" AND ITS CONSEQUENCES

In more ways than one, Athenian freedom rested on the servitude of others. Slaves performed much of the labor at home, and Athens' allies in the Delian League provided the resources that supported Athenian greatness. Without the surplus wealth flowing into Athens from the league, none of the projects Pericles undertook—pay for political participation, massive building projects, the patronage of Athenian drama—would have been possible. These projects kept Athens rich, its democracy vibrant, and Pericles in power. But ultimately, Athens' foreign policy and imperial ambitions undermined these achievements.

Since the 470s, as we noted above, Athens had begun crushing those allies who attempted to break from its control. By the early 440s, its only rival for supremacy in the Greek world was Sparta. Rather than attempting to maintain a balance of power, however, Pericles determined on a more aggressive policy: he made formal peace with Persia to ensure that available military resources would be directed toward any future Spartan opposition. But this undermined the sole purpose of the Delian League, which had been the defense of Greece against Persian aggression. Athens now had no justification for compelling the league members to maintain their allegiance. Many remained loyal nonetheless, paying their contributions and enjoying the economic benefits of warm relations with Athens. Others, however, did not, and Athens found itself increasingly having to force its reluctant allies back into line, often installing Athenian garrisons and planting Athenian colonists—who retained their Athenian citizenship—to ensure continued loyalty.

In the context of recent history and longstanding Greek values, such behavior was disturbing. The Delian League had been established to preserve Greek independence. Now Athens itself was becoming an oppressive, imperial power. Foremost among its critics were the Corinthians, whose own economic standing was threatened by Athenian dominance. The Corinthians were close allies of the Spartans, who in turn were the dominant power in what historians call the Peloponnesian League. (The Greeks called it simply the "Spartans and their allies.") When war finally erupted between Athens and Sparta, Thucydides—himself an Athenian—ascribed it to the growing power of Athens and the anxiety this inspired in other poleis. No modern historian has improved on Thucydides' thesis. Yet for the Athenians and their leaders, there could be no question of relinquishing their empire or the dream of dominating the Mediterranean world. For Sparta and its allies, meanwhile, the prospect of relinquishing their own culture and independence was equally unthinkable. Two very different ideas of Greek superiority were about to fight to the death.

## The Peloponnesian War Begins

When the Athenians and Spartans found themselves at war with one another in 431 B.C.E., both sides believed a conclusion would come quickly—a delusion common to many of history's pivotal wars. Instead, the war dragged on for twenty-seven years. Thucydides, writing about it in exile, recalled that he knew from the time of its outbreak that it was going to be "the greatest war in history," amounting to the first world war, because by the time it was over it would involve the entire Mediterranean. He also meant that it was the worst, so devastating to both sides that it partially destroyed the Greeks' proud heritage of freedom. By the time Athens was forced to concede defeat, all the poleis were weakened to such an extent that never again were they able to withstand outside threats.

From the beginning, Athens knew that it could not defeat Sparta on land; and neither Sparta nor its allies had a fleet capable of facing the Athenians at sea. Pericles therefore developed a bold strategy: he would pull the entire population of Attica within the walls of Athens and its harbor and not attempt to defend the countryside against Sparta. For sustenance, Athens would rely on supplies shipped in by its fleet, which would also be deployed to ravage the coasts of the Peloponnesus.

The Spartans duly plundered the farms and pastures of Attica, frustrated that the Athenians would not engage them in battle. Meanwhile, the Athenians inflicted significant destruction on Spartan territory in a series of raids and by successfully encouraging rebellion among the helots. The advantage appeared to be on Athens' side, but in 429 B.C.E. the crowded conditions of the besieged city gave rise to a typhus epidemic that killed over a third of the population, including the aged Pericles. Pericles' death revealed that he had been the only man capable of managing the political forces he had unleashed. His successors were mostly demagogues, ambitious men who played to the worst instincts of the demos. The most successful of these was Cleon, a particular target of Aristophanes' ridicule, who refused a Spartan offer of peace in 425 B.C.E. and continued the war

until his own death in battle four years later. It was under Cleon that Thucydides was given the impossible task of liberating a city under Spartan control; his failure in 423 led to his exile.

After the death of Cleon, a truce with Sparta was negotiated by an able Athenian leader named Nikias. But Athenians continued to pursue a "dirty war" by preying on poleis that it feared might support the Spartans. This led to atrocities such as the destruction of Melos, an island that had been colonized by the Spartans but had maintained its neutrality since the beginning of the war. When the inhabitants of Melos refused to compromise this position by accepting Athenian rule, Athens had the entire male population slaughtered and every woman and child sold into slavery. Thereafter, Athens' policy of preemptive warfare proved destructive to itself. In 415 B.C.E., a charismatic young aristocrat named Alkibiades (*al-kih-BY-uh-dees*) convinced the Athenians to attack the powerful Greek city of Syracuse in Sicily, which was allegedly harrying Athenian allies in the western Mediterranean. The expedition failed disastrously, ending with the death or enslavement of thousands of Athenian warriors.

News of the Syracusan disaster shattered the Athenians. Many political leaders were driven from the polis as scapegoats, and in 411 B.C.E. a hastily convened assembly of citizens voted democracy out of existence, replacing it with an oligarchy ("rule of the few") consisting of 400 members, many of whom had been present at this vote. The remains of the Athenian fleet, then stationed at Samos on the Ionian coast, responded by declaring a democratic government in exile under the leadership of none other than Alkibiades. The oligarchy proved to be brief, and democracy was restored to Athens by 409. But a pattern of self-destruction had been established, making it difficult for anyone in Athens or outside it to believe in the possibility of restored greatness.

## THE FAILURE OF ATHENIAN DEMOCRACY

The Spartans, too, despaired of bringing the war to an end. Even in its weakened condition, the Athenian fleet was still invincible. Finally, Sparta turned to the Persians, who were glad to avenge themselves on Athens and agreed to supply the gold and expertise necessary to train an effective Spartan navy. Meanwhile, the Athenians were turning against each other, making the Spartans' task easier. In 406 B.C.E., a rare Athenian naval victory at Arginusae (*ar-geh-NOO-si*)

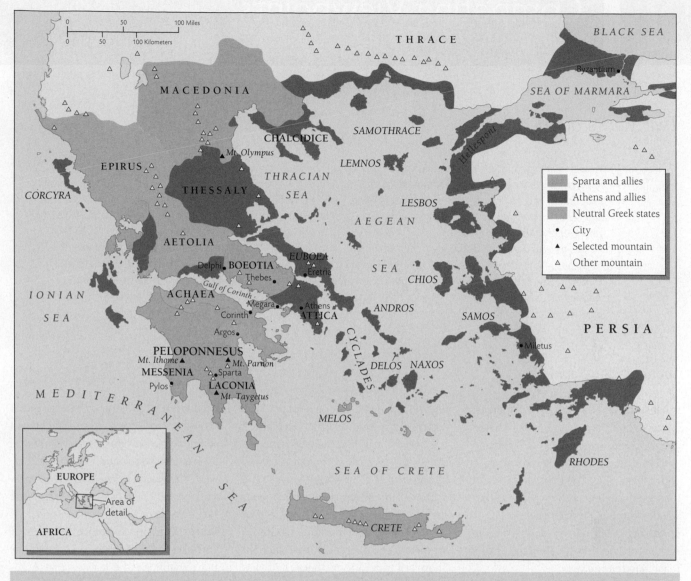

**THE PELOPONNESIAN WAR.** This map shows the patchwork of colonies and alliances that bound together the supporters of Sparta and Athens at the outbreak of the Peloponnesian War. ▪ *Which side had the geographical advantage?* ▪ *Which neutral powers might have been able to tip the balance by entering the war on one side or the other?* ▪ *What strategic and military choices did geography impose on the two combatants and their allies?*

ended in a sudden storm that prevented the Athenian commanders from rescuing the sailors whose ships had been wrecked. A firestorm of protest was fanned by demagogues who insisted on making an example of those generals brave enough to return to Athens. One of these was Pericles' son Pericles, who was executed: thereby dying a victim of his father's policies. Through such measures, the Athenians killed or exiled the last of their able commanders.

The result was tragic. The poorly led Athenian fleet was destroyed in 404 B.C.E. Without ships, the Athenians could neither feed themselves nor defend their city. The Spartans sailed the Aegean unopposed, installing pro-Spartan oligarchies to rule former Athenian allies. Finally,

they besieged Athens, which surrendered. Corinth and Thebes, remembering the ruthless treatment of Melos, called for Athens' annihilation. The Spartans refused but imposed harsh terms: the dismantling of Athens' defensive walls, the scrapping of its fleet, and the acceptance of an oligarchy under Spartan supervision. These so-called Thirty Tyrants confiscated private property and murdered their political opponents. Their excesses drove committed democrats to plan a desperate coup, a bloodbath averted only through the intervention of the Spartan kings. By the end of 401 B.C.E., Athens had restored a semblance of democratic governance, but it was never more than a shadow of its former self.

# Two Views of Socrates

> Most people regard Socrates as the sage thinker who challenged the prevailing prejudices of his day. During his own time,
> however, he was not so universally admired. In the first excerpt, from Aristophanes' comedy The Clouds, the protagonist,
> Strepsiades, goes to Socrates and his "Thought Shop," asking that Socrates make him and his son, Pheidippides, orators
> capable of winning lawsuits and growing rich. Aristophanes implies throughout that Socrates is a charlatan who teaches
> word games and tricks for hire.
>
> In the second excerpt, according to his pupil Plato, Socrates spent the last days of his life in conversation with
> his friends and followers, some of whom urged him to escape from captivity and live in exile. In the dialogue Crito,
> a young aristocrat of that name argues that the very laws that have condemned Socrates are unjust, and that by
> choosing to obey them Socrates is giving them legitimacy they do not deserve. But halfway through the debate,
> Socrates turns the tables on him.

## Socrates as a Sophist

**STREPSIADES:** See that he [Pheidippides] learns your two Arguments, whatever you call them—oh yes, Right and Wrong—the one that takes a bad case and defeats Right with it. If he can't manage both, then at least Wrong—that will do—but that he must have.

**SOCRATES:** Well, I'll go and send the Arguments here in person, and they'll teach him themselves.

**STREPSIADES:** Don't forget, he's got to be able to argue against any kind of justified claim at all.

**RIGHT:** This way. Let the audience see you....

**WRONG:** Sure, go wherever you like. The more of an audience we have, the more soundly I'll trounce you.

**RIGHT:** What sort of trick will you use?

**WRONG:** Oh, just a few new ideas.

**RIGHT:** Yes, they're in fashion now, aren't they, [to the audience] thanks to you idiots.... [to Pheiddipides] You don't want to be the sort of chap who's always in the agora telling stories about other people's sex lives, or in the courts arguing about some petty, filthy little dispute....

**WRONG:** People here at the Thought Shop call me Wrong, because I was the one who invented ways of proving anything wrong, laws, prosecutors, anything. Isn't that worth millions—to have a really bad case and yet win? . . . Suppose you fall in love with a married woman—have a bit of fun—and get caught in the act. As you are now, without a tongue in your head, you're done for. But if you come and learn from me, then you can

do whatever you like and get away with it . . . and supposing you do get caught with someone's wife, you can say to him. . . . "What have I done wrong? Look at Zeus; wasn't he always a slave of his sexual passions? And do you expect a mere mortal like me to do any better than a god?" . . .

**STREPSIADES [to Socrates]:** I wonder if you'd accept a token of my appreciation? But my son, has he learned that Argument we were listening to a moment ago?

**SOCRATES:** Yes, he has.

**STREPSIADES:** Holy Fraud, how wonderful!

**SOCRATES:** Yes, you'll now be able to win any case at all.

Source: Aristophanes, *The Clouds*, trans. Alan H. Sommerstein (New York: 1973), pp. 148–50, 154, 159–60 (slightly revised).

## Socrates and the Laws of Athens

**SOCRATES:** I should like you to consider whether we are still satisfied on this point: that the really important thing is not to live, but to live well.

**CRITO:** Why, yes.

**SOCRATES:** And that to live well means the same thing as to live honorably, or rightly?

**CRITO:** Yes.

**SOCRATES:** Then in light of this agree-

ment we must consider whether or not it is right for me to try to get away without an official pardon. If it turns out to be right, we must make the attempt; if not, we must let it drop. . . .

**CRITO:** I agree with what you say, Socrates....

**SOCRATES:** Well, here is my next point, or rather question. Ought one to fulfill all one's agreements, provided they are right, or break them?

**CRITO:** One ought to fulfill them.

**SOCRATES:** Then consider the logical consequence. If we leave this place without first persuading the polis to let us go . . . are we or are we not abiding by our just agreements?

**CRITO:** I can't answer your question, Socrates. I am not clear in my mind.

**SOCRATES:** Look at it this way. Suppose that while we were preparing to run away (or however one should describe it), the Laws of Athens were to come and confront us with this question: "Now, Socrates, what are your proposing to do? Can you deny that by this act which you are contemplating you intend, so far as you have the power, to destroy us, the Laws, and the whole polis as well? Do you imagine that a city can continue to exist and not be turned upside down, if the legal judgments which are pronounced in it have no force but are nullified and destroyed by private persons?"—How shall we answer this question, Crito, and others of the same kind? . . . Shall we say, "Yes, I do intend to destroy the Laws, because the polis has wronged me by passing a faulty judgment at my trial"? Is this to be our answer, or what?

**CRITO:** What you have just said, by all means, Socrates.

**SOCRATES:** Then supposing the Laws say, "Was there provision for this in the agreement between you and us, Socrates? Or did you pledge to abide by whatever judgments the polis pronounced? . . . [I]f you cannot persuade your country you must do whatever it orders, and patiently submit to any punishment it imposes, whether it be flogging or imprisonment. And if it leads you out to war, you must comply, and it is right that you should do so; you must not give way or retreat or abandon your position. Both in war and in the law courts you must do whatever your city and your country commands."

Source: Plato, *Crito*, excerpted (with modifications) from *The Last Days of Socrates*, trans. Hugh Tredennick (New York: 1969), pp. 87–91.

## Questions for Analysis

1. Socrates actually refused to teach the art of "making the weaker argument defeat the stronger." But in *The Clouds*, Aristophanes shows him teaching how "to win any case at all." Why were the powers of persuasion considered potentially dangerous in democratic Athens? Why would Aristophanes choose to represent Socrates in this way?

2. How do the arguments of Plato's Socrates compare with those of Aristophanes' character?

3. How does Socrates' sense of honor and his duty toward the polis compare with those of Tyrtaeus of Sparta (page 85)?

---

With its victory, Sparta succeeded Athens as the arbiter of the Greek world. But this was a thankless job, made worse by the losses the Spartans themselves had suffered during the war and the fact that they were even more aggressive in their control of the Aegean than the Athenians had been. Ironically, indeed, the Spartans found themselves in a position they had avoided throughout their history, because their far-flung interests now sapped their manpower and undermined their control over the helots. They also faced a reinvigorated Persian Empire, which took advantage of the Greeks' fratricidal struggles to increase its naval presence in the Aegean.

These were the circumstances in which the Athenian philosopher Socrates (469–399 B.C.E.) attempted to reform his city's ethical and political traditions. To understand something of his accomplishments, and to assess the reasons for his tragic death, we must trace briefly the history of philosophical speculation in the half century before his birth.

## The Pythagoreans and the Sophists

After the Persian conquest of Ionia, many Milesian philosophers fled to southern Italy. Philosophical speculation thus continued in the Greek "far west." A major proponent was Pythagoras, who founded a philosophical community in the Italian city of Croton. Pythagoras and his followers regarded the speculative life as the highest good, but

**SOCRATES.** According to Plato, Socrates looked like a goatman but spoke like a god.

edge. Their teachings are best exemplified by Protagoras (*pro-TAG-or-ahs*), an older contemporary of Socrates. His famous dictum, "Man is the measure of all things," means that goodness, truth, and justice are relative concepts, adaptable to the needs and interests of human beings. In other words, values are not moral imperatives established by the gods. Instead, Protagoras declared that no one could know whether the gods existed or, if they did, what they wanted. He concluded that there could be no absolute standards of right and wrong. Empirical facts, established by the perceptions of the senses, were thus the only source of knowledge. And because each man experienced the world in a different way, there could be only individual truths valid for the individual knower.

Such teachings struck many Greeks as dangerous. Sophists such as Protagoras made everyday life a subject for philosophical discussion, but their relativism could too easily degenerate into a conviction that the wise man (or the wise state) was the one best able to manipulate others and gratify individual desires. In both personal and collective terms, this conviction could rationalize monstrous acts of brutality—such those committed by Athens in the case of Melos. Indeed, the lessons of the Peloponnesian War went a long way toward demonstrating the disastrous consequences of this self-serving logic: if justice is merely relative, then neither individual morality nor society can survive. This ethical conviction led to the growth of a new philosophical movement grounded in the theory that absolute standards *do* exist and that human beings can determine what these are through the exercise of reason. The initiator of this trend was Socrates.

## The Life and Thought of Socrates

Socrates was not a professional teacher, as the Sophists were. He may have trained as a stonemason, and he certainly had some sort of livelihood that enabled him to maintain his status as a citizen and hoplite. Having fought in three campaigns as part of the Athenian infantry during the war with Sparta, he was both an ardent patriot and a sincere critic of Athenian policy. His method of instruction was conversation: through dialogue with passersby, he submitted every presumed truth to rigorous examination in order to establish a firm foundation for further inquiry. Everything we know about Socrates' teachings comes from the writings of younger men who considered themselves his pupils and participated in these conversations. The most important of these followers was Plato.

According to Plato, Socrates sought to show that all supposed certainties are merely unexamined prejudices

they believed that one must be purified of fleshly desires to achieve this. Just as the essence of life lay in the mind, they believed that the essence of the universe was to be found not in the natural world but in the study of abstracts, and so they concentrated on mathematics and musical theory. The Pythagoreans established the key properties of odd and even numbers and also proved an old Babylonian hypothesis in geometry, known today as the Pythagorean theorem. Even though they shunned the material world, they still exhibited the characteristic Greek quest for regularity and predictability in that world.

Meanwhile, philosophy as it developed in mainland Greece was more attuned to questions of ethics and politics than mathematics. The increasing power of individual citizens begged the question of how a man should conduct himself, in public and private life, so as to embrace "the beautiful and the good"—or at least to advance himself by the use of his wits. To answer this question, a new group of teachers arose. They were known as the Sophists, a term meaning "wise men."

Unlike the Milesian philosophers or the Pythagoreans, however, the Sophists made a living by selling their knowl-

**SOCRATES AS THE IDEAL EDUCATED MAN.** This image of Socrates features on a Roman funerary monument known as the Sarcophagus of the Muses, made in the second century C.E. The sarcophagus advertises its owner-occupant's desire to be viewed (even in death) as a highly cultivated man, the companion of the Nine Muses of Greek mythology and the companion of Socrates, who taught that the practice of philosophy helped to prepare the soul for immortality.

inherited from others. Socrates always said that he himself knew nothing, because this was a more secure place from which to begin the learning process. He sought to base his speculations on sound definitions of key concepts—justice, virtue, beauty, love—that he and his pupils could arrive at only by investigating their own assumptions. And he focused his attention on practical ethics rather than the study of the physical world (as the Milesians did) or mathematical abstractions (as the Pythagoreans did). He urged his listeners to reflect on the principles of proper conduct, both for their own sakes and for that of society as a whole. He taught that one should consider the meaning and consequences of one's actions at all times and be prepared to take responsibility for them. According to one of his most memorable sayings, "The unexamined life is not worth living."

It is bitterly paradoxical that Socrates, the product of Athenian democracy, should have been put to death by democratic processes. Shortly after the end of the Pelopon-

nesian War in 399 B.C.E., when Athens was reeling from both the shock of defeat and the violent internal upheavals, a democratic faction decided that Socrates was a threat to the state. A democratic court agreed, condemning him to death for denying the gods, disloyalty to the polis, and "corrupting the youth." Although his friends made arrangements for him to flee the city and thus evade punishment, Socrates insisted on abiding by the laws and remaining in prison, thus proving himself true to his own principles and setting an example for future citizens. He died calmly by the prescribed method: self-administered poison.

According to Socrates, the goal of philosophy is to help human beings understand and *apply* standards of absolute good, rather than mastering a series of mental tricks that facilitate personal gain at the expense of others. The circumstances of his death, however, show that it is difficult to translate this philosophy into principles that can be widely accepted. This would be the task of Plato, who would lay the groundwork for all subsequent Western philosophy (see Chapter 4).

## CONCLUSION

There are many striking similarities between the civilization of ancient Greece and our own—and many stark differences. Perhaps the most salient example of both is the concept of democracy, which the people of ancient Greece would have defined as a rule by a class of privileged male citizens supported by slavery. In theory and in practice, this amounted to only a small percentage of the population in Athens, and in Sparta the vast majority were subject to the rule of an even smaller class of Spartiates. Moreover, the growth of Athenian power meant, increasingly, the exploitation of other poleis and the spread of imperialism, a ruinous policy of preemptive warfare, and greater intolerance and paranoia. Socrates was not the only man put to death for expressing his opinions. Finally, the status of women in this "golden age" was lower than it had been in earlier periods of Greek history, and women had fewer personal rights than in any of the ancient societies we have studied so far.

And yet the profound significance of Greek experiments with new forms of governance and new ideas about the world is undeniable. This can be seen with particular clarity if we compare the Greek poleis with the empires and kingdoms of the Bronze Age, in which the typical political regime, as we have seen, was a monarchy supported by a powerful priesthood. In this context, cultural achievements were mainly instruments to enhance the prestige of rulers, and economic life was controlled by palaces and temples. By contrast, the core values of the Greeks were the primacy of the human male and the principles of competition, individual achievement, and human freedom and responsibility. (The very word for freedom—*eleutheria*—cannot be translated into any other ancient language, not even Hebrew.) In his history, Herodotus records a conversation between a Greek (in this case a Spartan) and a Persian, who expresses surprise that the Greeks should raise spears against the supposedly benign rule of his emperor. The Spartan retorts, "You understand how to be a slave, but you know nothing of freedom. Had you tasted it, you would advise us to fight not only with spears but with axes." How the Greeks came to turn those spears on each other within a few generations of their united victory is a story worthy of one of their own tragedies.

# After You Read This Chapter

 Go to **INQUIZITIVE** to see what you've learned—and learn what you've missed—with personalized feedback along the way.

## REVIEWING THE OBJECTIVES

- The Greek polis was a unique form of government. What factors led to its emergence?
- Hoplite warfare had a direct effect on the shaping of early democracy. Why?
- Poleis could develop in very different ways. What are some of the reasons for this?
- In what ways did Athenian culture, philosophy, and art reflect democratic ideals?
- The Persian and Peloponnesian Wars affected Greek civilization in profound ways. Describe some of the consequences of Athens' victory in the former and its defeat in the latter.

Another way of appreciating the enduring importance of Greek civilization is to recall the essential vocabulary we have inherited from it: not only the word *democracy* but also *politics, philosophy, theater, history.* How would we think without these concepts? The very notion of humanity comes to us from the Greeks. For them, the fullest development of one's potential should be the aim of existence: every free man is the sculptor of his own monument. This work of growing from childishness to personhood is what the Greeks called *paideia,* from which our term *pedagogy* is derived; the Romans called it *humanitas.* How this and other ideas came to be disseminated beyond Greece, to be adopted by the peoples and places of a much wider world, is the subject of Chapter 4.

## PEOPLE, IDEAS, AND EVENTS IN CONTEXT

- How did the epics of **HOMER** transmit the values of the Bronze Age to the **ARISTOCRACY** of the new Greek **POLEIS**?

- How did the spread of Greek culture transform the Mediterranean, even as the adoption of **HOPLITE** military tactics transformed Greek politics?

- Compare and contrast the historical circumstances that led to the development of **ATHENS**, **SPARTA**, and **MILETUS**. What were the main differences among them?

- What were the different motives for the invasions by **DARIUS** and **XERXES**? By what methods did the Greek poleis manage to emerge victorious from the **PERSIAN WARS**?

- What were the triumphs and limitations of **DEMOCRACY** in **PERICLEAN ATHENS**?

- How did the **PELOPONNESIAN WAR** transform Athens and affect the balance of power in the Mediterranean?

## THINKING ABOUT CONNECTIONS

- The trial and execution of Socrates can be seen as a referendum on the relationship between the individual and the state. What does this incident reveal about the limitations of personal power and individual rights? To what degree was this incident a product of Athenian losses during the Peloponnesian War? To what extent does it reflect long-term trends in the Greek world?

- We like to think that we can trace our democratic ideals and institutions back to Athens, but does this mean that the failings of Athenian democracy also mirror those of our own? What parallels can you draw between the cultures of fifth-century Athens and today's United States? What are some key differences?

## STORY LINES

- After the Peloponnesian War, divisions within and among the Greek poleis eventually made them vulnerable to the imperial ambitions of King Philip II of Macedonia and his son, Alexander the Great.

- Alexander's conquest of the Persian Empire and Egypt united the civilizations of antiquity under Greco-Macedonian rule. Even after his untimely death, a shared language and culture continued to bind these civilizations together in a new Hellenistic ("Greek-like") world.

- Ease of travel, trade, and communication throughout this Hellenistic world fostered urbanization on an unprecedented scale. The resulting cosmopolitan culture challenged traditional social, economic, and political norms, giving rise to new social classes, forms of wealth, and technological innovations.

- The unique art forms and intellectual inquiries of Greece were thus disseminated throughout this world and transformed by it.

## CHRONOLOGY

| | |
|---|---|
| 404 B.C.E. | Sparta defeats Athens in the Peloponnesian War |
| 401 B.C.E. | Xenophon and the Ten Thousand begin their Persian expedition |
| 395–338 B.C.E. | The struggle for Greek dominance (Thebes, Athens, Sparta) |
| 371 B.C.E. | Epaminondas of Thebes defeats the Spartans at Leuctra |
| 356 B.C.E. | Philip II becomes king of Macedonia |
| 338 B.C.E. | Macedonia defeats Thebes and Athens at Chaeronea |
| 336–323 B.C.E. | Reign and campaigns of Alexander |
| 323–c. 275 B.C.E. | Formation of the Hellenistic kingdoms |
| 323–c. 225 B.C.E. | The Greek diaspora |
| c. 300 B.C.E. | Formation of the Aetolian and Achaean Leagues |
| 300–270 B.C.E. | Rise of Stoicism and Epicureanism |
| c. 300–200 B.C.E. | The Hellenistic scientific revolution |
| 203–120 B.C.E. | Lifetime of the historian Polybius |

## Before You Read This Chapter

# The Greek World Expands, 400–150 B.C.E.

............................................................

## CORE OBJECTIVES

- **EXPLAIN** the reasons for Macedonia's rise to power and its triumph over the Greek poleis.

- **DESCRIBE** Alexander's methods of conquest, colonization, and governance.

- **IDENTIFY** the three main Hellenistic kingdoms and their essential differences.

- **DEFINE** the main characteristics of the Hellenistic world.

- **UNDERSTAND** how new philosophies and artistic movements reflect historical changes.

When the young Alexander of Macedonia set out for Persia in 334 B.C.E., he brought along two favorite books. The first was a copy of the *Iliad* that his teacher Aristotle had given him. The second was the *Anabasis*, "The Inland Expedition," by an Athenian called Xenophon (*ZEN-oh-fon*; 430–354 B.C.E.). Both choices are significant. The *Iliad* recounts the story of a much earlier Greek assault on Asia, and its protagonist is the hero Achilles—a consummate warrior, a favorite of the gods, a man who inspired passionate loyalty—a figure with whom Alexander identified. It is also full of information useful to someone planning a long campaign in foreign lands against a formidable enemy, with a fractious army drawn from all parts of Greece and little prospect of bringing them home safely or soon. The *Anabasis* was an even more practical choice. Its author had been one of 10,000 Greek mercenaries hired by a Persian prince to overthrow his older brother, the Great King. The attempted coup failed, but Xenophon's book made the prince, Cyrus, another role model for Alexander. It told, in detail, how Persians fought, how they lived, how they were governed, and what the terrain of their vast empire was like. Moreover, it showed what a dedicated army of hoplites could accomplish on Persian soil. This book would be Alexander's bible for the next ten years as he cut a victorious swath through the ancient civilizations of western Asia and North Africa.

An avid student of history, Alexander recognized that the golden age of the Greek polis had ended in the war of attrition between Athens and Sparta (discussed in Chapter 3). The fifty years prior to his own birth in 356 B.C.E. had merely continued this trend on a smaller scale, as the dominant poleis—first Sparta, then Thebes, then Athens—jockeyed for prominence. Meanwhile, social and economic problems were mounting. Faith in the old ideals of democracy were compromised by the vast gulf that now opened up between the rich and the poor. Increasingly, the wealthy withdrew from politics altogether, while free citizens were reduced to debt slavery. As the values of the polis decayed, a new generation of intellectuals argued about what had gone wrong, and they tried to imagine how Greece could be saved. One of these philosophers was Aristotle, a pupil of Plato and Alexander's own teacher.

Under the circumstances, no one would have been able to predict that the era of greatest Greek influence lay ahead. For rather suddenly, the stalemate of the weakened poleis was shattered by the rise to prominence of a tiny kingdom on their northern borders. Beginning in the reign of King Philip II, Macedonia came to control the Greek mainland. Then, under Philip's remarkable son, a united Greek and Macedonian army extended Greek culture and Greek governance from Egypt to the frontiers of India.

This personal empire, the empire of Alexander, could not last; but a cultural empire built on it did. For a thousand years, a Hellenistic ("Greek-like") civilization united the disparate lands and peoples of a vast region, forming the basis of the more lasting Roman Empire and mirroring, in uncanny ways, the cosmopolitan, globalized culture of our own time. How this happened is the subject of Chapter 4.

## THE DOWNFALL OF THE GREEK POLIS

The Peloponnesian War had left Sparta the dominant power in the Greek world, but the Spartans showed little talent for their new preeminence. At home, Spartan politicians remained deeply divided over the wisdom of sending forces beyond their frontiers; abroad, Spartan armies showed even less restraint than the Athenians had in subduing cities that should have been their allies. In 395 B.C.E., a significant portion of Greece—including such sworn enemies as Athens, Argos, Corinth, and Thebes—aligned themselves against Sparta in the so-called Corinthian War (395–387 B.C.E.). After years of stalemate, the Spartans could win the war only by turning once again to Persia, as they had done in the final stages of the Peloponnesian War. The Persians brokered a peace, which they were also prepared to enforce, one that left Sparta in control of Greece. This pattern of Greek-on-Greek violence, temporarily halted by the intervention of Persia, was repeated time and again over the next fifty years, during which the advantage shifted steadily toward Persia.

## The Struggle for Dominance

After the Corinthian War, the Spartans punished the most dangerous of their rivals, Thebes, by occupying the city for four years. This subjugation to a military garrison

**HONORING THE THEBAN SACRED BAND.** According to ancient historians, all 300 of the Band's sworn lovers fell at the Battle of Chaeronea in 338 B.C.E., when Thebes was defeated by Macedonian forces led by King Philip II and his son, Alexander. An excavation undertaken at this site in 1890 uncovered the remains of only 254 warriors, but it is possible that some were buried elsewhere. This monument is a modern reconstruction of the one originally erected by the citizens of Thebes toward the end of the fourth century B.C.E.

was intended and received as an act of humiliation, and when the Thebans regained their autonomy, they elected as their leader a fierce patriot who was also a military genius, Epaminondas (*eh-pa-min-OHN-das*; c. 410–362 B.C.E.).

For decades, various poleis had been experimenting with the basic form of the hoplite phalanx, adding light skirmishers and archers to enhance its effectiveness. Epaminondas now went further. In imitation of the Spartan system, he formed an elite hoplite unit known as the Theban Sacred Band, made up of 150 male couples, sworn lovers who had pledged to fight to the death for their polis and for each other's honor. Epaminondas also trained a corps of lighter-armed, fast-moving infantry. By the early 370s, he was ready for another trial of strength with the Spartans.

The Theban and Spartan armies met at Leuctra in 371 B.C.E. Epaminondas defied convention by placing his best troops (the Sacred Band) on the left-hand side of his formation, and by stacking this phalanx fifty rows deep, making a narrow wedge of ten men abreast whose hidden depth of strength he further disguised under a cover of arrows and javelin attacks. When the two sides met, the weight of the Theban left drove through the Spartan right flank, breaking it in two and collapsing it. Epaminondas followed his victory by marching through Messenia and freeing the helots. Spartan power—and the unique social system that had supported it—was at an end. Almost overnight, Epaminondas had reduced Sparta to a small, provincial polis and launched what has often been called the Theban Hegemony.

But as Theban power grew, so did the animosity of the other Greek poleis. In 371 B.C.E., Athens had supported Thebes against Sparta, its ancient enemy, but when the Thebans and Spartans squared off again in 362 B.C.E. at the Battle of Mantinea, the Athenians allied themselves with

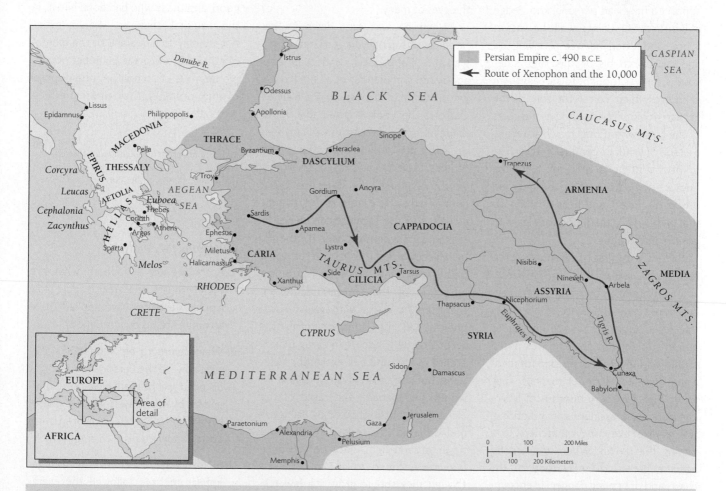

**THE INLAND EXPEDITION OF THE TEN THOUSAND.** This map shows the route taken by Xenophon and his fellow Greek mercenaries during their Persian campaigns, when they supported the failed coup of Cyrus against his brother Artaxerxes II and then fought their way home through enemy territory (as the *Anabasis* records). Follow Xenophon's route with your finger. ▪ *Where did it start and end?* ▪ *Compare this route with that of Alexander on page 125. How closely was Alexander following it?* ▪ *When and how did he diverge from it?* ▪ *Why would this journey of Greek mercenaries have provided Alexander with an important model?*

# Analyzing Primary Sources

## Xenophon Describes an Ideal Leader

*In his history of "The Inland Expedition" undertaken by the Ten Thousand, Xenophon (430–354 B.C.E.) mourns the death of Cyrus the Younger, whom he believes would have made a better Great King of Persia than the brother he challenged, Artaxerxes II. The following description of the prince's character and leadership became very famous in its time, often circulating as a separate booklet. It is likely to have influenced the young Alexander.*

hus then died Cyrus, a man who, of all the Persians since Cyrus the elder, was the most princely and the most worthy of rule, as is agreed by all who appear to have had personal knowledge of him. In the first place, while he was yet a boy, and when he was receiving his education with his brother and other youths, he was thought to surpass them all in everything. For all the sons of the Persian nobles are educated at the gates of the king, where they may learn many a lesson of virtuous conduct, but can see or hear nothing disgraceful. Here the boys see some honored by the king, and others disgraced, and hear of them, so that in their very childhood they learn to govern and to obey.

Here Cyrus, first of all, showed himself most remarkable for modesty among those of his own age, and for paying more ready obedience to his elders than even those who were inferior to him in station; and next, he was noted for his fondness for horses, and for managing them in a superior manner. They found him, too, very desirous of learning, and most assiduous in practicing, the warlike exercises of archery, and hurling the javelin. When it suited his age, he grew extremely fond of the chase, and of braving dangers in encounters with wild beasts. On one occasion, he did not shrink from a she-bear that attacked him, but, in grappling with her, was dragged from off his horse, and received some wounds, the scars of which were visible on his body, but at last killed her. The person who first came to his assistance he made a happy man in the eyes of many.

When he was sent down by his father, as satrap of Lydia and Great Phrygia and Cappadocia, and was also appointed commander of all the troops whose duty it is to muster in the plain of Castolus, he soon showed that if he made a league or compact with anyone, or gave a promise, he deemed it of the utmost importance not to break his word. Accordingly the states that were committed to his charge, as well as individuals, had the greatest confidence in him; and if anyone had been his enemy, he felt secure that if Cyrus entered into a treaty with him, he should suffer no infraction of the stipulations. When, therefore, he waged war against Tissaphernes, all the cities, of their own accord, chose to adhere to Cyrus in preference to Tissaphernes, except the Milesians; but they feared him, because he would not abandon the cause of the exiles; for he both showed by his deeds and declared in words that he would never desert them, since he had once become a friend to them, not even though they should grow still fewer in number, and be in a worse condition than they were.

Whenever anyone did him a kindness or an injury, he showed himself anxious to go beyond him in those respects; and some used to mention a wish of his that he desired to live long enough to outdo both those who had done him good, and those who had done him ill, in the requital that he should make. Accordingly to him alone of the men of our days were so great a number of people desirous of committing the disposal of their property, their cities, and their own persons.

Source: Excerpted from Xenophon, *Anabasis*, ed. M. I. Finley, in *The Portable Greek Historians* (New York: 1959), pp. 383–84.

### Questions for Analysis

1. According to Xenophon, what are the attributes of a great leader? How would Alexander have applied these attributes to his own situation?

2. What seems to be Xenophon's attitude toward the Persians? How might his portrayal of them have been influenced by his travels among them? How might it have been colored by his attitude toward his own countrymen?

3. In what ways does Cyrus the Younger appear to have followed the example of his ancestor, Cyrus the Great (page 64)?

the weaker Spartans. Although the Theban army again carried the day, the brilliant Epaminondas fell in battle, crippling Thebes' leadership. Athens then attempted to fill the vacuum by establishing a naval confederacy, organized more equitably than the Delian League had been, but the Athenians quickly reverted to manipulating and abusing their allies, and the confederacy dissolved in rebellions. Greece was thus reduced to a constellation of petty warring states, increasingly debilitated by their struggles with each other.

## Social and Economic Crises

Meanwhile, individual poleis were also riven by internal turmoil. Athens was spared the political revolutions many other cities suffered, mostly because the memory of the Thirty Tyrants had discredited the cause of oligarchy there; but elsewhere in the Greek world, strife between democrats and oligarchs worsened. Incessant warfare, combined with these political struggles, profoundly affected the Greek world's economic and social infrastructures. Many ordinary people were driven from their homes or reduced to slavery. Country towns had been ravaged, some repeatedly, as had farmlands throughout Greece. The destruction of orchards and vineyards was particularly devastating because of the long time it takes grapevines and olive trees to mature, 40 or 50 years in the latter case. So when an invading army cut down an olive grove, it was destroying a staple crop for two generations. Even arable land was exhausted and less productive than it had been earlier. As a result, prices rose around 50 percent while standards of living declined because wages remained more or less stagnant, and taxes increased. In Athens, the wealthiest private citizens now became the sponsors of public theaters and buildings, as well as the patrons who maintained roads and warships. Even so, the kind of ambitious civic spending undertaken by the tyrants or by Pericles was unknown in the fourth century B.C.E.

Unemployment was also widespread, especially among the growing population of the cities, which were swollen with refugees from the political collapse of the countryside and overseas colonies. During wartime, men might find employment as rowers or soldiers in the service of their city; but when their city was at peace, many turned to mercenary service. The Greek states of Sicily and Italy began to hire mercenaries from the mainland, as did Sparta, to supplement its own campaigns. As we have noted, the brother of the Persian emperor Artaxerxes II, Cyrus, even hired a Greek mercenary force of 10,000 men in an attempt to seize the throne in 401 B.C.E.—although

he did not reveal this aim until the army was deep in Persian territory and suddenly confronted with an enemy far more formidable than the tribal bands it had originally agreed to fight. Cyrus was killed in battle, and shortly thereafter, the Ten Thousand's Spartan general was murdered by agents of Artaxerxes. The army—marooned in a hostile country—had to fight its way out under elected leaders, one of whom was Xenophon, who later wrote his account of these adventures. Finally, the veterans reached the Black Sea and made their way back to Greece, where many (including Xenophon) settled in Sparta. Despite all these hardships, this episode was a stunning demonstration of what a professional Greek army could achieve, and it would fire Alexander's imagination.

# REIMAGINING THE POLIS: THE ARTISTIC AND INTELLECTUAL RESPONSE

We might take 399 B.C.E., the year of Socrates' execution, to mark the end of an era: that of the polis. This basic engine of Greek life had continued to drive innovation and cultural production even during the Peloponnesian War, both in support of the war and in opposition to it. In Athens alone, the historians Herodotus (in his final years) and Thucydides were at work, as were the tragic poets Sophocles and Euripides, the comic playwright Aristophanes, and scores of talented statesmen, poets, sculptors, and artisans. But it's hard not to see the death of Socrates as symbolic of democracy's failure. Thereafter, the evident breakdown of society during the fourth century had a profound impact on the arts, philosophy, and political thought.

## The Arts of the Fourth Century

As we observed in Chapter 3, the painters and sculptors of the fifth century B.C.E. were already working to achieve a heightened appearance of realism. This experimentation continued in the fourth century, especially in the relatively new art of portraiture. During this era, painters and sculptors tried to render both objects and people as they actually looked—for better or for worse—and to convey the illusion of movement, trends that would continue in subsequent centuries. They also grew bolder in their use of sophisticated techniques, such as the casting of full-size statues in bronze, which combined high levels of artistry with advanced metallurgy. This was a medium in which the era's most famous sculptor, Praxiteles, excelled. Praxiteles (*prak-SIT-el-ees*) was bold, too, in his choice of subjects, and he is widely regarded as the first artist to create full-size female nudes, an innovation that sparked controversy in his own day as well as in other eras (see *Interpreting Visual Evidence* on page 118).

The forms and functions of drama also changed considerably. In large part, this was because tragedy and comedy were no longer mounted as part of publicly funded festivals but were instead paid for by private patrons who could exercise greater control over the content of performances. As a result, fourth-century playwrights did not have the freedom to use drama as a vehicle for political and social critique. Nor did the comic genius Aristophanes have any true fourth-century successors. His biting, satirical wit gave way to a milder, less provocative style that bears some resemblance to early television sitcoms. It was this "New Comedy" that laid the groundwork for comedy that developed over the next several centuries: it came to rely more and more on mistaken identities, tangled familial relationships, humorous misunderstandings, and breaches of etiquette. The most famous comic playwright of this age was Menander (c. 342–292 B.C.E.), whose work survives today only in fragments but who directly inspired the comedians of the Roman theater. They in turn inspired medieval and then early modern playwrights such as Shakespeare. Similar trends toward escapism and frivolity are also apparent in a new literary genre that emerged during the fourth century: the prose novel, in which star-crossed lovers undergo extraordinary trials and perilous adventures before reuniting happily after a long separation. These pleasant fictions targeted an increasingly literate audience, including (as for modern novels) an audience of women.

**BRONZE YOUTH.** This lithe statue, dating from the years 340–330 B.C.E., was found in the sea near Marathon and has been identified as a work by the master sculptor Praxiteles (or one of his pupils). Compare this male nude with those discussed in Chapter 3. ■ *How might changes in the style of sculpture parallel cultural changes in society at large?*

## Philosophy after Socrates: The Schools of Plato and Aristotle

The intellectual and political work undertaken by Socrates was carried forward by his most talented student, Plato. Born in Athens to an aristocratic family around 429 B.C.E., Plato joined Socrates' circle as a young man and witnessed first hand the persecution, trial, and death of his mentor. For the next fifty years, to the time of his own death around 349 B.C.E., Plato usually shunned direct political involvement and strove instead to vindicate Socrates by constructing a philosophical system based on his teacher's unwritten precepts. Socrates had taught through dialectical conversation and by example; he mistrusted writing and resisted developing a coherent set of principles. Plato's mission was therefore to transmit his legacy in a way that captured the liveliness and charm of the Socratic method but within a more structured framework.

He did this in two ways: first, by founding an informal school called the Academy, which had no tuition or set curriculum; and later, by writing a series of dialogues that wrapped weighty philosophical content in a witty and accessible dramatic format, with Socrates as the central character. Most dialogues are known by the names of Plato's contemporaries, the original students who had

**PLATO AND ARISTOTLE IN THE SCHOOL OF ATHENS.** Although many artistic representations of Plato and Aristotle were made in antiquity, the image that best captures the essential difference between their philosophies is this one, the focal point of a fresco by the Renaissance painter Raphael (1483–1520 C.E.; discussed further in Chapter 12). Plato is the older man (center left), who points with his right hand to the heavens; Aristotle is the younger man (left), gesturing with an open palm to the earth. ▪ *How does this double portrait reflect these philosophers' teachings and perspectives?*

engaged Socrates in discussion (such as Crito, whose imagined dialogue with Socrates is excerpted in Chapter 3, on page 104). One dialogue, the *Symposium*, actually re-creates the conversation at a drinking party, where a tipsy Socrates, the comedian Aristophanes, and other Athenian worthies debate the nature of love.

The longest and most famous of Plato's dialogues is now known by its Latin title, the *Republic*. In Greek, it is the *Politeía* ("Polis-governance" or even "Policy"), the first treatise on political philosophy written in the West. In it, Plato argues—through the character of Socrates—that social harmony and order are more important than individual liberty or equality. He imagines an ideal polis in which most people—farmers, artisans, traders—are governed by a superior group of "guardians" chosen in their youth for their natural attributes of intelligence and character.

These prospective guardians would serve the polis first as soldiers, living together without private property. Those found to be the wisest would then receive more education, and a few would ultimately become "philosopher-kings." These enlightened rulers would in turn choose the next generation of guardians.

This utopian system actually bears an intriguing resemblance to the social order of Sparta, as well as containing elements of a benign tyranny, and is clearly a response to the failures of Athenian democracy in Plato's youth. But whether Plato himself believed in this system—he never voices his own opinion—is open to interpretation. Indeed, the students of Socrates who are represented as discussing it with him voice many objections. The most obvious of these is "Who will guard the guardians?" For such a system presumes that properly educated rulers will never be

## Reconstructing an Ideal of Female Beauty

The lost statue known as the Aphrodite of Knidos was considered the most beautiful in the ancient world, but we can study it only by looking at later copies. It was the work of the fourth century's most renowned sculptor, Praxiteles, who was reputed to have modeled it after the Athenian courtesan known as Phryne, a renowned beauty who inspired several contemporary artists and a whole series of apocryphal stories. The most reliable of these tales concerns the riches she accrued. Apparently she became so wealthy that she

offered to finance the rebuilding of Thebes in 336 B.C.E.—on the condition that the slogan "destroyed by Alexander, restored by Phryne the Courtesan" be prominently displayed on the new walls. (Her offer was rejected.)

Praxiteles' original statue is thought to have been the first monumental female nude fashioned in antiquity. According to one authority, Praxiteles initially received a commission from the island of Kos, for which he fashioned both clothed and naked versions of Aphrodite. Apparently, the scandalized citizens approved only the draped version and refused to pay for the nude. It was

purchased instead by the city of Knidos on Cyprus, where it was displayed in an open-air temple so that it could be seen from all sides. It quickly became a tourist attraction and was widely copied and emulated. Two of the more faithful replicas, made by later artists working in Rome, are pictured here.

### Questions for Analysis

1. As we have seen, the male nude was a favorite subject of Greek artists from the Archaic Period onward. Recall your knowledge of contemporary Greek culture and society. Why was it not until the fourth century B.C.E. that a life-size female nude could be publicly displayed? Were there any precedents for statues like this?

2. Compare and contrast the ideal of female beauty suggested by the Knidian Aphrodite with the male ideals discussed in Chapter 3. What can you conclude about the relationship between these ideals and the different expectations of male and female behavior in Greek society? Why, for example, would ancient sources insist that the model for this statue was a courtesan?

3. Among the Romans, a statue like the Knidian Aphrodite was called a *Venus pudica*, a "modest Venus" (image A). Yet the citizens of Kos were allegedly shocked by its indecency, and old photographs of the copy in the Vatican Museum (image B) show that it was displayed until 1932 with additional draperies made of tin. How do you account for these very different standards of decency? To what degree do they suggest that concepts of "beauty" or "modesty" are historically constructed?

A. Roman copy of the Aphrodite of Knidos.

B. Second century C.E. copy of the Aphrodite of Knidos.

corrupted by power or wealth, a proposition that has yet to be sustained in practice.

The more practical applications of philosophy would be the preoccupation of Plato's own student Aristotle (384–322 B.C.E.). Aristotle, the son of a physician, learned from his father the importance of observing natural phenomena. Although receptive to Plato's training, Aristotle geared his own philosophical system toward understanding the workings of the world through the rational analysis of empirical knowledge—that is, information gained through sensory experience. In contrast to Plato, who taught that everything we see and touch is an untrustworthy reflection of some intangible ideal, Aristotle advocated the rigorous investigation of real phenomena, in order to uncover the natural order of the universe and of human beings' place within it. His method of instruction was also different. Unlike Socrates and Plato, whose dialogues were often playful, Aristotle delivered lectures on which his students took detailed notes, and eventually these notes became the basis of separate but interrelated treatises on politics, ethics, logic, metaphysics, and poetics. Aristotle also established rules for the syllogism, a form of reasoning in which certain premises inevitably lead to a valid conclusion, and developed precise categories that could be used to further philosophical and scientific analysis.

With respect to ethics, Aristotle taught that the highest good consists in the harmonious functioning of the individual human mind and body. Since humans differ from animals by virtue of their rational capacities, he argued, they find happiness by exercising these capacities appropriately. Good conduct is therefore rational conduct, and consists in acting moderately: showing courage rather than rashness or cowardice, temperance rather than excessive indulgence or self-denial. And whereas Plato conceived of politics as a means to an end that could never be achieved in this life, Aristotle thought of politics as an end in itself: the collective exercise of moderation.

But Aristotle also took it for granted that some people—such as barbarians—are not fully human and so are intended by nature to be slaves. He also believed that women were not endowed with a full measure of humanity and so could never achieve the good life, either as individuals or as participants in the public sphere of the polis. So when Aristotle asserted that "man is by nature a political animal" (or, to be more faithful to the Greek, "a creature of the polis"), he meant only Greek males of privileged status. He also did not believe that the best form of government is a democracy. Like Plato, Aristotle saw democracy as a debased form of government. What he preferred was the polity, in which monarchical, aristocratic, and democratic elements are combined by means of checks and balances. Only this form of government, he posited, would allow free men to realize their rational potential.

## Men of Thought and Action

For all their brilliance and originality, Plato and Aristotle offered few prescriptions for reforming their own societies. Both imagined the perfect polis as one made up of a few thousand households, largely engaged in agriculture and living together in a single community. Although Greek civilization had begun in such a world, the realities of fourth-century political life were very different. Plato and Aristotle recognized this to some extent, yet for both the answer was a reorganization of existing institutions, not something entirely new.

But other intellectuals at this time were considering more radical alternatives. One was Xenophon, that veteran of the Ten Thousand, who was another product of the Socratic tradition and an exact contemporary of Plato. After his return from Persia, he went on to fight for the Spartan king Agesilaus (ah-geh-si-LA-uhs), who became a trusted friend. Thoroughly disillusioned by the failures of Athenian democracy, Xenophon spent most of his adult life in exile. It is mostly thanks to his admiring account that we know anything about the Spartiate system described in Chapter 3, which he intended to be a rebuke to Athens. We also have his own view of Socrates' teaching, which he related in a series of memoirs and treatises on kingship and household management (the *Oikonomikos*, the root of our word *economics*). He loved horses and dogs and wrote a treatise on training them for the hunt, as well. All the while, he watched as the Theban leader Epaminondas crippled the state he so admired, Sparta. (Xenophon hated him so much that he refused to mention his name in the history he was compiling.)

The Athenian orator Isocrates (436–338 B.C.E.) was another direct contemporary of Plato and was also convinced that something had gone horribly awry as a result of the Peloponnesian War. Rather than imagining that a solution lay in the reform of the polis, he proposed instead that the Greeks rediscover their lost unity by staging a massive invasion of Persia. This assault, he prophesied, would be led by a man of vision and ability, someone who could unite the Greek world behind his cause. Isocrates spent most of his life casting about to find such a leader. Finally, he began to think that the man for the job was someone whom most Greeks considered no Greek at all: the king of Macedonia, Philip II.

## Aristotle's Justification of Slavery

*Like* The Republic *of his teacher Plato, Aristotle's treatise* Politics *attempts to define and rationalize various methods of governance. Early in this work, Aristotle grappled with the fact that all ancient societies were highly dependent on slave labor and answered objections that the forcible subjugation of some men to the will of others goes against the laws of nature and the ideals of his own society.*

But is there anyone thus intended by nature to be a slave, and for whom such a condition is expedient and right, or rather is not all slavery a violation of nature? There is no difficulty in answering this question, on grounds both of reason and of fact. For that some should rule and others be ruled is a thing not only necessary, but expedient; from the hour of their birth, some are marked out for subjection, others for rule. . . .

But that those who take the opposite view have in a certain way right on their side, may be easily seen. For the words *slavery* and *slave* are used in two senses. There is a slave or slavery by law as well as by nature. The law of which I speak is a sort of convention—the law by which whatever is taken in war is supposed to belong to the victors. But this right many jurists impeach, as they would an orator who brought forward an unconstitutional measure: they detest the notion that, because one man has the power of doing violence and is superior in brute strength, another shall be his slave and subject.

Even among philosophers there is a difference of opinion. The origin of the dispute, and what makes the views invade each other's territory, is as follows: in some sense virtue, when furnished with means, has actually the greatest power of exercising force; and as superior power is only found where there is superior excellence of some kind, power seems to imply virtue, and

the dispute to be simply one about justice (for it is due to one party identifying justice with goodwill while the other identifies it with the mere rule of the stronger). If these views are thus set out separately, the other views have no force or plausibility against the view that the superior in virtue ought to rule, or be master. Others, clinging, as they think, simply to a principle of justice (for law and custom are a sort of justice), assume that slavery in accordance with the custom of war is justified by law, but at the same moment they deny this. For what if the cause of the war be unjust?

And again, no one would ever say he is a slave who is unworthy to be a slave. Were this the case, men of the highest rank would be slaves and the children of slaves if they or their parents chance to have been taken captive and sold. Wherefore Hellenes [Greeks] do not like to call Hellenes slaves, but confine the term to barbarians. Yet, in using this language, they really mean the natural slave of whom we spoke at first; for it must be admitted that some are slaves everywhere, others nowhere.

The same principle applies to nobility. Hellenes regard themselves as noble everywhere, and not only in their own country, but they deem the barbarians noble only when at home, thereby implying that there are two sorts of nobility and freedom, the one absolute, the other relative. . . .

We see then that there is some foundation for this difference of opinion, and that all are not either slaves by nature or

freemen by nature, and also that there is in some cases a marked distinction between the two classes, rendering it expedient and right for the one to be slaves and the others to be masters: the one practicing obedience, the others exercising the authority and lordship which nature intended them to have. The abuse of this authority is injurious to both; for the interests of part and whole, of body and soul, are the same, and the slave is a part of the master, a living but separated part of his bodily frame. Hence, where the relation of master and slave between them is natural they are friends and have a common interest, but where it rests merely on law and force the reverse is true.

Source: Excerpted from Aristotle, *Politics*, Book I: v–vi, trans. Benjamin Jowett (Oxford: 1920), pp. 32–37.

### Questions for Analysis

1. According to Aristotle, how does one become a slave? Why is the question of slavery's justice related to that of the just war?

2. Aristotle posits that some people are slaves by nature, others by some unfortunate circumstances (such as being captured in battle). For example, he says that Hellenes (Greeks) do not admit that they can be slaves; that is possible only for barbarians. What are the implications of this argument?

# THE RISE OF MACEDONIA

Isocrates had a point. By the middle of the fourth century, the Greek poleis had become so embroiled in military, political, and socioeconomic turmoil that they barely noticed the powerhouse on their northern frontier. Until the fourth century, Macedonia (or Macedon) had been a weak kingdom, regarded as a throwback to the "dark ages" before the emergence of enlightened poleis, ruled by a royal dynasty barely strong enough to control its own nobility and beset by intrigue and murderous ambition. As recently as the 360s, Macedonia had teetered on the edge of collapse, nearly succumbing to the even smaller kingdoms and predatory tribes that surrounded it.

Despite the efforts of a few Macedonian kings to add a gloss of Hellenic culture to their courts—one had successfully invited Euripides and Sophocles to his palace—the Greeks considered them nearly as barbaric as their northern neighbors. It is still not known whether the ancient Macedonians were Greek-speakers during this period, although the royal family and nobility, at least, would have spoken Greek as a second language; and Macedonians seem to have participated in the Olympic Games, which were open only to Greeks. But they were definitely perceived as dangerous outsiders. Therefore, when a young and energetic king named Philip consolidated the southern Balkans under his rule, many Greeks saw it as a development no less troubling than the approach of the Persians in the fifth century.

**PHILIP II OF MACEDONIA.** This tiny ivory head was discovered in a royal tomb at Vergina and is almost certainly a bust of the king himself. Contemporary sources report that Philip the Great had his right eye blinded by a catapult bolt, a deformity visible here—and testimony to the unflinching realism of Greek portraiture in the fourth century B.C.E.

## The Reign of Philip II (359–336 B.C.E.)

Philip II of Macedonia was not supposed to be its ruler. Born in 382 B.C.E., he was the third and youngest son of King Amyntas III and considered so dispensable that he was sent to Thebes as a hostage when he was fourteen, at the time of the Theban Hegemony. This turned out to be the making of him: he became the protégé of the brilliant Epaminondas and may even have trained alongside the general Pelopidas (*pel-OH-pi-das*) in the Theban Sacred Band. By the time he returned to the Macedonian capital of Pella in 364 B.C.E., three years later, he had received a more thorough education in Greek culture and military tactics than any Macedonian before him.

He was also ambitious, and may already have laid great plans for the future. So when both of his older brothers died in battle, one after the other, Philip was not content with the role of regent for an infant nephew. By 356 B.C.E., he had supplanted his nephew and was reigning as king, the same year that his queen, Olympias, bore him an heir.

The boy was given the dynastic name Alexandros, meaning "leader of men."

The first problem of Philip's reign was the fragility of Macedonia's northern borders. Through a combination of warfare and diplomacy, he subdued the tribes of the southern Balkans and incorporated their territory into his kingdom—losing an eye in the process. His success in this had much to do with his reorganization of Macedonian warriors into a hoplite infantry along Theban lines. The mineral resources to which he now had access also helped, since he used that new wealth to pay and equip a standing professional army; just one of his gold mines produced as much in one year as the Delian League at its height had collected annually.

Philip also organized an elite cavalry squad—the Companions—who fought with and beside the king, an innovation that may have been designed to emulate the camaraderie of the Sacred Band and was intended to counter the Persian reliance on cavalry. These young men were

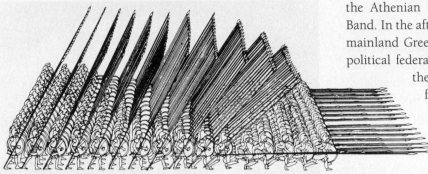

**MACEDONIAN PHALANX.** Philip of Macedonia's hoplite infantry—the model for Alexander's—was armed with two-handed pikes of graduated lengths, from thirteen to twenty-one feet, and was massed in squares sixteen rows deep and wide. Members of the phalanx were trained to wheel quickly in step formation and to double the width of their front rank as needed by filing off in rows of eight. The reach of their spears, called *sarissas*, extended the phalanx's fighting range.

the Athenian forces and destroying the Theban Sacred Band. In the aftermath, Philip called delegates from around mainland Greece to Corinth, where he established a new political federation. The main purpose of this federation, the League of Corinth, was to provide forces for the invasion of Persia and to maintain peace among the rival poleis.

Philip never realized his dream of Persian conquest. Two years later, in 336 B.C.E., he was assassinated during a festival at Pella, purportedly by a vengeful former lover. The kingship now fell to Alexander. Among the Greeks, he would be known as Alexander, the Sacker of Cities. To the Romans, impressed by his ruthless military genius, he was Alexander the Great.

drawn exclusively from the nobility, and Philip thereby hoped to inspire their deeper loyalty; in fact, under the guise of recruiting future Companions, he gained valuable young hostages to ensure the good conduct of aristocratic rivals. Their sons were now being brought up alongside Alexander and sharing his lessons with Aristotle, who had arrived at the Macedonian court in 343 B.C.E. Through a series of strategic marriages, Philip also managed to gain the goodwill and alliance of many neighboring kingdoms—although his open polygamy was, in Greek eyes, another irregularity that called to mind the barbarians of Persia.

Eventually, the increasing strength of Macedonia began to impinge on the consciousness of some Greeks, most notably the Athenians. But whereas Isocrates saw in Philip a potential savior of Greece, many Athenians believed that Philip's ultimate aim was to conquer and subjugate them. They may have misunderstood Philip's goals: his northward expansion was designed to secure his frontiers and the resources necessary to support an invasion of Persia, not of Greece. From 348 B.C.E. on, Philip was actually trying to forge an alliance with Athens, whose fleet could facilitate such an invasion by sea; in return, he promised to support Athens' old claim to hegemony over Greece. But the Athenians took the advice of an orator called Demosthenes and refused to cooperate.

This miscalculation would prove disastrous. Philip's inability to reach a peaceful understanding with Athens, despite strenuous diplomatic efforts, ultimately led to war, which sent the Athenians scrambling to ally with their former enemy, Thebes, and a number of smaller poleis. Their fate was sealed at the battle of Chaeronea (*kie-ROH-nee-ah*) in 338 B.C.E., when an army led jointly by Philip and Alexander (aged seventeen) won a narrow victory, decimating

## THE CONQUESTS OF ALEXANDER (336–323 B.C.E.)

By the time of Alexander's early death at the age of thirty-two, a monumental legend had already built up around him. This makes it all the more ironic and frustrating that no contemporary account of his life and achievements survives. So when we try to reconstruct the history of Alexander, we are relying on the writings of men who lived and worked under the Roman Empire, notably Plutarch (46–120 C.E.) and Arrian (c. 86–160 C.E.), both of whom were separated from their subject by a distance of 400 years. Luckily, there is good reason to believe that they were basing their histories on sources derived from two (lost) firsthand accounts, one written by Alexander's general (and alleged half brother) Ptolemy (*TOHL-eh-mee*; c. 367–c. 284 B.C.E.), who founded a new dynasty of Egyptian pharaohs, and another by Æschines Socraticus (c. 387–322 B.C.E.), an Athenian statesman. Nevertheless, it is a salutary reminder of how fragile the historical record of antiquity is, that sources for the life of the era's most famous man are so hard to come by.

### The Conquest of Persia

When Alexander succeeded his father Philip in 336 B.C.E., he could not begin to carry out his plans of conquest until he had put down the revolts that erupted immediately after Philip's death—notably at Thebes, an uprising that he punished by destroying its famous walls. Two years later, he

**ALEXANDER DEFEATS KING DARIUS OF PERSIA AT THE BATTLE OF ISSUS (333 B.C.E.).** This Roman mural, discovered at Pompeii (see Chapter 5), shows Darius fleeing from the battlefield in his chariot on the right, pursued by Alexander, the mounted figure on the far left.

was crossing the Hellespont at the head of a hoplite army to challenge the Great King of Persia, Darius III.

From the beginning, Darius was no match for Alexander. He was a minor member of the royal family who had taken the dynastic name when he was placed on the throne after a palace coup, at the relatively old age of forty-five—the same year that Alexander became king at age twenty. Darius and his advisers failed to take the Macedonian threat seriously, despite the Persians' past history of defeat at the hands of Greek armies—even on Persian soil and within living memory. Perhaps they assumed that the enormous forces they could rally in defense of their empire would easily overwhelm a comparatively small army of 42,000; or perhaps they misunderstood Alexander's aims, which would reveal themselves over time to be far-reaching indeed. In any event, the Persian army of Darius III was made up of mercenaries or poorly paid conscripts under the command of inexperienced generals.

As a result, Alexander achieved a series of extraordinary victories, beginning in northwest Anatolia, near the epic field of Troy, and continuing down the Ionian coastline. In 333 B.C.E., Darius was persuaded to engage Alexander personally, at the head of a force that significantly outnumbered that of his opponent. But the chosen site, on the banks of a river near Issus, favored Alexander's fast-moving infantry, not the heavy cavalry and chariots of the Persians, which had no room to maneuver and were hampered by mud. No warrior himself, Darius shamefully fled the battlefield, abandoning not only his army but his entire household, which included his wife and his mother. They were captured by Alexander's troops and treated by him with great respect.

Darius spent the remainder of his life running from Alexander's advancing army, until his decisive defeat at

Gaugamela (near Mosul in modern Iraq) in 331 B.C.E., when he was killed by a local chieftain who hoped to win Alexander's favor. Instead, Alexander—acting as the new Great King—had the chieftain executed for treason against his former enemy and predecessor. The next spring, Alexander destroyed the royal capital of Persepolis, lest it serves as a rallying point for Persian resistance.

Meanwhile, in the two years that had passed since Darius's humiliation at Issus, Alexander had completed his conquest of the Persian Empire. One by one, the cities of Syria and Palestine surrendered after Alexander made a powerful statement by destroying the wealthy Phoenician capital at Tyre. Following the example of Cyrus the Great, whose tactics he increasingly came to emulate, Alexander developed a policy of offering amnesty to cities that submitted peacefully—but dealing mercilessly with those that resisted. The fortified city of Gaza, the last Persian stronghold on the Egyptian border, provides an example: its commander, Batis, not only refused to surrender but seemed determined to fight to the death, inflicting severe losses on the troops besieging his city and seriously wounding Alexander himself. When the fortress was finally taken, Alexander's troops slew all the adult males and enslaved the women and children. According to a later Roman historian, Alexander also dragged the body of Batis around the city's walls behind his chariot, imitating Achilles' treatment of his fallen rival Hector.

## Alexander in Egypt

After this, Alexander marched into Egypt unopposed. In fact, he was welcomed: Egypt had been governed as a Persian satrapy (principality) since 525 B.C.E., when Cambyses, son of Cyrus the Great, had deposed the last pharaoh of

Philip but by Zeus. Alexander, ever mindful of precedent and the historical significance of his own actions, seems to have decided at this point that Egypt should be the capital of his new empire. Persia had been the goal, and parts of it still remained to be conquered, piece by piece; but it was in Egypt that he would build his shining new city of Alexandria. In the end, he had time only to lay out a plan for the streets and central spaces before he marched north to the reckoning with Darius at Gaugamela. When he finally returned, he was in his sarcophagus.

## Alexander's Final Campaigns

Over the ensuing five years, Alexander campaigned in the far reaches of the Persian Empire, in the mountainous regions that had been only loosely yoked together with the more settled lands of Mesopotamia. This is the region encompassed today by Afghanistan, a terrain famous for defeating every attempt at conquest or control. There, in the mountains of Bactria, Alexander and his army experienced

the reigning dynasty (see Chapter 2). Now Alexander himself was hailed as pharaoh and given the double crown of Upper and Lower Egypt, becoming the latest in a succession of rulers reaching back 3,000 years to the time of King Narmer (see Chapter 1).

Something about this feat seems to have amazed even Alexander himself. The "barbarian" chieftain of a backwater kingdom in the Balkan foothills had become pharaoh of the oldest civilization on earth and heir to its immense riches and extraordinary history—a history that the Greeks knew, thanks to the writings of Herodotus. Whereas the Persians and (before them) the Medes had long been the Greeks' traditional enemies, the Egyptians had always been too far away to pose a threat; indeed, they were an object of awe and source of inspiration.

This may help explain Alexander's response to the oracle of Ammon, the name the Greeks gave to the Egyptian sun god Amun-Ra, whom they identified with Zeus. At the oracle's desert oasis of Siwa, Alexander was reportedly told that he was the "son of Ammon" and a god himself, a pronouncement that gave weight to a story already in circulation among his men: that he had been fathered not by

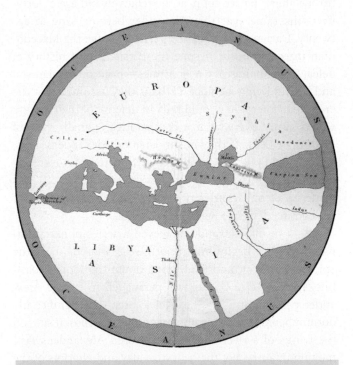

the hardest fighting of their long campaign. Indeed, they never succeeded in getting more than a tenuous hold on the territory, despite Alexander's marriage to Roxane, the daughter of a local Bactrian chieftain. Thereafter, Alexander moved down through what is now Pakistan to the Indus Valley, meeting stiff resistance from its warlords but eventually defeating their leader, Porus, at the Battle of Hydaspes (*heed-AH-spes*) in 326 B.C.E.

This was to be the last major battle of his career, and the one in which his famous warhorse, Bucephalus, was killed. (He was buried nearby, and a city was founded in his name.) It was here in India that Alexander's exhausted army refused to go on, thousands of miles and eight years from home, and he was forced to turn back. Rather than attempting to recross the mountains of the Hindu Kush or the foothills of the Himalayas, he pressed southward to the shores of the Arabian Sea—what was then known as Ocean, and the end of the world. The ensuing march through the Gedrosian Desert, combined with a decade of continuous fighting, weakened him and his army considerably.

But Alexander still had great plans for the future, and when he reached the royal palace of Susa, he took steps that indicate how he would have tried to combine his Greco-Macedonian Empire with that of Persia, had he lived. He announced that he would begin training Persian youths to fight alongside Greeks and Macedonians, so as to begin an integration of the two armies. He arranged a mass marriage between hundreds of his officers and a corresponding number of Persian noblewomen, and he made an example of men who had been caught desecrating the nearby tomb of Cyrus the Great. Most controversially, he showed respect for his Persian subjects by adopting Persian dress—considered by Greeks to be symbolic of their enemies' barbarism—and by encouraging those around him to perform the ritual of *proskynesis* (*pros-kin-EE-sis*).

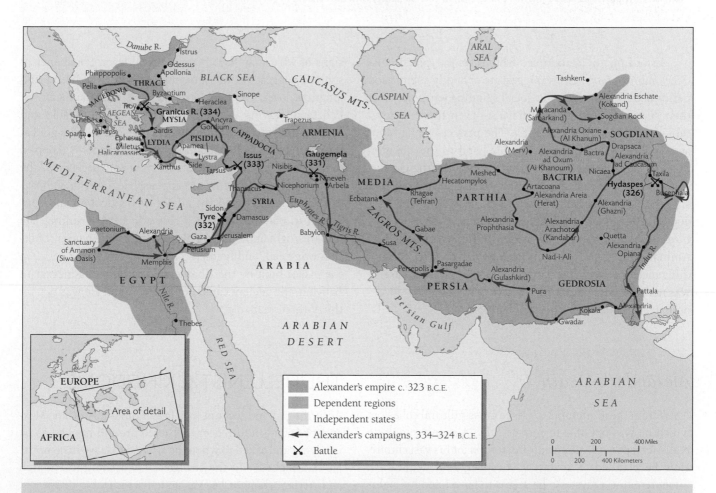

**THE CAMPAIGNS OF ALEXANDER.** The conquests of Alexander the Great brought Greek culture to the vast expanse of the former Persian Empire, as far east as the Indus River. ▪ *Trace Alexander's route with your finger. Where did he start and end?* ▪ *What was the farthest point east that he traveled on his conquests?* ▪ *Why might Alexander have chosen to found so many cities named after himself, and what can you conclude about the purposes of these cities, on the basis of their locations?*

**LESSER KINGS OF PERSIA APPROACH THE GREAT KING TO PERFORM** *PROSKYNESIS.* ▪ *Why would Alexander's Greek and Macedonian soldiers have balked at the suggestion that they show their solidarity with the Persians by performing this ritual?*

According to Herodotus, who gave the practice its Greek name, *proskynesis* was a gesture of bodily submission performed by those of lesser social standing when they met their superiors, and by all Persians—even those of royal rank—to honor the Great King. The person paying homage would bow deeply and kiss his hand to the emperor, in some cases prostrating himself entirely. To the Greeks, this practice was not only humiliating but blasphemous: it suggested that the Persians worshiped their emperor as a god. To Alexander and his close advisers, *proskynesis* may have seemed an appropriate tribute to his status as "son of Ammon," but it was more likely intended to level cultural differences between Persians and Greeks. In any case, it was not a success, and it fueled a mutiny among the Macedonians that Alexander himself had to quell.

## Alexander's Death

Apart from these attempts to create cross-cultural cohesion, which he was not able to pursue fully, Alexander took no realistic steps to create an administration for his vast empire. How he planned to govern it effectively and bequeath it intact remains a mystery; he seems to have fixed his sights more clearly on further conquests, perhaps in Arabia, perhaps toward "Greater Greece" (Italy and Sicily)—we will never know. In late May of 323 B.C.E., he began to show signs of what may have been malarial fever. Some ancient sources suggest he was poisoned; his closest friend and longtime lover, Hephaistion, had died the year before at Ecbatana, leaving Alexander without his most able and vigilant bodyguard. (Emulating Achilles' passionate grief at the death of Patroclus, the mourning Alexander is reported to have built an enormous funeral pyre and "sacrificed" the residents of a nearby town to appease Hephaistion's ghost.) But Alexander ignored the advice of his doctors and continued to play the part of a Homeric hero, drinking late into the night and exerting himself incautiously. His condition worsened, and he died on June 10 or 11, 323 B.C.E., in the palace built by the Chaldean king Nebuchadnezzar in Babylon, the ancient capital of Hammurabi. He was not yet thirty-three years old.

## THE HELLENISTIC KINGDOMS

According to one account by a later Roman historian, Alexander's friends and officers gathered around his bed as he lay dying and asked to whom he wished to leave his empire. He had replied, "To the strongest." According to Plutarch and Arrian, though, he was actually incapable of speech. According to still other late sources, he silently gave his signet ring to a Macedonian general called Perdiccas, the leader of his cavalry.

# Analyzing Primary Sources

## Alexander Puts Down a Mutiny

*The following account comes from the history of Alexander's campaigns by the Greek-speaking Roman historian Arrian (c. 86–160 C.E.), who lived in the Roman province of Bythinia in northern Anatolia. This is the closest thing we have to a primary source, since histories written by Alexander's own contemporaries have not survived. The following passage describes Alexander's response to a mutiny among his troops after his return from India in 324 B.C.E.*

My countrymen, you are sick for home—so bc it! I shall make no attempt to check your longing to return. Go wherever you will; I shall not hinder you. But if go you must, there is one thing I would have you understand—what I have done for you, and in what coin you have repaid me. . . .

"[M]arching out from a country too poor to maintain you decently, [I] laid open for you at a blow, and in spite of Persia's naval supremacy, the gates of the Hellespont. My cavalry crushed the satraps of Darius, and I added all Ionia and Aeolia, the two Phrygias and Lydia to your empire. . . . I took them and gave them to you for your profit and enjoyment. The wealth of Egypt and Cyrene, which I shed no blood to win, now flows in your hands; Palestine and the plains of Syria and Mesopotamia are now your property; Babylon and Bactria and Susa are yours; you are the masters of the gold of Lydia, the treasures of Persia, the wealth of India—yes, and the seas beyond India, too. You are my captains, my generals, my governors of provinces.

"From all this that I have labored to win for you, what is left for me myself except the purple and the crown? I keep nothing for my own. . . . Perhaps you will say that, in my position as your commander, I had none of the labors and distress which you had to endure to win me what I have won. . . . Come now—if you are wounded, strip and show your wounds, and I will show mine. There is no part of my body but my back which does not have a scar; not a weapon a man may grasp or fling, the mark of which I do not carry on me . . . and all for your sakes: for your glory and your gain. Over every land and sea, across river, mountain, and plain, I led you to the world's end, a victorious army. I marry as you marry, and many of you will have children related by blood to my own. . . . But you all wish to leave me. Go then! And when you reach home, tell them that Alexander your king, who vanquished the Persians and Medes and Bactrians . . . tell them, I say, that you deserted him and left him to the mercy of barbarian men, whom you yourselves conquered. . . ."

On the Macedonians, the immediate effect of Alexander's speech was profound. . . . But when they were told [three days later that] . . . command was being given to Persian officers, foreign troops drafted into Macedonian units, a Persian corps of Guards called by a Macedonian name, Persian infantry units given the coveted title of Companions . . . every man of them hurried to the palace . . . and [they] swore they would not stir from the spot until Alexander took pity on them.

Source: Arrian, *The Campaigns of Alexander*, trans. Aubrey de Selincourt (New York: 1958), pp. 360–65 (slightly modified).

### Questions for Analysis

1. What qualities of leadership does Alexander display in this speech? How do these qualities compare with those of Cyrus the Younger, in Xenophon's description of him (page 114)?

2. Given the circumstances that precipitated this mutiny, why does Alexander use the term *barbarians* to describe the Persians and other conquered peoples? What does he hope to convey by using this word and then by reorganizing his forces to replace Macedonians with Persians?

3. Histories written well into the nineteenth century of our era feature speeches that were allegedly spoken by historical characters on momentous occasions. How closely do you think Arrian's reconstruction of this speech reflects historical reality? How might you go about arguing that it is, in fact, an accurate reflection of what Alexander actually said?

Throughout its history, the Persian dynasty founded by Seleucus (known as the Seleucids) struggled with the problem of keeping the disparate parts of the realm together. The dynasty's hold on the easternmost provinces was especially tenuous, but Seleucus solved part of this problem by ceding much of the Indus Valley to the great Indian warrior-king Chandragupta, in exchange for peace and a squad of war elephants. By the middle of the third century B.C.E., the Seleucids had also lost control of Bactria, where a series of Indo-Greek states were emerging with a uniquely complex culture of their own. (One Greco-Bactrian king, Menander, is memorialized in Buddhist tradition.) The Seleucid heartland became northern Syria, parts of Anatolia, Mesopotamia, and the western half of Persia—still a great, wealthy kingdom but far less than what Alexander had left.

Like the Ptolemies, the Seleucids presented two faces to their subjects, one looking to ancient Mesopotamian traditions and the other looking to Greece. In his proclamations, Antiochus used terms reminiscent of Sargon, Hammurabi, and Cyrus: "I am Antiochus, Great King, legitimate king . . . king of Babylon, king of all countries." But on his coins, he wore his hair short in the fashion of the Greeks and styled himself *basileus* (the Greek word for "king"). Although the Seleucids' bureaucracy was less organized than that of the Ptolemies, even haphazard tax collection could reap huge rewards in an empire of 30 million inhabitants. However, the Seleucids seldom converted their gains into public-works projects or capital investments. Instead, they hoarded their wealth in great state treasuries. All the same, they had more than enough cash to defend their borders through the third century, a period of regular warfare with Egypt. It was not until the second century, when Antiochus III lost a costly war with the Romans, that he had to plunder temples and private wealth to pay off the indemnity imposed on him.

## Antigonid Macedonia and Greece

The Macedonian homeland did not possess the vast wealth of the new kingdoms carved from Alexander's conquests in Egypt and Asia. It also remained highly unstable from the time of Alexander's death until 276 B.C.E., when a general named Antigonus (*an-TIG-on-uhs*) was finally able to establish his rule over the area and his own dynasty (known as the Antigonids). Thereafter, Macedonia drew its strength from considerable natural resources and its influence over Aegean trade, as well as its king's status as overlord of Greece. The Macedonians also continued to field the most effective army of any of the successor states, and these warriors owned coveted bragging rights as the heirs of Alexander's unconquered army.

Antigonus was influenced by a philosophical outlook called Stoicism (discussed later in this chapter) and viewed kingship as a form of noble servitude: an office to be endured rather than enjoyed. This perspective, combined with his modest resources, convinced him not to compete with the Seleucids and Ptolemies for dominance. Instead, Antigonid policy was to keep these other two powers at war with one another and away from the Macedonian sphere of influence. Antigonus and his successors thus pursued a strategy more reminiscent of Philip II than of his son. They secured the northern frontiers; maintained a strong, standing army; and kept the divided Greeks at arm's length.

The Greeks, however, were restive under the Antigonids, and two emergent powers within the Greek world became rallying points for those who resented "barbarian" rule. These two forces, the Aetolian League and the Achaean League, embodied a new form of Greek political organization. Unlike the defensive alliances of the classical period, each of these two leagues constituted a true political entity, with some centralization of governance. Citizens of the member poleis participated in councils of state that dealt with foreign policy and military affairs, trials for treason, and the annual election of a league general (also the chief executive officer) and his deputy. New members were admitted on an equal footing with existing members, and all citizens of the various poleis enjoyed joint citizenship throughout the league. The same laws, weights and measures, coinage, and judicial procedures also applied throughout each federation. So impressive was this degree of cooperation that James Madison, John Jay, and Alexander Hamilton employed the Achaean League as one of their models in advocating federalism in the United States.

# FROM POLIS TO COSMOPOLIS

So what became of the polis, that building block of classical Greek civilization? As we have seen, the changes of the fourth century B.C.E. were already disrupting the traditional patterns of social and political life well before Alexander's conquests. But these conquests hastened the process of transformation and opened up a wider world—a world that, within a few generations, came to admire all things Greek. During the third century B.C.E., a common

# Past and Present

## Mass Migration and the Challenges of Assimilation

The Greek diaspora ("dispersion") that bound the Hellenistic kingdoms together eventually led to the emergence of distinctive new hybrid cultures. The mosaic on the left comes from an ancient synagogue and shows Jewish ritual objects (including a menorah and a shofar) accompanied by a Greek inscription. The image on the right shows a rally in support of refugees from the ongoing war in Syria, in 2015. In Belgium and other European countries, the challenges of integrating newcomers has since led to violence and xenophobia.

**Watch related author interview on the Student Site**

Hellenistic culture encompassed the eastern Mediterranean and western Asia, transcending political and geographical boundaries. It was fueled by the hundreds of thousands of adventurers who joined the Greek *diaspora* ("dispersion") and whose emigration reduced the population of the Greek mainland by as much as 50 percent in the century between 325 and 225 B.C.E.

This exciting, urbane world was made up of interconnected cities whose scale dwarfed anything imaginable in Periclean Athens. During the fifth century B.C.E., direct participation in government had meant that every male citizen of a Greek polis had some share and stake in his society—its institutions, its gods, its army, and its cultural life. If we transpose this outlook onto a typical cosmopolitan Hellenistic city, which would have been at least three times larger, we can appreciate the magnitude of the change. Two centuries later, all these ways of defining one-

self were no longer relevant. The individual male's intimate connection with the political life of the state was broken, as was his nexus of social and familial relationships. An average Greek in one of the Hellenistic cities might have only his immediate family to rely on, if that; very often, he was alone. What resulted was a traumatic disjunction between the traditional values and assumptions of Greek life and the social and political realities of the day—and a host of entirely new opportunities.

## Commerce and Urbanization

The Hellenistic world was prosperous, owing to the freedom of long-distance trade, the development of financial networks, and the enormous growth of cities. Alexander's death or any other supernatural phenomena. The Epicureans thus came by a very different route to the same general conclusion as the Stoics: nothing is better than tranquility of mind.

The moral teachings and political goals of the Epicureans reflected this worldview. In contrast to the Stoics, they did not insist on virtue as an end in itself or on the fulfillment of one's duties. For an Epicurean, the only duty a person has is to the self, and the only reason to act virtuously is to increase one's own happiness. Similarly, Epicureans also denied that there is any such thing as justice: laws and political institutions are "just" only insofar as they contribute to the welfare of the individual. Yes, every society has found certain rules to be necessary in every society for the maintenance of order, but these rules should be obeyed solely because it is to one's advantage. The state is, at best, a mere convenience, and the wise man should take no active part in politics. Instead, he should withdraw to study philosophy and enjoy the fellowship of a few congenial friends. Modern libertarian movements share many characteristics with Epicureanism.

## Extreme Doubt: Skepticism

The most pessimistic philosophy generated by the Hellenistic era was propounded by the Skeptics, whose name derives from a Greek word meaning "those on the lookout" or "the spies." Skepticism reached the zenith of its popularity in the second century under the influence of Carneades (*kar-NEE-ah-dees*; c. 214–129 B.C.E.), a man born in the Greek city of Cyrene, in North Africa, and who spent his youth in Athens. The chief source of his inspiration was the teaching (filtered through Aristotle) that all knowledge is based on sense perception and is therefore limited and relative. From this, the Skeptics concluded that no one can truly know or prove anything. Because the impressions of our senses can deceive us, we cannot even be certain about the truth of whatever empirical knowledge we think we have gained by observation of the world. All we can say is that things *appear* to be such and such; we do not know that they really *are* that way. It follows, furthermore, that we can have no definite knowledge of the supernatural, the meaning of life, or the right and wrong.

The only sensible course for the Skeptic is therefore to suspend judgment: this alone can lead to happiness. If a person abandons the fruitless quest for truth and ceases to worry about good conduct and the existence of evil, he can at least attain a certain peace of mind—the highest satisfaction that an uncertain life affords. Needless to say, the Skeptics were even less concerned than the Epicureans with political and social problems, from which they felt wholly alienated. Their ideal was one of escape from an incomprehensible world. In some key respects, they anticipated modern existentialism and nihilism.

## The Varieties of Religion

Like Epicureanism and Skepticism, Hellenistic religion tended to offer vehicles of escape from political commitments. When we think back to the link between Greek selfhood and politics, down to the middle of the fourth century B.C.E.—"man is a creature of the polis"—we can begin to appreciate what a radical change had occurred in just a few generations. In the classical age of the polis, as in all the societies we have studied so far, religion was wholly interconnected with politics. Divine worship centered on the gods who protected a community and furthered its interests. Hence, the most serious of the charges brought against Socrates was that he had "denied the gods of the polis" and thus committed treason. Religious crimes were political crimes, and piety was the same as patriotism.

Although this sense of a vital connection between a place and its gods persisted to a certain extent during the Hellenistic period, civic-oriented worship was compromised by the rootless multiculturalism of the third and second centuries B.C.E. In its place, some elite members of society gravitated toward one of the philosophies discussed above. Ordinary people, though, were more likely to embrace religious cults that offered emotional gratification or the diversion of colorful rituals, as well as some assurance of an afterlife, which the new philosophies did not.

In Greek-speaking communities especially, cults that stressed extreme methods of atonement for sin, ecstatic mystical union with the divine, or contact with supernatural forces attracted many followers. Among these mystery religions—so called because their membership was select and their rites secret—one of the most popular was the cult of Dionysus, which celebrated the cyclical death and resurrection of that Greek god. The Egyptian cult of Isis, drawing on the story of Osiris (see Chapter 1), also revolved around rituals of death and rebirth. So, too, did Zoroastrianism (see Chapter 2), which became increasingly dualistic: its magi taught that the material world was entirely evil and urged believers to adopt ascetic practices that would purify their souls and prepare them for ethereal joy in the afterlife.

# Analyzing Primary Sources

## A Jewish Response to Hellenization

*Greek culture became a powerful force throughout the Hellenistic world, even among Jews. In the second century B.C.E., the Hellenized ways of the Jewish elites in Jerusalem led to a revolt by a native Hebrew dynasty known as the Maccabees, who decried the effects of Hellenization on Jewish life. These events are recorded in two apocryphal books of the Hebrew Bible. In the passage that follows, note that even the High Priest of the Temple bears a Greek name, Jason.*

n those days, lawless men came forth from Israel and misled many, saying, "Let us go and make a covenant with the Gentiles [Greeks] round about us, for since we separated from them many disasters have come upon us." . . .

[This happened when] Antiochus [IV, 175–164 B.C.E.] who was called Epiphanes had succeeded to the kingdom, [and] Jason the brother of Onias obtained the high priesthood by corruption. . . . [H]e at once shifted his countrymen over to the Greek way of life . . . and he destroyed the lawful ways of living and introduced new customs contrary to the law. For with alacrity he founded a gymnasium right under the citadel, and he induced the noblest of the young men to wear the Greek hat [and not the traditional head covering]. There was such an extreme of Hellenization and increase in the adoption of foreign ways . . . that the priests were no longer intent upon the services of the altar. Despising the sanctuary and neglecting the sacrifices, they hurried to take part in the unlawful proceedings in the wrestling arena after the signal for the discus-throwing, disdaining the honors prized by their ancestors and putting the highest value upon Greek forms of prestige. . . . When the quadrennial games were being held at Tyre and the king was present, the vile Jason sent envoys . . . to carry three hundred silver drachmas for the sacrifice to Heracles. . . .

Not long after this, the king sent an Athenian senator to compel the Jews to forsake the laws of their fathers and cease to live by the laws of God, and also to pollute the temple in Jerusalem and call it the temple of Olympian Zeus. . . . Harsh and utterly grievous was the onslaught of evil. For the temple was filled with debauchery and reveling by the Gentiles, who dallied with prostitutes and had intercourse with women within the sacred precincts, and besides brought in things for sacrifice that were unfit. The altar was covered with abominable offerings that were forbidden by the laws. A man could neither keep the Sabbath nor observe the feasts of his fathers, nor so much as confess himself to be a Jew.

Source: Excerpted from 1 Maccabees 1:11; 2 Maccabees 4:10–18 and 6:1–6, in *The New Oxford Annotated Bible* (Oxford: 1994).

### Questions for Analysis

1. Given the history of their ancestors (see Chapter 2), why would Hellenistic culture be particularly threatening to the Jews?

2. What, specifically, are the offensive actions and activities described here? Why, for example, would the building of a gymnasium (a Greek academy and athletic facility) in Jerusalem be problematic?

---

Like the peoples who worshiped them, the gods of the Hellenistic world were often immigrants from other lands. Temples to Greek gods and goddesses were dedicated throughout western Asia and Egypt; conversely, temples to Egyptian and Mesopotamian divinities were constructed in cities of the Greek homeland. In Alexandria, scholars of religion collected anecdotes about exotic mythologies, which were recorded and reformulated for Greek-speaking audiences. People throughout the Hellenistic world had a dazzling variety of religious choices.

Even among the Jews of Palestine, who resisted assimilation and the adoption of foreign customs, Hellenistic culture put down deep roots. This was especially true among Jewish elites and Jews living outside Palestine, who outnumbered the Palestinian population by a considerable margin by the end of the second century B.C.E.

# Competing Viewpoints

## Debating the Education and Role of Women

The drastic political, social, and economic changes of the fourth century led philosophers to reimagine the traditional structures of the polis and to debate the proper role of women within these structures. Meanwhile, the cosmopolitan culture of the expanding Hellenistic world made it increasingly difficult to limit women's access to public spaces. The following excerpts represent two philosophical responses to these problems. The first comes from Plato's treatise on "Polis-matters" (Politeía), known to us as The Republic, the longest of his philosophical dialogues and the most influential work of political thought in history. Its conceptual narrator and protagonist is Socrates, who engages in a series of debates with his pupils. The second excerpt is taken from a philosophical treatise attributed to a female follower of Pythagoras (see Chapter 3), but it was really written by a man around 200 B.C.E. in Hellenistic Italy.

### Plato, The Republic, c. 380 B.C.E.

**SOCRATES:** For men born and educated like our citizens, the only way, in my opinion, of arriving at a right conclusion about the possession and use of women and children is to follow the path on which we originally started, when we said that the men were to be the guardians and watchdogs of the herd.

**GLAUCON:** True.

**SOCRATES:** Let us further suppose the birth and education of our women to be subject to similar or nearly similar regulations; then we shall see whether the result accords with our design.

**GLAUCON:** What do you mean?

**SOCRATES:** . . . The education which was assigned to the men was music and gymnastic[s].

**GLAUCON:** Yes.

**SOCRATES:** Then women must be taught music and gymnastic[s] and also the art of war, which they must practice like the men?

**GLAUCON:** That is the inference, I suppose.

**SOCRATES:** I should rather expect . . . that several of our proposals, if they are carried out, being unusual, may appear ridiculous.

**GLAUCON:** No doubt of it.

**SOCRATES:** Yes, and the most ridiculous thing of all will be the sight of women

naked in the palaestra, exercising with the men, especially when they are no longer young; they certainly will not be a vision of beauty, any more than the enthusiastic old men who in spite of wrinkles and ugliness continue to frequent the gymnasia. . . . . [Yet] not long ago, as we shall remind them, the Hellenes were of the opinion, which is still generally received among the barbarians, that the sight of a naked man was ridiculous and improper; and when first the Cretans and then the Lacedaemonians [Spartans] introduced the custom, the wits of that day might equally have ridiculed the innovation.

**GLAUCON:** No doubt. . . .

**SOCRATES:** First, then, whether the question is to be put in jest or in earnest, let us come to an understanding about the nature of woman: Is she capable of sharing either wholly or partially in the actions of men, or not at all? And is the art of war one of those arts in which she can or cannot share? That will be the best way of commencing the enquiry, and will probably lead to the fairest conclusion. . . .

**GLAUCON:** I suppose so. . . .

**SOCRATES:** And if . . . the male and female sex appear to differ in their fitness for any art or pursuit, we should say that

such pursuit or art ought to be assigned to one or the other of them; but if the difference consists only in women bearing and men begetting children, this does not amount to a proof that a woman differs from a man in respect of the sort of education she should receive; and we shall therefore continue to maintain that our guardians and their wives ought to have the same pursuits.

**GLAUCON:** Very true.

**SOCRATES:** Next, we shall ask . . . how, in reference to any of the pursuits or arts of civic life, the nature of a woman differs from that of a man? . . .

**GLAUCON:** By all means.

**SOCRATES:** . . . [W]hen you spoke of a nature gifted or not gifted in any respect, did you mean to say that one man will acquire a thing easily, another with difficulty; a little learning will lead the one to discover a great deal; whereas the other, after much study and application, no sooner learns than he forgets? Or again, did you mean, that the one has a body which is a good servant to his mind, while the body of the other is a hindrance to him? Would not these be the sort of differences which distinguish the man gifted by nature from the one who is ungifted?

**GLAUCON:** No one will deny that.

**SOCRATES:** And can you mention any pursuit of mankind in which the male sex has not all these gifts and qualities in a higher degree than the female? Need I waste time in speaking of the art of weaving, and the management of pan- cakes and preserves, in which woman- kind does really appear to be great, and in which for her to be beaten by a man is of all things the most absurd?

**GLAUCON:** You are quite right . . . in maintaining the general inferiority of the female sex: although many women are in many things superior to many men, yet on the whole what you say is true.

Source: Excerpted from Plato, *The Republic*, Book V, trans. Benjamin Jowett (New York: 1982), pp. 170–76.

## Treatise attributed to Phintys, Third/Second Century B.C.E.

Now some people think that it is not appropriate for a woman to be a philosopher, just as a woman should not be a cavalry officer or a politician. . . . I agree that men should be generals and city officials and politicians, and women should keep house and stay inside and receive and take care of their husbands. But I believe that courage, justice, and intelligence are qualities that men and women have in common. . . . Courage and intelligence are more appropriately male qualities because of the strength of men's bodies and the power of their minds. Chastity is more appropriately female.

Accordingly, a woman must learn about chastity and realize what she must do quantitatively and qualitatively to be able to obtain this womanly virtue. I believe that there are five qualifications: (1) the sanctity of her marriage bed, (2) the cleanliness of her body, (3) the manner in which she chooses to leave her house, (4) her refusal to participate in secret cults . . . , (5) her readiness and modera- tion in sacrificing to the gods.

Of these, the most important qual- ity for chastity is to be pure in respect of the marriage bed, and for her not to have affairs with men from other house- holds. If she breaks the law in this way she wrongs the gods of her family and provides her family and home not with its own offspring but with bastards. . . .

She should also consider the following: that there is no means of atoning for this sin; no way she can approach the shrines or the altars of the gods as a pure woman. . . . The greatest glory a freeborn woman can have—her foremost honor— is the witness her own children will give to her chastity toward her husband, the stamp of the likeness they bear to the father whose seed produced them. . . .

As far as adornment of her body is concerned . . . [h]er clothes should not be transparent or ornate. She should not put on silken material, but moderate, white-colored clothes. In this way, she will avoid being over-dressed or luxu- rious or made-up, and not give other women cause to be uncomfortably envi- ous. . . . She should not apply imported or artificial coloring to her face—with her own natural coloring, by washing only with water, she can ornament herself with modesty. . . .

Women of importance leave the house to sacrifice to the leading divin- ity of the community on behalf of their husbands and their households. They do not leave home at night nor in the evening, but at midday, to attend a reli- gious festival or to make some purchase, accompanied by a single female servant or decorously escorted by two servants at most. . . . They keep away from secret cults . . . particularly because these forms of worship encourage drunkenness and ecstasy. The mistress of the house and head of the household should be chaste and untouched in all respects.

Source: From Mary R. Lefkowitz and Maureen B. Fant, eds. *Women's Life in Greece & Rome: A Source Book in Translation*, 2nd ed. (Baltimore, MD: 1992), pp. 163–64.

### Questions for Analysis

**1.** Follow the steps of the argument made by Socrates. How does he go about proving that women and men are dif- ferent and so should have different roles in society? Are there flaws in this argument? How would you refute it?

**2.** How does the author of the treatise seem to define "chastity," and why does she (or he) say that it corre- sponds to more masculine qualities of courage and intelligence? Why would this author have wanted to attribute these reflections to female members of the community founded by the phi- losopher Pythagoras (c. 570–c. 495) three centuries earlier? How might this treatise be a response to the changes brought about by the expan- sion of the Greek world in the fourth and third centuries B.C.E.?

**3.** What are the main points on which these two perspectives agree? How might ideas like those expressed here have influenced contemporary ideas of female beauty (see **Interpreting Visual Evidence** on page 118)?

## Urban Architecture and Sculpture

Hellenistic architecture drew on Greek models, but it was also influenced by standards and tastes more characteristic of Egypt and Persia. Two examples (both of which no longer survive) are the great lighthouse of Alexandria, which rose to a height of nearly 400 feet and was daringly composed of three diminishing stories topped by eight slender columns supporting the light; and the citadel of Alexandria, built of stone and covered with blue-tinted plaster, described by a contemporary as seeming to float in mid-air. The best-surviving example, though, comes from Pergamon, a city on the coast of Anatolia that became the capital of a new kingdom wrested from the Seleucids' control in the second century B.C.E. It boasted an enormous altar dedicated to Zeus that crowned the heights of the city, below which an open-air theater was built into the steep slope of the hill. In Ephesus, not far away, the streets were not only paved, but paved with marble.

Perhaps the most influential of all Hellenistic arts was sculpture, which moved further away from classical ideals and placed even more emphasis on realism than the fourth-century sculptures discussed earlier in this chapter. Sculptors now prided themselves on faithfully reproducing facial furrows, muscular distortions, and complex folds of drapery. Awkward human postures offered the greatest technical challenges, to such an extent that sculptors might prefer to show people stretching themselves or balancing on one leg in ways that hardly ever occur in real life.

**THE CITADEL OF PERGAMON.** An artist's reconstruction of Pergamon in the second century B.C.E., based on the work of nineteenth-century German archaeologists. High atop the hill is the massive altar of Zeus (now in the Pergamon Museum in Berlin), and below it slope the tiers of the theater. Other features include fortifications, terraces, and artificial landscaping for public gardens. ▪ *How does this complex of buildings compare with that of another citadel, the Acropolis of Athens (see page 76)?*

**THE MARBLE STREETS OF EPHESUS.** Ephesus was already a splendid city when it was incorporated into the Persian Empire, along with other Greek settlements in Ionia. In the Hellenistic era, it became more splendid still.

Because monumental sculpture of this kind was executed for wealthy private patrons, it is clear that the goal was to create something unique in both conception and craftsmanship—something a collector could show off as the only one of its type. It is not surprising, therefore, that complexity came to be admired for its own sake, and extreme naturalism sometimes teetered on the brink of caricature. To our eyes, such works frequently appear familiar because of the influence they exerted on later sculptors like Michelangelo (see Chapter 12) and Auguste Rodin. Three of the most famous examples are pictured here, each exhibiting different aesthetic qualities and artistic techniques: the *Dying Gaul*, made in Pergamon around 220 B.C.E.; the *Winged Victory of Samothrace*, dating from around 200 B.C.E.; and the *Laocoön* group, from the first century B.C.E.

## Literary Fantasy and Historical Reality

In the sixth century B.C.E. it was the lyric, in the fifth century it was tragedy, and in the fourth century it was the novel; but in the Hellenistic era, the new literary genre was pastoral verse. These poems tapped into a strong vein of nostalgia for rural pastimes and simple pleasures, a make-believe world of shepherds and wood nymphs. The most important pastoral poet of the age was Theocritus (*thee-AW-krit-uhs*), who flourished around 270 B.C.E. in the big-city environment of Alexandria. Theocritus was a merchant of escapism. In the midst of urban bustle and within sight of overcrowded slums, he celebrated the charms of country life and lazy summer afternoons, putting into the mouths of his rustic characters unlikely sentiments expressed in ornate language. He thereby founded

**DYING GAUL.** The original (now lost) statue on which this Roman copy was based was sculpted in Pergamon around 220 B.C.E. The sculptor clearly wished to exhibit his skill in depicting an unusual subject: the Gauls were a Celtic people about whom very little was known in this era. ■ *How does this sympathetic representation of a "barbarian" express the new values of Hellenistic philosophy?*

**THE WINGED VICTORY OF SAMOTHRACE (LEFT).** This marble sculpture of the goddess Nike (Victory) may originally have been displayed on the prow of a monumental ship. It formed part of a temple complex on the island of Samothrace in the northern Aegean, and dates to around the year 200 B.C.E. It is now in the Louvre Museum, Paris. **LAOCOÖN AND HIS SONS (RIGHT).** In sharp contrast to the serene and confident *Winged Victory* is this famous sculpture group from the first century B.C.E. According to legend, Laocoön warned the Trojans not to accept the wooden horse sent by the Greeks and was accordingly punished by the sea god Poseidon, who sent two serpents to kill him and his sons. The intense physicality of this work was an important influence on Michelangelo, a millennium and a half later. It is now in the Vatican Museum, Rome.

an enduring tradition that would be taken up by poets from the Roman Virgil to the Englishman (and classical scholar) A. E. Housman, and that which has continuously provided a wealth of themes for the visual arts. Musical composers such as Beethoven and Debussy also owe a debt to Theocritus.

By contrast, Hellenistic prose literature was dominated by historians and biographers who consciously modeled their work on earlier pioneers, especially Thucydides. By far the most important was Polybius (*poh-LIB-ee-uhs*; c. 203–120 B.C.E.), a well-born Greek from the mainland whose father was a prominent politician active in the Achaean League. Polybius himself was trained as a horseman and cavalry officer, and both his vocation and his family connections gave him ample opportunity to observe the workings of government, diplomacy, and military strategy. This was at a time when the Achaean League was trying to position itself favorably in ongoing wars between the rising republic of Rome and the various warring kingdoms of northern Greece, notably Macedonia and Epiros. In 168 B.C.E., the Romans became suspicious of the Achaeans' declared neutrality and demanded that a thousand noble hostages be sent from Greece to Rome as a guarantee of the League's good behavior.

Polybius was one of those hostages, and he spent the next seventeen years living in Rome. There, he became a fervent admirer of Roman customs and especially of Rome's unique form of government. He also formed warm friendships with high-ranking Roman families, including the descendants of Scipio Africanus, a prominent Roman general. He kept up these contacts after his release, traveling to North Africa during the Third Punic War and witnessing firsthand the destruction of Carthage in 146 B.C.E. (see Chapter 5).

The result of this colorful career was a series of histories that glorified the achievements of Rome and its political system. Polybius also attempted to account for the patterns he discerned in the history of Greece since the Peloponnesian War. He argued that historical developments follow regular cycles, and that nations pass inevitably through stages of growth and decay. Hence, it should be possible to predict exactly where a given state is heading if one knows what happened to it in the past. Yet he also argued that the special character of Rome's constitution would allow it to break free from this cycle, because it combined all the different forms of government, which Aristotle had outlined in his *Politics*. This view of history galvanized the framers of the U.S. Constitution, directly influencing their conception of our own political institutions.

# CONCLUSION

Judged from the perspective of classical Greece, Hellenistic civilization seems alien and exotic. The autocratic governments of the age that followed Alexander's conquests would probably appear repugnant to a staunch proponent of Athenian democracy, and the Hellenistic love of extravagance and display can contrast strikingly with the more austere tastes of the fifth century B.C.E. Yet Hellenistic civilization had its own achievements that the classical age could not match, achievements that make it in some ways more familiar to us. Most Hellenistic cities offered a greater range of public facilities than any Greek cities of the previous period, and the numerous advances in science and technology are astonishing when compared with anything that came before or even after.

But the most important contribution of the Hellenistic era to subsequent historical developments was its role as an intermediary between the nascent empire of Rome and the older civilizations of Mesopotamia, Egypt, and Greece. The example set by Alexander, in particular, was one that the Romans would emulate, and the economic and political infrastructures that were put in place after his conquests would form the framework of Roman imperial government. The Romans would also take advantage of the common language and cultural expectations that bound together the far reaches of the Greek-speaking world. Their own Latin language became acceptable for cultivated conversation and literary expression only toward the very end of the first century B.C.E., and it would never supplant Greek as the preeminent language of scholarship and administration in the eastern portions of their empire.

The Hellenistic era must also be recognized as the bridge that connects us to the earlier ages of antiquity: most of what is contained in the first four chapters of this textbook is known to us only because older texts and inscriptions and artifacts were collected and copied by the scholars of Alexandria and other Hellenistic cities. This era also bridges the gap between the tastes and ideals and customs of classical Greece and those that would be more characteristic of Rome. It was Hellenistic art and architecture, Hellenistic city planning and civic culture that the Romans strove to emulate and export to their own colonies, not those of Periclean Athens. The same can be said of drama and poetry.

For us, two further aspects of Hellenistic culture deserve special mention: its cosmopolitanism and its modernity. The word *cosmopolitan* itself comes from a Greek word meaning "universal city," and it was the Greeks of the Hellenistic period who came closest to turning this ideal of globalization into reality. Around 250 B.C.E., a Greek tourist could have traveled from Sicily to the borders of India—the two known ends of the earth—and never cease to be among people who spoke his language and shared his basic outlook. Nor would this tourist have identified himself in ethnic or nationalist terms, or felt any exclusive loyalty to a city-state or kingdom; he would have considered himself a citizen

# After You Read This Chapter

 Go to **INQUIZITIVE** to see what you've learned—and learn what you've missed— with personalized feedback along the way.

## REVIEWING THE OBJECTIVES

- Macedonia's successful conquest of the Greek poleis can be attributed to several factors. What are they?
- Alexander the Great's imperial policies were influenced by his own upbringing, the different cultures he encountered, and some key historical precedents. Give at least one example of each type of influence.
- Explain how the three Hellenistic kingdoms reflect the differences among the three main civilizations we have studied so far.
- Why is the Hellenistic world described as "cosmopolitan"? How did this urban culture differ from that of the Greek poleis?
- The philosophies of Plato and Aristotle both derive from the teachings of Socrates, but they diverge in some important ways. What are those main differences?

of the world. He would also have considered himself a modern man, not bound by the old prejudices and superstitions of the past. It is for these reasons that Hellenistic civilization seems so closely related to our own. It was a world of stark contrasts and infinite possibilities, where economic instability, extremism, and authoritarian regimes existed side by side with unprecedented prosperity, rational inquiry, and extraodinary freedoms. In Chapter 5, we will see how this world adapted itself to the dominion of a single Italian city.

## PEOPLE, IDEAS, AND EVENTS IN CONTEXT

- In what ways were the military strategies of **PHILIP II** of Macedonia variations on older forms of hoplite warfare? How did the rise of mercenary armies and of Thebes further change military strategies in the fourth century?

- How did the philosophies of **PLATO** and **ARISTOTLE** respond to the crisis of the polis?

- To what degree did the conquests of **ALEXANDER THE GREAT** unite Mesopotamia, Egypt, and Greece?

- Why and how did the three **HELLENISTIC KINGDOMS** emerge? How were the **AETOLIAN AND ACHAEAN LEAGUES** new models for governance and cooperation in Greece?

- In what ways were **STOICISM, EPICUREANISM**, and other new philosophies a response to **COSMOPOLITANISM** and the breakdown of traditional societies and values?

- What were the driving forces behind the **SCIENTIFIC REVOLUTION OF ANTIQUITY**? What were its main achievements?

- What are some essential characteristics of **HELLENISTIC ART**? In what ways did it differ from that of the fifth century B.C.E. (see Chapter 3)?

## THINKING ABOUT CONNECTIONS

- "The history of the world is but the biography of great men": so the Scottish historian Thomas Carlyle (1795–1881) summarized the impact of figures such as Alexander the Great. How would you construct an argument in support of this proposition, using what you've learned in this chapter? How would you refute it?

- In what ways do Alexander's actions demonstrate his own knowledge of history as well as a capacity to apply that knowledge to his own circumstances? Can you identify leaders of our own day who have mobilized their understanding of history in similar ways?

- In your view, which civilization more resembles our own: classical Athens or the Hellenistic world? Why? What characteristics make an era seem "modern"?

## STORY LINES

- The Romans were proud of their unique history, especially the legend that they had overthrown their kings. They clung to this story even when individual men came to wield kingly powers.

- Roman identity, religion, and politics were intimately bound up in the worship of ancestors, especially male ancestors. As a result, fathers (living and dead) wielded extraordinary power in early Rome.

- Roman women enjoyed many more freedoms than women of ancient Greece, but were nevertheless subject to the authority of their male relatives.

- Paradoxically, the Romans celebrated their farming heritage even as they built a highly urbanized society. At the same time, they regarded Greek culture as both superior and dangerous.

- The Roman army had unprecedented strength and importance in this civilization, but the army's relationship to Roman politics and society changed drastically as Rome's empire grew.

## CHRONOLOGY

| | |
|---|---|
| 753 B.C.E. | Legendary founding of Rome |
| c. 509 B.C.E. | Roman Republic established |
| c. 450 B.C.E. | Law of the Twelve Tables |
| 287 B.C.E. | "Struggle of the Orders" ends |
| 264–146 B.C.E. | Punic Wars |
| 134–104 B.C.E. | Slave revolts in Sicily |
| 133–122 B.C.E. | Reforms of the Gracchi |
| 107–86 B.C.E. | Consulship of Marius |
| 82–79 B.C.E. | Dictatorship of Sulla |
| 73–71 B.C.E. | Rebellion of Spartacus |
| 52–48 B.C.E. | Struggle of Pompey and Caesar |
| 48–44 B.C.E. | Dictatorship of Caesar |
| 44–30 B.C.E. | Rivalry of Octavian and Antony |
| 27 B.C.E.–14 C.E. | Principate of the Emperor Augustus |
| 27–180 C.E. | Flowering of the *Pax Romana* |
| 79 C.E. | Eruption of Mount Vesuvius destroys (and preserves) Pompeii |
| 117 C.E. | Roman Empire reaches its greatest territorial extent under Trajan |

Before You Read This Chapter

# The Civilization of Ancient Rome

## CORE OBJECTIVES

- **IDENTIFY** the factors that influenced the formation of the Roman Republic.

- **UNDERSTAND** the basic elements of Roman identity.

- **ANALYZE** the competing interests of the different classes of people who struggled for power in Rome.

- **DESCRIBE** the impact of territorial expansion on Roman society.

- **TRACE** the events leading up to the establishment of the Principate and **UNDERSTAND** the significance of this new form of autocratic government.

"Could anyone be so indifferent or slow-witted as not to care how, and under what system of government, the Romans managed to bring nearly the whole inhabited world under their rule? Can anything be more important than understanding this?" So the Greek soldier Polybius (c. 203–120 B.C.E.) addresses Greek readers in a history celebrating the achievements of the Roman Republic. Polybius had witnessed some of these achievements firsthand: on the battlefield, in Rome itself as a hostage and a guest, and on a visit to the newly conquered city of Carthage. What better testament could there be to the success of a small Italian city than the admiration of a cultivated Greek aristocrat who, having been subjected to Roman authority, wholeheartedly embraced it? None, unless we cite the equally enthusiastic endorsement of the same Jews who had rebelled against Greek influence in 164 B.C.E. They, too, could not say enough in praise of the Romans, and they willingly placed themselves under Roman protection:

> Those whom they wish to help and to make kings, they make kings, and those whom they wish they depose;

147

and they have been greatly exalted. Yet for all that, not one of them has put on a crown or worn purple as a mark of pride, but they have built for themselves a senate chamber and every day three hundred and twenty senators constantly deliberate concerning the people, to govern them well. (1 Maccabees 8:12–15)

The only people who could say more in praise of Rome were the Romans themselves. To them, the enormous success of their empire meant that they were divinely chosen to colonize the world. This was the message conveyed by the poet Virgil (70–19 B.C.E.), commissioned by the emperor Augustus to tell the story of Rome's rise to glory in a manner imitating the epics of Homer. In one key passage of this monumental poem, the father of Aeneas, Virgil's epic hero, "foretells" the future and addresses posterity: "Remember, Roman, you whose power rules / all peoples, that these are your arts: plant peace, / make law, spare subjects, and put down the proud" (*Aeneid*, Book VI, lines 851–53).

While the Greeks struggled against the Persians and each other, a new civilization had emerged beyond the far fringes of the Greek world, on the banks of the river Tiber in central Italy. By 300 B.C.E., Rome was the dominant power on the Italian peninsula. Two centuries later, it had conquered Greece itself. For the next three centuries after that—an unprecedented period of sustained expansion—its power steadily increased. In the first century of our era, it ruled the former Hellenistic kingdoms as well as a vast region that Greek culture had never touched: northwestern Europe. Eventually, Rome's empire united the entire Mediterranean world and most of western Asia, while at the same time embracing provinces that are now parts of France, Spain, Portugal, Britain, Belgium, Germany, Switzerland, and the Balkan states. Rome thus built a historical arc that enabled Europe to share in a rich heritage reaching back to ancient Mesopotamia and Egypt: a heritage that gives meaning to the concept of "western civilization." Without Rome, European culture as we know it would not exist, and neither would the political and legal institutions that formed the United States. To echo Polybius: "Can anything be more important than understanding this?"

## THE TIME OF THE KINGS

The Romans looked back uneasily on their early history, for this was the time when they were ruled by kings. It may have been necessary in those days: the Romans had never

been peaceful settlers, and their land did not yield an easy living. Although Italy had sizable forests and much more fertile land than Greece, it has few mineral resources aside from excellent supplies of marble. Its extensive coastline boasts only a few good harbors, and most of these are on the western side, away from the commercial hubs of the Mediterranean; nor does the length of this coastline offer secure natural defenses. In short, Italy was rich enough to be attractive but not rich enough to be easily defended. So the Romans were a warlike people from the first, continually obliged to fortify their hard-won lands against other invaders and needing strong leaders to spearhead their efforts.

## Early Influences

When the Romans arrived in Italy, the dominant inhabitants of the peninsula were a people whom the Greeks called Tyrrhenians. To the Romans, they were Etruscans; to us, they remain mysterious, despite the rich archaeological record they left behind. This is because their language (not a branch of Indo-European) has never been fully deciphered, even though the Etruscans used an alphabet borrowed from the Greeks, with whom they were in frequent contact. By the sixth century B.C.E., the Etruscans had established a confederation of independent city-states in north-central Italy. They were skilled metalworkers, artists, and architects, from whom the Romans later took their knowledge of the arch and the vault, among much else, including the bloody sport of gladiatorial combat and the practice of foretelling the future by studying the entrails of animals and the flight of birds.

The two most important foundation myths told by the Romans also were derived from Etruscan tradition: the story of Aeneas's escape from Troy, which became the basis of Virgil's *Aeneid;* and the story of the infant twins Romulus and Remus, abandoned at birth and then raised by a maternal wolf, afterward founding a city on the slopes of the Palatine Hill. Rome's politicians and historians mined both legends for their metaphorical significance and added further details to increase their relevance for a changing audience. For example, the story of Aeneas's seduction and abandonment of Dido, queen of Carthage, reflected Rome's defeat of that powerful North African civilization. And for many Roman commentators, the murder of Remus at the hands of his brother Romulus epitomized an all-too-familiar pattern in Roman politics.

One aspect of Etruscan culture was of more limited influence. In marked contrast to women in Greek society, Etruscan women enjoyed very high status and played

**AN ETRUSCAN COUPLE.** This sarcophagus lid dates from the middle of the fourth century B.C.E. and depicts a deceased couple as they lie together in bed, emphasizing with their intimate embrace the closeness of their marital bond. (Photograph © 2017 Museum of Fine Arts, Boston.)

important roles in public life. They participated in politics and sporting events, they attended dramatic performances and athletic competitions (forbidden to Greek women), and they danced in ways that shocked both the Greeks and the Romans. Etruscan wives also ate meals with their husbands, another departure from both Greek and Roman custom, and reclined with them on the same couch at banquets. After death, these devoted couples were buried together in the same mortuary vaults, and their tombstones and sarcophagi often emphasize their mutual affection. Etruscan families even traced their descent through the female line. Some of these practices certainly affected the Romans, since Roman women were less sequestered than

their Greek counterparts. Yet they did not enjoy the same freedoms as Etruscan women until very late in Roman history, and by then these freedoms were condemned as signs of Rome's decadence.

The Romans also borrowed ideas from the Greek settlers who had begun to colonize southern Italy and Sicily in large numbers during the eighth century B.C.E. From them, Romans derived their alphabet, many of their religious beliefs, and much of their art. But the Romans downplayed Greek influence in their founding mythology, preferring to emphasize their alleged descent from the Trojans and also tracing their ancestry back to an Italic people called the Sabines, whose women (according to legend) Romulus and his men had forcibly abducted. This was a practice Romans would continue, in one form or another, as the legions planted new colonies and intermarried with indigenous populations from the Persian Gulf to the lowlands of Scotland.

## The Founding of Rome

The real founders of Rome were a tribe called the Latins, descendants of a cluster of Indo-European-speaking peoples who crossed the Alps into Italy during the second millennium B.C.E. Recent archaeological research has pushed the origins of the city back to at least the tenth century, several centuries earlier than 753 B.C.E., which the Romans themselves calculated as the year of their city's foundation.

Rome's position on the Tiber was advantageous. Trading ships (but not large war fleets) could navigate the river as far as the city, but no farther; thus Rome could be a commercial port but was not threatened by attack from the sea. Rome also sat astride the first good ford across the Tiber, making it a major crossroads. This was particularly important in its early years, when all roads did *not* lead to Rome, and the city was just a trading post on the frontier between Latium (the territory of the Latins) and Etruria (the Etruscan homeland). The seven hills that ringed the settlement, among which Rome was nestled, also offered strategic advantages. Eventually, Rome's central marketplace—the *forum* or "open space"—would become the beating heart of the world's most populous and powerful city, with approximately a million people crowded into an area of five square miles.

The topography of Latium—a broad, flat plain with few natural obstacles—also influenced the way the Romans dealt with neighboring communities, because it was not a terrain with defensible natural boundaries. At an early date, they negotiated a series of agreements with their neighbors that were known collectively as the Latin Right: a trading pact called the *commercium*; provisions for intermarriage called the *connubium*; and the *migratio*, which allowed a Latin resident of one settlement to emigrate to another and, after a year's residence, have the full rights of a citizen there. These privileges contrast strongly with the rigid isolationism and mutual suspicion that divided the city-states of ancient Mesopotamia or Greece. Indeed, the Romans' later willingness to extend the Latin Right far beyond Latium was a key factor in the success of their empire.

According to their own legends, the Romans' early government was a monarchy that mirrored the structure of Roman households, with a patriarchal king who exercised power that was checked only by a council of elders, the Senate (a word derived from the Latin *senex*, "old man"). Seven kings, including Romulus, are said to have ruled in succession. The last, Tarquinius Superbus (Tarquin the Arrogant), is reputed to have been an Etruscan who paved the way for Rome's imperial expansion by dominating Latium and the agriculturally wealthy district of Campania to the south. But his power came at the price of Roman freedom and dignity, as was made clear when Tarquin's son raped a virtuous Roman wife, Lucretia, around 510 B.C.E. When she committed suicide to avoid dishonor, the Romans—led by Lucretia's kinsman, Lucius Junius Brutus—rose up in rebellion, overthrowing not only the Etruscan dynasty but rejecting the very idea of monarchy as a legitimate form of government. Henceforth, any claim to royal authority in Rome was considered anathema, and the very word *rex* ("king") was a term of insult. The Brutus who would be instrumental in the assassination of Julius Caesar nearly five centuries later, was a descendant of that same Brutus who had driven out the Tarquin kings, something he and his contemporaries never forgot.

## THE TRIUMPH OF THE EARLY REPUBLIC

The story of Lucretia's defilement and death, whether or not it occurred as it was remembered, remained a rallying theme of patriotic myth and was also a potent statement of Roman attitudes toward female chastity and family honor. And it coincided with a radical change in Roman governance. This change was so radical, in fact, that it did not match any of Aristotle's political categories (see Chapter 4) but instead combined elements of them all. The Romans themselves didn't know what to call their political system: they spoke of it merely as *res publica* (the "public thing").

## The Territorial Expansion of Rome

The early Roman republic was marked by almost constant warfare, initially defensive but soon aimed at stitching together a patchwork of valuable territories that could support Rome's growing population. Gradually, the Romans came to control all the Latin hinterland and the valuable port of Ostia at the mouth of the Tiber, about twenty miles from their city. They also pushed northward toward Etruscan territory, and southward to Naples, another good port. By 300 B.C.E., Romans had absorbed or allied themselves with all of central Italy and had begun to look even further south, to the wealthy Greek colonies of Sicily.

Their rapid success is remarkable when compared with the patterns familiar to us from our study of classical Greece, the only corollary (and not a close one) being Philip II of Macedonia's subjugation of the poleis earlier in that same century. What was the secret of Roman success? For one thing, the Romans did not impose heavy burdens of taxation and tribute on the settlements they conquered. More often, they demanded that their allies contribute only soldiers to the Roman army. Rome also extended the Latin Right to many of these conquered territories, giving them a further stake in its continued political and military expansion.

Rome thus gained for itself nearly inexhaustible reserves of fighting men. By the middle of the third century B.C.E., its army may have counted as many as 300,000—a huge force even by modern standards, and all the more formidable due to the soldiers' rigorous training. As we have seen, the Greeks had eventually turned to paid soldiers out of economic necessity, but they fought in smaller numbers; Xenophon's army was 10,000 and Alexander's 100,000. The Great King of Persia, at the height of his powers, could claim to muster a million men, but these were private or tribal armies commanded by his satraps, not a standing army loyal to him. The Romans, in contrast, devoted themselves to the discipline of warfare in ways the Greeks (except for the Spartans) and the Persians did not. In this, although not in their tactics, they resemble the Hittites of the late Bronze Age and the Neo-Assyrians of the eighth century B.C.E. (see Chapter 2).

Although the Romans originally borrowed the phalanx formation from the Greeks, they quickly replaced it with smaller, more flexible divisions that could adjust to the varied geographical conditions of central Italy. Although the major unit of the Roman army was always the legion (5,000 men), the basic combat unit was the *maniple* ("handful"), a group of about 120 infantrymen who trained together and who often performed specialized tasks or used special weaponry. The Greek Polybius could not say enough in praise of this system, which made the army adaptable

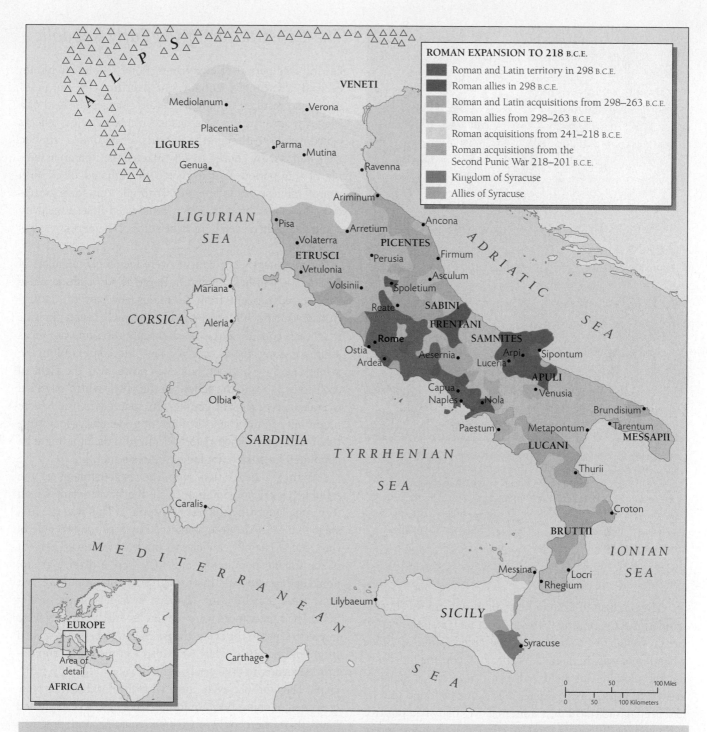

**ROMAN EXPANSION TO 218 B.C.E.**

- Roman and Latin territory in 298 B.C.E.
- Roman allies in 298 B.C.E.
- Roman and Latin acquisitions from 298–263 B.C.E.
- Roman allies from 298–263 B.C.E.
- Roman acquisitions from 241–218 B.C.E.
- Roman acquisitions from the Second Punic War 218–201 B.C.E.
- Kingdom of Syracuse
- Allies of Syracuse

**ROMAN EXPANSION IN ITALY, 485–218 B.C.E.** This map illustrates early Roman expansion in the peninsula. ▪ *What is the geographical relationship between Roman and Etruscan territory?* ▪ *What seem to have been the most attractive avenues for Roman expansion?* ▪ *What powers might have threatened Rome after its transformation into the dominant power on the peninsula after 265 B.C.E.?*

to climate, terrain, and the deployment of new military technologies.

The republic's early history reinforced not only the military character of the Roman state but also its commitment to agriculture as the only proper peacetime employment for a Roman. The acquisition of new lands made it possible for needy citizens to maintain themselves as farmers in the new colonies around Rome. By accommodating an increasing population in this way, the Romans were able to remain staunchly agricultural for a surprisingly long time. As a result, they developed an interest in shipping and commerce fairly late when compared with the Greeks or Phoenicians. And they would continue—even at the height of their empire—to valorize rural life over that of the city.

## The Constitution of the Early Republic

During this period of expansion, Rome's political system evolved accordingly. Initially, the overthrow of the monarchy had resulted in only moderate changes: instead of a king, the government was headed by two elected officers called *consuls*. Although the consuls of the infant republic were supposedly chosen by all citizens, the Roman assembly of this period actually voted in affiliated blocs with shared interests, economic or territorial. And since groups consisting of the wealthiest citizens voted first, a majority could be reached even before the votes of the poorer groups were cast.

Consequently, the consuls were inevitably members of aristocratic families, known in Rome as *patricians* because they traced descent from a famous ancestor or "father" (*pater*). During his term of office, which lasted for one year, each consul exercised essentially the same power as a king: dealing justice, making law, and commanding the army. The only limit on consular power was the right of each consul to veto the actions of the other, which often led to stalemate or violent conflict. In such cases, the Senate might have to arbitrate. In times of grave emergency (like that resulting in Cincinnatus's election), a dictator might be appointed for a term not longer than six months.

Within a generation after the establishment of the republic, patrician dominance of the government began to be challenged by the *plebs* ("people"). This was the first stage in a centuries-long contest known as the Struggle of the Orders. The plebeian classes made up nearly 98 percent of the Roman population, and they were a diverse group. Some had grown wealthy through trade or agriculture, but most were smallholding farmers, artisans, or the urban poor. Their grievances were numerous. Although they were forced to serve in the army, they were nevertheless excluded from holding office. They were also victims of discriminatory decisions in civil trials, which were judged by patricians. They did not even know what legal rights they were supposed to enjoy, because Rome had as yet no established laws: there were only unwritten customs and practices whose meaning was interpreted by the patricians to their own advantage. The plebeians were also, like the poorer citizens of Greek poleis, threatened with debt slavery.

These wrongs prompted a rebellion in the early fifth century B.C.E., when plebeians refused to join in the military defense of Rome and instead seceded from the city, camping out on the Aventine hill (see the map of Rome on page 176). This general strike of military labor forced the patricians to allow the people to elect their own officers, who were known as *tribunes* (tribal leaders). The job of each tribune was to protect his constituents from patrician injustice.

**CINCINNATUS THE STATESMAN-FARMER.** This bronze statue of Cincinnatus is prominent in Cincinnati, Ohio, which was named after the Roman hero (and in honor of George Washington) in 1790. In his right hand he holds the *fasces*, symbolizing his powers as dictator. In his left, he grasps the handle of a plow. ■ *Why would this figure have fired the imagination of Americans during their War of Independence?*

The paragon of Roman heroism in this era was Lucius Quinctius Cincinnatus (519–c. 430 B.C.E.), a stout-hearted citizen-farmer who reluctantly accepted political office when Rome was threatened by attack. According to legend, he was plowing his fields when a delegation of senators arrived to bring him to Rome. In the city, he found that he had been named *dictator*, a word that originally had positive connotations (like *tyrant* in Greece). This was a position of power to which the Romans elected one man during times of crisis. And as the term implies, the dictator's job was to tell everyone what they should do in a tough situation requiring decisive leadership. As legend has it, Cincinnatus dutifully performed this role, led Rome in its wars with hostile neighbors—and then went back to his farm. If Lucretia was the Roman epitome of matronly fortitude, Cincinnatus was the paradigm of manly virtue: willing to turn his hand to politics or warfare when necessary but preferring to put it to the plow. George Washington was frequently compared with him, to his own satisfaction.

Moreover, the plebeians guaranteed the safety of these officers by vowing to kill any person who hindered them from exercising their powers.

The plebs' victory led to the codification of the Law of the Twelve Tables, proclaimed around 450 B.C.E. and inscribed on wooden tablets (hence "tables"). Although this law would be regarded by later Romans as a charter of liberties, it was really a perpetuation of ancient custom. Nevertheless, the fact that the law was now *defined* was a significant improvement. Plebeians were also made eligible to hold elected offices, and they gradually gained access to the Senate. A further victory came in 287 B.C.E., when the plebeians succeeded in passing a law that made decisions enacted in their own assembly, the *concilium plebis*, binding on the Roman government—whether the Senate approved them or not. It was at this time that the phrase *Senatus Populusque Romanum* came into regular use, abbreviated *SPQR* and designating any decree or decision made by "the Senate and People of Rome." (Visitors to Rome will still find *SPQR* emblazoned on everything from public buildings to the manhole covers of Rome's sewers.)

These reforms had several important consequences over the long term. Successful plebeians could now work their way into the upper reaches of Roman society, which loosened the hold of patrician families on the exercise of power. At the same time, laws preventing wealth from becoming a controlling factor in Roman politics barred senators from engaging directly in commerce. This restriction had the effect of creating a new social order, that of the equestrians ("horsemen" or knights): men who chose a life of business rather than politics and whose wealth made it possible for them to own and equip warhorses and thus to provide Rome's cavalry. But the equestrians

and the senators were never wholly distinct. Often, some members of an important family would stay aloof from politics while underwriting the political careers of their brothers and cousins. Those families who managed to win election by such means, generation after generation, became increasingly prestigious and influential. Meanwhile, patricians who chose politics over wealth became impoverished and resentful. By the first century B.C.E., many such men felt excluded from political influence and were tempted to pursue their private agendas by styling themselves champions of the people (see below).

Later Roman patriots would regard this era as a golden age of shared government, but Rome never was a democracy. A republic differs from a monarchy only in that power is exercised by officers who are in some way responsible to citizens, and whose offices are not (at least in theory) hereditary. A republic, in short, is a political system designed to preserve the power of an oligarchy or privileged group. This is what the republic had been founded to achieve: kings were driven out, but patricians reigned. The constitution that emerged in these key centuries therefore broadened and stabilized oligarchy by the balance it struck among competing governmental institutions: the assembly, the Senate, and executive officeholders. Thanks to this distribution of powers, no single individual or clique could become overwhelmingly strong; but neither could direct expressions of the popular will—that is, democracy—affect Roman policy.

For the Greek historian Polybius, this was an ideal system because it combined elements of a monarchy (executive officeholders, the consuls), an aristocracy (the Senate), and a polity (the people's assembly and the tribunes). For the framers of the U.S. Constitution, it was a model for the three branches of a new government designed to *prevent* the vast majority of Americans from participating directly in politics, while allowing some citizens (originally, white men with sufficient property) a say in choosing their representatives. Polybius prophesied that such a system would break the political cycle that had destroyed the Greek poleis and that it would last forever. He was wrong.

**SENATUS POPULUSQUE ROMANUM.** The proud stamp of the "Senate and People of Rome" can be found even on public works and buildings in modern Rome. It is shown here on a manhole cover.

## THE ESSENCE OF ROMAN IDENTITY

The slow unfolding of the early republic ensured, in part, its success: Romans were conservatives who accepted new things reluctantly but then preserved them fiercely. The prevailing principle behind their institutions was the *mos*

**A ROMAN PATRICIAN OF THE FIRST CENTURY** B.C.E. This man, who wears the toga of an aristocrat, displays his piety by holding the busts of his ancestors. Busts, like the funerary masks described by Polybius (see page 155), commemorated the dead and were the focus for family worship in household shrines. ■ *How does the Roman attitude toward age and death differ from that of the Greeks (see the image on page 82)?* ■ *What do these differences suggest about the broader values of these two societies?*

*maiorum* (*MOHS my-OR-um*), "the code of the elders" or "the custom of the ancestors" or even, to use the word derived from the Latin *mos*, "morality." This unwritten code was sacrosanct and essential to Roman identity. It accounts for the remarkable coherence of Roman culture, religion, and law, all of which rested on ancestor worship. The Latin word *pietas* ("piety") meant reverence for family traditions and for one's fathers—living and dead. What made the legendary Aeneas "pious Aeneas" was his devotion to his father, Anchises (*an-KIE-sees*), whom he carried to safety on his back while Troy burned. In a metaphorical sense, this meant that Aeneas was the carrier of tradition, a man willing to shoulder the burdens of his ancestors and carry them forever.

This helps to explain why the Romans, in the ensuing centuries of their world domination, continued to identify so strongly with their homeland and its customs. To a Roman, "going native" in a foreign place was a terrible betrayal of the *mos maiorum*; patriotism, after all, is dedication to the fatherland. It also explains the extraordinary maxim of *patria potestas* (*PAH-tree-a poh-TEST-ahs*; "fatherly power") upheld by the Twelve Tables. A Roman father, no matter what his social class, had absolute authority within his household, including the power of life and death. If he was too poor to raise a child, he could expose it (leaving it to perish or to charity) or sell it into slavery. If his wife or child dishonored him, he could kill with impunity. Paternal supremacy was upheld in theory and in legends like that of Lucretia: had she not killed herself, her father could have killed her with his own hands.

These values set the Romans apart from everyone in the Hellenistic world. The Greeks, for example, never condoned anything like *patria potestas*: when a father kills his children in Greek mythology, he is inevitably killed in revenge by another member of his own family, or by the gods. And although pride in one's ancestry is a very human attribute, and patriarchy common to every known civilization, the Romans' contemporaries were awed by their extreme devotion to these principles. This devotion was one of the things that made the Romans so admirable in the eyes of those Jews disgusted by the loose morals of Hellenistic civilization (see Chapter 4). For the Greek Polybius, it was the key to Roman success. In addition to describing the workings of the Roman government and army in minute detail, he reports (with anthropological interest) on the conduct of Roman funeral processions and the Romans' practice of wearing the death-masks of their ancestors, which on other days were hung in special household shrines.

In some respects, Rome's public religion resembled that of the Greeks: Jupiter corresponded to Zeus as god of the skies, Neptune to Poseidon as god of the seas, Venus

## Polybius Describes the Romans' Worship of Their Ancestors

*The Law of the Twelve Tables forbade excessive display at funerals, especially displays of wealth and grief by women. Instead, funerals were supposed to be occasions for the display of family piety. In the following passage, the Greek historian Polybius—who had spent a formative fourteen years of his life in Rome—describes Roman burial customs and these rites' relationship to the strength of republican ideals.*

 quote just one example to illustrate the pains taken by the Roman state to produce men who will endure anything to win a reputation for valor in their country. Whenever one of their celebrated men dies . . . his body is carried with every kind of honor into the Forum, . . . sometimes in an upright position so as to be conspicuous, or else, more rarely, recumbent. The whole mass of the people stand round to watch, and his son, if he has one of adult age who can be present, or if not some other relative, then . . . delivers an address which recounts the virtues and successes achieved by the dead man during his lifetime. By these means the whole populace . . . are involved in the ceremony, so that when the facts of the dead man's career are recalled . . . their sympathies are so deeply engaged that the loss

seems . . . to be a public one which affects the whole people. Then, after the burial of the body and the performance of the customary rites, they place the image of the dead man in the most conspicuous position in the house, where it is enclosed in a wooden shrine. This image consists of a mask which is fashioned with extraordinary fidelity . . . to represent the features of these dead men. On occasions when public sacrifices are offered, these masks are displayed and decorated with great care. And when any distinguished member of the family dies, the masks are taken to the funeral, and are worn by men who are considered to bear the closest resemblance to the original, both in height and their general appearance and bearing. . . .

It would be hard to imagine a more impressive scene for a young man who aspires to win fame and practice virtue. For who could remain unmoved at the

sight of the images of all these men who have won renown in their time, now gathered together as if alive and breathing? What spectacle could be more glorious than this?

Source: Polybius, *The Rise of the Roman Empire*, trans. Ian Scott-Kilvert (New York: 1979), pp. 346–47.

### Questions for Analysis

**1.** Why does Polybius place so high a premium on the Romans' conduct at funerals? How can such rites be related to republican ideals?

**2.** Compare this analysis of Roman funerary rites with the image of a Roman patrician and his ancestors on page 154. How do they complement each other?

---

to Aphrodite as goddess of beauty and sexuality, Mars to Ares as god of war. But in keeping with the Roman equation of religion with family, this entire pantheon functioned as family gods of the Roman state. The republic was essentially a giant, timeless household run by "elders" (senators) and "father figures" (patricians), some of whom traced their ancestry back to gods; the mother of Aeneas was Venus. Like a Roman household, the Roman state could flourish only if these father- and mother-gods lent their continuing and active support to its enterprises. Committees of priests therefore functioned as branches of the government and tended to the worship of the city's temples. And in stark contrast to

priests in other ancient societies, these priests were not full-time professionals who formed a special caste but prominent men who rotated in and out of office while serving as leaders of the Senate. Their dual roles made religion even more integral to political life in Rome than it had been in Greece—similar in some ways to the integration of religion and politics in ancient Mesopotamia (see Chapter 1).

The Roman man's primary duty to honor his ancestors also bolstered the prestige of the Roman army, because soldiers were supposed to sacrifice themselves for the public good and to fear disgrace above all things. The all-important sense of ancestral duty is further reflected in Roman naming practices, another custom that separated them from other ancient cultures. Most free men in antiquity were known by a given name and their father's name only: Alexander, before he was "the Great," was "son of Philip." A free-born Roman, in contrast, had at least two names. The name by which he was formally known—the name that mattered— was the name of his earliest ancestor, the man from whom his family descended. Gaius Julius Caesar, to take a famous example, would have entered public life as Julius, a member of the family of the Julii, who claimed ancestry from Iulus, the son of Aeneas. His forename, Gaius, was the most common name in Rome, the equivalent of "Joe" or "John." He would never be addressed by this name in public, except perhaps by very intimate friends or family members. His third name, Caesar, which means "Hairy" (probably a joke), was a nickname he acquired in the course of his career. And because it was the most distinctive of his names—the name he didn't share with an ancestor or with average Romans—it became the name by which he was commonly known. The same goes for Marcus Tullius Cicero (Cicero means "chickpea"). The illustrious Cincinnatus was actually "Curly."

What's in a name? Everything, if you were a Roman man. And nothing, at least nothing of personal significance, if you were a Roman woman. Lucretia's name was not her own but her father's or forefather's: the feminine version of Lucretius. If she had a sister, they would both be called Lucretia, differentiated only as Major and Minor ("big/elder" and "little/younger") Lucretia. If there were two more girls, they would be Tertia and Quarta ("Third" and "Fourth") Lucretia, and so on. The only people in Rome who had personal names were slaves (who were named by their masters, like pets) or very low-born Romans and immigrants who had no lineage that mattered.

## FROM REPUBLIC TO EMPIRE

For more than two centuries after the founding of the republic, warfare and agriculture remained the chief occupations of most Romans. A few artisans could be found in cities, and some minor attempts were made to establish trading networks. But the fact that Rome had no standard system of coinage until 289 B.C.E. suggests strongly that commerce was an insignificant component of its economy. Apparently, Romans didn't rely on portable wealth; when they weren't fighting, they wanted to be home on the farm, not gadding about the world. If they had money, they put it into real estate: land or slaves.

All of this changed rapidly when Romans began to look beyond Italy. In 265 B.C.E., they completed their absorption of Etruscan territory and could claim to control most of the peninsula. A year later, they were already embroiled in a war overseas. For a home-loving people who had now secured ample resources for their own support, this seems paradoxical. Indeed, historians continue to argue about the motives for Roman expansion. Did Rome constantly seek to extend its rule as a matter of policy, to feed a collective appetite for warfare and plunder? Or was it an accidental empire, built up in a series of reactions to changing pressures at home as well as in response to threats—real and imagined—from abroad? No definitive answer is yet possible, but it was in this crucial period that the Roman Republic began to transform Western civilizations, and itself, into the Roman Empire.

## The Punic Wars, 264–146 B.C.E.

In 265 B.C.E., Roman territory extended to the tip of Italy's "boot," but there it ended. Just off its coast, the large islands of Corsica and Sardinia and the western half of Sicily were part of another state, much older and far wealthier. This was the great maritime empire of Carthage, which stretched along the northern coast of Africa from modern-day Tunisia through the Straits of Gibraltar and into modern Spain. Carthage itself was a vital port city at the northeastern tip of Africa, founded around 800 B.C.E. as a Phoenician colony (see Chapter 2) but now independent and powerful. It had the largest and most effective navy of its day, and it commanded the vast resources of commercial networks that reached as far north as Britain and deep into Egypt. In almost every respect but one it was far superior to Rome. Yet that one factor was decisive: although the Carthaginian fleet was unrivaled, Carthage had no standing army. It relied on mercenaries bankrolled by the enormous profits of its merchants.

The epic struggle between Rome and Carthage for dominance of the Mediterranean lasted well over a century. It crystallized in three periods of concentrated warfare known as the Punic Wars, because the Romans called their enemies the Poeni ("Phoenicians"). The first of these wars began in 264 B.C.E., when Rome sent a garrison to occupy the independent city of Messina (originally a Greek colony) on the eastern tip of Sicily, directly across from the Italian mainland. Carthage, in response, took advantage of the local enmity between Messina and Syracuse (another Greek city), and sent warships to protect Syracuse from what it saw as Roman aggression. Twenty-three years of bitter fighting ensued, protracted because the Carthaginians needed to suffer only one defeat in a land battle before resolving to engage the Romans solely at sea. There they had the advantage—until

**CARTHAGINIAN COIN.** This coin was issued by Hannibal's family around 230 B.C.E. and circulated in the Carthaginian colonies of Spain. Its face shows the Carthaginian god Melqart in the guise of Hercules (notice the club over his shoulder). The reverse features a war elephant with a mounted rider, like the ones that Hannibal used against Rome.

the Romans built their own navy, virtually from scratch. In 241 B.C.E., Carthage was beaten down and forced to cede all of its Sicilian lands to Rome and to pay a large indemnity. Sicily thus became Rome's first overseas province. It was shortly followed by Corsica and Sardinia, which the Roman Senate contrived to seize on the grounds that Carthage had defaulted on the payment of reparations.

Thereafter, the Carthaginians had ample reason to harbor resentment against Rome, while the Romans were determined not to let Carthage revive its maritime power. So when Carthage attempted to expand its presence in Spain, leaders of the Senate interpreted this as a threat to Roman interests and declared a new war that lasted for sixteen years: the Second Punic War. This time, however, Rome was thrown entirely off its guard by the brilliant exploits of the Carthaginian commander Hannibal (247–183 B.C.E.), who very nearly defeated the Romans at their own game and on their own soil. No one had imagined that a Carthaginian attack could come by land, from the north. But in a daring strategy, Hannibal raised an army in Spain, heavily manned by cavalry in order to counter the superior infantry of Rome, and equipped it with dozens of war elephants and siege engines. He then led this entire force across the Pyrenees into Gaul (now southern France) and then over the Alps into Italy. There, he harried Roman forces in their own territories for nearly sixteen years, from 218 to 202 B.C.E.

In the end, Hannibal was challenged more by the rigors of campaigning and the difficulty of supplying his army in hostile terrain than by the Romans themselves. (He had lost many of his elephants and some important equipment in the icy mountain passes of the Alps.) He also seems to have counted on winning the support of the Italian territories that Rome had conquered, but Rome's generous treatment of its Latin allies kept them loyal. As a result, Rome could call on vast human resources while Hannibal had only his exhausted army, with no reserves forthcoming from Carthage. Nevertheless, he won several

amazing victories in Italy before retreating—technically undefeated—in 202 B.C.E. He also won the admiration of the Romans themselves, whose own histories frankly acknowledge his tactical genius. Indeed, this phase of warfare ended only when a Roman general, Publius Cornelius Scipio, took a leaf out of Hannibal's book. He had been campaigning in Spain against the army of Hannibal's brother, Hasdrubal. In 201 B.C.E., having seized a number of key Carthaginian strongholds, he crossed into Africa and met Hannibal at Zama, near Carthage. Scipio's victory ended the Second Punic War and won him a new name, "Africanus," in honor of his conquest.

Carthage was now compelled to abandon all of its possessions except the city itself and its immediate hinterlands, and to pay an indemnity three times greater than the already crippling reparations Rome had demanded after the First Punic War. Yet Roman suspicion of Carthage remained obsessive, and warmongers in the Senate read every sign of its recovery as a threat. By the middle of the second century, some hard-liners were urging a preemptive strike. Among the most vocal was an elderly patrician, Marcus Porcius Cato, famous for his stern obedience to Roman custom and his virulent xenophobia. Cato ended every speech he gave—no matter what the topic—with the words: "And furthermore, I strongly advise that Carthage be destroyed." This won him the nickname Cato the Censor, from the Latin verb meaning "to advise."

Eventually, the Senate was persuaded. In 149 B.C.E., it seized on a minor pretext to demand that the Carthaginians abandon their city and settle at least ten miles from the coast, where they would have no access to the sea. Of course, this absurd mandate amounted to a death sentence for a city dependent on commerce, and it was refused—as the Romans knew it would be. The result was the Third Punic War and the siege of Carthage, which ended in 146 B.C.E. when the Romans breached the walls and butchered the population. Those who survived the massacre were sold into slavery, and their once-magnificent city was razed to the ground. The legend that the Romans sowed the land with salt (to make it infertile) is not a real tactic but a poetic way of describing the successful eradication of an entire civilization. It would stand as a warning to Rome's other potential enemies.

## Roman Control of the Hellenistic World

Rome's victories over Carthage enormously increased Roman territory, leading to the creation of new colonial provinces in Sicily, North Africa, and Hispania (Spain). This not only brought Rome great new wealth (above all,

access to Sicilian and African grain supplies and the silver mines of the Iberian Peninsula) but it was also the beginning of the westward expansion that became Rome's defining influence on the history of Europe.

At the same time, Rome's overseas expansion brought it into conflict with eastern Mediterranean powers, paving the way for further conquests. During the Second Punic War, Philip V of Macedonia had entered an alliance with Carthage; soon afterward, he moved aggressively into Greece and was rumored to have designs on Egypt. Rome sent an army to stop him and later foiled the plans of the Achaean League (see Chapter 4). This was when Polybius was sent to Rome as a hostage. He became a guest-friend in the family descended from Scipio Africanus and later witnessed the destruction of Carthage. Rome also thwarted similar efforts by the Seleucid

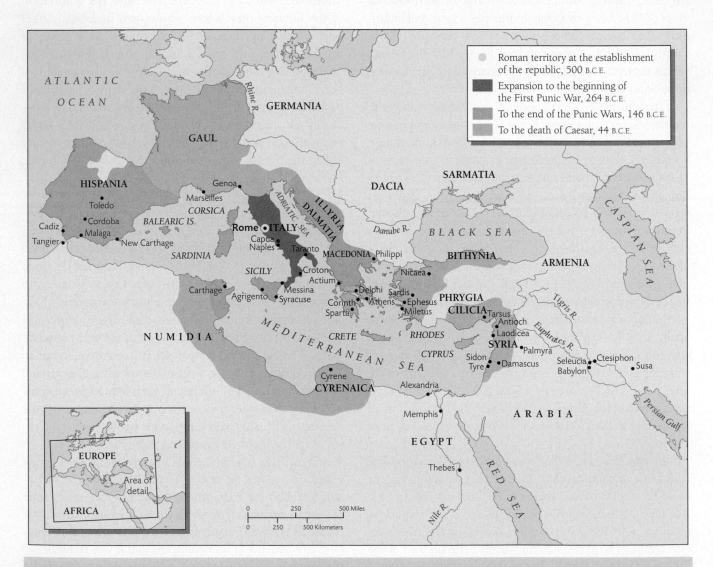

**THE FURTHER EXPANSION OF ROME, 264–44 B.C.E.** The rapid increase of Rome's territories opened up new opportunities and challenges. ▪ *Examine the phases of expansion on this map. In what directions did Roman dominion move?* ▪ *Why was this the case?* ▪ *What particular problems might have been created by the eventual extension of Roman rule into Gaul, well beyond the "Roman lake" of the Mediterranean?*

monarch Antiochus III. In neither of these cases did Rome set out to conquer the eastern Mediterranean on purpose. By 146 B.C.E., however, both Greece and Macedonia had become Roman provinces, Seleucid Asia had lost most of its territories, and Ptolemaic Egypt had largely become a pawn of Roman commercial and political interests.

## THE CONSEQUENCES OF IMPERIALISM

Rome's seemingly inadvertent conquest of Greece and western Asia transformed the economic, social, and cultural life of the republic. New wealth poured in, increasing the inequalities within Roman society and challenging the traditional values of frugality and self-sacrifice. Small farmers left the land and swelled the impoverished urban population, unable to compete with the huge new plantations owned by aristocrats and worked by gangs of slaves. Slaves also played an increasing role in Roman cities as artisans, merchants, and household servants. Roman rule over the Hellenistic world had a particularly pervasive impact on cultural life— so much so that many Romans considered themselves to have been intellectually "conquered" by Greece. Hitherto self-assured and self-satisfied, they now felt that their own language, history, and customs were uncouth and barbaric compared with those of their cultivated colonial subjects.

### Economic Change and Social Upheaval

Like all peoples of the ancient world, the Romans took slavery for granted. But nothing in Rome's earlier experience prepared it for the huge increase in the number of slaves that resulted from its western and eastern conquests. In 146 B.C.E., 55,000 Carthaginians were enslaved after the destruction of their city; not long before, 150,000 Greek prisoners of war had met the same fate. By the end of the second century B.C.E., there were a million slaves in Italy alone. Rome's became one of the most slave-based economies in history, rivaling ancient Egypt or the antebellum American South.

The majority of Roman slaves worked as agricultural laborers on the vast (and growing) estates of the Roman aristocracy. Some of these estates were the result of earlier Roman conquests within Italy itself. But others were consolidated by aristocrats who bought up the holdings of peasant farmers. Soldiers in particular, who might be required to serve for years at a time on foreign campaigns,

often found it impossible to maintain their farms. Instead, they moved to the city—where free men had no way to sustain themselves except through trade or violence. With abundant, cheap slaves to do all the rough work, moreover, there was no impetus for technological innovation. Meanwhile, expensive slaves did the specialized jobs: they were secretaries, bookkeepers, personal assistants, playwrights, musicians, sculptors, and artists. The Romans had almost no incentive to employ paid labor at all or even to train in these arts, as the Greeks had. By the first century B.C.E., as a result, a third of Rome's one million inhabitants were receiving free grain from the state, partly to keep them alive and partly to keep them quiet. The poet Juvenal would later satirize the plebs as needing only "bread and circuses" to stay satisfied and docile.

As we have seen, the Roman economy had remained fundamentally agrarian until the mid–third century B.C.E. During the following century, however, Rome's eastern conquests brought it fully into the sophisticated commercial sphere of the Hellenistic world. The principal beneficiaries of this change were the equestrian class. As overseas merchants, they profited handsomely from Rome's voracious appetite for foreign luxury goods. And as representatives of the Roman government in the provinces, they operated mines, built roads, and collected taxes, always with an eye toward their own profits. They were also the principal moneylenders to the Roman state and to distressed individuals. Interest rates were high, and when the state could not pay its bills, the moneylenders were often allowed to repay themselves by exploiting the populations of the provinces.

Commoners who lost their lands suffered from these economic changes, but the principal victims of Rome's transformation were its slaves. Even though some were cultivated foreigners—mainly Greek-speaking—taken as prisoners of war, the standard policy of their owners was to get as much work out of them as possible until they died of exhaustion or were "freed" in old age to fend for themselves. The same irascible Cato the Censor who had demanded the destruction of Carthage even wrote a "how-to" book on this subject. The ready availability of slaves also made Roman slavery a far more impersonal and brutal institution than it had been in many other ancient civilizations. Of course, there were exceptions. Some domestic slaves were treated as trusted family members, and slave secretaries vital to the business of Roman governance and the arts could even win fame or earn enough to buy their freedoms. Some slave artisans were permitted to run their own businesses, keeping some of the profits.

But the general lot of slaves was horrendous. Some businessmen owned slaves whom they trained as gladiators to be mauled by wild animals or by other gladiators for

## Spectator Sports

Like the Romans' love for gladiatorial combat, Americans' love of football is inextricably tied to a sense of shared identity and fascination with violence and warfare. Although American football is not a blood sport in a technical sense, part of its allure stems from the very great physical risks taken by its players, whose careers are often cut short by injury. Both pastimes form the core of far-reaching entertainment economies that would be dismantled by any attempts at reform: concessions, advertising, merchandising, and an array of other moneymaking activities.

 **Watch related author interview on the Student Site**

the amusement of a paying public. The luxurious lifestyles of the wealthy meant that dozens of slaves in every household were trapped in a cycle of menial tasks as doorkeepers, litter-bearers, couriers, valets, wet nurses, and childminders. In some great households, designated slaves had no other duties than to rub down the master after his bath or to keep track of the mistress's social engagements. It was a life that debased both slave and owner, according to many Roman critics, thus undermining the values of the republic.

## New Money, New Values

In the early republic, as we have seen, Roman men had nearly absolute powers over their individual households. During the second century B.C.E., however, two innovations greatly altered this pattern of patriarchal control. One was the introduction of new laws that allowed married women to manage their own property instead of handing that wealth over to their husbands; if a married woman died, her possessions would then revert to her father or her father's heirs if she had no children of her own. Alongside this new law came more liberal laws that allowed women to initiate divorce proceedings.

These changes were intended to safeguard family wealth, but they eventually resulted in greater independence for women. A woman now had much more authority within the household because she contributed to its upkeep. If her husband did not show respect, she could leave him and deprive him of income. It was ironic that the growth of Rome's slave system also gave women greater freedom, for slaves took over the traditional work of child rearing, household maintenance, and the endless tasks of spinning and weaving. Women from well-to-do families now spent more time away from the home and began to engage in a range of social, intellectual, and artistic activities. Indeed, women were among the chief consumers of the new Hellenistic fashions, commodities, and ideas available in Rome.

In earlier centuries, Romans had taken pride in the simplicity of their lives, their language, and their moral code. Now, however, elite Romans began to indulge in creature comforts and cultivate Hellenistic habits as proof of their refinement. Bilingualism became increasingly common, and Greek literature became the standard against which Roman authors measured themselves. Latin was fine for business or politics or farming, but if one wanted to express lofty or beautiful thoughts one did so in Greek, which was far more flexible and sophisticated. Latin was not yet a literary language.

Well-educated Greek slaves were therefore at a premium: to lend social cachet, to act as secretaries and personal assistants, and to tutor Roman children. The popularity of Greek plays, mostly comedies, was such that they quickly spawned Latin imitations, such as those of Plautus (257?–184 B.C.E.) and Terence (195/185–159 B.C.E.). Terence's career path is suggestive of a larger pattern: a Greek-speaker of Libyan descent, he was sold into slavery as a boy in Carthage and bought by a wealthy Roman called Terentius, who took him back to Rome and cultivated his talents, which he marketed under his own name. Six of Terence's Latin adaptations of Greek comedies survive, enjoyed enormous popularity well into the Middle Ages, and eventually influenced the plays of Shakespeare.

Many Romans nursed an inferiority complex with respect to Greek culture. But others (including Cato) regarded these foreign influences with disgust. For them, the good old ways of paternal authority and stern military discipline were giving way to effeminacy and the decadence of soft living. Accordingly, conservative politicians deplored these new trends and passed laws that would restore "family values" and regulate the conspicuous consumption of luxuries, especially by women—but these measures were ineffectual. Rome was being irreversibly transformed from a republic of self-reliant farmers into a complex metropolitan empire reliant on foreign slaves, foreign grain, and foreign luxuries, in which the gap between rich and poor was widening and traditional behavioral constraints were giving way to new morals and ideas.

## Philosophy and Spirituality in the Late Republic

The late republic was deeply influenced by Hellenistic philosophy, and both Epicureanism and Stoicism found strong adherents in Rome. The former was popularized by Lucretius (98–55 B.C.E.), the author of a book-length philosophical poem, *On the Nature of Things*. But more congenial to Roman values was Stoicism, which soon numbered among its converts many powerful public figures. The most influential of these was Cicero (106–43 B.C.E.), famous in his day as an orator, statesman, and staunch defender of republican values. Cicero based his ethical teachings on the Stoic premises that virtue is happiness and tranquility of mind the highest good. The ideal man is therefore rational and indifferent to sorrow and pain. Yet Cicero diverged from the Stoics in his approval of the

**ROMAN MYSTERY RITES.** One of the Roman houses preserved at Pompeii features an astonishing cycle of wall paintings, executed around 50 B.C.E., that give the house its name: Villa of the Mysteries. The exact meaning of these images is still debated, but some scholars have argued that they depict a succession of ritual practices. Here a young woman is being whipped, perhaps as part of an initiation ceremony, while another woman performs a dance.

active, political life. He became an advocate for the revival of Roman tradition through service to the state. His elegant prose style also advanced the use of Latin as a language of eloquence and became the standard model for Latin composition: students learning Latin today still learn to read with Cicero.

The religious practices of Rome also changed markedly in this era. The most pronounced innovation was the spread of exotic mystery cults, which satisfied a need for more emotionally intense spiritual experiences than did traditional forms of Roman worship—again, especially for women, who were largely excluded from the rites of the patriarchal state religion. From Egypt came the cults of Isis and Osiris, while from Asia came the worship of the Great Mother, all emphasizing the power of female sexuality and reproduction. Despite the attractions of these new cults, Romans continued to honor their traditional gods alongside these new deities. Roman polytheism could absorb them all, so long as the ancestor gods of the household and of the city were paid due reverence.

# "RESTORING THE REPUBLIC": THE STRUGGLE FOR POWER

In Rome itself, the period from the end of the Third Punic War in 146 to about 30 B.C.E. was one of turbulence. Politically motivated murders, bloody competition among rival dictators, wars, and insurrections were common occurrences. Slave uprisings also added to the general disorder. In 134 B.C.E., some 70,000 slaves defeated a Roman army in Sicily before being put down by emergency reinforcements. Slaves ravaged Sicily again in 104 B.C.E. But the most threatening revolt of all was led by Spartacus, a Thracian captive who was being trained as a gladiator. Along with a band of 200 fellow slaves from a gladiatorial training camp—all bought by a wealthy entrepreneur—they escaped, heavily armed, from Capua (near Naples; see the map on page 151) to the slopes of Mount Vesuvius, where their cause attracted a huge host of other fugitives.

From 73 to 71 B.C.E., this desperate army defeated trained Roman forces of as many as 10,000 men and overran much of southern Italy before Spartacus himself was killed. The Senate, terrified of the precedent set by the near victory of the rebels, ordered 6,000 of the captured slaves to be crucified along the length of the road from Capua to Rome (about 150 miles) as a warning to future insurgents. Crucifixion was a form of punishment reserved for slaves and non-Roman rebels, and it meant a slow, terrible, and public death from gradual suffocation and exposure.

## The Reforming Efforts of the Gracchi

Meanwhile, these waves of rural rebellion were being mirrored by urban unrest in various forms, as the poorer classes of Rome were finding new champions among some progressive aristocrats. In 133 B.C.E., a grandson of Scipio Africanus, Tiberius Gracchus, was elected a tribune of the people. He took his office very seriously and proposed to remedy the growing rift between rich and poor Romans by instituting major reforms, including the redistribution of property. As we have noted, small farmers had been losing their lands to patricians and equestrians whose new wealth allowed them to amass giant estates. To counter this, Gracchus invoked older laws that had limited the amount of land a single individual could own.

The motives behind the proposed reforms were both populist and practical. The Roman army had been forced to expand its presence into far-reaching territories and needed more manpower to handle uprisings such as that of Spartacus. Since a man had to meet certain property qualifications to serve in the Roman army, the available pool of citizen soldiers was shrinking along with the wealth of average citizens. Gracchus saw that the army could be strengthened if more of Rome's inhabitants could qualify for citizenship. With the support of his brother Gaius, Tiberius Gracchus accordingly proposed that estates be no larger than 300 acres per citizen, plus 150 acres for each child in his family. Since many aristocratic estates exceeded these measures, the excess land could then be divided among poor settlers. But since most senators stood to lose from this legislation, they worked to ensure that it would be vetoed by Gracchus's fellow tribunes. Gracchus retaliated, arguing that tribunes who opposed the people's interests were betraying their offices, and planned to stand for reelection when his term expired. This enabled a conservative faction to allege that Gracchus had his sights set on a dictatorship, and with this excuse, they attacked and murdered him and his supporters.

Ten years later, Gaius Gracchus renewed his older brother's struggle after being elected to the same office. Although some land reforms had finally been enacted by the Senate after the assassination of Tiberius Gracchus, Gaius wanted to enact more laws for the benefit of the poor by stabilizing the price of grain in Rome and checking the abuses of the senatorial class by giving the equestrians greater powers. He also imposed controls on provincial governors suspected of exploiting their subjects for personal gain. Most controversial, Gaius proposed to extend full Roman citizenship to all the allied states of Italy: a move that would have kept the army well supplied with new soldiers but would also create new citizens whose collective power would challenge existing elites. Senate aristocrats arranged to have Gaius Gracchus proclaimed an outlaw. In the ensuing conflict, he and several thousand of his supporters became the victims of a violent political purge.

## Rivalry among Rome's Generals

The attempted reforms of the Gracchi exposed the degree to which the republic's constitution—intended to ensure a balance of power among competing classes—was being compromised by the undue influence of a wealthy elite. But the popularity of the Gracchi among the plebs suggested a new path to power for ambitious men willing to court the favor of the people. Most of these men were former army commanders who traded on their military victories and the wealth they had gained from plunder to win popular support.

The first of these ambitious generals was Gaius Marius, a soldier from an obscure provincial family who had fought a successful and well-publicized campaign against Jugurtha of Numidia, whose small kingdom had threatened Rome's hard-won supremacy in the former Punic territories of North Africa. In 107 B.C.E., Marius's popularity—and his command of several legions—enabled him to secure election to the office of consul, an office that he would hold six more times in the course of his career. This set a powerful precedent, because it showed that a man with no family connections or political experience could override opposition from older political elites if he had an army to help him intimidate those elites. A successful army command could therefore be an alternative path to power, bypassing the traditional routes through which senators usually obtained high office.

Marius further influenced the future of Rome by reorganizing and expanding the army. Desperate for more men to fight in Africa and in Gaul, which Rome was slowly infiltrating, Marius abolished the property qualification that had hitherto limited military service; the potential pool of soldiers now included the urban poor and landless peasants. As a result, a career as a Roman legionnaire became an end in itself, rather than a matter of routine citizen service to the state. This meant, further, that a soldier's loyalty was more directed toward his commander, whose success would win rewards for his men, than driven by an abstract ideal of patriotism.

Moreover, this change meant that factional fighting among political rivals could lead to full-blown civil war, if legions loyal to one general were pitted against those of another. And indeed, this happened in Marius's own lifetime. An aristocratic general named Lucius Cornelius Sulla had fought with distinction in the so-called Social War of 91–88 B.C.E.: a conflict between Rome and its Italian allies that resulted in the extension of Roman citizenship throughout the peninsula. Sulla seemed the likely person to lead Rome's army to war in Anatolia. Marius, however, forced the Senate to deny Sulla's claim. Sulla's response was to rally the five victorious legions that had just fought under his command and, with a Roman army at his back, to march onto Rome.

This was a disturbing move: strong taboos had long prevented any armed force from entering the city limits of Rome. But Sulla argued that his actions were in keeping with the *mos maiorum*, which Marius and the Senate had betrayed. When the Senate conceded and awarded him the coveted army command, Marius again defied the Senate and seized control of the city with his own legions. When Marius died soon afterward, a conservative backlash against his popular rule led the aristocracy to appoint Sulla to the office of dictator—but not for the traditional six months, as under the early republic. Sulla's term had no limits, and he used his powers to exterminate his opponents and pack the Senate with men loyal to himself while curtailing the authority of the peoples' tribunes. Then, after three years of autocratic rule, he retired to a life of luxury on his country estate.

## Caesar's Triumph—and His Downfall

The purpose and effect of Sulla's dictatorship was to empower the aristocracy and terminally weaken the power of the plebs. Soon, however, new leaders emerged to espouse the people's cause, once again using the army as their tool of influence. The most prominent of these were Gnaeus Pompeius Magnus (106–48 B.C.E.) and Gaius Julius Caesar (100–44 B.C.E.). Initially, they cooperated in a plot to gain control of the government and "restore the republic" by forming an alliance with a third general, Marcus Junius Crassus, the man credited with finally defeating Spartacus. This alliance was known as a *triumvirate (tri-UM-vir-et)*, meaning "rule of three men," but it soon dissolved into open rivalry. Pompey (as Pompeius is known in English) had won fame as the conqueror of Syria and Palestine, while Caesar devoted his energies to a series of campaigns in Gaul. It was under his authority that the territories encompassing modern France, Belgium, and western Germany were added to the Roman Empire, extending its northern border along the length of the Rhine.

Caesar himself advertised these conquests in a series of self-congratulatory dispatches published in book form—*On the War in Gaul*—which secured his reputation at home and cemented the loyalty of his army. These victories also put him in a strong political position. It had become accepted that the best general should be the leader of Rome, and the example of Sulla had made it possible for that leader to be a dictator for life, a king in all but name. But it was Pompey, not Caesar, who was actually in Rome and in a position to influence the Senate directly. Indeed, in the face of tremendous popular protest, and even some opposition from the aristocracy, Pompey had managed to get himself elected sole consul. Essentially, this meant that he could act as dictator. Using this authority, he declared that Caesar, who was still stationed in Gaul, was an enemy of the republic and that his ambition was to make himself king.

The result was a pervasive and deadly civil war. In 49 B.C.E., Caesar took up Pompey's challenge and crossed the Rubicon River, the northern boundary of Rome's Italian territories, thereby signaling his intention to take Rome by force. Pompey fled to the east in the hope of gathering an army large enough to confront Caesar's legions. Caesar pursued him and, in 48 B.C.E., the two Roman armies met at Pharsalus in Greece. Pompey was defeated and fled to Alexandria, where he was murdered by a Roman officer attached to the court of Ptolemy XIII (62/61–47? B.C.E.).

**BUST OF JULIUS CAESAR.** Caesar's nickname meant "hairy," but it has come to be synonymous with imperial rule. It was the title preferred by the German kings of the late nineteenth and twentieth centuries, who called themselves *kaisers*, and by the tsars of Russia. In classical Latin, the "C" sound is hard, which means that the pronunciations of *caesar*, *kaiser*, and *tsar* are very similar.

This young pharaoh, a descendant of Alexander's general Ptolemy, was then about fourteen years old and engaged in a civil war of his own—against his elder sister and co-ruler, Cleopatra VII (69–30 B.C.E.). He must have thought that he could curry favor with Caesar by encouraging the murder of Pompey; but instead, Caesar threw his support on the side of the twenty-one-year-old queen. The two must have become lovers soon after their first meeting, since their son Caesarion ("Little Caesar") was born just nine months later. After a brief struggle, Ptolemy was defeated and mysteriously drowned in the Nile. Cleopatra then took as consort her even younger brother, known as Ptolemy XIV, but she ruled as pharaoh of Egypt in her own right, much as Hatshepsut had done nearly a millennium and a half before (see Chapter 2).

After that, Caesar returned to Rome in triumph—literally. A *triumph* was a spectacular honor awarded to a victorious Roman general by the Senate and was the only occasion on which (unarmed) soldiers were legally allowed to parade in the streets of Rome. Triumphs had been celebrated since the earliest days of the republic, and they featured columns of prisoners and spoils of war, chained captives (often enemy kings) led in humiliation to their public executions, floats featuring live tableaux commemorating the achievements of the triumphant man, and thousands upon thousands of cheering Romans, who received extra rations of grain and gathered up coins thrown by the handful. Through it all, Caesar would have ridden in a chariot with a golden wreath held above his head while a slave stood behind him, murmuring in his ear the words *Memento mori* ("Remember: you will die"). A triumph was so glorious and—under the republic—so rarely granted that those thus honored might forget their own mortality.

Caesar may well have done so, since his power seemed absolute. In 46 B.C.E., he was named dictator for ten years; two years later, this was changed to a lifetime appointment. In addition, he assumed nearly every other title that could augment his power. He obtained from the Senate full authority to make war and peace and to control the revenues of the state. He even governed the reckoning of time, something that was regarded as controversial. In imitation of the Egyptian calendar (slightly modified by a Greek astronomer), he revised the Roman calendar to make a 365-day year with an extra day added every fourth year. This Julian calendar (as adjusted by Pope Gregory XIII in 1582) is still observed, and the seventh month is still named after Julius.

Caesar also took important steps toward eliminating the distinction between Italians and provincials within the empire by conferring citizenship on residents of Hispania (Spain) and the newly annexed provinces in Gaul. Moreover, by settling many of his army veterans and some of the

**CLEOPATRA VII AS EGYPTIAN PHARAOH AND HELLENISTIC RULER.** Like her ancestor Ptolemy I, Cleopatra represented herself as both enlightened Greek monarch and pharaoh. It was perhaps owing to her example that Julius Caesar was the first Roman leader to issue coins impressed with his own image. ■ *How does Cleopatra's self-representation compare to that of Hatshepsut (see page 44) or Ptolemy (see page 129)?*

urban poor in these lands, he relieved economic inequities and furthered colonization. Even more important was his farsighted resolve to focus efforts in northwestern Europe. Whereas Pompey, and before him Alexander, went east to gain fame and fortune, Caesar followed only the Phoenicians in recognizing the potential of the wild West. By incorporating Gaul into the Roman world, he brought in a much-needed source of food and natural resources and created a new outlet for the spread of Roman settlement and culture.

In the eyes of many contemporaries, however, Caesar's achievements were signs that he actually did intend to make himself king: a hateful thought to those who still cherished the *mos maiorum* and glorified the early days of the republic. Indeed, it was around a descendant of Lucretia's avenger, Lucius Junius Brutus, that a faction of the Senate crystallized into an assassination conspiracy. On the Ides of March in 44 B.C.E.—the midpoint of the month, according to his own calendar—Caesar was attacked on the floor of the Senate chamber and stabbed to death by a group of men. His body was later autopsied (the first forensic medical examination in recorded history) and was found that he had sustained twenty-three wounds.

**IDES OF MARCH COIN.** This coin celebrates the assassination of Julius Caesar by Marcus Junius Brutus, who is shown on the face; on the reverse, a cap of liberty (customarily worn by freed slaves) is flanked by two daggers, and below it is the legend *EID-MAR*, the Latin abbreviation for "Ides of March." ■ *Given that Caesar drew criticism for depicting himself on Roman coinage, what do you think is the significance of Brutus's image being shown in this way?*

## THE PRINCIPATE AND THE PAX ROMANA, 27 B.C.E.–180 C.E.

In his will, Caesar had adopted his grandnephew Gaius Octavius (or Octavian; 63 B.C.E.–14 C.E.), then a young man of eighteen serving in Illyria, across the Adriatic Sea. On learning of Caesar's death, Octavian hastened home to claim his inheritance and avenge his slain "father," whose name he took: he now called

**OCTAVIAN.** Caesar's adopted heir was later granted the title *augustus* ("worthy of honor") by the Senate and was also known as *princeps* ("first man"). He was worshiped as a god in Rome's provinces, and idealized statues like this one were erected in temples and public places throughout the empire.

himself Gaius Julius Caesar the Younger. He soon found that he had rivals among those supporters of Caesar who had not been implicated in the plot to kill him, most notably Marcus Antonius (Mark Antony; 83–30 B.C.E.), who had served under Caesar's command in Gaul and had ambition to make himself governor of that whole province.

Octavian engineered his own election to the office of consul (though he was far too young for this honor) and used his power to have Caesar's assassins declared outlaws. He then pursued Antony to Gaul, at the head of an army, where Antony's forces were overwhelmed. In 43 B.C.E., Antony and Octavian reconciled and formed an alliance, bringing in a third man, a senator named Marcus Aemilius Lepidus, to make up a second triumvirate. They then set about crushing the political faction responsible for Caesar's murder.

The methods they employed were brutal: prominent members of the opposition were hunted down and their property confiscated. The most notable of these victims was Cicero, who was murdered by Mark Antony's hired thugs. (This was a revenge killing, because Cicero had actively sought to undermine Antony and had branded him a public enemy.) Meanwhile, the masterminds behind Caesar's assassination—Marcus Junius Brutus and Gaius Cassius—left Rome and raised an army of legions from Greece and Anatolia. But they were defeated by the united forces of Antony and Octavian on a battlefield near the Macedonian town of Philippi (founded by Alexander's father, Philip II) in 42 B.C.E. There, both Brutus and Cassius committed suicide.

With their mutual enemies effectively destroyed, tensions mounted between Antony and Octavian, whose friendship had never been firm. Antony went to Egypt and made an alliance with Cleopatra, plotting to use the resources of her realm against Octavian. Octavian, meanwhile, reestablished himself in Rome, where he skillfully portrayed Antony as having been seduced and emasculated by his foreign lover. He reminded the people that the Egyptian queen's son, Caesarion, threatened his own position as Caesar's rightful heir.

For ten years, Antony played the king in Egypt, fathering three of Cleopatra's children and making big plans for annexing Rome's eastern provinces. Octavian, claiming that he had seen a copy Antony's will, alleged that Antony had transferred his allegiance to Egypt and was a traitor to Rome. This enabled Octavian to argue that a war with Cleopatra's Egypt was not a civil war with another Roman general.

In 31 B.C.E., Octavian's superior forces defeated those of Antony and Cleopatra in the naval battle of Actium, off the coast of Greece. Soon afterward, both Antony and Cleopatra committed suicide. Their children were taken back to Rome—Caesarion disappeared under suspicious circumstances—and although their lives were spared, they were paraded through the streets as captives. This marked the end of Egypt's long independence: Cleopatra had been its last pharaoh. After more than 3,000 years of self-rule, Egypt was now another province in Rome's empire.

## The Government of Augustus

The victory at Actium ushered in a new period of Roman history. Octavian, now "Gaius Julius Caesar the Younger," was the only claimant to power left standing. With no rivals left, he had no further need for political purges. For the first time in nearly a century, Rome was not embroiled in civil war.

## Antony and Cleopatra

*In his* Parallel Lives, *the Greek intellectual Plutarch (c. 46–120 C.E.) paired the biographies of famous Greeks with those of famous Romans, always to the disadvantage of the latter. For example, Julius Caesar suffers in comparison with Alexander the Great, as Romulus does when set up against Theseus. The following excerpt is from Plutarch's* Life of Mark Antony, *in which the Hellenistic ruler of Egypt, Cleopatra, plays a starring role.*

aesar and Pompey knew Cleopatra when she was still a girl, and ignorant of the world, but it was a different matter in the case of Antony, because she was ready to meet him when she had reached the time of life when women are most beautiful and have full understanding. So she prepared for him many gifts and money and adornment, of a magnitude appropriate to her great wealth and prosperous kingdom, but she put most of her hopes in her own magical arts and charms. . . . For (as they say), it was not because her beauty in itself was so striking that it stunned the onlooker, but the inescapable impression produced by daily contact with her: the attractiveness in the persuasiveness of her talk, and the character that surrounded her conversation was stimulating. It was a pleasure to hear the sound of her voice, and she tuned her tongue like a many-stringed instrument expertly to whatever language she chose, and only used interpreters to talk to a few

foreigners. . . . She is said to have learned the languages of many peoples, although her predecessors on the throne did not bother to learn Egyptian, and some had even forgotten how to speak the Macedonian dialect.

She took such a hold over Antony that, while his wife Fulvia was carrying on the war in Rome against Octavian on his behalf, and the Parthian army . . . was about to invade Syria, Antony was carried off by Cleopatra to Alexandria, and amused himself there with the pastimes of a boy . . . and whether Antony was in a serious or a playful mood she could always produce some new pleasure or charm, and she kept watch on him by night and day and never let him out of her sight. She played dice with him and hunted with him and watched him exercising with his weapons and she roamed around and wandered about with him at night when he stood at people's doors and windows and made fun of people inside, dressed in a slave-woman's outfit; for he also attempted to dress up like a slave. He returned from these expedi-

tions having been mocked in return, and often beaten, although most people suspected who he was. But the Alexandrians got pleasure from his irreverence . . . enjoying his humor and saying that he showed his tragic face to the Romans and his comic one to them.

Source: Plutarch, *Life of Marcus Antonius*, cc. 25–29, excerpted in *Women's Life in Greece and Rome: A Sourcebook in Translation*, eds. Mary R. Lefkowitz and Maureen B. Fant (Baltimore, MD: 1992), pp. 147–49.

### Questions for Analysis

1. How do Cleopatra's behavior and accomplishments, in Plutarch's description of her, compare with those of Roman women?

2. Given what you have learned about the values of the Roman Republic, how would a Roman reader respond to this description of Antony's behavior under the influence of the Egyptian queen? What do you think were Plutarch's motives in portraying him in this light?

---

But Rome was also no longer a republic. Even though Octavian maintained the fiction that he was governing as a mere citizen, his rule was entirely autocratic. For four years, he ruled as sole consul, and then adopted the titles of *imperator* ("victorious commander") and *augustus* ("worthy of honor"). Although these honorifics had been in use under the republic, they now became attached to the person of the sole ruler. So although Rome had been an empire for centuries, not until now did it have a single emperor. To avoid confusion, historians therefore refer to this phase of Rome's

history as the Principate, from the title Augustus himself preferred: *princeps*, "prince" or "first man."

Because Augustus was determined not to be regarded as a tyrant or (worse) a king, he left most of Rome's republican institutions in place—but he gradually emptied them of their power. In theory, the emperor served at the will of "the Senate and People of Rome" (*SPQR*). In practice, though, he controlled the army, which meant that he also controlled the city and its government. Fortunately, Augustus was an able ruler. He introduced a range of public services, including a police

# Competing Viewpoints

## Two Views of Augustus's Rule

> The emperor Augustus was a master propagandist with an unrivaled capacity for presenting his own actions in the best possible light. This list of his deeds below was written by Augustus himself and was displayed on two bronze pillars set up in the Roman forum. The second excerpt is by the senatorial historian Tacitus (c. 56–117 C.E.). Writing in the first decades of the second century C.E., he began his chronicle of imperial rule, Annals, with the death of Augustus a century earlier.

### Augustus Speaks for Himself

Below is a copy of the accomplishments of the deified Augustus by which he brought the whole world under the empire of the Roman people, and of the moneys expended by him on the state and the Roman people.

1. At the age of nineteen, on my own initiative and at my own expense, I raised an army by means of which I liberated the Republic, which was oppressed by the tyranny of a faction.

2. Those who assassinated my father I drove into exile, avenging their crime by due process of law.

3. I waged many wars throughout the whole world by land and by sea, both civil and foreign....

* * *

5. The dictatorship offered to me . . . by the people and by the Senate . . . I refused to accept.... The consulship, too, which was offered to me . . . as an annual office for life, I refused to accept.

6. [T]hough the Roman Senate and people together agreed that I should be elected sole guardian of the laws and morals with supreme authority, I refused to accept any office offered me which was contrary to the traditions of our ancestors.

7. I have been ranking senator for forty years.... I have been *pontifex maximus*, augur, member of the college of fifteen for performing sacrifices, member of the college of seven for conducting religious banquets, member of the Arval Brotherhood, one of the *Titii sodales*, and a *fetial* [all priestly offices].

* * *

9. The Senate decreed that vows for my health should be offered up every fifth year by the consuls and priests. . . . [T]he whole citizen body, with one accord, . . . prayed continuously for my health at all the shrines.

* * *

17. Four times I came to the assistance of the treasury with my own money . . . providing bonuses for soldiers who had completed twenty or more years of service.

* * *

20. I repaired the Capitol and the theater of Pompey with enormous expenditures on both works, without having my name inscribed on them. I repaired . . . the aqueducts which were falling into ruin in many places.... I repaired eighty-two temples.... I reconstructed the Flaminian Way....

* * *

34. [H]aving attained supreme power by universal consent, I transferred the state from my own power to the control of the Roman Senate and people.... After that time I excelled all in authority, but I possessed no more power than the

---

ended in a massacre of indigenous tribes and cost the lives of thousands of Britons. Another rebellion was violently quashed in Judea, the most restive of all the Roman provinces, leading to the destruction of the Temple at Jerusalem in 70 C.E. In 135 C.E., a second Jewish rebellion completed the destruction of the city. Although it was refounded by Hadrian as Aelia Capitolina, a colony for veterans of Rome's army, Jews were forbidden to settle there (see Chapter 6).

Such rebellions were not the norm, however. Although the Roman Empire had been achieved by conquest, it was not maintained by force. Instead, Rome controlled its territories by offering incentives for assimilation. Local

others who were my colleagues in each magistracy.

**35.** At the time I wrote this document I was in my seventy-sixth year.

Source: "Res Gestae Divi Augusti," in *Roman Civilization, Sourcebook II: The Empire,* eds. Naphtali Lewis and Meyer Reinhold (New York: 1966), pp. 9–19.

## The Historian Tacitus Evaluates Augustus's Reign

Intelligent people praised or criticized Augustus in varying terms. One opinion was as follows. Filial duty and a national emergency, in which there was no place for law-abiding conduct, had driven him to civil war—and this can be neither initiated nor maintained by decent methods. He had made many concessions to Antony and to Lepidus for the sake of vengeance on his father's murderers. When Lepidus grew old and lazy, and Antony's self-indulgence got the better of him, the only possible cure for the distracted country had been government by one man. However, Augustus had put the State in order not by making himself king or dictator but by creating the Principate. The empire's frontiers were on the ocean, or on distant rivers. Armies, provinces, fleets, the whole system was interrelated. Roman citizens were protected by the law. Provincials were decently treated. Rome itself had been lavishly beautified. Force had been sparingly used—merely to preserve peace for the majority.

The opposite view went like this. Filial duty and national crisis had been merely pretexts. In actual fact, the motive of Octavian, the future Augustus, was lust for power. Inspired by that, he had mobilized ex-army settlers by gifts of money, raised an army—while he was only a half-grown boy without any official status—won over a consul's brigade by bribery, pretended to support Sextus Pompeius [the son of Pompey], and by senatorial decree usurped the status and rank of a praetor. Soon both consuls . . . had met their deaths—by enemy action; or perhaps in the one case by the deliberate poisoning of his wound, and in the other at the hand of his own troops, instigated by Octavian. In any case, it was he who took over both their armies. Then he had forced the reluctant Senate to make him consul. But the forces given him to deal with Antony he used against the State. His judicial murders and land distributions were distasteful even to those who carried them out. True, Cassius and Brutus died because he had inherited a feud against them; nevertheless, personal enmities ought to be sacrificed to the public interest. Next he had cheated Sextus Pompeius by a spurious peace treaty, Lepidus by spurious friendship. Then Antony, enticed by treaties and his marriage with Octavian's sister, had paid the penalty of that delusive relationship with his life. After that, there had certainly been peace, but it was a bloodstained peace. . . . And gossip did not spare his personal affairs—how he had abducted [Livia] the wife of Tiberius Claudius Nero, and asked the priests the farcical question whether it was in order for her to marry while pregnant. Then there was the debauchery of his friend Publius Vedius Pollio. But Livia was a real catastrophe, to the nation, as a mother and to the house of the Caesars as a stepmother.

Source: Tacitus, *Annals* i.9–10. Based on *Tacitus: The Annals of Imperial Rome,* trans. Michael Grant (New York: 1989), pp. 37–39.

### Questions for Analysis

**1.** How does Augustus organize his list, and why? What does he leave out, and what does he choose to emphasize?

**2.** Tacitus presents two contrasting views of Augustus's motives. Which does he himself seem to believe? How does his account complement or undermine that of Augustus himself?

**3.** Could you write a new account of Augustus's life making use of both sources? How would you strike a balance between them? What would your own conclusion be?

elites were encouraged to adopt Roman modes of education, behavior, and dress in order to gain access to political office. Local gods became Roman gods and were adopted into the Roman pantheon of divinities.

Tens of thousands of army veterans settled in the provinces, marrying local women and putting down local roots. It was common for soldiers born in Syria or North Africa to end their days peacefully in northern Gaul or Pannonia (modern Hungary). In Camulodunum (now Colchester, England), the gravestone of a legionnaire called Longinus sketches a typical career: born in Serdica (modern Sofia, in Bulgaria) to a local man named Szdapezematygus, he rose through the ranks to become a sergeant of the First Thracian Cavalry under Claudius and one of the first Roman colonists of Britannia.

Rights of citizenship were also extended, and able provincials could rise far in the imperial government. Some, like the emperors Trajan and Hadrian—both raised in Hispania—came to control it. Even the outer fringes of the empire, areas not incorporated into provinces, need to be understood as part of Rome's orbit. Although historians speak of the empire's "borders" for the sake of convenience, these were permeable zones of intensive interaction. Roman influence reached far beyond these fluid frontiers, into the heartland of Germania and lands far to the east. By the middle of the third century C.E., when some frontier garrisons were withdrawn to take part in wars within the empire itself, many of these peoples moved into the empire's settled provinces and became aspiring Romans (see Chapter 6).

## Imperial Infrastructure and the Environment

Augustus liked to boast that he had found Rome a city of clay and left it a city of marble. It is certainly true that ambitious public works projects were initiated under the Principate; but in reality, marble was too precious to be used in common construction. Instead, marble panels or ornaments were added to the facings of buildings otherwise made of concrete. The Romans had discovered how to make this hard and reliable building material from a mixture of quicklime, volcanic ash, and pumice; and it was this—along with superior engineering skills—that allowed them to build massive structures such as the Colosseum, which could accommodate 50,000 spectators at gladiatorial combats.

Roman engineers also excelled in the building of roads and bridges, many of which were constructed by Rome's armies as they moved into new territories. Like the Persian Royal Road of the sixth century B.C.E. (or the German Autobahn of the 1930s and the interstate highways of the United States begun in the 1950s), roads have always been, first and foremost, a device for moving armies, and secondarily, for moving goods and people. Many of these Roman roads still survive or form the basis for modern European highways. In Britain, for example, the only major thoroughfares before the building of the high-speed motorways were Roman roads, to which the motorways now run parallel.

The inhabitants of Roman cities also enjoyed the benefits of a public water supply. By the early decades of the second century C.E., eleven aqueducts brought water into Rome from the nearby hills and provided the city with 300 million gallons per day—for drinking and bathing and for flushing a well-designed sewage system. These amenities were common in cities throughout the empire, and the homes of the wealthy even had indoor plumbing and central heating. Water was also funneled into the homes of the rich for private gardens, fountains, and pools. The emperor Nero built a famous Golden House with special pipes that sprinkled his guests with perfume, baths supplied with medicinal waters, and a pond "like a sea." In addition, a spherical ceiling in the banquet hall revolved day and night like the heavens. "At last," said Nero on moving day, "I can live like a human being."

Throughout the empire, new Roman cities were constructed on a similar model and boasted the same amenities: public baths and fountains, amphitheaters, and paved roads. But not all would have had ready access to the resources, especially the water, required to supply them. Depending on the local climate and landscape, the need to provide imperial subjects with these amenities led to vast projects: swamps were drained, forests felled, mountains leveled, and valleys filled in. In the process, Roman urban planners and engineers temporarily or permanently altered the environment (see **Interpreting Visual Evidence** on page 176).

## Imperial Entertainments

The cultural and intellectual developments that began in Rome during the late republic came to fruition during the Principate and are richly reflected in its literature. For the first time in its already long history, Latin began to replace Greek as a language of learning and poetry. Roman literature of this era is conventionally divided into two periods: the Golden Age of writings produced under the more or less direct

**FEMALE GLADIATORS.** Like men, enslaved women also fought as gladiators. This marble relief commemorates the freeing of two such fighters, "Amazon" and "Achillia," presumably as a reward for their successes in the arena.

influence of Augustus, and the Silver Age of the first and early second centuries C.E. Most Golden Age literature is, not surprisingly, propagandistic, the purpose of which was to advertise and justify Augustus's achievements. The poetry of Publius Virgilius Maro (Virgil; 70–19 B.C.E.) is typical, and we have already noted his strategic use of "prophecy" to link the reign of Augustus to the story of Aeneas (see page 148). Other major poets of this age were Quintus Horatius Flaccus (Horace; 65–8 B.C.E.) and Publius Ovidius Naso (Ovid; 43 B.C.E.–17 C.E.): the former, a master of the lovely, short lyric; and the latter, our major source for Greek mythology, which he retold in a long poem, *Metamorphoses* ("Transformations"). Ovid was also a satirist, and his frank advice to his readers on the best way to attract women at the race course and his own (probably fictional) strategy for conducting an adulterous affair with the wife of a senator are exemplary of the writings that resulted in his banishment.

After Augustus's death, Roman authors had more license and became incisive cultural critics. The tales of Petronius and Apuleius describe the more bizarre and sometimes sordid aspects of Roman life, and the satirist Juvenal (60?–140 C.E.) wrote with savage wit about the moral degeneracy he saw in his contemporaries. A similar attitude toward Roman society characterizes the writings of Tacitus (55?–117? C.E.), an aristocratic historian who describes the events and people of his age largely for the purpose of passing judgment on them. His *Annals* offer a subtle but devastating portrait of the political system constructed by Augustus and ruled by his heirs; his *Germania* contrasts the manly virtues of northern barbarians with the effeminate vices of decadent fellow Romans. Like Juvenal, Tacitus was a master of ironic wit. He has a barbarian chieftain say, referring to Rome's conquests, "They create a wilderness and call it peace."

To many people today, the most repellent—or most fascinating and familiar—aspect of Roman culture during the Principate was its spectacular cruelty, exhibited (literally) in the public arenas erected in every Roman town. Gladiatorial contests were not new, but they were now presented in amphitheaters built to hold thousands. Everyone, even emperors, attended these events, and they became

**THE COLOSSEUM.** Constructed between 75 and 80 C.E., this was the first amphitheater in Rome purposely built to showcase gladiatorial combats. Prior to this, gladiators would often fight in improvised arenas in the Forum or other public places. ▪ *How does the fact of the Colosseum's relatively late construction change your perception of Roman history?*

## The Architecture of Roman Water Management

*The following excerpt comes from a remarkable handbook authored by Marcus Vitruvius Pollio (c. 75–c.14 B.C.E.), a Roman architect and civil engineer. In* On Architecture, *Vitruvius offered a practical guide to all aspects of construction, from the choice of building site, to design, to contracting, to decoration. He described the proper way to plan a city and lay out its streets, the proper acoustics for a theater, and the best type of central heating for a house. In this section, Vitruvius tackles one of the most vital and difficult aspects of urban planning: the supply and distribution of water.*

here are three methods of conducting water: in channels through masonry conduits, or in lead pipes, or in pipes of baked clay. If using conduits, the masonry should be as solid as possible and the bed of the channel should have a gradient of not less than a quarter of an inch for every hundred feet; and the masonry structure should be arched over, so that the sun may not strike the water at all.

When the water has reached the city, build a reservoir with a distribution tank with three compartments to receive the water. . . . From this first compartment, pipes will be laid to all the basins and fountains in the city; from the second, to public baths which yield an annual income to the state; and from the third, to private houses, so that water for public use will not run short. For people will be unable to divert water illegally if they have only their own supplies from headquarters. This is the reason why I have made these divisions, and also in order that individuals who take water into their houses may by their taxes help to maintain the conducting of the water by the contractors.

If, however, there are hills between the city and the source of supply, subterranean channels must be dug, and brought to a level at the gradient mentioned above. If the bed is of tufa or other stone, let the channel be cut in it; but if it is of earth or sand, there must be vaulted masonry walls for the channel, and the water should thus be conducted, with shafts built at every two hundred and forty feet.

But if the water is to be conducted in lead pipes, first build a reservoir at the source; then, let the pipes have an interior area corresponding to the amount of water, and lay these pipes from this reservoir to the reservoir which is inside the city walls. . . . If there is a regular fall from the source to the city, without any intervening hills that are high enough to interrupt it, but with depressions in it, then we must build substructures to bring it up to the level as in the case of channels and conduits. If the distance round such depressions is not great, the water may be carried round circuitously; but if the valleys are extensive, the course will be directed down their slope. On reaching the bottom, a low substructure is built so that the water level there may continue as long as possible. It is also effective to build reservoirs at intervals of 24,000 feet, so that if a break occurs anywhere, it will not completely ruin the whole work, and the place where it has occurred can easily be found. . . .

But if we wish to spend less money, we must proceed as follows. Clay pipes with a skin at least two digits thick should be made, but these pipes should be tongued at one end so that they can fit into and join one another. . . . Clay pipes for conducting water have the following advantages. In the first place, if anything happens to them, anybody can repair the damage. Secondly, water from clay pipes is much more wholesome than that which is conducted through lead pipes, because lead is found to be harmful for the reason that white lead is derived from it, and this is said to be hurtful to the human system. . . . Hence, water ought by no means to be conducted in lead pipes, if we want to have it wholesome. That the taste is better when it comes from clay pipes may be proved by everyday life, for though our tables are loaded with silver vessels, yet everybody uses earthenware for the sake of purity of taste.

Source: Adapted from Vitruvius, *Ten Books on Architecture*, trans. M. H. Morgan (Cambridge, MA, 1916), pp. 244–47.

### Questions for Analysis

1. Why does Vitruvius advise urban planners to distribute water in three separate ways? What does he reveal about the demand for water in a Roman city, and the tensions among different segments of the population? How do these revelations illuminate our understanding of Roman society?

2. Roman water management took an enormous toll on the environment. From your reading of Vitruvius, how do you think the construction of reservoirs and aqueducts affected the landscape? What might have been the unintended consequences of these engineering projects?

increasingly bloody and brutal as people demanded more and more innovative violence. Individual gladiators fought to the death with swords or the exotic weapons of their homelands. Teams of gladiators fought pitched battles, often reenacting historic Roman victories. Occasionally, a wealthy entrepreneur would fill an arena with water to stage a naval battle. Hundreds of men and women would die in these organized slaughters. On other occasions, hundreds of half-starved animals imported from Africa, India, or the forests of Germania would tear each other (or human victims) apart. When a fighter went down with a disabling wound, the crowd would be asked to decide whether to spare his life or kill him. If the arena floor became too slippery with blood, the action would stop—but only so that a fresh layer of sand could be spread over the gore so that the performance could continue.

## Roman Visual Arts

Like Latin literature, Roman art assumed a distinctive character during the Principate. Before this time, most artworks displayed in Roman homes and public places were imported from Hellenistic capitals. Conquering armies also brought back wagonloads of statues, reliefs, and marble columns as plunder from Greece, Egypt, and western Asia. These

**A ROMAN FLOOR MOSAIC.** This fine mosaic from the Roman city of Londinium (London) shows Bacchus (Dionysus), the god of wine and revelry, mounted on a tiger. Tigers, native to India, were prized by animal collectors and were also imported for gladiatorial shows.

**ROMAN AQUEDUCT IN SOUTHERN GAUL (PROVENCE).** The massive arches shown here were originally part of a thirty-one-mile-long complex that supplied water to the city of Nemausus (Nîmes). It is now known as the Pont du Gard (Bridge of the Gardon), reflecting the use to which it was put after the aqueduct ceased to function, some eight centuries after its construction in the first century C.E. Some Roman aqueducts remained operational into the modern era: the one at Segovia, Spain, was still in use at the end of the twentieth century. ■ *What does the magnitude and longevity of such projects tell us about Roman power and technology?*

## Roman Urban Planning

**P**rior to Roman imperial expansion, most cities in the ancient world were not planned cities—with the exception of the new settlements established by Alexander the Great; notably, Alexandria in Egypt. Rome itself was not carefully planned but grew up over many centuries, expanding outward and up the slopes of its seven hills from the nucleus of the Forum. By the time of Augustus, it was a haphazard jumble of buildings and narrow streets. Outside of Rome, however, the efficiency of Roman government was in large part due to the uniformity of imperial urban planning. As their colonial reach expanded, the Romans sought to ensure that travelers moving within their vast domain would encounter the same amenities in every major city. They also wanted to convey, through the organization of urban landscape, the ubiquity of Roman authority and majesty.

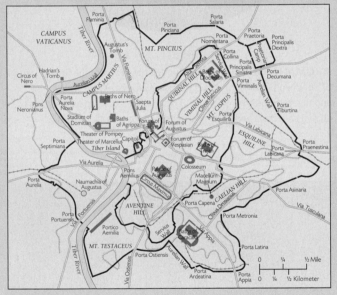

A. Imperial Rome

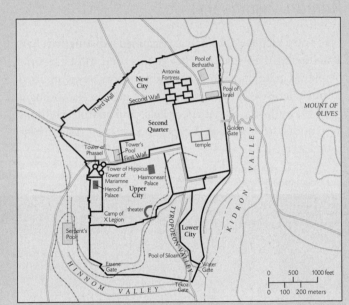

B. Roman settlement in Aelia Capitolina (Jerusalem) after 135 C.E.

became the property of the wealthy, and as the demand for such works increased, hundreds of copies were made by Roman artisans. In many cases, these copies proved more durable than their originals. (In Chapter 4, we were able to examine the lost Aphrodite of Knidos, courtesy of Roman sculptors.)

Encouraged by the patronage of Augustus and his successors, artists began to experiment with more distinctively Roman styles and subjects. The relief sculpture of this period is particularly notable for its delicacy and naturalism, and sculptors also became adept at portraiture. On their coins, emperors were portrayed very much as they looked in real life; and since the matrices for coins were recut annually, we can trace on successive issues a ruler's receding hairline or his advancing double chin.

Painting and mosaic, however, were the Romans' most original and intimate arts. Romans loved intense colors, and those who could afford it surrounded themselves with brilliant wall paintings and mosaics made of tiny fragments of glass and stone, which were often set into the floors of houses and public baths or formed the centerpieces of gardens. Lavish mosaics have been found in the remains of Roman villas in all the territories of the empire, and similar design features indicate that many were mosaic "kits" that could be ordered from a manufacturer, who would ship out all the necessary components along with a team of workmen to assemble them.

## Questions for Analysis

**1.** Look closely at the map of Rome (map A). How did topographical features—such as the river Tiber and the seven hills—determine the shape and layout of the city? What are the major buildings and public areas? What were the functions of these spaces? What do they reveal about Roman society and values?

**2.** Compare the plan of Rome with those of Roman London (map C) and Roman Jerusalem (map B). Which features do all three have in common, and why? Which features are unique to each place? What might these unique features reveal about the different regions of the empire and the needs of the different cities' inhabitants?

**3.** Given that all Roman cities share certain features, what message(s) were Roman authorities trying to convey to inhabitants and travelers through urban planning? Why, for example, would they have insisted on rebuilding Jerusalem as a Roman city after the rebellion of 135 C.E.?

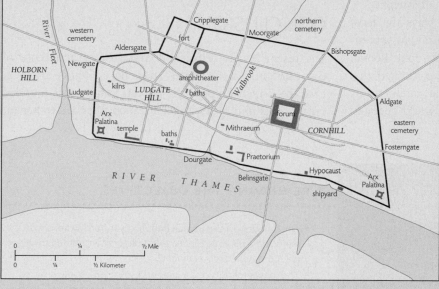

C. London under the Romans, c. 200 C.E.

## The Reach of Roman Law

As impressive and ingenious as Roman architecture and engineering are, the most durable and useful of this civilization's legacies is its system of law. Over the course of several centuries, the primitive legal code of the Twelve Tables was largely replaced by a series of new precedents and principles. These reflect the changing political climate of Rome and the needs of its diverse and ever-growing population. They also reveal the influence of new philosophies, especially Stoicism; the decisions of specific judges; and the edicts of magistrates called *praetors*, who had the authority to define and interpret law in particular cases and issue instructions to judges.

The most sweeping legal changes occurred during the Principate. This was partly because the reach of Roman law had to match the reach of the empire, which now extended over a much wider field of jurisdiction. But the major reason for the rapid development of Roman legal thinking during these years was the fact that Augustus and his successors appointed a small number of eminent jurists to deliver opinions on the issues raised by cases under trial in the courts. The five most prominent of these jurists flourished in the second century C.E.: Gaius (only this most common of his names is known), Domitius Ulpianus (Ulpian), Modestinus, Aemelianus Papinianus (Papinian), and Paulus. Although most of them came to hold high offices, they gained their reputations primarily as lawyers and commentators. Taken together, their legal opinions constitute the first philosophy of law and the foundation for all subsequent jurisprudence, a word derived from the Latin phrase meaning "legal wisdom."

As developed by the jurists, Roman law comprised three great branches or divisions: civil law, the law of nations, and natural law. Civil law was the law of Rome and its citizens, both written and unwritten. It included the statutes of the Senate, the decrees of the emperor, the edicts of magistrates, and ancient customs that had the force of law (such as the *mos maiorum*). The law of nations was not specific to Rome but extended to all people of the world regardless of their origins and ethnicity. It was the precursor of international law. This law authorized and regulated slavery; protected private ownership of property; and defined the mechanisms of purchase and sale, partnership, and contract. It was not superior to civil law but supplemented it. It applied especially to those inhabitants of the empire who were not citizens, as well as to all foreigners.

The most interesting—and in many ways the most important—branch of Roman law was natural law, a product not of judicial practice but of legal philosophy. Roman Stoics, following in the footsteps of Cicero, posited that nature itself is rationally ordered and that careful study will reveal the laws by which the natural world operates, including the nature of justice. They affirmed that all men are by nature equal and entitled to certain basic rights that governments have no authority to transgress. "True law," Cicero had said, "is right reason consonant with nature, diffused among all men, constant, eternal." Accordingly, no person or institution has the authority to infringe on this law, repeal it, or ignore it. This law supersedes any state or ruler, and a ruler who transgresses it is a tyrant.

Although jurists did not regard the philosophical concept of natural law as an automatic limitation on the workings of civil law, they did uphold it as an ideal. The practical law applied in local Roman courts often bore little resemblance to the law of nature, yet the development of the concept of abstract justice as a fundamental principle was one of the noblest achievements of Roman civilization. It gave us the doctrine of human rights—even if it did not end abuses of those rights.

## CONCLUSION

The resemblances between Rome's history and those of Great Britain and the United States have often been noted. Like the British Empire, the Roman Empire was founded on conquest and overseas colonization intended to benefit

## After You Read This Chapter

 Go to **INQUIZITIVE** to see what you've learned—and learn what you've missed—with personalized feedback along the way.

### REVIEWING THE OBJECTIVES

- The founding of the Roman Republic was both a cherished myth and a series of events. What factors contributed to this unique system of government?
- The shared identity and values of the Roman people differed in many ways from those of other ancient civilizations. What were some of these major differences?
- Rome's population was divided among classes of people who often struggled with each other for power. Identify these classes and their points of contention.
- The expansion of Rome's empire had a profound impact on Roman society. Why?
- The establishment of the Principate ushered in a new era in the history of Rome. What events led to this change?

both the homeland and its colonial subjects, who were seen as beneficiaries of the metropolis's "civilizing mission." Like America's economy, the Roman economy evolved from agrarianism to a complex system of domestic and foreign markets, leading to problems of unemployment, gross disparities of wealth, and vulnerability to financial crisis. And like both the British and the American empires, the Roman Empire justified itself by celebrating the peace its conquests allegedly brought to the world.

Ultimately, however, such parallels break down when we remember that Roman civilization differed profoundly from any society of the modern world. It was not an industrialized society. Its government never pretended to be representative of all its citizens. Roman class divisions are not directly comparable with ours. The Roman economy rested on slavery to a degree unmatched in any modern state. As a result, technological advances were not encouraged, social stratification was extreme, and gender relations were profoundly unequal. Religious practice and political life were inseparable.

Nevertheless, the civilization of ancient Rome continues to structure our everyday lives in ways so profound that they can go unnoticed. Our days are mapped onto the Roman calendar. The Constitution of the United States is largely modeled on that of the republic, and Roman architecture survives in the design of our public buildings. Roman law forms the basis of most European legal codes, and American judges still cite Gaius and Ulpian. Virtually all modern commemorative sculpture is inspired by Roman sculpture, and Roman authors continue to set the standards for prose composition in many Western countries. Indeed, most European languages are either derived from Latin (Romance languages are so called because they are "Roman-like") or have borrowed Latin grammatical structures or vocabulary (German, for example). As we shall see in the following chapters, the organization of the Roman Catholic Church can be traced back to the structure of the Roman state. Even today, the pope bears the title of Rome's high priest, *pontifex maximus*.

Perhaps the most significant of all Rome's contributions was its role as mediator between Europe and the civilizations of the ancient Mediterranean world and western Asia. Had Rome's empire not come to encompass much of Europe, there would be no such thing as the concept of Western civilization and no shared ideas and heritage to link us to those distant places and times. Although we will pursue the history of Rome's fragmentation and witness the emergence of three different civilizations in the territories once united by its empire, we will see that they all shared a common cultural inheritance. In that sense, the Roman Empire did not collapse but was transformed, and the factors driving that transformation will be the subject of Chapter 6.

## PEOPLE, IDEAS, AND EVENTS IN CONTEXT

- In what ways were the early Romans influenced by their **ETRUSCAN** neighbors and by their location in central Italy?
- What were the components of the **ROMAN REPUBLIC**'s constitution? What was the relationship between **ROMAN CITIZENSHIP** and the **ROMAN ARMY** in this era?
- How do the stories of **AENEAS, LUCRETIA**, and **CINCINNATUS** reflect core Roman values? How did those values, summarized in the phrase *MOS MAIORUM*, set the Romans apart from the other civilizations we have studied?
- Why did the Romans come into conflict with **CARTHAGE**? How did the **PUNIC WARS** and Rome's other conquests change the balance of power in the Mediterranean?
- How did imperialism and contact with **HELLENISTIC CULTURE** affect the core values of Roman society, its economy, and its political system? What role did **SLAVERY** play in this civilization?
- What were the major crises of the late republic? What were the means by which ambitious men gained power? How did **JULIUS CAESAR** emerge triumphant, and why was he assassinated?
- In what ways did the **PRINCIPATE** differ from the **ROMAN REPUBLIC**? What were the new powers of the **EMPEROR**, and how did **AUGUSTUS** use these powers?
- How did the Romans consolidate their **EMPIRE** during the **PAX ROMANA**? By what means did they spread Roman culture?

## THINKING ABOUT CONNECTIONS

- Polybius believed that the Roman Republic would last forever, because it fused together aspects of monarchy, aristocracy, and polity. What were the chief factors that led to its demise in the first century B.C.E.? Could these have been avoided? If so, how?
- In what ways does the Roman Empire share the characteristics of earlier empires, especially that of Alexander? In what ways does it differ from them?
- The Roman Empire could be said to resemble our own civilization in different ways. What features does the United States share with the republic today? With the Principate? What lessons can we draw from this resemblance?

CONSTANTINVS MAIOR IMPERATOR
HERACLII ET TIBERII IMPERATOR

PRIVILEGIA C

AR
COP
VS

## STORY LINES

- In a little over three centuries, Christianity grew from obscure beginnings in a small Roman province to become the official religion of the empire.

- Meanwhile, the Roman Empire was becoming too large and diverse to be governed by a single, centralized authority. Significant political, military, and economic changes occurred during the third century in response to these challenges.

- In the fourth century, the founding of a new capital at Constantinople shifted the focus of imperial administration to the eastern territories of the Roman Empire, while mass migrations of frontier peoples created new settlements within the western half of the empire.

- Christianity's eventual association with political power changed the religion in profound ways. At the same time, Christian intellectuals adapted Rome's traditional culture to meet Christian needs.

## CHRONOLOGY

| | |
|---|---|
| c. 4 B.C.E.– c. 30 C.E. | Lifetime of Jesus |
| 46–67 C.E. | Paul's missionary career |
| 66–70 C.E. | Jewish rebellion |
| 132–135 | Expulsion of Jews from Jerusalem |
| 203 | Death of Perpetua at Carthage |
| 235–284 | Rule of the "barracks emperors" |
| 284–305 | Diocletian divides the empire |
| 312 | Constantine's victory at the Milvian Bridge |
| 313 | Edict of Milan |
| 325 | Council of Nicea convened |
| c. 370–430 | Careers of Jerome, Ambrose, and Augustine |
| c. 376 | Frontier migrations begin |
| 391 | Pagan religion outlawed |
| 410 | Visigoths sack Rome |
| 476 | Odovacar deposes Romulus Augustulus |
| 493–526 | Rule of Theodoric the Ostrogoth |
| c. 500–583 | Careers of Boethius, Benedict, and Cassiodorus |

# The Transformation of Rome

## CORE OBJECTIVES

- **IDENTIFY** the historical factors that shaped early Christianity.

- **DESCRIBE** the pressures on Roman imperial administration during the third century.

- **TRACE** the ways that Christianity changed after it became a legal religion.

- **EXPLAIN** how barbarian migrations affected the empire.

- **UNDERSTAND** the difference between traditional Roman and Christian worldviews.

n the year 203 C.E., a young woman, Vivia Perpetua, was brought before the Roman governor at Carthage. She was twenty-two years old, well educated, and from a respectable family. At the time of her arrest she had an infant child she was still nursing. She also had two brothers (one of whom was arrested with her) and a father who doted on her. She must have had a husband, one presumes, but he is conspicuously absent from the firsthand account of her experiences. Perpetua herself says nothing about him, though she says a great deal about her father's grief and the efforts he made to intercede on her behalf. Not only did he beg the judge for mercy, he begged his daughter to confess so that her life could be spared. He admitted to having loved her more than her brothers and blamed himself for the liberal education he had given her. Clearly, he had failed as a father, for a Roman *paterfamilias* should never suffer humiliation through a daughter's conduct; he should kill her with his own hands if she has disgraced the family. For Perpetua's crime was terrible: it was not only treason against the Roman state but also an act of gross impiety toward her father, her family, and her ancestors. Worse, it was punishable by a death so debasing that it was reserved for slaves, barbarian prisoners, and hardened criminals. It was inconceivable that a respectable Roman matron would be stripped naked before a holiday crowd and mauled by wild beasts in the arena of her own city. But that was the death Perpetua died. Perpetua was a Christian.

Early Christianity posed a challenge to the Roman Empire and its core values at almost every level, a challenge exemplified by Vivia Perpetua. To be a Christian was to be, by definition, an enemy of Rome, because Christians refused to venerate the emperor as the embodiment of Rome's gods; denying his association with divinity meant denying his authority. Moreover, the Christ whom Christians worshiped had himself been declared a criminal, a political insurgent, and had been duly tried and put to death by the Roman state. Also disturbing was the way Christians flouted the conventions of Roman society. Perpetua was young, yet she disobeyed her father and ancestors. She was well born, yet she chose to endure the filth of a common jail. She was a woman, yet she denied the authority of men and renounced her femininity, dying in the dust like a gladiator. If this was what it meant to be a Christian, then being a Christian was incompatible with being a Roman.

How, then, did a Roman emperor become a Christian just a few centuries after Christ's death—and just a century or so after Perpetua's? What changes did both Rome and Christianity have to undergo for this to happen? And what other forces were at work, within the empire and beyond its borders, that helped bring this about?

The Rome in which Perpetua was raised stretched from central Asia to the British Isles, from the Rhine to her own province of North Africa. But as we shall see, the governance of this enormous state and its diverse population was straining the bureaucracy that had been built on the foundations of the old republic. By the end of the third century C.E., it was increasingly obvious that Rome's western and eastern provinces could not be controlled by a single centralized authority. During the fourth century, Rome itself ceased to be the capital and hub of the empire; it now shared its prestige with the new city of Constantinople, named by the Christian emperor who founded it. At the same time, Rome's settled provinces were coming under increased pressure from groups of people who had long lived along its borders but were now moving from the periphery to the center. These peoples would challenge what it meant to be Roman and contribute to the transformation of the Roman world.

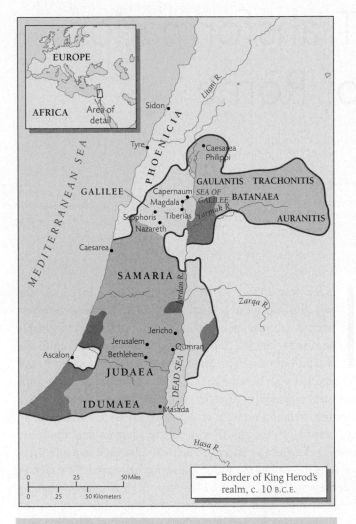

**JUDEA AND GALILEE IN THE TIME OF JESUS.** Judea was a Roman colony and Galilee was a province ruled by a client king, Herod, loyal to Rome. ▪ *What were the major cities in first-century C.E. Judea?* ▪ *What do they indicate about the effects of Roman occupation on the lives of Jews?* ▪ *Given what you have learned about their history, why do you think some Jews would resist Roman rule?*

## THE CHALLENGE OF CHRISTIANITY

Like the Hebrew monotheism that undergirds Judaism or the central tenets of Zoroastrianism (see Chapter 2), Christianity was—and is—the product of historical processes. It began with the teachings of Jesus, who lived and worked among his fellow Jews in rural Judea and his native Galilee around the year 30 C.E. It took root, however, in the Hellenistic world we studied in Chapter 4: the cosmopolitan, Greek-speaking cities around the eastern Mediterranean, which had now been absorbed into the Roman Empire.

### The Career of Jesus

Yeshua bar Yosef (Joshua, son of Joseph), known to the Greeks as Jesus, is one of the few figures of the ancient world—certainly one of the few commoners—about whose life we know a great deal. The earliest writings that mention Jesus specifically are the letters of his follower Paul of Tarsus, a Hellenized Jew who was active during the 50s and 60s C.E. (see below). There are also many different narratives of Jesus's life and teachings, most written between c. 70 and 100 C.E. Eventually, four such accounts were included in the "New Testament," a collection of Christian scriptures appended to the Greek text of the Hebrew Bible, which Christians call the "Old Testament." In their original Greek, these accounts were called *evangelia* ("good messages"); we know them as *Gospels*, an Old English word that means the same thing.

Jesus was born around the year 4 B.C.E. (He was not born precisely in the first year of the Common Era as we now reckon it, because when a Christian monk called Dionysius Exiguus first began to reckon time "in the year of Our Lord," or *Anno Domini*, during the sixth century, he made some mistakes.) When Jesus was around thirty years old, he was endorsed by a Jewish preacher of moral reform, John the Baptist, whom some considered to be a prophet. Thereafter, Jesus traveled widely around the rural areas of Galilee (his home province) and Judea, preaching and displaying unusual healing powers. He accumulated a number of disciples, some of whom had political ambitions.

Around the year 30 C.E., Jesus staged an entry into Jerusalem during Passover, a major religious holiday that brought large crowds to the city. This move was interpreted as a bid for political power by the Roman colonial government and the high-ranking Jews of the Temple. Three of the Gospel accounts state that Jesus also drew attention to himself by attacking merchants and moneychangers associated with the Temple. The city's religious leaders therefore arrested him and turned him over to the Roman governor, Pontius Pilatus (Pilate), for sentencing.

Pilate's main concern was to preserve peace during a volatile religious festival. He knew that his authority depended on maintaining good relations with local Jewish elites and with Herod Antipas, who ruled the province of Galilee as a client king of the empire. Because Jesus was a resident of Galilee, not a citizen of Roman Judea, Pilate sent Jesus to Herod for sentencing. But Herod promptly sent him back, indicating that dealing with Jesus fell under Roman jurisdiction. Pilate was thus in a tough position. It had been rumored that Jesus planned to lead a rebellion, and something similar had happened in the second century B.C.E., when a group of Jews had overthrown the rule of the Persian Seleucid empire and established Judea as an autonomous kingdom. Judea had come under Roman control only in 63 B.C.E., and many Jews resented Roman subjugation.

Pilate, who would have been mindful of all this, chose to make an example of Jesus and condemned him to death by crucifixion, which was the standard criminal penalty for non-Romans found guilty of sedition against Rome. Jesus's execution might have been the end of the story if not for his followers, who asserted that he had risen from the dead before being taken up into heaven. Moreover, they said that Jesus had promised to return again at the end of time.

## Interpreting the Life and Death of Jesus

In 1947, an extraordinary cache of ancient parchment and papyrus scrolls was discovered in a cave near Qumran, on the shores of the Dead Sea. Over the course of the next decade, eleven more caves were found to house similar texts. Only since the mid-1980s, however, have these Dead Sea Scrolls been widely available to scholars. Written in Hebrew, Greek, and Aramaic, at various times between 100 B.C.E. and 70 C.E., they have revolutionized our understanding of Judaism in the lifetime of Jesus: a period known as "Second Temple" Judaism, in reference to the Jewish traditions and culture that had emerged after the reconstruction of the Temple at Jerusalem in the sixth century B.C.E. (see Chapter 2). What these documents show is the diversity of religious practice and the competition among groups of Jews during this period.

When Jesus was born, Roman rule in Palestine was relatively new and still controversial, as we noted above. Many Jews were content to live under Rome's protection—especially the urban elite, who had been Hellenized for generations and reaped the rewards of participation in the Roman economy and administration. But many rural communities and the urban poor were rebellious, disadvantaged by Roman rule, and hoped for a *messiah*: a divinely inspired leader who would establish a new, autonomous Jewish kingdom. The most extreme were the Zealots, who eventually led two armed revolts against Roman rule. The first, between 66 and 70 C.E. (a generation after Jesus's death), ended in the Romans' destruction of the Temple. The second, in 132–135 C.E., caused the destruction of Jerusalem itself: the Romans expelled the entire Jewish population and razed the city to the ground. On its ruins, they built the colony of Aelia Capitolina (see Chapter 5).

This historical framework is essential to understanding the very different ways that the words and actions of Jesus were interpreted during his lifetime and after his death—especially since all the accounts of his life were written down after the destruction of the Temple in 70 C.E. and further influenced by later events.

In addition to the social and political unrest within the Jewish community at this time, there were significant religious divisions. The Temple priesthood was hereditary and controlled by a group known as the Sadducees. These elites collaborated closely with Rome (the high priest was

**SPOILS FROM JERUSALEM.** A bas-relief inside the triumphal Arch of Titus in the Roman Forum shows plundered treasures of the Temple at Jerusalem, including the menorah, being carried through Rome in triumph after the quashing of a Jewish rebellion in 70 C.E. ▪ *What message(s) did this image convey to viewers?*

even appointed by the Senate), and as a result of their overt political agenda, many Jews regarded them with suspicion. Their chief rivals were the Pharisees, preachers of religious doctrine who considered themselves heirs of the prophetic tradition of the ancient Hebrews. While the Sadducees claimed the right to control the interpretation of the Torah, the five books attributed to Moses, the Pharisees argued that Yahweh had given Moses an oral Torah as well as a written one, and that this oral traditon, handed down to them, taught how the laws of the Torah should be applied in daily life.

The Pharisees, accordingly, were quite flexible in their interpretation of religious law. For example, in order to allow neighbors to dine together on the Sabbath, when Jews were forbidden to work and could not even carry food outside their homes, the Pharisees ruled that an entire neighborhood could constitute a single household. They also believed in a life after death, a day of judgment, and the damnation or reward of individual souls. They actively sought out converts through preaching and looked forward to the imminent arrival of the promised messiah. The Sadducees, who had a vested interest in maintaining their privileged political status, interpreted the Torah more strictly and considered Judaism closed to anyone who had not been born a Jew.

Countering both of these dominant groups were the Essenes, a quasi-monastic faction that sought salvation through repentance, asceticism, and separation from their fellow Jews. Although some scholars see Essene influence behind the career of Jesus, his Jewish contemporaries probably saw Jesus as some sort of Pharisee: Jesus's emphasis on the ethical requirements of the law rather than its literal interpretation is reflected in many of his teachings. His apparent belief in life after death and the imminent coming of the "kingdom of God" also fits within a Pharisaic framework, as does his willingness to reach out to people beyond the Jewish community.

But Jesus seems to have carried these principles considerably further than did the Pharisees. For most ordinary Jews, religious observance consisted of going up to the Temple on holy days; paying the annual Temple tax; reciting the morning and evening prayers; and observing certain fundamental laws, such as circumcision (for men), ritual purity (especially for women), and prohibitions on the consumption of certain foods. Jesus deemphasized such observances, and it may have seemed that he wished to abolish them. But what made him most controversial was his followers' claim that he was the messiah sent to deliver Israel from its enemies.

After his death, these claims grew more assertive, yet they never persuaded more than a small minority of Jews. But

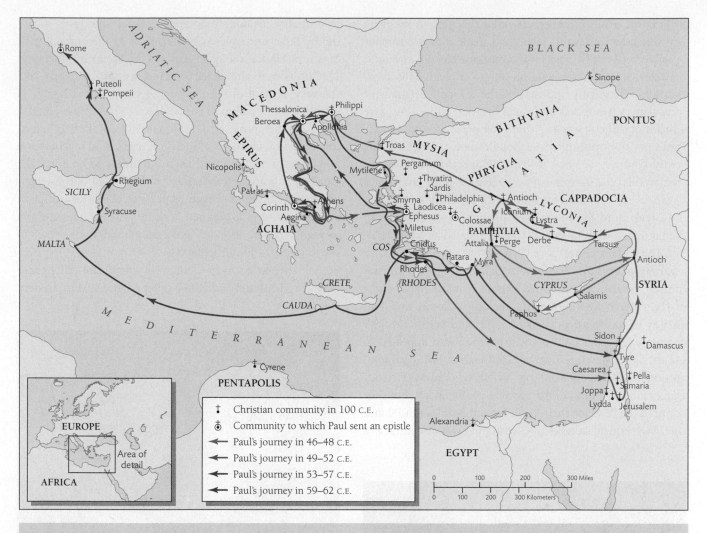

**PAUL'S MISSIONARY JOURNEYS.** Quite apart from its theological importance, Paul's career offers fascinating glimpses into the life of a Hellenized Roman citizen from one of the empire's eastern provinces. ▪ *What were the main phases of Paul's travels in the eastern Mediterranean?* ▪ *How were his itineraries shaped by geography and by various modes of transport?* ▪ *What conclusions about his mission can you draw from the extent of his travels and his major destinations?*

when his followers began to preach to non-Jewish audiences, they found many willing listeners. So they began to represent Jesus in terms that made sense to the Greek-speaking communities of the Hellenistic world, preaching that Jesus was not merely a messiah for the Jews but was the *Christos* ("anointed one" in Greek), the divine son of God who had suffered and died for the sins of all humanity. He had conquered death itself by rising from his tomb and, after appearing to his followers several times, ascended into heaven. He would soon return to judge all the world's inhabitants, and those who believed in him would be given eternal life.

## Christianity in the Hellenistic World

This new understanding of Jesus's divinity was largely developed by his younger contemporary, Paul of Tarsus

(c. 10–c. 67 C.E.). Born in the capital city of the Roman province of Cilicia (now south-central Turkey) to a family of Pharisees, he was given the name Saul. The Acts of the Apostles, the continuation of Luke's Gospel and a major source for Saul's early life, records that he was dedicated to stamping out the cult of the crucified Jesus. But at some point in his mid-twenties—a few years after Jesus's death—he underwent a dramatic conversion experience. He changed his name to Paul and devoted the rest of his life to spreading the new faith to Greek-speaking, mainly non-Jewish, communities.

Unlike Peter and some other early apostles (from the Greek word meaning "one who is sent forth"), Paul had never met Jesus. Instead, he claimed to have received a direct revelation of Jesus's teachings. This led to a number of major disputes, because Peter and his companions believed that followers of Jesus had to be Jews or converts to Judaism. Paul, however, declared that Jewish religious law was now irrelevant; Jesus had made a new covenant possible between God and humanity, and the old covenant between God and the Jews no longer applied. This position was vehemently opposed by the Jewish Christians of Jerusalem, a group led by Jesus's brother, James. But after a series of difficult debates that took place around 49 C.E., Paul's position triumphed. Although some early Christians would continue to obey Jewish law, most of the converts who swelled the movement were Gentiles (non-Jews). Paul began to call this new community of believers an *ekklesia*, the Greek word for a legislative assembly (see Chapter 3); the Latinized form of this word is translated as "church."

The earliest converts to Christianity were attracted for a variety of reasons. Some were Hellenized Jews like Paul himself. Jewish communities existed in most major cities of the eastern Mediterranean, including Rome, and had already begun to adapt their lifestyles and beliefs through contact with other cultures. Christianity also appealed to groups of non-Jews, known as "God-fearers," who gathered around these Greek-speaking Jewish communities. God-fearers did not follow all the precepts of Jewish law, but they admired the Jews for their loyalty to ancestral tradition and their high ethical standards. Christianity was also attractive

to ordinary cosmopolitan Greeks. Some saw Jesus as living by Stoic principles (Chapter 4) or as the embodiment of Ahura-Mazda, the good god of Zoroastrianism (Chapter 2). Others were already devotees of mystery religions, like the very old cult of the Egyptian goddess Isis (Chapter 1) or the newer worship of the warrior god Mithras, popular among Rome's professional soldiers. Both of these religions revolved around stories of sacrifice, death, and regeneration and would have prepared their adherents to embrace the worship of Jesus. It was largely for the benefit of these converts that Christians began to practice elaborate initiation ceremonies such as baptism, a ritual purification common to many ancient religions and exemplified among Jews in the ministry of John the Baptist.

At the same time, there were significant differences between Christianity and these other religions. Most mystery

**PAUL OF TARSUS.** Many ancient images of Paul survive, and all depict him with the same features: a gaunt face, balding head, pointed black beard, and intense dark gaze. In the summer of 2009, archaeologists working in the catacombs of Thekla (named after a holy woman and follower of Paul) discovered this faded fresco. It has been identified as the oldest known portrait of this formative Christian figure and can be dated to the fourth century C.E.

**A FRESCO FROM THE CATACOMBS OF ROME.** This image shows a *catachumen* (Greek for "instructed one") being baptized by the Holy Spirit in the form of an eagle. It is one of many paintings to be found in the ancient catacombs around Rome: subterranean burial and meeting places where Christians also hid during times of persecution. ▪ *Why were such images important?*

**A CHRISTIAN LOVE FEAST.** This fresco, another image from the catacombs, shows Christians celebrating a ritual feast. The inscription above it reads, "I join with you in love."
▪ *How would a Roman viewer interpret this scene?* ▪ *How might this interpretation differ from that of a Christian?*

cults stressed the rebirth of the individual through spiritual transformation, but Christianity emphasized the importance of community. By the middle of the second century, the Christian church at Rome had a recognizable structure, headed by a bishop (in Greek, *episcopos,* or "overseer") and lesser officeholders, including priests, deacons, confessors, and exorcists. Women were extremely prominent in these churches, not only as patrons and benefactors (a role Roman women often played in religious cults) but also as officeholders.

This high status accorded to women was unusual. In other ancient religions, women could be priests and officeholders—but only in cults open solely to women; they never took precedence over men. Many cults, such as Mithraism, denied them access entirely. The fact that Christianity drew its adherents from a broad range of social classes also distinguished it from other cults, which were accessible mainly to those with money and leisure. In time, these unusual features were distorted by Christianity's detractors, who alleged that Christians were political insurgents like the Jesus they worshiped, that they engaged in illicit acts during "love feasts," or that they practiced human sacrifice and cannibalism.

As both Christianity and Judaism redefined themselves during the second and third centuries C.E., they grew further apart. Judaism was adapting to the Romans' destruction of the Temple and the mass exile of Jews from Jerusalem and surrounding provinces. By and large, the scholars who reshaped it during these difficult years ignored Christianity.

It simply did not matter to them any more than did the cults of Mithras or Isis. Christians, however, could not ignore Judaism. Their religion rested on the belief that Jesus was the savior promised by God to Israel in the Hebrew Bible. The fact that so few Jews accepted this claim was a standing rebuke to their faith, one that threatened to undermine the credibility of the Christian message.

More Christians could have responded as did Marcion, a second-century Christian scholar, who declared that Jewish religious practices and the entire Hebrew Bible could be ignored. Most Christians, however, refused to abandon their religion's Jewish foundation. For them, the heroes of Jewish scripture prefigured Jesus, while the major events of Hebrew history could be read, allegorically, as Christian paradigms. Christ was the new Adam, reversing man's original sin; wood from the fateful Tree in Eden became the wood of the Cross on which Christ died. Christ, like Abel, had been slain at the hands of a brother, and his blood continued to cry out from the ground. Christ was the new Noah, saving Creation from its sins. Christ was prefigured in Isaac, in Joseph, in Moses. Furthermore, according to Christians, all the words of the Hebrew prophets point to Jesus, as do the Psalm and the Proverbs.

In short, Christian theologians argued that the Christian church was the true Israel and that when the Jews rejected Jesus, God rejected the Jews and made Christians his new chosen people. The Hebrew Bible was henceforth the Old Testament, vital to understanding Christianity but superseded by the New Testament. At the end of time, the Jews would see the error of their ways and convert. Until then, their only reason for existing was to testify to the truth of Christianity. From a Christian perspective, the Jews' own impiety had caused their exile from the Holy Land and would continue to bring suffering down on their descendants.

## Christianity and the Roman State

As long as Christianity remained a minority religion within the Roman Empire, such attitudes had no effect on the position of Jews under Roman rule. Judaism remained a legally recognized religion, and many Jews were further protected by their Roman citizenship. Indeed, the biblical

# Analyzing Primary Sources

## The Prosecution of a Roman Citizen

*The Acts of the Apostles was written by the same author as Luke's Gospel and was intended as a continuation of that book. It recounts the adventures and ministry of Jesus's original disciples and also follows the career of Paul, a Hellenized Jew who became a missionary to the Gentiles throughout the Roman world. It offers fascinating glimpses into the workings of the Roman legal system because Paul, depicted here as a Roman citizen, had special rights under Roman law (as Jesus had not). In this passage, Paul, accused of treason against the emperor by a group of Pharisees, has been sent to Felix, the governor of Judea. These events took place between 57 and 59 C.E.*

 o the soldiers, according to their instructions, took Paul and brought him by night to [the city of] Antipatris. The next day, they let the horsemen go on with him, while they returned to the barracks. When they came to Caesarea and delivered the letter to the governor, they presented Paul also before him. On reading the letter, he asked what province he belonged to, and when he learned that he was from Cilicia he said, "I will give you a hearing when your accusers arrive." Then he ordered that he be kept under guard in Herod's headquarters.

Five days later, the high priest Ananias came down with some elders and an attorney, a certain Tertullus, and they reported their case against Paul to the governor. When Paul had been summoned, Tertullus began to accuse him, saying: "Your Excellency, because of you we have long enjoyed peace, and reforms have been made for this people because of your foresight. We welcome this in every way and everywhere with utmost gratitude. But, to detain you no further, I beg you to hear us briefly with your customary graciousness. We have, in fact, found this man a pestilent fellow, an agitator among all the Jews throughout the world, and a ringleader of the sect of the Nazarenes. He even tried to profane the temple, and so we seized him. By examining him yourself you will be able to learn from him concerning everything of which we accuse him." The Jews also joined in the charge by asserting that all this was true.

When the governor motioned to him to speak, Paul replied: "I cheerfully make my defense, knowing that for many years you have been a judge over this nation. As you can find out, it is not more than twelve days since I went up to worship in Jerusalem. They did not find me disputing with anyone in the temple or stirring up a crowd either in synagogues or throughout the city. Neither can they prove to you the charge that they now bring against me. But this I admit to you, that according to the Way, which they call a sect, I worship the God of our ancestors, believing everything laid down according to the law or written in the prophets. I have hope in God—a hope that they themselves also accept—that there will be a resurrection of both the righteous and the unrighteous. Therefore I do my best always to have a clear conscience toward God and all people. . . ."

But Felix, who was rather well informed about the Way, adjourned the hearing with the comment, "When Lysias the tribune comes down, I will decide your case." Then he ordered the centurion to keep him in custody, but to let him have some liberty and not to prevent any of his friends from taking care of his needs.

When some days later Felix came with his wife Drusilla, who was Jewish, he sent for Paul and heard him speak concerning faith in Christ Jesus. And as he discussed justice and self-control and future judgment, Felix was alarmed and said, "Go away for the present; when I have an opportunity I will summon you." At the same time he hoped that money would be given him by Paul. So he sent for him often and conversed with him. But when two years had elapsed, Felix was succeeded by Porcius Festus; and desiring to do the Jews a favor, Felix left Paul in prison.

Source: Acts of the Apostles 23:31–24:27, in *The New Oxford Annotated Bible*, New Revised Standard Version, ed. Bruce M. Metzger and Roland E. Murphy (New York: 1994).

### Questions for Analysis

1. According to this account, what legal procedures are in place for dealing with any Roman citizen accused of a crime?

2. What seems to be the relationship between the Jewish elite of Judea and the Roman governor? What is the role of their spokesman, Tertullus?

3. What is the nature of the accusation against Paul, and how does he defend himself?

book known as the Acts of the Apostles represents Paul as a Roman citizen who could not be summarily put to death (as the noncitizen Jesus had been) when brought up on charges of treason. Instead, Acts follows his progress through the Roman judicial system, until he is finally brought to trial at Rome and executed (by beheading) under Nero. Even after their rebellion, the Jews of the diaspora were allowed to maintain the special status they had always had under Roman rule and were not required, as other subject peoples were, to offer sacrifices to the emperor. As we have seen, nothing was more important to the Romans than *pietas* and respect for one's ancestors, and the Romans understood the Jews' traditions as a remarkable form of ancestor worship.

Christianity, in contrast, was a novelty religion. It carried neither the patina of antiquity nor the sanction of tradition—quite the contrary. It raised suspicions on many levels: it encouraged women and slaves to hold office and therefore to rise above their proper stations; it revolved around the worship of a criminal condemned by the Roman state; its secret meetings could be breeding grounds for rebellion. Nevertheless, the official attitude of the Roman state toward Christians was largely one of indifference. There were not enough of them to matter and only a few had any political power. During the first and second centuries C.E., therefore, Christians were tolerated by Roman officials, except when local magistrates chose to make an example of someone who flagrantly flouted authority.

# THE CHALLENGE OF IMPERIAL EXPANSION

The emergence of Christianity within the Roman Empire coincided with the empire's most dramatic period of growth and with a growing variety of challenges. For a long time, Rome's emperors and administrators clung to the methods of governance that had been put in place under Augustus, methods based on a single centralized authority. The reality, however, was that Rome's empire was no longer centered on Rome, or even on Italy. It embraced ecosystems, linguistic groupings, ethnicities, cultures, economies, and political systems of vastly different kinds. More and more people could claim to be Roman citizens, and more and more people wanted a share of Rome's power. This placed enormous stress on the imperial administration as the centrifugal forces of Rome's own making constantly pulled resources into her far-flung provinces, where cities had to be built, people governed, and communications maintained. The fact that the empire had few defensible borders was another problem.

Hadrian had attempted to establish one after 122 C.E. by building a wall between Roman settlements in southern Britannia and the badlands of the northern tribes (see Chapter 5), but this act was more symbolic than effective.

For much of the second century, such stresses were masked by the peaceful transfer of power among the so-called Five Good Emperors: Nerva, Trajan, Hadrian, Antoninus Pius, and Marcus Aurelius. This harmonious state of affairs was partly accidental, being that none of these first four rulers had a surviving male heir, and so a custom developed whereby each adopted a young man of good family and trained the successor in the craft of government. This sensible practice changed with the death of Marcus Aurelius in 180 C.E. Although he was the closest Roman equivalent to Plato's ideal of the philosopher-king, Marcus was not wise enough to recognize that his own son, Commodus, lacked the capacity to rule effectively. After his father's death, Commodus alienated the army by withdrawing from costly wars along the Danube. This move was also unpopular with the Senate, as were Commodus's violent tendencies and his scorn for the traditional norms of aristocratic conduct, including an alleged appearance as a gladiator in the Colosseum. In 192 C.E., a conspiracy was hatched inside his own palace, where he was strangled by his wrestling coach.

## The Empire of the Severan Dynasty

Because Commodus had no obvious successor, the armies stationed in various provinces of the empire raised their own candidates. Civil war ensued, as it had during the crises of the late republic and in 68 C.E., when three men had struggled for imperial power. In this case, there were five major contenders. The eventual victor was a North African general, Septimius Severus (r. 193–211 C.E.).

Under Severus (*SEH-ver-uhs*) and his successors, the administration of Rome's empire changed to a greater extent than it had since the time of Augustus. In many respects, these changes were long overdue. Even the "Five Good Emperors" had been somewhat insulated from the realities of colonial rule. Many of them were able commanders, but they were not professional soldiers as Severus was. Another major difference was the fact that Severus had been born and raised in the North African town of Leptis Magna (now in Libya) and identified strongly with his father's Punic ancestors, seemingly more than with his mother's patrician family. Unlike Trajan and Hadrian, who had also grown up in the provinces, Severus did not regard Rome as the center of the universe, and the time he spent in the imperial capital as a young man seems to have convinced him that little could be accomplished there.

# Competing Viewpoints

## The Development of an Imperial Policy toward Christians

> It was not until the third century that the Roman imperial government began to initiate full-scale investigations into the activities of Christians. Instead, the official position was akin to a policy of "don't ask, don't tell." Local administrators handled only occasional cases, and they were often unsure as to whether the behavior of Christians was illegal or criminal. The following letter was sent to the emperor Trajan by Gaius Plinius Caecilius Secundus (Pliny the Younger), the governor of Bithynia-Pontus (Asia Minor), around 112 C.E. Pliny was anxious to follow proper procedures in dealing with the new sect and wanted advice about this. His letter indicates what Romans did and didn't know about early Christian beliefs and practices.

### From Pliny to Trajan

It is my regular custom, my lord, to refer to you all questions which cause me doubt, for who can better guide my hesitant steps or instruct my ignorance? I have never attended hearings concerning Christians, so I am unaware what is usually punished or investigated, and to what extent. . . . In the meantime, this is the procedure I have followed in the cases of those brought before me as Christians. I asked them whether they were Christians. If they admitted it, I asked them a second and a third time, threatening them with execution. Those who remained obdurate I ordered to be executed, for I was in no doubt . . . that their obstinacy and inflexible stubbornness should at any rate be punished. Others similarly lunatic were Roman citizens, so I registered them to be sent back to Rome.

Later in the course of the hearings, as usually happens, the charge rippled outwards, and more examples appeared. An anonymous document was published containing the names of many. Those who denied that they were or had been Christians and called upon the gods after me, and with incense and wine made obeisance to your statue . . . and who moreover cursed Christ . . . I ordered to be acquitted.

Others, who were named by an informer, stated that they were Christians and then denied it. They said that they had been, but had abandoned their

---

In fact, Severus represents the degree to which the Roman Empire had succeeded in making the world Roman—succeeded so well that Rome itself was becoming practically irrelevant. One could be as much a Roman in Britannia or Africa as in central Italy. Severus's second wife, Julia Domna, exemplifies this trend in a different way. Descended from the Aramaic aristocracy who ruled the Roman client kingdom of Emesa (Syria), her father was the high priest of its sun god, Ba'al. She was highly educated and proved an effective governer during her husband's almost perpetual absence from Rome.

Severus largely ignored the politics of the Senate and slighted what remained of its powers. He preferred to rule through the army, which he reorganized and expanded. Two of his reforms had long-term consequences. The first was a drastic raise in army pay, probably as much as 100 percent, which had the effect of securing the soldiers' absolute loyalty

and diminishing their need to augment their wages through plunder. The second was a relaxation of the long-standing rule forbidding soldiers to marry while still in service. This dispensation encouraged men to put down roots in local communities, but it also made them reluctant to move when their legion was called up. On the one hand, this domesticated the army (hitherto a highly mobile fighting machine) and may have made it less effective. On the other hand, it gave the army a stake in the peaceful governance of Rome's colonies and further contributed to the decentralization of power.

Severus spent most of his imperial career with his army. He died at Eboracum (York, England) in 211 C.E., after conducting a series of successful negotiations with Pictish tribes north of Hadrian's Wall. On his deathbed, he is reported to have said to his sons, "Get along together, keep the soldiers rich, and don't bother about anyone else." His elder son, Caracalla, didn't heed the first of these

allegiance some years previously.... They maintained, however, that all that their guilt or error involved was that they were accustomed to assemble at dawn on a fixed day, to sing a hymn antiphonally to Christ as God, and to bind themselves by an oath ... to avoid acts of theft, brigandage, and adultery.... When these rites were completed, it was their custom to depart, and then reassemble again to take food, which was, however, common and harmless. They had ceased, they said, to do this following my edict, by which in accordance with your instructions I had outlawed the existence of secret brotherhoods. So I thought it all the more necessary to ascertain the truth from two maidservants [i.e., slaves], who were called deaconnesses, even by employing torture. I found nothing other than a debased and boundless superstition....

## From Trajan to Pliny

You have followed the appropriate procedures, my Secundus.... [N]o general rule can be laid down which would establish a definite routine. Christians are not to be sought out. If brought before you and found guilty, they must be punished, but in such a way that a person who denies that he is a Christian, and demonstrates this by his action ... may obtain pardon for his repentance, even if his previous record is suspect. Documents published anonymously must play no role in any accusation, for they give the worst example, and are foreign to our age.

Source: Excerpted from *Pliny the Younger: The Complete Letters*, trans. P. G. Walsh (Oxford: 2006), pp. 278–79 (X.96–97).

## Questions for Analysis

1. How does Pliny's treatment of Christians differ according to their social class? How does it differ from Felix's treatment of Paul (page 188)?

2. Why would Trajan insist that anonymous accusations, such as those Pliny mentions, not be used as evidence? Why was this "foreign to our age"?

3. What do you conclude from this exchange about the relationship between religion and politics under the Roman Empire?

injunctions for long. By the end of the year, he had assassinated his brother, Geta, then attempted to erase him from the historical record by declaring a *damnatio memoriae* (literally, "a condemnation of memory"), banning the mention of Geta's name and defacing his image on public monuments. The second of his father's orders he obeyed in a certain sense, by extending the rights of Roman citizenship to everyone in the empire. This included the entire army in the franchise and increased the tax base. Such a move was beneficial in some respects, but it may also have cheapened Roman citizenship, which was no longer a prize to be won through service or the adoption of Roman values and manners. Another indication of Caracalla's populism was his sponsorship of the largest public baths ever constructed in Rome, an enormous complex that would have rivaled St. Peter's Basilica had it survived. (The sprawling remains can still be seen.) His father's final piece of advice helped to

**THE EMPRESS JULIA DOMNA.** This Roman coin, dating from about 200 C.E., is one of several issued in the name of Severus's powerful wife. As the coin's legend shows, she ruled as "Julia Augusta," names associated with the imperial family since the time of Augustus Caesar.

shorten Caracalla's reign significantly, since it exacerbated his already pronounced tendency to alienate everyone who disagreed with him. He was assassinated in 217 C.E.

Caracalla's true successor was his mother's sister, Julia Maesa, who ruled through his nominal heir and cousin, her adolescent grandson. This youth was known as Heliogabalus (or Elagabalus; r. 218–222 C.E.) because of his devotion to Ba'al. But when Heliogabalus caused controversy by attempting to replace Jupiter, Rome's patron god, with a Latinized version of this eastern deity, Sol Invictus ("Invincible Sun"), his own grandmother engineered

his assassination. Another of her grandsons, Alexander Severus (r. 222–235 C.E.), took his place. Alexander, in turn, was ruled by his mother Julia Mamea, the third in a succession of strong women behind the Severan dynasty, who even traveled with him on military campaigns. This eventually proved fatal for both. The new prominence of the army made Rome's legions engines of political advancement, even more than they had been under the dictators of the late republic. Many aspiring generals could harness this power and with it the support of their legions' provincial bases. In 235 C.E., in consequence, Alexander and his mother were murdered at Moguntiacum (Mainz) in Upper Germania, when the army of the region turned against them. Fifty years of civil unrest ensued.

## The Test of Rome's Strength

From 235 to 284 C.E., there were no fewer than twenty-six "barracks emperors" in Rome: military commanders who, backed by a few loyal legions, struggled with each other and an array of problems. This period is sometimes called the "Third-Century Crisis" and interpreted as a time when the Roman Empire was nearly destroyed. It is more accurately interpreted as a time when the consequences of Roman imperialism made themselves acutely felt. Those aspects of the empire that were strong survived, while those that had always been fragile were further strained.

For example, the disruptions of the mid-third century exposed weaknesses in the economic and administrative infrastructures. Inflation, caused by the devaluation of currency under Severus, drained Roman coinage of its value. Meanwhile, aspiring emperors levied exorbitant taxes on civilians in their provinces, as warfare among rival claimants and their armies destroyed crops and interrupted trade, causing food shortages. Because Rome itself was almost entirely dependent on Egyptian grain and other goods shipped in from the East, its inhabitants suffered accordingly. Poverty and famine even led to a new form of slavery in Italy, as free artisans, local businessmen, and small farmers were forced to labor on the estates of large landholders in exchange for protection and food.

In 251 C.E., a terrible plague, probably smallpox, swept through the empire's territories and recurred in some areas for almost two decades. A similar plague had ravaged Rome a century earlier, but its effects had been mitigated by sound governance. Now, with an estimated 5,000 people dying every day in the crowded city, people sought local scapegoats, and Christians were among those targeted. Beginning in the short reign of Decius (r. 249–251 C.E.), all Roman citizens were required to swear a public oath

**THE EMPEROR SEPTIMIUS SEVERUS.** This statue, carved during the emperor's lifetime, emphasizes his career as a military commander, showing him in the standard-issue uniform of a Roman legionnaire. How does this image of Severus compare with that of Augustus (see page 166)? ■ *What do these differences suggest about the emperor's new role in the third century?*

affirming their loyalty to Rome, which meant worshiping Rome's gods. Those who did so received a certificate testifying to this fact, which they had to produce on demand. Large numbers of Christians were implicated when this edict was put into effect. The enlightened policies of earlier emperors were abandoned.

## The Reorganized Empire of Diocletian

As it happens, the most zealous persecutor of Christians was also responsible for reining in these destructive forces. Diocletian (*die-oh-KLEE-shan*; r. 284–305 C.E.) was a cavalry officer from the Roman province of Dalmatia (modern Croatia) who had risen through the ranks. He could have been another "barracks emperor," but he was determined not to be a victim of the cycle. Instead, he embraced the reality of Rome as a multicultural entity that could not be governed from one place by one person with one centralized bureaucracy. He appointed a fellow officer, Maximian, as co-emperor, putting him in charge of the western half of the empire and retaining the wealthier eastern half for himself. In 293 C.E., he delegated new authority to two junior emperors, or "caesars": Galerius and Constantius. The result was a tetrarchy, a "rule of four," with each man governing a quarter of the empire, further subdivided into administrative units called *dioceses*. This system not only responded to the challenges of imperial administration but was designed to secure a peaceful transfer of power, since the two young "caesars" were being groomed to take the place of the two senior "augusti."

Diocletian apparently recognized that disputes over succession had been a fatal flaw of the Augustan system. Also unlike Augustus, who had cloaked the reality of his personal power in the trappings of the republic, Diocletian presented himself as an undisguised autocrat. His title was not *princeps* ("first man"), but *dominus* ("lord"). In fact, his style of imperial rule borrowed more from the Persian model than it did from the Roman. Gone were the days of republican simplicity and the scorn of kingly pomp. Diocletian wore a diadem and a purple gown of silk interwoven with gold, and he introduced Persian-style ceremonies at his court. Under the Principate, the emperor's palace had been run like the household of any well-to-do Roman, only on a large scale. Diocletian, however, remained physically removed behind a maze of doorways, rooms, and curtains. Those lucky enough to gain an audience with him had to prostrate themselves, while a privileged few could kiss his robe. Too much familiarity with their soldiers had bred contempt for the "barracks emperors," and as a soldier-turned-emperor himself, Diocletian was keen to avoid this mistake.

**THE TETRARCHY: DIOCLETIAN AND HIS COLLEAGUES.** This grouping, carved from a valuable purple stone called porphyry, shows the two augusti, Diocletian and Maximian, embracing their younger caesars, Galerius and Constantius. ▪ *Why do you think that these rulers are portrayed with identical facial features and military regalia?* ▪ *What message does this convey?*

Although Diocletian retained close personal control over the army, he took steps to separate military from civilian chains of command; never again would Roman armies make and unmake emperors. To control the devastatingly high rates of inflation that were undermining the economy, Diocletian stabilized the currency, attempted to fix prices and wages, and reformed the tax system. He even moved the administrative center of the empire from Italy to Nicomedia in the Roman province of Bithynia (modern Turkey). Rome remained the symbolic capital of the empire, not least because the Senate continued to meet there, but Diocletian had little need for the Senate's advice and the real power lay elsewhere.

This new emphasis on orthodoxy (Greek for "correct teaching") was another major consequence of Christianity's conversion. The beliefs of early Christians had been fairly simple: there is one God; Jesus is the anointed one who suffered and died for the sins of mankind and who was raised from the dead; in order to be saved, his followers must renounce sin. But beginning in the fourth century, Christian theology became ever more complex. Christian intellectuals had to demonstrate that their beliefs could withstand intense philosophical scrutiny and that Christianity was superior to Hellenistic philosophy. Just as there were many different schools of Greek and Roman thought, so there arose many different interpretations of Christian doctrine. Before Christianity became a legal religion, any doctrinal disputes could only be addressed informally, by small groups of bishops meeting at local councils that had no power to enforce their decisions. In the fourth century, however, doctrinal disputes had real political consequences.

As a result, the Roman state became increasingly enmeshed in the governance of the Church. Constantine began this process in 325 C.E., when he summoned Christian representatives to the first ecumenical ("worldwide") meeting of the Christian community, the Council of Nicea, where Arianism was condemned and discrepancies in the books included in the Christian Bible were resolved. Constantine's successors carried this intervention much further. Gradually, they claimed to preside over Church councils as Christ's representatives on earth, which entitled them to decide what Christian doctrine should be. Some even violently suppressed Christian groups who refused to accept imperial mandates, labeled them heretical, and subjected them to ecclesiastical penalties—condemnation and excommunication from the Church—as well as criminal prosecution. Essentially, these imperial interventions were an extension of Augustan policies, which had made the emperor *pontifex maximus*, Rome's high priest. In the fourth century, it began to look as though this trend would continue, and that secular and spiritual authority would be combined in the person of the emperor. But this would change in later centuries, as we shall see.

## New Attitudes toward Women and the Body

Women were conspicuously absent from the new hierarchy of the Church and were also barred from the decision-making process at Nicea. Even though they had long been deacons and may even have performed priestly duties, women were now firmly and completely excluded from any position of power.

This was an enormous change, more fundamental than any other aspect of Christianity's conversion. Women had been leaders of many early churches. Jesus had included many women among his close followers—yet one of the early gospels rejected from the biblical canon at the Council of Nicea was ascribed to Mary Magdalene. Paul had relied on women to organize and preside over churches and to finance his missionary journeys; he had declared in one letter (Galatians 3:28) that there should be no distinctions of gender, rank, or ethnicity among Christians. Women such as Perpetua were prominent among the martyrs and were often regarded as prophets. These strong roles had always been controversial because they set Christianity apart from the traditional values of Roman society—but that had also been one of Christianity's main attractions.

What accounts for this drastic change? Three factors can be clearly identified. When Christianity was absorbed into the staunch patriarchy of Rome, it could no longer promote the authority of women effectively. As the Church came to mirror the imperial administration, it replicated the structures of governance that had been the province of men since the founding of the republic. The Church now had the capacity to exclude or censor writings that represented women as the companions of Jesus and founders of the religion based on his teachings. These efforts were so successful that it was not until the very end of the nineteenth century that a gospel attributed to Mary Magdalene was known to exist.

The second factor leading to the marginalization of women was the growing identification of Christianity with Roman cults that emphasized masculinity, particularly the worship of Sol Invictus and the soldiers' god Mithras. This was a deliberate strategy on the part of the Church. It is easier to convert people to a new religion if that religion is not wholly new and embraces elements of other religions. In common with these two cults, as well as with many of the other religions we have studied, such as the worship of Osiris in Egypt, Christianity emphasized the heroic suffering and death of a male god and his eventual victory over death itself. Christ was increasingly identified with Sol Invictus, and his birthday came to be celebrated on December 25, the Roman holiday that marked the passing of the winter solstice and the return of lengthening days.

The third factor contributing to women's exclusion from power was the Christian emphasis on asceticism ("self-denial"), which changed attitudes toward the body. As we noted above, Neoplatonism taught that the goal of life was to liberate the soul from the tyranny of bodily desires, a teaching that it shared with Stoicism. None of this was emphasized in the teachings of Christ. Quite the contrary: the body was celebrated as God's creation, and Christ himself had encouraged feasting, touching, bathing,

## Resisting Imperialism

Attempts at conquest are always met with resistance. In the Roman province of Britannia, a Celtic warrior queen named Boudica led an armed uprising against the imperial army that is still celebrated as a proud example of British independence—as this modern statue in London indicates. A more peaceful uprising against American imperialism took place in Manila on the eve of President Barack Obama's first inauguration in 2008.

Ⓢ **Watch related author interview on the Student Site**

and marriage. His followers insisted that he had been bodily resurrected, and that the bodies of all the faithful would be resurrected, too. Although early Christians had to be willing to sacrifice their lives for their faith, if need be, they were not required to renounce earthly pleasures.

After Christianity became legal, however, there were few opportunities to "bear witness" to the faith through martyrdom. Instead, some Christians began to practice asceticism as an alternative path to sanctity. This meant renunciation of the flesh, especially sex and eating, activities both associated with women, who were in charge of any household's food supply and who were (obviously) sexual partners. A new spiritual movement called monasticism also took hold, providing an alternative lifestyle for men who wanted to reject the world entirely; the word for this movement comes from the Greek word *monos*, "alone." Early monks lived as hermits and practiced extraordinary feats of self-abasement. Some grazed in the fields like cows, others penned themselves into small cages, still others

hung heavy weights around their necks. A monk named Cyriacus would stand for hours on one leg, like a crane. Another, Simeon "the Stylite," lived on top of a high pillar for thirty-seven years, punishing his lice-infested flesh while crowds gathered below to marvel.

This extreme denial of the body was a departure not only from most previous Christian practices but also from the practices of many civilizations up to this point—not to mention the realities of human existence. Ancient religions often celebrated sexuality as a delight, as well as a necessity. Even Roman religion had a place for priestesses and female prophets. Moreover, marriage was so important a marker of social respectability that unmarried men were objects of deep suspicion. Furthermore, Romans had regarded citizens' bodies as being at the service of the state: men as soldiers and fathers, women as mothers and wives. Now, however, some Christians were asserting that their bodies belonged not to the state but to God, and that to serve God fully meant no longer serving the state—or posterity—by bearing children.

## Christians and Pagans

The urban focus of Christianity is reflected in the Latin word referring to a non-Christian: *paganus*, meaning someone who lives in the countryside. The implication is that only someone with a hopelessly rustic outlook would cling to the old Roman religion and so spoil his chances of advancement in society. As Christians came to occupy positions of power within the empire, men with political ambitions were increasingly forced to convert—or at least conform—to Christian norms.

Constantine had retained both pagan and Christian officials in his court, and was careful to speak in terms that embraced a non-Christian audience. But his successors were less inclined to tolerate competing faiths. An interesting exception was Constantine's nephew Julian "the Apostate" (r. 360–363 C.E.), who rejected Christianity and attempted to revive traditional Roman piety. But when Julian was killed in a battle with the Persians, his pro-pagan edicts were allowed to lapse. By 391 C.E., the emperor Theodosius (r. 379–395 C.E.) had prohibited pagan worship of any sort within the empire. This meant that within three generations, Christianity had gone from being a persecuted faith to a persecuting religion. Theodosius even removed the sacred altar of the goddess Victory from the Senate chamber in Rome, prompting pagan loyalists to prophesy the end of the empire. Fifteen years later, Rome fell to a barbarian army.

# SHIFTING CENTERS AND MOVING FRONTIERS

In 324 C.E., Constantine broke ground for the capital city he named after himself. It was built on the site of a settlement called Byzantium, chosen for its strategic location at the mouth of the Black Sea and the crossroads between Europe and Asia: the Hellespont ("bridge to Greece"). This site gave Constantinople commanding advantages as a center for communications and trade. It also made the city readily defensible, because it was surrounded on three sides by water and protected by walls on land. It would remain the political and economic center of the Roman Empire until 1453, when the city was conquered by the Ottoman Turks (see Chapter 11).

## East or West?

The founding of Constantinople epitomizes the shift in Rome's center of gravity from Italy and western Europe to the eastern Mediterranean. It also signaled Constantine's

**SAINT SIMEON "THE STYLITE."** This gold plaque dating from the sixth century depicts the exertions of the ascetic saint who defied the devil (shown as a huge snake) by abusing his own body. Admirers wishing to speak to the saint could climb the ladder shown on the left. ■ *What do you make of the relationship between the luxurious medium of this image (gold) and the message it conveys?*

Virginity for both men and women was accordingly preached as the highest spiritual standard, with celibacy for those who had once been married valued almost as highly. Marriage remained acceptable for average people, the laity, but was often characterized as a second-best option whose purpose was to prevent weak-minded people from being consumed by desire. Moreover, because pseudoscientific theories stemming back to Aristotle posited that women were inherently more lustful than men, the denigration of sexuality had a disproportionately negative effect on attitudes toward women.

# Analyzing Primary Sources

## A Senator Defends the Traditional Religion of Rome

*In 382 C.E., the emperor Theodosius ordered the removal of the ancient altar dedicated to the goddess of Victory (Nike) from the Senate chamber in Rome, as part of his efforts to make Christianity the dominant religion in the empire. This controversial move sparked heated debate and elicited strong protests from Rome's senatorial elites. The following statement of their case was made by Quintus Aurelius Symmachus (c. 345–402 C.E.), who was at that time prefect of the city of Rome. It is principally addressed to the young western emperor, Valentinian.*

 o what is it more suitable that we defend the institutions of our ancestors, and the rights and destiny of our country . . . than to the glory of these times, which is all the greater when you understand that you may not do anything contrary to the custom of your ancestors? We demand then the restoration of that condition of religious affairs which was so long advantageous to the state. . . . Who is so friendly with the barbarians as not to require an Altar of Victory? . . . But even if the avoidance of such an omen were not sufficient, it would at least have been seemly to abstain from injuring the ornaments of the Senate House. Allow us, we beseech you, as old men to leave to posterity what we received as boys. The love of custom is great. . . . Where shall we swear to obey your laws and commands? By what religious sanction shall the false mind be terrified, so as not to lie in bearing witness? All things are indeed filled with God, and no place is safe for the perjured, but to be urged in the very presence of religious forms has great power in producing a fear of sinning. That altar preserves the concord of all, that altar appeals to the good faith of each, and nothing gives more authority to our decrees than that the whole of our order issues every decree as it were under the sanction of an oath. . . .

Let us now suppose that Rome is present and addresses you in these words: "Excellent princes, fathers of your country, respect my years to which pious rites have brought me. Let me use the ancestral ceremonies, for I do not repent of them. Let me live after my own fashion, for I am free. This worship subdued the world to my laws, these sacred rites repelled Hannibal from the walls, and the Senones [Gauls] from the capitol. Have I been reserved for this, that in my old age I should be blamed? I will consider what it is thought should be set in order, but tardy and discreditable is the reformation of old age." We ask, then, for peace for the gods of our fathers and of our country. It is just that all worship should be considered as one. We look on the same stars, the sky is common, the same world surrounds us. What difference does it make by what pains each seeks the truth? We cannot attain to so great a secret by one road; but this discussion is rather for persons at ease, we offer now prayers, not conflict.

Source: Excerpted from *A Select Library of the Nicene and Post-Nicene Fathers,* 2nd Series (New York: 1896), vol. X, pp. 411–14.

### Questions for Analysis

1. How does Symmachus's defense exemplify the traditional values of the Roman Republic?

2. How does Symmachus justify the coexistence of Christianity and Rome's state religion? How would a Christian refute his position?

3. Less than a decade after the altar's removal, Theodosius outlawed all religions but Christianity. From your reading of this letter, how do you think this edict would have affected Romans such as Symmachus?

---

intention to abandon the political precedents set by Diocletian, including the institution of the tetrarchy. Instead, the imperial succession became hereditary. Constantine thus embraced a principle of dynastic monarchy that the Romans had rejected 800 years earlier. Even more ominous, he divided the empire among his three sons, resulting in a civil war, made more bitter because each of these men supported a different faction within the Christian Church. In the meantime, the empire became more and more fragmented. The last ruler who could claim to govern a united Rome was the same Theodosius who outlawed its venerable religion; but then he, too, divided the empire between his sons.

As we have seen, there had always been linguistic and cultural differences between the Greek- and Latin-speaking

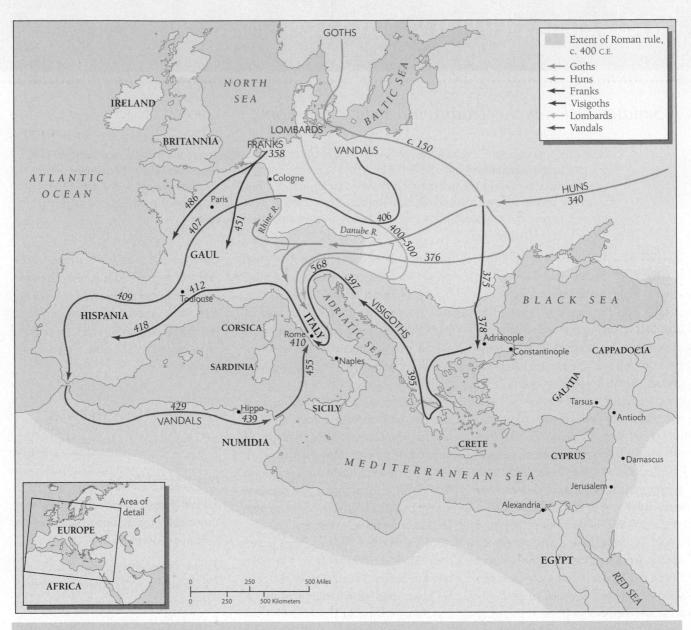

THE MIGRATIONS OF ROME'S FRONTIER PEOPLES. ▪ *What do the routes followed by these different peoples suggest about their destinations and motives?* ▪ *Why did so many converge on Rome, although the city was no longer the capital even of the western Roman Empire?* ▪ *Why did the Romans refer to these migrants as "barbarians"?*

peoples under Roman rule. Now, however, these differences became heightened. The eastern empire was becoming more populous, more prosperous, and more central to imperial policy, while the western provinces were becoming poorer and more peripheral. Many western cities now relied on transfers of funds from their eastern counterparts, and suffered when these funds dried up, trade or communication failed, or Roman legions were transferred elsewhere. Rome itself, which had been demoted to provincial status under Diocletian, now lost even that nominal position. The Italian city of Ravenna on the Adriatic coast became the new capital of the region and a more convenient stopping place for

emperors and ambassadors traveling from Constantinople to the administrative centers of Milan and Trier (in what is now Germany). Only two of Constantine's successors ever visited Rome itself, and none of them lived there.

## Internal and External Pressures

The shifting center of the empire and the widening gap between the eastern and western provinces were not the only fault lines emerging in this period. Secessionist movements arose among many residents of Britannia, Gaul,

Hispania, and Germania. The residents of Egypt were particularly afflicted by high levels of taxation, which targeted their rich agricultural lands. Meanwhile, North Africans and other citizens living in the empire's interior regions were increasingly ignored by authorities. The Italians resented their new status as provincial subjects of Constantinople. Beneath the surface of imperial autocracy, the fourth-century empire was slowly dissolving into its constituent parts.

The empire was also coming under renewed pressure from its borders. Since the third century, the growing power of a new Persian dynasty, the Sassanids, had prompted a shift of Roman military weight to the eastern frontier, reducing the number of troops stationed elsewhere. Partly as a result of this, the northwestern territories suffered a devastating series of raids along the porous frontier of Germania. During the fourth century, relations between assimilated Romans and their barbarian neighbors were generally peaceful. But starting in the early fifth century, a new wave of settlers moved into the empire's oldest provinces, permanently altering their histories and cultures.

## From the Periphery to the Center

In the eyes of many Romans, the tribes that lived along the empire's northern frontiers were barbarians in the pure sense of that (Greek) term: they did not speak either of the empire's civilized languages and did not live in cities. But in no sense were they savage peoples. They were sophisticated agriculturalists and metalworkers who had enjoyed trading relationships with the Roman world for centuries. Many had been settled within Roman provinces for generations as farmers and craftsmen. Legionnaires from the hinterlands of Germania were core components in Roman armies. In some frontier areas, entire tribes had become Roman *foederati*: allied troops who reinforced Roman garrisons or took their places when legions were withdrawn. By the end of the fourth century, many of these tribes had even adopted the form of Christianity preached by disciples of Arius. Although this made them heretics from the perspective of the institutional Church, it tied them more closely to Roman civilization. One general of mixed descent, Flavius Stilicho (359–408 C.E.), was the military leader of the western empire under Theodosius.

What altered this relatively peaceful coexistence? Our study of many previous civilizations has prepared us to answer this question: the arrival of new peoples and the subsequent struggle for land and resources. During the mid-fourth century, a group of nomadic herdsmen known as the Huns began to migrate westward from central Asia, into the region north and east of the Black Sea. Around 370 C.E., their arrival forced a number of other groups, notably the Goths,

to migrate south and west—and in a hurry. Within a few years, they had reached the Roman frontier along the Danube River. The Goths had been clients of the Roman state for several centuries, but now they were refugees and too numerous and too desperate to repel by force. The Romans therefore permitted them to cross the Danube and settle within the empire. In return for food and other supplies, they were to guard the region against other migrant groups.

Local officials, however, failed to uphold their end of the bargain. Instead, they forced the starving Goths to sell themselves and their children into slavery in return for food. In 378 C.E., the Goths revolted, and the Roman army sent to suppress them was defeated at the battle of Adrianople. Peace was restored when the Romans accommodated the Goths' demands for goods and farmland and enrolled them in the Roman army under their own military leaders. But when Theodosius divided the empire between his two young sons, their military advisers—including Stilicho, father-in-law of the emperor Honorius, the de facto ruler—constantly undermined one another. This provided an opening for Alaric, a young leader of the Goths, to advance his own agenda. Targeting the wealthier eastern provinces, he led his army into Greece, looting or capturing many ancient cities, including Athens.

In a desperate attempt to halt these incursions, Alaric was offered a Roman military command and encouraged to move to Italy: the price of peace in the eastern empire was Rome itself. Meanwhile, the Huns had arrived in the region corresponding to modern-day Hungary, forcing several other peoples westward toward the Rhine. On New Year's Eve in the year 406 C.E., a people known as the Vandals crossed the frozen Rhine and invaded Gaul. To repulse them, Stilicho (whose own father had been a Vandal) made an alliance with Alaric and his Goths. But Stilicho fell from imperial favor just a few months later, and the imperial government could no longer exercise any restraint on Alaric's actions.

Like Stilicho, Alaric seems to have wanted to win a permanent place for himself in the imperial hierarchy. But unlike Stilicho—and many Roman generals before him—he did not understand how to use violence as a means toward that end. His assault on Rome did not make him Rome's conqueror but its destroyer. In 410 C.E., after a protracted period of siege, Alaric's army captured and sacked the city. But by now, Rome had little to offer in the way of either food or spoils. So many of the Goths moved on, eventually settling in southern Gaul and Hispania, where they established what came to be known as the Visigothic (Western Gothic) kingdom. Others, later labeled Ostrogoths (Eastern Goths), remained in Italy. The Vandals set out for the Iberian Peninsula, too, but ultimately crossed the Strait of Gibraltar to settle in North Africa. Other tribes, including the Franks

**THEODORIC THE OSTROGOTH.** This coin shows the king in Roman dress but with the long hair characteristic of a barbarian nobleman. The inscription reads *Rex Theodericvs pivs princis*, "King Theodoric, pious prince." ▪ *How does this image compare with that of Constantine (see page 196)?*

and the Burgundians, followed the Vandals across the Rhine into Gaul and established kingdoms of their own.

A generation later, the Huns—whose migrations had set all of these gears in motion—themselves invaded Roman territory under the leadership of their warlord, Attila. Meanwhile, Britannia had been abandoned by its remaining legions, which were hastily withdrawn in 410 C.E. There, a mixed population of Romans and Celts eventually intermingled with invaders from northwestern Germania and Scandinavia: Angles, Saxons, and Jutes. These tribes were so efficient that they dominated all but the westernmost and northern portions of the island within a few generations. Many Celts retreated to the regions where Celtic languages are still spoken today, including Wales and Scotland. The rest of Britain would become Angle-land: England.

The last western Roman emperor was an ineffectual usurper derisively known as Romulus Augustulus ("Little Romulus Augustus"). In 476 C.E., he was deposed by Odovacar, a chieftain who headed a mixed band of barbarians, Huns, and disgruntled Romans. Viewed from the perspective of Constantinople, this event was decisive: it was now not only "New Rome," it was the only viable capital. And the best way for its imperial agenda to be carried forward in the western provinces was through a strong barbarian ruler. Luckily, the emperor Zeno (r. 474–491 C.E.) knew just the man: Theodoric, the son of a Gothic king, who had been sent to Constantinople as a hostage and raised in the civilized surroundings of the imperial court. After a decade of fierce fighting, Theodoric and his imperially equipped Gothic army managed to drive the Huns from Italy and establish a kingdom based in Ravenna, which he ruled—with imperial support—until his death in 526.

## The Impact of the Fifth-Century Migrations

The events of the fifth century increased the porosity of the empire's northern frontiers and penetrated to its core provinces: Italy, Gaul, Hispania, and North Africa. Yet the groups that moved through these territories were small. They were joined by refugees and desperados, but they were never more than war bands. So why couldn't long-established imperial cities sustain themselves?

By the beginning of the fifth century, many Roman armies were already weakened. The best legions had been withdrawn from frontier provinces to protect the richer eastern ones. Those that remained tended to be integrated into local civilian populations, staffed by married men who grew their own food and lived with their families, making it difficult to move troops even in an emergency. Furthermore, there was no mechanism for increasing the revenues needed to support the army. And even if the citizens of Rome's western provinces had been able to maintain a crack fighting force on the frontier, they would have had little reason to think that such an expenditure was necessary. Their "barbarian" neighbors hadn't seemed threatening for generations, and many were so Romanized that differences between the groups are difficult to detect in surviving archaeological evidence.

In the eastern Roman Empire, by contrast, a thriving economy made it easier to equip and maintain a strong fighting force. Cities remained centers of commerce and industry, which meant that citizens possessed greater taxable wealth and so could sustain the burdens of the imperial bureaucracy more easily. Moreover, potential invaders could be bought off or bribed to direct their attention elsewhere—as Alaric had been. For all these reasons, the eastern empire prospered during the fifth century C.E., while the western empire floundered. After the fifth-century migrations, these differences were exacerbated. Every territory that was plundered or occupied represented tax revenues lost, and the scale of these losses was enormous. Ten years after the Goths sacked Rome, the area was capable of producing only 15 percent of the revenues it had generated in 407 C.E. Similar reductions in revenues resulted from attacks on Gaul and Hispania. After 420 C.E. or so, as the newcomers began to set up their own kingdoms, these areas ceased to pay any taxes at all to imperial authorities.

When the Vandals captured North Africa in 439 C.E., the richest of all Rome's western provinces was lost.

The consequences of these structural changes were far-reaching. In the year 400 C.E., the economy of the western Roman Empire was characterized by the mass production of low-cost, high-quality consumer goods that circulated in massive quantities. Although regional and local systems of exchange continued after 500 C.E., long-distance trade in bulk goods could be sustained only in the Mediterranean. As markets disappeared in northwestern provinces, skilled artisans had to find other ways to make a living, or emigrate. Standards of living gradually declined, and so did the overall population. Indeed, it is likely that the population of western Europe did not return to its fourth-century levels for a thousand years, until just before the Black Death (see Chapter 10).

Other aspects of Roman life in these regions changed, too, but almost imperceptibly. Roman bureaucracies often survived, although the proceeds from taxes now went into the purses of the new barbarian rulers or Christian bishops. Roman agricultural patterns continued in most areas, frequently under the same landlords. Local Roman elites continued to dominate civic life, and Roman cities continued to dominate their surrounding regions, especially in southern Gaul and Hispania. The invasions did not even bring an end to Roman culture or the influence of Roman values. As King Theodoric the Goth was fond of remarking: "An able Goth wishes to be like a Roman; but only a poor Roman would want to be like a Goth."

# THE SHAPING OF A NEW WORLDVIEW

Throughout this time of change, Christian intellectuals were formulating a new outlook on the world that would remain dominant for over a thousand years. As the empire sustained attack from external forces and began to fragment along old fault lines, it seemed clearer than ever that a new age was beginning. Christ had promised to come again at the end of time, when all human souls would be judged. How, then, should Christians live in this new world and prepare for that imminent event? The men who forged answers to this question were contemporaries who knew and influenced one another, though they did not always agree. They are now regarded as saints and "fathers" of the Church: Jerome (c. 340–420 C.E.), who came from the northeastern edge of Italy, near the port of Aquilea; Ambrose (c. 340–397), who grew up in Trier and was eventually named bishop of Milan; and Augustine (354–430), who was born and raised in North Africa, where he became a bishop in later life.

## Jerome: Translating the Christian Message

Jerome's signal contribution to the culture of the Roman West was his translation of the Bible from Hebrew and Greek into Latin. Known as the Vulgate or "common" version, it was not the first attempt to produce a Latin Bible but it quickly became the standard, and it remained so until the sixteenth century (see Chapter 13). Jerome's translation is vigorous, colloquial, and clear; its powerful prose and poetry influenced Latin authors for centuries. Jerome was also an influential commentator on the Bible's interpretation, encouraging readings that emphasized a passage's symbolic or allegorical significance, as well as its literal or historical meaning.

Jerome was not a notably original thinker, but he was an eloquent and effective translator of others' ideas as well as of others' words. He was among the first to argue that pagan learning could and should be studied by Christians as long as it was thoroughly adapted to Christian aims. The perennial problem, of course, was that one was always tempted to appreciate classical literature for its own sake, and not for the light it shed on Christian truths. Jerome himself never succeeded in subordinating his love for pagan authors, especially Cicero, to his love for God. He liked to tell a story about a dream he'd experienced, in which he arrived at the gates of heaven and was asked by God if he was a Christian. When he replied that he was, God retorted, "You're not a Christian; you're a Ciceronian." Perhaps in an effort to compensate for this, Jerome became a rigorous ascetic and a fervent promoter of monasticism. He also held a narrow view of women's roles that exercised a strong influence on some later Christian teachers.

## Ambrose and the Authority of the Church

Jerome was primarily a scholar, but Ambrose, by contrast, was an aristocrat and man of the world who helped to define the relationship between the sacred authority of the Church and the secular authority of worldly rulers. As patriarch of the imperial administrative capital at Milan, he fearlessly rebuked the pious emperor Theodosius for a mismanaged massacre of innocent civilians in the Greek city of Thessalonia. Theodosius may have been the emperor, but until he did penance for his sins, Ambrose refused to admit him into his church. On matters of faith, he declared, "The emperor is within the Church, not above the Church." Eventually, Theodosius capitulated

## Roman or Barbarian?

*These two letters from Sidonius Apollinaris (c. 430–c. 480) illustrate the ways in which cultural assimilation was rapidly blurring the distinctions between "Roman" and "barbarian" in the West. Sidonius was himself the descendant of an illustrious Roman provincial family in Gaul. He was one of the most admired Latin stylists of his day, and although he eventually became a bishop and was regarded as a saint, his letter collection (from which these extracts are taken) tells us much more about the literary culture of Romano-Visigothic Gaul than it does about Christianity. His two correspondents also exemplify this new hybrid culture: Arbogastes (ahr-go-BAHS-tees) was the Frankish governor of the Roman city of Trier (in what is now Germany), and Syagrius (sigh-AG-ree-uhs) was from an ancient Roman family and became, effectively, the king of a large region now corresponding to northern France and Belgium.*

### Letter 4:17: Sidonius to His Friend Arbogastes

My honored Lord, your friend Eminentius has handed me a letter written by your own hand, a really literary letter, replete with the grace of a three-fold charm. The first of its merits is certainly the affection which prompted such condescension to my lowly condition, for if not a stranger I am in these days a man who courts obscurity; the second virtue is your modesty. . . . In the third place comes your urbanity, which leads you to make a most amusing profession of clumsiness, when as a matter of fact you have drunk deep from the spring of Roman eloquence and, dwelling by the Moselle, you speak the true Latin of the Tiber: you are intimate with the barbarians but are innocent of barbarisms, and are equal in tongue, as also in strength of arm, to the leaders of old, I mean those who were wont to handle the pen no less than the sword. Thus the splendor of the Roman speech, if it still exists anywhere, has survived in you, though it has long been wiped out from the Belgian and Rhenic lands: with you and your eloquence surviving, even though Roman law has ceased at our border, the Roman speech does not falter. For this reason . . . I rejoice greatly that at any rate in your illustrious breast there have remained traces of our vanishing culture. If you extend these by constant reading you will discover for yourself as each day passes that the educated are no less superior to the unlettered than men are to beasts.

---

the Romans," and his goal was to preserve the best aspects of ancient learning by compiling a series of handbooks and anthologies that packaged and explained classical texts in ways that were appropriate for Christian readers.

Boethius devoted special attention to logic, translating several of Aristotle's treatises from Greek to Latin. Because Roman philosophers had never been much interested in logic, Boethius thus forged a crucial link between classical Greek thought and the new intellectual culture of Christianity. This is most evident in *The Consolation of Philosophy*, which he wrote in prison after Theodoric condemned him to death for treason. (The justice of the charge is unclear.) In this treatise, Boethius concludes that happiness is not found in earthly rewards such as riches or fame but in the "highest good," which is God. Yet he comes to this realization not through any reference to Christian revelation but through a series of imaginary conversations with "Lady Philosophy,"

the embodiment of wisdom. For the next millennium, Boethius's *Consolation* was one of the most read and imitated books in the West—the ultimate example of classical philosophy's absorption into the Christian worldview.

## Monastic Education

The vital work of preserving selected classics and interpreting their meaning was increasingly performed by monks, whose way of life had undergone some significant changes during the fourth century. Leaders of the monastic movement recognized that few men were capable of ascetic feats, and some disapproved of such showmanship. Rather, they advocated a more moderate approach and emphasized the benefits of communal life. In the Roman East, the most important figure in this new monasticism was Basil of Caesarea (c. 330–379).

## Letter 5:5: Sidonius to his Friend Syagrius

**Y**ou are the great-grandson of a consul, and in the male line too—although that has little to do with the case before us; I say, then, you are descended from a poet, to whom his literary glory would have brought status had not his magisterial glories done so . . . and the culture of his successors has not declined one whit from his standard, particularly in this respect. I am therefore inexpressibly amazed that you have quickly acquired a knowledge of the German tongue with such ease.

And yet I remember that your boyhood had a good schooling in liberal studies and I know for certain that you often declaimed with spirit and eloquence before your professor of oratory. This being so, I should like you to tell me how you managed to absorb so swiftly into your inner being the exact sounds of an alien race, so that now after reading Virgil under the schoolmaster's cane and toiling and working the rich fluency of [Cicero] . . . you burst forth before my eyes like a young falcon from an old nest.

You have no idea what amusement it gives me, and others too, when I hear that in your presence the barbarian is afraid to perpetrate a barbarism in his own language. The bent elders of the Germans are astounded at you when you translate letters, and they adopt you as umpire and arbitrator in their mutual dealings. . . . And although these people are stiff and uncouth in body and mind alike, they welcome in you, and learn from you, their native speech combined with Roman wisdom.

Only one thing remains, most clever of men: continue with undiminished zeal, even in your hours of ease, to devote some attention to reading; and, like the man of refinement that you are, observe a just balance between the two languages: retain your grasp of Latin, lest you be laughed at, and practice the other, in order to have the laugh of them. Farewell.

Source: Reprinted by permission of the publishers and the Trustees of the Loeb Classical Library. From *Sidonius: Volume II–Letters,* Loeb Classical Library, vol. 420, prepared by W. H. Semple and E. H. Warmington from material left by W. B. Anderson, pp. 127–29, 181–83, Cambridge, MA: Harvard University Press. Copyright © 1965 by the President and Fellows of Harvard College. Loeb Classical Library® is a registered trademark of the President and Fellows of Harvard College.

### Questions for Analysis

**1.** For what qualities does Sidonius praise Arbogastes? What might have been the motive behind his extravagant compliments?

**2.** For what different qualities does Sidonius praise Syagrius? Given that Syagrius controlled much of the former Roman province of northern Gaul, what would have been his reasons for learning the local language?

---

Basil's guidelines prohibited monks from engaging in prolonged fasts or extreme discipline of the flesh, and instead encouraged useful work and silent meditation.

In the Roman West, the most influential proponent of the monastic movement was a contemporary of Boethius, Benedict of Nursia (c. 480–c. 547), the son of a Roman aristocrat. Benedict founded a monastery at Monte Cassino, southeast of Rome, where he urged his followers to adopt a "simple rule for beginners." Adapted from a much harsher set of precepts called *The Rule of the Master,* Benedict's *Rule* is notable for its brevity, flexibility, and practicality. It established a carefully defined cycle of daily prayers, lessons, and communal worship. It laid down guidelines for what monks should eat (a sufficiency of simple food, a small amount of wine, meat only for the sick or on special occasions), and how the work of the monastery should be performed. Physical labor was encouraged—idleness, Benedict declared, was "an enemy of the soul"—but the monks also had time for private study and contemplation. In all such matters, Benedict left much to the discretion of the leader of the monastery, whom all the monks were expected to obey without hesitation. This man was the abbot, from the Syriac word *abba* ("father").

## Cassiodorus and the Classical Canon

Benedict was no admirer of classical pagan culture, but he did believe that monks must study the Bible in order to perform their daily cycle of prayers properly and to participate fully in a life of worship. This meant that they had to be educated along the lines prescribed by Augustine. And because many monks entered religious life as children, the monastery would need to provide schooling. Through this somewhat roundabout path, classical learning entered the monastic curriculum.

**CASSIODORUS.** This frontispiece from a Bible, produced in a monastery in Britain around the year 700, depicts Cassiodorus as a copyist and keeper of books. Monasteries were instrumental in changing the form of the book from the ancient scroll to the modern codex. Because their parchment pages were heavy, codices were customarily stored in cupboards, lying flat, as we see them here.

The man largely responsible for this was Flavius Magnus Aurelius Cassiodorus Senator (c. 490–c. 583), a younger contemporary of Benedict. Like Boethius, Cassiodorus (*cass-ee-oh-DOHR-uhs*) was attached to Theodoric's court and was for many years the secretary in charge of the king's correspondence. He also wrote a *History of the Goths*, which depicted Theodoric's people as part of Rome's history. After Theodoric's death, Cassiodorus founded an important monastery at Vivarium in southern Italy. There he composed commentaries on the Psalms as well as his most influential work, *Institutes*.

Inspired by Augustine and his own classical education, Cassiodorus believed that the study of classical literature was an essential preliminary to a proper understanding of the Bible. The *Institutes* is essentially a syllabus, a list of readings arranged so that a student would begin with simpler, straightforward works of pagan literature before moving on to more difficult works, and finally to the demanding study of theology. Cassiodorus thereby defined a classical canon that formed the basis of Christian education in the Roman West.

In order to ensure that his monks had access to the necessary readings, Cassiodorus encouraged the copying of books. He argued that this was precisely the sort of manual labor that Benedict had advocated. Under his influence, monasteries thus became engines for the collection, preservation, and transmission of knowledge. It is important to note that nearly all the Greek and Latin texts on which we rely for our study of western civilizations survived because they were copied in monasteries.

# After You Read This Chapter

🐰 Go to **INQUIZITIVE** to see what you've learned—and learn what you've missed—with personalized feedback along the way.

## REVIEWING THE OBJECTIVES

- A number of historical factors shaped the way Jesus's teachings were received. Describe the most important of these factors.
- The expansion of Rome and the strain on its central government posed significant challenges in the third century. How did Roman emperors respond?
- Christianity's legalization changed it in profound ways. Why was this?
- During the fourth and fifth centuries, a new wave of migrations penetrated to the very heart of the empire. What made this possible?
- The differences between traditional Roman and Christian cultures were gradually reconciled through the efforts of Christian intellectuals. Why was this considered necessary?

Monasteries also developed and disseminated an important new information technology: the codex. For millennia, the standard book had been a scroll, a clumsy format that made searching for a particular passage difficult and confined the reader to one passage at a time. The codex facilitates indexing (from the Latin word for "finger") because a reader can flip back and forth among various pages, with a finger in one place while looking at another. Codices also store information more safely and efficiently because they compress many hundreds of pages within protective bindings. They are less wasteful, too, because texts can be copied on both sides of a page. They even make finding a given book easier because titles can be written on the codex's spine. It's arguable, in fact, that the invention of the codex was more revolutionary than the invention of printing a thousand years later. Unless you are scrolling through a digital version of this book, your copy of *Western Civilizations* is a codex.

# CONCLUSION

Ever since the English historian Edward Gibbon published the first volume of *The Decline and Fall of the Roman Empire* in 1776 (a year when Britain's own empire suffered a setback), more has been written about the "fall of Rome" than on the passing of any other civilization. Gibbon himself blamed Christianity, depicting it as a debilitating disease that sapped the empire's strength. Others have accused the barbarians whose movements put pressure on Rome's frontiers. But even in the time of Julius Caesar, Roman moralists had already declared that Rome was in decline. Indeed, any self-respecting Roman republican would say that Rome fell when Augustus came to power.

More recent scholarship has influenced the narrative offered in this chapter, which views *transformation* as a more accurate way of understanding this period. No civilization is static and unchanging; civilizations, like human beings, are living organisms. Therefore, any evidence of Rome's decline can also be read as evidence of its adaptability. The imperial policies of Septimius Severus and Diocletian were responses to the realities of Rome's size and diversity. The settlement of frontier peoples in Rome's western provinces gave rise to hybrid polities that found new uses for Roman buildings, political offices, and laws. Through Christianity, the language, administrative structures, and culture of ancient Rome were preserved and extended. The flexibility of the Roman political system made this possible, because it was inclusive to a degree no modern empire has ever matched.

Still, this transformation changed what it meant to be Roman, to the extent that historians now call this period "late antiquity" to distinguish it from the classical world that preceded it. By the seventh century, so much had changed that the contours of three distinctive civilizations can be discerned, each one exhibiting different aspects of Roman influence and crystallizing around different regions of the former empire. We will explore each of these civilizations in Chapter 7.

## PEOPLE, IDEAS, AND EVENTS IN CONTEXT

- What were the main differences between **JESUS** and other Jewish leaders of his day?
- How did **PAUL OF TARSUS** reach out to the peoples of the Hellenistic world? How did his teachings influence the development of early Christianity?
- In what ways did **DIOCLETIAN**'s division of the empire and his institution of the **TETRARCHY** respond to longstanding problems?
- How and why was Christianity changed under **CONSTANTINE**? What effects did this have on attitudes toward women and their role in the church?
- How did the relocation of the imperial capital to **CONSTANTINOPLE** contribute to the growing divide between the **GREEK EAST** and the **LATIN WEST**? How did the mass migrations of frontier peoples transform the Latin West?
- What were the key contributions of **JEROME**, **AMBROSE**, and **AUGUSTINE** to the development of a specifically Christian outlook by the end of the fourth century c.e.?
- How did **BOETHIUS**, **BENEDICT**, and **CASSIODORUS** reshape classical culture in the fifth century c.e.?

## THINKING ABOUT CONNECTIONS

- In your opinion, which phenomenon had a more profound impact on Rome: the overextension of imperial power, or the mass migration of peoples from Rome's frontier? Why?
- Few historians would now agree with the judgment of Edward Gibbon, who posited that Christianity destroyed the Roman Empire. But to what extent did Christianity alter the traditional values and infrastructure of the Roman state? Were these alterations inevitable? Why or why not?

## STORY LINES

- Justinian's attempt to reconquer the western territories of the Roman Empire was ultimately more destructive than the mass migrations of the previous centuries.

- Byzantine culture combined Roman legal and political systems with the learning of classical Greece but was most acutely shaped by Orthodox Christianity.

- The close connections among religion, military conquest, and commerce helped to drive the rapid expansion of Islam in the eighth century.

- In western Europe, the disintegration of Roman political and economic infrastructures had a destabilizing effect, but this was countered by the success of the Frankish kingdom and the spread of monasticism.

- The empire of Charlemagne unified vast portions of northwestern Europe under a single centralized government, fostering important administrative, economic, and cultural developments.

## Before You Read This Chapter

## CHRONOLOGY

| | |
|---|---|
| 481–511 | Reign of Clovis, king of the Franks |
| 527–565 | Reign of Justinian |
| 570–632 | Lifetime of Muhammad and early Muslim conquests |
| 590–604 | Papacy of Gregory the Great |
| 636–651 | Arab conquests of Persia, Palestine, Egypt, and North Africa |
| 661–750 | Dominion of the Umayyad dynasty in the Islamic world |
| 717–787 | Iconoclast Controversy in Byzantium |
| 717–751 | The Carolingian dynasty shares power with Merovingian kings |
| 730 | The Venerable Bede completes his history of the English church |
| 750–930 | Dominion of the Abassid dynasty in Baghdad and the Umayyad dynasty in Al-Andalus (Spain) |
| 751 | Pepin becomes king of the Franks |
| 768–814 | Reign of Charlemagne |
| 800–1000 | Period of Viking invasions |
| 871–899 | Reign of Alfred the Great in England |

# Rome's Three Heirs, 500–950

## CORE OBJECTIVES

- **EXPLAIN** why Justinian's efforts to reunite the Roman Empire proved destructive.

- **DEFINE** and **EXPLAIN** the distinctive features of Byzantine culture.

- **IDENTIFY** the reasons for the rapid success of the Arab conquests and Islam's expansion.

- **DESCRIBE** the relationship between monasticism and secular power in early medieval Europe.

- **UNDERSTAND** the importance of the Carolingian Empire.

Around the year 600, Anglo-Saxon tribes that had settled on the island of Britain were approached by missionaries sent from Rome. These Latin-speaking evangelists faced an enormous challenge: they had to find a way to convert tribal leaders and translate the central ideas of their Christian faith into languages and concepts that made sense in a new cultural context. They also needed to look for ways to meld Roman practices with pagan ones by building churches on sacred sites and gradually turning the worship of traditional gods into the rituals of Christianity. An account of these negotiations comes down to us in a remarkable book written several generations later. In *The History of the English Church and People*, a monk named Bede (c. 672–735) describes how Celtic and Anglo-Saxon peoples were uneasily united under the Roman Church and came to adopt Latin as a language of learning and worship. He also shows how, in the process, Roman Christian ideals were changed and adapted to meet new needs and express a new worldview.

This is but one example of the ways in which Rome's legacy was transmitted and transformed during the pivotal period known as the Middle Ages. This term is a problematic one, and it doesn't begin to express the diverse realities—or perceptions—of the generations of people who lived during this thousand-year

# Competing Viewpoints

## Debating the Power of Icons

> The Iconoclast Controversy of the eighth century divided Byzantine society and was a factor in the growing division between the Latin Church of Rome and the Greek Orthodox Church. The excerpts below are representative of the two main arguments voiced at the time. The first is from a treatise by John of Damascus (c. 675–749), a Christian in the service of the Muslim Umayyad caliphs. The second is an official report issued from the synod convened by the emperor Constantine V (r. 741–775) in 754. Constantine was carrying forward the iconoclastic policies of his father, Leo III.

### John of Damascus on Holy Images

Now adversaries say: God's commands to Moses the lawgiver were, "Thou shalt adore the Lord thy God, and thou shalt worship him alone, and thou shalt not make to thyself a graven thing that is in heaven above, or in the earth beneath." . . .

These injunctions were given to the Jews on account of their proneness to idolatry. Now we, on the contrary, are no longer in leading strings. . . . We have passed the stage of infancy, and reached the perfection of manhood . . . and know what may be imaged and what may not. . . . An image is a likeness of the original with a certain difference, for it is not an exact reproduction of the original. Thus, the Son is the living,

substantial, unchangeable Image of the invisible God, bearing in Himself the whole Father, being in all things equal to Him, differing only in being begotten by the Father. . . . That which is divine is immutable; there is no change in Him, nor shadow of change. . . . God has noted and settled all that He would do, the unchanging future events before they came to pass. In the same way, a man who wished to build a house, would first make and think out a plan. Again, visible things are images of invisible and intangible things, on which they throw a faint light. Holy Scripture clothes in figure God and the angels. . . . If, therefore, Holy Scripture, providing for our need, ever putting before us what is intangible,

clothes it in flesh, does it not make an image of what is thus invested with our nature, and brought to the level of our desires, yet invisible? . . . For the invisible things of God since the creation of the world are made visible through images. We see images in creation which remind us faintly of God, as when, for instance, we speak of the holy and adorable Trinity, imaged by the sun, or light, or burning rays, or by a running fountain, or a full river, or by the mind, speech, or the spirit within us, or by a rose tree, or a sprouting flower, or a sweet fragrance. . . .

Source: Excerpted from *St. John Damascene on Holy Images*, trans. Mary H. Allies (London: 1898), pp. 6–12.

schools based their instruction on classical Greek literature, in marked contrast to the more tentative attitude toward classical learning in western Europe (see Chapter 6). Educated people around the Byzantine court who quoted only a single line of Homer could expect their listeners to recognize the entire passage from which it came. In the English-speaking world, only the King James Bible has ever achieved the same degree of cultural saturation. Indeed, Homeric epics were a kind of sacred text in Byzantium as were the surviving tragedies of Athenian dramatists of the fifth century B.C.E.

Byzantine scholars intensively studied the philosophy of Plato and the historical prose of Thucydides. In

contrast, Aristotle's works were less well known, and many other philosophical traditions of antiquity were deemed dangerous. Although Justinian had presided zealously over the codification of ancient Roman (and thus pagan) law, he registered his distrust of Greek (pagan) philosophy by shutting down the Athenian academies that had existed since Plato's day. The practice of Greek scientific inquiry and the advances of Hellenistic science were also neglected. Tradition was more highly prized than originality, as was preservation over innovation. The benefit of this, for posterity, is that Byzantium rescued Greek and Hellenistic writings for later ages. The vast majority of ancient Greek texts known

## Canons of the Synod of 754

t is the unanimous doctrine of all the holy Fathers and of the six Ecumenical Synods, that no one may imagine any kind of separation or mingling in opposition to the unsearchable, unspeakable, and incomprehensible union of the two natures in the one *hypostasis* or person. What avails, then, the folly of the painter, who from sinful love of gain depicts that which should not be depicted—that is, with his polluted hands he tries to fashion that which should only be believed in the heart and confessed with the mouth? He makes an image and calls it Christ. The name *Christ* signifies *God and man*. Consequently it is an image of God and man, and consequently he has in his foolish mind, in his representation of the created flesh, depicted the Godhead which cannot be represented, and thus mingled what should not be mingled. Thus he is guilty of a double blasphemy—the one in making an image of the Godhead, and the other by mingling the Godhead and manhood . . . like the Monophysites, or he represents the body of Christ as not made divine and separate and as a person apart, like the Nestorians.

The only admissible figure of the humanity of Christ, however, is bread and wine in the holy Supper. This and no other form, this and no other type, has he chosen to represent his incarnation. Bread he ordered to be brought, but not a representation of the human form, so that idolatry might not arise. And as the body of Christ is made divine, so also this figure of the body of Christ, the bread, is made divine by the descent of the Holy Spirit; it becomes the divine body of Christ by the mediation of the priest who, separating the oblation from that which is common, sanctifies it.

Source: Excerpted from *The Seven Ecumenical Councils of the Undivided Church*, trans. H. R. Percival, in *Nicene and Post-Nicene Fathers*, 2nd Series, ed. P. Schaff and H. Wace (repr. Grand Rapids, MI: 1955), pp. 543–44.

### Questions for Analysis

1. With what other phenomena does John of Damascus compare the making of images? How do these comparisons help him make his argument in favor of them?

2. With what phenomena do the theologians of the synod compare the making of images? Why do they declare the bread and wine of the Eucharist to be the only legitimate representations of Christ?

3. What is the significance of the fact that John of Damascus did not live under the jurisdiction of the Byzantine emperor, but that of the Muslim Umayyad caliph? How might that have influenced his writing?

---

today survive only because they were copied by Byzantine scribes.

In further contrast to western Europe, as we shall see, the Byzantine educational system was inclusive, open to the laity and even to women. Although most girls from aristocratic or prosperous families were educated at home by private tutors, they nevertheless mingled freely with their male counterparts at court or on social occasions, and many female intellectuals were praised for their erudition. There were even female physicians, another extraordinary departure from both ancient tradition and the practices of western Europe until the latter part of the nineteenth century.

## Byzantine Art and Architecture

Byzantine achievements in the realms of architecture and art are exemplified by the church of Hagia Sophia ("Holy Wisdom") in Constantinople, constructed at enormous cost under the patronage of Justinian. It quickly came to define an architectural style unique to Byzantium. Its purpose was not to express pride in human accomplishment but rather to symbolize the mysteries of the Christian faith and the holy knowledge imparted by Christ to the soul of the believer. For this reason, the architects paid little attention to the external appearance of the building.

**HAGIA SOPHIA.** This great monument to the artistry, engineering skill, and spirituality of Byzantium was built during the reign of Justinian. The four minarets at its corners were added in 1453, after Constantinople (now Istanbul) was absorbed into the empire of the Ottoman Turks. Hagia Sophia is now a mosque and a museum.

The interior, however, was decorated with richly colored mosaics, gold leaf, colored marble columns, and bits of tinted glass set on edge to refract rays of sunlight like sparkling gems, making it appear that light is generated from within. The magnificent dome over its central square was an unprecedented engineering feat: it was upheld by four great arches springing from pillars at the four corners of the square. The result was an architectural framework both marvelously strong and delicate. Its effect is heightened by the many windows placed around the dome's rim, which convey the impression that it floats in midair.

Many aspects of Byzantine arts and learning exerted strong influence on the artisans and scholars of western Europe through continued economic and cultural contact. The basilica of San Marco in Venice (c. 1063) reflects this influence distinctly, as do medieval mosaics in such cities as Ravenna and Palermo. Greek-speaking monasteries in southeastern Italy maintained especially close ties with

**DOME OF HAGIA SOPHIA.** The revolutionary structure of the church, shown here, made it appear as if the enormous dome floated on light and air.

their counterparts in the eastern empire, and many were allowed to practice the rituals of the Orthodox Church; many Greek books, including the comedies of Aristophanes (Chapter 4), were copied and preserved there. But much of the heritage of Western civilizations that was cultivated in Byzantium was largely inaccessible elsewhere in Europe, because the knowledge of Greek became increasingly rare.

# MUHAMMAD AND THE TEACHINGS OF ISLAM

In many ways, the civilization that formed around the religion of Islam mirrors the Roman Empire in its global reach and longevity; in this, it is truly one of Rome's heirs. Islam (Arabic for "submission") also calls to mind the early republic of Rome in that it demands adherence from its followers—not just to common forms of worship, but also to certain social and cultural norms. But whereas the Roman Empire came to undergird Christianity, elevating it to the status of a major faith, the Muslim faith was itself an engine of imperial expansion.

## The Revelations of Muhammad

Islam emerged in Arabia, a desert land considered so forbidding that neither the Romans nor the Persians sought to conquer it. Arabian society was tribal and did not revolve around urban settlements. Many Arabs were herdsmen, living off the milk of their camels and the produce of desert oases. But as with the Hittites in the second millennium B.C.E. (Chapter 1), their very mobility, ingenuity, and pioneering spirit made them excellent explorers and long-distance traders. In the second half of the sixth century, when protracted wars between Byzantium and Persia made travel dangerous for merchants, the Arabs quickly established themselves as guides, couriers, and guardians of transit routes between Africa and Asia.

As part of this process, towns began to emerge. The most prominent of these was Mecca, an ancient sacred site that lay at the crossroads of major caravan routes. Mecca was home to the Kaaba (*KAH-ah-bah*), a shrine housing the Black Stone worshiped by many Arabian tribes. (It may be a meteorite, and hence of celestial origin.) The Quraysh (*kur-AYSH*), the tribe that controlled this shrine, thus came to dominate the economic and religious life of the whole region, forming an aristocracy of traders and entrepreneurs.

Muhammad, the founder of Islam, was a member of this tribe. He was born in Mecca about 570. Orphaned early in life, he entered the service of a rich widow whom he later married, thereby attaining financial security. Until middle age, he lived as a prosperous trader, little different from his fellow townsmen. But around 610, he experienced a spiritual epiphany. At this time, the Arab tribes worshiped many gods. Yet, like the ancient Hebrews, they also acknowledged one god as more powerful. For the Hebrews, God was Yahweh; for the Arabs, Allah. But whereas the Hebrews' embrace of monotheism was a long and gradual process, Muhammad's conversion was sudden, the immediate consequence of revelation. Thereafter, Muhammad received further revelations that became the basis for his teachings and by which he was persuaded to accept the calling of a prophet and proclaim the new faith to his tribe.

## The Beginnings of Islam

Yet Muhammad was not successful in gaining converts among his own people. In Mecca, tribal leaders of the Quraysh feared that his teachings would diminish the importance of the Kaaba. Some residents of the town of Yathrib, however, saw an opportunity to increase their prestige and invited Muhammad to live among them to serve as judge and arbiter in local rivalries. Muhammad and a few loyal friends accepted this invitation in 622. Because this emigration—in Arabic, the *Hijra* (*HIJ-ruh*)—marks the beginning of Muhammad's wider influence, Muslims regard it as the beginning of time. Just as Christians date all events according to the birth of Jesus (see Chapter 6), Muslims begin their dating system with the Hijra.

Muhammad changed the name of Yathrib to Medina ("City of the Prophet") and established himself as the town's ruler. He did not, however, abandon his desire to exercise authority among his own people. He and his followers began a series of military raids of Quraysh caravans traveling beyond Mecca. An important early victory occurred in 624 at the Battle of Badr in western Arabia, where a small number of loyal adherents to Islam defeated a much larger force sent out from Mecca to defend a valuable trading caravan. Muhammad's men killed the expedition's leader and took valuable booty and prisoners. The success of this enterprise sent a powerful message to the Quraysh and inspired many men to join Muhammad. But there was further opposition to Islam, not only from Mecca, but from Jewish tribes in the region who joined forces with Muhammad's Arab enemies. This led Muhammad to denounce the Jews as faithless to their own prophets and to expel all but one wealthy Jewish clan from Medina and its surrounding region.

In 627, the Quraysh assembled a large coalition force to attack Medina, hoping that the remaining Jews there—who had

## A Sura from the Qur'an

*The Qur'an preserves the teachings of Muhammad in a series of* suras, *or chapters. Composed in verse forms that draw on much older traditions of Arabic poetry, they are meant to be sung or chanted. Indeed, the word* Qur'an *means "recitations," referring both to Muhammad's method of teaching and the Muslim practice of memorizing and repeating portions of scripture.*

### Sura 81: The Overturning

In the Name of God the Compassionate the Caring

When the sun is overturned
When the stars fall away
When the mountains are moved
When the ten-month pregnant
    camels are abandoned
When the beasts of the wild
    are herded together   5
When the seas are boiled over
When the souls are coupled
When the girl-child buried alive
is asked what she did to deserve
    murder
When the pages are folded out   10
When the sky is flayed open
When Jahím [the Day of Reckoning]
    is set ablaze

When the garden is brought near
Then a soul will know what it
    has prepared
I swear by the stars that slide,   15
stars streaming, stars that sweep
    along the sky
By the night as it slips away
By the morning when the fragrant
    air breathes
This is the word of a messenger
    ennobled,
empowered, ordained before
    the lord of the throne,   20
holding sway there, keeping trust
Your friend [Muhammad] has not
    gone mad
He saw him on the horizon clear
He does not hoard for himself
    the unseen
This is not the word of a satan
    struck with stones   25

Where are you going?
This is a reminder to all beings
For those who wish to walk straight
Your only will is the will of God lord
    of all beings

Source: From *Approaching the Qur'an: The Early Revelations*, trans. Michael Sells (Ashland, OR: 1999), pp. 48–50.

### Questions for Analysis

1. What impressions of Arab culture emerge from this sura? What does the litany of unlikely or mystical events reveal about the values of Muhammad's contemporaries?

2. How does Muhammad speak of himself and his role in society?

reason to distrust Muhammad—would join forces with them. In response, Muhammad decided to risk a siege of his own city and caused a deep defensive trench to be dug around it, slowing the enemy's advance. The Meccan army had not come equipped for an extended battle and eventually dispersed: an ignominious defeat known as the Battle of the Trench. And even though the Jews of Medina had not joined forces with the Meccans, the Muslims charged them with treason and executed all the men and enslaved the women and children.

By 630, Muhammad's successes had persuaded his kinsmen to submit to his authority and teachings. Muhammad, for his part, ensured that the Kaaba's shrine would be revered as Islam's holiest place, a status it maintains today. And because Mecca had long been a pilgrimage site and gathering place for tribes throughout Arabia, many

more people were exposed to Muhammad's teachings and inspired by his military prowess, which promised prosperity for his people in the years to come. At the time of his death in 632, Islam had become an established faith.

## Muhammad and the Qur'an

As its name indicates, the faith of Islam calls for submission to Allah, whom Muslims identify as being the same as the Jews' Yahweh and the Christian God. (The Muslim saying "there is no god but Allah" is more accurately translated as "there is no god but God.") For Muslims, the history and prophecies of the Jews are therefore important components of their religion, as are the teachings of Jesus, who is

**LEAVES FROM THE OLDEST EXTANT COPY OF THE QUR'AN.** In 2015, scholars at the University of Birmingham (England) announced that two leaves of a Qur'an manuscript had been carbon dated to the years 568–645 C.E. (Carbon dating is only accurate for a range of years and cannot pinpoint a single date.) This extraordinary discovery suggests that at least some of Muhammad's teachings were written down much earlier than had been previously thought—possibly even during his lifetime, and certainly within a decade or so after his death. The implications of this evidence will be debated by Arabic scholars and historians of Islam for years to come.

regarded as a great prophet. But Muhammad is regarded as the greatest prophet, whose teachings established the rituals and practices essential to Islam.

These teachings are preserved in the sacred scripture of the Qur'an (*kuhr-AHN*), an Arabic word meaning "recitations," because Muhammad is said to have recited his revelations orally. Eventually, they were gathered together and transcribed, a process that continued after Muhammad's death. So unlike the Christian Gospels, which offer different perspectives on Jesus's ministry and were recorded a generation or two after his crucifixion, the Qur'an is considered to be a direct link with Muhammad. It is also unlike most books of the Bible because it takes the form of poetry, drawing on ancient genres of Arabic song.

Islam teaches that a day of judgment is coming—and soon. On this day, the righteous will be granted eternal life in a paradise of delights, but wrongdoers will be damned to a realm of eternal fire. Therefore all people are offered a fundamental choice: to begin a new life of divine service or to follow their own path. If they choose to follow God, they will be blessed; if they do not, God will turn away from them. Thus, the only sure means of achieving salvation is to observe the Five Pillars of the faith: submission to God's will as described in the teachings of Muhammad, frequent prayer, ritual fasting, giving alms, and annual pilgrimage to Mecca (the *Hajj*).

Unlike Christianity, Islam is a religion without priests. In this, it more closely resembles Rabbinic Judaism as it developed after the destruction of the Second Temple, which made a Temple priesthood obsolete. Instead, as we noted above, Jewish communities gathered around a master teacher, the rabbi. Similarly, Muslims often rely on a community leader (*imam*), a scholar qualified to comment on matters of faith who may also act as a judge in disputes. Like Judaism, Islam also emphasizes the inextricable connection between religious observance and daily life, between spirituality and politics. There is no opposition of sacred and secular authority, as in Christianity. But in marked contrast to Judaism, Islam is a religion that aspires to unite the world in a shared faith. This means that Muslims, like Christians, consider it their duty to engage in the work of conversion.

# THE WIDENING ISLAMIC WORLD

As we have frequently noted, the death of any charismatic leader precipitates a series of crises. Muhammad and Alexander the Great represent different types of leadership, but both were visionaries whose military and political successes inspired intense loyalty; and neither designated his own successor, leaving behind a number of close followers who disagreed as to the proper uses of the power they inherited.

## The Arab Conquest of the West

Muhammad's closest followers were his father-in-law Abu Bakr (*ah-boo BAHK-uhr*) and an early convert named Umar. After Muhammad's death, they took the initiative in providing a leader for the Muslims of Arabia by naming Abu Bakr as *caliph*, a word meaning "deputy" or "representative" of Muhammad. But many tribes were unwilling to accept this aged man's authority as Muhammad's successor, leading to a new phase of warfare. As armies loyal to Abu Bakr moved northward, their successes encouraged even more men to embrace Islam and join the fight to establish the faith. When they came to the Arabian frontier they kept going, meeting only minimal resistance from the Byzantine and Persian armies as they moved west.

When Abu Bakr died two years later, Umar succeeded him as caliph, and he continued to direct the growing Muslim forces against Byzantium and Persia. In the following years, victories were virtually continuous. In 636, they routed a Byzantine army in Syria and then quickly swept over the entire area, occupying the leading cities of Antioch, Damascus, and Jerusalem. In 637, they destroyed the main army of the Persians and took the Persian capital of Ctesiphon. By 651, the Arabian conquest of the entire Persian Empire was virtually complete.

Arab forces, now increased by newer converts to Islam, then turned toward North Africa, capturing Roman Egypt by 646 and extending their control throughout the rest of North Africa during the following decades. Only Ethiopia, far to the south, remained an independent Christian kingdom. Although attempts to capture Constantinople were not successful, as we noted above, Muslim forces crossed from North Africa into Visigothic Spain in 711, quickly absorbing most of the Iberian Peninsula. In less than a century, followers of Islam had conquered the oldest civilizations of western Asia and much of the Roman Mediterranean. In the process, the desert-dwelling Arabs had transformed themselves into the world's most daring seafarers.

How can we explain this prodigious achievement? On a basic level, what motivated the Arabs had motivated the Sumerians, Neo-Assyrians, Greeks, Macedonians, and Romans: the search for richer territory and new wealth. The Muslim identity that was bound up with military successes also played a crucial role, since the teachings of Muhammad and the shared study of the Qur'an forged common allegiances among tribes hitherto at war with one another.

This Muslim identity must have been further strengthened by the absence of any organized opposition to the Arabs' advancement; it was regarded as a mark of their religious superiority. Missionary fervor may also have played a role, although there is little evidence that Muslims actively

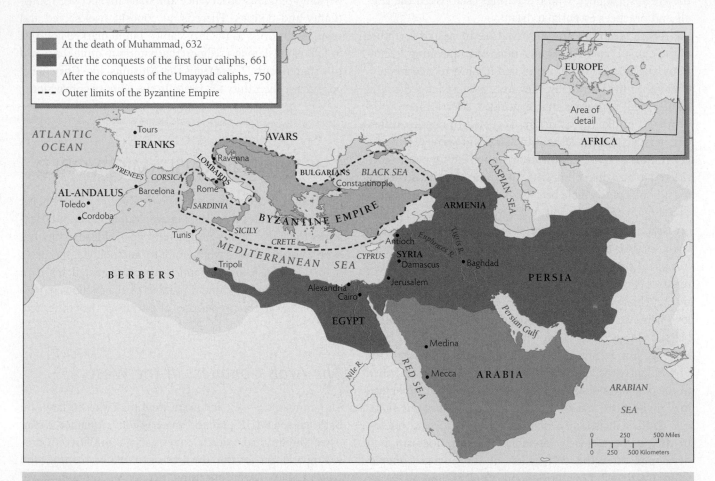

**THE EXPANSION OF ISLAM TO 750.** This map shows the steady advance of Islam through Arab conquests from the time of Muhammad to the middle of the eighth century. ■ *What was the geographical extent of Muslim rule in 750?* ■ *Compare this map to the map of Justinian's empire on page 214. Which of these territories had formerly belonged to Rome? What resources would have been available to the Muslim conquerors as they moved into these territories?*

converted their new subjects to the faith of Islam at this time. Instead, they established themselves as a ruling class, with a grasp of the sophisticated workings of governance and finance that matched their military acumen. Non-Muslims living under Muslim rule were expected to pay the taxes that had been due to the previous Persian or Byzantine authorities, as well as a poll tax (*jizya*). In many places, those conquered by the Muslims preferred their rule to that of their Byzantine and Persian predecessors.

## The Shi'ite–Sunni Schism

As this wave of conquests widened the reach of Islam, disputes continued to divide the original Muslims of Mecca. When the caliph Umar died in 644, he was replaced by Uthman, a member of the Umayyad (*oo-MY-yad*) family: a wealthy clan that had long resisted Muhammad's authority. Opponents of Uthman accordingly rallied around Muhammad's cousin and son-in-law, Ali, whose family ties to Muhammad made him seem a more appropriate choice. When Uthman was murdered in 656, Ali's supporters declared him the new caliph—but Uthman's powerful family refused to accept him. When Ali, too, was murdered, another member of the Umayyad family replaced him. From 661 to 750, this Umayyad dynasty ruled the Islamic world, establishing its capital at Damascus in Syria.

Ali's followers, however, did not accept defeat. They formed a separate group known as the Shi'ites (from *shi'a*, the Arabic word for "faction"). The Shi'ites insisted that only descendants of Ali and his wife, Muhammad's daughter Fatimah, could legitimately rule the Muslim community. Moreover, the Shi'ites did not accept the customary religious practices (*sunna*) that had developed under the first two caliphs who succeeded Muhammad, his father-in-law Abu Bakr and his disciple Umar. Hence, those Muslims who supported the Umayyad family and who *did* regard these customs as binding were called Sunnis. This division between Shi'ites and Sunnis lasts until the present day. Often persecuted by the Sunni majority as heretics, Shi'ites consider themselves the only true exponents of Islam. Today, Shi'ites predominate in Iran and are the largest single Muslim group in Iraq, yet they constitute only one-tenth of the world's Muslims.

**THE GREAT UMAYYAD MOSQUE AT DAMASCUS.** This mosque was built by Caliph al-Walid between 705 and 715. Byzantine influence is apparent in its arched colonnades, mosaics, and series of domes, all of which were replicated in many subsequent Islamic architecture. The mosaic over the central doorway, shown here, indicates that the visitor is entering paradise. The mosque was constructed on the foundations of a Roman temple and also incorporates a later Christian shrine dedicated to Saint John the Baptist. ▪ *Why would the caliph have chosen this site for his mosque?*

## The Umayyad and Abbasid Dynasties

The political triumph of the Umayyads in 661 and the military conquests of their supporters created a strong state centered on Damascus, formerly an administrative capital of the Roman Empire. And in many ways, the Umayyad caliphate functioned as a Roman successor state: it even continued to employ Greek-speaking bureaucrats trained in the techniques of Roman governance. Through these means, the Umayyads dominated the Mediterranean for several generations.

But the failure of the Umayyads' two massive attacks on Constantinople checked their power, which was also being challenged by a rival dynasty, the Abbasids, who claimed descent from one of Muhammad's uncles and regarded the Umayyads as usurpers. In 750, the Abbasids led a successful rebellion, with the help of the Persians, forcing the Umayyads to retreat to their territories in Al-Andalus (Muslim Spain).

In contrast with the Umayyads, the Abbasid caliphate stressed Persian elements over Roman ones. Symbolic of this change was the shift in capitals from Damascus to Baghdad, where the second Abbasid caliph, al-Mansur (r. 754–775), built a new city near the ruins of the old Persian capital. The Abbasid caliphs also modeled their behavior on that of

Persian princes and their administration on the autocratic rule of the former Persian Empire, imposing heavy taxation to support a large professional army and presiding over an extravagantly luxurious court. This is the world described in the *Arabian Nights*, a collection of stories written in Baghdad under the Abbasids. The dominating presence in these stories is Harun al-Rashid, who ruled from 786 to 809. His reign marked the height of Abbasid power.

Meanwhile, the Umayyad dynasty continued to rule in Al-Andalus and continued to claim that it was the only legitimate successor of Muhammad. Relations between the Umayyads of Spain and the Abbasids of Persia were therefore very cold; but because their realms were far apart, the hostility between them rarely erupted into war. Instead, the two courts competed for preeminence through literary and cultural patronage, much as the Hellenistic kingdoms had done. Philosophers, artists, and especially poets flocked to both. The *Arabian Nights* was one product of this rivalry in Baghdad. Not to be outdone, the caliphs at the Spanish capital of Córdoba amassed a library of more than 400,000 volumes—at a time when a monastery in western Europe that possessed 100 books qualified as a major center of learning. Nothing remotely comparable had been seen in the Mediterranean since the time of the Ptolemies in Alexandria.

## Commerce and Industry in the Islamic World

Alongside its political and military triumphs, the transformation of tiny settlements into thriving metropolitan commercial centers is one of early Islam's most remarkable achievements. So is the Arabs' capacity to adapt themselves to life in highly urbanized regions and to build on the long-established commercial infrastructures of Egypt, Syria, and Persia. By the tenth century, Arab merchants had penetrated into southern Russia and equatorial Africa, and had become masters of the caravan routes that led eastward to India and China. Ships from the Islamic world established new trade routes across the Indian Ocean, the Persian Gulf, and the Caspian Sea, and for a time dominated the Mediterranean as well.

The growth of commerce during this period was driven and sustained by a number of important new industries. Mosul in Iraq was a center for the manufacture of cotton cloth; Baghdad specialized in glassware, jewelry, pottery, and silks; Damascus was famous for its fine steel and its woven-figured silk known as "damask"; Morocco and portions of Al-Andalus were noted for leatherworking; and Toledo produced excellent swords. Drugs, perfumes, carpets,

tapestries, brocades, woolens, satins, metal goods, and a host of other products turned out by skilled artisans were carried throughout the Mediterranean world, and also into central Asia along the network of roads to China that came to be known as the Silk Road—after the most prized commodity for which these goods were traded. With these precious goods went the Islamic faith, which took root among some peoples in what are now India, Pakistan, and Afghanistan.

## The Power of Paper

One commodity in particular deserves special mention: paper. Both Arabs and Persians learned papermaking from the Chinese and became masters of the art in their own right. By the end of the eighth century, Baghdad alone had more than a hundred shops where blank paper or books written on paper were sold. Paper was cheaper to produce, easier to store, and far easier to use than papyrus (the chief writing material of antiquity) or parchment (widely used in northern Europe). As a result, paper replaced papyrus in the Islamic world by the early eleventh century—even in Egypt, the heartland of papyrus production for almost 4,000 years.

The ready availability of paper brought about a revolution. Many of the characteristic features of Islamic civilization—bureaucratic record keeping, high levels

**ARABIC CALLIGRAPHY.** Muslim artists experimented with the art of calligraphy to make complex designs, sometimes abstract but often representing natural forms. This ink drawing on paper actually incorporates Arabic words. It dates from the seventh century and also demonstrates the Muslim mastery of papermaking.

of literacy and book production (especially copies of the Qur'an), even the standard form of cursive Arabic script known as Kufic—would have been impossible without the widespread availability of paper. Western Europeans began to practice papermaking only in the thirteenth century, but they would still continue to rely on the more durable parchment made from animal hides for the copying of most books and documents. And it was not until the advent of print that paper began to replace parchment as the reading and writing material of western Europe (see Chapter 12).

## Mobility, Opportunity, and Status

As the reach of Islam extended through conquest and commerce, so Muslim culture became highly cosmopolitan, blending Arab customs with the civilizations of Byzantium and Persia, which were themselves the heirs of ancient empires stretching back to the time of Hammurabi's Babylon. The preeminence of trade and ease of travel increased geographical mobility, and with it social mobility. (Muhammad's teachings further encouraged this, because the Qur'an stressed the equality of all Muslim men.) At the courts of Baghdad and Córdoba, careers were open to men of talent, regardless of birth or wealth. Because literacy was remarkably widespread, many could rise through education and achieve top offices through enterprise and skill. Even slaves could achieve high status through these means. Slave women (non-Muslim or Muslim) who bore male children to Muslim men often shared some of the privileges of their legitimate sons.

For those men wishing instead to embrace the religious life, Islam offered two main alternatives. One was that of the *ulama*, a learned man whose studies qualified him to offer advice on aspects of religious law and practice. These men often exerted great influence on the conduct of public life. Complementary to them were the *Sufis*, mystics who might be equated with Christian monks were it not for the fact that they seldom withdrew from the life of the community. Whereas the ulamas stressed adherence to religious law, the Sufis stressed individual contemplation and the cultivation of spiritual ecstasy. Some Sufis were "whirling dervishes," so known in the West because of their mystical dances; others were *faqirs*, associated in the West with snake charming; still others were quiet, meditative men. Sufis were usually organized into brotherhoods and eventually made many successful efforts to convert the peoples of Africa and India to Islam. Sufism also provided a channel for the most intense religious impulses. The ability of the ulamas and the Sufis to coexist is testimony to the cultural pluralism of the Islamic world.

There were no comparable careers for religious women, a reminder of the limits often imposed by gender. There are significant exceptions, of course. Muhammad's favored wife, Aisha (*ah-EE-sha*; d. 678), was revered as a scholar and played an important role in the creation and circulation of the *hadith* (Arabic for "narrative"): stories and sayings that shed light on the Prophet's life and teachings. But in general, women were mainly considered valuable as indicators of a man's wealth and status. The Qur'an allowed any Muslim man to marry as many as four wives, which often meant that the number of women available for marriage was far smaller than the number of men who desired to marry. This made for intense competition, and men who had wives and daughters needed to ensure that their prized assets were safeguarded. So women were usually kept from the sight of men who were not members of the family or trusted friends. Along with female servants and the enslaved concubines also owned by wealthy men, they were housed in a segregated part of the residence called the *haram* ("forbidden place"). Following Persian custom, they were often guarded by eunuchs (men, usually sold as slaves, who had been castrated prior to adolescence). Within these enclaves, women vied with each other for precedence and worked to advance the fortunes of their children—often the only form of power they could exercise.

## Islam's Neighbors

For the inhabitants of Byzantium, the triumph of the Abbasid caliphate in the eighth century released the Mediterranean from the pressures of Umayyad expansion. Farther west, the Franks of Gaul also benefited from the advent of the Abbasids. Because an Umayyad dynasty controlled Al-Andalus, the great Frankish ruler Charlemagne (*SHAHR-leh-mayn*; r. 768–814) could counter neighboring Muslims' power by maintaining strong diplomatic and commercial relations with the more distant Abbasid caliphate. The most famous symbol of this connection was an elephant called Abul Abbas, a gift from Harun al-Rashid to Charlemagne. More important, however, was the flow of silver that found its way from the Abbasid Empire north through the Baltic into the Rhineland, where it was exchanged for Frankish exports of furs, wax, honey, leather, and especially slaves—Europeans, often Slavic peoples, who were captured and sold for profit by other Europeans. Through these channels, jewels, silks, spices, and other luxury goods from India and the Far East flowed north and west into Frankish territory. These trading links with the Abbasid world helped fund the extraordinary achievements of Charlemagne's own empire, which had a lasting effect on the culture and politics of Europe.

# Past and Present

## *The Meanings of Medievalism*

Joan of Arc Saved France

W.S.S. **WOMEN OF AMERICA SAVE YOUR COUNTRY** *Buy* **WAR SAVINGS STAMPS** UNITED STATES TREASURY DEPARTMENT

*The return of Sir Lancelot*

The people who lived during the thousand-year period that we call the Middle Ages didn't think of themselves as "medieval." And indeed, this modern term tends to be used to describe modern phenomena—whether things that we seek to condemn (terrorism, persecution) or to glorify. The romantic image of Joan of Arc on the left was used to rally Americans to the cause of France and its allies during World War I. The image on the right shows warfare as imagined by the game *Arthur II*.

**Watch related author interview on the Student Site**

## THE CONVERSION OF NORTHWESTERN EUROPE

At the end of the sixth century, the Frankish chronicler Gregory of Tours (c. 538–594) considered himself to be a Roman, living in a Roman world of towns, trade, and local administration. Gregory was proud of his family's senatorial rank and took it for granted that he and his male relatives should be bishops who ruled, by right of birth and status, over their cities and the surrounding countryside. Like others of his class, Gregory still spoke and wrote Latin—a different Latin from the polished prose of Cicero, but one that would certainly have been comprehensible to the Romans of the republic. Although Gregory was aware that the western territories of the Roman Empire were now ruled by Frankish, Visigothic, and Lombard kings, he regarded at least some of these kings as Roman successors because

they ruled in accordance with Roman models. In the case of the Franks, the king even ruled with the approval of the Roman emperor in Constantinople. It was also a source of satisfaction to Gregory that all these barbarian kings had converted to Roman Christianity and no longer embraced the heresy of Arianism, which reinforced their *romanitas* and lent legitimacy to their rule.

Two hundred years later, the greatest of all Frankish kings, Charlemagne (742–814), was crowned as a new kind of Roman emperor in the West. But by this time, people no longer felt a sense of direct continuity with the earlier Roman world or a sense of obligation to the Roman emperor in Byzantium. When intellectuals at Charlemagne's court set out to reform the political, religious, and cultural life of their time, their goal was to revive the Roman Empire from which they considered themselves estranged. They sought a *renovatio Romanorum imperii* ("a renewal of the empire of the Romans"). This awareness of a break with the Roman past developed during the seventh century as a consequence of profound economic, religious, and cultural changes.

## Economic and Political Instability

Even though the economy of the Roman Empire had become increasingly regionalized from the third century C.E. onward (see Chapter 6), the Mediterranean remained a crucial nexus of trade and communication. Gold coinage continued to circulate in both the eastern and the western provinces; a luxury trade in silks, spices, swords, and jewelry continued to move west; and slaves, wine, grain, and leatherwork still moved east from Gaul, Hispania, and North Africa toward Constantinople, Egypt, and Syria. By about 650, however, this Mediterranean world disintegrated further. This was partly a result of Justinian's failed efforts to reconquer the empire's western territories, and imperial overtaxation of agricultural land, especially in Egypt and North Africa, also played a role.

But the most significant causes of economic instability in northwestern Europe were internal, not external. The cities of Italy, Gaul, and Hispania could no longer maintain their walls, public buildings, and urban infrastructures as they had done under the Roman Empire. Although Christian bishops and their aristocratic kinsmen still governed from these cities and continued to provide a market for certain kinds of luxury goods, barbarian kings and their nobles were moving to the countryside during the seventh century, living as much as possible from the produce of their own estates rather than purchasing their supplies in the marketplace. At the same time, much agricultural land was passing out of cultivation. The slaves or servile peasants who had farmed the large plantations for hundreds of years had no efficient Roman state to enforce their obedience. They were able to become more independent, yet also less effective, working just a few acres by themselves. Productivity declined, as did revenues from tolls and taxes.

The systems of coinage that circulated in western Europe were also breaking down, which means that wealth ceased to be readily portable, hindering long-distance exchange. The Arab conquests may have further reduced the supply of gold available, because it was now being channeled eastward. But in any case, gold coins were too valuable to be useful in a local market economy. When we find evidence of such coins at this time, they are more likely to have been plundered, hoarded, or given as gifts rather than used to facilitate commerce. By the 660s, rulers who were still in a position to mint coins and guarantee their value had shifted from gold to silver coinage. Indeed, Europe would remain a silver-based economy for the next thousand years, until the supply of gold from European conquests in Africa and America once again made a gold standard viable (see Chapter 12).

## Lordship and Its Limitations

As a result of these processes, western Europe came to rely on a two-tier economy, a kind that had not been necessary in any Western civilization since the Lydians introduced a standardized currency in the sixth century B.C.E. (see Chapter 2). Gold, silver, and luxury goods circulated among the very wealthy, but most people relied on barter and various substitute currencies to facilitate transactions. Local lords collected rents from their peasants in food or labor, but then found it difficult to convert these in-kind payments into weapons, jewelry, and silks that brought prestige in aristocratic society. This was problematic not only for social reasons but also for political ones: the power of lords depended on their ability to bestow rich gifts on their followers (see *Interpreting Visual Evidence* on page 232). When they could not acquire these items through trade, they had to win them through plunder and extortion; either way, the process led to violence.

The successful chieftains of this era therefore tended to be those whose areas of influence adjoined wealthy but poorly defended territories that could easily be attacked or blackmailed. Such "soft frontiers" provided warlords and kings with land and booty that they could then distribute to their followers. Successes of this sort would bring more followers to a lord's service, allowing him to further extend his influence; and as long as more conquests were made, the process of amassing power and wealth would continue. But power acquired through plunder and conquest was inherently fragile: a few defeats might speedily reverse the fortunes of the lords reliant on it, leaving their followers to seek plunder elsewhere.

Another factor contributing to the instability of power in this world was the difficulty of ensuring its peaceful transfer. The barbarian rulers who established themselves during the mass migrations of the fifth and sixth centuries did not come from the traditional royal families of their peoples, and thus faced opposition from many of their own warriors. Moreover, the groups who took possession of territories within the western Roman Empire during these years were rarely (if ever) composed of a single affinity group; they were usually made up of many different tribes, including a sizable number of displaced Romans. Such unity was largely the creation of the charismatic chieftain who led them, and this charisma was not easily passed on by inheritance.

## The Ship Burial of Sutton Hoo

Two of the most impressive finds in the history of British archaeology have been made by amateurs. The most recent, in the summer of 2009, was the largest hoard of worked gold and silver ever found in one place, more than 5 kilograms of gold and 2.5 kilograms of silver (image A). It was discovered by a man in Staffordshire walking over a neighbor's farm with a metal detector. The hoard's extraordinary value and range of artifacts—and their historical implications—can only be guessed at now; even the dating is inconclusive.

The other find, made in 1939, was a royal gravesite dating from the seventh century (image B), which many scholars believe to be the tomb of King Redwald of East Anglia, described by Bede as a baptized Christian who refused to give up the worship of his ancestral gods. The king's body was placed in a wooden structure in the middle of a ninety-foot-long ship that had been dragged to the top of a bluff (a *hoo*), eleven miles from the English Channel. The ladder in the photograph of the original excavation reaches into the burial chamber.

The contents of the grave included:

- a lamp and a bronze bucket that had been suspended from a chain

A. The Straffordshire hoard, found in 2009.

B. The original excavation of the burial chamber at Sutton Hoo, found in 1939.

## The Prosperous Kingdom of the Franks

Of all the groups that set up kingdoms in western Europe during the fifth and sixth centuries, only the Franks succeeded in establishing a single dynasty from which leaders would be drawn for the next 250 years. This dynasty reached back to Clovis (r. c. 481–511), a warrior-king who established an alliance between his family and the powerful bishops of Gaul by converting to Roman Christianity—emulating the example of Constantine on many levels. Clovis's family came to be known as the Merovingians, after his legendary grandfather Merovech, who was said to have been fathered by a sea monster—meaning that no one really knew where Merovech came from. Clovis's own name proved even longer lasting than the dynasty he founded. As the language of the Franks merged with the

- a ceremonial helmet (image C) modeled on those worn by Roman cavalry officers just before the withdrawal of the legions from Britain in 410, but decorated like helmets found in eastern Sweden

- a sword and a large circular shield, resembling those found in Swedish burial sites

- exquisitely crafted belt buckles and shoulder clasps (image D) made of gold and garnets and worked with designs

- a pair of silver spoons with long handles, possibly crafted in Byzantium, and inscribed in Greek with the names PAULOS and SAULOS (Paul and Saul)

- a large silver dish (72 cm in diameter) made in Byzantium between 491 and 518

- a bronze bowl from the eastern Mediterranean

- a six-stringed lyre in a bag made of beaver skin, similar to lyres found in Germany

- a purse containing thirty-seven gold coins, each from a different Merovingian mint, the most recent datable to the 620s

- heaps of armor, blankets, cloaks, and other gear

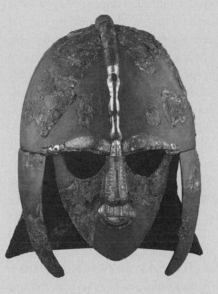

C. Sutton Hoo helmet.

### Questions for Analysis

*1.* What do these artifacts, and the contexts in which they were found, reveal about the extent of Anglo-Saxon contact with the rest of the world? Which regions are represented, and why?

*2.* From this evidence, what conclusions can you draw about Anglo-Saxon culture and values?

*3.* Do any of these graves' goods indicate that the occupant was a Christian king? Why or why not?

D. Sutton Hoo buckles.

Latin of Gaul to become French, the name "Clovis" lost its hard *C*, and the pronunciation of the *V* was softened. Thus "Clovis" became "Louis," the name borne by French kings up to the time of the French Revolution over a millennium later (see Chapter 18).

The Merovingians were not the only noble family in Gaul with a claim to kingship, but they were more successful in defending it than their counterparts in Visigothic Spain, Lombard Italy, and both the Anglo-Saxon and Celtic territories of Britain. In part, this was due to their capacity to transfer power from one generation to another. In early medieval Europe, the right of inheritance was not limited to the eldest male claimant of each competing royal family. When it came to property or power, all the king's sons—and frequently all his male cousins and nephews, and even his daughters—could consider themselves rightful heirs.

## From Anglo-Saxon Slave Girl to Frankish Queen

*The Anglo-Saxon Saint Balthild rose to prominence as the wife of the Merovingian king Clovis II (r. 639–657), but she began her life as a slave. After the king's death, she was left in a precarious position at the Frankish court as regent for her son, Clothar III, and eventually was forced to enter the convent she had founded at Chelles, near Paris. The following excerpt from her Latin vita ("life") describes her speedy ascent to a position of power. It was probably written by a nun of Chelles.*

raise should first be sung of Him Who made the humble great and raised the pauper from the dung-hill and seated him among the princes of his people. Such a one is the woman present to our minds, the venerable and great lady Balthild the queen. Divine Providence called her from across the seas. She, who came here as God's most precious and lofty pearl, was sold at a cheap price. Erchinoald, a Frankish magnate and most illustrious man, acquired her and in his service the girl behaved most honorably. . . . For she was kind-hearted and sober and prudent in all her ways, careful and plotting evil for none. . . . And since she was of the Saxon race, she was graceful in form with refined features, a most seemly woman with a smiling face and serious gait. And she so showed herself just as she ought in all things, that she pleased her master and found favor in his eyes. So he determined that she should set out the drinking cup for him in his chamber and, honored above all others as his house-keeper, stand at his side always ready to serve him. . . . She gained such happy fame that, when the said lord Erchino-ald's wife died, he hoped to unite him-self to Balthild, that faultless virgin, in a matrimonial bed. . . .

[But] when she was called to the master's chamber she hid herself secretly in a corner and threw some vile rags over herself so that no one could guess that anyone might be concealed there. . . . She hoped that she might avoid a human marriage bed and thus merit a spiritual and heavenly spouse. . . . Thereafter it happened, with God's approval, that Balthild, the maid who escaped marriage with a lord, came to be espoused to Clovis, son of the former king Dagobert. Thus by virtue of her humility she was raised to a higher rank.

Source: Excerpted from *Sainted Women of the Dark Ages,* ed. and trans. John E. Halborg, Jo Ann McNamara, and E. Gordon Whatley (Chapel Hill, NC: 1992), pp. 268–70.

### Questions for Analysis

**1.** Judging from what you have learned about the prevalence of the slave trade in ancient and early medieval civilizations, what might you speculate about Balthild's actual role in Erchino-ald's household?

**2.** Balthild would have been a contemporary of the king buried at Sutton Hoo. Is it likely that she would have been a Christian when she was sold into slavery in England? Why or why not?

**3.** In light of Balthild's later status as a queen and regent for her son, why would her biographer stress that she was "careful and plotting evil for none"? To what allegations or incidents might the author of this life be responding?

---

So even when the rule of any family was not threatened by outsiders, the transfer of power was almost always bloody.

In Gaul, however, the often brutal conflicts between rival Merovingian kings did not materially disrupt the strength and sophistication of their governance. Many elements of late Roman local administration survived throughout this period. Latin literacy, fostered by a network of monasteries linked to the Frankish court, remained an important element in this administration, providing a foundation on which Charlemagne would later build. Even the cultural revival associated with the reign of Charlemagne (see below) really began in the late seventh century at the monastic foundations fostered by members of the Merovingian family and other powerful lords. Such monasteries grew remarkably during the seventh century, becoming the engines that made Merovingian Gaul wealthier and more stable than other regions of northwestern Europe. Approximately 550 monasteries were thriving by the year 700, more than 300 of which had been established in the preceding century alone. Frankish bishops also prospered along with their cities, amassing most of their landed possessions by the end of the seventh century, possessions from which their successors would continue to profit until the time of the French Revolution.

This massive redistribution of wealth reflected a fundamental shift in the economic center of gravity of the Frankish kingdom. In the year 600, the wealth of Gaul was still concentrated in the south, where it had been throughout the late Roman period. By the year 750, however, the economic center of the kingdom lay north of the Loire, in the territories that extended from the Rhineland westward to the North Sea. It was here that most of the new monastic foundations of the seventh century were established.

Behind this shift in prosperity lay a long effort to bring under cultivation the rich, heavy soils of northern Europe. This effort was largely engineered by the new monasteries, which harnessed the peasant workforce and pioneered agricultural technologies adapted to the climate and terrain. The most important invention was a heavy, wheeled plow capable of cutting and turning grassland sod and clay, soils very different from those of the Mediterranean. This innovation in turn necessitated the development of more efficient devices for harnessing animals (particularly oxen) to these plows. Gradually warming weather (see Chapter 8) also improved the fertility of the wet northern soils, lengthening the growing season and so making possible more efficient crop-rotation systems. As food became more plentiful, the population began to expand. Although much of Frankish Gaul remained a land of scattered settlements separated by dense forests, it was far more populous by 750 than it had been in the time of Clovis. All these developments would continue during the reign of Charlemagne and beyond.

## The Power of Monasticism

As we have just seen, the seventh century witnessed a rapid increase in the foundation of monastic houses all over northwestern Europe. Although monasteries had existed in Gaul, Italy, and Hispania since the fourth century, most were located in highly Romanized areas. In the fifth century, a powerful monastic movement began in Ireland as well, and eventually spread to the Celtic regions of Britain and from there to the Continent. The Irish missionary Columbanus (540–615), for example, was the founder of Merovingian monasteries at Luxeuil and Fontaine. Important monasteries were also established on the island of Iona, off the western coast of what is now Scotland, and at Lindisfarne, off Britain's northeastern coast. In all of these cases, close ties were forged between monks and local tribal leaders or powerful families, much to the political and economic gain of all parties.

**ABBEY CHURCH, ISLAND OF IONA.** This tiny island off Scotland's west coast is the site of many Iron Age forts and has been home to a monastic community since the sixth century. Missionaries from Iona were instrumental in converting the Celtic tribes of northern Britain to Christianity.

Most monastic foundations of the seventh century were deliberately located in rural areas and at strategic trading crossroads, where they played a crucial role in trade and governance. Indeed, the material advantages of monastic innovation were a powerful incentive toward Christian conversion in the communities with improved living conditions. Prosperity was also a powerful advertisement for authority: a lord or chieftain who had the support of a monastery and the beneficent Christian God was obviously worthy of loyalty. Because monasteries played such a key role in economic development and political order, lords often granted them special privileges, helping to free them from the control of local bishops and giving them jurisdiction over their own lands. Thus, monasteries became politically powerful, not only because they had been founded by powerful men but because they were lordships in their own right.

Frequently, these new foundations were double monasteries that accommodated women as well as men; but often, they were established for women only. In either case, they were usually ruled by abbesses drawn from noble or royal families. Monasticism thus became a road to political power for women, too. It also gave women—commoners as well as queens—freedoms they did not have elsewhere, or at any other time in history up to this point. Within the monastery, women had more control over their own minds and bodies. They could wield enormous influence, promoting their families' diplomatic and dynastic interests without the dangers and uncertainties of pregnancy. And they were guaranteed salvation, at a time when salvation outside the cloister seemed a perilously uncertain prospect. Moreover, the prayers of holy women were regarded as particularly effective in securing divine support or retribution. This further enriched convents through donations of land and wealth, although it could not always safeguard them from violence, or their inhabitants from abduction and rape.

Monasteries for women also served the interests of men, which is why kings and lords supported them. They were dynamic repositories of prayer, regarded as essential to furthering the ambitions of their male benefactors and protecting them from harm. They provided a dignified place of retirement for inconvenient but politically powerful women, such as the sisters and daughters of rivals or the widow of a previous ruler. And by limiting the number of powerful women who could reproduce, female monasteries also reduced the number of male claimants to power. Establishing aristocratic and royal women in such convents was thus an important way of controlling successions and managing political disputes.

Monasticism played an important role in missionary activity, too. As noted above, the work of Irish monks was crucial to the spread of Christianity in northern parts of Britain and in other areas of northern Europe virtually untouched by the Roman Empire. Missionaries were also sponsored by the fledgling papacy in Rome and by the Merovingian royal family—especially its women. The best example of this is the conversion of Britain's Anglo-Saxon tribes, which we glimpsed in the opening paragraph of this chapter. In 597, a group of forty Benedictine monks were sent by Pope Gregory I (r. 590–604) to the southeastern kingdom of Kent, where their efforts were assisted by Frankish translators—and by the fact that the local king, Æthelbehrt (*ETH-el-behrt*), had married a Frankish princess who was already a Christian. This pattern of influence repeated itself all over southern and eastern Britain. Writing a hundred years later in the monastery of Monkwearmouth in Northumbria, the historian Bede could claim that the tribes of England were now united in their shared allegiance to the Roman Church and its English archbishop, whose seat was the cathedral in Æthelbert's capital at Canterbury. Bede credited the Roman pope for initiating this remarkable achievement, and the monastic rule under which he himself lived for bringing it to fruition.

## The Papacy of Gregory the Great

Pope Gregory I, also known as Gregory the Great, was the first bishop of Rome to envision a new role for the papacy in northwestern Europe. We have seen that the Roman *papa* had begun to assert his superiority over other patriarchs throughout the Christian world; but in reality, he was subordinate to the emperors in Constantinople and the greater prestige of its patriarch. As Byzantine power in Italy declined, however, Gregory sought to create a more autonomous Latin Church by focusing attention on the untapped resources of the wild West. An influential theologian, he is considered the intellectual successor of Jerome, Ambrose, and Augustine (see Chapter 6) because he greatly extended the applicability of their teachings to the world outside the Romanized Mediterranean.

Among Gregory's doctrinal contributions were an emphasis on the necessity of penance for the forgiveness of sins and the concept of Purgatory as a place where the soul could be purified before being admitted into heaven—instead of being sent immediately to perpetual damnation. Alongside this emphasis on penance, Gregory emphasized the importance of pastoral care: the proper instruction, encouragement, and control of the laity. He also sought to increase the affective power of Christian worship by promoting the performance of music. Song has always been essential to religious ritual, but Gregory encouraged it to such a degree that the very style of singing that emerged in this period is known as Gregorian chant.

**THE LINDISFARNE GOSPELS.** This page from one of the astonishing illuminated ("light-filled") books produced by the monastery at Lindisfarne shows the opening of the Gospel of John. ▪ *Why would monastic scribes have devoted so much time, energy, and skill to the decoration of this text? How do these artistic motifs compare with those featured on the metalwork found at Sutton Hoo (see page 232)?* ▪ *What conclusions can you draw from these similarities?*

**THE COVER OF THE LINDAU GOSPELS.** This book, bound in gilded silver and encrusted with jewels and ivory cameos, was presented by Pope Gregory the Great to a Lombard queen around the year 600. ▪ *Given what you have learned about the economic and cultural circumstances of northern Europe, what is the significance of this rich gift?* ▪ *What would Gregory have been attempting to achieve by giving it?*

Gregory was also a statesman and leader in the model of his Roman forebears. Within Italy, he ensured the survival of the papacy against Lombard invaders by clever diplomacy and expert management of papal estates and revenues. He maintained good relations with Byzantium while asserting his authority over the other bishops of the Roman Church. His support of communities living under the *Rule* of Saint Benedict (see Chapter 6) helped make Benedictine monasticism the predominant monastic force in the West. Yet Gregory's influence was not always benign. He was the first prominent theologian to articulate the Church's official policy toward Jews, which became increasingly negative. Building on Gregory's example, later popes would insist that the Jews' alleged role in Christ's crucifixion and their denial of his divinity had deprived them of their rights in a Christian world.

## THE EMPIRE OF CHARLEMAGNE

Toward the end of the seventh century, tensions among noble families in the Merovingian heartland of Neustria and in the Frankish border region of Austrasia were increasing (see map on page 238). The Austrasian nobles had profited from their steady push into the "soft frontier" east of the Rhine, acquiring wealth and military power in the process, while the Merovingians, settled in Neustria, had no such easy conquests at their disposal. Moreover, Merovingians had given a considerable portion of their land to monasteries during the course of the seventh century, which decreased their wealth and their capacity to attract followers. A succession of short-lived kings then opened the door to a series of civil wars, and finally to a decisive challenge to the dynasty.

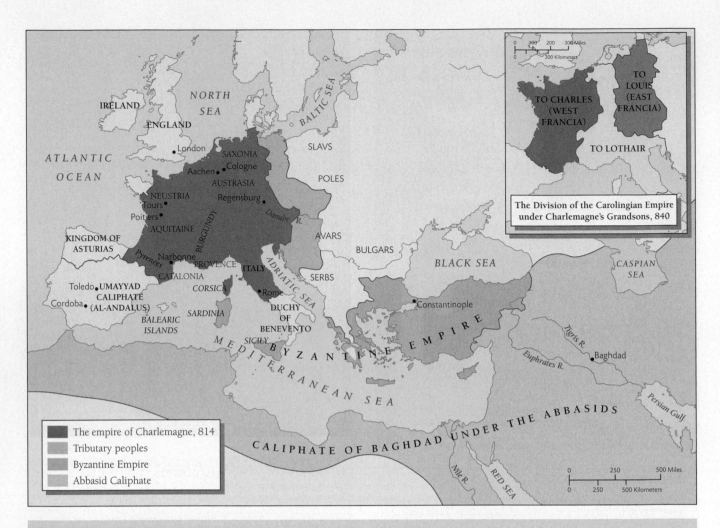

**THE EMPIRE OF CHARLEMAGNE IN 814.** When Charlemagne died in 814, he had created an empire that embraced a large portion of the lands formerly united under the western Roman Empire. ▪ *What were the geographical limits of his power?* ▪ *How were these limits dictated by the historical forces we have been studying?* ▪ *Along what lines was Charlemagne's empire divided after his death?*

## Kings and Kingmakers

In 687, an Austrasian nobleman called Pepin (635/45–714) came to power by making himself the Frankish king's right-hand man and enforcer. He took the title *maior domus* ("great man of the house") and began to exercise royal authority while maintaining the fiction that he was merely a royal servant. He did this effectively for more than twenty-five years. After his death, his illegitimate son Charles Martel ("the Hammer"; 688–741) further consolidated control over both the Merovingian homeland and the Frankish royal administration. For two generations, the Merovingian kings were largely figureheads in a realm ruled by Charles Martel and his sons.

Charles Martel is sometimes considered the second founder (after Clovis) of the Frankish kingdom. His claim to this title is twofold. First, in 733 or 734, he repelled a Muslim

army sent by the Umayyad caliphate in Al-Andalus, which was attempting to expand its reach across the Pyrenees and into the rich farmlands of Aquitaine (the Bordeaux region of modern France). Charles and his forces met them in battle between the cities of Poitiers and Tours, some 150 miles from the Merovingian stronghold at Paris. This victory won him great prestige, and he successfully advanced Frankish power southward toward the Muslim-held region of Narbonne.

At the same time, Charles was fostering an alliance with Benedictine missionaries from England, who were attempting to convert the Low Countries and central Germany to Christianity. Charles's family had long been active in the drive to conquer and settle these areas, and he understood clearly how missionary work and Frankish expansion could go hand in hand, and so assisted these conversion efforts. In return, the leader of the English Benedictines, Boniface (c. 672–754), brought him into contact with the papacy.

Although Charles never sought to become king himself, he was so clearly the effective ruler of Gaul that the Franks did not bother to choose a new king when the reigning Merovingian ruler died in 737. But then Charles himself died in 741, and his sons Carloman and Pepin were forced to allow the election of a new king while they exercised power behind the scenes. This compromise did not last long, however. In 750, Carloman withdrew from public life by entering a monastery, and Pepin decided to seize the throne for himself. This turned out to be harder than he may have expected. Even though the reigning king was ineffectual, Frankish identity was bound up with loyalty to Clovis's descendants; and although tribal leaders had the power to elect a new king, they were reluctant to do so.

Pepin therefore turned to the Frankish bishops, who were also unwilling to support him without backing from Rome. To gain this support, Pepin traded on his family's support of the monastic movement. The pope, for his part, saw that a powerful leader of the Franks could be a potential ally in his political struggle with the Byzantine emperors over iconoclasm (which the papacy opposed), and in his military struggle against the Lombard kings for control of central Italy.

So Boniface, acting as papal emissary, anointed Pepin king of the Franks in 751. Anointing was a new ritual, but it had a powerful biblical precedent: the ceremony by which the prophet Samuel had made Saul the first king of Israel, by anointing his head with holy oil (see Chapter 2). Indeed, the significance of the Old Testament precedent would grow under Pepin's son Charlemagne (associated with David) and his grandson Louis the Pious (associated with Solomon).

To contemporary observers, however, the apparent novelty of these proceedings underscored the uncertainty of the times: a legitimate king had been deposed and a new king elevated. And as we will see, this king-making process was the first step on a long road that would ultimately limit the power of later medieval kings and modern constitutional monarchs alike. It eventually established the principle that kingship is an office that can be occupied, at least theoretically, by anyone; and by extension, if a ruler is ineffectual or tyrannical, he can be deposed and replaced.

## The Reign of Charlemagne

The Franks benefited from Pepin's military leadership. In 759, he finally defeated the Muslims of Narbonne and extended Frankish control to the Mediterranean coast. But his grip on the title of king was a tenuous one; and when he died in 768, it seemed likely that the Frankish kingdom would break up into mutually hostile regions: Austrasia, Neustria, and the new region of Aquitaine. That it did not was the work of Pepin's son, Charles: known to the French as Charlemagne and to the Germans as Karl der Grosse ("Charles the Great") because both modern nations claim him as their founding father. It is from him, as well as from his grandfather Charles Martel, that this new Frankish dynasty takes the name "Carolingian" (from *Carolus*, the Latin form of "Charles").

When Charlemagne came to power in 768, he managed to unite the Franks by the tried and true method of attacking a common, outside enemy. In a series of conquests, the Franks succeeded in annexing the Lombard kingdom of northern Italy, most of what is now Germany, portions of central Europe, and—taking advantage of the weakened Umayyad caliphate—Catalonia, just beyond the Pyrenees. These conquests seemed to set a seal of divine approval on the new Carolingian dynasty. More important, they provided the victorious Franks with spoils of war and vast new lands that enabled Charlemagne to reward his closest followers.

Many of the peoples Charlemagne conquered were already Christians. In the northern territory of Saxony, however, Charlemagne's armies campaigned for twenty years before subduing the pagan inhabitants and forcing their conversion. This created a precedent that linked military conquest with conformity of belief, and it would be repeated by Charlemagne's successors in Baltic and Slavic lands.

To rule his new empire, Charlemagne enlisted the help of the Frankish warrior class he had enriched and elevated to positions of prominence. These counts (*comites* in Latin, "followers") supervised local governance within their territories. Among their many duties were the administration of justice and the raising of armies. Charlemagne also established a network of other local officials who convened courts, established tolls, administered royal lands, and collected taxes. To facilitate transactions and trade, he created a new coinage system based on a division of the silver pound into units of twenty shillings, each worth twelve pennies: a system that would last into the 1970s in parts of continental Europe and in Britain (when it was replaced by a decimal-based currency). As noted above, much of the silver for this new coinage originated in the Abbasid caliphate, and was payment for furs, cloth, and especially slaves captured in Charlemagne's wars, who were now being transported to Baghdad. The silver, in turn, circulated as far north as Scandinavia and the Baltic Sea region.

Like Carolingian administration generally, this new monetary system depended on the regular use of written records, which means that the sources supporting historical research on Charlemagne's empire are numerous. But

# Analyzing Primary Sources

## The Capitularies of Charlemagne

*Charlemagne's careful governance of his domains set a high standard for other rulers far into the future. One of the means by which this governance was carried out was through capitularies (from a Latin word denoting a document divided into chapters), which contained instructions issued by the central administration of the court to local elites known as counts (or comites in Latin)—hence the word "county" to describe an administrative area. The following are directives addressed in 785 to the administrators of Saxony, a region Charlemagne had recently conquered and whose pagan inhabitants were converted to Christianity.*

### Capitulary Concerning the Parts of Saxony

**1.** Decisions were taken first on the more important items. All were agreed that the churches of Christ which are now being built in Saxony and are consecrated to God should have no less honor than the temples of idols had, but rather a greater and more surpassing honor.

**2.** If anyone takes refuge in a church, let no one presume to drive him out of that church by force; rather let him be in peace until he is brought to plead his case, . . . and after this let him be brought to the presence of our lord the king. . . .

**3.** If anyone makes forcible entry to a church, and steals anything from it by violence or stealth, or if he sets fire to the church, let him die.

**4.** If anyone in contempt of the Christian faith should spurn the holy Lenten fast and eat meat, let him die; but let the priest enquire into the matter, lest it should happen that someone is compelled by necessity to eat meat.

\* \* \*

**6.** If anyone is deceived by the devil, and believes after the manner of pagans that some man or some woman is a witch and eats people, . . . let him pay the penalty of death.

**7.** If anyone follows pagan rites and causes the body of a dead man to be consumed by fire, . . . let him pay with his life.

**8.** If there is anyone of the Saxon people lurking among them unbaptized, and if he scorns to come to baptism, . . . let him die.

**9.** If anyone sacrifices a man to the devil, . . . let him die.

\* \* \*

**12.** If anyone rapes the daughter of his lord, he shall die.

**13.** If anyone kills his lord or his lady, he shall be punished in the same way.

\* \* \*

**18.** On Sundays there are to be no assemblies or public gatherings, except in cases of great need or when an enemy is pressing; rather let all attend church to hear the word of God. . . .

\* \* \*

**33.** With regard to perjury, the law of the Saxons is to apply.

**34.** We forbid the Saxons to come together as a body in public gatherings, except on those occasions when our *missus* [messenger] assembles them on our instructions; rather, let each and every count hold court and administer justice in his own area. And the clergy are to see to it that this order is obeyed.

Source: From *The Reign of Charlemagne: Documents on Carolingian Government*, ed. and trans. H. R. Loyn and John Percival (New York: 1975), pp. 51–54.

### Questions for Analysis

**1.** What types of behavior does this capitulary attempt to regulate? What seem to be the major challenges faced by Charlemagne's administrators in this new territory?

**2.** In only one case does this capitulary mention the laws of the Saxon people themselves, in the clause relating to perjury (number 33). Why would Charlemagne's administrators consider it advisable to punish this particular crime in accordance with Saxon custom?

**3.** How would you characterize Charlemagne's method of dealing with a conquered people? In your estimation, is this policy likely to be effective? Why or why not?

Charlemagne did not rely on the written word alone to make his will felt. Periodically, his court sent special messengers, known as *missi*, on tours through the countryside to relay his instructions and report back on the conduct of local administrators. This was the most thorough system of governance known in Europe since the height of the Roman Empire, reaching many parts of the Continent that the Romans had never occupied. It set a standard for royal administration that would be emulated and envied for centuries.

## Christianity and Kingship

In keeping with the traditions established by his father and grandfather, Charlemagne took his responsibilities as a Christian king seriously. Moreover, as his empire expanded, he came to see himself as the leader of a unified Christian society, Christendom, which he was obliged to defend. Like his contemporaries in Byzantium and the Muslim world—as well as his Roman predecessors—he recognized no distinction between religion and politics. Indeed, he conceived kingship as a sacred office created by God to protect the Church and promote the salvation of Christian people. Religious reforms were therefore no less central to proper kingship than were justice and defense. In some ways, a king's responsibilities for his kingdom's spiritual welfare were more important than his other, secular responsibilities.

These ideas were not new in the late eighth century, but they took on a new importance because of the extraordinary power Charlemagne wielded. Like other rulers of this period, Charlemagne was able to appoint and depose bishops and abbots, just as he did his counts and other officials who administered his realm. He extended his authority by changing the liturgy of Frankish churches, reforming the rules of worship in Frankish monasteries, declaring the tenets of Christian belief, ruthlessly prohibiting pagan practices, and forcibly imposing basic Christian observances on the conquered peoples of Saxony. As the dominant political power in central Italy, Charlemagne was also the protector of the papacy. Although he acknowledged the pope as the spiritual leader of Christendom, Charlemagne dealt with the bishop of Rome much as he did other bishops in his empire. He supervised and approved papal elections, and also protected the pope from his many enemies. To Charlemagne, such measures were clearly required if God's new chosen people, the Franks, were to avoid the fate that befell biblical Israel whenever Hebrews turned away from obedience to God.

## The Carolingian Renaissance

Similar political motivations lay behind the phenomenon known as the Carolingian Renaissance, a cultural and intellectual flowering that took place around the Carolingian court. Like their biblical exemplars David and Solomon, Charlemagne and his son Louis the Pious considered it a crucial part of their role to be patrons of learning and the arts. In doing so, they created an ideal of the court as an intellectual and cultural center: an ideal that would profoundly influence western European cultural life until the First World War (see Chapter 24).

Behind the Carolingians' support for scholarship was the conviction that learning was the foundation on which Christian wisdom rested, and that such wisdom was essential to the salvation of God's people. Charlemagne therefore recruited intellectuals from all over Europe to further the cause of scholarship. Foremost among these was the Anglo-Saxon monk Alcuin, whose command of classical Latin established him as the intellectual leader of Charlemagne's court. Under Alcuin's direction, Carolingian scholars produced much original Latin poetry and an impressive number of theological and pastoral tracts. But their primary efforts were devoted to collating, correcting, and recopying ancient Latin texts, including, most important, the text of the Latin Bible, which had accumulated many generations of copyists' mistakes in the 400 years since Jerome's translation (see Chapter 6).

**CHARLEMAGNE'S IMAGE OF AUTHORITY.** A silver penny struck between 804 and 814 in Mainz (as indicated by the letter *M* at the bottom) represents Charlemagne in a highly stylized fashion, as a Roman emperor with a military cloak and laurel wreath. The inscription reads *KAROLUS IMP AVG* (Charles, Emperor, Augustus) and his portrait is closely modeled on both Hellenistic and Roman coins.

**ROMAN HISTORY IN CAROLINGIAN MINUSCULE.** The very survival of Livy's history of the Roman Republic, originally written during the reign of Augustus Caesar, is due to the Carolingian Renaissance. Furthermore, the clear layout and beautifully formed script of this manuscript copy helped readers without detailed knowledge of Latin to make out the words. For example, the first two words of the heading near the bottom are *Incipit Liber* ("[Here] begins the book"), and the sentence following it begins with a reference to the Carthaginian general Hannibal.

To detect and correct these errors, Alcuin and his associates gathered as many different versions of the biblical text as they could find and compared them, word by word. After determining the correct version among all the variants, they made a new, corrected copy and destroyed the other versions. They also developed a new style of handwriting, with simplified letter forms and spaces inserted between words, so as to reduce the likelihood that subsequent copyists would misread the corrected texts. Reading was further facilitated by the addition of punctuation. This new style of handwriting, known as Carolingian minuscule, is the foundation for the typefaces of most modern books—including this one.

## The Revival of the Western Roman Empire

On Christmas Day in the year 800, Charlemagne was crowned emperor by Pope Leo III. Centuries later, popes would cite this epochal event as precedent for the political superiority they claimed over the ruler of the "Holy Roman Empire," as it came to be called (see Chapter 9). In the year 800, however, Pope Leo was entirely under Charlemagne's control. Yet Charlemagne's biographer, Einhard, later claimed that the coronation was planned without the emperor's knowledge. Why, then, did he accept the title and, in 813, transfer it to his son Louis? For one thing, it

was certain to anger the imperial government in Byzantium, with which Charlemagne had strained relations. And the imperial title did not add much to Charlemagne's position since he was already the de facto emperor in his own right.

Historians still debate this question. What is clear, in any case, is the symbolic significance of the action. Although the Romans of Byzantium no longer influenced western Europe directly, they continued to regard it (somewhat vaguely) as an outlying province of their empire. Moreover, the emperor in Constantinople claimed to be the political successor of Caesar Augustus. Charlemagne's assumption of the title Emperor of the Romans was therefore a clear slight to the reigning empress Irene (r. 797–802), whose occupation of the imperial throne was controversial because she was a woman. It also deepened Byzantine suspicion of Charlemagne's cordial relationship with Byzantium's enemy, Harun al-Rashid, the Abbasid caliph of Baghdad. But for Charlemagne's followers—and for all the medieval rulers who came after him—the assumption of the imperial title was a declaration of independence and superiority. With only occasional interruptions, western Europeans continued to crown Roman emperors until the nineteenth century, while territorial claims and concepts of national sovereignty continued to rest on Carolingian precedent. Whatever his own motives may have been, Charlemagne's revival of the western Roman Empire was crucial to the developing self-consciousness of western Europe.

# DISPUTED LEGACIES AND NEW ALLIANCES

When Charlemagne died in 814, his empire descended intact to his only surviving son, Louis the Pious. Under Louis, however, the empire disintegrated and was eventually divided among his three sons in 840. Western Francia (the core of modern France) went to Charles the Bald; eastern Francia (which became key principalities of Germany) went to Louis the German; and a third kingdom (stretching from the Rhineland to Rome) went to Lothair, along with the imperial title. But when Lothair's line died out in 856, this fragile compromise dissolved into open warfare, as the East and West Franks fought over Lothair's former territories and the imperial power that went with them. The heartland of this disputed domain, known to the Germans as Lotharingia and to the French as Alsace-Lorraine, would continue to be a site of bitter contention until the end of the Second World War (see Chapter 26).

## The Collapse of the Carolingian Empire

Louis the Pious faced an impossible situation of a kind we have studied many times before: the task of holding together an artificial constellation of territories united by someone else. Charlemagne's empire had been built on successful conquests; however, by 814, he had pushed the borders of his empire beyond the practical limits of his administration. To the southwest, he now faced the Umayyad rulers of Al-Andalus, and to the north, the pagan inhabitants of Scandinavia. In the east, his armies were too preoccupied with settling the territories they had already conquered to secure the Slavic lands that lay beyond. At the same time, the pressures that had driven these conquests—the need for land and plunder to cement the allegiance of followers—had become ever more pronounced as a result of their very success. The number of counts had tripled, from approximately 100 to 300, and each of them wanted more wealth and power.

Frustrated by the new emperor's inability to reward them, the Frankish aristocracy turned against him and on each other. Smoldering hostilities among Austrasians, Neustrians, and Aquitanians—which Charlemagne had stifled by directing their energies elsewhere—flared up again. As centralized authority broke down, the vast majority of the empire's free inhabitants found themselves increasingly dominated by local lords who treated them as

if they were serfs. At the same time, internal troubles in the Abbasid Empire caused a breakdown in the commercial system through which Scandinavian traders brought Abbasid silver into Carolingian domains. Deprived of their livelihood, these traders turned to raiding, which is what the Norse word *viking* means. Under these combined pressures, the Carolingian Empire fell apart, and a new map of Europe began to emerge.

## The Impact of the Viking Invasions

Scandinavian traders were already familiar figures in the North Sea and Baltic ports of Europe when Charlemagne came to power. They had begun to establish strategic settlements from which they navigated down the rivers to Byzantium (through the Black Sea) and the Abbasid caliphate (through the Caspian Sea). But when the power of the Abbasids declined, Viking raiders turned to plunder, ransom, tribute collection, and slaving. At first, these were small-scale operations; but soon, some Viking attacks involved organized armies numbering in the thousands. The small tribal kingdoms of the Anglo-Saxons and Celts made the British Isles easy targets, as were the divided kingdoms of the Franks.

By the tenth century, the Vikings controlled independent principalities in eastern England, Ireland, the islands of Scotland, and the region of France that is still called "Norseman-land" (Normandy). A Viking people known as the Rus' established the beginnings of a kingdom that would become Russia. At the end of the tenth century, Vikings ventured farther west and colonized Iceland, Greenland, and a distant territory they called Vinland (Newfoundland, Canada). In 1016, a Viking army placed a Danish king on the English throne.

The threat of Viking attacks began to diminish after Scandinavia's conversion to Christianity, which proceeded rapidly from the late tenth century onward. But it was more effectively mitigated by the fact that Viking populations quickly assimilated into the cultural and political world of northwestern Europe. By 1066, when the "Norsemen" of Normandy conquered England, the English—many of whom were descended from Vikings themselves—perceived them to be French. Driving this rapid assimilation may have been the raids of the Magyars, a non-Indo-European people who crossed the Carpathian Mountains around 895 and carried out a number of devastating campaigns throughout continental Europe before settling in what is now Hungary. The disparate inhabitants of the new Viking colonies may have been forced to unite

**PATTERNS OF VIKING ACTIVITY AND SETTLEMENT, c. 800–1100.** The Vikings were instrumental in maintaining commercial contacts among northern Europe, Byzantium, and Islam until the eighth century, when changing historical forces turned them into raiders and colonists. ▪ *What area was the original homeland of the Vikings?* ▪ *What geographic region did the Vikings first conquer, and why?* ▪ *The areas marked in green show territories that were later targeted by pillagers. Why would the Vikings have avoided settlement in these areas?*

against this common enemy, and thus may have come to share a sense of common identity.

The overall effect of the Viking diaspora and settlement on Europe continues to be a matter of scholarly controversy. The destruction caused by raiding is undeniable, and many of the monasteries of Frankish, Anglo-Saxon, and Celtic lands were destroyed—along with countless precious books and historical artifacts. Yet the Vikings were not the only source of disorder in the ninth and tenth centuries. The civil wars and local political rivalries that had replaced the centralized states of Charlemagne and the Islamic caliphates contributed mightily to the chaos of the post-Carolingian world and made the Vikings' successes easily won. Nor were the Vikings a source of disorder alone. In Ireland and eastern England, Vikings founded a series of new towns. And as long-distance traders, they transported large quantities of silver into western Europe, fueling the European economy.

## Alfred the Great and the Unification of England

In those few regions where people did succeed in fending off Viking attacks, the unifying force of victory was strong. The best example of this phenomenon is England, which had never been part of Charlemagne's empire and had remained divided into small kingdoms at war with one other—despite Bede's wishful history of an "English church and people." Yet in a direct response to the Viking threat, a loosely unified kingdom emerged for the first time under Alfred the Great (r. 871–899). His success in defending his own small kingdom from Viking attacks, combined with the destruction of every other competing royal dynasty, allowed Alfred and his heirs to assemble effective armed forces, institute mechanisms of local government, found new towns, and codify English laws. In

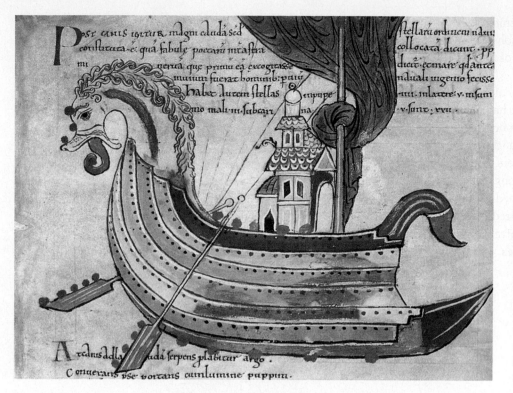

**A DRAGON-PROWED VIKING LONGBOAT.** This manuscript illumination—from a book copied in Anglo-Saxon England—depicts one of the vessels terrifyingly well known to the shore-dwelling peoples of northwestern Europe. Concerted efforts to ward off Viking invasions led to the establishment of the first unified English kingdom.

addition, Alfred established a court school and fostered a distinctive Anglo-Saxon literary culture. Although the Anglo-Saxon vernacular had been a written language since the time of the Roman missions, it now came to rival Latin as a language of administration, history, scholarship, and spirituality. Moreover, oral traditions of poetic composition and storytelling were preserved and extended, as exemplified by the epic *Beowulf*. Until the eleventh century, Anglo-Saxon was the only European vernacular used for regular written communication.

## The Disintegration of the Islamic World

As noted above, the declining power of the Abbasid dynasty in Persia was one of the forces that contributed to the escalation of Viking raids. A major cause of this decline was the gradual impoverishment of the Abbasids' economic base, the agricultural wealth of the ancient Tigris-Euphrates basin, due to ecological crises and a devastating revolt by the enslaved African workforce there. Tax revenues from the Abbasid caliphate also declined as provincial Muslim rulers in North Africa, Egypt, and Syria retained larger and larger portions of those revenues for themselves. As their sources of income became depleted, the Abbasids were unable to support their large civil service and the mercenary

army on which they relied for defense. This army consisted largely of slaves and hired troops whose loyalties lay with the individual rulers who employed them, not the caliphs. Massively expensive building projects, including the construction of the new Abbasid capital at Baghdad, further exacerbated the fiscal, military, and political crisis.

Behind the Abbasid collapse lay two fundamental developments of great significance for the future of the Islamic world: the growing power of regional rulers and the sharpening religious divisions between Sunnis and Shi'ites, and among the Shi'ites themselves. In 909, regional and religious hostilities came together when a local Shi'ite dynasty known as the Fatimids seized control of the Abbasid province of North Africa. In 969, the Fatimids succeeded in conquering Egypt as well. Meanwhile, another Shi'ite group, rivals of both the Fatimids and the Abbasids, attacked Baghdad in 927 and Mecca in 930, seizing the Kaaba. Although an Abbasid caliphate would continue to exist in Baghdad until 1258, when invading Mongol armies dissolved it (see Chapter 10), its empire had effectively disappeared by the 930s. In its place, a new order began to emerge, centered around an independent Egyptian kingdom and a new Muslim state based in Persia.

In Al-Andalus, disputes over succession within the Umayyad dynasty were matched by new external pressures. In the mid-ninth century, the small Christian kingdoms of northern and eastern Iberia began to encroach on Muslim territory, increasing the internal difficulties of the

Umayyad caliphate. By the opening years of the eleventh century, the caliphate had dissolved, to be replaced by a host of smaller kingdoms, some of which paid tribute to the Christian rulers of the north.

The fractured political unity of the Islamic world deepened the religious divisions that had always existed among Muslim groups. Whereas Islamic rulers were relatively tolerant of religious and cultural differences when dealing with Jews and Christians, dissent within Islam itself was another matter. Under the strong rule of the caliphates, some different groups had learned to coexist; but with the disappearance of these centralized states, it became difficult to reconcile the ideal of universality with the realities of regional and ethnic differences.

## CONCLUSION

The three civilizations that emerged as Rome's heirs each exhibit aspects of Roman civilization, which was itself a product of older civilizations. Which civilization was the true heir of the older empire? The answer depends on the criteria used to make this evaluation. If we argue that imperial Rome's most fundamental characteristics were the maintenance of legal and political institutions, the answer is Byzantium. If we are looking for a civilization that combines the rich legacies of ancient Mesopotamia, Egypt, and the Hellenistic world, the answer is Islam, which also emulated Rome in promoting commerce and culture. If we associate Rome chiefly with the city itself and the Latin

## After You Read This Chapter

Go to **INQUIZITIVE** to see what you've learned—and learn what you've missed—with personalized feedback along the way.

### REVIEWING THE OBJECTIVES

- Justinian's attempted reunification of the Roman Empire proved destructive. What were its effects in the East? In the West?
- Byzantine culture was distinctive in many ways. What were some of its important features?
- The rapid expansion of Islam can be explained with reference to several historical factors. What were they?
- What accounts for the close relationship between monasticism and secular power in early medieval Europe?
- What was the Carolingian Empire? Why is it important?

language of the first Romans, or with the Christian patriarchy of Rome, the answer is northwestern Europe.

There are also many connections to be drawn among these three successors. All took on their defining characteristics during the sixth and seventh centuries and, by the eighth century, had developed their own unique strengths and weaknesses. Moreover, they had fruitful—if uneasy—relationships with each other, and many mutual dependencies: Italian traders were active in Constantinople, Muslim traders were common in the ports of southern Italy and Gaul, Anglo-Saxon merchants were regular visitors to the Mediterranean, Jewish merchants in the Rhineland carried on an active trade with the communities of Muslim Egypt, and Viking traders had opened trade routes from the Baltic to the Black Sea and were busily founding cities from Novgorod to Dublin.

But the developments of the ninth and tenth centuries would disrupt these networks and create new centers of power. Western Europeans began to share a sense of common Christian identity: within the vast territory that extended from the Baltic to the Mediterranean, and from the Pyrenees to Poland, every ruler was (or would soon be) looking to the Roman Church for spiritual guidance and to his fellow rulers for aid and alliance. At the same time, western Europe became a society mobilized for war to a degree unmatched in either Byzantium or the Islamic world. In the centuries to come, this militarization would prove to be a decisive factor in the shifting relationship among Rome's heirs.

## PEOPLE, IDEAS, AND EVENTS IN CONTEXT

- In what ways do **JUSTINIAN'S CODE OF ROMAN LAW** and the building of **Hagia Sophia** reflect his desire to revive the glories of ancient Rome?
- What were **BYZANTIUM'S** sources of stability, and of dissent? What effect did the **ICONOCLAST CONTROVERSY** have on Byzantine society?
- What factors contributed to **MUHAMMAD'S** rise to power? What are the **FIVE PILLARS OF ISLAM**? What is the role of the **QUR'AN**?
- To what extent were the **UMAYYAD** and **ABBASID CALIPHATES** heirs of Rome? What made Islamic culture of this period distinctive?
- How did the **MEROVINGIAN** kings of the Franks acquire and hold power? How did **BENEDICTINE MONASTICISM** contribute to the economy of western Europe? How was it linked to politics?
- How did **CHARLEMAGNE** build an empire? How did the **CAROLINGIAN RENAISSANCE** revive and extend **CLASSICAL LEARNING**?
- How did the **VIKINGS** contribute to the developments of the ninth and tenth centuries?

## THINKING ABOUT CONNECTIONS

- Arguably, each of these three civilizations could claim the mantle of the Roman Empire. In your view, which one has the strongest claim to carrying forward the legacies of the classical past?
- How do the historical circumstances in which Islam emerged compare with those that shaped early Christianity? What are some key similarities and differences?

## STORY LINES

- Around the year 1000, a warming climate and new agricultural technologies and social groupings transformed the economy and landscape of Europe. Meanwhile, new kingdoms emerged in Scandinavia and eastern Europe.
- The rejuvenation of towns and trade created new opportunities for advancement. But at the same time, the decentralization of political power led to violent rule by lords who could harness human and material resources to their own advantage.
- Meanwhile, a reforming movement within the Roman Church increased the authority of the papacy, which attempted to assert its supremacy over secular rulers and to control violence by directing it against Europe's neighbors.
- One manifestation of this Church-sanctioned violence was the First Crusade, which began when Muslim warriors' attack on Byzantium became the pretext for a holy war.
- Crusading broadened cultural and economic contacts with the East, but also led to increased intolerance of "others," both outside and within Europe.

## CHRONOLOGY

| | |
|---|---|
| 900–1050 | Monastic reform movement |
| 911–989 | The peoples of Rus' are converted by missionaries from Byzantium |
| 930 | Establishment of the Althing in Iceland |
| 936–973 | Reign of Otto I "the Great" |
| 980–1037 | Lifetime of Avicenna |
| 1035 | Death of Cnut the Great |
| 1050 | Medieval agricultural revolution at its height |
| 1066–1087 | Reign of William the Conqueror in England |
| 1073–1085 | Papacy of Gregory VII |
| 1075–1122 | Investiture Conflict |
| 1081–1118 | Reign of Alexius Comnenus in Byzantium |
| 1095–1099 | First Crusade |
| c. 1100 | The *Song of Roland* is written down |

Before
You
Read
This
Chapter

# The Expansion of Europe, 950–1100

## CORE OBJECTIVES

- **EXPLAIN** the reasons for the diffusion of political power throughout most of Europe during this period.

- **IDENTIFY** the most important outcomes of the medieval agricultural revolution.

- **DESCRIBE** the effects of the reforming movement within the Church.

- **UNDERSTAND** the motives behind the Crusades.

- **TRACE** the political, economic, intellectual, and cultural effects of the Crusades.

In the version of history popularized by medieval minstrels, Charlemagne and his knights defeat a Muslim army on the mountainous borderlands of Al-Andalus (Spain). They then face only one remaining obstacle: the castle of a Muslim king whose stalwart courage commands the Christians' respect. So when ambassadors from the king promise his conversion in exchange for the safety of his people, Charlemagne readily agrees. One of his men must now negotiate the terms of surrender. Roland, Charlemagne's noblest knight, suggests that his stepfather Ganelon be the chosen messenger. But Ganelon is furious, certain that the mission will end in his death. Secretly, he resolves to betray both his stepson and his liege lord, and convinces the Muslim king that Charlemagne intends to trick him. Ganelon incites the king to attack the Christian warriors as they travel homeward through the mountain passes of the Pyrenees. Because Roland is the bravest knight, Ganelon knows that he will volunteer to command the rear guard.

And so it happens. Roland's men are ambushed and his sworn companion, Olivier, urges him to call for help. But Roland refuses. He will never endanger his lord by any such dishonorable deed; instead, he will fight to the death. With his last ounce of strength, he breaks his sword, Durandal, for it would never do to have this sacred gift of Charlemagne—made holier still by the relic in its pommel—fall into the hands of heathens. As Roland reminds Olivier, "We must not be the theme of mocking songs." The worst thing imaginable is shame; the best, to become the hero of just such an epic.

Like Homer's *Iliad*, the *Song of Roland* is the product of an oral storytelling tradition that took shape over hundreds of years. Written down around the year 1100, it reflects the many ways in which the world had changed since the time of Charlemagne. Its very language exemplifies one such change: the language we call French, no longer the Frankish tongue of Charlemagne. In Charlemagne's time, moreover, there was no such thing as knighthood or chivalry, no major castles, and no holy war against the followers of Islam. All of these features were added to the story over time, to mirror a new reality and, most immediately, the ethos of the First Crusade (1095–1099).

In this chapter, we will begin to trace the processes that transformed western Europe from an economic backwater and political patchwork into the premier power among the three successor civilizations of the Roman Empire. With the increased authority and prestige of the Roman Church, European Christendom came to embrace the formerly outlying territories of Scandinavia, Hungary, Poland, and Bohemia. Christian colonists and missionaries also pushed into the Baltic and the Balkans. And allied Christian armies advanced into formerly Islamic territories in Spain and established (and eventually lost) a Latin kingdom centered on Jerusalem. This expansion would be accompanied by a revolution in agricultural production, urbanization, and a growing population. It would foster the growth of monarchies, create a wealthy but highly stratified new social order, and spur remarkable intellectual and cultural achievements.

# A TOUR OF EUROPE AROUND THE YEAR 1000

The mapmakers of antiquity (see Chapter 4) had used the term *Europe* to refer to one of the three known continents, and they divided it from Asia by the river Don and from Africa by the Straits of Gibraltar. We have seen that many of Europe's territories were gradually brought into the orbit of Western civilizations through trade, imperial conquest, the Jewish diaspora, and the spread of Christianity and Islam. Meanwhile, waves of immigration from the steppes of Central Asia increased the already rich ethnic and cultural diversity of Europe, as did the movements of the Vikings

and their interactions with both newer and more established groups. Although Charlemagne (see Chapter 7) had tried to promote an idea of a Europe as unified and Christian, Europe was not (and could never be) wholly Christian; and it was certainly not unified. So what was it?

This chapter is titled "The Expansion of Europe" for two main reasons: first, because the idea of Europe gained increasing coherence during this pivotal period; and second, because Europeans' conquest of new frontier territories and the Mediterranean was a crucial development. Indeed, historians argue that Europe was really invented in this era, through an ongoing process of internal and external colonization. That is, new kingdoms were being created by conquest and settlement within Europe—complicating ethnic identities, kinship networks, and tribal loyalties—as well as beyond it. Europeans were becoming the agents of imperialism, not its targets. This is a striking change. The West's center of gravity had always been the Mediterranean and its adjacent lands in Anatolia, western Asia, and North Africa; it was from there that influences flowed to the less civilized lands of the farther West. The movements of peoples, too, had usually been westward. But now, that trajectory was being reversed.

## Viking Initiatives

In the aftermath of the Viking invasions, new political entities began to emerge in northern Europe. Some, on the far-flung fringes of the known world, were formed when the Vikings themselves became colonists in Iceland, Greenland, and (briefly) Newfoundland. Indeed, Iceland can claim to be Europe's oldest state and the world's first parliamentary democracy. Its political institutions date back to the year 930, when settlers formed a legislative assembly called the Althing, a Norse word with the same meaning as the Latin *res publica*. Icelanders built one of the most culturally distinctive polities of the Middle Ages and produced a fascinating and influential body of poetic forms and literary entertainments, notably the *sagas*: sprawling family histories that unfold over generations, feature diverse casts of characters, and range from the hilarious to the ruthless (often both at once). Modern action films and epics are heavily indebted to the sagas and their historical contexts.

In regions where Vikings settled among more established groups—in Francia, the British Isles, Scandinavia, and the Low Countries—they both absorbed and affected these cultures. In Normandy, for example, the descendants of Vikings maintained marriage alliances and ties of kinship with the rest of the Norse world while intermarrying with the Franks and adopting their language.

**LINGSBERG RUNESTONE.** This is one of two commemorative runestones erected at Lingsberg, Sweden, at the beginning of the eleventh century. The runic inscription records that a woman named Holmfríðr had it placed there in memory of her husband, Halfdan, whose father had been a Viking raider in England. Runic alphabets were in use among Germanic-speaking peoples of the North prior to the adoption of the Latin alphabet. Few runic letters survive in Anglo-Saxon and Old Norse, including the *edh* and the letter ð (in the name Holmfríðr), which is pronounced *th* (as in *the*).

## The Rise of Rus'

One group of Vikings established an important kingdom on the broad steppes of Eurasia, at the heart of a region that still bears a version of their name: Russia. Originally from Sweden, the Rus' were active raiders and traders in the Baltic region, where they came to dominate the Finns and Slavic peoples who lived along the seaboard. Gradually, they extended their reach through the navigation of Eurasian waterways while moving farther inland, to Novgorod. By the year 1000, they had conquered the fortress of Kiev.

Kiev (now in western Ukraine) was a key outpost of the frontier region influenced by the Khazars, a Turkic people who had established an empire along the Silk Road to China, and whose assimilation extended their influence still further. (Many had embraced a form of Judaism centuries before.) From Kiev, on the shores of the river Dneiper, the Rus' had easy access to the Black Sea and thence to Constantinople and Baghdad. They were thus in a position to trade directly with the eastern Roman Empire in Byzantium, as well as with Arabic, Persian, and Turkic peoples who had access to China. Moreover, through a series of strategic intermarriages, they forged further connections with many of the royal and aristocratic dynasties of western Europe. This placed the land of Rus' at the heart of economic and political activity in the medieval world.

## The New Kingdoms of East-Central Europe

The rise of Rus' was countered by the crystallization of independent Balkan and Slavic kingdoms. Serbia and Croatia in the south, on the Adriatic, grew within long-settled provinces of the old Roman Empire. When the empire divided along religious and cultural lines, the ruling families of Croatia, who were near neighbors of the Venetians, embraced the Latin Christianity of Rome. The Serbians, however, were loyal to Byzantine Orthodoxy.

Hungary, comprising the old Roman province of Pannonia and stretching eastward toward the Carpathian mountains, had been conquered by the Huns in the late fourth century and had since attracted numerous other immigrants. The most recent arrivals were the Magyars, a nomadic people from the region of the Urals whose language, like that of the Finns, is non-Indo-European (Chapter 7). The Magyars were expert herdsmen and horsemen, and also served as mercenaries fighting for various warring kings in western Europe and for the emperor in Byzantium. Around 895, they united under their leader Arpád and took control of the fertile land of the Danube river basin, where they became farmers and cattle ranchers. Arpád's descendants later embraced Latin Christianity and worked to integrate the kingdom of Hungary into western Europe through dynastic marriages and diplomacy.

Bohemia (now part of the Czech Republic) and Poland were also in the process of conversion, actively encouraged by Rome. Here, as in Anglo-Saxon England and the Frankish kingdom, allegiance with Rome was politically advantageous for ambitious would-be kings, who could legitimize their claims to power by receiving papal approval. And as Europe's economy revived, the towns of this region were tied into an expanding web of overland and waterborne trade.

## New Scandinavian Kingdoms and the Empire of Cnut the Great

While Rus' was on the rise, other groups of Vikings were establishing territorial control over parts of their Scandinavian homeland—borrowing forms of governance that drew on Carolingian and Byzantine models and embracing Latin Christianity as a way of legitimizing their rule. Around the year 1000, three strong kingdoms had emerged: Norway, Sweden, and Denmark. Each built on the legacy of powerful Viking forebears who had already established Norse settlements in the lands of the Franks, the Anglo-Saxons, and the Irish through their reputation for fearlessness in battle and generosity afterward, their capacity to dominate seas and riverways—and thereby to supply the lifeblood (silver and gold currency) of the medieval economy—and their canny practices of adaptation and intermarriage.

What made these new states special was their rulers' very deliberate manipulation of this heritage, blended with the strategic decision to convert their followers to Christianity and to the political conventions of the Continent. They simultaneously glorified their own distinctive culture and economic achievements while tying them to newer models of government. For these reasons, scholars have often spoken of this period as Europe's "Viking Age," and it exemplifies the cross-currents of colonial enterprise mentioned above. On the one hand, older western civilizations can be said to have colonized Scandinavia; on the other hand, it was really Scandinavians who were doing the colonizing.

The empire forged by King Cnut (*kuh-NOOT*) of Denmark is a good example of this. At the time of his death in 1035, Cnut the Great ruled over Norway, much of Sweden, and England, as well as his native land; had a controlling interest in large parts of Ireland and portions of the Low Countries; and had diplomatic and family ties to the independent principalities of Flanders and Normandy, the new kingdom of Poland (through his mother, a Polish princess), and the imperial family of Germany (through his daughter, who became empress). Although his was, in many ways, a personal empire that came apart after his death—like that of Alexander—it had long-term effects on the political organization of northwestern Europe. Most notably, it set the stage for the Norman conquest of England (see **Interpreting Visual Evidence** on page 264). Cnut's empire could only have been brought together as a result of the initiatives that had made

**BENEDICTINE ABBEY OF TYNIEC (POLAND).** High above the river Vistula—one of the most important waterways in Central Europe—is the abbey of Tyniec (*TIN-y-ech*), founded on the site of an ancient Paleolithic fortress by King Casimir I of Poland, around the year 1040. It was just upriver of the newly established royal capital at Kraków, and its monks were assigned the task of helping the king convert local pagans to Christianity. ▪ *Why would Casimir have chosen this site?*

raiding Vikings into settled kings who were able to exploit the far-flung networks of trade, influence, and kinship that had allowed their forebears to flourish in earlier times.

## Mediterranean Microcosms

The dynamism of the new states of eastern Europe, Rus', and Scandinavia stands in contrast to the very different dynamics that governed relations in an older part of western civilizations: the Mediterranean. If the map below struggles to capture the patchwork of principalities and polities of Europe's mainland, it fails utterly to convey the contours of political, religious, cultural, and economic interactions in this maritime world. It is useful, in fact, to imagine the Mediterranean coastal regions and islands as interlocking components of a different zone entirely, and to imagine further that a community on the shores of North Africa—say,

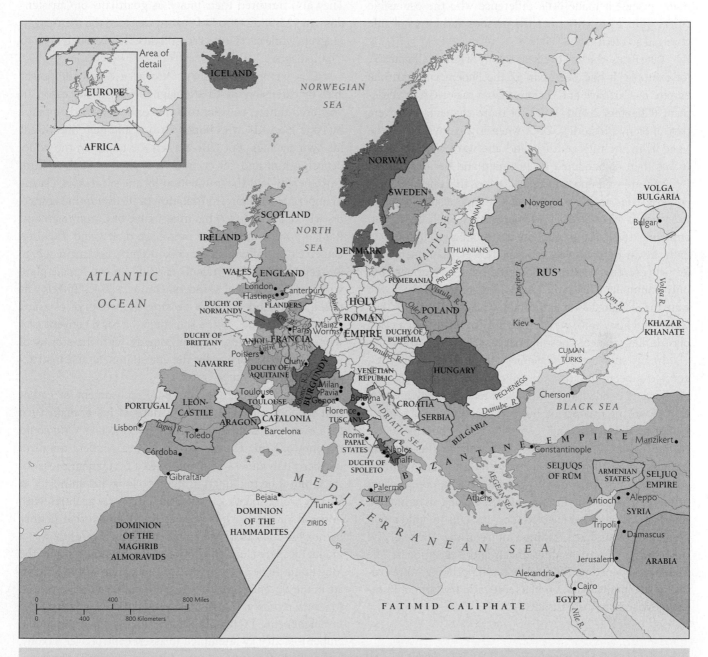

**EUROPE, c. 1000.** This map shows the patchwork of political power in western Europe after the millennium, although it cannot accurately illustrate the degree of fragmentation within these major territories, especially those of the Holy Roman Empire. ▪ *What factors account for the close relationship between Italy and the German principalities?* ▪ *How are they related to the northwestern regions of the Continent and the British Isles?* ▪ *Which geopolitical entities would you expect to emerge as dominant in the following centuries?*

Muslim Tunis—would have more in common, and more contact, with Christian Barcelona than with another African Muslim community farther inland.

Indeed, it is extremely tricky (and probably futile) to pin down the identity and allegiances of any one group or individual in this zone. The medieval Mediterranean was a complex organism made up of diverse microcosms whose contours and interrelationships were determined more by geography, prevailing winds, trading patterns, and climate than by the vaunted control of a particular ruler. In many places, it made little difference who the ostensible rulers were, especially since the persons and forms of rule changed so often.

Take Sicily, the first overseas colony of Rome (Chapter 5), for example. It had been part of the Phoenician maritime empire of Carthage and, before that, a major Greek settlement (Chapters 2 and 3). All of those elements still were part of Sicily's historical DNA when it was invaded by the Vandals in the fifth century, and afterward by the Goths. It was then reconquered by Justinian and became part of Byzantium—so important a part, in fact, that one Byzantine emperor tried to move the capital from Constantinople to Palermo. In the course of the tenth century, Sicily became an emirate of the Fatimid caliphate based in Egypt. In the eleventh, it was progressively infiltrated by Norman mercenaries who eventually succeeded in establishing a Norman (but only nominally Christian) kingdom there in 1072. So who were the Sicilians? More important, who did they think they were? And how stable was that identity over this long period of continual change? These are not easy questions to answer.

In any such case, it is better to think in terms of influences, connections, and orbits of exchange than about stable borders or identities; this holds true of many areas of Europe during this period but is especially true of regions joined by water. Gaining "control" of any constellation of Mediterranean communities—constantly in flux—meant harnessing its inherent complexity and commercial power, something not best done through violent conquest or military occupation. Indeed, an exemplary light-handed interference was what enabled the Venetians to build a successful and long-lived trading empire in the Adriatic, and then in the eastern Mediterranean and Aegean Seas. The Venetians opened up the sea lanes and ports that were crucial to the implementation of a more military form of European expansion: the Crusades.

## The Heirs of Charlemagne

What of Europe's heartland, which had become the empire of Charlemagne (Chapter 7)? The most powerful monarchs on the Continent were the Saxon kings of eastern Francia (in what is now Germany). Like the Anglo-Saxon kings of England, they modeled themselves on Charlemagne, but drew on different aspects of his rule. Whereas England was becoming an effective administrative monarchy with centralized financial and judicial systems, royal power on the Continent rested on the profits of continual expansion. So just as the Carolingians had built their power on the conquest of Saxony in the eighth century, the Saxon kings now built theirs on the conquests of Slavic lands to the east. They also nurtured their image as guardians of Christendom: in 955, King Otto I of Saxony defeated the then-pagan Magyars while carrying a sacred lance that had belonged to Charlemagne.

This victory established Otto as a dominant power and, by extension, as Charlemagne's worthy successor. In 962, accordingly, he went to Rome to be crowned emperor by Pope John XII, who hoped Otto would help him defeat his own enemies. But Otto turned the tables on the pope, deposing him and selecting a new pope to replace him. Otto thereby laid the foundation for his successors' claims to imperial autonomy, in imitation of the Byzantine emperors. He also advertised his inheritance of Carolingian and Roman power through his patronage of arts and learning. Under Otto's influence, the Saxon court became a refuge for men and women of talent. The first known female playwright, Hrotsvitha of Gandersheim (c. 935–c. 1002), was raised there, and grew up hearing the works of classical authors read aloud. When she entered a royal convent, she wrote plays blending Roman comedy with the stories of early Christian martyrs for the entertainment and instruction of her fellow nuns.

Otto also presided over the establishment of cathedral schools and helped the bishops of his domain turn their own courts into cultural centers. However, Otto could not control either the papacy or the independent towns of northern Italy unless he maintained a permanent presence there. But if he remained in Italy too long, his authority in Saxony would break down. Balancing local realities with imperial ambitions thus presented a dilemma that neither he nor his successors were able to solve. The result was a gradually increasing rift between the local elites and the king in his guise as emperor. This alienation would accelerate in the eleventh century when the imperial crown passed to a new dynasty, the Salians, centered not in Saxony but in neighboring Franconia. By the 1070s, when the Salian emperor Henry IV attempted to assert control over Saxony, he touched off a war that was to have momentous repercussions (see below).

Aspects of Charlemagne's legacy also survived in the Mediterranean world. In Catalonia, counts descended from

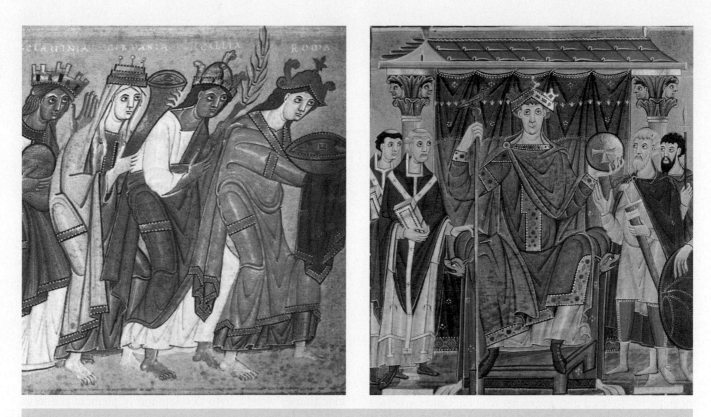

**EMPEROR OTTO THE GREAT.** In this opening from a deluxe set of Gospels he commissioned for himself, Otto is shown seated on a throne, vested with the regalia of imperial and royal authority, and surrounded by clerical and secular counselors. On the left, a procession of deferential women offer him tribute, representing the four regions and peoples that Otto aspired to rule: Roma (Romans), Gallia (Franks), Germania (Germans), and Sclavinia (Slavs). Compare this image to that of Emperor Justinian on page 216. • *In what ways is Otto making use of similar iconography?* • *What claims to power is he thereby making?*

Carolingian appointees continued to administer justice in public courts of law throughout the tenth century, and to draw revenues from tolls and trade. The city of Barcelona grew rapidly as both a long-distance and a regional market under the protection of these counts. In Aquitaine also, the counts of Poitiers and Toulouse continued to rest their authority on Carolingian foundations.

In Charlemagne's own Frankish kingdom, however, Carolingian rule collapsed under the combined weight of Viking raids, economic disintegration, and the growing power of local lords. A few Carolingian institutions—such as public courts and a centrally minted coinage—survived in some regions, but they were used to build up new, autonomous principalities, such as Anjou and Flanders. The Norse-Frankish rulers of Normandy used these techniques effectively. But in the Franks' traditional heartland, even this modicum of Carolingian authority disappeared. The Franks still had a king, but this king was no longer a descendant of Charlemagne. Moreover, his domain had been reduced to the tiny region around Paris, the only territorial remnant that the local count, Hugh Capet, had managed to defend against the Vikings. In 987, this modest feat earned him the title "King of the Franks." Marooned on this Île-de-France (literally, "island of France"), the Capetian kings clung to the fiction that they were the heirs of Charlemagne's greatness. It would be another 200 years before one of them made this fiction a political reality (see Chapter 9).

# THE AGRICULTURAL REVOLUTION OF THE MEDIEVAL WARM PERIOD

Prior to the late twentieth century, when human activity began to have a measurable effect on the global climate, the warmest period of the last two millennia occurred between 950 and 1250. It is known as the Medieval Warm Period or Medieval Climate Optimum, because it optimized the conditions for agricultural and economic growth, especially in the Northern Hemisphere. Archaeological evidence from the Americas to Europe to Asia shows similar patterns of human adaptation to this new environment, when average global temperatures are estimated to have risen by about 1°C or 2°C (3.6°F)—the same increment as the present level of human-caused warming today. This climate anomaly made it possible to raise crops as far north as Greenland and to produce wine in southern England. Moreover, the warming climate benefited northern Europe by drying the soil and lengthening the growing season, with hotter summers and diminishing rainfall harming Mediterranean agriculture in equal measure.

## New Technologies and Conditions for Growth

As noted in Chapter 7, Europe's agricultural boom had already begun in the eighth century, fostered by monastic inventions such as the new heavy-wheeled plow, fitted with an iron-tipped coulter and dragged by a team of oxen or horses, that could cut and turn the rich soil of northern Europe far more effectively than traditional Mediterranean plows. Related improvements in collars and harnesses enhanced the efficiency of draft animals, making it possible for these animals to pull heavy loads without choking. The development of iron horseshoes (around 900) and the tandem harnessing of paired teams (around 1050) made the use of horses more effective not only in the field but also for transporting agricultural goods to new markets.

Labor-saving devices further increased productivity. Since most work was done by individuals using hand tools, the more widespread use of iron for hoes, pitchforks, shovels, and scythes made work faster and easier. The wheelbarrow was a crucial invention, as was the harrow, drawn over the field after plowing to level the earth and mix in the seed. Water mills were another major innovation. The Romans had relied mainly on human- and animal-powered wheels to grind grain into flour or crush olives for oil, but the need for greater efficiency and the lack of slave labor led medieval monastic engineers to experiment with various ways of harnessing water power. Secular landowners followed suit, recognizing the mill as a source of economic and political power to which they could control access. Indeed, mills would remain the world's only source of mechanical power for manufacturing until the invention of the steam engine powered the Industrial Revolution (see Chapter 19).

## Harnessing People

These new technologies became more widespread after the settlement of Viking and Magyar peoples decreased the threat of invasion and the consequent disruption of planting cycles and damage to crops. Left in relative peace, monasteries were able to develop and implement the tools described above, which were then copied by local lords who saw the benefits of managing their own lands more efficiently—rather than raiding others'. It became clear to entrepreneurial peasants, too, that investment in agricultural improvements would yield surpluses and profits. Productivity was also linked to increased population, fundamental changes in patterns of settlement, and the organization of the peasant workforce.

In the centuries after the fragmentation of Roman imperial power, most farmers in northern Europe lived on individual plots of land worked by themselves and their

**LIGHT PLOW AND HEAVY PLOW.** Compare these two contemporary depictions of plowing: the one on the left is taken from a Greek manuscript copied in Byzantium and shows the light plow in use throughout the Mediterranean since antiquity; the one on the right shows the heavy wheeled plow adapted to northern Europe. Note that the peasant using the light plow has to press his foot on it to give it added weight. Another major innovation of the heavy European plow was the long moldboard, which turned over the ground after the plowshare cut into it; and the padded horse collar allowed horses to throw their full weight into pulling.

families. Starting in the ninth century, however, many of these individual holdings merged into large, common fields that could be farmed collectively by the inhabitants of entire villages; the resulting complex is sometimes called a *manor* (from the Latin verb *manere*, meaning "to dwell"). In many cases, the impetus for the consolidation of manors came from the peasants themselves. Large fields could be farmed more efficiently than small fields, and investment costs were lower and could be shared equally: a single plow and a dozen oxen might suffice for an entire village, obviating the need for every farmer to maintain his own plow and team. Common fields were potentially more productive, too, allowing villagers to experiment with new crops and support larger numbers of animals on common pastures. In time, prosperous peasants might be able to establish a parish church, a communal oven, a blacksmith, a mill, and a tavern. They could also converse, socialize, and assist their neighbors. In a difficult and demanding natural environment, these were important considerations.

In other cases, a manor could be created or co-opted by a local lord or lordly monastery. Manors were attractive because their greater productivity meant that lords could take a larger share of the peasants' surplus; it was also easier to control and exploit peasants who lived together in villages and were bound to each other by ties of kinship and dependence. Over time, some lords were therefore able to reduce formerly free peasants to serfs who could not leave the land without permission. Like slaves, serfs inherited their servile status; but unlike slaves, they were not supposed to be sold apart from the lands they worked. In practical terms, there may have been little difference between a serf and a free peasant—indeed, some serfs may have been better off. But as we have seen, social mobility is often tied to geographical mobility; and the inability of serfs to move freely prevented them from achieving the liberties of those workers who could (see below).

## The Conquest of the Land

The manor's organization of labor opened up more land for cultivation and made that cultivation more efficient. For centuries, farmers had known that if they sowed the same crop in the same field year after year, they would eventually exhaust the soil. The traditional solution was to divide the land, planting half in the fall to harvest in the spring, and leaving the other half to lie fallow. In the dry, thin soils of the Mediterranean, this remained the most common cropping pattern throughout the Middle Ages. In the more fertile soils of northern Europe, however, farmers slowly discovered that a three-field crop-rotation system could produce a sustainable increase in overall production. One-third of the land would lie fallow or be used as pasture, so that manure would fertilize the soil; one-third would be planted with winter wheat or rye, sown in the fall and harvested in the early summer; and one-third would be planted in the spring with another crop to be harvested in the fall. These fields were then rotated over a three-year cycle.

This system increased the amount of land under cultivation from 50 to 67 percent, while the two separate growing seasons provided some insurance against loss due to natural disasters or inclement weather. The system also produced higher yields per acre, particularly if legumes or fodder crops such as oats were a regular part of the crop-rotation pattern and replaced the nitrogen that wheat and rye leach out of the soil. Both humans and animals could eat oats, and legumes provided a source of protein to balance the intake of carbohydrates from bread and beer, the two main staples of the peasant diet in northern and central Europe. Additional fodder supported more and healthier animals, increasing the efficiency of plow beasts, diversifying the economy of the manor, and providing an additional source of protein through meat and milk. The new crop-rotation system also helped spread labor more evenly over the course of the year.

## THE GROWTH OF TOWNS AND TRADE

As we observed in Chapter 7, the urban infrastructure of the western Roman Empire was weakened over the course of the fifth and sixth centuries. A few Roman cities continued to thrive under the lordship of bishops, but many—including Rome itself—began to crumble as their depleted populations could no longer maintain public buildings, services, and defensive walls. In most areas in northwestern Europe, monasteries replaced cities as the nuclei of civilization. Then, under Charlemagne and his imitators, towns came to be planted as centers for markets and administration by royal initiative. In Anglo-Saxon England, too, King Alfred and his successors established new towns in strategic locations, while at the same time reviving older Roman cities. They also issued a reliable and well-regulated currency that encouraged commerce.

## Fostering Commerce

Although many towns were devastated by the Viking raids of the tenth century, the agricultural revolution helped to

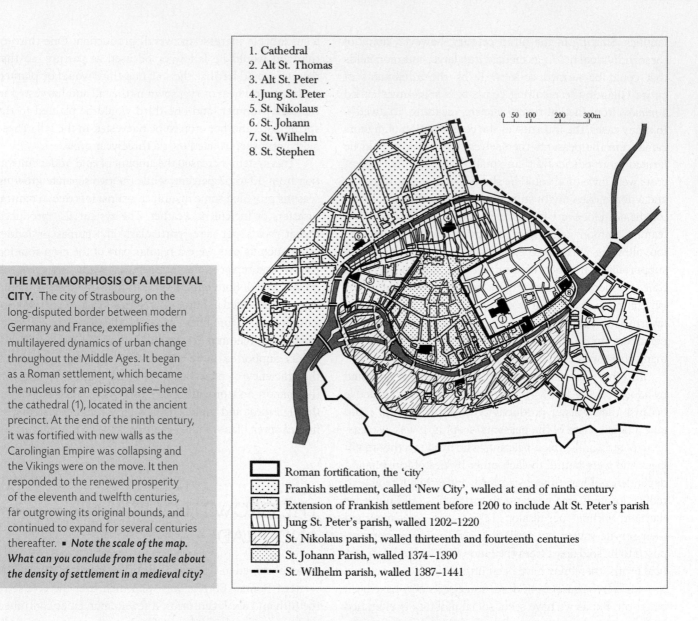

1. Cathedral
2. Alt St. Thomas
3. Alt St. Peter
4. Jung St. Peter
5. St. Nikolaus
6. St. Johann
7. St. Wilhelm
8. St. Stephen

0  50  100      200      300m

☐ Roman fortification, the 'city'
⋯ Frankish settlement, called 'New City', walled at end of ninth century
▨ Extension of Frankish settlement before 1200 to include Alt St. Peter's parish
▥ Jung St. Peter's parish, walled 1202–1220
▧ St. Nikolaus parish, walled thirteenth and fourteenth centuries
⋮ St. Johann Parish, walled 1374–1390
∎∎∎ St. Wilhelm parish, walled 1387–1441

**THE METAMORPHOSIS OF A MEDIEVAL CITY.** The city of Strasbourg, on the long-disputed border between modern Germany and France, exemplifies the multilayered dynamics of urban change throughout the Middle Ages. It began as a Roman settlement, which became the nucleus for an episcopal see—hence the cathedral (1), located in the ancient precinct. At the end of the ninth century, it was fortified with new walls as the Carolingian Empire was collapsing and the Vikings were on the move. It then responded to the renewed prosperity of the eleventh and twelfth centuries, far outgrowing its original bounds, and continued to expand for several centuries thereafter. ▪ *Note the scale of the map. What can you conclude from the scale about the density of settlement in a medieval city?*

revitalize them—as did the influx of silver and gold set in circulation by the Vikings themselves. The rapid urbanization of Europe during the eleventh and twelfth centuries was also fostered by the initiatives of monasteries and secular lords who saw the economic advantages to be gained from providing safe havens for travelers and trade. This was especially true in the principalities of the Rhineland, the Low Countries, and the independent counties of Flanders and Champagne. Many towns grew up around monasteries, which provided protection and encouraged innovation. In southwestern Europe, existing towns prospered from their status as ports or their location along the overland routes connecting the Mediterranean with the Atlantic. In Italy, which had been decimated by five centuries of warfare and invasion, the growth of towns gave rise to especially dramatic changes.

Initially, the renewed prosperity of Italy depended on the Byzantine emperors' suppression of piracy in the eastern Mediterranean. Hence, the most successful cities around the turn of the millennium were situated in the Byzantine-controlled areas of the peninsula: Venice in the north and Amalfi, Naples, and Palermo in the south. These were the trading posts that brought silks, spices, and other luxuries from the East into western Europe. In the eleventh century, however, the Norman invasions of southern Italy frequently disrupted this trade, while Turkish invasions of Anatolia turned Byzantium's attention to the empire's eastern frontier. This opened new opportunities for the northern ports of Genoa and Pisa, whose merchant navies took over the task of policing the Mediterranean.

From Italy and other Mediterranean ports, exotic goods flowed northward to the towns of Flanders and the organized system of fairs—international markets convened at certain times of the year—that enriched the county of Champagne. Flemish towns, in turn, kept up a brisk trade with England, processing English wool into cloth, which

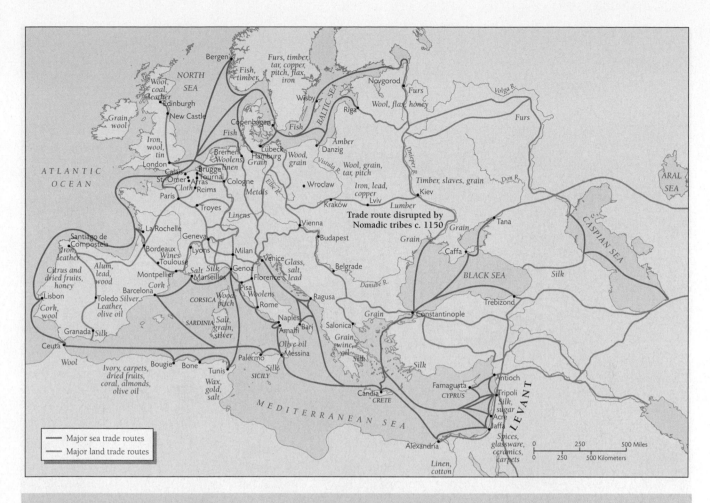

**MEDIEVAL TRADE ROUTES.** ▪ *What does this map reveal about the relationship between waterways and overland routes during the eleventh and twelfth centuries?* ▪ *Which regions appear to be most extensively interconnected, and why?* ▪ *How does the trade in certain specialized goods create certain commercial patterns?*

was the staple commodity of medieval Europe, alongside wheat and wine. Eventually, merchants would succeed in opening up a direct route by sea between Italy and the Atlantic ports of northern Europe, after which it became practical to import raw wool directly from England to towns such as Florence, which began producing its own cloth.

It would be misleading, however, to overemphasize the role of long-distance trade in the urbanization of medieval Europe. Some towns that were dependent on such commerce, such as Venice and Genoa, attracted populations approaching 100,000 by 1300. But others that grew to be as large, including Paris and London, drew primarily on the wealth of their surrounding hinterlands for food, raw materials, and the bulk of their population. Furthermore, towns large and small existed in a symbiotic relationship with the countryside, providing markets for the food surplus of outlying farms and transforming raw materials into marketable goods through manufacturing.

## "Town Air Makes You Free"

To modern eyes, most medieval towns would still have seemed half rural. (Indeed, New York City would have seemed so until the end of the nineteenth century.) Streets were often unpaved, houses had gardens for raising vegetables, and animals were everywhere. (In the early twelfth century, the heir to the throne of France was killed when his horse tripped over a pig running loose in the streets of Paris.) Sanitary conditions were poor and the air reeked of excrement, both animal and human. (This was also true of New York even in 1900, where 150,000 horses produced 45,000 tons of manure each month.) Under these conditions, disease could spread rapidly, and fire was another omnipresent danger because wooden and thatched buildings were clustered close together.

But these inconveniences were far outweighed by the advantages of urban life, not least of which was that towns provided a means of escape from the strictures of the

**THE MARKET SQUARE OF KRAKÓW (POLAND).** This view of the *rynek* (or the main market square) of Kraków was taken from the medieval tower of St. Mary's Basilica. It emphasizes the extraordinary scale of commercial activity that has taken place here since the eleventh century. Measuring around 430,000 square feet, it is one of the largest medieval town squares in Europe and a symbol of urban prosperity and pride. Although the handsome Cloth Hall in the center was not built until the fifteenth century, it stands on the site of market stalls dating back to the foundation of the city. Recent excavations of the square itself have revealed artifacts from numerous artisanal workshops. ▪ *Compare the scale of this market with the plan of Strasbourg on page 258.* ▪ *What historical factors might account for the far more generous proportions of this newer medieval town?*

countryside. As a German adage puts it, "Town air makes you free" ("*Stadtluft macht frei*"). This is because the citizens of most medieval towns were not subject to the arbitrary jurisdiction of a lord—or if they were, the lord realized that rewarding initiative with further freedoms fostered still more initiatives and more wealth.

Many Catalonian and Flemish towns accordingly received charters of liberty from the counts of these regions and were given the right to govern themselves. Others seized that right: In 1127, the people of Arras, on the Franco-Flemish border, declared that they were no longer the serfs of the local monastery that had nurtured the growth of their town in the first place. They banded together to form a commune, swearing to maintain solidarity with

one another and setting up their own form of representative government. The monastery was forced to free them, and then free to tax them. This arrangement was mutually beneficial, and by the end of the century, Arras was the wealthiest and most densely populated town in northern Europe.

Urban areas further expanded through the constant immigration of free peasants and escaped serfs in search of a better life. Once a town had established its independence, newcomers could claim the status of citizens after a year and a day; thereafter, the only authority to which they were subject was that of the town's officials. For this reason, some powerful lords and rulers resisted the efforts of towns to claim independence. Almost inevitably, though, they paid a high price for this. In Rome, the pope's claim to secular authority over the city led to frequent uprisings. In the French city of Laon, the bishop who asserted his lordship over a newly formed commune was murdered in 1112. And in 1127, the count of Flanders, Charles the Good (r. 1119–1127), was assassinated by a family of powerful officials who resented his claims that they were, in fact, his serfs.

## Portable Wealth: Money and Credit

The growth of towns and trade depends on more than surplus goods, initiative, and mobility; it also depends on money, a reliable supply of cash and the availability of credit. It is no accident that the earliest participants in the commercial revolution of the Middle Ages were cities located in regions whose rulers minted and regulated a strong currency: Byzantium, Al-Andalus, and the Christian kingdoms of Spain, the old Roman region of Provence (southern France), Anglo-Saxon England, and Flanders. Yet precisely because there were so many currencies in circulation, the economy also depended on moneychangers and bankers who could extend credit to merchants, thus obviating the need to travel roads and waterways with bags full of cash.

Most of the sophisticated financial mechanisms for extending credit and making investments had long been in place throughout the Islamic world and Byzantium, but in western Europe, much of this crucial activity was carried forward by Jewish bankers situated within the network of close-knit Jewish communities that connected cities such as Constantinople, Baghdad, and Córdoba to the burgeoning cities of the north. In many regions, Jews had a virtual monopoly on these activities, because Christians were technically forbidden to lend money at interest or make a profit from investments. This practice was called *usury* (from the Latin word for "interest"), and Christian theologians cited various passages from the Old and New Testaments that seemed to condemn it. But in practice, the Roman Church turned a blind eye to such practices. Indeed, many prominent churchmen, including bishops, made fortunes lending money, as did many laymen—especially in towns such as Arras and Florence.

Still, the moral stigma attaching to this necessary practice meant that Jews were often the ones targeted at times of crisis, just as they were the people to whom rulers would turn most readily when they needed funds—helping to explain why many kings, princes, and bishops protected the Jewish communities in their realms and often extended special privileges to them in exchange for money. The

unfortunate result of this Christian hypocrisy was the circulation of conspiracy theories harmful to Jews, who were perceived as exercising control over Christians through secret channels of communication and maintaining a stranglehold on finance. Jewish communities' reliance on the protection of powerful men also made them vulnerable when those men withdrew their support or were incapable of controlling the violence unleashed by their own policies.

# VIOLENCE, LORDSHIP, AND MONARCHY

The new wealth of western Europe fostered social mobility, yet it also created a more stratified society. In the Carolingian period, the nobility comprised a relatively small number of ancient families that counted each other as equals and married among themselves. During the tenth and eleventh centuries, however, new families began to emerge as territorial lords and princes, rivaling and sometimes surpassing the old aristocracy in power and wealth. Some of these new families were descended from lesser officeholders in the Carolingian administration, men who had established independent powers after the empire collapsed and who used their public offices for private gain. Others were successful interlopers who had seized control of undefended manors and sustained war-bands of treasure-hungry young men.

## Tools of Power: Castles and Knights

The predatory lords who emerged during this period protected their territories, families, and followers by building strongholds: castles (from the Latin word *castellum*, "little fortress"). These structures, seldom known in Europe before the Viking invasions, came to dominate the landscape during the eleventh and twelfth centuries. A castle was both defensive and offensive. It rendered its owner more secure from arson and attack—though it was vulnerable to siege—and it enabled him to dominate the surrounding countryside. Indeed, castles often formed the nucleus of a new town by providing protection for the peasants and merchants who clustered their dwellings close to its walls. In case of attack, these outliers could move inside.

Although most early castles were modest structures built of wood, situated on earthwork mounds surrounded by a ditch or moat, stone walls and keeps (fortified towers) soon replaced wooden palisades as the level of competitive

**YORK CASTLE (ENGLAND).** This fortification exemplifies some of the major phases of medieval castle building. The large mound is the remains of an earthwork erected on the orders of William the Conqueror in 1068, when it would have been crowned by a wooden palisade: this most basic type of construction is called a motte-and-bailey castle. York's castle remained a wooden tower until it was destroyed by fire and rebuilt in stone after 1245. It is now known as Clifford's Tower, after the rebel leader Sir Roger Clifford, who was held prisoner there prior to his execution in 1322.

violence increased. In Italy, rival families even built castles and towers in the middle of towns. Eventually, some castellans ("castle-holders") acquired enough power and booty to challenge more established lords, laying claim not only to property and influence but also to rank. These new lords didn't descend from Roman senators or Carolingian counts; instead, they boasted of lineages reaching back to successful warlords, such as Rollo the Viking, whom the Normans claimed to be their first duke (from the Latin word *dux*, "leader").

In addition to castle holding, both the older aristocracy and these self-made lords needed the help of warriors to enforce their claims to power. Accordingly, each lord maintained a private army of men heavily equipped with the new weaponry and armor that the widespread availability of iron—and new techniques for smelting it—made possible. These men fought on horseback, and were therefore called "horsemen" (in French, *chevaliers*; in English, *knights*).

Knighthood was a career that embraced men of widely varying status. Some eleventh-century knights were the younger sons of lords who sought to increase their chances of winning wealth by attaching themselves to the households of greater lords. Others were youths recruited from the peasantry, mounted and armed. All that bound them together was their function, which was the violent prosecution of their lord's interests. Gradually,

though, knights came to regard themselves as belonging to a special military caste with its own rules of conduct. The beginnings of this process are discernible in the *Song of Roland*, and further developments would transform the meaning of *chivalry*, from "horsemanship" (*cheval* in French), to something very different (see below).

## Kings and Lords

Despite the emergence of self-governing cities and predatory lordships, the idea of kingship was still a powerful one in Europe. For example, the weak Capetian rulers of Paris kept alive the pretense that everyone dwelling in the lands once ruled by more powerful Frankish kings still owed allegiance to them, while the Ottonians claimed to be kings in northern Italy as well as in their own Saxon domain. In practice, however, neither was able to control the territories they claimed to rule. Effective political and military power lay in the hands of dukes, counts, castellans, and knights, all of whom channeled the increasing wealth of the countryside into their own hands. From their castles, these lords (*domini*) constructed dominions: lordships within which they exercised not only property rights but also the rights to mint money, judge legal cases, raise troops, wage war, collect taxes, and impose tolls.

## The Problem of "Feudalism"

This highly diffused distribution of power is conventionally known as *feudalism*. But this vague term is unsatisfactory for several reasons. First and foremost, it is a modern concept not used in the period being discussed. Moreover, it has been used by different people to mean different things. For example, scholars influenced by the work of Karl Marx (1818–1883; see Chapter 20) use the term to describe an economic system in which wealth is entirely agricultural and cities have not yet formed; as we have seen, this does not reflect the historical reality of the eleventh and twelfth centuries. For other scholars, feudalism has been construed as an aristocratic social order in which propertied men are bound together by kinship and shared interests; again, this does not explain the varieties of power wielded in this period. Still others have spoken of feudalism as a system of landholding in which lesser men hold land from greater men in return for services of various kinds; but it was not always the greater men who held the most land. The term also has been used to refer to a system whereby great lords and kings grant land in order to raise troops.

Because all these definitions of feudalism are anachronistic, most recent historians of the Middle Ages have questioned or abandoned the use of the term. If, however, we look for a common denominator, we can say that feudalism denotes the abuse of official privileges for personal gain: making use of public resources or institutions for private purposes. In this case, there is general agreement that such practices took shape in Frankish lands after the disintegration of the Carolingian Empire, and later spread to other areas of Europe, changing as they adapted to different circumstances. In some regions, these customs fed a developing ideology that justified new kinds of dominion by which kings were supposed to be able to subordinate other powerful men. In this sense, feudalism legitimated royal power and helped to lay the groundwork for the emergence of European nation-states.

## Fief and Vassals

Although the people living at this time would never have heard the term "feudalism," they would have understood the word at its root: *feudum*, usually translated as "fief" (FEEF). A fief is a gift or grant that creates a kind of contractual relationship between the giver and receiver. This gift could be land, but it could also be the revenues from a toll or a mill, or an annual sum of money. In return, the recipient owed the giver loyalty or services of some kind. In many cases, the gift implied that the recipient was subordinate to the giver and had in fact become the giver's *vassal* (from a Celtic

word meaning "boy"). This relationship was dramatized in an act of *homage*, a powerful ceremony that made the vassal the *homme* ("man" in French) of his lord. Typically, the vassal would kneel and place his hands together in a position of prayer, and the lord would cover the clasped hands with his own. He would then raise up his new "man" and exchange a kiss with him. The symbolic importance of these gestures is clear: the lord (*dominus*) was literally the dominating figure. He could protect and raise up his man and also discipline him. The role of the vassal, meanwhile, was to support the lord and do nothing to incur his displeasure.

In regions where no centralized authority existed, such personal relationships were essential to creating and maintaining order. However, these relationships were not understood in the same ways all over Europe. Many castellans and knights held their lands freely, owing no service whatsoever to the count or duke within whose territories their lands lay. Nor were these relationships neatly hierarchical: "feudalism" created no "feudal pyramids," in which knights held fiefs from counts, and counts held fiefs from kings, all in an orderly fashion. Sometimes, kings would insist that the world *should* be structured this way, but they were seldom able to make this wish a reality.

## A New Type of Monarchy: England

The first place where we can begin to observe the efforts of a particular line of kings to establish a monarchy that dominated other powerful lordships is England. In 1066, Duke William of Normandy claimed that he was the rightful successor of the English king, Edward the Confessor, who had just died. But the English elected a new king, Harold, ignoring his claim. So William crossed the English Channel to take the kingdom by force, defeating Harold at the Battle of Hastings (see **Interpreting Visual Evidence** on page 264). Now, William had to subjugate all the other chieftains who held power in England, many of whom also aspired to be king.

William accomplished this, first, by asserting that he was king by imperial conquest as well as by succession, and that all the land of England thereby belonged to him. Then William rewarded his Norman followers with fiefs: extensive grants of land taken from their English holders, which the Norman lords were allowed to exploit and subdue. In return, William received their loyalty and a share of their revenues.

The Norman conquerors of England were already accustomed to holding land in return for service to their duke back in Normandy. But in England, their subordination to the king was further enforced by the effective machinery of the Anglo-Saxon state and longstanding customs that

# Interpreting Visual Evidence

## The Graphic History of the Bayeux Tapestry

One of the most famous historical documents of all time is not a document at all, but an embroidered strip of linen 231 feet long (originally much longer) and 20 inches wide. It is also not an actual tapestry, as its name misleadingly implies, but an elaborate exercise in needlepoint. It tells the story of the Norman conquest of England and the events leading up to it. The circumstances of its making remain a mystery, but it was certainly commissioned by someone close to William the Conqueror (1027–1087), the Norman duke who claimed the throne of England in 1066. Indeed, its purpose was to demonstrate the truth of William's claim and to justify his invasion of England when Harold Godwinson (c. 1022–1066; image A) was crowned king of England in his place (image B). One likely patron was Queen Edith of England, the widow of the late King Edward (r. 1042–1066) and sister of Harold, who became a friend and adviser to William. Edith was noted for her skill in embroidery as well as for her political acumen, and she would have been able to oversee the making of this visual history by the women of her household. Two of its evocative scenes, with translations of accompanying Latin texts, are reproduced here.

**A. Harold Sails the Sea.** In this scene, from the first portion of the Tapestry, Harold has been sent on an embassy by King Edward. He feasts with friends in a hall on the English coast before crossing the Channel.

**B. Harold Is Seated, King of the English.** Although Harold may have promised to relinquish his claim to the English throne in William's favor, the central scene of the tapestry is his coronation. Stigant, the archbishop of Canterbury, stands on his right. Outside the cathedral, the people of London look on curiously. Some appear to be surprised or alarmed.

### Questions for Analysis

1. Like a graphic novel or a comic strip, the Bayeux Tapestry tells its story through images, and words (in very simple Latin) play a minor role. What do the Tapestry's artists choose to express exclusively through visualization? When do they choose to state something verbally? What might be the motivation behind these choices? What is left out of the story, or left ambiguous? What might be the reason(s) for this?

2. In addition to being a source for political and military historians, the Bayeux Tapestry provides us with fascinating glimpses into the daily life and material culture of the Middle Ages. What, for example, can you conclude about the necessary preparations for a voyage by sea? About the history of clothing, weaponry, or animals?

3. If Queen Edith was responsible for commissioning and helping to make the Tapestry, it would constitute one of the few surviving historical accounts by a woman prior to the twentieth century. Would the creator's gender change your perception of this artifact or of these particular scenes? Why or why not?

had the force of law. As king of England, therefore, William was able to exercise a variety of public powers that he could not have enjoyed in Normandy. In England, only the king could coin money, and only the king's money was allowed to circulate. As kings of England, William and his successors also inherited the right to collect a national land tax, supervise justice in royal courts, and raise an army. They even retained the Anglo-Saxon officers of local government, known as sheriffs, to help them administer and enforce their rights.

William was thereby able to insist that all the people of England owed ultimate loyalty to the king, even if they did not hold a scrap of land directly from him. William's kingship thus represented a powerful fusion of Carolingian-style traditions of public power with the new forms of lordship that had grown up in the tenth and eleventh centuries, bolstered by indigenous Anglo-Saxon forms of governance. It was a new type of monarchy.

## The Struggle for Imperial Power

We can contrast the wide-ranging powers of the new Anglo-Norman kings of England with those of Germany. No German king could claim to rule more than a single principality, and his imperial authority over a host of other rulers was maintained only through a close alliance with the Church. For this reason, the emperor relied heavily on ecclesiastical leaders: his chief administrators were archbishops and bishops whom the emperor himself had appointed and installed in their sacred offices, just as Charlemagne had done. Even the pope was frequently an imperial appointee. The fact that leading churchmen were often members of the imperial family also helped to counter the power of regional rulers.

But during the latter half of the eleventh century, this close cooperation between sacred and secular authority was fractured, as was the ultimate power of the German monarch. In 1056, the six-year-old Henry IV (1050–1106) succeeded his father as king and emperor; and, as we will frequently note, political competition among the advisers of underage rulers often escalates into larger conflicts. In this case, the German princes of various regions—led by the disenfranchised Saxon nobility—tried to gain control of the royal government at the expense of Henry's regents. When Henry began to rule in his own right, in 1073, these hostilities escalated into a civil war.

At the same time, the newly elected pope, Gregory VII (r. 1073–1085), began to insist that no laymen—not even royal ones—should have any influence within the Church. (This would become a core contention in a movement toward increased papal power, to be discussed in the next section.) King Henry, of course, resisted any initiative that would prohibit him from selecting his own bishops and abbots, for these were the key players in the administration of his realm. So Pope Gregory allied himself with the rebellious Saxon nobility, and together they moved to depose Henry. To save his crown, Henry was forced to acknowledge the pope's superiority by begging forgiveness.

Crossing the Alps into Italy in 1077, in the depths of winter, Henry found Gregory installed at the castle of Canossa under the protection of one of Europe's most powerful rulers, Matilda of Tuscany. Encouraged by Matilda, who interceded on his behalf, Henry performed an elaborate ritual of penance: standing for three successive days

**MATILDA OF TUSCANY MEDIATES BETWEEN EMPEROR AND POPE.** Matilda was one of the most powerful rulers in eleventh-century Europe, controlling many strategic territories in northern Italy. Fluent in German as well as Latin and Italian, she was a key mediator in the struggle between the emperor and the pope, and a supporter of the reforming movement within the Church. The Latin inscription accompanying this manuscript miniature reads: "The King entreats the Abbot [i.e., the pope] and even humbles himself before Matilda." ▪ *How does this image represent the relationships among these figures?* ▪ *Which appears to be the most powerful, and why?*

outside the gates of the castle, barefoot, stripped of his imperial trappings, clad in the sackcloth of a supplicant. This performance of subjection and servitude forestalled Henry's deposition, but it did not resolve his dispute with the nobility of German lands. And it also symbolically reversed the relationship between secular power and religious power. Since the time of Constantine, popes had been dependent on the rulers who protected them; but now, an emperor had been bested by the pope. For the other kings and lords of Europe, Henry's humiliation was a chilling example of what could happen when a king let himself be made a vassal.

## RELIGIOUS REFORM AND PAPAL POWER

The increased power of the papacy in the eleventh century was a result of the processes we have been surveying in this chapter, but it was a development that would have been hard to foresee at the time of Charlemagne's death. Yet, in the wake of the Viking invasions and the redistribution of power within the former Carolingian Empire, no ruler could maintain Charlemagne's hold on the Church. Many parish churches had been abandoned or destroyed; and those that survived were often regarded as the personal property of some local family, whose responsibility for protecting parishioners could become an excuse to oppress them. Bishoprics, too, were co-opted by families who regarded Church lands and offices as their private property. Monasteries underwent a further process of privatization, becoming safe havens for aristocratic younger sons and daughters with little inclination for religious life. Meanwhile, the holders of papal office were its worst abusers, most of whom were incompetent or corrupt and the sons of powerful Roman families. Many

fathered sons who themselves succeeded to high ecclesiastical office, including that of pope. As the guardian of the tombs of Peter and Paul, the bishop of Rome had long occupied a privileged position. Now, however, the papacy's credibility had been severely compromised.

## The Monastic Reform Movement

The first successful attempt to restore the spiritual authority of the Roman Church can be traced to the founding of a new kind of monastery in Burgundy (now southeastern France). In 910, a Benedictine abbey called Cluny freed itself from any obligation to local families by placing itself under the direct protection of the papacy. And although it had a wealthy benefactor, that benefactor relinquished control over Cluny's property; instead, Duke William of Aquitaine and his family gained the spiritual support and prayers of the monks, whose intercessions might help save warlike men from eternal damnation.

This arrangement would set a new precedent for the relationship between monasteries and powerful families for centuries to come, as Cluny began to sponsor other monasteries on the same model. Indeed, the foundation of these daughter houses was another innovation: prior to this, all Benedictine monasteries had been independent of each other, united only by their observance of Benedict's *Rule*. Now, Cluny established a network of Cluniac clones across Europe, all of which remained subordinate to the mother house. By 1049, there were sixty-seven such Cluniac priories, as the daughter monasteries were called, each one performing the same elaborate round of prayer and worship for which Cluny became famous—and each one entirely free from the control of local lords who hoped to reap spiritual rewards from their support of the pious monks.

**THE ABBEY CHURCH AT CLUNY.** Its extraordinary wealth and power made Cluny a major target during the French Wars of Religion, and again during the French Revolution, when locals who had been subjected to its lordship for centuries razed most of the buildings to the ground (see Chapters 14 and 18). This artist's reconstruction shows the vast abbey church as it might have looked by the twelfth century, after several extensive building campaigns. In its day, Cluny was one of the largest structures in Europe and a quintessential example of the architectural style known as Romanesque.

Cluniac influence was strongest in the former Frankish territories and in Italy, where the virtual absence of effective kingship allowed monastic reforms to thrive unchecked. In Germany and England, by contrast, fostering monastic reform emerged as an essential responsibility of Christian rulers whose role model was the pious Charlemagne. These rulers, too, followed Cluniac example by insisting on the strict observance of poverty, chastity, and obedience within the monastery, and on the performance of liturgical prayer. Yet, because they were the guarantors of the monasteries' freedom from outside interference, it was they who appointed the abbots, just as they also appointed the bishops of their kingdoms. As a result of this trend, and the concurrent Norman conquest of England, future kings of England would have more direct control over Church lands than other European rulers. In Germany, a prince's right to appoint spiritual leaders was the central cause of strife with the papacy (see below).

Despite the differences in sponsorship, these parallel reforming movements made monasticism the dominant spiritual model for Latin Christianity. The peaceful, orderly round of daily worship in monasteries and convents was regarded as mirroring a perfect celestial harmony, and monastic prayers were considered uniquely effective because of nuns' and monks' holy way of life. Monasteries also had an important influence on the piety of ordinary people, because many monastic communities maintained parishes that ministered directly to the laity. The spiritual practices that had been unique to monks and nuns in earlier centuries, therefore, came to influence daily life outside the cloister.

## Relics and Pilgrims

One potent example of this new popular spirituality was the growing devotion to relics. Monasteries were often the repositories of cherished objects associated with saints, such as fragments of bone or pieces of cloth cut from the garments of some holy person. These souvenirs were believed to possess special protective and curative powers. Hence, a relic was always buried beneath the altar of a church during the ceremony of its consecration, to render the church building sacrosanct. Reliquaries made of precious metals and studded with jewels were casings that reflected and augmented the value of the holy objects contained within them. They were also collected and displayed.

Indeed, relics were so valuable that monasteries and cathedrals competed with one another for their acquisition and even plotted the "holy theft" of a particularly prized treasure. For instance, the relics of Nicholas, a fourth-century bishop of Myra (in Turkey), were stolen from the saint's tomb during the eleventh century. These were brought to Bari in southeastern Italy, where Benedictine monks built a magnificent church to house them. It became a major—and lucrative—destination for pilgrims.

The possession and display of relics thus became a way for monasteries to attract attention and generate revenue, since those who sought cures or favors at the shrine of a saint would often make a donation to the monastery in the saint's honor. If a saint was especially famous for a particular type of miracle, pilgrims might travel thousands of miles to visit a shrine. Saint Nicholas was famous for increasing the wealth of his suppliants, and for bestowing gifts—hence his later incarnation as Santa Claus. The relics of Sainte Foy ("Saint Faith") of Conques (southern France) were renowned for their power to rectify injustices, restore order, and heal the maladies that afflicted the poor. Those of the apostle James at Compostela (northern Spain) became the chief destination on a major pilgrimage route, rivaling even the holy sites of Rome and Jerusalem in its popularity. Pilgrimage was another of the important ways in which the new patterns of Christian piety that developed in monasteries began to spread to the laity.

## The Reform of the Secular Clergy

By the eleventh century, the movement toward spiritual renewal in the monasteries of Europe began to embrace the sees of bishops. This was a major change. Bishops and the priests who served in their dioceses were secular clergy, living in the world (*saeculum* in Latin), and it had long been expected that they would share some of the worldly preoccupations and lifestyles of their parishioners. But as the values and priorities of monasticism began to spread outward, abbots were more often appointed to episcopal office. Meanwhile, even nonmonastic bishops were forced to adopt stricter standards of personal conduct. Bishops also began to rebuild and expand their cathedral churches to make them more suitable reflections of divine majesty, in accordance with Cluniac example.

As their influence grew, the monasteries under the sway of Cluny began to lobby for even larger reforms, amounting to a fundamental dismantling of customs that reached back to the organization of the Church under Constantine, seven centuries earlier. They centered their attacks on the practice of simony (SIGH-mony), a term describing any use of ecclesiastical office for personal gain, including the purchase or sale of a bishopric or a priest's living (i.e., house, goods, and annual salary). In other words, the reform movement targeted the very structure of the Church as a network of

## A Miraculous Reliquary

*Although pilgrimages had been a part of Christian religious practice for centuries, they became much more central elements of popular piety from the tenth century on. Pilgrims brought money and spiritual prestige to the monasteries and cathedrals that housed miracle-working relics, and competition among monastic houses sometimes led one house to steal the relics of another. But some critics worried that these newly popular shrines were encouraging idolatry. Bernard of Angers (c. 960–1028) was one such critic. His account of a visit to the shrines of several saints, including that of Sainte Foy ("Saint Faith") at Conques, reveals the negative impression that ornate reliquaries made on him—and the power of wonder-working relics to correct that impression.*

t is an ancient custom in all of Auvergne, Rodez, Toulouse, and the neighboring regions that the local saint has a statue of gold, silver, or some other metal . . . [that] serves as a reliquary for the head of the saint or for a part of his body. The learned might see in this a superstition and a vestige of the cult of demons, and I myself . . . had the same impression the first time I saw the statue of Saint Gerard . . . resplendent with gold and stones, with an expression so human that the simple people . . . pretend that it winks at pilgrims whose prayers it answers. I admit to my shame that turning to my friend Bernerius and laughing, I whispered to him in Latin, "What do you think of the idol? Wouldn't Jupiter or Mars be happy with it?" . . .

Three days later we arrived at [the shrine of] St. Faith. . . . We approached [the reliquary] but the crowd was such that we could not prostrate ourselves like so many others already lying on the floor. Unhappy, I remained standing, fixing my view on the image and murmuring this prayer, "St. Faith, you whose relics rest in this sham, come to my assistance on the day of judgment." And this time I looked at my companion . . . because I found it outrageous that all of these rational beings should be praying to a mute and inanimate object. . . .

Later I greatly regretted to have acted so stupidly toward the saint of God. This was because among other miracles [that] Don Adalgerius, at that time dean and later . . . abbot [of Conques], told me [was] a remarkable account of a cleric named Oldaric. One day when the venerable image had to be taken to another place, . . . he restrained the crowd from bringing offerings and

The Reliquary of Saint Faith, Early Tenth Century.

he insulted and belittled the image of the saint. . . . The next night, a lady of imposing severity appeared to him: "You," she said, "how dare you insult my image?" Having said this, she flogged her enemy with a staff. . . . He survived only long enough to tell the vision in the morning.

Thus there is no place left for arguing whether the effigy of St. Faith ought to be venerated since it is clear that he who reproached the holy martyr nevertheless retracted his reproach. Nor is it a spurious idol where nefarious rites of sacrifice or of divination are conducted, but rather a pious memorial of a holy virgin, before which great numbers of faithful people decently and eloquently implore her efficacious intercession for their sins.

Source: Bernard of Angers, "The Procession of Saint Foy," in *Readings in Medieval History*, 5th edition, ed. and trans. Patrick J. Geary (University of Toronto Press: 2016), pp. 290–91 (slightly modified).

### Questions for Analysis

1. Why does Bernard initially object to the display of relics in ornate reliquaries? Why would he consider this practice blasphemous? How does he become reconciled to it?

2. Can you think of present-day practices that resemble the medieval fascination with collecting, displaying, and venerating relics? What do such practices reveal about any society?

independent lordships held by powerful men in trust for their families.

Even more radical was the reformers' demand that secular clergy share the lifestyles of monks, taking vows not only of personal poverty but of celibacy. Although some early councils of the Church had attempted to regulate the marriage of bishops and priests, none had been successful, for good reason: the task of ministering to the laity was very different from the monk's task of perpetual prayer and communal life. For a thousand years, it had been conceded that the demands of priestly celibacy were unreasonable, and would deprive a priest's parishioners of an additional resource and ministry—that of his wife. In the year 1000, therefore, the vast majority of parish priests all across Europe were married, and in the eastern Orthodox Church they would remain so. Married bishops were rare, but not unknown. In Brittany, the archbishop of Dol and his wife publicly celebrated the marriages of their daughters, endowing them with lands belonging to the bishopric. In Milan, the archbishops flatly rejected reformers' calls for celibacy, declaring that their patron saint, Ambrose (see Chapter 6), had been married, too.

## The Reform of the Papacy

In Rome, the most powerful bishopric of all remained resolutely unreformed until 1046, when the German emperor Henry III deposed three rival Roman nobles who claimed to be pope and appointed in their place his own relative, a monk who adopted the name Leo IX (r. 1049–1054). Leo and his supporters took control of the papal court and began to promulgate decrees against simony and clerical marriage. They then took steps to enforce these decrees by traveling throughout Christendom, disciplining or removing from office priests deemed guilty of simony or obstinately determined not to "put away" their wives—whom the reformers insisted on calling "concubines" as a way of discrediting these respectable relationships.

Implicit in Leo's reforming efforts was a new vision of the Roman Church as a type of monarchy, with the pope at the apex of a spiritual pyramid. This was an ideal difficult for any secular ruler to realize, and one that would severely limit the power of other ecclesiastical officeholders. It was not surprising, therefore, that Leo and his successors met considerable opposition from powerful leaders within the Church itself, and they could only enforce their claims in regions where they had the support of secular rulers. Chief among these was the pious emperor Henry III, whose protection insulated papal reformers from the Roman nobility, who would otherwise have deposed or assassinated them.

But when Henry III died in 1056, the regents of his child heir Henry IV (whose reign we discussed above) were neither able nor willing to stand behind the reforming movement. In 1058, the Roman aristocracy seized this opportunity to install one of their own men on the papal throne. By this time, however, the reform movement had gathered momentum; and a year later, a new pope had been installed who was determined to counter any interference from either the German or Italian nobility. To this end, Nicholas II (r. 1059–1061) created a new legislative body, the College of Cardinals (from the Latin for "collection" of "hinges"). Hitherto, local bishops around Rome had served the papacy as advisers and assistants, but now the college became the nexus for the creation of papal policy. It also ensured the continuity of the papal office by overseeing the selection of new popes, a role it still plays today.

Needless to say, this novel arrangement infuriated the advisers of the young Henry IV, since it denied the emperor's prerogative to oversee the process of papal elections himself. And it set the stage for the confrontations that were to follow.

## The Investiture Conflict

A few years after Henry IV began to rule in his own right, the new College of Cardinals selected as pope a zealous reformer, a Cluniac monk of Tuscan origins who had been a protégé of Leo IX. He took the name Gregory VII. Initially, pope and emperor treated one another with deference. Henry IV's position in Germany had been weakened by his wars with the Saxon nobility, and he needed papal backing to restore his authority. In his letters to the new pope, he therefore blamed the advisers of his youth for the troubles that had arisen between his own court and that of Rome, and he promised to make amends. Gregory, in turn, spoke of pope and emperor as the two eyes of a single, Christian body. On the surface, it appeared that harmony might be restored.

Two years later, however, relations between papacy and empire were riven by a conflict that would permanently alter the relationship between spiritual and temporal rulers in western Europe. Superficially, the issue that divided Gregory and Henry was that of investiture, the right to appoint bishops and to equip them with the trappings of office. Since the time of the Carolingians, this had been the prerogative of the emperor—as it was in Byzantium. But to Gregory, this practice smacked of simony, since a lay lord would obviously choose bishops who would be politically useful to him, regardless of their spiritual qualifications.

The real issue, however, was not the political power of bishops but the control of that power. The papal reform movement, as it developed under Gregory, was predicated paradoxically on liberating the Church from powerful worldly influences in order that the Church itself might become more worldly and powerful. This was the principle that lay behind discouraging clerical marriage, too: Church offices and Church property had to be protected by the Church for the Church; and allowing priests to marry might encourage the handing down of offices to sons, just as allowing rulers to appoint bishops encouraged these bishops to act as the rulers' agents. These practices tainted the austere authority that the pope was trying to cultivate, and it also threatened to alienate property and power that the papacy wanted to harness for its own purposes.

Gregory therefore took the reform movement to a new level, insisting that adherence to these principles was not just a matter of policy but of religious dogma, a term defined as a "truth necessary for salvation." When Henry IV refused to accept Gregory's reforms and proceeded to invest the new archbishop of Milan, Gregory reminded him that, as the successor of Saint Peter and the representative of Christ on earth, he himself had the power to save or damn all souls. To drive the point home, Gregory excommunicated a number of Henry's advisers, including several of the bishops who had participated in the investiture at Milan. Henry thereupon renounced his obedience to Gregory, calling on him to resign, to which Gregory responded by excommunicating Henry, along with his supporters.

In itself, the excommunication of a king was not terribly unusual. Gregory, however, went much further by equating excommunication with deposition, declaring that since Henry was no longer a faithful son of the Church, he was no longer king either, and so his subjects had a sacred duty to rebel against him. It was this declaration that occasioned Henry's humiliating penance at Canossa in January of 1077. But the story does not end there, because Henry used his restored powers to crush his Saxon opponents and eventually to drive Gregory himself from Rome; the aged pope died in exile in southern Italy in 1085. By then, however, he had established the principles on which papal governance would be based for the remainder of the Middle Ages.

In 1122, the conflict over investiture was provisionally resolved at the Concordat of Worms (*VOHRMS*) in Germany. Its terms declared that the emperor was forbidden to invest prelates with the *religious* symbols of their office but was allowed to invest them with the symbols of their rights as *temporal* rulers, in his capacity as their overlord. In practice, then, the rulers of Europe retained a great deal of influence over ecclesiastical appointments, but they had to acknowledge that bishops were now part of a clerical hierarchy headed by the pope, and that they were supposed to be loyal to the Church in Rome and not to the ruler of the region in which they lived.

## CRUSADING CAUSES AND OUTCOMES

Gregory VII's equation of excommunication with deposition had given the pope a powerful new weapon to use against wayward rulers. Indeed, according to a series of pronouncements issued in his name, Gregory insisted that the pope has the power to judge all men but cannot himself be judged by any earthly authority. Moreover, he has the power to free any man from obligations to his lord, because every Christian owes ultimate loyalty to the pope, the arbiter of eternal life or death. These were big claims. How could they be realized? Gregory's immediate successors would soon be driven to great lengths in their efforts to establish the credibility of the newly powerful papacy. In the end, it took the appeal of a Byzantine emperor and the preaching of a crusade against Muslims to unite western Christendom under the papal banner.

### The Expansion and Fragility of Byzantium

As Europe expanded and changed, the eastern Roman Empire was undergoing its own series of transformations. The decline of the Abbasid caliphate in Baghdad had relieved some of the pressures on its borders in the course of the ninth century. But at the same time, Byzantium was facing some new threats. In the mid-ninth century, Muslims from North Africa captured the Byzantine islands of Sicily and Crete. Meanwhile, the migration of pagan Slavs into the Balkans was rapidly undermining Byzantine control of that region. And a formidable power had emerged in the north, as the Viking Rus' established themselves along the river systems that fed into the Black and Caspian Seas. The most important trading partner of the Rus' was the Abbasid caliphate, with which they exchanged slaves, honey, wax, and furs for silver, Indian spices, and Chinese silks. But the Rus' knew their way to Constantinople, too. In 860, while the Byzantine emperor and his army were busy on the eastern frontier, a fleet of them sailed into the Black Sea and sacked the capital.

The best that the emperors in Byzantium could do was to make these newer enemies their allies. Greek-speaking missionaries began the process by converting some of the Balkan Slavs to Orthodox Christianity, devising for them a written language known as Old Church Slavonic and creating the Cyrillic alphabet still used today in Bulgaria, Serbia, and Russia. As we have often seen, domination went hand in glove with conversion. The empire also fostered a military and commercial alliance with the kingdom of Rus' centered around Kiev. In 911, hundreds of Rus' served with the Byzantine navy in an attack on Muslim Crete. In 957, a Kievan princess named Olga was lavishly entertained on a state visit to Constantinople. And in 989, the emperor Basil II turned to Vladimir, prince of Kiev, for the troops he needed to win a civil war against an imperial rival. In return for Vladimir's help, Basil married him to his sister Anna, and Vladimir, along with his people, accepted baptism into the Orthodox Church. (Russia remains strongly Orthodox to this day, despite Soviet efforts to dismantle the Russian Orthodox Church during the twentieth century.)

During the tenth century, the eastern Roman Empire further strengthened its position by launching a series of successful campaigns against the Abbasids, reconquering territories that had been lost since the first wave of Muslim conquests in seventh century. But although most of the peoples of this region had remained Christian through three centuries of Islamic rule, the Armenians and the Syrians in particular had their own distinctive Christian traditions that were at odds, both doctrinally and linguistically, with the Greek-speaking church at Constantinople. Reincorporating these "heretics" into the empire strained the limits of Orthodoxy to a considerable degree, and these efforts created a center of power that lay outside the imperial capital at Constantinople. Accordingly, rivalries divided the eastern nobility and the imperial court, eventually erupting into warfare after one aristocratic family attempted a coup.

Meanwhile, projects of reconquest and expansion were overextending the Byzantine military and its treasury. In an effort to raise cash, some emperors in the mid-eleventh century began to debase the gold coinage that had kept the empire competitive with the Islamic caliphate, thus undermining Byzantine commerce at the very moment when Venice, Genoa, and Pisa were consolidating their control in the

**THE BYZANTINE EMPIRE, c. 1025.** ▪ *According to the map, what political challenges faced the Byzantine Empire in the eleventh century?* ▪ *How was the long-standing influence of Muslims in the Near East likely to affect the character of Byzantine culture?* ▪ *How did the domain of Rus' potentially create additional economic and military pressure on Byzantium, directly as well as indirectly?*

## Preaching the First Crusade: Two Accounts

> We owe the following account of Urban II's call for a crusade to Fulcher of Chartres, a priest who was present at the Council of Clermont in 1095 and later served as a chaplain to Baldwin, the first Norman king of Jerusalem. It forms part of Fulcher's contemporary chronicle of the First Crusade. The second account of the motives behind the Crusade comes from a biography of the Byzantine emperor Alexius Comnenus, written by his daughter Anna (1083–1153), who also lived through these events.

### Pope Urban II's Call at Clermont, November 1195

Most beloved brethren: Urged by necessity, I, Urban, by the permission of God chief bishop and prelate over the whole world, have come into these parts as an ambassador with a divine admonition to you, the servants of God. . . .

Although, O sons of God, you have promised more firmly than ever to keep the peace among yourselves and to preserve the rights of the Church, there remains still an important work for you to do. Freshly quickened by the divine correction, you must apply the strength of your righteousness to another matter which concerns you as well as God. For your brethren who live in the east are in urgent need of your help, and you must hasten to give them the aid which has often been promised them. For, as most of you have heard, the Turks and Arabs have attacked them and have conquered the territory of Romania [the Byzantine Empire] as far west as the shore of the Mediterranean and the Hellespont. . . . They have occupied more and more of the lands of those Christians, and have overcome them in seven battles. They have killed and captured many, and have destroyed the churches and devastated the empire.

If you permit them to continue thus for a while with impunity, the faithful of God will be much more widely attacked by them. On this account I, or rather the Lord, beseech you as Christ's heralds to publish this everywhere and to persuade all people of whatever rank, footsoldiers and knights, poor and rich, to carry aid promptly to those Christians and to destroy that vile race from the lands of our friends. I say this to those who are present, but it is meant also for those who are absent. Moreover, Christ commands it.

All who die by the way, whether by land or by sea, or in battle against the pagans, shall have immediate remission of sins. This I grant them through the power of God with which I am invested. O what a disgrace, if such a despised and base race, which worships demons, should conquer a people which has the faith of omnipotent God and is made glorious with the name of Christ! With what reproaches will the Lord overwhelm us if you do not aid those who, with us, profess the Christian religion!

Let those who have been accustomed to wage unjust private warfare against the faithful now go against the infidels and end with victory this war which should have been begun long ago. Let those who for a long time have been robbers now become knights. Let those who have been fighting against their brothers and relatives now fight in a proper way against the barbarians. Let those who have been serving as mercenaries for small pay now obtain the eternal reward. Let those who have been wearing themselves out in both body

eastern Mediterranean and taking over the lucrative trade between Muslim North Africa (including Egypt) and western Europe.

A failing economy, ongoing dynastic civil war, the weakened condition of the army, and uneasy relations with the new kingdoms of the Balkans (especially Hungary) proved nearly fatal to Byzantine sovereignty. And then the empire was confronted with yet another threat. The Seljuq Turks, a powerful dynasty of Sunni Muslims who were building their own empire based in Persia, began to move westward in the latter part of the eleventh century. In 1071, they captured Armenia and moved swiftly into

and soul now work for a double honor. Behold! On this side will be the sorrowful and poor, on that, the rich; on this side, the enemies of the Lord, on that, his friends. Let those who go not put off the journey, but rent their lands and collect money for their expenses; and as soon as winter is over and spring comes, let them eagerly set out on the way with God as their guide.

Source: S. J. Allen and Emilie Amt, eds., *The Crusades: A Reader*, 2nd ed. (University of Toronto: 2014), pp 34–35.

## Anna Comnena Describes the Beginnings of the First Crusade

[A]lexius] had no time to relax before he heard a rumour that countless Frankish armies were approaching. He dreaded their arrival, knowing as he did their uncontrollable passion, their erratic character and their irresolution, not to mention . . . their greed for money. . . . So far from despairing, however, he made every effort to prepare for war if need arose. What actually happened was more far-reaching and terrible than rumour suggested, for the whole of the West and all the barbarians who lived between the Adriatic and the Straits of Gibraltar migrated in a body to Asia, marching across Europe country by country with all their households. The reason for this mass movement is to be found more or less in the following events. A certain Kelt, called Peter [the Hermit] . . . left to worship at the Holy Sepulchre and after suffering much ill-treatment at the hands of the Turks and Saracens who were plundering the whole of Asia, he returned home with difficulty. Unable to admit defeat, . . . he worked out a clever scheme. He decided to preach in all the Latin countries. A divine voice, he said, commanded him to proclaim to all the counts in France that all should depart from their homes, set out to worship at the Holy Shrine, and . . . strive to liberate Jerusalem. . . . Surprisingly, he was successful. . . . Full of enthusiasm and ardour they thronged every highway, and with these warriors came a host of civilians, outnumbering the sand of the sea shore or the stars of heaven, carrying palms and bearing crosses on their shoulders. There were women and children, too, who had left their own countries. . . .

The upheaval that ensued as men *and* women took to the road was unprecedented within living memory. The simpler folk were in very truth led on by a desire to worship at Our Lord's tomb and visit the holy places, but the more villainous characters . . . had an ulterior purpose, for they hoped on their journey to seize the capital [Jerusalem] itself, looking upon its capture as a natural consequence of the expedition. . . .

Source: Excerpted from Anna Comnena, *The Alexiad*, trans. E. R. A. Sewter (New York: 1969), pp. 308–11.

### Questions for Analysis

1. Given Urban II's explanation of the problems confronting the Byzantine Empire, how do you account for the fact that the Crusades were directed toward the Holy Land and not the relief of Byzantium?

2. How does Anna Comnena represent the motives of Peter the Hermit and the crusaders? What distinctions does she make among the participants?

3. Are there points of comparison between these two accounts? On what do they agree? How would you explain the differences between them?

the Byzantine heartland of Anatolia (Turkey), where they destroyed a Byzantine army sent to deflect them.

At a blow, the wealthiest and most productive part of the empire fell into Muslim hands—and not those of the Abbasids with whom the Byzantines had contended for centuries. In the same year, the Seljuqs captured Jerusalem, which had been part of a Shi'ite caliphate based in Egypt, ruled by the Fatimids. By 1081, when the eastern nobility of Byzantium finally emerged triumphant in their ongoing bid for the imperial throne, the new emperor Alexius Comnenus (r. 1081–1118) found himself at the head of a crippled state.

# Past and Present

## Ideas of Crusade

The launching of the First Crusade was the beginning of a trend that reshaped the relations between western Europeans and their neighbors—one that continues today. The very use of the word "crusade" is likely to cause trouble, as when President George W. Bush spoke of "this crusade, this war on terrorism" to which he pledged the United States after the attacks of September 11, 2001.

 **Watch related author interview on the Student Site**

## The Call for a Crusade

Alexius was an able emperor. In the first decade of his rule, he managed to shore up the failing economy and secure his hold over territory in the Balkans. He then began to plan a campaign against the Seljuqs. But with what forces? The Byzantine army had been decimated in Greece by a far superior cavalry of Norman knights in 1085. For by this time, the Normans had established independent principalities in southern Italy and Sicily and were moving farther east, taking advantage of the perpetual power vacuum in the Mediterranean and showcasing the effective tactics of chivalry. As it happened, this encounter between the Byzantine emperor and western Europe's most formidable warriors was historically significant. It convinced Alexius that such heavily armed horsemen would be successful if pitted against the lightly armored Seljuqs.

It was in the hopes of recruiting a mercenary force, therefore, that Alexius approached Pope Urban II (r. 1088–1099). This was a move that played into the hands of the reformed papacy. Urban was trying hard to realize some of the powerful claims that his recent predecessors had made on behalf of papal authority, and this seemed like a golden opportunity. By coming to the aid of the eastern Roman Empire, he would show the restive princes of western Europe that the papacy was a force to be reckoned with. At the same time, he hoped to show that Latin military and spiritual might was greater than that of the weakened Greeks, thereby healing the schism between Orthodox and Roman Churches and realizing the centuries-old dream of a universal Christian Church based in Rome, with the pope at its head. In addition, Urban would thereby show support for another reforming effort that had gained momentum in recent years: a peace movement that was attempting to quell the endemic violence unleashed by competitive bands of knights and their rapacious lords. What better way to defuse the situation than to ship those violent energies overseas, deploying them against a common enemy?

So Alexius received a favorable reply, but he got far more than he had asked for—or wanted. He had needed a modest contingent of a few thousand knights to help him reconquer Anatolia. Instead, what he got was a vast army of 100,000 men, charged by Urban II to retake the holy city of Jerusalem for Christendom. For Urban decided to interpret Alexius's request very loosely (see **Competing Viewpoints** on page 272). Speaking before an assembled crowd at an ecclesiastical council at Clermont (central France) in 1095, Urban announced that he fully supported the peace movement. He said, furthermore, that any knights who wished to fight, pillage, and wreak havoc could do so for a just and Christian cause by liberating the Holy Land from its Muslim rulers. At home, said Urban, most knights were riffraff and marauders, destined for hellfire and damnation; but abroad, by fighting or dying in the service of Christ, they would win absolution for their sins. By taking up the cross (*crux*, hence "crusade"), a warrior stood to win glory, booty, and salvation.

## The Motives of Crusaders

The Crusade was an irresistible trifecta for many pious, ambitious, or opportunistic men. Consequently, the ultimate response to Urban's call exceeded all expectations. Indeed, his message was amplified by other preachers, including a zealous priest called Peter the Hermit, who claimed (falsely) that he had been prevented by the Seljuqs from visiting the Holy Land. Within a year, tens of thousands of warriors, many of them new to battle, were on the march toward Constantinople, where they intended to gather before departing for Jerusalem.

As with any large enterprise, the participants' motives must have varied. A few might have hoped to win principalities for themselves. Others were drawn by the prospect of adventure. Many were the dependents of greater men and had no choice but to accompany their lords; some hoped to free themselves from dependence by fighting. Most probably had no idea how long the journey would be or knew anything about the places for which they were destined.

But the dominant motive for joining this First Crusade was religious. Except for a few of the greatest lords—mostly Normans from Sicily and southern Italy—the prospect of winning new lands was both unlikely and undesired. Indeed, one of the greatest challenges facing the Christian kingdom that was established in Jerusalem after 1099 was the fact that crusaders so rarely wanted to stay. After

fulfilling their vows, the vast majority went home. So why did they go in the first place? The risks of dying on such a journey were high, and the costs of embarking were enormous. Crusading knights needed a minimum of two years' revenues in hand to finance the journey; to raise such sums, most were forced to mortgage lands and borrow heavily from family, friends, monasteries, and merchants. They then had to find some way to pay back these loans if and when they returned home. By any rational assessment, the Crusade was a fool's errand.

The seeming irrationality of this endeavor underscores the importance of reckoning with the crusaders' piety, and even their desire to emulate legendary heroes such as Roland. Crusading was the ultimate pilgrimage, the holy places of Jerusalem the ultimate Christian shrines. If anyone could receive special blessings by traveling to Compostela, Conques, or Bari, how much more blessed would be those who fought through to the Holy Land! Urban II made this

**ROLAND AS A CRUSADING KNIGHT.** The association between knighthood and crusading helped to raise the social status of knights, and contributed to the refinement of a chivalric ethos. Here, Roland, as a crusading knight, dressed head to foot in expensive chain mail, is shown kneeling in homage to his lord, God.

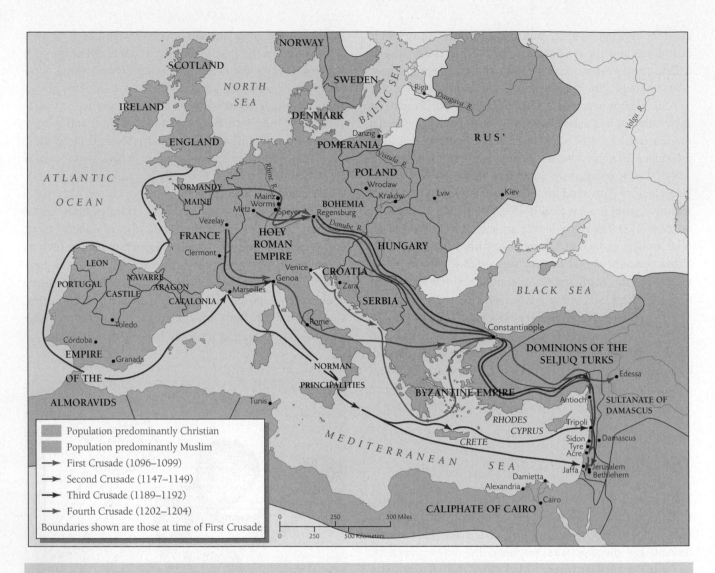

**THE ROUTES OF THE CRUSADERS, 1096–1204.** Compare the routes followed by the majority of participants in the first three Crusades. ■ *What were the three main routes followed?* ■ *What geographical and political factors appear to be determining these trajectories?* ■ *Why was the Fourth Crusade so different?*

point explicit at Clermont, promising that crusaders would be freed from all penances imposed by the Church. Some zealots went even further, promising that crusaders would be entirely freed from otherworldly punishments for all sins committed up to that point in their lives, and that the souls of those who died on a crusade would go straight to heaven.

Crusade preaching also emphasized the vengeance that Christ's soldiers should exact on his pagan enemies. So to some crusaders, it seemed absurd to wait until they arrived in the Holy Land to undertake this aspect of their mission. Muslims might hold Jesus's property at Jerusalem, but Christian theology held Jews responsible for the death of Jesus himself. Assaults against Jewish communities therefore began in the spring of 1096 and quickly spread eastward with the crusaders. Hundreds of Jews were killed in the German towns of Mainz, Worms, Speyer, and Cologne,

and hundreds more were forcibly baptized as the price for escaping death at the hands of crusading knights. Many individual churchmen attempted to prevent these attacks, among them the bishops in whose dioceses Jews lived, but the Church's own negative propaganda thwarted these efforts, and pogroms (organized attacks) against Europe's Jews would remain a regular and predictable feature of Christian crusading—and its modern manifestations.

## The Christian Conquest of Jerusalem

Surprised by the nature and scale of the response to his appeal, Emperor Alexius did his best to move the crusaders quickly through Constantinople and into Anatolia. But differences in outlook between the crusaders and the Byzantine

# Analyzing Primary Sources

## An Arab Aristocrat Encounters the Crusaders

*Usama ibn Munqidh (1095–1188) was an Arab Muslim from Syria, whose family maintained a prominent place in the local administration even after the conquests of the Seljuqs and the Christian crusaders. He traveled widely and worked in various Islamic cities as a diplomat and scholar. He ended his life in the service of Salah ad-Din (Saladin), the great Muslim leader who reconquered Jerusalem the year before Usama's death. The following excerpt is from Usama's memoir, which he called* The Book of Contemplation. *The Templars mentioned in the account are the Christian military order of the Knights of the Temple, who dedicated themselves to protecting pilgrims in Jerusalem and guarding the holy sites. Their headquarters were in the main mosque of the city, which stood on the Temple Mount.*

 nyone who is recently arrived from the Frankish lands is rougher in character than those who have become acclimated and have frequented the company of Muslims. Here is an instance of their rough character (may God abominate them!):

Whenever I went to visit the holy sites in Jerusalem, I would go in and make my way up to the al-Aqsa Mosque, beside which stood a small mosque that the Franks had converted into a church. When I went into the al-Aqsa Mosque—where the Templars, who are my friends, were—they would clear out that little mosque so that I could pray in it. One day, I went into the little mosque, recited the opening formula "God is great!" and stood up in prayer. At this, one of the Franks rushed at me and grabbed me and turned my face towards the east, saying, "Pray like *this*!"

A group of Templars hurried towards him, took hold of the Frank and took him away from me. I then returned to my prayers. The Frank, that very same one, took advantage of their inattention and returned, rushing upon me and turning my face to the east, saying, "Pray like *this*!"

So the Templars came in again, grabbed him and threw him out. They apologized to me, saying, "This man is a stranger, just arrived from the Frankish lands sometime in the past few days. He has never before seen anyone who did not pray towards the east."

"I think I've prayed quite enough," I said and left. I used to marvel at that devil, the change of his expression, the way he trembled and what he must have made of seeing someone praying towards Mecca.

Source: Usama ibn Munqidh, *The Book of Contemplation: Islam and the Crusades*, trans. Paul M. Cobb (New York: 2008), p. 147.

### Questions for Analysis

**1.** What does Usama's account reveal about the variety of relationships among Christians and Muslims in the crusader kingdom of Jerusalem?

**2.** Who is the true outsider in this scenario? What does Usama's treatment by the Templars suggest about the policy of Christian leaders toward the city's Muslim residents?

---

emperor quickly became apparent. Alexius had little interest in an expedition to Jerusalem, and insisted that the crusaders promise to restore to him any territory they captured. From his standpoint, the crusader army was a threat, not least because it was headed by several of the Norman knights who had attempted to infiltrate his empire only ten years earlier. To the crusaders—whose mission had been shaped by Pope Urban's policies, not those of Alexius—this seemed like treachery. The crusaders, furthermore, did not understand the Byzantine emperor's willingness to make alliances with some Muslim rulers (the Shi'ite Fatimids of Egypt and the Abassids of Baghdad) against other Muslim rulers (the Sunni Seljuqs). They ignorantly concluded that the Byzantines were working to undermine the crusading effort, perhaps even supporting the Muslims against them. Such suspicions contributed to their growing conviction that the eastern Roman Empire was itself an obstacle to the successful recovery of Jerusalem.

Viewed from the perspective of Alexius, the Crusade was a disaster; but from that of the papacy and the crusaders themselves, it was a triumph. In 1098, crusaders captured the old Hellenistic city of Antioch and with it most of the Syrian coast. At the end of 1099, they took Jerusalem, indiscriminately slaughtering its Muslim, Jewish, and Christian inhabitants. Their quick success stemmed mainly from the fact that their Muslim opponents were at that moment divided among themselves: the Fatimids had in fact recaptured Jerusalem just months before the crusaders arrived, and the defeated Seljuqs were at war with each other. Western military tactics, in particular the dominance of heavily armored knights, also played an important role in the crusaders' success. Equally critical was the naval support offered by Genoa and Pisa, whose merchant adventurers hoped—if the papacy's cause was successful—to control the Indian spice trade that passed through the Red Sea and on to Alexandria in Egypt. The Crusade thereby contributed to the further decline of Byzantine commerce and decisively altered the balance of power between Byzantium and western Europe.

## The Consequences of Crusade

For Byzantium, then, the consequences of the First Crusade were tragic, and they would worsen in the course of the ensuing century of intensified crusading movements (see Chapter 9). On the Muslim world, however, its impact was more modest. The crusader kingdoms established by victorious Norman and Frankish warlords were never more than a sparsely settled cluster of colonies along the coastline of Syria and Palestine. Because the crusaders did not control the Red Sea, the main routes of Islamic commerce with India and the Far East were unaffected by the change in Jerusalem's religious allegiance.

In any case, those crusaders who remained to settle in the region did not *want* to interfere with the overland caravan routes that wound through their new territories. Trade brokered by Arab, Persian, and Jewish merchants therefore continued despite periodic interruptions. The greatest economic gains for western Europeans therefore went to the Italian maritime republics of Venice and Genoa, and the western markets now open to Muslim merchants for their goods. Both sides also gained in military terms: western Europeans learned new techniques of fortification, and Muslims learned new methods of siege warfare and new respect for the uses of heavy cavalry.

The larger impact of the First Crusade on western Europe is more difficult to assess. From one standpoint, the establishment of the short-lived crusader states represents the limits of Europe's expansion during this otherwise extraordinary period of growth. Trade with the Islamic world, and beyond it with India and the Far East, brought enormous prosperity to some, but these trading links had existed before the Crusades and continued long after they ended.

Of course, the longest-lasting consequence of the First Crusade has also proved the deadliest in the long run. Both Christian and Islamic doctrines of holy war—which had developed in earlier centuries—continue to be destructive in the twenty-first century. Almost immediately, crusading rhetoric would dictate the terms of western Europeans' attitudes toward the wider world and even toward each other, as we shall see in the following chapters. It fostered a new political and religious ethos that would inform the "reconquest" of the Iberian Peninsula by the Christian rulers of Spain and lead to the massacre or forced conversion of Muslims and Jews. Crusading rhetoric underlay English wars against the Welsh and the Scots, and justified the massacre and dispossession of "heretics" in southern France by northern French imperialists. It justified the conquest of the Baltic region and, later, the subsequent conquest of the Americas and the colonization of Asia, Africa, and Australia. And it has continued to exacerbate global animosities to this day.

# THE CULTURE OF THE MUSLIM WEST

It would be misleading to assert that all the consequences of the First Crusade were negative. The positive outcomes were hugely important, too. Increased intellectual and cultural contact between the Latin West and the Islamic world had an enormous impact on western European learning, literature, music, and art. Perhaps most important, the study and practical applications of mathematics were revolutionized when Europeans adopted Arabic numerals and the concept of zero—first promoted beyond the Islamic world, not surprisingly, by the son of a Pisan merchant who grew up in Algeria, Leonardo Fibonacci (c. 1170–c. 1250).

Even Christian theology was transformed by contact with Islam. For one thing, Muslim scholars were the ones who had inherited, preserved, and developed not only Hellenistic medicine and science but the philosophy of Aristotle, which would form the basis of a new Christian philosophy in the twelfth and thirteenth centuries (see Chapter 9). For another, Europeans had been almost entirely ignorant of Muslim beliefs prior to the Crusades, assuming that Muslims were pagans who worshiped a god called Mahomet or Mahoun. But by 1143, Robert of Ketton (c. 1100–c. 1160), a scholar originally from a small town in England, had completed a Latin translation of the Qur'an while working in Spain, with the encouragement of the abbot of Cluny. In the 1130s, he and a friend, Hermann of Carinthia (in Slovenia), had traveled to Byzantium and the crusader kingdoms, where they became students of Arabic. They exemplify the world of possibilities that had opened up to northwestern Europeans as a result of the processes we have been studying in this chapter.

## Muslim Philosophy and Christian Theology

The scholars of Byzantium took a conservative approach to Greek philosophy, in every sense of the word (see Chapter 7). The dialogues of Plato and some works of Aristotle were copied and studied, but the latter's ideas were so hard to reconcile with Orthodox theology that Emperor Alexius Comnenus eventually banned the teaching of Aristotelian logic altogether. It was ironic, then, that the cultures that provided the most direct access to Greek learning were Arabic-speaking, and it was through Arabic translations that western European intellectuals became acquainted with these ideas—thanks to the labor of Arabists such as Robert and Hermann.

Even before the rise of Islam, a number of Greek philosophical texts had been translated into Syriac, a Semitic language closely related to Arabic. Arabic translations soon followed, many sponsored by the Abbasid court at Baghdad, which established a special school for this purpose, known as the House of Wisdom. By the end of the tenth century, Arabic translations of Plato, Aristotle, Plotinus, and other Greek authors were widely available and intensively studied throughout the Muslim world. Even in the remote Persian city of Bukhara, the great Muslim philosopher and physician Avicenna (Ibn Sina; 980–1037) was able to read all of Aristotle's works before reaching the age of eighteen.

Like their counterparts in Byzantium, Muslim philosophers strove to reconcile Greek and Hellenistic philosophical traditions with each other and with the tenets of their theology. Reconciling Aristotelianism and Neoplatonism was the easier task. Many of the translations and commentaries of Aristotle from which Muslim philosophers worked had already been filtered through the philosophical traditions of Alexandria and Rome. Moreover, Aristotle and the

Neoplatonists shared a number of common assumptions, including the eternity of the world and the capacity of the human mind to understand the rational principles that govern the world's workings. Both traditions also stressed the freedom of individual humans to choose between good and evil.

Combining Greek philosophy with Islamic theology was more difficult. Like Judaism and Christianity, Islam holds that a single omnipotent God created the world as an act of pure will and that the world will continue to exist only so long as God wills it. This runs counter to the classical Greek view of the world as eternal. Moreover, both Christian and Islamic theology rest on the immortality of the individual human soul, another doctrine flatly in conflict with Aristotelian and Neoplatonic thought. There were also conflicts over the concept of free will; and again, Muslims and Christians had more in common with one another than with the ancient Greek tradition. Although medieval theologians strongly emphasized the individual responsibility of believers to choose between good and evil, virtually all Muslims—like most Christians—believed that nothing good could occur unless God actively willed it. Islamic philosophers adopted an array of different intellectual tactics to deal with these challenges and, in doing so, laid the groundwork for the Christian theologians who relied on them (see Chapter 9).

**ARISTOTLE TEACHING ARAB ASTRONOMERS.** In this Arabic manuscript from the thirteenth century, Aristotle is represented as a contemporary of the astronomers he is instructing. ■ *What does this illustration suggest about Muslims' attitude toward Greek philosophy?*

## Muslim Science, Medicine, and Mathematics

Many Muslim philosophers were also distinguished physicians and scientists. The study of philosophy could bring a man renown (or censure) but few tangible rewards, whereas successful physicians and astrologers might rise to positions of wealth and power. Both astrology and medicine were applied sciences that relied on careful and accurate observation of natural phenomena. Indeed, Muslim observations of the heavens were so accurate that a few astronomers corroborated the findings of Hellenistic scientists (see Chapter 4): that the earth must rotate on its axis and revolve around the sun. But because these theories conflicted with the (mistaken) assumptions of Aristotle—that the earth remained stationary with the sun and planets revolving around it—they were not generally accepted in the Islamic world or in Europe. Yet they may have influenced Nicolaus Copernicus (1473–1543), who is usually credited as the first to suggest that the earth orbited the sun (see Chapter 16).

Muslim accomplishments in medicine were equally remarkable. Avicenna discovered the contagious nature of tuberculosis, described pleurisy and several varieties of nervous ailments, and noted that diseases could spread through contaminated water and soil. His *Canon of Medicine* remained an authoritative textbook in the Islamic world and western Europe until the seventeenth century. Later Islamic physicians learned the value of cauterization and styptic agents, diagnosed cancer of the stomach, prescribed antidotes in cases of poisoning, and made notable progress in treating eye diseases. They also recognized the infectious character of plague, pointing out that it could be transmitted by clothing.

Muslim physicians were pioneers in organizing hospitals and licensing medical practitioners. At least thirty-four great hospitals were located in the principal cities of Persia, Syria, and Egypt; each with separate wards for particular illnesses, a dispensary for giving out medicine, and a library. Chief physicians and surgeons lectured to students and graduates, examined them, and issued licenses to practice medicine. Even the owners of leeches (used for bloodletting, a standard medical practice of the day) had to submit their medicinal worms for inspection at regular intervals.

Islamic scientists made important advances in optics and chemistry, as well as mathematics. Using Arabic numerals—which Muslim scholars adopted from the Hindus—mathematicians developed a decimal arithmetic based on place values and hinging on the concept of the zero. Their work enabled fundamental advances in entirely new areas, both of which bear Arabic names: algebra and algorithms. Building on Greek geometry and their own astronomical observations, they also made great progress in spherical trigonometry.

Muslim mathematicians thus brought together and pushed forward all the areas of mathematical knowledge that were later adopted and developed in western Europe from the sixteenth century on. And they made an indispensable contribution to the burgeoning European economy, because the sophisticated accounting systems that supported commerce would have been impossible if merchants and bankers had continued to use the clumsy numerals adopted by the Romans. (Try balancing your checking account in Roman numerals!) Thanks to Arabic mathematics, western Europeans could now add, subtract, divide, and multiply quickly and accurately, with or without the help of another Muslim invention, the abacus.

## Muslim Literature and Art

Poetry was integral to Muslim culture. It had been a highly developed art form long before the emergence of Islam. It then became even more important to the development and dissemination of Muslim identity, because it was the form in which Muhammad framed the Qur'an (see Chapter 7).

Like medicine and astronomy, poetry was also a route to advancement. Not all poetry was composed in Arabic; particularly around the Abbasid court, poets writing in Persian enjoyed great renown. The best known of these is Umar Khayyam (d. 1123), whose *Rubaiyat* was turned into a popular English verse cycle by the Victorian poet Edward Fitzgerald (1809–1883). Although Fitzgerald's translation distorts much, the lush sensuality of Umar's poetic imagery ("a jug of wine, a loaf of bread—and thou") faithfully reflects themes that were common to much Muslim poetry. Many such poems was addressed by men to other men, a fact that occasioned no concern within the elite circles in which they were composed and performed. Jews also participated in this elite literary world, especially in Al-Andalus, where they wrote similarly sensuous, playful lyrics in both Hebrew and Arabic, praising wine, sexual intimacy, and their own songs. Muslim Spain saw a great flowering of Jewish intellectual life, which paralleled and intersected with that of the surrounding Muslim society.

Perhaps the most distinctive of Islamic arts are architectural and decorative, the arts that created the spaces in which poets and scientists interacted with their patrons. Many characteristic elements of Muslim architecture—the dome, the column, and the arch—were adapted from Byzantine models, but then combined with the intricate

## A Hebrew Poem from Muslim Spain

*In the courts of tenth- and eleventh-century Muslim Spain, Jewish poets began to write a new style of Hebrew verse closely modeled on contemporary Arabic examples. Samuel the Nagid was perhaps the most remarkable of this group of poets. He became the military leader of the Muslim kingdom of Granada as well as the head of the Jewish community there. In addition to his three volumes of poetry, he also wrote treatises on Hebrew grammar and religious law.*

Your debt to God is
righteously to live,
    And His to you,
    your recompense to
    give.
Do not wear out your days in
serving God;
    Some time devote to Him, some to
yourself.
    To Him give half your day, to work
the rest;
    But give the jug no rest throughout
the night.

Put out your lamps! Use crystal cups
for light.
    Away with singers! Bottles are better
than lutes.
    No song, nor wine, nor friend
beneath the sward—
    These three, O fools, are all of life's
reward.

Source: Raymond P. Scheindlin, ed. and trans.,
*Wine, Women, and Death: Medieval Hebrew Poems
on the Good Life* (Philadelphia: 1986), p. 47.

### Questions for Analysis

**1.** What values does this poem express? What is its perspective on the relationship among devotion to God, duty, and pleasure?

**2.** What does the career of Samuel the Nagid—poet, general, scholar—suggest about Jewish identity in this place and time? What does it suggest about the relations between Jewish and Muslim communities in medieval Spain?

---

tracery and ambitious scale of Persian buildings to form a new architectural vocabulary. Building styles were further inflected by the many different cultures that embraced Islam, from Spain to Egypt to India and beyond. Muslim artistry was also expressed in the magnificent gardens and fountains that adorned palaces, and in the more portable magnificence of gorgeous carpets, tooled leather, brocaded silks and tapestries, inlaid metalwork, enameled glassware, and painted pottery—all decorated with Arabic script, interlacing geometric designs, plants, fruits, flowers, and fantastic animal figures (another Persian influence). These complex designs can often seem strikingly modern, precisely because they anticipate the abstract forms that were considered new in the twentieth century.

**IVORY PYXIS FROM AL-ANDALUS.** Fashioned in the tenth century, this little round box is made from a segment of elephant tusk and would have had a matching lid (now lost). Such boxes usually held spices or incense. Its decorative motifs are echoed in Islamic architecture on a larger scale, reminding us that medieval Islam did not prohibit the representation of natural and fanciful figures, as is often supposed.

## STORY LINES

- The power of Europe's new monarchies and of the papacy depended on new methods of oversight, administration, and documentation.

- Schools and universities were crucial to the development of these institutions, and they also provided ambitious men with unprecedented intellectual, social, and political opportunities.

- Crusading movements continued in the twelfth and thirteenth centuries, intensifying contacts between Latin Christendom and the Muslim world while posing a threat to many minority groups within Europe, as well as to the Byzantine Empire.

- The Church's presence in the daily lives of the laity produced vibrant forms of spirituality, yet placed strict limitations on women, religious dissidents, and non-Christians.

- Meanwhile, Europe's princely courts, wealthy towns, universities, and cathedrals fostered new forms of entertainment, art, and architecture.

## CHRONOLOGY

| | |
|---|---|
| 1079–1142 | Lifetime of Peter Abelard |
| c. 1090–c. 1164 | Lifetime of Heloise |
| 1098–1179 | Lifetime of Hildegard of Bingen |
| 1099 | First Crusade ends |
| 1122–1204 | Lifetime of Eleanor of Aquitaine |
| c. 1140 | Gratian's *Concordance of Discordant Canons* |
| 1152–1190 | Reign of Frederick II Barbarossa |
| 1180–1223 | Reign of Philip II Augustus |
| 1187 | Muslim reconquest of Jerusalem |
| 1192–1194 | Alfonso II of Aragon compiles the *Liber feudorum maior* |
| 1198–1216 | Reign of Pope Innocent III |
| 1204 | Capture and sack of Constantinople |
| 1209 | Franciscan order established |
| | Beginning of the Albigensian Crusade |
| 1215 | Magna Carta and the canons of the Fourth Lateran Council are both formulated |
| 1216 | Dominican order established |
| 1240 | Battle of the Neva |

Before You Read This Chapter

# The Consolidation of Europe, 1100–1250

## CORE OBJECTIVES

- **IDENTIFY** the differences among Europe's emerging monarchies.

- **DESCRIBE** the ongoing effects of crusading.

- **UNDERSTAND** the connections between new religious movements and the power of the papacy.

- **DEFINE** scholasticism and trace its development.

- **EXPLAIN** the changing meaning of *chivalry*.

At the turn of the twelfth century, the eldest son of a nobleman did something unusual: he traded lordship for scholarship. His name was Peter Abelard. By his own estimation, he was the smartest man in the world, and the most attractive. He was certainly one of the most ambitious. After leaving his father's lands in Brittany and besting all the established teachers in Paris, he was appointed to the position of master in the cathedral school, one of the highest academic posts then available. There he met Heloise, the niece of a priest called Fulbert.

Heloise had received an excellent education in a nearby convent, but the normal path of intellectual advancement—Abelard's school—was closed to her. So Fulbert arranged for her to become Abelard's private pupil. She soon became more than that: his intellectual partner, lover, and wife. This last step was particularly problematic, because marriage was no longer an option for clerics and would ruin Abelard's chances of a brilliant career in the Church. So it remained a secret, as did Heloise's subsequent pregnancy and the birth of their son. But her uncle eventually found out and took revenge on Abelard, sending some local thugs to castrate him. Heloise and Abelard lived out

**ABELARD AND HELOISE.** This image from a thirteenth-century manuscript shows Abelard in a scholar's gown and cap and Heloise wearing a nun's habit; their gestures indicate that they are engaged in a lively debate. The story of their fervent attraction and doomed marriage was already famous during their lifetimes, and by the time this manuscript was copied, theirs had become the ultimate example of star-crossed love.

the remainder of their lives in isolation from one another, and most of what we know about their relationship comes from letters they exchanged years later, when Heloise was the leader of a new religious community and Abelard was laying the intellectual foundations of the first university.

The developments of the twelfth and thirteenth centuries altered Europe in profound and lasting ways, affecting individuals, communities, and entire regions. This period witnessed the emergence of large-scale, territorial monarchies and the papacy as dominant forces. Cathedral schools and universities turned out larger and larger cohorts of the professional men needed to run the bureaucracies that supported secular and religious authority. New opportunities for social advancement and new spiritual practices transformed daily life, many of them the direct and indirect consequences of the Crusades. Also as a result of the Crusades and medieval Europe's new engagement with the Islamic world, both ancient texts and novel ideas generated the intellectual revolution in which Abelard and Heloise

participated. Artistic and technological influences were galvanizing forces, too, financed by prelates and kings, princely courts, and wealthy towns engaged in an integrated and far-reaching economy. Moreover, new literary forms took shape as the spoken vernaculars of Europe came to challenge Latin, becoming languages of learning, devotion, and entertainment. By the middle of the thirteenth century, the political institutions and cultural identities that still define Europe today had been formed.

# THE MAKING OF MEDIEVAL MONARCHIES

As we learned in Chapter 8, independent medieval towns and powerful lords often refused to acknowledge royal authority, and kings could no longer rely on traditional, close-knit kin groups or the broad imperial powers wielded by a ruler such as Charlemagne. How, then, did some European rulers build the foundations of states that continue to exist today? Crucially, the *idea* of a national state—a state that consolidates its people's sense of a shared identity and destiny—was an idea forged in the twelfth and thirteenth centuries. It would endure to become the basis that still supports the political system of our world.

Not all attempts at state formation were equally robust. The France that emerged in the twelfth century would almost collapse 200 years later (see Chapter 10). Other European states would not be consolidated until the nineteenth century (Germany, for example) and, even then, *political* unification could not hide the continued cultural and linguistic diversity (as evident in Italy, Belgium, and Switzerland to this day). Yet it became so vital for modern European states to trace their origins to the medieval past that those states without a medieval pedigree would eventually be obliged to invent one.

## England: From Conquest to Consolidation

The imperial conquest of England in 1066 allowed the first Norman king, William, to experiment with a new type of kingship. In theory, he commanded the allegiance of every person dwelling in his kingdom. In practice, he needed to impose his will on his new subjects, often in the form of violence. His will was also expressed through the highly effective administrative structures of his Anglo-Saxon predecessors, which his administrators adapted to their own needs.

This process was carried forward by William's sons, especially Henry I (r. 1100–1135), whose approach to kingship was unusual in its focus on effective governance rather than warfare. Henry strengthened the Anglo-Norman system of local administration and instituted a system of traveling judges to administer royal justice. His biggest innovation was the introduction of a method of financial accounting carried out by an office known as the Exchequer, so called because clerks moved counters around on a checkered cloth to calculate receipts and expenditures. Yet Henry's hands-on approach to royal lordship was unpopular. Then, as now, those opposed to "big government" could react violently against it. After Henry's death, those reactions provoked a civil war—until the people of England began to long for a king who would bring back the good old days of centralized rule.

They found him in Henry's grandson, Henry of Anjou (r. 1154–1189), who at the age of twenty-one was already the duke of Normandy and the lord of two other independent French counties, Anjou and Maine. He also controlled the Aquitaine, thanks to his recent marriage to its powerful and brilliant ruler, Eleanor (1122–1204), who had annulled her first marriage to the French king Louis VII in order to marry Henry.

As King Henry II of England, Henry of Anjou restored his grandfather's administration and began, steadily, to extend its reach. He ordered reliable local men, organized into juries (from the Latin *jus*, meaning both "law" and "oath"), to report every major crime that occurred in their districts, and also empowered them to investigate civil cases. These innovations are the origin of the modern Anglo-American legal system. Henry II also made it easier for common people to seek justice in the royal courts. All of these measures brought an unprecedented number of average people into the exercise of government, and thus increased their sense of loyalty to the king.

But these innovations also brought Henry into conflict with the Church, because the extension of royal justice impinged on the ecclesiastical courts: tribunals overseen by bishops that claimed the exclusive right to try and sentence clergy accused of committing crimes—even capital crimes such as murder. Henry, in contrast, declared that clerics convicted of serious crimes in Church courts should lose their clerical status and be handed over to the royal court for sentencing. The principle underlying this aimed to promote a sense of shared identity and accountability: clerics should be English subjects before they were servants of the Roman Church.

Opposition to this policy came from an unexpected quarter: Thomas Becket, a longtime friend and supporter of Henry's who was now the archbishop of Canterbury. Thomas was a self-made man, a son of immigrants who had benefited from the social mobility of town life in London, and who was able to obtain an education and rise through the ranks of the Church. He saw the advantages to maintaining the independence of ecclesiastical procedures, and feared that Henry's goal was to undermine the power of the clergy.

Henry responded by exiling Thomas from England for several years. And when Thomas returned in 1170, he was assassinated in his own cathedral by four of Henry's knights, who claimed to be acting on the king's orders. Thomas was quickly proclaimed a martyr and a saint, and his tomb at Canterbury became one of the most important pilgrimage sites in Europe. Henry, for his part, was compelled to visit the tomb as a barefoot penitent and ask the saint's forgiveness for his sins.

In the long run, Henry II did not win the right to sentence clerics in royal courts, but he did retain the right to

**THE MURDER OF THOMAS BECKET.** In this illumination from a thirteenth-century prayer book, one of the knights has struck the archbishop so violently that he has broken his sword. ■ *How might a contemporary viewer have interpreted this symbolism?*

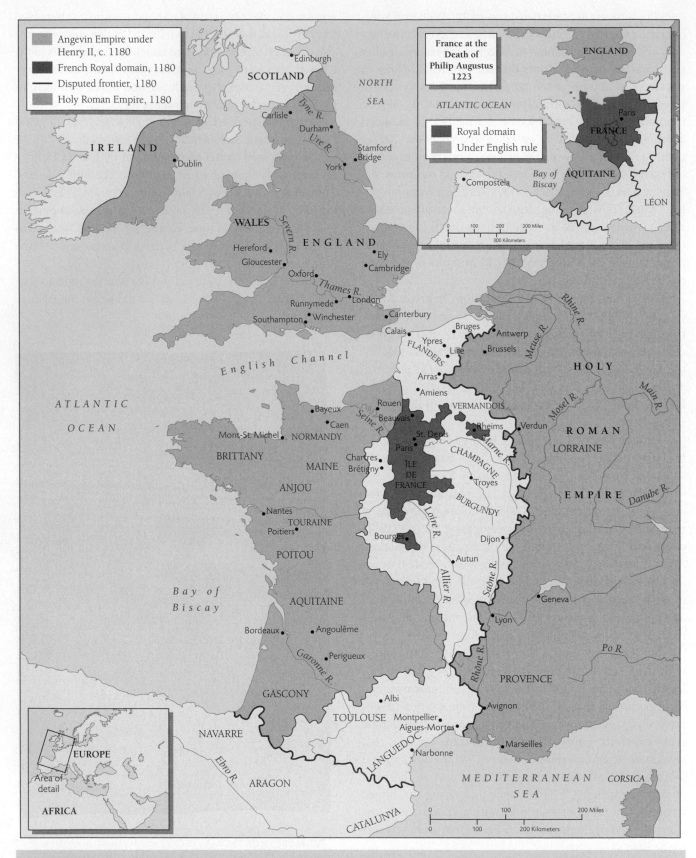

**Legend (main map):**
- Angevin Empire under Henry II, c. 1180
- French Royal domain, 1180
- Disputed frontier, 1180
- Holy Roman Empire, 1180

**Inset map:**

France at the Death of Philip Augustus 1223

- Royal domain
- Under English rule

ENGLAND

ATLANTIC OCEAN

Paris

FRANCE

AQUITAINE

Bay of Biscay

Compostela

LÉON

0    100    200    300 Miles

0            300 Kilometers

**Main map labels:**

SCOTLAND · Edinburgh · Carlisle · Durham · Tyne R. · Ure R. · Stamford Bridge · York

NORTH SEA

IRELAND · Dublin

WALES · Hereford · Gloucester · ENGLAND · Oxford · Ely · Cambridge · Thames R. · London · Runnymede · Winchester · Southampton · Canterbury · Severn R.

ATLANTIC OCEAN

English Channel

Calais · Ypres · Bruges · Antwerp · FLANDERS · Lille · Brussels · Arras · Amiens · Meuse R. · Rhine R.

HOLY ROMAN EMPIRE · LORRAINE

Bayeux · Caen · Rouen · Beauvais · VERMANDOIS · Rheims · Verdun · Mosel R. · Main R.

Mont-St. Michel · NORMANDY · Seine R. · St. Denis · Paris · ÎLE DE FRANCE · Marne R. · CHAMPAGNE

BRITTANY · MAINE · Chartres · Brétigny · Troyes · BURGUNDY · Danube R.

ANJOU · Nantes · TOURAINE · Poitiers · Bourges · Loire R. · Autun · Dijon · Saône R.

POITOU · Allier R.

Bay of Biscay

AQUITAINE · Bordeaux · Angoulême · Perigueux · Garonne R.

Geneva · Lyon · Rhône R. · Po R. · PROVENCE

GASCONY · Albi · Avignon · Marseilles

NAVARRE · TOULOUSE · Montpellier · Aigues-Mortes · LANGUEDOC · Narbonne

ARAGON · Ebro R. · CATALUNYA

MEDITERRANEAN SEA · CORSICA

0    100    200 Miles

0    100    200 Kilometers

**Locator inset:**
EUROPE · Area of detail · AFRICA

**HENRY II'S EMPIRE AND THE KINGDOM OF FRANCE, 1180–1223.** ▪ *What areas did Henry II's empire control in 1180?* ▪ *What advantages would the king of France have when challenging English control over Continental territories—even though his own power was confined to the "island" (Île) of France around Paris?*

nominate clerics to high office and thereby exercise a large measure of control over those courts' personnel. The most concrete proof of Henry II's success is that his government continued to work efficiently even after his death—to the extent that his crusading son Richard "the Lionheart" (r. 1189–1199) could rule his father's empire for ten years, while spending only about six months in England during that time.

## The Meaning of Magna Carta

After Richard was killed while besieging a castle, he was succeeded by his brother John (r. 1199–1216), an efficient administrator. But by 1204, military and legal losses had forced John to cede nearly all of his father's Continental possessions to the powerful young king of France, Philip II; only the Aquitaine—the inheritance of his mother, Eleanor—remained. This was politically disastrous for John. Not only did it deplete his resources, it also angered the most powerful lords of England, nearly all of whom were of Norman descent and who thus lost their ancestral lands when John lost Normandy. John's response was an attempt to recover the lost territories by raising taxes to equip an army, which angered the nobility further. In 1215, they forced John to set his seal to Magna Carta, a "great charter" that defined the barons' rights while limiting those of the king.

Magna Carta established some important principles that would continue to shape the laws of England and, eventually, its colonies. It stipulated that the king could levy no taxes without the consent of the kingdom at large, that no free man could be punished until he had been judged guilty by a jury of his peers in accordance with the law, that no one could be arrested and imprisoned without a warrant, and that no unqualified or ignorant person should hold public office. The charter also established a representative body of barons: Parliament (a word derived from the French "talking together"). Above all, Magna Carta expressed the extraordinary idea that a king is bound by the law.

We have frequently noted the achievements of various powerful lawgivers whose contributions have been essential to Western civilizations, starting with Hammurabi (Chapter 1). But for the most part, those lawgivers held themselves to be above the law. Although medieval monarchs—in England and elsewhere—attempted to behave as though this were true for them as well, ultimately they were forced to concede the rule of law itself. Magna Carta thus normalized the idea that strong, representative government was a good thing. In time, Parliament became a legislative body that

could help govern the kingdom. And since Magna Carta had demanded that no taxation be imposed without the common consent of the realm, kings had to convene Parliament to explain why such taxation was necessary. Meetings of Parliament were also used to hear judicial cases, review local administration and complaints of injustice, and promulgate new laws. Gradually, England was changing from a conquered territory within a larger Norman empire into a constitutional monarchy grounded in government and ruled by law.

## The Emergence of France

Compared with the Anglo-Saxon and Anglo-Norman kings of England, the king of the Franks presided over a minuscule territory over which he exercised little control: the immediate hinterland of Paris. Here, most of Charlemagne's institutions of governance had collapsed and been further weakened by Viking raids or by ongoing pressure from the Viking state of Normandy. When Henry II's empire was at its height, the kingdom of Louis VII (r. 1137–1180)—who had lost both his wife, Eleanor, and her lands to that same Henry—was tiny and insignificant.

But in many ways the Capetian dynasty, which had been founded during the Viking raids (Chapter 8), was fortunate. Against all biological odds, it managed to produce an unbroken line of able male heirs for over 300 years (from 987 to 1328)—men who were also long lived. (On average, each Capetian king ruled for 30 years, which contributed greatly to political stability.) And this kingdom, though small, was a rich center of agriculture and trade, which provided a steadily increasing source of income. The prestige of the Capetians was also enhanced by their patronage of the new University of Paris founded by Abelard, which made the royal city the intellectual capital of Europe (see below). Beyond all this, the Capetians proved to be shrewd politicians, carefully husbanding their strengths while more powerful enemies overreached themselves.

The epitome of these strengths was Philip II (r. 1180–1223), a man who styled himself "Augustus" and the first to use the title "king of France": king of a sovereign state, rather than "king of the Franks," a tribe of people. Philip came to the throne at the age of eighteen, having witnessed the struggles of his father, Louis VII. He understood that he could not win a direct confrontation with either Henry or his son Richard; however, John—known to his detractors as "Soft Sword" and "Lack Land"—was another matter. Philip declared that John owed him homage and allegiance in return for Normandy and its adjacent territories, and then took advantage of his position as John's overlord to undermine John's control over these lands. When John objected, Philip declared all John's lands to be forfeit to the French crown and backed this declaration with armies that won decisive victories in 1204 and 1214.

With Normandy and other formerly English territories added to his domain, Philip had the resources to build an effective system of local administration. He wisely chose to maintain the bureaucratic structures established by generations of Anglo-Norman rulers, but he appointed royal overseers, known as bailiffs, who had full judicial, administrative, and military authority. Philip drew these men from among the needy knights and lesser nobility of his own domain and rotated them frequently from region to region, which ensured their loyalty to him and prevented them from developing personal ties to the regions they governed. This administrative strategy recognized regional diversity while promoting centralized royal control, and it continued to characterize French royal government down to the time of the French Revolution (see Chapter 18). Philip's son, Louis VIII (r. 1223–1226), also extended this strategy to newly conquered territories in the southeast.

## German Kingship and the Holy Roman Empire

We have seen (in Chapter 8) that the struggles between the German emperor Henry IV and the papacy ultimately led to the weakening of imperial authority. But in the middle of the twelfth century, a newly elected emperor made an ambitious attempt to restore the power of the German monarchy and to free it from papal control. This emperor was Frederick, later known as Barbarossa ("Red Beard"; r. 1152–1190). Frederick coined the term "Holy Roman Empire" to describe his realm—thereby asserting that its holiness derived from the blessing of God and did not depend on the intervention of the pope, with whom he was constantly at odds.

Frederick forged a close alliance with other German princes by supporting their efforts to control their own territories. In exchange, he exacted their support for his efforts to reassert imperial control over the wealthy cities of northern Italy. This strategy worked, but it sparked a series of destructive wars. Led by Milan and sanctioned by the pope, the cities of northern Italy formed an alliance, the Lombard League, which put up a staunch resistance to Frederick and finally forced him to guarantee their independence in return for large cash payments. Meanwhile, Frederick attempted to bypass the power of the papacy by supporting a series of papal pretenders, or "antipopes." This move was successfully countered by the reigning pope, Alexander III

(r. 1159–1181), who drove a shrewd bargain with Frederick: if Frederick would concede the sovereignty of the pope's rule within Rome and its adjacent territories—lands that came to be known as the Papal States—then Alexander would concede the emperor's sovereignty within his domains and even his overlordship of the Church within those domains. Frederick eventually agreed, thereby gaining the pope's support for his rule in northern Italy.

When Frederick left for the Holy Land in 1189—joining Richard the Lionheart of England and Philip Augustus of France on a (failed) crusade to reconquer Jerusalem—he left his realm in a powerful position. Although he died on that venture, his careful planning bore fruit in the reign of his son, Henry VI, who succeeded to his father's throne without opposition and enjoyed a huge income from the north Italian towns. Henry ultimately became the king of Sicily, too, which strengthened the empire's position even further. But when Henry died in 1197, he left only a three-year-old son, the future Frederick II, as his heir apparent. Two decades of civil war followed.

By the time Frederick II came of age, the German princes had become so entirely autonomous that all he could do was recognize their privileges in exchange for their loyalty. In Italy, the cities of the Lombard League had ceased to pay their taxes, and the powerful administrative structure of Sicily had fallen into chaos. Frederick tackled all these problems and eventually restored control over the disparate territories of his empire. But he made the mistake of asserting a right to rule the northern Italian cities directly, bypassing their own independent governments. The result was another Lombard League and another lengthy war, which continued until Frederick's death in 1250. The papacy took every advantage of this situation, even excommunicating Frederick and, after his death, denying the rights of his heirs. When Frederick's last legitimate son died in 1254, the prospect of effective imperial rule died with him. For the next 500 years, until the founding of the modern German and Italian states, political power in the lands of the Holy Roman Empire would be divided among several hundred territorial princes and independent cities.

## The States of Central and Eastern Europe

As all of these examples show, the making of medieval monarchies was a gradual, nonlinear process. The states that formed, shifted, and reformed were fragile—much more fragile than modern nationalist mythologies will admit.

## THE HOLY ROMAN EMPIRE AND CENTRAL AND EASTERN EUROPE, c. 1200.

This map approximates the borders of the region's major territories. ▪ *Identify the kingdoms and principalities discussed in this chapter.* ▪ *If you were the ruler of one of them, what opportunities do you see for the expansion of your power? What limitations?* ▪ *Why would the prospect of a single heir to the Holy Roman Empire and to the kingdom of the Two Sicilies be a threat to the papacy?*

Moreover, many powerful and effective states were not kingdoms at all, but cities and principalities. The new territorial powers that were emerging in central and eastern Europe offer further alternative examples of state formation in this era.

Like many of the other principalities that made up the (highly disunified) Holy Roman Empire, Bohemia was a nonhereditary monarchy whose rulers were elected by powerful families. That changed at the end of the twelfth century, however, when Ottokar I (r. 1192–1230) managed to secure papal and imperial support for the establishment of a dynasty. Bohemia also extended its rule into the province of Moravia, which it governed as a frontier principality. During the thirteenth century, when the Holy Roman Emperor's attention was fixed on Italy and the alliances among German territories were weak, Bohemia emerged as one of the strongest states in central Europe.

The kings of Hungary, meanwhile, with their close ties to the Roman Church and papacy, cultivated a strong and relatively centralized royal authority. They also expanded Hungarian influence into the regions of Transylvania and Croatia, whose natural resources included rich silver mines. As a result, the wealth of King Béla III (r. 1172–1196) far exceeded that of his contemporaries elsewhere in Europe. He also adopted many of the techniques favored by these contemporaries, including the use of written records to aid in royal governance.

Poland, which had achieved a remarkable territorial unity at an early date (Chapter 8), was carved into several smaller dukedoms after 1138, when King Boleslaw III (r. 1107–1138) divided his extensive lands among his sons. This led to competition among members of the same dynasty, and spurred Polish dukes to seek out new opportunities for advancing their interests. Duke Conrad of Masovia (r. 1229–1232), for example, forged an alliance with a crusading order, the Teutonic Knights, who were attempting to conquer and colonize the pagan peoples of the Baltic (see below). Conrad's own northern frontier territories were subject to raids by the pagan Prussians, and he saw this as an expedient measure. Nevertheless, the knights were not content merely to fight the pagans and often clashed with Polish troops as well.

Other Polish rulers successfully pursued more inclusive methods of strengthening their principalities. In the wake of the First Crusade, which had led to pogroms against Jewish communities in the Rhineland, violent attacks against Jews were becoming increasingly common in northwestern Europe, while their legal rights were also being curtailed. But Polish dukes were eager to encourage Jewish settlements, knowing that their cities would benefit from the expertise of Jewish merchants and craftsmen, and from being woven into the banking networks that were crucial to the medieval economy. By the thirteenth century, thousands of Jews—entire families and communities—were making their way to Poland to take advantage of these favorable conditions.

A glimpse of these can be seen in the Statute of Kalisz (*KAH-leesh*), issued by Duke Boleslaw the Pious in 1264. Often regarded as a foundational document in the history of human rights, it granted the Jews of Greater Poland extensive legal privileges, including freedom of movement and worship; equal rights under the law; and the right to prosecute Christians who insulted, harmed, or stole from them. As a result of these extraordinary initiatives, Poland became a magnet for Jews for the remainder of the Middle Ages, taking in still more refugees from the wave of expulsions suffered by the Jews of England, France, and Spain (see Chapters 10 and 12).

## Rus' and the Novgorod Republic

The trading settlements established by the Viking Rus' in the eleventh century had been centered on the city of Kiev and had benefited from a vibrant system of commercial networks, kinship ties with many of Europe's royal families, and a close spiritual and political alliance with the eastern Roman Empire. But as subsequent crusading movements weakened Byzantium and disrupted trade with the Islamic world (see below), the powerful position of Kiev was also undermined. The center of gravity began to move north, to the city of Novgorod, which was already economically powerful and ideally placed to take advantage of the trade with the peoples of the Baltic region and Scandinavia via the Volga and Dnieper Rivers. Novgorod functioned as a powerful city-state and the center of an entity often called the Novgorod Republic, because the power of Novgorod's prince and its aristocratic families and prominent churchmen was countered by urban elites and a network of occasional public assemblies that gave voice to merchants and craftsmen.

Novgorod was also affected by the changing fortunes of Byzantium. In 1204, when Constantinople was besieged and captured by crusaders loyal to Rome, many German and Scandinavian warlords began to make the Orthodox Christians of Rus' another target of crusading fervor. In a series of wars, the Swedes successfully invaded Novgorod's northern frontier, and there were constant skirmishes with the Danes and Germans as well. In 1240, according to later Russian sources, a Swedish army attempted to gain control of the Neva River to establish control over a major trade route. But the invasion was routed by a force led by a young prince of Novgorod, Alexander (b. 1221–1263), who thereafter took the surname Nevsky (victor of the Neva). Alexander is also credited with the defeat of the Teutonic knights at Lake Peipus in the early spring of 1242, when the lake was still frozen; hence its iconic name, the Battle on the Ice. Although the importance of this battle, like that of the Neva, is questionable, the event and its hero have become enshrined in Russian cultural memory. This is thanks in large part to the great nationalist epic *Alexander Nevsky* (1938) by the Soviet filmmaker Sergei Eisenstein, in which the Teutonic Knights represent the more modern menace of Nazi Germany (see Chapter 26).

## The "Reconquest" of Spain

The small Christian kingdoms of the Iberian Peninsula were even more distinct from each other than the principalities of Germany and Eastern Europe. And yet, a unified kingdom of Spain would emerge as the most powerful monarchy in Europe and the wider Atlantic world by the end of the Middle Ages (a process we will continue to trace in later chapters). The key to this extraordinary development lay in the successful alliances forged among the peninsula's Christian rulers and their eventual defeat of neighboring wealthy and well-governed Muslim kingdoms. This

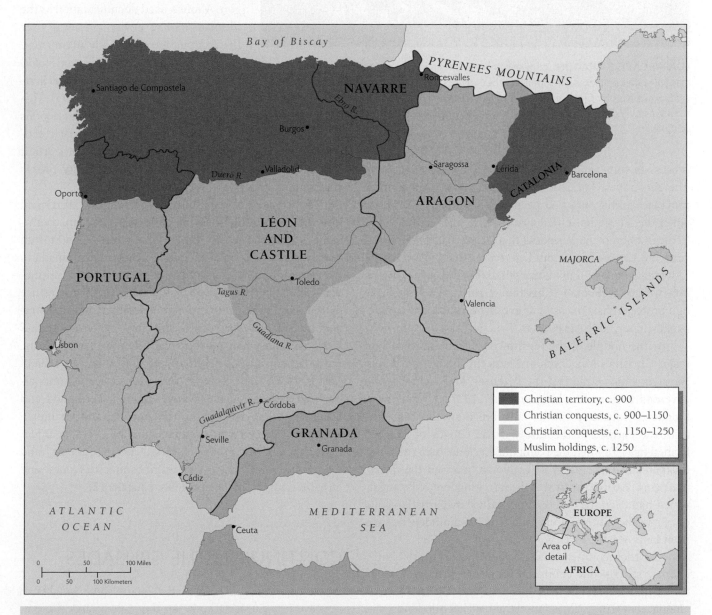

**THE "RECONQUEST" OF SPAIN, 900–1250.** ▪ *Where were the frontiers of the Christian kingdoms in 900? 1150? 1250?* ▪ *What geographical factors might have helped to sustain these small kingdoms?* ▪ *Why might Castile eventually have become the largest of the Christian kingdoms?* ▪ *How could Aragon and Catalonia have maintained important positions as wealthy and significant powers?*

**LOARRE CASTLE, ARAGON.** No single photograph can capture the size or setting of this massive castle complex in the foothills of the Pyrenees. Initially fortified in the eleventh century as a base for Christian expansion into Muslim territory, it was further enlarged in the twelfth century. The encircling wall and towers were added in the thirteenth and fourteenth centuries.

process is somewhat misleadingly termed the *reconquista* (the "reconquest") of Christian lands. In reality, the Roman province of Hispania had been only nominally Christian when the Visigoths settled there in the fifth century (see Chapter 6), and the Visigoths themselves had barely converted to Latin Christianity before the Muslims arrived in 711 (see Chapter 7). But conceptualizing this struggle as a holy war to "reconquer" Christian territory allowed Christian propagandists to cast it as another crusade and so earn papal support for their efforts.

By the middle of the twelfth century, there were four major Christian kingdoms in Iberia. In the far north was Navarre, which straddled the Pyrenees, and León-Castile, governed as a united kingdom after 1037. Beyond these kingdoms' southern frontier lay a broad swath of Muslim territory. Farther to the east was the Crown of Aragon, formed in 1137 when the count of Barcelona, who ruled the independent principality of Catalonia, married the queen of Aragon. Farthest west was the new kingdom of Portugal, which had been the first territory gained by Christian conquests in the ninth century, and which won independence from León-Castile in 1139.

Like their counterparts elsewhere in Europe, the kings of Spain struggled to control the power of great lords. Centuries of warfare between Muslims and Christians and among competing Christian clans had left the landscape sown with enormous castles. Even those nominally controlled by kings were in fact the property and power bases of castellans (castle-keepers). A ruler seeking to establish control thus had to use a combination of force and cunning to bring these rival powers to heel. Indeed, the kings of this region came to deploy a combination of tactics that we have already seen at work in England: a mixture of violent conquest and the development of effective administrative structures that made royal power a fact of everyday life.

This strategy is exemplified by King Alfonso II of Aragon (r. 1162–1196), who was also the count of Barcelona and the first to rule the united Crown of Aragon. Alfonso used documentation as the ultimate tool of power, presiding over the compilation of a richly illuminated "big book of fiefs" (*Liber feudorum maior*) between 1192 and 1194 (see **Interpreting Visual Evidence** on page 295). This book recounted property transactions and family lineages dating back centuries, citing documents in the royal archives. Alfonso thereby grounded his authority on his command of history and written records.

Throughout the remainder of the twelfth century and into the thirteenth, Christian influence in Spain continued to spread southward until all that remained of Muslim dominion was the small kingdom centered on Granada in the extreme south. Castile became by far the largest kingdom, although it was rivaled in wealth and consequence by the more urbanized and commercially connected Aragon. Indeed, wars between Castile and Aragon kept either kingdom from achieving supremacy for the next 200 years, until the marriage of Ferdinand of Aragon and Isabella of Castile joined the two lands in a unified Spanish monarchy that also included Navarre. In 1492, Ferdinand and Isabella's united army captured Granada, and an Italian adventurer named Christopher Columbus set sail under their flag. The first event completed the "reconquest," and the second began Spain's successful conquest of a new and hitherto undreamed-of world (see Chapter 12).

## CONTINUING THE CRUSADES

When Pope Urban II urged the quarrelsome knights of northwestern Europe to take up the cross against the enemies of Christ in 1095, he was responding to the Byzantine emperor's request for reinforcements in his war with the Seljuk Turks, with the aim of recapturing imperial

# Interpreting Visual Evidence

## Picturing Legal Transactions

Between the years 1192 and 1194, King Alfonso II of Aragon (r. 1162–1196) and his court scribes compiled a remarkable book. The codex known today as the "big book of fiefs" (*Liber feudorum maior*) may have been made to assist Alfonso and his descendants in legitimizing their authority over the many areas they controlled, but it was also a way of expressing that authority: its very existence represented a new claim to royal power. In its original form, it consisted of 888 parchment folios (1,776 pages) on which 903 separate documents were copied.

This "big book" represents a new trend in Europe. In most places, claims to property were made on the basis of custom and memory, not documentation. When property changed hands, the chief witnesses were people, and when questions arose, it was these people (or their heirs) whose testimony proved ownership. In Catalonia, the habit of documenting things had a long history, and it was not unusual for individual families to keep archives of documents. At the same time, however, documentation was never sufficient on its own: verbal exchanges of agreement and the public performance of transactions constituted legally binding ceremonies meaningful to the entire community, and the validity of these actions was not dependent on the making of a written record.

With all this in mind, it is striking that seventy-nine of the documents copied into the book are accompanied by images that convey important messages about documentation and its limitations.

On the book's opening frontispiece (image A), King Alfonso consults with his chief archivist, Ramón de Caldes. Ramón discusses one of the charters taken from a large pile at his elbow, while a scribe makes copies behind him—perhaps to aid in the compilation of the "big book." The king is backed by men who look on approvingly.

One of the charters copied into the "big book" is accompanied by another image (image B). It records that the Viscount of Nîmes betrothed his daughter, Ermengarde of Carcassone, to the Count of Roussillon. Ermengarde, her flowing hair uncovered as a sign of her maidenhood, stands between her bearded father and her seated mother, Cecilia of Provence.

## Questions for Analysis

1. Why would a book designed to document property transactions contain images, too? What functions could they have served?

2. Why would the artist of the "big book" have depicted the king consulting his archivist in the very first image? How does he depict the relationship between them? Why does he include a group of men as witnesses to their discussion?

3. Women figure prominently in many of the book's images, including image B. On what basis could you argue that their active presence is crucial to the transactions being described?

A. King Alfonso and Ramón de Caldes.

B. Betrothal of Ermengarde of Carcassone to the Count of Roussillon.

territories in Anatolia. But the pope's own conception of the crusaders' mission was broader and extended beyond the frontiers of Byzantium to the great cities of Antioch and Jerusalem, which had been in the hands of Muslims for centuries. And, as we saw in Chapter 8, many crusaders acted on a still broader interpretation of their mission by attacking "enemies of Christ": the Jewish communities of Europe.

From the first, then, both the reason for crusading and the target of Christian aggression were ideologically malleable. Even though the papacy never officially sanctioned violence against Jews, in the centuries following the First Crusade individual popes authorized the use of force against many different kinds of people who could be construed as "enemies of Christ" because they stood in opposition to the Roman Church. Although historians, for convenience, often speak of the Crusades as divided into seven or more

distinct phases (the Second Crusade, the Third Crusade, etc.), the people of the time—both aggressors and victims—experienced crusading as a continuous, snowballing movement. It was (and is still) a powerful and deadly force.

## Crusader States and Crusading Orders

The military successes of the First Crusade were due not only to the might of the crusaders but also to the diversity of (and divisions among) the many peoples who inhabited the coastline of the eastern Mediterranean. This is an area we have been studying since Chapter 1, formed by successive waves of colonization over the course of many millennia. The principalities known as the Crusader States should therefore be understood as laying a thin veneer of European influence on top of a deep, complex culture that withstood any superficial changes.

Those Europeans who stayed and flourished here were those who were able to adapt. Most probably retained some aspects of their former identities—as Normans or Franks, as loyal to the Roman Church—but they and their descendants became intertwined with the local populations, intermarrying and adopting their fashions, food, and outlook. In time, they had more in common with their immediate neighbors—Syrian and Armenian Christians, adherents of Greek Orthodoxy, Shi'ite and Sunni Muslims—than with their distant families "back home." Second- and third-generation settlers might never visit western Christendom in the course of their lives.

Because of all these factors, the four principal Crusader States were very different from the territorial monarchies that were being consolidated in parts of Europe at this time. They were more like the loosely configured and combative lordships of the tenth and eleventh centuries than like burgeoning bureaucratic realms. As such, they were mostly short lived. The largest, the inland county of Edessa, was founded in 1098. It stretched as far east as the Tigris River and had to be heavily fortified against constant internal uprisings and external threats. Its European Christian population was always a tiny minority, and by 1150 it had been mostly subsumed into the Seljuk Empire, with some portions reverting to Byzantium.

Edessa's position was made even more precarious because its Frankish rulers had friendlier relations with their Armenian subjects (with whom they largely intermarried) than with the crusader principality of Antioch to the west, which comprised parts of what are now Syria and Turkey. Although Antioch was named a patriarchate of the Roman Church, it also had a tiny European Christian population. After the fall of Edessa, it was largely dependent on Constantinople, and later Armenia, for protection from the Seljuk Turks. Antioch

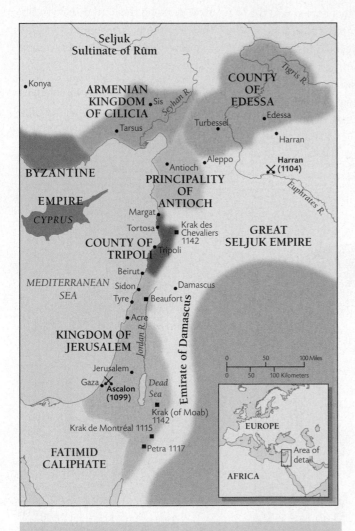

**THE CRUSADER STATES.** This map shows the fragile colonies known as the Crusader States at their greatest extent, around 1100. ■ *What geographical, political, and military factors would make these states vulnerable?*

**KRAK DES CHEVALIERS.** The necessity of securing hard-won territory in the Holy Land led to the construction of enormous castles such as this one, built by the Knights Hospitaller in the early twelfth century when crusading movements were also being launched in Europe itself. Similar castles were built to subjugate peoples deemed rebellious or heretical.

ceased to exist in 1268, when its lands became part of the vast new empire of the Mongols (see Chapter 10).

The third major state, the county of Tripoli, was founded in 1109 and it linked the northern states of Edessa and Antioch with the kingdom of Jerusalem. Tripoli's strategic commercial position exposed it to constant raids and threats of invasion, which led its rulers to entrust most of the frontier to one of the military orders dedicated to perpetual pursuit of the crusading effort: the Knights Hospitaller. Originally charged with the care of pilgrims in the Hospital of St. John at Jerusalem, founded in 1023, members of this religious order became militarized after 1099 and came to control the islands of Rhodes and Malta, as well as the many strategic fortifications in the eastern Mediterranean. Their fortress, the massive Krak des Chevaliers ("Knights' Castle," in a mixture of Arabic and French), survives as a monument to their might. In fact, the Hospitallers long outlived the Crusader States, maintaining a sovereign presence in the region into the early nineteenth century; the order is now headquartered in Rome.

## The Kingdom of Jerusalem and the Conquest of Saladin

The kingdom of Jerusalem, the fourth and most symbolically important of the Crusader States, was really a network of cities and fortresses that constantly changed hands, as much the target of rival crusaders as of Muslim raiders. Its cosmopolitan population was a testament to the number of peoples who claimed the Holy Land for their own, with major concentrations of Muslims (both Sunni and Shi'a) and Orthodox Christians (Greek and Syrian), alongside smaller communities (Jews, Samaritans)—all of whom dwarfed the European Christian population of the region. As a result, those who claimed kingship in Jerusalem were greatly dependent on support from other Crusader States as well as from various European princes. Yet the cachet of Jerusalem was such that any contingent of reinforcements sent by an ambitious ally could be attempting to seize power there. Defense of the kingdom therefore came to rest heavily on another of the new crusading orders, the Knights Templar. Founded during the reign of King Baldwin II of Jerusalem (r. 1118–1131), the Templars were based in a wing of the captured al-Aqsa Mosque, which was now the royal palace and thought to be part of King Solomon's original Temple complex (Chapter 2)—hence the order's name.

Although the kingdom of Jerusalem persisted in theory until 1291, it ceased to have any purchase on Jerusalem itself after 1187. In this year, a remarkable Kurdish chieftain, Salāh ad-Dīn (c. 1138–1193), who had become the Sunni sultan of both Egypt and Syria, rallied Muslim opposition to the occupying crusader forces and succeeded in recapturing the Holy City. Saladin (as he was called by Europeans) became the target of a renewed crusading effort (the Third Crusade, 1189–1192), which, as we noted above, spurred three kings to take the cross: England's Richard the Lionheart, France's Philip Augustus, and the Holy Roman Empire's Frederick Barbarossa. But Frederick was killed, Philip left early, and Richard was captured on the way home.

Meanwhile, the victorious Saladin became celebrated not only by Muslims but also among crusaders, who considered him a paragon of chivalry. Richard even considered arranging a marriage between his sister, Joan of Sicily, and Saladin's brother, thereby establishing allied rule in Jerusalem. This never happened though, and Jerusalem remained in Muslim hands. The city of Acre (Akko, in northern Israel) then became the new capital of the Christian kingdom, until its fall in 1291 marked the end of any viable European presence in the region—that is, until the short-lived conquests of Napoleon at the end of the eighteenth century (see Chapter 18).

## The Extension of Crusading Ideas into European Colonial Projects

Once unleashed, the crusading ethos could not be contained by efforts to liberate the Holy Land. The promise that those who killed the "enemies of Christ" with papal approval would be absolved of their sins and win eternal salvation, while potentially winning lands and riches in the process, was soon applied to a host of other initiatives—especially those that could open new lands for settlement and bring more peoples into the orbit of the Roman Church.

Beginning in the 1160s, accordingly, the rulers of Denmark and the German duchy of Saxony began to colonize the Baltic coast and the lands between the Elbe and Oder Rivers. This effort was represented as a missionary movement, but it was also an attempt to control trading and raiding activities in that region. And it was not carried forward peacefully; those who spearheaded it (literally) were members of the military crusading order of the Teutonic Knights. In 1202, they managed to carve out a new bishopric around Riga (present-day Latvia), where they set about the violent conversion of the indigenous inhabitants. We have already noted the Knights' subsequent clashes with the peoples of Poland and Rus'.

Meanwhile, the English were launching crusades against the "infidel" Irish and Welsh, who were actually Christian, justifying this action on the grounds that the Celts were barbarians who would benefit from the civilizing influence of their superior overlords. It had been a short step from the calling of crusades against foreigners to those aimed at fellow Europeans and Christians.

## The Crusade against Constantinople and the Revenge of Venice

The First Crusade (1095–1099) had begun as an attempt to aid Constantinople. The Fourth Crusade (1202–1204) ended in its destruction. The object of this expedition, which had been called by Pope Innocent III at the time of his election in 1198, was Egypt, where Saladin's successors continued to rally Muslim opposition to European colonial efforts. This meant launching an attack by sea, because the remaining crusader outposts of the Holy Land had become too weak and scattered to enable the movement of armies by land. The natural embarkation point was Venice.

A major player in maritime trade since the ninth century, Venice had already benefited enormously from the Crusades. Venice furnished the ships and supplies that

transported and sustained the waves of aspiring conquerors while reaping the benefits of closer ties with Byzantium, with which this Italian city-state shared many interests. But relations with Constantinople worsened throughout the twelfth century, as the Crusades increasingly damaged Byzantine trade and threatened its security. In 1182, popular anticrusading sentiment had even led enraged citizens of Constantinople to massacre enclaves of Italian merchants and seamen; those who were not killed were banished, the Venetians among them.

The Venetians therefore had a reason to resent the Byzantines. And they were now overrun by an army of eager and impoverished crusaders who could not pay for the passage to Cairo; it would cost the Venetians enormously in time, money, and men to ship them there. So in the end, the crusaders paid the Venetians with the services they could render. Rather than sailing for Egypt, the crusading expedition was diverted to Zara on the Dalmatian coast of the Adriatic, a former Venetian port that had rebelled and sought the protection of the king of Hungary (it is now Zadar in Croatia). Despite the fact that Hungary was loyal to Rome, the city was attacked and taken.

From Zara, the crusaders moved on to Constantinople. After a terrible siege, the city was savagely overrun and sacked in 1204, its people killed or left homeless, its churches and public buildings severely damaged, and its books and artworks consigned to flames or seized as loot. (For example, the stolen porphyry statue of the Roman tetrarchs, shown on page 193, is still in Venice.) In the aftermath, the Venetians were able to colonize the city itself, controlling the shipping in and around Constantinople as well as the island of Crete and many cities on the Greek mainland. Only in 1261 was Byzantine rule reestablished in the capital. But by that time, the empire had shrunk to a fraction of its former size. Meanwhile, crusading efforts continued within western Christendom.

## Innocent III's Crusade for a Unified Christendom

Although Pope Innocent III expressed alarm at the turn taken by the crusade he had called, he accepted the spoils of war that were offered to him and set his seal of approval on the Latin occupation of Greek territory. He was an ambitious man. Elected to the papal dignity at the age of thirty-seven, probably the youngest holder of the office in history, his goal was to unify all Christendom—and the wider world—under papal

## Medieval Plots and Modern Movies

From westerns to science fiction to action movies to romantic comedies, most of the films that draw big audiences today are based loosely or closely on literary genres that were popularized during the Middle Ages: tales of chivalry and heroism, forbidden love, supernatural events, and magical adventures.

**Watch related author interview on the Student Site**

dominion. Unlike Gregory VII (Chapter 8), Innocent never questioned the right of kings and princes to rule in their own secular spheres. Instead, he saw the pope's role as regulatory and disciplinary, which meant that when rulers sinned, they should be reprimanded or excommunicated by the pope—who could thereby call into question the legitimacy of their rule. Moreover, Innocent was even more insistent than his predecessors on the obligation of every Christian to obey the pope as Jesus Christ's representative on earth.

Innocent sought to achieve this goal in many different ways. He made the papacy financially and politically independent by expanding and consolidating papal territories in central Italy. (Vatican City is now the last surviving remnant of these territories, and it continues to function as an independent state within Rome and Italy.) He loudly proclaimed his power as kingmaker and king breaker by

brokering the selection of the Holy Roman Emperor. He also disciplined both Philip Augustus of France, for marital misconduct, and John of England, who at one point was compelled to grant England itself to the pope as its overlord. Innocent further claimed, with varying degrees of success, a comparable lordship over Aragon, Sicily, and Hungary. He even levied the first income tax on the clergy in order to support the crusade that brought Orthodox Christians to heel.

The crowning achievement of Innocent's pontificate was the ratification of his agenda at a representative assembly of the Roman Church, the Fourth Lateran Council of 1215, so called because it was held in the Roman palace of St. John Lateran. This council defined the central dogmas of Latin Christianity, one of which was the acknowledgment of papal supremacy. Since a dogma is defined as a "truth necessary for salvation," this meant that all Christians had

## The Crusade against Heresy

Innocent's reign achieved the height of papal power, but it also fomented violence and sowed seeds of dissent. Future popes continued to centralize the government of the Church, but they also became involved in protracted political and military struggles that compromised the papacy's credibility. Because the Papal States bordered on the kingdom of Sicily, Innocent's successors quickly came into conflict with Emperor Frederick II, who became an inveterate opponent of papal monarchy. But instead of excommunicating him and calling for his deposition, as Innocent might have done, they called a crusade against him.

Innocent himself had paved the way for this by launching a series of crusades against heretics, now defined as any group or individual who did not fall into line with the papacy's policies—and who were, by association, "enemies of Christ." The most notorious of these campaigns was the Albigensian (*al-bih-JEN-see-an*) Crusade, launched in 1209. Ostensibly, the crusade was directed against a heretical sect called the Cathars; but in reality, it justified the colonization of what is now southern France by land-hungry knights from northern France.

Although the Albigensian Crusade can be said to have ended by 1255, it created lasting tensions within the forcibly enlarged French kingdom that would lead the inhabitants of this devastated region to ally with the English during the Hundred Years' War (see Chapter 10), and continue to make southern France particularly susceptible to violent religious warfare during and after the Reformation (see Chapter 13). Indeed, the language, culture, and political orientation of southern France are still very different from those of Paris and its environs.

In order to understand how all of this happened, we must turn to some larger religious developments within Europe.

## UNITY AND DISSENT IN THE WESTERN CHURCH

The Investiture Conflict (Chapter 8) engaged both clergy and laity in debates over the essential meaning of Jesus Christ's life and teachings. Many regions of Europe supported the papacy's claim to supremacy, but others saw marked resistance to its encroachment on centuries-old practices and social networks. After all, bishops had been members of the aristocracy since the time of Constantine, and it was customary for bishoprics to be controlled by certain families. Meanwhile, priests had been married men

**THE JEWISH BADGE.** The distinctive apparel that marked Jews as different from their Christian neighbors varied from region to region. In some places it was pointed hats, like those worn by the Old Testament Jews in this manuscript illumination from a fourteenth-century French vernacular Bible. This type of hat later became associated with witchcraft or idiocy, as in the dunce's cap or the witch's peaked hat. In other regions, Jews wore a distinctive patch on their clothing, often colored yellow to make it more visible.

to acknowledge the pope's ultimate power; those unwilling to do so (including the Christians of Byzantium) were, by definition, heretics—and as heretics, they could be prosecuted and punished.

In a further effort to achieve unity and uniformity within Christendom, the Fourth Lateran Council took an unprecedented interest in the religious education and habits of every Christian. It responded to the urbanization of Europe by establishing free primary schools (for boys) in all the major cities, requiring bishops to recruit effective preachers, and outlawing all kinds of misbehavior on the part of the clergy. It also sought to increase the distance between Christians and their Muslim and Jewish neighbors by discouraging social relationships, economic exchanges, and intermarriage. Most disturbing, Innocent's council mandated that "infidels" be visibly distinguished from Christians by wearing distinctive clothing, the origins of the infamous "Jewish badge" (see Chapter 26).

since the establishment of the first Christian churches; and the wives of priests were not only their husbands' partners, they were also ministers to the communities in which they lived. When the papacy preached against "fornicating priests" and their "concubines," it delegitimized relationships that had been essential to local communities for generations. No wonder, then, as one contemporary reported, that nothing else was talked about "even in the women's spinning rooms and the artisans' workshops."

On the one hand, the reforms of Pope Gregory VII and his successors gave the common people an important role to play, by urging them to reject certain practices and to retaliate against offenders. Combined with the fervor that had been whipped up by the Crusades, the result was a more widespread interest in spiritual matters and a greater participation in religious life—as well as increased violence. On the other hand, however, the reforming movement severely limited the ways in which the laity were allowed to express their spirituality or to participate meaningfully in the life of the Church.

## The New Monasticism and the Mass

One of the first manifestations of the new popular piety was the growth and diversification of monastic movements. The abbey of Cluny had revived the observance of Benedict's *Rule* during the tenth century and, at the same time, had kept Cluny and its daughter houses independent of local lords. So these monasteries became lordships in their own right, acquiring extensive lands and enormous wealth. Those seeking to reject worldliness, therefore, had to look elsewhere. The result, beginning in the late eleventh century, was the founding of new monastic orders.

The order that became most widespread was founded at the French monastery of Cîteaux in 1098. Cistercian monks followed Benedict's *Rule*, but in the purest and most austere way possible. They founded new monasteries in wildernesses and remote areas, far from worldly temptations. They also shunned all unnecessary decoration and elaborate liturgical rites. Instead, they practiced contemplation and private prayer, and committed themselves to hard manual labor. Under the charismatic leadership of Bernard of Clairvaux

(1090–1153), a spellbinding preacher and one of the most influential personalities of his age, the Cistercian order grew exponentially, from 5 houses in 1115 to 343 by 1153. This astonishing increase meant that many more men and women were becoming professional religious, and that still more pious people were donating funds and lands to support monasteries and thereby participating indirectly in their life of devotion.

Another manifestation of popular piety was a new focus on the sacrament of the Mass, the liturgical reenactment of Christ's last meal with his disciples. This celebration, also known as the Eucharist, had always been an important part of Christian religion and social practice (see Chapter 6), but only in the twelfth century did it become the central act of worship in the western Church. Bernard of Clairvaux was instrumental in making it so, by developing and preaching the doctrine of transubstantiation. According to this doctrine, every Mass is a miraculous event because the priest's blessing transforms the bread and wine on the altar into the body and blood of Christ; hence the term *transubstantiation*, since earthly substances become the substance of Christ's divine body.

Popular reverence for the Eucharist became so great that the Church initiated the practice of elevating the consecrated bread, known as the Host, so that the whole congregation could see it. Not incidentally, this new theology of the Eucharist further enhanced the prestige of the priesthood by seeming to endow it with wonder-working powers.

**THE CISTERCIAN ABBEY OF SULEJÓW (POLAND).** Founded in 1176, this abbey was part of a vast European network of new monastic houses connected to each other and to the original Cistercian abbey at Cîteaux in France. Like this one, most were founded in remote rural areas and formed the nuclei of new towns. The abbey church of Sulejów (*SOO-lay-uf*) was dedicated to the English saint Thomas Becket, who had been canonized as a saint just three years before its foundation. ■ *How does this Polish abbey's dedication to St. Thomas Becket exemplify the transnational interconnectivity of Cistercian monasteries?*

# Analyzing Primary Sources

## The Canons of the Fourth Lateran Council

*In 1215, Innocent III presided over an ecumenical assembly of Church leaders in the papal palace and church of St. John Lateran in Rome. The resulting canons (rules) both reaffirmed older legislation and introduced a number of new laws in response to widespread social, economic, and cultural changes. Published the same year as Magna Carta, they too became a standard set of principles and continued to be applied within the Church until they were modified by the Council of Trent in the sixteenth century.*

### Canon 1

. . . There is one Universal Church of the faithful, outside of which there is absolutely no salvation. In which there is the same priest and sacrifice, Jesus Christ, whose body and blood are truly contained in the sacrament of the altar under the forms of bread and wine; the bread being changed (*transubstantiation*) by divine power into the body, and the wine into the blood, so that to realize the mystery of unity we may receive of Him what He has received of us. And this sacrament no one can effect except the priest who has been duly ordained in accordance with the keys of the Church, which Jesus Christ Himself gave to the Apostles and their successors. . . .

\* \* \*

### Canon 3

We excommunicate and anathematize every heresy that rises against the holy, orthodox, and Catholic faith . . . condemning all heretics under whatever names they may be known, for while they have different faces they are nevertheless bound to each other by their tails, since in all of them vanity is a common element. Those condemned, being handed over to the secular rulers of their bailiffs, let them be abandoned, to be punished with due justice, clerics being first degraded from their orders.

\* \* \*

### Canon 9

Since in many places within the same city and diocese there are people of different languages having one faith but various rites and customs, we strictly command that the bishops of these cities and dioceses provide suitable men who will, according to the different rites and languages, celebrate the divine offices for them, administer the sacraments of the Church and instruct them by word and example.

### Canon 10

. . . It often happens that bishops, on account of their manifold duties or bodily infirmities, or because of hostile invasions or other reasons, to say nothing of lack of learning, which must be absolutely condemned in them and is not to be tolerated in the future, are themselves unable to minister the word of God to the people, especially in large and widespread dioceses. Wherefore we decree that bishops provide suitable men, powerful in work and word, to exercise with fruitful result the office of preaching; who in place of the bishops, since these cannot do it, diligently visiting the people committed to them, may instruct them by word and example. . . .

### Canon 11

Since there are some who, on account of the lack of necessary means, are unable to acquire an education or to meet opportunities for perfecting themselves, the Third Lateran Council in a salutary decree provided that in every cathedral church a suitable benefice be assigned to a master who shall instruct *gratis* the clerics of that church and other poor students, . . . we, confirming the aforesaid decree, add that, not only in every cathedral church but also in other churches where means are sufficient, a competent master be appointed . . . who shall instruct *gratis* and to the best of his ability the clerics of those and other churches in the art of grammar and in other branches of knowledge.

\* \* \*

### Canons 14–16

That the morals and general conduct of clerics may be better, let all strive to live chastely and virtuously, particularly those in sacred orders, guarding against every vice of desire . . .

. . . All clerics shall carefully abstain from drunkenness. . . .

We forbid hunting and fowling to all clerics; wherefore, let them not presume to keep dogs and birds for these purposes. . . .

Clerics shall not hold secular offices or engage in secular and, above all, dishonest pursuits. They shall not attend the performances of mimics and buffoons, or theatrical representations. They shall not visit taverns except in case of necessity, namely, when on a journey.

They are forbidden to play games of chance or be present at them. They must have a becoming crown and tonsure and apply themselves diligently to the study of the divine offices and other useful subjects. Their garments must be worn clasped at the top and neither too short nor too long. They are not to use red or green garments or curiously sewed-together gloves, or beak-shaped shoes . . .

\* \* \*

## Canon 68

In some provinces a difference in dress distinguishes the Jews or Saracens [Muslims] from the Christians, but in certain others such a confusion has grown up that they cannot be distinguished by any difference. Thus it happens at times that through error Christians have relations with the women of Jews or Saracens, and Jews and Saracens with Christian women. Therefore, that they may not, under pretext of error of this sort, excuse themselves in the future for the excesses of such prohibited intercourse, we decree that such Jews and Saracens of both sexes in every Christian province and at all times shall be marked off in the eyes of the public from other peoples through the character of their dress. . . .

Moreover, during the last three days before Easter and especially on Good Friday, they shall not go forth in public at all, for the reason that some of them on these very days, as we hear, do not blush to go forth better dressed and are not afraid to mock the Christians who maintain the memory of the most holy Passion by wearing signs of mourning. . . .

Source: Excerpted from H. J. Schroeder, *Disciplinary Decrees of the General Councils: Text, Translation and Commentary* (St. Louis, MO: 1937), pp. 236–96.

## Questions for Analysis

1. On the basis of this selection of canons, how would you characterize the main concerns of the Fourth Lateran Council? What is it attempting to regulate, and why? What changing historical circumstances do the canons reflect?

2. In what ways do the canons distinguish between clergy and laity? How does legislation work to maintain those distinctions?

3. Why do the canons place so much emphasis on clothing and appearance? Why would it be important for both clerics and "infidels" (Jews and Muslims) to dress in distinctive ways?

In later centuries, the Latin words spoken at the consecration of the Host, *Hoc est enim corpus meum* ("This is my body"), were understood as a magical formula, *hocus pocus*.

## Holy Women, Human and Divine

Popular devotion to the Eucharist was matched by another new and hugely influential religious practice: the veneration of Jesus's mother, Mary. In this development, too, Bernard of Clairvaux played an important role, traveling around Europe to promote a theology that made Mary central to Christianity, the very embodiment of the Church. Eventually, Catholic teaching would hold that not only had Mary given birth to Jesus while still a virgin, but that she remained a virgin even after Jesus's birth; and, more radically, that she herself had been conceived without sin. This made Mary the exact opposite of Eve—the woman whose disobedience had (according to Judeo-Christian tradition) brought sin into the world for the first time— for through God's grace, she had given birth to Christ, a second Adam, whose obedient sacrifice of himself atoned for that original sin.

New doctrines also raised Mary from the position of God's humble handmaid to that of heaven's queen, with the power to intercede on behalf of all, even the worst sinners. Her soaring reputation as a miracle worker and advocate is amply testified by the thousands of devotional images created during this period, the many stories and hymns celebrating her virtues and miracles, and the fact that practically all the magnificent new cathedrals of the age were dedicated to "Our Lady," such as the many churches of Notre Dame in France, the Frauenkirchen of Germany, and so on.

The burgeoning cult of the Blessed Virgin had two contradictory effects. On the one hand, it elevated a female figure to a prominent place in the official Church for the first time, and thereby celebrated virtues associated with femininity: motherhood, healing, nourishment, mercy, kindness, and so on. On the other hand, it made Mary an unattainable, paradoxical model of female perfection: she

# Competing Viewpoints

## Two Conversion Experiences

*Both Peter Waldo (or Waldes), later branded a heretic, and Francis of Assisi, later declared a saint, were moved to take up a life of preaching and poverty after undergoing a process of conversion. Their experiences exhibit some striking similarities despite their different fates. The first account is that of an anonymous chronicler in Peter's home town of Lyons; the second is by Francis's contemporary and hagiographer, Thomas of Celano (c. 1200–c. 1260/70).*

### The Conversion of Peter Waldo

At about this time, in 1173, there was a citizen of Lyons named Peter Waldo, who had made a great deal of money by the evil means of usury. One Sunday he lingered by a crowd that had gathered round a traveling storyteller, and was much struck by his words. He took him home with him, and listened carefully to his story of how St. Alexis had died a holy death in his father's house. Next morning Waldo hastened to the schools of theology to seek advice about his soul. When he had been told of the many ways of coming to God he asked the master whether any of them was more sure and reliable than the rest. The master quoted to him the words of the Lord, "If thou wilt be perfect go sell what thou hast and give it to the poor and thou shalt have treasure in heaven. And come follow me."

Waldo returned to his wife and gave her the choice between having all his movable wealth or his property in land. . . . She was very upset at having to do this and chose the property. From his movable wealth he returned what he had acquired wrongly, conferred a large portion on his two daughters, whom he placed in the order of Fontevrault without his wife's knowledge, and gave a still larger amount to the poor.

At this time a terrible famine was raging through Gaul and Germany. . . . Waldo generously distributed bread, soup and meat to anyone who came to him. On the [Feast of the] Assumption of the Virgin [August 15] he scattered money among the poor in the streets saying, "You cannot serve two masters, God and Mammon." The people around thought he had gone out of his senses. Then he stood up on a piece of high ground and said, "Friends and fellow-citizens, I am not mad as you think. . . . I know that many of you disapprove of my having acted so publicly. I have done so both for my own sake and for yours: for my sake, because anybody who sees me with money in future will be able to say that I am mad; for your sake, so that you may learn to place your hopes in God and not in wealth." . . .

1177 Waldo, the citizen of Lyons whom we have already mentioned, who had vowed to God that he would possess neither gold nor silver, and take no thought for the morrow, began to make converts to his opinions. Following his example they gave all they had to the poor, and willingly devoted themselves to poverty. Gradually, both in public and in private they began to inveigh against both their own sins and those of others. . . .

1178 Pope Alexander III held a council at the Lateran palace. . . . The council condemned heresy and all those who fostered and defended heretics. The pope embraced Waldo, and applauded the vows of voluntary poverty which he had taken, but forbade him and his companion to assume the office of preaching except at the request of the priests. They obeyed this instruction for a time, but later they disobeyed, and affronted many, bringing ruin on themselves.

Source: Excerpted from *Chronicon universale anonymi Laudunensis*, ed. and trans. Robert I. Moore, in *The Birth of Popular Heresy* (London: 1975), pp. 111–13 (slightly modified).

### The Conversion of Francis of Assisi

There was a man by the name of Francis, who from his earliest years was brought up by his parents proud of spirit, in accordance with the vanity of the world. . . . These are the wretched circumstances among which the man whom we venerate today as a saint, for he is truly a saint, lived in his youth; and almost up to the twenty-fifth year of his age, . . . he outdid all his contemporaries in vanities and he came to be a promoter of evil and was

more abundantly zealous for all kinds of foolishness. . . . And while, not knowing how to restrain himself, he was . . . worn down by a long illness, [he] began to think of things other than he was used to thinking upon. When he had recovered somewhat and had begun to walk about the house with the support of a cane to speed the recovery of his health, he went outside one day and began to look about at the surrounding landscape with great interest. But the beauty of the fields, the pleasantness of the vineyards, and whatever else was beautiful to look upon, could stir in him no delight. He wondered therefore at the sudden change that had come over him. . . . From that day on, therefore, he began to despise himself. . . .

Now since there was a certain man in the city of Assisi whom he loved more than any other because he was of the same age as the other, and since the great familiarity of their mutual affection led him to share his secrets with him; he often took him to remote places, places well-suited for counsel, telling him that he had found a certain precious and great treasure. This one rejoiced and, concerned about what he heard, he willingly accompanied Francis whenever he was asked. There was a certain grotto near the city where they frequently went and talked about this treasure. The man of God, who was already holy by reason of his holy purpose, would enter the grotto, while his companion would wait for him outside; and filled with a new and singular spirit, he would pray to his Father in secret. . . .

One day, however, when he had begged for the mercy of God most earnestly, it was shown to him by God what

he was to do. . . . He rose up, therefore, fortified himself with the sign of the cross, got his horse ready and mounted it, and taking with him some fine cloth to sell, he hastened to the city called Foligno. There, as usual, he sold everything he had with him . . . and, free of all luggage, he started back, wondering with a religious mind what he should do with the money. . . . When, therefore, he neared the city of Assisi, he discovered a certain church . . . built of old in honor of St. Damian but which was now threatening to collapse because it was so old. . . . And when he found there a certain poor priest, he kissed his sacred hands with great faith, and offered him the money he had with him, . . . begging the priest to suffer him to remain with him for the sake of the Lord. . . .

When those who knew him . . . compared what he was now with what he had been . . . they began to revile him miserably. Shouting out that he was mad and demented, they threw the mud of the streets and stones at him. . . . Now . . . the report of these things finally came to his father . . . [who] shut him up mercilessly in a dark place for several days . . . It happened, however, when Francis' father had left home for a while on business and the man of God remained bound in the basement of the house, his mother, who was alone with him and did not approve of what her husband had done, spoke kindly to her son. . . . and loosening his chains, she let him go free. . . .

He [the father] then brought his son before the bishop of the city, so that, renouncing all his possessions into his hands, he might give up everything he had. . . . Indeed, he [Francis] did not wait for any words nor did he speak any,

but immediately putting off his clothes and casting them aside, he gave them back to his father. Moreover, not even retaining his trousers, he stripped himself completely naked before all. The bishop, however, sensing his disposition and admiring greatly his fervor and constancy, arose and drew him within his arms and covered him with the mantle he was wearing. . . .

Source: Excerpted from Thomas of Celano, "The First Life of Saint Francis" in *Saint Francis of Assisi: Writings and Biographies*, ed. Marion A. Habiq (Chicago: 1973), pp. 229–41.

## Questions for Analysis

1. How do the conversions of Peter and Francis reflect the social and economic changes of the twelfth century? What new sources of tension and temptation are evident?

2. How do these two accounts describe the new converts' relationship(s) with their families, communities, and Church authorities? What are the similarities and differences? Why would these be important factors in determining the sanctity of either?

3. The story of Peter's conversion is written by an anonymous chronicler of Lyons, that of Francis by his follower and official biographer. How do these different perspectives shape the two accounts? Which is the more reliable, and why?

originated from the teachings of a merchant named Peter Waldo, or Waldes. Waldensians were laypeople who wished to imitate the life of Christ to the fullest. They were active in the vernacular translation and study of the Gospels and dedicated to lives of poverty and preaching. None of this contradicted any contemporary doctrines, and for a while the Church did not interfere with the Waldensians' ministry. But when they began to preach without authorization, they were condemned as heretics. In response, they began to articulate a more radical opposition to the established hierarchy. Incidentally, many of their leaders, too, were women.

At the same time, however, Innocent embraced two other popular movements and turned them into two new religious orders: the Dominicans and the Franciscans. Like the Waldensians, the friars ("brothers") of these orders imitated the life of Jesus and his apostles by wandering through the countryside and establishing missions in Europe's growing towns, preaching and offering spiritual and material assistance to the poor. They also embraced poverty and begged for a living, hence their categorization as *mendicants*, from the Latin verb *mendicare* ("to beg"). In the end, the only thing that separated them from the Waldensians was their willingness to subject themselves to papal authority.

The Dominican order, formally known as the Order of Preachers, was founded by the zealous Dominic of Osma (1170–1221), a Castilian theologian. Approved in 1216, it was particularly dedicated to the prosecution of heretics and the conversion of Jews and Muslims. At first, the Dominicans hoped to achieve these ends by preaching and public debate; and to further these goals, many of its members pursued academic careers in the nascent universities, and thus contributed to the development of philosophy and theology (see below). The most influential intellectual of the Middle Ages, Thomas Aquinas (1225–1274), was a Dominican. But they soon became associated with the use of other persuasive techniques through the administration of the Inquisition, which became formalized in the thirteenth century. (It is now called the Congregation for the Doctrine of the Faith and is still staffed by members of the order.)

The Franciscans, formally known as the Order of the Friars Minor ("Little Brothers"), were committed less to doctrine and discipline than to the welfare of the poor and the cultivation of personal spirituality. Whereas Dominic and his earliest followers were ordained priests, the founder of the Franciscans was the ne'er-do-well son of an Italian merchant, Francis of Assisi (1182–1226), who eventually rebelled against the materialistic values of his father. Stripping himself (literally) of all his worldly possessions, he put on the tattered garb of a beggar and began to preach salvation in town squares. Unlike Dominic, Francis did this without official approval, thereby risking papal censure. Indeed, the pope might well have rejected Francis as a heretic. But when he showed himself willing to profess obedience in 1209, Innocent granted Francis and his followers permission to preach.

Although the rapid growth of the Franciscan order would eventually necessitate more administrative stability and doctrinal training for all its members, many Franciscans continued to engage in revivalistic outdoor preaching and to offer a model for apostolic living. This was not, however, an approved religious lifestyle for women. Francis's most important female follower, Clare of Assisi (1194–1253), wanted to found an order along the same lines, the Order of Poor Ladies (also known as the Poor Clares). But its members were not allowed to work directly among the people, as men did, and instead lived in cloistered convents supported by charitable donations.

Their counterparts in northern Europe were the Beguines, communities of laywomen who lived in loosely organized communal quarters and ministered directly to the poor. Their relationship with Church officials was strained, because the Beguines embraced many of the precepts and practices associated with the Waldensians, including the unauthorized translation and study of the Bible. And the fact that they were women made them even more suspect.

## Christians against Jews

Although violence and exploitation continued to beset Europe's Jewish communities, the Church's official position never explicitly endorsed the view that Jews posed a threat to Christians—yet it did little to combat such attitudes, either. As a result, many ordinary people came to believe that their Jewish neighbors were agents of evil who routinely crucified Christian children, consumed Christian blood, profaned the body of Christ in the Eucharist, and spread disease in Christian communities by poisoning wells. Fanciful stories of Jewish wealth added an economic element to the development of anti-Semitism, as did the fact that the Jews' social and cultural networks were the engine of the medieval economy. From this fact, conspiracy theorists inferred the existence of organized Jewish plots to undermine Christian society, which they regularly cited as justifications for mass executions and other atrocities.

The precarious position of Europe's Jews worsened throughout the twelfth and thirteenth centuries as both secular and ecclesiastical authorities devised more systematic mechanisms for policing undesirable segments of society: "heretics" as well as the indigent poor, prostitutes, "sodomites," and lepers. The canons of the Fourth Lateran

Council had mandated that Jews be exposed through the wearing of the Jewish badge, making them easier targets in times of unrest. At the same time, the protections that Europe's rulers had once extended to their Jewish subjects were gradually withdrawn. In Spain, the Reconquista had absorbed many of the Muslim kingdoms in which Jews had enjoyed a measure of tolerance, and the Jews were not easily accommodated within the emerging monarchies of Christian Spain.

Starting in the 1280s, rulers elsewhere in Europe began to expel their Jewish subjects from their kingdoms altogether, in most cases because they could no longer pretend to repay the enormous sums they had extorted from Jewish moneylenders; this was the case in the kingdoms of Sicily (1288), England (1290), and France (1306). Further expulsions followed during the fourteenth century in the Rhineland, and in 1492 from Spain. By 1500, only northern Italy and various eastern European regions (encompassed today by Poland, Belarus, and Ukraine) were home to sizable Jewish communities—where they would survive until the dreadfully efficient persecutions of the Nazi Holocaust eradicated them (see Chapter 26).

## AN INTELLECTUAL REVOLUTION

The Fourth Lateran Council responded to the growing urbanization of Europe by mandating the education of the laity and insisting on more rigorous training for all clergy. These measures responded to a number of factors that were transforming the cultural landscape of Europe and to the new opportunities opening up for advancement through education. The growth of towns had led to the growth of schools in those towns, for the most part founded by local bishops or monasteries. Meanwhile, the Crusades became conduits for the transmission of Muslim learning and, through Muslim mediation, the precepts of ancient Greek philosophy.

The infusion of these new ideas created an extraordinary new forum for intellectual endeavor: the university. In much the same way that ease of travel and communication had fostered a scientific revolution in the cities of the Hellenistic world (see Chapter 4), so the conditions that gave rise to the university marked the beginning of a revolution in the intellectual history of Europe.

**TWO CONCEPTIONS OF ELEMENTARY EDUCATION.** In the illustration on the left, an illumination from a fourteenth-century manuscript, a master of grammar points to the day's lesson in a book while simultaneously keeping order with a cudgel. The illustration on the right, a later woodcut, represents education as more benign: Lady Wisdom shows an eager schoolboy how to learn his letters while unlocking the door of knowledge, while scholarly men in a multi-tiered tower representing the different branches of learning smile out at him.

## Access to Education

Around 800, Charlemagne had ordered that primary schools be established in every city and monastery of his realm. But it was not until the economic revival of the late eleventh century that educational opportunities became more widely available. By 1179, Pope Alexander III decreed that all cathedrals should set aside income for at least one schoolteacher, whose task would be to accept all comers, rich or poor, without fee. He predicted, correctly, that this measure would increase the number of well-trained clerics and administrators, supplying the growing bureaucracy of the Church. The recently martyred Thomas Becket had been an early beneficiary of such schooling.

At first, cathedral schools existed almost exclusively for the training of parish priests, but their curriculum was soon broadened as the growth of both ecclesiastical and secular governments escalated demand for trained men with more sophisticated skills. The most fundamental elements of this curriculum were known as the *trivium* ("three ways"): grammar, logic, and rhetoric. This meant a thorough grounding in Latin through the study of classical Roman authors, such as Cicero and Virgil, and training in the formulation and expression of sound arguments. Students who mastered the trivium were fit to perform basic clerical tasks, but those who wanted to achieve the reputation and advantages of scholars had to master the remaining branches of learning, the *quadrivium* (or "four ways"): arithmetic, geometry, astronomy, and music. Together, these seven liberal arts—so called because they liberated those who acquired them from menial labor—were the prerequisites for advanced study in philosophy, theology, law, and medicine.

Until about 1200, most students in urban schools belonged to the minor orders of the clergy, meaning they took vows of obedience and were immune from prosecution by secular authorities—but not required to remain celibate, unlike priests and bishops, who belonged to major orders. Even men who hoped to become lawyers or bureaucrats usually found it advantageous to "take orders" in case powerful ecclesiastical offices became open to them. Heloise tried to discourage Abelard from marrying her for this very reason, because it would destroy his chances of being appointed a bishop or papal legate. Abelard, a nobleman's son, was by no means typical of the men who rose to prominence in this era through education. His contemporary and rival, Suger, was more representative. An orphan of obscure origins, he became abbot of the royal monastery of Saint-Denis and de facto chancellor of France.

By the thirteenth century, most boys who entered schools were not members of the clergy and never intended to be. Some were children of wealthy families, which regarded Latin literacy as a badge of status and a practical necessity. Others were future notaries, estate managers, and merchants who needed to be literate and numerate in order to succeed in their careers. Many alternative schools were eventually established to cater to these vocational students and became largely independent of ecclesiastical control. In some of these schools, Latin ceased to be the language of instruction and was replaced by the vernacular language of the region.

Although formal schooling remained restricted to males, many girls and women became highly educated, too, especially those reared in convents or princely courts. Heloise had an unusual degree of access to the educational milieu of Paris, but she clearly had received excellent preparatory training in the convent before she began her studies with Abelard. Most laywomen, however, were taught at

**THE TOMB OF ELEANOR OF AQUITAINE.** Eleanor probably commissioned the tomb effigies representing herself, her husband Henry II, and her son Richard the Lionheart—both of whom died years before she did. She was eventually buried alongside them in the vault of the convent of Fontevrault in Anjou, where she spent the last years of her life. ▪ *Notice that Eleanor's effigy shows her reading a book. How does this reinforce or challenge what we have learned about women's access to education?*

## Peter Abelard Critiques Theological Contradictions

*In 1120, Abelard published the* Sic et Non *("So and Not So"), a pioneering work of dialectic theology and a model for the development of later scholastic methods. In it, he arranged passages from scripture as well as the writings of the church fathers that had bearing on important doctrinal issues and appeared to offer contradictory views. His eventual aim, as the prologue to this work indicates, was to reconcile these differences through the use of critical analysis.*

There are many seeming contradictions and even obscurities in the innumerable writings of the church fathers. Our respect for their authority should not stand in the way of an effort on our part to come at the truth. The obscurity and contradictions in ancient writings may be explained upon many grounds, and may be discussed without impugning the good faith and insight of the fathers. A writer may use different terms to mean the same thing, in order to avoid a monotonous repetition of the same word. Common, vague words may be employed in order that the common people may understand; and sometimes a writer sacrifices perfect accuracy in the interest of a clear general statement. Poetical, figurative language is often obscure and vague. . . .

Doubtless the fathers might err; even Peter, the prince of the apostles, fell into error; what wonder that the saints do not always show themselves inspired? The fathers did not themselves believe that they, or their companions, were always right. Augustine found himself mistaken in some cases and did not hesitate to retract his errors. He warns his admirers not to look upon his letters as they would upon the Scriptures, but to accept only those things which, upon examination, they find to be true.

All writings belonging to this class are to be read with full freedom to criticise, and with no obligation to accept unquestioningly; otherwise the way would be blocked to all discussion, and posterity be deprived of the excellent intellectual exercise of debating difficult questions of language and presentation. But an explicit exception must be made in the case of the Old and New Testaments. In the Scriptures, when anything strikes us as absurd, we may not say that the writer erred, but that the scribe made a blunder in copying the manuscripts, or that there is an error in interpretation, or that the passage is not understood. The fathers make a very careful distinction between the Scriptures and later works. They advocate a discriminating, not to say suspicious, use of the writings of their own contemporaries.

In view of these considerations, I have ventured to bring together various dicta of the holy fathers, as they came to mind, and to formulate certain questions which were suggested by the seeming contradictions in the statements. These questions ought to serve to excite tender readers to a zealous inquiry into truth and so sharpen their wits. The master key of knowledge is, indeed, a persistent and frequent questioning. Aristotle, the most clear-sighted of all the philosophers, was desirous above all

things else to arouse this questioning spirit, for in his *Categories* he exhorts a student as follows: "It may well be difficult to reach a positive conclusion in these matters unless they be frequently discussed. It is by no means fruitless to be doubtful on particular points." By doubting we come to examine, and by examining we reach the truth.

Source: Peter Abelard, prologue to the *Sic et Non*, trans. James Harvey Robinson, in *Readings in European History*, 2 vols. (Boston: 1904), vol. 1, pp. 450–51.

### Questions for Analysis

1. According to Abelard, on what grounds can religious authorities be challenged? What distinctions does he make between criticism of the scriptures and of other authorities, and why?

2. In this work, Abelard did not attempt to resolve the contradictions among his sources. Based on what you have learned, why would have his project seemed threatening to the authority of the Church?

home, sometimes by private tutors but more often by other women. In fact, laywomen were more likely to be literate than laymen, and it is for this reason that women were often the patrons of poets and the primary readers and owners of books. It is significant that the effigy that Eleanor of Aquitaine commissioned for her own tomb shows her lying awake reading, flanked by her sleeping husband and son, till Judgment Day.

## The Development of Scholasticism

The educational revolution that began in the eleventh century led to the development of new critical methods for framing and resolving complex theological and philosophical problems. These methods are collectively known as *scholasticism*, because they had their origins in the pedagogy of medieval schools. Scholastic methods are highly systematic and respectful of authority, but they also rely on rigorous questioning and argumentation. They therefore place great emphasis on evidence derived from reason. Indeed, scholasticism can be defined as a way of reconciling various forms of knowledge through logical debate, often called *dialectic*.

The earliest practitioner of the scholastic method is often considered to be Anselm of Canterbury (1033–1109), a Benedictine monk from northern Italy who became archbishop of Canterbury. The central premise of Anselm's teaching was that the human mind can combine knowledge gained through education and experience with divine revelation— as long as one has faith in God and careful scholastic training. As he put it, "I believe in order to understand," so that belief can be enriched and strengthened by understanding.

Building on the writings of Augustine and Boethius (see Chapter 6), and so (indirectly) on the teachings of Plato (see Chapter 4), Anselm developed various rational proofs for the underlying truths of Christian doctrine. The most famous of these is his proof for the existence of God, known as the ontological proof ("proof from the fact of existence") because it reasons that human beings could not have ideas of goodness, truth, or justice unless some higher being had instilled those ideas in us. He further reasoned that God, as the essence of all ideals, must be "that than which nothing greater can be conceived," and as such must exist, or else God could not be the greatest thing conceivable.

Anselm's writings were influential, but the philosopher who popularized the scholastic method was Abelard. It was largely thanks to him that Paris became the intellectual capital of Europe. As a cathedral city and the seat of the French monarchy, it already boasted a number of schools, but it was only after Abelard was appointed to the school-

master's chair at Notre Dame that Paris became a magnet for ambitious young men, many of whom were attracted to Abelard's unorthodox teaching style. We can glimpse it through his audacious treatise the *Sic et Non* ("Yes and No" or "So and Not So"). In this book, Abelard gathered a collection of seemingly contradictory statements from the Church Fathers, organized around 150 key theological problems. Like his contemporary Gratian, the codifier of canon law, Abelard's ultimate ambition was to show that these divergent authorities could be reconciled—in this case, through the skillful use of dialectic.

Yet Abelard did not propose any solutions in the *Sic et Non*, and the work therefore caused grave concern. More inflammatory still were Abelard's meditations on the doctrine of the Trinity, which circulated in a book of lectures that was denounced and burned in 1121. Twenty years later, Bernard of Clairvaux had Abelard brought up on another charge of heresy at the Council of Soissons, where he was condemned a second time. Bernard's own mystic spirituality stood in direct opposition to Abelard's tireless quest for reasoned understanding.

Abelard, for his part, found no solace in the monastic life beloved by Bernard. For Abelard, teaching was the activity that nurtured his faith. Luckily, teaching also expanded his fame and allowed him to train many pupils who eventually vindicated his teachings. After Abelard's death, his student Peter Lombard asked the same fundamental questions, but he took care to resolve the tensions that the *Sic et Non* left open. His great work, known as the *Sentences*, became the standard theological textbook of the medieval university, and all aspirants to the doctorate were required to comment on it.

## The Invention of the University

The emergence of the university—a unique public forum for advanced study, questioning of received ideas, and creation of new knowledge—was the natural extension of Abelard's teachings. His reputation and that of his students attracted many intellectuals to Paris, and together they began to offer more varied forms of instruction than anything obtainable in the average cathedral school. By 1200, this loose association of teachers had formed themselves into a *universitas* ("corporation" in Latin), and the resulting faculty began to collaborate in the higher academic study of the liberal arts, with a special emphasis on theology. At about the same time, students of law in Bologna came together in a *universitas* whose specialty was law.

Paris and Bologna provided the two models on which all medieval universities were based. In southern Europe,

CENTURY UNIVERSITY
WAS FOUNDED

- ■ Twelfth century
- ■ Thirteenth century
- □ Fourteenth century
- ■ Fifteenth century
- — Boundaries c. 1500

| 0 | 100 | 200 | 300 Miles |
| 0 | 100 | 200 | 300 Kilometers |

**THE SPREAD OF UNIVERSITIES.** This map shows the geographical distribution of Europe's major universities and their dates of foundation. ▪ *Where were the first universities founded, and why?* ▪ *Notice the number and location of the universities founded in the fourteenth and fifteenth centuries. What pattern do you see in these later foundations?* ▪ *What might explain this pattern?*

such universities as Montpellier, Salamanca, and Naples were patterned after Bologna, where the students themselves constituted the corporation: they hired the teachers, paid their salaries, and fined or discharged them for poor instruction. The universities of northern Europe were like that of Paris, consisting of guilds of teachers who governed themselves and established rules of conduct and fees for tuition. They eventually embraced four faculties—liberal arts, theology, law, and medicine—each headed by a dean. By the end of the thirteenth century, the northern universities also expanded to include separate, semiautonomous colleges, which usually provided housing for poorer students and were often endowed by private benefactors. Over time, these colleges became centers of instruction as well as residences. The universities of Oxford and Cambridge still retain this pattern of organization: the colleges of which they are composed are semi-independent educational units.

Most of the academic degrees granted in our modern universities derive from those awarded in the Middle Ages, even though the actual courses of study are very different. No university curriculum included history or vernacular languages or anything like the social sciences prior to the nineteenth century. The medieval student was assumed to know Latin grammar thoroughly before entering a university, which he would have learned in the primary (or "grammar") schools discussed above. On admission, he was required to spend about four years studying the basic liberal arts, which meant doing advanced work in Latin rhetoric and mastering the rules of logic. If he passed his examinations, he received the preliminary degree of bachelor of arts (the prototype of our BA). But to ensure himself a place in professional life, he had to devote additional years to the pursuit of an advanced degree, the master of arts (MA) or the doctor of laws, medicine, or theology. This was accomplished by reading and commenting on standard texts such as Peter Lombard's *Sentences* (theology), Gratian's *Decretum* (law), or Aristotle's *Physics* (medicine). The requirements for the degree of doctor of philosophy (PhD) included even more specialized training, and those for the doctorate in theology were particularly arduous: by the end of the Middle Ages, it took twelve or thirteen years to earn this degree, over and above the eight years required to earn the MA. University degrees of all grades were recognized as standards of attainment and became pathways to a variety of careers.

Student life in medieval universities was rowdy. Because many students began their studies between the ages of twelve and fifteen, they were working through all the challenges of adolescence and early adulthood as they worked toward their degrees; this explains the many injunctions against drunkenness, gambling, and other pursuits included among the canons of the Fourth Lateran Council. Moreover, university students generally believed that they constituted an independent and privileged community, apart from the local communities in which they lived. This often led to riots or even pitched battles between "town" and "gown."

That said, the time devoted to actual study was very intensive. Because books were prohibitively expensive, the primary mode of instruction was the lecture (Latin for "reading") in which a master would read an authoritative work aloud to his students and comment on it while they took notes. As students advanced in their disciplines, they were expected to develop their own skills of analysis and interpretation in formal, public disputations. Advanced disputations could become extremely complex and abstract, and sometimes might last for days. Often, they sparked public debates of great magnitude. The Ninety-Five Theses posted by Martin Luther in 1517 were actually a set of debating points organized along these lines (see Chapter 13).

## Classical Thought, Muslim Learning, and Scholastic Theology

The intellectual revolution of the Middle Ages was hugely indebted to the intellectual legacy of Islam, which was filtering into Europe via the Crusades. As we saw in Chapter 8, Muslim philosophers had been honing an array of different techniques to deal with the challenge of reconciling classical thought with Islamic belief, and these techniques contributed fundamentally to the development of Christian theology.

The most influential of these Muslim philosophers was Ibn Rushd, known to his Christian disciples as Averroës (*ah-VAIR-oh-ayz*; 1126–1198). Born in the Andalusian capital of Córdoba, in Muslim Spain, Averroës single-handedly advanced the study of Aristotelian logic by publishing a series of careful commentaries that sought to purge the Greek philosopher's works of all later (and confusing) influences, to allow for their proper analysis and interpretation. Soon translated from Arabic into Latin, these commentaries were received in western Christendom alongside new translations of Aristotle's texts, also conveyed to Latin readers via Arabic, and thus fundamentally influenced the way all subsequent European scholars understood Aristotle. The prestige of Averroës was so great that Christian intellectuals called him simply "the Commentator," just as they called Aristotle "the Philosopher," as if there were no others.

By far the greatest accomplishments in this endeavor were made by Thomas Aquinas (1225–1274), who became the leading theologian at the University of Paris. As a member of the Dominican order, Thomas was committed to the defense of the Roman Church. But he also believed that the study of the physical world was a legitimate way of gaining knowledge of the divine, because God had created both the world and the many ways of knowing it. Imbued with a deep confidence in the value of both human reason and human experience, Thomas worked quietly and steadily on his two great summaries of theology, the *Summa contra gentiles* (a compendium of the arguments for refuting non-Christian religions) and the comprehensive *Summa theologiae*. The theology of the modern Roman Catholic Church still rests on Thomistic methods, doctrines, and principles.

**THE INFLUENCE OF AVERROÈS.** This portrait of the Muslim polymath Averroès is featured in a fourteenth-century fresco celebrating the achievements of the Christian theologian Thomas Aquinas (c. 1225–1274). ■ *What does his inclusion in this context indicate about the relationship between Muslim and Christian intellectual traditions?*

Ultimately, Averroès's learning was suppressed by the new Muslim dynasty that came to power in his lifetime, the Almohads, who demanded that all philosophical inquiry be subordinated to orthodox Muslim belief. After burning several of Averroès's works, they exiled him to Morocco. Thereafter, Islamic philosophy may have had more impact on Europe than in some Islamic kingdoms.

The greatest Jewish scholar of this period, Moses Maimonides (*my-MAHN-eh-dees*; c. 1137–1204), was also driven into exile by the Almohads. He traveled first to North Africa and then to Egypt, where he became a famous teacher, jurist, and physician. Also like Averroès, he exercised great influence on Christian theologians through his systematic exposition of Jewish law in his *Mishneh Torah*, which earned him the nickname the "second Moses."

Because many aspects of the rabbinic tradition, Greek philosophy, and Arabic learning were not readily compatible with Christian faith, they had to be filtered through the dialectical methods pioneered by Abelard and his pupils.

## COURTS, CITIES, AND CATHEDRALS

In the eleventh century, it was possible to describe European society as divided among "those who worked, those who prayed, and those who fought." By 1200, such a description no longer bore much relationship to reality. New elites had emerged in the burgeoning cities of Europe. The wealthiest members of society were merchants and bankers, and aristocrats either had to best them (by engaging in trade themselves) or join them through strategic intermarriage. The aristocracy still fought, but so did upwardly mobile knights, urban crossbowmen, longbowmen, citizen militias, and peasant levies. Meanwhile, such lines as existed between town and countryside were easily crossed, and the pupils of the new schools made up a growing professional class that further defied neat categorization. We have noted that careers in the Church or royal bureaucracies were particularly open to self-made, educated men, but medieval courts and cities also provided opportunities for advancement.

## From Chevalerie to Chivalry

The ennoblement of chivalry and the emergence of medieval court culture were connected to the growing wealth of Europe, the competition among states and princes, and the contemporary developments in military technology brought about by the Crusades. In 1100, a knight could get by with a woolen tunic and leather corselet, a couple of horses, a groom, and a sword. A hundred years later, a knight needed a full-body armor made of iron, a visored helmet, a broadsword, a lance, a shield, and several warhorses capable of carrying all this gear. By 1250, a knight also had to keep up appearances at tournaments, which meant maintaining a string of horses, sumptuous silk clothing for himself and caparisons for his steeds, and a retinue of liveried squires and servants. As the costs of a warrior's equipment rose, the number of men who could personally afford it dramatically declined, making knightly display something increasingly prized by nobles and upstart merchants alike. Knights who did not inherit or gain sufficient property to support themselves had to seek wealthy brides or the protection of a lord who could afford to equip them.

Still other factors contributed to the prestige of knighthood. As part of a larger effort to control the violent competition for land and wealth, both secular and ecclesiastical rulers began to promote a new set of values that would come to redefine chivalry: bravery, loyalty, generosity, and civility. This new chivalry appealed to knights because it distinguished them from all the other "new men" who were emerging as powerful figures in this period, especially merchants and clerics. It also appealed to the nobility, whose status in this socially mobile world no longer depended on descent from high-born ancestors; families who *did* have such ancestors did not necessarily have the wealth to maintain a noble lifestyle, whereas many families who lived as nobility did not have prestigious ancestors.

What, then, was *nobility*? To the older aristocracy, it was a visible sign of good breeding. To professional warriors, such as many crusaders, and the merchants and bureaucrats who later adopted its language and customs, chivalry offered a way of legitimizing social positions attained through bravery or skill. As a result, mounted combat—whether on the battlefield, in tournaments, or in the hunt—would remain the defining pastime of European gentlemen until the end of the First World War (see Chapter 24).

## The Aristocratic Landscape and Its Environmental Effects

In previous centuries, warriors had hunted to supplement their diets or to protect their households from predators. But as more and more land was placed under cultivation or devoted to raising sheep and cattle, and as many species of wild animals (notably wolves, bears, and boar) were hunted to near extinction in Europe, hunting ceased to be a necessity and became a symbol of noble status. Not only did hunting require a good horse, a pack of trained dogs and servants, and an array of weapons, it also required elites to enclose certain areas of protected land so that they could be stocked with game. These protected spaces were called forests—regardless of whether or not they were wooded—and they were governed by a "law of the forest," which stipulated that only the lord who owned or controlled the forest could hunt or allow others to hunt there.

Forest law forbade peasants from hunting game and prescribed heavy penalties for poaching (stealing). Such laws also prohibited foraging or cutting down trees for construction or firewood. In England, for example, only dead twigs and branches small enough to be pulled down with a pruning hook or a shepherd's crook could be harvested: hence the expression "by hook or by crook." In fact, after the Norman Conquest, the kings of England had

**MAKING A KNIGHTLY APPEARANCE.** The costs of maintaining a chivalric lifestyle mounted steeply in the twelfth and thirteenth centuries, not only because a knight needed the most up-to-date equipment but also because he was expected to cut a gallant figure at tournaments and dazzle female spectators. This image is one of many sumptuous full-page illuminations in the Manesse Codex, made in Zurich in the early fourteenth century and preserving the compositions of earlier courtly poets.

so increased the amount of land that was deemed "royal forest" that Magna Carta contained a series of provisions demanding that this land be "disaforrested" and returned to common use. In 1217, the young King Henry III issued a companion document, the Charter of the Forest, to reestablish his subjects' rights to these lands.

As in so many other arenas, the Crusades had an impact on hunting and the environment, too. Crusaders were impressed and inspired by the elegance and elaborate engineering of the gardens and parks they saw in the Holy Land, North Africa, and the Muslim kingdoms of Spain. So during the thirteenth century, many European aristocrats embarked on major projects designed to turn their own forests into hunting parks, and also to create habitats friendly to new species of birds and animals. The natural landscape of Europe was decisively altered as a result. Fallow deer (*Dama dama*), which were native only to Anatolia and had been brought to the Mediterranean by the Romans, were now introduced in England and France, where they were bred for hunting.

Rabbits, originally native to Spain and North Africa, were also newcomers in northern Europe, prized for their meat and pelts; but they had an unexpectedly devastating effect on native plants and quickly became invasive pests.

Herons, native to northern Europe, were now aggressively cultivated and bred to stock heronries, which meant that many low-lying arable lands were removed from peasant control and artificially flooded to provide the proper habitat and sources of food—such as carp, which were imported from southeastern Europe and Anatolia. Herons, in turn, fed the new aristocratic mania for hunting with birds of prey: these large, graceful birds would be forced to fly from their nests while expensively trained hawks, falcons, and peregrines were loosed to catch and kill them. Emperor Frederick II, having grown up in Sicily at the heart of the multicultural Mediterranean, drew on Arabic sources for his important treatise on falconry. He also maintained a menagerie of exotic animals. For him, as for his peers, demonstrating control over the environment became a new source of aristocratic identity.

***ON THE ART OF HUNTING WITH BIRDS.*** This beautifully illuminated manuscript of Frederick II's famous treatise on falconry was commissioned by his son Manfred shortly after his father's death in 1250. It is now in the Vatican Library in Rome.

## The Culture of the Court

Closely linked to this new aristocratic identity and the ideology of chivalry was an emphasis on *courtoisie* ("courtliness"), the refined behavior appropriate to a court. This stemmed in part from practical necessity: those great lords who could support a knightly retinue had households full of energetic, lusty young men whose appetites had to be controlled. Hence, the emerging code of chivalry encouraged its adherents to view noblewomen as objects of veneration who could be wooed and won only by polished manners, poetry, and valiant deeds; in other words, they had to be courted. (Non-noblewomen, though, were fair game and could be taken by force if they did not yield willingly to the desires of a knight.)

Whole new genres of poetry, song, and storytelling emerged in the twelfth century to celebrate the allied cultures of chivalry and courtliness. These genres stand in marked contrast to the older entertainments of Europe's warrior class, the heroic epics that are often the earliest literary artifacts of various vernacular languages: the Anglo-Saxon *Beowulf*, the French *Song of Roland*, the Norse sagas, the German *Song of the Nibelungs*, and the Spanish *Poem of the Cid*. These epics portray a virile, violent society where gore flows freely and skulls are cleaved; manly valor, honor, and loyalty are the major themes. If women are mentioned, it is usually as prizes to be won in battle.

The courtly entertainments introduced in the twelfth century were of very different style, subject, and authorship.

Many of them were addressed to, and commissioned by, women. In some cases, they were even composed by women or were composed in close collaboration with a female patron. An example of the former is the collections of *lais* (versified stories) of Marie de France, who was active during the reigns of Henry II and Eleanor of Aquitaine, and who may have been an abbess as well as a member of the Anglo-Norman aristocracy. An example of the latter is one of the Arthurian tales composed by Marie's contemporary, Chrétien de Troyes (*KRAY-tyan duh TWAH*; fl. 1165–1190), who spent some time working under the patronage of Eleanor's daughter (by her first husband, Louis VII), Marie of Champagne.

Romances were engaging tales of love and adventure, often focusing on the exploits of King Arthur and his knights or some other heroic figure of the past, such as Alexander the Great. But they were also attuned to the interests and concerns of women: threats to women's independence, enforced or unhappy marriages, disputed inheritances, fashion, and fantasies of power. The heroine of one anonymous romance is a woman who dresses as a knight and travels the world performing valiant deeds. Other heroines accompany their husbands on crusades or quests, defend their castles against attack, or have supernatural powers. Following in Chrétien's footsteps, the German poets Wolfram von Eschenbach and Gottfried von Strassburg vied to produce romances that retained the scope and complexity of heroic epics while featuring women in strong, central roles. Both Wolfram's *Parzival*, the story of the search for the Holy Grail, and Gottfried's *Tristan*, which retold the Celtic story of the adulterous love between Tristan and Isolde, inspired the operatic reconceptions of Richard Wagner (1813–1883).

The poetic tradition initiated by the southern French troubadours and the northern French trouvères (terms deriving from the verbs *trobar/trouver*, "to discover, to invent") also contributed to the culture of chivalry and inspired the work of German *minnesänger* ("love singers"). Much troubadour poetry displays sensitivity to feminine beauty and the natural world, and pays eloquent tribute to the political and sexual powers of women. Take, for example, a lyric of Bernart de Ventadorn (c. 1135–1195), one of Eleanor's protégés:

> When leaves and grass are lush with renewed
> growth
> The beauty of my lady blossoms forth . . .
> I am her slave, her vassal, she my lord;
> I pay her homage, hope to have a word
> Of kindness, or of love, exchanged for mine
> But she is cruel: she will not make a sign.

Other troubadour songs celebrate old-fashioned warlike virtues, as in the verses of Bernart's contemporary, Bertran de Born (c. 1140–1214), a friend of Eleanor's son, Richard the Lionheart:

> It pleases me to hear the mirth and song
> Of birds, filling the wood the whole day long.
> But more it pleases me to see the fields
> All planted thick with tents, to see the shields
> And swords of my companions ranged for war,
> To hear the screams, to see the blood and gore.

To what extent do the entertainments of the court reflect the reality of noblewomen's status? Certainly, there were women throughout this period who wielded tremendous power, particularly in Scandinavia and parts of southern Europe, where women could inherit property, rule in their own right, and were treated as lords in fact and in name (as in Bernart's song). Queen Urraca ruled the combined kingdom of León-Castile from 1109 until 1126. Ermengarde of Narbonne (c. 1127–1197) ruled her strategically placed county from early adolescence to the time of her death. Eleanor remained sole ruler of Aquitaine throughout her long life and played a crucial role in the government of England at various times. The strong-willed Blanche of Castile (1188–1252), Eleanor's granddaughter, ruled France during the minority of her son Louis IX, and again when he went on a crusade.

Queens are not, of course, typical, but their activities during this period reflect some of the opportunities open to other well-born women—and the freedoms that set most European women apart from their counterparts in the Byzantine and Muslim worlds. A striking symbol of this is the figure of the queen in the game of chess. In the Muslim courts where the game originated, the equivalent of the queen was a male figure, the king's chief minister, who could move only diagonally and one square at a time. In twelfth-century Europe, however, this piece became the queen: the only figure powerful enough to move all over the board.

## Urban Opportunities and Inequalities

In 1174, a cleric named William FitzStephen wrote a biography of his late employer, Thomas Becket, who had recently been canonized. In it, William went out of his way to extol the urban culture of London that had produced this saintly man and other "men of superior quality," as well as all the splendid sights and pastimes to be had there: feasting, churchgoing, ice skating, bear baiting, plays, sports—and,

# Analyzing Primary Sources

## Illicit Love and the Code of Chivalry

*Little is known about Marie de France, the author of a series of popular verse tales that are among the earliest chivalric romances. She may have been a nun or abbess living in the Anglo-Norman realm of Henry II and Eleanor of Aquitaine. The following excerpt is from her* Lais, *adapted from stories told in the Franco-Celtic county of Brittany (Abelard's home).*

he Bretons, who lived in Brittany, were fine and noble people. In days gone by these valiant, courtly and noble men composed lays for posterity and thus preserved them from oblivion. . . . One of them, which I have heard recited, should not be forgotten. It concerns Equitan, a most courtly man, lord of Nantes, justiciary and king.

Equitan enjoyed a fine reputation and was greatly loved in his land. He adored pleasure and amorous dalliance: for this reason he upheld the principles of chivalry. Those who lack a full comprehension and understanding of love show no thought for their lives. Such is the nature of love that no one under its sway can retain command over reason. Equitan had a seneschal, a good knight, brave and loyal, who took care of his entire territory, governing it and administering its justice. Never, except in time of war, would the king have forsaken his hunting, his pleasures or his river sports, whatever the need might have been.

As his wedded wife the seneschal had a woman who was to bring great misfortune to the land. She was a lady of fine breeding and extremely beautiful with a noble body and good bearing. Nature had spared no pains when fashioning her: her eyes sparkled, her face and mouth were beautiful and her nose was well set. She had no equal in the kingdom, and the king, having often heard her praised, frequently sent her greetings and gifts. . . . He went hunting in her region on his own and on returning from his sport took lodging for the night in the place where the seneschal dwelt, in the very castle where the lady was to be found. He had ample occasion to speak with her, to express his feelings and display his fine qualities. He found her most courtly and wise, beautiful in body and countenance. . . .

That night he neither slept nor rested, but spent his time reproaching and reprimanding himself. "Alas," he said, "what destiny brought me to this region? Because of this lady I have seen, my heart has been overwhelmed by a pain so great that my whole body trembles. I think I have no option but to love her. Yet, if I did love her, I should be acting wrongly, as she is the seneschal's wife. I ought to keep faith with him and love him, just as I want him to do with me. . . ."

Source: From "Equitan," in *The Lais of Marie de France*, trans. Glyn S. Burgess and Keith Busby (Harmondsworth, UK: 1985), pp. 56–57.

### Questions for Analysis

1. Despite the king's initial misgivings, he and the seneschal's wife eventually have an affair and plot to murder her husband, only to be caught in their own trap. Knowing this outcome, how would you interpret Marie's remarks about courtliness and "the code of chivalry"? What are the tenets of this code, according to the king?

2. What social tensions does this story reflect? How might it shed light on historical realities? What moral might contemporary readers draw from it?

of course, the pleasures of moneymaking. Towns were crucibles of activity, and as such became cultural as well as economic powerhouses, the launching pads for the careers of ambitious men.

As we noted in Chapter 8, many of the towns that emerged in the eleventh century were governed by associations of citizens who undertook a wide variety of civic responsibilities. But urban governance was likely to fall into the hands of oligarchs, a trend that became increasingly

marked during the thirteenth century, when the enormous wealth generated by some forms of commerce led to marked social inequalities, much as in the Greek poleis (Chapter 3). In Italy, some cities even sought to control the resulting violence by turning to an outsider who would rule as a dictator for a (supposedly) limited term. Other cities adopted the model of Venice and became formal oligarchies, casting off all pretense of democracy. Some cities remained republics in principle, as did Florence, but became increasingly oligarchical in practice. Aristocratic families lived in fortified towers surrounded by houses of their supporters, and their rivalries often produced a violent culture of vendetta.

But even in places where town governance was controlled by a powerful few, there were many meaningful opportunities for collective activity. Urban manufacturing was regulated by professional associations known as guilds or (in some regions) confraternities. Guilds promoted the interests of their members by trying to preserve monopolies and limit competition. To these ends, terms of employment and membership were strictly regulated. If an apprentice or a journeyman worker (from the French *journée*, meaning "day" and, by extension, "day's work") wished to become a master, he had to produce a "masterpiece" to be judged by the masters of the guild. If the market was considered too weak to support additional master craftsmen, even a masterpiece would not secure a craftsman the coveted right to set up his own shop and thus earn enough to marry. Most guilds were closed to Jews and Muslims, and they also restricted the opportunities available to women, who had little influence over the terms and conditions under which they worked.

Guilds and confraternities were therefore instruments of economic control, but they were also important social, political, and cultural institutions. Most combined the functions of religious association, drinking club, and benevolent society, looking after members and their families in hard times, supporting the dependents of members who died, and helping to finance funerals. Guilds also empowered their members in much the same way that unions do today, providing them with political representation and raising their social status. The wealthy town of Arras even had a guild of professional entertainers, the confraternity of *jongleurs*, which became the most powerful organization in the town by 1250.

## Varieties of Vernacular Entertainment

Like courts, towns fostered new kinds of vernacular entertainment during the twelfth and thirteenth centuries. Even the genres of Latin poetry, song, and drama produced in this period can be considered "vernacular" because they made use of vernacular elements (such as rhyme, which is not a feature of classical Latin poetry), dealt with current events, and were popular with a wide audience. In one of Heloise's letters to Abelard, she recalls that he was so renowned for the beauty of his love songs that "every street and tavern resounded with my name." It is possible that some of Abelard's songs were sung in French, but more probable that they used the edgy, colloquial Latin popular among the student singer-songwriters known as "goliards," which means something like "daredevils." Their lyrics celebrated the carefree life of the open road, the pleasures of drinking and dice, the joys of love, and the agonies of poverty.

Perhaps the genre most representative of urban culture is the *fabliau*, a "fable" or short story with a salacious, irreverent, or satirical twist. Fabliaux drew attention to the absurdities of urban life and lampooned the different types of people striving to reinvent themselves in the permissive world of the town: the oafish peasant, the effete aristocrat, the corrupt priest, the sex-starved housewife, the wily student, the greedy merchant, and the con man. Gender-bending and reversals of fortune are also common themes. In one fabliau, a young noble woman is forced by her impoverished father to marry a buffoonish shopkeeper who thereby gains knighthood; to shame him, she dresses herself as a knight and beats her husband in a jousting match. In another, a priest tricks a poor peasant out of his cow by promising that God will reward him by doubling his "investment" in the work of the Church; when the cow breaks out of the priest's pasture and runs for home, bringing the priest's cow, too, the peasant is delighted by the fulfillment of the promised miracle.

## The Medieval Cathedral

The cathedrals constructed in Europe's major cities during this period exemplify the ways in which the cultural communities of the court, the schools, and the town came together. For although any cathedral-building campaign would have been spearheaded by a bishop looking to glorify his episcopal see, it could not be completed without the support of the nobility, the resources of the wealthy, the learning of trained theologians, and the talents of urban craftsmen. And cathedrals were not merely edifices: they were theaters for the performance of liturgy, music, drama, and preaching.

Cathedrals were not, in themselves, new: the seat of a bishop had long been known as his *cathedra*, his throne, and the church that housed it was the principal church of the diocese. But the size, splendor, and importance of cathedrals increased exponentially in the twelfth and thirteenth centuries, alongside the growing power of the Church, the population of cities, and the wealth and knowledge necessary for their construction. Indeed, the cathedrals of this period are readily distinguishable from their predecessors by their architectural style, which came to be called "Gothic," whereas the style of earlier buildings is known as "Romanesque."

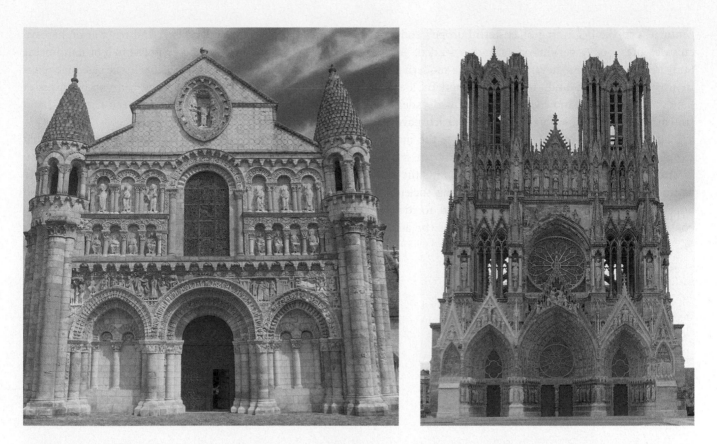

**ROMANESQUE AND GOTHIC.** Some distinguishing features of the Romanesque and Gothic styles are shown in these two churches, both dedicated to the Virgin Mary and built within a century of one another. On the left is the west front of the Church of Notre-Dame-la-Grande in Poitiers, the ancestral domain of Eleanor of Aquitaine. Constructed between 1135 and 1145, it featured rounded arches, strong stone walls, massive supporting pillars, and small windows. On the right is the cathedral of Notre-Dame at Reims in Champagne, built between 1220 and 1299. Here, the emphasis on stolid horizontal registers is replaced by soaring vertical lines. The gabled portals, pointed arches, and bristling pinnacles all accentuate the height of this structure, while the multitude of stained-glass windows—chiefly the enormous rose window—flood the vast interior with colored light.

As the term suggests, Romanesque buildings use the basic elements of public architecture under the Roman Empire: the rounded arch, massive stone walls, and sturdy supporting columns. These features convey regularity and stability, and they also made churches places of refuge that could be fortified and defended in troubled times. By contrast, the structural elements of Gothic architecture are the pointed arch, groined and ribbed vaulting, and the flying buttress, an external support that strengthened the much thinner stone walls and enormous stained-glass windows, whose light illuminated elaborate decorative programs that made the cathedral a microcosm of the medieval world and an encyclopedia of medieval knowledge.

These new Gothic cathedrals were not buildings that could be defended in wartime and, it was thought, would never have to be. They were manifestations of urban pride, expressions of practical and intellectual genius, and symbols of a triumphant and confident Church. Their builders would have been dismayed to learn that the modern term *gothic* was actually intended to be derogatory, the name for art forms that Renaissance artists—who favored Roman models—considered barbaric (see Chapter 12). They would have been still more shocked to learn that cathedrals were among the first monuments targeted for destruction during the Reformation, the revolutions of the eighteenth and nineteenth centuries, and the wars of the twentieth. One of the prime examples of Gothic architecture, the cathedral dedicated to the Virgin Mary at Reims (shown above), was largely destroyed during World War I; what visitors see today is a reconstruction.

## CONCLUSION

A century ago, the American historian Charles Homer Haskins described the intellectual, religious, and cultural changes of this era as the "Renaissance of the twelfth century" and the beginning of western Europe's enduring cultural prestige. A generation later, his student Joseph Strayer located the "medieval origins of the modern state" in this same period and, with them, modern ideas of national sovereignty and identity. In recent decades, the British historians R. I. Moore and Robert Bartlett have also argued that this era marks the beginning of the modern world—but not in positive ways. Moore sees the growth of strong institutions such as the Church and the state as leading to the "formation of a persecuting society," in which governmental bureaucracies are used to identify, control, and punish groups of people deemed threatening to those in power through a never-ending "war on heresy." Bartlett views this era as the key phase in a brutal process of "conquest and colonization" visible in the eastern expansion of the Holy Roman Empire, the Norman conquest of England, the growth of papal power, the Crusades, and other movements.

Common to all of these paradigms is a recognition that the expansion of European power and influence that began around the year 1000 continued into the twelfth century and consolidated in the thirteenth. By 1250, Europe had taken on the geographic, political, linguistic, and cultural characteristics that continue to define it today. Whether

# After You Read This Chapter

 Go to **INQUIZITIVE** to see what you've learned—and learn what you've missed—with personalized feedback along the way.

## REVIEWING THE OBJECTIVES

- The emerging monarchies of Europe shared certain features but differed from each other in significant ways. What were the major similarities and differences of kingship in England, France, and Iberia?
- How did the meaning and purposes of crusading change in the twelfth and thirteenth centuries?
- The growth of papal power made religion an important part of Christians' daily life in unprecedented ways, but how did it at the same time limit lay spirituality and the rights of non-Christians?
- Scholasticism was the method of teaching and learning fostered by medieval schools, but it was also a method of debating and resolving problems. How did scholasticism assist in the reconciliation of classical and Christian thought?
- Why did the meaning of chivalry change in the twelfth century? What new literary genres and art forms were fostered by courts, universities, and towns?

or not a direct line runs between the developments of this period and the world in which we live, many European nations look to these centuries for their origins and for the monuments of their cultural heritage. Magna Carta is still cited as a foundational document of English law and English constitutional monarchy. The territories united under the rule of the French kings still form the nation of France. The doctrines crystallized in medieval canon law and scholastic theology have become the core doctrines of the modern Roman Catholic Church, and devotion to the Virgin Mary is still central to the piety of millions. The religious orders that emerged to educate and curb a burgeoning medieval population continue their ministries. The daughter houses of medieval monastic orders continue to proliferate in lands unknown to medieval Europeans: Japan, Australia, New Zealand, and the Americas. Students still pursue the degrees first granted in medieval universities, and those who earn them wear the caps and gowns of medieval scholars. Meanwhile, poets aspire to the eloquence of troubadours, singers record the music of Hildegard, and Hollywood films are based on chivalric romances and the tragic love of Abelard and Heloise. It is difficult to tell where the Middle Ages end and the modern world begins.

## PEOPLE, IDEAS, AND EVENTS IN CONTEXT

- What was at stake in the clash between **HENRY II** of England and **THOMAS BECKET**?
- What was **MAGNA CARTA**? Why was it formulated? How did **PHILIP AUGUSTUS** consolidate royal authority in France? Why were the German emperors unable to do so?
- Why were the **CRUSADER STATES** short lived and fragile? How did the **RECONQUISTA** continue the Crusades?
- What were the main goals of **INNOCENT III**? How did the **FRANCISCANS** and the **DOMINICANS** advance his agenda?
- How do the **CULT OF THE VIRGIN** and the careers of **HILDEGARD OF BINGEN** and **HELOISE** exemplify the ideals and realities of women's roles in the Church?
- What is **SCHOLASTICISM**? How did **THOMAS AQUINUS** respond to the influence of Classical and Muslim philosophies?
- Why were **PETER ABELARD**'s teachings condemned by the Church? In what sense can he be considered the founder of the **UNIVERSITY OF PARIS**?
- How did noblewomen such as **ELEANOR OF AQUITAINE** contribute to the emergence of a new vernacular culture? What types of entertainment were characteristic of medieval cities?

## THINKING ABOUT CONNECTIONS

- The growth of towns, monarchies, and the Church increased the degree of control that those in power could exercise; yet this growth also increased access to education and new forms of social mobility. Is this a paradox, or are these two phenomena related?
- The U.S. Constitution is based on the legal principles and institutions that emerged in medieval England, but it also drew on Roman models. Which do you consider to be more influential, and why?
- Some historians have argued that the extent and methods of persecution discernible in the Middle Ages are unprecedented in the history of Western civilizations. How would you support or refute this thesis? For example, does the persecution of Jews in medieval Europe differ from their treatment under the neo-Assyrians and Chaldeans, or under the Roman Empire? Why or why not?

## STORY LINES

- The Mongol Empire widened channels of communication, commerce, and cultural exchange between Europe and the Far East. At the same time, Europeans were extending their reach into the Atlantic Ocean.

- Western civilizations' integration with this wider medieval world led to new ways of mapping, measuring, and describing that world.

- Despite these broadening horizons, most Europeans' lives were bounded by their communities and focused on the parish church.

- Meanwhile, the growing strength of the kings of France and England drew them into territorial disputes that led to the Hundred Years' War.

- As global climate change affected the ecosystems of Europe and caused years of famine, the integrated networks of the medieval world facilitated the rapid transmission of the Black Death.

## CHRONOLOGY

| | |
|---|---|
| 1206–1260 | Rapid expansion of the Mongol Empire under Genghis Khan and his heirs |
| 1240 | The territory of Rus' is dominated by the Mongols |
| | Mongol Khanate of the Golden Horde established |
| 1260–1294 | Reign of Kublai Khan, Great Khan, and emperor of China |
| 1271–1295 | Travels of Marco Polo |
| 1309 | "Babylonian Captivity" of the papacy in Avignon begins |
| 1315–1322 | The Great Famine in Europe |
| 1320 | The Declaration of Arbroath proclaims Scotland's independence from England |
| 1326–1354 | The travels of Ibn Battuta |
| 1337 | Beginning of the Hundred Years' War |
| 1347–1353 | Spread of the Black Death |
| 1352 | Circulation of Mandeville's *Book of Marvels* |

Before
You
Read
This
Chapter

# The Medieval World, 1250–1350

## CORE OBJECTIVES

- **DESCRIBE** the effects of the Mongol conquests.

- **IDENTIFY** the key characteristics of the medieval world system and the responses to it.

- **UNDERSTAND** the reasons for the papacy's loss of prestige and the rise of strong secular monarchs.

- **DEFINE** the concept of sovereignty and its importance.

- **EXPLAIN** the rapid spread of the Black Death in this historical context.

W hen Christopher Columbus set out to find a new trade route to the East, he carried with him two influential travel narratives written centuries before his voyage. One was *The Book of Marvels*, composed around 1350 and attributed to John de Mandeville, an English adventurer (writing in French) who claimed to have reached the far horizons of the globe. The other was Marco Polo's *Description of the World*, an account of that Venetian merchant's journey through the vast Eurasian realm of the Mongol Empire to the court of the Great Khan in China. He had dictated it to an author of popular romances around 1298, when both men (Marco Polo and his ghostwriter) were in prison—coincidentally, in Columbus's own city of Genoa. Both books were the product of an extraordinary era of unprecedented interactions among the peoples of Europe, Asia, and the interconnected Mediterranean world. And both became highly influential, inspiring generations of mercantile adventurers, ambitious pilgrims, and armchair travelers. Eventually, they would fuel the imaginations of those future mariners who launched a further age of discovery (see Chapter 12).

In many ways, these narratives were as fantastical as they were factual, making them problematic sources for historians. But they are representative of an era that seemed wide open to every sort of influence. This was a time when ease of communication and commercial exchange made Western civilizations part of an interlocking network that had the potential to span the globe. Although this network would prove fragile in the face of a large-scale demographic crisis, the Black Death, it created a lasting impression of infinite possibilities. Indeed, it was only *because* of this network's connective channels that the Black Death wreaked such devastation in the years around 1350. Looking back, we can see the century leading up to this near-worldwide crisis as the beginning of a new global age.

Europeans' integration with this widening world not only put them into contact with unfamiliar cultures and commodities but it also opened up new ways of looking at the world they already knew. Novel artistic and intellectual responses are discernible in this era, as are a host of new inventions and technologies. At the same time, involvement in this wider world placed new pressures on long-term developments within Europe, notably the growing tensions among large territorial monarchies, and between these secular powers and the authority of the papacy. By the early fourteenth century, the papal court was literally held hostage by the king of France. A few decades later, the king of England openly declared his own claim to the French throne. The ensuing struggles for sovereignty would have a profound impact on the balance of power in Europe, and further complicate Europeans' relationships with one another and with their far-flung neighbors.

# THE MONGOL EMPIRE AND THE REORIENTATION OF THE WEST

In our long-term survey of Western civilizations, we have frequently noted the existence of strong links between the Mediterranean world and the Far East. Trade along the network of trails known as the Silk Road can be traced far back into antiquity, and we have seen that such overland networks were extended by Europe's waterways and by the sea. But it was not until the late thirteenth century that Europeans were able to establish direct connections with India, China, and the so-called Spice Islands of the Indonesian archipelago. For Europeans, these connections would prove profoundly important, as much for their impact on the European imagination as for their economic significance. For the peoples of Asia, however, the more frequent appearance of Europeans was less consequential than the events that made these journeys possible: the rise of a new empire that encompassed the entire continent.

## The Expansion of the Mongol Empire

The Mongols were among many nomadic peoples inhabiting the vast steppes of Central Asia. Although closely connected with the Turkish populations with whom they frequently intermarried, the Mongols spoke their own distinctive language and had their own homeland, located to the north of the Gobi Desert in what is now known as Mongolia. Essentially, the Mongols were herdsmen whose daily lives and wealth depended on the sheep that provided shelter (sheepskin tents), woolen clothing, milk, and meat; but they were also highly accomplished horsemen and raiders. Indeed, it was to curtail their raiding ventures that the Chinese had fortified their Great Wall many centuries before. Primarily, though, China defended itself from the Mongols by attempting to ensure that the Mongols remained internally divided, with their energies turned against each other.

In the late twelfth century, however, a Mongol chief named Temujin (c. 1162–1227) began to unite the various tribes under his rule. He did so by incorporating the warriors of each defeated tribe into his own army, gradually building up a large and terrifyingly effective military force. In 1206, his supremacy over all these tribes was reflected in his new title: Genghis Khan (from the Mongol words meaning "universal ruler"). This new name also revealed his wider ambitions and, in 1209, Genghis Khan began to direct his enormous army against the Mongols' neighbors.

Taking advantage of the fact that China was then divided into three warring states, Genghis Khan launched an attack on the Chin Empire of the north and managed to penetrate deep into its interior by 1211. These initial attacks were probably looting expeditions rather than deliberate attempts at conquest, but their aims were soon sharpened under Genghis Khan's successors. Shortly after his death in 1227, a full-scale invasion of both northern and western China was under way. In 1234, these regions also fell to the Mongols. By 1279, one of Genghis Khan's numerous grandsons, Kublai Khan, would complete the conquest by adding southern China to the empire.

For the first time in centuries, China was reunited, although under Mongol rule. It was also connected to western and central Asia in ways unprecedented in its long history, because Genghis Khan had brought crucial commercial cities and the Silk Road trading posts (Tashkent, Samarkand, and Bukhara) into his empire. Building on

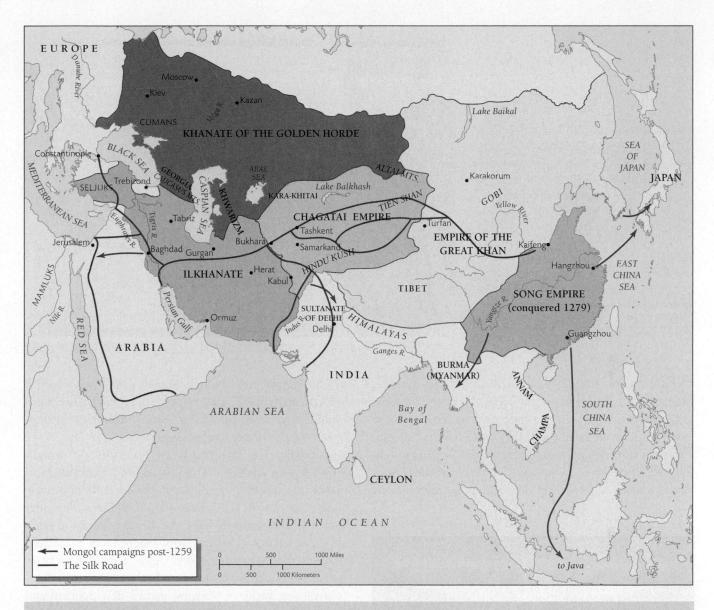

**THE STATES OF THE MONGOL EMPIRE.** Like Alexander's, Genghis Khan's empire was swiftly assembled and encompassed vast portions of Europe and Asia. ▪ *How many different Mongol khanates were there after 1260, when Kublai Khan came to power? Were these domains mapped onto older divisions within Western civilizations?* ▪ *How might the Mongol occupation of the Muslim world have aided the expansion of European trade?* ▪ *At the same time, why would it have complicated the efforts of crusader armies in the Holy Land?*

these achievements, one of his sons, Ögedei (*EHRG-uh-day*), laid plans for an even farther-reaching expansion of Mongol influence. Between 1237 and 1240, the Mongols under his command conquered the Rus' capital at Kiev and then launched a two-pronged assault directed at the rich lands of the European frontier. The smaller of the two Mongol armies swept through Poland toward Germany; the larger army went southwest toward Hungary. In April 1241, the smaller Mongol force met a hastily assembled army of Germans and Poles at the battle of Legnica in southern Poland, where the Mongols were driven back at the cost of many lives on both sides. Two days later, the larger Mongol army

annihilated the Hungarian army at the river Sajo. It could have moved even deeper into Europe after this important victory, but it withdrew when Ögedei Khan died in December of that year.

## Muscovy and the Mongol Khanate

As we have seen in previous chapters, the capital of Rus' at Kiev had fostered crucial diplomatic and trading relations with both western Europe and Byzantium, as well as

THE BATTLE OF LEGNICA, 1241. This image from a fourteenth-century chronicle shows heavily armored knights from Poland and Germany (on the right) confronting the swift-moving mounted archers of the Mongol cavalry (on the left). Mongol warriors often had the advantage over Europeans because their smaller, faster horses carried lighter loads and they could shoot down their opponents at long range. ▪ *Which army appears to be gaining the upper hand here?*

with the Islamic Caliphate at Baghdad. But that dynamic changed with the arrival of the Mongols, who shifted the locus of power from Kiev to their own settlement on the lower Volga River. From there, they extended their dominion over a vast terrain, stretching from the Black Sea to central Asia. It became known as the Khanate of the Golden Horde, a name that captures the striking impression made by the Mongol tents, which literally shone with wealth because many were hung with cloth of gold. (The word *horde* derives from the Mongol word meaning "encampment" and the related Turkish word *ordu*, "army.")

Initially, the Mongols ruled Rus' directly, installing their own administrative officials and requiring local princes to show their obedience to the Great Khan by traveling in person to the Mongol court in China. But after Kublai Khan's death in 1294, the Mongols began to tolerate the existence of several semi-independent principalities from which they demanded regular tribute. Kiev never recovered its dominant position, but one of these principalities, the duchy of Moscow, gained new political and economic prominence due to its strategic geographical location. Moscow became the tribute-collecting center for the Mongol Khanate, and so was supplied with resources to defend itself against attack. Its dukes were even encouraged to extend their lordship to neighboring territories in the region in order to increase its security. Eventually, the Muscovite dukes came to control the khanate's tax-collecting mechanisms. As a reflection of these extended powers, Duke Ivan I (r. 1325–1340) gained the title Grand Prince of Rus'. When the Mongol Empire began to disintegrate, the Muscovites were therefore in a strong position to supplant their former overlords.

A MONGOL ROBE IN CLOTH OF GOLD. The majestic term *Khanate of the Golden Horde* captures both the power and the splendor of the Mongol warriors who conquered Rus' and many other lands. The robe depicted here dates from the late thirteenth or early fourteenth century and was made from cloth of gold: silk woven with gold (and sometimes silver) thread, a precious but surprisingly durable material that was also used for banners and even tents. A robe similar to this one was sold at auction in 2011 for nearly a quarter of a million dollars.

## The Making of the Mongol Ilkhanate

As Ögedei Khan moved into the lands of Rus' and eastern Europe, Mongol armies were also sent to subdue the vast territory that had been encompassed by the former Persian Empire, then those by the empires of Alexander and Rome. Indeed, the strongest state in this region was known as the sultanate of Rûm (the Arabic word for "Rome"). This Sunni Muslim sultanate had been founded by the Seljuk Turks in 1077, just prior to the launching of the First Crusade, and consisted of Anatolian provinces formerly belonging to the eastern Roman Empire. It had successfully withstood waves of European crusading aggression while capitalizing on the further misfortunes of Byzantium, taking over several key ports on the Mediterranean and the Black Sea as well as cultivating a flourishing overland trade.

But in 1243, the Seljuks of Rûm were forced to surrender to the Mongols, who had already succeeded in occupying what is now Iraq, Iran, portions of Pakistan and Afghanistan, and the Christian kingdoms of Georgia and Armenia. Thereafter, the Mongols easily found their way into regions weakened by centuries of Muslim infighting and Christian crusading movements. Byzantium, as we noted in Chapter 9, had been fatally weakened by the Fourth Crusade. Constantinople was now controlled by the Venetians, and Byzantine successor states centered on Nicaea (in Anatolia) and Epirus (in northern Greece) were hanging on by their fingertips. The capitulation of Rûm left remaining Byzantine possessions in Anatolia without a buffer, and most of these were absorbed by the Mongols.

In 1261, emperor Michael VIII Paleologus (r. 1259–1282) managed to regain control of Constantinople and its immediate hinterland, but the depleted empire he ruled was ringed by hostile neighbors. The crusader principality of Antioch, which had been founded in 1098, finally succumbed to the Mongols in 1268. The Mongols themselves were halted in their drive toward Palestine only by the Mamluk Sultanate of Egypt, established in 1250 and

**THE MONGOL RULER OF MUSLIM PERSIA, HIS CHRISTIAN QUEEN, AND HIS JEWISH HISTORIAN.** Hulagu Khan (1217–1265) was a grandson of Genghis and a brother of Kublai. He consolidated Persia and its neighboring regions into the Ilkhanate. This image shows him with his wife, Dokuz Khatun, who was a Turkic princess and a Christian. It comes from the *Compendium of Chronicles* by Rashid al-Din (1247–1318), a Jewish convert to Islam, whose work exemplifies the pluralistic culture encouraged by Mongol rule: written in Persian and often translated into Arabic, it embeds the achievements of the Mongol ruler within the long history of Islam. ■ *Why would Rashid al-Din have wanted to place the new Mongol dynasty in this historical context?*

ruled by a powerful military caste of non-Arab Muslims. The name of this dynasty reflects the fact that its founders were originally Turkic slaves (in Arabic, *mamlūk* means "an enslaved person").

All of these disparate territories came to be called the Ilkhanate, the "subordinate khanate," meaning that its Mongol rulers paid deference to the Great Khan. The first Ilkhan was Hulagu, a brother of China's Kublai Khan. His descendants would rule this realm for another eighty years, eventually converting to Islam but remaining hostile toward the Mamluk Muslims, who were their chief rivals.

## The Pax Mongolica and Its Price

Although the Mongols' expansion of power into Europe had been checked, their combined conquests made them masters of lands that stretched from the Black Sea to the Pacific Ocean: one-fifth of the earth's surface, the largest land empire in history. No single Mongol ruler's power was absolute within this domain. Kublai Khan (1260–1294), who took the additional title *khagan* (or "Great Khan"), never claimed to rule all the Mongol khanates directly. In his own domain of China and Mongolia, his power was highly centralized and built on the intricate (and ancient) imperial bureaucracy of China; but elsewhere, Mongol governance was directed at securing a steady tribute payment from subject peoples, which meant that local rulers could retain much of their power.

This distribution of authority made Mongol rule flexible and adaptable to local conditions, and in this, it resembled the Persian Empire (see Chapter 3) and also could be regarded as building on Hellenistic and Roman examples. But if their empire resembled those of antiquity in some respects, the Mongol khans differed from most contemporary European rulers in that they were highly tolerant of

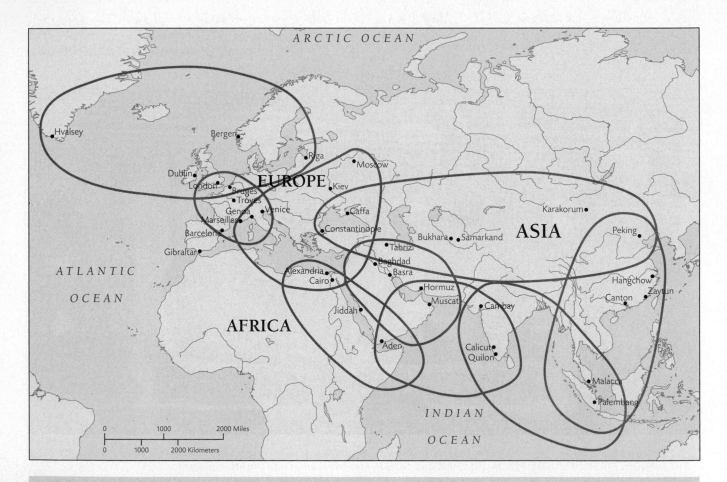

**THE MEDIEVAL WORLD SYSTEM, c. 1300.** At the turn of the fourteenth century, Western civilizations were more closely connected to each other and to the rest of the world than ever before: waterways and overland routes stretched from Greenland to the Pacific coast of Southeast Asia. ▪ *How did Europe's relationship with its neighbors change as a result of its integration into this wider world?* ▪ *How were seemingly marginal territories (such as Rus' or Hungary, Scotland, or Norway) central to one or more interlocking components of this system?*

all religious beliefs. This was an advantage in governing peoples who observed an array of Buddhist, Christian, and Muslim practices, not to mention Hindus, Jews, and the many itinerant groups and individuals whose languages and beliefs reflected a melding of many cultures.

This acceptance of cultural and religious difference, alongside the Mongols' encouragement of trade and love of rich things, created ideal conditions for some merchants and artists. Hence, the term *Pax Mongolica* ("Mongol Peace") is often used to describe the century from 1250 to 1350, a period in many ways analogous to the one fostered by the Roman Empire at its greatest extent (Chapter 5). No such term should be taken at face value, however, because this peace was bought at a great price. Indeed, the artists whose varied talents created the gorgeous textiles, utensils, and illuminated books prized by the Mongols were not all willing participants in a peaceful process. Many were captives or slaves subject to ruthless relocation. The Mongols would often transfer entire families and communities of craftsmen from one part of the empire to another, directly and indirectly encouraging a fantastic blend of artistic techniques, materials, and motifs. The result was an intensive period of cultural exchange that might combine Chinese, Persian, Venetian, and Hungarian influences (among many others) in a single work of art. These objects encapsulate the many legacies of the Mongols' empire.

The Mongol Peace was also achieved at the expense of many flourishing Muslim cities that were devastated or crippled during the bloody process of Mongol expansion—cities that had preserved the heritage of even older civilizations. The city of Heràt, situated in one of Afghanistan's few fertile valleys and described by the Persian poet Rumi as the "pearl in the oyster," was entirely destroyed by Genghis Khan in 1221 and did not fully recover for centuries. Baghdad, the splendid capital of the Abbasid Caliphate and a haven for artists and intellectuals since the eighth century (Chapter 8), was savagely besieged and sacked by the Mongols in 1258. Amid many other atrocities, the capture of the city resulted in the destruction of the House of Wisdom, the library and research center where Muslim scientists, philosophers, and translators preserved classical knowledge and advanced cutting-edge scholarship in such fields as mathematics, engineering, and medicine.

Baghdad's destruction is held to mark the end of Islam's golden age, since the establishment of the Mongol Ilkhanate in Persia eradicated a continuous zone of Muslim influence that had blended cultures stretching from southern Spain and North Africa to India.

## Bridging East and West

To facilitate the movement of people and goods within their empire, the Mongols began to control the caravan routes that led from the Mediterranean and the Black Sea through Central Asia and into China, policing bandits and making conditions safer for travelers. They also encouraged and streamlined trade by funneling many exchanges through the Persian city of Tabriz, on which both land and sea routes from China converged. These measures accelerated and intensified the possible contacts between the Far East and the West. Prior to Mongol control, such commercial networks had been inaccessible to most European merchants. The Silk Road was not so much a highway as a tangle of trails and trading posts, with few outsiders who understood its workings. Now travelers at both ends of the route found their way smoothed.

Among the first travelers from the West were Franciscan missionaries whose journeys were bankrolled by

**VENETIAN AMBASSADORS TO THE GREAT KHAN.** Around 1270, the Venetian merchant brothers Niccolò and Matteo Polo returned to Europe after their first prolonged journey through the empire of the Great Khan, bearing with them an official letter to the Roman pope. This image, from a manuscript of Marco Polo's *Description of the World*, shows his father and uncle at the moment of their arrival in the Great Khan's court, to which they have seemingly brought a Christian cross and a Bible. ▪ *Knowing what you've learned about the Mongols and the medieval world, do you think it is plausible that the Polo brothers would have carried these items with them?*

# Competing Viewpoints

## Two Travel Accounts

> Two of the books that influenced Christopher Columbus and his contemporaries were travel narratives describing the exotic worlds that lay beyond Europe—worlds that may or may not have existed as they are described. The first excerpt below is taken from the account dictated by Marco Polo of Venice in 1298. The young Marco had traveled overland from Constantinople to the court of Kublai Khan in the early 1270s, together with his father and uncle. He became a gifted linguist and remained at the Mongol court until the early 1290s, when he returned to Europe after a journey through Southeast Asia and Indonesia, and across the Indian Ocean. The second excerpt is from the Book of Marvels, attributed to John de Mandeville. This is an almost entirely fictional account of wonders that also became a source for European ideas about Southeast Asia. This particular passage concerns a legendary Christian figure named Prester ("Priest") John, who is alleged to have traveled to the East and became a great ruler.

### Marco Polo's Description of Java

Departing from Ziamba, and steering between south and south-east, fifteen hundred miles, you reach an island of very great size, named Java. According to the reports of some well-informed navigators, it is the greatest in the world, and has a compass above three thousand miles. It is under the dominion of one king only, nor do the inhabitants pay tribute to any other power. They are worshipers of idols.

The country abounds with rich commodities. Pepper, nutmegs, spikenard, galangal, cubebs, cloves and all the other valuable spices and drugs, are the produce of the island; which occasion it to be visited by many ships laden with merchandise, that yields to the owners considerable profit.

The quantity of gold collected there exceeds all calculation and belief. From thence it is that . . . merchants . . . have imported, and to this day import, that metal to a great amount, and from thence also is obtained the greatest part of the spices that are distributed throughout the world. That the Great Khan [Kublai] has not brought the island under subjection to him, must be attributed to the length of the voyage and the dangers of the navigation.

Source: *The Travels of Marco Polo*, trans. William Marsden, rev. and ed. Manuel Komroff (New York, 1926), pp. 267–68.

### John de Mandeville's Description of Prester John

This emperor Prester John has great lands and has many noble cities and good towns in his realm and many great, large islands. For all the country of India is separated into islands by the great floods that come from Paradise, that divide the land into many parts. And also in the sea he has many islands. . . .

European rulers. In 1253, the friar William of Rubruck was sent by King Louis IX of France as his ambassador to the Mongol court, with letters of introduction and instructions to make a full report of his findings. Merchants quickly followed. The most famous are three Venetians: the brothers Niccolò and Matteo Polo, and Niccolò's son, Marco (1254–1324). Marco Polo's account of his travels (which began when he was seventeen) includes a report of his twenty-year sojourn in the service of Kublai Khan, and the story of his journey home through the Spice Islands, India, and Persia. As we noted above, this book had an enormous effect on the European imagination; Christopher Columbus's copy still survives.

Even more impressive in scope than Marco's travels are those of the Muslim adventurer Ibn Battuta (1304–1368), who left his native Morocco in 1326 to go on the sacred pilgrimage to Mecca—but then kept going. By the time he returned home in 1354, he had been to China and

This Prester John has under him many kings and many islands and many varied people of various conditions. And this land is full good and rich, but not so rich as is the land of the Great Khan. For the merchants do not come there so commonly to buy merchandise as they do in the land of the Great Khan, for it is too far to travel to. . . .

[Mandeville then goes on to describe the difficulties of reaching Prester John's lands by sea.]

This emperor Prester John always takes as his wife the daughter of the Great Khan, and the Great Khan in the same way takes to wife the daughter of Prester John. For these two are the greatest lords under the heavens.

In the land of Prester John there are many diverse things, and many precious stones so great and so large that men make them into vessels such as platters, dishes, and cups. And there are many other marvels there that it would be too cumbrous and too long to put into the writing of books. But of the principal islands and of his estate and of his law I shall tell you some part.

This emperor Prester John is Christian and a great part of his country is

Christian also, although they do not hold to all the articles of our faith as we do. . . .

And he has under him 72 provinces, and in every province there is a king. And these kings have kings under them, and all are tributaries to Prester John.

And he has in his lordships many great marvels. For in his country is the sea that men call the Gravelly Sea, that is all gravel and sand without any drop of water. And it ebbs and flows in great waves as other seas do, and it is never still. . . . And a three-day journey from that sea there are great mountains out of which flows a great flood that comes out of Paradise. And it is full of precious stones without any drop of water. . . .

He dwells usually in the city of Susa [in Persia]. And there is his principal palace, which is so rich and so noble that no one will believe the report unless he has seen it. And above the chief tower of the palace there are two round pommels of gold and in each of them are two great, large rubies that shine full brightly upon the night. And the principal gates of his palace are of a precious stone that men call sardonyxes [a type of onyx], and the frames and the bars are made of ivory. And the windows of the halls and cham-

bers are of crystal. And the tables upon which men eat, some are made of emeralds, some of amethyst, and some of gold full of precious stones. And the legs that hold up the tables are made of the same precious stones. . . .

Source: *Mandeville's Travels*, ed. M. C. Seymour (Oxford: 1967), pp. 195–99 (language modernized from Middle English by R. C. Stacey).

## Questions for Analysis

1. What does Marco Polo want his readers to know about Java, and why? What does this suggest about the interests of these intended readers?

2. What does Mandeville want his readers to know about Prester John and his domains? Why are these details so important?

3. Which of these accounts seems more trustworthy, and why? Even if we cannot accept one or both at face value, what insight do they give us into the expectations of Columbus and the other European adventurers who relied on these accounts?

sub-Saharan Africa, as well as to the ends of both the Muslim and Mongolian worlds: a journey of over 75,000 miles.

The window of opportunity that made such journeys possible was relatively narrow, however. By the middle of the fourteenth century, hostilities among and within various components of the Mongol Empire were making travel along the Silk Road perilous. The Mongols of the Ilkhanate, who dominated the ancient trade routes that ran through Persia, came into conflict with merchants from Genoa, who controlled trade

at the western ends of the Silk Road, especially in the transport depot of Tabriz. Mounting pressures finally forced the Genoese to abandon Tabriz, thereby breaking one of the major links in the commercial chain forged by the Mongol Peace. Then, in 1346, the Mongols of the Golden Horde besieged the Genoese colony at Caffa on the Black Sea. This event simultaneously disrupted trade while becoming a conduit for the Black Death, which passed from the Mongol army to the Genoese defenders, who returned with it to Italy (see below).

Over the next few decades, the European economy would struggle to overcome the devastating effects of the massive depopulation caused by the plague, which made recovery from these setbacks slower and harder. In the meantime, in 1368, the last Mongol rulers of China were overthrown, and most Westerners were now denied access to its borders; the remaining Mongol warriors were restricted to cavalry service in the imperial armies of the new Ming dynasty. The conditions that had fostered an integrated trans-Eurasian cultural and commercial network were no longer sustainable. Yet the view of the world that had been fostered by Mongol rule continued to exercise a lasting influence. European memories of the Far East would be preserved and embroidered, and the dream of reestablishing close connections between Europe and China would survive to influence a new round of commercial and imperial expansion in the centuries to come.

## THE EXTENSION OF EUROPEAN COMMERCE AND SETTLEMENT

Western civilizations' increased access to the riches of the Far East during the Pax Mongolica ran parallel to a number of ventures that were extending Europeans' presence in the Mediterranean and beyond. These endeavors were both mercantile and colonial, and in many cases resulted in the control of strategic trade routes or islands by representatives of a single adventurous state.

The language of crusading, with which we have become familiar, now came to be applied to these economic and political initiatives, whose often violent methods could be justified on the grounds that they were supporting papally sanctioned Christian causes. To take one prominent example, the strategic goal of the crusades that targeted North Africa in this era was to cut the economic lifelines that supported Muslim settlements in the Holy Land. Yet the only people who stood to gain from this were the merchants who dreamed of controlling the commercial routes that ran through Egypt, not only those that connected North Africa to the Silk Road but also the conduits of the sub-Saharan gold trade.

### The Quest for African Gold

European commerce in African gold was not new. It had been going on for centuries, facilitated by Muslim traders whose caravans brought a steady supply from the Niger River to the North African ports of Algiers and Tunis. In the early thirteenth century, rival bands of merchants from Catalonia and Genoa had established trading colonies in Tunis to expedite this process, exchanging woolen cloth from northern Europe for both North African grain and sub-Saharan gold.

But the medieval demand for gold accelerated during the late thirteenth and fourteenth centuries and could not be met by these established trading relationships. The luxuries coveted by Europeans were now too costly to be bought solely with bulk goods, which were, in any case, a cumbersome medium of exchange. Although precious textiles (usually silk) were a form of wealth the Mongols valued, the burgeoning economy of the medieval world demanded a reliable and abundant supply of more portable currency. For a long time, the rich silver mines of Poland and Bohemia had enabled the circulation of coinage in Europe and had furnished the means for rulers in Rus' to pay the tributes due to the Mongols. But silver production dropped markedly during the 1340s, as European engineers reached the limits of their technological capacity to extract ore from ever deeper mines; and this depletion of sources of silver could lead to a serious cash-flow problem.

Gold was therefore an obvious alternative currency for large transactions, and in the thirteenth century some European rulers began minting gold coins. But Europe itself had few natural gold reserves, and so maintaining and expanding these currencies required new sources of gold. The most obvious source was Africa, especially Mali and Ghana—which was called the "Land of Gold" by Muslim geographers.

### Models of Mediterranean Colonization: Catalonia, Genoa, and Venice

The heightened European interest in the African gold trade, which engaged the seafaring merchants of Genoa and Catalonia in particular, coincided with these merchants' creation of entrepreneurial empires in the western Mediterranean. During the thirteenth century, Catalan adventurers conquered and colonized a series of western Mediterranean islands, including Majorca, Ibiza, Minorca, Sardinia, and Sicily. Except in Sicily, which already had a large and diverse population that included many Christians (Chapter 8), the pattern of Catalan conquest was largely the same on all these islands: expulsion or extermination of the existing population, usually Muslim; the extension of economic concessions to attract new settlers; and a heavy reliance on slave labor to produce food-stuffs and raw materials for export.

These Catalan colonial efforts were mainly carried out by private individuals or companies operating under royal charters; the state did not actively sponsor them. They therefore contrast strongly with the established colonial practices of the Venetian maritime empire, whose strategic ventures were focused mainly on the eastern Mediterranean, where the Venetians dominated the trade in spices and silks. Venetian colonies were administered directly by the city's rulers or by their appointed colonial governors. These colonies included long-settled civilizations such as Greece, Cyprus, and the cities of the Dalmatian coast, meaning that Venetian administration laid just another layer on top of many other economic, cultural, and political structures.

The Genoese, to take yet another case, also had extensive interests in the western Mediterranean, where they traded bulk goods such as cloth, hides, grain, timber, and sugar. They too established trading colonies, but these tended to consist of family networks that were closely integrated with the peoples among whom they lived, whether in North Africa, Spain, or the shores of the Black Sea.

**THE CHURCH AT HVALSEY, GREENLAND.** Located on the southern tip of Greenland, Hvalsey was originally a farmstead established in the late tenth century by the uncle of Eirik the Red, father of the explorer Leif Eiriksson. The church at Hvalsey, pictured here, was built in the twelfth century and was roofed with turf. It was the site of the last documented event in the history of Norse settlement on the island: a wedding that took place in 1408. By that time, the population had largely died out due to starvation and disease.

## From the Mediterranean to the Atlantic

For centuries, European maritime commerce had been divided between this Mediterranean world and a very different northeastern Atlantic world, which encompassed northern France, the Low Countries, the British Isles, and Scandinavia. Starting around 1270, however, Italian merchants began to sail through the Straits of Gibraltar and on up to the wool-producing regions of England and the Low Countries. This was a step toward the extension of Mediterranean patterns of commerce and colonization into the Atlantic Ocean. Another step was the discovery (or possibly the rediscovery) of the Atlantic island chains known as the Canaries and the Azores, which Genoese sailors reached in the fourteenth century.

Efforts to colonize the Canary Islands, and to convert and enslave their inhabitants, began almost immediately.

Eventually, the Canaries would become the focus of a new wave of colonial settlement sponsored by the Portuguese, and the base for Portuguese voyages down the west coast of Africa. They would also be the jumping-off point from which Christopher Columbus would sail westward across the Atlantic Ocean in the hope of reaching Asia (see Chapter 12).

There was also a significant European colonial presence in the northern Atlantic, and had been for centuries. Viking settlers had begun to colonize Greenland in the late tenth century, and had established a settlement in a place they called Vinland (the coast of Newfoundland in present-day Canada) around 1000. According to the sagas that tell the story of these explorations, written down in the late twelfth and thirteenth centuries, a band of adventurers led by Leif Eiriksson had intended to set up a permanent colony there. Numerous expeditions resulted in the construction of houses, a fortification, and even attempts to domesticate livestock transported from Scandinavia. Yet North America did not become home to a permanent European population at this time; the sagas report that relations with indigenous peoples were fraught, and there may have been other factors hindering settlement.

However, Norse settlers did build a viable community on Greenland, which eventually formed part of the kingdom of Norway. This was facilitated by the warming of the earth's climate between 800 and 1300—the same phenomenon that partly enabled the agricultural revolution discussed in Chapter 8. For several centuries, these favorable climatic conditions made it possible to sustain some farming activities on the southern coastline of that huge island, supplemented by fishing, hunting, and foraging. But with the gradual cooling of the climate in the fourteenth century, which caused famines even in the rich farmlands of Europe, this fragile ecosystem was gradually eroded and the Greenlanders died out.

# WAYS OF KNOWING AND DESCRIBING THE WORLD

The success of European commercial and colonial expansion in this era both drove and depended on significant innovations in measuring and mapping. It also coincided with intellectual, literary, and artistic initiatives that aimed to capture and describe the workings of this wider world, and to imagine its celestial (or infernal) counterparts.

## Economic Tools: Balance Sheets, Banks, Charts, and Clocks

The economic boom that resulted from the integration of European and Asian commerce called for the refinement of existing business models and accounting techniques. New forms of partnership and the development of insurance contracts helped to minimize the risks associated with long-distance trading. Double-entry bookkeeping, widely used in Italy by the mid-fourteenth century, gave merchants a much clearer picture of their profits and losses by ensuring that both credits and debits were clearly laid out in parallel columns, a practice that facilitated the balancing of accounts. The Medici family of Florence established branches of its bank in each of the major cities of Europe and were careful that the failure of one would not bankrupt the entire firm as earlier branch-banking arrangements had done. Banks also experimented with advanced credit techniques borrowed from Muslim and Jewish financiers, allowing their clients to transfer funds without any real money changing hands—and without endangering their capital by carrying it with them. Such transfers were carried out by written receipts, the direct ancestors of the check, money order, and currency transfer.

Other late medieval technologies kept pace in different ways with the demands for increased efficiency and accuracy. Eyeglasses, first invented in the 1280s, were perfected in the fourteenth century, extending the careers of those who made a living by reading, writing, and accounting. The use of the magnetic compass helped ships sail farther away from land, making longer-distance Atlantic voyages possible for the first time. And as more and more mariners began to sail waters less familiar to them, pilots began to make and use special charts that mapped the locations of ports; called *portolani*, these charts also took note of prevailing winds, potential routes, good harbors, and known perils.

Among the many implements of modern daily life invented in this era, the most familiar are clocks. Mechanical clocks came into use shortly before 1300 and proliferated immediately thereafter. They were too large and expensive for private purchase, but towns vied with each other to install them in prominent public buildings, thus advertising municipal wealth and good governance. Mechanical

**DEVIL WITH EYEGLASSES.** Spectacles were most commonly worn by those who made a living by reading and writing, notably bureaucrats and lawyers. In this conceptualization of hell, the devil charged with keeping track of human sins wears eyeglasses. ▪ *What might this image reveal about popular attitudes toward record keeping and the growing legal and administrative bureaucracies of the later Middle Ages?*

**PORTOLAN CHART.** Accurate mapping was essential to the success of maritime colonial ventures in the thirteenth and fourteenth centuries. The chart shown here is the oldest surviving example of a map used by mariners to navigate between Mediterranean ports (the word *portolan* is the term for such charts). It dates from the end of the thirteenth century, and its shape clearly indicates that it was made from an animal hide. Although parchment was extremely durable, it would slowly have worn away due to prolonged exposure to salt water and other elements—hence the rarity of this early example.

timekeeping had two profound effects. One was the further stimulation of interest in complex machinery of all sorts, an interest already awakened by the widespread use of mills in the eleventh and twelfth centuries (see Chapter 8).

Another, more significant outcome, was the way that clocks regulated daily life. Until the advent of clocks, time was flexible. Although days had been *theoretically* divided into hours, minutes, and seconds since the time of the Sumerians (Chapter 1), people never had a way of mapping these temporal measurements onto an actual day. Now, clocks relentlessly divided time into exact units, giving rise to new expectations about labor and productivity. People were expected to start and end work "on time," to make the most of the time spent at work, and even to equate time with money. Like the improvements in bookkeeping, time-keeping made some kinds of work more efficient, but it also created new tensions and anxieties.

## Knowledge of the World and of God

In the mid-thirteenth century, Thomas Aquinas had constructed a theological view of the world as rational, organized, and comprehensible to the inquiring human mind (Chapter 9). But confidence in this picture began to wane during the fourteenth century, even before the Black Death posed a new challenge to it. Philosophers such as William of Ockham (d. c. 1348), an English member of the Franciscan order, denied that human reason could prove fundamental theological truths such as the existence of God. He

argued that human knowledge of God—and hence, salvation—depends entirely on what God himself has chosen to reveal through scripture, and urged humans to investigate the natural world and better understand its laws—without positing any necessary connection between the observable properties of nature and the unknowable essence of divinity.

This philosophical position, known as nominalism, had its roots in the philosophy of Plato (see Chapter 4) and has had an enormous impact on modern thought. The nominalists' distinction between the rational comprehensibility of the real world and the spiritual incomprehensibility of God encourages investigation of nature without reference to supernatural explanations: one of the most important foundations of the modern scientific method (see Chapter 16). Nominalism also encourages empirical observation, since it posits that knowledge of the world should rest on sensory experience rather than abstract theories. The philosophical principles laid down by these observers of the medieval world are thus fundamental to modern science.

## Creating God's World in Art

Just as a fascination with the natural world informed developments in medieval science, the artists of this era were paying close attention to the way plants, animals, and human beings really looked. Carvings of leaves and flowers were increasingly made from direct observation and are clearly recognizable to modern botanists as distinct species. Statues of humans also became more realistic in their portrayals of facial expressions and bodily proportions. According to a story in circulation around 1290, a sculptor working on a likeness of the German emperor allegedly made a hurried return trip to study his subject's face a second time, because he had heard that a new wrinkle had appeared on the emperor's brow.

This trend toward naturalism extended to manuscript illumination and painting as well. The latter was, to a large extent, a new art. As we saw in Chapter 1, wall paintings are among the oldest forms of artistic expression in human history, and throughout antiquity and the Middle Ages artists had decorated the walls of public and private buildings with frescoes (paintings executed on "fresh," wet plaster). Italian artists in the thirteenth century began to adapt the techniques used by icon painters in Byzantium, making freestanding pictures on pieces of wood or canvas using tempera (pigments mixed with water and natural gums) in addition to frescoes. Because these altarpieces, devotional

## Vikings Encounter the Natives of North America

*Although Norse voyagers had explored and settled the coast of Newfoundland around the year 1000, written accounts of these exploits were not made or widely circulated until the thirteenth century. The excerpt below comes from one of these narrative histories, the* Grænlendinga Saga *(Greenlanders' Saga). Its hero is Thorfinn Karlsefni, a Norwegian adventurer who arrives in Greenland and marries Gudrid, the twice-widowed sister-in-law of the explorer Leif Eiriksson. Leif had established the original colony of Vinland but had since returned to Greenland.*

here was still the same talk about Vinland voyages as before, and everyone, including [his wife] Gudrid, kept urging Karlsefni to make the voyage. In the end he decided to sail and gathered a company of sixty men and five women. He made an agreement with his crew that everyone should share equally in whatever profits the expedition might yield. They took livestock of all kinds, for they intended to make a permanent settlement there if possible.

Karlsefni asked Leif if he could have the houses in Vinland; Leif said that he was willing to lend them, but not to give them away.

They put to sea and arrived safe and sound at Leif's houses and carried their hammocks ashore. Soon they had plenty of good supplies, for a fine big rorqual* was driven ashore; they went down and cut it up, and so there was no shortage of food.

The livestock were put out to grass, and soon the male beasts became very frisky and difficult to manage. They had brought a bull with them.

Karlsefni ordered timber to be felled and cut into lengths for a cargo for the ship, and it was left out on a rock to season. They made use of all the natural resources of the country that were available, grapes and game of all kinds and other produce.

The first winter passed into summer, and then they had their first encounter with Skrælings,† when a great number of them came out of the wood one day. The cattle were grazing near by and the bull began to bellow and roar with great vehemence. This terrified the Skrælings and they fled, carrying their packs which contained furs and sables and pelts of all kinds. They made for Karlsefni's houses and tried to get inside, but Karlsefni had the doors barred against them. Neither side could understand the other's language.

Then the Skrælings put down their packs and opened them up and offered their contents, preferably in exchange for weapons; but Karlsefni forbade his men to sell arms. Then he hit on the idea of telling the women to carry milk out to the Skrælings, and when the Skrælings saw the milk they wanted to buy nothing else. And so the outcome of their trading expedition was that the Skrælings carried their purchases away in their bellies, and left their packs and furs with Karlsefni and his men.

After that, Karlsefni ordered a strong wooden palisade to be erected round the houses, and they settled in.

images, and portraits were portable, they were also more commercial. As long as artists could afford the necessary materials, they did not have to wait for specific commissions. This meant that they had more freedom to choose their subject matter and to put an individual stamp on their work—one of the reasons that we know the names of many more artists from this era.

One of these, Giotto di Bondone of Florence (c. 1267–1337), painted both walls and portable wooden panels. Like some of his contemporaries, Giotto (*gee-OHT-toh*) was preeminently an imitator of nature. Not only do his human beings and animals look lifelike, they seem to do natural things. When Christ enters Jerusalem on Palm Sunday, boys climb trees to get a better view; when Saint Francis is laid out in death, someone checks to see whether he has really received the *stigmata* (the marks of Christ's wounds); and when the Virgin's parents, Joachim and Anna, meet after a long separation, they embrace and kiss one another tenderly. Although many of the artists who came after Giotto moved away from naturalism, this style would become the norm by 1400. It is for this reason that Giotto is often regarded as the first painter of the Renaissance (see Chapter 11).

About this time Karlsefni's wife, Gudrid, gave birth to a son, and he was named Snorri.

Early next winter the Skrælings returned, in much greater numbers this time, bringing with them the same kind of wares as before. Karlsefni told the women, "You must carry out to them the same produce that was most in demand last time, and nothing else." . . .

[B]ut a Skræling was killed by one of Karlsefni's men for trying to steal some weapons. The Skrælings fled as fast as they could, leaving their clothing and wares behind . . .

"Now we must devise a plan," said Karlsefni, "for I expect they will pay us a third visit, and this time with hostility and in greater numbers. This is what we must do: ten men are to go out on the headland here and make themselves conspicuous, and the rest of us are to go into the wood and make a clearing there, where we can keep our cattle when the Skrælings come out of the forest. We shall take our bull and keep him to the fore."

The place where they intended to have their encounter with the Skrælings had the lake on one side and the woods on the other.

Karlsefni's plan was put into effect, and the Skrælings came right to the place that Karlsefni had chosen for the battle. The fighting began, and many of the Skrælings were killed. There was one tall and handsome man among the Skrælings and Karlsefni reckoned that he must be their leader. One of the Skrælings had picked up an axe, and after examining it for a moment he swung it at a man standing beside him, who fell dead at once. The tall man then took hold of the axe, looked at it for a moment, and then threw it as far as he could out into the water. Then the Skrælings fled into the forest as fast as they could, and that was the end of the encounter.

Karlsefni and his men spent the whole winter there, but in the spring he announced that he had no wish to stay there any longer and wanted to return to Greenland. They made ready for the voyage and took with them much valuable produce, vines and grapes and pelts. They put to sea and reached Eiriksfjord safely and spent the winter there.

* A kind of whale, the largest species of which is a blue whale.

† A Norse word meaning "savages," applied to the different indigenous peoples of Greenland and of North America.

Source: Magnus Magnusson and Herman Palsson, *The Vinland Sagas: The Norse Discovery of America* (Penguin, 1965), pp. 65–67.

## Questions for Analysis

1. What policies did the Norse settlers adopt toward the native peoples they encountered on the coast of New-foundland? How effective were they?

2. Knowing their extensive preparations for colonization and the success of their early efforts, why do you think Karlsefni and his companions abandoned their settlement in North America? Can you find clues in the text?

3. Compare this encounter with the sources describing other interactions between Europeans and the indigenous inhabitants of the New World after 1492 (see Chapters 12 and 14). How do you account for any similarities? What are some key differences?

## A Vision of the World We Cannot See

An exact contemporary of Giotto's had a different way of capturing the spiritual world in a naturalistic way, and he worked in a different medium. Dante Alighieri (1265–1321) of Florence pioneered what he called a "sweet new style" of poetry in his native tongue, which was now so different from the Latin of antiquity that it had become a language in its own right. Yet, as a scholar and devotee of classical Latin verse, Dante also strove to make this Italian vernacular an instrument for serious political and social critique. His great work, known in his own day as the *Comedy* (called the *Divine Comedy* by later admirers) was composed during the years he spent in exile from his beloved city, after the political party he supported was ousted from power in 1301.

The *Comedy* describes the poet's imaginary journey through hell, purgatory, and paradise; a journey that begins in a "dark wood," a metaphor for the personal and political crises that threatened Dante's faith and livelihood. In the poem, the narrator is led out of this forest and through the first two realms (hell and purgatory) by the Roman

# Interpreting Visual Evidence

## Seals: Signs of Identity and Authority

**F**or much of human history, applying a seal to a document was the way to certify its legality and identify the people who had ratified it. During antiquity and the early Middle Ages, those people were only powerful men—kings, bishops, heads of monasteries—and occasionally powerful women. But as participation in documentary practices became more and more common, seals were increasingly used by corporations (such as universities and crusading orders), towns, and many individuals. The devices (images) and legends (writing) on these seals were carefully chosen to capture central attributes of their owners' personalities or status. A seal was made by pressing a deeply incised lead matrix onto hot wax or resin, which would quickly dry to form a durable impression. The images reproduced here are later engravings that make the features of the original seals easier to see.

**A. Seal of the town of Dover, 1281.** Dover has long been one of the busiest and most important port cities of England because of its strategic proximity to France; indeed, the Dover Strait that separates this town from Calais, just across the English Channel, is only twenty-one miles wide. In 1281, when this seal was used, ferries and other ships like the one depicted here made this crossing several times a day. The legend around the edges of the seal reads (in Latin) "Seal of the commune of barons of Dover." It reflects the high status accorded to the free men of Dover by the English crown: because of their crucial role in the economy and defense of the kingdom, they were considered a corporate body and entitled to representation in Parliament alongside individual barons.

**B. Personal seal of Charles II, king of Naples and Sicily, 1289.** Charles II (b. 1254; r. 1285–1309) was the son and heir of Charles of Anjou, who became King Charles I of Sicily in 1266 and died in 1285. This means that Charles II had succeeded his father and had reigned as king for four years before he used this seal to ratify an agreement to his daughter's marriage in 1289. Yet the seal shown here was clearly made for him when he was a young man—probably when he was first knighted. It depicts him as count of Anjou (see the heraldic fleurs-de-lys, a lily representing the French monarchy) and gives him his other princely titles, including "Son of King Charles of Sicily." Although he was thirty-five years old, a king in his own right, and a father, he was still using this older seal!

## Questions for Analysis

**1.** Medieval towns represented themselves in a variety of ways on their seals: sometimes showing a group portrait of town councilors, sometimes a local saint, sometimes a heraldic beast, and sometimes distinctive architectural features. Why would Dover choose this image? What messages does this seal convey?

**2.** Think carefully about the mystery of Charles II's seal. Usually, an important agreement such as a marriage contract (with the son of the French king, no less!) would have carried a king's official, royal seal. What are all the possible reasons that Charles would still have been using this outdated seal? What are the possible ramifications of this choice? In your role as historian-detective, how would you go about solving this mystery?

**3.** The seals of medieval women were almost always shaped like almonds (pointed ovals; the technical term is *vesica-shaped*). Yet Ingeborg's seal is round, like the seals of men and corporations. Why might that be the case?

**4.** In general, what is the value of seals for the study of history? What are the various ways in which they function as sources?

**C. Seal of Ingeborg Håkansdotter, Duchess of Sweden, 1321.** Ingeborg (1301–1361) was the daughter of King Håkon V of Norway and was betrothed to a Swedish duke, Erick Magnusson, when she was only eleven years old. After a dramatic series of events that left her a young widow, she became the regent for her son, Magnus, who was elected king of both Norway and Sweden in 1319. Ingeborg herself was barely eighteen at the time. The legend on her seal reads "Ingeborg by the Grace of God Duchess of Norway," her official title.

**THE MEETING OF JOACHIM AND ANNA BY GIOTTO.**
According to legend, Anna and Joachim were an aged and infertile couple who were able to conceive their only child, Mary, through divine intervention. Hence, this painting may portray the moment of her conception—but it also portrays the affection of husband and wife. ▪ *What human characteristics and values does this painting convey to the viewer?*

poet Virgil (Chapter 5), who represents the best of classical culture. But Dante can be guided toward knowledge of the divine in Paradise only by his deceased beloved, Beatrice, who symbolizes Christian wisdom.

In the course of this visionary pilgrimage, Dante's narrator meets the souls of many historical personages and contemporaries, and questions them closely, inviting them to explain why they met their fates. This was Dante's ingenious way of commenting on current events and passing judgment on his enemies. In many ways, this monumental poem is a fusion of classical and Christian cultures, Latin learning and vernacular artistry.

# PAPAL POWER AND POPULAR PIETY

Dante's *Comedy* was a creative response to the political turmoil that engulfed Italy during his lifetime, a situation that was transforming the papacy in ways that he condemned. Indeed, many of the men whom Dante imaginatively placed

in Hell were popes, those who had held high offices in the Church, foreign rulers (such as the Holy Roman Emperor) who sought to subjugate Italian territories, or rapacious Italian princes and factional leaders who fought among themselves—all who were creating a state of permanent warfare among and within cities, as in Dante's native Florence. But despite the weakening authority of the papal office, which caused violent divisions within the Church, popular piety arguably achieved its strongest expressions during this era.

## The Limits of Papal Power

As we saw in Chapter 9, the power of the papacy reached a new height at the beginning of the thirteenth century, as holders of the office continued to centralize the government of the Church. But they also attempted to extend their influence further into the secular sphere, which led to protracted political struggles that ultimately compromised the papacy's credibility.

For example, the Italian territories under papal lordship shared a border with the kingdom of Sicily, which comprised the important city of Naples, all of southern Italy, and the island of Sicily. The ruler of these territories was also the German emperor Frederick II (Chapter 9), who proved a formidable opponent of the papacy's expanded powers. The reigning pope, therefore, called a crusade against him. But in order to implement this crusade, the pope needed to find a military champion willing to lead an army against a fellow Christian ruler—someone with little to lose and everything to gain.

This turned out to be Charles of Anjou, the youngest brother of the French king, who had few resources of his own. Charles was eventually crowned king of Sicily, but he made matters in southern Italy worse by antagonizing his own subjects, who instead offered their allegiance to the king of Aragon. The papacy then made Aragon the target of yet another crusade, resulting in a disastrous war among Christian princes and their armies on European soil. In the wake of this debacle, the French king Philip IV (r. 1286–1314) resolved to punish the papacy for abusing its powers.

In 1300, Pope Boniface VIII (r. 1294–1303) called for the celebration of a papal jubilee, asserting that Rome was the center of the Christian world and that the pope was the arbiter of all power. But just a few years later, Rome had ceased to matter. The new capital of the Christian world was now in France, because Philip IV had challenged Boniface to prove that he could exercise real power—not just the power of propaganda. Following a heated dispute about the king's capacity to intervene in the affairs of the Church, Philip sent his thugs to the papal residence, where Boniface (then in his seventies) was so mistreated that he died a month later. Philip then pressed his advantage. He forced the new pope, Clement V, to thank him publicly for his zealous defense of the faith and then, in 1309, moved the entire papal court from Rome to Avignon (*AH-vee-nyon*), a city near the southeastern border of his own realm.

The papacy's capitulation to French royal power illustrates the enormous gap that had opened up between rhetoric and reality in the centuries since the Investiture Conflict (Chapter 8). Although Boniface was merely repeating the old claim that kings ruled only by divine approval as recognized by the Church, the Church now exercised its authority only by bowing to the superior power of a king.

## The Babylonian Captivity of the Papacy

The papacy would remain in Avignon for nearly seventy years, until 1378 (see Chapter 11). This period is often called the "Babylonian Captivity" of the papacy, recalling the Jews' exile in Babylon during the sixth century B.C.E. (Chapter 2). Even though the move was probably supposed to be temporary, it was not reversed after Philip IV's death in 1314. Perhaps many papal suppliants found that doing business in Avignon was easier than in Rome. Not only was Avignon closer to the major centers of power in northwestern Europe, it was now far removed from the tumultuous politics of Italy and safe from the aggressive attentions of German emperors.

All of these considerations were important for a succession of popes closely allied with the aims of the French monarchy. In time, Avignon began to feel like home to them. In fact, it *was* home for all the popes elected there, who were natives of the region, as were nearly all the cardinals whom they appointed. This further cemented their loyalty to the French king. And the longer the papacy stayed in Avignon, the larger its bureaucracy grew and the harder it was to contemplate moving it.

Although the papacy never abandoned its claims to the overlordship of Rome and the Papal States, making good on these claims required decades of diplomacy and a great deal of money. The Avignon popes accordingly imposed new taxes and obligations on the wealthy dioceses of France, England, Germany, and Spain. Judicial cases from ecclesiastical courts also brought large revenues into the papal coffers. Most controversially, the Avignon popes claimed the right to appoint bishops and priests to vacant offices anywhere in Christendom, directly bypassing the rights of individual dioceses and allowing the papacy to collect huge fees from successful appointees.

By these and other measures, the Avignon popes further strengthened administrative control over the Church. But they also further weakened the papacy's moral authority. Stories of the court's unseemly luxury circulated widely, especially during the reign of the notoriously corrupt Clement VI (r. 1342–1352), who openly sold spiritual benefits for money (boasting that he would appoint a jackass to a bishopric if he thought it would turn a profit), and who insisted that his sexual transgressions were therapeutic. His reign also coincided with the Black Death, whose terrifying and demoralizing effects were not alleviated by the quality of his leadership.

**THE PAPAL PALACE AT AVIGNON.** The work on this great fortified palace was begun in 1339 and symbolizes the apparent permanence of the papal residence in Avignon. ▪ *Why was it constructed as a fortress as well as a palace?*

## Uniting the Faithful: The Power of Sacraments

Despite the centralizing power of the papacy, which came to fruition under Innocent III, most medieval Christians experienced the Church at a local level, within their communities. In something of a paradox, this was another of Innocent III's legacies: nearly all of Europe was covered by a network of parish churches by the end of the thirteenth century because he had insisted that all people should have access to religious instruction. In these churches, parish priests not only taught the elements of Christian doctrine but also administered the sacraments: rituals that conveyed the grace of God to individual Christians by marking significant moments in the life cycle of every person and significant times in the Christian calendar.

Medieval piety came to revolve around these sacraments, which included baptism, confession of sins (also known as Penance), Extreme Unction (last rites for the dying), the ordination of priests, and the Eucharist or Mass. Baptism, a ceremony of initiation that had been administered to adults in the early centuries of Christianity (Chapter 6), had become a sacrament administered to infants as soon as possible after birth to safeguard their souls in case of an early death. Periodic confession of sins to a priest was thought to guarantee God's forgiveness, for if a sinner did not perform appropriate acts of penance, he or she would have to complete atonement in Purgatory—the netherworld between Paradise and Hell that Dante explored. Purgatory's existence was made a matter of Church doctrine for the first time in 1274.) In Extreme Unction, a priest anointed the forehead of a dying person with holy oil, signifying the final absolution of all sins and thus offering a last assurance of salvation. Another sacrament, marriage, was increasingly emphasized but very seldom practiced as a ceremony at this time; in reality, marriage required only the exchange of promises and was often formed simply by an act of sexual intercourse or by cohabitation.

This sacramental system was the foundation on which the practices of medieval popular piety rested. Pilgrimages, for example, were a form of penance and could shorten the pilgrim's time in purgatory. Crusading was a kind of extreme pilgrimage that promised complete fulfillment of all penances the crusader might owe for all the sins of his life. Many other pious acts—saying a series of prayers or giving alms to the poor—could also serve as penance for one's sins, while constituting good works that would help the believer in his or her journey toward salvation.

## The Miracle of the Eucharist

Of these sacraments, the one most central to the religious lives of medieval Christians was the Eucharist, or Mass. As we noted in Chapter 9, the ritual power of the Mass was greatly enhanced in the twelfth century, when the Church began promoting the doctrine of transubstantiation. Christians attending Mass were taught that when the priest spoke the ritual words "This is my body" and "This is my blood," the substances of bread and wine on the altar were miraculously transformed into the body and blood of Jesus Christ. To consume one or both of these substances was to ingest holiness. So powerful was this idea that most

**"THIS IS MY BODY": THE ELEVATION OF THE HOST.**
This fresco from a chapel in Assisi was painted by Simone Martini in the 1320s. It shows the moment in the Mass when the priest raises the eucharistic host so that it can be seen by the faithful. The Latin phrase spoken at this moment, *Hoc est enim corpus meum* ("This is my body"), came to be regarded as a magical formula (*hocus pocus*) because it could transform one substance into another. ▪ *Since medieval Christians believed that the sight of the host was just as powerful as ingesting it, how would they have responded to this life-size image of the elevation?* ▪ *What does the appearance of angels (above the altar) signify?*

Christians received the sacramental bread just once a year, at Easter; some holy women, however, attempted to sustain themselves by consuming only the single morsel of bread consecrated at daily Mass.

To share in the miracle of the Eucharist, one did not even have to consume it. One had only to witness the elevation of the host, the wafer of bread raised up by the priest, which "hosted" the real presence of Jesus Christ. Daily attendance at Mass simply to view the consecration of the host was therefore a common form of devotion, and this was facilitated by the practice of displaying a consecrated wafer in a special reliquary called a monstrance ("showcase"), which could be set up on an altar or carried through the streets. Believers sometimes attributed astonishing properties to the eucharistic host, feeding it to sick animals or rushing from church to church to see the consecrated bread as many times as possible in a day. The Church criticized some of these practices as superstitious, but by and large, these expressions of popular piety were encouraged and fervently practiced by many.

## The Pursuit of Holiness

The fundamental theme of preachers in this era, that salvation lay open to any Christian who strove for it, helps to explain the central place of the Mass and other sacraments in daily life. It also led many to seek out new paths that could lead to God. As we noted in Chapter 9, some believers who sought to achieve a mystical union with God (through rigorous prayer, penance, and personal sacrifice) were ultimately condemned for heresy because they did not subordinate themselves to the authority of the Church. But even less radical figures might find themselves treading on dangerous ground, especially if they published their ideas.

For example, the German preacher Master Eckhart (c. 1260–1327), a Dominican friar, taught that there is a "spark" deep within every human soul and that God lives in this spark. Through prayer and self-renunciation, any person could therefore retreat into this inner recess of his or her being and access divinity. This conveyed the message that laypeople could attain salvation through their own efforts, without the intervention of a priest or any of the sacraments he alone could perform. As a result, many of Eckhart's teachings were condemned. But such views found support in the teachings of popular preachers after the Black Death, when close-knit communities revolving around the parish church were broken up or weakened (see Chapter 11).

# STRUGGLES FOR SOVEREIGNTY

When the French king Philip IV transplanted the papal court from Rome to Avignon, he was not just responding to previous popes' abuse of power, he was bolstering his own. By the middle of the thirteenth century, the growth of strong territorial monarchies, combined with the increasing sophistication of royal justice, taxation, and propaganda, had given some secular rulers greater power than any European ruler had wielded since the time of Charlemagne (see Chapter 7).

Meanwhile, monarchs' willingness to support the Church's crusading efforts not only yielded distinct economic and political advantages but also allowed them to assert their commitment to the moral and spiritual improvement of their realms. Although a king still needed to be anointed with holy oil at the time of his coronation in order to claim that he ruled "by the grace of God"—a rite that required a bishop and, by extension, papal support—a king's authority in his own realm rested on the acquiescence of the aristocracy and on the popular perception of his reputation for justice, piety, and regard for his subjects' prosperity. On the wider stage of the medieval world, it also rested on his successful assertion of his kingdom's sovereignty.

## The Problem of Sovereignty

*Sovereignty* can be defined as an inviolable authority over a defined territory. In Chapter 9, we learned that Philip Augustus was the first monarch to call himself "king of France" and not "king of the French." In other words, he was defining his kingship in geographical terms, claiming that there was an entity called France and that he was king within that area.

But what was France? Was it the tiny "island" (Île-de-France) around Paris, which had been his father's domain? If so, France was very small—and very vulnerable, which would make it hard to maintain a claim to sovereignty. Or did France include any region, such as Champagne or Normandy, whose lord was willing to do homage to the French king? In that case, the king would need to enforce his rights of lordship constantly and, if necessary, exert his rule directly—as Philip did when he took Normandy away from England's King John in 1214.

But what if some of France's neighboring lords ruled in their own right, as did the independent counts of Flanders, thus threatening the security of France's borders? In that case, the king would need either to forge an alliance with these borderlands or to negate their independence. He would need to assert his sovereignty by absorbing these regions into an ever-growing kingdom.

This is the problem: a claim to sovereignty is credible only if it can be backed up with real power, and a state's or ruler's power must never seem stagnant or passive. The problem of sovereignty, then, is a zero-sum game: one state's sovereignty is won and maintained by diminishing that of other states. Although many French citizens today would assert that France has, in some mystical way, always existed in its present form, the fact is that France and every other modern European state was being cobbled together during the medieval period through a process of annexation and colonization—just as the United States was assembled at the expense of the empires that had colonized North America (the British, French, and Spanish), not to mention the killing or displacement of autonomous native peoples.

The process of achieving sovereignty is thus an aggressive and often violent one, affecting not only the rulers of territories but their peoples, too. In Spain, the "reconquest" of Muslim lands, which had accelerated in the twelfth century, continued apace in the thirteenth and fourteenth to the detriment of these regions' Muslim and Jewish inhabitants. German princes continued to push northward into the Baltic, where they responded with brutal force to native peoples' resistance. Meanwhile, the Scandinavian kingdoms that had been forming in the eleventh and twelfth centuries warred among themselves and their neighbors for the control of contested regions and resources. Italy and the Mediterranean became a constant battleground, as we have observed.

Among all these emerging states, the two most strident and successful in their assertion of sovereignty were France and England.

## The Prestige of France: The Saintly Kingship of Louis IX

After the death of Philip Augustus in 1223, the heirs to the French throne continued to pursue an expansionist policy, pushing the boundaries of their influence out to the east and south. There were significant pockets of resistance, though,

**A CONTAINER FOR THE CROWN OF THORNS.** The Sainte-Chapelle, built by Louis IX, was a giant reliquary for the display of this potent artifact and a symbol of Christ's divine majesty, which increased the prestige of the king of France.

notably from the southwestern lands that the kings of England had inherited from Eleanor of Aquitaine (see Chapter 9) and from the independent towns of Flanders that had escaped conquest under Philip Augustus. In 1302, citizen militias from several of these towns, fighting on foot with farming implements and other unconventional weapons, managed to defeat the heavily armed French cavalry. This victory at the Battle of Courtrai (Kortrijk) is still celebrated as a national holiday in Belgium (although its ultimate meaning is currently at the center of a divisive controversy between French- and Flemish-speaking Belgians).

This defeat was a setback for Philip IV of France, but we have already observed that he had other ways of asserting the power of French sovereignty. Much of that power derived from his grandfather, Louis IX (r. 1226–1270), who probably would have been horrified by the ways his grandson used it. Louis was famous for his piety and his conscientious exercise of his kingly duties. Unlike most of his fellow princes, Louis not only pledged to go on a crusade—he actually went. And although both of his campaigns were notorious failures (he died on the second, in 1270), they cemented his saintly reputation and political clout.

First, Louis's willingness to risk his life (and those of his brothers) in the service of the Church would give him tremendous influence in papal affairs—a key factor in making his youngest brother, Charles of Anjou, the king of Naples and Sicily. Second, the necessity of ensuring the good governance of his kingdom during his years of absence prompted Louis to invent or reform many key aspects of royal governance, which made France the bureaucratic rival of England for the first time. Third, Louis's first crusading venture was seen as confirmation that the king of France had inherited the mantle of Charlemagne as the protector of the Church and the representative of Christ on earth.

Although it was a military fiasco, this crusade found lasting artistic expression in the Sainte-Chapelle (Holy Chapel), a gorgeous jewel box of a church that Louis built in Paris for his collection of Passion relics—artifacts thought to have been used for the torture and crucifixion of Christ (the Latin *passio* means "suffering"). The most important of these was the Crown of Thorns, intended by Pilate as a mocking reference to "the king of the Jews" (see Chapter 6). Now that this holy crown belonged to Louis and was housed in Paris, it could be taken as a sign that Paris was the new Jerusalem.

Widely regarded as a saint in his lifetime, Louis was formally canonized in 1297, by the same Pope Boniface VIII who was brought down by Philip IV. Indeed, Boniface partly intended this gesture as a rebuke to the saint's grandson, but Philip turned it to his advantage. He even used his grandfather's pious reputation as a cloak for his frankly rapacious treatment of the Knights Templar, whose military order he suppressed in 1314 so that he could confiscate its extensive property and dissolve his own debts to the order. He had expelled the Jews from his realm in 1306 for similar reasons.

his father to suppress them. When Edward himself became king in 1272, he took steps to ensure that there would be no further revolts on his watch by tightening his control on the aristocracy and their lands, diffusing their power by strengthening that of Parliament, reforming the administration of the realm, and clarifying its laws.

Having seen to the internal affairs of England, Edward looked to its borders. Since Welsh chieftains had been major backers of the barons who had rebelled against his father, he was determined to clean up the border region and bring "wild Wales" within the orbit of English sovereignty. He initially attempted to do this by making treaties with various Welsh princes, but none of these arrangements were stable or gave him the type of control he wanted. Edward accordingly embarked on an ambitious and ruthless campaign of castle building, ringing the hilly country with enormous fortifications on a scale not seen in most of Europe—they were more like crusader castles—and treated the Welsh (who were actually his fellow Christians) as infidels. Indeed, he treated conquered Wales like a crusader state, making it a settler colony and subjecting the Welsh to the overlordship of his own men. When his son, the future Edward II, was born in 1284 at the great castle he had built at Caernarvon, he gave the infant the title "Prince of Wales," a title usually borne by a Welsh chieftain.

## Castles and Control: Edward I and the Expansion of English Rule

The expulsion of Jews who depended on a king's personal protection had actually been a precedent set by Philip's contemporary and kinsman, Edward I of England (r. 1272–1307). Unlike Philip, Edward had to build up the sovereignty of his state almost from scratch—for his father, Henry III (r. 1216–1272), had a long but troubled reign. Henry inherited the throne as a young boy, shortly after his father John's loss of Normandy and capitulation to Magna Carta (Chapter 9). From the first, he had to contend with factions among his regents and, later, the restive barons of his realm who rose against him on several occasions. His son Edward even sided with the rebels at one point, but later worked alongside

**CAERNARVON CASTLE.** One of many massive fortifications built by Edward I, this castle was the birthplace of the first English Prince of Wales and the site where the current Prince of Wales, Charles, was formally invested with that title in 1969. ■ *Castles of this size and strength had been constructed in the Crusader States and on the disputed frontiers of Muslim and Christian Spain, but never before in Britain (see the photos on pages 294 and 297). What does their construction reveal about Edward's attitude toward the Welsh?*

## A Declaration of Scottish Independence

*In April 1320, a group of powerful Scottish lords gathered at the abbey of Arbroath to draft a letter to Pope John XII in Avignon. The resulting Declaration of Arbroath petitioned the exiled pope (a Frenchman loyal to the French king) to recognize the Scots as a sovereign nation and to support their right to an independent kingdom that would be free from encroachment by the English. The Scots' elected king, Robert the Bruce, had been excommunicated by a previous pope who had upheld English claims to lordship in Scotland. The letter therefore makes a number of different arguments for the recognition of the Scots' right to self-governance.*

We know, most holy father and lord, and have gathered from the deeds and books about men in the past, that ... the nation of the Scots has been outstanding for its many distinctions. It journeyed from the lands of Greece and Egypt by the Tyrrhenian Sea and the Pillars of Hercules, ... but could not be subdued anywhere by any peoples however barbaric.... It took possession of the settlements in the west which it now desires, after first driving out the Britons and totally destroying the Picts, and although often attacked by the Norwegians, Danes and English. Many were its victories and innumerable its efforts. It has held these places always free of all servitude, as the old histories testify. One hundred and thirteen kings of their royal lineage have reigned in their kingdom, with no intrusion by a foreigner.

If the noble qualities and merits of these men were not obvious for other reasons, they shine forth clearly enough in that they were almost the first to be called to his most holy faith by the King of Kings and Lord of Lords, our Lord Jesus Christ, after his Passion and Resurrection, even though they were settled on the most distant boundaries of the earth....

Thus our people lived until now in freedom and peace ..., until that mighty prince Edward [I] king of England (the father of the present king) in the guise of a friend and ally attacked our kingdom in hostile fashion, when it had no head and the people were not harbouring any evil treachery, nor were they accustomed to wars or attacks. His unjust acts, killings, acts of violence, pillagings, burnings, imprisonments of prelates, burnings of monasteries, robbings and killings of regular clergy, and also innumerable other outrages, which he committed against the said people, sparing none on account of age or sex, religion or order—no one could write about them or fully comprehend them who had not been instructed by experience.

From these countless ills we have been set free, with the help of Him who follows up wounds with healing and cures, by our most energetic prince, king and lord Sir Robert [the Bruce; r. 1306–1329]. ... By divine providence his succession to his right according to our laws and customs which we intend to maintain to the death, together with the due consent and assent of us all, have made him our prince and king. ... But if he should give up what he has begun,

Edward then turned to Scotland, England's final frontier. Until now, control of Scotland had not been an English concern. The Scottish border had been peaceful for many years, and the Scottish kings did homage to the English king for some of their lands. In 1290, however, the succession to the Scottish throne was disputed among many rival claimants, none of whom had enough backing to secure election. Edward intervened, pressing his own claim to the kingdom and seemingly prepared to take Scotland by conquest. To avoid this, the Scots forged an alliance with the French, but this did not prevent Edward's army from fighting its way through to Scone Abbey in 1296.

Scone was a symbolic target: the site of the Stone of Destiny on which Scottish kings were traditionally enthroned. So Edward seized this potent symbol, brought it back to Westminster Abbey in London, and embedded it in the coronation chair of his namesake, Edward the Confessor, the last Anglo-Saxon king of England (Chapter 8). Save for a brief hiatus in 1950, when the stone was stolen from the abbey by Scottish nationalists—students at the University of Glasgow—it would remain there until 1996 as a sign that the sovereignty of Scotland had yielded to that of England. (It will be temporarily returned to London when the next British monarch is crowned.)

seeking to subject us or our kingdom to the king of the English, . . . we would immediately strive to expel him as our enemy and a subverter of his right and ours, and we would make someone else our king, who is capable of seeing to our defence. For as long as a hundred of us remain alive, we intend never to be subjected to the lordship of the English, in any way. For it is not for glory in war, riches or honours that we fight, but only for the laws of our fathers and for freedom, which no good man loses except along with his life.

Therefore, most holy father and lord, we implore your holiness with all vehemence in our prayers that you . . . look with paternal eyes on the troubles and difficulties brought upon us and the church of God by the English. And that you deign to admonish and exhort the king of the English, who ought to be satisfied with what he has (since England was formerly enough for seven kings or more), to leave us Scots in peace, living as we do in the poor country of Scotland beyond which there is no dwelling place, and desiring nothing but our own. . . .

It is important for you, holy father, to do this, since you see the savagery of the heathen raging against Christians (as the sins of Christians require), and the frontiers of Christendom are being curtailed day by day, and you have seen how much it detracts from your holiness's reputation if (God forbid!) the church suffers eclipse or scandal in any part of it during your time. Let it then rouse the Christian princes who are covering up their true motivation when they pretend that they cannot go to the assistance of the Holy Land on account of wars with their neighbours. The real reason that holds them back is that in warring with their smaller neighbours they anticipate greater advantage to themselves and weaker resistance. . . .

But if your Holiness too credulously trusts the tales of the English fully, or does not leave off favouring the English to our confusion, then we believe that the Most High will blame you for the slaughter of bodies. . . . Dated at our monastery at Arbroath in Scotland 6 April 1320 in the fifteenth year of our said king's reign.

Source: Walter Bower, *Scotichronicon*, vol. 7, ed. A. B. Scott and D. E. R. Watt (Aberdeen, Scotland: 1996).

## Questions for Analysis

1. On what grounds does this letter justify the political independence of the Scots? What different arguments does it make? Which in your view is the most compelling?

2. Why does this letter mention crusading? What are the Scottish lords implying about the relationship between Europe's internal conflicts and the ongoing wars with external adversaries?

3. Imagine that you are an adviser to the pope. Applying your knowledge of the papacy's situation at this time, would you advise him to do as this letter asks? Why or why not?

Edward considered the subjugation of Scotland to be England's manifest destiny. He called himself the "Hammer of the Scots," and when he died he charged his son Edward II (r. 1307–1327) with the completion of his task. But the younger Edward, unlike his father, was not a ruthless and efficient advocate of English expansion. He also had to contend with a rebellion led by his own queen, Isabella of France, who also engineered his abdication and murder. Their son, Edward III (r. 1327–1377), eventually renewed his grandfather's expansionist policies, but his main target was France, not Scotland—thus launching Europe's two strongest monarchies into a war that would last over a hundred years.

## The Outbreak of the Hundred Years' War

The Hundred Years' War was the largest, longest, and widest-ranging military conflict since Rome's wars with Carthage in the third and second centuries B.C.E. (Chapter 5). Although England and France were its principal antagonists, almost all major European powers became involved at some stage. Active hostilities began in 1337 and lasted until 1453, interrupted by truces of varying lengths.

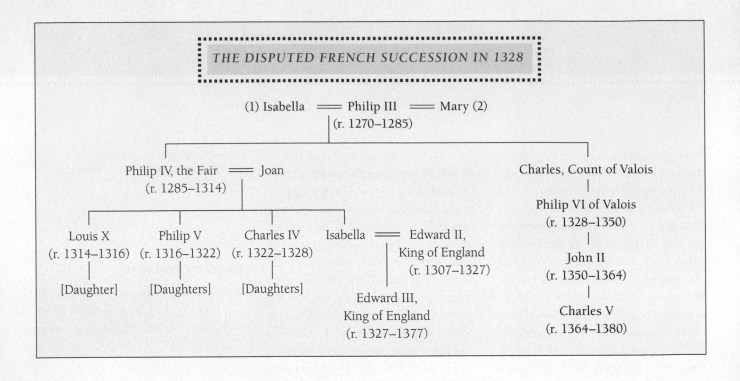

**THE DISPUTED FRENCH SUCCESSION IN 1328**

(1) Isabella === Philip III === Mary (2)
(r. 1270–1285)

Philip IV, the Fair === Joan
(r. 1285–1314)

Charles, Count of Valois

Philip VI of Valois
(r. 1328–1350)

Louis X
(r. 1314–1316)

Philip V
(r. 1316–1322)

Charles IV
(r. 1322–1328)

Isabella === Edward II,
King of England
(r. 1307–1327)

[Daughter]

[Daughters]

[Daughters]

Edward III,
King of England
(r. 1327–1377)

John II
(r. 1350–1364)

Charles V
(r. 1364–1380)

The most fundamental source of conflict, and the most difficult to resolve, was the fact that the kings of England held the duchy of Gascony as vassals of the French king; this had been part of Eleanor of Aquitaine's domain, which was added to the Anglo-Norman Empire in 1154 (Chapter 9). In the twelfth and thirteenth centuries, when the French kings had not yet absorbed this region into their domain, this fact had seemed less of an anomaly. But as Europe's territorial monarchies began to claim sovereignty on the basis of the free exercise of power within the "natural" boundaries of their domains, the English presence in "French" Gascony became more and more problematic. The fact that England also had close commercial links, through the wool trade, with Flanders—which consistently resisted French imperialism—added fuel to the fire; as did the French alliance with the Scots, who continued to resist English imperialism.

Complicating this volatile situation was the disputed succession of the French crown. In 1328, the last of Philip IV's three sons died without leaving a son to succeed him: the Capetian dynasty, founded by the Frankish warlord Hugh Capet in 987 (Chapter 8) had finally exhausted itself. A new dynasty, the Valois, came to the throne—but only by insisting that women could neither inherit royal power nor pass it on. For otherwise, the heir to France was Edward III of England, whose ambitious mother, Isabella, was Philip IV's only daughter. When his claim was initially passed over, Edward was only fifteen and in no position to protest. In 1337, however, when the disputes over Gascony and Scotland erupted into war, Edward raised the stakes by claiming

to be the rightful king of France, a claim that subsequent English kings would maintain until the eighteenth century.

Although France was richer and more populous than England by a ratio of at least three to one, the English crown was more effective in mobilizing the entire population, for reasons we discussed in Chapter 9. Edward III was therefore able to levy and maintain a professional army of seasoned and well-disciplined soldiers, cavalrymen, and archers. The huge but virtually leaderless armies assembled by the French proved no match for the tactical superiority of these smaller English forces. English armies pillaged the French countryside at will, while civil wars broke out between embattled French lords. A decade after the declaration of war, French knights were defeated in two humiliating battles at Crécy (1346) and Calais (1347). The English seemed invincible—but they were no match for an adversary approaching from the Far East.

# FROM THE GREAT FAMINE TO THE BLACK DEATH

By 1300, Europe was connected to Asia and the lands between by an intricate network that fostered connections of all kinds. At the same time, Europe was reaching its own ecological limits. Between 1000 and 1300, the population had tripled; a sea of grain fields stretched, almost unbroken, from Ireland to Ukraine; and forests had been cleared,

# Past and Present

## Global Pandemics

Although advances in medical science have made the causes of disease less mysterious, the rapid spread of new viruses is still terrifying and the variety of human responses to the possibility of sudden infection have changed little over time. The image on the left shows citizens from the town of Tournai (now in Belgium) marching in a procession to ward off the plague: they are praying and doing penance for their sins by beating their own bodies with whips, a practice called *flagellation*. The image on the right shows health care workers donning hazmat suits to protect themselves from the deadly Ebola virus outbreak of 2014–2015.

 **Watch related author interview on the Student Site**

marshes drained, and pastureland reduced by generations of peasants performing lifetimes of backbreaking labor. Yet Europe was barely able to feed its people. At the same time, the Medieval Warm Period (Chapter 8) was coming to an end, and with it the favorable climatic conditions that had enabled the agricultural revolution of the previous three centuries. Even a reduction of one or two degrees Centigrade is enough to cause substantial changes in rainfall patterns, shorten growing seasons, and decrease agricultural productivity. So it did in Europe, with disastrous consequences.

## Evil Times: The Seven Years' Famine

Between the years 1315 and 1322, the cooling climate caused nearly continuous adverse weather conditions in northern Europe. Winters were extraordinarily severe: in 1316, the Baltic Sea froze over and ships were trapped in the ice. Rains prevented planting in spring or summer, and when a crop did manage to struggle through it would be dashed by rain and hail in autumn. Amid these natural calamities, dynastic warfare continued in the sodden wheat fields, as the princes of Scandinavia and the Holy Roman Empire fought for supremacy and succession. In the once-fertile fields of Flanders, French armies slogged through mud in continued efforts to subdue the Flemish population. On the Scottish and Welsh borders, uprisings were ruthlessly suppressed and the paltry storehouses of the natives were pillaged to feed the English raiders.

The result was human suffering more devastating than that caused by any famine affecting Europe since that time; hence the name "Great Famine" to describe this terrible

## The Code of Chivalry: Putting Honor before Plunder

*The Hundred Years' War between England and France pitted these two countries' warrior aristocracies against each other. Yet these knights had a great deal in common: they all spoke French, many were closely related, and they were supposed to share a common set of values. The following excerpt is taken from* The Book of Chivalry, *written in French by Geoffroi de Charny, a French nobleman and veteran of this war's first major battles who ultimately died in combat at Poitiers in 1356. Because the war was fought almost entirely on French soil, Geoffroi was keenly aware of the toll it took on the land and its people. In the following passage, he addresses the problem of how a knight can sustain his honor when he is driven to acquire booty for himself through the theft of others' property.*

### Those Who Are Brave but Too Eager for Plunder

I now need to consider yet another category of men-at-arms, who deserve praise, who are strong and skillful, bold and sparing no effort, some of whom always want to be at the forefront, riding as foragers to win booty or prisoners or other profit from the enemies of those on whose side they fight. And they know well how to do it skillfully and cleverly; and because they are so intent on plunder, it often happens that on the entry into a town won by force, those who are so greedy for plunder dash hither and thither and find themselves separated from those of their companions who have no thought for gain but only for completing their military undertaking. And it often happens that such men, those who ride after and hunt for great booty, are killed in the process—frequently it is not known how, sometimes by their enemies, sometimes through quarrels in which greed for plunder sets one man against another. It often occurs that through lack of those who chase after plunder before the battle is over, that which is thought to be already won can be lost again and lives or reputations as well. It can also happen in relation to such people who are very eager for booty that when there is action on the battlefield, there are a number of men who pay more attention to taking prisoners and other profit, and when they have seized them and other winnings, they are more anxious to safeguard their captives and their booty than to help to bring the battle to a good conclusion. And it may well be that a battle can be lost in this way. And one ought instead to be wary of the booty which results in the loss of honor, life, and possessions. In this vocation one should therefore set one's heart and mind on winning honor, which endures for ever, rather than on winning profit and booty, which one can lose within one single hour. And yet one should praise and value those men-at-arms who are able to make war on, inflict damage on, and win profit from their enemies, for they cannot do it without strenuous effort and great courage. But again I shall repeat: he who does best is most worthy.

Source: *The Book of Chivalry of Geoffrey de Charny: Text, Context, and Translation*, trans. Richard W. Kaeuper and Elspeth Kennedy (Pennsylvania: 1996), p. 99.

### Questions for Analysis

1. How does Geoffroi justify the act of plundering? What insights into contemporary military tactics does this passage provide?

2. Given that Geoffroi must have seen Englishmen pillaging French lands, do you find his justification of this activity surprising? Why or why not?

crisis. Weakened by years of malnutrition and relentless efforts to counteract the climatic effects on the landscape, between 10 and 15 percent of the population of northern Europe perished. Many starved, while others fell victim to epidemic diseases that affected both animals and people. In southern Europe, around the shores of the Mediterranean, the effects of climate change were more muted, and food could be distributed through different channels. Nonetheless, the overall health of this region also suffered from the disruption of trade and the shortage of some staple goods, as well as from the highly unstable political situation we have discussed.

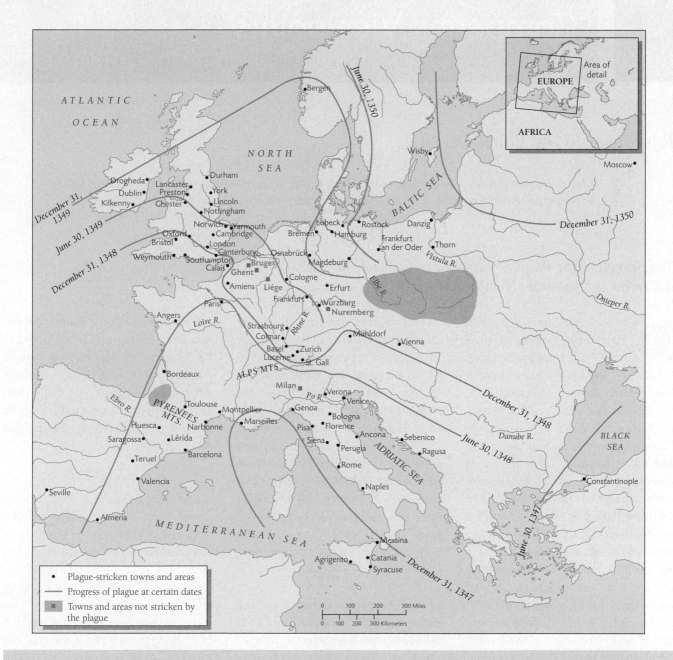

**EUROPEAN OUTBREAKS OF THE BLACK DEATH, 1347–1350.** ▪ *What trajectories did the Black Death follow once it arrived in Europe?* ▪ *How might have the growth of towns, trade, and travel contributed to the spread of the Black Death?* ▪ *Would such a rapid advance have been likely during the early Middle Ages or even in the ancient world? Why or why not?*

As food grew scarcer, prices climbed unpredictably, making even staple goods unobtainable by the poor. Plans for future crops, which kept hope alive, would be dashed when spring arrived and flooded fields prevented seeds from germinating. People then spent cold summers and autumns foraging for food. Hunting was restricted to the nobility (Chapter 9), but even those who risked the death penalty for poaching found little game. Wages did not keep pace with rising costs, and so those who lived in towns and depended on markets had less to spend on scarce provisions. Only a year after the famine began, townspeople were dying of ailments that would not have been fatal in good years.

The effects of the famine were especially devastating for children, since even those who survived were highly susceptible to disease, owing to the severe impairment of their immune systems. It may have been the Great Famine, then, that paved the way for the even more horrific destruction of the Black Death.

# Competing Viewpoints

## Responses to the Black Death

> Many chroniclers, intellectuals, and private individuals left accounts of the plague in which they attempt to understand why it had occurred, how it spread, and how communities should respond to it.

### The Spread of the Plague According to Gabriele de' Mussi (d. 1356), a Lawyer in Piacenza (Northern Italy)

Oh God! See how the heathen Tartar races, pouring together from all sides, suddenly infested the city of Caffa [on the Black Sea] and besieged the trapped Christians there for almost three years. . . . But behold, [in 1346] the whole army was affected by a disease which overran the Tartars and killed thousands upon thousands every day. It was as though arrows were raining down from heaven to strike and crush the Tartars' arrogance. All medical advice and attention was useless; the Tartars died as soon as the signs of disease appeared on their bodies: swellings in the armpit or groin caused by coagulating humours, followed by a putrid fever.

The dying Tartars, stunned and stupefied by the immensity of the disaster brought about by the disease, and realising that they had no hope of escape, lost interest in the siege. But they ordered corpses to be placed in catapults and lobbed into the city in the hope that the intolerable stench would kill everyone inside. What seemed like mountains of dead were thrown into the city, and the Christians could not hide or flee or escape from them, although they dumped as many of the bodies as they could in the sea. And soon the rotting corpses tainted the air and poisoned the water supply. . . . Moreover one infected man could carry the poison to others, and infect people and places with the disease by look alone. No one knew, or could discover, a means of defence.

Thus almost everyone who had been in the East . . . fell victim . . . through the bitter events of 1346 to 1348—the Chinese, Indians, Persians, Medes, Kurds, Armenians, Cilicians, Georgians, Mesopotamians, Nubians, Ethiopians, Turks, Egyptians, Arabs, Saracens and Greeks. . . .

* * *

As it happened, among those who escaped from Caffa by boat were a few sailors who had been infected with the poisonous disease. Some boats were bound for Genoa, others went to Venice and to other Christian areas. When the sailors reached these places and mixed with the people there, it was as if they had brought evil spirits with them. . . .

* * *

Scarcely one in seven of the Genoese survived. In Venice, where an inquiry was held into the mortality, it was found that more than 70 percent of the people had died. . . . The rest of Italy, Sicily and Apulia and the neighbouring regions maintain that they have been virtually emptied of inhabitants. . . . The Roman Curia at Avignon, the provinces on both sides of the Rhône, Spain, France, and the Empire cry up their griefs. . . .

* * *

Everyone has a responsibility to keep some record of the disease and the deaths, and because I am myself from Piacenza I have been urged to write more about what happened there in 1348. . . .

I don't know where to begin. Cries and laments arise on all sides. Day after day one sees the Cross and the Host being carried about the city, and countless dead being buried. . . . The living made preparations for their [own] burial, and because there was not enough room for individual graves, pits had to be dug in colonnades and piazzas, where nobody had ever been buried before. It often happened that man and wife, father and son, mother and daughter, and soon the whole household and many neighbours, were buried together in one place. . . .

Source: From Rosemary Horrox, ed. and trans., *The Black Death* (Manchester, 1994), pp. 16–21, 219–20.

## A Letter from the Town Council of Cologne to the Town Council of Strasbourg (Germany), 12 January 1349

Very dear friends, all sorts of rumours are now flying about against Judaism and the Jews prompted by this unexpected and unparalleled mortality of Christians. . . . Throughout our city, as in yours, many-winged Fame clamours that this mortality was initially caused, and is still being spread, by the poisoning of springs and wells, and that the Jews must have dropped poisonous substances into them. When it came to our knowledge that serious charges had been made against the Jews in several small towns and villages on the basis of this mortality, we sent numerous letters to you and to other cities and towns to uncover the truth behind these rumours, and set a thorough investigation in train. . . .

If a massacre of the Jews were to be allowed in the major cities (something which we are determined to prevent in our city, if we can, as long as the Jews are found to be innocent of these or similar actions) it could lead to the sort of outrages and disturbances which would whip up a popular revolt among the common people—and such revolts have in the past brought cities to misery and desolation. In any case we are still of the opinion that this mortality and its attendant circumstances are caused by divine vengeance and nothing else. Accordingly we intend to forbid any harassment of the Jews in our city because of these flying rumours, but to defend them faithfully and keep them safe, as our predecessors did—and we are convinced that you ought to do the same. . . .

### Questions for Analysis

1. How does Gabriele de' Mussi initially explain the causes of the plague? How does his understanding of it change as he traces its movements from East to West, and closer to Italy?

2. Why does the Council of Cologne wish to quell violence against the Jews? How does this reasoning complement or challenge what we have learned so far about the treatment of Jews in medieval Europe?

3. In your view, do these two perspectives display a rational approach to the horrors of the Black Death? Why or why not?

## A Crisis of Connectivity: Tracking the Black Death

The Black Death is the name given to a deadly global pandemic—an epidemic affecting "all people" (Greek: *pan + demos*)—that spread from China to Mongolia, northern India, and western Asia during the 1330s and 1340s. By 1346, the plague had reached the Black Sea, where it was transmitted to the Genoese colonists at Caffa (as noted above). From there, in 1347, Genoese ships inadvertently brought it to Sicily, North Africa, and northern Italy. From Italy, it spread westward along trade routes, first striking seaports, then turning inland with the travelers who carried it. It moved with astonishing rapidity, advancing about two miles per day, summer or winter. By 1350, it had reached Scandinavia and northern Russia, then spread southward again until it linked up with the original waves of infection that had brought it from Central Asia to the Black Sea. In Europe, it continued to erupt in local epidemics until the eighteenth century. In Asia and Africa, it was still causing devastating losses of life into the nineteenth century.

Although the absolute (total) mortality caused by other global pandemics has been greater—including the influenza pandemic of 1918–1919 and the ongoing HIV/AIDS pandemic—the *percentage* of the population affected by the Black Death was higher. In the space of a few decades, 40 to 60 percent of all people in these affected areas had died. The tremendous consequences of this catastrophe and the survivors' responses to the world left behind will be explored in Chapter 11. But what caused it?

In 2011, scientists confirmed that the Black Death bacterium was the deadly microbe *Yersinia pestis*, and that it almost certainly originated in China, on the

Tibetan-Qinghai Plateau. In 2013, another team of scientists proved that this medieval pandemic was actually the *second* plague caused by *Y. pestis*: an earlier strain had resulted in the Justinianic Plague of the sixth century C.E. (Chapter 7). This microbe is especially virulent because it can be contracted and manifested in so many ways, including bubonic plague and its even deadlier cousins, septicemic plague and pneumonic plague.

In its *bubonic* form, the plague microbe is carried by fleas that can live and travel on the backs of many kinds animals, including rats, marmots, hamsters, rabbits, camels, and even birds. Humans bitten by an infected flea or animal contract the plague through their lymphatic systems, resulting in the eruption of enormous and painful swellings (buboes) that appear in the lymph nodes of the groin, neck, and armpits. *Septicemic* plague occurs when an infected flea introduces the microbe directly into the human bloodstream, causing death within hours, usually before any symptoms of the disease are obvious. *Pneumonic* plague, perhaps the most frightening variation, results when *Y. pestis* infects the lungs, allowing the contagion to spread silently and invisibly, in the same ways as the common cold.

One of the things that made the Black Death so terrifying, therefore, was that it was mysteriously inconsistent. Those afflicted by the hideous bubonic plague might actually recover, whereas others—seemingly untouched—might die suddenly, from no apparent cause. Immediate reactions to the plague thus ranged from panic to anger to resignation. Observers quickly realized that the plague was contagious, but precisely how it spread remained unknown. Some believed that it was caused by breathing "bad air" and so urged people to flee from stricken areas, which caused the disease to spread even faster. Another response was the flagellant movement, so called because of the whips (*flagella*) with which traveling bands of penitents lashed themselves in order to appease the wrath of God. The unruly and sometimes hysterical mobs that gathered around the flagellants aroused the concern of both ecclesiastical and secular authorities, and the movement was suppressed by papal order.

Still others looked for scapegoats and revived old conspiracy theories that implicated Jews in the poisoning of communal water sources. Scores of Jewish communities were attacked and thousands of their inhabitants massacred in parts of the Rhineland, southern France, and the Christian kingdoms of Spain. For example, an important archaeological and forensic study published in 2014 reveals that hundreds of Jews—including children, the elderly, and the disabled—were brutally clubbed and hacked to death by their Christian neighbors in the small Catalonian town of Tárrega. The papacy and some local authorities tried to halt such attacks, but these efforts usually came too late.

# After You Read This Chapter

Go to **INQUIZITIVE** to see what you've learned—and learn what you've missed—with personalized feedback along the way.

## REVIEWING THE OBJECTIVES

- How did the conquests of the Mongols significantly impact Europe?
- The expansion of commerce and communication between eastern and western civilizations created a new world system. What were some key characteristics of this system? What kinds of exchange did it enable?
- What is *sovereignty*? What were the effects of competition for sovereign among European rulers?
- What were the short- and long-term causes for the papacy's loss of prestige? Why was the papal court moved to Avignon?
- What caused the Black Death? In what sense can it be seen as a product of the new world system that began with the Mongol conquests?

# CONCLUSION

The century between 1250 and 1350 was a time of significant change within all Western civilizations. The growing power of some monarchies led to encroachments on territories and cities that had once been independent, fueling resistance to these internal acts of colonization. The papacy, whose power had seemed so secure at the turn of the thirteenth century, would itself become a pawn in the keeping of the French king by the beginning of the fourteenth. Rome thereby lost its last source of authority while the New Rome, Constantinople, struggled to rebuild its prestige in the face of Mongol expansion. Yet, for the Mongol khans and the merchants they favored, for seafaring cities such as Venice and Genoa, for ambitious students at the universities, and for men on the make, the opportunities for advancement and mobility were great.

Other factors were in play during this era. Even in good times, Europe's population had outgrown its capacity to produce food; and when the climate grew cooler, years of cold summers and heavy rainfall took an enormous toll. Those regions most closely tied to the new global networks were densely settled and urban, which made the shortage of food and the spread of disease more acute there. In short, the benefits and drawbacks of increased globalization were already beginning to manifest themselves in the early fourteenth century—700 years ago. The Black Death can be understood as the ultimate example of medieval connectivity.

The scale of mortality caused by this pandemic is almost unimaginable, to us as to those who survived it; at least a third, and probably half, of Europe's people died between 1347 and 1353. In the countryside, entire villages disappeared. Cities and towns, overcrowded and unsanitary, were particularly vulnerable to plague and, thereafter, to outbreaks of violence. The immediate social consequences were profound, as were the economic ones. Crops rotted in the fields, manufacturing ceased, and trade came to a standstill in affected areas. Basic commodities became scarcer and prices rose higher, prompting ineffectual efforts to control prices and to force the remaining able-bodied laborers to work.

These were the short-term effects. How did the Black Death matter to those who survived it—including ourselves? According to Ibn Khaldun (1332–1406), a Muslim historian who is considered one of the founders of modern historical methods, it marked the end of the old world and the beginning of a new one that would require new systems of government, bodies of knowledge, and forms of art. Was he right? We will begin to answer that question in Chapter 11.

## PEOPLE, IDEAS, AND EVENTS IN CONTEXT

- What accounts for the success of **GENGHIS KHAN** and his successors? What circumstances enabled **MARCO POLO**'s travels to China? To what extent does the term *PAX MONGOLICA* describe this era in history?

- How did seafaring communities such as **GENOA** rise to prominence in this era? Why were new navigational aids such as **PORTOLAN CHARTS** necessary?

- How do the paintings of **GIOTTO** capture contemporary attitudes toward the world? How does **DANTE**'s artistry respond to the religious and political trends of his day?

- What was at stake in the controversy between **BONIFACE VIII** and **PHILIP IV**? Why was the papacy's residency at **AVIGNON** called the **BABYLONIAN CAPTIVITY**? What is a **SACRAMENT**? Why were these rites so important?

- In what different ways did **LOUIS IX** of France and **EDWARD I** of England contribute to the **SOVEREIGNTY** of their respective kingdoms? What was the relationship between claims to sovereignty and the causes of the **HUNDRED YEARS' WAR**?

- How did climate change contribute to the outbreak of the **GREAT FAMINE**?

- What were the long- and short-term causes of the **BLACK DEATH**?

## THINKING ABOUT CONNECTIONS

- If the Mongol khan Ögedei had not died in 1241, the Mongols could conceivably have continued their westward movement into Europe. Knowing what you have learned about Mongol rule, how do you think this might have changed the history of the world?

- How do the patterns of conquest and colonization discussed in this chapter compare with those of earlier periods, particularly those of antiquity? How many of these developments were new in 1250–1350?

- We live in a world in which the global circulation of people, information, goods, and bacteria is rapid—hence the dangers of emerging viruses such as Ebola and Zika. How does the medieval system compare with ours? What features seem familiar?

## STORY LINES

- The Black Death altered Europe in profound ways. The opportunities and challenges of this era are dynamically reflected in an array of developments.

- Some of these developments are associated with a new artistic and cultural movement known as the Renaissance, which began in Italy.

- Here, renewed appreciation of the classics and of Greek was facilitated by the flight of Greek-speaking intellectuals from Byzantium, as the Ottoman Turks absorbed the remaining lands of the eastern Roman Empire.

- Meanwhile, the competing territorial claims of Europe's sovereign powers led to large-scale warfare.

- Even after the papacy's return to Rome from Avignon, the failure of internal reform efforts led to the further decline of papal credibility. Consequently, a number of influential religious leaders sought more radical reforms.

## CHRONOLOGY

| | |
|---|---|
| 1304–1374 | Lifetime of Petrarch |
| 1351 | Black Death at its height |
| | The English Parliament passes the Statute of Laborers |
| 1377 | The papacy returns to Rome from Avignon |
| 1378 | The Great Schism begins |
| 1381 | Rebellions culminate in the English Peasants' Revolt |
| 1414–1418 | The Council of Constance is convened to end the Great Schism |
| | Jan Hus burned at the stake in 1415 |
| 1429–1431 | The career of Joan of Arc |
| 1431–1449 | The Council of Basel fails to check papal power |
| 1440 | Lorenzo Valla debunks "The Donation of Constantine" |
| 1453 | The Hundred Years' War ends |
| | Constantinople falls to the Ottoman Turks |

Before
You
Read
This
Chapter

# Rebirth and Unrest, 1350–1453

n June 1381, thousands of laborers from the English countryside rose up in rebellion against local authorities. Most were peasants or village artisans who were dismissed as ignorant by contemporary chroniclers. Yet the revolt was carefully coordinated. Plans were spread in coded messages circulated by word of mouth and by the followers of a renegade Oxford professor, John Wycliffe, who had called for the redistribution of Church property and taught that common people should be able to read the Bible in their own language.

The rebellion's immediate catalyst had been a series of exorbitant taxes levied by Parliament for the support of the ongoing war with France. But its more fundamental cause was an epidemic that had occurred thirty years earlier. The Black Death had reduced the entire population of Europe by 40 to 60 percent and drastically altered the world of those who survived it. In this new world, workers were valuable and could stand up to those who paid them poorly or treated them like slaves. During that fateful summer of 1381, the workers of England even vowed to kill representatives of both the Church and the government—to kill (as they put it) all the lawyers—and destroy all the documents that had been used to keep them in subjection. It was a

and the minute details of everyday life (see **Interpreting Visual Evidence** on page 368). Just as contemporary saints such as Francis of Assisi saw divinity in material objects, so too could an artist portray the Virgin and Child against a background vista of ordinary life, such as people going about their business or a man urinating against a wall. This was not blasphemous; on the contrary, it conveyed the message that the events of the Bible are constantly present, here and now. Such artworks suggest, for example, that Christ is our companion, not a distant figure whose life and outlook are irrelevant to us.

The same immediacy is also evident in medieval drama. Plays were often devotional exercises that involved the efforts of an entire community and celebrated that community. In the English city of York, for example, an annual series of pageants reenacted the entire history of human salvation from the Creation to the Last Judgment in a single summer day, beginning at dawn and ending late at night. Each pageant was produced by a particular craft guild and showcased that guild's special talents: "The Last Supper" was performed by the bakers, whose bread was a key element in their reenactment of the first Eucharist, whereas "The Crucifixion" was performed by the nail makers and the painters, whose wares were thereby put on prominent display in the depiction of Christ's bloody death on the cross.

In Italy, confraternities (brotherhoods) competed with each another to honor the saints with songs and processions. In Catalonia and many regions of Spain, there were elaborate dramas celebrating the life and miracles of the Virgin. One of these dramas is still performed every year in the Basque town of Elche and is the oldest European play in continuous production. In northern France, the Low Countries, and German-speaking lands, civic spectacles were performed over a period of several days, celebrating local history or the place of the community in the sacred history of the Bible. But not all plays were pious. Some honored visiting kings and princes, while others celebrated the flouting of social conventions, featuring cross-dressing and the reversal of hierarchies, which were further expressions of the topsy-turvy world created by the Black Death.

## THE BEGINNINGS OF THE RENAISSANCE IN ITALY

Rummaging through some old books in a cathedral library, an Italian bureaucrat attached to the papal court at Avignon was surprised to find a manuscript of Cicero's letters—letters that no living person had known to exist. They had probably been copied in the time of Charlemagne and had then been forgotten for hundreds of years. How many other works of this great Roman orator had been lost to posterity? Clearly, Francesco Petrarca (1304–1374) thought he was living in an age of ignorance. A great gulf seemed to open up between his own time and that of the ancients: a middle age that separated him from those well-loved models.

**PETRARCH'S COPY OF VIRGIL.** Petrarch's devotion to the classics of Roman literature prompted him to commission this new frontispiece for his treasured volume of Virgil's poetry. It was painted by the Sienese artist Simone Martini, who (like Petrarch) was attached to the papal court at Avignon. It is an allegorical depiction of Virgil (top right) and his poetic creations: the hero Aeneas, wearing armor (top left); and the farmer and shepherd, whose humble labors are celebrated in Virgil's lesser-known works. The figure next to Aeneas is the fourth-century scholar Servius, who wrote a famous commentary on Virgil. He is shown drawing aside a curtain to reveal the poet in a creative trance. The two scrolls proclaim (in Latin) that Italy was the country that nourished famous poets, and that Virgil helped it to achieve the glories of classical Greece. ■ *How does this image encapsulate and express Petrarch's devotion to the classical past?*

For centuries, Christian intellectuals had regarded the "dark ages" as the time between Adam's expulsion from Eden and the birth of Christ. But now, Petrarch (anglicized as Petrarca) redefined that concept and applied it to his own era. According to him, it was not the pagan past but the time that separated him from direct communion with the classics. And he wanted desperately to bridge this gap, "I would have written to you long ago," he said in a Latin letter to the Greek poet Homer (dead for over 2,000 years), "had it not been for the fact that we lack a common language."

Petrarch was famous in his own day as an Italian poet, a Latin stylist, and a tireless advocate for the resuscitation of the classical past. The values that he and his followers began to espouse would give rise to a new intellectual and artistic movement in Italy, a movement strongly critical of the present and admiring of a past that had disappeared with the fragmentation of Rome's empire and the end of Italy's greatness. We know this movement as the Renaissance, from the French word for "rebirth," a term that was invented in the eighteenth century and popularized in the nineteenth (when the term *medieval* was also invented). It has since become shorthand for the epoch *following* the Middle Ages—but it was really part of that same era.

## Renaissance Classicism

Talking about "the Renaissance," then, is a way of talking about some significant changes in education and artistic outlook that began to transform the culture of northern Italy in the late fourteenth century—and that eventually influenced the rest of Europe in important ways. This term has often been taken literally, as though the cultural accomplishments of antiquity had ceased to be appreciated and needed to be "reborn." Yet we have been tracing the enduring influence of classical civilization in many chapters and have constantly noted the reverence accorded to the heritage of antiquity, not to mention the persistence of Roman law and Roman institutions.

That said, the concept of "renaissance" helps to explain some of the key developments of this era. For example, the ancient texts that had long been preserved in monastic libraries came to be more widely available to secular scholars such as Petrarch. Their "discovery" of works by Livy, Tacitus, and Lucretius expanded the classical canon considerably, supplementing the well-studied works of Virgil, Ovid, and Cicero. Even more important was the expanded access to ancient Greek literature. As we noted in Chapters 8 and 9, Greek scientific and philosophical works became available to western Europeans in the twelfth and thirteenth centuries thanks to increased contact with Islam, via Latin translations of Arabic translations of the original Greek. And yet no Greek poems or plays were yet available in Latin translations, and neither were the major dialogues of Plato. Moreover, only a handful of western Europeans could read the language of classical Greece. But as the Mongols and, after them, the Ottoman Turks put increasing pressure on the shrinking borders of Byzantium (see below), more and more Greek-speaking intellectuals fled to Italy, bringing their books and their knowledge with them.

Some Italian intellectuals not only had increased access to more classical texts but they also used these texts in new ways. For centuries, Christian scholars had worked to bring ancient writings and values into line with their own beliefs (Chapter 6). But the new reading methods pioneered by Petrarch and others fostered an increased awareness of the conceptual gap that separated their contemporary world from that of antiquity. This awareness awakened a determination to recapture truly ancient worldviews and value systems. In the second half of the fifteenth century, especially, classical models also contributed strikingly to the distinctive artistic style that is most strongly associated with the Renaissance, something we will address in Chapter 12.

Another distinguishing feature of this new perspective on the classical past was the way that it became commercialized. Competition among and within Italian city-states fostered a culture of display that used the symbols and artifacts of ancient Rome as pawns in an endless power game. Meanwhile, the relative weakness of the Church contributed to the growth of claims to power based on classical models—even by Italian bishops and Church-sponsored universities. When the papacy was eventually restored to Rome, it too had to compete in this Renaissance arena, by patronizing the artists and intellectuals who espoused these aesthetic and political ideals.

## Renaissance Humanism

A crucial feature of this new intellectual and political agenda is summarized in the term *humanism*. This was a program of study that aimed to replace the scholastic emphasis on logic and theology—central to the curriculum of medieval universities—with the study of ancient literature, rhetoric, history, and ethics. That is, the goal of a humanist education was the understanding of the human experience through the lenses of the classical past. In contrast, a scholastic education filtered human experience through the teachings of scripture and the Church Fathers, with human salvation as the ultimate goal.

## Realizing Devotion

These two paintings by the Flemish artist Rogier van der Weyden (*FAN der VIE-den*; c. 1400–1464) capture some of the most compelling characteristics of late medieval art, particularly the trend toward realistic representations of holy figures and sacred stories. In image A, the artist depicts himself as the evangelist Luke, regarded in Christian tradition as a painter of portraits. He is sketching the Virgin nursing the infant Jesus in a townhouse overlooking a Flemish city. In image B, van der Weyden imagines the entombment of the body of Christ by his followers, including the Virgin (left), Mary Magdalene (kneeling), and the disciple John (right). Here he makes use of a motif that became increasingly prominent in the later Middle Ages: Christ as the Man of Sorrows, displaying his wounds and inviting the viewer to share in his suffering. In both paintings, van der Weyden emphasizes the humanity of his subjects rather than their iconic status (see Chapter 7), and places them in the urban and rural landscapes of his own world.

### Questions for Analysis

1. How are these paintings different from the sacred images of the earlier Middle Ages (see, for example, pages 304 and 342)? What messages does the artist convey by setting these events in his own immediate present?

2. In what ways do these paintings reflect broad changes in popular piety and medieval devotional practices? Why, for example, would the artist display the dead body of Christ, covered with wounds, rather than depicting him as resurrected and triumphant, or as an all-seeing creator and judge?

3. In general, how would you interpret these images as evidence of the worldview of the fifteenth century? What do they tell us about people's attitudes, emotions, and values?

A. Saint Luke drawing the portrait of the Virgin.

B. The Deposition.

Humanists accordingly preferred ancient writings to those of more recent authors, including their own contemporaries. And although some humanists wrote in Italian as well as Latin, most regarded vernacular literature as a lesser diversion suitable only for the uneducated; serious scholarship and praiseworthy poetry could be written only in Latin or Greek. Proper Latin, moreover, had to be the classical Latin of Cicero and Virgil, not the evolving language common to universities, international diplomacy, law, and the Church.

Renaissance humanists therefore condemned the living Latin of their day as a barbarous departure from classical (and therefore "correct") standards of Latin style. And ironically, their determination to revive this older language actually killed the lively Latin that had continued to flourish in Europe. By insisting on outmoded standards of grammar, syntax, and diction, they turned Latin into a fossilized discourse that ceased to have any direct relevance to daily life. They thus contributed, unwittingly, to the ultimate triumph of the various European vernaculars they despised and the demise of Latin as a common medium of communication.

Because humanism was an educational program designed to produce virtuous citizens and able public officials, it largely excluded women, because women were largely excluded from Italian public life. In a political context, humanism could be made to serve either the ideals of citizenship as exemplified by the Roman Republic, or the authoritarian agendas of autocratic rulers who wanted to emulate Roman imperial power.

## Why Italy?

These new attitudes toward education and the ancient past were fostered in northern Italy for historically specific reasons. After the Black Death, this region was the most densely populated part of Europe; other urban areas, notably northeastern France and Flanders, had been decimated by the Great Famine as well as by the plague. This region also differed from the rest of urbanized Europe because aristocratic families customarily lived in cities rather than in rural castles, and consequently, they became more fully involved in public affairs than their counterparts north of the Alps. Moreover, many town-dwelling aristocrats were engaged in banking or mercantile enterprises, while many rich mercantile families imitated the manners of the aristocracy. The Florentine ruling family, the Medici, originally made their fortune in banking and commerce, yet they were able to assimilate into the nobility.

These developments help to explain the emergence of humanist education. Newly wealthy families were not content to have their sons learn only the skills necessary to become successful businessmen; they sought teachers who would impart the knowledge and finesse that would enable them to cut a figure in society, mix with their noble neighbors, and speak with authority on public affairs. Consequently, Italy produced and attracted a large number of independent intellectuals who were not affiliated with monasteries, cathedral schools, or universities. Many of these intellectuals served as schoolmasters for wealthy young men while acting as cultural consultants and secretaries for their families. And they advertised their learning by producing political and ethical treatises and works of literature that would attract the attention of wealthy patrons or reflect well on the patrons they already had. As a result, Italian schools and private tutors turned out the best-educated laymen in Europe, men who constituted a new generation of wealthy, knowledgeable patrons ready to invest in the cultivation of new ideas and new forms of literary and artistic expression.

A second reason that late-medieval Italy was the birthplace of the Renaissance movement had to do with its vexed political situation. Unlike France and England, or the kingdoms of Spain, Scandinavia, and eastern Europe, Italy had no unifying political institutions. Italians therefore looked to the classical past for their time of glory, dreaming of a day when Rome would be, again, the center of the world. They boasted that ancient Roman monuments were omnipresent in their landscape and that classical Latin literature referred to cities and sites they recognized as their own.

Northern Italians were particularly intent on reappropriating their classical heritage because they were seeking to establish an independent cultural identity that could help oppose the intellectual and political supremacy of France. The removal of the papacy to Avignon had heightened antagonism between the city-states of Italy and the powerful nation-state beyond the Alps. This also explains the Italians' rejection of the scholasticism taught in northern Europe's universities and the humanists' embrace of intellectual alternatives. As Roman literature and learning took hold in the imaginations of Italy's intellectuals, so too did Roman art and architecture; ancient Roman models could help Italians create an artistic alternative to the dominant French school of Gothic architecture, just as ancient Roman learning offered an intellectual alternative to the scholasticism of Paris.

Finally, this Italian Renaissance could not have occurred without the underpinning of Italian wealth gained through the commercial ventures described in Chapter 10. This wealth meant that talented men seeking employment and patronage were more likely to stay at home, fueling the artistic and intellectual competition that arose from the intensification of urban pride and the concentration of

## A Renaissance Attitude toward Women

*Italian society of the fourteenth and fifteenth centuries was characterized by marriage patterns whereby men in their late twenties or thirties married women in their mid- to late teens. This demographic fact probably contributed to the widely shared belief that wives were essentially children who could not be trusted with important matters and who were best trained by being beaten. Renaissance humanism did little to change such attitudes, and in some cases, even reinforced them. The following is an excerpt from a treatise* On the Family *by Leon Battista Alberti (1404–1472), a Genoese architect and intellectual who also wrote an important treatise* On Painting. *He is often regarded as typifying the "Renaissance man."*

After my wife had been settled in my house a few days, and after her first pangs of longing for her mother and family had begun to fade, I took her by the hand and showed her around the whole house. I explained that the loft was the place for grain and that the stores of wine and wood were kept in the cellar. I showed her where things needed for the table were kept, and so on, through the whole house. At the end there were no household goods of which my wife had not learned both the place and the purpose. . . .

Only my books and records and those of my ancestors did I determine to keep well sealed. . . . These my wife not only could not read, she could not even lay hands on them. I kept my records at all times . . . locked up and arranged in order in my study, almost like sacred and religious objects. I never gave my wife permission to enter that place, with me or alone. . . .

[Husbands] who take counsel with their wives . . . are madmen if they think true prudence or good counsel lies in the female brain. . . . For this very reason I have always tried carefully not to let any secret of mine be known to a woman. I did not doubt that my wife was most loving, and more discreet and modest in her ways than any, but I still considered it safer to have her unable, and not merely unwilling, to harm me. . . . Furthermore, I made it a rule never to speak with her of anything but household matters or questions of conduct, or of the children.

Source: Leon Battista Alberti, "On the Family," in *The Family in Renaissance Florence,* ed. and trans. Renée N. Watkins (Columbia, SC: 1969), pp. 208–13, as abridged in Julie O'Faolain and Lauro Martines, eds., *Not in God's Image: Women in History from the Greeks to the Victorians* (New York: 1973), pp. 187–88.

### Questions for Analysis

1. For what reasons did Alberti argue that a wife should have no access to books or records?

2. Would you have expected humanism to make attitudes toward women more liberal and "modern"? How do views such as Alberti's challenge such assumptions?

3. Compare Alberti's view of women to that of Christine de Pisan (page 365). How do you think Christine would have responded to this passage?

---

individual and family wealth in urban areas. Cities themselves became the primary patrons of art and learning in the fourteenth century.

### Florentine Civic Ideals

Petrarch's personal goal was a solitary life of contemplation and asceticism. But subsequent Italian intellectuals, especially those of Florence, developed a different vision of life's true purpose. For them, the goal of classical education was civic enrichment. Humanists such as Leonardo Bruni (c. 1370–1444) and Leon Battista Alberti (1404–1472) taught that man's nature equips him for action, for usefulness to his family and society, and for serving the state—ideally a city-state after the Florentine model. In their view, ambition and the quest for glory were noble impulses that ought to be encouraged and channeled toward these ends. They also refused to condemn the accumulation of material possessions, arguing that the history of human progress is inseparable from the human dominion of the earth and its resources.

Many of the Florentine humanists' civic ideals are expressed in Alberti's treatise *On the Family* (1443) (see **Analyzing Primary Sources** on page 370), in which he presents the nuclear family as the fundamental unit of the city-state. Alberti accordingly argued that the family should mirror the city-state's organization, thereby consigning women—who, in reality, governed the household—to childbearing, child rearing, and subservience to men even within this domestic realm. He asserted, furthermore, that women should play no role whatsoever in the public sphere. Although actual women fiercely resisted such dismissals of women's abilities, the humanism of the Renaissance was characterized by a pervasive denigration of them—a denigration often mirrored in the works of classical literature that these humanists so admired.

## New Ways of Reading Ancient Texts

The humanists of northern Italy were aided by a number of Byzantine scholars who had migrated to northern Italy in the first half of the fifteenth century and gave instruction in the ancient form of their own language. Wealthy, well-connected men increasingly aspired to acquire Greek masterpieces, which often involved journeys back to Constantinople. In 1423, one adventurous bibliophile managed to bring back 238 manuscript books, among them rare works of Sophocles, Euripides, and Thucydides. These were quickly paraphrased in Latin and so made accessible to medieval Europeans for the first time.

This influx of new classical texts spurred a new interest in the critical reading of ancient sources. A pioneer in this activity was Lorenzo Valla (1407–1457). Born in Rome and active as a secretary to the king of Naples and Sicily, Valla had no allegiance to the republican ideals of the Florentine humanists. Instead, he turned his skills to the painstaking analysis of Greek and Latin writings to show how the historical study of language could discredit old assumptions and even unmask some texts as forgeries. For example, papal propagandists argued that the papacy's claim to secular power in Europe derived from rights granted to the bishop of Rome by the emperor Constantine in the fourth century, enshrined in a document known as the "Donation of Constantine." By analyzing the language of this text, Valla proved that it could not have been written in the time of Constantine because it contained more recent Latin usages and vocabulary.

This demonstration not only threatened to discredit more traditional scholarly methods, it alerted scholars to the necessity of avoiding anachronism in the study of history—that is, the intellectual vigilance needed to avoid projecting present values and expectations onto the past. Valla even applied his expert knowledge of Greek to elucidate the meaning of Saint Paul's letters, which he believed had been mangled by Jerome's Latin translation (Chapter 6). Valla's work was to prove an important link between Renaissance humanism and the Christian humanism that fueled the Reformation (see Chapter 13).

# THE END OF THE EASTERN ROMAN EMPIRE

The Greek-speaking refugees who arrived in Italy after the Black Death were responding to the succession of calamities that had reduced the once-proud eastern Roman Empire to a scattering of embattled provinces. As we have noted, when Constantinople fell to western European crusaders in 1204, the surrounding territories of Byzantium were severed from the capital that had held them together (Chapter 9). When the Latin presence in Constantinople was finally expelled in 1261, imperial power had been so weakened that it extended only into the immediate hinterlands of the city and to parts of the Greek Peloponnese. The rest of the empire had become a collection of small principalities that existed in precarious alliance with the Mongols, and indeed depended on the Pax Mongolica for survival (Chapter 10). Then, with the coming of the Black Death, the imperial capital suffered the loss of half its inhabitants and shrank still further. Meanwhile, the disintegration of the Mongol Empire laid the larger region of Anatolia open to a new set of invaders.

## The Rise of the Ottoman Turks

When the Mongols arrived in northwestern Anatolia, the Turks—originally a nomadic people—were already established there and were being converted to Islam by the resident Muslim powers of the region: the Seljuk sultanate of Rūm and the Abbasid caliphate of Baghdad. But when the Mongols toppled these older powers, they eliminated the two traditional authorities that had kept the Turkish chieftains in check. So now the Turks were free to raid, unhindered, along the soft frontiers of Byzantium. At the same time, the Turks remained far enough from the centers of Mongol power to avoid being destroyed themselves. One of their chieftains, Osman Gazi (1258–1326), even managed

**TIMUR THE LAME.** This bust of the Mongol leader, known in the West as Tamerlane, is based on a forensic reconstruction of his exhumed skull.

In 1402, another attack on Constantinople was deflected—this time, by a more potent foe with ambitions to match those of the Ottomans. Timur the Lame (Tamerlane, as he was called by European admirers) was born to a family of small landholders in the Mongol Khanate of Chagatai (named after its first ruler, the second son of Genghis Khan). While still a young man, he rose to prominence as a military leader and gained a reputation for tactical genius. He never officially assumed the title of khan in any of the territories he dominated, but instead moved ceaselessly from conquest to conquest, becoming the master of lands stretching from the Caspian Sea to the Volga River, as well as most of Persia. For a time, it looked briefly as if the Mongol Empire might be reunited under his reign. But Timur died in 1405, on his way to invade China, and his various conquests fell to local rulers. In Anatolia, the Ottoman Turks were able to regain their dominant position.

## The Fall of Constantinople

As Ottoman pressure increased on Constantinople during the 1420s and 1430s, monasteries and schools that had been established since the time of Constantine found themselves in the path of an advancing army. A steady stream of scholars fled westward, carrying a millennium's worth of books preserving the heritage of ancient Greece and the Hellenistic world. Then, in 1451, the Ottoman sultan Mehmet II turned his full attention to the conquest of the imperial city. In 1453, after a brilliantly executed siege, his army succeeded in breaching its walls. The Byzantine emperor was killed in the assault, the city itself was plundered, and its remaining population was sold into slavery.

The Ottoman conquest of Constantinople administered an enormous shock to European rulers and intellectuals. Yet its actual political and economic impact was minor. Ottoman control may have reduced European access to the Black Sea, but the bulk of the Eastern luxury trade with Europe had never passed through Black Sea ports in the first place. Europeans got most of their spices and silks through Venice, which imported them from Alexandria and Beirut, and these two cities did not fall to the Ottomans until the 1520s. Moreover, as we saw in Chapter 10, the Europeans already had colonial ambitions and significant trading interests in Africa and the Atlantic that connected them to far-reaching networks.

But if the practical effects of the Ottoman conquest were modest where Europe was concerned, the effects on

to establish his own kingdom, and eventually, his name became that of the Turkish dynasty that controlled the entire region for six centuries: the Ottomans.

By the mid-fourteenth century, Osman's successors had solidified their preeminence by capturing a number of important cities. These successes brought the Ottomans to the attention of the Byzantine emperor, who hired a contingent of them as mercenaries in 1345. They were extraordinarily successful, so much so that the eastern Roman Empire could not control their movements. The Turks struck out on their own and began to extend their control westward. In 1370, their holdings stretched all the way to the Danube. In 1389, they defeated a powerful coalition of Serbian forces at the battle of Kosovo, which enabled them to begin subduing Bulgaria, the Balkans, and eventually Greece. In 1396, the Ottoman army even attacked Constantinople itself, although it withdrew to repel an ineffectual crusading force that had been hastily sent by the papacy.

## Slavery and Social Advancement in the Ottoman Empire

To manage its continual expansion, the size of the Ottoman army and administration grew exponentially during this era, drawing more and more manpower from conquered territories. And because both army and bureaucracy were largely composed of slaves, the demand for more soldiers and administrators could best be met through further conquests that would capture yet more slaves. Those conquests, however, required a still larger army and an even more extensive bureaucracy—and so the cycle continued. It mirrors, in many respects, the dilemma of the Roman Empire in the centuries of its rapid expansion beyond Italy (Chapter 5), which also created an insatiable demand for slaves.

Not only were slaves the backbone of the Ottoman state, they were also critical to the lives of the Turkish upper class. An important measure of status was the number of slaves in one's household, with some elites maintaining households in the thousands. By the sixteenth century, the sultan alone possessed more than 20,000 slave attendants, not including his bodyguard and elite infantry units, both of which also comprised slaves.

Where did all of these slaves come from? Many were captured in war and many others were taken on raiding forays into Poland and Ukraine and then sold to slave merchants who shipped their captives from the Crimea to the slave markets of Istanbul. But slaves were also recruited from rural areas of the Ottoman Empire itself. Most were coerced, but some may have gone willingly. Because the vast majority of slaves were household servants and administrators rather than laborers, some men willingly accepted enslavement, believing that they would be better off as slaves in Istanbul than as impoverished peasants in the countryside. In the Balkans especially, many people were enslaved as children, handed over by their families to pay the "child tax" the Ottomans imposed on areas too poor to pay a monetary tribute. Although an excruciating experience for families, this practice opened up opportunities for social advancement. Special academies were created at Istanbul to train the ablest of the enslaved male children to act as administrators and soldiers, some of whom rose to become powerful figures in the Ottoman Empire.

For this reason, slavery carried relatively little social stigma. The sultans themselves were most often the sons of enslaved women. Because Muslims were not permitted to enslave other Muslims, the vast majority of Ottoman slaves were Christian—although many eventually converted to Islam. And because so many of the elite positions within the

**SULTAN MEHMET II, "THE CONQUEROR" (R. 1451–1481).** This portrait, executed by the Ottoman artist Siblizade Ahmed, exhibits stylistic features characteristic of both Central Asia and Europe. The sultan's pose—his aesthetic appreciation of the rose, his elegant handkerchief—are indicative of the former, as is the fact that he wears the white turban of a scholar and the thumb ring of an archer. But the subdued coloring and three-quarter profile may reflect the influence of Italian portraits. ■ *What did the artist achieve through this blending of styles and symbols?* ■ *What messages does this portrait convey?*

the Turks themselves were transformative. Vast new wealth poured into Anatolia, which the Ottomans increased by carefully tending the industrial and commercial interests of their new capital city, Constantinople, which they also called Istanbul, the Turkish pronunciation of the Greek phrase *eis tan polin* ("in the city"). Trade routes were redirected to feed the capital, and the Ottomans became a naval power in the eastern Mediterranean as well as in the Black Sea. As a result, Istanbul's population grew rapidly, from fewer than 100,000 in 1453 to more than 500,000. By 1600, it was the largest city in the world outside of China.

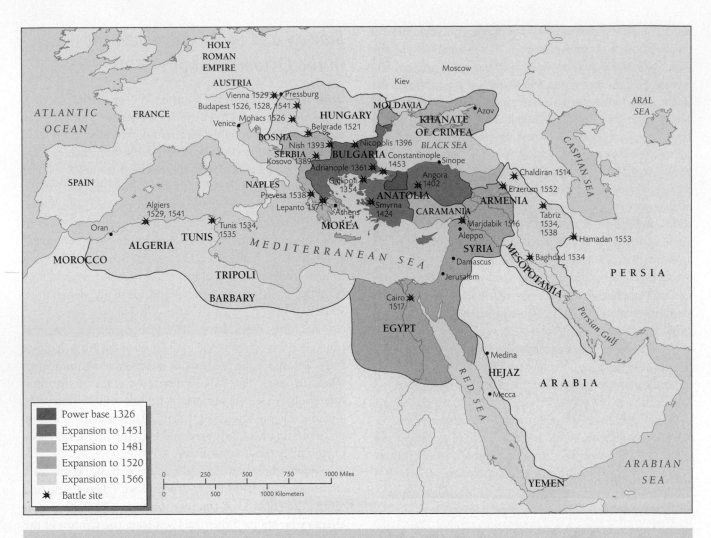

**THE GROWTH OF THE OTTOMAN EMPIRE.** Consider the patterns of Ottoman expansion revealed in this map. ▪ *Where is Constantinople (Istanbul), and how might its capture in 1453 have facilitated further conquests?* ▪ *Compare the extent of the Ottoman Empire in 1566 with that of the Byzantine Empire under Justinian (see the map on page 214). How would you account for their similarities?*

Ottoman government were held by these slaves, the paradoxical result was that Muslims, including the Turks themselves, were effectively excluded from the main avenues of social and political influence in the Ottoman Empire. Avenues to power were therefore remarkably open to men of ability and talent, most of them non-Muslim slaves.

This power was not limited to the government and the army, as commerce and business also remained largely in the hands of non-Muslims, most frequently Greeks, Syrians, and Jews. Jews in particular found in the Ottoman Empire a welcome refuge from the persecutions and expulsions that had characterized Jewish life in late-medieval Europe. After their expulsion from Spain in 1492 (see Chapter 12), more than 100,000 Spanish (Sephardic) Jews ultimately immigrated to the territories of the Ottoman Empire.

Because the Ottoman sultans were Sunni Muslims, they often dealt harshly with other Muslim sects and did not tolerate any forms of polytheism. But they accommodated their fellow monotheists, Christians and Jews, who were organized into legally recognized units and were permitted some rights of self-government. The authority of the Greek Orthodox patriarch of Constantinople was also tolerated, allowing Orthodox Christianity to maintain a presence in the capital founded by Constantine.

## WARFARE AND NATION BUILDING

War has always been an engine for the development of new technologies, something we have noted since Chapter 1. But in the era after the Black Death, the pace and scale of warfare escalated to an unprecedented degree—as did the deployment of new weapons. Explosives had been invented

**A FIFTEENTH-CENTURY SIEGE WITH CANNONS.** Cannons were an essential element in siege warfare during the Hundred Years' War.

twentieth, governments claimed new powers to tax their subjects and to recruit them as soldiers. Armies became larger and military technology deadlier. Wars became more destructive and society more militarized. As a result of these developments, the most successful European states were aggressively expansionist, and they aggressively engaged in creating an idea of national identity that would bind their peoples together against a common enemy.

## The Hundred Years' War Resumes

The Hundred Years' War can be divided into three main phases (see the map on page 376). The first phase dates from the initial declaration of war in 1337 (see Chapter 10), after which the English won a series of startling military victories before the Black Death put a temporary halt to hostilities. The war then resumed in 1356, with another English victory at Poitiers. Four years later, in 1360, Edward III decided to leverage his strong position, and renounced his larger claim to the French throne, in return for a guaranteed full sovereignty over a greatly enlarged duchy of Gascony, in southwestern France.

But the terms of the treaty were never honored, nor did it resolve the underlying issues that had led to the war itself, namely the problem of making good on any claim to sovereignty in contested territory and the question of the English king's place in the French royal succession. The French king continued to treat the English king as his vassal, while Edward and his heirs quickly renewed their claim to the throne of France.

Although there were no pitched battles in France itself for two decades after 1360, a destabilizing proxy war developed during the 1360s and 1370s, which spread violence to neighboring regions. Both the English troops (posted in Gascony) and the French troops (eager to avenge previous losses) were reluctant to settle down. Many organized into "Free Companies" of mercenaries and hired themselves out in the service of hostile factions in Castile and competing city-states in northern Italy. By 1376, when the conflict between England and France reignited, the Hundred Years' War had become a Europe-wide phenomenon.

in China, where they were used in fireworks displays, but they were first used to devastating and destructive effect in Europe. And although the earliest cannons were as dangerous to those who fired them as to those they targeted, they revolutionized the nature of warfare. In 1453, heavy artillery played a leading role in the outcomes of two crucial conflicts: when the Ottoman Turks breached the ancient defenses of Constantinople with cannon fire, and when the French captured the English-held city of Bordeaux, bringing an end to the attenuated conflict known as the Hundred Years' War.

Thereafter, cannons made it more difficult for rebellious aristocrats to hole up in their stone castles, and so consequently they aided in the consolidation of national monarchies. Cannons placed aboard ships made Europe's developing navies more effective. A handheld firearm, the pistol, was also invented during the fourteenth century; and around 1500, the musket ended forever the military dominance of heavily armored cavalry, giving the advantage to foot soldiers recruited from the ranks of average citizens.

Indeed, there is a symbiotic relationship between warfare and nation building, as well as between warfare and technology. Because Europeans were almost constantly at war from the fourteenth century to the middle of the

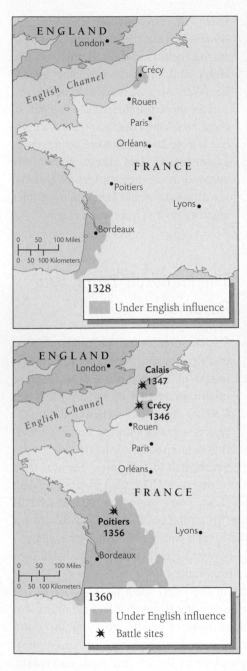

**THE PHASES OF THE HUNDRED YEARS' WAR.** Here we see three snapshots of the political geography of France during the Hundred Years' War. ▪ *In what areas of France did England make its greatest territorial gains before 1360?* ▪ *How and why did this change in the period leading up to 1429?* ▪ *What geographic and strategic advantages did the French monarchy enjoy after 1429 that might help explain its success in recapturing the French kingdom from the English?*

## The Brief Victory of Henry V

During this second phase of the war, the tide quickly shifted in favor of France. The new king, Charles V (r. 1364–1380), imposed a series of taxes to fund the raising of an army, restored order by disbanding the Free Companies, and hired the leader of one of these bands as the commander of his army. He thereby created a professional military that could match the English in discipline and tactics. By 1380, English territories in France had been reduced to a core area around the southwestern city of Bordeaux and the port of Calais in the extreme northeast.

Meanwhile, the aging Edward III had been succeeded by his nine-year-old grandson, Richard II (r. 1377–1399), who was too young to resume armed conflict in France. This was problematic, because the war had been extremely popular in England. Indeed, mismanagement by Richard's advisers was one of the issues that triggered the Peasants' Revolt in 1381. And when Richard came of age and showed no signs of warlike ambition, many of his own relatives turned against him. Richard retaliated against the ringleader of this faction, his cousin Henry of Lancaster, sending him into exile and confiscating his property. Henry's supporters used this as pretext for rebellion, and in 1399, Richard was deposed by Henry and eventually murdered.

As a usurper whose legitimacy was always in doubt, Henry IV (r. 1399–1413) struggled to maintain his authority in the face of rebellions and other challenges to his kingship. The best way to unite the country would have been to renew the war against France, but Henry was frequently ill and in no position to lead an army. However, when his son Henry V succeeded him in 1413, the new king immediately began to prepare for an invasion. His timing was excellent: the French royal government was foundering, owing to the insanity of the reigning king, Charles VI (r. 1380–1422). A brilliant diplomat as well as a capable soldier, Henry V sealed an alliance with the powerful Duke of Burgundy, who was allegedly loyal to France but stood to gain from its defeat. Henry also made a treaty with the German emperor, who agreed not to come to France's aid.

When he crossed the English Channel with his troops in the autumn of 1415, Henry thus faced a much-depleted French army that could not rely on reinforcements. Although it was still vastly larger and boasted hundreds of mounted knights, it was undisciplined. It was also severely hampered by bad weather and deep mud when the two armies clashed at Agincourt on October 25 of that year—conditions that favored the lighter English infantry. Henry's men managed to win a crushing victory. Then, over the next five years, Henry conquered most of northern France. In 1420, the ailing Charles VI was forced to recognize him as heir to the throne, thereby disinheriting his own son, whose ceremonial title was *Dauphin* ("dolphin"), from the heraldic device of the borderland province he controlled. Henry sealed the deal by marrying the French princess, Catherine, and fathering an heir to the joint kingdom of England and France.

## Joan of Arc's Triumph and Betrayal

Unlike his great-grandfather Edward III, who had claimed the French throne largely as a bargaining chip to secure sovereignty over Gascony (Chapter 10), Henry V honestly believed himself to be the rightful king of France. And his astonishing success in capturing the kingdom seemed to put the stamp of divine approval on that claim. But Henry's successes in France also transformed the nature of the conflict, turning it from a profitable war of conquest and plunder into an extended and expensive military occupation. It might have been sustainable had Henry been as long lived as many of his predecessors, but he died early in 1422, just short of his thirty-sixth birthday. And King Charles VI died only a few months later, leaving the infant Henry VI

(r. 1422–1461) to be crowned the first—and last—king of both England and France.

Meanwhile, English armies continued to press southward into territories held by the Dauphin, who was determined to win back his inheritance. Yet French confidence in his right to the throne had been shattered by his own mother's declaration that he was illegitimate. It began to look as though England would once again rule an empire comprising much of France, as it had for a century and a half after the Norman conquest.

But in 1429, a peasant girl from Lorraine (a territory only nominally part of France) made her way to the Dauphin's court and announced that an angel had told her that he, Charles, was the rightful king, and that she, Joan, should drive the English out of France. The very fact that Joan of Arc even got a hearing underscores the hopelessness of the Dauphin's position—as does the extraordinary fact that he gave her a contingent of troops. With this force, Joan liberated the strategic city of Orléans, then under siege by the English. She then led her army to a series of victories that culminated in the coronation of the Dauphin as King Charles VII in the cathedral of

**JOAN OF ARC.** A contemporary sketch of Joan was drawn in the margin of this register, documenting official proceedings at the Parlement of Paris in 1429.

## The Condemnation of Joan of Arc by the University of Paris, 1431

*After Joan's capture by the Burgundians, she was handed over to the English and tried for heresy at an ecclesiastical court set up in Rouen. It was on this occasion that the theology faculty of Paris pronounced the following verdict on her actions.*

You, Joan, have said that, since the age of thirteen, you have experienced revelations and the appearance of angels, of St. Catherine and St. Margaret, and that you have very often seen them with your bodily eyes, and that they have spoken to you. As for the first point, the clerks of the University of Paris have considered the manner of the said revelations and appearances. . . . Having considered all . . . they have declared that all the things mentioned above are lies, falsenesses, misleading and pernicious things and that such revelations are superstitions, proceeding from wicked and diabolical spirits.

Item: You have said that your king had a sign by which he knew that you were sent by God, for St. Michael, accompanied by several angels, some of which having wings, the others crowns, with St. Catherine and St. Margaret, came to you at the chateau of Chinon. All the company ascended through the floors of the castle until they came to the room of your king, before whom the angel bearing the crown bowed. . . . As for this matter, the clerks say that it is not in the least probable, but it is rather a presumptuous lie, misleading and pernicious, a false statement, derogatory of the dignity of the Church and of the angels. . . .

Item: you have said that, at God's command, you have continually worn men's clothes, and that you have put on a short robe, doublet, shoes attached by points, also that you have had short hair, cut around above the ears, without retaining anything on your person which shows that you are a woman, and that several times you have received the body of Our Lord dressed in this fashion, despite having been admonished to give it up several times, the which you would not do. You have said that you would rather die than abandon the said clothing, if it were not at God's command, and that if you were wearing those clothes and were with the king, and those of your party, it would be one of the greatest benefits for the kingdom of France. You have also said that not for anything would you swear an oath not to wear the said clothing and carry arms any longer. And all these things you say you have done for the good and at the command of God. As for these things, the clerics say that you blaspheme God and hold him in contempt in his sacraments; you transgress Divine Law, Holy Scripture, and canon law. You err in the faith. You boast in vanity. You are suspected of idolatry and you have condemned yourself in not wishing to wear clothing suitable to your sex, but you follow the custom of Gentiles and Saracens.

Source: Carolyne Larrington, ed. and trans., *Women and Writing in Medieval Europe* (New York: 1995), pp. 183–84.

### Questions for Analysis

1. Paris was in the hands of the English when this condemnation was issued. Is there any evidence that its authors were coerced into making this pronouncement?

2. On what grounds was Joan condemned for heresy?

3. In what ways does Joan's behavior highlight larger trends in late medieval spirituality and popular piety?

---

Reims, where French kings had been crowned for nearly a thousand years.

Despite her miraculous successes, Charles and the aristocratic generals of his army regarded Joan as an embarrassment: a peasant leading the nobility, a woman dominating men, and a commoner who claimed to have been commissioned by God. Her very charisma made her dangerous. So when the Burgundians captured her in battle a few months later and handed her over to the English as a prisoner of war, the French king she had helped to crown did nothing to save her. Accused of witchcraft, condemned by the theologians of Paris, and tried for heresy by an English ecclesiastical court, Joan was burned to death in the market square at Rouen in 1431. She was nineteen years old.

The French forces whom Joan had inspired, however, continued on the offensive. In 1435, the duke of Burgundy withdrew his alliance with the English, whose young king, Henry VI, proved to be first incompetent and then insane. Finally, a series of French victories culminated in the capture of Bordeaux. After 1453, English control over French territory was limited to the port of Calais on the French coast of the English Channel.

## The Long Shadow of the Hundred Years' War

The Hundred Years' War challenged the very existence of France. The disintegration of that kingdom—first during the 1350s and 1360s, and again between 1415 and 1435—glaringly revealed the fragility of the bonds that tied the king to his people and the royal capital of Paris to the kingdom's outlying regions. Nonetheless, the king's power had increased by the war's end, laying the foundations on which the power of the French state would be built.

The Hundred Years' War also had dramatic effects on the English monarchy. When English armies in France were successful, the king rode a wave of popularity that fueled an emerging sense of English identity. When the war turned against the English, defeats abroad undermined support for the monarch at home. Of the nine English kings who ruled England between 1307 and 1485, five were deposed and murdered by factions. This was a consequence of England's peculiar form of kingship, whose strength depended on the king's ability to mobilize popular support through Parliament while maintaining the support of his nobility through successful wars. Failure to maintain this balance was even more destabilizing in England than it would have been elsewhere, precisely because royal power was so centralized.

In France, the nobility could endure the insanity of Charles VI because his government was not powerful enough to threaten them. In England, by contrast, neither the nobility nor the nation could afford the weak kingship of Henry VI. The result was an aristocratic rebellion that led to a full-blown civil war: the Wars of the Roses, so called because of the floral emblems (red and white) adopted by the two competing noble families, Lancaster and York. It ended only when a Lancastrian claimant, Henry Tudor (r. 1485–1509), resolved the dynastic feud by marrying Elizabeth of York, and ruling as Henry VII, establishing a new dynasty whose symbol was a rose with both white and red petals. His second son would become Henry VIII (see Chapter 13).

In spite of England's ultimate defeat, the Hundred Years' War strengthened English identity in several ways.

First, it equated national identity with the power of the state and its king. Second, it fomented a strong anti-French sentiment that led to the triumph of the English language over French for the first time since the Norman conquest, over 300 years earlier; the first English court to speak English was that of Richard II, a patron of Geoffrey Chaucer. And having lost its continental possessions, England became, for the first time, a self-contained island nation that looked to the sea for defense and opportunity—not to the Continent. This would later prove to be an advantage in many ways.

## Conflict in Italy and the Holy Roman Empire

Elsewhere, the perpetual warfare that began to characterize the history of Europe during this period was even more destructive than it had proved to be in the struggle between England and France. In northern and central Italy, the second half of the fourteenth century was marked by incessant conflict. With the papacy based in Avignon, Rome was torn by factional violence. Warfare among northern Italian city-states added to the violence caused by urban rebellions in the wake of the plague. Finally, around 1400, Venice, Milan, and Florence succeeded in stabilizing their differing forms of government: Venice was now ruled by an oligarchy of merchants, Milan by a family of despots, and Florence was ruled as a republic but dominated by the influence of a few wealthy clans, especially the Medici banking family. Having settled their internal problems, these three cities then began to expand their influence by subordinating other cities to their rule.

Eventually, almost all the towns of northern Italy were allied with one or another of these powers. An exception was Genoa, which had its own trading empire in the Mediterranean and Atlantic (Chapter 10). The papacy, meanwhile, reasserted its control over central Italy when it was restored to Rome in 1377. The southern kingdom of Naples and Sicily persisted as a separate entity, but a constantly unstable one, riven by local warfare and poor government. After 1453, when the Hundred Years' War had ended and Ottoman expansion had been checked at Istanbul, an uneasy peace was achieved. But diplomacy and frequently shifting alliances did little to check the ambitions of any one state for further expansion or change the fact that none of these small-scale states could oppose the powerful national monarchies that were emerging north of the Alps.

In the lands of the Holy Roman Empire, meanwhile, armed conflict among territorial princes significantly weakened all combatants. Periodically, a powerful emperor would emerge to play a role, but the dominant trend was toward the continuing dissolution of power, with German princes dividing their territories among their heirs while free cities and local lords strove to shake off the princes' rule. Between 1350 and 1450, near anarchy prevailed in many regions. Only in the eastern regions of the empire were the rulers of Bavaria, Austria, and Brandenburg-Prussia able to strengthen their authority, mostly by supporting the efforts of the nobility to subject their peasants to serfdom and conquering and colonizing new territories on their eastern frontiers.

## King Jadwiga of Poland and the Jagiellonian Dynasty

During the thirteenth century (see Chapter 9), Poland had been culturally and economically enriched by its willingness to welcome the Jewish communities, which were being expelled from other parts of Europe. In the fourteenth century, Polish towns also benefited from a wave of German immigrants, mostly merchants, with ties to the Hanseatic League and to independent cities in the Holy Roman Empire. In order to attract and accommodate these newcomers, the rulers of Poland and other eastern European kingdoms granted special charters to the towns in which they settled. These charters granted citizens the rights of self-governance, collectively known as Magdeburg Law (named after a major German mercantile city).

In the centuries after the Black Death, more and more towns and villages were able to take advantage of these privileges, promoting the rapid urbanization of the once rural region of central and eastern Europe and creating a web of prosperous, ethnically and religiously diverse cities that generated enormous wealth. Lviv, now in western Ukraine, is a splendid example: ruled by Polish kings and governed by German town law, it fostered a large population of Armenians, Jews, Serbians, and Hungarians, among many others.

Alongside the commercial benefits of these burgeoning towns were the intellectual benefits. Just as medieval universities flourished in western Europe during the economic boom of the twelfth century, they now came to be established in central and eastern Europe, too. The first of these institutions was founded in the Bohemian capital of Prague in 1347, by Emperor Charles IV. The Polish king Casimir III (r. 1333–1370) followed his lead by establishing a fledgling university in Kraków in 1364. Universities in Vienna and Pécs (Hungary) were also established in the next few years. The university at Kraków soon came to be known as the Jagiellonian University, after the new dynasty that endowed it as a permanent institution.

The Jagiellonian dynasty was formed when the young female ruler of Poland, Jadwiga (*yahd-VEE-gah*), married the Grand Duke of Lithuania, Jagiello (*yahg-ee-EL-oh*). It was an extraordinary match. Jadwiga had been crowned king (not queen) in 1384, when she was barely ten years old. The Polish lords who acted as her advisers had insisted on the title because they did not want to see her eventual husband ruling over them. In search of a suitable match, they turned their gaze to the neighboring northern territory of Lithuania, which would give Poland more access to the Baltic Sea and more support against ongoing encroachments from the east by the Teutonic Knights of Prussia. Jadwiga agreed to the match even though Duke Jagiello was not only thirty years her senior but also a pagan. They were married after Jagiello's conversion to the Roman Church in 1386, when he received the royal baptismal name Wladyslaw II.

Thereafter, Jadwiga and Wladyslaw II Jagiello ruled their realms jointly, tripling the size of Poland-Lithuania

**WAWEL CATHEDRAL (KRAKÓW).** King Jadwiga of Poland and her infant daughter are entombed in the royal burial chamber of this magnificent church, which combines elements of medieval Romanesque, Gothic, and Byzantine architecture. It is surrounded by the royal castle on the Wawel (*VAH-vel*) Hill, overlooking the River Vistula.

and making it the largest and most powerful state in central Europe. Their patronage of the new university at Kraków turned it into one of Europe's intellectual powerhouses. It would later nurture such great Polish scholars as Nicolaus Copernicus (1473–1543) (see Chapter 16) and Karel Wojtyła (1920–2005), who became Pope John Paul II. Jadwiga also promoted Polish as a literary language, even encouraging the translation of the Bible into the vernacular. When she died in 1399, after a difficult childbirth, her husband married the wife she had chosen for him. In 1997, she was canonized as a saint of the Catholic Church.

**THE ROYAL CHAPEL OF KING WLADYSLAW II JAGIELLO.** This image captures only some of the hundreds of magnificent paintings that decorate the walls of the chapel in Lublin (Poland). This cycle of frescoes, which depict scenes from the Bible, was commissioned by King Jagiello after the death of his royal wife Jadwiga. The paintings, completed in 1418, were executed by a team of master artists from Ukraine, who combined eastern Orthodox imagery and styles with those of western Europe.
■ *Based on that you have learned about Jagiello, why would he have chosen to decorate his chapel in this way?*

## The Growth of National Monarchies

In France, England, Poland, Hungary, as well as in smaller kingdoms such as Scotland and Portugal, the later Middle Ages saw the emergence of more cohesive states than any that had existed before. The political patterns established in the formative twelfth and thirteenth centuries had made this possible, yet the active construction of a sense of national identity in these territories, and the fusion of that identity with kingship, were new phenomena. Forged by war and fueled by the growing cultural importance of vernacular languages, this fusion produced a new type of political organization: the national monarchy.

The advantages of a national monarchy over older forms of political organization—such as the empire, the principality, or the city-state—are significant. When the armies of France invaded the Italian peninsula at the end of the fifteenth century, neither the militias of the city-states nor the far-flung resources of Venice were a match for them. The German lands and the Low Countries endured similar invasions only a few generations later and, along with Italy, would remain battlegrounds for competing armies until the middle of the nineteenth century. But the new national monarchies brought significant disadvantages, too. They guaranteed the prevalence of warfare in Europe as they continued their struggles for sovereignty and territory, and eventually, they would export their rivalry through imperial ventures in Africa and the New World.

## THE CHALLENGES OF THE ROMAN CHURCH

Although the century after the Black Death witnessed the papacy's return to Rome, it also witnessed changes in the Church that would have far-reaching consequences in the centuries to come. Like other large landowners, the monasteries of Europe suffered from the economic changes brought about by the new world order, as did the Church's bishops who confronted the same dilemmas as the secular nobility. But no ecclesiastical institution suffered more severe trials than the papacy, which endured almost seventy years of exile from Rome followed by a debilitating forty-year schism. It then faced a protracted battle with reformers who sought to reduce the pope's role in Church governance. Even though the papacy won this battle in the short term, the renewed abuse of papal power would, in the long run, bring about the permanent schism caused by the Reformation of the sixteenth century (see Chapter 13).

## The Great Western Schism

In the decades that were transforming European society in so many other ways, calls for the papacy's return to Rome grew more insistent. It was eventually brought about by the letter-writing campaign of the nun and mystic Catherine of Siena (1347–1380), whose teasing but pious missives to Gregory XI (r. 1370–1378) alternately shamed and coerced him. In 1377, he was persuaded to make the move.

But the papacy's restoration was short lived. A year after Gregory's return to Rome, he died. His cardinals—many of them Frenchmen—struggled to interpret the wishes of the volatile Romans, whose habit of expressing themselves through violence was unsettling to outsiders. Later, the cardinals would claim that they capitulated to the Roman mob when they elected an Italian candidate, Urban VI. When Urban fell out with them soon afterward, the cardinals fled the city and, from a safe distance, declared his

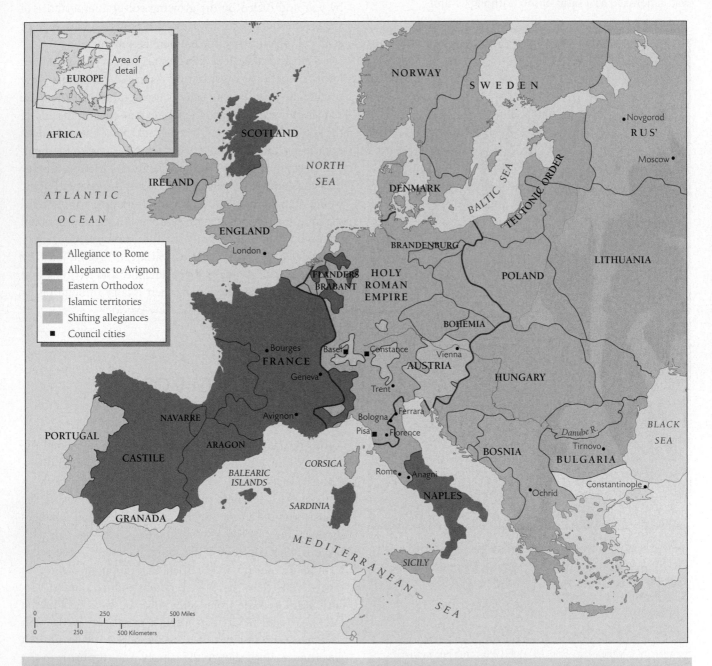

**THE GREAT SCHISM, 1378–1417.** During the Great Western Schism, the various territories of Europe were divided in their allegiances.
■ *According to the map key, what choices were the peoples of these regions making?* ■ *What common interests would have united the supporters of the Avignon pope or of the Roman pope?* ■ *Why would areas such as Portugal and Austria waver in their support?*

# Past and Present

## Replacing "Retired" Popes

When Pope Benedict XVI decided to retire from office in February 2013, pundits and theologians alike struggled to find a precedent for this extraordinary decision. Most reached back to the year 1417, when Pope Martin V was elected at the Council of Constance (left) to replace the "retired" Gregory XII. But in this case, the retirement was not voluntary, and it was accompanied by the enforced resignation of a rival pope and the excommunication of yet another. The installation mass of Pope Francis in March 2013 (right) was much more universally celebrated and much more public than that of his medieval predecessor.

S Watch related author interview on the Student Site

reign invalid because they had elected him under duress. They then elected a new pope, a Frenchman who took the name Clement VII. Urban retaliated by naming a new and entirely Italian College of Cardinals and refusing Clement access to the city. The French pope and his cardinals withdrew ignominiously to the papal palace in Avignon, while the Italian pope remained in Rome.

The resulting rift is known as the Great Schism (or, more specifically, the Great Western Schism, to distinguish it from the Great East–West Schism between the Roman and Orthodox Churches). Between 1378 and 1417, the Roman Church was divided between two—and, ultimately, three—competing papacies, each claiming to be legitimate and each denouncing the heresy of the others.

It is not surprising that Europe's religious allegiances fractured along political lines drawn by the ongoing Hundred Years' War: France and its allies Scotland, Castile, Aragon, and Naples recognized the pope in Avignon; whereas England, Germany, northern Italy, Scandinavia, Bohemia,

Poland, and Hungary recognized the Roman pope. There was no obvious way to end this embarrassing state of affairs, and the two rival Colleges of Cardinals continued to elect successors every time a pope died, perpetuating the problem. Finally, in 1409, some cardinals from both camps met at Pisa, where they ceremonially declared the deposition of both popes and named a new one from among their number. But neither of the popes reigning in Rome and Avignon accepted that decision, and there were now three rival popes excommunicating each other instead of two.

## The Council of Constance and the Failure of the Conciliar Movement

This debacle was ultimately addressed between 1414 and 1418 at the Council of Constance, the largest and longest ecclesiastical gathering since the Council of Nicea over a

# Council or Pope?

> The Great Schism spurred a fundamental and far-reaching debate about the nature of authority within the Church. Arguments for papal supremacy rested on traditional claims that the popes were the successors of Saint Peter, to whom Jesus Christ had delegated his own authority. Arguments for the supremacy of a general council had been advanced by many intellectuals throughout the fourteenth century, but it was only during the circumstances of the schism that these arguments found a wide audience. The following documents trace the history of the controversy, from the declaration of conciliar supremacy at the Council of Constance (Haec Sancta Synodus), to the council's efforts to guarantee regular meetings of general councils thereafter (Frequens), to the papal condemnation of appeals to the authority of general councils issued in 1460 (Execrabilis).

## Haec Sancta Synodus *(1415)*

This holy synod of Constance . . . declares that being lawfully assembled in the Holy Spirit, constituting a general council and representing the Catholic Church Militant, it has its power directly from Christ, and that all persons of whatever rank or dignity, even a Pope, are bound to obey it in matters relating to faith and the end of the Schism and the general reformation of the church of God in head and members.

Further, it declares that any person of whatever position, rank, or dignity, even a Pope, who contumaciously refuses to obey the mandates, statutes, ordinances, or regulations enacted or to be enacted by this holy synod, or by any other general council lawfully assembled, relating to the matters aforesaid or to other matters involved with them, shall, unless he repents, be . . . duly punished.

Source: L. R. Loomis, ed. and trans., *The Council of Constance* (New York: 1961), p. 229.

## Frequens *(1417)*

The frequent holding of general councils is the best method of cultivating the field of the Lord, for they root out the briars, thorns, and thistles of heresies, errors, and schisms, correct abuses, make crooked things straight, and prepare the Lord's vineyard for fruitfulness and rich fertility. Neglect of general councils sows the seeds of these evils and encourages their growth. This truth is borne in upon us as we recall times past and survey the present.

Therefore by perpetual edict we . . . ordain that henceforth general councils shall be held as follows: the first within the five years immediately following the end of the present council, the second within seven years from the end of the council next after this, and subsequently every ten years forever. . . . Thus there will always be a certain continuity. Either a council will be in session or one will be expected at the end of a fixed period.

Source: L. R. Loomis, ed. and trans., *The Council of Constance* (New York: 1961), pp. 246–47.

---

thousand years before (Chapter 6). Its chief mission was to remove all rival claimants for papal office before agreeing on the election of a new pope, an Italian who took the name Martin V. But many of the council's delegates had even farther-reaching plans for the reform of the Church, ambitions that stemmed from the legal doctrine that gave the council the power to depose and elect popes in the first place.

This doctrine, known as conciliarism, holds that supreme authority within the Church rests not with the pope but with a representative general council—and not just the council convened at Constance but also any future council. The delegates at Constance thus decreed that general councils should meet regularly to oversee the governance of the Church and to act as a check on the unbridled abuse of papal power.

Had conciliarism triumphed, the Reformation of the following century might not have occurred. But, perhaps predictably, Martin V and his successors did everything they could to undermine this doctrine, precisely because it limited their power. When the next general council met at

## Execrabilis (1460)

An execrable abuse, unheard of in earlier times, has sprung up in our period. Some men, imbued with a spirit of rebellion and moved not by a desire for sound decisions but rather by a desire to escape the punishment for sin, suppose that they can appeal from the Pope, Vicar of Jesus Christ—from the Pope, to whom in the person of blessed Peter it was said, "Feed my sheep" and "whatever you bind on earth will be bound in heaven"—from this Pope to a future council. How harmful this is to the Christian republic, as well as how contrary to canon law, anyone who is not ignorant of the law can understand. For . . . who would not consider it ridiculous to appeal to something which does not now exist anywhere nor does anyone know when it will exist? The poor are heavily oppressed by the powerful, offenses remain unpunished, rebellion against the Holy See is encouraged, license for sin is granted, and all ecclesiastical discipline and hierarchical ranking of the Church are turned upside down.

Wishing therefore to expel this deadly poison from the Church of Christ, and concerned with the salvation of the sheep committed to us . . . with the counsel and assent of our venerable brothers, the Cardinals of the Holy Roman Church, together with the counsel and assent of all those prelates who have been trained in canon and civil law who follow our Court, and with our own certain knowledge, we condemn appeals of this kind, reject them as erroneous and abominable, and declare them to be completely null and void. And we lay down that from now on, no one should dare . . . to make such an appeal from our decisions, be they legal or theological, or from any commands at all from us or our successors.

Source: Reprinted by permission of the publisher from Gabriel Biel, *Defensorium Obedientiae Apostolicae et Alia Documenta*, ed. and trans. Heiko A. Oberman, Daniel E. Zerfoss, and William J. Courtenay (Cambridge, MA: 1968), pp. 224–27. Copyright © 1968 by the President and Fellows of Harvard College.

### Questions for Analysis

1. On what grounds does *Haec Sancta Synodus* establish the authority of a council? Why would this be considered a threat to papal power?

2. Why did the Council of Constance consider it necessary for councils to meet regularly (*Frequens*)? What might have been the logical consequences of such regular meetings?

3. On what grounds does *Execrabilis* condemn the appeals to future councils that have no specified meeting date? Why would it not have condemned the conciliar movement altogether?

---

Siena in 1423, Pope Martin duly sent representatives—who then turned around and went back to Rome. (The Council of Constance had specified that councils must meet frequently but had not specified how long those meetings should last.) The following year, the delegates to a general council at Basel took steps to ensure that the pope could not dismiss it, and a lengthy struggle for power ensued between the advocates of papal monarchy and the conciliarists. Twenty-five years later, in 1449, the Council of Basel dissolved itself, bringing to an end a radical experiment in conciliar government—and dashing the hopes of those who thought it would lead to an internal reformation thorough enough to keep the Roman Church intact.

## Spiritual Challenges

We have noted that the spiritual and social lives of medieval Christians were inextricably intertwined; indeed, any distinction between the two would have made little sense to the people of this era. The parish church stood literally at the center of their lives. Churchyards were communal meeting places, sometimes even the sites of markets; church buildings were a refuge from attack and a gathering place for parish business; church's holidays marked the passage of the year; and church's bells marked the hours of the day. The church was holy, but it was also essential to daily life.

Yet, in the wake of the Black Death, when many parishes ceased to exist and many communities were decimated, an increasing number of medieval Christians were not satisfied with these conventional practices and developed forms of piety that were distinctly controversial. Many of them are regarded today as saints, but this was not necessarily the case during their lifetimes. Indeed, the distinction between the superhuman powers of a saint and those of a witch could be difficult to distinguish. As Joan of Arc's predicament reveals, medieval women found it particularly challenging to find outlets for their piety that would not earn them the condemnation of the Church. (Executed as a heretic, Joan was officially exonerated a generation later. But she would not be canonized as a saint until 1920, when belief in her holiness gained wide support during World War I and was considered a decisive factor in the victory of France and its allies.)

Many women therefore internalized their devotional practices or confined them to the domestic sphere—sometimes to the inconvenience of their families and communities. For example, the young Catherine of Siena (who later convinced the pope to return to Rome) refused to help with the housework or to support her working-class family; instead, she took over one of the house's two rooms for her own private prayers, confining her parents and a dozen siblings to the remaining room. Julianne of Norwich (1342–1416) withdrew from the world into a small cell built next to her local church, where she spent the rest of her life in prayer and contemplation. Her younger contemporary, the housewife Margery Kempe (c. 1372–c. 1439), resented the fact that she could not take such a step because she had a husband, several children, and a household to support. In later life, she renounced her domestic duties and devoted her life to performing acts of histrionic piety that alienated many of those who came into contact with her. For example, she was so moved by the contemplation of Jesus's sufferings on the cross that she would cry hysterically for hours, disrupting the Mass; and when on a pilgrimage in Rome, she cried at the sight of babies that reminded her of the infant Jesus or young men whom she thought resembled him.

The extraordinary piety of such individuals could be inspiring, but it could also threaten the Church's control over religious life and the links that bound individuals to their communities. It could, therefore, be regarded as dangerous. More safely orthodox was the practical mysticism preached by Thomas à Kempis, whose *Imitation of Christ* (c. 1427) taught readers how to appreciate aspects of the divine in their everyday lives. Originally written in Latin, *Imitation* was quickly translated into many vernacular languages and is now more widely read than any other Christian book except the Bible.

## Popular and Intellectual Reformers

For the most part, the threat of dissenting movements was less dangerous to the Church than the corruption of the papacy. But in the kingdoms of England, Bohemia (the modern Czech Republic), and Poland, some reform movements posed serious challenges because they were galvanized by respected intellectuals. In Poland, a professor at the new Jagiellonian University in Kraków, Paulus Vladimiri (Pawel

**WYCLIFFE'S ENGLISH BIBLE.** Although John Wycliffe was not directly responsible for this translation of the Bible, it was made in the later fourteenth century by his followers. Written in the same Middle English vernacular that Geoffrey Chaucer used for his popular works, it was designed to be accessible to lay readers who did not understand Latin. This page shows the beginning of the Gospel of Mark: "The bygyn-/nyng of Þe gos-/pel of Ihesu Crist/ Þe sone of god. . . ." (Note that the old English letter Þ stands for *th*.) ▪ *What might have been the impact of this translation on readers and listeners in the late fourteenth century?* ▪ *How would this English Bible have helped to further the reforming efforts of Wycliffe and his disciples?*

Wlodkowic; c. 1370–1435), wrote a treatise that criticized papal and imperial efforts to convert the peoples of eastern Europe and the Baltic by force through their support of the Teutonic Knights. He argued that neither had the power or the right to do so, and further argued that pagans and Christians could coexist in peace. He advanced these radical arguments as the Polish representative to the Council of Constance.

The Oxford theologian John Wycliffe (c. 1330–1384) was the central figure in both the English and Bohemian reform movements. A survivor of the Black Death and an outspoken critic of the papacy, he asserted that the empty sacraments of a corrupt Church could not save anyone, and therefore urged the English king to confiscate ecclesiastical wealth and to replace corrupt priests and bishops with men who would live according to apostolic standards of poverty and piety.

Some of Wycliffe's followers, known to their detractors as Lollards (from a word meaning "mumblers" or "beggars"), went even further, dismissing the sacraments as fraudulent attempts to extort money from the faithful. Lollard preachers advocated for direct access to the scriptures and promoted an English translation of the Bible sponsored by Wycliffe himself. Wycliffe's teachings also played an important role in the Peasants' Revolt of 1381, and Lollardy gained numerous adherents in the decades after his death. This movement was even supported by a number of aristocratic families, who found the idea of dissolving the Church's wealth attractive. But after a failed Lollard uprising in 1414, both the movement and its supporters went underground.

In Bohemia and other regions of central Europe, Wycliffe's ideas lived on and put down even deeper roots. They were powerfully adopted by Jan Hus (c. 1373–1415), a charismatic teacher at the Charles University in Prague. In contrast to the Lollards, who had scornfully dismissed the Mass and thereby lost much popular support, Hus emphasized the centrality of the Eucharist to Christian piety. Indeed, he demanded that the laity be allowed to receive not only the consecrated bread but also the consecrated wine, which was usually reserved solely for priests. This demand became a rallying cry for the Hussite movement. Influential nobles also supported Hus, partly in the hope that the reforms he demanded might restore revenues they had lost to the Church over the previous century.

Accordingly, most of Bohemia was behind him when Hus traveled to the Council of Constance to publish his views and urge the assembled delegates to undertake sweeping reforms. But rather than giving him a hearing, the other delegates to the council convicted Hus of heresy and had him burned at the stake. Back home, Hus's supporters raised the banner of open revolt, and the aristocracy took advantage of the situation to seize Church property. Between 1420 and 1424, armed bands of fervent Hussites resoundingly defeated several armies, as priests, artisans, and peasants rallied to pursue Hus's goals of religious reform and social justice.

These victories increased popular fervor but they also made radical reformers increasingly volatile. Accordingly, in 1434, a more conservative arm of the Hussite movement

**THE TEACHINGS OF JAN HUS.** An eloquent religious reformer, Jan Hus was burned at the stake in 1415 after he was found guilty of heresy at the Council of Constance. This lavishly illustrated booklet of his teachings was published over a century later in his native Bohemia and includes texts in the Czech vernacular and in Latin. ■ *What does this booklet's later publication suggest about how Hus's image and theology were put to use during the Protestant Reformation?*

was able to negotiate a settlement with the Bohemian church. By the terms of this settlement, Bohemians could receive both the bread and the wine of the Mass, which thus placed them beyond the pale of Latin orthodoxy and effectively separated the Bohemian national church from the Church of Rome.

Lollardy and Hussitism exhibit a number of striking similarities. Both began in the university and then spread to the countryside, both called for the clergy to live in simplicity and poverty, and both attracted noble support, especially in their early days. Both movements were also strongly nationalistic, employing their own vernacular languages (English and Czech) and identifying themselves with the English or Czech people in opposition to a "foreign" Church. And both relied on vernacular preaching and social activism. In all these respects, they established patterns that would emerge again in the vastly larger currents of the Protestant Reformation (see Chapter 13).

## CONCLUSION

The century after the Black Death was a period of tremendous creativity and revolutionary change. The effects of the plague were catastrophic, but the resulting food surpluses, opportunities for expansion, and labor shortages encouraged experimentation and opened up broad avenues for enrichment. Europe's economy diversified and expanded, and increasing wealth and access to education produced new forms of art and new ways of looking at the world. Hundreds and perhaps thousands of new schools were established, and scores of new universities would emerge as a result. Women were still excluded from formal schooling, but nevertheless they became active—and in many cases dominant—participants in literary endeavors, cultural life, and religious movements. Average men and women not only became more active in cultivating their own worldly goals, they also took control of their spiritual destinies at a

## After You Read This Chapter

Go to **INQUIZITIVE** to see what you've learned—and learn what you've missed—with personalized feedback along the way.

### REVIEWING THE OBJECTIVES

- The Black Death had short- and long-term effects on the economy and societies of Europe. What were some of the most important changes?

- The later "Middle Ages" and the "Renaissance" are often perceived to be two different periods, but the latter was actually part of the former. Explain why.

- What were some of the intellectual, cultural, and artistic innovations of this era in Italy and elsewhere in Europe?

- How did some European kingdoms become stronger and more centralized during this period? What were some examples of national monarchies?

- How did the conciliar movement seek to limit the power of the papacy? Why was this movement unsuccessful?

time when the institutional Church provided little inspiring leadership.

Meanwhile, some states were growing stronger and more competitive, whereas other regions remained deeply divided. The rising Ottoman Empire eventually absorbed many of the oldest territories of Western civilizations, including the venerable Muslim caliphate at Baghdad, the western portions of the former Mongolian Empire, the Christian Balkans and Greece, and—above all—the surviving core of the eastern Roman Empire at Constantinople. As a result, Greek-speaking refugees streamed into Italy, many bringing with them classic works of Greek philosophy and literature hitherto unknown in Europe. Fueled by new ideas and a fervid nostalgia for the ancient past, Italians began to experiment with new ways of reading ancient texts, advocating a return to classical models while at the same time trying to counter the political and cultural authority of the more powerful kingdoms north of the Alps.

In contrast to Italy, these emerging national monarchies cultivated shared identity through the promotion of a common vernacular language and allegiance to a strong, more centralized state. These tactics allowed kingdoms such as Poland and Scotland to increase their territories and influence, while led France and England into an epic battle for sovereignty and hegemony. The result, in all cases, was the escalation of armed conflict as incessant warfare drove more powerful governments to harvest a larger percentage of their subjects' wealth through taxation, which they proceeded to invest in ships, guns, and the standing armies made possible by new technologies and more effective administration.

In short, the generations that survived the calamities of famine, plague, and warfare seized the opportunities their new world presented. In the latter half of the fifteenth century, they stood on the verge of an extraordinary period of expansion and conquest that enabled them to dominate the globe.

## PEOPLE, IDEAS, AND EVENTS IN CONTEXT

- Compare and contrast the **BLACK DEATH**'s effects on rural and urban areas.
- In what ways do rebellions such as the **ENGLISH PEASANTS' REVOLT** reflect the changes brought about by the plague? How do the works of **GIOVANNI BOCCACCIO, GEOFFREY CHAUCER**, and **CHRISTINE DE PISAN** exemplify the culture of this era?
- What was **HUMANISM**? How was it related to the artistic and intellectual movement known as the **RENAISSANCE**?
- How did the **OTTOMAN EMPIRE** come to power? What were some of the consequences of its rise?
- What new military technologies were deployed during the **HUNDRED YEARS' WAR**? How did this conflict affect other parts of Europe, beyond England and France? What role did **JOAN OF ARC** play?
- How did the **COUNCIL OF CONSTANCE** respond to the crisis of the **GREAT SCHISM**?
- Why did **CONCILIARISM** fail? How did **JOHN WYCLIFFE** and **JAN HUS** seek to reform the Church?

## THINKING ABOUT CONNECTIONS

- In the year 2000, a group of historians was asked to identify the most significant historical figure of the past millennium. Rather than selecting a person (e.g., Martin Luther, Shakespeare, Napoleon, Adolf Hitler), they chose the microbe *Yersinia pestis*, which caused the Black Death. Do you agree with this assessment? Why or why not?
- In your view, which was more crucial to the formation of the modern state: the political and legal developments surveyed in Chapter 9 or the emergence of national identities discussed in this chapter? Why?
- Given what we have learned about the history of the Roman Church, do you think the conciliar movement was doomed to fail? Why or why not? How far back do we need to go to trace the development of disputes over ecclesiastical governance?

## STORY LINES

- The invention of the printing press enabled the widespread dissemination of information, including reports on the riches of the New World.

- Competition for power in Italy led to increased violence as well as to the increase of artistic patronage, providing opportunities to a new breed of Renaissance men.

- The humanist approach to education that had developed in Italy spread to other parts of Europe, influencing new approaches to biblical scholarship and new political philosophies.

- Spain, the newest and the most powerful European state, completed its "reconquest" of the Iberian Peninsula in 1492 and then looked to counter the successful colonial ventures of the Portuguese. This led to the early beginnings of a Spanish Empire in the Americas.

## CHRONOLOGY

| | |
|---|---|
| 1454–1455 | Gutenberg's printed Bible completed |
| 1488 | Bartolomeu Dias rounds the Cape of Good Hope (Africa) |
| 1492 | Christopher Columbus reaches the West Indies |
| 1494 | Treaty of Tordesillas divides the New World |
| | Charles VIII of France invades Italy |
| 1498 | Vasco da Gama reaches India |
| 1509 | Erasmus publishes *The Praise of Folly* |
| 1511 | Portuguese ventures to Indonesia |
| 1512 | Michelangelo completes painting the ceiling of the Sistine Chapel |
| 1513 | Niccolò Machiavelli completes *The Prince* |
| | Vasco Núñez de Balboa reaches the Pacific Ocean |
| 1516 | Thomas More publishes *Utopia* |
| 1519–1522 | Magellan's fleet circumnavigates the globe |
| 1533 | Aztec wars enable Cortés's conquest of Mexico |
| | Pizarro's conquest of the Inca Empire |

Before You Read This Chapter

# 12

# Innovation and Exploration, 1453–1533

## CORE OBJECTIVES

- **UNDERSTAND** the relationship between Renaissance ideals and the political and economic realities of Italy.

- **IDENTIFY** the key characteristics of Renaissance arts and learning during this period.

- **DEFINE** the term *reconquista* and its meaning in Spain.

- **DESCRIBE** the methods and motives of European colonization during this period.

- **EXPLAIN** why Europeans were able to dominate the peoples of the New World.

hat if exact copies of an idea could circulate quickly, all over the world? What if the same could be done for the latest news, the oldest beliefs, the most beautiful poems, or the most exciting—and deadly—discoveries? It would do for knowledge what the invention of coinage did for wealth: making it portable, so easier to use and disseminate. Indeed, it's no accident that the man who developed such a technology, Johannes Gutenberg of Mainz (c. 1398–1468), was the son of a goldsmith who made coins for the bishop of that German city. Both crafts were based on the same principle and used the same basic tools. Coins are metal disks, each stamped with identical words and images impressed on them with a reusable matrix. The pages of the first printed books—and later newspapers, leaflets, and pamphlets—were stamped with ink spread on rows of movable type (lead or cast-iron letter forms and punctuation marks) slotted into frames to form lines of words. Once a set of pages was ready, a press could make hundreds of copies in a matter of hours, many hundreds of times faster than the same page being copied by hand. Afterward, the type could be reused.

## Printing, Patriotism, and the Past

> The printing press helped to create new communities of readers by standardizing national languages and even promoting patriotism. And even as it enabled authors of new works to reach larger audiences, it also allowed printers to popularize older writings that had previously circulated in manuscript. The two sources presented here exemplify two aspects of this trend. The first is a preface by William Caxton of London, a printer who specialized in publishing books that glorified England's history and heritage. The preface is to a version of the legend of King Arthur, originally written by the English soldier Sir Thomas Malory, who completed it in 1470. It was printed for the first time in 1485 and quickly became a bestseller. The second excerpt is from the concluding chapter of Machiavelli's treatise The Prince. Like the book itself, these remarks were originally addressed to Lorenzo de' Medici, head of Florence's most powerful family. But when The Prince was printed in 1532, five years after Machiavelli's death, the author's passionate denunciation of foreign "barbarians" and his lament for Italy's lost glory resonated with a wider Italian-speaking public.

### William Caxton's preface to Thomas Malory's Le Morte d'Arthur ("The Death of Arthur"; printed 1485)

After I had accomplished and finished diverse histories, both of contemplation and of other historical and worldly acts of great conquerors and princes, . . . many noble and diverse gentlemen of this realm of England came and demanded why I had not made and imprinted the noble history of the Holy Grail, and of the most renowned Christian king and worthy, King Arthur, which ought most to be remembered among us Englishmen before all other Christian kings. . . . The said noble gentlemen instantly required me to imprint the history of the said noble king and conqueror King Arthur, and of his knights, with the history of the Holy Grail . . . considering that he was a man born within this realm, and king and emperor of the same: and that there be, in French, diverse and many noble volumes of his acts, and also of his knights. To whom I answered that diverse men hold opinion that there was no such Arthur, and that all such books as have been made of him be feigned and fables, because some chronicles make of him no mention. . . . Whereto they answered, and one in special said, that in him that should say or think that there was never such a king called Arthur might well be accounted great folly and blindness. . . . For in all places, Christian and heathen, he is reputed and taken for one of the Nine Worthies, and the first of the three Christian men. And also, he is more spoken of beyond the sea, and there are more books made of his noble acts than there be in England, as well in Dutch, Italian, Spanish, and Greek, as in French. . . . Wherefore it is a marvel why he is no more renowned in his own country. . . .

Then all these things aforesaid alleged, I could not well deny but that there was such a noble king named Arthur, reputed one of the Nine Worthies, and first and chief of the Christian men. And many noble volumes be made of him and of his noble knights in French, which I have seen and read beyond the sea, which be not had in our maternal tongue. . . . Wherefore, among all such [manuscript] books as have late been drawn out briefly into English I have . . . undertaken to imprint a book of the noble histories of the said King Arthur, and of certain of his knights, after a copy unto me delivered—which copy Sir Thomas Malory did take out of certain books of French, and reduced it into English. And I, according to my copy, have done set it in print, to the intent that noble men may see and learn the noble acts of chivalry, the gentle and virtuous deeds that some knights used in those days, by which they came to honor, and how they that were vicious were punished and oft put to shame and rebuke; humbly beseeching all noble

lords and ladies (with all other estates of what estate or degree they be) that shall see and read in this said book and work, that they take the good and honest acts to their remembrance, and follow the same. . . . For herein may be seen noble chivalry, courtesy, humanity, friendliness, hardiness, love, friendship, cowardice, murder, hate, virtue, and sin. Do after the good and leave the evil, and it shall bring you to good fame and renown.

Source: Sir Thomas Malory, *Le Morte d'Arthur* (London: 1485) (text and spelling slightly modernized).

## From the conclusion of Niccolò Machiavelli, The Prince (completed 1513; printed 1532)

Reflecting in the matters set forth above and considering within myself where the times were propitious in Italy at present to honor a new prince and whether there is at hand the matter suitable for a prudent and virtuous leader to mold in a new form, giving honor to himself and benefit to the citizens of the country, I have arrived at the opinion that all circumstances now favor such a prince, and I cannot think of a time more propitious for him than the present. If, as I said, it was necessary in order to make apparent the virtue of Moses, that the people of Israel should be enslaved in Egypt, and that the Persians should be oppressed by the Medes to provide an opportunity to illustrate the greatness and the spirit of Cyrus, and that the Athenians should be scattered in order to show the excellence of Theseus, thus at the present time, in order to reveal the valor of an Italian spirit, it was essential that Italy should fall to her present low estate, more enslaved than the Hebrews, more servile than the Persians, more disunited than the Athenians, leaderless and lawless, beaten, despoiled, lacerated, overrun and crushed under every kind of misfortune. . . . So Italy now, left almost lifeless, awaits the coming of one who will heal her wounds, putting an end to the sacking and looting in Lombardy and the spoliation and extortions in the Realm of Naples and Tuscany, and cleanse her sores that have been so long festering. Behold how she prays God to send her some one to redeem her from the cruelty and insolence of the barbarians. See how she is ready and willing to follow any banner so long as there be someone to take it up. Nor has she at present any hope of finding her redeemer save only in your illustrious house [the Medici] which has been so highly exalted both by its own merits and by fortune and which has been favored by God and the church, of which it is now ruler. . . .

This opportunity, therefore, should not be allowed to pass, and Italy, after such a long wait, must be allowed to behold her redeemer. I cannot describe the joy with which he will be received in all these provinces which have suffered so much from the foreign deluge, nor with what thirst for vengeance, nor with what firm devotion, what solemn delight, what tears! What gates could be closed to him, what people could deny him obedience, what envy could withstand him, what Italian could withhold allegiance from him? THIS BARBARIAN OCCUPATION STINKS IN THE NOSTRILS OF ALL OF US. Let your illustrious house then take up this cause with the spirit and the hope with which one undertakes a truly just enterprise. . . .

Source: Niccolò Machiavelli, *The Prince*, ed. and trans. Thomas G. Bergin (Arlington Heights, IL: 1947), pp. 75–76, 78.

### Questions for Analysis

1. What do these two sources reveal about the relationship between patriotism and the awareness of a nation's past? Why do you think Caxton looks back to a legendary medieval king, whereas Machiavelli's references are all to ancient examples? What do both excerpts reveal about the value placed on history in the popular imagination?

2. How does Caxton describe the process of printing a book? What larger conclusions can we draw from this about the market for printed books in general?

3. Why might Machiavelli's treatise have been made available in a printed version nearly twenty years after its original appearance in manuscript? How might his new audience have responded to its message?

## The Politics of Italy and the Philosophy of Machiavelli

But not all Florentines were galvanized by Platonic ideals. Indeed, the most influential philosopher of this era—and one of the most widely read authors of all time—was a thoroughgoing realist, who spent more time studying ancient Roman history than Greek philosophy: Niccolò Machiavelli (1469–1527). Machiavelli's writings reflect the unstable political situation of his home city, as well as his wider aspirations for a unified Italy that could revive the glory of Rome. We have observed that Italy had been in political disarray for centuries, a situation exacerbated by the "Babylonian Captivity" of the papacy and the controversies raging after its return to Rome (Chapters 10 and 11). Now, Italy was becoming the arena where bloody international struggles were being played out. The kings of France and Spain both had claims to territory in Italy, and each claimed to be the rightful champion of the papacy. Accordingly, both sent invading armies into the peninsula while busily competing for the allegiance of the various city-states, which in turn were torn by internal dissension.

In 1498, Machiavelli became a prominent official in the government of a new Florentine republic, set up four years earlier when a French invasion of the region led to the expulsion of the ruling Medici family. His duties largely involved diplomatic missions to other Italian city-states. While in Rome, he became fascinated with the attempt by Cesare Borgia, the son of Pope Alexander VI, to create his own principality in central Italy, and noted with approval Borgia's ruthlessness and his complete subordination of personal ethics to political ends. Machiavelli remembered his example in 1512, when the Medici returned to overthrow the Florentine republic and he was deprived of his position, imprisoned, tortured, and exiled. He now devoted his energies to the articulation of a political philosophy suited to the times and to the tastes of the family that had ousted him from his job.

On the surface, Machiavelli's two great works of political analysis appear to contradict each other. In his *Discourses on Livy*, which drew on the works of that Roman historian (Chapter 5), he praised the ancient Roman Republic as a model for his own contemporaries, lauding constitutional government, equality among citizens, and the subordination of religion to the service of the state. There is little doubt, in fact, that Machiavelli was a committed believer in the free city-state as the ideal form of human government. Yet Machiavelli also wrote *The Prince*, a "handbook for tyrants" in the eyes of his critics, and dedicated this work to Lorenzo, the son of Piero de' Medici, whose family had overthrown the Florentine republic that he had served.

**THE STATES OF ITALY, c. 1494.** This map shows the divisions of Italy on the eve of the French invasion in 1494. Contemporary observers often described Italy as being divided among five great powers: Milan, Venice, Florence, the Papal States, and the united kingdoms of Naples and Sicily. ▪ *Which of these powers seems most capable of expanding their territories?* ▪ *Which neighboring states would be most threatened by such attempts at expansion?* ▪ *Why would Florence and the Papal States so often find themselves in conflict with each other?*

Because *The Prince* has been so much more widely read than *Discourses*, it has often been interpreted as an endorsement of power for its own sake. But Machiavelli's real position was quite different. In the political chaos of early sixteenth-century Italy, he saw the likes of Cesare Borgia as the only hope for revitalizing the spirit of independence among his contemporaries, and thus making Italy fit, eventually, for self-governance. However dark his vision of human nature, Machiavelli never ceased to hope that his contemporaries would rise up, expel the French and Spanish occupying forces, and restore ancient traditions of liberty and equality. He regarded a period of despotism as a necessary step toward that end, not as a permanently desirable form of government.

Machiavelli continues to be a controversial figure. Some modern scholars, like many of his own contemporaries, represent him as disdainful of conventional morality and interested solely in the acquisition and exercise of power; others see him as an Italian patriot. Still others see him as a realist influenced by Saint Augustine (Chapter 6), who understood that, in a fallen world populated by sinful people, a ruler's good intentions do not guarantee that his policies will have good results. Accordingly, Machiavelli insisted that a prince's actions must be judged by their consequences and not by their intrinsic moral quality. He argued that the "necessity of preserving the state will often compel a prince to take actions which are opposed to loyalty, charity, humanity, and religion." As we shall see in later chapters, many subsequent political philosophers would go even further than Machiavelli in arguing that the preservation of the state—and the avoidance of political chaos—does indeed warrant the exercise of absolute power on the part of the ruler (see Chapters 14 and 15).

## The Ideal of the Courtier

Machiavelli's political theories were informed by years of diplomatic service in the courts of Italy, and so was his engaging literary style. Indeed, he never abandoned his interest in the literary arts of the court and continued to write poems, plays, and adaptations of classical comedies. In this he resembled another poet-courtier, Ludovico Ariosto (1474–1533), who undertook diplomatic missions for the Duke of Ferrara and some of Rome's most powerful prelates. His lengthy verse narrative, *Orlando Furioso* ("The Madness of Roland"), was a retelling of the heroic exploits celebrated in the French *Song of Roland* (Chapter 8)—but without the heroism. Although very different in form and tone from *The Prince*, it shared that work's skepticism of political or chivalric ideals. It emphasized the comedy of its lovers' passionate exploits and sought to charm an audience that found consolation in pleasure and beauty.

Thus a new Renaissance ideal was born, one that promoted the arts of pleasing the powerful secular and ecclesiastical princes who were in a position to employ clever men such as Machiavelli and Ariosto: the ideal of the courtier. The components of this ideal were embodied by their contemporary, the diplomat and nobleman Baldassare Castiglione (*bahl-dahs-SAH-re kah-stig-lee-OH-neh*; 1478–1529), who later wrote a manual for those who aspired to acquire these skills. If *The Prince* was a forerunner of modern self-help books, *The Book of the Courtier* was an early handbook of etiquette—and both stand in sharp contrast to the treatises on public virtue composed in the previous century. Whereas Bruni and Alberti (Chapter 11) had taught the sober virtues of strenuous service on behalf of the city-state, Castiglione taught how to attain the elegant and seemingly effortless skills necessary for advancement in princely courts.

More than anyone else, Castiglione articulated and popularized the set of talents still associated with the "Renaissance man": one accomplished in many different pursuits, witty, cultured, and stylish—but also an aspirant to Platonic ideals and human perfection. In many ways, Castiglione's courtiers (who were women as well as men) represent a *rejection* of the older ideals associated with the Renaissance as a rebirth of classical education for public men. Castiglione also rejected the misogyny of the humanists by stressing the ways in which court ladies could rise to influence and prominence through the graceful exercise of their womanly powers. Widely read throughout Western civilizations, his *Courtier* set the standard for polite behavior until the First World War.

## The Dilemma of the Artist

Without question, the most enduring legacy of the Italian Renaissance has been the contributions of its artists, particularly those who embraced new media and new attitudes toward the human body. For example, the creative and economic opportunities afforded by painting on canvas or wood panels freed artists from having to work on site and entirely on commission. Because such paintings are portable—unlike wall paintings—and can be displayed in different settings, they can reach different markets and be more widely distributed. We have also noted (Chapter 11) that the use of oil paints, pioneered in Flanders, further revolutionized painting styles.

To these benefits, the artists of Italy added an important technical ingredient: mastery of a vanishing (one-point) perspective, which gave an illusion of three-dimensional

**THE IMPACT OF PERSPECTIVE.** Masaccio's painting *The Trinity with the Virgin* illustrates the startling sense of depth, made possible by observing the rules of one-point perspective. Notice how the figure of the crucified Christ seems to be thrust forward toward the viewer.

result of this trend, because princes and merchants alike sought to glorify themselves and their families, as well as to compete with their neighbors and rivals. An artist therefore had to study the techniques of the courtier and the new artistic techniques in order to succeed in winning a patron. He also had to be ready to perform other services for which he had to cultivate other talents: overseeing the building and decoration of palaces; designing tableware, furniture, fanciful liveries (uniforms) for servants and soldiers; and even decorating firearms. Some artists, such as Leonardo da Vinci, were prized as much for their capacity to invent deadly weapons as for their paintings and sculptures.

## New Illusions and the Career of Leonardo

For much of the fifteenth century, the majority of the great painters were Florentines who followed in the footsteps of the precocious Masaccio (1401–1428), who died prematurely at the age of twenty-seven. His lasting legacy was the pioneering use of one-point perspective and dramatic lighting effects. Both are evident in his painting of the Trinity, where the body of the crucified Christ appears to be thrust forward by the impassive figure of God the Father, while the Virgin's gaze directly engages the viewer. Masaccio's most famous successor was Sandro Botticelli (1445–1510), who excelled in depicting graceful motion and the sensuous pleasures of nature. He is known today for paintings that evoke classical mythology.

The most adventurous and versatile artist of this period was Leonardo da Vinci (1452–1519). Leonardo personifies the Renaissance ideal: he was a painter, architect, musician, mathematician, engineer, and inventor. The illegitimate son of a notary, he had set up an artist's shop in Florence by the time he was twenty-five and gained the patronage of the Medici ruler Lorenzo the Magnificent. Yet Leonardo had a weakness: he worked slowly and had difficulty finishing anything. This naturally displeased Lorenzo and other Florentine patrons, who regarded artists as craftsmen who worked on specific projects and on their patrons' time, not their own. Leonardo, however, strongly objected to this view, considering himself to be an inspired, independent innovator. He therefore left Florence in 1482 and went to work for the Sforza dictators of Milan, whose favor he courted by emphasizing his skills as a maker of bombs, heavy ordnance, and siege engines. He remained there until the French invasion of 1499, then wandered about until finally accepting the patronage of the French king, under whose auspices he lived and worked until his death.

space. They also experimented with effects of light and shade, and intently studied the anatomy and proportions of the human body. These techniques also influenced the sculptors of this age. In visual terms, they were extensions of the values that Petrarch and other humanists had embraced in the fourteenth century and expressed through poetry and rhetoric: they recaptured the symmetry of classical art and placed the human subject (the viewer)—rather than God—at the center of artistic experience.

Behind all the beautiful artworks created in this era, which led to the glorification of the artist as a new type of hero, lie the harsh political and economic realities within which these artists worked. Increasing private wealth and the growth of lay patronage opened up new markets and created a huge demand for commodities—whether ornate buildings or beautiful objects—that could increase the status of those grappling for prestige. Portraiture was a direct

**THE BIRTH OF VENUS.** This painting was executed by Sandro Botticelli in Florence and is typical of the artist's imaginative treatment of stories from ancient mythology. Here, he depicts the moment when Aphrodite, the goddess of love, is spontaneously engendered from the foam of the sea by Chronos, the god of time.

Paradoxically, considering his skill in fashioning deadly weapons, Leonardo was convinced of the essential divinity of all living things. He was a vegetarian—unusual at the time—and went to the marketplace to buy caged birds only to release them to their native habitat once he had finished observing them. His approach to painting was that it should be the most accurate imitation possible of nature. He made careful studies of blades of grass, cloud formations, a waterfall; and he obtained human corpses for dissection and reconstructed them by drawing the minutest features of the anatomy. He carried this knowledge over to his paintings: *The Virgin of the Rocks* typifies not only his technical skill but also his passion for science and belief in the universe as a well-ordered place. The figures are arranged geometrically, with every stone and plant depicted in accurate detail.

In *The Last Supper*, painted on the refectory walls of a monastery in Milan (now in an advanced state of decay), Leonardo displayed his equally keen studies of human psychology. In this image, a serene Christ has just announced to his disciples that one of them will betray him. Leonardo succeeds in portraying the mingled emotions of surprise,

**THE VIRGIN OF THE ROCKS.** This painting reveals Leonardo's interest in the variety of human faces and facial expressions, and in natural settings.

# Analyzing Primary Sources

## Leonardo da Vinci Applies for a Job

*Few sources illuminate the tensions between Renaissance ideals and realities better than the résumé of accomplishments submitted by Leonardo da Vinci to a prospective employer, Ludovico Sforza of Milan. In the following letter, Leonardo explains why he deserves to be appointed chief architect and military engineer in the duke's household administration. He got the job and moved to Milan in 1481.*

1. I have the kind of bridges that are extremely light and strong, made to be carried with great ease, and with them you may pursue, and, at any time, flee from the enemy; . . . and also methods of burning and destroying those of the enemy.

2. I know how, when a place is under attack, to eliminate the water from the trenches, and make endless variety of bridges . . . and other machines. . . .

3. . . . I have methods for destroying every rock or other fortress, even if it were built on rock, etc.

4. I also have other kinds of mortars [bombs] that are most convenient and easy to carry. . . .

5. And if it should be a sea battle, I have many kinds of machines that are most efficient for offense and defense. . . .

6. I also have means that are noiseless to reach a designated area by secret and tortuous mines. . . .

7. I will make covered chariots, safe and unattackable, which can penetrate the enemy with their artillery. . . .

8. In case of need I will make big guns, mortars, and light ordnance of fine and useful forms that are out of the ordinary.

9. If the operation of bombardment should fail, I would contrive catapults, mangonels, trabocchi [trebuchets], and other machines of marvelous efficacy and unusualness. In short, I can, according to each case in question, contrive various and endless means of offense and defense.

10. In time of peace I believe I can give perfect satisfaction that is equal to any other in the field of architecture and the construction of buildings. . . . I can execute sculpture in marble, bronze, or clay, and also in painting I do the best that can be done, and as well as any other, whoever he may be.

Having now, most illustrious Lord, sufficiently seen the specimens of all those who consider themselves master craftsmen of instruments of war, and that the invention and operation of such instruments are no different from those in common use, I shall now endeavor . . . to explain myself to your Excellency by revealing to your Lordship my secrets.

Source: Excerpted from Leonardo da Vinci, *The Notebooks*, in *The Italian Renaissance Reader*, eds. Julia Conaway and Mark Mosa (Harmondsworth, UK: 1987), pp. 195–96.

### Questions for Analysis

1. Judging from the qualifications Leonardo highlights in this letter, what can you conclude about the political situation in Milan and the priorities of its duke? What can you conclude about the state of military technologies during this period and the conduct of warfare?

2. What do you make of the fact that Leonardo mentions his artistic endeavors only at the end of the letter? Does this fact alter your opinion or impression of him? Why or why not?

The first great master of Renaissance sculpture was Donatello (c. 1386–1466). His bronze statue of David, triumphant over the head of the slain Goliath, is the first freestanding nude of the period. Yet this *David* is clearly an agile adolescent rather than the muscular Greek athlete of Michelangelo's *David*, which was executed in 1501 as a public expression of Florentine civic life: not merely graceful but heroic. Michelangelo regarded sculpture as the most exalted of the arts because it allowed the artist to imitate God most fully in re-creating human forms. Furthermore, in Michelangelo's view, the most godlike sculptor disdained slavish naturalism: anyone could make a plaster cast of a human figure, but only an inspired creative genius could endow his sculpted figures with a sense of life.

Accordingly, in his sculptures, Michelangelo subordinated reality to the force of his imagination and sought to express his ideals in ever more astonishing forms. He also insisted on working in marble—the "noblest" sculptural material—and creating figures twice as large as life. By sculpting a serenely confident young man at the peak of physical fitness, Michelangelo celebrated the Florentine republic's own determination to resist tyrants and uphold ideals of civic justice.

Yet the serenity seen in his *David* is no longer prominent in the works of Michelangelo's later life, when (as in his painting) he began to explore the use of anatomical distortion to create effects of emotional intensity. Although his statues remained awesome in scale, they began to communicate rage, depression, and sorrow. The culmination of this trend is his unfinished but intensely moving *Descent from the Cross*, a depiction of an old man (the sculptor himself) grieving over the distorted, slumping body of the dead Christ.

## Renaissance Architecture

Renaissance architecture had its roots in the classical past to a much greater extent than either sculpture or painting, The Gothic style pioneered in northern France (see Chapter 9) had not found a welcome reception in Italy. Most of the buildings constructed in Italy were Romanesque in style, and the great architects influenced by the Renaissance movement generally adopted their building plans from these structures—some of which they believed (mistakenly) to be ancient. They also copied decorative devices from the authentic ruins of ancient Rome. But above all, they derived their influence from the writings of Vitruvius (fl. c. 60–15 B.C.E.), a Roman architect and engineer whose multivolume *On Architecture* was among the humanists' rediscovered ancient texts (Chapter 5). The governing principles laid out by Vitruvius were popularized by Leon Battista Alberti in his book *On the Art of Building*, which began to circulate in manuscript around 1450.

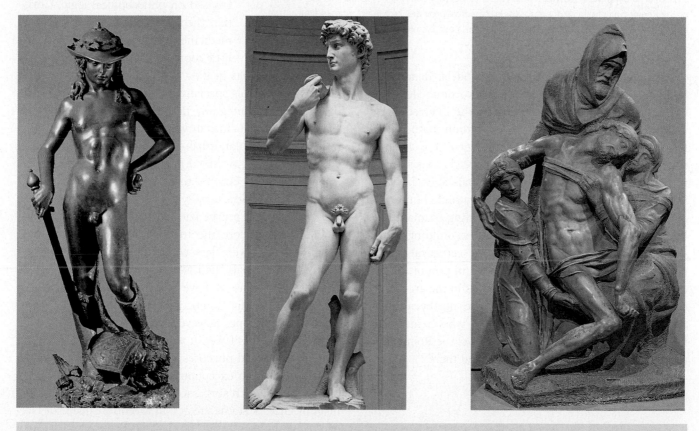

**THE POWER AND VULNERABILITY OF THE MALE BODY.** Donatello's *David* (left) was the first freestanding nude executed since antiquity. It shows the Hebrew leader as an adolescent youth and is a little over five feet tall. In contrast, Michelangelo's *David* (center) stands thirteen feet high and was placed prominently in front of Florence's city hall to proclaim the city's power and humanistic values. Michelangelo's *Descent from the Cross* (right), which shows Christ's broken body in the arms of the elderly Nicodemus (the sculptor himself), was made for Michelangelo's own tomb. (The Gospels describe Nicodemus as a Pharisee who became a follower of Jesus, and who was present at his death.) ▪ *Why would Michelangelo choose to represent himself as Nicodemus?* ▪ *How does his representation of David, and the context in which this figure was displayed, compare with that of Donatello's sculpture?*

**ST. PETER'S BASILICA, ROME.** This eighteenth-century painting shows the massive interior of the Renaissance building. If not for the perspective provided by the tiny human figures, the human eye would be fooled into thinking this was a much smaller space.

and financiers were familiar figures at northern cities and courts; students from all over Europe studied at Italian universities in Bologna or Padua; northern poets, including Geoffrey Chaucer (Chapter 11), and their works traveled to and from Italy; and northern soldiers were frequent combatants in Italian wars. Yet not until the very end of the fifteenth century did the innovative artistry and learning of Italy begin to be exported across the Alps into northern Europe and across the Mediterranean into Spain.

Historians have offered a variety of explanations for this delay. Northern European intellectual life in the later Middle Ages was dominated by universities such as those of Paris, Oxford, Kraków, and Prague, whose curricula focused on philosophical logic, Christian theology, and (to a lesser extent) medicine. These rigorous courses left little room for the study of classical literature. Universities in Italy, by contrast, were more often professional schools specializing in law and medicine, and they were more integrally tied to the nonacademic intellectual lives of the cities in which they were situated. As a result, a more secular, urban-oriented educational tradition took shape, as we saw in our previous discussion of humanism. In northern Europe, those scholars who *were* influenced by Italian ideas usually worked outside the university system, under the private patronage of kings and princes.

Moreover, before the turn of the sixteenth century, northern rulers were less committed to patronizing artists and intellectuals than were the city-states and princes of Italy. In Italy, as we have seen, such patronage was an important arena for competition between political rivals. In northern Europe, however, political units were larger, and political rivals fewer. It was therefore less necessary to use art for political purposes in a kingdom than it was in a city-state—a major exception being the independent duchy of Burgundy, which surpassed even the French court in its magnificence. A statue erected in a central square of Florence could be seen by all the city's residents; in Paris, such a statue would be seen by only a tiny minority of the French king's subjects. But as royal courts became more firmly established in royal capitals—and so became showcases for royal power—kings needed to impress townspeople, courtiers, and visitors. Consequently, they relied more and more on artists and intellectuals to advertise their wealth and taste.

In keeping with these classical models, Renaissance buildings emphasized geometrical proportion. These aesthetic values were also reinforced by the interest in Platonic philosophy, which taught that certain mathematical ratios reflect the harmony of the universe. For example, the proportions of the human body are the basis for the proportions of the quintessential Renaissance building: St. Peter's Basilica in Rome. Designed by some of the most celebrated architects of the time, including Bramante and Michelangelo, it is still one of the largest buildings in the world. Yet it seems smaller than a Gothic cathedral because it is built to human scale. The same artful proportions are evident in smaller-scale buildings too, as in the aristocratic country houses later designed by the northern Italian architect Andrea Palladio (1508–1580), who created secular miniatures of ancient temples, such as the Roman Pantheon, to glorify the aristocrats who lived there.

## THE RENAISSANCE NORTH OF THE ALPS

Despite Italian resentment at the political encroachment of foreign monarchs, contacts between Italy and northern Europe were close throughout this period. Italian merchants

## Christian Humanism and the Career of Erasmus

In general, then, the Renaissance movement in northern Europe differed from that in Italy because it grafted certain Italian ideals onto preexisting traditions, rather than sweeping away older forms of knowledge and artistry. This can be seen very clearly in the case of the intellectual development known as Christian humanism. Although northern scholars shared the Italian humanists' scorn for scholasticism's limitations, northern humanists were more committed to seeking ethical guidance from biblical and religious precepts, as well as from Cicero or Virgil. Like their Italian counterparts, they embraced the wisdom of antiquity, but the antiquity they favored was Christian as well as classical: the antiquity of the New Testament and the early Church. Similarly, although northern artists were inspired by the accomplishments of Italian masters and copied their techniques, they depicted classical subjects less frequently and almost never portrayed completely nude human figures.

Any discussion of Christian humanism must begin with the career of Desiderius Erasmus (c. 1469–1536). The illegitimate son of a priest, Erasmus was born near Rotterdam in the Netherlands. Later, as a result of his wide travels, he became a virtual citizen of all Europe. Forced into a monastery against his will when he was a teenager, the young Erasmus found little useful instruction there—but plenty of freedom to read what he liked. He devoured all the classics he could get his hands on, alongside the writings of the Church Fathers (Chapter 6). When he was about thirty years old, he obtained permission to leave the monastery and enroll in the University of Paris, where he completed the requirements for a bachelor's degree in divinity.

But Erasmus subsequently rebelled against what he considered the arid learning of Parisian academe, and he never served actively as a priest. Instead, he made his living from teaching, writing, and the proceeds of various ecclesiastical offices that required no pastoral duties. Ever on the lookout for new patrons, he traveled often to England, stayed for three years in Italy, and resided in several different cities in Germany and the Low Countries, before settling finally, toward the end of his life, in Basel (Switzerland). By means of a voluminous correspondence with learned friends, Erasmus became the leader of a humanist coterie. And through the popularity of his numerous publications, he also became the arbiter of northern European cultural tastes during his lifetime.

Erasmus's many-sided intellectual activity may be assessed from two different points of view: the literary and the doctrinal. As a Latin prose stylist, Erasmus was unequaled since the days of Cicero. Extraordinarily eloquent and witty, he reveled in tailoring his mode of discourse to fit his subject, creating dazzling verbal effects and coining puns that took on added meaning if the reader knew Greek as well as Latin. Above all, Erasmus excelled in the deft use of irony, poking fun at everything, including himself. For example, in his *Colloquies* (*Discussions*) he has a fictional character lament the evils of the times: "Kings make war, priests strive to line their pockets, theologians invent syllogisms, monks roam outside their cloisters, the commons riot, and Erasmus writes colloquies."

But although Erasmus's urbane Latin style and humor earned him a wide audience on those grounds alone, he intended everything he wrote to promote what he called the "philosophy of Christ." He believed that the society of his day had lost sight of the Gospels' teachings. Accordingly, he offered his contemporaries three different kinds of writings: clever satires in which people could recognize their own foibles, serious moral treatises meant to offer guidance

***ERASMUS*, BY HANS HOLBEIN THE YOUNGER.** This is generally regarded as the most evocative portrait of the preeminent Christian humanist.

## The Reputation of Richard III

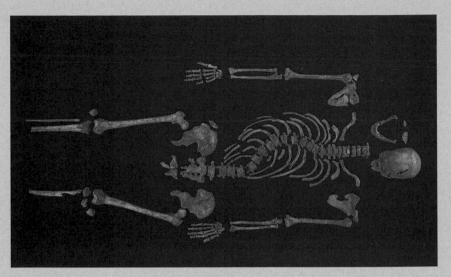

The name of England's King Richard III (r. 1483–1485) has been a byword for villainy since the time of his death, when Sir Thomas More and other propagandists working for his successor, Henry VII, alleged that his physically deformed body was matched by the depravity of his actions. Historians have debated the truth of both claims for centuries. Was Richard really a hunchback? And a murderer? In 2012, the stunning discovery of Richard's body (under a parking lot near the medieval battlefield where he died) confirmed that he had indeed suffered from severe scoliosis. The other claim has yet to be proven.

 **Watch related author interview on the Student Site**

toward proper Christian behavior, and scholarly editions of basic Christian texts.

In the first category belong the works of Erasmus that are still widely read today: *The Praise of Folly* (1509), in which he ridiculed pedantry and dogmatism, ignorance and gullibility—even within the Church; and the *Colloquies* (1518), in which he held up contemporary religious practices for examination, couching a serious message in the ironic tone we have just noted. In these books, Erasmus let fictional characters do the talking, so his own views on any given topic can only be determined by inference. But in his second mode, Erasmus spoke clearly in his own voice. In *Handbook of the Christian Knight* (1503), he used the popular language of chivalry as a means to encourage a life of inward piety; in *Complaint of Peace* (1517), he argued movingly for Christian pacifism. Erasmus's pacifism was

one of his most deeply held values, and he returned to it again and again in his published works.

Despite the success of these writings, Erasmus considered textual scholarship his greatest achievement. Revering the authority of the earliest Christian teachers, he brought out reliable printed editions of works by Augustine, Jerome, and Ambrose. He also used his extraordinary command of Latin and Greek to produce a more accurate edition of the New Testament. After reading Lorenzo Valla's *Notes on the New Testament* in 1504, Erasmus became convinced that nothing was more imperative than divesting the Christian scriptures of the myriad errors in transcription and translation that had piled up over the course of preceding centuries. He therefore spent ten years comparing all the early Greek biblical manuscripts he could find in order to establish an authoritative text. When it finally appeared in 1516, Erasmus's Greek

New Testament, published together with explanatory notes and his own new Latin translation, became one of the most important scholarly landmarks of all time—and it would play a critical role in the early stages of the Reformation in the hands of Martin Luther (see Chapter 13).

## The Influence of Erasmus

One of Erasmus's closest friends, and a close second to him in distinction among Christian humanists, was the Englishman Sir Thomas More (1478–1535). In later life, following a successful career as a lawyer and speaker of the House of Commons in Parliament, More was appointed lord chancellor of England in 1529. He was not long in this position, however, before he opposed King Henry VIII's plan to establish a national church under royal control that would deny the supremacy of the pope (see Chapter 13). He was eventually executed and is now revered as a Catholic martyr.

Much earlier, in 1516, More published his most famous book, *Utopia* (from Greek meaning *No Place*). Purporting to describe an ideal community on an imaginary island, the book is really an Erasmian critique of contemporary culture: disparities between poverty and wealth, drastic punishments, religious persecution, and the senseless slaughter of war. In contrast to Europeans, the inhabitants of the fictional Utopia hold all their goods in common, work only six hours a day (so that all may have leisure for intellectual pursuits), and practice the natural virtues of wisdom, moderation, fortitude, and justice. Although More did not advance explicit arguments in favor of Christianity, he may have meant to imply that if the Utopians could manage their society so well without the benefit of Christian revelation, Europeans who knew the Gospels ought to be able to do even better.

Erasmus and More head a long list of energetic and eloquent northern humanists who made signal contributions to the collective enterprise of revolutionizing the study of early Christianity, and their achievements had a direct influence on Protestant reformers (as we will see in the next chapter). Yet very few of them were willing to join Luther and other Protestant leaders in rejecting the fundamental principles on which the power of the Roman Church was based. Most tried to remain within its fold while still espousing an ideal of inward piety and scholarly inquiry. But as the leaders of the Church grew less and less tolerant of dissent, even mild criticism came to seem like heresy. Erasmus died early enough to escape persecution, but several of his less fortunate followers did not.

**SIR THOMAS MORE, BY HANS HOLBEIN THE YOUNGER.** Holbein's skill in rendering the gravity and interiority of his subject is matched by his masterful representation of the sumptuous chain of office, furred mantle, and velvet sleeves that indicate the political and professional status of Henry VIII's lord chancellor.

## The Literature of the Northern Renaissance

Although Christian humanism would be severely challenged by the Reformation, the artistic Renaissance in the North flourished. Poets in France and England vied with one another to adapt the elegant lyric forms pioneered by Petrarch and popularized by many subsequent poets, including Michelangelo. The sonnet was particularly influential and would become one of the verse forms embraced by William Shakespeare (1554–1616) (see Chapter 14). Another English poet, Edmund Spenser (c. 1552–1599), drew on the literary innovation of Ariosto's *Orlando Furioso*. Spenser's *Faerie Queene* is a similarly long chivalric romance that revels in sensuous imagery.

Meanwhile, the more satirical side of Renaissance humanism was embraced by the French writer François Rabelais (*RAH-beh-lay*; c. 1494–1553). Like Erasmus, whom he greatly admired, Rabelais began his career in the Church, but soon left the cloister to study medicine.

A practicing physician, Rabelais interspersed his professional activities with literary endeavors, the most enduring of which are the twin books *Gargantua* and *Pantagruel*: a series of "chronicles" describing the lives and times of giants whose fabulous size and gross appetites serve as vehicles for much lusty humor. Like Erasmus, Rabelais also satirized religious hypocrisy, scholasticism, superstition, and bigotry. But unlike Erasmus, who wrote in a highly cultivated classical Latin style comprehensible only to learned readers, Rabelais chose to address a different audience by writing in extremely crude French and glorifying every human appetite as natural and healthy.

## Northern Architecture and Art

Although many architects in northern Europe continued to build in the flamboyant Gothic style of the later Middle Ages, the classical values of Italian architects can be seen in some of the splendid new castles constructed in France's Loire valley—châteaux too elegant to be defensible—and in

***SAINT JEROME IN HIS STUDY*, BY DÜRER.** Jerome, the biblical translator of the fourth century (Chapter 6), was a hero to both Dürer and Erasmus, and the paragon of inspired Christian scholarship. Note how the scene exudes contentment, even down to the sleeping lion, which seems more like an overgrown tabby cat than a symbol of Christ.

the royal palace of the Louvre in Paris (now the museum), which replaced an old twelfth-century fortress. The influence of Renaissance ideals are also visible in the work of the German artist Albrecht Dürer (*DIRR-er*; 1471–1528). Dürer was the first northerner to master the techniques of proportion and perspective, and he shared with contemporary Italians a fascination with nature and the human body. He also took advantage of the printing press to circulate his work to a wide audience, making his delicate pencil drawings into engravings that could be mass produced.

But Dürer never really embraced classical subjects, instead drawing inspiration from more traditional Christian legends and the Christian humanism of Erasmus. For example, Dürer's serenely radiant engraving of Saint Jerome seems to express the scholarly absorption that Erasmus would have enjoyed while working quietly in his study. Indeed, Dürer aspired to immortalize Erasmus himself in a major portrait, but the paths of the two men crossed only once. Instead, the accomplishment of capturing Erasmus's pensive spirit in art was left to another northern artist, the German Hans Holbein the Younger (1497–1543). Holbein also painted an acute portrait of Erasmus's friend, Sir Thomas More. These two portraits, in themselves, exemplify a Renaissance emphasis on the making of naturalistic likenesses that express human individuality.

## Tradition and Innovation in Music

Like the visual arts, the lovely music produced during this era was nourished by patrons' desire to surround themselves with beauty. Yet unlike painting and sculpture, musical practice did not reach back to classical antiquity, but instead drew on well-established medieval conventions. Even before the Black Death, a musical movement called *ars nova* ("new art") was already flourishing in France and spread to Italy during the lifetime of Petrarch; its outstanding composers were Guillaume de Machaut (c. 1300–1377) and Francesco Landini (c. 1325–1397).

The part-songs and ballads composed by these musicians and their successors expanded on earlier genres of secular music, but their greatest achievement was a highly complicated yet delicate contrapuntal style adapted for the liturgy of the Church. Machaut's polyphonic (harmonized) setting of the major sections of the Mass is the earliest by a single composer. In the fifteenth century, the dissemination of this new musical aesthetic combined with a host of French, Flemish, and Italian elements in the multicultural courts of Europe, particularly that of Burgundy. By the beginning of the sixteenth century, Franco-Flemish composers dominated many important courts and cathedrals, creating a variety of new forms and styles that bear a close affinity to Renaissance art and poetry.

Throughout Europe, the general level of musical proficiency during this era was very high. The singing of part-songs was a popular pastime in homes and at informal social gatherings, and the ability to read a part at sight was considered part of an elite education. Aristocratic women, in particular, were expected to display mastery of the new musical instruments that had been developed to add nuance and texture to existing musical forms, including the lute, the viol, the violin, and a variety of woodwind and keyboard instruments such as the harpsichord.

Although most composers of this period were men trained in the service of the Church, they rarely made sharp distinctions between sacred and secular music. Like sculpture, music was coming into its own as a serious, independent art. As such, it would become an important medium for the expression of both Catholic and Protestant ideals during the Reformation, and also one of the few art forms equally acceptable to all.

# THE POLITICS OF CHRISTIAN EUROPE

We have already observed how the intellectual and artistic activity of the Renaissance was both fueled and hindered by the political developments of the later fifteenth century—within Italy, and throughout Europe. In 1453, France had emerged victorious in the Hundred Years' War, whereas England plunged into three decades of bloody civil conflict that touched every corner of that kingdom. The French monarchy, therefore, was able to rebuild its power and prestige while at the same time extending its control over regions long controlled by the English that were now part of an enlarged kingdom of France.

In 1494, the French king Charles VIII acted on his plan to expand his reach even farther, into Italy. Leading an army of 30,000 well-trained troops across the Alps, and aided by an alliance with the duchy of Milan, he intended to press his ancestral claim to the kingdom of Naples. By the time Charles left a year later, however, this effort yielded only a tenuous hold on Naples, while solidifying Italian opposition to French occupation—as we noted above in our discussion of Machiavelli.

The rulers of Spain, whose territorial claims on Sicily also extended to Naples, were spurred by Charles's expansionism to forge an uneasy alliance among the Papal States, some principalities of the Holy Roman Empire, Milan, and Venice. But the respite was brief, for Charles's successor,

Louis XII, launched a second French invasion in 1499. For over a generation, until 1529, warfare in Italy was virtually uninterrupted. Alliances and counteralliances among city-states became further catalysts for violence and made Italy a magnet for mercenaries who could barely be kept in check by the generals who employed them.

Meanwhile, the northern Italian city-states' virtual monopoly of trade with Asia, which had been one of the chief economic underpinnings of artistic and intellectual patronage, was being gradually eroded by the shifting of trade routes from the Mediterranean to the Atlantic (Chapters 10 and 11). It was also hampered by the increasing power of the Ottoman Empire, and even by the imperial pretensions of a new Russian ruler.

## The Power of Ivan the Great

In Chapter 10, we noted that Moscow had emerged as an administrative capital under the Mongols, and then had become the center of an independent principality, the Grand Duchy of Muscovy. In this era, its exponential growth was driven by its ruler Ivan III (r. 1462–1505), also known as Ivan the Great, the first Muscovite prince to adopt a distinctive imperial agenda.

Ivan launched a series of conquests that annexed all the independent principalities between Moscow and the border of Poland-Lithuania. After invading Lithuania in 1492 and 1501, he even succeeded in bringing parts of that domain (portions of modern Belarus and Ukraine) under his control. Meanwhile, he married the niece of the last Byzantine emperor: an alliance that inspired later Russian rulers to claim that Moscow was the "third Rome" and they were heirs of the Caesars—hence the title *czar* or *tsar*. Ivan also rebuilt his fortified Moscow residence, known as the Kremlin, in magnificent Italianate style. By the time of his death in 1505, Muscovy was firmly established as a dominant power on the frontier of eastern Europe.

## The Growth of National Churches

At the same time that Muscovy laid claim to the mantle of Roman imperial power, the papacy was pouring resources into the glorification of the original Rome and the aggrandizement of the papal office. But neither the city nor its rulers could keep pace with their political and religious rivals. Following the Council of Constance (Chapter 11), the papacy's victory over the conciliarists was a costly one. To win the support of Europe's kings and princes, various popes negotiated a series of religious treaties known as "concordats," which granted these rulers extensive authority

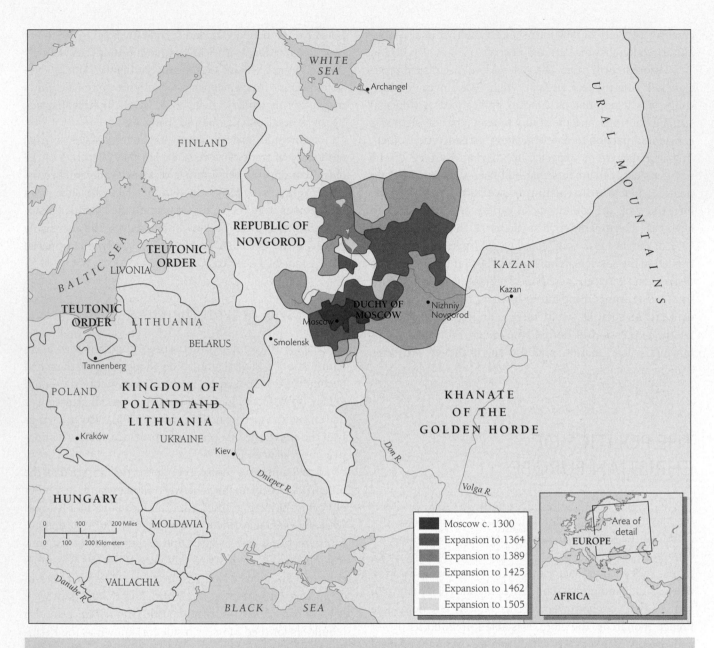

**THE EXPANSION OF MUSCOVITE TERRITORY TO 1505.** The Grand Duchy of Moscow (also known as Muscovy) was the heart of what would become an empire. ▪ *With what other empires and polities did the Muscovites have to compete during this period of expansion?*

over churches within their domains. Under the terms of these concordats, kings now received many of the revenues that had previously gone to the papacy and acquired new powers to appoint candidates to Church offices. The papacy thus secured its theoretical supremacy at the expense of its real power, and strengthened the national monarchies that were emerging during this era. Such changes were, in many ways, a drastic reversal of the hard-won reforms of the eleventh and twelfth centuries that had created such a powerful papacy in the first place.

Having given away so many sources of revenue and authority, the popes of the late fifteenth century became even more dependent on their own territories in central Italy. But to tighten their hold on the Papal States, they had to rule like other Italian princes: leading armies, jockeying for alliances, and undermining their opponents by every possible means—including covert operations and assassinations. By secular standards of the day, these efforts paid off: the Papal States became one of the better-governed and wealthiest principalities in Italy. But such methods did nothing to enhance the popes' reputation for piety, and disillusionment with the papacy as a force for the advancement of spirituality became even more widespread.

**AN ITALIAN RENAISSANCE CATHEDRAL IN MUSCOVITE RUS'.** Ivan the Great commissioned the Italian architect Aristotele Fioravanti to build this cathedral, dedicated to the Blessed Virgin and honoring her Assumption into heaven. It is now part of the Kremlin palace complex in Moscow. ▪ *Why would Ivan choose to build this cathedral and commission this particular architect?* ▪ *What messages might he have been trying to convey?*

The solution to the disputed succession that had caused the war in Aragon ultimately lay in the blending of two powerful royal families. In 1469, Prince Ferdinand of Aragon was recognized as the undisputed heir to that throne and, in the same year, secured this position by marrying Isabella, the heiress of Castile. Isabella became queen in 1474 and Ferdinand became king in 1479. Although Castile and Aragon continued to be ruled as separate kingdoms until 1714 (there are tensions between the two former kingdoms even now), the marriage of Ferdinand and Isabella enabled them to pursue several ambitious policies. In particular, their union allowed them to spend their combined resources on the creation of Europe's most powerful army, which was initially employed to conquer the last remaining principality—Granada—of what had been al-Andalus, Muslim Spain. That principality fell in 1492.

With both papal authority and Rome's spiritual prestige in decline, kings and princes became the primary figures to whom both clergy and laity looked for religious and moral guidance. Many secular rulers responded to such expectations aggressively, closing scandal-ridden monasteries, suppressing alleged heretics, and prohibiting the lower classes from dressing like the nobility. By these and other such measures, rulers could present themselves as champions of moral reform even as they strengthened their political power. The result was an increasingly close link between national monarchies and national churches, a link that would become even stronger after the Reformation.

## The Triumph of the Reconquista

The kingdoms of the Iberian Peninsula were also in constant conflict during this period. In Castile, civil war and incompetent governance allowed the Castilian nobility to gain greater control over the peasantry and greater independence from the monarchy. In Aragon, royal government benefited from the extended commercial influence of Catalonia, which was under Aragonese authority. But after 1458, Aragon too became enmeshed in a civil war, a war that involved both France and Castile.

## The End of the Convivencia and the Expulsion of the Jews

For more than seven relatively peaceful centuries, many of Spain's Jewish communities had enjoyed the privileges extended by their Muslim rulers, who were also relatively tolerant of their Christian subjects. Indeed, scholars often refer to this period of Spain's history as a time of *convivencia*, a word that means "living together" or "coexistence." Although relations among various religious and ethnic groups were not always uniformly peaceful or positive, the policies of Muslim rulers in al-Andalus had enabled an extraordinary hybrid culture to flourish.

The aims of the Spanish *reconquista* were diametrically opposed to those of "living together." The crusading ideology of "reconquest" sought to forge a single, homogenous community based on the fiction that Spain had once been entirely Christian and should be restored to its former purity. The year 1492, therefore, marks not only the end of Muslim rule in medieval Spain but also the culmination of Jewish exclusion, a process that had accelerated in the late thirteenth century (Chapter 9). Within this history, the Spanish expulsion of the Jews stands out for the staggering scope of the displacements and destruction it entailed: at least 100,000, and possibly as many as 200,000, men,

**FERDINAND AND ISABELLA HONORING THE VIRGIN.** In this contemporary Spanish painting, the royal couple are shown with two of their children and two household chaplains, in the company of the Blessed Virgin, the Christ Child, and saints from the Dominican order. (The Dominicans were instrumental in conducting the affairs of the Spanish Inquisition.) ▪ *How clear is the distinction between these holy figures and the royal family?* ▪ *What message is conveyed by their proximity?*

women, and children were deprived of their homes and livelihoods.

The Christian monarchs' motives for ordering this expulsion are still debated. Tens of thousands of Spanish Jews had converted to Christianity between 1391 and 1420, many as a result of coercion but some from sincere conviction. And for a generation or so, it seemed possible that these converts, known as *conversos*, might successfully assimilate into Christian society. But the same civil wars that led to the union of Ferdinand and Isabella made the *conversos* targets of discriminatory legislation. Conflicts may also have fueled popular suspicions that these converts remained Jews in secret. To make "proper" Christians out of the *conversos*, the "Most Catholic" monarchs (as they were now called) may have concluded that they needed to remove any potentially seditious influences that might stem from the continuing presence of a Jewish community in Spain.

What became of the Spanish Jews? Some traveled north, to the Rhineland towns of Germany or to Poland and eastern Europe. But most settled in Muslim regions of the Mediterranean and Middle East, where many found a haven in the Ottoman Empire. As we already noted, there were many opportunities for advancement in the Ottoman imperial bureaucracy, while the Ottoman economy benefited from the highly skilled labor of Jewish artisans and the vast trading networks of Jewish merchants. In time, new forms and expressions of Jewish culture would emerge, and new communities would form. And although the extraordinary opportunities afforded by the *convivencia* could never be revived, the descendants of these Spanish Jews—known as Sephardic Jews, or Sephardim—still treasure the traditions and customs formed in Spain over a thousand year period.

## The Extension of the Reconquista

Although the Christian kingdoms of Iberia had been devoted for centuries to the "reconquest" of territory, the victory over the Muslims of Granada and the expulsion of the Jews in 1492 were watershed events. They mark the beginning of a sweeping initiative to construct a new basis for the precariously united kingdoms of Aragon and Castile, one that could transcend rival regional identities. Like other contemporary monarchs, Ferdinand and Isabella strengthened their emerging nation-state by constructing an exclusively Christian identity for its people and attaching that new identity to the crown and promoting a single national language: Castilian Spanish. They also succeeded in capturing and redirecting another language: the rhetoric of crusade.

The crusading ethos, as we have seen, always seeks new outlets. With the creation of a new, exclusively Christian, Spanish kingdom through the defeat of all external enemies and internal threats, where could the energies harnessed by the *reconquista* be directed? The answer came from an unexpected quarter. Just a few months after Ferdinand and Isabella marched victoriously into Granada, the queen granted three ships to a Genoese adventurer who promised to reach India by sailing westward across the Atlantic Ocean, and to claim any new lands he found for Spain. Columbus never reached India, but he did help to extend the tradition of reconquest and the ethos of crusading to the New World—with far-reaching consequences.

## NEW TARGETS AND TECHNOLOGIES OF CONQUEST

The Spanish monarchs' decision to underwrite a voyage of exploration was spurred by their desire to counter the successful Portuguese ventures of the past half century. It was becoming clear that the tiny kingdom on the northwestern tip of the Iberian Peninsula would soon dominate the sea-lanes if rival entrepreneurs did not attempt to find alternate routes and establish equally lucrative colonies. This competition with Portugal was another reason that Isabella turned to a Genoese sea captain—not to a Portuguese one—when she sought to expand Spain's wealth and global influence.

## Prince Henry the Navigator and Portuguese Colonial Initiatives

Although Portugal had been an independent Christian kingdom since the twelfth century (Chapter 9), it was never able to compete effectively with its more powerful neighbors—Muslim or Christian—on land. But when the focus of European economic expansion began to shift toward the Atlantic (Chapter 10), Portuguese mariners were well placed to take advantage of this trend.

A central figure in the history of Portuguese maritime imperialism is Prince Henry (1394–1460), later called "the Navigator," a son of King João I of Portugal and his English queen, Philippa of Lancaster, the sister of England's Henry IV. Prince Henry was fascinated by the sciences of cartography and navigation, and he helped to ensure that Portuguese sailors had access to the latest charts and navigational instruments. He was also inspired by the stories told by John de Mandeville and Marco Polo—particularly the legend of Prester John, a mythical Christian king dwelling somewhere at the end of the earth, whom Europeans believed would be their ally against the Muslims if only they could locate him. Indeed, Prince Henry was Grand Master of a new crusading order, the Order of Christ, whose mission was to drive the Muslims out of Africa. He also had ambitions to extend Portuguese control into the Atlantic, to tap into the burgeoning market for slaves in the Ottoman Empire, and to establish direct links with sources of African gold.

Prince Henry played an important part in organizing the Portuguese colonization of Madeira, the Canary Islands, and the Azores. In the process, he also pioneered the Portuguese slave trade, which almost entirely eradicated the population of the Canaries before targeting Africa. By the 1440s, Portuguese explorers had reached the Cape Verde Islands. In 1444, they landed on the African mainland, in the area that became known as the Gold Coast, where they began to collect cargoes of gold and slaves for export back to Portugal.

Prince Henry personally directed eight of the thirty-five Portuguese voyages to Africa that took place during his lifetime. Also, in order to outflank the cross-Saharan gold trade, largely controlled by the Muslims of North Africa and mediated by the Genoese, he decided to intercept this trade at its source by building a series of forts along the African coastline. This was also his main reason for colonizing the Canary Islands, which he saw as a staging ground for expeditions into the African interior.

## From Africa to India and Beyond: An Empire of Spices

By the 1470s, Portuguese sailors had rounded the western coast of Africa and were exploring the Gulf of Guinea. In 1483, they reached the mouth of the Congo River. In 1488, the Portuguese captain Bartolomeu Dias was inadvertently blown around the southern tip of Africa by a gale, after which he named the point "Cape of Storms." But King João II (r. 1481–1495), taking a more optimistic view of Dias's achievement, renamed it the Cape of Good Hope and began planning a naval expedition to India. In 1497–1498, Vasco da Gama rounded the cape and then, with the help of a Muslim navigator named Ibn Majid, crossed the Indian Ocean to Calicut, on the southwestern coast of India. This voyage opened a viable sea route between Europe and the Far Eastern spice trade for the first time. Although da Gama lost half his fleet and one-third of his men on this two-year voyage, his cargo of spices was so valuable that these losses were deemed insignificant. His heroism became legendary, and his story became the basis for the Portuguese national epic, the *Lusiads*.

Now masters of the quickest route to riches in the world, the Portuguese swiftly capitalized on their decades of accomplishment. Not only did their trading fleets sail regularly to India, they attempted to monopolize the entire spice trade. In 1509, the Portuguese defeated an Ottoman fleet and then blockaded the mouth of the Red Sea, attempting to cut off one of the traditional routes by which spices had traveled to Alexandria and Beirut. By 1510, Portuguese military forces had established a series of forts along the western Indian coastline, including their headquarters at Goa. In 1511, Portuguese ships seized Malacca, a center of the spice trade on the Malay Peninsula. By 1515, they had reached the Spice Islands (East Indies) and the coast of China. So completely did the Portuguese now dominate the spice trade that even the Venetians were forced to buy their pepper in the Portuguese capital of Lisbon.

## Naval Technology and Navigation

The Portuguese caravel—the workhorse ship of those first voyages to Africa—was based on ship and sail designs that had been in use among Portuguese fishermen since the thirteenth century. Starting in the 1440s, however, Portuguese shipwrights began building larger caravels of about 50 tons displacement and equipped with two masts, each carrying a triangular (lateen) sail. Columbus's *Niña* was a ship of this design, although it was refitted with two square sails in the Portuguese-held Canary Islands to enable it to sail more efficiently before the wind during the Atlantic crossing. Such ships required much smaller crews than did the multi-oared galleys still commonly used in the Mediterranean. By the end of the fifteenth century, even larger caravels of around 200 tons were being constructed, with a third mast and a combination of square and lateen sails.

Europeans were also making significant advances in navigation during this era. Quadrants, which could calculate latitude in the Northern Hemisphere by the height of the North Star above the horizon, were in widespread use by the 1450s. As sailors approached the equator, however, the quadrant became less and less useful, and navigators instead made use of astrolabes, which reckoned latitude by the height of the sun. Like quadrants, astrolabes had been in use for centuries; but it was not until the 1480s that they became practical instruments for seaborne navigation, thanks to the standard tables for the calculation of latitude, whose preparation was sponsored by the Portuguese crown. Compasses, too, were coming into more widespread use during the fifteenth century. Longitude, however, remained impossible to calculate accurately until the eighteenth century, when the invention of the marine chronometer finally made it possible to keep accurate time at sea. In this prior age of discovery, Europeans sailing east or west across the oceans generally had to rely on their skill at dead reckoning to determine where they were.

European sailors also benefited from a new interest in maps and navigational charts. Especially important were books known as *rutters* or *routiers*. These contained detailed sailing instructions and descriptions of the coastal landmarks a pilot could expect to encounter en route to a variety of destinations. Mediterranean sailors had used similar portolan charts since the thirteenth century, mapping the ports along the coastlines, tracking prevailing winds and tides, and indicating dangerous reefs and shallow harbors (see Chapter 10). During the fifteenth century, these map-making techniques were extended to the Atlantic Ocean. And by the end of the sixteenth century, the accumulated knowledge contained in rutters spanned the globe.

## Artillery and Empire

Larger, more maneuverable ships and improved navigational aids made it possible for the Portuguese and other European mariners to reach Africa, Asia, and—eventually—the Americas. But fundamentally, these European commercial empires were military achievements that capitalized on what Europeans had learned in their wars against each other. Perhaps the most critical military advance was the increasing sophistication of artillery, a development made possible not only by gunpowder but also by improved metallurgical techniques for casting cannon barrels. By the middle of the fifteenth century, as we observed in Chapter 11, the use of artillery pieces had rendered the stone walls of medieval castles and towns obsolete, a fact brought home in 1453 by the successful French siege of Bordeaux (which ended the Hundred Years' War), and by the Ottoman siege of Constantinople (which ended the Byzantine Empire).

**SPANISH GALLEON.** The larger, full-bottomed ships that came into use during the fifteenth century became engines of imperial conquest and the vessels that brought the riches of those conquests back to Europe. This wooden model was made for the Museo Storico Navale di Venezia (Naval History Museum) in Venice, Italy.

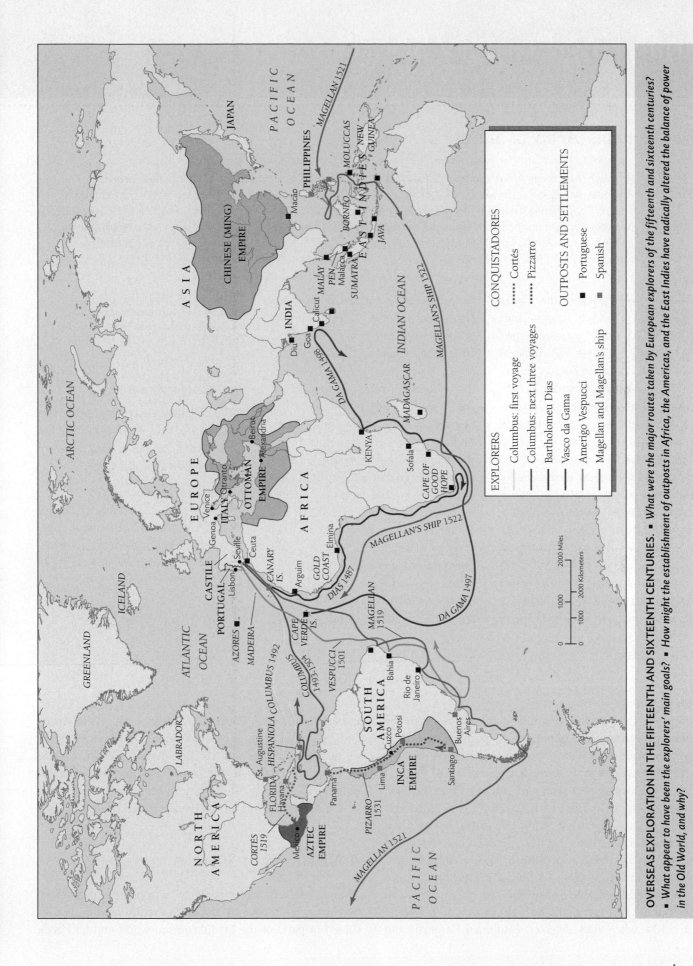

**OVERSEAS EXPLORATION IN THE FIFTEENTH AND SIXTEENTH CENTURIES.** ▪ What were the major routes taken by European explorers of the fifteenth and sixteenth centuries? ▪ What appear to have been the explorers' main goals? ▪ How might the establishment of outposts in Africa, the Americas, and the East Indies have radically altered the balance of power in the Old World, and why?

## The Ottomans' Army of Slaves

*Although the growing African slave trade was creating a newly racialized idea of slavery in the Caribbean and the Americas, slavery in Europe was not tied to race. Indeed, slavery could be a path to upward mobility in the Ottoman Empire. The following account is from a memoir written by Konstantin Mihailovic, a Serbian Christian who was captured as a youth by the army of Sultan Mehmet II. For eight years, he served in the Ottoman janissary ("gate-keeper") corps. In 1463, the fortress he was defending for the sultan was captured by the Hungarians, after which he recorded his experiences for a Christian audience.*

 henever the Turks invade foreign lands and capture their people, an imperial scribe follows immediately behind them, and whatever boys there are, he takes them all into the janissaries and gives five gold pieces for each one and sends them across the sea [to Anatolia]. There are about two thousand of these boys. If, however, the number of them from enemy peoples does not suffice, then he takes from the Christians in every village in his land who have boys, having established what is the most every village can give so that the quota will always be full. And the boys whom he takes in his own land are called *cilik*. Each one of them can leave his property to whomever he wants after his death. And those whom he takes among the enemies are called *pendik*. These latter after their deaths can leave nothing; rather, it goes to the emperor, except that if someone comports himself well and is so deserving that he be freed, he may leave it to whomever he wants. And on the boys who are across the sea the emperor spends nothing; rather, those to whom they are entrusted must maintain them and send them where he orders. Then they take those who are suited for it on ships and there they study and train to skirmish in battle. There the emperor already provides for them and gives them a wage. From there he chooses for his own court those who are trained and then raises their wages.

Source: Konstantin Mihailovic, *Memoirs of a Janissary* (Michigan Slavic Translations 3), trans. Benjamin Stolz (Ann Arbor, MI: 1975), pp. 157–59.

### Questions for Analysis

1. Why might the Ottoman emperor have established this system for "recruiting" and training janissaries? What are its strengths and weaknesses?

2. Applying your knowledge of Western civilizations, how unusual would you deem this method of raising troops? How does it compare with the strategies of other rulers we have studied?

Indeed, the new ship designs—first caravels, then the heavier galleons—were important in part because their larger size made it possible to mount more effective artillery pieces. European vessels were now conceived as floating artillery platforms, with scores of guns mounted in fixed positions along their sides and swivel guns mounted fore and aft. These guns were vastly expensive, as were the ships that carried them, but for rulers who could afford them, such ships made it possible to back mercantile ventures with military power. As we already noted, Vasco da Gama had been able to sail into the Indian Ocean in 1498, but the Portuguese did not gain control of that ocean until 1509, when they defeated combined Ottoman and Indian naval forces. Portuguese trading outposts in Africa and Asia were essentially fortifications, built not so much to guard against the attacks of native peoples as to ward off assaults from other Europeans. Without this essential military component, the European maritime empires that were emerging in this period could not have existed.

## A New Kind of Slavery

Although slavery had effectively disappeared in much of northwestern Europe by the early twelfth century, it continued in parts of the Mediterranean world and had been introduced into some regions of central and eastern Europe after the Black Death. But this slavery existed on a very small scale; there were no slave-powered factories or large-scale agricultural systems in this period. The only major slave markets and slave economies were in the Ottoman Empire, and there, slaves ran the vast Ottoman bureaucracy and staffed the army. In all these cases, as in antiquity, no aspect of slavery was racially based. In Italy and elsewhere in the medieval Mediterranean world, slaves were often captives from an array of locales. In eastern Europe, they were functionally serfs. Most Ottoman slaves were European Christians, predominantly Poles, Ukrainians, Greeks, and Bulgarians. In the early Middle Ages, Germanic and Celtic peoples had been widely enslaved. And under the Roman Empire, slaves had come from every part of the known (and unknown) world.

What was new about the slavery of the late fifteenth century was its increasing racialization—an aspect of modern slavery that has made an indelible impact on our own society. To Europeans, African slaves were visible in ways that other slaves were not, and it became convenient for those who dealt in them to justify the mass deportation of entire populations by claiming their racial inferiority and their "natural" fitness for a life of bondage. This nefarious ideology has had long-lasting and tragic consequences that still afflict the civilizations of our own world.

In Lisbon, which became a significant market for enslaved Africans during Prince Henry's lifetime, something on the order of 15,000 to 20,000 African captives were sold within a twenty-year period. In the following half century, by about 1505, the numbers amounted to 150,000. For the most part, the purchasers of these slaves regarded them as status symbols; it became fashionable to have African footmen, pageboys, and ladies' maids. In the Atlantic colonies—Madeira, the Canaries, and the Azores—land was still worked mainly by European settlers and sharecroppers. Slave labor, if it was employed at all, was generally used only in sugar mills. On Madeira and the Canaries, where sugar became the predominant cash crop during the last quarter of the fifteenth century, some slaves were introduced as agricultural laborers. But even sugar production did not lead to the widespread use of slavery on these islands.

However, a new kind of slave-based sugar plantation began to emerge in Portugal's eastern Atlantic colonies in the 1460s, starting on the Cape Verde Islands and then extending southward into the Gulf of Guinea. These islands were not populated when the Portuguese began to settle them, and their climate generally discouraged most Europeans from living there. They were ideally located, however, along the routes of slave traders venturing outward from the nearby West African coast. It is this plantation model that would be exported to Brazil by the Portuguese and to the Caribbean islands of the Americas by their Spanish conquerors, with incalculable consequences for the peoples of Africa, the Americas, and Europe (see Chapter 14).

# EUROPEANS IN A NEW WORLD

Like his contemporaries, Christopher Columbus (1451–1506) understood that the world was a sphere; and also like them, he thought it was much smaller. (As we saw in Chapter 4, the accurate calculation of the globe's circumference made in ancient Alexandria had been suppressed centuries later by Roman geographers.) Furthermore, it had long been accepted that there were only three continents—Europe, Asia, and Africa—hence Columbus's decision to reach Asia by sailing west, a plan that seemed even more plausible after the discovery and colonization of the Canary Islands and the Azores.

The existence of these islands reinforced a new hypothesis that the Atlantic was dotted with similar lands all the way to Japan. This emboldened Columbus's royal patrons, Ferdinand and Isabella of Spain, who were convinced the Genoese mariner could reach China in about a month, after a stop for provisions on the Canaries. This turned out to be a kind of self-fulfilling prophecy, for when Columbus reached the Bahamas and the island of Hispaniola after only a month's sailing, he reported that he had reached the outer islands of Asia.

## The Shock of Discovery

Of course, Columbus was not the first European to set foot on the American continents. As we have already learned, Viking sailors briefly settled present-day Newfoundland, Labrador, and perhaps even portions of New England around the year 1000 (Chapter 8). But knowledge of these Viking landings had been forgotten or ignored outside of Iceland for hundreds of years. It wasn't until the 1960s that the stories of these expeditions were corroborated by archaeological evidence. (In 2016, a new site of Norse settlement was identified on the coast of Baffin Island.) Moreover, the tiny Norwegian colony on Greenland—technically part of the North American landmass—had been abandoned in the fifteenth century, when the cooling of the climate (Chapter 10) destroyed the fragile ecosystems that barely sustained the lives of Norse settlers there.

Although Columbus did not return with spices to prove that he had found an alternate route to Asia, he did

# Interpreting Visual Evidence

## America as an Object of Desire

Under the influence of popular travel narratives that had circulated in Europe for centuries, Columbus and his fellow voyagers were prepared to find the New World full of cannibals. They also assumed that the indigenous peoples' custom of wearing little or no clothing—not to mention their "savagery"—would render their women sexually available. In a letter sent back home in 1495, one of Columbus's men recounted a notable encounter with a "cannibal girl" whom he had taken captive in his tent and whose naked body aroused his desire. He was surprised to find that she resisted his advances so fiercely that he had to tie her up—which of course made it easier for him to "subdue" her. In the end, he cheerfully reports, the girl's sexual performance was so satisfying that she might have been trained, as he put it, in a "school for whores."

The Flemish artist Jan van der Straet (1523–1605) would have heard many such reports of the encounters between (mostly male) Europeans and the peoples of the New World. This engraving, based on one of his drawings, is among the thousands of mass-produced images that circulated widely in Europe, thanks to the invention of printing. It imagines the first encounter between a male "Americus" (such as Columbus or Amerigo Vespucci himself) and the New World "America," depicted as a voluptuous, available woman. The Latin caption reads: "America rises to meet Americus; and whenever he calls her, she will always be aroused."

### Questions for Analysis

**1.** Study the details of this image carefully. What does each detail symbolize? How do they work together as an allegory of conquest and colonization?

**2.** On what stereotypes of indigenous peoples does this image draw? Notice, for example, the cannibalistic campfire of the group in the background and the posture of "America."

**3.** Why is the New World itself ("America") imagined as female in this image? What messages might this—and the suggestive caption—have conveyed to a European viewer?

AMERICA.

*Americen Americus retexit, & Semel vocauit inde semper excitam.*

Ioan. Stradanus inuent.
Theodor. Galle sculp.

return with some small samples of gold and few indigenous people—whose existence gave promise of entire tribes that might be "saved" by conversion to Christianity, and whose lands could provide homes for Spanish settlers seeking new frontiers after the *reconquista*. This provided sufficient incentive for the "Most Catholic" monarchs to finance three more expeditions by Columbus and many more by other adventurers, missionaries, and colonists.

Meanwhile, the Portuguese, who had already obtained a papal decree granting them (hypothetical) ownership of all lands south of the Canaries, rushed to establish their own claims. After two years of wrangling and conflicting papal pronouncements, the Treaty of Tordesillas (1494) sought to demarcate Spanish and Portuguese possession of as-yet-undiscovered lands. The Spanish would ultimately emerge as the big winners in this gambling match: within a decade, the coasts of two hitherto unknown continents were identified, as were clusters of new islands, most on the Spanish side of the meridian.

Gradually, Europeans reached the conclusion that the voyages of Columbus and his immediate successors had revealed an entirely "New World." And, shocking to Europeans, this world had not been foretold by either the teachings of Christianity or the wisdom of the ancients. Among the first to champion the fact of two new continents' existence was the Italian explorer and geographer Amerigo Vespucci (1454–1512), whose name was soon adopted as a descriptor for them. Eventually, those who came to accept this fact were forced to question the reliability of the key sources of knowledge on which Western civilizations had hitherto hinged (see Chapter 14).

At first, the realization that the Americas (as they were now called) were not an outpost of Asia came as a disappointment to the Spanish, because it meant that two major land masses and two vast oceans disrupted their plans to beat the Portuguese to the Spice Islands. But new possibilities gradually became clear. In 1513, the Spanish explorer Vasco Núñez de Balboa first viewed the Pacific Ocean from the Isthmus of Panama, and news of the narrow divide between two vast oceans prompted Ferdinand and Isabella's grandson to renew their dream. This young monarch, Charles V (1500–1556), ruled not only Spain but also a huge patchwork of territories encompassed by the Holy Roman Empire. In 1519, he accepted Ferdinand Magellan's proposal to see whether a route to Asia could be found by sailing around South America.

Yet Magellan's voyage demonstrated beyond question that the world was simply too large for any such plan to be feasible at that time. Of the five ships that left Spain under his command, only one returned, three years later, having been forced to circumnavigate the globe. Out of a crew of 265 sailors, only 18 survived, most having died of scurvy or starvation. Magellan himself had been killed in a skirmish with native peoples in the Philippines.

This fiasco ended all hope of discovering an easy southwest passage to Asia—although the deadly dream of a northwest passage survived and motivated many European explorers of North America into the twentieth century. It has been revived today, in our age of global warming. The retreat of Arctic pack ice has led to the opening of new shipping lanes, and in 2008, the first commercial voyage successfully traversed the Arctic Ocean.

## The Dream of Gold and the Downfall of Empires

Although the unforeseen size of the globe made a westward passage to Asia untenable, given the technologies then available, Europeans were quick to capitalize on the sources of wealth that the New World itself could offer. What chiefly fired the imagination were those small samples of gold that Columbus had initially brought back to Spain. Although rather paltry in themselves, they nurtured hopes that gold might lie piled in ingots somewhere in these vast new lands, ready to enrich any adventurer who discovered them. Rumor fed rumor, until a few freelance Spanish soldiers really did strike it rich beyond their most avaricious imaginings.

Their success, though, had little to do with their own efforts. Within a generation after Columbus's first ships had landed, European diseases had spread rapidly among the indigenous peoples of the Caribbean and the coastlines of the Americas. These diseases—especially measles and smallpox—were not fatal to those who carried them, because

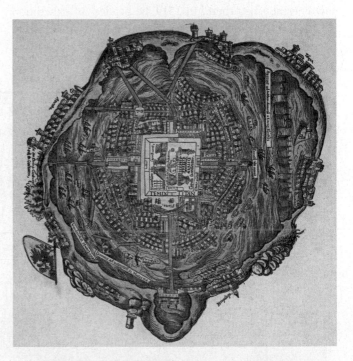

***THE AZTEC CITY OF TENOCHTITLÁN.*** The Spanish conquistador Bernal Díaz del Castillo (1492–1585) took part in Hernán Cortés's conquest of the Aztec Empire and later wrote an account of his adventures. His admiring description of the Aztec capital at Tenochtitlán records that the Spaniards were amazed to see such a huge city built in the midst of a vast lake, with gigantic buildings arranged in a meticulous urban plan around a central square and broad causeways linking the city to the mainland. This hand-colored woodcut was included in an early edition of Cortés's letters to Emperor Charles V, printed at Nuremberg (Germany) in 1524.

Europeans had developed immunities over many generations. But to the peoples of this New World, they were extremely deadly: there were probably 250,000 people living on Hispaniola when Columbus first arrived, but within thirty years—a single generation—70 percent had perished from disease.

The new waves of *conquistadores* (conquerors) were also assisted by the complex political, economic, and military rivalries that already existed among the highly sophisticated societies they encountered. The Aztec Empire of Mexico rivaled any European state in its power, culture, and wealth—and like any successful empire it had subsumed many neighboring territories in the course of its own conquests. Its capital, Tenochtitlán (*ten-och-tit-LAN*; now Mexico City), amazed its European assailants, who had never seen anything like the height and grandeur of its buildings or the splendor of its public works. This splendor was itself evidence of the Aztecs' imperial might, which was resisted by many of the peoples from whom they demanded tribute.

The Aztecs' eventual conqueror, Hernán Cortés (1485–1547), arrived in Hispaniola as a young man, in the wake of Columbus's initial landing. He had received a land grant from the Spanish crown and acted as magistrate of one of the first towns established there. In 1519, he headed an expedition to the mainland, which had been the target of some earlier exploratory missions but had not resulted in any permanent settlements, owing largely to the tight control of the Aztecs, whose imperial domain extended far beyond Tenochtitlán.

When Cortés arrived on the coast of the Aztec realm, he formed an intimate relationship with a native woman known as La Malinche. She became his consort and interpreter in the Nahua language, which was a lingua franca among the many different ethnic groups within the empire. With her help, he discovered that some peoples subjugated by the Aztecs were rebellious, and so he began to form strategic alliances with their leaders. Cortés himself could only muster a force of a few hundred men, but his native allies numbered in the thousands.

These strategic alliances were crucial. Although Cortés and his men had potentially superior weapons—guns and horses—these were more effective for their novelty than their utility. In fact, the rifles were of inferior quality, while gunpowder dampened by the humid climate had a tendency to misfire or fail to ignite altogether. So Cortés adopted the tactics and weaponry of his native allies in his dealings with the Aztec king Montezuma II (r. 1502–1520) and in his assaults on the fortifications of Tenochtitlán. In the end, though, it was European bacteria, not European technology or cunning, that led to his victory. The Aztecs were devastated by

**SPANISH CONQUISTADORS IN MEXICO.** This sixteenth-century drawing of conquistadors slaughtering the Aztec aristocracy emphasizes the advantages that plate armor and steel swords gave to the Spanish soldiers.

## A Spanish Critique of New World Conquest

*Not all Europeans approved of European imperialism or its "civilizing" effects on the peoples of the New World. One of the most influential contemporary critics was Bartolomé de las Casas (1484–1566) of Spain. In 1502, when Bartolomé was eighteen years old, he and his father joined an expedition to Hispaniola. In 1510, he became the first ordained priest in the Americas and eventually bishop of Chiapas (Mexico). Although he was a product of his times—he owned many slaves—he was also prescient in discerning the devastating effects of European settlement in the West Indies and Central America, and he particularly deplored the exploitation and extermination of indigenous populations. The following excerpt is from one of the many eloquent manifestos he published in an attempt to gain the sympathies of the Spanish crown and to reach a wide readership. It was printed in 1542, but it draws on the impressions and opinions he had formed since his arrival in New Spain as a young man.*

God made all the peoples of this area, many and varied as they are, as open and as innocent as can be imagined. The simplest people in the world—unassuming, long-suffering, unassertive, and submissive—they are without malice or guile, and are utterly faithful and obedient both to their own native lords and to the Spaniards in whose service they now find themselves. . . . They are innocent and pure in mind and have a lively intelligence, all of which makes them particularly receptive to learning and understanding the truths of our Catholic faith and to being instructed in virtue; indeed, God has invested them with fewer impediments in this regard than any other people on earth. . . .

It was upon these gentle lambs . . . that from the very first day they clapped eyes on them the Spanish fell like ravening wolves upon the fold, or like tigers and savage lions who have not eaten meat for days. The pattern established at the outset has remained unchanged to this day, and the Spaniards still do nothing save tear the natives to shreds, murder them and inflict upon them untold misery, suffering and distress, tormenting, harrying and persecuting them mercilessly. . . .

When the Spanish first journeyed there, the indigenous population of the island of Hispaniola stood at some three million; today only two hundred survive.

The island of Cuba, which extends for a distance almost as great as that separating Valladolid from Rome, is now to all intents and purposes uninhabited; and two other large, beautiful and fertile islands, Puerto Rico and Jamaica, have been similarly devastated. Not a living soul remains today on any of the islands of the Bahamas . . . even though every single one of the sixty or so islands in the group . . . is more fertile and more beautiful than the Royal Gardens in Seville and the climate is as healthy as anywhere on earth. The native population, which once numbered some five hundred thousand, was wiped out by forcible expatriation to the island of Hispaniola, a policy adopted by the Spaniards in an endeavour to make up losses among the indigenous population of that island. . . .

At a conservative estimate, the despotic and diabolical behaviour of the Christians has, over the last forty years, led to the unjust and totally unwarranted deaths of more than twelve million souls, women and children among them. . . .

The reason the Christians have murdered on such a vast scale and killed anyone and everyone in their way is purely and simply greed. . . . The Spaniards have shown not the slightest consideration for these people, treating them (and I speak from first-hand experience, having been there from the outset) not as brute animals—indeed, I would to God they had done and had shown them the consideration they afford their animals—so much as piles of dung in the middle of the road. They have had as little concern for their souls as for their bodies, all the millions that have perished having gone to their deaths with no knowledge of God and without the benefit of the Sacraments. One fact in all this is widely known and beyond dispute, for even the tyrannical murderers themselves acknowledge the truth of it: the indigenous peoples never did the Europeans any harm whatever.

Source: Bartolomé de las Casas, *A Short Account of the Destruction of the Indies*, trans. Nigel Griffin (Harmondsworth, UK: 1992), pp. 9–12.

### Questions for Analysis

*1.* Given his perspective on the behavior of his countrymen, how might Bartolomé de las Casas have justified his own presence in New Spain (Mexico)? What do you think he may have hoped to achieve by publishing this account?

*2.* What comparisons does Bartolomé make between New Spain (Mexico) and the Old, and between indigenous peoples and Europeans? What is he trying to convey?

*3.* Compare this account with the contemporary print on page 418. What new light does this excerpt shine on that visual allegory? How might a reader-viewer of the time have reconciled these two very different pictures of European imperialism?

an outbreak of the plague that had arrived along with Cortés and his men. In 1521, the Aztec Empire fell.

In 1533, another lucky conquistador, Francisco Pizarro, would manage to topple the highly centralized empire of the Incas, based in what is now Peru, by similar voluntary and involuntary means. In this case, he took advantage of an ongoing civil war that had weakened the reigning dynasty; he was also assisted by an epidemic of smallpox. Like Cortés, Pizarro promised his native allies liberation from an oppressive regime. Those former subjects of the Aztecs and Incas would soon be able to judge how sincere these promises were.

## The Price of Conquest

The astonishing conquests of Mexico and Peru gave the conquistadors access to hoards of gold and silver that had been accumulated for centuries by Aztec and Inca rulers. And almost immediately, a search for the sources of these precious metals was launched by agents of the Spanish crown. The first gold deposits were discovered in Hispaniola, where surface mines were speedily established using native laborers who were already dying in appalling numbers from disease, and who were now further decimated by brutality and overwork. The population soon dwindled further, to a mere 10 percent of its Pre-Columbian strength.

The loss of so many workers made the mines of Hispaniola uneconomical to operate, so European colonists turned instead to cattle raising and sugar production. Modeling their sugarcane plantations on those of the Cape Verde Islands and St. Thomas (São Tomé) in the Gulf of Guinea, colonists began to import thousands of African slaves to labor in the new industry. Sugar production was, by its nature, a capital-intensive undertaking. The need to import slave labor added further to its costs, guaranteeing that control over the new industry would fall into the hands of a few extremely wealthy planters and financiers.

Despite the establishment of sugar production in the Caribbean and cattle ranching on the Mexican mainland—whose devastating effects on the fragile ecosystem of Central America will be discussed in Chapter 14—it was mining that would shape the Spanish colonies most fundamentally in this period. If gold was the lure that had initially inspired the conquest, silver became its most lucrative export. Even before the discovery of vast silver deposits, the Spanish crown had taken steps to assume direct control over all colonial exports. It was therefore to the Spanish crown that the profits of the empire were channeled. Europe's silver shortage, which had been acute for centuries, came to an end.

Yet this massive infusion of silver into the European economy created more problems than it solved, because it accelerated inflation that had already begun in the late fifteenth century. Initially, inflation had been driven by the renewed growth of the European population, an expanding

# After You Read This Chapter

🐰 Go to **INQUIZITIVE** to see what you've learned—and learn what you've missed—with personalized feedback along the way.

## REVIEWING THE OBJECTIVES

- The artists of Italy were closely tied to those with political and military power. How did this relationship affect the kinds of work these artists produced?
- Which aspects of Renaissance artistry and learning were adopted in northern Europe?
- What was the *reconquista*, and how did it lead to a new way of thinking about Spanish identity?
- Europeans, especially the Portuguese, developed new technologies and techniques that enabled exploration and colonial ventures in this period. What were they?
- The "discovery" of the New World had profound effects on the indigenous peoples and the environment of the Americas. Describe some of these effects.

colonial economy, and a relatively fixed supply of food. Thereafter, thanks to the influx of New World silver, inflation was driven by the vastly increased supply of coinage. As we shall see, this abundance of coinage led to the doubling and quadrupling of prices in the course of the sixteenth century and the collapse of this inflated economy—which paradoxically drove a wave of impoverished Europeans to settle in the New World in ever greater numbers.

# CONCLUSION

The connection between the Mediterranean world into the Atlantic, which had begun in the thirteenth century, was the essential preliminary to Columbus's voyages and to the rise of European empires in Africa, India, the Caribbean, and the Americas. Other events and innovations we have surveyed in this chapter played a key role, too: the relatively rapid communications facilitated by the printing press; the struggle for power in Italy that led to the development of ever deadlier weapons; the navigational and colonial initiatives of the Portuguese; and the success of the Spanish *reconquista*, which displaced Spain's venerable Jewish community and drove Spanish rulers and adventurers to seek their fortunes overseas.

For the indigenous peoples and empires of the Americas, the results were cataclysmic. Within a century of Europeans' arrival, between 50 and 90 percent of some native populations had perished from disease, massacre, and enslavement. Moreover, Europeans' capacity to further their imperial ambitions—wherever ships could sail and guns could penetrate—profoundly destabilized Europe and its neighbors, sharpening the divisions among competing kingdoms and empires.

The ideals of the humanists and the artistry associated with the Renaissance often stand in sharp contrast to the harsh realities alongside which they coexisted and in which they were rooted. Artists could thrive in the atmosphere of competition and one-upmanship that characterized this period, but they could also find themselves reduced to the status of servants in the households of the wealthy and powerful—or forced to subordinate their artistry to the demands of warfare, espionage, and slavery. Meanwhile, intellectuals and statesmen looked to the precedents and glories of the past for inspiration.

But to which aspects of the past? Some humanists may have wanted to revive the principles of the Roman Republic, but many of them worked for ambitious despots who modeled themselves on Rome's dictators. The theories that undergirded European politics and colonial expansion were being used to legitimize many different kinds of power, including that of the papacy, and a newly racialized industry of enslavement. All these trends would be carried forward into the sixteenth century and would have a role to play in the upheaval that shattered Europe's fragile religious unity. It is to this upheaval—the Reformation—that we turn in Chapter 13.

## PEOPLE, IDEAS, AND EVENTS IN CONTEXT

- Why was **GUTENBERG**'s invention of the **PRINTING PRESS** such a significant development?
- How did **NICCOLÒ MACHIAVELLI** respond to Italy's political situation within Europe? In what ways do artists such as **LEONARDO DA VINCI** and **MICHELANGELO BUONARROTI** exemplify the ideals and realities of the Renaissance?
- How did northern European scholars such as **DESIDERIUS ERASMUS** and **THOMAS MORE** apply humanist ideas to Christianity? How were these ideas expressed in art?
- What is significant about **IVAN THE GREAT**'s use of the title **TSAR**?
- How did **ISABELLA OF CASTILE** and **FERDINAND OF ARAGON** succeed in creating a unified Spain through the **RECONQUISTA**?
- How does **PRINCE HENRY THE NAVIGATOR** exemplify the motives for pursuing overseas expansion? Why were the Portuguese so successful in establishing colonies during this period?
- What were the expectations that launched **COLUMBUS**'s voyage? What enabled the Spanish **CONQUISTADORS** to subjugate the peoples of the **AMERICAS**?

## THINKING ABOUT CONNECTIONS

- Phrases such as "Renaissance man" and "Renaissance education" are still part of our common vocabulary. Given what you have learned in this chapter, how has your understanding of such phrases changed? How would you explain their true meaning to others?
- How do the patterns of conquest and colonization discussed in this chapter compare with those of earlier periods, such as the era of the Crusades or the empires of antiquity? How many of these developments were new?
- Although the growth of the African slave trade resulted in a new racialization of slavery in the Atlantic world, the justifications for slavery had very old roots. How might Europeans have used Greek and Roman precedents in defense of these new ventures (see Chapters 4 and 5)?

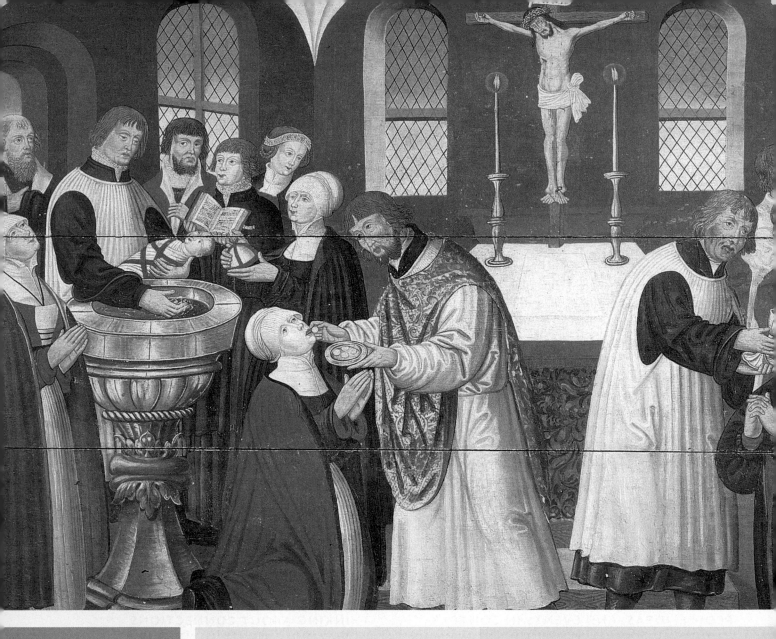

## Before
## You
## Read
## This
## Chapter

### STORY LINES

- The movement catalyzed by Martin Luther's challenge to the Roman Church grew out of much earlier attempts at reform, but it was also a response to more recent religious and political developments.

- Within a decade after Luther's excommunication, religious dissent was widespread and a number of different Protestant faiths were taking hold in various regions of Europe.

- Forms of Protestantism transformed not only the political landscape of Europe but also basic structures of the family and attitudes toward marriage and sexuality that still shape our lives today.

- These changes also affected the structures and doctrine of the Roman Catholic ("universal") Church, which reemerged as an institution different in many ways from the medieval Church, and more similar to that of today.

### CHRONOLOGY

| | |
|---|---|
| 1517 | Luther posts the Ninety-Five Theses |
| 1520s | Lutheranism becomes the official religion of Scandinavian countries |
| 1521 | Luther is excommunicated at the Diet of Worms |
| 1525 | Swabian peasants' revolt |
| 1529 | Luther breaks with Zwingli |
| 1534 | Henry VIII establishes the Church of England |
| 1534 | Ignatius Loyola founds the Society of Jesus (the Jesuits) |
| 1541 | Geneva adopts a theocratic government based on Calvinism |
| 1545–1563 | Council of Trent is convened |
| 1555 | Peace of Augsburg |
| 1553–1558 | Mary Tudor attempts to restore the Catholic faith in England |
| 1559 | Elizabeth reestablishes Protestantism in England |
| 1564 | Papal Index of Forbidden Books is published for the first time |

# The Age of Dissent and Division, 1500–1564

## CORE OBJECTIVES

- **DEFINE** the main premises of Lutheranism.

- **EXPLAIN** why some rulers and/or regions embraced forms of Protestant Christianity and why others did not.

- **IDENTIFY** the ways in which family structures and values changed during the Reformation.

- **UNDERSTAND** the reasons behind England's unusual Protestant faith.

- **DESCRIBE** the Roman Catholic Church's response to the challenge of Protestantism.

In 1517, on the night before the Feast of All Saints—All Hallows' Eve (or Halloween)—a professor of theology at a small university in northern Germany posted a list of debating points on the door of Wittenberg's Castle Church (part of the princely palace of the local ruler, the elector of Saxony; it also served as the university's chapel). This was not a prank; it was the usual method of announcing a scholarly disputation. Yet Martin Luther's choice of an evening traditionally associated with mischief making was appropriate, because the posting of these Ninety-Five Theses was a subversive act. For one thing, the sheer number of propositions that Dr. Luther offered to debate was unusual. But what really caught the attention of his fellow scholars was their unifying theme: the corruption of the Roman Church and, in particular, the office of the pope. It was a topic very much in vogue at the time, but it had seldom been dissected so clearly by a licensed theologian who was also a monk, an ordained priest, and a charismatic teacher.

This document, and the wider controversy it stimulated, soon spread far beyond Wittenberg. By the time the papacy formally retaliated in 1520, religious dissent was mounting—and not only among academics. Many of Europe's rulers saw

## Decoding Printed Propaganda

The printing press has been credited with helping to spread the teachings of Martin Luther and thus securing the success of the Protestant Reformation. But even before Luther's critiques were published, reformers were using the new technology to disseminate images that attacked the corruption of the Church. After Luther rose to prominence, both his supporters and detractors vied to disseminate propaganda that appealed visually to a lay audience and can be understood even by those who could not read.

The first pair of images below is really a single printed artifact dated to around 1500, an early example of a "pop-up" card. It shows Pope Alexander VI (r. 1492–1503) as a stately pontiff (image A) whose true identity is concealed by a flap, but when the flap is raised, he is revealed as a devil (image B). The Latin texts read: "Alexander VI, *pontifex maximus*" and "I am the pope," respectively.

The other two examples represent both sides of the debate as it had developed by 1530, and they do so with

A. Pope Alexander VI as pontiff.

B. Pope Alexander VI as a devil.

reference to the same image: the seven-headed beast mentioned in the Book of Revelation. Image C, a Lutheran engraving, shows the papacy as the beast with seven heads, representing seven orders of Catholic clergy. The sign on the cross (referring to the sign hung over the head of the crucified Christ) is in German, and reads: "For money, a sack full of indulgences"; the Latin words on either side say "Reign of the Devil." By contrast, image D, a Catholic engraving produced in Germany, shows Luther as Revelation's beast, with its seven heads labeled: "Doctor–Martin–Luther–Heretic–Hypocrite–Fanatic–Barabbas," the last alluding to the thief who should have been executed instead of Jesus, according to the Gospels.

## Questions for Analysis

**1.** Given that the attack on Pope Alexander VI precedes Martin Luther's critique of the Church by nearly two decades, what can you conclude about its intended audience? To what extent can it be read as a barometer of popular disapproval? What might have been the reason(s) for using the concealing flap?

**2.** What do you make of the fact that both Catholic and Protestant propagandists used the same imagery? What do you make of the key differences, such as the fact that the seven-headed papal beast sprouts out of an altar on which a Eucharistic chalice is displayed, while the seven-headed Martin Luther is reading a book?

**3.** All of these printed images make use of words. Would the message of each image be clear without the texts? Why or why not?

C. The seven-headed papal beast.

D. The seven-headed Martin Luther.

of wars. Leo X (r. 1513–1521) was a self-indulgent member of the Medici family of Florence. In *The Praise of Folly*, first published in 1511 and frequently reprinted (Chapter 12), Erasmus had declared that the popes of his day were incapable of leading Christlike lives as their office required. In *Julius Excluded*, published anonymously in 1517, Erasmus imagines a conversation at the gates of heaven between Saint Peter and Julius II, in which Peter refuses to admit the armored, vainglorious pope who claims to be his own earthly representative.

In Germany, resentment of the papacy ran especially high because there were no special agreements (concordats) limiting papal authority in its principalities, as there were in Spain, France, Bohemia, and England (Chapter 12). German princes complained that papal taxes were so high that the country was drained of its wealth, and yet Germans had almost no influence over papal policy. Frenchmen, Spaniards, and Italians dominated the College of Cardinals and the papal bureaucracy, and the popes were almost invariably Italian (as they would continue to be until 1978, when the Polish John Paul II was elected). As a result, graduates from the rapidly growing German and central European universities almost never found employment in Rome; instead, many joined the throngs of Luther's supporters, to become leaders of the new religious movement.

**THE EMPEROR CHARLES V.** This portrait by the Venetian painter Titian depicts Europe's most powerful ruler sitting quietly in a chair, dressed in simple clothing of the kind worn by judges or bureaucrats. ▪ *Why might Charles have chosen to represent himself this way, rather than in the regalia of his many royal, imperial, and princely offices?*

## Emperor Charles V and the Condemnation at Worms

In 1520, Pope Leo X issued a papal edict condemning Luther's publications as heretical and threatening him with excommunication if he did not recant. Luther's response was defiant: rather than acquiescing to the pope's demand, he staged a public burning of the document. Thereafter, his heresy confirmed, he was formally given over for punishment to his lay overlord, Frederick III "the Wise" of Saxony. Frederick, however, proved a supporter of Luther and a critic of the papacy. Rather than burning Luther at the stake, he declared that Luther had not yet received a fair hearing. Early in 1521, he therefore brought Luther to the city of Worms (*VORMS*) to be examined by a select representative assembly known as a "diet."

At Worms, the diet's presiding officer was the newly elected Holy Roman Emperor Charles V, a member of the Habsburg family who had been born and bred in his ancestral holding of Flanders, at that time part of the Netherlands. By 1521, through the unpredictable workings of dynastic inheritance, marriage, and election, he had become not only the ruler of the Netherlands but also the king of Germany, Holy Roman emperor, duke of Austria, duke of Milan, and ruler of the Franche-Comté. And as the grandson of Ferdinand and Isabella on his mother's side, he was also the king of Spain; king of Naples, Sicily, and Sardinia; and ruler of all the Spanish possessions in the New World. Governing such an extraordinary combination of territories posed enormous challenges, especially since this empire had no capital or centralized administrative institutions and shared no common language or culture or geographically contiguous borders.

Because of the diversity of his empire, Charles could not tolerate threats to the fundamental force that held it together: Catholicism, as the religion of Rome was coming to be called. There was, therefore, little doubt that the Diet of Worms would condemn Martin Luther for heresy. And when Luther refused to back down, thereby endangering

**THE EUROPEAN EMPIRE OF CHARLES V, c. 1526.** Charles V ruled a vast variety of widely dispersed territories in Europe and the New World, and as Holy Roman emperor he was also the titular ruler of Germany. ▪ *What were the main countries and kingdoms under his control?* ▪ *Which regions were most threatened by Charles's extraordinary power, and where might the rulers of these regions turn to for allies?* ▪ *How might the expansion of the Ottoman Empire have complicated the political and religious struggles within Christian Europe?*

his life, his lord Frederick the Wise intervened once more, arranging for Luther to be "kidnapped" and hidden for a year at the elector's castle of the Wartburg, where he was kept out of harm's way. Although Charles proclaimed Luther an outlaw at Worms, this edict was never enforced; instead, he left Germany for a war with France. A year later, in 1522, Luther returned in triumph to Wittenberg, where the changes he had called for had already been put into practice by his university supporters. When several German princes formally converted to Lutheranism, they brought their territories with them. In a little over a decade, a new form of Christianity had been established.

**THE WARTBURG, EISENACH (GERMANY).** This medieval stronghold became the refuge of Martin Luther after his condemnation at the Diet of Worms in 1520. His room in the castle has since been preserved.

## The German Princes and the Lutheran Church

Why did some German princes decide to embrace Lutheran religious practices? This is an important development, because popular support for Luther would not have been enough to ensure the success of his teachings had they not been embraced by a number of powerful rulers and free cities. Indeed, it was only in those territories where Lutheranism was formally established that the new religion prevailed. Elsewhere in Germany, Luther's sympathizers were forced to flee, face death, or conform to Catholicism.

The power of individual lords to control the practice of religion in their lands reflects developments we have noted in previous chapters. Rulers had long sought to control appointments to Church offices in their own realms, to restrict the flow of money to Rome, and to limit the independence of ecclesiastical courts. But in Germany, as noted above, neither the emperor nor the princes were strong enough to secure special treatment. This situation changed, however, as a result of Luther's initiatives. In one of the pamphlets published in 1520, Luther explicitly encouraged German princes to confiscate the wealth of the Church, as an incentive for gaining aristocratic support. At first, the princes bided their time, but when they realized that Charles V could not act

swiftly enough, several moved to introduce Lutheranism. Personal piety surely played a role in individual cases, but political and economic considerations were generally more decisive. Protestant princes could consolidate authority by naming their own religious officials, cutting off fees to Rome, and curtailing the jurisdiction of Church courts. They could also guarantee that the political and religious boundaries of their territories would now coincide; no longer would a rival ecclesiastical prince (such as a bishop or archbishop) be able to use his spiritual office to undermine a secular prince's sovereignty.

Similar considerations also moved a number of free cities to adopt Lutheranism. Acting independently, town councils could establish themselves as the supreme governing authorities within their jurisdictions, cutting out local bishops or powerful monasteries. Given the added fact that under Lutheranism monasteries and convents could be shut down and their lands appropriated by the newly sovereign secular authorities, the practical advantages of the new faith were overwhelming.

Once safely ensconced in Wittenberg under princely protection, Luther began to express his political and social views more vehemently, views which tended toward the strong support of the new political order. In a treatise of 1523, he insisted that "godly" (Protestant) rulers must be obeyed in all things and that even "ungodly" ones should never be targets of dissent because tyranny "is not to be resisted but endured." In 1525, when peasants throughout Germany rebelled against their landlords, Luther responded with intense hostility. In his vituperative pamphlet *Against the Thievish, Murderous Hordes of Peasants*, he urged readers to hunt the rebels down as though they were mad dogs: to "strike, strangle, stab secretly or in public, and remember that nothing can be more poisonous than a man in rebellion." After the ruthless suppression of this revolt, which may have cost as many as 100,000 lives, the firm alliance of Lutheranism with state power helped preserve and sanction the existing social order.

In his later years, Luther concentrated on debating with younger, more radical religious reformers who challenged his political conservatism. Never tiring in his prolific literary activity, he wrote an average of one treatise every two weeks for twenty-five years.

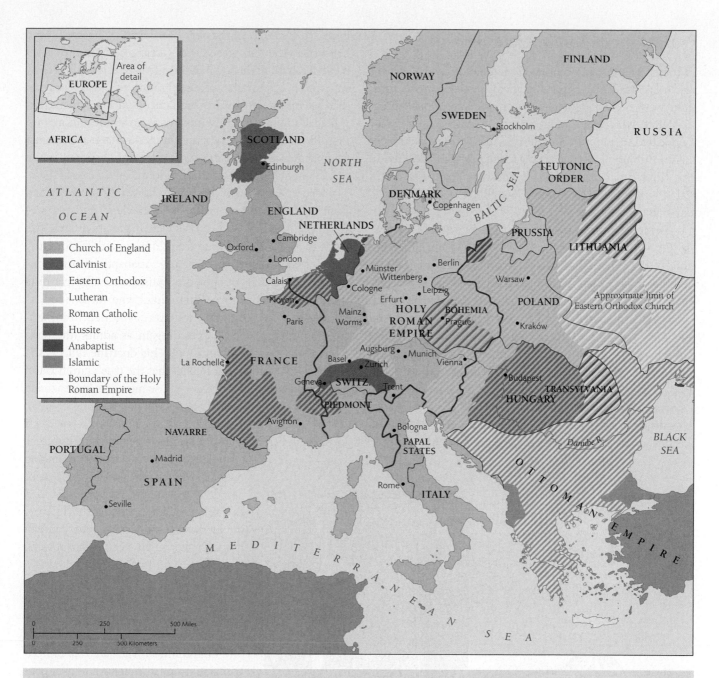

**Legend:**
- Church of England
- Calvinist
- Eastern Orthodox
- Lutheran
- Roman Catholic
- Hussite
- Anabaptist
- Islamic
- Boundary of the Holy Roman Empire

**CONFESSIONAL DIFFERENCES, c. 1560.** The religious affiliations (confessions) of Europe's territories had become very complicated by the year 1560, roughly a generation after the adoption of Lutheranism in some areas. ▪ *Which major countries and kingdoms had embraced a form of Protestantism by 1560?* ▪ *To what extent do these divisions conform to political boundaries?* ▪ *To what extent did the divisions complicate the political situation?* ▪ *Why might Lutheranism have spread north into Scandinavia, but not south into Bavaria or west across the Rhine?*

# THE MANY FORMS OF PROTESTANTISM

Originating as a term applied to Lutherans who "protested" the Catholic authority of Charles V, the word *Protestant* was soon applied to a much wider range of dissenting forms of Christianity. Lutheranism planted lasting roots in northern Germany and Scandinavia, where it became the state religion of Denmark, Norway, and Sweden as early as the 1520s. But other early Lutheran successes in southern Germany, Poland, and Hungary were eventually rolled back. Elsewhere in Europe, meanwhile, competing forms of Protestantism soon emerged from the seeds Luther had sown.

## Protestantism in Switzerland

In the early sixteenth century, Switzerland was ruled neither by kings nor territorial princes; instead, prosperous cities were either independent or on the verge of becoming so. Hence, when the leading citizens of a Swiss municipality decided to adopt Protestant reforms, no one could stop them. Although religious arrangements varied from city to city, three main forms of Protestantism emerged in Switzerland between 1520 to 1550: Zwinglianism, Anabaptism, and Calvinism.

Zwinglianism, founded in Zürich by Ulrich Zwingli (*TSVING-lee*; 1484–1531), was the most theologically moderate of the three. Zwingli had just begun his career as a Catholic priest when his humanist study of the Bible convinced him that Catholic theology and practice conflicted with the Gospels, which eventually led him to condemn religious images and hierarchical authority within the Church. Yet he did not speak out publicly until Luther set a precedent. In 1522, Zwingli began attacking the authority of Rome, and soon much of northern Switzerland had accepted his religious leadership.

Although Zwingli's reforms closely resembled those of the Lutherans in Germany, Zwingli differed from Luther in regard to the theology of the Eucharist. Whereas Luther believed in the real presence of Christ's body in the sacrament, for Zwingli the Eucharist conferred no grace at all and was simply a reminder and celebration of Christ's historic sacrifice on the cross. This fundamental disagreement prevented Lutherans and Zwinglians from uniting in a common Protestant front. When Zwingli died in battle against Catholic forces in 1531, his movement was absorbed by the more systematic Protestantism of John Calvin (see below).

Before Calvinism prevailed, however, more radical form of Protestantism arose in Switzerland and parts of Germany. The first Anabaptists were members of Zwingli's circle in Zürich who broke from him around 1525 on the issue of infant baptism. Because Anabaptists were convinced that the sacrament of Baptism was effective only when administered to willing adults who understood its significance, they required followers who had been baptized as infants to be baptized again as adults (the term *Anabaptism* means "rebaptism"). This doctrine reflects the Anabaptists' fundamental belief that the true church was a small community of believers whose members had to make a deliberate, inspired decision to join it.

No other Protestant groups were prepared to go so far in rejecting the medieval Christian view of the Church as a single vast body to which all members of society belonged from birth. And in an age when almost everyone assumed that religious and secular authority were inextricably connected, Anabaptism was rejected by all established powers, both Protestant and Catholic. It was a movement that appealed to sincere religious piety in calling for pacifism, strict personal morality, and extreme simplicity of worship.

This changed when a group of Anabaptist extremists managed to gain control of the German city of Münster in 1534. These zealots were driven by millenarianism, the belief that God intends to institute a completely new order of justice and spirituality throughout the world before the end of time. Determined to help God bring about this goal, the extremists attempted to turn Münster into a new Jerusalem. A former tailor named John of Leyden assumed the title "king of the New Temple" and proclaimed himself the successor of the Hebrew king David. Under his leadership, Anabaptist religious practices were

**THE ANABAPTISTS' CAGES, THEN AND NOW.** After the three Anabaptist leaders of Münster were executed in 1535, their corpses were prominently displayed in cages hung from a tower of the marketplace church. As can be seen from the photo on the right, their bones are gone, but the iron cages remain. ▪ *What would be the purpose of keeping these cages on display?* ▪ *What different messages might this sight convey?*

made obligatory, private property was abolished, and even polygamy was permitted based on Old Testament precedents. Such practices were deeply shocking to Protestants and Catholics alike. Accordingly, Münster was besieged and captured by Catholic forces little more than a year after the Anabaptist takeover. The new "David," together with two of his lieutenants, was put to death by torture, and the three bodies were displayed in iron cages in the town square.

Thereafter, even moderate Anabaptists throughout Europe were ruthlessly persecuted on all sides. The few who survived banded together in the Mennonite sect, named after its founder, the Dutchman Menno Simons (c. 1496–1561). This sect, dedicated to pacifism and the simple "religion of the heart" of original Anabaptism, is still particularly strong in the central United States.

## John Calvin's Reformed Theology

A year after the events in Münster, a twenty-six-year-old Frenchman, Jean Calvin (1509–1564), published the first version of his *Institutes of the Christian Religion*, the most influential formulation of Protestant theology ever written. Born in Noyon, in northern France, Calvin had originally trained for the law; but by 1533, he was studying the Greek

and Latin classics while living off the income from a priestly benefice. As he later wrote, he was "obstinately devoted to the superstitions of popery" until he experienced a miraculous conversion. He became a Protestant theologian and propagandist, eventually fleeing the Swiss city of Basel to escape persecution.

Although some aspects of Calvin's early career resemble those of Luther, the two men were very different. Luther was an emotionally volatile personality and a lover of controversy. He responded to theological problems as they arose or as the impulse struck him, and never attempted to systematize his beliefs. Calvin, however, was a coolly analytical legalist, who resolved in his *Institutes* to set forth all the principles of Protestantism comprehensively, logically, and systematically. After several revisions and enlargements, the definitive edition of *Institutes* appeared in 1559, and it became the Protestant equivalent of Thomas Aquinas's *Summa Theologiae* (Chapter 9).

Calvin's austere and stoical theology started with the omnipotence of God. For Calvin, the entire universe depends utterly on the will of the Almighty, who knows all things present and to come. Because of man's original fall from grace, all human beings are sinners by nature, bound to an evil inheritance they cannot escape. Yet God (for reasons of his own) predestined some for eternal salvation

**JEAN CALVIN.** This recently discovered portrait by an anonymous artist shows the young Protestant reformer as a serene and authoritative figure. It places the grotesque caricature of Calvin (right) in perspective.

**CALVIN AS SEEN BY HIS ENEMIES.** In this image, which circulated among Calvin's Catholic detractors, the reformer's facial features are a disturbing composite of fish, toad, and chicken.

and damned the rest to the torments of hell. There is nothing that individuals can do to alter their fate; all souls are stamped with God's blessing or curse before they are born. Nevertheless, Christians cannot be indifferent to their conduct on earth. If they are among the elect, God will implant in them the desire to live according to his laws. Upright conduct is thus a sign that an individual has been chosen to sit at the throne of glory. Membership in the Reformed Church (as Calvinist churches are more properly known) is another presumptive sign of election to salvation. Most of all, Calvin urged Christians to conceive of themselves as chosen instruments of God, charged to work actively to fulfill God's purposes on earth. Because sin offends God, Christians should do all they can to prevent it; God's glory is diminished if sin is allowed to flourish unchecked.

Calvin always acknowledged a great theological debt to Luther, but his religious teachings diverged from those of the Wittenberg reformer in several essentials. First, Luther's attitude toward proper Christian conduct in the world was much more passive than Calvin's. For Luther, a Christian should endure the trials of this life through suffering, whereas for Calvin the world was to be mastered through unceasing labor for God's sake. Calvin's religion was also more controlling than Luther's. Although Luther insisted that his followers attend church on Sunday, he did not demand that during the remainder of the day they refrain from all pleasure or work. Calvin, however, issued stern strictures against worldliness of any sort on the Sabbath and forbade all sorts of minor self-indulgences even on non-Sabbath days.

The two men also differed on fundamental matters of church governance and worship. Although Luther broke from the Catholic system of hierarchical church government, Lutheran district superintendents exercised some of the same powers as bishops, including the supervision of parish clergy. Luther also retained many features of traditional Christian worship, including altars, music, and ritual. Calvin, however, rejected everything that smacked of "popery." He argued for the elimination of all traces of hierarchy within the church; each congregation should elect its own ministers, and assemblies of ministers and "elders" (laymen responsible for maintaining proper religious conduct among the faithful) should govern the Reformed Church as a whole. Calvin also insisted on the utmost simplicity in worship, prohibiting (among much else) vestments, processions, instrumental music, and religious images of any sort, including stained-glass windows. He also dispensed with all remaining vestiges of Catholic sacramental theology by making the sermon, rather than the Eucharist, the centerpiece of reformed worship. As a sign of this change, pulpits were frequently moved to the center of the church sanctuary.

## Calvinism in Geneva

Consistent with his theological convictions, Calvin was intent on putting his religious teachings into practice. Sensing an opportunity in the French-speaking Swiss city of Geneva—then in the throes of political and religious upheaval—he moved there late in 1536 and immediately began to preach and organize. In 1538, his activities caused him to be expelled by the city council, but he returned in 1541 and brought the city under his sway.

With Calvin's guidance, Geneva's government became a theocracy, under the "rule of God." Supreme authority was vested in a "consistory," or assembly, composed of twelve lay elders and between ten and twenty pastors whose weekly meetings Calvin dominated. In addition to passing legislation, the consistory's main function was to supervise morality, both public and private. To this end, Geneva was divided into districts, and a committee of the consistory visited every household, without prior warning, to check on the behavior of its members. Dancing, card playing, attending the theater, and working or playing on the Sabbath were all outlawed as works of the devil. Innkeepers were forbidden to allow anyone to consume food or drink without first saying grace, or to permit any patron to stay up after nine o'clock. Adultery, witchcraft, blasphemy, and heresy all became capital crimes, and penalties for lesser crimes were severe. During the first four years after Calvin gained control in Geneva, there were no fewer than fifty-eight executions in a city whose total population was only 16,000.

As rigid as such a regime may seem today, Calvin's Geneva was a beacon of light to thousands of Protestants throughout Europe in the mid-sixteenth century. Calvin's disciple John Knox (c. 1514–1572), who brought the reformed religion to Scotland, declared Geneva the "most perfect school of Christ that ever was on earth since the days of the Apostles." Converts such as Knox flocked to Geneva for refuge or instruction, then returned home to become ardent proselytizers for the new religion. Geneva thus became the center of an international movement dedicated to spreading reformed religion to France and the rest of Europe through organized missionary activity and propaganda.

These efforts were remarkably successful. By the end of the sixteenth century, Calvinists were a majority in Scotland (where they were known as Presbyterians) and Holland (where they founded the Dutch Reformed Church). They were also influential in England, although the Church of England adopted reformed theology but not reformed worship. (Calvinists who sought further reforms in worship were known as Puritans.) There were also substantial

Calvinist minorities in France (where they were called Huguenots), Germany, Hungary, Lithuania, and Poland. By the end of the sixteenth century, Calvinism had spread to the New World.

## The Beginnings of Religious Warfare in Divided Europe

Less than a generation after Luther's challenge to the Church, wars between Catholic and Protestant rulers began. In Germany, Charles V attempted to establish Catholic unity by launching a military campaign against several German princes who had instituted Lutheran worship in their territories. But despite several notable victories, his efforts to defeat the Protestant princes failed. In part, this was because Charles was also involved in wars against France; primarily, however, it was because the Catholic princes of Germany worked against him, fearing that any suppression of Protestant princes might diminish their own independence. As a result, the Catholic princes' support for the foreign-born Charles was only lukewarm; at times, they even joined with the Protestants in battle against him. Meanwhile, the French looked beyond Christian Europe, forming a powerful alliance with the Muslim sultan Suleiman the Magnificent (r. 1520–1566), who protected France from Charles V and brought the Ottoman Empire into the military and diplomatic sphere of Europe.

Regional religious warfare sputtered on and off until a compromise settlement was reached via the Peace of Augsburg in 1555. Its governing principle was *cuius regio, eius religio* ("as the ruler, so the religion"). This meant that in those principalities where Lutherans ruled, Lutheranism would be the sole state religion; but where Catholic princes ruled, the people of their territories would be Catholic. In some regions, this rule was not needed or enforced, because local rulers permitted religious diversity. In Transylvania, a province under the overlordship of Hungary (now in Romania), Catholics lived alongside three different Protestant groups in relative peace. In Poland and Lithuania, Eastern Orthodox Christianity expanded its influence alongside Catholicism and was eventually tolerated. But these were rare exceptions.

For better and for worse, the Peace of Augsburg was a historical milestone. For the first time since Luther had been excommunicated, Catholic rulers were forced to acknowledge the legality of Protestantism. Yet the peace set a dangerous precedent, because it established the premise that no sovereign state can tolerate religious diversity. Moreover, it excluded Calvinism entirely and thus spurred German and Scots Calvinists to become aggressive opponents of the status quo. As a result, Europe was riven by religious warfare for another century and exported sectarian violence to the New World (see Chapter 14).

# THE DOMESTICATION OF REFORM

Within two decades, Protestantism had become a diverse revolutionary movement whose radical claims for the spiritual equality of all Christians had the potential to undermine the political, social, and even gender hierarchies on which European society rested. Luther himself did not anticipate that his ideas might have such implications, and he was by no means the only staunchly conservative Protestant. Indeed, most of the prominent early Protestant leaders were not radicals, and they depended on the support of existing elites: territorial princes, as well as the ruling elites of towns. As a result, the Reformation movement was speedily "domesticated" in two senses. Its revolutionary potential was toned down—Luther himself rarely spoke about the "priesthood of all believers" after 1525—and there was an increasing emphasis on the patriarchal family as the central institution of reformed life.

## Reform and Discipline

As we have seen, injunctions to lead a more disciplined and godly life had been a frequent message of previous religious reform movements, especially after the Black Death (Chapter 11). Many of these efforts had been actively promoted by princes and town councils, most famously perhaps in Florence, where the Dominican preacher Girolamo Savonarola led the city on an extraordinary but short-lived campaign of puritanism and moral reform between 1494 and 1498. And there are numerous other examples of rulers legislating against sin. When Desiderius Erasmus called on secular authorities to think of their territories as giant monasteries, he was sounding an already familiar theme.

Protestant rulers, however, took the need to enforce godly discipline with particular seriousness, because the depravity of human nature was a fundamental tenet of Protestant belief. Like Saint Augustine at the end of the fourth century (Chapter 6), Protestants believed that people would inevitably turn out to be bad unless they were compelled to be good. It was therefore the responsibility

# Competing Viewpoints

## Marriage and Celibacy: Two Views

These two selections illustrate strong contrasting views on the spiritual value of marriage versus celibacy as embraced by Protestant and Catholic religious authorities. The first selection is part of Martin Luther's more general attack on monasticism, which emphasizes his contention that marriage is the natural and divinely intended state for all human beings. The second selection, from the cannons of the Council of Trent (1545–1563), restates traditional Church teaching on the holiness of marriage but also emphasizes the spiritual superiority of virginity to marriage and the necessity of clerical celibacy. Celibacy for all clergy (not only monks and nuns) had been instituted for the first time in the eleventh century (Chapter 8), but it had never been fully accepted, especially in Britain and Scandinavia, or universally practiced.

### Luther's Views on the Impossibility of Celibacy (1535)

Listen! In all my days I have not heard the confession of a nun, but in the light of Scripture I shall hit upon how matters fare with her and know I shall not be lying. If a girl is not sustained by great and exceptional grace, she can live without a man as little as she can without eating, drinking, sleeping, and other natural necessities.

Nor, on the other hand, can a man dispense with a wife. The reason for this is that procreating children is an urge planted as deeply in human nature as eating and drinking. That is why God has given and put into the body the organs, arteries, fluxes, and everything that serves it. Therefore what is he doing who would check this process and keep nature from running its desired and intended course? He is attempting to keep nature from being nature, fire from burning, water from wetting, and a man from eating, drinking, and sleeping.

Source: E. M. Plass, ed., *What Luther Says*, vol. 2 (St. Louis, MO: 1959), pp. 888–89.

### Church Canons on the Sacrament of Matrimony (1563)

Canon 1: If anyone says that matrimony is not truly and properly one of the seven sacraments . . . instituted by Christ the Lord, but has been devised by men in the Church and does not confer grace, let him be anathema [cursed].

Canon 9: If anyone says that clerics constituted in sacred orders or regulars [monks and nuns] who have made solemn profession of chastity can contract marriage . . . and that all who feel that they have not the gift of chastity, even though they have made such a vow, can contract marriage, let him be anathema [cursed], since God does not refuse that gift to those who ask for it rightly, neither does he suffer us to be tempted above that which we are able.

Canon 10: If anyone says that the married state excels the state of virginity or celibacy, and that it is better and happier to be united in matrimony than to remain in virginity or celibacy, let him be anathema.

Source: H. J. Schroeder, *Canons and Decrees of the Council of Trent* (St. Louis, MO: 1941), pp. 181–82.

### Questions for Analysis

1. On what grounds does Luther attack the practice of celibacy? Do you agree with his basic premise? Why or why not?

2. How do the canons of the Catholic Church respond to Protestant views such as Luther's? What appears to be at stake in this defense of marriage and celibacy?

of secular and religious leaders to control and punish the misbehavior of their people, because otherwise their evil deeds would anger God and destroy human society. It was also essential that all people receive godly education.

Protestant godliness began with the discipline of children. Luther himself wrote two catechisms (instructional tracts) designed to teach children the tenets of their faith and the obligations—toward parents, masters, and rulers—that God imposed on them. Luther also insisted that all children, boys and girls alike, be taught to read the Bible in their own languages. Schooling thus became a characteristically Protestant preoccupation and rallying cry. Even the Protestant family was designated a "school of godliness," in which fathers were expected to instruct and discipline their wives, children, and household servants.

But family life in the early sixteenth century still left much to be desired in the eyes of Protestant reformers. Drunkenness, domestic violence, illicit sexual relations, lewd dancing, and the blasphemous swearing of oaths were frequent topics of reforming discourse. Various methods of discipline were attempted, including private counseling, public confessions of wrongdoing, public penance and shaming, exclusion from church services, and even imprisonment. All these efforts met with varying, but generally modest, success. Creating godly Protestant families and enforcing godly discipline on entire communities were going to require the active cooperation of godly authorities.

## Protestantism, Government, and the Family

The domestication of the Reformation in this sense took place principally in the free towns of Germany, Switzerland, and the Netherlands. From those regions it spread westward to North America. Protestant attacks on monasticism and clerical celibacy found a receptive audience among townsmen who resented the immunity of monastic houses from taxation and regarded clerical celibacy as a subterfuge for the seduction of their own wives and daughters. Protestant emphasis on the depravity of the human will and the consequent need for that will to be disciplined by authority also resonated powerfully with guilds and town governments, which were anxious to maintain and increase the control exercised by urban elites (mainly merchants and master craftsmen) over the apprentices and journeymen who made up the majority of the male population. By eliminating the competing jurisdictional authority of the Catholic Church, Protestantism allowed town governments to consolidate all authority within the city into their own hands.

Meanwhile, Protestantism reinforced the control of individual males over their own households by emphasizing the family as the basic unit of religious education. In place of a priest, an all-powerful father figure was expected to assume responsibility for instructing and disciplining his household according to the precepts of reformed religion. At the same time, Protestantism introduced a new religious ideal for women. No longer was the virginal nun the exemplar of female holiness; in her place stood the married and obedient Protestant "goodwife." As one Lutheran prince wrote in 1527, "Those who bear children please God better than all the monks and nuns singing and praying." To this extent, Protestantism resolved the tensions between piety and sexuality that had long characterized Christian teachings, by declaring the holiness of marital sex.

But this did not promote a new view of women's spiritual potential or elevate their social and political status. Quite the contrary: Luther regarded women as even more sexually driven than men and less capable of controlling their desires. His opposition to convents rested on his belief that it was impossible for women to remain chaste, so sequestering them simply made their illicit behavior inevitable. To prevent sin, it was necessary that all women be married, preferably at a young age, and placed under the governance of a godly husband.

For the most part, Protestant town governments were happy to cooperate in shutting down female monasteries, since a convent's property went to the town. But conflicts did arise between Protestant reformers and town fathers over marriage and sexuality, especially over the reformers' insistence that both men and women should marry young as a restraint on lust. In many towns, men were traditionally expected to delay marriage until they had achieved the status of master craftsman—an expectation that had become increasingly difficult to meet as guilds sought to restrict the number of journeymen permitted to become masters. In theory, then, apprentices and journeymen were not supposed to marry, but instead were expected to frequent brothels and taverns—a legally sanctioned outlet for extramarital sexuality long viewed as necessary to men's physical well-being—which Protestant reformers now deemed morally abhorrent.

Towns responded in a variety of ways to these opposing pressures. Some instituted special committees to police public morals, of the sort we have noted in Calvin's Geneva. Some abandoned Protestantism altogether. And others, such as the German town of Augsburg, alternated between Protestantism and Catholicism for several decades. Yet regardless of a town's final choice of religious allegiance, by the end of the sixteenth century a revolution had taken place with respect to governments' attitudes toward public morality. In their competition with each other, neither Catholics nor Protestants wished to be seen as soft on sin. The result was the widespread closing of publicly licensed brothels, the outlawing of prostitution, and far stricter governmental supervision of many other aspects of private life than had ever been the case in any Western civilization.

## The Control of Marriage

Protestantism also increased parents' control over their children's choice of marital partners. The medieval Church had defined marriage as a sacrament, but one that did not require the involvement of a priest. The mutual free consent of two individuals, even if given without witnesses or parental approval, was enough to constitute a legally valid marriage in the eyes of the Church. Opposition to this doctrine had long come from many quarters, especially from wealthy families who stood to lose from this liberal doctrine, because marriage involved rights of inheritance to property. For this reason, it was regarded as too important a matter to be left to the choice of adolescents. Instead, elite parents wanted the power to prevent unsuitable matches and, in some cases, to force their children to accept the marriage arrangements their families might negotiate on their behalf. For them, Protestantism offered an opportunity to obtain such control. Luther had declared marriage to be a purely secular matter, not a sacrament at all, and one that could be regulated however the governing authorities thought best. Calvin largely followed suit, although Calvinist theocracy drew less of a distinction between the powers of church and state than did Lutheranism.

Even the Catholic Church was eventually forced to give way. Although it never abandoned its insistence that both members of a couple must freely consent to their marriage, the Church's new doctrine required formal public notice of intent to marry and insisted on the presence of a priest at the wedding ceremony. Both rules were efforts to prevent elopements, allowing families time to intervene before an unsuitable marriage was concluded. Individual Catholic countries sometimes went even further in trying to assert parental control over their children's choice of marital partners. In France, for example, although couples might still

marry without parental consent, those who did so forfeited their rights to inherit their families' property. In somewhat different ways, both Protestantism and Catholicism moved to strengthen the control parents could exercise over their children—and, in the case of Protestantism, husbands over their wives.

# THE REFORMATION IN ENGLAND

In England, the Reformation took a rather different course than it did in Continental Europe. Although a long tradition of popular reform survived into the sixteenth century, the number of dissidents was too small and their influence too limited to play a significant role. England was also not particularly oppressed by the papal exactions and abuses that roiled Germany. At the start of the sixteenth century, English monarchs already exercised close control over Church appointments within the kingdom and received the lion's share of the papal taxes collected. Thus the power of ecclesiastical courts did not inspire any particular resentments. On the contrary, these courts would continue to function in Protestant England until the eighteenth century. Why, then, did sixteenth-century England become a Protestant country at all?

## "The King's Great Matter"

In 1527, King Henry VIII of England had been married to Ferdinand and Isabella's daughter, Catherine of Aragon, for eighteen years. Yet all the offspring of this union had died in infancy, with the exception of a daughter, Mary. Because Catherine was now past childbearing age and Henry needed a male heir to preserve the peaceful succession to the throne, he had political reasons to propose a change of wife. He also had a more personal motive, having become infatuated with a lady-in-waiting named Anne Boleyn.

Henry therefore appealed to Rome to annul his marriage to Catherine, arguing that because she had previously been married to his older brother Arthur, who had died in adolescence, his marriage to Catherine had been invalid from the beginning. As Henry's representatives pointed out, the Bible pronounced it "an unclean thing" for a man to take his brother's wife and cursed such a marriage with childlessness (Leviticus 20:31). Even a papal dispensation, which Henry and Catherine had long before obtained for their marriage, could not exempt them from

**HENRY VIII OF ENGLAND.** Hans Holbein the Younger executed several portraits of the English king. This one depicts him in middle age, confident of his powers.

such a clear prohibition—as the marriage's childlessness proved.

Henry's petition put Pope Clement VII (r. 1523–1534) in an awkward position. Both Henry and Clement knew that popes in the past had granted annulments to reigning monarchs on far weaker grounds than the ones Henry was alleging. But if the pope granted Henry's annulment, he would cast doubt on the validity of all papal dispensations. More seriously, he would provoke the wrath of the emperor Charles V, Catherine of Aragon's nephew, whose armies were in firm command of Rome and who at that moment held the pope himself in captivity. Clement was trapped, and all he could do was procrastinate and hope that the matter would resolve itself. For two years, he allowed Henry's case to proceed in England without ever reaching a verdict. Then, suddenly, he transferred the case to Rome, where the legal process began all over again.

Exasperated by these delays, Henry began to increase pressure on the pope. In 1531, he compelled an assembly of English clergy to declare him "protector and only supreme head" of the Church in England. In 1532, he encouraged Parliament to produce an inflammatory list of grievances against the English clergy and used this threat to force them to concede his right, as king, to approve or deny all Church legislation. In January 1533, Henry married Anne Boleyn (already pregnant) even though his marriage to Catherine still had not been annulled. The new archbishop of Canterbury, Thomas Cranmer, later provided the required annulment in May, acting on his own authority.

In September, Princess Elizabeth was born; her father, disappointed again in his hopes for a son, refused to attend her christening. Nevertheless, Parliament settled the succession to the throne on the children of Henry and Anne, redirected all papal revenues from England into the king's hands, prohibited appeals to the papal court, and formally declared the "King's Highness to be Supreme Head of the Church of England." In 1536, Henry executed his former tutor and chancellor, Sir Thomas More (Chapter 12), for his refusal to endorse this declaration of supremacy, and took the first steps toward dissolving England's many monasteries. By the end of 1539, the monasteries and convents were emptied and their lands and wealth confiscated by the king, who distributed them to his supporters.

These measures, largely masterminded and engineered by Henry's Protestant adviser Thomas Cromwell (c. 1485–1540), broke the bonds that linked the English Church to Rome. But they did not make England a Protestant country. Although certain traditional practices (such as pilgrimages and the veneration of relics) were prohibited, the English Church remained overwhelmingly Catholic in organization, doctrine, ritual, and language. The Six Articles promulgated by Parliament in 1539 at Henry VIII's behest left no room for doubt as to the official orthodoxy: oral confession to priests, masses for the dead, and clerical celibacy were all confirmed; the Latin Mass continued; and Catholic Eucharistic doctrine was not only confirmed but its denial was made punishable by death. To most English people, only the disappearance of the monasteries and the king's own continuing matrimonial adventures (he married six wives in all) were evidence that their Church was no longer in communion with Rome.

## The Reign of Edward VI

For truly committed Protestants, and especially those who had visited Calvin's Geneva, the changes Henry VIII enforced on the English Church did not go nearly far enough. And in 1547, the accession of the nine-year-old king Edward VI (Henry's son by his third wife, Jane Seymour)

# Analyzing Primary Sources

## The Six Articles of the English Church

*Although Henry VIII withdrew the Church of England from obedience to the papacy, he continued to reject most Protestant theology. Some of his advisers, most notably Thomas Cromwell, were committed Protestants, and the king allowed his son and heir, Edward VI, to be raised as a Protestant. But even after several years of rapid (and mostly Protestant) change in the English Church, Henry reasserted a set of traditional Catholic doctrines in the Six Articles of 1539. These remained binding on the Church of England until the king's death in 1547.*

First, that in the most blessed sacrament of the altar, by the strength and efficacy of Christ's mighty word, it being spoken by the priest, is present really, under the form of bread and wine, the natural body and blood of our Savior Jesus Christ, conceived of the Virgin Mary, and that after the consecration there remains no substance of bread or wine, nor any other substance but the substance of Christ, God and man;

Secondly, that communion in both kinds is not necessary for salvation, by the law of God, to all persons, and that it is to be believed and not doubted ... that in the flesh, under the form of bread, is the very blood, and with the blood, under the form of wine, is the very flesh, as well apart as though they were both together;

Thirdly, that priests, after the order of priesthood received as afore, may not marry by the law of God;

Fourthly, that vows of chastity or widowhood by man or woman made to God advisedly ought to be observed by the law of God. . . .

Fifthly, that it is right and necessary that private masses be continued and admitted in this the king's English Church and congregation . . . whereby good Christian people . . . do receive both godly and goodly consolations and benefits; and it is agreeable also to God's law;

Sixthly, that oral, private confession is expedient and necessary to be retained and continued, used and frequented in the church of God.

Source: *Statutes of the Realm*, vol. 3 (London: 1810–1828), p. 739 (modernized).

### Questions for Analysis

1. Three of these six articles focus on the sacrament of the Eucharist (the Mass). Given what you have learned in this chapter, why would Henry have been so concerned about this sacrament? What does this reveal about his values and those of his contemporaries?

2. Given Henry's insistence on these articles, why might he have allowed his son to be raised a Protestant? What does this suggest about the political situation in England?

---

gave them the opportunity to finish the task of reform. Henry's last wife, Catherine Parr, was a Lutheran sympathizer and, as the teacher of the royal children, contributed greatly to further reforms that stripped many Roman practices from the English Church. Edward's government permitted priests to marry; English services replaced Latin ones; the veneration of images was discouraged, and the images themselves were defaced or destroyed; prayers for the dead were declared useless, and endowments for such prayers were confiscated; and new articles of belief were drawn up, repudiating all sacraments except Baptism and Communion and affirming the Protestant creed of justification by faith alone. Most important, *The Book of Common Prayer* by Archbishop Cranmer, considered one of the great landmarks of English literature, defined precisely how the new English-language services of the church were to be conducted.

Edward's successor, however, was his pious Catholic and much older half sister Mary (r. 1553–1558), granddaughter of the "Most Catholic monarchs" of Spain, Ferdinand and Isabella (Chapter 11). Mary speedily reversed her half brother's religious policies, restoring the Latin Mass and requiring married priests to give up their wives. She even prevailed on Parliament to vote a return to papal allegiance. Hundreds of Protestant leaders fled abroad, many to Geneva; others, including Archbishop Cranmer, were burned at the stake for refusing to abjure their Protestantism. News of the martyrdoms spread and shocked Protestant Europe, but in England Mary's policies sparked relatively little resistance. After two decades of religious upheaval, most English men

**QUEEN MARY AND QUEEN ELIZABETH.** The two daughters of Henry VIII, Queen Mary (left) and Queen Elizabeth (right), were the first two queens regnant of England; that is, the first women to rule in their own right. Despite the similar challenges they faced, they had strikingly different fates and have been treated very differently in popular histories. ■ *How do these two portraits suggest differences in the queens' personalities and their self-representation as rulers?*

and women were probably hoping that Mary's reign would bring some stability to their lives.

This, however, Mary could not do. The executions she ordered were insufficient to wipe out religious resistance; instead, Protestant propaganda about "Bloody Mary" caused widespread unease, even among those who welcomed the return of traditional religious forms. She also could not restore monasticism, because too many leading families had profited from Henry VIII's dissolution of the monasteries for her to reverse this policy. Mary's marriage to her cousin Philip, Charles V's son and heir to the Spanish throne, was another miscalculation. Although the marriage treaty stipulated that Philip could not succeed her in the event of her death, her English subjects never trusted him. When she allowed herself to be drawn by Philip into a war with France on Spain's behalf—in which England lost Calais, its last foothold on the European continent—many people became highly disaffected.

Ultimately, however, what doomed Mary's policies was simply an accident of biology: she was unable to conceive an heir. When she died after only five years of rule, her throne passed to her Protestant half sister, Elizabeth.

## The Elizabethan Settlement

The daughter of Henry VIII and Anne Boleyn, Elizabeth (r. 1558–1603) was predisposed in favor of Protestantism by the circumstances of her parents' marriage as well as by her upbringing. But Elizabeth was no zealot and recognized that supporting radical Protestantism in England might provoke bitter sectarian strife. Accordingly, she presided over what is often known as the "Elizabethan settlement" or compromise. By a new Act of Supremacy (1559), she repealed Mary's Catholic legislation, prohibiting foreign religious powers (the pope) from exercising any authority within England and declaring herself "supreme governor" of the English church—a more Protestant title than Henry VIII's "supreme head," since most Protestants believed that Christ alone was the head of the Church. She also adopted many of the Protestant liturgical reforms instituted by her half brother Edward, including Cranmer's revised version of *The Book of Common Prayer*.

But Elizabeth retained vestiges of Catholic practice, too, including bishops, church courts, and vestments for the clergy. On most doctrinal matters, including predestination and free will, Elizabeth's Thirty-Nine Articles of Faith (approved in 1562) struck a decidedly Protestant, even Calvinist, tone. Still, this prayer book was more moderate and, on the critical issue of the Eucharist, deliberately ambiguous. By combining Catholic and Protestant interpretations ("This is my body. . . . Do this in remembrance of me") into a single declaration, for example, the prayer book permitted an enormous latitude for competing interpretations of the service by priests and parishioners alike.

Yet religious tensions persisted in Elizabethan England, not only between Protestants and Catholics, whose opposition to Protestant elements in England was absolute, but also between moderate and more extreme Protestants. On the one hand, the queen was obliged to continue Mary's practice of persecuting heretics—in this case, Catholics—and executing them for treason. On the other hand, her attempts to promote a "middle way" among competing forms of Christianity caused dissatisfaction among hardliners of all stripes.

In the long run, what preserved the "Elizabethan settlement" was the extraordinary length of the queen's reign, along with the fact that, for much of that time, Protestant England was at war with Catholic Spain. Under Elizabeth, Protestantism and English forms of nationalism gradually fused into a potent conviction that God himself had chosen England for greatness. After 1588, when English naval forces won an improbable victory over the Spanish Armada (see Chapter 14), Protestantism and Englishness became nearly indistinguishable to most of Queen Elizabeth's subjects. Laws against Catholic practices became increasingly severe, and although an English Catholic tradition did survive, its adherents were a persecuted minority. Significant, too, was the situation in Ireland, where the vast majority of the people remained Catholic despite the government's efforts to impose Protestantism. As a result, Irishness would be as firmly identified with Catholicism as was Englishness with Protestantism—but it was the Protestants who were in power in both countries.

# THE REBIRTH OF THE ROMAN CATHOLIC CHURCH

So far, our emphasis on the spread of Protestantism has cast the spotlight on dissident reformers such as Luther and Calvin. But there was also a powerful internal reform movement within the Church in the same decades, which resulted in the birth (or rebirth) of a Catholic ("universal") faith.

For some, this movement is the "Catholic Reformation"; for others, it is the "Counter-Reformation." Those who prefer the former term emphasize that the Church was continuing significant reforming movements that can be traced back to the eleventh century (Chapter 8) and that gained new momentum in the wake of the Great Schism (Chapter 11). Others insist that most Catholic reformers of this period were reactionaries, inspired primarily by the urgent need to resist Protestantism and strengthen the power of the Roman Church in opposition.

## Catholic Reforms

Even before Luther's challenge to the Church, there was a strong movement for moral and institutional reform within some religious orders, as we have seen. And while the papacy showed little interest in them, these efforts received support from several secular rulers. In Spain, for example, reforming activities directed by Cardinal Francisco Jiménes de Cisneros (1436–1517) led to the imposition of strict rules of behavior and the elimination of abuses prevalent among the clergy. Jiménes (he-MEN-ez) also helped to regenerate the spiritual life of the Spanish Church. In Italy, meanwhile, earnest clerics labored to make the Italian Church more worthy of its prominent position. Reforming existing institutions was a difficult task, not least because the papal court set such a poor example. Yet some new religious orders, dedicated to high ideals of piety and social service, were emerging. In northern Europe, Christian humanists such as Erasmus and Thomas More played a role in this Catholic reform movement, criticizing abuses and editing sacred texts (Chapter 12).

These internal reforms were inadequate, however, as a response to the concerted challenges posed by Protestantism. Starting in the 1530s, therefore, a more aggressive phase of reform began to gather momentum under a new style of vigorous papal leadership. The leading Counter-Reformation popes Paul III (r. 1534–1549), Paul IV (r. 1555–1559), Pius V (r. 1566–1572), and Sixtus V (r. 1585–1590) were the most zealous reformers of the Church since the eleventh century. All led upright lives; some, indeed, were so grimly ascetic that contemporaries longed for the bad old days. As a Spanish councilor wrote of Pius V in 1567, "We should like it even better if the present Holy Father were no longer with us, however great, inexpressible, unparalleled, and extraordinary His Holiness may be." In confronting Protestantism, however,

# Past and Present

## Controlling Consumption

Although laws regulating the conspicuous consumption of expensive commodities—especially status-conscious clothing—were common during the later Middle Ages, it was not until after the Reformation that both Protestant and Catholic leaders began to criminalize formerly acceptable behaviors and stimulants. New theories of sensory perception, the availability of new consumer goods such as coffee and tobacco, and a new push to internalize reform led some authorities to outlaw prostitution (hitherto legal) and to ban normal social practices such as drinking and dancing. The image on the left shows the militant Catholic League, which was founded in sixteenth-century France to combat Protestantism and promote strict religious observance. The image on the right shows Czech protesters calling for the decriminalization of marijuana.

 **Watch related author interview on the Student Site**

an excessively holy pope was vastly preferable to a self-indulgent one. And these Counter-Reformation popes were not merely holy men but also accomplished administrators, reorganizing papal finances and filling ecclesiastical offices with bishops and abbots who were no less renowned for austerity and holiness than the popes themselves.

Papal reform efforts intensified at the Council of Trent, a general meeting of the entire Church convoked by Paul III in 1545 and that met at intervals thereafter until 1563. The decisions made at Trent, a provincial capital of the Holy Roman Empire (in modern-day Italy), provided the foundations on which a new Catholic Church would be erected. Although the council began by debating some form of compromise with Protestantism, it ended by reaffirming all the Catholic tenets challenged by Protestant critics. "Good works" were affirmed as necessary for salvation, and all seven sacraments were declared indispensable means of grace, without which salvation was impossible. Transubstantiation, purgatory, the invocation of saints, and the rule of celibacy for the clergy were all confirmed as dogmas—essential elements—of the Catholic faith. The Bible, in its imperfect Vulgate translation, and the traditions of apostolic teaching were held to be of equal authority as sources of Christian truth. Papal supremacy over every bishop and priest was expressly maintained, and the supremacy of the pope over any Church council was taken for granted outright, signaling a final defeat of the still-active conciliar movement. The Council of Trent even reaffirmed the doctrine of indulgences that had touched off the Lutheran revolt, although it condemned the worst abuses connected with their sale.

*The Rebirth of the Roman Catholic Church* | 447

**THE COUNCIL OF TRENT.** This fresco depicts the General Council of the Catholic Church, which met at intervals for nearly twenty years between 1545 and 1563 in the city of Trent (in modern-day Italy) to enact significant internal reforms.

***THE INSPIRATION OF SAINT JEROME*, BY GUIDO RENI (1635).** The Council of Trent declared Saint Jerome's Latin translation of the Bible, the Vulgate, to be the Catholic Church's official version. Biblical scholars had known since the early sixteenth century that Saint Jerome's translation contained numerous mistakes, so Catholic defenders of the Vulgate insisted that even his mistakes had been divinely inspired.

■ *How does this painting attempt to make this point?*

The decrees issued at Trent were not confined to matters of doctrine. To improve pastoral care of the laity, bishops and priests were forbidden to hold more than one spiritual office. To address concerns that priests were not sufficiently prepared for their tasks, a theological seminary was to be established in every diocese. The council also suppressed a variety of local religious practices and saints' cults, replacing them with new cults authorized and approved by Rome. To prevent heretical ideas from corrupting the faithful, the council further decided to censor or suppress dangerous books.

In 1564, a specially appointed commission published the first Index of Prohibited Books, an official list of writings forbidden to faithful Catholics. It was ironic that all of Erasmus's works were immediately placed on the Index, even though he had been a chosen champion of the Church against Martin Luther only forty years before. A permanent agency known as the Sacred Congregation of the Index was later set up to revise the list, which was maintained until 1966, when it was abolished after the Second Vatican Council (1962–1965). For centuries, it symbolized the doctrinal intolerance that characterized sixteenth-century Christianity, both in Catholic and Protestant varieties.

## Ignatius Loyola and the Society of Jesus

In addition to the concerted activities of popes and the legislation of the Council of Trent, a third main force propelling the Counter-Reformation was the foundation of the Society of Jesus (commonly known as the Jesuits) by

## The Demands of Obedience

*The necessity of obedience in the spiritual formation of monks and nuns can be traced back to the* Rule of Saint Benedict *in the early sixth century, and beyond. In keeping with the mission of its founder, Ignatius of Loyola (1491–1556), the Society of Jesus brought renewed fervor to this old ideal, dedicating its members to superior intellectual achievements, teaching, and missionary work. Below are excerpts from two of the order's founding texts, the* Spiritual Exercises *of Ignatius and the* Jesuit *Constitutions.*

### Rules for Thinking with the Church

**1.** Always to be ready to obey with mind and heart, setting aside all judgment of one's own, the true spouse of Jesus Christ, our holy mother, our infallible and orthodox mistress, the Catholic Church, whose authority is exercised over us by the hierarchy.

**2.** To commend the confession of sins to a priest as it is practised in the Church; the reception of the Holy Eucharist once a year, or better still every week, or at least every month, with the necessary preparation....

\* \* \*

**4.** To have a great esteem for the religious orders, and to give the preference to celibacy or virginity over the married state....

\* \* \*

**6.** To praise relics, the veneration and invocation of Saints: also the stations, and pious pilgrimages, indulgences, jubilees, the custom of lighting candles in the churches, and other such aids to piety and devotion....

\* \* \*

**9.** To uphold especially all the precepts of the Church, and not censure them in any manner; but, on the contrary, to defend them promptly, with reasons drawn from all sources, against those who criticize them.

**10.** To be eager to commend the decrees, mandates, traditions, rites, and customs of the Fathers in the Faith or our superiors....

**11.** That we may be altogether of the same mind and in conformity with the Church herself, if she shall have defined anything to be black which to our eyes appears to be white, we ought in like manner to pronounce it to be black. For we must undoubtingly believe, that the Spirit of our Lord Jesus Christ, and the Spirit of the Orthodox Church His Spouse, by which Spirit we are governed and directed to salvation, is the same....

### From the Constitutions of the Jesuit Order

Let us with the utmost pains strain every nerve of our strength to exhibit this virtue of obedience, firstly to the Highest Pontiff, then to the Superiors of the Society; so that in all things ... we may be most ready to obey his voice, just as if it issued from Christ our Lord ... leaving any work, even a letter, that we have begun and have not yet finished; by directing to this goal all our strength and intention in the Lord, that holy obedience may be made perfect in us in every respect, in performance, in will, in intellect; by submitting to whatever may be enjoined on us with great readiness, with spiritual joy and perseverance; by persuading ourselves that all things [commanded] are just; by rejecting with a kind of blind obedience all opposing opinion or judgment of our own.

Source: Henry Bettenson, ed., *Documents of the Christian Church*, 2nd ed. (Oxford: 1967), pp. 259–61.

### Questions for Analysis

**1.** How might Loyola's career as a soldier have inspired the language used in his "Rules for Thinking with the Church"?

**2.** In what ways do these Jesuit principles respond directly to the challenges of Protestant reformers?

Ignatius Loyola (1491–1556). In the midst of a career as a mercenary, this young Spanish nobleman was wounded in battle in 1521, the same year in which Luther defied authority at the Diet of Worms. While recuperating, he turned from the reading of chivalric romances to a romantic vernacular retelling of the life of Jesus, and the impact of this experience convinced him to become a spiritual soldier of Christ.

For ten months, Ignatius lived as a hermit in a cave near the town of Manresa, where he experienced ecstatic visions and worked out the principles of his subsequent guidebook, the *Spiritual Exercises*. This manual, completed in 1535 and first published in 1541, offered practical advice on how to master one's will and serve God through a systematic program of meditations on sin and the life of Christ. It eventually became the basic handbook for all Jesuits and has been widely studied by Catholic laypeople as well. Indeed, Loyola's *Spiritual Exercises* ranks alongside Calvin's *Institutes* as the most influential religious text of the sixteenth century.

The Jesuit order originated as a group of six disciples who gathered around Loyola during his belated career as a student in Paris. They vowed to serve God in poverty, chastity, and missionary work and were formally constituted by Pope Paul III in 1540. By the time of Loyola's death, the Society of Jesus already numbered some 1,500 members. It was by far the most militant of the religious orders fostered by the Catholic reform movements of the sixteenth century. It was not merely a monastic society but a company of soldiers sworn to defend the faith; their weapons were not bullets and swords but eloquence, persuasion, and instruction in correct doctrines.

But the Society also became accomplished in more worldly methods of exerting influence. Its organization was patterned after that of a military unit, whose commander in chief enforced the iron discipline of all members; individuality was suppressed, and a stoical obedience was required from the rank and file. Indeed, the Jesuit general, sometimes known as the "black pope" (from the color of the order's habit), was elected for life and answered only to the pope in Rome; all senior Jesuits took a special vow of strict obedience to him, by which all Jesuits were held to be at the pope's disposal at all times.

The activities of the Jesuits consisted primarily of proselytizing and establishing schools, which meant that they were ideal missionaries. Accordingly, Jesuits were soon dispatched to preach to non-Christians in India, China, and Spanish America. One of Loyola's closest associates, Francis Xavier (ZAY-vyer; 1506–1552), baptized thousands of people and traveled thousands of miles in South and East Asia. Although Loyola had not at first conceived of his society as a battalion of "shock troops" in the fight against Protestantism, that is what it primarily became. Through preaching and diplomacy—sometimes at the risk of their lives—Jesuits in the second half of the sixteenth century helped to colonize the world. In many places, they were instrumental in keeping rulers and their subjects loyal to Catholicism; in others, they met martyrdom; and in still others, notably Poland and parts of Germany and France, they succeeded in regaining territory previously lost to followers of Luther and Calvin. Wherever they were allowed to settle, they set up schools and colleges on the grounds that only a vigorous Catholicism nurtured by widespread literacy and education could combat Protestantism.

## A New Catholic Christianity

The greatest achievement of these reform movements was the revitalization of the Church. Had it not been for such determined efforts, Catholicism would not have swept over the globe during the seventeenth and eighteenth centuries—or reemerged in Europe as a vigorous spiritual force. The reforms had other consequences, such as the rapid advancement of lay literacy in Catholic countries and the growth of intense concern for acts of charity. Because Catholicism continued to emphasize good works as well as faith, charitable activities took on an extremely important role.

There was also a renewed emphasis on the role of religious women. Reformed Catholicism did not exalt marriage as a route to holiness to the same degree as Protestantism, but it did encourage the piety of the female religious elite. For example, it embraced the mysticism of Saint Teresa of Ávila (1515–1582) and her renewal of religious women's spirituality by establishing new orders of nuns, such as the Ursulines and the Sisters of Charity. Both Protestants and Catholics continued to exclude women from the priesthood or ministry, but Catholic women could pursue religious lives with at least some degree of independence, and the convent continued to be a route toward spiritual and even political advancement in Catholic countries.

The reformed Catholic Church did not, however, perpetuate the tolerant Christianity of Erasmus. Instead, Christian humanists lost favor with the papacy, and even scientists such as Galileo were regarded with suspicion (see Chapter 16). Yet contemporary Protestantism was just as intolerant and even more hostile to the cause of rational

**TERESA OF ÁVILA.** Teresa of Ávila (1515–1582), canonized in 1622, was one of many female religious figures who played an important role in the reformed Catholic Church. This image is dated 1576, and the Latin wording on the scroll unfurled above Teresa's head reads, "I will sing forever of the mercy of the Holy Lord."

thought. Indeed, because Catholic theologians turned for guidance to the scholasticism of Thomas Aquinas, they tended to be much more committed to the dignity of human reason than were their Protestant counterparts, who emphasized the literal interpretation of the Bible and the importance of unquestioning faith. It is no coincidence that René Descartes, one of the pioneers of rational philosophy ("I think, therefore I am"), was educated by Jesuits.

It would be wrong, therefore, to claim that the Protestantism of this era was more forward-looking or progressive than Catholicism. Both were, in fact, products of the same troubled time. Each variety of Protestantism responded to specific historical conditions and the needs of specific peoples in specific places, while carrying forward certain aspects of the Christian tradition considered valuable by those communities. The Catholic Church also responded to new spiritual, political, and social realities—to such an extent that it must be regarded as distinct from either the early Church of the later Roman Empire or the ever-evolving Church of the Middle Ages. That is why the phrase "Roman Catholic Church" has not appeared in this book prior to this chapter; the Roman Catholic Church as we know it emerged for the first time in the sixteenth century.

## CONCLUSION

The Reformation grew out of the complex historical processes that we have been tracing in the last few chapters. Foremost among these was the increasing power of Europe's sovereign states. As we have seen, the German princes who embraced Protestantism were moved to do so by their desire for sovereignty. The kings of Denmark, Sweden, and England followed suit for many of the same reasons. Protestantism bolstered state power because Protestant leaders preached absolute obedience to godly rulers, and the state in Protestant countries assumed direct control of its churches. Yet the power of the state had been growing for a long time prior to the Reformation, especially in such countries as France and Spain, where Catholic kings already exercised most of the same rights that were seized by Lutheran authorities and by Henry VIII of England in the course of their own reformations. Those rulers who aligned themselves with Catholicism, then, had the same need to bolster their sovereignty and power.

Ideas of national identity, too, were already influential and thus available for manipulation by Protestants and Catholics alike. Religion thus became a new source of both identity and disunity. Prior to the Reformation, peoples in different regions of Germany spoke such different dialects that they had difficulty understanding each other. But Luther's Bible gained such currency that it eventually became the linguistic standard for all these disparate regions, which began to conceive of themselves as part of a single nation. Yet religion alone could not achieve the political unification of Germany, which did not occur for another 300 years (see Chapter 21); and, indeed, it contributed to existing divisions by cementing the opposition of Catholic princes and peoples. Elsewhere in Europe—as in the Netherlands, where Protestants fought successfully against a foreign, Catholic overlord—religion created a shared identity where politics could not. In England, where it is arguable that a sense of nationalism had already been fostered before the Reformation, membership in the Church of England became a new, but not uncontested, attribute of "Englishness."

Ideals characteristic of the Renaissance also contributed something to the Reformation and the Catholic responses to it. The criticisms of Christian humanists helped to prepare Europe for the challenges of Lutheranism, and close textual study of the Bible led to the publication of the newer, more accurate editions used by Protestant reformers. For example, Erasmus's improved edition of the Latin New Testament enabled Luther to reach some crucial conclusions concerning the meaning of penance, and became the foundation for Luther's own translation of the Bible. However, Erasmus was not a supporter of Lutheran principles and most other Christian humanists shunned Protestantism as soon as it became clear to them what Luther was actually teaching. Indeed, in certain basic respects, Protestant doctrine was completely at odds with the principles, politics, and beliefs of most humanists, who became staunch supporters of the Catholic Church.

# After You Read This Chapter

 Go to **INQUIZITIVE** to see what you've learned—and learn what you've missed— with personalized feedback along the way.

## REVIEWING THE OBJECTIVES

- The main premises of Luther's theology had religious, political, and social implications. What were they?
- Switzerland fostered a number of different Protestant movements. Why was this the case?
- The Reformation had a profound effect on the basic structures of family life and on the attitudes toward marriage and morality. Describe these changes.
- The Church of England was established in response to what specific political situation?
- How did the Catholic Church respond to the challenge of Protestantism?

In the New World and Asia, both Protestantism and Catholicism became forces of imperialism and new catalysts for competition. The race to secure colonies and resources now became a race for converts, as missionaries of both faiths fanned out over the globe. In the process, the confessional divisions of Europe were mapped onto these regions, often with violent results. Over the course of the ensuing century, newly sovereign nation-states would struggle for hegemony at home and abroad, setting off a series of religious wars that would cause as much destruction as any plague. Meanwhile, Western civilizations' extension into the Atlantic would create new kinds of ecosystems, forms of wealth, and types of bondage.

## PEOPLE, IDEAS, AND EVENTS IN CONTEXT

- How did **MARTIN LUTHER**'s attack on **INDULGENCES** tap into a more widespread criticism of the papacy? What role did the printing press and the German vernacular play in the dissemination of his ideas?

- Why did many German principalities and cities rally to Luther's cause? Why did his condemnation at the **DIET OF WORMS** not lead to his execution on charges of heresy?

- How did the Protestant teachings of **ULRICH ZWINGLI, JOHN CALVIN**, and the **ANABAPTISTS** differ from one another and from those of Luther?

- What factors made some of Europe's territories more receptive to **PROTESTANTISM** than others? What was the meaning of the principle **CUIUS REGIO, EIUS REGIO**, established by the Peace of Augsburg?

- How did the **REFORMATION** alter the status and lives of women in Europe? Why did it strengthen male authority in the family?

- Why did **HENRY VIII** break with Rome? How did the **CHURCH OF ENGLAND** differ from other Protestant churches in Europe?

- What decisions were made at the **COUNCIL OF TRENT**? What were the founding principles of **IGNATIUS LOYOLA**'s **SOCIETY OF JESUS**, and what was its role in the **COUNTER-REFORMATION** of the **CATHOLIC CHURCH**?

## THINKING ABOUT CONNECTIONS

- Our study of Western civilizations has shown that reforming movements are nothing new, and Christianity has been continuously reformed throughout its long history. What made this Reformation so different?

- Was a Protestant break from the Catholic Church inevitable? Why or why not?

- The political, social, and religious structures put in place during this era continue to shape our lives in such profound ways that we scarcely notice them—or we assume them to be inevitable and natural. In your view, what is the farthest-reaching consequence of this age of dissent and division? Why? In what ways has it formed your own values and assumptions?

## STORY LINES

- By the middle of the sixteenth century, the Atlantic Ocean had become a central space for colonization, migration, and settlement, as the peoples of this Atlantic world confronted each other.

- In the wake of the Reformation, Europe itself remained politically unstable, and devastating religious wars were waged on the Continent. In England, mounting pressures caused a crisis that resulted in civil war and the execution of the reigning king.

- At the same time, competition in the wider Atlantic world exported these political and religious conflicts to the new European colonies.

- This widening world and its pervasive violence caused many Europeans to question the beliefs of earlier generations. Intellectuals and artists sought new sources of authority and new ways of explaining the complex circumstances of their time.

## CHRONOLOGY

| | |
|---|---|
| 1562–1598 | French wars of religion |
| 1588 | Destruction of the Spanish Armada |
| 1566–1609 | Dutch wars with Spain |
| 1598 | Henry IV issues the Edict of Nantes |
| 1607 | English colony of Jamestown founded |
| 1608 | French colony in Québec founded |
| 1611 | William Shakespeare's play *The Tempest* performed in London |
| 1618 | Thirty Years' War begins |
| 1621 | Dutch West India Company founded |
| 1642–1649 | English Civil War |
| 1648 | Beginning of the Fronde rebellions Thirty Years' War ends |
| 1660 | Restoration of the English monarchy |

Before
You
Read
This
Chapter

# Europe in the Atlantic World, 1550–1660

## CORE OBJECTIVES

- **TRACE** the new linkages between Western civilizations and the Atlantic world, and **EXPLAIN** their consequences.

- **DESCRIBE** the different forms of unfree labor that developed in European colonies during this period.

- **IDENTIFY** the monarchies that dominated Europe and the Atlantic world and the newer powers whose influence was expanding.

- **EXPLAIN** the reasons for Europe's religious and political instability and its consequences for Europe's monarchies and the Atlantic world.

- **UNDERSTAND** how artists and intellectuals responded to the crises and uncertainties of this era.

The Atlantic Ocean thrashes the western shores of Europe and Africa with wind-driven waves that have traveled thousands of miles from the American coasts. Its immense area links continents shaped by a wide variety of climates, including the arid desert of the Sahara, the more temperate zones of Europe and North America, the tropical islands of the Gulf of Mexico and the Caribbean, and the rain forests of the Amazon basin in South America. This ecological diversity, and the hitherto infrequent and limited movement of peoples on opposite sides of the ocean, meant that each region nurtured its own forms of plant and animal life, and its own unique microbes and pathogens.

In the sixteenth century, the emergence of the Atlantic world as an arena of cultural and economic exchange broke down the isolation of these ecosystems. Transatlantic commerce and migration now eclipsed the importance of the Mediterranean, which had been the crucial connector of Western civilizations since the Bronze Age (Chapter 2). Populations of humans, animals, and plants on once-remote shores came into frequent and intense contact. On the one hand, Europeans brought diseases that devastated the peoples of the Americas,

455

along with gunpowder and a hotly divided Christianity. On the other hand, the huge influx of silver from South America transformed (and eventually exploded) the cash-starved European economy, while the arrival of American stimulants such as tobacco, sugar, and chocolate fostered new consumer appetites that could be satisfied only by new regimes of unfree labor.

Eventually, the need for slaves to power the plantations that supplied these consumer products fostered a vast industry of human trafficking, which led to the forcible removal of nearly 11 million people from Africa over the course of three centuries. Colonial settlement in North and South America also created new social hierarchies and new forms of inequality, which unsettled even long-established structures in Europe. The peoples of the Americas were forced to deal with the presence of newly arrived settlers, and the settlers in turn confronted both indigenous peoples and the meddling interference of distant imperial bureaucracies.

Meanwhile, European states were riven by internal dissent and engaged in deadly competitions among themselves—and these, too, were exported to the Atlantic world. Galvanized by the crisis of the Reformation (Chapter 13), the Roman Catholic Church sought to redress the loss of religious dominance in Europe by spreading its influence to the Americas and Asia through the work of new missionary orders. The Spanish crown, which controlled the most developed colonial empire of the time, was also the most zealous defender of the Catholic faith—thus the wars within Spain's Protestant Dutch provinces and with Protestant England affected colonial politics, too. Similar attempts by the Catholic Habsburg monarchy to enforce religious uniformity among the varied territories of central Europe led to the Thirty Years' War, one of the longest and bloodiest conflicts in western history. In both direct and indirect ways, these deadly disputes stimulated the migration of persecuted minorities across the Atlantic, replanting and propagating these rivalries.

But religion was not the only cause of conflict within Europe. Tension was growing between powerful monarchs and landowning elites who disputed the right of their rulers and administrators to raise revenues through increased taxation. Supporting colonial expansion in the Atlantic world and fighting wars within Europe were expensive projects that strained traditional alliances and ideas of kingship. Political and moral philosophers accordingly struggled to redefine the role of government in a world of religious pluralism and to articulate new political ideologies that did not necessitate violence among people of different faiths. Intellectuals and artists also strove to reassess the place for Europeans in this expanding Atlantic world, to process the flood of new information and commodities, and to make sense of the profound changes in daily life.

# THE EMERGENCE OF THE ATLANTIC WORLD

With the few exceptions we have noted in previous chapters, even the most skilled of Europe's sailors were limited to coastal cruising along the Atlantic's eastern shores until the fifteenth century. But after the Portuguese and Spanish established settlements on the Canary Islands, this archipelago off the northwestern coast of Africa became a permanent base of operations for successive exploratory ventures. From here, generations of Portuguese sailors learned to navigate the West African coast, after which they successfully rounded the Cape of Good Hope and began to establish trading colonies in the Indian Ocean (see Chapter 12). During these years, Portuguese sailors also launched the first kidnapping raids for slaves along the Atlantic coast of Senegal. When they found that some African chieftains were willing to facilitate the capture of people from rival tribes, the Portuguese began to set up coastal outposts where they could trade livestock, foodstuffs, cotton, copper, and iron for ivory, gold, finished textiles, and human beings.

## Competing Colonial Ventures

Spanish successes in Mexico soon encouraged other European kingdoms to attempt imperial ventures of their own. Finding that Spanish and Portuguese holds on the Caribbean and South America were firm, northern European explorers targeted the North American coast. Protestant rulers were obviously not bound by the Treaty of Tordesillas (1494) and all subsequent papal pronouncements that favored Catholic colonial ventures. In 1497–1498, the Italian-born explorer John Cabot was hired by the English crown to explore the mouth of the St. Lawrence River. But it was nearly a century later, in 1585, that Walter Raleigh attempted to start an English colony just north of Spanish Florida. The settlement at Roanoke Island (present-day North Carolina) was intended to solidify English claims to the territory of Virginia, named for England's "Virgin Queen" Elizabeth. It originally encompassed the North American seaboard from South Carolina to Maine, including Bermuda.

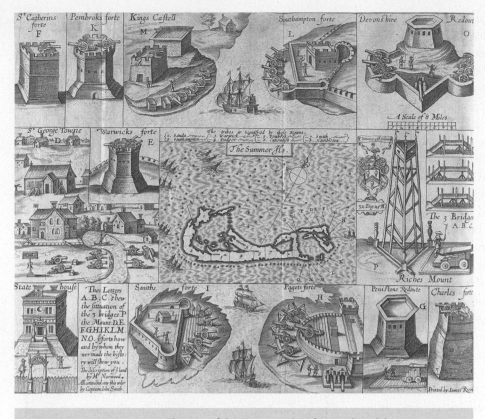

**THE ISLAND OF BERMUDA.** This map of the "Summer Isle" of Bermuda and the accompanying images of its major fortifications and sites were drawn by Captain John Smith and published in *The Generall Historie of Virginia, New-England, and the Summer Isles* (1624). ■ *Why would such features be of interest to readers of this pamphlet?*

continent. Bitter conflicts and occasional cooperation between newcomers and indigenous peoples are part of a larger history of intermittent struggle and coexistence that began the moment Columbus first landed on Hispaniola. Especially in the early years of colonization, when the number of European immigrants was small, some Native American peoples sought to take advantage of these new contacts to trade for goods otherwise unavailable to them. European settlers, for their part, often behaved with a combination of paternalism and contempt for the peoples they encountered. Some hoped to convert them to Christianity, while others sought to use them as labor for their economic enterprises. Ultimately, however, the balance was tipped by larger environmental, biological, and demographic factors that lay outside the control of individuals.

This ill-conceived experiment ended with the disappearance of the first colonists, but it was followed by Christopher Newport's expedition to the Chesapeake Bay in 1606, a voyage funded by a private London firm, the Virginia Company. Newport and his followers did not conceive of themselves as empire builders. They were not sponsored by the English king, and they probably did not intend to settle permanently in the New World. They were "gentleman planters" whose goal was to provide agricultural goods for the European market and so make their fortunes before returning home. Nevertheless, with the Spanish model much in mind, Newport's band reserved the right to subdue any peoples who proved uncooperative. So when Native Americans of the Powhatan tribe killed one-third of the settlers during a raid in 1622, the colonists responded by crushing the Powhatans and seizing their lands.

For decades thereafter, the native populations of North America remained capable of both threatening and fostering the survival of fragile settlements on the American coast

## The Columbian Exchange and Its Environmental Effects

The accelerating rate of global connections in the sixteenth century precipitated an extraordinary movement of peoples, plants, animals, goods, cultures, and diseases. This movement is known as the "Columbian exchange," a term coined by the historian Alfred Crosby in 1972 with reference to Columbus's voyage. Yet this exchange soon came to encompass lands that still lay far beyond the purview of Columbus and his contemporaries—not just the African and Eurasian landmass and the vast terrain of the Americas but also Australia and the Pacific Islands.

Because of its profound consequences for human populations and the environment, the Columbian exchange is considered a fundamental turning point in both human history and the history of the earth's ecology. The exchange put new agricultural products into circulation, introduced new species of domesticated animals, and accidentally encouraged the spread of deadly diseases and the devastating invasions of nonnative plants and animals. Both natural ecosystems and human immune systems around the world were destroyed or transformed. For example, the introduction of pigs and dogs to islands in the Atlantic and Pacific resulted in the extinction of indigenous animals and birds. The landscapes of Central America and southwestern North America were denuded of vegetation after Spanish settlers turned to large-scale herding and ranching operations. Honeybees displaced native insect populations and fostered the propagation of harmful plant species. Then there were the unintended exchanges: gray squirrels and raccoons from North America found their way to Britain and the European Continent, and brown rats and even some species of earthworms were transported to the Americas. Insects from all over the world traveled to new environments and spread unfamiliar forms of bacteria and pollen.

Obviously, the transfer of human populations in the form of settlers, soldiers, merchants, sailors, indentured servants, and slaves accelerated the process of change. Some groups were wiped out through violence, forced resettlement, and bacteria. As much as 90 percent of the pre-Columbian population of the Americas died from communicable diseases such as smallpox, cholera, influenza, typhoid, measles, malaria, and bubonic plague—all brought from Europe. Syphilis, in contrast, appears to have been brought to Europe from the Americas. Some scholars have even asserted that it was Columbus's own sailors who transmitted the disease across the Atlantic.

Meanwhile, the importation of foodstuffs from one part of the world to another, and their cultivation in new habitats, revolutionized the diets of local populations. The American potato, which could be grown in substandard soil and stored for long periods, eventually became the staple diet of the European poor. American tomatoes, although not widely consumed in Europe until the nineteenth century, are today an essential ingredient in many regional Italian dishes.

Indeed, the foods and flavors that characterize modern-day iconic cuisines are, to an extraordinary degree, the result of the Columbian exchange, because many new, exotic foods quickly become fashionable and then habitual. Who can imagine an English meal without potatoes? Switzerland or Belgium without chocolate? Thai food without chili peppers? On the other side of the Atlantic, Hawaii without pineapples? Florida without oranges? Colombia without coffee? Of the ingredients that make up the quintessential American hamburger—ground-beef patties on a bun with lettuce, tomato, pickles, onion, and (if you like) cheese—only one component is indigenous to America: tomato. Everything else is from the Old World: beef, wheat for the bun, cucumber for the pickle, onion, and lettuce. Even the name is European, a reference to the town of Hamburg in Germany.

---

## THE COLUMBIAN EXCHANGE

The following are just a few of the commodities and contagions that moved between the Old World and the New World in this era.

| *Old World →*<br>*New World* | *New World →*<br>*Old World* |
|---|---|
| • Wheat | • Corn |
| • Sugar | • Potatoes |
| • Bananas | • Beans |
| • Rice | • Squash |
| • Wine vines | • Pumpkins |
| • Horses | • Tomatoes |
| • Pigs | • Avocados |
| • Chickens | • Chili peppers |
| • Sheep | • Pineapples |
| • Cattle | • Cocoa |
| • *Smallpox* | • Tobacco |
| • *Measles* | • *Syphilis* |
| • *Typhus* | |

---

## Colonial Populations Compared

Compared to the more than 7 million slaves who were taken from Africa to labor and die on plantations across the Atlantic, only about 1.5 million Europeans immigrated to the Americas in the two centuries after Columbus's first voyage. The total number who initially emigrated from Spain is estimated at 200,000 to 250,000—most of whom were men. By 1570, given the high mortality of migrants and some returns to Europe, the population had reduced to about 150,000. The Spanish crown did what it could to encourage a new wave of settlement, but even in a period of demographic growth, the number of those who chose to seek their fortunes abroad remained relatively small. Transatlantic travel was expensive and uncertain, and the demand for a European labor force remained low as long as Native Americans could be conscripted and enslaved.

The population of the Spanish Americas thus remained largely urban during this period, with most colonists living in the military and administrative centers of the empire. Even the owners of large plantations lived in cities, corresponding from afar with the foremen who managed their estates. Only those who had been granted *encomiendas* tended to live on the lands entrusted to them by the Spanish crown (the Spanish verb *encomendar* means "to trust"). The *encomienda* system reveals how Spanish conquests in the New World were an extension of the earlier Reconquista (Chapter 12) of Spain itself. Originally set up to manage Muslim populations in territories captured by Christian crusaders, this arrangement made the *encomenderos* agents of the crown. Technically, the lands they oversaw were still owned by native peoples; but in practice, many *encomenderos* were able to exploit the land for their own profit, treating native workers like serfs. Some of the *encomenderos* were descendants of the first conquistadors. Others were drawn from Aztec and Inca elites, many of whom were women, like the daughters of the Aztec emperor Montezuma, who had been given extensive lands to hold in trust after their father's capitulation to Cortés.

In North America, by contrast, English colonies in New England and the Chesapeake Bay were small and rural. But they grew more quickly, with settlers numbering about 250,000 by 1700. Part of the reason for this growth was the greater impetus for emigration caused by overpopulation in the British Isles. The persecution of various Protestant groups also played an important role in driving immigration, especially to the New England colonies where relocation of entire families and even communities was common. The colonies in Virginia offered additional incentive by granting 100 acres to each settler.

But these factors did not swell the numbers of migrants so much as the encouragement of indentured servitude, a practice that brought thousands of "free" European laborers across the Atlantic to work under terms that made them little different from the slaves. Perhaps 75 to 80 percent of the people who arrived in the Chesapeake colony in the 1600s were indentured servants, nearly a quarter of whom were women. The successful use of indentured servants to grow tobacco in North America led some landowners to try the same system on plantations in the Caribbean islands. Ultimately, however, the plantation system earned its greatest profits through the labor of African slaves.

## New Social Hierarchies in New Spain

After the conquests of the Aztec and Inca Empires (Chapter 12), the Spanish established colonial governments in Mexico and Peru, under the control of a central bureaucracy in Madrid. This centralization was facilitated by the highly organized structure of the Aztec society in Mexico and the Incas in Peru. For the most part, native peoples already lived in large, well-regulated villages and towns. The Spanish government could therefore work closely with local elites to maintain order. Indeed, the *encomienda* system was initially effective because it was built on these existing structures and did not attempt to uproot or eliminate existing native cultures; it focused, instead, on controlling and exploiting native labor, especially for extracting mineral resources. Although farming and ranching were encouraged in Central and South America, and later in Florida and California, mining dominated the Spanish colonial economy for a century and a half.

The Spanish collected tributes from all the communities of their empire and worked to convert native peoples to Catholicism, but they did not attempt to change basic patterns of life. The result was a widespread cultural assimilation by the relatively small numbers of (usually male) settlers, which was assisted by the normality of intermarriage between (male) colonizers and (female) colonial subjects. This pattern gave rise to a complex and distinctive caste system in New Spain, with a few "pure-blooded" Spanish immigrants at the top, a very large number of Creoles (peoples of mixed descent) in the middle, and Native Americans at the bottom.

In theory, these racial categories corresponded to class distinctions, but in practice, race and class did not always coincide. Racial concepts and practices were extremely flexible, and prosperous individuals or families of mixed descent often found ways to establish their "pure" Spanish ancestry by adopting the social practices of the new Spanish colonial elites. The lingering effects of this complicated stratification are still evident in Latin America today.

## Sugar, Slaves, and the Transatlantic Triangle

The Europeans who settled in the Americas faced a major problem: labor. Mining and plantation agriculture required many workers, and the indigenous labor supply of the Americas was limited. As we have seen, the introduction of new diseases resulted in the deaths of millions of Native Americans in only a few decades. Meanwhile, the return of the plague in Europe in the seventeenth century, along with the slowing population growth due to the wars of religion, meant that colonists could not look to Europe to satisfy their labor needs. Colonial agents thus began to import slaves from Africa to bolster the labor force and produce the wealth they so avidly sought. And overwhelmingly, that wealth was derived not from gold or silver but from a new commodity for which there was an insatiable appetite in Europe: sugar.

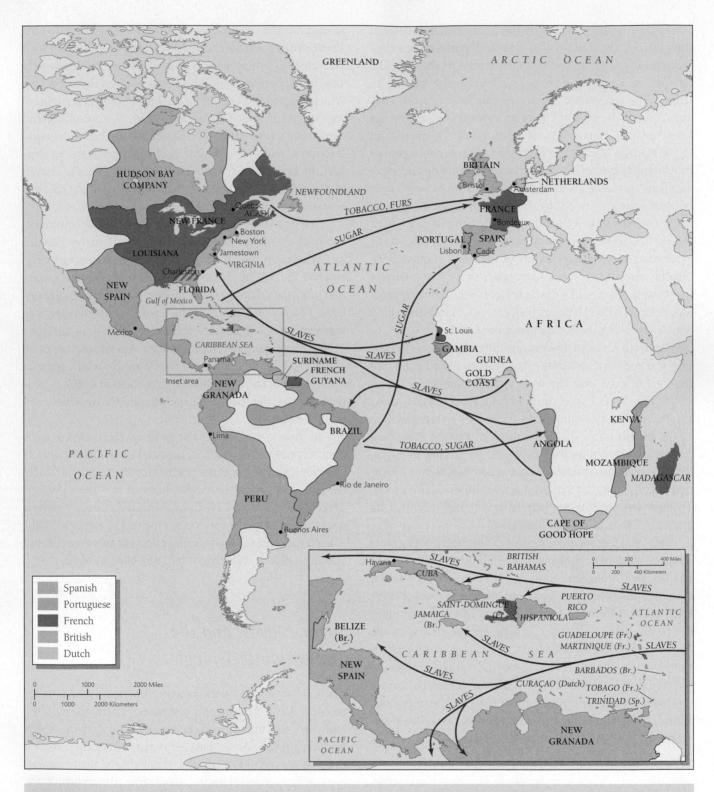

**THE ATLANTIC WORLD AND THE TRIANGULAR TRADE.** ▪ *Trace the routes of the triangular trade. What products did French and British colonies in North America provide to the European market?* ▪ *Which colonies were most dependent on slave labor and what products did they produce?* ▪ *How did these products enter into the triangle?*

## Enslaved Native Laborers at Potosí

*The Spanish crown received one-fifth of all revenues from the mines of New Spain, as well as maintaining a monopoly over the mercury used to refine the silver ore into silver, so it had an important stake in ensuring the mines' productivity. To this end, the crown granted colonial mine owners the right to conscript native peoples and gave them considerable freedom in the treatment of their workers. This account, dated to about 1620, describes the conditions endured by these native laborers at Potosí (discussed in Chapter 12).*

According to His Majesty's warrant, the mine owners on this massive range [at Potosí] have a right to the conscripted labor of 13,300 Indians in the working and exploitation of the mines, both those [mines] which have been discovered, those now discovered, and those which shall be discovered. It is the duty of the *Corregidor* [municipal governor] of Potosí to have them rounded up and to see that they come in from all the provinces between Cuzco . . . and as far as the frontiers of Tarija and Tomina. . . .

The conscripted Indians go up every Monday morning to the . . . foot of the range; the *Corregidor* arrives with all the provincial captains or chiefs who have charge of the Indians assigned him for his miner or smelter; that keeps him busy till 1 P.M., by which time the Indians are already turned over to these mine and smelter owners.

After each has eaten his ration, they climb up the hill, each to his mine, and go in, staying there from that hour until Saturday evening without coming out of the mine; their wives bring them food, but they stay constantly underground, excavating and carrying out the ore from which they get the silver. They all have tallow candles, lighted day and night; that is the light they work with, for as they are underground, they have need for it all the time. . . .

These Indians have different functions in the handling of the silver ore; some break it up with bar or pick, and dig down in, following the vein in the mine; others bring it up; others up above keep separating the good and the poor in piles; others are occupied in taking it down from the range to the mills on herds of llamas; every day they bring up more than 8,000 of these native beasts of burden for this task. These teamsters who carry the metal are not conscripted, but are hired.

Source: Antonio Vázquez de Espinosa, *Compendium and Description of the West Indies*, trans. Charles Upson Clark (Washington, DC: 1968), p. 62.

### Questions for Analysis

**1.** From the tone of this account, what do you think was the narrator's purpose in writing it? Who is his intended audience?

**2.** Reconstruct the conditions in which these laborers worked. What would you estimate to be the human costs of a week's labor? Why, for example, would a fresh workforce be needed every Monday?

Sugar was at the center of the "triangular trade" that linked markets for goods in Africa, the Americas, and Europe—all of which were driven by slave labor. For example, slave ships that transported African slaves to the Caribbean might trade their human cargo for molasses made on the sugar plantations of the islands. These ships would then proceed to New England, where the molasses would be traded to distillers who used the sugary syrup to make rum. Loaded up with a consignment of rum, the slavers would return to the African coast to repeat the process. An alternative triangle might see cheap manufactured goods move from England to Africa, where they would be traded for slaves. Those slaves would then be shipped to Virginia and exchanged for tobacco, which would be shipped back to England to be processed and distributed.

Although the transatlantic slave trade was theoretically controlled by the governments of European colonial powers, private entrepreneurs and working-class laborers were active at every stage of the supply chain: in the ports of West Africa, where captured slaves cast their eyes on their homelands for the last time; on the ships, where these captives were imprisoned; and in the slave markets of the

Americas, where agents for the landowners and merchants bid against one another to purchase the human chattel that had survived the terrible voyage. (Britain officially entered this trade in 1564, the year of William Shakespeare's birth.)

Many other branches of the economy in Europe and the Americas were also linked to the slave trade: investors in Amsterdam, London, Lisbon, and Bordeaux who financed the slave trader's journey; insurance brokers who negotiated complex formulas for protecting these investments; financial agents who offered a range of credit instruments; and those seeking to enter into the expensive and risky business of transatlantic trade. And this is to say nothing of the myriad ways in which the everyday lives of average people were bound to slavery. All who bought the commodities produced by slave labor or who manufactured the implements and weapons that enabled enslavement were also implicated. The slave trade was not, as is sometimes assumed, a venture carried forward by a few unscrupulous men. It created wealth and prestige for every sector of European society, not merely for those who had direct contact with it. It was the engine that created the modern globalized economy.

## The Human Cost of the Slave Trade

The Portuguese were the first to bring African slaves to their sugarcane plantations in Brazil, in the 1540s. By this time, slavery was already crucial to the domestic economies of West African kingdoms. In the following decades, however, the ever-increasing demand for slaves would cause the permanent disintegration of the political order in this region by creating an incentive for war and raiding among rival tribes. Moreover, the increased traffic in human beings called for more highly systematized methods for corralling, sorting, and shipping them. By the end of the sixteenth century, accordingly, the Portuguese government established a fortified trading outpost on an island known as Luanda on the central African coast (near what is now Angola). Additional trading posts were then established at multiple places along the coast to assist with processing the increasing number of captives.

On board the ships, enslaved humans were shackled below decks in spaces barely wider than their own bodies, without sanitary facilities of any kind. It might seem

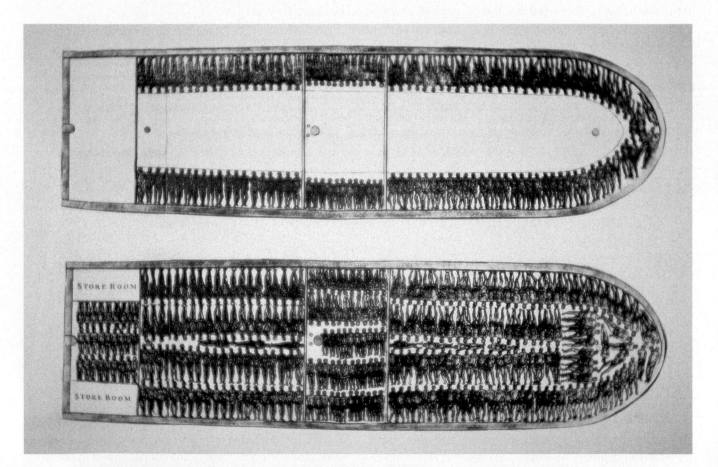

**HOW SLAVES WERE STOWED ABOARD A SHIP DURING THE MIDDLE PASSAGE.** Men were "housed" on the right, women on the left, and children in the middle. The human cargo was jammed onto platforms six feet wide without sufficient headroom to permit an adult to sit up. This diagram is from evidence gathered by English abolitionists in 1788 and depicts conditions on the Liverpool slave ship *Brookes*.

surprising that the mortality rate on these voyages was relatively low (probably 10 or 11 percent), but this was only because the slaves chosen for transport were healthy to begin with, and slave traders were anxious to maintain their goods so as to sell at a profit. Those Africans who were transported, then, were already the toughened survivors of unimaginable hardships. To place the above statistic in a larger context, we need to consider how many people would have died before the ships were ready to transport them. One historian estimated that 36 out of 100 people captured in the African interior would perish in the six-month-long forced march to the coast of Angola, and another dozen or so would die in the prisons there. Eventually, perhaps 57 of the original 100 captives would be taken aboard a slave ship, and some 51 would survive the journey and be sold into slavery on arrival. If the destination was Brazil's sugar plantations, only 40 would still be alive after two years. In other words, the actual mortality rate of these new slaves was closer to 60 percent—and this doesn't begin to account for their life expectancy.

The people consigned to this fate struggled against it, and their initiatives helped to shape the emerging Atlantic world. When the opportunity presented itself, slaves banded together in revolt—a perpetual possibility that haunted slave owners and led to draconian regimes of violence and punishment (as in ancient Rome; see Chapter 5). When revolt was impossible, slaves resorted to other forms of resistance, among them suicide and infanticide. Above all, slaves sought to escape; almost as soon as the slave trade escalated, communities of escaped slaves sprang up throughout the Americas. Many of these independent settlements were large enough to assert and defend their autonomy. One such community, founded in 1603 in the hinterlands of Brazil's Pernambuco Province, persisted for over a century and had as many as 20,000 inhabitants. Most others were much smaller and more ephemeral, but their existence testifies to the limits of imperial authority at the fringes of the new American colonies.

# CONFLICT AND COMPETITION IN EUROPE AND THE ATLANTIC WORLD

Most of Europe had enjoyed steady economic growth since the middle of the fifteenth century. The colonization of the Americas seemed to promise further prosperity for the decades to come, while providing an outlet for European expansion and aggression. But in the second half of the sixteenth century, prolonged political, religious, and economic crises destabilized Europe. These crises were, in essential ways, the products of long-term developments within and between Europe's most powerful states, but they were exacerbated by the imperial ambitions of those states. Inevitably, European conflicts spread to European colonial holdings, and eventually the outcome of these conflicts determined which European powers were best positioned to enlarge their presence in the Atlantic world—and beyond.

## New World Silver and Old World Economies

In the latter half of the sixteenth century, an unprecedented inflation in prices profoundly destabilized the European economy. And because nothing on this scale had ever happened before, it caused widespread panic. Although the twentieth century would see more dizzying inflations, suddenly skyrocketing prices were a terrifying novelty in this era, causing what some historians have termed a "price revolution."

**PEASANTS HARVESTING WHEAT, SIXTEENTH CENTURY.** The inflation that swept through Europe in the late sixteenth century affected poorer workers most acutely. The abundant labor supply damped wages while the cost of food rose because of poor harvests.

Two developments in particular underlay this phenomenon. The first was demographic: after the plague-induced decline of the fourteenth century (Chapter 11), Europe's population grew from roughly 50 million people in 1450 to 90 million in 1600—that is, it increased by nearly 80 percent in a relatively short span of time. Yet Europe's food supply remained nearly constant, causing food prices to rise steeply by the increased population's higher demand for basic commodities. Meanwhile, the enormous influx of silver and gold from Spanish America flooded Europe's previously cash-poor economy (Chapter 12), and this sudden availability of ready coin drove prices higher still.

About 10 million ducats' worth of silver, roughly equivalent to 10 billion U.S. dollars in today's currency, passed through the Spanish port of Seville in just four years, from 1556 to 1560. (A single gold ducat, the standard unit of monetary exchange for long-distance trade, would now be worth nearly a thousand dollars.) Consequently, the market was flooded with coins whose originally high worth quickly downgraded due to the large

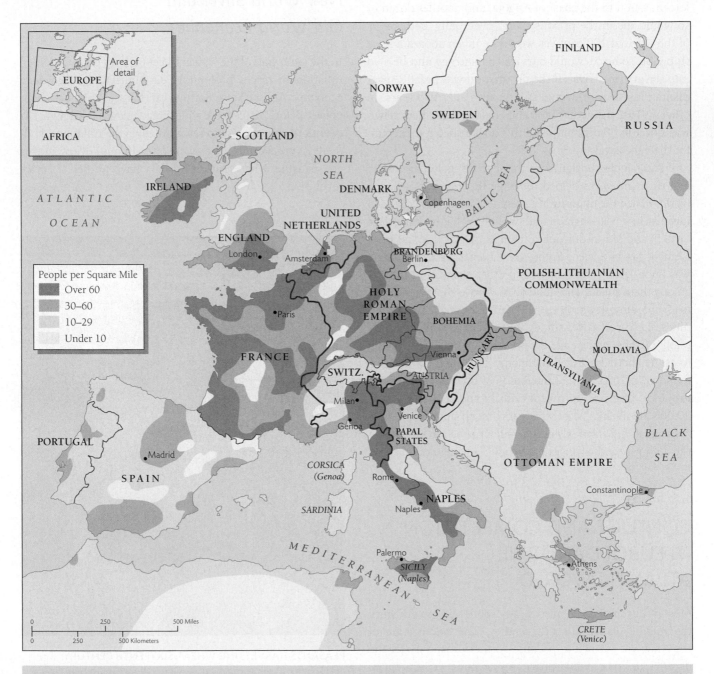

**POPULATION DENSITY, c. 1600.** ▪ *In what regions was the population most dense?* ▪ *Why were the largest gains in population on the coasts?* ▪ *How would urbanization affect patterns of life and trade?*

amount in circulation; and still silver poured in, cheapening the coinage even more. Between 1576 and 1580, the amount of imported silver doubled, becoming 20 million ducats; and between 1591 and 1595, it more than quadrupled. Most of this money was used by the Spanish crown to pay its armies and the many creditors who had financed its imperial ventures, so a huge volume of coinage was put quickly into circulation through European banks, making the problem of inflation even more widespread. Since some people suddenly had more money to pay for goods and services, those who supplied these commodities charged higher and higher prices. But at the same time, the value of the coinage itself was plummeting. "I learned a proverb here," said a French traveler in Spain in 1603. "Everything costs a lot, except silver."

## The New European Poor

In this climate, aggressive entrepreneurs profited from financial speculation, landholders from the rising prices of agricultural produce, and merchants from increasing demand for luxury goods. But laborers were caught in a vise: prices were rising steeply but wages were not keeping pace, owing to the population boom that kept labor relatively cheap. As the cost of food staples rose, poor people had to spend an ever-greater percentage of their paltry incomes on necessities. In Flanders, for example, the cost of wheat tripled between 1550 and 1600; in Paris, grain prices quadrupled; and in England, the overall cost of living more than doubled in Shakespeare's lifetime. When disasters such as wars or bad harvests drove grain prices out of reach, as happened frequently, the poor starved to death.

The price revolution also placed new pressures on the sovereign states of Europe. Inflation depressed the real value of money, so fixed incomes derived from taxes and rents yielded less and less actual wealth. Governments therefore were forced to raise taxes merely to keep their revenues constant. Yet most states needed more revenue than before because they were engaging in more wars, and because warfare was becoming increasingly expensive. The only recourse, then, was to raise taxes precipitously. Hence, governments faced continuous threats of defiance and even armed resistance from their citizens who could not afford to foot these bills.

Although prices rose less rapidly after 1600, as both the population growth and the flood of silver began to slow, the ensuing decades were a time of economic stagnation. A few areas—notably the Netherlands (see below)—bucked the trend, and the rich usually were able to hold their own, but the laboring poor made no advances, since wages continued

to rise far more slowly than prices. Indeed, the lot of the poor in many places deteriorated further, as helpless civilians were plundered by rapacious tax collectors, looting soldiers, or sometimes both. In England, peasants who had been dispossessed of property or driven off once-common lands were branded as vagrants, and vagrancy itself became a criminal offense. It was this population of newly impoverished Europeans who became the indentured servants or deported criminals of the American colonies.

## Wars of Religion in France

Compounding these economic problems were the wars that erupted within many European states. As we began to observe in Chapter 9, most medieval kingdoms were created through the colonization of smaller, traditionally autonomous territories—either by conquest or through marriage alliances with ruling families. Now these enlarged monarchies began to make ever-greater financial claims on their citizens while at the same time demanding religious uniformity among them. The result was regional and civil conflict, as local populations and even elites rebelled against the centralizing demands of monarchs who often embraced a different religion than that of their subjects.

France was the first of these kingdoms to be enflamed by religious warfare. Calvinist missionaries from Geneva had made significant headway there (Calvin himself was French), assisted by the conversion of many aristocratic Frenchwomen, who in turn converted their husbands. By the 1560s, French Calvinists, known as Huguenots (HEW-guh-nohz), made up between 10 and 20 percent of the population. But there was no open warfare until dynastic politics led factions within the government to break down along religious lines, pitting the (mostly southern) Huguenots against the (mostly northern) Catholic aristocracy. In some places, mobs incited by members of the clergy on both sides took this opportunity to settle local scores.

Although the Huguenots were not strong enough to win any major battle, there were too many of them to be ignored. In 1572, accordingly, the two sides almost brokered a truce: the presumptive heir to the throne, Prince Henry of Navarre—who had become a Protestant—was to marry the Catholic sister of the reigning king, Charles IX. But this compromise was undone by the Queen Mother, Catherine de Medici, whose Catholic faction plotted to kill all the Huguenot leaders while they were assembled in Paris for her daughter's wedding. In the early morning of Saint Bartholomew's Day (August 24), most of these Protestant aristocrats were murdered in their beds, and thousands of humble Protestants were slaughtered in the streets

**HENRY IV OF FRANCE.** The reign of Henry of Navarre (r. 1589–1610) founded the Bourbon dynasty that would rule France until 1792, and ended the bitter civil war between Catholic and Huguenot factions.

of local autonomy in southwestern France, in spite of the monarchy's centralized power. The success of this effort can be measured by the fact that peace was maintained in France even after Henry IV was assassinated by a Catholic in 1610.

The wars of religion may be one reason that France did not enter the competition for Atlantic wealth until the seventeenth century, despite its early involvement in North American explorations. It was not until 1608 that French colonial settlements received royal support, after which Catholic (but not Huguenot) immigration to "New France" (Canadian Québec) was encouraged. Meanwhile, there were three failed attempts to establish French outposts in Portuguese Brazil, the last of which (in 1612–1615) resulted only in the export of six Amazonian villagers to France, where they aroused great curiosity in an organized tour of French towns. The Brazilians' Catholic hosts even arranged for them to be baptized publicly as part of an attempt to bolster support for the Catholic cause: an episode that further illustrates the strong connection between the expansion of European influence abroad and the politics of religion at home.

## The Revolt of the Netherlands and the Dutch Trading Empire

Warfare between Catholics and Protestants also broke out in the Netherlands during this period. Controlled for almost a century by the same Habsburg family that ruled Spain and its overseas empire, the Netherlands had prospered through intense involvement with trade in the Atlantic world. The Dutch had the highest per capita wealth in all of Europe, and the metropolis of Antwerp (now in Belgium) was northern Europe's leading commercial and financial center. So when the Spanish king Philip II (r. 1556–1598) attempted to tighten his hold there in the 1560s, the fiercely independent Dutch cities resented this imperial intrusion and were ready to fight it.

This conflict took on a religious dynamic because Calvinism had spread into the Netherlands from France, and Philip, an ardent defender of the Catholic faith, could not tolerate this combination of political and religious disobedience. When crowds began ransacking and desecrating Catholic churches throughout the country, Philip dispatched an army of 10,000 Spanish soldiers to wipe out Protestantism in his Dutch territories. A reign of terror ensued, with some 12,000 people rounded up on charges of heresy or sedition, thousands of whom were convicted and executed for treason.

or drowned in the Seine. When word of the Parisian massacre spread to the provinces, local massacres proliferated.

Henry of Navarre escaped, along with his bride, but the war continued for more than two decades. Finally, Catherine's death in 1589 was followed by that of her son, Henry III, who had produced no heir to supplant Henry of Navarre; he became Henry IV, and renounced his Protestant faith to placate France's Catholic majority. In 1598, Henry made a landmark effort to end the conflict by issuing the Edict of Nantes, which recognized Catholicism as the official religion of the realm but permitted Protestants to practice their religion in specified places. This was an important step toward a policy of religious tolerance. For the first time, French Protestants were allowed to hold public office, enroll in universities, and work in hospitals, and they were even allowed to fortify some towns for their own military defense. Because the religious divide in France had a regional component, the edict also reinforced a tradition

**PROTESTANTS RANSACKING A CATHOLIC CHURCH IN THE NETHERLANDS.**
Protestant destruction of religious images provoked a stern response from Philip II.
- *Why would Protestants have smashed statuary and other devotional artifacts?*

These events catalyzed the Protestant opposition. A Dutch aristocrat, William of Orange, emerged as the anti-Spanish leader and sought help from religious allies in France, Germany, and England. In response, organized fleets of Protestant privateers (that is, privately owned ships) began harassing the Spanish navy in the waters of the North Atlantic. In 1572, William's Protestant army seized control of the Netherlands' northern provinces. Although William was assassinated in 1584, his efforts were instrumental in forcing the Spanish crown to recognize the independence of a northern Dutch Republic in 1609. Once united, these seven northern provinces became wholly Calvinist. But the southern region, still largely Catholic, remained under Spanish rule.

After gaining its independence, the new Dutch Republic emerged as the most prosperous European commercial empire of the seventeenth century. Indeed, its reach extended well beyond the Atlantic world, targeting the Indian Ocean and East Asia as well. In general, the Dutch colonial project owed more to the strategic "fort and factory" model of expansion favored by the Portuguese, than to the Spanish technique of territorial conquest and settlement. For example, the Dutch established a colony on the Cape of Good Hope at the southern tip of Africa, which facilitated the eastward spread of their influence. Many early initiatives were spurred by the establishment of the Dutch East India Company, a private mercantile corporation that came to control Sumatra, Borneo, and the Moluccas (the so-called Spice Islands). This meant that the Dutch

had a lucrative monopoly on the European trade in pepper, cinnamon, nutmeg, mace, and cloves. The company also secured an exclusive right to trade with Japan, and maintained military and trading outposts in China and India.

In the Atlantic world itself, the Dutch did not have significant presence. They did, however, establish an outpost in North America, the colony known as New Amsterdam (until it was surrendered to the English in 1667 and renamed New York). Their remaining territorial holdings in the Atlantic were Dutch Guyana (present-day Surinam) on the coast of South America and the islands of Curaçao and Tobago in the Caribbean. Although the Dutch did not match the Spanish or the English in their accumulation of land, the establishment of a second merchant enterprise, the Dutch West India Company, allowed them to dominate the Atlantic slave trade with Africa after 1621.

In constructing this new transoceanic trading empire in slaves and spices, the Dutch pioneered a new financial mechanism for investing in colonial enterprises: the joint-stock company. The Dutch East and West India Companies were early examples, raising cash by selling shares to individual investors whose liability was limited to the sum of their investment. These investors were not part of the company's management, but they were entitled to a share in the profits. Originally, the Dutch East India Company intended to pay off its investors within ten years, but when that period was up, it convinced the investors—who wanted to realize their profits immediately—to sell their shares on the open market. The creation of a market in shares, which we now call a stock market, was an innovation that spread quickly. Arguably, stock markets now control the world's economy.

## The Struggle between England and Spain

Religious strife could spark civil war (as in France) or political rebellion (as in the Netherlands), as well as provoke warfare between sovereign states, as in the struggle between England and Spain. In this case, religious conflict was entangled with both dynastic claims and economic competition in the Atlantic world.

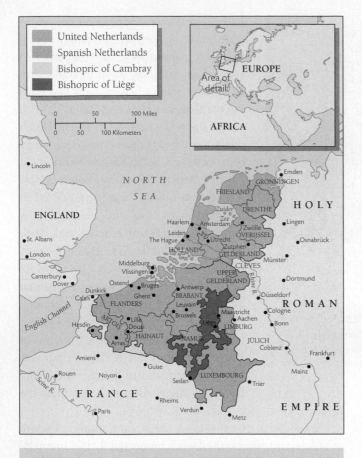

these measures created the deep ethnic and religious conflicts that still trouble the island today.

England's conflict with Spain, meanwhile, was worsened by the fact that English economic interests were directly opposed to those of Spain. English traders were making steady inroads into Spanish commercial networks in the Atlantic, as English sea captains such as Sir Francis Drake and Sir John Hawkins plundered Spanish vessels on the high seas. In a particularly dramatic exploit lasting from 1577 to 1580, prevailing winds and a lust for booty propelled Drake all the way around the world, to return with stolen Spanish treasure worth twice as much as Queen Elizabeth's annual revenue.

After suffering numerous such attacks over a period of two decades—and after Elizabeth's government openly supported the Dutch rebellion against Spain in 1585—King Philip finally resolved to fight back. In 1588, he dispatched an enormous fleet, confidently called the "Invincible Armada," whose mission was to invade England. But the invasion never occurred: after an indecisive initial encounter between the two fleets, a fierce storm—hailed as a "Protestant wind" by the lucky English—drove the Spanish galleons off course, leaving many of them wrecked off the coast of Ireland. The shattered flotilla eventually limped home with almost half its ships lost after a disastrous circumnavigation of the British Isles. Meanwhile, Elizabeth took credit for her country's miraculous escape. In subsequent years, continued threats from Spain and sporadic skirmishes nurtured a renewed sense of English nationalism and fueled anti-Catholic sentiment in that realm.

## England's Colonial Ambitions

During the early decades of the seventeenth century, the English challenge to Spanish supremacy in the Atlantic began to bear fruit. Unlike New Spain, England's North American colonies had no significant mineral wealth; instead, as we noted above, English colonists sought to profit from the establishment of large-scale agricultural settlements in North America and the Caribbean. The first permanent colony was founded at Jamestown, Virginia, in 1607. Although this settlement was not particularly successful, more than twenty autonomous settlements were planted over the next forty years by a total of about 80,000 English immigrants.

Many of the colonists were motivated by a desire for religious freedom—hence the name we still give to the Pilgrims who landed at Plymouth, Massachusetts, in 1620. These radical Protestants, known as Puritans, were also political dissidents, so they were almost as unwelcome as Catholics

The dynastic competition came from the English royal family's division along confessional lines. The Catholic queen Mary (r. 1553–1558), eldest daughter of Henry VIII and granddaughter of Ferdinand and Isabella of Spain (Chapter 13), had married her cousin Philip II of Spain in 1554, and she ruled at a time of great strife between Catholics and Protestants in England. After Mary's death, her Protestant half sister Elizabeth (r. 1558–1603) came to the throne, and relations with Spain rapidly declined. They declined further when Catholic Ireland—an English colony—rose in rebellion in 1565, with Spain quietly supporting the Irish. Although it took almost thirty bloody years, English forces eventually suppressed the rebellion. Elizabeth then cemented the Irish defeat by encouraging intense colonial settlement in Ireland. Somewhat ironically, she did so in conscious imitation of Spanish policy in the Americas, sending thousands of Protestant English settlers to occupy land in Ireland in the hope of creating a colonial state with a largely English identity. Instead,

**THE DUTCH EAST INDIA COMPANY WAREHOUSE AND TIMBER WHARF AT AMSTERDAM.** The substantial warehouse, the stockpiles of lumber, and the company ship under construction in the foreground illustrate the degree to which overseas commerce could stimulate the economy of the mother country.

**THE "ARMADA PORTRAIT" OF ELIZABETH.** This is one of several royal portraits that commemorated the defeat of the Spanish Armada in 1588. Through the window on the left, an English flotilla sails serenely on sunny seas; on the right, Spanish ships are wrecked by a "Protestant wind." Elizabeth's right hand rests protectively—and commandingly—on the globe. ▪ *How would you interpret this image?*

in England, where the church was an extension of the monarchy. English colonists, however, showed little interest in trying to convert Native American peoples to Christianity. Missionizing played a much larger role in Spanish efforts to colonize Central and South America, and in French efforts to penetrate the North American hinterlands.

Another difference between Spanish and English colonialism is the fact that these English colonies did not begin as royal enterprises. They were private ventures, farmed either by individual landholders (as in Maryland and Pennsylvania) or managed by joint-stock companies (as in Virginia and the Massachusetts Bay Colony). Building on their experience in Ireland, where colonies had been called "plantations," many English settlers established plantations (planned communities) that attempted to replicate as many features of English life as possible. Geography largely dictated the foundational locations of these English settlements, which were established along the northeast Atlantic coast and on rivers and bays that provided good harbors. Aside from the Hudson, there were no great rivers to lead colonists far inland, so the English colonies clung to the coastline and to each other. The densely populated corridor along the Atlantic seaboard today is a direct result of these early settlement patterns.

Because most land in the Old World was owned by royal and aristocratic families, the accumulation of wealth through the control of land was a new and exciting prospect for small- and medium-scale landholders in the new English colonies. This helps to explain the colonies' rural, agricultural character—in contrast to the great cities of New Spain. But this focus on agricultural holdings was also due to the demographic catastrophe that had decimated native populations in this region, as in so many others. By the early seventeenth century, a great deal of rich land had been abandoned by native farmers simply because there were so few of

**PLIMOTH PLANTATION.** An English settlement was established at Plimoth (now Plymouth) in the Massachusetts Bay Colony in 1620. This image shows a reconstruction of the village as it might have looked in 1627. Although speculative, this reconstruction captures the plantation's diminutive fragility and isolation.

lands that had felt the first divisive effects of the Reformation and the Counter-Reformation (Chapter 13). Not only was this period of warfare one of the longest in European history, it was one of the bloodiest and most widespread, engulfing most of the Continent before it ended thirty years later, in 1648. Although it began as a religious conflict, it quickly became an international struggle for dominance in which these initial provocations were all but forgotten. In the end, some 8 million people died, and entire regions were devastated by the rapacity of crisscrossing armies. The populations of several regions never recovered, and most of the great powers that fought the war were impoverished and weakened—with the exception of France, which emerged as the preeminent power in Europe.

them to till it. As a result, indigenous peoples who had not already succumbed to European diseases were now under threat from colonists who wanted complete and exclusive control over these lands.

To this end, the English soon set out to eliminate, through expulsion and massacre, the former inhabitants of the region. There were a few exceptions, such as in the Quaker colony of Pennsylvania, where colonists and Native Americans maintained friendly relations for more than half a century. But in the Carolinas, by contrast, there was widespread enslavement of native peoples, either for sale to the West Indies or for work on the rice plantations along the coast. In another contrast to the Spanish and French colonies, intermarriage between English colonists and native populations was rare, creating a nearly unbridgeable racial divide in these North American colonies.

## THE THIRTY YEARS' WAR AND ITS OUTCOMES

With the promulgation of the French Edict of Nantes in 1598, the end of open hostilities between England and Spain in 1604, and the truce between Spain and the Dutch Republic in 1609, religious warfare in Europe came briefly to an end. In 1618, however, a new series of wars broke out in central Europe, in some of the German-speaking

### The Beginnings of the Thirty Years' War and the Downfall of Bohemia

Like the number and variety of the combatants involved, the causes of the Thirty Years' War are complicated. On one level, it was an outlet for deeper aggressions and tensions that had been building up since the Peace of Augsburg in 1555. On another level, it grew out of even longer-standing disputes among rulers and territories in the patchwork of provinces that made up the Holy Roman Empire, disputes into which allied powers were drawn. On still another level, it was an opportunity for players on the fringes of power to rise to prominence.

The catalyst came in 1618, when the Austrian Habsburg (Catholic) prince Ferdinand, who also ruled Hungary and the united Polish-Lithuanian Commonwealth, was named heir to the throne of Protestant Bohemia. This prompted a rebellion among the Bohemian aristocracy. A year later, the complex dynastic politics of central Europe resulted in Ferdinand's election as Holy Roman Emperor, a title that gave him access to an imperial (Catholic) army, which he sent to crush the Protestant revolt. The Bohemians, meanwhile, were bolstered by the support of some Austrian nobility—many of whom were also Protestant—who saw a way to recover power from the Habsburg ruling family.

In 1620, the war escalated further when the Ottomans threw their support behind the Protestants and, in so doing, touched off a war with staunchly Catholic Poland

## The Devastation of the Thirty Years' War

*The author of the following excerpt, Hans Jakob Christoph von Grimmelshausen (GRIM-mill-show-sen; 1621–1676), barely survived the horrors of the Thirty Years' War. His parents were killed, probably when he was thirteen years old, and he himself was kidnapped the following year and forced into the army. By age fifteen, he was a soldier. His darkly satiric masterpiece,* Simplicissimus *("The Simpleton"), drew heavily on these experiences and, although technically a fictional memoir, portrays with brutal accuracy the terrible realities of this era.*

 lthough it was not my intention to take the peaceloving reader with these troopers to my dad's house and farm, seeing that matters will go ill therein, yet the course of my history demands that I should leave to kind posterity an account of what manner of cruelties were now and again practised in this our German war: yes, and moreover testify by my own example that such evils must often have been sent to us by the goodness of Almighty God for our profit. For, gentle reader, who would ever have taught me that there was a God in Heaven if these soldiers had not destroyed my dad's house, and by such a deed driven me out among folk who gave me all fitting instruction thereupon? . . .

The first thing these troopers did was, that they stabled their horses: thereafter each fell to his appointed task: which task was neither more nor less than ruin and destruction. For though some began to slaughter and to boil and to roast so that it looked as if there should be a merry banquet forward, yet others there were who did but storm through the house above and below stairs. Others stowed together great parcels of cloth and apparel and all manner of household stuff, as if they would set up a frippery market. All that

they had no mind to take with them they cut in pieces. Some thrust their swords through the hay and straw as if they had not enough sheep and swine to slaughter: and some shook the feathers out of the beds and in their stead stuffed in bacon and other dried meat and provisions as if such were better and softer to sleep upon. Others broke the stove and the windows as if they had a never-ending summer to promise. Houseware of copper and tin they beat flat, and packed such vessels, all bent and spoiled, in with the rest. Bedsteads, tables, chairs, and benches they burned, though there lay many cords of dry wood in the yard. Pots and pipkins must all go to pieces, either because they would eat none but roast flesh, or because their purpose was to make there but a single meal.

Our maid was so handled in the stable that she could not come out, which is a shame to tell of. Our man they laid bound upon the ground, thrust a gag into his mouth, and poured a pailful of filthy water into his body: and by this, which they called a Swedish draught, they forced him to lead a party of them to another place where they captured men and beasts, and brought them back to our farm, in which company were my dad, my mother, and our Ursula.

And now they began: first to take the flints out of their pistols and in place

of them to jam the peasants' thumbs in and so to torture the poor rogues as if they had been about the burning of witches: for one of them they had taken they thrust into the baking oven and there lit a fire under him, although he had as yet confessed no crime: as for another, they put a cord round his head and so twisted it tight with a piece of wood that the blood gushed from his mouth and nose and ears. In a word each had his own device to torture the peasants, and each peasant his several tortures.

Source: Hans Jakob Christoph von Grimmelshausen, *Simplicissimus*, trans. S. Goodrich (New York: 1995), pp. 1–3, 8–10, 32–35.

### Questions for Analysis

1. The first-person narrator here recounts the atrocities committed "in this our German war," in which both perpetrators and victims are German. How believable is this description? What lends it credibility?

2. Why would Grimmelshausen have chosen to publish his account as a satirical fiction rather than as a straightforward historical narrative or an autobiography? How would this choice have affected readers' response to scenes such as he describes?

## Cardinal Richelieu on the Common People of France

*Armand Jean du Plessis, duke of Richelieu and cardinal of the Roman Catholic Church, was the effective ruler of France from 1624 until his death in 1642. His* Political Testament *was assembled after his death from historical sketches and from memoranda of advice he had prepared for King Louis XIII, the ineffectual monarch whom he served. This book was eventually published in 1688, during the reign of Louis XIV.*

All students of politics agree that when the common people are too well off it is impossible to keep them peaceable. The explanation for this is that they are less well informed than the members of the other orders in the state, who are much more cultivated and enlightened, and so if not preoccupied with the search for the necessities of existence, find it difficult to remain within the limits imposed by both common sense and the law.

It would not be sound to relieve them of all taxation and similar charges, since in such a case they would lose the mark of their subjection and consequently the awareness of their station. Thus being free from paying tribute, they would consider themselves exempted from obedience. One should compare them with mules, which being accustomed to work, suffer more when long idle than when kept busy. But just as this work should be reasonable, with the burdens placed upon these animals proportionate to their strength, so it is likewise with the burdens placed upon the people. If they are not moderate, even when put to good public use, they are certainly unjust. I realize that when a king undertakes a program of public works it is correct to say that what the people gain from it is returned by paying the *taille* [a heavy tax imposed on the peasantry]. In the same fashion it can be maintained that what a king takes from the people returns to them, and that they advance it to him only to draw upon it for the enjoyment of their leisure and their investments, which would be impossible if they did not contribute to the support of the state.

Source: *The Political Testament of Cardinal Richelieu,* trans. Henry Bertram Hill (Madison, WI: 1961), pp. 31–32.

### Questions for Analysis

1. According to Cardinal Richelieu, why should the state work to subjugate the common people? What assumptions about the nature and status of "common people" underlie this argument?

2. What theory of the state emerges from this argument? According to Richelieu, what is the relationship between the king and the state and between the king and the people?

## The Policies of Cardinal Richelieu

This expansion of French power can be credited, in part, to Henry IV's de facto successor, Armand Jean du Plessis, Cardinal Richelieu (*REESH-eh-lyuh*). The real king of France, Henry's son Louis XIII (r. 1610–1643), had come to the throne at the age of nine. Richelieu, as his chief minister of state, dominated his reign. His chief aim was to centralize royal bureaucracy while exploiting opportunities to foster French influence abroad.

Within France, Richelieu amended the Edict of Nantes so that it no longer supported the military and political rights of the Huguenots. He also prohibited these French Protestants from settling in Québec. Yet considering that he owed his political power (in part) to his ecclesiastical position in the Catholic Church, the fact that he allowed the edict to stand at all reflects his larger interest in fostering a sense of French national identity that centered on the monarchy. In keeping with this policy, he imposed direct taxation on powerful provinces that had retained their financial autonomy since then. Later, to make sure taxes were efficiently collected, Richelieu instituted a new system of local government that empowered royal officials to put down provincial resistance.

These policies made the French royal government more powerful than any in Europe. It also doubled the crown's income, allowing France to engage in the Thirty Years' War, which expanded its power on the Continent. But this increased centralization of royal authority also provoked challenges from aristocratic elites in the years after Richelieu's death—eventually, leading to the French Revolution (see Chapter 18).

## The Challenge of the Fronde

A more immediate response to Richelieu's policies was a series of uncoordinated revolts known collectively as the *Fronde* (from the French word for a sling used to hurl stones). In 1643, just after the death of Richelieu, Louis XIII was succeeded by his five-year-old son, Louis XIV. The young king's regents were his mother, Anne of Austria, and her alleged lover, Cardinal Jules Raymond Mazarin. Both were foreigners—Anne was a Habsburg and Mazarin was an Italian by birth—and both were despised by many extremely powerful nobles. The nobles also hated the way that Richelieu's government had curtailed their authority in their own ancestral provinces. Popular resentments were aroused as well, because the costs of the ongoing Thirty Years' War were now combined with several consecutive years of bad harvests. So when cliques of nobles expressed their disgust for Mazarin, they found much popular support.

In 1648, the levy of a new tax had protesters on the streets of Paris, armed with slings and projectiles. However, neither the aristocratic leaders of the Fronde nor the commoners who joined them claimed to be resisting the young king; their targets were the corruption and mismanagement of Mazarin. Some of the rebels insisted that part of Mazarin's fault lay in his pursuit of Richelieu's centralizing policy, but most aristocrats wanted to become part of this centralizing process. Years later, when Louis XIV began to rule in his own right in 1651, the memory of these early turbulent years haunted him, and he resolved never to let the aristocracy or their provinces get out of hand. To this aim, he became the most effective absolute monarch in Europe (see Chapter 15).

# THE CRISIS OF KINGSHIP IN ENGLAND

Of all the crises that shook Europe in this era, the most radical in its consequences was the English Civil War. The causes of this conflict were similar to those that had sparked trouble in other countries: hostilities between the component parts of a composite kingdom, religious animosities between Catholics and Protestants, struggles for power among competing factions of aristocrats at court, and a fiscal system that could not keep pace with the increasing costs of government, much less those of war. But in England, these developments led to the unprecedented criminal trial and execution of a king, an event that sent shock waves throughout Europe and the Atlantic world.

## The Origins of the Civil War

The chain of events that led to a civil war in England can be traced to the last decades of Queen Elizabeth's reign. The expenses of England's defense against Spain, rebellion in Ireland, widespread crop failures, and the inadequacies of the antiquated English taxation system drove the queen's government deeply into debt. When Elizabeth was succeeded by her cousin, James Stuart—King James VI of Scotland, James I of England—bitter factional disputes at court were complicated by the financial crisis. When the English Parliament rejected James's demands for more taxes, he raised what revenues he could without parliamentary approval, imposing new tolls and selling trading monopolies to favored courtiers. These measures aroused resentment against the king and made voluntary grants of taxation from Parliament even less likely.

James also struggled with religious divisions among his subjects. His own kingdom of Scotland had been firmly Calvinist since the 1560s. England, too, was Protestant—but of a very different kind, because the Church of England retained many of the rituals, hierarchies, and doctrines of the medieval Church (Chapter 13). Indeed, a significant number of English Protestants, the Puritans, wanted to bring this church more firmly into line with Calvinist principles. Although James was largely successful in mediating these conflicts, he stirred up trouble in staunchly Catholic Ireland by encouraging thousands of Scottish Calvinists to settle in the northern Irish province of Ulster. In doing so, he exacerbated a situation that had already become violent under Elizabeth.

## Parliament versus the King

English politics became more volatile in 1625, when James was succeeded by his surviving son, Charles. Charles alarmed his Protestant subjects by marrying the Catholic sister of France's Louis XIII; he then launched a new war with Spain, straining his already slender financial

**CHARLES I.** King Charles I of England was a connoisseur of the arts and a patron of artists. He was adept at using portraiture to convey the magnificence of his tastes and the grandeur of his conception of kingship. ▪ *How does this portrait by Anthony van Dyck compare to the engravings of the "martyred" king in* **Interpreting Visual Evidence** *on page 482?*

To meet the Scottish threat, Charles was forced to summon Parliament, whose members were determined to impose radical reforms on the king's government before they would consider granting him funds to raise an army. The Scottish Calvinists even found support among some Puritans in Parliament. To avoid dealing with this difficult political situation, Charles tried to arrest Parliament's leaders and force his own agenda. When this failed, he withdrew from London to raise his own army. Parliament responded by mustering a separate military force and voting itself the taxation to pay for it. By the end of 1642, open warfare had erupted between the English king and the English government: something that was inconceivable in neighboring France, where the king and the government were inseparable.

Arrayed on the king's side were most of England's aristocrats and largest landowners, many of whom owned lands in the Atlantic colonies as well. The parliamentary forces were made up of smaller landholders, tradesmen, and artisans, many of whom were Puritan sympathizers. The king's royalist supporters were commonly known by their aristocratic name of Cavaliers. They derisively called their opponents, who cut their hair short in contempt for the fashionable custom of wearing long curls, Roundheads. After 1644, when the parliamentary army was effectively reorganized, the royalist forces were badly beaten; and in 1646, the king was compelled to surrender. Soon thereafter, the episcopal hierarchy of the Church of England was abolished and a Calvinist-style church was mandated throughout England and Wales.

The struggle might have ended here had not a quarrel developed within the parliamentary party. The majority of its members were ready to restore Charles to the throne as a limited monarch, under an arrangement whereby a uniformly Calvinist faith would be imposed on both Scotland and England as the state religion. But a radical minority of Puritans, commonly known as Independents, insisted on religious freedom for themselves and all other Protestants. Their leader was Oliver Cromwell (1599–1658), who had risen to command the Roundhead army, which he reconstituted as the "New Model Army."

resources. When Parliament refused to grant him funds, he demanded forced loans from his subjects and punished those who refused by lodging soldiers in their homes and imprisoning others without trial. Parliament responded in 1628 by imposing the Petition of Right, which declared that taxes not voted on by Parliament were illegal, condemned arbitrary imprisonment, and prohibited the quartering of soldiers in private houses.

Thereafter, Charles tried to rule England without Parliament—something that had not been attempted since the establishment of that body 400 years earlier (Chapter 9). He also ran into trouble with his Calvinist subjects in Scotland because he began to favor the most Catholic-leaning elements in the English Church. The Scots rebelled in 1640, and a Scottish army marched south into England to demand the withdrawal of Charles's "Catholicizing" measures.

## The Fall of Charles Stuart and Oliver Cromwell's Commonwealth

Taking advantage of the dissension within the ranks of his opponents, Charles renewed the war in 1648. But he was forced to surrender after a brief campaign, and Cromwell seized control of the government. To ensure that the

**OLIVER CROMWELL AS PROTECTOR OF THE COMMON-WEALTH.** This coin, minted in 1658, shows the Lord Protector wreathed with laurel garlands like a classical hero or a Roman consul. It also proclaims him to be "by the Grace of God Protector of the Commonwealth." ■ *What mixed messages does this imagery convey?*

Puritan agenda would be carried out, Cromwell ejected all the moderates from Parliament by force. This "Rump" (remaining) Parliament then proceeded to put the king on trial and eventually to condemn him to death for treason against his own subjects.

Charles Stuart was publicly beheaded on January 30, 1649—marking the first time in history that a reigning king had been legally deposed and executed. Europeans reacted to his death with horror, astonishment, or rejoicing, depending on their political convictions (see **Interpreting Visual Evidence** on page 482). After the king's execution, his son—the future King Charles II—joined with the remaining royalist forces in an attempt to restore the monarchy. But he was defeated by Cromwell's army and fled to France.

With the heir to the English throne in exile, Cromwell and his supporters abolished Parliament's hereditary House of Lords and declared England a Commonwealth: an English translation of the Latin *res publica*. Technically, the Rump Parliament continued as the legislative body; but Cromwell, with the army at his command, possessed the real power. And he soon became exasperated by legislators' attempts to enrich themselves by confiscating their

opponents' property. In 1653, he marched a detachment of troops into the Rump Parliament and disbanded it.

The short-lived Commonwealth was thus replaced by the "Protectorate," a thinly disguised autocracy established under a constitution drafted by officers of the army. Called the *Instrument of Government*, this text is the nearest approximation to a written constitution that England has ever had. Extensive powers were given to Cromwell as Lord Protector for life, and his office was made hereditary.

## The Restoration of the Monarchy

Many intellectuals noted the similarities between these events and those that had given rise to the Principate of Augustus after the death of Julius Caesar (Chapter 5). Among the people, Cromwell's Puritan military dictatorship was growing unpopular, not least because it prohibited public recreation on Sundays and closed London's theaters. Many became nostalgic for the milder and more tolerant Church of England and began to hope for a restoration of the old royalist regime.

The opportunity came with Cromwell's death in 1658. His son Richard had no sooner succeeded to the office of Lord Protector when a faction within the army removed him from power. As groups of royalists plotted an uprising, a new Parliament was organized. In April 1660, it declared that King Charles II had been the ruler of England since his father's execution in 1649. Almost overnight, England became a monarchy again.

Charles II (r. 1660–1685) revived the Church of England but was careful not to return to the provocative religious policies of his father. Quipping that he did not wish to "resume his travels," he agreed to respect Parliament and to observe the Petition of Right that had so enraged Charles I. He also accepted all the legislation passed by Parliament immediately before the outbreak of civil war in 1642, including the requirement that Parliament be summoned at least once every three years. England thus emerged from its civil war as a limited monarchy, in which power was exercised by "the king in Parliament." It remains a constitutional monarchy to this day.

## The English Civil War and the Atlantic World

These tumultuous events had a significant influence on the development of a new political sensibility within England's Atlantic colonies. The English landed aristocracy had sided

## Debating the English Civil War

> The English Civil War raised fundamental questions about political rights and responsibilities, many of which are addressed in the two excerpts below. The first comes from a lengthy debate held within the General Council of Cromwell's army in October 1647. The second is taken from the speech given by King Charles I, moments before his execution in 1649.

### The Army Debates, 1647

Colonel Rainsborough: Really, I think that the poorest man that is in England has a life to live as the greatest man, and therefore truly, sir, I think it's clear, that every man that is to live under a government ought first by his own consent to put himself under that government, and I do think that the poorest man in England is not at all bound in a strict sense to that government that he has not had a voice to put himself under . . . insomuch that I should doubt whether I was an Englishman or not, that should doubt of these things.

General Ireton: Give me leave to tell you, that if you make this the rule, I think you must fly for refuge to an absolute natural right, and you must deny all civil right, and I am sure it will come to that in the consequence. . . . For my part, I think it is no right at all. I think that no person has a right to an interest or share in the disposing of the affairs of the kingdom, and in determining or choosing those that shall determine what laws we shall be ruled by here, no person has a right to this that has not a permanent fixed interest in this kingdom, and those persons together are properly the represented of this kingdom who, taken together, and consequently are to make up the representers of this kingdom. . . .

We talk of birthright. Truly, birthright there is. . . . [M]en may justly have by birthright, by their very being born in England, that we should not seclude them out of England. That we should not refuse to give them air and place and ground, and the freedom of the highways and other things, to live amongst us, not any man that is born here, though he in birth or by his birth there come nothing at all that is part of the permanent interest of this kingdom to him. That I think is due to a man by birth. But that by a man's being born here he shall have a share in that power that shall dispose of the lands here, and of all things here, I do not think it is a sufficient ground.

Source: David Wootton, ed., *Divine Right and Democracy: An Anthology of Political Writing in Stuart England* (New York: 1986), pp. 286–87 (language modernized).

with the king during this conflict, but many in the colonies had sympathized with Parliament and its claims to protect the liberties of small landowners who bore a disproportionate share of taxation. Even after the Restoration of the monarchy in 1660, many colonial leaders maintained an antimonarchist and antiaristocratic bias.

The fact that the government had been almost entirely concerned with the business of putting down rebellion meant that England's colonies had become used to a large degree of independence at an early stage. As a result, once the monarchy was restored, all of Parliament's efforts to extend more control over the colonies caused greater and greater friction (see Chapter 15). Slogans declaring the rights of "free-born Englishmen" would echo among farmers, and "free trade" became a rallying cry against royal interference in colonial commerce. The bitter religious conflicts that had divided the more radical Puritans from the Church of England also forced the colonies to come to grips with the problem of religious diversity. Some, like Massachusetts, took the opportunity to impose their own brand of Puritanism on settlers, and others experimented with forms of religious toleration that sometimes went beyond the forms of religious freedom that existed back in England.

Paradoxically, though, the spread of ideas about the protection of liberties and citizens' rights coincided with

## Charles I on the Scaffold, 1649

I think it is my duty, to God first, and to my country, for to clear myself both as an honest man, a good king, and a good Christian.

I shall begin first with my innocence. In truth I think it not very needful for me to insist long upon this, for all the world knows that I never did begin a war with the two Houses of Parliament, and I call God to witness, to whom I must shortly make an account, that I never did intend to incroach upon their privileges. . . .

As for the people—truly I desire their liberty and freedom as much as anybody whatsoever. But I must tell you that their liberty and freedom consists in having of government those laws by which their lives and goods may be most their own. It is not for having share in government. That is nothing pertaining to them. A subject and a sovereign are clean different things, and therefore, until they do

that—I mean that you do put the people in that liberty as I say—certainly they will never enjoy themselves.

Sirs, it was for this that now I am come here. If I would have given way to an arbitrary way, for to have all laws changed according to the power of the sword, I needed not to have come here. And therefore I tell you (and I pray God it be not laid to your charge) that I am the martyr of the people.

Source: Brian Tierney, Donald Kagan, and L. Pearce Williams, eds., *Great Issues in Western Civilization* (New York: 1967), pp. 46–47.

### Questions for Analysis

**1.** What fundamental issues are at stake in both excerpts? How do the debaters within the parliamentary army (first excerpt) define "natural" and "civil" rights?

**2.** How does Charles defend his position? What is his theory of kingship? How does it compare with that of Cardinal Richelieu (see page 476)? How does it conflict with the ideas expressed in the army's debate?

**3.** It is interesting that none of the participants in these debates seems to have recognized the implications that their arguments might have for the political rights of women. Why would that have been the case?

---

a rapid and considerable expansion of unfree labor in the colonies. Prior to the 1640s, the English colonies in North America and the Caribbean had been assured of a steady stream of immigrants, such as the Puritan Pilgrims of Massachusetts in 1620. The outbreak of civil war in 1642, and the subsequent triumph of the Puritans under Cromwell, caused a drop in this migration, because many who might have thought about emigrating decided to stay in England. In North America, the decline in the arrival of new settlers was so sudden that it caused a depression in local economies.

Meanwhile, the demand for labor was increasing rapidly owing to the expansion of tobacco plantations in

Virginia and sugar plantations in Barbados and Jamaica, which the British captured from the Spanish in 1655. These plantations, with their punishing working conditions and high mortality rates from disease, were insatiable in their demand for workers. Plantation owners thus sought to meet this demand by investing ever more heavily in forms of unfree labor, including indentured servants and African slaves. The social and political crisis unleashed by the English Civil War also led to the forced migration of paupers and political prisoners, especially from Scotland, Wales, and Ireland: a pattern that continued during Cromwell's reign. These exiles, many without resources, swelled the ranks of the unfree and the very

# Interpreting Visual Evidence

## The Execution of a King

This allegorical engraving (image A) accompanied a pamphlet called *Eikon Basilike* ("The Kingly Image"), which began to circulate in Britain just weeks after the execution of King Charles I. It was purported to be an autobiographical account of the king's last days, and a justification of his royal policies. It was intended to arouse widespread sympathy for the king and his exiled heir, Charles II; it succeeded admirably, as the cult of Charles "King and Martyr" became increasingly popular. Here, the Latin inscription on the shaft of light suggests that Charles's piety will beam "brighter through the shadows," while the scrolls on the left proclaim "virtue grows beneath weight" and "unmoved, triumphant." Charles's earthly crown (on the floor at his side) is "splendid and heavy," whereas the crown of thorns he grasps is "bitter and light"; this heavenly crown is "blessed and eternal." Even people who could not read these and the other Latin mottoes would have known that Charles's last words were: "I shall go from a corruptible to an incorruptible Crown, where no disturbance can be."

At the same time, broadsides showing the moment of execution (image B) circulated in various European countries with explanatory captions. This one was printed in Germany, with almost identical versions surviving from the Netherlands. It shows members of the crowd fainting and turning away at the sight of blood spurting from the king's neck while the executioner holds up the severed head.

### Questions for Analysis

1. How would you interpret the message of image A? How might it have been read differently by Catholics and Protestants within Britain and Europe?

2. What might have been the political motives underlying the publication and display of these images? For example, would you expect the depiction of the king's execution to be supportive of monarchy or antiroyalist? Why?

3. Given what you have learned about the political and religious divisions in Europe at the time of the king's execution, where do you think image A would have found the most sympathetic audiences? Why might it be significant that image B circulated more widely in Germany and the Netherlands than in France or Spain?

A. King Charles I as a martyr.

B. The execution of King Charles I.

poor in England's Atlantic colonies, spurring the formation of new social hierarchies, as earlier arrivals sought to distance themselves from more recent immigrants, whom they regarded as inferiors. The crisis of kingship in England thus led to a substantial increase in the African slave trade and a sharpening of social and economic divisions in the English colonies.

# AN AGE OF DOUBT AND THE ART OF BEING HUMAN

On the first day of November 1611, a new play by William Shakespeare premiered in London. *The Tempest* takes place on a remote island, where an exiled duke from the Italian city-state of Milan has used his magical arts to subjugate the island's inhabitants. The plot drew on reports from the new European colonies of the Atlantic, especially the Caribbean, where slaves were called Caribans—hence the name Shakespeare chose for the play's rebellious slave, Caliban, who seeks to take revenge on the magician Prospero, his oppressive master. When reminded that he owes his knowledge of the English language to the civilizing influence of Prospero's daughter, Miranda, Caliban retorts, "You taught me language, and my profit on't is, I know how to curse." According to Caliban, the benefits of a European education could not outweigh the evils of colonization—but could, in fact, be used to resist it. Shakespeare's audience was thus confronted with the spectacle of their own colonial ambitions gone awry.

The doubt and uncertainty caused by Europe's extension into the Atlantic world were primary themes and motivators of this era's creative arts, which both documented and critiqued contemporary trends while emphasizing the redemptive qualities of human suffering and compassion. Another example of this artistic response is the novel *Don Quixote*, which its author, Miguel de Cervantes (*sehr-VAHN-tehs*; 1547–1616), composed largely in prison. It recounts the adventures of an idealistic Spanish gentleman, Don Quixote of La Mancha, who becomes deranged by his constant reading of chivalric romances and sets out to have delusional adventures of his own. His sidekick, Sancho Panza, is his exact opposite: a plain, practical man content with modest bodily pleasures. Together, they represent different facets of human nature. On the one hand, *Don Quixote* is a devastating satire of Spain's decline. On the other, it is a sincere celebration of the human capacity for optimism and goodness.

Throughout the long century between 1550 and 1660, Europeans confronted a world in which all that they had once taken for granted was cast into confusion. Vast continents had been discovered, populated by millions of people whose very existence challenged Western civilizations' former parameters and Europeans' most basic assumptions. Not even religion seemed an adequate foundation on which to build new certainties, for European Christians now disagreed about the fundamental truths of their faith. Political allegiances were similarly under threat, as intellectuals and common people alike began to assert a right to resist princes with whom they disagreed. The very notions of morality and custom were beginning to seem arbitrary. There was a sometimes desperate search for new bases on which to construct some measure of certainty in the face of such challenges.

## Witchcraft and the Power of the State

Contributing to the anxiety of the age was the widespread conviction that witchcraft was a new and increasing threat. Although the belief that certain individuals could heal or harm through the practice of magic was not new, it was not until the late fifteenth century that authorities began to insist that such powers could derive only from some kind of satanic bargain. In 1484, Pope Innocent VIII had ordered papal inquisitors to use all means at their disposal, including torture, to detect and eliminate witchcraft. Predictably, torture increased the number of accused witches who "confessed" to their alleged crimes, and as more accused witches "confessed," more witches were "discovered," tried, and executed—even in places such as England and Scotland, where torture was not legal and the Catholic Church had no influence. Both Luther and Calvin had also urged that accused witches be tried and sentenced with less leniency than ordinary criminals.

When religious authorities' efforts to detect witchcraft were backed by the coercive powers of secular governments, the fear of witches escalated into persecutions. It was therefore through this fundamental agreement between Catholics and Protestants, with the complicity of modern secular states, that an early modern "witch craze" claimed tens of thousands of victims in this era. The final death toll will never be known, but we do know that the vast majority of the victims were women. In the 1620s, there were 100 burnings a year, on average, in the German cities of Würzburg and Bamberg; around the same time, it was said that the town square of Wolfenbüttel "looked like a little forest, so crowded were the stakes." When accusations of witchcraft diminished in Europe, they became endemic in some European colonies, as at the English settlement of Salem in the Massachusetts Bay Colony.

This hunt for witches resulted in part from fears that traditional religious remedies (prayer, the sacraments) were no longer adequate to guard against the evils of the world. It also reflects Europeans' growing conviction that only the state had the power to protect them. Even in Catholic countries, where witchcraft prosecutions began in Church courts, these cases were transferred to the state's courts for final judgment and punishment because Church courts could not carry out capital penalties. In most Protestant countries, the entire process of detecting, prosecuting, and punishing suspected witches was carried out under state supervision.

## The Search for a Source of Authority

The crisis of religious and political authority in Europe also spurred more rational approaches to the problem of uncertainty. The French nobleman Michel de Montaigne (*mohn-TEHN-yeh*; 1533–1592), the son of a Catholic father and a Huguenot mother of Jewish ancestry, applied a searching skepticism to all traditional ways of knowing the world and adopted instead a practice of profound introspection. His *Essays* (from the French word for "attempts" or "trials") were composed during the French wars of religion and proceed from one basic question: *Que sais-je?* ("What do I know?").

The *Essays'* first premise is that every human perspective is limited. For example, in the famous essay "On Cannibals," Montaigne argued that what may seem indisputably true and moral to one group of people may seem absolutely false to another, because "everyone gives the title of barbarism to everything that is not of his usage." From this follows Montaigne's second main premise: the need for moderation. Because all people think they follow the true religion or have the best form of government, he concludes that no religion or government is really perfect, and consequently no belief is worth fighting or dying for. People should, instead, accept the teachings of religion on faith and obey the governments constituted to rule over them, but without resorting to fanaticism in either sphere.

Another French philosopher, Blaise Pascal (*pahs-KAHL*; 1623–1662), confronted the problem of doubt by embracing an extreme form of puritanical Catholicism known as Jansenism, named after its Flemish founder, Cornelius Jansen. Until his death, he worked on a highly ambitious philosophical-religious project meant to establish the truth of Christianity by appealing simultaneously to the intellect and the emotion. In his posthumous work, *Pensées* ("Thoughts"), Pascal argued that only faith could resolve the contradictions of the world because "the heart has its reasons, of which reason itself knows nothing."

*Pensées* expresses Pascal's own anguish and awe in the face of evil and uncertainty, but presents that awe as evidence for the existence of God. Pascal's hope was that, on this foundation, some measure of confidence in humanity and its capacity for self-knowledge could be rediscovered.

## The Science of Politics

Montaigne's immediate contemporary, the French jurist Jean Bodin (*boh-DAN*; 1530–1596), took a more practical approach to the problem of uncertain authority and found a solution in the power of the state. Like Montaigne, Bodin was troubled by the upheavals of the religious wars. He had witnessed the Saint Bartholomew's Day Massacre of 1572 and, in response, developed a theory of absolute sovereignty that would (he surmised) put an end to such catastrophes. In his monumental *Six Books of the Commonwealth* (1576), he argued that the state has its origins in the needs of family-oriented communities, and its paramount duty is to maintain order. He defined sovereignty as the "most high, absolute, and perpetual power over all subjects," meaning that a sovereign head of state could make and enforce laws without the consent of those governed: precisely what King Charles of England later argued when he tried to dispense with Parliament—and precisely what his subjects ultimately rejected. Even if the ruler proved a tyrant, Bodin insisted that subjects had no right to resist, for any resistance would open the door to anarchy, "which is worse than the harshest tyranny in the world."

In England, experience of the Civil War led Thomas Hobbes (1588–1679) to propose a different theory of state sovereignty in his treatise *Leviathan* (1651). Whereas Bodin assumed that sovereign power should be vested in a monarch, Hobbes argued that any form of government capable of protecting its subjects' lives and property might act as an all-powerful sovereign.

Hobbes's conviction of the need for a strong state arose from his pessimistic view of human nature. The "state of nature" that existed before government, he wrote, was "war of all against all." Because man naturally behaves as "a wolf" toward other men, human life without government is "solitary, poor, nasty, brutish, and short." To escape such consequences, people must surrender their liberties to a sovereign state, in exchange for the state's obligation to keep the peace. Bodin saw the ultimate goal of the state as the protection of property, whereas Hobbes saw it as the preservation of people's lives, even at the expense of their liberties.

## Montaigne on Cannibals

*The* Essays *of Michel de Montaigne (1533–1592) reflect his attempts to grapple with the contradictions of his own time. In this famous passage, he contrasts the barbarism of the European wars of religion and conquest with the reported behavior of peoples in the New World.*

had with me for a long time a man who had lived ten or twelve years in that other world which has been discovered in our time.... This discovery of so vast a country seems to me worth reflecting on. I should not care to pledge myself that another may not be discovered in the future, since so many greater men than we have been wrong about this one....

[And] I do not believe, from what I have been told about [the] people [of this land] that there is anything barbarous or savage about them, except that we call barbarous anything that is contrary to our own habits. Indeed we seem to have no other criterion of truth and reason than the type and kind of opinions and customs current in the land where we live.... These people are wild in the same way ... that fruits are wild, when nature has produced them by herself and in her ordinary way; whereas, in fact, it is those that we have artificially modified, and removed from the common order, that we ought to call wild....

These [people], then, seem to me barbarous in the sense that they have received very little moulding from the human intelligence, and are still very

close to their original simplicity.... They are in such a state of purity that it sometimes saddens me to think that we did not learn of them earlier ... when there were men who were better able to appreciate them than we....

[For example,] they have their wars against the people who live further inland, on the other side of the mountains; and they go to them quite naked, with no other arms but their bows or their wooden swords, pointed at one end.... [And after] treating a prisoner well for a long time, and giving him every attention he can think of, his captor assembles a great company of his acquaintances. He then ties a rope to the prisoner's arms, holding him by the other end, at some yards' distance for fear of being hit, and gives his best friend the man's other arm, to be held in the same way; and these two, in front of the whole assembly, dispatch him with their swords. This done, they roast him, eat him all together, and send portions to their absent friends....

I am not so anxious that we should note the horrible savagery of these acts as concerned that, whilst judging their faults so correctly, we should be so blind to our own. I consider it more barbarous to eat a man alive than to eat him dead;

to tear by rack and torture a body still full of feeling, to roast it by degrees, and then give it to be trampled and eaten by dogs and swine—a practice which we have not only read about but seen within recent memory, not between ancient enemies, but between neighbours and fellow-citizens and, what is worse, under the cloak of piety and religion—than to roast and eat a man after he is dead.

Source: Michel de Montaigne, *Essays,* trans. J. M. Cohen (Harmondsworth: 1958), pp. 105–13.

### Questions for Analysis

*1.* How does Montaigne regard the "barbarous" people of the New World? How does he (re)define that concept?

*2.* How does Montaigne critique the assumptions and values of his own time in this passage?

*3.* Montaigne compares the reported behavior of cannibals to the behavior of Europeans during the ongoing wars of religion. What is he trying to achieve by making this comparison?

# Past and Present

## Shakespeare's Popular Appeal

Although the plays of William Shakespeare are frequently described as elite entertainments, their enduring appeal can hardly be explained in those terms. In fact, Shakespeare wrote for a diverse audience and for a group of actors who would have been more likely to see the inside of a prison than a royal court. His plays combine high politics, earthy comedy, and deeply human stories that still captivate and move audiences at the reconstructed Globe Theatre in London (left). They also lend themselves to inventive adaptations that comment on our contemporary world, as in the recent film *Coriolanus* (right).

Ⓢ **Watch related author interview on the Student Site**

Hobbes and Bodin developed such theories in response to their firsthand experience of political and social upheavals resulting from the breakdown of traditional authorities. Their different political philosophies thus reflect a practical preoccupation with the observation and analysis of actual occurrences (empirical knowledge) rather than abstract or theological arguments. Because of this practical bent, they are seen as early examples of a new kind of discipline: what we now call political science.

## Poetry and Theater

In the late sixteenth century, the construction of public playhouses (enclosed theaters) made drama an especially effective mass medium for the formation of public opinion, the dissemination of ideas, and the articulation of national identities. A pioneering poet and playwright in Poland, Jan Kochanowski (1530–1584), was the first to write a tragedy in the Polish vernacular. He also invented genres and verse forms that are still influential today. Indeed, his series of moving laments for his beloved daughter Ursula, who died before her third birthday, are exemplars of the human need to find meaning even in the most dreadful situation.

Theater was an especially influential medium in England during the last two decades of Elizabeth's reign and that of her successor, James. Among the large number of playwrights at work in London during this era, the most noteworthy are Christopher Marlowe (1564–1593), Ben Jonson (c. 1572–1637), and William Shakespeare (1564–1616). Marlowe, who may have been a spy for Elizabeth's government and who was mysteriously murdered in a tavern brawl, was extremely popular in his day. In plays such as *Tamburlaine*, about the life of the Mongolian warlord Timur the Lame (Chapter 12), and *Doctor Faustus*, he created heroes who pursue larger-than-life ambitions only to be felled by their own human limitations. In contrast to the heroic tragedies of Marlowe, Ben Jonson wrote dark comedies that expose human vices and foibles. In *The Alchemist*, he balanced an attack on pseudoscientific quackery with admiration for resourceful lower-class characters who cleverly take advantage of their supposed betters.

William Shakespeare was born into a family of a tradesman in the provincial town of Stratford-upon-Avon, where he attained a modest education before moving to London around the age of twenty. There, he composed or collaborated on an unknown number of plays, of which some forty survive in whole or in part. They owe their longevity to the author's unrivaled gifts of verbal expression, humor, and psychological insight. Those written during the playwright's early years reflect the political, religious, and social upheavals of the late sixteenth century, including many history plays that recount episodes from England's medieval past and the struggles that

***VIEW OF TOLEDO*, BY EL GRECO.** This is one of El Greco's many landscape paintings depicting the hilltop city that became his home in later life. Its supple style almost defies historical periodization.

established the Tudor dynasty of Elizabeth's grandfather, Henry VII. They also include the lyrical tragedy *Romeo and Juliet*, and a number of comedies that explore fundamental problems of identity, honor and ambition, love and friendship. The plays from Shakespeare's second period, like other contemporary artworks, are characterized by a troubled individual searching into the mysteries and the meaning of human existence; they showcase the perils of indecisive idealism (*Hamlet*) and the abuse of power (*Macbeth* and *King Lear*). The plays composed toward the end of his career emphasize the possibilities of reconciliation and peace, even after years of misunderstanding and violence (*The Tempest*).

## The Artists of Southern Europe

The ironies and tensions inherent in this age also found expression in the visual arts. In Italy and Spain, many painters cultivated a highly dramatic style sometimes known as "Mannerism." The most unusual of these artists was El Greco ("the Greek"; c. 1541–1614), a pupil of the Venetian master Tintoretto (1518–1594). Born Domenikos Theotokopoulos on the Greek island of Crete, El Greco

absorbed some of the stylized elongation characteristic of Byzantine icon painting (Chapter 7) before traveling to Italy, then settling in Spain. Many of his paintings were too strange to be truly appreciated in his day, and even now appear so avant-garde as to be almost surreal. His *View of Toledo*, for example, is a transfigured landscape, mysteriously lit from within. Equally amazing are his swirling biblical scenes and the stunning portraits of gaunt, dignified saints who radiate austerity and spiritual insight.

In the seventeenth century, the dominant artistic style of southern Europe was the Baroque, a school whose name has become a synonym for elaborate, highly wrought sculpture and architectural details. This style originated in Rome during the Counter-Reformation and promoted a glorified Catholic worldview. Its most imaginative and influential figure was the architect and sculptor Gianlorenzo Bernini (1598–1680), a frequent employee of the papacy who created a magnificent celebration of papal grandeur in the sweeping colonnades leading up to St. Peter's Basilica. Breaking with the more serene classicism of Renaissance styles (Chapter 12), Bernini's work drew inspiration from the restless motion and artistic bravado of Hellenistic statuary (Chapter 4).

**DAVID, BY GIANLORENZO BERNINI.** Whereas the earlier conceptions of David by the Renaissance sculptors Donatello and Michelangelo were serene and dignified (see page 403), the Baroque sculptor Bernini chose to portray the young hero at the peak of physical exertion. ■ *Can you discern the influence of Hellenistic sculpture (see Chapter 4) in this work?* ■ *What are some shared characteristics?*

Characteristics of this Baroque style can also be found in paintings, such as those of the great Spanish master Diego Velázquez (*vay-LAH-skez*; 1599–1660), who served the Spanish Habsburg court in Madrid. Although many of his canvases display a Baroque attention to motion and drama, those most characteristic of his own style are more conceptually thoughtful and daring. An example is *The Maids of Honor (Las Meniñas),* a masterpiece of self-referentiality, completed around 1656. It shows the artist himself at work on a double portrait of the Spanish king and queen, but the scene is dominated by the children and servants of the royal family.

## Dutch Painting in the Golden Age

Southern Europe's main rival in the visual arts was the Netherlands, where many exemplary painters explored the theme of man's greatness and wretchedness to the full. Pieter Bruegel the Elder (*BROY-ghul*; c. 1525–1569) exulted

**THE MAIDS OF HONOR (LAS MENIÑAS), BY DIEGO VELÁZQUEZ.** The artist himself (standing on the left) is shown working at his easel and gazing out at the viewer—or at the subjects of his double portrait, the Spanish king and queen, depicted in the distant mirror. The real focus of the painting is the delicate, impish princess in the center, flanked by two young ladies-in-waiting, a dwarf, and another royal child, as courtiers in the background look on.

in portraying the busy, elemental life of the peasantry. Most famous in this respect are his rollicking *Peasant Wedding* and *Peasant Wedding Dance*, as well as his spacious *Harvesters*, in which field hands are taking a well-deserved break under the noonday sun. But late in his career, Bruegel became appalled by the intolerance and bloodshed he witnessed during the Calvinist riots and the Spanish repression of the Netherlands. He expressed his criticism in works such as *The Massacre of the Innocents*. From a distance, this painting looks like a snug scene of village life; but, in fact, soldiers are methodically breaking into homes and slaughtering helpless infants—as Herod's soldiers once did after the birth of Jesus, and as warring armies did in Bruegel's own day.

Another Dutch painter, Peter Paul Rubens (1577–1640), was inspired by very different politics. A native of Antwerp, part of the Spanish Netherlands, Rubens was a staunch Catholic who glorified the Roman Church and the local aristocrats who supported the Habsburg regime. Even when his intent was not propagandistic, Rubens reveled in the sumptuous extravagance of the Baroque style. (He is most famous today for the pink and rounded flesh of his well-nourished nudes.) Although he celebrated martial valor for most of his career, his late painting *The Horrors of War* movingly captures what he called "the grief of unfortunate Europe, which, for so many years now, has suffered plunder, outrage, and misery."

***THE MASSACRE OF THE INNOCENTS*, BY PIETER BRUEGEL THE ELDER.** This painting shows how effective art can be as a means of political and social commentary. Here, Bruegel depicts the suffering of the Netherlands at the hands of the Spanish in his own day, with reference to the biblical story of Herod's slaughter of Jewish children after the birth of Jesus—thereby collapsing the two historical incidents.

***THE CONSEQUENCES OF WAR*, BY PETER PAUL RUBENS.** In his old age, Rubens took a far more critical view of war than he had done for most of his career. Here, the war god Mars casts aside his mistress Venus, goddess of love, and threatens humanity with death and destruction.

**SELF-PORTRAITS.** Self-portraits became common during the sixteenth and seventeenth centuries, reflecting the intense introspection of the period. Rembrandt painted more than sixty self-portraits; this one on the left, dating from around 1660, captures the artist's creativity, theatricality (note the costume), and honesty of self-examination. Judith Leyster, shown on the right, was a contemporary of Rembrandt, who pursued a successful career during her early twenties before she married. Respected in her own day, she was all but forgotten for centuries thereafter, but is once again the object of much attention.

# After You Read This Chapter

Go to **INQUIZITIVE** to see what you've learned—and learn what you've missed—with personalized feedback along the way.

## REVIEWING THE OBJECTIVES

- How were the peoples and ecosystems of the Americas, Africa, and Europe intertwined during this period? What were some of the consequences of these new linkages?

- Why did the colonies of the Spanish, the English, and the Dutch differ from each other? How did these differences affect the lives and labor of colonists, both free and unfree?

- Which European powers came to dominate the Atlantic world? What factors led to the decline of Spain and the rise of France?

- What forms did religious and political conflict take in France, the Netherlands, and Germany? What were the causes of the English Civil War? What impact did this event have on the English colonies?

- How do the arts and the political philosophies of this period reflect the turmoil of Europe and the Atlantic world?

In some ways a blend of Bruegel and Rubens, Rembrandt van Rijn (*vahn REEN*; 1606–1669) defies all attempts at easy characterization. Living across the border from the Spanish Netherlands, in the staunchly Calvinist Dutch Republic, Rembrandt managed to put both realistic and Baroque traits to new uses. Early in his career, he gained fame and fortune as a painter of biblical scenes, and was also active as a portrait painter who knew how to flatter his subjects—to the great advantage of his purse. But as personal tragedies mounted in his middle and declining years, the painter's art gained dignity, subtlety, and mystery. His later portraits, including several self-portraits, are highly introspective and suggest that only part of the story is being told. Equally fearless is the frank gaze of Rembrandt's slightly younger contemporary, Judith Leyster (1609–1660), who looks out of her own self-portrait with a refreshingly optimistic and good-humored expression.

# CONCLUSION

It would take centuries for Europeans to adapt themselves to the changes brought about by their integration into the Atlantic world and to grasp its implications. Finding new lands and cultures unknown to the ancients and unmentioned in the Bible had exposed the limitations of Western civilizations' accumulated knowledge, and called for new ways of knowing and explaining the world. The Columbian exchange of people, plants, livestock, and pathogens that had previously been isolated from each other had a profound and lasting effect on populations and ecosystems throughout the Atlantic zone. The distribution of new agricultural products transformed the lives of the European poor and rich alike.

The transatlantic slave trade, which made all this possible, brought Africans and their cultures into a world of growing global connections under the worst possible circumstances for those who were enslaved—yet this did not prevent them from actively shaping this new world. Meanwhile, the influx of silver from New Spain precipitated the great price inflation of the sixteenth and seventeenth centuries, which bewildered contemporary observers and contributed to the atmosphere of crisis in a post-Reformation Europe already riven by religious and civil warfare. The response was a trend toward stronger centralized states, justified by theories of absolute government. Led by the French monarchy of Louis XIV, these absolutist regimes would reach their apogee in the coming century.

## PEOPLE, IDEAS, AND EVENTS IN CONTEXT

- What was the **COLUMBIAN EXCHANGE**? How did it affect the relations among the peoples of the Americas, Africa, and Europe during this period?
- What circumstances led to the development of the **TRIANGULAR TRADE**?
- What were the main sources of instability in Europe during the sixteenth century? How did the **PRICE REVOLUTION** exacerbate this instability?
- How did **HENRY IV** of France and **PHILIP II** of Spain deal with the religious conflict that beset Europe during these years?
- What were the origins of the **THIRTY YEARS' WAR**? Was it primarily a religious conflict? Why or why not?
- How did the policies of **CARDINAL RICHELIEU** strengthen the power of the French monarchy?
- What policies of England's **CHARLES I** were most detested by his subjects? Why was his execution so momentous?
- In what ways did the **WITCH CRAZE** of early modern Europe reveal the religious and social tensions of the sixteenth and seventeenth centuries?
- What were the differences between **JEAN BODIN**'s theory of absolute sovereignty and that of **THOMAS HOBBES**?
- How did philosophers such as **MONTAIGNE** and **PASCAL** respond to the uncertainties of the age? How were contemporary trends reflected in the works of **SHAKESPEARE** and in the visual arts?

## THINKING ABOUT CONNECTIONS

- The emergence of the Atlantic world can be seen as the *cause* of new developments as well as the *result* of historical processes. What long-term political, economic, and demographic circumstances drove the expansion of European influence into the Atlantic? What subsequent historical developments can be attributed to the creation of this interconnected world?
- The political crises of this era reveal the tensions produced by sectarian religious disputes as well as by a growing rift between powerful centralizing monarchies and landholding elites who are unwilling to surrender their authority and independence. What other periods in history are marked by similar tensions? How do those periods compare with the one we have studied in this chapter?
- The intellectual currents of this era reveal that a new generation was challenging the assumptions of its predecessors. In what other historical eras do we find similar phenomena? What social and political circumstances tend to produce consensus, and what tend to produce dissent, skepticism, and doubt?

### STORY LINES

- After 1660, many European rulers invoked an absolutist definition of sovereignty in order to expand the power of the monarchy. The most successful absolutist kings, such as Louis XIV of France or Peter the Great of Russia, limited the power of traditional aristocratic elites and the independence of religious institutions.

- Absolutism was not universally successful. Efforts by English monarchs to create an absolutist regime in England after the Civil War were resisted by political opponents of the Crown in Parliament. Other regimes in Europe that found alternatives to absolutism included the Dutch Republic and the Polish Lithuanian Commonwealth.

- Absolutism reinforced the imperial ambitions of European monarchies and led to frequent wars that were increasingly fought both in Europe and in colonial spaces in other parts of the world. The pressures of war favored dynasties capable of building strong centralized states with reliable sources of revenue from trade and taxation.

### CHRONOLOGY

| | |
|---|---|
| 1643–1715 | Reign of Louis XIV of France |
| 1660 | Restoration of the Stuart kings in England |
| 1685 | Revocation of the Edict of Nantes |
| 1683 | Ottoman siege of Vienna |
| 1688 | Glorious Revolution in England |
| 1688–1697 | War of the League of Augsburg |
| 1690 | Publication of John Locke's *Two Treatises of Government* |
| 1689–1725 | Reign of Peter the Great of Russia |
| 1702–1713 | War of the Spanish Succession |
| 1713 | Treaty of Utrecht |

Before You Read This Chapter

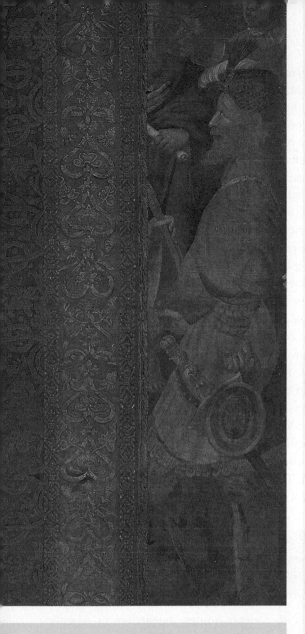

# European Monarchies and Absolutism, 1660–1725

## CORE OBJECTIVES

- **DEFINE** *absolutism,* **UNDERSTAND** its central principles as a theory of government, and **IDENTIFY** the major absolutist rulers in Europe during this period.

- **DEFINE** *mercantilism* and its relation to absolutist rule.

- **EXPLAIN** the alternatives to absolutism that emerged, most notably in England, the Dutch Republic, and Poland-Lithuania.

- **DESCRIBE** how the wars between 1661 and 1715 changed the balance of power in Europe and in the colonial spheres of the Atlantic world.

- **UNDERSTAND** the reforms undertaken by Peter the Great in Russia and **COMPARE** his regime with the absolutist kingdoms of western and central Europe.

I n the mountainous region of south-central France known as the Auvergne in the 1660s, the Marquis of Canillac had a notorious reputation. His noble title gave him the right to collect minor taxes on special occasions, but he insisted that these small privileges be converted into annual tributes. To collect these payments, he housed twelve accomplices in his castle whom he called his apostles. Their other nicknames—one was known as Break Everything—gave a more accurate sense of their activities in the local villages. The marquis imprisoned those who resisted and forced their families to buy their freedom. In an earlier age, the marquis might have gotten away with this profitable arrangement. In 1662, however, he ran up against the authority of a king, Louis XIV, who was determined to demonstrate that the power of the central monarch was absolute. The marquis was brought up on charges before a special court of judges from Paris, was found guilty, and forced to pay a large fine. The king then confiscated his property and had his castle destroyed.

Louis XIV's special court in the Auvergne heard nearly a thousand civil cases over four months in 1662. It convicted 692 people, many of whom, like the Marquis of Canillac, were noble.

493

The verdicts were an extraordinary example of Louis XIV's ability to project his authority into the remote corners of his realm, and to do so in a way that diminished the power of other elites. During his long reign (1643–1715), Louis XIV systematically pursued such policies on many fronts, asserting his power over the nobility, the clergy, and the provincial courts. Increasingly, these elites were forced to look to the crown to guarantee their interests, and their own power became more closely connected with the sacred aura of the monarchy itself. Louis XIV's model of kingship was known as *absolute monarchy*—a system of government that invested all authority in the king—and his reign was seen as the most successful application of this model. In recognition of the influence of Louis XIV's political system, the period from around 1660 (when the English monarchy was restored and Louis XIV began his personal rule in France) to 1789 (when the French Revolution erupted) is traditionally known as the age of absolutism. This is a crucial period in the development of modern, centralized, bureaucratic states in Europe.

*Absolutism* was a political theory that encouraged rulers to claim complete sovereignty within their territories. An absolute monarch could make law, dispense justice, create and direct a bureaucracy, declare war, and levy taxation without the approval of any other governing body. Assertions of absolute authority were buttressed by claims that

rulers governed by divine right, just as fathers ruled over their households (see *Competing Viewpoints* on page 498). After the chaos and religious wars of the previous century, many Europeans came to believe that only by exalting the sovereignty of absolute rulers could order be restored to European life.

European monarchs also continued to project their power abroad during this period. By 1660, as we have seen, the French, Spanish, Portuguese, English, and Dutch had all established important colonies in the Americas and Asia. These colonies created trading networks that brought profitable new consumer goods such as sugar, tobacco, and coffee to a wide public in Europe. They also encouraged the colonies' reliance on slavery to produce these goods. Rivalry among colonial powers to control the trade in slaves and consumer goods was intense and often led to wars that were fought both in Europe and in contested colonies. These wars, in turn, increased the motivation of absolutist rulers to extract as much revenue as they could from their subjects and encouraged the development of institutions that enhanced their power such as armies, navies, tax systems, tariffs and customs controls.

Absolutism was not universally successful during this period. The English monarchy, restored in 1660 after the turbulent years of the Civil War, attempted to impose absolutist rule but met resistance from parliamentary leaders who insisted on more inclusive institutions of government. After 1688, England, Scotland, the Dutch Republic, Switzerland, Venice, Sweden, and Poland-Lithuania were all either limited monarchies or republics. In Russia, on the other hand, an extreme autocracy emerged that gave the tsar a degree of control over his subjects' lives and property far beyond anything imagined by western European absolutists. But even in Russia, absolutism was never unlimited in practice. So, too, the most absolute monarchs could rule effectively only with the consent of their subjects (particularly the nobility). When serious opposition erupted, even powerful kings were forced to back down. King George III of Britain discovered this when his North American colonies declared their independence in 1776, forming the United States of America. In 1789, a more sweeping revolution began in France, and the entire structure of absolutism came crashing to the ground (see Chapter 18).

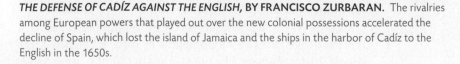

*THE DEFENSE OF CADÍZ AGAINST THE ENGLISH,* **BY FRANCISCO ZURBARAN.** The rivalries among European powers that played out over the new colonial possessions accelerated the decline of Spain, which lost the island of Jamaica and the ships in the harbor of Cadíz to the English in the 1650s.

# THE APPEAL AND JUSTIFICATION OF ABSOLUTISM

Absolutism's promise of stability and order was an appealing alternative to the disorder of the "iron century" that preceded it. The early theorists of absolutism, such as Jean Bodin and Thomas Hobbes, looked to strong royal governments as an answer to the violence of religious wars and the crises of the sixteenth and seventeenth centuries (see Chapter 14). Louis XIV himself was profoundly disturbed by an aristocratic revolt that occurred while he was still a child. When marauding Parisians entered his bedchamber one night in 1651, Louis saw the intrusion as an affront not only to his own person but to the majesty of the French state. Such experiences convinced him that he needed to rule assertively and without limits to his power.

Absolutist monarchs sought control of the state's armed forces and its legal system, and they demanded the right to collect and spend the state's financial resources at will. To achieve these goals, they also needed to create an efficient, centralized bureaucracy that owed its allegiance directly to the monarch. Creating and sustaining such a bureaucracy was expensive but necessary in order to weaken the special interests that hindered the free exercise of royal power. The nobility and the clergy, with their traditional legal privileges; the political authority of semiautonomous regions; and representative assemblies such as parliaments, diets, or estates-general were all obstacles—in the eyes of absolutists—to strong, centralized monarchical government. The history of absolutism is the history of kings who attempted to bring such institutions to heel.

In most Protestant countries, the power of the church had already been subordinated to the state when the age of absolutism began. Even where Roman Catholicism remained the state religion, such as in France, Spain, and Austria, absolutist monarchs now devoted considerable attention to bringing the Church and its clergy under royal control. Louis XIV took an active role in religious matters, appointing his own bishops and encouraging the repression of religious dissidents, but unlike his predecessors, he rarely appointed members of the clergy to offices within his administration.

The most important potential opponents of royal absolutism were not churchmen, however, but nobles. Louis XIV deprived the French nobility of political power in the provinces but increased their social prestige by making them live at his lavish court at Versailles (*vuhr-SY*). Peter the Great of Russia (1689–1725) forced his nobles into life-long government service. Successive monarchs in Brandenburg-Prussia managed to co-opt the powerful aristocracy by granting them immunity to taxation and giving them the right to enserf their peasants; in exchange, they ceded administrative control to the increasingly bureaucratized Prussian state. In most European monarchies, including Spain, France, Prussia, and England, the nobility retained their preponderant role within the military.

Struggles between monarchs and nobles frequently affected relations between local and central government. In France, the requirement that nobles live at the king's court undermined the provincial institutions that the nobility had used to exercise their political power. In Spain, the monarchy, based in Castile, battled the independent-minded nobles of Aragon and Catalonia. Prussian rulers asserted control over formerly "free" cities by claiming the right to police and tax their inhabitants. The Habsburg emperors tried, unsuccessfully, to suppress the largely autonomous nobility of Hungary. Rarely was the path of confrontation between crown and nobility successful in the long run. The most effective absolutist monarchies of the eighteenth century continued to trade privileges for allegiance, so that nobles came to see their own interests as tied to those of the crown. For this reason, wary cooperation between kings and nobles was more common than open conflict during the eighteenth century.

# THE ABSOLUTISM OF LOUIS XIV

In Louis XIV's state portrait, it is almost impossible to discern the human being behind the facade of the absolute monarch dressed in his coronation robes and surrounded by the symbols of his authority. That facade was artfully constructed by Louis, who recognized, more fully than any other early modern ruler, the importance of theater to effective kingship. Louis and his successors deliberately staged spectacular demonstrations of their sovereignty to enhance their position as rulers endowed with godlike powers.

## *Performing Royalty at Versailles*

Louis's most elaborate staging of his authority took place at his palace at Versailles, outside Paris. The main facade of the palace was a third of a mile in length. Inside, tapestries and paintings celebrated French military victories and royal triumphs; and mirrors reflected shimmering light throughout the building. In the vast gardens outside, statues of the Greek god Apollo, god of the sun, recalled Louis's claim to be the "Sun King" of France. Noblemen vied to

# Interpreting Visual Evidence

## The Performance and Display of Absolute Power at the Court of Louis XIV

istorians studying the history of absolutism and the court of Louis XIV in particular have emphasized the Sun King's brilliant use of symbols and display to demonstrate his personal embodiment of sovereignty. Royal portraits, such as that painted by Hyacinthe Rigaud in 1701 (shown below), vividly illustrate the degree to which Louis's power was based on a studied performance. His pose, with his exposed and shapely calf, was an important indication of power and virility, necessary elements of legitimacy for a hereditary monarch. In the elaborate rituals of court life at Versailles, Louis often placed his own body at the center of attention, performing in one instance as the god Apollo in a ballet before his assembled courtiers. His movements through the countryside, accompanied by a retinue of soldiers, servants, and aristocrats, were another occasion for highly stylized ritual demonstrations of his quasi-divine status. Finally, of course, the construction of his palace at Versailles, with its symmetrical architecture and sculpted gardens, was a demonstration that his power extended over the natural world as easily as it did over the lives of his subjects.

### Questions for Analysis

1. Who was the intended audience for the king's performance of absolute sovereignty?

2. Who were Louis's primary competitors in this contest for eminence through the performance of power?

3. What possible political dangers might lie in wait for a regime that invested so heavily in the sumptuous display of semidivine authority?

A. Hyacinthe Rigaud's 1701 portrait of Louis XIV.

B. Louis XIV as the Sun King.

C. *The Royal Procession of Louis XIV,* by Adam Franz van der Meulen (1664).

D. Louis XIV arrives at the Palace of Versailles.

## Absolutism and Patriarchy

*These selections show how two political theorists justified royal absolutism by deriving it from the absolute authority of a father over his household. Bishop Jacques-Bénigne Bossuet (1627–1704) was a famous French preacher and the tutor to the son of King Louis XIV of France before becoming bishop of Meaux. Sir Robert Filmer (1588–1653) was an English political theorist. Filmer's works attracted particular attention in the 1680s, when John Locke directed the first of his* Two Treatises of Government *to refute Filmer's views on the patriarchal nature of royal authority.*

### Bossuet on the Nature of Monarchical Authority

There are four characteristics or qualities essential to royal authority. First, royal authority is sacred; Secondly, it is paternal; Thirdly, it is absolute; Fourthly, it is subject to reason. . . . All power comes from God. . . . Thus princes act as ministers of God, and his lieutenants on earth. It is through them that he exercises his empire. . . . In this way . . . the royal throne is not the throne of a man, but the throne of God himself. . . .

We have seen that kings hold the place of God, who is the true Father of the human race. We have also seen that the first idea of power that there was among men, is that of paternal power; and that kings were fashioned on the model of fathers. Moreover, all the world agrees that obedience, which is due to public power, is only found . . . in the precept which obliges one to honor his parents. From all this it appears that the name "king" is a father's name, and that goodness is the most natural quality in kings. . . .

Royal authority is absolute. In order to make this term odious and insupportable, many pretend to confuse absolute government and arbitrary government. But nothing is more distinct, as we shall make clear when we speak of justice. . . . The prince need account to no one for what he ordains. . . . Without this absolute authority, he can neither do good nor suppress evil: his power must be such that no one can hope to escape him. . . . [T]he sole defense of individuals against the public power must be their innocence. . . .

One must, then, obey princes as if they were justice itself, without which there is neither order nor justice in affairs. They are gods, and share in some way in divine independence. . . . It follows from this that he who does not want to obey the prince . . . is condemned irremissibly to death as an enemy of public peace and of human society. . . . The prince can correct himself when he knows that he has done badly; but against his authority there can be no remedy. . . .

Source: Jacques-Bénigne Bossuet, *Politics Drawn from the Very Words of Holy Scripture*, trans. Patrick Riley (Cambridge: 1990), pp. 46–69, 81–83.

attend him when he arose from bed, ate his meals (usually stone cold after having traveled the distance of several city blocks from kitchen to table), strolled in his gardens (even the way the king walked was choreographed by the royal dancing master), or rode to the hunt. France's leading nobles were required to reside with Louis at Versailles for a portion of the year; the splendor of Louis's court was deliberately calculated to blind them to the possibility of disobedience while raising their prestige by associating them with himself (see **Interpreting Visual Evidence** on page 496).

At the same time, the almost impossibly detailed rules of etiquette at court left these privileged nobles in constant suspense, forever fearful of offending the king by committing some trivial violation of proper manners.

Of course, the nobility did not surrender social and political power entirely. The social order was still hierarchical, and noblemen retained enormous privileges and rights over local peasants within their jurisdiction. The absolutist system forced the nobility to depend on the crown, but it did not seek to undermine their superior place in society.

## Filmer on the Patriarchal Origins of Royal Authority

The first government in the world was monarchical, in the father of all flesh, Adam being commanded to multiply, and people the earth, and to subdue it, and having dominion given him over all creatures, was thereby the monarch of the whole world; none of his posterity had any right to possess anything, but by his grant or permission, or by succession from him. . . . Adam was the father, king and lord over his family: a son, a subject, and a servant or a slave were one and the same thing at first. . . .

I cannot find any one place or text in the Bible where any power . . . is given to a people either to govern themselves, or to choose themselves governors, or to alter the manner of government at their pleasure. The power of government is settled and fixed by the commandment of "honour thy father"; if there were a higher power than the fatherly, then this commandment could not stand and be observed. . . .

All power on earth is either derived or usurped from the fatherly power, there being no other original to be found of any power whatsoever. For if there should be granted two sorts of power without any subordination of one to the other, they would be in perpetual strife which should be the supreme, for two supremes cannot agree. If the fatherly power be supreme, then the power of the people must be subordinate and depend on it. If the power of the people be supreme, then the fatherly power must submit to it, and cannot be exercised without the licence of the people, which must quite destroy the frame and course of nature. Even the power which God himself exercises over mankind is by right of fatherhood: he is both the king and father of us all. As God has exalted the dignity of earthly kings . . . by saying they are gods, so . . . he has been pleased . . . [t]o humble himself by assuming the title of a king to express his power, and not the title of any popular government.

Source: Robert Filmer, "Observations upon Aristotle's Politiques," in *Divine Right and Democracy: An Anthology of Political Writing in Stuart England,* ed. David Wootton (Harmondsworth, UK: 1986), pp. 110–18. First published 1652.

### Questions for Analysis

1. Bossuet's definition of *absolutism* connected the sacred power of kings with the paternal authority of fathers within the household. What consequences does he draw from defining the relationship between king and subjects in this way?

2. What does Filmer mean when he says, "All power on earth is either derived or usurped from the fatherly power"? How many examples does he give of paternal or monarchical power?

3. Bossuet and Filmer make obedience the basis for order and justice in the world. What alternative political systems did they most fear?

In this sense, the relationship between Louis XIV and the nobility was more of a negotiated settlement than a complete victory of the king over other powerful elites. Louis XIV understood this, and in a memoir that he prepared for his son on the art of ruling, he wrote, "The deference and the respect that we receive from our subjects are not a free gift from them but payment for the justice and the protection that they expect from us. Just as they must honor us, we must protect and defend them." In their own way, absolutists depended on the consent of those they ruled.

## Administration and Centralization

Louis defined his responsibilities in absolutist terms: to concentrate royal power so as to produce domestic tranquility. In addition to convincing the nobility to cede political authority, he also recruited the upper bourgeoisie as royal intendants, administrators responsible for running the thirty-six *generalités* into which France was divided. Intendants usually served outside the region where they were born and thus were unconnected with the local elites

# Past and Present

## The Persistence of Monarchies in a Democratic Age

In the past, monarchs such as Louis XIV (left) often ran roughshod over tradition as they sought ways to increase their power. Today, twelve European states still have reigning monarchs such as England's Queen Elizabeth II (right), but their popularity probably would be called into question if they sought an active role in government.

 **Watch related author interview on the Student Site**

over whom they exercised authority. They held office at the king's pleasure and were clearly his men. Other administrators, often from families newly ennobled as a reward for their service, assisted in directing affairs of state from Versailles. These men were not actors in the theater of Louis the Sun King; rather, they were the hardworking assistants of Louis the royal custodian of his country's welfare.

Louis's administrators devoted much of their time and energy to collecting the taxes necessary to finance the large standing army on which his aggressive foreign policy depended. Absolutism was fundamentally an approach to government by which ambitious monarchs could increase their own power through conquest and display. As such, it was enormously expensive. In addition to the *taille* (land tax), which increased throughout the seventeenth century, Louis's government introduced *capitation* (head tax) and

pressed successfully for the collection of indirect taxes on salt (the *gabelle*), wine, tobacco, and other goods. Because the nobility was exempt from the taille, its burden fell most heavily on the peasantry, whose local revolts Louis easily crushed.

Regional opposition was curtailed but not eliminated during Louis's reign. By removing the provincial nobility to Versailles, Louis cut them off from their local sources of power and influence. To restrict the powers of regional parlements (law courts), Louis decreed that members of any parlement who refused to approve and enforce his laws would be summarily exiled. The Estates General, the French representative assembly that met at the king's pleasure to act as a consultative body for the state, was last summoned in 1614. It did not meet at all during Louis's reign and, in fact, was not convened again until 1789.

## Louis XIV's Religious Policies

For both reasons of state and personal conscience, Louis was determined to impose religious unity on France, regardless of the economic and social costs.

Although the vast majority of the French population was Roman Catholic, French Catholics were divided among Quietists, Jansenists, Jesuits, and Gallicans. Quietists preached retreat into personal mysticism, emphasizing a direct relationship between God and the individual human heart. Such doctrine, dispensing as it did with the intermediary services of the Church, was suspect in the eyes of absolutists wedded to the doctrine of *un roi, une loi, une foi* ("one king, one law, one faith"). Jansenism—a movement named for its founder, Cornelius Jansen, a seventeenth-century bishop of Ypres—held to an Augustinian doctrine of predestination that could sound and look surprisingly like a kind of Catholic Calvinism. Louis vigorously persecuted Quietists and Jansenists, offering them a choice between recanting and prison or exile. At the same time, he supported the Jesuits in their efforts to create a Counter-Reformation Catholic Church in France. Louis's support for the Jesuits upset the traditional Gallican Catholics of France, however, who desired a French church independent of papal, Jesuit, and Spanish influence. As a result of this dissension among Catholics, the religious aura of Louis's kingship diminished during the course of his reign.

Against the Protestant Huguenots Louis waged unrelenting war. Protestant churches and schools were destroyed, and Protestants were banned from many professions. In 1685, Louis revoked the Edict of Nantes, the legal foundation of the toleration the Huguenots had enjoyed since 1598. Protestant clerics were exiled, laymen were sent to the galleys as slaves, and their children were forcibly baptized as Catholics. Many families converted, but 200,000 Protestant refugees fled to England, Holland, Germany, and America, bringing with them their professional and artisanal skills. This migration was an enormous loss to France. Huguenots fleeing Louis XIV's persecution, for example, established the silk industries of Berlin and London.

## Colbert and Royal Finance

Louis's drive to unify France depended on a vast increase in royal revenues engineered by Jean-Baptiste Colbert, the king's finance minister from 1664 to 1683; Colbert died in office. Colbert tightened the process of tax collection and eliminated wherever possible the practice of tax farming, which permitted collection agents to retain for themselves a percentage of the taxes they gathered for the king. When Colbert assumed office, only about 25 percent of the taxes collected throughout the kingdom reached the treasury. By the time he died, that figure had risen to 80 percent. Under Colbert's direction, the state sold public offices, including judgeships and mayoralties, and guilds purchased the right to enforce trade regulations. Colbert also tried to increase the nation's income by controlling and regulating foreign trade. As a confirmed mercantilist, Colbert believed France's wealth would grow if it reduced its imports and increased its exports. He therefore imposed tariffs on foreign goods imported into France, while using state money to promote the domestic manufacture of formerly imported goods, such as silk, lace, tapestries, and glass. He was especially anxious to create domestic industries capable of producing the goods France would need for war. To encourage domestic trade, he improved France's roads, bridges, and waterways.

Despite Colbert's efforts to increase crown revenues, his policies ultimately foundered on the insatiable demands of Louis XIV's wars (see page 508). Colbert himself foresaw this result when he lectured the king in 1680: "Trade is the source of public finance and public finance is the vital nerve of war. . . . I beg your Majesty to permit me only to say to him that in war as in peace he has never consulted the amount of money available in determining his expenditures." Louis, however, paid him no heed. By the end of Louis's reign, his aggressive foreign policy lay in ruins, and his country's finances had been shattered by the unsustainable costs of war.

## French Colonialism under Louis XIV

Finance Minister Colbert regarded overseas expansion as an integral part of the French state's economic policy, and with his guidance, Louis XIV's absolutist realm emerged as a major colonial power. Recognizing the profits to be made in responding to Europe's growing demand for sugar, Colbert encouraged the development of sugar-producing colonies in the West Indies, the largest of which was Saint-Domingue (present-day Haiti). Sugar, virtually unknown in Christian Europe during the Middle Ages, became a popular luxury item in the late fifteenth century (see Chapter 14). It took the slave plantations of the Caribbean to turn sugar into a mass-market product. By 1750, slaves in Saint-Domingue produced 40 percent of the world's sugar (and 50 percent of its coffee), exporting more sugar than Jamaica, Cuba, and Brazil combined. By 1700, France also dominated the interior of the North American continent, where French traders brought furs to the Native Americans and missionaries preached Christianity in a vast territory that stretched from Québec to Louisiana. The financial returns from North America were never large, however. Furs, fish, and tobacco were exported to European markets but never matched the profits from the Caribbean sugar colonies or from the trading posts that the French maintained in India.

Like the earlier Spanish colonies (see Chapter 14), the French colonies were established and administered as direct crown enterprises. French colonial settlements in North America were conceived mainly as military outposts and trading centers, and they were overwhelmingly populated by men. The elite of French colonial society were military officers and administrators sent from Paris. Below their ranks were fishermen, fur traders, small farmers, and common soldiers who constituted the majority of French settlers in North America. Because the fishing and the fur trades relied on cooperative relationships with native peoples, a mutual economic interdependence grew between the French colonies and the peoples of the surrounding region. Intermarriage, especially between French traders and native women, was common. These North American colonies remained dependent on the wages and supplies sent to them from the mother country. Only rarely did they become truly self-sustaining economic enterprises.

The phenomenally successful sugar plantations of the Caribbean had their own social structure, with slaves at the bottom, people of mixed African and European descent forming the middle layer, and wealthy European plantation owners at the top, controlling the lucrative trade with the outside world. Well over half of the sugar and coffee sent to France was resold and sent elsewhere to markets throughout Europe. Because the monarchy controlled the prices that colonial plantation owners could charge French merchants for their goods, traders in Europe who bought the goods for resale abroad could also make vast fortunes. Historians estimate that as many as 1 million of the 25 million inhabitants of France in the eighteenth century lived off the money flowing through this colonial trade, making the slave colonies of the Caribbean a powerful force for economic change in France. The wealth generated from these colonies added to the prestige of France's absolutist system of government.

# ALTERNATIVES TO ABSOLUTISM

Although absolutism was the dominant model for seventeenth- and eighteenth-century European monarchs, it was by no means the only system by which Europeans governed themselves. A republican oligarchy continued to rule in Venice. In the Polish-Lithuanian Commonwealth, the monarch was elected by the nobility and governed alongside a parliament that met every two years. In the Netherlands, the territories that had won their independence from Spain during the early seventeenth century combined to form the United Provinces, the only truly new country to take shape in Europe during the early modern era. England, which had suffered through a violent civil war between 1642 and 1651, followed by the tumultuous years of Oliver Cromwell's Commonwealth and the Protectorate (see Chapter 14), also took a different path during these years, eventually arriving at a constitutional settlement that gave a larger role to Parliament and admitted a degree of participation by non-nobles in the affairs of state. Arriving at this settlement was not easy, however. The end of the civil wars and the collapse of Cromwell's Protectorate had made it clear that England would be a monarchy and not a republic, but what sort of monarchy England would be remained an open question. Two issues were paramount: the religious question and the relationship between Parliament and the king.

## The Restoration Monarchy in England

The king who took the throne following the Restoration of the Stuarts in 1660, Charles II (r. 1660–1685), was initially welcomed by most English, despite being the son of the beheaded and much-despised Charles I (see Chapter 14). He restored bishops to the Church of England, but he did not initially return to the provocative religious policies of his father. He declared limited religious toleration for Protestant "dissenters" who were not members of the Church of England. He promised to observe the Magna Carta and the Petition of Right, which comforted members of Parliament. He also accepted the legislation passed by Parliament immediately before the outbreak of civil war in 1642, including the requirement that Parliament be summoned at least once every three years. England thus emerged from its civil war as a limited monarchy, in which power was exercised by the "king in Parliament." Meanwhile, the unbuttoned moral atmosphere of Charles II's court, with its risqué plays, dancing, and sexual licentiousness, may have reflected a public desire to forget the restraints of the Puritan past.

During the 1670s, however, Charles began openly to model his kingship on the absolutism of Louis XIV. As a result, the great men of England soon came to be publicly divided between Charles's supporters (known as "Tories," a popular nickname for Irish Catholic bandits) and his opponents (called "Whigs," a nickname for Scottish Presbyterian rebels). In fact, both sides feared absolutism as well as a return to the bad old days of the 1640s when resistance to the Crown had led to civil war and ultimately to republicanism. What they could not agree on was which possibility frightened them more.

Charles's known sympathy for Roman Catholicism (he converted on his deathbed in 1685) also generated fodder for the opposition Whigs. During the 1670s, he briefly suspended civil penalties against Catholics and Protestant dissenters by asserting his right as king to ignore parliamentary legislation, retreating only in the face of public protest. The Whigs, meanwhile, rallied support by targeting Charles's Catholic brother James, the heir to the throne. The result was a series of Whig electoral victories between 1679 and 1681. A group of radical Whigs tried and failed to exclude James from succeeding his brother by law, and thereafter Charles found that his rising revenues from customs duties, combined with a secret subsidy from Louis XIV, enabled him to govern without relying on Parliament for money. Charles further alarmed Whig politicians by executing several of them on charges of treason and remodeling local government to make it more amenable to royal control. Charles died in 1685 with his power enhanced, but left behind a political and religious legacy that was to be the undoing of his less able and adroit successor.

James II was the very opposite of his worldly brother. A zealous Catholic convert, James admired the French monarchy's Gallican Catholicism, which sought to further the work of the Church by harnessing it to the power of an absolutist bureaucratic state. His commitment to absolutism also led him to build up the English army and navy, which in turn led him to search for innovative solutions to the problems of taxation and the quartering of troops. To make the tax system more efficient he created new revenue agencies in many English towns. His quest for more accurate intelligence about political opponents led him to take control over the country's new post office, which made domestic surveillance routine, and his government also stepped up its efforts to prosecute seditious speech and writings. For the Whigs, James's policies were all that they had feared.

Meanwhile, James's Catholicism also alienated his Tory supporters, who were close to the established Church of England. Religion was not the only cause of his unpopularity, but resistance to his policies was often mixed with resentment against a perception that he favored Catholics. His decision to appoint Catholics as officers in the army was unpopular, but even more so was his decision to maintain a standing army in peacetime. Towns that were asked to quarter troops resented the expense and the disruptive presence of soldiers in their midst. In June 1688, when he ordered all Church of England clergymen to read his decree of religious toleration from their pulpits, seven bishops refused and were promptly imprisoned. At their trial, however, they were declared not guilty of sedition, to the enormous satisfaction of the Protestant English populace.

The trial of the bishops was one event that galvanized the growing opposition to James. The other was the unexpected birth of a son in 1688 to James and his second wife, Mary of Modena. This child, who was to be raised a Catholic, replaced James's much older Protestant daughter Mary Stuart as heir to the thrones of Scotland and England. So unexpected was this birth that there were widespread rumors that the child was not in fact James's son at all but had been smuggled into the royal bedchamber in a warming pan.

With the birth of the "warming-pan baby," events moved swiftly toward a climax. A delegation of Whigs and

**CHARLES II OF ENGLAND (r. 1660–1685) IN HIS CORONATION ROBES.** This full frontal portrait of the monarch, holding the symbols of his rule, seems to confront the viewer personally with overwhelming authority of the sovereign's gaze. Compare this classic image of the absolutist monarch with the very different portraits of William and Mary, who ruled after the Glorious Revolution of 1688 (page 504). ■ *What had changed between 1660, when Charles II came to the throne, and 1688, when the more popular William and Mary became the rulers of England?*

Tories crossed the channel to Holland to invite Mary Stuart and her Protestant husband, William of Orange, to cross to England with an invading army to preserve English Protestantism and English liberties by summoning a new Parliament. As the leader of a continental coalition, then at war with France, William also welcomed the opportunity to make England an ally against Louis XIV's expansionist foreign policy.

## The Glorious Revolution

Following William and Mary's invasion, James fled the country for exile in France. Parliament declared the throne vacant, clearing the way for William and Mary to succeed him as joint sovereigns. The Bill of Rights, passed by Parliament and accepted by the new king and queen in 1689, reaffirmed English civil liberties, such as trial by jury, *habeas corpus* (a guarantee that no one could be imprisoned unless charged with a crime), and the right to petition the monarch through Parliament. The Bill of Rights also declared that the monarchy was subject to the law of the land. The Act of Toleration also passed in 1689, granting Protestant dissenters the right to worship freely, though not to hold political office. And in 1701, the Act of Succession ordained that every future English monarch must be a member of the Church of England. Queen Mary died childless, and the throne passed from William to Mary's Protestant sister Anne (r. 1702–1714) and then to George, the elector of the German principality of Hanover and the Protestant great-grandson of James I. In 1707, the formal Act of Union between Scotland and England ensured that in the future, the Catholic heirs of King James II would have no more right to the throne of Scotland than they did to the throne of England.

The English soon referred to the events of 1688 and 1689 as the "Glorious Revolution," because it firmly established England as a mixed monarchy governed by the "king in Parliament" according to the rule of law. Although William and Mary and their successors continued to exercise a large measure of executive power, after 1688, no English monarch attempted to govern without Parliament, which has met annually from that time on. Parliament, and especially the House of Commons, also strengthened its control over taxation and expenditure. Although Parliament never codified the legal provisions of this form of monarchy into one constitutional document, historians consider the settlement of 1688 as a founding moment in the development of a constitutional monarchy in Britain.

Yet 1688 was not all glory. Contrary to many historical accounts, the revolution of 1688 was not "bloodless."

**WILLIAM AND MARY.** In 1688, William of Orange and his wife, Mary Stuart, became Protestant joint rulers of England in a coup that took power from her father, the Catholic James II. Compare this contemporary print with the portraits of Louis XIV (page 496) and Charles II (page 503). ■ *What relationship does this portrait seem to depict between the royal couple and their subjects?* ■ *What is the significance of the gathered crowd in the public square in the background?* ■ *How is this different from the spectacle of divine authority projected by Louis XIV or the image of Charles II looking straight at the viewer?*

The accession of William and Mary was accompanied by violence in many parts of England, Scotland, and Ireland. Angry Whigs attacked royal troops in York, Hull, Carlisle, Chester, and Portsmouth. James's revenue agencies were also attacked, as were his newly founded Catholic schools. Historians now see this violence as motivated as much by antiabsolutism as by religious bigotry. Popular anger against James II focused not so much on his defense of tradition but on his innovations, specifically his attempts to strengthen the power of the bureaucratic state. Furthermore, the revolution of 1688 consolidated the position of large property holders, whose control over local government had been threatened by the absolutist policies of Charles II and James II. It thus reinforced the power of a wealthy class of English elites in Parliament who would soon become even wealthier from government patronage and the profits of war. It also brought misery to the Catholic minority in Scotland and to the Catholic majority in Ireland. After 1690, when King William won a decisive victory over James II's forces at the Battle of the Boyne, power in Ireland would lie firmly in the hands of a "Protestant Ascendancy," whose dominance over Irish society would last until modern times.

At the same time, however, England's Glorious Revolution also established a climate that favored the growth and political power of the English commercial classes, especially the increasing number of people concentrated in English cities whose livelihood depended on international commerce in the Atlantic world and beyond. In the decades to come, trade became a political issue, and merchant's associations began to lobby Parliament for favorable legislation. Whigs in Parliament became the voice of this newly influential pressure group of commercial entrepreneurs, who sought to challenge the monopoly enjoyed by the East India Company (founded with a royal charter in 1600) and open up colonial trade to competitors. They also argued that royal charter companies discouraged English manufacture by importing cheaper goods from abroad. The Whigs also argued for revisions to the tax code that would benefit those engaged in manufacturing and trade, rather than the landed elites who had benefited from the tax regime under the Stuarts. In 1694, the Whigs succeeded in establishing the Bank of England, with the explicit goal of facilitating the promotion of English power through the generation of wealth, inaugurating a financial revolution that would make London the center of a vast network of international banking and investment in the eighteenth century.

**JOHN LOCKE (1632–1704).** Locke was an important foundational thinker in the liberal political tradition. He had a profound influence on the Glorious Revolution of 1688 in England, as well as on the American Revolution and the French political theory during the Enlightenment. His debate with Robert Filmer, a defender of absolutism, led him to elaborate a theory of government as a contract between the ruler and the ruled.

## John Locke and the Contract Theory of Government

The Glorious Revolution was the product of unique circumstances, but it also reflected antiabsolutist theories of politics that were taking shape in the late seventeenth century in response to the ideas of writers such as Bodin, Hobbes, Filmer, and Bossuet. Chief among these opponents of absolutism was the Englishman John Locke (1632–1704), whose *Two Treatises of Government* were written before the Glorious Revolution but published for the first time in 1690.

Locke maintained that humans had originally lived in a state of nature characterized by absolute freedom and equality, with no government of any kind. The only law was the law of nature (which Locke equated with the law of reason), by which individuals enforced for themselves their natural rights to life, liberty, and property. Soon, however, humans perceived that the inconveniences of the state of nature outweighed its advantages. Accordingly, they agreed

first to establish a civil society based on absolute equality, and then to set up a government to arbitrate the disputes that might arise within this civil society. But they did not make government's powers absolute. All powers not expressly surrendered to the government were reserved to the people themselves; as a result, governmental authority was both contractual and conditional. If a government exceeded or abused the authority granted to it, society had the right to dissolve it and create another.

Locke condemned absolutism in every form. He denounced absolute monarchy, but he was also critical of claims for the sovereignty of parliaments. Government, he argued, had been instituted to protect life, liberty, and property; no political authority could infringe these natural rights. The law of nature was therefore an automatic and absolute limitation on every branch of government.

In the late eighteenth century, Locke's ideas would resurface as part of the intellectual background of both the American and French Revolutions. Between 1690 and 1720, however, they served a far less radical purpose. The landed gentry who replaced James II with William and Mary read Locke as a defense of their conservative revolution. Rather than protecting their liberty and property,

James II had threatened both; hence, the magnates were entitled to overthrow the tyranny he had established and replace it with a government that would defend their interests by preserving these natural rights. English government after 1689 was dominated by Parliament; Parliament in turn was controlled by a landed aristocracy that was firm in the defense of its common interests, and that perpetuated its control by determining that only men possessed of substantial property could vote or run for office. During the beginning of the eighteenth century, then, both France and Britain had solved the problem of political dissent and social disorder in their own way. The emergence of a limited monarchy in England after 1688 contrasted vividly with the absolutist system developed by Louis XIV, but both systems, in fact, worked well enough to contain the threats to royal authority posed by powerful landed nobles and religious dissent.

## The Dutch Republic

Another exception to absolutist rule in Europe was the Dutch Republic of the United Provinces, which had gained its independence from Spanish rule in 1648, after a long period of struggle (see Chapter 14). The seven provinces of the Dutch Republic (also known as the Netherlands) carefully preserved their autonomy with a federal legislature known as the States General, made up of delegations from each province. Through this flexible structure, the inhabitants of the republic worked hard to prevent the reestablishment of hereditary monarchy in the Dutch Republic. They were all the more jealous of their independence because several Catholic provinces of the southern Low Countries, including present-day Belgium and Luxembourg, remained under Spanish control.

The princes of the House of Orange served the Dutch Republic with a special title, *stadtholder*, or steward. The stadtholder did not technically rule and had no power to make laws, though he did exercise some influence over the appointments of officials and military officers. Instead, powerful merchant families in the United Provinces exercised real authority, through their dominance of the legislature. It was from the Dutch Republic that the stadtholder William of Orange launched his successful bid to become the king of England in the Glorious Revolution of 1688.

The Dutch United Provinces were not, perhaps, the first place that one would choose as a base for a commercial trading empire. Much of the territory of the Dutch Republic was below sea level, and the water was kept out only by an elaborate system of dikes that protected the land from floods. But the Dutch made good use of their proximity to the sea. By 1670, the prosperity of the Dutch Republic was strongly linked to trade: grains and fish from eastern Europe and the Baltic Sea; spices, silks, porcelains, and tea from the Indian Ocean and Japan; and slaves, silver, coffee, sugar, and tobacco from the Atlantic world. With a population of nearly 2 million and a capital, Amsterdam, that was an international hub for goods and finance, the Dutch Republic's commercial network was global (see Chapter 14). Trade brought with it an extraordinary diversity of peoples and religions, as Spanish and Portuguese Jews, French Huguenots, English Quakers, and Protestant dissidents from central Europe all sought to take advantage of the relative spirit of toleration that existed in the Netherlands. This toleration did have limits, however. Jews were not required to live in segregated neighborhoods, as in many other European capitals, but they were prohibited from joining guilds or trade associations. Tensions between Calvinists and Catholics were a perennial issue, with Calvinists living in the western provinces and Catholics concentrated to the east and south.

The last quarter of the seventeenth century witnessed a decline in Dutch power, as the Low Countries were increasingly squeezed between the military strength and territorial ambitions of absolutist France to the south and competition from the maritime empire of the British in the Atlantic and Indian Oceans. The turning point came in 1672, when the French king, Louis XIV, put together a coalition that surrounded the United Provinces, threatening an invasion. The English took advantage of this moment of vulnerability to attack a major Dutch convoy returning from the eastern Mediterranean. Louis XIV invaded and quickly overran all but two of the Dutch provinces. Popular anger at the failures of Dutch leadership turned violent, and in response, the panicked assemblies named William of Orange the new stadtholder of Holland, giving him the power to organize the defense of the republic and quell internal dissent. William opened the dikes that held back the sea, and the French armies were forced to retreat in the face of rising waters. Soon after, the Spanish entered the war on the side of the Dutch, which caused Louis XIV to abandon his plans to conquer the United Provinces. After the Glorious Revolution of 1688 in England, which brought William of Orange to the English throne, the Dutch joined an alliance with the English against the French. This alliance protected the republic against further aggression from France, but it also forced the Dutch into heavy expenditures on fortifications and defense and involved them in a series of costly wars (see below). As a result, the dynamic and flexible political institutions that had been part of the strength of the Dutch Republic became more rigid and inflexible over time. Meanwhile, both the French and the British continued to pressure the Dutch commercial fleet at sea. In the eighteenth century, the Dutch no longer exercised the same influence abroad.

## The Polish-Lithuanian Commonwealth

The Commonwealth of Poland and Lithuania was a vast state that ruled over much of present-day Poland, Lithuania, Latvia, Estonia, Belarus, and Ukraine between 1569 and 1795. At its greatest extent, during the second decade of the seventeenth century, the Commonwealth reached from the Baltic coast nearly to the Black Sea. The kings of the Commonwealth allied themselves with Austria to challenge attempts by the Ottoman Empire to expand its control over the territory in southeastern Europe.

Unlike Austria, Prussia, France, and Russia, however, the Commonwealth had a tradition of limits to monarchical authority that make it an important exception to the trend toward absolutist rule in seventeenth-century Europe. Poland and Lithuania had been governed by a single ruler since 1386, and this personal connection between the two lands was given more formal status by the Union of Lublin in 1569. The political system of the Commonwealth was unusual in its commitment to a principle of representative institutions that could act as a check on the authority of the king. This makes the Commonwealth a striking early example of a central European state that committed itself to a separation of powers.

The limits to royal authority in Poland-Lithuania in the seventeenth and eighteenth centuries were largely enforced by the relatively numerous landowning gentry. These nobles elected members to seats in smaller provincial assemblies and in a parliament known as the Sejm. It was generally accepted by all that the king could not outfit an army or raise taxes without consulting the Sejm. In the seventeenth and eighteenth centuries, the Sejm consisted of two chambers, a smaller Senate with representatives of the Church and the State and the Chamber, which received representatives or envoys from each provincial assembly. The custom after 1569 was

for the Chamber and the Senate to meet for a six-week session at least every two years. When the king died, the Sejm supervised the process by which the landowning aristocracy elected a new ruler. Parliamentary authority was not at all complete, however, and the crown retained considerable power. One sixth of the land in the Commonwealth remained under the direct control of the king, and this gave him considerable economic wealth, which in turn increased his military authority and his ability to gain support through patronage.

This unusual balance of power between the landed gentry and the crown in the Commonwealth of Poland and Lithuania was exceptional in central and eastern Europe, but it also demonstrates that the most important dynamic influencing the development of state institutions during this period remained the relationship between the landed elites and dynastic rulers. In some European forms of government—the Restoration monarchy of England after 1688, the Dutch Republic, and the Polish-Lithuanian Commonwealth—circumstances allowed for greater power to remain in the hands of the gentry. In France, Prussia, and Russia (see below), on the other hand, absolutist rulers eventually succeeded in imposing their will on the aristocrats who remained their most powerful rivals for authority.

A. *The Present King in his Throne.*
BB. *The ten Crown Officers.*
C. *The A Bp. of Gnesna with y Cross born behind him.*
DDDD. *The other Ecclesiasticall Senators.*
EEEEE *Forreign Embassadors admitted only to y Diet of Election.*
FFFFFF. *The Palatins & Castellans in y three Rows on each side.*
GGGGGG. *The Deputys in the two back Rows on each side.*
H. *The Nuncio Marshall or Speaker of Deputys.*
IIII. *Vacant seats for such others as are sometimes admitted.*
1. *The Arms of Poland.*  2. *The Arms of Lithuania.*

**THE POLISH SEJM.** This was the representative body of the Polish-Lithuanian Commonwealth between 1569 and 1793, whose approval the king needed to pass legislation. Through most of its history it met for six weeks every two years, usually in Warsaw. Compare this with the Estates General in France, which did not meet at all between 1614 and 1789.

# WAR AND THE BALANCE OF POWER, 1661–1715

By the beginning of the eighteenth century, Europe was being reshaped by wars whose effects were also felt far beyond Europe's borders. The initial causes of these wars lay in the French monarch's efforts to challenge his main European rivals: the Habsburg powers in Spain, the Spanish Netherlands, and the Holy Roman Empire. Louis XIV's personal rule began in 1661 (he had come to the throne as a child in 1643), and he first invaded the Spanish Netherlands in 1667. Through his continued campaigns in the Low Countries, he expanded his territory, eventually taking Strasbourg (1681), Luxembourg (1684), and Cologne (1688). In response, William of Orange organized the League of Augsburg, which over time included Holland, England, Spain, Sweden, Bavaria, Saxony, the Rhine Palatinate, and the Austrian Habsburgs. The resulting Nine Years' War between France and the League extended from Ireland to India to North America (where it was known as King William's War), demonstrating the broadening imperial reach of European dynastic regimes and the increasing significance of French and English competition in the Atlantic world.

These wars were signs of both the heightening power of Europe's absolutist regimes and their growing vulnerability. Financing the increasingly costly wars of the eighteenth century would prove to be one of the central challenges faced by all of Europe's absolutist regimes, and the pressure to raise revenues from their subjects through taxation would eventually strain European society to a breaking point. By the end of the eighteenth century, popular unrest and political challenges to absolutist and imperial states were widespread, both on the European continent and in the colonies of the Atlantic world.

## From the League of Augsburg to the War of the Spanish Succession

The League of Augsburg reflected the emergence of a new diplomatic goal in western and central Europe: the preservation of a balance of power. This goal would animate European diplomacy for the next 200 years, until the balance-of-power system collapsed with the outbreak of the First World War. The main proponents of balance-of-power diplomacy were England, the United Provinces (Holland), Prussia, and Austria. By 1697, the League forced Louis XIV to make peace, because France was exhausted by war

and famine. Louis gave back many of his recent gains but kept Strasbourg and the surrounding territory of Alsace. In North America, the borders between French and English colonial territories remained unchanged for the time being (see below). Louis was nevertheless looking at the real prize: a French claim to succeed to the throne of Spain and so control the Spanish Empire in the Americas, Italy, the Netherlands, and the Philippines.

In the 1690s, it became clear that King Charles II of Spain (r. 1665–1700) would soon die without a clear heir, and both Louis XIV of France and Leopold I of Austria (r. 1658–1705) were interested in promoting their own relatives to succeed him. Either solution would have upset the balance of power in Europe, and several schemes to divide the Spanish realm between French and Austrian candidates were discussed. Meanwhile, King Charles II's advisers sought to avoid partition by passing the entire Spanish Empire to a single heir: Louis XIV's grandson Philip of Anjou. Philip was to renounce any claim to the French throne in becoming king of Spain, but these terms were kept secret. When Charles II died, Philip (r. 1700–1746) was proclaimed King Philip V of Spain, and Louis XIV rushed troops into the Spanish Netherlands while also sending French merchants into the Spanish Americas to end Spain's monopoly on trade from the region. Immediately the War of the Spanish Succession broke out, pitting England, the United Provinces, Austria, and Prussia against France, Bavaria, and Spain. Although the English king, William of Orange, died in 1702, just as the war was beginning, his generals led an extraordinary march deep into the European continent, inflicting a devastating defeat on the French and their Bavarian allies at Blenheim (1704). Soon after, the English captured Gibraltar, establishing a commercial foothold in the Mediterranean. The costs of the campaign nevertheless created a chorus of complaints from English and Dutch merchants, who feared the damage that was being done to trade and commerce. Queen Anne of England (Mary's sister and William's successor) gradually grew disillusioned with the war, and her government sent out peace feelers to France.

In 1713, the war finally came to an end with the Treaty of Utrecht. Its terms were reasonably fair to all sides. Philip V, Louis XIV's grandson, remained on the throne of Spain and retained Spain's colonial empire intact. In return, Louis agreed that France and Spain would never be united under the same ruler. Austria gained territories in the Spanish Netherlands and Italy, including Milan and Naples. The Dutch were guaranteed protection of their borders against future invasions by France, but the French retained both Lille and Strasbourg. The most significant consequences of the settlement, however, were played out in the Atlantic world, as the balance of powers among Europe's colonial empires underwent a profound shift.

## Imperial Rivalries after the Treaty of Utrecht

The fortunes of Europe's colonial empires changed dramatically owing to the wars of the late seventeenth and early eighteenth centuries. Habsburg Spain proved unable to defend its early monopoly over colonial trade, and by 1700, although Spain still possessed a substantial empire, it lay at the mercy of its more dynamic rivals. Portugal, too, found it impossible to prevent foreign penetration of its colonial empire. In 1703, the English signed a treaty with Portugal allowing English merchants to export woolens duty free into Portugal and allowing Portugal to ship its wines duty free into England. Access to Portugal also led British merchants to trade with the Portuguese colony of Brazil, an important sugar producer and the largest of all the American markets for African slaves.

The 1713 Treaty of Utrecht opened a new era of colonial rivalries. The French retained Québec and other territories in North America, as well as their small foothold in India. The biggest winner by far was Great Britain, as the combined kingdoms of England and Scotland were known after 1707. The British kept Gibraltar and Minorca in the Mediterranean and also acquired large chunks of French territory in the New World, including Newfoundland, mainland Nova Scotia, the Hudson Bay, and the Caribbean island of St. Kitts. Even more valuable, however, Britain also extracted from Spain the right to transport and sell African slaves in Spanish America. As a result, the British were now poised to become the principal slave merchants and the dominant colonial and commercial power of the eighteenth-century world.

The Treaty of Utrecht thus reshaped the balance of power in the Atlantic world in fundamental ways. Spain's collapse was already precipitous, and by 1713, it was complete. Spain would remain the "sick man of Europe" for the next two centuries. The Dutch decline was more gradual, but by 1713, Dutch merchants' inability to compete with the British in the slave trade diminished their economic clout. In the Atlantic, Britain and France were now the dominant powers. Although they would duel for another half century for control of North America, the balance of colonial power tilted decisively in Britain's favor after Utrecht. Within Europe, the myth of French military supremacy had been shattered. Britain's navy, not France's army, would rule the new imperial and commercial world of the eighteenth century.

**THE TREATY OF UTRECHT, 1713.** This illustration from a French royal almanac depicts the treaty that ended the War of Spanish Succession and reshaped the balance of power in western Europe in favor of Britain and France.

# THE REMAKING OF CENTRAL AND EASTERN EUROPE

The decades between 1680 and 1720 also were decisive in reshaping the balance of power in central and eastern Europe. As Ottoman power waned, the Austro-Hungarian Empire of the Habsburgs emerged as the dominant power in central and southeastern Europe. To the north, Brandenburg-Prussia was also a rising power. The most dramatic changes, however, occurred in Russia, which emerged from a long war with Sweden as the dominant power in the Baltic Sea and would soon threaten the combined kingdom of Poland-Lithuania. Within these regimes, the main tension

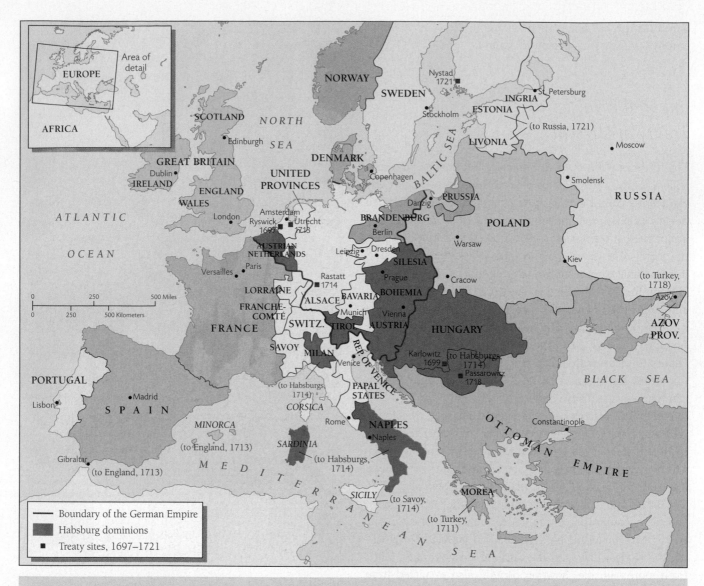

**EUROPE AFTER THE TREATY OF UTRECHT (1713).** ▪ *What were the major Habsburg dominions?* ▪ *What geographical disadvantage faced the kingdom of Poland as Brandenburg-Prussia grew in influence and ambition?* ▪ *How did the balance of power change in Europe as a result of the Treaty of Utrecht?*

came from ambitious monarchs who sought to increase the power of the centralized state at the expense of other elites, especially aristocrats and the Church. In Brandenburg-Prussia and in tsarist Russia, these efforts were largely successful, whereas in Habsburg Austria, regional nobilities retained much of their influence.

## The Austrian Habsburg Empire

In the second half of the seventeenth century, as Louis XIV of France demonstrated the power of absolutism in western Europe, the Austrian Habsburg Empire, with its capital in Vienna, must have seemed increasingly like a holdover from a previous age. Habsburg Austria was the largest state within what remained of the medieval Holy Roman Empire, a complex federal association of nearly 300 nominally autonomous dynastic kingdoms, principalities, duchies, and archbishoprics that had been created to protect and defend the papacy. Some, such as the kingdom of Bavaria, were large and had their own standing armies. Each Holy Roman emperor was chosen by seven "electors" who were either of noble rank or archbishops—in practice, the emperor was always from the Habsburg family. Through strategic marriages with other royal lines, earlier generations of Habsburg rulers had consolidated their control over a substantial part of Europe, including Austria, Bohemia, Moravia, and Hungary in central Europe; the Netherlands and Burgundy in the west; and, if one included the Spanish branch of the Habsburg family, Spain and its vast colonial empire as well. After 1648, when the Treaty of Westphalia granted individual member states within the Holy Roman Empire the right to conduct their own foreign policy, the influence of the Austrian Habsburgs waned, at precisely the moment when they faced challenges from France to the west and the Ottoman Empire to the east.

The complicated structure of the Holy Roman Empire limited the extent to which a ruler such as Leopold I of Austria could emulate the absolutist rule of Louis XIV in France. Every constituent state within the empire had its own local political institutions and its own entrenched nobilities, each with a strong interest in resisting any attempt to centralize crucial functions of government, such as taxation or the raising of armies. Even if direct assertion of absolutist control was impossible, Habsburg rulers found ways of increasing their authority. In Bohemia and Moravia, the Habsburgs encouraged landlords to produce crops for export by forcing peasants to provide three days of unpaid work per week to their lords. In return, the landed elites of these territories permitted the emperors to reduce the political independence of their traditional legislative estates. In Hungary, however, the powerful and independent nobility resisted such compromises. In 1679, when the Habsburgs began a campaign against Hungarian Protestants, an insurrection broke out that forced Leopold to grant concessions to Hungarian nobles in exchange for their assistance in restoring order. When the Ottoman Empire sought to take advantage of this disorder to press an attack against Austria from the east, the Habsburgs survived only by enlisting the help of a Catholic coalition led by the Polish king John Sobieski (r. 1674–1696).

In 1683, the Ottomans launched their last assault on Vienna, but after their failure to capture the Habsburg capital, Ottoman power in southeastern Europe declined. By 1699, Austria had reconquered most of Hungary from the Ottomans, and by 1718, it controlled all of Hungary and also Transylvania and Serbia. With these victories, Austria became one of the arbiters of the European balance of power. The same obstacles to the development of centralized absolutist rule persisted, however, and Austria was increasingly overshadowed in central Europe by the rise of another German-speaking state: Prussia.

## The Rise of Brandenburg-Prussia

After the Ottoman defeat, the main threat to Austria came from the rising power of Brandenburg-Prussia. Like Austria, Prussia was a composite state made up of several geographically divided territories acquired through inheritance by a single royal family, the Hohenzollerns. Their two main holdings were Brandenburg, centered on its capital city, Berlin, and the duchy of East Prussia. Between these two territories lay Pomerania (claimed by Sweden) and an important part of the kingdom of Poland, including the port of Gdansk (Danzig). The Hohenzollerns' aim was to unite their state by acquiring these intervening territories. Over the course of more than a century of steady state building, they finally succeeded. In the process, Brandenburg-Prussia became a dominant military power and a key player in the balance-of-power diplomacy of the mid-eighteenth century.

The foundations for Prussian expansion were laid by Frederick William, the "Great Elector" (r. 1640–1688). He

**PRUSSIANS SWEARING ALLEGIANCE TO THE GREAT ELECTOR AT KÖNIGSBERG, 1663.** On this occasion, the Prussian estates first acknowledged the overlordship of their ruler. This ceremony marked the beginning of the centralization of the Prussian state.

# Analyzing Primary Sources

## The Siege of Vienna (1683)

*In 1683, the armies of the Ottoman Empire besieged the city of Vienna, the capital of the Austrian Habsburg monarchy, which was defended by forces of the Holy Roman Empire of the German Nations, led by King John III Sobieski of the Polish-Lithuanian Commonwealth. The battle marked the high point of Ottoman expansion into southeastern Europe, and the Ottoman defeat was celebrated by many in Europe as a victory of Christianity over Islam. The reality was more complicated, however, as Protestant armies in Hungary allied with anti-Habsburg forces had received arms and support from the Ottoman Empire in the years before the battle, apparently in exchange for a promise that Hungary would control Vienna in the event of an Ottoman victory. This source, published in 1684 in English in Cologne and London, contains enough details to allow one to assume that it was, at least in part, informed by eyewitnesses of the events.*

### Emperor Leopold I Flees Vienna for Passau

The Emperor who had receiv'd a fierce alarm by the suddain irruption of the Infidels, and who consider'd that after the revolt of the Hungarians, he could no longer remain at Vienna in surety, bethought himself at the same time of leaving it. But first augmented the privileges of the Scholars, which were already very great, and considerable, that having receiv'd them as a recompence of their Courage which they shew'd heretofore against Solyman [the Ottoman Emperor Suleiman the Magnificent], when he besieg'd the City [in 1529] this should be a fresh incitement to defend it with the same resolution. He gave also to the Shoomakers Apprentices their Freedom, who were to the number of about 1500, in case they took Arms, and did any thing considerable for the Country.

\* \* \*

Every one wept at his departure, and this Prince had much ado to forbear himself. So greatly was he afflicted to be thus constrained to abandon his people to the mercy of the Infidels. In the mean time each one endeavor'd to follow him, to avoid the being expos'd to those mischiefs which they represented. In fine, there being not Coaches enough to carry all those that offer'd 'emselves, several Women of Quality got behind like Lacques [servants]; so that one might have seen the first Prince in the World, follow'd by all the flower of the German Nobility, to go as an exul [exile] amidst the screeches and lamentations of his people, who presented 'emselves in his passage with showr's of tears...

\* \* \*

The Emperor all this while marched with a countenance sad and dejected like his fortune. Others kept a mournful silence, and although each had left their estates behind 'em 'twas not known whether their own mishap or that of the Prince was to be most lamented. In fine, this march much resembled a Funeral Pomp, when another spectacle encreas'd the dolour and compassion. For they beheld the other side of the *Danube* all in fire, and the Emperor having caused his Coach to stop, knowing not at first what it was, soon perceived 'twas the *Turks*, who shew'd there new testimonies of their barbarous cruelty. He could not withhold his tears at the sight of a thing so much needing his compassion, and although he did all he could to refrain his grief, he could not effect it.

### Disease Afflicts the Defenders of Vienna

And having made his retreat, and taken great care of the wounded, [Stahrenberg, the military commander of Vienna] made a review of those Forces he had left him; which he found diminish'd by a third part, not so much by Sallies, and in this last occasion, as by the Dysentery or Flux which began to rage in the Town, as well amongst the Citizens and Soldiers. In effect the fatigues together with the bad food they eat, had so heated the bloud of most of 'em, that they fell sick every day. And it being impossible for 'em after this to do service, the rest, whose weariness increased as fast as the number of the others dimnish'd, were soon in the same condition, or at least so tir'd out with labour and watching, that they were all ready to drop down as they march'd....

\* \* \*

But that which contributed to render this malady more incurable was the Airs being so infected by the stench of the dead Bodies which lay unburied, that it could not be more dangerous in a time of Plague. The cause of this stench was that Stahrenberg would not yield to any terms of a Truce propos'd by the Visier

[Vizier], to take away those of his party, who had been kild in so many several skirmishes, hoping that besides the displeasure he would receive thereby, this would be a spectacle to damp the Courage of the Soldiers, when in marching up to the Charge, they should see before their Eyes the fortune of their Companions, which would be a presage to them of the like. Howsoever whether 'twas this infection or something else, which brought this grievous sickness into the Town, they were so greatly incommodated [sic] by it, that they would willingly have been deliver'd from of it at the cost of a greater danger from the enemy. Yet did this distemper rage as well in the Camp of the Turks, of which there dyed every day near 300, but which was scarce perceivable, because they continually receiv'd fresh supplies, which made up their losses.

Source: Anonymous, *The History of the late war with the Turks, during the siege of Vienna, and the great victory obtain'd against them at the raising the siege* (Cologne and London, 1684), pp. 33–86.

## Questions for Analysis

1. How did Emperor Leopold encourage the people of the city to defend themselves even as he retreated to a safer location?

2. What is the significance of the term *Infidels*, which the author uses to describe the Ottomans?

3. What does this description tell us about the effects of the siege on military and civilian populations? What explanations does the author give for the spread of disease in the city and among the attacking armies?

---

obtained East Prussia from Poland in exchange for help in a war against Sweden. Behind the elector's diplomatic triumphs lay his success in building an army and mobilizing the resources to pay for it. He gave the powerful nobles of his territories, known as "Junkers" (*YUN-kurs*), the right to enserf their peasants and guaranteed immunity from taxation. In exchange, they staffed the officer corps of his army and supported his highly autocratic taxation system. Secure in their estates and made increasingly wealthy in the grain trade, the Junkers surrendered management of the Prussian state to the elector's newly reformed bureaucracy, which set about its main task of increasing the size and strength of the Prussian army.

By supporting Austria in the War of the Spanish Succession, the Great Elector's son, Frederick I (r. 1688–1713) earned the right to call himself king of Prussia from the Austrian emperor. He too was a crafty diplomat, but his main attention was devoted to developing the cultural life of his new royal capital, Berlin. His son, Frederick William I (r. 1713–1740), however, focused on building the army like his grandfather. During his reign, the Prussian army grew from 30,000 to 83,000 men, becoming the fourth largest army in Europe, after those of France, Austria, and Russia. To support his army, Frederick William I increased taxes and shunned the luxuries of court life. For him, the theater of absolutism was not the palace but the office, where he personally supervised his army and the growing bureaucracy that sustained it. Frederick William's son, known as Frederick the Great, would use this Prussian army and the bureaucracy that sustained it to transform the kingdom into a major power in central Europe after 1740 (see Chapter 17).

Thus, in both Prussia and Habsburg Austria, the divided nature of the respective realms and the entrenched strength of local nobilities forced the rulers of each to grant significant concessions to noble landowners in exchange for incremental increases in the power of the centralized state. Whereas the nobility in France increasingly sought to maximize their power by participating in the system of absolutist rule at the court of Louis XIV, and wealthy landowners in England sought to exercise their influence through Parliament, the nobilities of Prussia and Habsburg Austria had more leverage to demand something in return for their cooperation. Often, what they demanded was the right to enserf or coerce labor from the peasantry in their domains. In both eastern and western Europe, therefore, the state became stronger. In eastern Europe, however, this increase in state power often came at the expense of an intensification of feudal obligations that the peasantry owed to their local lords.

**THE CITY OF STETTIN UNDER SIEGE BY THE GREAT ELECTOR FREDERICK WILLIAM IN THE WINTER OF 1677–1678 (c. 1680).** This painting depicts the growing sophistication and organization of military operations under the Prussian monarchy. Improvements in artillery and siege tactics forced cities to adopt new defensive strategies, especially the zones of battlements and protective walls that became ubiquitous in central Europe during this period. ▪ *How might these defensive developments have shaped the layout of Europe's growing towns and cities?* ▪ *How might this emphasis on the military and its attendant bureaucracy have affected the relationship between the monarchy and the nobility, or between the king and his subjects?*

into contact with western Europe, but his policies were decisive in making Russia a great European power.

## The Early Years of Peter's Reign

Like Louis XIV of France, Peter came to the throne as a young boy, and his minority was marked by political dissension and court intrigue. In 1689, however, at the age of seventeen, he overthrew the regency of his half sister Sophia and assumed personal control of the state. Determined to make Russia into a great military power, the young tsar traveled to Holland and England during the 1690s to study shipbuilding and to recruit skilled foreign workers to help him build a navy. But while he was abroad, his elite palace guard (the *streltsy*) rebelled, attempting to restore Sophia to the throne. Peter quickly returned home from Vienna and crushed the rebellion with striking savagery. About 1,200 suspected conspirators were summarily executed, many of them gibbeted outside the walls of the Kremlin, where their bodies rotted for months as a graphic reminder of the fate awaiting those who dared challenge the tsar's authority.

## AUTOCRACY IN RUSSIA

An even more dramatic transformation took place in Russia under Tsar Peter I (r. 1672–1725). Peter's official title was "autocrat of all the Russias," but he was soon known as Peter the Great. His imposing height (six feet eight inches) and his mercurial personality (jesting one moment, raging the next) added to the outsize impression he made on his contemporaries. Peter is most remembered for his controversial efforts to make Russians emulate aspects of western European culture he admired. He demanded that the aristocracy shave their beards and adopt Western forms of etiquette, and called upon them to educate themselves and read books from abroad. To showcase his ambitions he built a modern capital city, St. Petersburg, along western European lines, and asserted control over the Russian Orthodox Church. Peter was not the first tsar to bring his country

## The Transformation of the Tsarist State

Peter is most famous as the tsar who attempted to westernize Russia by imposing a series of social and cultural reforms on the traditional Russian nobility: ordering noblemen to cut off their long beards and flowing sleeves; publishing a book of manners that forbade spitting on the floor and eating with one's fingers; encouraging polite conversation between the sexes; and requiring noblewomen to appear, together with men, in Western garb at weddings, banquets, and other public occasions. The children of Russian nobles were sent to western European courts for their education. Thousands of western European

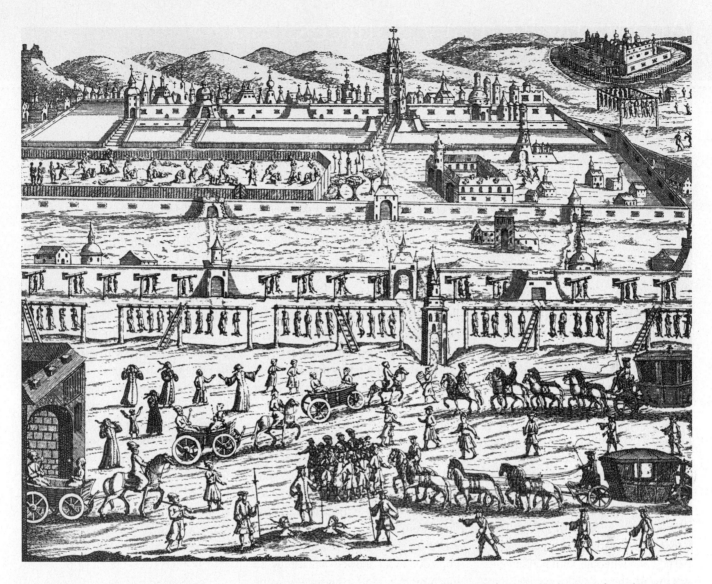

**EXECUTION OF THE STRELTSY (1698).** A contemporary woodcut showing how Peter the Great ordered the public hanging of guard regiments who rebelled against his authority. How does this display of autocratic power compare with the spectacle of power so carefully orchestrated by Peter's contemporary Louis XIV of France?

experts were brought to Russia to staff the new schools and academies Peter built; to design the new buildings he constructed; and to serve in the tsar's army, navy, and administration.

These measures were important, but the tsar was not motivated primarily by a desire to modernize or westernize Russia. Peter's policies transformed Russian life in fundamental ways, but his real goal was to make Russia a great military power, not to remake Russian society. For example, while his new taxation system (1724), which assessed taxes on individuals rather than on households, rendered many of the traditional divisions of Russian peasant society obsolete, it was created to raise more

money for war. His Table of Ranks, imposed in 1722, had similar impact on the nobility. By insisting that all nobles must work their way up from the (lower) landlord class to the (higher) administrative class and to the (highest) military class, Peter reversed the traditional hierarchy of Russian noble society, which had valued landlords by birth above administrators and soldiers who had risen by merit. This created a powerful new incentive to lure his nobility into administrative and military service to the tsar.

As "autocrat of all the Russias," Peter the Great was the absolute master of his empire to a degree unmatched elsewhere in Europe. After 1649, Russian peasants were legally

## The Revolt of the Streltsy and Peter the Great

*The streltsy were four regiments of Moscow guards that became involved in a conspiracy in support of Peter the Great's older sister Sophia, who had earlier made claim to the throne while Peter was still a child. Approximately 4,000 of the rebels were defeated in June 1698 by troops loyal to Peter. Peter himself was abroad during the fighting, and although his officers had already tortured many of the streltsy to determine the involvement of other nobles, he ordered a more far-reaching investigation on his return. Over 1,000 of the streltsy were executed after being tortured again. Afterward, their bodies were put on display in the capital. Johann Georg Korb, an Austrian diplomat in Moscow, recorded his observations of the power wielded by the Russian autocrat.*

 ow sharp was the pain, how great the indignation to which the Czar's Majesty was mightily moved, when he knew of the rebellion of the Strelitz [*streltsy*], betrayed openly a mind panting for vengeance. [*sic*] . . . Going immediately to Lefort (the only person almost that he condescended to treat with intimate familiarity), he thus indignantly broke out: "Tell me, Francis, son of James, how I can reach Moscow, by the shortest way, in a brief space, so that I may wreak vengeance on this great perfidy of my people, with punishments worthy of their flagitious crime. Not one of them shall escape with impunity. Around my royal city, of which, with their impious efforts, they meditated the destruction, I will have gibbets and gallows set upon the walls and ramparts, and each and every of them will I put to a direful death." . . .

His first anxiety, after his arrival [in Moscow] was about the rebellion. In what it consisted? What the insurgents meant? Who had dared to instigate such a crime? And as nobody could answer accurately upon all points, and some pleaded their own ignorance, others the obstinacy of the Strelitz, he began to have suspicions of everybody's loyalty, and began to cogitate about a fresh investigation. The rebels that were kept in custody . . . were all brought in by four regiments of the guards, to a fresh investigation and fresh tortures. Prison, tribunal, and rack, for those that were brought in, was in Bebraschentsko. No day, holy, or profane, were the inquisitors idle; every day was deemed fit and lawful for torturing. As many as there were accused there were knouts, and every inquisitor was a butcher. Prince Feodor Jurowicz Romadonowski showed himself by so much more fitted for his inquiry, as he surpassed the rest in cruelty. He put the interrogatories, he examined the criminals, he urged those that were not confessing, he ordered such Strelitz as were more pertinaciously silent, to be subjected to more cruel tortures; those that had already confessed about many things were questioned about more; those who were bereft of strength and reason, and almost of their senses, by excess of torment, were handed over to the skill of the doctors, who were compelled to restore them to strength, in order that they might be broken down by fresh excruciations. The whole month of October was spent in butchering the backs of the culprits with knout and with flames: no day were those that were left alive exempt from scourging or scorching, or else they were broken upon the wheel, or driven to the gibbet, or slain with the axe—the penalties which were inflicted upon them as soon as their confessions had sufficiently revealed the heads of the rebellion.

Source: Johann Georg Korb, *Diary of an Austrian Secretary of Legation at the Court of Czar Peter the Great*, trans. Count MacDonnell (London: 1863), vol. 2, pp. 85–87.

### Questions for Analysis

*1.* Why was it important for Korb to begin this account with a description of the monarch's pain?

*2.* What does this episode reveal about Peter's conception of his own person and of the loyalty that his subjects owed him? Does it show that his power was fragile, immense, or both?

*3.* What does it mean to describe torture as an "investigation" even while also describing it as "vengeance"?

**PETER THE GREAT CUTS THE BEARD OF AN OLD BELIEVER.**
This woodcut depicts the Russian emperor's enthusiastic policy of westernization, as he pushed everybody in Russia who was not a peasant to adopt western styles of clothes and grooming. The Old Believer (a member of a religious sect in Russia) protests that he has paid the beard tax and should therefore be exempt. ■ *Why would an individual's choices about personal appearance be so politically significant in Peter's Russia?* ■ *What customs were the target of Peter's reforms?*

the property of their landlords; by 1750, half were serfs and the other half were state peasants who lived on lands owned by the tsar himself. (In contrast, many peasants in western Europe owned their own land, and very few were serfs.) State peasants could be conscripted to serve as soldiers in the tsar's army, as workers in his factories (whose productive capacity increased enormously during Peter's reign), or as forced laborers in his building projects. Serfs could also be taxed by the tsar and summoned for military service, as could their lords. All Russians, of whatever rank, were expected to serve the tsar, and all Russia was considered in some sense to belong to him. Russia's autocracy thus went even further than the absolutism of Louis XIV.

To consolidate his power further, Peter replaced the Duma—the tsar's handpicked council of noble elites—with a smaller handpicked senate, a group of nine administrators who supervised military and civilian affairs. In religious matters, he took direct control over the Russian Orthodox Church by appointing an imperial official to manage its affairs. To cope with the demands of war, he also fashioned a new, larger, and more efficient administration, for which he recruited both nobles and non-nobles. The rank in the new bureaucracy did not depend on birth. One of his principal advisers, Alexander Menshikov, began his career as a cook and finished as a prince. This degree of social mobility would have been impossible in any contemporary western European country. In Russia, more so than in western Europe, noble status depended on government service, with all nobles expected to participate in Peter's army or administration. Peter was not entirely successful in enforcing this requirement, but the administrative machinery he devised furnished Russia with its ruling class for the next 200 years.

## Russian Imperial Expansion

The goal of Peter's foreign policy was to secure year-round ports for Russia on the Black Sea and the Baltic Sea. In the Black Sea, his enemy was the Ottoman Empire. Here, however, he had little success, and Russia would not secure its position in the Black Sea until the end of the eighteenth century. Nevertheless, Peter continued to push against the Ottoman Empire in the North Caucasus region throughout his reign. This mountainous area on Russia's southern flank became an important site for Russia's experiments in colonial expansion into central Asia, which began during the sixteenth century and would later mirror the process of colonial conquest undertaken by European powers and the United States in North and South America. Like those of France and Britain, the Russian state bureaucracy was built during a period of ambitious colonialism; and as in Spain, the monarchy's identity was shaped by a long contest with Muslim power on its borders.

Since the late sixteenth century, successive Russian leaders had extended their control over bordering territories of central Asia. Although merchants helped fund early expeditions into Siberia, this expansion was primarily motivated by geopolitical concerns; the tsar sought to gain access to the populations of Russia's border areas and bring them into the service of the expanding Russian state. In this sense, Russian colonialism during this period differed from western European expansion into the Atlantic world, which had primarily been motivated by hopes of commercial gain.

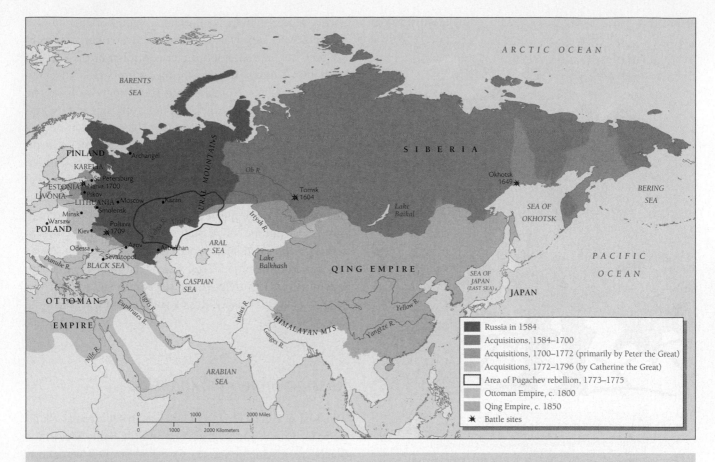

**THE GROWTH OF THE RUSSIAN EMPIRE.** ▪ *How did Peter the Great expand the territory controlled by Russia?* ▪ *What neighboring dynasties were most affected by Russian expansion?* ▪ *How did the emergence of a bigger, more powerful Russia affect the European balance of power?*

In its early stages, as successive Russian emperors moved Russian troops eastward into Asia, they relied on a process of indirect rule, often seeking to co-opt local elites. Later in the eighteenth century, they had more success settling Russians in border regions to rule directly over local populations. Religion also provided a cover for expansion, and Peter and his successors funded missionary work by Georgian Christians among Muslims in the Caucasus. Efforts to convert Muslim populations to Orthodox Christianity had little effect, and in fact the opposite occurred: the region's commitment to Islam was continuously renewed through contact with different strains of Islamic practice coming from neighboring Ottoman lands and Persia.

Peter could point to more concrete success to the north. In 1700, he began what would become a twenty-one-year war with Sweden, then the dominant power in the Baltic Sea. By 1703, Peter had secured a foothold on the Gulf of Finland and immediately began to build a new capital

city there, which he named St. Petersburg. For Peter, the new capital became a vehicle for his drive for international recognition: seen primarily as a naval port and a bulwark against the Swedish at first, it became a model for what he believed Russia could become.

After 1709, when Russian armies decisively defeated the Swedes at the battle of Poltava, work on Peter's new capital city accelerated. An army of serfs was now conscripted to build the new city, whose centerpiece was a royal palace designed to imitate and rival Louis XIV's Versailles. Conditions for the laborers were grueling and deaths were frequent. Peter's elaborate building sites required armed guards to maintain order. He insisted on western designs for all the buildings in the new city, and in 1714, he forced one thousand aristocrats to move into the new capital with their families, ignoring their protests. In the end, Peter's model city was equipped with remarkable amenities: street lighting, regular waste collection, and a fire brigade.

But resentment at his autocratic methods remained for generations afterwards.

The Great Northern War with Sweden ended in 1721 with the Peace of Nystad. This treaty marked a realignment of power in eastern Europe comparable with that effected by the Treaty of Utrecht in the West. Sweden lost its North Sea territories to Hanover, its Baltic German territories to Prussia, and its eastern territories, including the entire Gulf of Finland, Livonia, and Estonia, passed to Russia. Sweden was now a second-rank power in the northern European world. Poland-Lithuania survived, but it too was a declining power; by the end of the eighteenth century, this kingdom would disappear altogether, its territories swallowed up by its more powerful neighbors (see Chapter 17). The victors at Nystad were the Prussians and the Russians. These two powers secured their position along the Baltic coast, positioning themselves to take advantage of the lucrative eastern European grain trade with western Europe. Peter's accomplishments came at enormous cost. Direct taxation in Russia increased 500 percent during his reign, and in the 1720s, his army numbered more than 300,000 men. Peter made Russia a force to be reckoned with on the European scene, but in so doing, he aroused great resentment, especially among his nobility. Peter's only son and heir, Alexis, became the focus for conspiracies against the tsar, until finally Peter had him arrested and executed in 1718. As a result, when Peter died in 1725, he left no son to succeed him. A series of ineffective tsars followed, mostly from the palace guard; under these rules, the resentful nobles reversed many of Peter the Great's reforms. In 1762, however, the crown passed to Catherine the Great, a ruler whose ambitions and determination were equal to those of her great predecessor (see Chapter 17).

# CONCLUSION

By the time of Peter the Great's death in Russia in 1725, the power of Europe's absolutist realms to reinvigorate European political institutions was visible to all. Government had become more bureaucratic; state service had been more professionalized; and administrators loyal to the kings had become more numerous, more efficient, and more demanding. Despite the increasing scope of government, the structure and principles of government changed relatively little. Apart from Great Britain, the Dutch Republic, and Poland-Lithuania, the great powers of eighteenth-century Europe were still governed by rulers who styled themselves as absolutist monarchs in the mold of Louis XIV, who claimed an authority that came directly from God and ruled over a society in which social hierarchies based on birth were taken for granted.

However, these absolutist regimes could not hide the fact that their rule depended on a kind of negotiated settlement with other powerful elites within European society, in particular with landed aristocrats and religious leaders. Louis XIV used his power to curb the worst excesses of nobles who abused their position, and to defend Catholic orthodoxy against dissident Catholics and Protestants. Nevertheless, his power depended on a delicate exchange of favors: French aristocrats surrendered their political authority to the state in exchange for social and legal privileges and immunity from many (but not all) forms of taxation, and the Church made a similar bargain. Peter the Great's autocratic rule in Russia worked out a slightly different balance of powers between his state and the Russian aristocracy, one that tied aristocrats more closely to an ideal of state service, a model that also worked well for the rulers of Brandenburg-Prussia. Even in England, the establishment of a limited constitutional monarchy and a king who ruled alongside Parliament was not really a radical departure from the European absolutist model. It was merely a different institutional answer to the same problem: What relationship should the monarchical state have with other elites within society?

The demands of state building during this period required kings to raise enormous revenues—for the sumptuous displays of their sovereignty in royal residences such as Louis XIV's palace at Versailles, for the sponsorship of royal academies and the patronage of artists, but most of all, for war. Expanding territory within Europe and holding on to colonial empires in the Atlantic world were costly. Distributing the burden of taxation to pay for these endeavors became an intensely fraught political issue for European monarchs during this period, and the financing of royal debt became an increasingly sophisticated art. Colbert's mercantilist policy was an attempt to harness the full power of the economy for the benefit of royal government; and the competition among Spain, Holland, England, and France to control the revenue flows coming from the Atlantic world forced Europe's monarchs to recognize that the balance of power was increasingly being played out on a global stage.

These themes—the expansion of state powers; conflicts between the monarchy and the aristocracy or with religious dissidents; the intensification of the tax burden on the population; and the opening up of Europe to ever more frequent interactions with other peoples in the Atlantic world, the Indian Ocean, and eventually, the Pacific—prompted many in eighteenth-century Europe to reflect on the consequences of these developments. What were the limits to state power, and by what criteria were the actions of rulers to be judged? What was the proper measure of economic prosperity, and who was it for? Could a well-ordered society tolerate religious diversity? Given Europe's growing awareness of cultures in other parts of the world with different religions, different political systems, and different ways of expressing their moral and ethical values, how might Europeans justify or measure their own beliefs and customs? The intellectuals who looked for answers to these questions were similar to earlier generations of

# After You Read This Chapter

🐛 Go to **INQUIZITIVE** to see what you've learned—and learn what you've missed—with personalized feedback along the way.

## REVIEWING THE OBJECTIVES

- Absolutist rulers claimed a monopoly of power and authority within their realms. What was absolutism? Who were the most successful absolutist monarchs?

- Mercantilism was an economic doctrine that guided the policies of absolutist rulers. What did mercantilists believe?

- Alternatives to absolutist government emerged in England, Holland, and Poland-Lithuania. What forms of government did these regimes develop? How did they differ from the absolutist and autocratic regimes of France, Prussia, and Russia?

- The wars begun by Louis XIV after 1680 drove his opponents to ally with each other to achieve a balance of power. What was the result of these conflicts in Europe and in the Atlantic world?

- Peter the Great embarked on an ambitious program of reform and territorial expansion in Russia. How did his autocratic government compare with absolutist regimes in western and central Europe?

scientific researchers in their respect for reason and rational thought, but they turned their attention beyond problems of natural philosophy and science to the messy world of politics and culture. Their movement—known as the Enlightenment—reached its peak in the middle decades of the eighteenth century and created the basis for a powerful critique of Europe's absolutist regimes. The Enlightenment itself emerged slowly from a revolution in scientific thinking that had begun earlier in the early modern period, and it is to this history that we now turn.

## PEOPLE, IDEAS, AND EVENTS IN CONTEXT

- What did **LOUIS XIV** of France and **PETER THE GREAT** of Russia have in common? How did they deal with those who resisted their attempts to impose absolutist rule?

- Compare the religious policies of **LOUIS XIV** of France with the religious policies of the English Stuart kings **CHARLES II** and **JAMES II**. In what way did religious disagreements limit their ability to rule effectively?

- How did European monarchies apply the economic theory known as **MERCANTILISM** to strengthen the power and wealth of their kingdoms? How did this theory influence **FRENCH COLONIALISM**?

- What was the **CONTRACT THEORY OF GOVERNMENT** according to the English political thinker **JOHN LOCKE**?

- What limits to royal power were recognized in Great Britain as a result of the **GLORIOUS REVOLUTION**?

- What was significant about the new **BALANCE OF POWER** that developed in Europe as a result of **LOUIS XIV**'s wars?

- What does the **TREATY OF UTRECHT** (1713) tell us about the diminished influence of Spain and the corresponding rise of Britain and France as European and colonial powers?

- What was different about the attempts by rulers in Habsburg Austria and Brandenburg-Prussia to impose **ABSOLUTISM** in central Europe?

- What innovations did **PETER THE GREAT** bring to Russia?

## THINKING ABOUT CONNECTIONS

- What makes absolutism different from older models of kingship in earlier periods?

- Was the absolutist monarchs' emphasis on sumptuous displays of their authority something new? Explain how the display of power under absolutism is different from the way that political power is represented in democratic societies today.

## STORY LINES

- After about 1550, new sciences in Europe questioned older beliefs about the physical universe. New methods of inquiry led to the development of astronomy, physics, biology, chemistry, geology, and new institutions that supported scientific research and education.

- The scientific revolution gave rise to theoretical breakthroughs in explaining the physical universe as well as advances in the practical knowledge of artisans who built mechanical devices such as telescopes or microscopes. This combination of scientific inquisitiveness and craft techniques encouraged technological developments that would later be useful in industrialization.

- The new sciences did not mark a clean rupture with older traditions of religious thinking. Most scientists of the 1600s remained essentially religious in their worldview. In any case, their work was accessible only to a small, literate minority who had access to books.

## CHRONOLOGY

| | |
|---|---|
| 1543 | Nicolaus Copernicus (1473–1543) publishes *On the Revolutions of the Heavenly Spheres* |
| 1576 | Tycho Brahe sets up Uraniborg observatory |
| 1609 | Johannes Kepler (1571–1643) publishes *Astronomia Nova* |
| 1610 | Galileo (1564–1642) publishes *The Starry Messenger* |
| 1620 | Francis Bacon (1561–1626) publishes *Novum Organum* |
| 1632 | Galileo publishes *Dialogue Concerning the Two Chief World Systems* |
| 1633 | Galileo's trial |
| 1637 | René Descartes (1596–1650) publishes *Discourse on Method* |
| 1660 | Royal Society of London founded |
| 1666 | French Academy of Sciences founded |
| 1687 | Isaac Newton (1642–1727) publishes *Principia Mathematica* |

Before
You
Read
This
Chapter

# The New Science of the Seventeenth Century

*Doubt thou the stars are fire,*
*Doubt that the sun doth move,*
*Doubt truth to be a liar,*
*But never doubt I love.*

Shakespeare, Hamlet, II.2

"**D**oubt thou the stars are fire" and "that the sun doth move." Was Shakespeare alluding to controversial ideas about the cosmos that contradicted the teachings of medieval scholars? *Hamlet* (c. 1600) was written more than fifty years after Copernicus had suggested, in his treatise *On the Revolutions of the Heavenly Spheres* (1543), that the sun did not move but the earth did, revolving around the sun. Shakespeare probably knew of such theories, although they circulated only among small groups of learned Europeans. As Hamlet's lovelorn speech to Ophelia makes clear, they were considered conjecture—or strange mathematical hypotheses. These theories were not exactly new: a heliocentric universe had been proposed as early as the second century B.C.E. by ancient Greek astronomers. But they flatly contradicted the consensus that had set in after Ptolemy

523

proposed an earth-centered universe in the second century C.E., and to Shakespeare's contemporaries, they defied common sense and observation. Learned philosophers, young lovers, shepherds, and sailors alike could watch the sun and the stars move from one horizon to the other each day and night—or so they thought.

Still, a small handful of thinkers did doubt. Shakespeare was born in 1564, the same year as Galileo. By the time the English playwright and the Italian natural philosopher were working, the long process of revising knowledge about the universe and discovering a new set of rules that explained how the universe worked was under way. By the end of the seventeenth century a hundred years later, the building blocks of the new view had been put in place. This intellectual transformation brought sweeping changes to European philosophy and to Western views of the natural world and of humans' place in it.

*Science* entails at least three things: a body of knowledge, a method or system of inquiry, and a community of practitioners and the institutions that support them and their work. The *scientific revolution* of the seventeenth century—usually understood to have begun in the mid-sixteenth century and culminated in 1687 with Newton's *Principia*—involved each of these three realms. As far as the content of knowledge is concerned, the scientific revolution saw the emergence and confirmation of a heliocentric (sun-centered) view of the planetary system, which displaced the earth—and humans—from the center of the universe. Even more fundamental, it brought a new mathematical physics that described and confirmed such a view. Second, the scientific revolution established a method of inquiry for understanding the natural world, a method that emphasized the role of observation, experiment, and the testing of hypotheses. Third, *science* emerged as a distinctive branch of knowledge. During the period covered in this chapter, people referred to the study of matter, motion, optics, or the circulation of blood as natural philosophy (the more theoretical term), experimental philosophy, medicine, and—increasingly—science. The growth of societies and institutions dedicated to what we now commonly call scientific research was central to the changes at issue here. Science required not only brilliant thinkers but also patrons, states, and communities of researchers; the scientific revolution was thus embedded in other social, religious, and cultural transformations.

The scientific revolution was not an organized effort. Brilliant hypotheses sometimes led to dead ends, discoveries were often accidental, and artisans grinding lenses for telescopes played a role in the advance of knowledge just as surely as did great abstract thinkers. Educated women also claimed the right to participate in scientific debate, but their efforts were met with opposition or indifference. Old and new worldviews often overlapped as individual thinkers struggled to reconcile their discoveries with their faith or to make their theories—about the movement of bodies in the heavens, or the age of the earth, for instance—consistent with received wisdom. Science was slow to work its way into popular understanding. It did not necessarily undermine religion, and it certainly did not intend to (figures such as Isaac Newton thought their work confirmed and deepened their religious beliefs). In short, change came slowly and fitfully. But as the new scientific method started to produce radical new insights into the workings of nature, it eventually came to be accepted well beyond the small circles of experimenters, theologians, and philosophers with whom it had begun.

## THE INTELLECTUAL ORIGINS OF THE SCIENTIFIC REVOLUTION

Much was new in the scientific breakthroughs of the sixteenth and seventeenth centuries, but these advances were rooted in earlier developments. Medieval artists and intellectuals had been observing and illustrating the natural world with great precision since at least the twelfth century. Medieval sculptors carved plants and vines with extraordinary accuracy, and fifteenth-century painters and sculptors devoted the same careful attention to the human face and form. The link among observation, experiment, and invention was not new to the sixteenth century either. The magnetic compass had been known in Europe since the thirteenth century; gunpowder since the early fourteenth; and printing—which permeated the intellectual life of the period and opened new possibilities for disseminating ideas quickly, collaborating more easily, and buying books and building libraries—since the middle of the fifteenth. "Printing, firearms, and the compass," wrote Francis Bacon, "no empire, sect or star appears to have exercised a greater power and influence on human affairs than these three mechanical discoveries." A fascination with light, which was a powerful symbol of divine illumination for medieval thinkers, encouraged the study of optics and, in turn, new techniques for grinding lenses. Lens grinders laid the groundwork for the seventeenth-century inventions of the telescope and microscope, creating reading glasses along the way. Astrologers were also active in the later Middle Ages, charting the heavens in the firm belief that the stars controlled the fates of human beings.

Behind these efforts to understand the natural world lay a nearly universal conviction that the natural world had been created by God. Religious belief spurred scientific study. One school of thinkers (the Neoplatonists) argued that nature was a book written by its creator to reveal the ways of God to humanity. Convinced that God's perfection must be reflected in nature, Neoplatonists searched for the ideal and perfect structures they believed must lie behind the "shadows" of the everyday world. Mathematics, particularly geometry, was an important tool in this quest. The mathematician and astronomer Johannes Kepler, for example, was deeply influenced by Neoplatonism.

Renaissance humanism also helped prepare the grounds for the scientific revolution. The humanists' educational program placed a low value on natural philosophy, directing attention instead toward the recovery and study of classical antiquity. Humanists revered the authority of the ancients. Yet the energies the humanists poured into recovering, translating, and understanding classical texts (the source of conceptions of the natural world) made many of those important works available for the first time to a wider audience. Previously, Arabic sources had provided Europeans with the main route to ancient Greek learning; Greek classics were translated into Arabic and then picked up by late medieval scholars in Spain and Sicily. The humanists' return to the original texts themselves—and the fact that the new texts could more easily be printed and circulated—encouraged new study and debate. Islamic scholars knew Ptolemy better than did Europeans until the humanist scholar and printer Johannes Regiomontanus recovered and prepared a new summary of Ptolemy's work. The humanist rediscovery of works by Archimedes—the great Greek mathematician who had proposed that the natural world operated on the basis of mechanical forces, like a great machine, and that these forces could be described mathematically—profoundly impressed important late-sixteenth- and seventeenth-century thinkers, including the Italian scientist Galileo, and shaped mechanical philosophy in the 1600s.

The Renaissance also encouraged collaboration between artisans and intellectuals. Twelfth- and thirteenth-century thinkers had observed the natural world, but they rarely tinkered with machines, and they had little contact with the artisans who developed expertise in constructing machines for practical use. During the fifteenth century, however, these two worlds began to come together. Renaissance artists such as Leonardo da Vinci were accomplished craftsmen; they investigated the laws of perspective and optics, they worked out geometric methods for supporting the weight of enormous architectural domes, they studied the human body, and they devised new and more effective weapons for war. The Renaissance brought a vogue for alchemy and astrology, and wealthy amateurs built observatories and measured the courses of the stars. This fusion of intellectual curiosity and skilled handiwork created new possibilities for research and encouraged the creation of new fields of knowledge.

What of the voyages of discovery? Sixteenth-century observers often linked the exploration of the globe to new knowledge of the cosmos. An admirer wrote to Galileo that he had kept the spirit of exploration alive: "The memory of Columbus and Vespucci will be renewed through you, and with even greater nobility, as the sky is more worthy

**PTOLEMAIC ASTRONOMICAL INSTRUMENTS.** Armillary sphere, 1560s, built to facilitate the observation of planetary positions relative to the earth, in support of Ptolemy's theory of an earth-centered universe. In the sphere, seven concentric rings rotated about different axes. When the outermost ring was set to align with a north–south meridian, and the next ring was set to align with the celestial pole (the North Star, or the point around which the stars seem to rotate), the user could determine the latitude where the instrument was located. The inner rings were used to track the angular movements of the planets, key measurements in validating the Ptolemaic system. ▪ *What forms of knowledge were necessary to construct such an instrument?* ▪ *How do they relate to the breakthrough that is known as the scientific revolution?*

# Past and Present

## Has Science Replaced Religion?

Galileo recanted his claims about the movement of heavenly bodies when challenged by the Church (left); but physicists persisted in their research, leading eventually to the development of modern particle accelerators. such as the one located in this lab in Grenoble, France (right). Few would say, however, that science has replaced religion in the modern world.

Ⓢ **Watch related author interview on the Student Site**

than the earth." The parallel does not work quite so neatly, however. Columbus had not been driven by an interest in science. Moreover, it took centuries for European thinkers to realize the New World's implications for different fields of study, and the links between the voyages of discovery and breakthroughs in science were largely indirect. The discoveries of new lands made the most immediate impact in the field of natural history, which was vastly enriched by travelers' detailed accounts of the flora and fauna of the Americas. Finding new lands and cultures in Africa and Asia and the revelation of the Americas—a world unknown to the ancients and unmentioned in the Bible—also laid bare gaps in Europeans' inherited body of knowledge. In this sense, the exploration of the New World dealt a blow to the authority of the ancients.

In sum, the late medieval recovery of ancient texts long thought to have been lost, the expansion of print culture and reading, the turmoil in the Church such as the fierce wars and political maneuvering that followed the Reformation,

and the discovery of a new world across the oceans to explore and exploit all shook the authority of older ways of thinking. What we call the scientific revolution was part of the intellectual excitement that surrounded these challenges. We can say in retrospect that the scientific revolution enhanced and confirmed the importance of these other developments.

## THE COPERNICAN REVOLUTION

Medieval cosmologists, like their ancient counterparts and their successors during the scientific revolution, wrestled with the contradictions between ancient texts and the evidence of their own observations. Their view of an earth-centered universe was particularly influenced by the teachings of Aristotle (384–322 B.C.E.), especially as they were systematized by Ptolemy of Alexandria (100–178 C.E.). In fact, Ptolemy's vision of an earth-centered universe contradicted an earlier proposal by Aristarchus of Samos (310–230 B.C.E.), who had deduced that the earth and other planets revolve around the sun. Like the ancient Greeks, Ptolemy's medieval followers used astronomical observations to support their theory, but the persuasiveness of this model for medieval scholars also derived from the ways that it fitted with their Christian beliefs (see Chapter 4). According to Ptolemy, the heavens orbited the earth in a carefully organized hierarchy of spheres. Earth and the heavens were fundamentally different, made of different matter and subject to different laws of motion. The sun, moon, stars, and planets were formed of an unchanging (and perfect) quintessence, or ether. The earth, by contrast, was composed of four elements (earth, water, fire, and air), and each of these elements had its natural place: the heavy elements (earth and water) toward the center and the lighter ones farther out. The heavens—first the planets, then the stars—traced perfect circular paths around the stationary earth. The motion of these celestial bodies was produced by a prime mover, whom Christians identified as God. The view fitted Aristotelian physics, according to which objects could move only if acted on by an external force, and with a belief that each fundamental element of the universe had a natural place. Moreover, the Ptolemaic view both followed from and confirmed the belief in the purposefulness of God's universe.

By the late Middle Ages astronomers knew that this cosmology, called the "Ptolemaic system," did not correspond exactly to what many had observed. Orbits did not conform to the Aristotelian ideal of perfect circles. Certain planets, Mars in particular, sometimes appeared to loop backward before continuing on their paths. Ptolemy had managed to account for these orbital irregularities, but with complicated mathematics. By the early fifteenth century, the efforts to make the observed motions of the planets fit into the model of perfect circles in a geocentric (earth-centered) cosmos had produced astronomical charts that were mazes of complexity. Finally, the Ptolemaic system proved unable to solve serious difficulties with the calendar. That practical crisis precipitated Nicolaus Copernicus's intellectual leap forward.

By the early sixteenth century, the old Roman calendar was significantly out of alignment with the movements of the heavenly bodies. The major saints' days, Easter, and the other holy days were sometimes weeks off where they should have been according to the stars. Catholic authorities tried to correct this problem, consulting mathematicians and astronomers all over Europe. One of these was a Polish church official and astronomer, Nicolaus Copernicus (1473–1543). Educated in Poland and northern Italy, he was a man of diverse talents. He was trained in astronomy, canon law, and medicine; he read Greek; he was well versed in ancient philosophy; and he was also a careful mathematician and a devout Catholic who did not believe that God's universe could be as messy as Ptolemy's model. His proposed solution, based on mathematical calculations, was simple and radical: Ptolemy was mistaken; the earth was neither stationary nor at the center of the planetary system; the earth rotated on its axis and orbited with the other planets around the sun. Reordering the Ptolemaic system simplified the geometry of astronomy and made the orbits of the planets comprehensible.

Copernicus was in many ways a conservative thinker. He did not consider his work to be a break with either the Church or the authority of ancient texts. He believed, rather, that he had restored a pure understanding of God's design, one that had been lost over the centuries. Still, the implications of his theory troubled him. His ideas contradicted centuries of astronomical thought, and they were hard to

**NICOLAUS COPERNICUS.** This anonymous portrait of Copernicus characteristically blends his devotion and his scientific achievements. His scholarly work (behind him in the form of an early planetarium) is driven by his faith (as he turns toward the image of Christ triumphant over death). ▪ *What relationship between science and religion is evoked by this image?*

reconcile with the observed behavior of objects on earth. If the earth moved, why was that movement imperceptible? Copernicus calculated the distance from the earth to the sun to be at least 6 million miles. Even by Copernicus's very low estimate, the earth was hurtling around the sun at the dizzying rate of many thousands of miles an hour. How did people and objects remain standing? (The earth is actually about 93 million miles from the sun, moving through space at 67,000 miles an hour and spinning on its axis at about 1,000 miles an hour!)

Copernicus was not a physicist. He tried to refine, rather than overturn, traditional Aristotelian physics, but his effort to reconcile that physics with his new model of a sun-centered universe created new problems and inconsistencies that he could not resolve. These frustrations and complications dogged Copernicus's later years, and he hesitated to publish his findings. Just before his death, he consented to the release of his major treatise, *On the Revolutions of the Heavenly Spheres* (*De Revolutionibus*), in 1543. To fend off scandal, the Lutheran scholar who saw his manuscript through the press added an introduction to the book declaring that Copernicus's system should be understood as an abstraction, a set of mathematical tools for doing astronomy and not a dangerous claim about the nature of heaven and earth. For decades after 1543, Copernicus's ideas were taken in just that sense—as useful but not realistic mathematical hypotheses. In the long run, however, as one historian puts it, Copernicanism represented the first "serious and systematic" challenge to the Ptolemaic conception of the universe.

## TYCHO'S OBSERVATIONS AND KEPLER'S LAWS

Within fifty years, Copernicus's cosmology was revived and modified by two astronomers also critical of the Ptolemaic model of the universe: Tycho Brahe (*TI-koh BRAH-hee*; 1546–1601) and Johannes Kepler (1571–1630). Each was considered the greatest astronomer of his day. Tycho was born into the Danish nobility, but he abandoned his family's military and political legacy to pursue his passion for astronomy. He was hotheaded as well as talented; at twenty, he lost part of his nose in a duel. Like Copernicus, he sought to correct the contradictions in traditional astronomy. But unlike Copernicus, who was a theoretician, Tycho championed observation and believed that careful study of the heavens would unlock the secrets of the universe. He first made a name for himself by observing a completely new star, a "nova," that flared into sight in 1572. The Danish

king Friedrich II, impressed by Tycho's work, granted him the use of a small island, where he built a castle specially designed to house an observatory. For over twenty years, Tycho meticulously charted the movements of each significant object in the night sky, compiling the finest set of astronomical data in Europe.

Tycho was not a Copernican. He suggested that the planets orbited the sun and that the whole system orbited a stationary earth. This picture of cosmic order, though clumsy, seemed to fit the observed evidence better than the Ptolemaic system, and avoided the upsetting physical and theological implications of the Copernican model. In the late 1590s, Tycho moved his work and his huge collection

**TYCHO BRAHE, 1662.** This seventeenth-century tribute shows the master astronomer in his observatory. ▪ *How much scientific knowledge does one need to understand this image?* ▪ *Is this image, which celebrates science and its accomplishments, itself a scientific statement?* ▪ *What can we learn about seventeenth-century science from such imagery?*

of data to Prague, where he became the court astronomer to the Holy Roman emperor Rudolph II. In Prague, he was assisted by a young mathematician from a troubled family, Johannes Kepler. Kepler was more impressed with the Copernican model than was Tycho, and he combined the study of Copernicus's work with his own interest in mysticism, astrology, and the religious power of mathematics.

Kepler believed that everything in creation, from human souls to the orbits of the planets, had been created according to mathematical laws. Understanding those laws would thus allow humans to share God's wisdom and penetrate the inner secrets of the universe. Mathematics was God's language. Kepler's search for the pattern of mathematical perfection took him through musical harmonies, geometric shapes nested inside the planets' orbits, and numerical formulas. After Tycho's death, Kepler inherited Tycho's position in Prague as well as his trove of observations and calculations. Those data demonstrated to Kepler that two of Copernicus's assumptions about planetary motion simply did not match observations. Copernicus, in keeping with Aristotelian notions of perfection, had believed that planetary orbits were circular. Kepler, however, calculated that the planets traveled in elliptical orbits around the sun (this finding became his First Law). Copernicus held that planetary motion was uniform. But Kepler stated that the speed of the planets varied with their distance from the sun (his Second Law). Kepler also argued that magnetic forces between the sun and the planets kept the planets in orbital motion, an insight that paved the way for Newton's law of universal gravitation, formulated nearly eighty years later at the end of the seventeenth century.

Each of Kepler's works, beginning with *Cosmographic Mystery* in 1596 and continuing with *Astronomia Nova* in 1609 and *The Harmonies of the World* in 1619, revised and augmented Copernicus's theory. His version of Copernicanism fitted with remarkable accuracy the best observations of the time (which were Tycho's). Kepler's search for rules of motion that could account for the earth's movements in its new position was also significant. More than Copernicus, Kepler broke down the distinction between the heavens and the earth that had been at the heart of Aristotelian physics.

# NEW HEAVENS, NEW EARTH, AND WORLDLY POLITICS: GALILEO

Kepler had a friend deliver a copy of *Cosmographic Mystery* to the "mathematician named Galileus Galileus," then teaching mathematics and astronomy at Padua, near Venice.

Galileo (1564–1642) thanked Kepler in a letter that nicely illustrates the Italian's views at the time (1597):

> So far I have only perused the preface of your work, but from this I gained some notion of its intent, and I indeed congratulate myself of having an associate in the study of Truth who is a friend of Truth. . . . I adopted the teaching of Copernicus many years ago, and his point of view enables me to explain many phenomena of nature which certainly remain inexplicable according to the more current hypotheses. I have written many arguments in support of him and in refutation of the opposite view—which, however, so far I have not dared to bring into the public light. . . . I would certainly dare to publish my reflections at once if more people like you existed; as they don't, I shall refrain from doing so.

Kepler replied, urging Galileo to "come forward!" Galileo did not answer.

At Padua, Galileo couldn't teach what he believed; Ptolemaic astronomy and Aristotelian cosmology were the established curriculum. By the end of his career, however, Galileo had provided powerful evidence in support of the Copernican model and laid the foundation for a new physics. What was more, he wrote in the vernacular (Italian) as well as in Latin. Kepler may have been a "friend of Truth," but his work was abstruse and bafflingly mathematical (as was Copernicus's). In contrast, Galileo's writings were widely translated and widely read, raising awareness of changes in natural philosophy across Europe.

Ultimately, Galileo made the case for a new relationship between religion and science, challenging in the process some of the most powerful churchmen of his day. His discoveries made him the most famous scientific figure of his time, but his work put him on a collision course with Aristotelian philosophy and the authority of the Catholic Church.

Galileo became famous by way of his discoveries with the telescope. In 1609, he heard reports from Holland of a lens grinder who had made a spyglass that could magnify very distant objects. Excited, Galileo quickly devised his own telescope. He trained it first on earthly objects to demonstrate that it worked, and then dramatically pointed it at the night sky. Galileo studied the moon, finding on it mountains, plains, and other features of an earthlike landscape. His observations suggested that celestial bodies resembled the earth, a view at odds with the concept of the

# Interpreting Visual Evidence

## Astronomical Observations and the Mapping of the Heavens

One (often-repeated) narrative about the scientific revolution is that it marked a crucial break, separating modern science from an earlier period permeated by an atmosphere of superstition and theological speculation. But, in fact, medieval scholars tried hard to come up with empirical evidence for beliefs that their faith told them must be true, and

without these traditions of observation, scientists like Copernicus would never have been led to propose alternative cosmologies (see "Ptolemaic Astronomical Instruments" on page 525).

The assumption that the "new" sciences of the seventeenth century marked an extraordinary rupture with a more ignorant or superstitious past is thus not entirely correct. It would be closer to the truth to suggest that works

such as that of Copernicus or Galileo provided a new context for assessing the relationship between observations and knowledge that came from other sources. Printed materials provided opportunities for early modern scientists to learn as much from each other as from more ancient sources.

The illustrations here are from scientific works on astronomy both before and after the appearance of Copernicus's

A. The Ptolemaic universe, as depicted in Peter Apian, *Cosmographia* (1540).

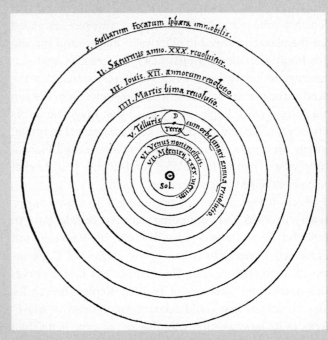

B. The Copernican universe (1543).

heavens as an unchanging sphere of heavenly perfection, inherently and necessarily different from the earth. He saw moons orbiting Jupiter, evidence that earth was not at the center of all orbits. And he saw spots on the sun. Galileo published these results, first in *The Starry Messenger* (1610) and then in *Letters on Sunspots* (1613). *The Starry Messenger*, with its amazing reports of Jupiter's moons, was short,

aimed at a wide reading audience, and bold. It only hinted at Galileo's Copernicanism, however. The *Letters on Sunspots* declared it openly.

A seventeenth-century scientist needed powerful and wealthy patrons. As a professor of mathematics, Galileo chafed at the power of university authorities who were subject to Church control. Princely courts offered an inviting

work. All of them were based on some form of observation and claimed to be descriptive of the existing universe. Compare the abstract illustrations of the Ptolemaic (image A) and Copernican (image B) universes with Tycho Brahe's (image C) attempt to reconcile heliocentric observations with geocentric assumptions, or with Galileo's illustration of sunspots (image D) observed through a telescope.

## Questions for Analysis

**1.** What do these illustrations tell us about the relationship between knowledge and observation in sixteenth- and seventeenth-century science? What kinds of knowledge were necessary to produce these images?

**2.** Are the illustrations A and B intended to be visually accurate, in the sense that they represent what the eye sees?

Can we say the same of illustration D? What makes Galileo's illustration of sunspots different from the others?

**3.** Are the assumptions about observation in Galileo's drawing of sunspots (image D) applicable to other sciences such as biology or chemistry? If yes, how so?

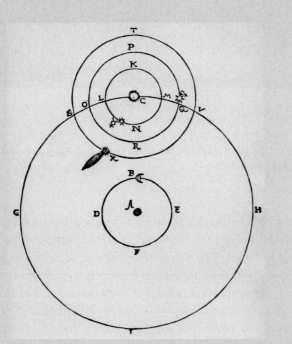

C. Brahe's universe (c. 1572; A [earth], B [moon], C [sun]).

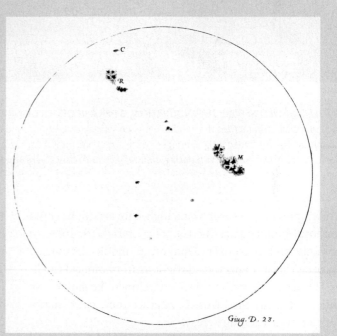

D. Galileo's sunspots, as observed through a telescope (1612).

alternative. The Medici family of Tuscany, like others, burnished its reputation and bolstered its power by surrounding itself with intellectuals as well as artists. Persuaded he would be freer at its court than in Padua, Galileo took a position as tutor to the Medicis and flattered and successfully cultivated the family. He addressed *The Starry Messenger* to them, and named the newly discovered moons of Jupiter the "Medicean stars." He was rewarded with the title of chief mathematician and philosopher to Cosimo de' Medici, the grand duke of Tuscany. Now well positioned in Italy's networks of power and patronage, Galileo was able to pursue his goal of demonstrating that Copernicus's heliocentric (sun-centered) model of the planetary system was correct.

***GALILEO GALILEI BEFORE THE INQUISITION, BY FRANÇOIS FLEURY-RICHARD.*** This nineteenth-century painting of Galileo before the Holy Office dramatizes the conflict between science and religion, and depicts the Italian natural philosopher as defiant. In fact, Galileo submitted but continued his work under house arrest and published, secretly, in the Netherlands. ▪ *Would Galileo himself have subscribed to the message of this much later painting, that religion and science were opposed to one another?*

This pursuit, however, was a high-wire act, for he could not afford to antagonize the Catholic Church. In 1614, an ambitious and outspoken Dominican monk denounced Galileo's ideas as dangerous deviations from biblical teachings. Other philosophers and churchmen began to ask Galileo's patrons, the Medicis, whether their court mathematician was teaching heresy.

Disturbed by the murmurings against Copernicanism, Galileo penned a series of letters to defend himself. He addressed the relationship between natural philosophy and religion, and argued that one could be both a sincere Copernican and a sincere Catholic (see *Analyzing Primary Sources* on page 533). The Church, Galileo said, did the sacred work of teaching scripture and saving souls, but accounting for the workings of the physical world was a task better left to natural philosophy, grounded in observation and mathematics. For the Church to take a side in controversies over natural science might compromise its spiritual authority and credibility. Galileo envisioned natural philosophers and theologians as partners in a search for truth, but with very different roles.

In a brilliant rhetorical moment, he quoted Cardinal Caesar Baronius in support of his argument: the purpose of the Bible was to "teach us how to go to heaven, not how heaven goes."

Nevertheless, in 1616, the Church moved against Galileo. The Inquisition ruled that Copernicanism was "foolish and absurd in philosophy and formally heretical." Copernicus's *De Revolutionibus* was placed on the Index of Prohibited Books, and Galileo was warned not to teach Copernicanism.

For a while, he did as he was asked. But when his Florentine friend and admirer Maffeo Barberini was elected pope as Urban VIII in 1623, Galileo believed the door to Copernicanism was (at least half) open. He drafted one of his most famous works, *A Dialogue Concerning the Two Chief World Systems*, which was published in 1632. The *Dialogue* was a hypothetical debate between supporters of the old Ptolemaic system, represented by a character he named Simplicio (simpleton) on the one hand, and proponents of the new astronomy on the other. Galileo gave the best lines to the Copernicans throughout. However, at the very end, to satisfy the letter of the Inquisition's decree, he had them capitulate to Simplicio.

## Galileo on Nature, Scripture, and Truth

*One of the clearest statements of Galileo's convictions about religion and science comes from his 1615 letter to the grand duchess Christina, the mother of Galileo's patron, Cosimo de' Medici, and a powerful figure in her own right. Galileo knew that others objected to his work. The church had warned him that Copernicanism was inaccurate and impious, that it could be disproved scientifically, and that it contradicted the authority of those who interpreted the Bible. Thoroughly dependent on the Medicis for support, he wrote to the grand duchess to explain his position. In this section of the letter, Galileo sets out his understanding of the parallel but distinct roles of the Church and natural philosophers. He walks a fine line between acknowledging the authority of the Church and standing firm in his convictions.*

Possibly because they are disturbed by the known truth of other propositions of mine which differ from those commonly held, and therefore mistrusting their defense so long as they confine themselves to the field of philosophy, these men have resolved to fabricate a shield for their fallacies out of the mantle of pretended religion and the authority of the Bible. . . .

Copernicus never discusses matters of religion or faith, nor does he use arguments that depend in any way upon the authority of sacred writings which he might have interpreted erroneously. He stands always upon physical conclusions pertaining to the celestial motions, and deals with them by astronomical and geometrical demonstrations, founded primarily upon sense experiences and very exact observations. He did not ignore the Bible, but he knew very well that if his doctrine were proved, then it could not contradict the Scriptures when they were rightly understood. . . .

I think that in discussions of physical problems we ought to begin not from the authority of scriptural passages, but from sense-experiences and necessary demonstrations; for the holy Bible and the phenomena of nature proceed alike from the divine Word, the former as the dictate of the Holy Ghost and the latter as the observant executrix of God's commands. It is necessary for the Bible, in order to be accommodated to the understanding of every man, to speak many things which appear to differ from the absolute truth so far as the bare meaning of the words is concerned. But Nature, on the other hand, is inexorable and immutable; she never transgresses the laws imposed upon her, or cares a whit whether her abstruse reasons and methods of operation are understandable to men. For that reason it appears that nothing physical which sense-experience sets before our eyes, or which necessary demonstrations prove to us, ought to be called in question (much less condemned) upon the testimony of biblical passages which may have some different meaning beneath their words. For the Bible is not chained in every expression to conditions as strict as those which govern all physical effects; nor is God any less excellently revealed in Nature's actions than in the sacred statements of the Bible. . . .

Source: Galileo, "Letter to the Grand Duchess Christina," in *The Discoveries and Opinions of Galileo Galilei*, ed. Stillman Drake (Garden City, NY: 1957), pp. 177–83.

### Questions for Analysis

1. How does Galileo deal with the contradictions between the evidence of his senses and biblical teachings?

2. For Galileo, what is the relationship between God, man, and nature?

3. Why did Galileo need to defend his views in a letter to Christina de' Medici?

The Inquisition banned the *Dialogue* and ordered Galileo to stand trial in 1633. Pope Urban, provoked by Galileo's scorn and needing support from Church conservatives during a difficult stretch of the Thirty Years' War, refused to protect his former friend. The verdict of the secret trial shocked Europe. The Inquisition forced Galileo to repent his Copernican position, banned him from working on or even discussing Copernican ideas, and placed him under house arrest for life. According to a story that began to circulate shortly afterward, as he left the court for house arrest he stamped his foot and muttered defiantly, looking down at the earth, "Still, it moves."

The Inquisition could not put Galileo off his life's work. He refined the theories of motion he had begun to develop early in his career. He proposed an early version of the theory of inertia, which held that an object's motion stays the same until an outside force changed it. He calculated that objects of different weights fall at almost the same speed and with a uniform acceleration. He argued that the motion of objects follows regular mathematical laws. The same laws that govern the motions of objects on earth (which could be observed in experiments) could also be observed in the heavens—again a direct contradiction of Aristotelian principles and an important step toward a coherent physics based on a sun-centered model of the universe. Compiled under the title *Two New Sciences* (1638), this work was smuggled out of Italy and published in Protestant Holland.

Galileo believed that Copernicanism and natural philosophy in general need not subvert theological truths, religious belief, or the authority of the Church. But his trial seemed to show the contrary: that natural philosophy and Church authority could not coexist. Galileo's trial silenced Copernican voices in southern Europe, and the Church's leadership retreated into conservative reaction. It was therefore in northwest Europe that the new philosophy Galileo had championed would flourish.

## DATING THE AGE OF THE EARTH: THE ORIGINS OF GEOLOGY AND THE ENVIRONMENTAL SCIENCES

Galileo's contention that celestial bodies were subject to the same laws of motion as matter on earth was a significant step toward modern science. In retrospect, it is not surprising that some within the Church perceived Galileo's teachings to be a threat to Christian scripture. At the same time, the split between religion and those who would explore the sciences of the heavens and earth was not at all absolute. The modern science of geology, for example, emerged gradually out of a long debate that moved back and forth between evidence compiled from religious and secular texts on the one hand, and data gathered by those who made observations about the physical landscape and the stones they collected while walking through the countryside on the other. The debate that fostered this discussion revolved around a fundamental question that had long provoked theologians: How old was the earth?

In 1654, twelve years after Galileo's death, James Ussher (1581–1656), the archbishop of Armagh in Ireland, published an account of the earth's creation based on a wide variety of textual sources, both biblical and secular. Ussher declared that according to his calculations, the world had been created on Saturday, October 22, 4004 B.C. Though modern authors often ridicule Ussher's work as an extreme example of biblical literalism, it is important to recognize that his thinking was very much rooted in the culture of his

time, and his estimate differed little from the assertions of many others who tried to answer the same question. Ussher's estimate became famous only because of an accident of history. After his death, his dates for the Creation story were included in subsequent editions of the King James Bible. Ussher's chronology was part of a larger intellectual attempt to construct a timeline for the history of the world that recorded both material events such as the appearance of comets, volcanic eruptions, or solar and lunar eclipses as well as sacred dates. His decision to treat the Bible as one source among many was in fact a significant departure from a purely religious approach, and his desire to divide the history of the earth into "epochs" or "eras" marked an important step toward a more historical approach to the earth's past.

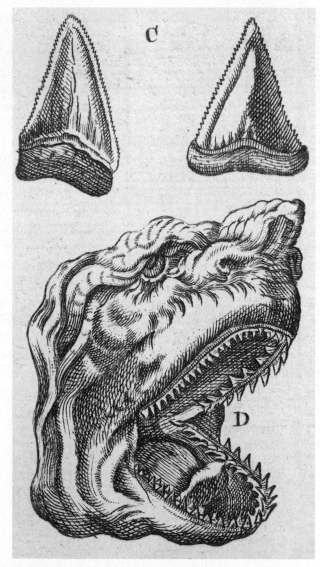

**PALEONTOLOGY IN THE SERVICE OF GEOLOGY.** An illustration from Nicolas Steno's 1667 paper comparing shark's teeth from a dissected specimen with petrified teeth found in rocky hillsides far from the ocean. He used such observations to demonstrate the changes that had taken place in the earth's crust over time, and to assert that deeper layers were a record of a more distant past.

James Ussher, like other early seventeenth-century writers, assumed that the earth's history and human history covered roughly the same length of time: following the story of Genesis, they assumed that humans appeared on earth soon after its creation. They also assumed that the stories told in the Bible about the natural environment—including the story of Noah and the Flood—had some basis in historical fact. A German Jesuit, Athanasius Kircher (1602–1680), suggested that the Flood story could be analyzed historically, and he attempted to calculate the amount of water that would have been required to cover the earth's mountains. He assumed that the physical landscape of the earth would have been transformed as the floodwaters drained away, and that the shapes of the continents and oceans must have changed as well. It was only later that natural philosophers realized the vast expanse of earth's history that predated human society, but they were already beginning to imagine that this history was accessible to human knowledge through observation.

**CABINET OF CURIOSITIES.** This illustration was the frontispiece of a book on natural history by a Danish doctor, Ole Wurm, who taught medicine, Latin, and Greek in Copenhagen after studying in Marburg. Wurm was a celebrated collector of objects, ranging from fossils and specimens of animals to artifacts of ethnographic interest. Such collections provided the principal data for those engaged in debates about the origins of fossils and the age of the earth.

Such speculation was also fueled by the work of natural philosophers who asked questions about the fossils that they found throughout the European countryside. As interest in natural philosophy developed in the seventeenth century, scholars began to assemble large collections of what they called "curiosities"—images and forms of animals and plants found in stones and seashells collected on mountaintops far from the ocean, as well as the bones and antlers of animals both recognizable and unknown. Some of these objects could be explained in terms of accepted biblical histories. Religious believers, for example, asserted that seashells on mountaintops could have been deposited by Noah's Flood. A Danish physician, Nils Stensen (more frequently referred to by his Latin name, Nicolas Steno), began a more systematic compilation of this evidence that pointed the way toward the science of geology. The key breakthrough was a paper he published in 1667 that demonstrated that shark's teeth, obtained through the dissection of a recently caught animal, were structurally similar, though smaller in size, to petrified teeth found bound in stone on land far from the sea. Steno began to believe that the physical landscape of Tuscany (where he was living at the time) constituted a visible record of a historical sequence that could be reconstructed through observation. He noted a tendency of broken hillsides to reveal strata of different stones, as if one layer had been laid down over the previous one. An English natural philosopher, Robert Hooke, writing at the same time in England, came to the same conclusion, asserting that the rocks and fossils were "documents" to be read in the book of nature.

The debate on the age of the earth continued into the eighteenth and nineteenth centuries, but the line from Steno's and Hooke's remarks to modern geological research is a direct one. In the space of little more than one or two generations in the seventeenth century, the earth sciences had emerged in a form that is recognizable to modern readers. From Galileo's claim that heavenly bodies and earthly matter were all subject to the same laws of motion, to Ussher's call for a chronology of earth's history that could be assembled from both secular and religious sources, to Steno's and Hooke's imaginative claim that the earth's landscape constituted a legible "monument" pointing to a distant and material past, the evolution of natural philosophy in the seventeenth century indicated new possibilities for a scientific understanding of the terrestrial environment.

# METHODS FOR A NEW PHILOSOPHY: BACON AND DESCARTES

Advances in the new sciences eventually became concentrated in northwest Europe, where thinkers began to spell out standards of practice and evidence. Sir Francis Bacon and René Descartes (*deh-KAHRT*) loom especially large in this development, setting out the methods or the rules that should govern modern science. Bacon (1561–1626) lived at roughly the same time as Kepler, Galileo—and Shakespeare; Descartes (1596–1650) was slightly younger. Both Bacon and Descartes came to believe that theirs was an age of profound change, open to the possibility of astonishing discovery. They were persuaded that knowledge could take the European moderns beyond the ancient authorities, and they set out to formulate a philosophy to encompass the learning of their age.

"Knowledge is power." This phrase is Bacon's and captures the changing perspective of the seventeenth century and its new confidence in the potential of human thinking. Bacon trained as a lawyer, serving in the Parliament and briefly as the lord chancellor to James I of England. His abiding concern was with the assumptions, methods, and practices he believed should guide natural philosophers and the progress of knowledge. The authority of the ancients should not constrain the ambition of modern thinkers, and deference to accepted doctrines could block innovation or obstruct understanding: "There is but one course left . . . to try the whole thing anew upon a better plan, and to commence a total reconstruction of sciences, arts, and all human knowledge, raised upon the proper foundations." Pursuing knowledge did not mean thinking abstractly and leaping to conclusions; it meant observing, experimenting, confirming ideas, or demonstrating points. If thinkers will be "content to begin with doubts," Bacon wrote, "they shall end with certainties." We thus associate Bacon with the gradual separation of scientific investigation from philosophical argument.

Bacon advocated an *inductive* approach to knowledge: amassing evidence from specific observations to draw general conclusions. In Bacon's view, many philosophical errors arose from beginning with assumed first principles. The traditional view of the cosmos, for instance, rested on the principles of a prime mover and the perfection of circular motion for the planets and the stars. The inductive method required accumulating data (as Tycho had done) and then, after careful review and experiment, drawing appropriate conclusions about the motions of heavenly bodies. Bacon argued that scientific knowledge was best tested through the cooperative efforts of researchers performing experiments that could be repeated and verified. The knowledge thus gained would be predictable and useful to philosophers and artisans alike, contributing to a wide range of endeavors from astronomy to shipbuilding.

Bacon's vision of science and progress is vividly illustrated by two images. The first, more familiar, is the title page of Bacon's *Novum Organum* (1620), shown on the left, with its bold ships sailing out beyond the Straits of Gibraltar, formerly the limits of the West, into the open sea, in pursuit of unknown but great things to come. The second is of Bacon's imagined factory of discovery, "Solomon's house," at the end of his utopian *New Atlantis* (1626). Inside the

**FRONTISPIECE TO BACON'S *NOVUM ORGANUM* (1620).** This illustration suggests that scientific work is like a voyage of discovery, similar to a ship setting out through uncharted waters. Compare this image with the fanciful image of Tycho Brahe at work in his observatory (page 528). ■ *What metaphors and allegorical imagery did scientists use during this period to characterize the significance of their work?*

factory, "sifters" would examine and conduct experiments, passing on findings to senior researchers who would draw conclusions and develop practical applications. The work of these scholars would be supplemented by accounts sent by their emissaries abroad, traveling ambassadors of science who would gather data and information about the natural world and human societies in other places. Bacon's utopian image of patient researchers and experimenters anticipated the modern university.

René Descartes was French, though he lived all over Europe. He was intellectually restless as well; he worked in geometry, cosmology, optics, and physiology—for a while dissecting cow carcasses daily. He was writing a (Copernican) book on physics when he heard of Galileo's condemnation in 1633, a ruling that impressed on him the dangers of "expressing judgements on this world." Descartes's *Discourse on Method* (1637), for which he is best known, began simply as a preface to three essays on optics, geometry, and meteorology. It is personal, recounting Descartes's dismay at the "strange and unbelievable" theories he encountered in his traditional education. His first response, as he described it, was to doubt systematically everything he had ever known or been taught. Better to clear the slate, he

believed, than to build an edifice of knowledge on received assumptions. His first rule was "never to receive anything as a truth which [he] did not clearly know to be such." He took the human ability to think as his point of departure, summed up in his famous and enigmatic *Je pense, donc je suis*, later translated into Latin as *cogito ergo sum* and into English as "I think, therefore I am." As the phrase suggests, Descartes's doubting led (quickly, by our standards) to self-assurance and truth: the thinking individual existed, reason existed, God existed. For Descartes, then, doubt was a ploy, or a piece that he used in an intellectual chess game to defeat skepticism. Certainty, not doubt, was the centerpiece of the philosophy he bequeathed to his followers.

Descartes, like Bacon, sought a "fresh start for knowledge," or the rules for understanding the world as it was. Unlike Bacon, however, he emphasized *deductive* reasoning, proceeding logically from one certainty to another. "So long as we avoid accepting as true what is not so," he wrote in *Discourse on Method*, "and always preserve the right order of deduction of one thing from another, there can be nothing too remote to be reached in the end, or too well hidden to be discovered." For Descartes, mathematical thought expressed the highest standards of reason, and his work contributed

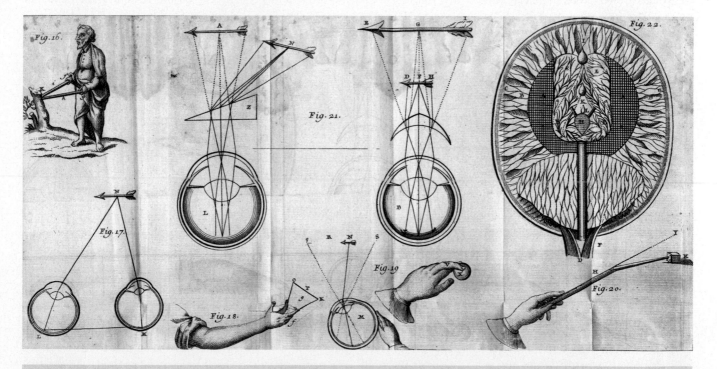

**FROM RENÉ DESCARTES, *L'HOMME* (1729; ORIGINALLY PUBLISHED AS *DE HOMINI*, 1662).** Descartes's interest in the body as a mechanism led him to suppose that physics and mathematics could be used to understand all aspects of human physiology, and his work had an important influence on subsequent generations of medical researchers. In this illustration, Descartes depicts the optical properties of the human eye. ▪ *How might such a mechanistic approach to human perception have been received by proponents of Baconian science, who depended so much on the reliability of human observations?*

# Competing Viewpoints

## The New Science and the Foundations of Certainty

> *Francis Bacon (1561–1626) and René Descartes (1596–1650) were both enthusiastic supporters of science in the seventeenth century, but they differed in their opinions regarding the basis for certainty in scientific argumentation. Bacon's inductive method emphasized the gathering of particular observations about natural phenomena, which he believed could be used as evidence to support more general conclusions about causes, regularity, and order in the natural world. Descartes, on the other hand, defended a deductive method. He believed that certainty could be built only by reasoning from first principles that one knew to be true, and he was less certain of the value of evidence that came from the senses alone.*

### Aphorisms *from* Novum Organum

#### XXXI

It is idle to expect any advancement in science from the super-inducing and engrafting of new things upon old. We must begin anew from the very foundations, unless we would revolve forever in a circle with mean and contemptible progress. . . .

#### XXXVI

One method of delivery alone remains to us which is simply this: we must lead men to the particulars themselves, and their series and order; while men on their side must force themselves for a while to lay their notions by and begin to familiarize themselves with facts. . . .

#### XLV

The human understanding of its own nature is prone to suppose the existence of more order and regularity in the world than it finds. And though there be many things in nature which are singular and unmatched, yet it devises for them parallels and conjugates and relatives which do not exist. Hence the fiction that all celestial bodies move in perfect circles. . . . Hence too the element of fire with its orb is brought in, to make up the square with the other three which the sense perceives. . . . And so on of other dreams. And these fancies affect not dogmas only, but simple notions also. . . .

#### XCV

Those who have handled sciences have been either men of experiment or men of dogmas. The men of experiment are like the ant, they only collect and use; the reasoners resemble spiders, who make cobwebs out of their own substance. But the bee takes a middle course: it gathers its material from the flowers of the garden and of the field, but transforms and digests it by a power of its own. Not unlike this is the true business of philosophy; for it neither relies solely or chiefly on the powers of the mind, nor does it take the matter which it gathers from natural history and mechanical experiments and lay it up in the memory whole . . . but lays it up in the understanding altered and digested. Therefore, from a closer and purer league between these two faculties, the experimental and the rational (such as has never yet been made), much may be hoped. . . .

Source: Michael R. Matthews, ed., *The Scientific Background to Modern Philosophy: Selected Readings* (Indianapolis: 1989), pp. 47–48, 50–52.

### From A Discourse on Method

Just as a great number of laws is often a pretext for wrongdoing, with the result that a state is much better governed when, having only a few, they are strictly observed; so also I came to believe that in the place of the great number of precepts that go to make up logic, the following four would be sufficient for my purposes, provided that I took a firm but unshakeable decision never once to depart from them.

The first was never to accept anything as true that I did not *incontrovertibly* know to be so; that is to say, carefully to avoid both *prejudice* and premature conclusions; and to include nothing in my judgments other than that which presented itself to my mind so *clearly* and *distinctly*, that I would have no occasion to doubt it.

The second was to divide all the difficulties under examination into as many parts as possible, and as many as were required to solve them in the best way.

The third was to conduct my thoughts in a given order, beginning with the *simplest* and most easily understood objects, and gradually ascending, as it were step by step, to the knowledge of the most *complex;* and *positing* an order even on those which do not have a natural order of precedence.

The last was to undertake such complete enumerations and such general surveys that I would be sure to have left nothing out.

The long chain of reasonings, every one simple and easy, which geometers habitually employ to reach their most difficult proofs had given me cause to suppose that all those things which fall within the domain of human understanding follow on from each other in the same way, and that as long as one stops oneself taking anything to be true that is not true and sticks to the right order so as to deduce one thing from another, there can be nothing so remote that one cannot eventually reach it, nor so hidden that one cannot discover it. . . .

[B]ecause I wished . . . to concentrate on the pursuit of truth, I came to think that I should . . . reject as completely false everything in which I could detect the least doubt, in order to see if anything thereafter remained in my belief that was completely indubitable. And so, because our senses sometimes deceive us, I decided to suppose that nothing was such as they lead us to imagine it to be. And because there are men who make mistakes in reasoning, even about the simplest elements of geometry, and commit logical fallacies, I judged that I was as prone to error as anyone else, and I rejected as false all the reasoning I had hitherto accepted as valid proof. Finally, considering that all the same thoughts which we have while awake can come to us while asleep without any one of them then being true, I resolved to pretend that everything that had ever entered my head was no more true than the illusions of my dreams. But immediately afterwards I noted that, while I was trying to think of all things being false in this way, it was necessarily the case that I, who was thinking them, had to be something; and observing this truth: *I am thinking therefore I exist,* was so secure and certain that it could not be shaken by any of the most extravagant suppositions of the sceptics, I judged that I could accept it without scruple, as the first principle of the philosophy I was seeking.

Source: René Descartes, *A Discourse on the Method,* trans. Ian Maclean (New York: 2006), pp. 17–18, 28.

## Questions for Analysis

1. Descartes's idea of certainty depended on a "long chain of reasonings" that departed from certain axioms that could not be doubted and rejected evidence from the senses. What science provided him with the model for this idea of certainty? What was the first thing that he felt he could be certain about? Did he trust his senses?

2. Bacon's idea of certainty pragmatically sought to combine the benefits of sensory knowledge and experience (gathered by "ants") with the understandings arrived at through reason (cobwebs constructed by "spiders"). How would Descartes have responded to Bacon's claims? According to Bacon, was Descartes an ant or a spider?

3. What do these two thinkers have in common?

greatly to the authority of mathematics as a model for scientific reasoning.

Descartes made a particularly forceful statement for *mechanism*, a view of the world shared by Bacon and Galileo and one that came to dominate seventeenth-century scientific thought. As the name suggests, mechanical philosophy proposed to consider nature as a machine. It rejected the traditional Aristotelian distinction between the works of humans and those of nature, and the view that nature, as God's creation, necessarily belonged to a different—and higher—order. In the new picture of the universe that was emerging from the discoveries and writings of the early seventeenth century, it seemed that all matter was composed of the same material and that all motion obeyed the same laws. Descartes sought to explain everything, including the human body, mechanically. As he put it firmly, "There is no difference between the machines built by artisans and the diverse bodies that nature alone composes." Nature operated according to regular and predictable laws and thus was accessible to human reason. This belief guided, indeed inspired, much of the scientific experiment and argument of the seventeenth century.

## The Power of Method and the Force of Curiosity: Seventeenth-Century Experimenters

For nearly a century after Bacon and Descartes, most of England's natural philosophers were Baconian, and most of their colleagues in France, Holland, and elsewhere in northern Europe were Cartesians (followers of Descartes). The English Baconians concentrated on performing experiments in many different fields, producing results that could then be debated and discussed. The Cartesians turned instead toward mathematics and logic. Descartes himself pioneered analytical geometry. Blaise Pascal (1623–1662) worked on probability theory and invented a calculating machine before applying his intellectual skills to theology. A Cartesian thinker, Christian Huygens (1629–1695) of Holland, combined mathematics with experiments to understand problems of impact and orbital motion. A Dutch Cartesian, Baruch Spinoza (1632–1677), applied geometry to ethics and believed he had gone beyond Descartes by proving that the universe was composed of a single substance that was both God and nature.

English experimenters pursued a different course. They began with practical research, putting the alchemist's tool, the laboratory, to new uses. They also sought a different kind of conclusion: empirical laws or provisional generalizations based on evidence rather than absolute statements of deductive truth. Among the many English laboratory scientists of this era were the physician William Harvey (1578–1657), the chemist Robert Boyle (1627–1691), and the inventor and experimenter Robert Hooke (1635–1703).

Harvey's contribution was enormous: he observed and explained that blood circulated through the arteries, heart, and veins. To do this, he was willing to dissect living animals (vivisection) and experiment on himself. Boyle performed experiments and established a law (known as Boyle's law) showing that at a constant temperature the volume of a gas decreases in proportion to the pressure placed on it. Hooke introduced the microscope to the experimenter's tool kit. The compound microscope had been invented in Holland early in the seventeenth century, but it was not until the 1660s that Hooke and others demonstrated its potential by using it to study the cellular structure of plants. Like the telescope before it, the microscope revealed an unexpected dimension of material phenomena. Examining even the most ordinary objects revealed detailed structures of perfectly connected smaller parts, and this persuaded many that with improved instruments they would uncover even more of the world's intricacies.

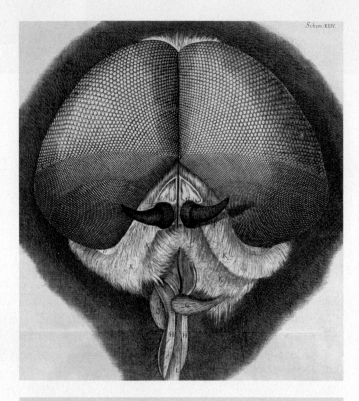

**ROBERT HOOKE'S *MICROGRAPHIA*.** Hooke's diagram of a fly's eye as seen through a microscope seemed to reveal just the sort of intricate universe the mechanists predicted. ▪ *Compare this image with that of Galileo's sunspots (page 531). What do these two images have in common?*

The microscope also provided what many regarded as new evidence of God's existence. The way each minute structure of a living organism, when viewed under a microscope, corresponded to its purpose testified not only to God's existence but also to God's wisdom. The mechanical philosophy did not exclude God but in fact could be used to confirm his presence. If the universe was a clock, there must be a clock maker. Hooke himself declared that only imbeciles would believe that what they saw under the microscope was "the production of chance" rather than of God's creation.

## The State, Scientific Academies, and Women Scientists

Seventeenth-century state building (see Chapter 14) helped secure the rise of science. In 1660, England's monarchy was restored after two decades of revolution and civil war. The newly crowned King Charles II granted a group of natural philosophers and mathematicians a royal charter (1662) to establish the Royal Society of London, for the "improvement of natural knowledge" and committed to experimentation and collaborative work among natural philosophers. The founders of the Royal Society, in particular Boyle, believed it could serve a political as well as an intellectual purpose. The Royal Society would pursue Bacon's goal of collective research, in which members would conduct formal experiments, record the results, and share them with other members. These members would in turn study the methods, reproduce the experiment, and assess the outcome. This enterprise would give England's natural philosophers a common sense of purpose and a system to reach reasoned, gentlemanly agreement on "matters of fact." Also, by separating systematic scientific research from the dangerous language of politics and religion that had marked the civil war, the Royal Society could help restore a sense of order and consensus to English intellectual life.

The society's journal, *Philosophical Transactions*, reached out to professional scholars and experimenters throughout Europe, and similar societies began to appear elsewhere. The French Academy of Sciences was founded in 1666, and it was also tied to seventeenth-century state building, in this case, Bourbon absolutism (see Chapter 15). Royal societies, devoted to natural philosophy as a collective enterprise, provided a state- (or prince-) sponsored framework for science, and an alternative to the important but uncertain patronage of lesser nobles or to the religious (and largely conservative, Aristotelian) universities. Scientific societies reached rough agreements about what constituted legitimate research; they established the modern scientific custom of crediting discoveries to those who were the first to publish results; and they enabled the easier exchange of information and theories across national boundaries, although philosophical differences among Cartesians, Baconians, and traditional Aristotelians remained very difficult to bridge. Science began to take shape as a discipline.

The early scientific academies did not have explicit rules barring women, but with few exceptions, they consisted only of men. This did not mean that women did not practice science, though their participation in scientific research and debate remained controversial. In some cases, the new science could itself become a justification for women's inclusion, as when the Cartesian philosopher François Poullain de la Barre used anatomy to declare in 1673 that "the mind has no sex." Since women possessed the same physical senses as men and the same nervous systems and brains, Poullain asked, Why should they not equally occupy the same roles in society? In fact, historians have discovered more than a few women who taught at European universities in the sixteenth and seventeenth centuries, above all in Italy. Elena Cornaro Piscopia received her doctorate of philosophy in Padua in 1678, the first woman to do so.

**OBSERVING THE TRANSIT OF VENUS (1673).** Elisabetha (1647–1693) and Johannes Hevelius (1611–1687) believed that precise observations about the timing of Venus's passage across the face of the sun when observed from different parts of the earth could be used to calculate the distance from the earth to the sun. This German-speaking husband-and-wife astronomy team from Gdansk (in present-day Poland) worked together on many of their projects. After Johannes's death, Elisabetha published their jointly written star catalog.

Laura Bassi became a professor of physics at the University of Bologna after receiving her doctorate there in 1733, and on the merits of her exceptional contributions to mathematics, she became a member of the Academy of Science in Bologna. Her papers—such as "On the Compression of Air" (1746), "On the Bubbles Observed in Freely Flowing Fluid" (1747), and "On Bubbles of Air That Escape from Fluids" (1748)—gained her a stipend from the academy.

Italy appears to have been an exception in allowing women to win formal recognition for their education and research in established institutions. Elsewhere, elite women could educate themselves by associating with learned men. The aristocrat Margaret Cavendish (1623–1673), a natural philosopher in England, gleaned the information necessary to start her career from her family and their friends, a network that included Thomas Hobbes and, while she was in exile in France during the 1640s, René Descartes. These connections were not enough to overcome the isolation she felt working in a world of letters that was still largely the preserve of men, but this did not prevent her from developing her own

## Gassendi on the Science of Observation and the Human Soul

*Pierre Gassendi (1592–1655) was a seventeenth-century French Catholic priest and philosopher. A contemporary of Descartes, Gassendi was part of a group of intellectuals in France who sought a new philosophy of nature that could replace the traditional teachings of Aristotle that Copernicus and his followers had so severely criticized. Gassendi had no doubt that his faith as a Christian was compatible with his enthusiasm for the new sciences of observation, but in order to demonstrate this to his contemporaries, he had to show that the mechanical explanations of the universe and the natural world did not necessarily lead to a heretical materialism or atheism. In the following passage, taken from his posthumously published work* Syntagma Philosophicum *(1658), Gassendi attempted to demonstrate that one might infer the existence of the human soul, even if it was not accessible to the senses.*

There are many such things for which with the passage of time helpful appliances are being found that will make them visible to the senses. For example, take the little animal the mite, which is born under the skin; the senses perceived it as a certain unitary little point without parts; but since, however, the senses saw that it moved by itself, reason had deduced from this motion as from a perceptible sign that this little body was an animal and because its forward motion was somewhat like a turtle's, reason added that it must get about by the use of certain tiny legs and feet. And although this truth would have been hidden to the senses, which never perceived these limbs, the microscope was recently invented by which sight could perceive that matters were actually as predicted. Likewise, the question had been raised what the galaxy in the sky with the name of the Milky Way was. Democritus, concerning whom it was said that even when he did not know something he was knowing, had deduced from the perceptible sign of its filmy whiteness that it was nothing more than an innumerable multitude of closely packed little stars which could not be seen separately, but produced that effect of spilt milk when many of them were joined together. This truth had become known to him, and yet

had remained undisclosed to the senses until our day and age, until the moment that the telescope, recently discovered, made it clear that things were in fact what he had said. But there are many such things which, though they were hidden from the ancients, have now been made manifest for our eyes. And who knows but a great many of those which are concealed in our time, which we perceive only through the intelligence, will one day also be clearly perceived by the senses through the agency of some helpful appliance thought up by our descendants? . . .

Secondly, if someone wonders whether a certain body is endowed with a soul or not, the senses are not at all capable of determining that by taking a look as it were at the soul itself; yet there are operations which when they come to the senses' notice, lead the intellect to deduce as from a sign that there is some soul beneath them. You will say that this sign belongs to the empirical type, but it is not at all of that type, for it is not even one of the indicative signs since it does not inform us of something that the senses have ever perceived in conjunction with the sign, as they have seen fire with smoke, but informs us instead of something that has always been impenetrable to the senses themselves, like our skin's pores or the mite's feet before the microscope.

You will persist with the objection that we should not ask so much whether there is a soul in a body as what its nature is, if it is the cause of such operations, just as there is no question that there is a force attracting iron in a magnet or that there is a tide in the sea, but there are questions over what their nature is or what they are caused by. But let me omit these matters which are to be fully treated elsewhere, and let it be enough if we say that not every truth can be known by the mind, but at least some can concerning something otherwise hidden, or not obvious to the senses themselves. And we bring up the example of the soul both because vital action is proposed by Sextus Empiricus as an example of an indicative sign and because even though it pertains not so much to the nature of the soul as to its existence, still a truth of existence of such magnitude as this, which it is most valuable for us to know, is made indisputable. For when among other questions we hear it asked if God is or exists in the universe, that is a truth of existence which it would be a great service to establish firmly even if it is not proven at the same time what he is or what his nature is. Although God is such that he can no more come under the perusal of the senses than the soul can, still we infer that the soul exists in the body from the actions that occur before the senses and are so peculiarly appropriate to a soul that if one were not present, they would not be either. In the same way we deduce that God exists in the universe from his effects perceived by the senses, which could not be produced by anything but God and which therefore would not be observed unless God were present in the world, such as the great order of the universe, its great beauty, its grandeur, its harmony, which are so great that they can only result from a sovereignly wise, good, powerful, and inexhaustible cause. But these things will be treated elsewhere at greater length.

Source: Craig B. Brush, ed., *The Selected Works of Pierre Gassendi* (New York: 1972), pp. 334–36.

## Questions for Analysis

*1.* What is the relationship between new knowledge and new scientific tools (the microscope and the telescope) in Gassendi's examples of the mite and the Milky Way? Is he a Baconian or a Cartesian?

*2.* What are the limitations of the senses when it comes to questions of the human soul, according to Gassendi?

*3.* Given these limitations, does Gassendi conclude that science will never be able to say anything about his religious faith?

speculative natural philosophy and using it to critique those who would exclude her from scientific debate. The "tyrannical government" of men over women, she wrote, "hath so dejected our spirits, that we are become so stupid, that beasts being but a degree below us, men use us but a degree above beasts. Whereas in nature we have as clear an understanding as men, if we are bred in schools to mature our brains."

The construction of observatories in private residences enabled some women living in such homes to work their way into the growing field of astronomy. Between 1650 and 1710, 14 percent of German astronomers were women, the most famous of whom was Maria Winkelmann (1670–1720). Winkelmann had collaborated with her husband, Gottfried Kirch, in his observatory, and when he died she had already done significant work, discovering a comet and preparing calendars for the Berlin Academy of Sciences. When Kirch died, she petitioned the academy to allow her to take her husband's place in that prestigious body but was rejected. Gottfried Leibniz, the academy's president, explained, "Already during her husband's lifetime the society was burdened with ridicule because its calendar was prepared by a woman. If she were now to be kept on in such capacity, mouths would gape even wider." In spite of this rejection, Winkelmann continued to work as an astronomer, training both her son and two daughters in the discipline.

Like Winkelmann, the entomologist Maria Sibylla Merian (1647–1717) also made a career based on observation. And like Winkelmann, Merian was able to carve out a space for her scientific work by exploiting the precedent of guild women who learned their trades in family workshops. Merian was a daughter of an engraver and illustrator in Frankfurt and served as his informal apprentice

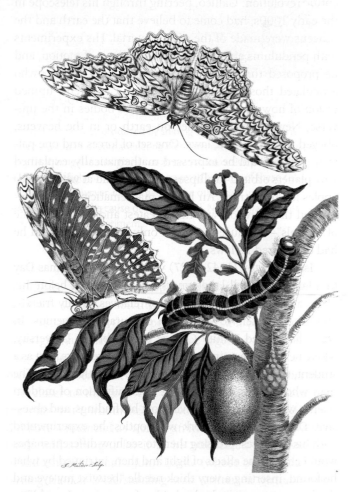

**FROM *METAMORPHOSIS OF THE INSECTS OF SURINAM*, BY MARIA SYBILLA MERIAN (1705).** Merian, the daughter of a Frankfurt engraver, learned in her father's workshop the skills necessary to become an important early entymologist and scientific illustrator and conducted her research on two continents.

## Newton on the Purposes of Experimental Philosophy

*When Newton added his* General Scholium *to the second edition of* Principia *in 1713, he was seventy-one, president of the Royal Society, and widely revered. Responding to Continental critics, he set out his general views on science and its methods, arguing against purely deductive reasoning and reliance on hypotheses about ultimate causes.*

Hitherto we have explained the phenomena of the heavens and of our sea by the power of gravity, but have not yet assigned the cause of this power. This is certain, that it must proceed from a cause that penetrates to the very centres of the sun and planets, without suffering the least diminution of its force; that operates not according to the quantity of the surfaces of the particles on which it acts (as mechanical causes used to do), but according to the quantity of the solid matter which they contain, and propagates its virtue on all sides to immense distances, decreasing always as the inverse square of the distances. . . . [H]itherto I have not been able to discover the cause of those properties of gravity from phenomena, and I frame no hypothesis; for whatever is not deduced from the phenomena is to be called an hypothesis and hypotheses, whether metaphysical or physical, whether of occult qualities or mechanical, have no place in experimental philosophy. In this philosophy particular propositions are inferred from the phenomena, and afterwards rendered general by induction. . . . And to us it is enough that gravity does really exist, and acts according to the laws which we have explained, and abundantly serves to account for all the motions of the celestial bodies, and of our sea.

Source: Michael R. Matthews, ed., *The Scientific Background to Modern Philosophy: Selected Readings* (Indianapolis: 1989), p. 152.

### Questions for Analysis

1. Why did Isaac Newton declare that "hypotheses, whether metaphysical or physical, whether of occult qualities or mechanical, have no place in experimental philosophy"?

2. Is Newton's thinking similar to Bacon's, or does he argue in ways similar to Descartes?

and was given a funeral at Westminster Abbey. The poet Alexander Pope expressed the awe that Newton inspired in some of his contemporaries in a famous couplet:

> Nature and nature's law lay hid in night;
> God said, "Let Newton be!" and all was light.

Voltaire, the French champion of the Enlightenment (discussed in the next chapter), was largely responsible for Newton's reputation in France. In this, he was helped by a woman who was a brilliant mathematician in her own right, Emilie du Châtelet. She coauthored a book with Voltaire introducing Newton to a French audience; and she translated *Principia*, a daunting scientific and mathematical task and one well beyond Voltaire's mathematical abilities. Newton's French admirers and publicists disseminated Newton's findings. In their eyes, Newton exemplified a cultural transformation, a turning point in the history of knowledge.

## Science and Cultural Change

From the seventeenth century on, science stood at the heart of what it meant to be "modern." It grew increasingly central to the self-understanding of Western culture, and scientific and technological power became one of the justifications for the expansion of Western empires and the subjugation of other peoples. For all these reasons, the scientific revolution was and often still is presented as a thoroughgoing break with the past, a moment when Western culture was recast. But as one historian wrote, "no house is ever built of entirely virgin materials, according to a plan bearing no resemblance to old patterns, and no body of culture is able to wholly reject its past. Historical change is not like that, and most 'revolutions' effect less sweeping changes than they advertise or than are advertised for them."

To begin with, the transformation we have considered in this chapter involved elite knowledge. Ordinary people inhabited a very different cultural world. Second, natural philosophers' discoveries—Tycho's mathematics and Galileo's observations, for instance—did not undo the authority of the ancients in one blow, nor did they seek to do so. Third, science did not subvert religion. Even when traditional concepts collapsed in the face of new discoveries, natural philosophers seldom gave up on the project of restoring a picture of a divinely ordered universe. Mechanists argued that the intricate universe revealed by the discoveries of Copernicus, Kepler, Galileo, Newton, and others was evidence of God's guiding presence. Robert Boyle's will provided funds for a lecture series on the "confutation of atheism" by scientific means, and Isaac Newton was happy to have his work contribute to that project. "Nothing," he wrote to one of the lecturers in 1692, "can rejoice me more than to find [*Principia*] usefull for that purpose." The creation of "the Sun and Fixt stars," "the motion which the Planets now have could not spring from any naturall cause alone but were imprest with a divine Agent." Science was thoroughly compatible with belief in God's providential design, at least through the seventeenth century.

The greatest scientific minds were deeply committed to beliefs that do not fit present-day notions of science. Newton,

again, is the most striking case in point. The great twentieth-century economist John Maynard Keynes was one of the first to read through Newton's private manuscripts. On the three hundredth anniversary of Newton's birth (the celebration of which was delayed because of the Second World War), Keynes offered the following reappraisal of the great scientist:

I believe that Newton was different from the conventional picture of him. . . .

In the eighteenth century and since, Newton came to be thought of as the first and greatest of the modern age of scientists, a rationalist, one who taught us to think on the lines of cold and untinctured reason.

I do not see him in this light. I do not think that any one who has pored over the contents of that box which he packed up when he finally left Cambridge in 1696 and which, though partly dispersed, have come down to us, can see him like that. Newton was not the first of the age of reason. He was the last of the magicians, the last of the Babylonians and Sumerians, the last great mind which looked out

***ESTABLISHMENT OF THE ACADEMY OF SCIENCES AND FOUNDATION OF THE OBSERVATORY, 1667.*** The 1666 founding of the Academy of Sciences was a measure of the new prestige of science and the potential value of research. Louis XIV sits at the center, surrounded by the religious and scholarly figures who offer the fruits of their knowledge to the French state. ■ ***What was the value of science for absolutist rulers such as Louis?***

on the visible and intellectual world with the same eyes as those who began to build our intellectual inheritance rather less than 10,000 years ago.

Like his predecessors, Newton saw the world as God's message to humanity, a text to be deciphered, and close reading and study would unlock its mysteries. This same impulse led Newton to read accounts of magic, investigate alchemy's claims that base metals could be turned into gold, and immerse himself in the writings of the Church fathers and the Bible, which he knew in intimate detail. If these activities sound unscientific from the perspective of the present, it is because the strict distinction between rational inquiry and belief in the occult or religious traditions simply did not exist in his time. Such a distinction is a product of a long history of scientific developments after the eighteenth century. Newton, then, was the last representative of an older tradition, and also, quite unintentionally, the first of a new one.

What, then, did the scientific revolution change? Seventeenth-century natural philosophers had produced new answers to fundamental questions about the physical world. Age-old questions about astronomy and physics had been recast and, to some extent (although it was not yet clear to what extent), answered. This process also brought about a new approach to amassing and integrating information in a systematic way, an approach that helped yield more insights into the workings of nature as time went on. During this period, too, the most innovative scientific work moved out of the restrictive environment of the Church and the universities. Natural philosophers began talking to and working with each other in lay organizations that developed standards of research. England's Royal Society spawned imitators in Florence and Berlin, and later, in Russia. The French Royal Academy of Sciences had a particularly direct relationship with the monarchy and the French state. France's statesmen exerted control over the academy and sought to share in the rewards of any discoveries made by its members.

New were beliefs about the purpose and methods of science. The practice of breaking a complex problem down into parts made it possible to tackle more and different questions

## After You Read This Chapter

Go to **INQUIZITIVE** to see what you've learned—and learn what you've missed—with personalized feedback along the way.

### REVIEWING THE OBJECTIVES

- The scientific revolution marked a shift toward new forms of explanation in descriptions of the natural world. What made the work of scientists during this period different from earlier forms of knowledge or research?

- The scientific revolution nevertheless depended on earlier traditions of philosophical thought. What earlier traditions proved important in fostering a spirit of scientific investigation?

- Observations of natural processes both in the heavens and on the earth played a central role in the scientific revolution. What technological innovations made new astronomical work possible? What questions led to the development of geology and the earth sciences?

- Central to the scientific revolution was the rejection of the Ptolemaic view of the universe and its replacement by the Copernican model. What was this controversy about?

- Francis Bacon and René Descartes held contrasting ideas about scientific method. What approach to science did each of these natural philosophers defend?

in the physical sciences. And mathematics assumed a more central role in the new science. Finally, rather than simply confirming established truths, the new methods were designed to explore the unknown and provide means to discover new truths. As Kepler wrote to Galileo, "How great a difference there is between theoretical speculation and visual experience, between Ptolemy's discussion of the Antipodes and Columbus's discovery of the New World." Knowledge itself was reconceived. In the older model, to learn was to read: reason logically, argue, compare classical texts, and absorb a finite body of knowledge. In the newer one, to learn was to discover, and what could be discovered was boundless.

## CONCLUSION

The pioneering natural philosophers remained circumspect about their abilities. Some sought to lay bare the workings of the universe, while others believed humans could only catalog and describe the regularities observed in nature. By unspoken but seemingly mutual agreement, the question of first causes was left aside. The new science did not say *why*, but *how*. Newton, for one, worked toward explanations that would reveal the logic of creation laid out in mathematics. Yet, in the end, he settled for theories explaining motions and relationships that could be observed and tested.

The eighteenth-century heirs to Newton were much more daring. Laboratory science and the work of the scientific societies largely stayed true to the experimenters' rules and limitations. But as we will see in the next chapter, the natural philosophers who began investigating the human sciences cast aside some of their predecessors' caution. Society, technology, government, religion, even the individual human mind seemed to be mechanisms or parts of a larger nature waiting for study. The scientific revolution overturned the natural world as it had been understood for a millennium; it also inspired thinkers more interested in revolutions in society.

## PEOPLE, IDEAS, AND EVENTS IN CONTEXT

- How did the traditions of **NEOPLATONISM**, **RENAISSANCE**, and **HUMANISM** contribute to a vision of the physical world that encouraged scientific investigation and explanation?

- In what way did the work of **NICOLAS COPERNICUS**, **TYCHO BRAHE**, **JOHANNES KEPLER**, and **GALILEO GALILEI** undermine the intellectual foundations of the **PTOLEMAIC SYSTEM**? Why did their work largely take place outside the traditional centers of learning in Europe, such as universities?

- What was the significance of **JAMES USSHER**'s claim that the earth was created in 4004 B.C.? How did **NICOLAS STENO** demonstrate that the different layers of the earth's surface were visible signs of the earth's history?

- What differences in scientific practice arose from **FRANCIS BACON**'s emphasis on observation and **RENÉ DESCARTES**'s insistence that knowledge could be derived only from unquestionable first principles?

- What were **ISAAC NEWTON**'s major contributions to the scientific revolution? Why have some suggested that Newton's interests and thinking were not all compatible with modern conceptions of scientific understanding?

- What was important about the establishment of institutions such as the British **ROYAL SOCIETY** or the French **ACADEMY OF SCIENCES** for the development of scientific methods and research?

- What prevented women from entering most of Europe's scientific academies? How did educated women such as **LAURA BASSI**, **MARGARET CAVENDISH**, **MARIA WINKELMANN**, and **MARIA SYBILLA MERIAN** gain the skills necessary to participate in scientific work?

## THINKING ABOUT CONNECTIONS

- How did ideas about the value of ancient scholarship and philosophy change after the development of new sciences of observation during the seventeenth century?

- What possible connections might be made between the intellectual developments in scientific thinking during the seventeenth century and the Reformation of the sixteenth century? Was the new science incompatible with religious faith?

# Rulers of Principal States

## THE CAROLINGIAN DYNASTY

Pepin of Heristal, mayor of the palace, 687–714
Charles Martel, mayor of the palace, 715–741
Pepin III, mayor of the palace, 741–751; king, 751–768
Charlemagne, king, 768–814; emperor, 800–814
Louis the Pious, emperor, 814–840

### West Francia

Charles the Bald, king, 840–877; emperor, 875–877
Louis II, king, 877–879
Louis III, king, 879–882
Carloman, king, 879–884

## HOLY ROMAN EMPERORS

### Saxon Dynasty

Otto I, 962–973
Otto II, 973–983
Otto III, 983–1002
Henry II, 1002–1024

### Franconian Dynasty

Conrad II, 1024–1039
Henry III, 1039–1056
Henry IV, 1056–1106
Henry V, 1106–1125
Lothair II (Saxony), 1125–1137

### Hohenstaufen Dynasty

Conrad III, 1138–1152
Frederick I (Barbarossa), 1152–1190
Henry VI, 1190–1197
Philip of Swabia, 1198–1208 } Rivals
Otto IV (Welf), 1198–1215 }

### Middle Kingdoms

Lothair, emperor, 840–855
Louis (Italy), emperor, 855–875
Charles (Provence), king, 855–863
Lothair II (Lorraine), king, 855–869

### East Francia

Ludwig, king, 840–876
Carloman, king, 876–880
Ludwig, king, 876–882
Charles the Fat, emperor, 876–887

Frederick II, 1220–1250
Conrad IV, 1250–1254

### Interregnum, 1254–1273

### Emperors from Various Dynasties

Rudolf I (Habsburg), 1273–1291
Adolf (Nassau), 1292–1298
Albert I (Habsburg), 1298–1308
Henry VII (Luxemburg), 1308–1313
Ludwig IV (Wittelsbach), 1314–1347
Charles IV (Luxemburg), 1347–1378
Wenceslas (Luxemburg), 1378–1400
Rupert (Wittelsbach), 1400–1410
Sigismund (Luxemburg), 1410–1437

### Habsburg Dynasty

Albert II, 1438–1439
Frederick III, 1440–1493

Maximilian I, 1493–1519
Charles V, 1519–1556
Ferdinand I, 1556–1564
Maximilian II, 1564–1576
Rudolf II, 1576–1612
Matthias, 1612–1619
Ferdinand II, 1619–1637
Ferdinand III, 1637–1657

Leopold I, 1658–1705
Joseph I, 1705–1711
Charles VI, 1711–1740
Charles VII (not a Habsburg), 1742–1745
Francis I, 1745–1765
Joseph II, 1765–1790
Leopold II, 1790–1792
Francis II, 1792–1806

## RULERS OF FRANCE FROM HUGH CAPET

### Capetian Dynasty

Hugh Capet, 987–996
Robert II, 996–1031
Henry I, 1031–1060
Philip I, 1060–1108
Louis VI, 1108–1137
Louis VII, 1137–1180
Philip II (Augustus), 1180–1223
Louis VIII, 1223–1226
Louis IX (Saint Louis), 1226–1270
Philip III, 1270–1285
Philip IV, 1285–1314
Louis X, 1314–1316
Philip V, 1316–1322
Charles IV, 1322–1328

### Valois Dynasty

Philip VI, 1328–1350
John, 1350–1364
Charles V, 1364–1380
Charles VI, 1380–1422
Charles VII, 1422–1461
Louis XI, 1461–1483
Charles VIII, 1483–1498
Louis XII, 1498–1515
Francis I, 1515–1547

Henry II, 1547–1559
Francis II, 1559–1560
Charles IX, 1560–1574
Henry III, 1574–1589

### Bourbon Dynasty

Henry IV, 1589–1610
Louis XIII, 1610–1643
Louis XIV, 1643–1715
Louis XV, 1715–1774
Louis XVI, 1774–1792

### After 1792

First Republic, 1792–1799
Napoleon Bonaparte, first consul, 1799–1804
Napoleon I, emperor, 1804–1814
Louis XVIII (Bourbon dynasty), 1814–1824
Charles X (Bourbon dynasty), 1824–1830
Louis Philippe, 1830–1848
Second Republic, 1848–1852
Napoleon III, emperor, 1852–1870
Third Republic, 1870–1940
Pétain regime, 1940–1944
Provisional government, 1944–1946
Fourth Republic, 1946–1958
Fifth Republic, 1958–

## RULERS OF ENGLAND

### Anglo-Saxon Dynasty

Alfred the Great, 871–899
Edward the Elder, 899–924
Ethelstan, 924–939
Edmund I, 939–946
Edred, 946–955
Edwy, 955–959
Edgar, 959–975

Edward the Martyr, 975–978
Ethelred the Unready, 978–1016
Canute, 1016–1035 (king of Denmark)
Harold I, 1035–1040
Hardicanute, 1040–1042
Edward the Confessor,
   1042–1066
Harold II, 1066

## House of Normandy

William I (the Conqueror), 1066–1087
William II, 1087–1100
Henry I, 1100–1135
Stephen, 1135–1154

## House of Plantagenet

Henry II, 1154–1189
Richard I, 1189–1199
John, 1199–1216
Henry III, 1216–1272
Edward I, 1272–1307
Edward II, 1307–1327
Edward III, 1327–1377
Richard II, 1377–1399

## House of Lancaster

Henry IV, 1399–1413
Henry V, 1413–1422
Henry VI, 1422–1461

## House of York

Edward IV, 1461–1483
Edward V, 1483
Richard III, 1483–1485

## House of Tudor

Henry VII, 1485–1509
Henry VIII, 1509–1547
Edward VI, 1547–1553
Mary I, 1553–1558
Elizabeth I, 1558–1603

## House of Stuart

James I, 1603–1625
Charles I, 1625–1649

## Commonwealth and Protectorate, 1649–1659

Oliver Cromwell, Lord protector, 1653–1658

## House of Stuart Restored

Charles II, 1660–1685
James II, 1685–1688
William III and Mary II, 1689–1694
William III alone, 1694–1702
Anne, 1702–1714

## House of Hanover

George I, 1714–1727
George II, 1727–1760
George III, 1760–1820
George IV, 1820–1830
William IV, 1830–1837
Victoria, 1837–1901

## House of Saxe-Coburg-Gotha

Edward VII, 1901–1910
George V, 1910–1917

## House of Windsor

George V, 1917–1936
Edward VIII, 1936
George VI, 1936–1952
Elizabeth II, 1952–

# RULERS OF AUSTRIA AND AUSTRIA-HUNGARY

*Maximilian I (archduke), 1493–1519
*Charles V, 1519–1556
*Ferdinand I, 1556–1564
*Maximilian II, 1564–1576
*Rudolf II, 1576–1612
*Matthias, 1612–1619
*Ferdinand II, 1619–1637
*Ferdinand III, 1637–1657
*Leopold I, 1658–1705
*Joseph I, 1705–1711
*Charles VI, 1711–1740
Maria Theresa, 1740–1780

*Joseph II, 1780–1790
*Leopold II, 1790–1792
*Francis II, 1792–1835 (emperor of Austria as Francis I after 1804)
Ferdinand I, 1835–1848
Francis Joseph, 1848–1916 (after 1867 emperor of Austria and king of Hungary)
Charles I, 1916–1918 (emperor of Austria and king of Hungary)
Republic of Austria, 1918–1938 (dictatorship after 1934)
Republic restored, under Allied occupation, 1945–1956
Free Republic, 1956–

*Also bore title of Holy Roman emperor

# RULERS OF PRUSSIA AND GERMANY

*Frederick I, 1701–1713
*Frederick William I, 1713–1740
*Frederick II (the Great), 1740–1786
*Frederick William II, 1786–1797
*Frederick William III, 1797–1840
*Frederick William IV, 1840–1861
*William I, 1861–1888 (German emperor after 1871)
Frederick III, 1888

*kings of Prussia

*William II, 1888–1918
Weimar Republic, 1918–1933
Third Reich (Nazi dictatorship), 1933–1945
Allied occupation, 1945–1952
Division into Federal Republic of Germany in west
    and German Democratic Republic in east,
    1949–1991
Federal Republic of Germany (united), 1991–

# RULERS OF RUSSIA

Ivan III, 1462–1505
Vasily III, 1505–1533
Ivan IV, 1533–1584
Theodore I, 1584–1598
Boris Godunov, 1598–1605
Theodore II, 1605
Vasily IV, 1606–1610
Michael, 1613–1645
Alexius, 1645–1676
Theodore III, 1676–1682
Ivan V and Peter I, 1682–1689
Peter I (the Great), 1689–1725
Catherine I, 1725–1727
Peter II, 1727–1730

Anna, 1730–1740
Ivan VI, 1740–1741
Elizabeth, 1741–1762
Peter III, 1762
Catherine II (the Great), 1762–1796
Paul, 1796–1801
Alexander I, 1801–1825
Nicholas I, 1825–1855
Alexander II, 1855–1881
Alexander III, 1881–1894
Nicholas II, 1894–1917
Russian Revolution and Civil War, 1917–1922
Union of Soviet Socialist Republics, 1922–1991
Russian Federation, 1991–

# RULERS OF UNIFIED SPAIN

Ferdinand { and Isabella, 1479–1504
            and Philip I, 1504–1506
            and Charles I, 1506–1516
Charles I (Holy Roman Emperor Charles V), 1516–1556
Philip II, 1556–1598
Philip III, 1598–1621
Philip IV, 1621–1665
Charles II, 1665–1700
Philip V, 1700–1746
Ferdinand VI, 1746–1759
Charles III, 1759–1788
Charles IV, 1788–1808
Ferdinand VII, 1808

Joseph Bonaparte, 1808–1813
Ferdinand VII (restored), 1814–1833
Isabella II, 1833–1868
Republic, 1868–1870
Amadeo, 1870–1873
Republic, 1873–1874
Alfonso XII, 1874–1885
Alfonso XIII, 1886–1931
Republic, 1931–1939
Authoritarian nationalist dictatorship under Francisco
    Franco, 1939–1975
Juan Carlos I, 1975–2014
Felipe VI, 2014–

# RULERS OF ITALY

Victor Emmanuel II, 1861–1878
Humbert I, 1878–1900
Victor Emmanuel III, 1900–1946

Fascist dictatorship under Benito Mussolini, 1922–1943
    (maintained in northern Italy until 1945)
Humbert II, May 9–June 13, 1946
Republic, 1946–

# PROMINENT AND RECENT POPES

Silvester I, 314–335
Leo I, 440–461
Gelasius I, 492–496
Gregory I, 590–604
Nicholas I, 858–867
Silvester II, 999–1003
Leo IX, 1049–1054
Nicholas II, 1058–1061
Gregory VII, 1073–1085
Urban II, 1088–1099
Paschal II, 1099–1118
Alexander III, 1159–1181
Innocent III, 1198–1216
Gregory IX, 1227–1241
Innocent IV, 1243–1254
Boniface VIII, 1294–1303
John XXII, 1316–1334
Nicholas V, 1447–1455
Pius II, 1458–1464
Alexander VI, 1492–1503

Julius II, 1503–1513
Leo X, 1513–1521
Paul III, 1534–1549
Paul IV, 1555–1559
Sixtus V, 1585–1590
Urban VIII, 1623–1644
Gregory XVI, 1831–1846
Pius IX, 1846–1878
Leo XIII, 1878–1903
Pius X, 1903–1914
Benedict XV, 1914–1922
Pius XI, 1922–1939
Pius XII, 1939–1958
John XXIII, 1958–1963
Paul VI, 1963–1978
John Paul I, 1978
John Paul II, 1978–2005
Benedict XVI, 2005–2013
Francis, 2013–

# Further Readings

## CHAPTER 1

Baines, J., and J. Málek. *Atlas of Ancient Egypt*. Rev. ed. New York, 2000. A reliable, well-illustrated survey, with excellent maps.

Bottéro, Jean. *Everyday Life in Ancient Mesopotamia*. Trans. Antonia Nevill. Baltimore, 2001. A wide-ranging, interdisciplinary account.

Bottéro, Jean. *Religion in Ancient Mesopotamia*. Chicago, 2001. An accessible, engaging survey.

Broodbank, Cyprian. *The Making of the Middle Sea: A History of the Mediterranean from Its Beginning to the Emergence of the Classical World*. Oxford, 2013. A landmark study of the Mediterranean world, beautifully written.

Foster, Benjamin R., and Karen Polinger Foster. *Civilizations of Ancient Iraq*. Princeton, NJ, 2011. A critically acclaimed survey that charts the history of this region from the earliest Sumerian civilization to the Arab conquests of the seventh century C.E.

Geller, Markham J. *Ancient Babylonian Medicine: Theory and Practice*. Malden, MA, 2010. Makes use of previously unstudied cuneiform sources to tell a new story about the relationship between medicine and magic.

George, Andrew, trans. *The Epic of Gilgamesh: A New Translation. The Babylonian Epic Poem and Other Texts in Akkadian and Sumerian*. New York and London, 1999. A reliable translation that carefully distinguishes the chronological "layers" of this famous text; also includes many related texts.

Hodder, Ian. *The Leopard's Tale: Revealing the Mysteries of Çatalhöyük*. London and New York, 2006. The most up-to-date account of this fascinating archaeological site, written for general readers by the director of the excavation.

Leick, Gwendolyn. *The Babylonians: An Introduction*. London and New York, 2002. A wide-ranging survey of Babylonian civilization across the centuries.

McDowell, A. G. *Village Life in Ancient Egypt: Laundry Lists and Love Songs*. Oxford, 1999. A fascinating collection of translated texts recovered from an Egyptian peasant village, dating from 1539 to 1075 B.C.E.

McGregor, Neil. *A History of the World in 100 Objects*. London, 2011. Based on an acclaimed BBC Radio program, this book features a range of artifacts from the collections of the British Museum, embeds them in their historical contexts, and explores the ways that they still hold meaning today.

Mithen, Steven, with Sue Mithen. *Thirst: Water and Power in the Ancient World*. Cambridge, MA, 2013. A new comparative history of water management and consumption throughout the ancient world.

Pollock, Susan. *Ancient Mesopotamia*. Cambridge, 1999. An advanced textbook that draws on theoretical anthropology to interpret Mesopotamian civilization up to 2100 B.C.E.

Redford, Donald B., ed. *The Oxford Encyclopedia of Ancient Egypt*. 3 vols. New York, 2001. An indispensable reference work, intended for both specialists and beginners.

Richardson, Seth. "Early Mesopotamia: The Presumptive State." *Past and Present* 215 (2012): 3–49. A powerful summary of the new methodologies and research questions that are challenging the traditional narrative of state building and urban life in Mesopotamia.

Roaf, Michael. *Cultural Atlas of Mesopotamia and the Ancient Near East*. New York, 1990. An informative, authoritative, and lavishly illustrated guide, with excellent maps.

Robins, Gay. *The Art of Ancient Egypt*. London, 1997. An excellent survey, now the standard account.

Shafer, Byron E., ed. *Religion in Ancient Egypt: Gods, Myths, and Personal Practice*. London, 1991. A scholarly examination of Egyptian belief and ritual, with contributions from leading authorities.

Shaw, Ian, ed. *The Oxford History of Ancient Egypt*. Oxford, 2000. An outstanding collaborative survey of Egyptian history from the Stone Age to c. 300 C.E., with excellent bibliographical essays.

Shryock, Andrew, and Daniel Lord Smail. Berkeley, 2012. *Deep History: The Architecture of Past and Present*. A fascinating fusion of historical, anthropological, and scientific research on what it means to be human.

Smail, Daniel Lord. *On Deep History and the Brain*. Berkeley, 2008. A pioneering introduction to the historical uses of neuroscience and evolutionary biology.

Snell, Daniel C., ed. *A Companion to the Ancient Near East*. Oxford, 2005. A topical survey of recent scholarly work, particularly strong on society, economy, and culture.

Wengrow, David. *The Archaeology of Early Egypt: Social Transformations in North-East Africa, 10,000 to 2650 B.C.* Cambridge, 2006. An authoritative account of archaeological evidence and its interpretation.

## CHAPTER 2

Aubet, Maria Eugenia. *Phoenicia and the West: Politics, Colonies, and Trade*. Trans. Mary Turton. Cambridge, 1993. An intelligent and thought-provoking examination of Phoenician civilization and its influence.

Blenkinsopp, Joseph. *David Remembered: Kingship and National Identity in Ancient Israel*. Cambridge, 2013. An accessible history of King David, his dynasty, and his historical legacy, authored by a noted biblical scholar.

Boardman, John. *Assyrian and Babylonian Empires and Other States of the Near East from the Eighth to the Sixth Centuries* B.C. New York, 1991. Scholarly and authoritative.

———. *Persia and the West*. London, 2000. A great book by a distinguished scholar, with a particular focus on art and architecture as projections of Persian imperial ideologies.

Boyce, Mary. *Textual Sources for the Study of Zoroastrianism*. Totowa, NJ, 1984. An invaluable collection of documents.

Bryce, Trevor. *The Kingdom of the Hittites*. Oxford, 1998; and *Life and Society in the Hittite World*. Oxford, 2002. An extraordinary synthesis, now the standard account of Hittite political, military, and daily life.

Collins, John J., and Daniel C. Harlow, eds. *The Eerdmans Dictionary of Early Judaism*. Cambridge, 2010. A comprehensive tool for students and researchers.

Cooney, Kara. *The Woman Who Would Be King: Hatshepsut's Rise to Power in Ancient Egypt*. New York, 2014. A blend of historical scholarship and informed, imaginative reconstruction.

Curtis, John. *Ancient Persia*. Cambridge, MA, 1990. Concise, solid, reliable.

Dever, William. *Who Were the Early Israelites and Where Did They Come From?* Grand Rapids, MI, 2003. A balanced, fair-minded account with excellent bibliographical guidance to recent work.

Dickinson, O. T. P. K. *The Aegean Bronze Age*. Cambridge, 1994. An excellent summary of archaeological evidence and scholarly argument concerning Minoan, Mycenaean, and other cultures of the Bronze Age Aegean basin.

Dothan, Trude, and Moshe Dothan. *Peoples of the Sea: The Search for the Philistines*. New York, 1992. The essential starting point for understanding Philistine culture and its links to the Aegean basin.

Drews, Robert. *The End of the Bronze Age: Changes in Warfare and the Catastrophe ca. 1200* B.C. Princeton, NJ, 1993. A stimulating analysis and survey, with excellent bibliographies.

Finkelstein, Israel, and Nadav Na'aman, eds. *From Nomadism to Monarchy: Archaeological and Historical Aspects of Early Israel*. Jerusalem, 1994. Scholarly articles on the Hebrews' transformation from pastoralists to a sedentary society focused on the worship of Yahweh.

Fitton, J. Lesley. *Minoans: Peoples of the Past*. British Museum Publications. London, 2002. A careful, reliable debunking of myths about the Minoans, written for nonspecialists.

Kamm, Antony. *The Israelites: An Introduction*. New York, 1999. A short, accessible history of the land and people of Israel up to 135 C.E., aimed at students and general readers.

Kemp, Barry. *The City of Akhenaten and Nefertiti: Amarna and Its People*. London, 2012. A cutting-edge study of this ancient site, based on decades of archaeological research.

Kuhrt, Amélie. *The Ancient Near East, c. 3000–330 B.C.* 2 vols. London and New York, 1995. An outstanding survey, written for students, that includes Egypt and Israel as well as Mesopotamia, Babylonia, Assyria, and Persia.

Marinatos, Nannos. *Minoan Kingship and the Solar Goddess: A Near Eastern Koine*. Champaign, IL, 2010. A rich new interpretation of Minoan culture and its wider connections and influence within the world of the late Bronze Age.

Metzger, Bruce M., and Michael D. Coogan, eds. *The Oxford Companion to the Bible*. New York, 1993. An outstanding reference work, with contributions by leading authorities.

Niditch, Susan. *Ancient Israelite Religion*. New York, 1997. A short introduction designed for students, emphasizing the diversity of Hebrew religious practices.

Prezioso, Donald, and Louise A. Hitchcock. *Aegean Art and Architecture*. Oxford, 2000. Archaic Greek artistic forms in their broader geographic and cultural context, from the fourth millennium to 1000 B.C.E.

Redford, Donald B. *Egypt, Canaan, and Israel in Ancient Times*. Princeton, NJ, 1992. An overview of the interactions between these peoples from about 1200 B.C.E. to the beginning of the Common Era.

Renfrew, Colin. *Archaeology and Language: The Puzzle of Indo-European Origins*. Cambridge, 1987. A masterful but controversial work by one of the most creative archaeologists of the twentieth century.

Sandars, Nancy K. *The Sea Peoples: Warriors of the Ancient Mediterranean*. Rev. ed. London, 1985. An introductory account for students and scholars.

Tubb, Jonathan N., and Rupert L. Chapman. *Archaeology and the Bible*. London, 1990. A good starting point for students that clearly illustrates the difficulties in linking archaeological evidence to biblical accounts of early Hebrew history and society.

Wood, Michael. *In Search of the Trojan War*. New York, 1985. Aimed at a general audience, this carefully researched and engagingly written book is an excellent introduction to the late–Bronze Age context of the Trojan War.

## CHAPTER 3

Penguin Classics and the Loeb Classical Library both offer reliable translations of Greek literary, philosophical, and historical texts.

Beard, Mary. *The Parthenon*. Cambridge, MA, 2003. Traces the successive stages of this monument's construction, deconstruction, reconstruction, and restoration.

Boardman, John, Jaspar Griffin, and Oswyn Murray, eds. *Greece and the Hellenistic World*. Oxford, 1988. A reprint of the Greek and Hellenistic chapters from *The Oxford History of the Classical World,* originally published in 1986. Classic surveys, accessible to a general audience.

Brunschwig, Jacques, and Geoffrey E. R. Lloyd. *Greek Thought: A Guide to Classical Knowledge*. Trans. Catherine Porter. Cambridge, MA, 2000. An outstanding work of reference.

Buckley, Terry, ed. *Aspects of Greek History, 750–323 B.C.: A Source-Based Approach*. London, 1999. A good collection of source materials.

Cartledge, Paul A. *The Spartans: An Epic History*. New York, 2003. A lively and authoritative history of Sparta from its origins to the Roman conquest.

Fantham, Elaine, Helene Foley, Natalie Kampen, Sarah B. Pomeroy, and H. A. Shapiro. *Women in the Classical World: Image and Text*. Oxford, 1994. Wide-ranging analysis drawing on both visual and written sources, covering both the Greek and the Roman periods.

Garlan, Yvon. *Slavery in Ancient Greece*. Ithaca, NY, 1988. Now the standard account.

Hanson, Victor Davis. *The Other Greeks: The Family Farm and the Agrarian Roots of Western Civilization*. New York, 1995. Polemical and idiosyncratic, but convincing in its emphasis on smallholding farmers as the backbone of Greek urban society.

Havelock, Eric A. *The Literate Revolution in Greece and Its Cultural Consequences*. Princeton, 1982. A now-classic account of the wide-ranging effects of writing on Greek society.

Jones, Nicholas F. *Ancient Greece: State and Society*. Upper Saddle River, NJ, 1997. A concise survey from the Minoans up to the end of the Classical period.

Krentz, Peter. *The Battle of Marathon*. New Haven, 2011. A fresh analysis of this landmark battle, paying special attention to the conditions in which hoplite warriors fought.

Lee, Mireille M. *Body, Dress, and Identity in Ancient Greece*. Cambridge, 2015. A major interdisciplinary contribution to our understanding of personal adornment, class, and gender identity.

Lefkowitz, Mary, and Maureen Fant. *Women's Life in Greece and Rome: A Source Book in Translation*. 3rd ed. Baltimore, 2005. A remarkably wide-ranging collection, topically arranged, invaluable to students.

Malkin, Irad. *A Small Greek World: Networks in the Ancient Mediterranean*. Oxford, 2011. A study showing how a Panhellenic identity developed during and because of widespread Greek settlement throughout the ancient world.

Nevett, Lisa C. *Domestic Space in Classical Antiquity*. Cambridge, 2010. Reassesses what we can know about the architecture of households in antiquity through a fresh assessment of archaeological evidence and material culture.

Pomeroy, Sarah. *Goddesses, Whores, Wives, and Slaves: Women in Classical Antiquity*. New York, 1995. The first historical survey of antiquity to place women at the center of the narrative, and still unrivaled in scope.

Price, Simon. *Religions of the Ancient Greeks*. Cambridge, 1999. Concise and authoritative, this survey extends from the Archaic Period up to the fifth century C.E.

Pritchard, David M., ed. *War, Democracy and Culture in Classical Athens*. Cambridge, 2010. A collection of scholarly essays on the close relationship between Athenian politics, culture, and military technology.

Robinson, Eric W. *Democracy beyond Athens: Popular Government in the Greek Classical Age*. Cambridge, 2011. An important contribution to the history of Greek political institutions in poleis other than Athens.

Seaford, Richard. *Money and the Greek Mind: Homer, Philosophy, Tragedy*. Cambridge, 2004. A provocative study of portable wealth and its far-reaching effects.

Strassler, Robert B., ed. *The Landmark Thucydides*. New York, 1996. Reprints the classic Richard Crawley translation with maps, commentary, notes, and appendices by leading scholars.

Thomas, Rosalind. *Oral Tradition and Written Record in Classical Athens*. Cambridge, 1989. A fascinating look at how oral epic, lyric, and drama were transmitted over time.

## CHAPTER 4

Penguin Classics and the Loeb Classical Library both offer reliable translations of scores of literary and historical texts from this period. Particularly important are historical works by Arrian (*Anabasis of Alexander*), Plutarch (*Life of Alexander*), and Polybius (*The Histories*).

Austin, M. M. *The Hellenistic World from Alexander to the Roman Conquest: A Selection of Ancient Sources in Translation*. Cambridge, 1981. A good collection of primary documents.

Aylward, William, ed. *Excavations at Zeugma*. 3 vols. Oxford, 2013. Available free online: http://zeugma.packhum.org. The results of a massive scholarly effort (undertaken between 1987 and 1988) to excavate and analyze the remains of Samosata and the palace of Antiochus I, the best-preserved royal palace in the Hellenistic world, before the site was submerged beneath a Turkish dam in 1989.

Borza, Eugene N. *In the Shadow of Olympus: The Emergence of Macedon*. Princeton, NJ, 1990. The standard account of the rise of Macedon up to the accession of Philip II.

Bosworth, A. B. *Conquest and Empire: The Reign of Alexander the Great*. Cambridge, 1988. A political and military analysis of Alexander's career that strips away the romance, maintaining a clear vision of the ruthlessness and human cost of his conquests.

————. *The Legacy of Alexander: Politics, Warfare, and Propaganda under the Successors*. Oxford, 2002. The most recent survey of the half century following Alexander's death and of the people who created the Hellenistic kingdoms of Egypt, Persia, and Macedon.

Burstein, Stanley M., ed. and trans. *The Hellenistic Age from the Battle of Ipsos to the Death of Kleopatra VII*. Cambridge, 1985. An excellent collection, with sources not found elsewhere.

Cartledge, Paul. *Agesilaus and the Crisis of Sparta*. Baltimore, 1987. A thorough but readable analysis of the social and political challenges besetting Sparta in the fourth century B.C.E.

————. *Alexander the Great: The Hunt for a New Past*. Woodstock, NY, 2004. A compelling account of Alexander's life, times, and influences.

Green, Peter. *Alexander of Macedon, 356–323 B.C.* Berkeley, 1991. Revised edition of the author's earlier biography; entertainingly written, rich in detail and insight.

————. *The Hellenistic Age: A Short History*. New York, 2007. An authoritative synthesis that carries the history of Greek influence into the fourth century C.E.

Hansen, Mogens H. *The Athenian Democracy in the Age of Demosthenes*. Oxford, 1991. An examination of the political institutions of Athens in the fourth century B.C.E.

Holt, Frank. L. *Into the Land of Bones: Alexander the Great in Afghanistan*. Repr. ed. Berkeley, 2012. A vivid, charged narrative that places the beginning of a current war in the distant past.

Johnstone, S. "A New History of Libraries and Books in the Hellenistic Period." *Classical Antiquity* 33 (2014): 347–93. A revolutionary and accessible review of the ancient evidence for the first public libraries.

Lloyd, Geoffrey, and Nathan Sivin. *The Way and the Word: Science and Medicine in Early China and Greece.* New Haven, 2002. An extraordinary comparative study.

McGing, Brian. *Polybius' Histories.* Oxford, 2010. A critical dissection of this influential ancient historian's techniques and historical philosophy.

Nicholas, G. L. *The Genius of Alexander the Great.* Chapel Hill, NC, 1998. A clear, authoritative, admiring account, distilling a lifetime of research on the subject.

Ober, Josiah. *Mass and Elite in Democratic Athens: Rhetoric, Ideology, and the Power of the People.* Princeton, NJ, 1989. An excellent study of the ideology of democracy in Athens that borrows from the insights of modern social science.

Pollitt, Jerome J. *Art in the Hellenistic Age.* New York, 1986. The standard account, blending cultural history with art history.

Sherwin-White, Susan, and Amélie Kuhrt. *From Samarkhand to Sardis: A New Approach to the Seleucid Empire.* London, 1993. A stimulating examination of the relationship between rulers and ruled in the vast expanses of the Seleucid Empire.

Shipley, Graham. *The Greek World after Alexander, 323–30 B.C.* New York and London, 2000. A study of the social, intellectual, and artistic changes in the Hellenistic era.

Thomas, Carol G. *Alexander the Great in His World.* Oxford and Malden, MA, 2007. A study of the contexts—familial, political, and social—that shaped Alexander's career.

Tripolitis, Antonia. *Religions of the Hellenistic-Roman Age.* Grand Rapids, MI, 2002. Survey of the variety of religious experience, ritual, and belief in the centuries before the emergence of Christianity.

Tritle, Lawrence A., ed. *The Greek World in the Fourth Century: From the Fall of the Athenian Empire to the Successors of Alexander.* New York, 1997. A wide-ranging collection of scholarly essays.

## CHAPTER 5

Translations of Roman authors are available in both the Penguin Classics series and in the Loeb Classical Library.

Arnason, Johann P., and Kurt A. Raaflaub, eds. *The Roman Empire in Context: Historical and Comparative Perspectives.* Malden, MA, 2011. One of the few books to place the formation of the Roman Empire in a comparative, global perspective.

Barker, Graeme, and Tom Rasmussen. *The Etruscans.* Oxford and Malden, MA, 1998. A fine survey, from the Blackwell *Peoples of Europe* series.

Beard, Mary. *SPQR: A History of Ancient Rome.* New York, 2015. A masterful narrative and critical history of the shift from republic to Principate.

———. *Pompeii: The Life of a Roman Town.* New York, 2010. A fascinating, cutting-edge study of daily life and of the archaeological work that uncovered it.

Cornell, T. J. *The Beginnings of Rome: Italy and Rome from the Bronze Age to the Punic Wars (c. 1000–264 B.C.).* London, 1995. An ambitious survey of the archaeological and historical evidence for early Rome.

Crawford, Michael. *The Roman Republic,* 2nd ed. Cambridge, MA, 1993. A lively, fast-paced survey of republican Rome. An excellent place to start.

Fantham, Elaine, Helene Peet Foley, Natalie Boymel Kampen, Sarah B. Pomeroy, and H. Alan Shapiro. *Women in the Classical World.* Oxford, 1994. An expert survey of both Greece and Rome.

Garnsey, Peter, and Richard Saller. *The Roman Empire: Economy, Society, and Culture.* Berkeley, 1987. A straightforward short survey.

Gruen, Erich S. *The Hellenistic World and the Coming of Rome.* 2 vols. Berkeley, 1984. A massive survey, focused on the unpredictable rise of Rome to a position of dominance within the Mediterranean world.

Harris, William V. *War and Imperialism in Republican Rome, 327–70 B.C.* Oxford, 1979. A challenging study arguing that Rome's need for military conquest and expansion was deeply embedded in the fabric of Roman life.

Hayes, Ian. *Blood of the Provinces: The Roman Auxilia and the Making of Provincial Society from Augustus to Severus.* Oxford, 2013. A new history of Roman warfare and its role in expanding imperial power, showing how archaeological evidence challenges written sources.

Krebs, Christopher. *A Most Dangerous Book: Tacitus's "Germania" from the Roman Empire to the Third Reich.* A history of this ancient ethnography's transmission and reception, and especially the political uses to which it was put in Nazi Germany.

Lancel, Serge. *Carthage: A History.* Trans. Antonia Nevill. Oxford, 1995. An account of Rome's great rival for control of the Mediterranean world.

Millar, Fergus G. B. *The Emperor in the Roman World, 31 B.C.–A.D. 337.* London, 1977. A classic work that showed (among much else) the importance of emperor worship to the religious outlook of the Roman Empire.

———. *The Crowd in Rome in the Late Republic.* Ann Arbor, MI, 1999. A revisionist account that emphasizes the reality of Roman democracy in the late republic, against those who would see the period's politics as entirely under the control of aristocratic families.

Watkin, David. *The Roman Forum.* London, 2009. A history of the successive buildings and archaeological excavations of this central Roman space.

Wells, Colin. *The Roman Empire,* 2nd ed. Cambridge, MA, 1992. An easily readable survey from the reign of Augustus to the mid–third century C.E., particularly useful for its treatment of the relationship between the Roman central government and its Italian provinces.

Wiseman, T. P. *Remembering the Roman People.* Oxford, 2009. A collection of studies devoted to popular politics in the late republic.

Woolf, Greg. *Becoming Roman: The Origins of Provincial Civilization in Gaul.* Cambridge, 1998. An exemplary study of how provincial elites made themselves "Roman."

———. *Rome: An Empire's Story.* Oxford, 2012. A masterful account of Rome's reconfiguration of the ancient world and its enduring impact; critically acclaimed by scholars and general readers.

_____. *Tales of the Barbarians: Ethnography and Empire in the Roman West*. Malden, MA, 2011. Applies modern ethnographic methodologies to a dissection of how Romans applied their own ethnographic theories to contemporary "others."

## CHAPTER 6

Augustine. *The City of God*. Trans. Henry Bettenson. Baltimore, 1972.

_____. *Confessions*. Trans. Henry M. Chadwick. Oxford, 1991.

_____. *On Christian Doctrine*. Trans. D. W. Robertson Jr. New York, 1958.

Boethius. *The Consolation of Philosophy*. Trans. R. Green. Indianapolis, 1962.

Bowersock, G. W., Peter Brown, and Oleg Grabar. *Late Antiquity: A Guide to the Postclassical World*. Cambridge, MA, 1999. An authoritative compilation. The first half is devoted to essays on the cultural features of the period; the second half is organized as an encyclopedia.

Brown, Peter. *Augustine of Hippo*. Berkeley, 1967. A great biography by the great scholar of late antiquity.

_____. *The Body and Society: Men, Women and Sexual Renunciation in Early Christianity*. New York, 1988. A revealing study of the fundamental transformations wrought by Christianity in the late antique world.

_____. *The Rise of Western Christendom: Triumph and Diversity, 200–1000*, 2nd ed. Oxford, 2002. An evocative picture of Christianity's spread eastward and northward from the Mediterranean world.

_____. *The World of Late Antiquity*. New York, 1971. Still the best short survey of the period, with excellent illustrations.

_____. *Through the Eye of a Needle: Wealth, the Fall of Rome, and the Making of Christianity in the West, 350–550 A.D.* Princeton, NJ, 2012. The most recent of this historian's magisterial dissections of late antiquity, focused on the relationship between religion, culture, power, and wealth (or its lack).

Cameron, Averil. *The Later Roman Empire, A.D. 284–430*. London, 1993. Now the standard account of its period, with an emphasis on imperial politics.

_____. *The Mediterranean World in Late Antiquity, A.D. 395–600*. London, 1993. Masterful, with excellent, succinct bibliographical essays.

Cassiodorus. *An Introduction to Divine and Human Readings*. Trans. L. W. Jones. New York, 1946.

Chadwick, Henry M. *Augustine*. Oxford, 1986. A short introduction to Augustine's thought.

_____. *Boethius*. Oxford, 1981. An intellectual biography of this important thinker.

Clark, Gillian. *Christianity and Roman Society*. Cambridge, 2004. A short, stimulating survey that places early Christianity firmly in its Roman social context.

_____. *Women in Late Antiquity*. Oxford, 1993. A clear, compact account of an important subject.

Ehrman, Bart D. *The New Testament: A Historical Introduction to the Early Christian Writings,* 4th ed. Oxford, 2008. The standard textbook by a leading authority.

Ehrman, Bart D., and Zlatko Pleše, eds. *The Aprocryphal Gospels: Texts and Translations* Oxford, 2011. The first scholarly edition and translation of all the apocryphal gospels, including Latin, Greek, and Coptic texts.

Eusebius. *The History of the Church*. Trans. G. A. Williamson. Baltimore, 1965. A contemporary account of Constantine's reign, written by one of his courtier-bishops.

_____. *Eusebius' Life of Constantine*. Trans. Averil Cameron and Stuart Hall. Oxford, 1999. An admiring biography that reflects Constantine's own vision of his religious authority.

Grig, Lucy, and Gavin Kelly, eds. *Two Romes: Rome and Constantinople in Antiquity*. Oxford, 2015. A set of comparative essays by noted scholars.

Hopkins, Keith. *A World Full of Gods: The Strange Triumph of Christianity*. New York, 1999. An imaginative study of religious pluralism in the Roman world and the context in which Christianity emerged.

Kulikowski, Michael. *Rome's Gothic Wars: From the Third Century to Alaric*. Cambridge, 2007. An authoritative and critical account.

Lane Fox, Robin. *Augustine: Conversions to Confessions*. New York, 2015. A beautifully written reconstruction of Augustine's early life in its historical context.

Lawrence, Clifford Hugh. *Medieval Monasticism*. 3rd ed. London, 2000. Concise, perceptive survey of monasticism from its beginnings to the end of the Middle Ages.

Pagels, Elaine. *The Gnostic Gospels*. New York, 1979. A pathbreaking study of the noncanonical gospels and the history of their exclusion from the Bible.

Potter, David. *The Roman Empire at Bay, A.D. 180–395*. London and New York, 2004. The most up-to-date account of the empire's reorganization and transformation in this era.

Rebillard, Éric. *Christians and Their Many Identities in Late Antiquity, North Africa, 200–450 C.E.* Ithaca, NY, 2012. In this book, as in his earlier works, the author argues that there was no special importance attached to being a "Christian" in late antiquity, and that religious identities are better understood as fluid and hybrid.

Sanders, E. P. *The Historical Figure of Jesus*. London and New York, 1993. A fine study of Jesus in his first-century Jewish context.

Shanks, Hershel, ed. *Christianity and Rabbinic Judaism: A Parallel History of Their Origins and Early Development*. Washington, DC, 1992. Accessible chapters written by top authorities, describing both Jewish and Christian developments from the first to the sixth centuries C.E.

Sherwin-White, A. N. *Roman Society and Roman Law in the New Testament*. Oxford, 1963. A fascinating reading of the New Testament in its historical context.

Traina, Giusto. *428 A.D.: An Ordinary Year at the End of the Roman Empire*. Princeton, NJ, 2011. An enlightening glimpse into the world of late antiquity, from the vantage point of a single "average" year.

Whittaker, C. R. *Frontiers of the Roman Empire: A Social and Economic Study*. Baltimore, 1994. A convincing picture of the frontiers of the Roman Empire as zones of intensive cultural interaction.

Williams, Stephen. *Diocletian and the Roman Recovery*. New York, 1997. Thorough and authoritative.

## CHAPTER 7

Translations of Arabic sources are now available in the *Library of Arabic Literature* series from New York University Press.

Arnold, Jonathan J. *Theoderic and the Roman Imperial Restoration.* Cambridge, 2014. An ambitious new reading of Theoderic's reign, arguing for the thoroughly Roman identity and ambitions of this Gothic ruler.

Bede. *A History of the English Church and People.* Trans. Leo Sherley-Price. Baltimore, 1955. The fundamental source for early Anglo-Saxon history.

Campbell, James, ed. *The Anglo-Saxons.* Oxford, 1982. An authoritative and splendidly illustrated volume.

Conant, Jonathan. *Staying Roman: Conquest and Identity in Africa and the Mediterranean, 439–700.* Cambridge, 2012. An exploration of what it meant to be "Roman" and the sources of identity in this tumultuous period.

Einhard and Notker the Stammerer. *Two Lives of Charlemagne.* Trans. Lewis Thorpe. Baltimore, 1969. Lively and entertaining works of contemporary biography.

Geanakoplos, Deno John, ed. *Byzantium: Church, Society and Civilization Seen through Contemporary Eyes.* Chicago, 1984. An outstanding source book.

Gregory, Timothy E. *A History of Byzantium.* Malden, MA, and Oxford, 2005. The most accessible of the recent textbooks on Byzantium. An excellent place to start.

Herrin, Judith. *Byzantium: The Surprising Life of a Medieval Empire.* Princeton, NJ, 2009. An accessible and comprehensive history of the eastern Roman Empire.

————. *The Formation of Christendom.* Princeton, NJ, 1987. A synthetic history of the Christian civilizations of Byzantium and western Europe from 500 to 800, written by a prominent historian.

Hodges, Richard, and David Whitehouse. *Mohammed, Charlemagne and the Origins of Europe.* London, 1983. A critical analysis of the "Pirenne thesis," reexamining the relationship between the Mediterranean world and northern Europe.

Hourani, Albert. *A History of the Arab Peoples.* New York, 1992. A sympathetic and clear survey written for nonspecialists.

Hoyland, Robert G. *In God's Path: The Arab Conquests and the Creation of the Islamic Empire.* Oxford, 2014. A highly acclaimed new study of Islam's rapid expansion as a product of Arab imperial ambitions.

Kazhdan, Alexander P., ed. *The Oxford Dictionary of Byzantium.* 3 vols. Oxford, 1991. An authoritative reference work.

Kennedy, Hugh. *The Prophet and the Age of the Caliphates.* 2nd ed. Harlow, UK, 2004. A lucid introduction to the political history of the Islamic world from the sixth through the eleventh centuries.

Krautheimer, Richard. *Early Christian and Byzantine Architecture.* 4th ed. New York, 1986. A classic work by one of the greatest Byzantine art historians of the twentieth century.

Little, Lester K., ed., *Plague and the End of Antiquity: The Pandemic of 541–750.* Cambridge, 2006. The first full-length scholarly history of the first global pandemic.

Mango, Cyril, ed. *The Oxford History of Byzantium.* Oxford and New York, 2002. Full of sharp judgments and attractively illustrated.

McCormick, Michael. *The Origins of the European Economy: Communications and Commerce* A.D. *300–900.* Cambridge, 2002. An astonishing reinterpretation of the evidence for the myriad contacts between Christian Europe and Islam.

McKitterick, Rosamond. *Charlemagne: The Formation of a European Identity.* Cambridge, 2008. A history of Charlemagne's career and its lasting impact by an eminent scholar of the Carolingian world.

————, ed. *The Uses of Literacy in Early Medieval Europe.* New York, 1990. A superb collection of essays.

McNamara, Jo Ann, and John E. Halborg, eds. *Sainted Women of the Dark Ages.* Durham, NC, 1992. Translated saints' lives from Merovingian and Carolingian Europe.

Murray, A. C., ed. *From Roman to Merovingian Gaul: A Reader.* Toronto, 2000. An excellent collection of sources.

Pelikan, Jaroslav. *The Christian Tradition.* Vol. 2, *The Spirit of Eastern Christendom.* Chicago, 1974. An outstanding synthetic treatment of the doctrines of Byzantine Christianity.

Procopius. *The Secret History.* Trans. G. A. Williamson. Baltimore, 1966. An "unauthorized" account of Justinian's reign, written by the emperor's offical historian.

Reuter, Timothy. *Germany in the Early Middle Ages, 800–1056.* New York, 1991. The best survey in English.

Sijpesteijn, Petra M. *Shaping a Muslim State: The World of a Mid-Eighth-Century Egyptian Official.* Oxford, 2013. Based on a cache of papyrus letters sent to a Muslim administrator, this book reveals how an Arab/Muslim state was established in a former province of the eastern Roman Empire.

Treadgold, Warren. *A History of the Byzantine State and Society.* Stanford, CA, 1997. A massive, encyclopedic narrative of the political, economic, and military history of Byzantium from 284 until 1461.

Wallace-Hadrill, John Michael. *Early Germanic Kingship in England and on the Continent.* Oxford, 1971. A classic analysis of changing ideas about kingship in early medieval Europe, emphasizing the links between Anglo-Saxon and Carolingian cultures.

————. *The Frankish Church.* Oxford, 1983. A masterful account that links the Merovingian and Carolingian churches.

Watt, W. Montgomery. *Islamic Philosophy and Theology.* 2nd ed. Edinburgh, 1985. The standard English account.

Wemple, Suzanne Fonay. *Women in Frankish Society: Marriage and the Cloister, 500–900.* Philadelphia, 1981. An influential account of changing attitudes toward marriage among the early Franks.

Whittow, Mark. *The Making of Orthodox Byzantium, 600–1025.* London, 1996. Emphasizes the centrality of orthodoxy in shaping Byzantine history. Particularly good on Byzantine relations with the peoples outside the empire.

Wickham, Chris. *Framing the Middle Ages: Europe and the Mediterranean, 400–800.* Oxford, 2007. An eye-opening history that spans the transitional periods of late antiquity and the early Middle Ages, paying careful attention to regional differences.

Wood, Ian. *The Merovingian Kingdoms, 450–751.* New York, 1994. A detailed study, but difficult for beginners.

## CHAPTER 8

Amt, Emily, ed. *Women's Lives in Medieval Europe: A Sourcebook.* New York, 1993. An excellent collection of primary texts.

*The Song of Roland.* Trans. Robert Harrison. New York, 1970. A lively translation.

Arnold, Benjamin. *Princes and Territories in Medieval Germany.* Cambridge and New York, 1991. The best such survey in English.

Berend, Nora, Przemysław Urbańczyk, and Przemysław Wisewski. *Central Europe in the High Middle Ages: Bohemia, Hungary and Poland, c. 900–c. 1300.* Cambridge, 2013. An accessible introduction to the medieval history of this region.

Boswell, John E. *Christianity, Social Tolerance, and Homosexuality: Gay People in Western Europe from the Beginning of the Christian Era to the Fourteenth Century.* Chicago, 1980. A pioneering account, hotly debated but highly respected.

Burman, Thomas E. *Reading the Qur'ān in Latin Christendom, 1140–1560.* Philadelphia, 2007. A fascinating account of the Qur'an's reception in medieval Europe.

Dunbabin, Jean. *France in the Making, 843–1180.* 2nd ed. Oxford and New York, 2000. An authoritative survey of the disparate territories that came to make up the medieval French kingdom.

Dyer, Christopher. *Making a Living in the Middle Ages: The People of Britain 850–1520.* New Haven, 2002. A splendid new synthesis that combines social, economic, and archaeological evidence.

Fossier, Robert. *The Ax and the Oath: Ordinary Life in the Middle Ages.* Princeton, NJ, 2010. A quirky, personal, and often insightful look at the daily lives and worldview of this era by a leading French historian.

Frankopan, Peter. *The First Crusade: The Call from the East.* Cambridge, MA, 2012. Analyzes the causes and catalysts of the crusading movement.

Hicks, Carola. *The Bayeux Tapestry: The Life Story of a Masterpiece.* London, 2006. An art historian's engrossing account of the making, reception, and interpretation of this amazing artifact.

Horden, Peregrine, and Nicholas Purcell. *The Corrupting Sea: A Study of Mediterranean History.* Malden, MA, 2000. An extraordinary attempt to encompass the history of the Mediterranean world over a span of three millennia.

Leyser, Henrietta. *Medieval Women: A Social History of Women in England, 440–1500.* New York, 1995. Although limited to one country, this is the best of the recent surveys treating medieval women.

McLaughlin, Megan. *Sex, Gender, and Episcopal Authority in an Age of Reform, 1000–1122.* Cambridge, 2010. A new interpretation of gendered discourse and politics during the Investiture Controversy.

Martin, Janet. *Medieval Russia, 980–1584.* 2nd ed. Cambridge, 2007. A concise history with a wide reach.

Miller, Maureen C. *Power and the Holy in the Age of the Investiture Conflict: A Brief History with Documents.* Boston, 2005. A stimulating approach to the eleventh-century conflicts over temporal and spiritual power, with many newly translated sources.

Moore, Robert I. *The First European Revolution, c. 970–1215.* Oxford and Cambridge, MA, 2000. A remarkable description of the ways in which European society was fundamentally reshaped during the eleventh and twelfth centuries.

Raffensperger, Christian. *Reimagining Europe: Kievan Rus' in the Medieval World.* Cambridge, MA, 2012. An exciting new study of early Rus' and its neighbors.

Reilly, Bernard F. *The Medieval Spains.* New York, 1993. A succinct account that covers the entire Iberian peninsula from 500 to 1500.

Reynolds, Susan. *Fiefs and Vassals: The Medieval Evidence Reinterpreted.* Oxford and New York, 1994. A detailed revisionist history of "feudalism."

Rubenstein, Jay. *Armies of Heaven: The First Crusade and the Quest for Apocalypse.* New York, 2011. An accessible narrative of the First Crusade, written for a general audience and arguing for a new interpretation of the crusaders' motives.

Sawyer, Peter, ed. *The Oxford Illustrated History of the Vikings.* Oxford, 1997. The best one-volume account, lavishly illustrated.

Sheingorn, Pamela, trans. *The Book of Sainte Foy.* Philadelphia, 1995.

Stillman, Norman A. *The Jews of Arab Lands: A History and Source Book.* Philadelphia, 1979. An essential resource.

Stow, Kenneth R. *Alienated Minority: The Jews of Medieval Latin Europe.* Cambridge, MA, 1992. An excellent survey.

Tierney, Brian. *The Crisis of Church and State, 1050–1300.* Toronto, 1988. An indispensable collection for both teachers and students.

Winroth, Anders. *The Conversion of Scandinavia: Vikings, Merchants, and Missionaries in the Remaking of Northern Europe.* New Haven, 2012. Argues that the peoples of Scandinavia were active participants in the cultural, economic, and political processes that accompanied their conversion to Christianity.

## CHAPTER 9

Abelard and Heloise. *The Letters and Other Writings.* Trans. William Levitan. Indianapolis, 2007. A beautiful and accurate translation of the correspondence and related documents, with a full introduction and notes.

Abulafia, David. *Frederick II: A Medieval Emperor.* London and New York, 1988. A reliable biography that strips away much of the legend that has hitherto surrounded this monarch.

Baldwin, John W. *The Government of Philip Augustus.* Berkeley and Los Angeles, 1986. A landmark scholarly account.

Barber, Malcolm. *The Crusader States.* New Haven, 2012. A new and comprehensive history by an esteemed historian.

Bartlett, Robert. *The Making of Europe: Conquest, Colonization and Cultural Change, 950–1350.* Princeton, NJ, 1993. A wide-ranging examination of the economic, social, and religious expansion of Europe, full of stimulating insights.

Bisson, Thomas N. *The Crisis of the Twelfth Century: Power, Lordship, and the Origins of European Government.* Princeton, NJ, 2009. A new interpretation of the evidence.

Bynum, Caroline Walker. *Holy Feast and Holy Fast: The Religious Significance of Food to Medieval Women.* Berkeley and Los Angeles, 1988. One of the most influential and important works of scholarship published in the late twentieth century.

Camille, Michael. *Gothic Art: Glorious Visions.* New York, 1996. A succinct and beautifully illustrated introduction to the art of the twelfth through fifteenth centuries in Europe.

Chrétien de Troyes. *Arthurian Romances*. Trans. W. W. Kibler. New York, 1991.

Clanchy, Michael T. *Abelard: A Medieval Life*. Oxford and Cambridge, MA, 1997. A great biography.

———. *From Memory to Written Record: England, 1066–1307*. Oxford, 1992. A fascinating and hugely influential account of a revolutionary shift toward documentation.

Fassler, Margot. *Gothic Song: Victorine Sequences and Augustinian Reform in Twelfth-Century Paris*. Cambridge, 1993. The emergence of new musical genres and their cultural context.

Gillingham, John. *The Angevin Empire*. 2nd ed. Oxford and New York, 2001. The best treatment by far of its subject, brief but full of ideas.

Gottfried von Strassburg. *Tristan*. Trans. A. T. Hatto. Baltimore, 1960.

Hallam, Elizabeth, and Judith Everard. *Capetian France, 987–1328*. 2nd ed. New York, 2001. A clear and well-organized account.

Haskins, Charles Homer. *The Renaissance of the Twelfth Century*. Cambridge, MA, 1927. A classic and influential study.

Jones, P. J. *The Italian City-State: From Commune to Signoria*. Oxford and New York, 1997. A fundamental reinterpretation of the evidence.

Jordan, William C. *Europe in the High Middle Ages*. Vol. 3 of the Penguin History of Europe. New York and London, 2003. An outstanding survey.

Kaeuper, Richard W. *Chivalry and Violence in Medieval Europe*. Oxford and New York, 1999. A darker view of chivalry than Keen's.

Keen, Maurice. *Chivalry*. New Haven, 1984. A comprehensive treatment of chivalry from its origins to the sixteenth century.

Lawrence, Clifford Hugh. *The Friars: The Impact of the Early Mendicant Movement on Western Society*. London and New York, 1994. The best short introduction to the early history of the Franciscans and the Dominicans.

Leclerq, Jean. *The Love of Learning and the Desire for God*. 3rd ed. New York, 1982. A beautiful interpretation of twelfth-century monastic culture and the influence of Bernard of Clairvaux.

Little, Lester. *Religious Poverty and Profit Economy in Medieval Europe*. Ithaca, NY, 1978. A fascinating study of the relationship between religious practice and economic reality.

Lopez, Robert S., and Irving W. Raymond, eds. *Medieval Trade in the Mediterranean World*. New York, 1990. A useful collection of source material.

Madden, Thomas F. *The New Concise History of the Crusades*. New York, 2005. An acclaimed and accessible survey for students.

Marie de France. *Lais*. Trans. Glyn S. Burgess and Keith Busby. Harmondsworth, UK, 1999. A compelling and entertaining prose translation.

Moore, R. I. *The War on Heresy*. Cambridge, MA, 2012. A courageous and searching revisionist history, based on decades of research and reflection. Moore argues for a radical reassessment of what "heresy" consisted of, and why those branded as "heretics" were persecuted during the Middle Ages.

Morris, Colin. *The Papal Monarchy: The Western Church from 1050 to 1250*. Oxford, 1989. An excellent scholarly survey, part of the Oxford History of the Christian Church series.

Newman, Barbara, ed. *Voice of the Living Light: Hildegard of Bingen and Her World*. Berkeley and Los Angeles, 1998. An introduction to Hildegard's life and work.

Nirenberg, David. *Neighboring Faiths: Christianity, Islam and Judaism in the Middle Ages and Today*. Chicago, 2014. A thoughtful and powerful study of interfaith relations and the challenges of coexistence, then and now.

Otto, Bishop of Freising. *The Deeds of Frederick Barbarossa*. Trans. C. C. Mierow. New York, 1953. A contemporary chronicle interesting enough to read from start to finish.

Smalley, Beryl. *The Study of the Bible in the Middle Ages*. 3rd ed. Oxford, 1983. The standard work, gracefully written and illuminating.

Strayer, Joseph R. *On the Medieval Origins of the Modern State*. With new forewords by Charles Tilly and William Chester Jordan. Princeton, NJ, 2005. This new edition of Strayer's series of lectures places them in their scholarly context.

Swanson, R. N. *The Twelfth-Century Renaissance*. Manchester, UK, 1999. An updated survey of the intellectual developments of the twelfth century.

Symes, Carol. *A Common Stage: Theater and Public Life in Medieval Arras*. Ithaca, NY, 2007. A study of a vibrant cultural hub.

Wakefield, Walter, and Austin P. Evans, eds. and trans. *Heresies of the High Middle Ages*. New York, 1969, 1991. A comprehensive collection of sources.

Wei, Ian. *Intellectual Culture in Medieval Paris: Theologians and the University, c. 1100–1330*. Cambridge, 2012. A fresh and compelling new history of medieval intellectual culture that ranges beyond Paris and pays attention to the contributions of medieval women.

Wolfram von Eschenbach. *Parzival*. Trans. H. M. Mustard and C. E. Passage. New York, 1961.

## CHAPTER 10

Abu-Lughod, Janet L. *Before European Hegemony: The World System A.D. 1250–1350*. Oxford and New York, 1989. A now classic study of the trading links among Europe, the Middle East, India, and China, with special attention to the role of the Mongol Empire; extensive bibliography.

Allsen, Thomas T. *Culture and Conquest in Mongol Eurasia*. Cambridge and New York, 2001. A synthesis of the author's earlier studies, emphasizing Mongol involvement in the cultural and commercial exchanges that linked China, Central Asia, and Europe.

Christian, David. *A History of Russia, Central Asia and Mongolia*. Vol. 1, *Inner Eurasia from Prehistory to the Mongol Empire*. Oxford, 1998. The authoritative English-language work on the subject.

Cole, Bruce. *Giotto and Florentine Painting, 1280–1375*. New York, 1976. A clear and stimulating introduction.

Crummey, Robert O. *The Formation of Muscovy, 1304–1613*. New York, 1987. The standard account.

Dante Alighieri. *The Divine Comedy*. Trans. Mark Musa. 3 vols. Baltimore, 1984–1986.

Dunn, Ross E. *The Adventures of Ibn Battuta: A Muslim Traveler of the Fourteenth Century*. Rev. ed. Berkeley, 2005. Places the writings and experiences of this far-reaching Muslim traveler in their historical and geographical contexts.

Dyer, Christopher. *Standards of Living in the Later Middle Ages: Social Change in England, c. 1200–1520.* Cambridge and New York, 1989. Detailed but highly rewarding.

Foltz, Richard. *Religions of the Silk Road: Premodern Patterns of Globalization.* 2nd ed. New York, 2010. A compelling and thought-provoking study of the varieties of religious experience and cross-cultural interaction in medieval Eurasia.

Green, Monica, ed. *Pandemic Disease in the Medieval World: Rethinking the Black Death.* Special inaugural issue, *The Medieval Globe*, 1, no. 1 (2014). Available online in an open-access format: http://scholarworks.wmich.edu/tmg/vol1/iss1/. A pathbreaking collection of articles synthesizing the most recent research in the history, epidemiology, microbiology, and archaeology of the plague.

Horrox, Rosemary, ed. *The Black Death.* New York, 1994. A fine collection of documents reflecting the impact of the Black Death, especially in England.

Jackson, Peter. *The Mongols and the West, 1221–1410.* Harlow, UK, 2005. A well-written survey that emphasizes the interactions among the Mongol, Latin Christian, and Muslim worlds.

Jordan, William Chester. *The Great Famine: Northern Europe in the Early Fourteenth Century.* Princeton, NJ, 1996. An outstanding social and economic study.

Keen, Maurice, ed. *Medieval Warfare: A History.* Oxford and New York, 1999. The most attractive introduction to this important subject. Lively and well illustrated.

Kitsikopoulos, Harry, ed. *Agrarian Change and Crisis in Europe, 1200–1500.* London, 2011. An up-to-date collection of scholarly essays that addresses a classic and complicated set of historical questions.

Komaroff, Linda, and Stefano Carboni, eds. *The Legacy of Ghenghis Khan: Courtly Art and Culture in Western Asia, 1256–1353.* New York, 2002. An informative and lavishly illustrated catalog of an acclaimed exhibition.

Larner, John. *Marco Polo and the Discovery of the World.* New Haven, 1999. A study of the influence of Marco Polo's *Travels* on Europeans.

*Memoirs of a Renaissance Pope: The Commentaries of Pius II.* Abridged ed. Trans. Florence A. Gragg, ed. Leona C. Gabel. New York, 1959. Remarkable insights into the mind of a particularly well-educated mid-fifteenth-century pope.

Morgan, David. *The Mongols.* 2nd ed. Oxford, 2007. An accessible introduction to Mongol history and its sources, written by a noted expert on medieval Persia.

Onon, Urgunge, trans. *The History and the Life of Chinggis Khan: The Secret History of the Mongols.* Leiden, 1997. A newer version of *The Secret History*, now the standard English version of this important Mongol source.

Polo, Marco. *The Description of the World.* Trans. Sharon Kinoshita. Indianapolis, 2016. A faithful and accessible new translation of the text, with authoritative notes and commentary.

Rossabi, Morris. *Khubilai Khan: His Life and Times.* Berkeley, 1988. The standard English biography.

Seymour, M. C., ed. *Mandeville's Travels.* Oxford, 1968. An edition of the *Book of Marvels* based on the Middle English version popular in the fifteenth century.

Swanson, R. N. *Religion and Devotion in Europe, c. 1215–c. 1515.* Cambridge and New York, 1995. An excellent study of late-medieval popular piety; an excellent complement to Oakley.

Vaughan, Richard. *Valois Burgundy.* London, 1975. A summation of the author's four-volume study of the Burgundian dukes.

## CHAPTER 11

Alberti, Leon Battista. *The Family in Renaissance Florence (Della Famiglia).* Trans. Renée Neu Watkins. Columbia, SC, 1969.

Allmand, Christopher T., ed. *Society at War: The Experience of England and France during the Hundred Years' War.* Edinburgh, 1973. An outstanding collection of documents.

Boccaccio, Giovanni. *The Decameron.* Trans. Mark Musa and P. E. Bondanella. New York, 1977.

Brucker, Gene. *Florence: The Golden Age, 1138–1737.* Berkeley and Los Angeles, 1998. A classic account of the city at the height of its influence.

Bruni, Leonardo. *The Humanism of Leonardo Bruni: Selected Texts.* Trans. Gordon Griffiths, James Hankins, and David Thompson. Binghamton, NY, 1987. Excellent translations, with introductions, to the Latin works of a key Renaissance humanist.

Burke, Peter. *The Renaissance.* New York, 1997. A brief introduction by an influential cultural historian.

Burkhardt, Jacob. *The Civilization of the Renaissance in Italy.* There are many editions of this nineteenth-century study, which first crystallized the concept of the "Renaissance."

Cassirer, Ernst, et al., eds. *The Renaissance Philosophy of Man.* Chicago, 1948. Excerpts from important original works by Petrarch, Ficino, and Pico della Mirandola, among others.

Castor, Helen. *Joan of Arc: A History.* London, 2015. An accessible and highly readable account of the ways that Joan was understood in her own time, and her changing reputation up to the present day.

Chaucer, Geoffrey. *The Canterbury Tales.* Trans. Nevill Coghill. New York, 1951. A modern English verse translation, lightly annotated.

Cohn, Samuel K., Jr. *Lust for Liberty: The Politics of Social Revolt in Medieval Europe, 1200–1425. Italy, France, and Flanders.* Cambridge, MA, 2006. An important and provocative study of social movements before and after the Black Death.

Coles, Paul. *The Ottoman Impact on Europe.* London, 1968. An excellent introductory text, still valuable despite its age.

Dobson, R. Barrie. *The Peasants' Revolt of 1381.* 2nd ed. London, 1983. A comprehensive source collection, with excellent introductions to the documents.

Fernández-Armesto, Felipe. *Before Columbus: Exploration and Colonisation from the Mediterranean to the Atlantic, 1229–1492.* London, 1987. An indispensible study of the medieval background to the sixteenth-century European colonial empires.

Froissart, Jean. *Chronicles.* Trans. Geoffrey Brereton. Baltimore, 1968. A selection from the most famous contemporary account of the Hundred Years' War to about 1400.

Goffman, Daniel. *The Ottoman Empire and Early Modern Europe.* Cambridge and New York, 2002. A revisionist account that presents the Ottoman Empire as a European state.

Hankins, James. *Plato in the Italian Renaissance*. Leiden and New York, 1990. A definitive study of the reception and influence of Plato on Renaissance intellectuals.

———, ed. *Renaissance Civic Humanism: Reappraisals and Reflections*. Cambridge and New York, 2000. An excellent collection of scholarly essays reassessing republicanism in the Renaissance.

Hobbins, Daniel, ed. and trans. *The Trial of Joan of Arc*. Cambridge, MA, 2007. An excellent translation of the transcripts of Joan's trial.

Inalcik, Halil. *The Ottoman Empire: The Classical Age, 1300–1600*. London, 1973. The standard history by the dean of Turkish historians.

———, ed. *An Economic and Social History of the Ottoman Empire, 1300–1914*. Cambridge, 1994. An important collection of essays, spanning the full range of Ottoman history.

*John Hus at the Council of Constance*. Trans. M. Spinka, New York, 1965. The translation of a Czech chronicle with an expert introduction and appended documents.

Kafadar, Cemal. *Between Two Worlds: The Construction of the Ottoman State*. Berkeley and Los Angeles, 1995. An important study of Ottoman origins in the border regions between Byzantium, the Seljuk Turks, and the Mongols.

Kaldellis, Anthony. *A New Herodotos: Laonikos Chalkokondyles on the Ottoman Empire, the Fall of Byzantium, and the Emergence of the West*. Washington, DC, 2014. This volume is the first full-length study of Laonikos Chalkokondyles, a historian from Athens who wrote a classical Greek history of his own times, tracing the fall of Constantinople.

Kempe, Margery. *The Book of Margery Kempe*. Trans. Barry Windeatt. New York, 1985. A fascinating personal narrative by an early fifteenth-century Englishwoman who hoped she might be a saint.

Lane, Frederic C. *Venice: A Maritime Republic*. Baltimore, 1973. An authoritative account.

Ormrod, W. Mark. *Edward III*. New Haven, 2012. A new biography of this English monarch by a leading social historian.

Normore, Christina. *A Feast for the Eyes: Art, Performance, and the Late Medieval Banquet*. Chicago, 2015. A fascinating study of the aristocratic feast and its meanings.

Shirley, Janet, trans. *A Parisian Journal, 1405–1449*. Oxford, 1968. A marvelous panorama of Parisian life recorded by an eyewitness.

Sumption, Jonathan. *The Hundred Years' War*. Vol. 1, *Trial by Battle*. Vol. 2, *Trial by Fire*. Philadelphia, 1999. The first two volumes of a massive narrative history of the war, carrying the story up to 1369.

## CHAPTER 12

Baxandall, Michael. *Painting and Experience in Fifteenth-Century Italy*. Oxford, 1972. A classic study of the perceptual world of the Renaissance.

Castiglione, Baldassare. *The Book of the Courtier*. Many editions. The translations by C. S. Singleton (New York, 1959) and by George Bull (New York, 1967) are both excellent.

Cellini, Benvenuto. *Autobiography*. Trans. George Bull. Baltimore, 1956. This Florentine goldsmith (1500–1571) is the source for many of the most famous stories about the artists of the Florentine Renaissance.

Columbus, Christopher. *The Four Voyages of Christopher Columbus*. Trans. J. M. Cohen. New York, 1992. Columbus's own self-serving account of his expeditions to the Indies.

Erasmus, Desiderius. *The Praise of Folly*. Trans. J. Wilson. Ann Arbor, MI, 1958.

Fernández-Armesto, Felipe. *1492: The Year the World Began*. London, 2010. A panoramic view of the world in a pivotal year, putting the voyage of Columbus in a broad historical perspective.

Flint, Valerie I. J. *The Imaginative Landscape of Christopher Columbus*. Princeton, NJ, 1992. A short, suggestive analysis of the intellectual influences that shaped Columbus's geographical ideas.

Fox, Alistair. *Thomas More: History and Providence*. Oxford, 1982. A balanced account of a man too easily idealized.

Grafton, Anthony, and Lisa Jardine. *From Humanism to the Humanities: Education and the Liberal Arts in Fifteenth- and Sixteenth-Century Europe*. London, 1986. An account that presents Renaissance humanism as the elitist cultural program of a self-interested group of pedagogues.

Grendler, Paul, ed. *Encyclopedia of the Renaissance*. New York, 1999. A valuable reference work.

Jardine, Lisa. *Worldly Goods*. London, 1996. A revisionist account that emphasizes the acquisitive materialism of Italian Renaissance society and culture.

Kanter, Laurence, Hilliard T. Goldfarb, and James Hankins. *Botticelli's Witness: Changing Style in a Changing Florence*. Boston, 1997. This catalog for an exhibition of Botticelli's works, at the Gardner Museum in Boston, offers an excellent introduction to the painter and his world.

King, Margaret L. *Women of the Renaissance*. Chicago, 1991. Deals with women in all walks of life and in a variety of roles.

Kristeller, Paul O. *Renaissance Thought: The Classic, Scholastic, and Humanistic Strains*. New York, 1961. Very helpful in defining the main trends of Renaissance thought.

Machiavelli, Niccolò. *The Discourses* and *The Prince*. Many editions. These two books must be read together if one is to understand Machiavelli's political ideas properly.

Mallett, Michael, and Christine Shaw. *The Italian Wars, 1494–1559: War, State, and Society in Early Modern Europe*. Boston, 2012. Argues that the endemic warfare of this period within Italy revolutionized European military tactics and technologies.

Mann, Charles. *C. 1491: New Revelations of the Americas before Columbus*. New York, 2006.

———. *1493: Uncovering the New World Columbus Created*. New York, 2012. Written for a popular audience, these are also engaging and well-informed syntheses of historical research.

Martines, Lauro. *Power and Imagination: City-States in Renaissance Italy*. New York, 1979. Insightful account of the connections among politics, society, culture, and art.

More, Thomas. *Utopia*. Many editions.

Olson, Roberta. *Italian Renaissance Sculpture*. New York, 1992. The most accessible introduction to the subject.

Parker, Geoffrey. *The Military Revolution: Military Innovation and the Rise of the West (1500–1800)*. 2nd ed. Cambridge and New York, 1996. A work of fundamental importance for understanding the global dominance achieved by early modern Europeans.

Perkins, Leeman L. *Music in the Age of the Renaissance*. New York, 1999. A massive study that needs to be read in conjunction with Reese.

Phillips, J. R. S. *The Medieval Expansion of Europe*. 2nd ed. Oxford, 1998. An outstanding study of the thirteenth- and fourteenth-century background to the fifteenth-century expansion of Europe. Important synthetic treatment of European relations with the Mongols, China, Africa, and North America. The second edition includes a new introduction and a bibliographical essay; the text is the same as in the first edition (1988).

Phillips, William D., Jr., and Carla R. Phillips. *The Worlds of Christopher Columbus*. Cambridge and New York, 1991. The first book to read on Columbus: accessible, engaging, and scholarly. Then read Fernández-Armesto's biography.

Rabelais, François. *Gargantua and Pantagruel*. Trans. J. M. Cohen. Baltimore, 1955. A robust modern translation.

Reese, Gustave. *Music in the Renaissance*. Rev. ed. New York, 1959. A great book; still authoritative, despite the more recent work by Perkins, which supplements but does not replace it.

Rice, Eugene F., Jr., and Anthony Grafton. *The Foundations of Early Modern Europe, 1460–1559*. 2nd ed. New York, 1994. The best textbook account of its period.

Rowland, Ingrid D. *The Culture of the High Renaissance: Ancients and Moderns in Sixteenth-Century Rome*. Cambridge and New York, 2000. Beautifully written examination of the social, intellectual, and economic foundations of the Renaissance in Rome.

Russell, Peter. *Prince Henry "The Navigator": A Life*. New Haven, 2000. A masterly biography by a great historian who has spent a lifetime on the subject. The only book one now needs to read on Prince Henry.

Scammell, Geoffrey V. *The First Imperial Age: European Overseas Expansion, 1400–1715*. London, 1989. A useful introductory survey, with a particular focus on English and French colonization.

Waltom, Nicholas. *Genoa, "La Superba": The Rise and Fall of a Merchant Pirate Superpower*. London, 2015. A history of the maritime city-state that shaped the career of Columbus and other adventurers.

## CHAPTER 13

Bainton, Roland. *Erasmus of Christendom*. New York, 1969. Still the best biography in English of the Dutch reformer and intellectual.

Benedict, Philip. *Christ's Churches Purely Reformed: A Social History of Calvinism*. New Haven, 2002. A wide-ranging recent survey of Calvinism in both western and eastern Europe.

Bossy, John. *Christianity in the West, 1400–1700*. Oxford and New York, 1985. A brilliant, challenging picture of the changes that took place in Christian piety and practice as a result of the sixteenth-century reformations.

Bouwsma, William J. *John Calvin: A Sixteenth-Century Portrait*. Oxford and New York, 1988. The best biography of this magisterial reformer.

Duffy, Eamon. *The Stripping of the Altars: Traditional Religion in England, c. 1400–c. 1550*. A brilliant study of religious exchange at the parish level.

————. *The Voices of Morebath: Reformation and Rebellion in an English Village*. New Haven, 2003. How the crises of this period affected and are reflected in the history of a single parish.

Hart, D. G. *Calvinism: A History*. New Haven, 2013. A new survey of this leading Protestant movement from its beginnings to the present day.

*John Calvin: Selections from His Writings*. Ed. John Dillenberger. Garden City, NY, 1971. A judicious selection, drawn mainly from Calvin's *Institutes*.

Koslofksy, Craig. *The Reformation of the Dead: Death and Ritual in Early Modern Germany*. Basingstoke, UK, 2000. How essential rituals and responses to death were reshaped during this period.

Loyola, Ignatius. *Personal Writings*. Trans. by Joseph A. Munitiz and Philip Endean. London and New York, 1996. An excellent collection that includes Loyola's autobiography, his spiritual diary, and some of his letters, as well as his *Spiritual Exercises*.

MacCulloch, Diarmaid. *Reformation: Europe's House Divided, 1490–1700*. London and New York, 2003. A definitive new survey; the best single-volume history of its subject in a generation.

Marshall, Peter, ed. *The Oxford Illustrated History of the Reformation*. Oxford, 2015. A compendium of new perspectives on the religious upheavals of the sixteenth century.

*Martin Luther: Selections from His Writings*, ed. John Dillenberger. Garden City, NY, 1961. The standard selection, especially good on Luther's theological ideas.

McGrath, Alister E. *Reformation Thought: An Introduction*. Oxford, 1993. A useful explanation, accessible to non-Christians, of the theological ideas of the major Protestant reformers.

Mullett, Michael A. *The Catholic Reformation*. London, 2000. A sympathetic survey of Catholicism from the mid-sixteenth to the eighteenth century that presents the mid-sixteenth-century Council of Trent as a continuation of earlier reform efforts.

Murray, Linda. *High Renaissance and Mannerism*. London, 1985. The place to begin a study of fifteenth- and sixteenth-century Italian art.

Oberman, Heiko A. *Luther: Man between God and the Devil*. Trans. by Eileen Walliser-Schwarzbart. New Haven, 1989. A biography stressing Luther's preoccupations with sin, death, and the devil.

O'Malley, John W. *The First Jesuits*. Cambridge, MA, 1993. A scholarly account of the origins and early years of the Society of Jesus.

————. *Trent: What Happened at the Council*. Cambridge, MA, 2012. A clear and comprehensive narrative of the Church council that gave birth to the modern Catholic Church.

Pettegree, Andrew, ed. *The Reformation World*. New York, 2000. An exhaustive multiauthor work representing the most recent thinking about the Reformation.

Pelikan, Jaroslav. *Reformation of Church and Dogma, 1300–1700*. Vol. 4 of *A History of Christian Dogma*. Chicago, 1984. A masterful synthesis of Reformation theology in its late-medieval context.

Roper, Lyndal. *The Holy Household: Women and Morals in Reformation Augsburg.* Oxford, 1989. A pathbreaking study of Protestantism's effects on a single town, with special attention to its impact on attitudes toward women, the family, and marriage.

Ryrie, Alex. *Being Protestant in Reformation Britain.* Oxford, 2015. A vivid portrait of daily life in a turbulent time.

Shagan, Ethan H. *Popular Politics and the English Reformation.* Cambridge, 2002. Argues that the English Reformation reflects an ongoing process of negotiation, resistance, and response.

Tracy, James D. *Europe's Reformations, 1450–1650.* 2nd ed. Lanham, MD, 2006. An outstanding survey, especially strong on Dutch and Swiss developments, but excellent throughout.

Williams, George H. *The Radical Reformation.* 3rd ed. Kirksville, MO, 1992. Originally published in 1962, this is still the best book on Anabaptism and its offshoots.

**CHAPTER 14**

Bonney, Richard. *The European Dynastic States, 1494–1660.* Oxford and New York, 1991. An excellent survey of continental Europe during the "long" sixteenth century.

Briggs, Robin. *Early Modern France, 1560–1715,* 2nd ed. Oxford and New York, 1997. Updated and authoritative, with new bibliographies.

———. *Witches and Neighbors: The Social and Cultural Context of European Witchcraft.* New York, 1996. An influential recent account of Continental witchcraft.

Cervantes, Miguel de. *Don Quixote.* Trans. Edith Grossman. New York, 2003. A splendid new translation.

Clarke, Stuart. *Thinking with Demons: The Idea of Witchcraft in Early Modern Europe.* Oxford and New York, 1999. By placing demonology into the context of sixteenth- and seventeenth-century intellectual history, Clarke makes sense of it in new and exciting ways.

Cochrane, Eric, Charles M. Gray, and Mark A. Kishlansky. *Early Modern Europe: Crisis of Authority.* Chicago, 1987. An outstanding source collection from the University of Chicago Readings in Western Civilization series.

Elliot, J. H. *The Old World and the New, 1492–1650.* Repr. ed. Cambridge, 1992. A brilliant and brief set of essays on the ways that the discovery of the Americas challenged European perspectives on the world and themselves.

———. *Empires of the Atlantic World: Britain and Spain in America, 1492–1830.* An illuminating comparative study. New Haven, 2007.

Geschwend, Annemarie Jordan, and K. J. P. Lowe, eds. *The Global City: On the Streets of Renaissance Lisbon.* London, 2015. A beautifully illustrated collection of essays by leading scholars.

Hibbard, Howard. *Bernini.* Baltimore, 1965. The basic study in English of this central figure of Baroque artistic activity.

Hirst, Derek. *England in Conflict, 1603–1660: Kingdom, Community, Commonwealth.* Oxford and New York, 1999. A complete revision of the author's *Authority and Conflict* (1986), this is an up-to-date and balanced account of a period that has been a historical battleground over the past twenty years.

Hobbes, Thomas. *Leviathan.* Ed. Richard Tuck. 2nd ed. Cambridge and New York, 1996. The most recent edition, containing the entirety of *Leviathan*, not just the first two parts.

Holt, Mack P. *The French Wars of Religion, 1562–1629.* Cambridge and New York, 1995. A clear account of a confusing time.

Ipsen, Pernille. *Daughters of the Trade: Atlantic Slavers and Interracial Marriage on the Gold Coast.* Philadelphia, 2014. A study that puts women and families at the heart of the story of African slavery.

Kors, Alan Charles, and Edward Peters *Witchcraft in Europe, 400–1700: A Documentary History.* 2nd ed. Philadelphia, 2000. A superb collection of documents, significantly expanded in the second edition, with up-to-date commentary.

Kingdon, Robert. *Myths about the St. Bartholomew's Day Massacres, 1572–1576.* Cambridge, MA, 1988. A detailed account of this pivotal moment in the history of France.

Kochanowski, Jan. *Laments.* Translated by Stanislaw Baranczak and Seamus Heaney. New York, 1995. A moving rendition of works by the great poet of Renaissance Poland.

Levack, Brian P. *The Witch-Hunt in Early Modern Europe,* 2nd ed. London and New York, 1995. The best account of the persecution of suspected witches; coverage extends from Europe in 1450 to America in 1750.

Levin, Carole. *The Heart and Stomach of a King: Elizabeth I and the Politics of Sex and Power.* Philadelphia, 1994. A provocative argument for the importance of Elizabeth's gender for understanding her reign.

Limm, Peter, ed. *The Thirty Years' War.* London, 1984. An outstanding short survey, followed by a selection of primary-source documents.

Lynch, John. *Spain, 1516–1598: From Nation-State to World Empire.* Oxford and Cambridge, MA, 1991. The best book in English on Spain at the pinnacle of its sixteenth-century power.

MacCaffrey, Wallace. *Elizabeth I.* New York, 1993. An outstanding traditional biography by an excellent scholar.

Martin, Colin, and Geoffrey Parker. *The Spanish Armada.* London, 1988. Incorporates recent discoveries from undersea archaeology with more traditional historical sources.

Mattingly, Garrett. *The Armada.* Boston, 1959. A great narrative history that reads like a novel; for more recent work, however, see Martin and Parker.

McGregor, Neil. *Shakespeare's Restless World.* London, 2013. Based on an acclaimed BBC Radio program, this book illuminates Shakespeare's life, times, and plays with reference to specific objects in the British Museum.

Newson, Linda A., and Susie Minchin. *From Capture to Sale: The Portuguese Slave Trade to Spanish South America in the Early Seventeenth Century.* London, 2007. Makes use of slave traders' own rich archives to track the process of human trafficking.

Parker, Geoffrey. *The Dutch Revolt.* 2nd ed. Ithaca, NY, 1989. The standard survey in English.

Pascal, Blaise. *Pensées* (French-English edition). Ed. H. F. Stewart. London, 1950.

Pestana, Carla. *Protestant Empire: Religion and the Making of the British Atlantic World.* Philadelphia, 2010. How the Reformation helped to drive British imperial expansion.

Roberts, Michael. *Gustavus Adolphus and the Rise of Sweden*. London, 1973. Still the authoritative English-language account.

Russell, Conrad. *The Causes of the English Civil War*. Oxford, 1990. A penetrating and provocative analysis by one of the leading "revisionist" historians of the period.

Schmidt, Benjamin. *Innocence Abroad: The Dutch Imagination and the New World, 1570–1670*. Cambridge, 2006. A cultural history of Europeans' encounter with the Americas that highlights the perspective and experience of Dutch merchants, colonists, and artists.

Strum, Daniel. *The Sugar Trade: Brazil, Portugal, and the Netherlands (1595–1630)*. Translated by Colin Foulkes, Roopanjali Roy, and H. Sabrina Gledhill. Stanford, CA, 2013. A close examination of the merchants, seafarers, and slaves who drove the economy of the Atlantic world.

## CHAPTER 15

Beik, William. *A Social and Cultural History of Early Modern France*. Cambridge, 2009. A broad synthesis of French history from the end of the Middle Ages to the French Revolution, by one of the world's foremost authorities on absolutism.

Clark, Christopher. *Iron Kingdom: The Rise and Downfall of Prussia, 1600–1947*. Cambridge, MA, 2009. A definitive account of Prussian history over nearly four centuries.

Jones, Colin. *The Great Nation: France From Louis XV to Napoleon*. New York, 2002. An excellent and readable scholarly account that argues that the France of Louis XV in the eighteenth century was even more dominant than the kingdom of Louis XIV in the preceding century.

Kishlansky, Mark A. *A Monarchy Transformed: Britain, 1603–1714*. London, 1996. An excellent survey that takes seriously its claim to be a "British" rather than merely an "English" history.

Klein, Herbert S. *The Atlantic Slave Trade*. Cambridge and New York, 1999. An accessible survey by a leading quantitative historian.

Lewis, William Roger, gen. ed. *The Oxford History of the British Empire*. Vol. I: *The Origins of Empire: British Overseas Enterprise to the Close of the Seventeenth Century*, ed. Nicholas Canny. Vol. II: *The Eighteenth Century*, ed. Peter J. Marshall. Oxford and New York, 1998. A definitive, multiauthor account.

Locke, John. *Two Treatises of Government*. Ed. Peter Laslett. Rev. ed. Cambridge and New York, 1963. Laslett has revolutionized our understanding of the historical and ideological context of Locke's political writings.

Massie, Robert. *Peter the Great, His Life and World*. New York, 1980. Prize-winning and readable narrative account of the Russian tsar's life.

Monod, Paul K. *The Power of Kings: Monarchy and Religion in Europe, 1589–1715*. New Haven, 1999. A study of the seventeenth century's declining confidence in the divinity of kings.

Quataert, Donald. *The Ottoman Empire, 1700–1822*. Cambridge and New York, 2000. Well balanced and intended to be read by students.

Riasanovsky, Nicholas V., and Steinberg, Mark D. *A History of Russia*. 7th ed. Oxford and New York, 2005. Far and away the best single-volume textbook on Russian history: balanced, comprehensive, and intelligent, with full bibliographies.

Saint-Simon, Louis. *Historical Memoirs*. Many editions. The classic source for life at Louis XIV's Versailles.

Snyder, Timothy. *The Reconstruction of Nations: Poland, Ukraine, Lithuania, Belarus, 1569–1999*. New Haven, 2004. Essential account of nation building and state collapse in eastern Europe with significant relevance to the region's contemporary situation.

Thomas, Hugh. *The Slave Trade: The History of the Atlantic Slave Trade, 1440–1870*. London and New York, 1997. A survey notable for its breadth and depth of coverage and for its attractive prose style.

Tracy, James D. *The Rise of Merchant Empires: Long-Distance Trade in the Early Modern World, 1350–1750*. Cambridge and New York, 1990. Important collection of essays by leading authorities.

White, Richard. *The Middle Ground: Indians, Empires and Republics in the Great Lakes Region, 1650–1815*. Cambridge, 1991. A path-breaking account of interactions between Europeans and Native Americans during the colonial period.

## CHAPTER 16

Biagioli, Mario. *Galileo, Courtier*. Chicago, 1993. Emphasizes the importance of patronage and court politics in Galileo's science and career.

Cohen, I. B. *The Birth of a New Physics*. New York, 1985. Emphasizes the mathematical nature of the revolution; unmatched at making the mathematics understandable.

Daston, Lorraine, and Elizabeth Lunbeck, eds. *Histories of Scientific Observation*. Chicago, IL, 2011. Field-defining collection of essays on the history of scientific observation from the seventeenth to the twentieth centuries.

Daston, Lorraine. *Wonders and the Order of Nature, 1150–1750*. Cambridge, MA, 2001. Erudite, sweeping account of the history of science in the early modern period, emphasizing the natural philosopher's awe and wonder at the marvelous, the unfamiliar, and the counterintuitive.

Dear, Peter. *Revolutionizing the Sciences: European Knowledge and Its Ambitions, 1500–1700*. Princeton, NJ, 2001. Among the best short histories.

Drake, Stillman. *Discoveries and Opinions of Galileo*. Garden City, NY, 1957. The classic translation of Galileo's most important papers by his most admiring modern biographer.

Feingold, Mardechai. *The Newtonian Moment: Isaac Newton and the Making of Modern Culture*. New York, 2004. An engaging essay on the dissemination of Newton's thought, with excellent visual material.

Gaukroger, Stephen. *Descartes: An Intellectual Biography*. Oxford, 1995. Detailed and sympathetic study of the philosopher.

Gleick, James. *Isaac Newton*. New York, 2003. A vivid and well-documented brief biography.

Grafton, Anthony. *New Worlds, Ancient Texts: The Power of Tradition and the Shock of Discovery*. Cambridge, MA, 1992. Accessible essay by one of the leading scholars of early modern European thought.

Jacob, Margaret. *Scientific Culture and the Making of the Industrial West*. Oxford, 1997. A concise examination of the connections between developments in science and the Industrial Revolution.

Kuhn, Thomas. *The Structure of Scientific Revolutions*. Chicago, 1962. A classic and much-debated study of how scientific thought changes.

Pagden, Anthony. *European Encounters with the New World*. New Haven and London, 1993. Subtle and detailed on how European intellectuals thought about the lands they saw for the first time.

Rudwick, Martin J. S. *Earth's Deep History: How It Was Discovered and Why It Matters* (Chicago, 2014). A fascinating account of the origins of the geological sciences and awareness of the earth's long history before the advent of human civilizations.

Scheibinger, Londa. *The Mind Has No Sex? Women in the Origins of Modern Science*. Cambridge, MA, 1989. A lively and important recovery of the lost role played by women mathematicians and experimenters.

Shapin, Steven. *The Scientific Revolution*. Chicago, 1996. Engaging, accessible, and brief—organized thematically.

Shapin, Steven, and Simon Schaffer. *Leviathan and the Air Pump*. Princeton, NJ, 1985. A modern classic, on one of the most famous philosophical conflicts in seventeenth-century science.

Stephenson, Bruce. *The Music of the Heavens: Kepler's Harmonic Astronomy*. Princeton, NJ, 1994. An engaging and important explanation of Kepler's otherworldly perspective.

Thoren, Victor. *The Lord of Uranibourg: A Biography of Tycho Brahe*. Cambridge, 1990. A vivid reconstruction of the scientific revolution's most flamboyant astronomer.

Westfall, Richard. *The Construction of Modern Science*. Cambridge, 1977.

_____. *Never at Rest: A Biography of Isaac Newton*. Cambridge, 1980. The standard work.

Wilson, Catherine. *The Invisible World: Early Modern Philosophy and the Invention of the Microscope*. Princeton, NJ, 1995. An important study of how the "microcosmic" world revealed by technology reshaped scientific philosophy and practice.

Zinsser, Judith P. *La Dame d Esprit: A Biography of the Marquise Du Châtelet*. New York, 2006. An excellent cultural history. Issued in paperback as *Emilie du Châtelet: Daring Genius of the Enlightenment* (2007).

# Glossary

**1973 OPEC oil embargo** Some leaders in the Arab-dominated Organization of the Petroleum Exporting Countries (OPEC) wanted to use oil as a weapon against the West in the Arab-Israeli conflict. After the 1972 Arab-Israeli war, OPEC instituted an oil embargo against Western powers. The embargo increased the price of oil and sparked spiraling inflation and economic troubles in Western nations, triggering in turn a cycle of dangerous recession that lasted nearly a decade. In response, Western governments began viewing the Middle Eastern oil regions as areas of strategic importance.

**Abbasid caliphate** (750–930) The Abbasid family claimed to be descendants of Muhammad, and in 750 they successfully led a rebellion against the Umayyads, seizing control of Muslim territories in Arabia, Persia, North Africa, and the Near East. The Abbasids modeled their behavior and administration on those of the Persian princes and their rule on that of the Persian Empire, establishing a new capital at Baghdad.

**Peter Abelard** (1079–1142) Highly influential philosopher, theologian, and teacher, often considered the founder of the University of Paris.

**absolutism** Form of government in which one person or body, usually the monarch, controls the right to make war, tax, judge, and coin money. The term was often used to refer to the state monarchies in seventeenth- and eighteenth-century Europe.

**abstract expressionism** The mid-twentieth-century school of art based in New York that included Jackson Pollock, Willem de Kooning, Franz Kline, and Helen Frankenthaler. It emphasized form, color, gesture, and feeling instead of figurative subjects.

**Academy of Sciences** This French institute of scientific inquiry was founded in 1666 by Louis XIV. France's statesmen exerted control over the academy and sought to share in the rewards of any discoveries its members made.

**Aeneas** Mythical founder of Rome, Aeneas was a refugee from the city of Troy whose adventures were described by the poet Virgil in the *Aeneid,* which was modeled on the oral epics of Homer.

**Aetolian and Achaean Leagues** These two alliances among Greek poleis were formed during the Hellenistic period in opposition to the Antigonids of Macedonia. Unlike the earlier defensive alliances of the classical period, each league was a real attempt to form a political federation.

**African National Congress (ANC)** Multiracial organization founded in 1912 whose goal was to end racial discrimination in South Africa.

**Afrikaners** Descendants of the original Dutch settlers of South Africa; formerly referred to as Boers.

**agricultural revolution** Numerous agricultural revolutions have occurred in the history of Western civilizations. One of the most significant began in the tenth century C.E. and increased the amount of land under cultivation as well as the productivity of the land. This revolution was made possible through the use of new technology, a rise in global temperatures, and more efficient methods of cultivation.

**AIDS** Acquired Immunodeficiency Syndrome. The final phase of HIV, AIDS first appeared in the 1970s and has developed into a global health catastrophe; it is spreading most quickly in developing nations in Africa and Asia.

**Akhenaten** (r. 1352–1336 B.C.E.) Pharaoh whose attempt to promote the worship of the sun god, Aten, ultimately weakened his dynasty's position in Egypt.

**Alexander the Great** (356–323 B.C.E.) The Macedonian king whose conquests of the Persian Empire and Egypt created a new Hellenistic world.

**Alexander II** (1818–1881) After the Crimean War, Tsar Alexander embarked on a program of reform and modernization, which included the emancipation of the serfs. A radical assassin killed him in 1881.

**Alexius Comnenus** (1057–1118) This Byzantine emperor requested Pope Urban II's help in raising an army to recapture Anatolia from the Seljuk Turks. Instead, Pope Urban II called for knights to go to the Holy Land and liberate it from its Muslim captors, launching the First Crusade.

**Algerian War** (1954–1962) The war between France and Algerians seeking independence. Led by the National Liberation Front (FLN), guerrillas fought the French army in the mountains and desert of Algeria. The FLN also initiated a campaign of bombing and terrorism in Algerian cities that led French soldiers to torture many Algerians, attracting world attention and international scandal.

**Dante Alighieri** (c. 1265–1321) Florentine poet and intellectual whose *Divine Comedy* was a pioneering work in the Italian vernacular and a vehicle for political and religious critique.

**Allied Powers** The First World War coalition of Great Britain, Ireland, Belgium, France, Italy, Russia, Portugal, Greece, Serbia, Montenegro, Albania, and Romania.

**al Qaeda** The radical Islamic organization founded in the late 1980s by former mujahidin who had fought against the Soviet Union in Afghanistan. Al Qaeda carried out the 9/11 terrorist attacks and is responsible as well for attacks in Africa, Southeast Asia, Europe, and the Middle East.

**Ambrose** (c. 340–397) One of the early church fathers, he helped define the relationship between the sacred authority of bishops and other Church leaders and the secular authority of worldly rulers. He believed that secular rulers were a part of the Church and therefore subject to it.

**Americanization** The fear of many Europeans, since the 1920s, that U.S. cultural products, such as film, television, and music, exerted too much influence. Many of the criticisms centered on America's emphasis on mass production and organization. Fears about Americanization were not limited to culture but extended to corporations, business techniques, global trade, and marketing.

**Americas** The name given to the two great landmasses of the New World, derived from the name of the Italian geographer Amerigo Vespucci. In 1492, Christopher Columbus reached the Bahamas and the island of Hispaniola, which began an era of Spanish conquest in North and South America. Originally, the Spanish had sought a route to Asia. Instead they discovered two continents whose wealth they decided to exploit. They were especially interested in gold and silver, which they either stole from indigenous peoples or mined, using indigenous peoples as labor. Silver became Spain's most lucrative export from the New World.

**Amnesty International** Nongovernmental organization formed in 1961 to defend "prisoners of conscience"—those detained for their beliefs, color, sex, ethnic origin, language, or religion.

**Anabaptism** Protestant movement that emerged in Switzerland in 1521; its adherents insisted that only adults could be baptized Christians.

**anarchism** In the nineteenth century, a political movement with the aim of establishing small-scale, localized, and self-sufficient democratic communities that could guarantee a maximum of individual sovereignty. Renouncing parties, unions, and any form of modern mass organization, the anarchists fell back on the tradition of conspiratorial violence.

**Anatolia** A region consisting of the peninsula linking Asia to Europe and reaching northward to the Black Sea, southward to the Mediterranean, and westward to the Aegean; often called "Asia Minor."

**Anthropocene** A term coined by geographers, geologists, and climate scientists to describe the era when human activities began to reshape earth's environment. Although some scholars contend that this epoch dates only as far back as the Industrial Revolution of the mid-nineteenth century, others date it from the Neolithic Revolution and the emergence of the earliest civilizations.

**Anti-Corn Law League** This organization successfully lobbied Parliament to repeal Britain's Corn Laws in 1846. The Corn Laws of 1815 had protected British landowners and farmers from foreign competition by establishing high tariffs, which kept bread prices artificially high for British consumers. The league saw these laws as unfair protection of the aristocracy and pushed for their repeal in the name of free trade.

**anti-Semitism** Anti-Semitism refers to hostility toward Jewish people. Religious forms of anti-Semitism have a long history in Europe, but during the nineteenth century anti-Semitism emerged as a potent ideology for mobilizing new constituencies in the era of mass politics. Playing on popular conspiracy theories about alleged Jewish influence in society, anti-Semites effectively rallied large bodies of supporters in France during the Dreyfus Affair, and then again during the rise of National Socialism in Germany after the First World War. The Holocaust would not have been possible without the acquiescence or cooperation of many thousands of people who shared anti-Semitic views.

**apartheid** The racial segregation policy of the Afrikaner-dominated South African government. Legislated in 1948 by the Afrikaner National Party, it existed in South Africa for many decades.

**appeasement** The policy pursued by Western governments in the face of German, Italian, and Japanese aggression leading up to the Second World War. The policy, which attempted to accommodate and negotiate peace with the aggressive nations, was based on the belief that another global war like the First World War was unimaginable, a belief that Germany and its allies had been mistreated by the terms of the Treaty of Versailles, and a fear that fascist Germany and its allies protected the West from the spread of Soviet communism.

**Thomas Aquinas** (1225–1274) Dominican friar and theologian whose systematic approach to Christian doctrine was influenced by Aristotle.

**Arab-Israeli conflict** Between the founding of the state of Israel in 1948 and the present, a series of wars has been fought between Israel and neighboring Arab nations: the war of 1948 when Israel defeated attempts by Egypt, Jordan, Iraq, Syria, and Lebanon to prevent the creation of the new state; the 1956 war between Israel and Egypt over the Sinai Peninsula; the 1967 war, when Israel gained control of additional land in the Golan Heights, the West Bank, the Gaza strip, and the Sinai; and the Yom Kippur War of 1973, when Israel once again fought with forces from Egypt and Syria. A particularly difficult issue in all of these conflicts has been the situation of the 950,000 Palestinian refugees made homeless by the first war in 1948 and the movement of Israeli settlers into the occupied territories (outside of Israel's original borders). In the late 1970s, peace talks between Israel and Egypt inspired some hope of peace, but an ongoing cycle of violence between Palestinians and the Israeli military has made a final settlement elusive.

**Arab nationalism** During the period of decolonization, secular forms of Arab nationalism, or pan-Arabism, found a wide following in many countries of the Middle East, especially in Egypt, Syria, and Iraq.

**Arianism** A variety of Christianity condemned as a heresy by the Roman Church, it derives from the teaching of a fourth-century priest named Arius, who rejected the idea that Jesus could be the divine equal of God.

**aristocracy** From the Greek word meaning "rule of the best." By 1000 B.C.E., the accumulated wealth of successful traders in Greece had created a new type of social class, which was based on wealth rather than warfare or birth. These men saw their wealth as a reflection of their superior qualities and aspired to emulate the heroes of old.

**Aristotle** (384–322 B.C.E.) A student of Plato, he based his philosophy on rational analysis of the material world. In contrast to his teacher, he stressed the rigorous investigation of real phenomena, rather than the development of universal ethics. He was, in turn, the teacher of Alexander the Great.

**Asiatic Society** A cultural organization founded in 1784 by British Orientalists who lauded native culture but believed in colonial rule.

**Assyrians** A Semitic-speaking people that moved into northern Mesopotamia around 2400 B.C.E.

**Athens** Athens emerged as the Greek polis with the most markedly democratic form of government through a series of political struggles during the sixth century B.C.E. After its key role in the defeat of two invading Persian forces, Athens became the preeminent naval power of ancient Greece and the exemplar of Greek culture. But it antagonized many other poleis, and became embroiled in a war with Sparta and its allies in 431 B.C.E. Called the Peloponnesian War, this bloody conflict lasted until Athens was defeated in 404 B.C.E.

**atomic bomb** In 1945, the United States dropped atomic bombs on Hiroshima and Nagasaki in Japan, ending the Second World War. In 1949, the Soviet Union tested its first atomic bomb, and in 1953 both superpowers demonstrated their new hydrogen bombs. Strategically, the nuclearization of warfare polarized the world. Countries without nuclear weapons found it difficult to avoid joining either the Soviet or American military pacts. Over time, countries split into two groups: the superpowers with enormous military budgets and those countries that relied on agreements and international law. The nuclearization of warfare also encouraged "proxy wars" between clients of superpowers. Culturally, the hydrogen bomb came to symbolize the age as well as both humanity's power and its vulnerability.

**Augustine** (c. 354–397) One of the most influential theologians of all time, Augustine described his conversion to Christianity in his autobiographical *Confessions* and articulated a new Christian worldview in *The City of God*, among other works.

**Augustus** (63 B.C.E.–14 C.E.) Born Gaius Octavius, this grandnephew and adopted son of Julius Caesar came to power in 27 B.C.E. His reign signals the end of the Roman Republic and the beginning of the Principate, the period when Rome was dominated by autocratic emperors.

**Auschwitz-Birkenau** The Nazi concentration camp in Poland that was designed for the systematic murder of Jews and Gypsies. Between 1942 and 1944 over one million people were killed in Auschwitz-Birkenau.

**Austro-Hungarian Empire** The dual monarchy established by the Habsburg family in 1867; it collapsed at the end of the First World War.

**authoritarianism** A centralized and dictatorial form of government, proclaimed by its adherents to be superior to parliamentary democracy. Authoritarian governments claim to be above the law, do not respect individual rights, and do not tolerate political opposition. Authoritarian regimes that have developed a central ideology such as fascism or communism are sometimes termed "totalitarian."

**Avignon** A city in southeastern France that became the seat of the papacy between 1305 and 1377, a period known as the "Babylonian Captivity" of the Roman Church.

**Aztecs** An indigenous people of central Mexico; their empire was conquered by Spanish conquistadors in the sixteenth century.

**baby boom** (1950s) The post–Second World War upswing in U.S. birth rates; it reversed a century of decline.

**Babylon** An ancient city between the Tigris and Euphrates Rivers, which became the capital of Hammurabi's empire in the eighteenth century B.C.E. and continued to be an important administrative and commercial capital under many subsequent imperial powers, including the Neo-Assyrians, Chaldeans, Persians, and Romans. It was here that Alexander the Great died in 323 B.C.E.

**Babylonian captivity** Refers both to the Jews' exile in Babylon during the sixth century B.C.E. and the period from 1309 to 1378, when papal authority was subjugated to the French crown and the papal court was moved from Rome to the French city of Avignon.

**Francis Bacon** (1561–1626) British philosopher and scientist who pioneered the scientific method and inductive reasoning. In other words, he argued that thinkers should amass many observations and then draw general conclusions or propose theories on the basis of these data.

**balance of powers** The principle that no one country should be powerful enough to destabilize international relations. Starting in the seventeenth century, this goal of maintaining balance influenced diplomacy in western and central Europe for two centuries until the system collapsed with the onset of the First World War.

**Balfour Declaration** A letter dated November 2, 1917, by Lord Arthur J. Balfour, the British foreign secretary, that promised a homeland for the Jews in Palestine.

**Laura Bassi** (1711–1778) She was accepted into the Academy of Science in Bologna for her work in mathematics, which made her one of the few women to be accepted into a scientific academy in the seventeenth century.

**Bastille** The Bastille was a royal fortress and prison in Paris. In June 1789, a revolutionary crowd attacked the Bastille to show support for the newly created National Assembly. The fall of the Bastille was the first instance of the people's role in revolutionary change in France.

**Bay of Pigs invasion** (1961) The unsuccessful invasion of Cuba by Cuban exiles, supported by the U.S. government. The rebels intended to incite an insurrection in Cuba and overthrow the communist regime of Fidel Castro.

**Cesare Beccaria** (1738–1794) An influential writer during the Enlightenment who advocated for legal reforms. He believed that the only legitimate rationale for punishments was to maintain social order and to prevent other crimes. He argued for the greatest possible leniency compatible with deterrence and opposed torture and the death penalty.

**Beer Hall Putsch** (1923) An early attempt by the Nazi party to seize power in Munich; Adolf Hitler was imprisoned for a year after the incident.

**Benedict of Nursia** (c. 480–c. 547) Benedict's rule for monks formed the basis of Western monasticism and is still observed in monasteries all over the world.

**Benedictine monasticism** This form of monasticism was developed by Benedict of Nursia. Its followers adhere to a defined cycle of daily prayers, lessons, communal worship, and manual labor.

**Berlin airlift** The transport in 1948 of vital supplies to West Berlin by air, primarily under U.S. auspices, in response to a blockade of the city that had been instituted by the Soviet Union to force the Allies to abandon West Berlin.

**Berlin Conference** At this conference in 1884, the leading colonial powers met and established ground rules for the partition of Africa by European nations. By 1914, 90 percent of African territory was under European control. The Berlin Conference ceded control of the Congo region to a private company run by King Leopold II of Belgium. The company agreed to make the Congo valleys open to free trade and commerce, to end the slave trade in the region, and to establish a Congo Free State. In reality, King Leopold II's company established a regime that was so brutal in its treatment of local populations that an international scandal forced the Belgian state to take over the colony in 1908.

**Berlin Wall** The wall built in 1961 by the East German Communists to prevent citizens of East Germany from fleeing to West Germany; it was torn down in 1989.

**birth control pill** This oral contraceptive became widely available in the mid-1960s. For the first time, women had a simple method of birth control that they could take themselves.

**Otto von Bismarck** (1815–1898) The prime minister of Prussia and later the first chancellor of a unified Germany, Bismarck was the architect of German unification and helped to consolidate the new nation's economic and military power.

**Black Death** The epidemic of bubonic plague that ravaged Europe, Asia, and North Africa during the fourteenth century, killing one third to one half of the population.

**Blackshirts** The troops of Mussolini's fascist regime; the squads received money from Italian landowners to attack socialist leaders.

**Black Tuesday** October 29, 1929, the day on which the U.S. stock market crashed, plunging the U.S. and international trading systems into crisis and leading to the Great Depression.

**William Blake** (1757–1827) Romantic writer who criticized industrial society and factories. He championed the imagination and poetic vision, seeing both as transcending the limits of the material world.

**Blitzkrieg** The German "lightning war" strategy used during the Second World War; the Germans invaded Poland, France, Russia, and other countries with fast-moving and well-coordinated attacks using aircraft, tanks, and other armored vehicles, followed by infantry.

**Bloody Sunday** On January 22, 1905, the Russian tsar's guards killed 130 demonstrators who were protesting the tsar's mistreatment of workers and the middle class.

**Giovanni Boccaccio** (1313–1375) Florentine author best known for his *Decameron*, a collection of prose tales about sex, adventure, and trickery written in the Italian vernacular after the Black Death.

**Jean Bodin** (1530–1596) A French political philosopher whose *Six Books of the Commonwealth* advanced a theory of absolute sovereignty, on the grounds that the state's paramount duty is to maintain order and that monarchs should therefore exercise unlimited power.

**Boer War** (1898–1902) Conflict between British and ethnically European Afrikaners in South Africa, with terrible casualties on both sides.

**Boethius** (c. 480–524) A member of a prominent Roman family, he sought to preserve aspects of ancient learning by compiling a series of handbooks and anthologies appropriate for Christian readers. His translations of Greek philosophy provided a crucial link between classical Greek thought and the early intellectual culture of Christianity.

**Bolsheviks** Former members of the Russian Social Democratic Party who advocated the destruction of capitalist political and economic institutions and started the Russian Revolution. In 1918, the Bolsheviks changed their name to the Russian Communist Party. Prominent Bolsheviks included Vladimir Lenin and Josef Stalin. Leon Trotsky joined the Bolsheviks late but became a prominent leader in the early years of the Russian Revolution.

**Napoleon Bonaparte** (1769–1821) Corsican-born French general who seized power and ruled as dictator and emperor from 1799 to 1814. After the successful conquest of much of Europe, he was defeated by Russian and Prussian forces and died in exile.

**Boniface VIII** During his pontificate (1294–1303), repeated claims to papal authority were challenged by King Philip IV of France. When Boniface died in 1309 (at the hands of Philip's thugs), the French king moved the papal court from Rome to the French city of Avignon, where it remained until 1378.

**Sandro Botticelli** (1445–1510) An Italian painter devoted to the blending of classical and Christian motifs by using ideas associated with the pagan past to illuminate sacred stories.

**bourgeoisie** Term for the middle class, derived from the French word for a town dweller, *bourgeois*.

**Boxer Rebellion** (1899–1900) Chinese peasant movement that opposed foreign influence, especially that of Christian missionaries; it was finally put down after the Boxers were defeated by a foreign army composed mostly of Japanese, Russian, British, French, and American soldiers.

**Tycho Brahe** (1546–1601) Danish astronomer who believed that the careful study of the heavens would unlock the secrets of the universe. For over twenty years, he charted the movements of significant objects in the night sky, compiling the finest set of astronomical data in Europe.

**Brexit** A public referendum in June 2016 in which the population of the United Kingdom, by a slim majority, voted to leave the European Union (EU). This marked the first time that a member nation chose to retreat from the goal of increased integration with other members of the EU. The Brexit vote was controversial in Scotland and Northern Ireland, because in these areas of the United Kingdom, a majority expressed a wish to remain in the EU.

**British Commonwealth of Nations** Formed in 1926, the Commonwealth conferred dominion status on Britain's white settler colonies in Canada, Australia, and New Zealand.

**Bronze Age** (3200–1200 B.C.E.) The name given to the era characterized by the discovery of techniques for smelting bronze (an alloy of copper and tin), which was then the strongest known metal.

**Brownshirts** Troops of young German men who dedicated themselves to the Nazi cause in the early 1930s by holding street marches, mass rallies, and confrontations. They engaged in beatings of Jews and anyone who opposed the Nazis.

**George Gordon, Lord Byron** (1788–1824) Writer and poet whose life helped give the Romantics their reputation as rebels against conformity. He was known for his love affairs, his defense of working-class movements, and his passionate engagement in politics, which led to his death in the war for Greek independence.

**Byzantium** A small settlement located at the mouth of the Black Sea and at the crossroads between Europe and Asia, it was chosen by Constantine as the site for his new imperial capital of Constantinople in 324. Modern historians use this name to refer to the eastern Roman Empire, which lasted in this region until 1453, but the inhabitants of that empire referred to themselves as Romans.

**Julius Caesar** (100–44 B.C.E.) The Roman general who conquered the Gauls, invaded Britain, and expanded Rome's territory in Asia Minor. He became the dictator of Rome in 46 B.C.E. His assassination led to the rise of his grandnephew and adopted son, Gaius Octavius Caesar, who ruled the Roman Empire as Caesar Augustus.

**caliphs** Islamic rulers who claim descent from the prophet Muhammad.

**John Calvin** (1509–1564) French-born theologian and reformer whose radical form of Protestantism was adopted in many Swiss cities, notably Geneva.

**Canary Islands** Islands off the western coast of Africa that were colonized by Portugal and Spain in the mid-fifteenth century, after which they became bases for further expeditions around the African coast and across the Atlantic.

**Carbonari** An underground organization that opposed the Concert of Europe's restoration of monarchies. They held influence in southern Europe during the 1820s, especially in Italy.

**Carolingian** Derived from the Latin name Carolus (Charles), this term refers to the Frankish dynasty that began with the rise to power of Charlemagne's grandfather, Charles Martel (688–741). At its height under Charlemagne (Charles "the Great"), this dynasty controlled what are now France, Germany, northern Italy, Catalonia, and portions of central Europe. The Carolingian Empire collapsed under the combined weight of Viking raids, economic disintegration, and the growing power of local lords.

**Carolingian Renaissance** A cultural and intellectual flowering that took place around the court of Charlemagne in the late eighth and early ninth centuries.

**Carthage** The great maritime empire that grew out of Phoenician trading colonies in North Africa and rivaled the power of Rome. Its wars with Rome, collectively known as the Punic Wars, ended in its destruction in 146 B.C.E.

**Cassidorus** (c. 490–c. 583) Member of an old senatorial family, he was largely responsible for introducing classical learning into the monastic curriculum and for turning monasteries into centers for the collection, preservation, and transmission of knowledge. His *Institutes*, an influential handbook of classical literature for Christian readers, was intended as a preface to more intensive study of theology and the Bible.

**Catholic Church** The "universal" (catholic) church based in Rome, which was redefined in the sixteenth century, when the Counter-Reformation resulted in the rebirth of the Catholic faith at the Council of Trent.

**Margaret Cavendish** (1623–1673) English natural philosopher who developed her own speculative natural philosophy. She used this philosophy to critique those who excluded her from scientific debate.

**Camillo Benso di Cavour** (1810–1861) Prime minister of Piedmont-Sardinia and founder of the Italian Liberal party; he played a key role in the movement for Italian unification under the Piedmontese king, Victor Emmanuel II.

**Central Powers** The First World War alliance between Germany, Austria-Hungary, Bulgaria, and Turkey.

**Charlemagne** (742–814) As king of the Franks (767–813), Charles "the Great" consolidated much of western Europe under his rule. In 800, he was crowned emperor by the pope in Rome, establishing a problematic precedent that would have wide-ranging consequences for western Europe's relationship with the eastern Roman Empire in Byzantium and for the relationship between the papacy and secular rulers.

**Charles I** (1625–1649) The second Stuart king of England, Ireland, and Scotland, Charles attempted to rule without the support of Parliament, sparking a controversy that erupted into civil war in 1642. The king's forces were ultimately defeated and Charles himself was executed by act of Parliament, the first time in history that a ruling king was legally deposed and executed by his own government.

**Charles II** Nominally king of England, Ireland, and Scotland after his father Charles I's execution in 1649, Charles II lived in exile until he was restored to the throne in 1660. Influenced by his cousin, King Louis XIV of France, he presided over an opulent royal court until his death in 1685.

**Chartism** A working-class movement in Britain that called for reform of the British political system during the 1840s. The Chartists were supporters of the "People's Charter," which had six demands: universal white male suffrage, secret ballots, an end to property qualifications as a condition of public office, annual parliamentary elections, salaries for members of the House of Commons, and equal electoral districts.

**Geoffrey Chaucer** (1340–1400) English poet whose collection of versified stories, *The Canterbury Tales*, features characters from a variety of classes.

**Christendom** A term used to denote an ideal vision of Christian unity—political and cultural, as well as spiritual—promoted by powerful Christian rulers, beginning with Charlemagne. The "Holy Roman Empire," a term coined by Frederick I Barbarossa, was an outgrowth of this idea. Christendom was never a united entity, but it was a powerful vision.

**Christine de Pisan** (c. 1364–c. 1431) Born in Italy, Christine spent her adult life attached to the French court and, after her husband's death, became the first laywoman to earn her living by writing. She was the author of treatises on warfare and chivalry as well as of books and pamphlets that challenged long-standing misogynistic claims.

**Church of England** Founded by Henry VIII in the 1530s, as a consequence of his break with the authority of the Roman pope.

**Winston Churchill** (1874–1965) British prime minister who led the country during the Second World War. He also coined the phrase "Iron Curtain" in a speech at Westminster College in 1946.

**Marcus Tullius Cicero** (106–43 B.C.E.) Influential Roman senator, orator, Stoic philosopher, and prose stylist. His published writings still form the basis of instruction in classical Latin grammar and usage.

**Lucius Quinctius Cincinnatus** (519–c. 430 B.C.E.) A legendary citizen-farmer of Rome who reluctantly accepted an appointment as dictator. After defeating Rome's enemies, he allegedly left his political office and returned to his farm.

**Civil Constitution of the Clergy** Issued by the French National Assembly in 1790, the Civil Constitution of the Clergy decreed that all bishops and priests should be subject to the authority of the state. Their salaries were to be paid out of the public treasury, and they were required to swear allegiance to the new state, making it clear that they served France rather than Rome. The Assembly's aim was to make the Catholic Church of France a truly national and civil institution.

**civilizing mission** The basis of an argument made by Europeans to justify colonial expansion in the nineteenth century. Supporters of this idea believed that Europeans had a duty to impose Western ideas of economic and political progress on the indigenous peoples they ruled over in their colonies. In practice, the colonial powers often found that ambitious plans to impose European practices on colonial subjects led to unrest that threatened the stability of colonial rule. By the early twentieth century most colonial powers were more cautious in their plans for political or cultural transformation.

**civil rights movement** The Second World War increased African American migration from the American South to northern cities, intensifying a drive for rights, dignity, and independence. By 1960, civil rights groups had started organizing boycotts and demonstrations directed at discrimination against blacks in the South. During the 1960s, civil rights laws passed under President Lyndon B. Johnson did bring African Americans some equality with regard to voting rights and, to a much lesser degree, school desegregation. However, racism continued in areas such as housing, job opportunities, and the economic development of African American communities.

**Civil War** (1861–1865) Conflict between the northern and southern states of America that cost over 600,000 lives; this struggle led to the abolition of slavery in the United States.

**classical learning** The study of ancient Greek and Latin texts. After Christianity became the only legal religion of the Roman Empire, scholars needed to find a way to make classical learning applicable to a Christian way of life. Christian monks played a significant role in resolving this problem by reinterpreting the classics for a Christian audience.

**Cluny** A powerful Benedictine monastery founded in 910 whose enormous wealth and prestige derived its independence from secular authorities as well as from its wide network of daughter houses (priories).

**Cold War** (1945–1991) Ideological, political, and economic conflict in which the USSR and Eastern Europe opposed the United States and Western Europe in the decades after the Second World War. The Cold War's origins lay in the breakup of the wartime alliance between the United States and the Soviet Union in 1945 and resulted in a division of Europe into two spheres: the West, committed to market capitalism; and the East, which sought to build socialist republics in areas under Soviet control. The Cold War ended with the collapse of the Soviet Union in 1991.

**collectivization** Stalin's plan for nationalizing agricultural production, begun in 1929. Twenty-five million peasants were forced to give up their land and join 250,000 large collective farms. Many who resisted were deported to labor camps in the Far East, and Stalin's government cut off food rations to those areas most marked by resistance to collectivization. In the ensuing human-caused famines, millions of people starved to death.

**Columbian exchange** The widespread exchange of peoples, plants, animals, diseases, goods, and culture between the African and Eurasian landmass (on the one hand) and the region that encompasses the Americas, Australia, and the Pacific Islands (on the other); precipitated by Christopher Columbus's voyage in 1492.

**Christopher Columbus** (1451–1506) A Genoese sailor who persuaded King Ferdinand and Queen Isabella of Spain to fund his expedition across the Atlantic, with the purpose of discovering a new trade route to Asia. His miscalculations landed him in the Bahamas and the island of Hispaniola in 1492.

**commercial revolution** A period of economic development in Europe lasting from c. 1500 to c. 1800. Advances in agriculture and handicraft production, combined with the expansion of trade networks in the Atlantic world, brought new wealth and new kinds of commercial activity to Europe. The commercial revolution prepared the way for the Industrial Revolution of the 1800s.

**Committee of Public Safety** Political body during the French Revolution that was controlled by the Jacobins, who defended the revolution by executing thousands during the Reign of Terror (September 1793–July 1794).

**commune** A community of individuals who have banded together in a sworn association, with the aim of establishing their independence and setting up their own form of representative government. Many medieval towns originally founded by lords or monasteries gained their independence through such methods.

***The Communist Manifesto*** Radical pamphlet by Karl Marx (1818–1883) that predicted the downfall of the capitalist system and its replacement by a classless, egalitarian society. Marx believed that this revolution would be accomplished by the workers (the proletariat).

**Compromise of 1867** Agreement between the Habsburgs and the peoples living in Hungarian parts of the empire that the Habsburg state would be officially known as the Austro-Hungarian Empire.

**Concert of Europe** (1814–1815) The body of diplomatic agreements designed primarily by the Austrian minister Klemens von Metternich between 1814 and 1848 and supported by other European powers until 1914. Its goal was to maintain a balance of power on the Continent and to prevent destabilizing social and political change in Europe.

**conciliarism** A doctrine developed in the thirteenth and fourteenth centuries to counter the growing power of the papacy, conciliarism holds that papal authority should be subject to a council of the Church at large. Conciliarists emerged as a dominant force after the Council of Constance (1414–1418) but were eventually outmatched by a rejuvenated papacy.

**Congress of Vienna** (1814–1815) International conference to reorganize Europe after the downfall of Napoleon and the French Revolution. European monarchies restored the Bourbon family to the French throne and agreed to respect each other's borders and to cooperate in guarding against future revolutions and war.

**conquistador** Spanish term for "conqueror," applied to the mercenaries and adventurers who campaigned against indigenous peoples in central and southern America.

**conservatives** In the nineteenth century, conservatives aimed to legitimize and solidify the monarchy's authority and the hierarchical social order. They believed that change had to be slow, incremental, and managed so that the structures of authority were strengthened and not weakened.

**Constantine** (275–337 C.E.) The first emperor of Rome to convert to Christianity, Constantine came to power in 312 C.E. In 324 C.E., he founded a new imperial capital, Constantinople, on the site of a maritime settlement known as Byzantium.

**Constantinople** Founded by the emperor Constantine on the site of a village called Byzantium, Constantinople became the new capital of the Roman Empire in 324 C.E. and continued to be the seat of imperial power after its capture by the Ottoman Turks in 1453. It is now known as Istanbul.

**contract theory of government** A theory of government written by Englishman John Locke (1632–1704) that posits that government authority is both contractual and conditional; therefore, if a government has abused its given authority, society has the right to dissolve it and create another.

**Nicholas Copernicus** (1473–1543) Polish astronomer who advanced the idea that the earth revolves around the sun.

**cosmopolitanism** Stemming from the Greek word meaning "universal city," the culture characteristic of the Hellenistic world challenged and transformed the narrower worldview of the Greek polis.

**cotton gin** Invented by Eli Whitney in 1793, this device mechanized the process of separating cotton seeds from cotton fibers, which sped up the production of cotton and reduced its price. This change made slavery profitable in the United States.

**Council of Constance** (1417–1420) A meeting of clergy and theologians in an effort to resolve the Great Schism within the Roman Church. The council deposed all rival papal candidates and elected a new pope, Martin V, but it also adopted the doctrine of conciliarism, which holds that the supreme authority within the Church rests with a representative general council and not with the pope. However, Martin V himself was an opponent of this doctrine and refused to be bound by it.

**Council of Trent** The name given to a series of meetings held in the Italian city of Trent (Trento) between 1545 and 1563, when leaders of the Roman Church reaffirmed Catholic doctrine and instituted internal reforms.

**Counter-Reformation** The movement to counter the Protestant Reformation, initiated by the Catholic Church at the Council of Trent in 1545.

**coup d état** French term for the overthrow of an established government by a group of conspirators, usually with military support.

**Crimean War** (1854–1856) War waged by Russia against Great Britain and France. Spurred by Russia's encroachment on Ottoman territories, the conflict revealed Russia's military weakness when Russian forces fell to British and French troops.

**Cuban missile crisis** (1962) Diplomatic standoff between the United States and the Soviet Union that was provoked by the Soviet Union's attempt to base nuclear missiles in Cuba; it brought the world closer to nuclear war than ever before or since.

*cuius regio, eius religio* A Latin phrase meaning "as the ruler, so the religion." Adopted as a part of the settlement of the Peace of Augsburg in 1555, it meant that those principalities ruled by Lutherans would have Lutheranism as their official religion and those ruled by Catholics must practice Catholicism.

**cult of domesticity** Concept associated with Victorian England that idealized women as nurturing wives and mothers.

**cult of the Virgin** The beliefs and practices associated with the veneration of Mary, the mother of Jesus, which became increasingly popular in the twelfth century.

**cuneiform** An early writing system that began to develop in Mesopotamia during the fourth millennium B.C.E. By 3100 B.C.E., its distinctive markings were impressed on clay tablets using a wedge-shaped stylus.

**Cyrus the Great** (c. 585–529 B.C.E.) As architect of the Persian Empire, Cyrus extended his dominion over a vast territory stretching from the Persian Gulf to the Mediterranean and incorporating the ancient civilizations of Mesopotamia. His successors ruled this Persian Empire as "Great Kings."

**Darius** (521–486 B.C.E.) The Persian emperor whose conflict with Aristagoras, the Greek ruler of Miletus, ignited the Persian Wars. In 490 B.C.E., Darius sent a large army to punish the Athenians for their intervention in Persian imperial affairs, but this force was defeated by Athenian hoplites on the plain of Marathon.

**Charles Darwin** (1809–1882) British naturalist who wrote *On the Origin of Species* and developed the theory of natural selection to explain the evolution of organisms.

**D-Day** (June 6, 1944) Date of the Allied invasion of Normandy, under General Dwight Eisenhower, to liberate Western Europe from German occupation.

**Decembrists** Nineteenth-century Russian army officers who were influenced by events in France and formed secret societies that espoused liberal governance. They were put down by Nicholas I in December 1825.

**Declaration of Independence** (1776) Historic document stating the principles of government on which the United States was founded.

**Declaration of the Rights of Man and of the Citizen** (1789) French charter of liberties formulated by the National Assembly during the French Revolution. The seventeen articles later became the preamble to the new constitution, which the assembly finished in 1791.

**democracy** In ancient Greece, this form of government allowed a class of propertied male citizens to participate in the governance of their polis; but it excluded women, slaves, and citizens without property from the political process. As a result, the ruling class amounted to only a small percentage of the entire population.

**René Descartes** (1596–1650) French philosopher and mathematician who emphasized the use of deductive reasoning.

**Denis Diderot** (1713–1784) French philosophe and author who was the guiding force behind the publication of the first encyclopedia. His *Encyclopedia* showed how reason could be applied to nearly all realms of thought and aimed to be a compendium of all human knowledge.

**Dien Bien Phu** (1954) Defining battle in the war between French colonialists and the Viet Minh that secured North Vietnam for Ho Chi Minh and his army and left the south to form its own government, which was supported by France and the United States.

**Diet of Worms** The select council of the Church that convened in the German city of Worms and condemned Martin Luther on a charge of heresy in 1521.

**Diocletian** (245–316 C.E.) As emperor of Rome from 284 to 305 C.E., Diocletian recognized that the empire could not be governed by one man in one place. His solution was to divide the empire into four parts, each with its own imperial ruler, but he himself remained the dominant ruler of the resulting tetrarchy ("rule of four"). He also initiated the Great Persecution, a time when many Christians became martyrs to their faith.

**Directory** (1795–1799) Executive committee that governed after the fall of Robespierre and held control until the coup of Napoleon Bonaparte.

***Discourse on Method*** Philosophical treatise by René Descartes (1596–1650) proposing that the path to knowledge was through logical deduction, beginning with one's own self: "I think, therefore I am."

**Dominican order** Also called the Order of Preachers, it was founded by Dominic of Osma (1170–1221), a Castilian preacher and theologian, and approved by Innocent III in 1216. The order was dedicated to the rooting out of heresy and the conversion of Jews and Muslims. Many of its members held teaching positions in European universities and contributed to the development of medieval philosophy and theology. Others became the leading administrators of the Inquisition.

**dominion in the British Commonwealth** Status granted to Canada after its promise to maintain fealty to the British crown, even after gaining independence in 1867; later applied to Australia and New Zealand.

**Dreyfus Affair** The 1894 French scandal surrounding accusations that a Jewish captain, Alfred Dreyfus, sold military secrets to the Germans. Convicted, Dreyfus was sentenced to solitary confinement for life. However, after a public outcry, it was revealed that the trial documents were forgeries, and Dreyfus was pardoned after a second trial in 1899. In 1906, he was fully exonerated and reinstated in the army. The affair revealed the depths of popular anti-Semitism in France.

**Alexander Dubček** (1921–1992) Communist leader of the Czechoslovakian government who advocated for "socialism with a human face." He encouraged debate within the party, academic and artistic freedom, and less censorship, which led to the "Prague spring" of 1968. People in other parts of Eastern Europe began to demonstrate in support of Dubček and demanded their own reforms. When Dubček tried to democratize the Communist party and did not attend a meeting of the Warsaw Pact, the Soviets sent tanks and troops into Prague and ousted Dubček and his allies.

**Duma** The Russian parliament, created in response to the revolution of 1905.

**Dunkirk** The French port on the English Channel where British and French forces retreated after sustaining heavy losses against the German military. Between May 27 and June 4, 1940, the Royal Navy evacuated over 300,000 troops in commercial and pleasure boats.

**Eastern Front** Battlefront between Berlin and Moscow during the First and Second World Wars.

**East India Company** (1600–1858) British charter company created to outperform Portuguese and Spanish traders in the Far East; in the eighteenth century the company became, in effect, the ruler of a large part of India. There was also a Dutch East India Company.

**Edict of Nantes** (1598) Issued by Henry IV of France in an effort to end religious violence. The edict declared France to be a Catholic country but tolerated some forms of Protestant worship.

**Edward I** King of England from 1272 to his death in 1307, Edward presided over the creation of new legal and bureaucratic institutions in his realm, violently subjugated the Welsh, and attempted to colonize Scotland. He expelled English Jews from his domain in 1290.

**Eleanor of Aquitaine** (1122–1204) Ruler of the wealthy province of Aquitaine and wife of Louis VII of France, Eleanor had her marriage annulled in order to marry the young count of Anjou, Henry Plantagenet, who became King Henry II of England a year later. The mother of two future kings of England, she was an important patron of the arts.

**Elizabeth I** (1533–1603) The Protestant daughter of Henry VIII and his second wife, Anne Boleyn, Elizabeth succeeded her sister Mary as the second queen regnant of England (1558–1603).

**emancipation of the serfs** (1861) The abolition of serfdom was central to Tsar Alexander II's program of modernization and reform, but it produced a limited amount of change. Former serfs now had legal rights. However, farmland was granted to village communes instead of to individuals. The land was of poor quality, and the former serfs had to pay installments for it to the village commune.

**emperor** Originally the term for any conquering commander of the Roman army whose victories merited celebration in an official triumph. After Augustus seized power in 27 B.C.E., it was the title borne by the sole ruler of the Roman Empire.

**empire** A centralized political entity consolidated through the conquest and colonization of other nations or peoples in order to benefit the ruler and/or his homeland.

**Enabling Act** (1933) Emergency act passed by the Reichstag (German parliament) that helped transform Hitler from Germany's chancellor, or prime minister, into a dictator, following the suspicious burning of the Reichstag building and a suspension of civil liberties.

**enclosure** Long process of privatizing what had been public agricultural land in eighteenth-century Britain; it helped to stimulate the development of commercial agriculture and forced many people in rural areas to seek work in cities during the early stages of industrialization.

*Encyclopedia* Joint venture of French philosophe writers, led by Denis Diderot (1713–1784), which proposed to summarize all modern knowledge in a multivolume illustrated work with over 70,000 articles.

**Friedrich Engels** (1820–1895) German social and political philosopher who collaborated with Karl Marx on many publications.

**English Civil War** (1642–1649) Conflicts between the English Parliament and King Charles I erupted into civil war, which ended in the defeat of the royalists and the execution of Charles on charges of treason against the crown. A short time later, Parliament's hereditary House of Lords was abolished and England was declared a Commonwealth.

**English Navigation Act of 1651** Act stipulating that only English ships could carry goods between the mother country and its colonies.

**Enlightenment** Intellectual movement in eighteenth-century Europe with a belief in human betterment through the application of reason to solve social, economic, and political problems.

**Epicureanism** A philosophical position articulated by Epicurus of Athens (c. 342–270 B.C.E.), who rejected the idea of an ordered universe governed by divine forces; instead, he emphasized individual agency and proposed that the highest good is the pursuit of pleasure.

**Desiderius Erasmus** (c. 1469–1536) Dutch-born scholar, social commentator, and Catholic humanist whose new translation of the Bible influenced the theology of Martin Luther.

**Estates General** The representative body of the three estates in France. In 1789, King Louis XVI summoned the Estates General to meet for the first time since 1614 because it seemed to be the only solution to France's worsening economic crisis and financial chaos.

**Etruscans** Settlers of the Italian peninsula who dominated the region from the late Bronze Age until the rise of the Roman Republic in the sixth century B.C.E.

**Euclid** Hellenistic mathematician whose *Elements of Geometry* (c. 300 B.C.E.) forms the basis of modern geometry.

**eugenics** A Greek term, meaning "good birth," referring to the project of "breeding" a superior human race. It was popularly championed by scientists, politicians, and social critics in the late nineteenth and early twentieth centuries.

**Eurasia** The preferred term for the geographical expanse that encompasses both Europe and Asia.

**European Common Market** (1957) The Treaty of Rome established the European Economic Community (EEC), or Common Market. The original members were France, West Germany, Italy, Belgium, Holland, and Luxembourg. The EEC sought to abolish trade barriers between its members and it pledged itself to common external tariffs, the free movement of labor and capital among the member nations, and uniform wage structures and social security systems to create similar working conditions in all member countries.

**European Union (EU)** Successor organization to the European Economic Community or European Common Market, formed by the Maastricht Treaty, which took effect in 1993. Currently twenty-eight member states compose the EU, which has a governing council, an international court, and a parliament. Over time, member states of the EU have relinquished some of their sovereignty, and cooperation has evolved into a community with a single currency, the euro.

**Exclusion Act of 1882** U.S. law prohibiting nearly all immigration from China to the United States; fueled by animosity toward Chinese workers in the American West.

**existentialism** Philosophical movement that arose out of the Second World War and emphasized the absurdity of human condition. Led by Jean-Paul Sartre and Albert Camus, existentialists encouraged humans to take responsibility for their own decisions and dilemmas.

**expulsion of the Jews** European rulers began to expel their Jewish subjects from their kingdoms beginning in the 1280s, mostly due to their inability to repay the money they had extorted from Jewish moneylenders but also as a result of escalating anti-Semitism in the wake of the Crusades. Jews were also expelled from the Rhineland during the fourteenth century and from Spain in 1492.

**fascism** The doctrine formulated by Benito Mussolini, which emphasized three main ideas: statism ("nothing above the state, nothing outside the state, nothing against the state"), nationalism, and militarism. Its name derives from the Latin *fasces*, a symbol of Roman imperial power adopted by Mussolini.

**Fashoda Crisis** (1898) Disagreements between the French and the British over land claims in North Africa led to a standoff between armies of the two nations at the Sudanese town of Fashoda. The crisis was solved diplomatically. France ceded southern Sudan to Britain in exchange for a stop to further expansion by the British.

**Federal Republic of Germany** Nation founded from the Allied zones of occupation of Germany after the Second World War; also known as West Germany.

***The Feminine Mystique*** Groundbreaking book by the feminist Betty Friedan (1921–2006), who tried to define *femininity* and explored how women internalized those definitions.

**Franz Ferdinand** (1863–1914) Archduke of Austria and heir to the Austro-Hungarian Empire; his assassination led to the beginning of the First World War.

**Ferdinand** (1452–1516) **and Isabella** (1451–1504) In 1469, Ferdinand of Aragon married the heiress to Castile, Isabella. Their union allowed them to pursue several ambitious policies, including the conquest of Granada, the last Muslim principality in Spain, and the expulsion of Spain's large Jewish community. In 1492, Isabella granted three ships to Christopher Columbus of Genoa (Italy), who went on to claim portions of the New World for Spain.

**Fertile Crescent** An area of fertile land comprising what are now Syria, Israel, Turkey, eastern Iraq, and western Iran that was able to sustain settlements due to its wetter climate and abundant natural food resources. Some of the earliest known civilizations emerged there between 9000 and 4500 B.C.E.

**feudalism** A problematic modern term that attempts to explain the diffusion of power in medieval Europe and the many different kinds of political, social, and economic relationships that were forged through the giving and receiving of fiefs (*feoda*). But because it is anachronistic and inadequate, this term has been rejected by most historians of the medieval period.

**financial crisis of 2008** A global economic crisis following the sudden collapse of real estate prices in many parts of the world in 2008. The effects of this crisis were magnified by the increased level of globalization in the world economy, particularly in banking and the financial industry. In order to prevent a complete collapse of the global economy, governments in the United States and in Europe provided bailouts to cash-strapped banks and financial institutions, funded by taxpayers.

**First Crusade** (1095–1099) Launched by Pope Urban II in response to a request from the Byzantine emperor Alexius Comnenus. Alexius had asked for a small contingent of knights to assist him in fighting Turkish forces in Anatolia, but Urban instead directed the crusaders' energies toward the Holy Land and the recapture of Jerusalem, promising those who took the cross (*crux*) that they would merit eternal salvation if they died in the attempt. This crusade prompted attacks against Jews throughout Europe and resulted in six subsequent—and unsuccessful—military campaigns.

**First World War** A total war from August 1914 to November 1918, involving the armies of Britain, France, and Russia (the Allies) against Germany, Austria-Hungary, and the Ottoman Empire (the Central Powers). Italy joined the Allies in 1915, and the United States joined them in 1917, helping to tip the balance in favor of the Allies, who also drew on the populations and raw materials of their colonial possessions. Also known as the Great War.

**Five Pillars of Islam** The Muslim teaching that salvation is assured only through observance of five basic precepts: submission to God's will as described in the teachings of Muhammad, frequent prayer, ritual fasting, the giving of alms, and an annual pilgrimage to Mecca (the Hajj).

**Five-Year Plan** Soviet effort launched under Stalin in 1928 to replace the market with a state-owned and state-managed economy in order to promote rapid economic development over a five-year period and thereby "catch and overtake" the leading capitalist countries. The First Five-Year Plan was followed by the Second Five-Year Plan (1933–1937) and so on, until the collapse of the Soviet Union in 1991.

**fly shuttle** Invented by John Kay in 1733, this device sped up the process of weaving.

**Fourteen Points** President Woodrow Wilson proposed these points as the foundation on which to build peace in the world after the First World War. They called for an end to secret treaties, "open covenants, openly arrived at," freedom of the seas, the removal of international tariffs, the reduction of arms, the "self-determination of peoples," and the establishment of a League of Nations to settle international conflicts.

**Franciscan Order** Also known as the Order of the Friars Minor. The earliest Franciscans were followers of Francis of Assisi (1182–1226) and strove, like him, to imitate the life and example of Jesus. The order was formally established by Pope Innocent III in 1209. Its special mission was the care and instruction of the urban poor.

**Frankfurt Parliament** (1848–1849) Failed attempt to create a unified Germany under constitutional principles. In 1849, the assembly offered the crown of the new German nation to Frederick William IV of Prussia, but he refused the offer and suppressed a brief protest. The delegates went home disillusioned.

**Frederick I** "Barbarossa" ("Red Beard"; r. 1155–1190) was the first of Charlemagne's successors to call his realm the Holy Roman Empire, thereby claiming its spiritual and political independence from Rome. He spent his long reign struggling with the papacy and the rebellious towns of northern Italy. He died during the Third Crusade.

**Frederick the Great** (1712–1786) Prussian ruler (1740–1786) who engaged the nobility in maintaining a strong military and bureaucracy and led Prussian armies to notable military victories. He also encouraged Enlightenment rationalism and artistic endeavors.

**French Revolution of 1789** In 1788, a severe financial crisis forced the French monarchy to convene the Estates General, an assembly representing the three estates of the realm: the clergy, the nobility, and the commons (known as the Third Estate). When the Estates General met in 1789, representatives of the Third Estate demanded major constitutional changes. When the king and his government proved uncooperative, the Third Estate broke with the other two estates and renamed itself the National Assembly, demanding a written constitution. The position of the National Assembly was confirmed by a popular uprising in Paris, forcing the king to accept the transformation of France into a constitutional monarchy. This constitutional phase of the revolution lasted until 1792, when the pressures of foreign invasion and the emergence of a more radical revolutionary movement caused the collapse of the monarchy and the establishment of a Republic in France.

**French Revolution of 1830** The French popular revolt against Charles X's July Ordinances of 1830, which dissolved the

French Chamber of Deputies and restricted suffrage to exclude almost everyone except the nobility. After several days of violence, Charles abdicated the throne and was replaced by a constitutional monarch, Louis Philippe.

**French Revolution of 1848** Revolution overthrowing Louis Philippe in February 1848, leading to the formation of the Second Republic (1848–1852). Initially enjoying broad support from both the middle classes and laborers in Paris, the new government became more conservative after elections in which the French peasantry participated for the first time. A workers' revolt was violently repressed in June 1848. In December 1848, Napoleon Bonaparte's nephew, Louis-Napoleon Bonaparte, was elected president. In 1852, Louis-Napoleon declared himself emperor and abolished the republic.

**Sigmund Freud** (1856–1939) Austrian physician who founded the discipline of psychoanalysis and suggested that human behavior was largely motivated by unconscious and irrational forces.

**Galileo Galilei** (1564–1642) Italian physicist and inventor; the implications of his ideas raised the ire of the Catholic Church, and he was forced to retract most of his findings.

**Gallipoli** (1915) During the First World War, a combined force of French, British, Australian and New Zealand troops tried to invade the Gallipoli Peninsula, in the first large-scale amphibious attack in history, and seize it from the Turks. After seven months of fighting, the Allies had lost 200,000 soldiers. Defeated, they withdrew.

**Mohandas K. (Mahatma) Gandhi** (1869–1948) The Indian leader who advocated nonviolent noncooperation to protest colonial rule and helped win home rule for India in 1947.

**Giuseppe Garibaldi** (1807–1882) Italian revolutionary leader who led the fight to free Sicily and Naples from the Habsburg Empire; those lands were then peaceably annexed by Sardinia to produce a unified Italy.

**Gaul** The region of the Roman Empire that was home to the Celtic people of that name, comprising modern France, Belgium, and western Germany.

**Geneva Peace Conference** (1954) International conference to restore peace in Korea and Indochina. The chief participants were the United States, the Soviet Union, Great Britain, France, the People's Republic of China, North Korea, South Korea, Vietnam, the Viet Minh party, Laos, and Cambodia. The conference resulted in the division of North and South Vietnam.

**Genoa** Maritime city on Italy's northwestern coast. The Genoese were active in trading ventures along the Silk Road and in the establishment of trading colonies in the Mediterranean. They were also involved in the world of finance and backed the commercial ventures of other powers, especially Spain.

**German Democratic Republic** Nation founded from the Soviet zone of occupation of Germany after the Second World War; also known as East Germany.

**German Social Democratic party** Founded in 1875, it was the most powerful socialist party in Europe before 1917.

**Gilgamesh** Sumerian ruler of the city of Uruk around 2700 B.C.E., Gilgamesh became the hero of one of the world's oldest epics, which circulated orally for nearly a millennium before being written down.

**Giotto** (c. 1266–1337) Florentine painter and architect who is often considered a forerunner of the Renaissance.

**glasnost** Introduced by the Soviet leader Mikhail Gorbachev in June 1987, glasnost was one of the five major policies that constituted *perestroika* ("reform" or "restructuring"). Often translated into English as "openness," it called for transparency in Soviet government and institutional activities by reducing censorship in mass media and lifting significant bans on the political, intellectual, and cultural lives of Soviet civilians.

**globalization** The term used to describe political, social, and economic networks that span the globe. These global exchanges are not limited by nation-states and in recent decades have become associated with new technologies, such as the Internet. Globalization is not new, however; human cultures and economies have been in contact with each other for centuries.

**Glorious Revolution** The overthrow of King James II of England and the installation of his Protestant daughter, Mary Stuart, and her husband, William of Orange, to the throne in 1688 and 1689. It is widely regarded as the founding moment in the development of a constitutional monarchy in Britain. It also established a more favorable climate for the economic and political growth of the English commercial classes.

**Mikhail Gorbachev** (1931–) Soviet leader who attempted to reform the Soviet Union through his programs of glasnost and perestroika in the late 1980s. He encouraged open discussions in other countries of the Soviet bloc, which helped inspire the velvet revolutions throughout Eastern Europe. Eventually the political, social, and economic upheaval he had unleashed led to the breakup of the Soviet Union.

**Gothic style** A type of graceful architecture emerging in twelfth- and thirteenth-century England and France. This style is characterized by pointed arches, delicate decoration, and large windows.

**Olympe de Gouges** (1748–1793) French political radical and feminist whose *Declaration of the Rights of Woman* demanded an equal place for women in France.

**Great Depression** Global economic crisis following the U.S. stock market crash on October 29, 1929, and ending with the onset of the Second World War.

**Great Famine** A period of terrible hunger and deprivation in Europe that peaked between 1315 and 1317, caused by a cooling of the climate and by soil exhaustion due to overfarming. It is estimated to have reduced the population of Europe by 10 to 15 percent.

**Great Fear** (1789) Following the outbreak of revolution in Paris, fear spread throughout the French countryside, as rumors circulated that armies of brigands or royal troops were coming. Some peasants and villagers organized into militias; others attacked and burned the manor houses in order to destroy the records of manorial dues.

**Great Schism** (1378–1417) Also known as the Great Western Schism, to distinguish it from the long-standing rupture between the churches of the Greek East and the Latin West. During the Great Schism, the Roman Church was divided between two (and, ultimately, three) competing popes. Each pope claimed to be legitimate, and each denounced the heresy of the others.

**Great Terror** (1936–1938) The systematic murder of nearly a million people and the deportation of another million and a half to labor camps by Stalin's regime in an attempt to consolidate power and remove perceived enemies.

**Greek East** After the founding of Constantinople, the eastern Greek-speaking half of the Roman Empire grew more populous, prosperous, and central to imperial policy. Its inhabitants considered themselves to be the true heirs of Rome and their own Orthodox Church to be the true manifestation of Jesus's ministry.

**Greek independence** Nationalists in Greece revolted against the Ottoman Empire and fought a war that ended in Greek independence in 1827. They received crucial help from British, French, and Russian troops as well as widespread sympathy throughout Europe.

**Pope Gregory I** (r. 590–604) Also known as Gregory the Great, he was the first bishop of Rome to successfully negotiate a more universal role for the papacy. His political and theological agenda widened the rift between the western Latin (Catholic) Church and the eastern Greek (Orthodox) Church in Byzantium. He also articulated the Church's official position on the status of Jews, promoted effective approaches to religious worship, encouraged the Benedictine monastic movement, and sponsored missionary expeditions.

**Guernica** The Basque town bombed by German planes in April 1937 during the Spanish Civil War. It is also the subject of Pablo Picasso's famous painting from the same year.

**guilds** Professional organizations in commercial towns that regulated business and safeguarded the privileges of those practicing a particular craft. Often identical to confraternities ("brotherhoods").

**Gulag** The vast system of forced labor camps under the Soviet regime. It originated in 1919 in a small monastery near the Arctic Circle and spread throughout the Soviet Union. Penal labor was required of both ordinary criminals and those accused of political crimes. Tens of millions of people were sent to the camps between 1928 and 1953; the exact figure is unknown.

**Gulf War** (1991) Armed conflict between Iraq and a coalition of thirty-two nations, including the United States, Britain, Egypt, France, and Saudi Arabia. The seeds of the war were planted with Iraq's invasion of Kuwait on August 2, 1990.

**Johannes Gutenberg** European inventor of the printing press. His shop in Mainz produced the first printed book—a Bible—between the years 1453 and 1455.

**Habsburg Dynasty** A powerful European dynasty that came to power in the eleventh century in a region now part of Switzerland. Early generations of Habsburgs consolidated their control over neighboring German-speaking lands. Through strategic marriages with other royal lines, later rulers eventually controlled a substantial part of Europe—including much of central Europe, the Netherlands, and even Spain and all its colonies for a time. In practice, the Holy Roman Emperor was chosen from a member of the Habsburg lineage. By the latter half of the seventeenth century, the Austrian Habsburg Empire was made up of nearly 300 nominally autonomous dynastic kingdoms, principalities, duchies, and archbishoprics.

**Hagia Sophia** The enormous church dedicated to "Holy Wisdom," built in Constantinople at the behest of the emperor Justinian in the sixth century C.E. When Constantinople fell to Ottoman forces in 1453, it became an important mosque.

**Haitian Revolution** (1802–1804) In 1802, Napoleon sought to reassert French control of Saint-Domingue, but stiff resistance and yellow fever crushed the French army. In 1804, Jean-Jacques Dessalines, a general in the army of former slaves, declared the independent state of Haiti (see **slave revolt in Saint-Domingue**).

**Hajj** The annual pilgrimage to Mecca; an obligation for Muslims.

**Hammurabi** Ruler of Babylon from 1792 to 1750 B.C.E., Hammurabi issued a collection of laws that were greatly influential in the Near East and that constitute the world's oldest surviving law code.

**Harlem Renaissance** Cultural movement in the 1920s that was based in Harlem, a part of New York City with a large African American population. The movement gave voice to black novelists, poets, painters, and musicians, many of whom used their art to protest racial subordination.

**Hatshepsut** (1479–1458 C.E.) As a pharaoh during the New Kingdom, she launched several successful military campaigns and extended trade and diplomacy. She was an ambitious builder who probably constructed the first tomb in the Valley of the Kings. Though she never pretended to be a man, she was routinely portrayed with a masculine figure and a ceremonial beard.

**Hebrews** Originally a pastoral people divided among several tribes, they were briefly united under the rule of David and his son, Solomon, who promoted the worship of a single god, Yahweh, and constructed the first temple at the new capital city of Jerusalem. After Solomon's death, the Hebrew tribes were divided between the two kingdoms of Israel and Judah, which were eventually conquered by the Neo-Assyrian and Chaldean empires. It was in captivity that the Hebrews came to define themselves through worship of Yahweh and to develop a religion, Judaism, that could exist outside of Judea. They were liberated by the Persian king Cyrus the Great in 539 B.C.E.

**Hellenistic art** The art of the Hellenistic period bridged the tastes, ideals, and customs of classical Greece and those that became more characteristic of Rome. The Romans strove to emulate Hellenistic city planning and civic culture, thereby exporting Hellenistic culture to their own far-flung colonies in western Europe.

**Hellenistic culture** The "Greek-like" culture that dominated the ancient world in the wake of Alexander's conquests.

**Hellenistic kingdoms** Following the death of Alexander the Great, his vast empire was divided into three separate states: Ptolemaic Egypt, under the rule of the general Ptolemy and his successors; Seleucid Asia, ruled by the general Seleucus and his heirs; and Antigonid Greece, governed by Antigonus of Macedonia. Each state maintained its independence, but the shared characteristics of Greco-Macedonian rule and a shared Greek culture and heritage bound them together in a united cosmopolitan world.

**Hellenistic world** The various Western civilizations of antiquity that were loosely united by shared Greek language and culture, especially around the eastern Mediterranean.

**Heloise** (c. 1090–1164) One of the foremost scholars of her time, she became the pupil and the wife of the philosopher and teacher Peter Abelard. In later life, she was the founder of a new religious order for women.

**Henry IV** King of Germany and Holy Roman Emperor from 1056—when he ascended the throne at the age of six—until his death in 1106. Henry's reign first was weakened by conflict with the Saxon nobility and later was marked by the Investiture Controversy with Pope Gregory VII.

**Henry VIII** (1491–1547) King of England from 1509 until his death, Henry rejected the authority of the Roman Church in 1534 when the pope refused to annul his marriage to his queen, Catherine of Aragon; Henry became the founder of the Church of England.

**Henry of Navarre** (1553–1610) Crowned King Henry IV of France, he renounced his Protestantism but granted limited toleration to Huguenots (French Protestants) through the Edict of Nantes in 1598.

**Prince Henry the Navigator** (1394–1460) A member of the Portuguese royal family, Henry encouraged the exploration and conquest of western Africa and the trade in gold and slaves.

**hieroglyphs** The writing system of ancient Egypt, based on a complicated series of pictorial symbols. It fell out of use when Egypt was absorbed into the Roman Empire and was deciphered only after the discovery of the Rosetta Stone in the early nineteenth century.

**Hildegard of Bingen** (1098–1179) A powerful abbess, theologian, scientist, musician, and visionary who claimed to receive regular revelations from God. Although highly influential in her own day, she was never officially canonized by the Church, in part because her strong personality no longer matched the changing ideal of female piety.

**Hiroshima** Japanese port devastated by an atomic bomb on August 6, 1945.

**Adolf Hitler** (1889–1945) The author of *Mein Kampf* and leader of the Nazis who became chancellor of Germany in 1933. Hitler and his Nazi regime started the Second World War and orchestrated the systematic murder of over 6 million Jews, hundreds of thousands of people with disabilities living in institutions, tens of thousands of Roma, and thousands of homosexuals.

**Hitler-Stalin Pact** (1939) Treaty between Stalin and Hitler that promised Stalin a share of Poland, Finland, the Baltic states, and Bessarabia in the event of a German invasion of Poland, which began shortly thereafter, on September 1, 1939.

**HIV epidemic** The first cases of HIV-AIDS appeared in the late 1970s. As HIV-AIDS became a global crisis, international organizations recognized the need for an early, swift, and comprehensive response to future outbreaks of disease.

**Thomas Hobbes** (1588–1679) English political philosopher whose *Leviathan* argued that any form of government capable of protecting its subjects' lives and property might act as an all-powerful sovereign. This government should be allowed to trample over both liberty and property for the sake of its own survival and that of his subjects. Hobbes argued that in his natural state, man was like "a wolf" toward other men.

**Holy Roman Empire** The loosely allied collection of lands in central and eastern Europe ruled by German kings from the twelfth century until 1806. Its origins are usually identified with the empire of Charlemagne, the Frankish king who was crowned emperor of Rome by the pope in 800. The term itself was promoted by Frederick I "Barbarossa" in the mid-twelfth century.

**homage** A ceremony in which an individual becomes the "man" (French: *homme*) of a lord.

**Homer** (fl. eighth century B.C.E.) A Greek rhapsode ("weaver" of stories) credited with merging centuries of poetic tradition in the epics known as the *Iliad* and the *Odyssey*.

**hoplite** A Greek foot-soldier armed with a spear or short sword and protected by a large round shield (*hoplon*). In battle, hoplites stood shoulder to shoulder in a close formation called a phalanx.

**Huguenots** French Protestants who endured severe persecution in the sixteenth and seventeenth centuries.

**humanism** A program of study associated with the movement known as the Renaissance, humanism aimed to replace the scholastic emphasis on logic and philosophy with the study of ancient languages, literature, history, and ethics.

**human rights** The rights of all people to legal equality, freedom of religion and speech, and the right to participate in government. Human rights laws prohibit torture, cruel punishment, and slavery.

**David Hume** (1711–1776) Scottish writer who applied Newton's method of scientific inquiry and skepticism to the study of morality, the mind, and government.

**Hundred Years' War** (1337–1453) A series of wars between England and France, fought mostly on French soil and prompted by the territorial and political claims of English monarchs.

**Jan Hus** (c. 1373–1415) A Czech reformer who adopted many of the teachings of the English theologian John Wycliffe, and who also demanded that the laity be allowed to receive both the consecrated bread and wine of the Eucharist. The Council of Constance burned him at the stake for heresy. In response, his supporters, the Hussites, revolted against the Church.

**Saddam Hussein** (1937–2006) The dictator of Iraq who invaded Iran in 1980 and started the eight-year-long Iran-Iraq war; invaded Kuwait in 1990, which led to the Gulf War of 1991; and was overthrown when the United States invaded Iraq in 2003. Involved in Iraqi politics since the mid-1960s, Hussein became the official head of state in 1979.

**Iconoclastic Controversy** (717–787) A serious and often violent theological debate that raged in Byzantium after Emperor Leo III ordered the destruction of religious art on the grounds that any image representing a divine or holy personage was likely to promote idol worship and blasphemy. *Iconoclast* means "breaker of icons." Those who supported the veneration of icons were called iconodules, "adherents of icons."

**Il-khanate** Mongol-founded dynasty in thirteenth-century Persia.

**Indian National Congress** Formed in 1885, this Indian political party worked to achieve Indian independence from British colonial control. The Congress was led by Gandhi during the 1920s and 1930s.

**Indian Rebellion of 1857** This uprising began near Delhi, when the military disciplined a regiment of Indian soldiers employed by the British for refusing to use rifle cartridges greased with pork fat—unacceptable to either Hindus or Muslims. Rebels attacked law courts and burned tax rolls, protesting debt and corruption. The mutiny spread through large areas of northwest India before being violently suppressed by British troops.

**Indo-Europeans** A group of people speaking variations of the same language and who moved into the Near East and Mediterranean region shortly after 2000 B.C.E.

**indulgences** Grants exempting Catholic Christians from the performance of penance, either in life or after death. The abusive trade in indulgences was a major catalyst of the Protestant Reformation.

**Inca Empire** The highly centralized South American empire that was toppled by the Spanish conquistador Francisco Pizarro in 1533.

**Innocent III** (1160/61–1216) As pope, he wanted to unify all of Christendom under papal hegemony. He furthered this goal at the Fourth Lateran Council of 1215, which defined one of the Church's dogmas as the acknowledgment of papal supremacy. The council also took an unprecedented interest in the religious education and habits of every Christian.

**Inquisition** Formalized in the thirteenth century, this tribunal of the Roman Church aims to enforce religious orthodoxy and conformity.

**International Monetary Fund (IMF)** Established in 1945 to ensure international cooperation regarding currency exchange and monetary policy, the IMF is a specialized agency of the United Nations.

**Investiture Conflict** The name given to a series of debates over the limitations of spiritual and secular power in Europe during the eleventh and early twelfth centuries, it came to a head when Pope Gregory VII and Emperor Henry IV of Germany both claimed the right to appoint and invest bishops with the regalia of office. After years of diplomatic and military hostility, it was partially settled by the Concordat of Worms in 1122.

**Irish potato famine** Period of agricultural blight from 1845 to 1849 whose devastating results produced widespread starvation and led to mass immigration to the United States.

**Iron Curtain** Term coined by Winston Churchill in 1946 to refer to the borders of Eastern European nations that lay within the zone of Soviet control.

**Islamic State (Daesh)** In 2014, following the outbreak of the civil war in Syria, a militant group of Muslim fundamentalists seized territory in northeastern Syria and northwestern Iraq and proclaimed themselves a new *caliphate*, the authority over all Muslims. Known as the Islamic State of Iraq and Syria (ISIS) or the Islamic State of Iraq and the Levant (ISIL), they are also called Daesh by Arabic-speaking critics of their violence and brutality. ("Daesh" is an Arabic acronym for the group's name, but it also sounds like a word that means to trample or crush something.) They have been designated a terrorist organization by the United Nations and many countries of the world, both for their actions in the Middle East and for their encouragement of terrorist acts in Europe, Africa, and North and South America.

**Italian invasion of Ethiopia** (1896) Italy invaded Ethiopia, the last major independent African kingdom. Menelik II, the Ethiopian emperor, soundly defeated the Italian forces.

**Ivan III, the Great** (1440–1505) Russian ruler who annexed neighboring territories and consolidated his empire's position as a European power.

**Jacobins** Radical French political group during the French Revolution that took power after 1792, executed the French king, and sought to remake French culture.

**Jacquerie** Violent 1358 peasant uprising in northern France, incited by disease, war, and taxes.

**James I** (1566–1625) Monarch who ruled Scotland as James VI and who succeeded Elizabeth I as king of England in 1603. He supervised the English vernacular translation of the Bible known by his name.

**James II** King of England, Ireland, and Scotland from 1685 to 1688 whose commitment to absolutism and Catholic zealotry led to his exile to France after the Glorious Revolution of 1688.

**Janissaries** Corps of enslaved soldiers recruited as children from the Christian provinces of the Ottoman Empire and trained to display intense personal loyalty to the Ottoman sultans, who used these forces to curb local autonomy and as their personal bodyguards.

**Jerome** (c. 340–420 C.E.) One of the early church fathers, he translated the Bible from Hebrew and Greek into a popular form of Latin—hence the name by which this translation is known: the Vulgate, or "vulgar" (popular), Bible.

**Jesuits** The religious order formally known as the Society of Jesus, founded in 1540 by Ignatius Loyola to combat the spread of Protestantism. The Jesuits became active in politics, education, and missionary work.

**Jesus** (c. 4 B.C.E.–c. 30 C.E.) A Jewish preacher and teacher in the rural areas of Galilee and Judea who was arrested for seditious political activity, tried, and crucified by the Romans. After his execution, his followers claimed that he had been resurrected from the dead and taken up into heaven. They began to teach that Jesus had been the divine representative of God, the Messiah foretold by ancient Hebrew prophets, and that he had suffered for the sins of humanity and would return to judge all the world's inhabitants at the end of time.

**Joan of Arc** (c. 1412–1431) A peasant girl from the province of Lorraine who claimed to have been commanded by God to lead French forces against the English occupying army during the Hundred Years' War. Successful in her efforts, she was betrayed by the French king and handed over to the English, who condemned her to death for heresy. Her reputation underwent a process of rehabilitation, but she was not officially canonized as a saint until 1920.

**Judaism** The religion of the Hebrews as it developed in the centuries after the establishment of the Hebrew kingdoms under David and Solomon, especially during the period of Babylonian Captivity.

**Justinian** (527–565) Emperor of Rome who unsuccessfully attempted to reunite the eastern and western portions of the empire. Also known for his important codification of Roman law, in the *Corpus Juris Civilis*.

**Justinian's Code of Roman Law** Formally known as the *Corpus Juris Civilis,* or "Body of Civil Law," this compendium consisted of a systematic compilation of imperial statutes, the writings of Rome's great legal authorities, a textbook of legal principles, and the legislation of Justinian and his immediate successors. As the most authoritative collection of Roman law, it formed the basis of canon law (the legal system of the Roman Church) and became essential to the developing legal traditions of every European state as well as of many countries around the world.

*Das Kapital* ("Capital") The 1867 book by Karl Marx that outlined the theory behind historical materialism and attacked the socioeconomic inequities of capitalism.

**Johannes Kepler** (1571–1630) Mathematician and astronomer who elaborated on and corrected Copernicus's theory and is chiefly remembered for his discovery of the three laws of planetary motion that bear his name.

**Keynesian Revolution** Postdepression economic ideas developed by the British economist John Maynard Keynes, whereby the state took a greater role in managing the market economy through monetary policy in order to maintain levels of unemployment during periods of economic downturn.

**KGB** Soviet political police and spy agency, first formed as the Cheka not long after the Bolshevik coup in October 1917. It grew to more than 750,000 operatives with military rank by the 1980s.

**Genghis Khan** (c. 1167–1227) "Oceanic Ruler," the title adopted by the Mongol chieftain Temujin, founder of a dynasty that conquered much of southern Asia.

**Khanate** The major political unit of the vast Mongol Empire. There were four Khanates, including the Yuan Empire in China, forged by Chingiz Khan's grandson Kubilai in the thirteenth century.

**Ruhollah Khomeini** (1902–1989) Iranian Shi'ite religious leader who led the revolution in Iran that resulted in the abdication of the shah in 1979. His government allowed some limited economic and political populism combined with strict constructions of Islamic law, restrictions on women's public life, and the prohibition of ideas or activities linked to Western influence.

**Nikita Khrushchev** (1894–1971) Leader of the Soviet Union during the Cuban missile crisis, Khrushchev came to power after Stalin's death in 1953. His reforms and criticisms of the excesses of the Stalin regime led to his fall from power in 1964.

**Kremlin** Once synonymous with the Soviet government, this word refers to Moscow's walled city center and the palace originally built by Ivan the Great.

**Kristallnacht** Organized attack by Nazis and their supporters on the Jews of Germany following the assassination of a German embassy official by a Jewish man in Paris. Throughout Germany, thousands of stores, schools, cemeteries, and synagogues were attacked on November 9, 1938. Dozens of people were killed, and tens of thousands of Jews were arrested and held in camps, where many were tortured and killed in the ensuing months.

**Labour party** Founded in Britain in 1900, this party represented workers and was based on socialist principles.

**Latin West** After the founding of Constantinople, the western Latin-speaking half of the Roman Empire became poorer and more peripheral, but it also fostered the emergence of new barbarian kingdoms. At the same time, the Roman pope claimed to have inherited both the authority of Jesus and the essential elements of Roman imperial authority.

**League of Nations** International organization founded after the First World War to solve international disputes through arbitration; it was dissolved in 1946 and its assets were transferred to the United Nations.

**Leonardo da Vinci** (1452–1519) Florentine inventor, sculptor, architect, and painter whose breadth of interests typifies the ideal of the "Renaissance man."

**Vladimir Lenin** (1870–1924) Leader of the Bolshevik Revolution in Russia (1917) and the first leader of the Soviet Union.

**Leviathan** A book by Thomas Hobbes (1588–1679) that recommended a ruler have unrestricted power.

**liberalism** Political and social theory that judges the effectiveness of a government in terms of its ability to protect individual rights. Liberals support representative forms of government, free trade, and freedom of speech and religion. In the economic realm, liberals believe that individuals should be free to engage in commercial or business activities without interference from the state or their community.

**lithograph** Art form that involves drawing or writing on stone and producing printed impressions.

**John Locke** (1632–1704) English philosopher and political theorist known for his contributions to liberalism. Locke had great faith in human reason and believed that just societies were those that infringed the least on the natural rights and freedoms of individuals. This led him to assert that a government's legitimacy depended on the consent of the governed, a view that had a profound effect on the authors of the United States' Declaration of Independence.

**Louis IX** King of France from 1226 to his death on crusade in 1270, Louis was famous for his piety and for his close attention to the administration of law and justice in his realm. He was officially canonized as Saint Louis in 1297.

**Louis XIV** (1638–1715) Called the "Sun King," he was known for his success at strengthening the institutions of the French absolutist state.

**Louis XVI** (1754–1793) Well-meaning but ineffectual king of France, finally deposed and executed during the French Revolution.

**Toussaint L'Ouverture** (1743–1803) A former slave who, after 1791, led the slaves of the French colony of Saint-Domingue in the largest and most successful slave insurrection in world history. After his capture and death in 1803, his followers succeeded in establishing an independent Haiti in 1804.

**Ignatius Loyola** (1491–1556) Founder of the Society of Jesus (commonly known as the Jesuits), whose members vowed to serve God through poverty, chastity, and missionary work. He abandoned his first career as a mercenary after reading an account of Christ's life written in his native Spanish.

**Lucretia** According to Roman legend, Lucretia was a virtuous Roman wife who was raped by the son of Rome's last king and who virtuously committed suicide in order to avoid bringing shame on her family.

**Luftwaffe** Literally "air weapon," this is the name of the German air force, which was founded during the First World War, disbanded in 1945, and reestablished when West Germany joined NATO in 1950.

*Lusitania* The British passenger liner that was sunk by a German U-boat (submarine) on May 7, 1915. Public outrage over the sinking contributed to the U.S. decision to enter the First World War.

**Martin Luther** (1483–1546) A German monk and professor of theology whose critique of the papacy launched the Protestant Reformation.

*ma'at* The Egyptian term for the serene order of the universe, with which the individual soul (*ka*) must remain in harmony. The power of the pharaoh was linked to *ma'at*, insofar as it ensured the prosperity of the kingdom. After the upheavals of the First Intermediate Period, the perception of the pharaoh's relationship with *ma'at* was revealed to be conditional, something that had to be earned.

**Niccolò Machiavelli** (1469–1527) As the author of *The Prince* and the *Discourses on Livy*, he looked to the Roman past for paradigms of greatness, at the same time hoping to win the patronage of contemporary rulers who would restore Italy's political independence.

**Magna Carta** The "Great Charter" of 1215, enacted during the reign of King John of England and designed to limit his powers. It is regarded now as a landmark in the development of constitutional government. In its own time, its purpose was to restore the power of great lords.

**Magyar nationalism** Lajos Kossuth led this national movement in the Hungarian region of the Habsburg Empire, calling for national independence for Hungary in 1848. With the support of Russia, the Habsburg army crushed the movement and all other revolutionary activities in the empire. Kossuth fled into exile.

**Moses Maimonides** (c. 1137–1204) Jewish scholar, physician, and scriptural commentator whose *Mishneh Torah* is a fundamental exposition of Jewish law.

**Thomas Malthus** (1766–1834) British political economist who believed that populations inevitably grew faster than the available food supply. Societies that could not control their population growth would be checked only by famine, disease, poverty, and infant malnutrition. He argued that governments could not alleviate poverty. Instead, the poor had to exercise "moral restraint," postpone marriage, and have fewer children.

**Nelson Mandela** (1918–2013) The South African opponent of apartheid who led the African National Congress and was imprisoned from 1962 until 1990. After his release from prison, he worked with Prime Minister Frederik Willem De Klerk to establish majority rule. Mandela became the first black president of South Africa in 1994.

**Manhattan Project** The secret U.S. government research project to develop the first nuclear bomb. The vast project involved dozens of sites across the United States, including New Mexico, Tennessee, Illinois, California, Utah, and Washington. The first test of a nuclear bomb was near Alamogordo, New Mexico, on July 16, 1945.

**manors** Common farmland worked collectively by the inhabitants of entire villages, sometimes on their own initiative, sometimes at the behest of a lord.

**Mao Zedong** (1893–1976) The leader of the Chinese Revolution who defeated the Nationalists in 1949 and established the Communist regime in China.

**Marne** A major battle of the First World War in September 1914; halted the German invasion of France and led to protracted trench warfare on the Western Front.

**Marshall Plan** Economic aid package given to Europe by the United States after the Second World War to promote reconstruction and economic development and to secure European countries from a feared communist takeover.

**Karl Marx** (1818–1883) German philosopher and economist who believed that a revolution of the working classes would overthrow the capitalist order and create a classless society. Author of *Das Kapital* and *The Communist Manifesto*.

**Marxists** Followers of the socialist political economist Karl Marx, who called for workers everywhere to unite and create an independent political force. Marxists believed that industrialization brought about an inevitable struggle between laborers and the class of capitalist property owners. This struggle would culminate in a revolution that would abolish private property and establish a society committed to social equality.

**Mary** See **cult of the Virgin**.

**Mary I** (1516–1558) Catholic daughter of Henry VIII and his first wife, Catherine of Aragon, Mary Tudor was the first queen regnant of England. Her attempts to reinstitute Catholicism in England met with limited success. After her early death, she was labeled "Bloody Mary" by the Protestant supporters of her half sister and successor, Elizabeth I.

**mass culture** The spread of literacy and public education in the nineteenth century created a new audience for print entertainment and a new class of media entrepreneurs to cater to this audience. The invention of radio, film, and television in the twentieth century carried this development to another level, as millions of consumers were now accessible to the producers of news, information, and entertainment. The rise of this "mass culture" has been celebrated as an expression of popular tastes but also criticized as a vehicle for the manipulation of populations through clever and seductive propaganda.

**Maya** Native American people whose culturally and politically sophisticated empire encompassed lands in present-day Mexico and Guatemala.

**Giuseppe Mazzini** (1805–1872) Founder of Young Italy and an ideological leader of the Italian nationalist movement.

**Mecca** Center of an important commercial network of the Arabian Peninsula and birthplace of the prophet Muhammad. It is now considered the holiest site in the Islamic world.

**Medici** A powerful dynasty of Florentine bankers and politicians whose ancestors were originally apothecaries ("medics").

**Meiji Empire** Empire created under the leadership of Mutsuhito, emperor of Japan from 1868 until 1912. During the Meiji period, Japan became a world industrial and naval power.

**Mensheviks** Within the Russian Social Democratic Party, the Mensheviks advocated slow changes and a gradual move toward socialism, in contrast to the Bolsheviks, who wanted to push for a proletarian revolution. The Mensheviks believed that a proletarian revolution in Russia was premature and that the country needed to complete its capitalist development first.

**mercantilism** A theory and policy for directing the economy of monarchical states between 1600 and 1800 based on the assumption that wealth and power depended on a favorable balance of trade (more exports and fewer imports) and the accumulation of precious metals. Mercantilists advocated forms of economic protectionism to promote domestic production.

**Maria Sybilla Merian** (1647–1717) A scientific illustrator and an important early entomologist. She conducted research on two continents and published the well-received *Metamorphosis of the Insects of Surinam*.

**Merovingian dynasty** A Frankish dynasty that claimed descent from a legendary ancestor called Merovic, the Merovingians were the only powerful family to establish a lasting kingdom in western Europe during the fifth and sixth centuries.

**Mesopotamia** The "land between the Tigris and the Euphrates rivers," where the civilization of Sumer, the first urban society, flourished.

**Klemens von Metternich** (1773–1859) Austrian foreign minister whose primary goals were to bolster the legitimacy of monarchies and, after the defeat of Napoleon, to prevent another large-scale war in Europe. At the Congress of Vienna, he opposed social and political change and wanted to check Russian and French expansion.

**Michelangelo Buonarroti** (1475–1564) A virtuoso Florentine sculptor, painter, and poet who spent much of his career in the service of the papacy. He is best known for the decoration of the Sistine Chapel and for his monumental sculptures.

**Middle East** Like "Near East," this term was invented in the nineteenth century. It usually describes a region stretching from North Africa and Egypt to the Arabian Peninsula and Anatolia.

**Middle Kingdom of Egypt** (2055–1650 B.C.E.) The period following the First Intermediate Period of dynastic warfare, which ended with the reassertion of pharaonic rule under Mentuhotep II.

**Miletus** A Greek polis and Persian colony on the Ionian coast of Asia Minor. Influenced by the cultures of Mesopotamia, Egypt, and Lydia, it produced several of the ancient world's first scientists and sophists. Thereafter, a political conflict between the ruler of Miletus, Aristagoras, and the Persian emperor, Darius, sparked the Persian Wars with Greece.

**John Stuart Mill** (1806–1873) English liberal philosopher whose faith in human reason led him to support a broad variety of civic and political freedoms for men and women, including the right to vote and the right to free speech.

**Slobodan Milosevic** (1941–2006) The Serbian nationalist politician who became president of Serbia and whose policies during the Balkan wars of the early 1990s led to the deaths of thousands of Croatians, Bosnian Muslims, Albanians, and Kosovars. After leaving office in 2000, he was arrested and tried for war crimes at the International Court in The Hague. The trial ended before a verdict with his death in 2006.

**Minoan Crete** A sea empire based at Knossos on the Greek island of Crete and named for the legendary King Minos. The Minoans dominated the Aegean for much of the second millennium B.C.E.

**modernism** There were several different modernist movements in art and literature, but they shared three key characteristics. First, modernists believed that the world had radically changed and that this change should be embraced. Second, they believed that traditional aesthetic values and assumptions about creativity were ill suited to the present. Third, they developed a new conception of what art could do that emphasized expression over representation and insisted on the value of novelty, experimentation, and creative freedom.

**Mongol people** A nomadic people from the steppes of Central Asia who were united under the ruler Genghis Khan. His conquest of China was continued by his grandson Kubilai and his great-grandson Ogedei, whose army also seized southern Russia and then moved through Hungary and Poland toward eastern Germany. The Mongol armies withdrew from eastern Europe after the death of Ogedei, but his descendants continued to rule his vast empire for another half century.

**Michel de Montaigne** (1533–1592) French philosopher and social commentator, best known for his *Essays*.

**Baron de Montesquieu** (1689–1755) An Enlightenment philosophe whose most influential work was *The Spirit of Laws*. In this work, he analyzed the structures that shaped law and categorized governments into three types: republics, monarchies, and despotisms. His ideas about the separation of powers among the executive, the legislative, and the judicial branches of government influenced the authors of the U.S. Constitution.

**Thomas More** (1478–1535) Christian humanist, English statesman, and author of *Utopia*. In 1529, he was appointed lord chancellor of England but resigned because he opposed King Henry VIII's plans to establish a national church under royal control. He was eventually executed for refusing to take an oath acknowledging Henry to be the head of the Church of England and has since been canonized by the Catholic Church.

**mos maiorum** Literally translated as the "code of the elders" or the "custom of ancestors." This unwritten code governed the lives of Romans under the Republic and stressed the importance of showing reverence to ancestral tradition. It was sacrosanct and essential to Roman identity and an important influence on Roman culture, law, and religion.

**Wolfgang Amadeus Mozart** (1756–1791) Austrian composer, famous at a young age as a concert musician and later celebrated as a prolific composer of instrumental music and operas that are seen as the apogee of the Classical style in music.

**Muhammad** (570–632 C.E.) The founder of Islam, regarded by his followers as God's last and greatest prophet.

**Munich Conference** (1938) Hitler met with the leaders of Britain, France, and Italy and negotiated an agreement that gave Germany a major slice of Czechoslovakia. The British prime minister Neville Chamberlain believed that the agreement would bring peace to Europe, but instead Germany invaded and seized the rest of Czechoslovakia.

**Muscovy** The duchy centered on Moscow whose dukes saw themselves as heirs to the Roman Empire. In the early fourteenth century, Moscow was under the control of the Mongol Khanate. After the collapse of the Khanate, the Muscovite grand duke, Ivan III, conquered all the Russian principalities between Moscow and the border of Poland-Lithuania, and then Lithuania itself. By the time of his death, Ivan had established Muscovy as a dominant power.

**Muslim learning and culture** The Crusades brought the Latin West in contact with the Islamic world, which influenced European culture in myriad ways. Europeans adapted Arabic numerals and mathematical concepts as well as Arabic and Persian words. Through Arabic translations, Western scholars gained access to Greek learning, which had a profound influence on Christian theology. European scholars also learned from the Islamic world's accomplishments in medicine and science.

**Benito Mussolini** (1883–1945) The Italian founder of the Fascist party who came to power in Italy in 1922 and allied himself with Hitler and the Nazis during the Second World War.

**Mycenaean Greece** (1600–1200 B.C.E.) The term used to describe the civilization of Greece during the late Bronze Age, when territorial kingdoms such as Mycenae formed around a king, a warrior caste, and a palace bureaucracy.

**Nagasaki** Second Japanese city on which the United States dropped an atomic bomb. The attack took place on August 9, 1945; the Japanese surrendered shortly thereafter, ending the Second World War.

**Napoleon Bonaparte** (1769–1821) French general who became First Consul (1799) and Emperor (1804–1814) of France. He came to power during the French Revolution, and his political innovations transformed the French state while also continuing a process of centralization that had begun under earlier monarchs. As a military leader he conquered much of Europe. He was finally defeated and sent into exile by a coalition of Russian, British, Prussian, and Austrian armies, setting the stage for the restoration of the Bourbon family on the French throne.

**Napoleon III** (1808–1873) The nephew of Napoleon Bonaparte, Napoleon III was elected president of the French Second Republic in 1848 and made himself emperor of France in 1852. During his reign (1852–1870), he rebuilt the French capital of Paris. Defeated in the France-Prussian War of 1870, he went into exile.

**Napoleonic Code** Legal code drafted by Napoleon in 1804 and based on Justinian's *Corpus Iuris Civilis*. It distilled different legal traditions to create one uniform law. The code confirmed the abolition of feudal privileges of all kinds and set the conditions for exercising property rights.

**Napoleon's military campaigns** In 1805, the Russians, Prussians, Austrians, Swedes, and British attempted to contain Napoleon, but he defeated them. Out of his victories, Napoleon created a new empire and affiliated states. In 1808, he invaded Spain, but fierce resistance prevented him from achieving a complete victory. In 1812, he invaded Russia, and his army was decimated as it retreated from Moscow during the winter. After the Russian campaign, the united European powers defeated Napoleon and forced him into exile. He escaped and reassumed command of his army, but the European powers defeated him for the final time at the Battle of Waterloo.

**Gamal Abdel Nasser** (1918–1970) President of Egypt and the most prominent spokesman for secular pan-Arabism. He became a target for Islamist critics, such as Sayyid Qutb and the Muslim Brotherhood, angered by the Western-influenced policies of his regime.

**National Assembly** Governing body of France that succeeded the Estates General in 1789 during the French Revolution. It was composed of, and defined by, the delegates of the Third Estate.

**National Association for the Advancement of Colored People (NAACP)** Founded in 1910, this U.S. civil rights organization is dedicated to ending inequality and segregation for black Americans.

**National Convention** The governing body of France from September 1792 to October 1795. It declared France a republic and then tried and executed King Louis XVI. The Convention also confiscated the property of the enemies of the revolution, instituted a policy of de-Christianization, changed marriage and inheritance laws, abolished slavery in its colonies, placed a cap on the price of necessities, and ended the compensation of nobles for their lost privileges.

**nationalism** Movement to unify a country under one government based on perceptions of the population's common history, customs, and social traditions.

**nationalism in Yugoslavia** In the 1990s, Slobodan Milosevic and his allies reignited Serbian nationalism in the former Yugoslavia, which led non-Serb republics in Croatia and Slovenia to seek independence. The country erupted into war, with the worst violence taking place in Bosnia, a multiethnic region with Serb, Croatian, and Bosnian Muslim populations. European diplomats proved powerless to stop attempts by Croatian and Serbian military and paramilitary forces to claim territory through ethnic cleansing and violent intimidation. Atrocities were committed on all sides, but pro-Serb forces were responsible for the most deaths.

**NATO** The North Atlantic Treaty Organization, a 1949 military agreement among the United States, Canada, Great Britain, and eight Western European nations, which declared that an armed attack against any one of the members would be regarded as an attack against all. Created during the Cold War in the face of the Soviet Union's control of Eastern Europe, NATO continues to exist today. Its twenty-eight countries include former members of the Warsaw Pact as well as Albania and Turkey.

**Nazi party** Founded in the early 1920s, the National Socialist German Workers' Party (NSDAP) gained control over Germany under the leadership of Adolf Hitler in 1933 and continued in power until Germany was defeated in 1945.

**Nazism** The political movement in Germany led by Adolf Hitler that advocated a violent anti-Semitic, anti-Marxist, pan-German ideology.

**Near East** Like "Middle East," a geographical term coined during the nineteenth century to describe western Asia and the eastern Mediterranean—that is, the parts of Asia nearest to Europe.

**Neo-Assyrian Empire** (883–859 B.C.E. to 612–605 B.C.E.) Assurnasirpal II laid the foundations of the Neo-Assyrian Empire through military campaigns against neighboring peoples. Eventually, the empire stretched from the Mediterranean Sea to western Iran. A military dictatorship governed the empire through its army, which it used to frighten and oppress both its subjects and its enemies. The empire's ideology was based on waging holy war in the name of its principal god, Assur, and the exaction of tribute through terror.

**neoliberalism** Neoliberals believe that free markets, profit incentives, and restraints on both budget deficits and social welfare programs are the best guarantee of individual liberties. Beginning in the 1980s, neoliberal theory was used to structure the policy of financial institutions such as the International Monetary Fund and the World Bank, which turned away from interventionist policies in favor of market-driven models of economic development.

**Neolithic Revolution** The "New" Stone Age, which began around 11,000 B.C.E., saw new technological and social developments, including managed food production, the beginnings of permanent settlements, and the rapid intensification of trade.

**Neoplatonism** A school of thought based on the teachings of Plato. Prevalent in the Roman Empire, it had a profound effect on the formation of Christian theology. Neoplatonists argued that nature is a book written by its creator to reveal the ways of God to humanity. Convinced that God's perfection must be reflected in nature, the Neoplatonists searched for the ideal and perfect structures that they believed must lie behind the "shadows" of the everyday world.

**New Deal** President Franklin D. Roosevelt's package of government reforms that were enacted during the depression of the 1930s to provide jobs for the unemployed, social welfare programs for the poor, and security to the financial markets.

**New Economic Policy** In 1921, the Bolsheviks abandoned war communism in favor of the New Economic Policy (NEP). Under the NEP, the state still controlled all major industry and financial concerns, while individuals could own private property, trade freely within limits, and farm their own land for their own benefit. Fixed taxes replaced grain requisition. The policy successfully helped Soviet agriculture recover from the civil war but was later abandoned in favor of collectivization.

**Isaac Newton** (1642–1727) One of the foremost scientists of all time, Newton was an English mathematician and physicist; he is noted for his development of calculus, work on the properties of light, and theory of gravitation.

**Nicholas II** (1868–1918) The last Russian tsar, who abdicated the throne in 1917. He and his family were executed by the Bolsheviks on July 17, 1918.

**Friedrich Nietzsche** (1844–1900) The German philosopher who denied the possibility of knowing absolute "truth" or "reality," since all knowledge comes filtered through linguistic, scientific, or artistic systems of representation. He also criticized Judeo-Christian morality for instilling a repressive conformity that drained civilization of its vitality.

**nongovernmental organizations (NGOs)** Private organizations such as the Red Cross that play a large role in international affairs.

*Novum Organum* Work by the English statesman and scientist Francis Bacon (1561–1626) that advanced a philosophy of study through observation.

**October Days** (1789) The high price of bread and the rumor that the king was unwilling to cooperate with the assembly caused the women who worked in Paris's large central market to march to Versailles along with their supporters to address the king. Not satisfied with their initial reception, they broke through the palace gates and called for the king to return to Paris from Versailles, which he did the following day.

**Old Kingdom of Egypt** (c. 2686–2160 B.C.E.) During this period, the pharaohs controlled a powerful and centralized bureaucratic state whose vast human and material resources are exemplified by the pyramids of Giza. This period came to an end as the pharaoh's authority collapsed, leading to a period of dynastic warfare and localized rule.

**OPEC (Organization of the Petroleum Exporting Countries)** Organization created in 1960 by oil-producing countries in the Middle East, South America, and Africa to regulate the production and pricing of crude oil.

**Operation Barbarossa** The code name for Hitler's invasion of the Soviet Union in 1941.

**Opium Wars** (1839–1842) Wars fought between the British and Qing China to protect the British trade in opium; resulted in the ceding of Hong Kong to the British.

**Oracle at Delphi** The most important shrine in ancient Greece. The priestess of Apollo who attended the shrine was believed to have the power to predict the future.

**Ottoman Empire** (c.1300–1923) During the thirteenth century, the Ottoman dynasty established itself as leader of the Turks. From the fourteenth to sixteenth centuries, the Ottomans conquered Anatolia, Armenia, Syria, and North Africa as well as parts of southeastern Europe, the Crimea, and areas along the Red Sea. Portions of the Ottoman Empire persisted up to the time of the First World War, but it was dismantled in the years following the war.

**Reza Pahlavi** (1919–1980) The West-friendly shah of Iran who was installed during a 1953 coup supported by Britain and the United States. After a lengthy economic downturn, public unrest, and personal illness, he retired from public life under popular pressure in 1979.

**Pan-African Conference** A 1900 assembly in London that sought to draw attention to the sovereignty of African people and their mistreatment by colonial powers.

**Panhellenism** The "all-Greek" culture that allowed ancient Greek colonies to maintain a connection to their homeland and to each other through their shared language and heritage. These colonies also exported their culture into new areas and created new Greek-speaking enclaves, which permanently changed the cultural geography of the Mediterranean world.

**pan-Slavism** Cultural movement that sought to unite native Slavic peoples within the Russian and Habsburg Empires under Russian leadership.

**Partition of India** (1947) At independence, British India was partitioned into the nations of India and Pakistan. The majority of the population in India was Hindu, and the majority of the population in Pakistan was Muslim. The process of partition brought brutal religious and ethnic warfare. More than 1 million Hindus and Muslims died, and 12 million became refugees.

**Blaise Pascal** (1623–1662) A Catholic philosopher who wanted to establish the truth of Christianity by appealing simultaneously to intellect and emotion. In his *Pensées*, he argued that faith alone can resolve the world's contradictions and that his own awe in the face of evil and uncertainty must be evidence of God's existence.

**Paul of Tarsus** Originally known as Saul, Paul was a Greek-speaking Jew and Roman citizen who underwent a miraculous conversion experience and became the most important proponent of Christianity in the 50s and 60s C.E.

**Pax Romana** (27 B.C.E.–180 C.E.) Literally translated as the "Roman Peace." During this time, the Roman world enjoyed an unprecedented period of peace and political stability.

**Peace of Augsburg** A settlement negotiated in 1555 among factions within the Holy Roman Empire, it formulated the principle *cuius regio, eius religio* ("he who rules, his religion"): the inhabitants of any given territory should follow the religion of its ruler, whether Catholic or Protestant.

**Peace of Paris** The 1919 Paris Peace Conference established the terms to end the First World War. Great Britain, France, Italy, and the United States signed five treaties with each of the defeated nations: Germany, Austria, Hungary, Turkey, and Bulgaria. The settlement is notable for the territory that Germany had to give up, including large parts of Prussia to the new state of Poland, and Alsace and Lorraine to France; the disarming of Germany; and the "war-guilt" provision, which required Germany and its allies to pay massive reparations to the victors.

**Peace of Westphalia** (1648) An agreement reached at the end of the Thirty Years' War that altered the political map of Europe. France emerged as the predominant power on the Continent. The Austrian Habsburgs had to surrender all the territories they had gained and could no longer use the office of the Holy Roman Emperor to dominate central Europe. Spain was marginalized, and Germany became a volatile combination of Protestant and Catholic principalities.

**Pearl Harbor** The American naval base in Hawaii that was bombed by the Japanese on December 7, 1941, bringing the United States into the Second World War.

**peasantry** Term used in continental Europe to refer to rural populations that lived from agriculture. Some peasants were free and could own land. Serfs were peasants who were legally bound to the land and subject to the authority of the local lord.

**Peloponnesian War** The name given to the series of wars fought between Sparta (on the Greek Peloponnesus) and Athens from 431 B.C.E. to 404 B.C.E., which ended in the defeat of Athens and the loss of its imperial power.

**perestroika** Introduced by Soviet leader Mikhail Gorbachev in June 1987, *perestroika* was the name given to economic and political reforms begun earlier in his tenure. It restructured the state bureaucracy, reduced the privileges of the political elite, and instituted a shift from the centrally planned economy to a mixed economy, combining planning with the operation of market forces.

**Periclean Athens** Following his election as strategos in 461 B.C.E., Pericles pushed through political reforms in Athens that gave poorer citizens greater influence in politics. He promoted the Athenians' sense of superiority through ambitious public works projects and lavish festivals to honor the gods, thus ensuring his continual reelection. But eventually, Athens' growing arrogance and aggression alienated it from the rest of the Greek world.

**Pericles** (c. 495–429) Athenian politician who occupied the office of strategos for thirty years and who presided over a series of civic reforms, building campaigns, and imperialist initiatives.

**Persian Empire** Consolidated by Cyrus the Great in 559, this empire eventually stretched from the Persian Gulf to the Mediterranean and also encompassed Egypt. Persian rulers were able to hold their empire together through a policy of tolerance and a mixture of local and centralized governance. This imperial model of government was adopted by many future empires.

**Persian Wars** (490–479 B.C.E.) In 501 B.C.E., a political conflict between the Greek ruler of Miletus, Aristagoras, and the Persian emperor, Darius, sparked the first of the Persian Wars when Darius sent an army to punish Athens for its intervention on the side of the Greeks. Despite being heavily outnumbered, Athenian hoplites defeated the Persian army at the plain of Marathon. In 480 B.C.E., Darius's son Xerxes invaded Greece but was defeated at sea and on land by combined Greek forces under the leadership of Athens and Sparta.

**Peter the Great** (1672–1725) Energetic tsar who transformed Russia into a leading European country by centralizing government, modernizing the army, creating a navy, and reforming education and the economy.

**Francesco Petrarca (Petrarch)** (1304–1374) Italian scholar who revived interest in classical writing styles and was famed for his vernacular love sonnets.

**pharaoh** A term meaning "household," which became the title borne by the rulers of ancient Egypt. The pharaoh was regarded as the divine representative of the gods and the embodiment of Egypt itself. The powerful and centralized bureaucratic state ruled by the pharaohs was more stable and long lived than any other civilization in world history, lasting (with few interruptions) for approximately 3,000 years.

**Pharisees** A group of Jewish teachers and preachers who emerged in the third century B.C.E. They insisted that all of Yahweh's (God's) commandments were binding on all Jews.

**Philip II** (382–336 B.C.E.) King of Macedonia and father of Alexander, he consolidated the southern Balkans and the Greek city-states under Macedonian domination.

**Philip II** King of Spain from 1556 to 1598 and briefly king of England and Ireland during his marriage to Queen Mary I of England. As a staunch Catholic, Philip responded with military might to the desecration of Catholic churches in the Spanish Netherlands in the 1560s. When commercial conflict with England escalated, Philip sent the Spanish Armada to conquer England in 1588, but it was largely destroyed by stormy weather.

**Philip II Augustus** (1165–1223) The first French ruler to use the title "king of France" rather than "king of the French." After he captured Normandy and its adjacent territories from the English, he built an effective system of local administration, which recognized regional diversity while promoting centralized royal control. This administrative pattern would characterize French government until the French Revolution.

**Philip IV** (1268–1314) King of France from 1285 until his death. Philip's conflict with Pope Boniface VIII led to the transfer of the papal court to Avignon from 1309 to 1378.

**Philistines** Descendants of the Sea Peoples who fled to the region that now bears their name, Palestine, after their defeat at the hands of the pharaoh Ramses III. They dominated their neighbors the Hebrews, who used writing as an effective means of discrediting them. (The Philistines themselves did not leave a written record to contest the Hebrews' views.)

**philosophe** During the Enlightenment, this word referred to a person whose reflections were unhampered by the constraints of religion or dogma.

**Phoenicians** A Semitic people known for their trade in exotic purple dyes and other luxury goods, they originally settled in present-day Lebanon around 1200 B.C.E. and from there established commercial colonies throughout the Mediterranean, notably Carthage.

**Plato** (429–349 B.C.E.) A student of Socrates, Plato dedicated his life to transmitting his teacher's legacy through the writing of dialogues on philosophical subjects in which Socrates himself plays the major role. The longest and most famous of these, known as the *Republic*, describes an idealized polis governed by a superior group of individuals chosen for their natural attributes of intelligence and character, and who rule as philosopher-kings.

**Plotinus** (204–270 C.E.) A Neoplatonist philosopher who taught that everything in existence has its ultimate source in the divine and that the highest goal of life should be the mystic reunion of the soul with this divine source, something that can be achieved through contemplation and asceticism. This outlook blended with that of early Christianity and was instrumental in the spread of that religion within the Roman Empire.

**poleis** One of the major political innovations of the ancient Greeks was the *polis*, or city-state (plural *poleis*). These independent social and political entities began to emerge in the ninth century B.C.E., organized around an urban center and fostering markets, meeting places, and religious worship. Frequently, poleis also controlled some surrounding territory.

**Marco Polo** (1254–1324) Venetian merchant who traveled throughout Asia for twenty years and published his observations in a widely read memoir.

**population growth** In the nineteenth century, Europe experienced a dramatic increase in population. During this period, the spread of rural manufacturing allowed men and women to marry younger and raise families earlier, which increased the size of the average family. As the population increased, the proportion of young and fertile people also increased, which reinforced population growth. By 1900, population growth was strongest in Britain and Germany and slower in France.

**portolan charts** Also known as *portolani*, these special charts were invented by medieval mariners during the fourteenth century and were used to map locations of ports and sea routes, while also taking note of prevailing winds and other conditions at sea.

**Potsdam Conference** (1945) At this conference, Truman, Churchill, and Stalin met to discuss their options at the conclusion of the Second World War, including making territorial changes to Germany and its allies and the question of war reparations.

**Prague spring** A period of political liberalization in Czechoslovakia between January and August 1968 that was initiated by Alexander Dubček, the Czech leader. This period of expanding freedom and openness in this Eastern-bloc nation ended on August 20, when the USSR and Warsaw Pact countries invaded with 200,000 troops and 5,000 tanks.

**pre-Socratics** A group of philosophers in the Greek city of Miletus who raised questions about humans' relationship with the natural world and the gods and who formulated rational theories to explain the physical universe they observed. Their name reflects the fact that they flourished prior to the lifetime of Socrates.

**Price Revolution** An unprecedented inflation in prices during the latter half of the sixteenth century, resulting in part from the enormous influx of silver bullion from Spanish America.

**Principate** Modern term for the centuries of autocratic rule by the successors of Augustus, who seized power in 27 B.C.E. and styled himself Rome's *princeps* (or "first man"). See **Roman Republic**.

**printing press** Developed in Europe by Johannes Gutenberg of Mainz in 1453–1455, this new technology quickly revolutionized communication and played a significant role in political, religious, and intellectual movements.

**Protestantism** The name given to the many dissenting varieties of Christianity that emerged during the Reformation in sixteenth-century western Europe. Although Protestant beliefs and practices differed widely, all were united in their rejection of papal authority and the dogmas of the Roman Catholic Church.

**provisional government** After the collapse of the Russian monarchy in February 1917, leaders in the Duma organized a government and hoped to establish a democratic system under constitutional rule. They also refused to concede military defeat in the First World War. It was impossible to institute domestic reforms and fight a war at the same time. As conditions worsened, the Bolsheviks gained support. In October 1917, they attacked the provisional government and seized control.

**Claudius Ptolomeus, called Ptolemy** (c. 85–165 C.E.) A Greek-speaking geographer and astronomer active in Roman Alexandria, he rejected the findings of previous Hellenistic scientists in favor of the erroneous theories of Aristotle, publishing highly influential treatises that promulgated these errors and suppressed, for example, the accurate findings of Aristarchus, who had discovered the heliocentric universe, and Erathosthenes, who had calculated the circumference of the earth.

**Ptolemaic system** Ptolemy of Alexandria promoted Aristotle's understanding of cosmology. In this system, the heavens orbit the earth in an organized hierarchy of spheres, and the earth and the heavens are made of different matter and subject to different laws of motion. A prime mover produces the motion of the celestial bodies.

**Ptolemy** (c. 367–c. 284 B.C.E.) One of Alexander the Great's trusted generals (and possibly his half brother), he became pharaoh of Egypt and founded a new dynasty that lasted until that kingdom's absorption into the Roman Empire in 30 B.C.E.

**public sphere** Between the official realm of state activities and the private realm of the household and individual lies the public sphere. The public sphere has a political dimension—it is the space of debate, discussion, and expressions of popular opinion. It also has an economic dimension—it is where business is conducted, where commercial transactions take place, where people enter into contracts, search for work, or hire employees.

**Punic Wars** (264–146 B.C.E.) Three periods of warfare between Rome and Carthage, two maritime empires that struggled for dominance of the Mediterranean. Rome emerged as the victor, destroyed the city of Carthage, and took control of Sicily, North Africa, and Hispania (Spain).

**pyramid** Constructed during the third millennium B.C.E., the pyramids were monuments to the power and divinity of the pharaohs entombed inside them.

**Qur'an (often Koran)** Islam's holy scriptures, comprising the prophecies revealed to Muhammad and redacted during his life and after his death.

**Raphael (Raffaelo Sanzio)** (1483–1520) Italian painter active in Rome. His works include *The School of Athens*.

**realism** Artistic and literary style that sought to portray common situations as they would appear in reality.

**Realpolitik** Political strategy based on advancing power for its own sake.

**reason** The human capacity to solve problems and discover truth in ways that can be verified intellectually. Philosophers distinguish the knowledge gained from reason from the teachings of instinct, imagination, and faith, which are verified according to different criteria.

**Reformation** Religious and political movement in sixteenth-century Europe that led to a break between dissenting forms of Christianity and the Roman Catholic Church; notable figures include Martin Luther and John Calvin.

**Reich** A term for the German state. The First Reich corresponded to the Holy Roman Empire (ninth century to 1806), the Second Reich lasted from 1871 to 1919, and the Third Reich lasted from 1933 through May 1945.

**Reign of Terror** (1793–1794) Campaign at the height of the French Revolution in which violence, including systematic executions of opponents of the revolution, was used to purge France of its "enemies" and to extend the revolution beyond its borders. Radicals executed as many as 40,000 people who were judged enemies of the state.

**Renaissance** From the French word meaning "rebirth," this term came to be used during the nineteenth century to describe the artistic, intellectual, and cultural movement that emerged in Italy after 1300 and that sought to recover and emulate the heritage of the classical past.

**Restoration** (1815–1848) European movement after the defeat of Napoleon to restore Europe to its pre–French Revolution status and to prevent the spread of revolutionary or liberal political movements.

**Cardinal Richelieu** (1585–1642) First minister to King Louis XIII, he is considered by many to have ruled France in all but name, centralizing political power and suppressing dissent.

**Roman army** Under the Republic, the Roman army was made up of citizen-soldiers who were required to serve in wartime. As Rome's empire grew, the need for more fighting men led to the extension of citizenship rights and, eventually, to the development of a vast, professional, standing army that numbered as many as 300,000 by the middle of the third century B.C.E. By that time, however, citizens were not themselves required to serve, and many legions were made up of paid conscripts and foreign mercenaries.

**Roman citizenship** The rights and responsibilities of Rome's citizens were gradually extended to the free (male) inhabitants of other Italian provinces and later to most provinces in the Roman world. In contrast to slaves and non-Romans, Romans had the right to be tried in an imperial court and could not be legally subjected to torture.

**Roman Republic** The Romans traced the founding of their republic to the overthrow of their last king and the establishment of a unique form of constitutional government, in which the power of the aristocracy (embodied by the Senate) was checked by the executive rule of two elected consuls and the collective will of the people. For hundreds of years, this balance of power provided the Republic with a measure of political stability and prevented any single individual or clique from gaining too much power.

**Romanticism** Beginning in Germany and England in the late eighteenth century and continuing until the end of the nineteenth century, Romanticism was a movement in art, music, and literature that countered the rationalism of the Enlightenment by placing greater value on human emotions and the power of nature to stimulate creativity.

**Jean-Jacques Rousseau** (1712–1778) Philosopher and radical political theorist whose *Social Contract* attacked privilege and inequality. One of the primary principles of Rousseau's political philosophy is that politics and morality should not be separated.

**Royal Society** The goal of this British society, founded in 1660, is to pursue collective research. Members would conduct experiments, record the results, and share them with their peers, who would study the methods, reproduce the experiment, and assess the results. This arrangement gave English scientists a sense of common purpose as well as a system for reaching a consensus on facts.

**Russian Revolution of 1905** After Russia's defeat in the Russo-Japanese War, Russians began clamoring for political reforms. Protests grew over the course of 1905, and the autocracy lost control of entire towns and regions as workers went on strike, soldiers mutinied, and peasants revolted. Forced to yield, Tsar Nicholas II issued the October Manifesto, which pledged individual liberties and provided for the election of a parliament (called the Duma). The most radical of the revolutionary groups were put down with force, and the pace of political change remained very slow in the aftermath of the revolution.

**Russo-Japanese War** (1904–1905) Japanese and Russian expansionist goals collided in Mongolia and Manchuria. Russia was humiliated after the Japanese navy sank its fleet, which helped provoke a revolt in Russia and led to an American-brokered peace treaty.

**sacrament** A sacred rite. In the Catholic tradition, the administration of the sacraments is considered necessary for salvation.

**Saint Bartholomew's Day Massacre** The mass murder of French Protestants (Huguenots) instigated by Queen Catherine de' Medici of France and carried out by Catholics. It began in Paris on August 24, 1572 (Saint Bartholomew's day) and spread to other parts of France, continuing into October of that year. More than 70,000 people were killed.

**salon** Informal gathering of intellectuals and aristocrats that allowed discourse about Enlightenment ideas.

**Sappho** (c. 620–c. 550 B.C.E.) One of the most celebrated Greek poets, she was revered as the "Tenth Muse" and emulated by many male poets. Ironically, though, only two of her poems survive intact, and the rest must be pieced together from fragments quoted by later poets.

**Sargon the Great** (r. 2334–2279 B.C.E.) The Akkadian ruler who consolidated power in Mesopotamia.

**SARS epidemic** (2003) The successful containment of severe acute respiratory syndrome (SARS) is an example of how international health organizations can effectively work together to recognize and respond to a disease outbreak. The disease itself, however, is a reminder of the dangers that exist in a globalized economy with a high degree of mobility of both populations and goods.

**Schlieffen Plan** Devised by the German general Alfred von Schlieffen in 1905 to avoid the dilemma of a two-front war against France and Russia. The Schlieffen Plan required that Germany attack France first through Belgium and secure a quick victory before wheeling to the east to meet the slower armies of the Russians on the Eastern Front. The Schlieffen Plan was put into ·operation on August 2, 1914, at the outset of the First World War.

**scientific revolution of antiquity** The Hellenistic period was the most brilliant age in the history of science before the seventeenth century C.E. Aristarchus of Samos posited the existence of a heliocentric universe. Eratosthenes of Alexandria accurately calculated the circumference of the earth. Archimedes turned physics into its own branch of experimental science. Hellenistic anatomists became the first to practice human dissection, which improved their understanding of human physiology. Ironically, most of these discoveries were suppressed by pseudoscientists who flourished under the Roman Empire during the second century C.E., notably Claudus Ptolomeus (Ptolemy) and Aelius Galenus (Galen).

**second industrial revolution** The technological developments in the last third of the nineteenth century, which included new techniques for refining and producing steel; increased availability of electricity for industrial, commercial, and domestic use; advances in chemical manufacturing; and the creation of the internal combustion engine.

**Second World War** Worldwide war that began in September 1939 in Europe, and even earlier in Asia (the Japanese invasion of Manchuria began in 1931), pitting Britain, the United States, and the Soviet Union (the Allies) against Nazi Germany, Italy, and Japan (the Axis). The war ended in 1945 with Germany and Japan's defeat.

**Seleucus** (d. 280 B.C.E.) The Macedonian general who ruled the Persian heartland of Alexander the Great's empire.

**Semitic language** The Semitic language family has the longest recorded history of any linguistic group and is the root of most languages of the Middle and Near East. Ancient Semitic languages include those of the ancient Babylonians and Assyrians, Phoenician, the classical form of Hebrew, early dialects of Aramaic, and the classical Arabic of the Qur'an.

**Sepoy Mutiny of 1857** See **Indian Rebellion of 1857**.

**serfdom** Peasant labor. Unlike slaves, serfs are "attached" to the land they work and are not supposed to be sold apart from that land.

**William Shakespeare** (1564–1616) An English playwright who flourished during the reigns of Elizabeth I and James I. Shakespeare received a basic education in his hometown of Stratford-upon-Avon and worked in London as an actor before achieving success as a dramatist and poet.

**Shi'ites** An often-persecuted minority within Islam, Shi'ites, from the Arabic word *shi'a* ("faction"), believe that only descendants of Muhammad's successor Ali and his wife Fatimah, Muhammad's daughter, can have any authority over the Muslim community. Today, Shi'ites constitute the ruling party in Iran and are numerous in Iraq but otherwise comprise only 10 percent of Muslims worldwide.

**Abbé Sieyès** (1748–1836) In 1789, he wrote the pamphlet "What Is the Third Estate?" in which he posed fundamental questions about the rights of the Third Estate and helped provoke its secession from the Estates-General. He was a leader at the Tennis Court Oath, but he later helped Napoleon seize power.

**Sinn Féin** The Irish revolutionary organization that formed in 1900 to fight for Irish independence.

**Sino-Japanese War** (1894–1895) Conflict over the control of Korea; China was forced to cede the province of Taiwan to Japan.

**slave revolt in Saint-Domingue** (1791–1804) In September of 1791, the largest slave rebellion in history broke out in Saint-Domingue, an important French colony in the Caribbean. In 1794, the revolutionary government in France abolished slavery in the colonies, though this act essentially only recognized the liberty that the slaves had seized by their own actions. Napoleon reestablished slavery in the French Caribbean in 1802 but failed in his attempt to reconquer Saint-Domingue. Armies commanded by former slaves succeeded in winning independence for a new nation, Haiti, in 1804, making the revolt in Saint-Domingue the first successful slave revolt in history.

**slavery** The practice of subjugating people to a life of bondage and of selling or trading these unfree people. For most of human history, slavery had no racial or ethnic basis and was widely practiced by all cultures and civilizations. Anyone could become a slave, for example, by being captured in war or by being sold for the payment of a debt. It was only in the fifteenth century, with the growth of the African slave trade, that slavery came to be associated with particular races and peoples.

**Adam Smith** (1723–1790) Scottish economist and liberal philosopher who proposed that competition between self-interested individuals led naturally to a healthy economy. He became famous for his influential book *The Wealth of Nations* (1776).

**Social Darwinism** Belief that Charles Darwin's theory of natural selection (evolution) was applicable to human societies and justified the right of the ruling classes or countries to dominate the weak.

**social democracy** The belief that democracy and social welfare go hand in hand and that diminishing the sharp inequalities of class society is crucial to fortifying democratic culture.

**socialism** Political ideology that calls for a classless society with collective ownership of all property.

**Society of Jesus** See **Jesuits**.

**Socrates** (469–399 B.C.E.) The Athenian philosopher and teacher who promoted the careful examination of all inherited opinions and assumptions on the grounds that "the unexamined life is not worth living." A veteran of the Peloponnesian War, he was tried and condemned by his fellow citizens for engaging in allegedly seditious activities and was executed in 399 B.C.E. His most influential pupils were the philosopher Plato and the historian and social commentator Xenophon.

**Solon** (d. 559 B.C.E.) Elected archon in 594 B.C.E., this Athenian aristocrat enacted a series of political and economic reforms that formed the basis of Athenian democracy.

**Somme** (1916) During this battle of the First World War, Allied forces attempted to take entrenched German positions from July to mid-November of 1916. Neither side was able to make any real gains despite massive casualties: 500,000 Germans, 400,000 British, and 200,000 French.

**Soviet bloc** International alliance that included the East European countries of the Warsaw Pact as well as the Soviet Union; it also came to include Cuba.

**soviets** Local councils elected by workers and soldiers in Russia. Socialists started organizing these councils in 1905, and the Petrograd soviet in the capital emerged as one of the centers of power after the Russian monarchy collapsed in 1917 in the midst of World War I. The soviets became increasingly powerful, pressing for social reform and the redistribution of land, and calling for Russian withdrawal from the war effort.

**Spanish-American War** (1898) War between the United States and Spain in Cuba, Puerto Rico, and the Philippines. It ended with a treaty whereby the United States took over the Philippines, Guam, and Puerto Rico; Cuba won partial independence.

**Spanish Armada** The supposedly invincible fleet of warships sent against England by Philip II of Spain in 1588 but vanquished by the English fleet and bad weather in the English Channel.

**Sparta** Around 650 B.C.E., after the suppression of a slave revolt, Spartan rulers militarized their society in order to prevent future rebellions and to protect Sparta's superior position in Greece, orienting their society toward the maintenance of their army. Sparta briefly joined forces with Athens and other poleis in the second war with Persia in 480–479 B.C.E., but these two rivals ultimately fell out again in 431 B.C.E. when Sparta and its Peloponnesian allies went to war against Athens and its allies. This bloody conflict lasted until Athens was defeated in 404 B.C.E., after Sparta received military aid from the Persians.

**Spartiate** A full citizen of Sparta, hence a professional soldier of the hoplite phalanx.

**spinning jenny** Invention of James Hargreaves (c. 1720–1774) that revolutionized the British textile industry by allowing a worker to spin much more thread than was possible on a hand spinner.

**SS (Schutzstaffel)** Formed in 1925 to serve as Hitler's personal security force and to guard Nazi party (NSDAP) meetings, the SS grew into a large militarized organization that became notorious for its participation in carrying out Nazi policies.

**Joseph Stalin** (1879–1953) The Bolshevik leader who succeeded Lenin as leader of the Soviet Union and ruled until his death in 1953.

**Stalingrad** (1942–1943) The turning point on the Eastern Front during the Second World War came when the German army tried to take the city of Stalingrad in an effort to break the back of Soviet industry. The German and Soviet armies fought a bitter battle, in which more than a half million German, Italian, and Romanian soldiers were killed and the Soviets suffered over a million casualties. The German army surrendered after over five months of fighting. After Stalingrad, the Soviet army launched a series of attacks that pushed the Germans back.

**Stoicism** An ancient philosophy derived from the teachings of Zeno of Athens (fl. c. 300) and widely influential within the Roman Empire; it also influenced the development of Christianity. Stoics believe in the essential orderliness of the cosmos and that everything that occurs happens for the best. Since everything is determined in accordance with rational purpose, no individual is master of his or her fate, and the only agency that human beings have consists in their response to good fortune or adversity.

**Sumerians** The ancient inhabitants of southern Mesopotamia (modern Iraq and Kuwait) whose sophisticated civilization emerged around 4000 B.C.E.

**Sunnis** Proponents of Islam's customary religious practices (*sunna*) as they developed under the first two caliphs to succeed Muhammad: his father-in-law Abu-Bakr and his disciple Umar. Sunni orthodoxy is dominant within Islam but is opposed by the Shi'ites.

**syndicalism** A nineteenth-century political movement that embraced a strategy of strikes and sabotage by workers. The syndicalists hoped that a general strike of all workers would bring down the capitalist state and replace it with workers' syndicates, or trade associations. Their refusal to participate in politics limited their ability to command a wide influence.

**tabula rasa** Latin for "clean slate." Term used by John Locke (1632–1704) to describe people's minds before they acquired ideas as a result of experience.

**Tennis Court Oath** (1789) Oath taken by representatives of the Third Estate in June 1789, pledging to form a National Assembly and write a constitution limiting the powers of the king.

**tetrarchy** The result of Diocletian's political reforms of the late third century C.E., which divided the Roman Empire into four quadrants.

**Theban Hegemony** The term describing the period when the polis of Thebes dominated the Greek mainland, which reached its height after 371 B.C.E., under leadership of the Theban general Epaminondas. It was in Thebes that the future King Philip II of Macedon spent his youth. Macedonian hegemony was forcefully asserted in the defeat of Thebes and Athens at the hands of Philip and Alexander at the Battle of Chaeronea in 338.

**theory of evolution** Darwin's theory linking biology to history. Darwin believed that competition among different organisms and their struggle with the environment were fundamental and unavoidable facts of life. In this struggle, those individuals who were better adapted to their environment survived, whereas the weak perished. This produced a "natural selection," or the favoring of certain adaptive traits over time, leading to a gradual evolution of different species.

**Third Estate** The population of France under the Old Regime was divided into three estates, corporate bodies that determined an individual's rights or obligations under royal law. The nobility constituted the First Estate, the clergy the Second, and the commoners (the vast majority of the population) made up the Third Estate.

**Third Reich** The German state from 1933 to 1945 under Adolf Hitler and the Nazi party.

**Third World** Those nations—mostly in Asia, Latin America, and Africa—that are not highly industrialized.

**Thirty Years' War** (1618–1648) Beginning as a conflict between Protestants and Catholics in Germany, this series of skirmishes escalated into a general European war fought on German soil by armies from Sweden, France, and the Holy Roman Empire.

**Timur the Lame** (1336–1405) Also known as Tamerlane, he was the last ruler of the Mongol Khans' Asian empire.

**Josip Broz Tito** (1892–1980) This Yugoslavian communist and resistance leader became the leader of Yugoslavia and fought to keep his government independent of the Soviet Union. In response, the Soviet Union expelled Yugoslavia from the communist countries' economic and military pacts.

**town** A center for markets and administration. Towns existed in a symbiotic relationship with the countryside. They provided markets for surplus food from outlying farms as well as produced manufactured goods. In the Middle Ages, towns tended to grow up around a castle or monastery that afforded protection.

**transatlantic triangle** The trading of African slaves by European colonists to address labor shortages in the Americas and the Caribbean. Slaves were treated like cargo, loaded onto ships and sold in exchange for molasses, tobacco, rum, and other precious commodities.

**Treaty of Brest-Litovsk** (1918) Separate peace between imperial Germany and the new Bolshevik regime in Russia. This treaty acknowledged the German victory on the Eastern Front and withdrew Russia from the war.

**Treaty of Utrecht** (1713) Resolution to the War of Spanish Succession that reestablished a balance of power in Europe, to the benefit of Britain and in ways that disadvantaged Spain, Holland, and France.

**Treaty of Versailles** Signed on June 28, 1919, this peace settlement ended the First World War and required Germany to surrender a large part of its most valuable territories and to pay huge reparations to the Allies.

**trench warfare** Weapons such as barbed wire and the machine gun gave tremendous advantages to defensive positions in the First World War, leading to prolonged battles between entrenched armies in fixed positions. The trenches eventually consisted of 25,000 miles of tunnels and ditches that stretched across the Western Front in northern France, from the Atlantic coast to the Swiss border. On the Eastern Front, the large expanse of territories made trench warfare less significant.

**triangular trade** The eighteenth-century commercial Atlantic shipping pattern that took rum from New England to Africa, traded it for slaves taken to the West Indies, and brought sugar back to New England to be processed into rum.

**Triple Entente** Alliance developed before the First World War that eventually included Britain, France, and Russia.

**Truman Doctrine** (1947) Declaration promising U.S. economic and military intervention to counter any attempt by the Soviet Union to expand its influence. Often cited as a key moment in the origins of the Cold War.

**tsar** Russian word for "emperor," derived from the Latin *caesar* and similar to the German *kaiser*. This was the title claimed by the rulers of medieval Muscovy and of the later Russian Empire.

**Ubaid culture** An early civilization that flourished in Mesopotamia between 5500 and 4000 B.C.E., it was characterized by large village settlements and temple complexes: a precursor to the more urban civilization of the Sumerians.

**Umayyad caliphate** (661–930) The Umayyad family resisted the authority of the first two caliphs who succeeded Muhammad but eventually placed a member of their own family in that position of power. The Umayyad caliphate ruled the Islamic world from 661 to 750, modeling its administration on that of the Roman Empire. But after a rebellion led by the rival Abbasid family, the power of the Umayyad caliphate was confined to its territories in al-Andalus (Spain).

**Universal Declaration of Human Rights** (1948) United Nations declaration that laid out the rights to which all human beings are entitled.

**University of Paris** The reputation of Peter Abelard and his students attracted many intellectuals to Paris during the twelfth century. Some of them began offering instruction to aspiring scholars. By 1200, this loose association of teachers had formed itself into a *universitas,* or corporation. The teachers began collaborating in the higher academic study of the liberal arts, with a special emphasis on theology.

**Urban II** (1042?–1099) Instigator of the First Crusade (1096–1099), this pope promised that anyone who fought or died in the service of the Church would receive absolution from sin.

**urban population** During the nineteenth century, urban populations in Europe increased sixfold. For the most part, urban areas had medieval infrastructures, which new populations and industries overwhelmed. As a result, many European cities became overcrowded and unhealthy.

*Utopia* A semisatirical social critique by the English statesman Sir Thomas More (1478–1535); the title derives from the Greek "best place" or "no place."

**Lorenzo Valla** (1407–1457) One of the first practitioners of scientific philology (the historical study of language). Valla's analysis of the so-called Donation of Constantine showed that this document could not possibly have been written in the fourth century C.E. but must have been forged centuries later.

**vassal** A person who pledges to be loyal and subservient to a lord in exchange for land, income, or protection.

**velvet revolutions** The peaceful political revolutions against the Soviet Union throughout Eastern Europe in 1989.

**Verdun** (1916) This battle between German and French forces lasted for ten months during the First World War. The Germans saw the battle as a chance to break French morale through a war of attrition, and the French believed the battle to be a symbol of France's strength. In the end, over 400,000 lives were lost, and the German offensive failed.

**Versailles Conference** (1919) Peace conference of the victors of the First World War, it resulted in the Treaty of Versailles, which forced Germany to pay reparations and to give up its colonies to the victors.

**Victoria** (1819–1901) Influential queen of Great Britain, who reigned from 1837 until her death. Victoria presided over the expansion of the British Empire as well as the evolution of English politics and social and economic reforms.

**Viet Cong** Vietnamese communist group formed in 1954; committed to overthrowing the government of South Vietnam and reunifying North and South Vietnam.

**Vikings** (800–1000) The collapse of the Abbasid caliphate disrupted Scandinavian commercial networks and turned traders into raiders. (The word *viking* describes the activity of raiding.) These raids often escalated into invasions that contributed to the collapse of the Carolingian Empire, resulted in the devastation of settled territories, and ended with the establishment of Viking colonies. By the tenth century, Vikings controlled areas of eastern England; Scotland; the islands of Ireland, Iceland, and Greenland; and parts of northern France. They had also established the beginnings of the kingdom that became Russia and made exploratory voyages to North America, founding a settlement in Newfoundland (Canada).

*A Vindication of the Rights of Woman* Noted work of Mary Wollstonecraft (1759–1797), an English republican who applied Enlightenment political ideas to issues of gender.

**Virgil** (70–19 B.C.E.) An influential Roman poet who wrote under the patronage of the emperor Augustus. His *Aeneid* was modeled on the ancient Greek epics of Homer and told the mythical tale of Rome's founding by the Trojan refugee Aeneas.

**Visigoths** The tribes of "west" Goths who sacked Rome in 410 C.E. and later established a kingdom in the Roman province of Hispania (Spain).

**Voltaire** Pseudonym of French philosopher and satirist François Marie Arouet (1694–1778), who championed the cause of human dignity against state and Church oppression. Noted deist and author of *Candide*.

**Lech Wałęsa** (1943–) Leader of the Polish labor movement Solidarity, which organized a series of strikes across Poland in 1980. The strikers protested working conditions, shortages, and high prices. Above all, they demanded an independent labor union. Solidarity's leaders were imprisoned and the union banned, but they launched a new series of strikes in 1988 that led to the legalization of Solidarity and open elections.

**war communism** The Russian civil war forced the Bolsheviks to take a more radical economic stance. They requisitioned grain from the peasantry and outlawed private trade in consumer goods as "speculation." They also militarized production facilities and abolished money.

**Wars of the Roses** Fifteenth-century civil conflict between the English dynastic houses of Lancaster and York, each of which was symbolized by the heraldic device of a rose (red and white, respectively). It was ultimately resolved by the accession of the Lancastrian king Henry VII, who married Elizabeth of York.

**Warsaw Pact** (1955–1991) Military alliance between the USSR and other communist states that was established in response to the creation of the NATO alliance.

*The Wealth of Nations* 1776 treatise by Adam Smith, whose laissez-faire ideas predicted the economic boom of the Industrial Revolution.

**Weimar Republic** The government of Germany between 1919 and the rise of Hitler and the Nazi party in 1933.

**Western Front** During the First World War, the military front that stretched from the English Channel through Belgium and France to the Alps.

**Whites** Refers to the "counterrevolutionaries" of the Bolshevik Revolution (1918–1921) who fought the Bolsheviks (the "Reds"); included former supporters of the tsar, Social Democrats, and large independent peasant armies.

**William the Conqueror** (1027–1087) Duke of Normandy who laid claim to the throne of England in 1066, defeating the Anglo-Saxon king Harold at the Battle of Hastings. William and his Norman followers imposed imperial rule in England through a brutal campaign of military conquest, surveillance, and the suppression of the indigenous Anglo-Saxon language.

**William of Ockham** (d. 1349) An English philosopher and Franciscan friar, he denied that human reason could prove fundamental theological truths, such as the existence of God. Instead, William argued that there is no necessary connection between the observable laws of nature and the unknowable essence of divinity. His theories, derived from the work of earlier scholastics, form the basis of the scientific method.

**Woodrow Wilson** (1856–1924) U.S. president who requested and received a declaration of war from Congress so that America could enter the First World War. After the war, his prominent role at the Paris Peace Conference signaled the rise of the United States as a world power. He also proposed the Fourteen Points, which influenced the peace negotiations.

**Maria Winkelmann** (1670–1720) German astronomer who worked with her husband in his observatory. Although she discovered a comet and prepared calendars for the Berlin Academy of Sciences, the academy would not let her take her husband's place within the body after he died.

**witch craze** The rash of persecutions that took place in both Catholic and Protestant countries of early modern Europe and their colonies, facilitated by secular governments and religious authorities.

**women's associations** Because European women were excluded from the workings of parliamentary and mass politics, some women formed their own organizations to press for political and civil rights. Some groups focused on establishing educational opportunities for women; others campaigned energetically for the vote.

**William Wordsworth** (1770–1850) Romantic poet whose central themes were nature, simplicity, and feeling. He considered nature to be the most trustworthy teacher and the source of sublime power that nourished the human soul.

**World Bank** International agency established in 1944 to provide economic assistance to war-torn nations and countries in need of economic development.

**John Wycliffe** (c. 1330–1384) A professor of theology at the University of Oxford, Wycliffe urged the English king to confiscate ecclesiastical wealth and to replace corrupt priests and bishops with men who would live according to the apostolic standards of poverty and piety. He advocated direct access to the scriptures and promoted an English translation of the Bible. His teachings played an important role in the Peasants' Revolt of 1381 and inspired the still more radical initiatives of a group known as Lollards.

**Xerxes** (519?–465 B.C.E.) Xerxes succeeded his father, Darius, as Great King of Persia. Seeking to avenge his father's shame and eradicate any future threats to Persian hegemony, he launched his own invasion of Greece in 480 B.C.E. An allied Greek army defeated his forces in 479 B.C.E.

**Yalta conference** Meeting among U.S. president Franklin D. Roosevelt, British prime minister Winston Churchill, and Soviet premier Joseph Stalin that occurred in the Crimea in 1945 shortly before the end of the Second World War in which the three leaders planned for the postwar order.

**Young Turks** The 1908 Turkish reformist movement that aimed to modernize the Ottoman Empire, restore parliamentary rule, and depose Sultan Abdul Hamid II.

**ziggurats** Temples constructed under the Dynasty of Ur in what is now Iraq, beginning around 2100 B.C.E.

**Zionism** A political movement dating to the end of the nineteenth century holding that the Jewish people constitute a nation and are entitled to a national homeland. Zionists rejected a policy of Jewish assimilation and advocated the reestablishment of a Jewish homeland in Palestine.

**Zollverein** In 1834, Prussia started a customs union, which established free trade among the German states and a uniform tariff against the rest of the world. By the 1840s, the union included almost all of the German states except German Austria. It is considered an important precedent for the political unification of Germany, which was completed in 1870 under Prussian leadership.

**Zoroastrianism** One of the three major universal faiths of the ancient world, alongside Judaism and Christianity, it was derived from the teachings of the Persian Zoroaster around 600 B.C.E. Zoroaster redefined religion as an ethical practice common to all, rather than as a set of rituals and superstitions that cause divisions among people. Zoroastrianism teaches that there is one supreme god in the universe, Ahura-Mazda (Wise Lord), but that his goodness will be constantly assailed by the forces of evil until the arrival of a final "judgment day." Proponents of this faith should therefore help good to triumph over evil by leading a good life and by performing acts of compassion and charity. Zoroastrianism exercised a profound influence over many early Christians, including Augustine.

**Ulrich Zwingli** (1484–1531) A former priest from the Swiss city of Zurich, Zwingli joined Luther and Calvin in attacking the authority of the Roman Catholic Church.

# Text Credits

**Leon B. Alberti:** "On the Family" from *The Family in Renaissance Florence*, edited and translated by Renée Neu Watkins (Columbia: University of South Carolina Press, 1969), pp. 208–13. Reprinted by permission of the translator.

**Aristophanes:** Excerpt from "The Clouds" from *Lysistrata and Other Plays* by Aristophanes, translated with an introduction by Alan H. Sommerstein (Penguin Classics, 1973). Copyright © Alan H. Sommerstein, 1973. Reproduced by permission of Penguin Books Ltd.

**Arrian:** Excerpts from *The Campaigns of Alexander* by Arrian, translated by Aubrey de Sélincourt, revised with an introduction and notes by J. R. Hamilton (Penguin Classics, 1958; Revised Edition, 1971). Copyright © the Estate of Aubrey de Sélincourt, 1958. Introduction and Notes copyright © J. R. Hamilton, 1971. Reproduced by permission of Penguin Books Ltd.

**Nels M. Bailkey (ed.):** From *Readings in Ancient History: Thought and Experience from Gilgamesh to St. Augustine*, Fifth Edition. © 1996 Wadsworth, a part of Cengage Learning, Inc. Reproduced by permission. www.cengage.com/permissions.

**Bernard of Angers:** "Miracles of Saint Foy" from *Readings in Medieval History*, Fifth Edition, edited and translated Patrick J. Geary, © University of Toronto Press. Reprinted by permission of the publisher.

**Henry Bettenson (ed.):** "Rules for Thinking with the Church" and "Obedience of the Jesuits" from *Documents of the Christian Church*, Second Edition (1967). Reprinted by permission of Oxford University Press.

**Bible. New Revised Standard Version:** Scripture quotations from Genesis 6–9, 1 Samuel 8–10, Acts of the Apostles 23–24, 1 Maccabees 1, and 2 Maccabees 4 and 6 from the New Revised Standard Version of the Bible, copyright © 1989 National Council of the Churches of Christ in the United States of America. Used by permission. All rights reserved.

**Gabriel Biel:** "Execrabilis." Reprinted by permission of the publisher from *Defensorium Obedientiae Apostolicae et alia Documenta* by Gabriel Biel, edited and translated by Heiko A. Oberman, Daniel E. Zerfoss, and William J. Courtenay, pp. 224–27, Cambridge, MA: The Belknap Press of Harvard University Press, Copyright © 1968 by the President and Fellows of Harvard College.

**Walter Bower:** "A Declaration of Scottish Independence," from *Scotichronicon*, Volume 7, by Walter Bower. Edited by B. Scott and D. E. R. Watt. Copyright © University of St. Andrews 1996. Reprinted by permission of Birlinn Ltd.

**Anna Comnena:** Excerpts from *The Alexiad of Anna Comnena*, translated by E.R.A. Sewter (Penguin Classics, 1969). Copyright © E.R.A. Sewter, 1969. Reproduced by permission of Penguin Books Ltd.

**Geoffrey de Charny:** From *The Book of Chivalry of Geoffroi de Charny: Text, Context, and Translation*, translated by Richard W. Kaeuper and Elspeth Kennedy, pp. 99. Copyright © 1996 University of Pennsylvania Press. Reprinted with permission of the University of Pennsylvania Press.

**Marie de France:** "Equitan" from *The Lais of Marie de France*, translated by Glyn S. Burgess and Keith Busby (Penguin Classics, 1986; Second Edition, 1999). Copyright © Glyn S. Burgess and Keith Busby, 1986, 1999. Reproduced by permission of Penguin Books Ltd.

**Bartolome de las Casas:** Excerpts from *A Short Account of the Destruction of the Indies* by Bartolome de las Casas, edited and translated by Nigel Griffin, introduction by Anthony Pagden (Penguin Classics, 1992). Translation and Notes copyright © Nigel Griffin, 1992. Introduction copyright © Anthony Pagden, 1992. Reproduced by permission of Penguin Books Ltd.

**Michel de Montaigne:** Excerpts from *Montaigne: Essays* by Michel de Montaigne, translated by J. M. Cohen (Penguin Classics, 1958). Copyright © J. M. Cohen, 1958. Reproduced by permission of Penguin Books Ltd.

**Christine de Pisan:** Excerpt from pages 11–13, in *The Book of the Deeds of Arms and of Chivalry*, edited by Charity Cannon Willard and translated by Sumner Willard, 1999. Copyright © 1999 by The Pennsylvania State University Press. Reprinted by Permission of The Pennsylvania State University Press.

**René Descartes:** From *A Discourse on the Method*, translated by Ian Maclean. Copyright © Ian Maclean 2006. Reprinted by permission of Oxford University Press.

**Armand Jean du Plessis:** From Henry Bertram Hill (trans.), *The Political Testament of Cardinal Richelieu*, pp. 31–32. © 1961 by the Board of Regents of the University of Wisconsin System. Reprinted by permission of The University of Wisconsin Press.

**Robert Filmer:** "Observations upon Aristotle's Politiques" (1652), in *Divine Right and Democracy: An Anthology of Political Writing in Stuart England*, edited by David Wootton, pp 110–18. Copyright © 1986. Reproduced by permission of Hackett Publishing.

**Galileo Galilei:** Excerpts from *Discoveries and Opinions of Galileo* by Galileo, translated by Stillman Drake, copyright © 1957 by Stillman Drake. Used by permission of Doubleday, an imprint of the Knopf Doubleday Publishing Group, a division of Penguin Random House LLC. All rights reserved.

**Pierre Gassendi:** From *The Selected Works of Pierre Gassendi*, edited by Craig B. Brush. (New York: Johnson Reprint Corporation, 1972), pp. 334–36.

**Homer:** *The Iliad*, translated by Stanley Lombardo, selections from pp. 115–18. Copyright Hackett Publishing Company, 1997. Reprinted with permission of the publisher.

**Rosemary Horrox (ed.):** Excerpts from *The Black Death*, translated and edited by Rosemary Horrox. © Rosemary Horrox, 1994. Reprinted by permission of Manchester University Press, Manchester, United Kingdom.

**Maureen Gallery Kovacs (trans.):** Excerpt from *The Epic of Gilgamesh*, with an Introduction and Notes by Maureen Gallery Kovacs, translator. Copyright © 1985, 1989 by the Board of Trustees of the Leland Stanford Junior University. All rights reserved. Reprinted by permission of the publisher, Stanford University Press, www.sup.org.

**Carolyne Larrington (trans.):** "The Condemnation of Joan of Arc by the University of Paris" from *Women and Writing in Medieval Europe: A Sourcebook*, by Carolyne Larrington, Copyright © 1995 Routledge. Reproduced with permission of Taylor & Francis Books, United Kingdom.

A47

[Page numbers in *italics* refer to illustrations, maps, and tables.]

Abbasid dynasty, 227–28, 229, 245–46, 270, 381
Abbey Church (Cluny), *266*
Abbey Church (Island of Iona), *235*
Abelard, Heloise, 285–86, *286*, 304, 310
Abelard, Peter, 285–86, *286*, 289, 310, 311, 312
absolutism, 492–521
    absolute monarchy, 494, 498
    alternatives to, 502–7, *503, 504, 505, 507*
    appeal and justification of, 495
    autocracy in Russia and, 514–19, *515, 517, 518*
    chronology, 492
    defined, 494
    of Louis XIV, 495–502, *496, 497, 500*
    overview, 493–94, *494*
    remaking of Central and Eastern Europe, 509–13, *510, 511, 514*
    war and balance of power (1661–1715) as result of, 508–9, *509*
Abu Bakr, 225–26
Abul Abbas (elephant), 229
Abydos, 23
Academy, 116–19
Achaean League, 130, 143
Acre, as Christian capital of Jerusalem, 297
Acropolis, *76, 80, 87, 88*
Act of Succession (England), 504
Act of Supremacy (1559), 445
Act of Toleration (England), 504
Acts of the Apostles, 185, 188, 189
Adam (biblical character), 70, 187, 206, 400, *401,* 498
Æthelbehrt (king of Kent), 236
Aegean civilization
    Minoan thalassocracy, 49–50, *50, 51*
    Mycenaean Greece, *49,* 50–51, *51, 52, 53*
    overview, 48–49
    Persian Empire and, 65
    Sea Peoples and end of Bronze Age, 51–54
Aeneas (Roman), 154
*Aeneid* (Virgil), 148, 207
Aeschylus (Greek playwright), 97
Aetolian League, 130
Afghanistan,
    Alexander the Great's final campaigns and, 124
Africa
    Cape of Good Hope, 456, 467

medieval demand for gold in, 334
Order of Christ, 413
slave trade and fifteenth-century exploration, 413, 416–17
slave trade and sixteenth-seventeenth century colonialism, 459–62, *460, 462*
Stone Age societies in, 4–5
Vandals' capture of North Africa, 205
*see also individual names of countries*
Africanus (Scipio), 157
*Against the Thievish, Murderous Hordes of Peasants* (Luther), 434
Agesilaus (Spartan king), 119
agora, 80
agriculture
    agricultural revolution of Medieval Warm Period, 255–57, *256*
    in ancient Athens, 88
    in ancient Egypt, 22
    Black Death and impact on, 360–61
    Climate Optimum, 255, 336
    "Columbia Exchange" and effects on, 457–58, *458*
    of early civilizations, 4, *6,* 6–7, 8
    feudalism and, 263
    Great Famine, 351–53
    during Hellenistic period, 132
    hunter-gatherer societies and, 5, 6, 7
    irrigation in ancient Egypt, *24*
    lunar calendar and, 15
    serfdom and, 243, 257, 260–61
    Ubaid culture, 8–9
Ahhotep (queen of Egypt), 43
Ahmose (pharaoh of Egypt), 42–43
Ahriman (Zoroastrianism counter-deity), 66
Ahura-Mazda (Zoroastrianism god), 66
Aisha (Muhammad's wife), 229
Akhaiwoi (Achaeans), 53
Akhenaten (pharaoh of Egypt), *46,* 46–47
Akhetaten (Egypt), 47
Akkadian Realm, *16,* 16–17
Alaric (king of the Visigoths), 203
Albert (bishop of Hohenzollern), 428
Alberti, Leon Battista, 370–71, 403
Albigensian Crusade, 300
*Alchemist, The* (Jonsen), 487
Alcuin (Anglo-Saxon monk), 241
Alexander III (pope), 290, 310
Alexander III (the Great; king of Macedonia)
    attempted mutiny against, 127

conquest of Persia by, 122–23, *123, 126*
death of, 126–28
in Egypt, 123–24
final campaigns of, *124,* 124–26, *125*
legacy and characterization of, 122, *124*
overview, 111–12
Philip II and, *121,* 121–22, *122*
Ptolemy and, 122, 128–29, *129*
successor kingdoms to Alexander's empire, *128,* 128–30
*Alexander Nevsky* (film), 293
Alexander VI (pope), 396, 429–32, *430*
Alexandria (Egypt), 176
Alexis, Saint, 306
Alexius Comnenus (Byzantine emperor), 272, 274–75, 276–78
Alfonso II (king of Aragon), 294, 295, *295*
Alfred the Great (king of England), 244–45
Alhambra palace, *282*
Ali (caliph), 227
*Almagest* (Ptolemy), 136
Almohads, 315
alphabet(s)
    Cyrillic, 271
    Etruscan, 148
    evolution of, *56*
    Latin, 251
    Phoenician, *56,* 79
    Roman, 149
    Runic, *251*
    Ugaritic alphabet (Syria), 47–48, 55
Ambrose, Saint, 205–6
Amenemhet (pharaoh of Egypt), 34
Amenhotep III (pharaoh of Egypt), 51
Amerigo Vespucci, 418, 419
Ammon, oracle of, 124
Ammonites, 58
Amon, Egyptian god, 45–46, 47
Amorites, *17,* 17–18, 18–21, *21*
Amos (Jewish prophet), 71
Amun-Ra (Egyptian god), 124
Amyntas III (king of Macedonia), 121
Anabaptism, *436,* 436–37
*Anabasis* (Xenophon), 111
analytical geometry, 540
Anatolia
    Alexander the Great in, 123
    ancient Greek civilization and, 49
    Byzantine Empire, 217
    before civilization, 4

Indo-European peoples, 41–42
 Mycenaeans and Hittites, 53
 Seleucids, 130
Anavyssos (Attica), 82
ancestor worship, by Romans, 154, *154*, 155, 189
Anchises (Roman), 154
Andalus, Al-, 243, 245–46, 249–50, 411
Anglo-Norman system
 emergence of France, 289–90
 Henry I and, 287
 Henry II and, 287–89, *288*
 Magna Carta and, 289
 William the Conqueror and, 263–65, *264*, 286–87
Anglo-Saxons, 213
animals
 animal figures, 281
 Bucephalus (Alexander the Great's warhorse), 125
 "Columbia Exchange" and, 457–58, *458*
 horses, 82, 83, *83*, 125
 hunter-gatherer societies, 5, 6, 7
 hunting in Middle Ages, 317, *317*
Anna (princess of Kiev), 271
Anna Comnena (daughter of Alexius Comnenus), 272
*Annals* (Tacitus), 173
Anne (queen of England), 504, 508
Anne of Austria, 477
Anselm of Canterbury, 312
Anthropocene epoch, 7
Antigonus (Macedonian ruler), 130
Antioch, 218, 296–97
Antiochus (Persian ruler), 130
Antiochus III (Persian ruler), 130
anti-Semitism
 development of, 308–9
Antoninus Pius (Roman emperor), 169, 189
Anubis (Egyptian goddess), 30
apella, 90
Aphrodite (Greek goddess), 86
Aphrodite of Knidos, 118, *118*
Apian, Peter, *530*
Apollo (Greek god), 195, 495–98, *496*, *496*
Apollo at Delphi, 64, 81–82
Apollo of Piombino, *99*
Apollo of Tenea, *99*
aqueduct (Roman Empire), *175*
Aquitaine, 287, *310*, 318, 319, 350
Arabs
 Byzantine Empire and, 217
 calligraphy, *228*
 conquest of West by, 225–27, *226*
 revelations of Muhammad, 223
 *see also individual names of countries*
Aragon
 "big book of fiefs" (King Alfonso II of Aragon), 205, 294, 295, *295*
 Renaissance in, 411–12
 *see also individual names of leaders*
Arbroath, abbey of, 348–49
Archaic Period (ancient Egypt), 24
Archilochus of Paros, 86–87

Archimedes of Syracuse, 137
architecture
 of Byzantine Empire, 221–23, *222*
 of classical Greece, 98–100, *99*
 Hellenistic period, *140*, 140–41, *141*
 Medieval cathedrals, 320–21, *321*
 Muslim, Middle Ages, 280–81, *282*
 of northern European Renaissance, 408, *408*
 public works projects of Roman Empire, 172, 174, *175*
 Renaissance, 403–4, *404*
 wall and tower of Jericho, 8
Arch of Titus, Roman Forum, *184*
Areopagus, 87
Arianism, 197–98
Ariosto, Ludovico, 397
Aristagoras, 93
Aristarchus of Samos, 136
aristocracy
 of Archaic Greece, 84–85
 Black Death and effect on, 362–63, *363*
 of High Middle Ages, 315–21, *316*, *317*
 nobility, defined, 315
Aristophanes (playwright), *94*, 104–5, 116
Aristotle
 astronomy and, 526–27
 on democracy, 85
 legacy of, 116–19, *117*, 120, 279, *279*, 314
 on physiology, 137
 on slavery, 119, 120
 on tragedy, 97
Ark of the Covenant, 56
"Armada Portrait" (Elizabeth I), *469*
Armenia, Christian traditions, 271
Army Debates (General Council of Cromwell's army), 480
Arrian (Roman), 122, 127
art
 Byzantine Empire, 221–23, *222*
 classical Greece, 98–100, *99*
 Dutch painting, seventeenth century, 488–90, *489*, *490*
 Egyptian sculpture, *30*
 entertainment in High Middle Ages, 320
 European-Atlantic world integration (sixteenth-seventeenth centuries), 483–91, *486*, *487*, *488*, *489*, *490*
 following Black Death, 364–66
 of fourth century B.C.E., 115–16, *116*, *118*
 Hellenistic period, *132*, 136, 141–42
 Late Middle Ages, 337–38
 Middle Ages, modern-day artistic renditions, *299*
 Muslim, Middle Ages, 280–81, *281*
 of northern European Renaissance, 408, *408*
 papermaking, *228*, 228–29
 Renaissance, 397–401, *398*, *399*, *400*, *401*, 402
 Roman Empire, *175*, 175–78
 southern Europe, seventeenth century, *487*, 487–88, *488*
 *see also individual titles of art*

Artaxerxes II (Persian emperor), 115
asceticism, 198–200
Ashdod (Philistine citadel), 56
Asherah (Canaanite goddess), 69, *70*
Ashkelon (Philistine citadel), 56
Asia
 European explorers' search for routes to, 415, 419
 Renaissance politics of Christian Europe and effect on, 409
 *see also individual names of countries*
Assurbanipal (Neo-Assyrian king), 63, *64*
Assurnasirpal II (king of Assyria), 59
Assyrian Empire
 Assyrian military-religious ethos, 62–63
 Esarhaddon (king), 68
 Neo-Assyrian government and administration, 60–61, *62*, *63*
 Neo-Assyrian legacy, 63–64
 overview, 41, *41*
 revival of, overview, 59–60
 transnational networks of, 47, 54
astronomy
 Copernican revolution, 526–28, *527*, 529, *530*
 education in Middle Ages, 310
 Hellenistic period, 136–37
 Ptolemaic system, *525*, 526–27, *530*
 Tycho and Kepler, *528*, 528–29, *531*
Athena Parthenos (Greek goddess), 99, *100*
Athens
 acropolis, 76, 80, 87, 88
 classical Greek culture and life, 96–101, *98*, *101*
 downfall of poleis and, 113–15
 Isocrates (Athenian orator), 119
 ostracism, 87, 88
 overview, 87, 87–89, *88*, 93
 Parthenon, *76*, 99, *100*
 Peloponnesian War ("greatest war in history"), 101–5, *103*
 Phryne (Athenian courtesan), 118
 Pnyx, 88, *88*
 rise of poleis and, 79–80
 trireme warships, *93*
Augustine, Saint, 206, 427, 439
Augustinian order, 427
Augustus (Roman emperor), 148, 170, 171, 193
Austrasia, 239
Austria
 absolutism, 509–14, *510*
 League of Augsburg, 508–9
 Siege of Vienna, 512–13
autocracy, of Peter the Great, 514–19
Averroès Ibn Rushd (1126–1198), 314–15, *315*
Avicenna, 280
Avignon, papacy in, *343*, 343–44, 379
Azores, 335
Aztec Empire of Mexico, *419*, 419–22, *420*, 459

Ba'al (Canaanite god), 69, 192
Babylon
    Babylonian Captivity of papacy, 343
    formation of Judaism and, 72
    Hammurabi's rule of, 18–21, *21*
Bacon, Sir Francis, 524, *536*, 536–40
Badr, battle of, 223
Baghdad
    as capital of Islam, 227
    Mongol destruction of, 331
Balboa, Vasco Núñez de, 419
Baldwin II (king of Jerusalem), 297
Balkans
    rise of Ottoman Empire and, 372
    Slavs' migration to, 270–71
Balthild, Saint, 234
baptism, 344, 429, 436
barbarians
    Greek concept, 76
    Roman concept, *202*, 203–5
Barbarossa (Frederick I, Holy Roman
    emperor), 290, 297
Barberini, Maffeo, 532
"barracks emperors" (Roman), 192, 193
Bartlett, Robert, 322
Basil II (Byzantine emperor), 271
Basil of Caesarea, 208–9
Bassi, Laura, 541
baths (Rome), 191–92
Bayeux Tapestry, 264, *264*
Becket, Thomas, 287, *287*, 310, 318
Bede (monk), 213, 244
Before the Common Era (B.C.E.), 4
Belgium
    battle of Courtrai, 346
Belisarius (Roman general), 215
Benedict, Saint
    Benedictine monasticism, 236, *252*
    as Benedict of Nursia, 209–10
    *Rule of the Master*, 209–10, 237, 266, 301
Benedictine Abbey of Tyniec, *252*
Benedictine monasticism, 236, *252*
Benedict XVI (pope), *383*
Benjamin, tribe of, 61
Bermuda, colonization and, *457*
Bernard of Clairvaux, Saint, 301, 305
Bernart de Ventadorn, 318
Bernini, Gianlorenzo, *488*
Berry, duke of, *363*
*biblia* (books), 54
"big book of fiefs" (King Alfonso II of Ara-
    gon), 205, 294, 295, *295*
Bill of Rights (England), 504
birds, hunting of (Middle Ages), 317, *317*
*Birth of Venus, The* (Botticelli), *399*
Black Death
    challenges to Roman Church following,
        381, 386
    early global exploration, 326, 333
    Eckhart's teachings and, 345
    events of, 350–56, *351*, *353*
    impact of, *360*, 360–66, *363*, *364*
Black Stone, 223
Blanche of Castile, 318

Blessed Mary, cult of, 303–5, *304*
Boccaccio, Giovanni, 364
Bodin, Jean, 484
Boethius, Anicius Manlius Severinus, 207–8
Bohemia
    High Middle Ages, 292
    new kingdoms of East-Central Europe, 251
    reform movements, Late Middle Ages, 386,
        387–88
    Thirty Years War, 470–73
Boleslaw III (king of Poland), 292
Boleslaw the Pious (duke), 292
Boleyn, Anne (queen of England), 442–43
Boniface, Saint, 238
Boniface VIII (pope), 342–43, 347
*Book of Chivalry, The* (Charny), 352
*Book of Common Prayer, The* (Cranmer), 444,
    445
*Book of Contemplation, The* (Usama), 277
Book of Deuteronomy, 71–72
Book of Joshua, 57
*Book of Marvels, The* (Mandeville), 325, 332
*Book of the City of Ladies* (Christine de Pisan),
    364, 365
*Book of the Courtier, The* (Castiglione), 397
*Book of the Deeds of Arms and of Chivalry, The*
    (Christine de Pisan), 365
books
    *biblia*, 54
    *see also individual titles of books*
books of the dead, 31
Borgia, Cesare, 396, 397
Bossuet, Jacques-Bénigne, 498
Botticelli, Sandro, 399
Boudica (Celtic warrior queen), 169–70, *199*
Bourbon dynasty, Henry of Navarre and, *466*
Boyle, Robert, 540
Bramante, Donato, 400, 404
Brandenburg-Prussia, 509–14, *511*
Brazil, Pernambuco Province, 463
Bretons, 319
Bronze Age
    bronze, defined, 15
    Late Bronze Age, 47–48
    maps of, *41*, *48*
    Mycenaean Greeks and, 51, *52*
    overview, 39–42
    Sea Peoples and end of, 51–52
Bruegel, Pieter (the Elder), 488, *489*
Bruni, Leonardo, 370–71
Brutus, Marcus Junius, 165
bubonic plague, 356
Bucephalus (Alexander the Great's warhorse),
    125
bull-leaping fresco (Minoan), *50*
bureaucracy
    absolutism and, 499–500
    of ancient Egypt, 25, 28–29
    of tsarist Russia, 517
Burgundians, 204, 377–79
Burgundy, duke of, 377, 379
Bush, George W., 274
busts, of Romans, 154, *154*
Byzantine Empire

art and architecture of, 221–23, *222*
Byzantium and, 200
consequences of First Crusade, 278
Crusades, 294–96
expansion and fragility and First Crusade,
    270–73, *271*
"Greek fire," 217, *217*
Iconoclasm legacy, 219–21
Orthodox Christianity and Iconoclasm,
    218–19, *219*
overview, 217
piracy issues of, 258
stability of, 218

*Cabinet of Curiosities* (Wurm), 535
Cabot, John, 456
Caernarvon Castle, 347, *347*
Caesar, Augustus (Octavian), 165–69, *166*
Caesar, Gaius Julius, 156, 163–65, *164*
Caesarion, 164
calendars
    Common Era (C.E.), concept, 10
    Before the Common Era (B.C.E.), concept, 4
    Julian, 32, 164
    lunar, 15
Caligula (Roman emperor), 168
calligraphy, Arabic, *228*
Calvin, John, 436, *437*, 437–38, 465
Calvinism
    inception of, 436–37
    James I (king of England) and, 477
    in Netherlands, 467
Cambridge University, 544
Cambyses II (king of Persia), 65, 123
Camulodunum, 171–72
Canaanites, 41, 54, 57, 69, 70, *70*
Canada
    French exploration of, 475
    Québec (New France), *466*
Canary Islands, 335, 414, 417, 456
Canillac, Marquis of, 493–94
cannons, 375, *375*, 414
*Canon of Medicine* (Avicenna), 280
Canons of the Synod, 221
Cape of Good Hope, 413, 467
Capetian dynasty, 289, 350
Cape Verde Islands, 417
capitularies, 240
Caracalla (Roman emperor), 190–92
Caribbean, Louis XIV (king of France) and
    colonization of, 501–2
Carneades (Greek Skeptic), 134
Carolingian Empire, 254–55, *255*
Cartesians, 540
Carthage
    Carthaginian coin, *157*
    Phoenicians in, 54–55
    Punic Wars and, 156–58, *158*
Casas, Bartolomé de las (bishop of Chiapas),
    421
Cassiodorus, 209–10, *210*
castellans, 294
Castiglione, Baldassare, 397
Castile, 294, 411–12

Castle Church (Wittenberg), 425
castles
    of High Middle Ages, 261–62, 262
    of Late Middle Ages, 347, 347–50
catacombs (early Christian images), 186, 187
catacombs (Thekla), 186
Çatalhöyük, 4, 7–8
Catalonia (Catalunya), 294, 334–36
Cathars, 300, 305
cathedrals, Medieval, 320–21, 321
Catherine of Aragon, 442–43
Catherine of Siena, Saint, 382, 386
Catholicism
    Catholic, defined, 426, 432
    Catholic reforms at time of Protestant
        Reformation, 446–48, 447
    Edict of Nantes, 466
    Galileo and, 532, 532–34
    Ignatius Loyola and Society of Jesus,
        448–50
    Jansenism, 484
    Mass, 301–3, 304, 344–45
    reformed Catholic Church of seventeenth
        and eighteenth centuries, 450–51, 451
    sacraments, 344, 429, 442
    witchcraft accusations and, 483–84
Catholic League, 447
Cato, Marcus Porcius, 157
Cavaliers, 478
Cavendish, Margaret, 541
cave paintings, of Lascaux, 5, 5
Caxton, William, 394–95
celibacy
    Gregory VII's reforms, 300–301
    Protestant Reformation and Council of
        Trent on, 440
    reform of secular clergy (eleventh century),
        269
    virtue of, 200
Cella Septichora, 197
Celtics
    Abbey Church (Island of Iona), 235
    Bede on, 213
    monasticism of seventh century, 235–36
Central Europe
    absolutism, 509–13, 510, 511, 514
    absolutism and, 509–14
    map, Holy Roman Empire, 291
    medieval monarchies of, 290–92, 291
    new kingdoms of (High Middle Ages), 251
    see also individual names of countries
centralization, absolutism and, 499–500
Cervantes, Miguel de, 483
Chaeronea, battle of, 112, 112, 122
Chaldeans, 63–64, 72, 126
Champlain, Samuel de, 475
Champollion, Jean François, 27
Chandragupta (Indian warrior-king), 130
chariots
    Archaic Greece, 83, 83
    Assyrian, 41
    Byzantine Empire, 218
    Sumerian, 14, 15
Charlemagne (Roman emperor)

access to education during reign of, 310
capitularies, 240
Carolingian Empire of, 237–42, 238, 241,
    242, 243
death of, 266
legacy of, 249–50, 267
Merovingians and, 234
overview, 229, 230–31
Charles I (Charles Stuart; king of England),
    477–80, 478, 481, 482, 482, 484
Charles II (king of England), 479, 502–3,
    503, 504, 540
Charles II (king of Naples and Sicily), 340,
    342
Charles II (king of Spain), 508
Charles II (the Bald; Holy Roman Emperor),
    243
Charles Martel (king of Franks), 238–39
Charles the Good (count of Flanders), 261
Charles University, 387
Charles V (Holy Roman emperor), 432,
    432–33, 433, 434, 434, 439
Charles V (king of France), 376
Charles V (king of Spain), 419
Charles VI (king of France), 364, 377, 379
Charles VII (king of France), 377–78, 409
Charny, Geoffroi de, 352
Chaucer, Geoffrey, 379
Chauvet (France), cave paintings of, 5
children
    enslavement of, in Ottoman Empire, 373
    Protestant Reformation on discipline of, 441
China
    Black Death origin and, 355–56
    exploration of fifteenth century and, 413
    Great Wall of, 326
chivalry, code of, 315–16, 319, 352
Chrétien de Troyes, 318
Christian Bible
    Council of Nicea, 198–200
    King James Bible, 534
    Luther's translation of, 427
    Vulgate, 205, 448
    Wycliffe's English Bible, 386
Christianity, 180–211, 212–47
    Augustine's influence on, 206–7
    background, 181–82
    Carolingian Empire, 237–42, 238, 241, 242
    Carolingian Empire, collapse, 243–46, 244,
        245
    Christ, defined, 221
    Christian kingdoms of Iberian Peninsula,
        High Middle Ages, 293, 293–94, 294
    chronology, 180, 212
    classical learning and, 207–11, 210
    Constantinople establishment and Roman
        Empire, 200–205, 202, 204
    conversion of Northwestern Europe, 230,
        230–37, 235, 237
    conversion to, in Roman Empire, 194–200,
        196, 197, 199, 200
    early Islam and, 223–29, 225, 226, 227, 228
    Eucharist, 344–45
    expulsion of Jews from Spain, 411–12

in Hellenistic world, 185–87, 186
Henry II and, 287
hierarchy of Church, 197
Innocent III's Crusade for a unified Chris-
    tendom, 298–300
Jesus' life and death, 182, 182–85, 185
Judaism and inception of, 184
Justinian and, 214, 214–17, 216
Mass inception, 301–3
missionary activity, seventh century, 236
monastic reform movement, 266, 266–67
Mongol Empire and, 332–33
as new worldview, fourth-fifth centuries
    C.E., 205–7, 207, 208–9
northern European Renaissance and
    humanism, 405, 405–7
Renaissance and politics of, 409–12, 410,
    411, 412
Renaissance politics of Christian Europe,
    409–12, 410, 411, 412
Roman Empire and Christianity as minority
    religion, 181–82, 186, 187, 187–93, 191,
    192, 193, 194
Roman Empire of Byzantium, 217, 217–23,
    219, 222, 232–33
Rome's legacy and, 213–14
sacraments ("holy rites"), power of, 344
Christina (grand duchess, Medici family),
    533
Christine de Pisan, 364, 364, 365
chronology
    absolutism, 492
    Christianity inception, 180
    colonialism (sixteenth-seventeenth centu-
        ries), 454
    early civilizations, 2
    European-Atlantic world integration
        (sixteenth-seventeenth centuries), 454
    Greece (ancient), 74
    High Middle Ages, 248, 284
    Iron Age, 38
    Late Middle Ages, 324, 358
    Protestant Reformation, 424
    Renaissance, 390
    Roman Republic and Roman Empire, 146
    scientific revolution, 522
Church of England
    Civil War (England) and, 478
    Edward VI and, 443–44
    Elizabeth I and, 443, 445, 445–46
    Henry VIII and, 442–43, 443, 444
    James II and, 503–4
    Restoration of Stuarts, 479, 502–4, 503
Cicero, Marcus Tullius, 156, 161–62, 166,
    205, 206, 366
Cimon (Delian League strategos), 97
Cincinnatus, Lucius Quinctius, 152, 152
Ciompi regime, 362
Cistercian order, 301, 301, 429
citadel of Pergamon, 140
citizenship
    Roman Empire, 172
    towns of eleventh century and, 260,
        319–20

*City of God* (Augustine), 207, *207*
City of Man, 207, *207*
*City of Stettin Under Siege by the Great Elector Frederick William in the Winter of 1677–1678, The,* 514
civic ideals, Florentine Renaissance, 370–71
civilization, defined, 4
civil law, of Roman Empire, 178
Civil War (England)
   absolutism and, 494
   effect on Atlantic colonies, 479–83
   fall of Charles Stuart and Oliver Cromwell's Commonwealth, 478–79, *479,* 480
   overview, 477
   Parliament *versus* Charles I, 477–78, *478,* 481
   restoration of monarchy, 479, 502–4, *503*
Clare of Assisi, 308
class
   in Babylonian society, 19
   in classical Greece, 97
   courts, cities, and cathedrals of High Middle Ages, 315–21
   downfall of poleis and social crises, 115
   education in Middle Ages and, 310–12
   farming by peasants, *256,* 256–57
   Islam and mobility, opportunity, status (Byzantine Empire), 229
   "junkers," 513
   nobility, following Black Death, 362–63
   in Roman Republic, 161
   scientific revolution and cultural change, 546–49
   social advancement in Ottoman Empire, 373–74
   Sparta and status, 92
classical learning
   Christianity and, 207–11, *210*
   High Middle Ages, 314–15
   Mongol Empire and, 331
   during Renaissance, 367
Claudius I (Roman emperor), 169
Claudius Ptolemaeus, 136
Cleisthenes, 89
Clement V (pope), 343
Clement VII (pope), 383, 443
Cleopatra (use of name, in Ptolemaic Egypt), 129
Cleopatra VII (Egyptian pharaoh), 129, 164, *165,* 166, 167
climate
   Climate Optimum, 255, 336
   Great Famine, 351–53
   Neolithic Revolution and, 6
Climate Optimum, Medieval, 255, 336
clocks, invention of, 336–37
Clothar III (Merovingian king), 234
clothing of nobility, Late Middle Ages, 363
*Clouds, The* (Aristophanes), 104–5
Clovis (warrior-king of Franks), 232–33
Clovis II (Merovingian king), 234
Clunaic monasticism, 301
Cluny, *266*
Cnut the Great (king of Denmark), 252–53

Code (Justinian legislation), 216
Code of Hammurabi, 18–19, 20–21, *21*
codex
   "big book of fiefs" (King Alfonso II of Aragon), 205, 295, *295*
   invention of, 209–10, *210*
coffee trade, Louis XIV (king of France) and colonization of Caribbean, 501–2
coffin texts, 31
coins/coinage
   African gold for, 334
   Byzantine Empire, 218, 230, 231, 233, 271
   Carthaginian, *157*
   of Charlemagne, 239, *241,* 255
   Egyptian, *129*
   Holy Roman Empire, 290
   invention of, 92
   Oliver Cromwell, *479*
   Persian, 64, *65,* 132
   Renaissance, 391, 405
   Roman, 156, *165,* 168, 176, *191,* 192, 196
   Seleucids, 130
   Spanish American gold for, 464–65
   Theodoric the Ostrogoth, *204*
   of William the Conqueror, 265
Colbert, Jean-Baptiste, 501
College of Cardinals, 269
Cologne, Town Council of, 355
colonialism
   absolutism and, 494
   archaic Greece, 80–82, *81*
   Civil War (England) and effect on Atlantic colonies, 479–83
   extension of Crusades into European colonialism, 298
   under Louis XIV (king of France), 501–2
   nation building and warfare, 375–76
colonialism (sixteenth-seventeenth centuries), 454–65
   chronology, 454
   colonial populations compared, 458–59
   "Columbia exchange" and environmental effects, 457–58, *458*
   competing colonialism ventures (sixteenth-seventeenth centuries), 456–57
   European-Atlantic world integration (sixteenth-seventeenth centuries), 455–65, *458, 460, 462, 463, 464*
   European colonialism and conflict, overview, *463,* 463–65, *464*
   European poverty, *463,* 463–65, *464*
   Europe in Atlantic world (1550–1660), overview, 455–56
   slavery and triangular trade, 459–63, *460, 462*
   social hierarchies of New Spain, 459
color spectrum, Newton on, 544–48, *545*
Colosseum (Rome), *173*
Columbanus (Irish missionary), 235
Columbus, Christopher, 325, 412, 417–19, 457–58, *458,* 526
*Comedy* (Dante), 339, 342, 364
*comites,* 238

commerce
   absolutism and, 494
   by Dutch Republic (seventeenth century), 506
   of early civilizations, 8
   European-Atlantic world integration (sixteenth-seventeenth centuries) and, 455–65, *458, 460, 462, 463, 464*
   fall of Constantinople and, 372
   founding of Rome, 149–50
   "free trade," 480
   Hellenistic period, 131–32
   in Iron Age, 40
   Islam during Byzantine Empire, 228
   Late Middle Ages, extension of European commerce and settlement, 334–42, *335, 336, 337, 340, 341, 342*
   Middle Ages urban growth and trade, 257–61, *258, 259, 260*
   Mongol Empire and, 326, 331–34
   Netherlands revolt and Dutch trading empire (sixteenth century), 466–67
   by Phoenicians, 54–55
   Sparta and, 91
   spice trade, 413, 417, 467
   Sumerian, 14–16
   transnational trade of Late Bronze Age, 47–48, *48*
   triangular trade and, 459–62, *460*
   *see also individual industry names*
*commercium,* 150
Commodus (Roman emperor), 189
Common Era (C.E.), 10
Commonwealth, England as, 479
Commonwealth of Poland and Lithuania (sixteenth-seventeenth centuries), 507, *507*
Companions, 121–22, *122*
conciliarism, 383–85
Concordat of Worms (WOHRMS), 270
*Confessions* (Augustine), 206
confraternities, 320, 366
*connubium,* 150
Conrad (duke of Masovia), 292
*consquitadores, 419,* 419–22, *420*
Constantine I (the Great; Roman emperor), 195–98
Constantinople
   Byzantine Empire and, 217, 218
   capture during Crusades, 292–93, 298
   establishment of, 200–205, *202, 204*
   fall of, 371, 372–73
Constantius (Roman emperor), 193, *193,* 195
constitutions
   Jesuit, 449
   Roman Republic, 152–53
consuls, 152
consumption
   doctrine of indulgences, 428–29, 447
   Protestant Reformation's effects on, *447*
*conversos,* 412
*convivencia,* 411–12, *412*
Copernicus, Nicolaus, 280, 526–28, *527, 529, 530*

copper, 14
Corinth, 81
Corinthian War, 112
*Coriolanus* (film), 486
*Corpus* (Justinian), 216–17
Cortés, Hernán, *419*, 420–22
*Cosmographia* (Apian), *530*
*Cosmographic Mystery* (Kepler), 529
cosmopolis, polis transition to, 130–36
Cossacks, Thirty Years' War and, 474
Council of Basil, 385
Council of Constance, *383*, 383–85, 409
Council of Nicea, 198–200
Council of Trent, 302, 440, 447–48, *448*
Counter-Reformation (Catholic Church), 446–47
courtier, as ideal, 397
Courtrai, battle of, 346
Cranach, Lucas "the Elder," *426*
Cranmer, Thomas (archbishop of Canterbury), 443, 444, 445
Crassus, Marcus Junius, 163
*Creation of Adam, The* (Michelangelo), 400, *401*
Creation story
    Adam (biblical character), 70, 187, 206, 498
    *The Creation of Adam* (Michelangelo), 400, *401*
    Genesis, 3, 12–13, 70, 535
    scientific revolution and, 534–35
Critian boy, *99*
Crito (*The Clouds* character), 104–5
Croatia, High Middle Ages, 292
Croesus (king of Lydia), 64, 82
Cromwell, Oliver, 478–79, *479*, 480, 481, 502
Cromwell, Richard, 479
Cromwell, Thomas, 443
Crosby, Alfred, 457
Crown of Aragon, 294
Crown of Thorns, *346*, 347
crucifixion, Roman Senate and, 162
Crusades
    Albigensian Crusade, 300
    background, 270
    Christian conquest of Jerusalem, 275–78
    against Constantinople, 292–93, 298
    Crusader States, *296*, 296–97, *297*
    culture of Muslim west and, 278–83, *279*, *281*, *282*
    expansion and fragility of Byzantium, 270–73, *271*
    extension of, into European colonialism, 298
    First Crusade, *274*, 274–75, 278, 298
    Fourth Crusade, 298, 329
    Innocent III and, 298–300
    intellectual revolution during, 286
    motives of crusaders, *275*, 275–76
    revenge of Venice and, 298
    routes of, *276*
    Urban II, 294–96
csar/tsar, terminology, 409
cuneiform, 10, *10*

Cyprus, Minoans and, 49
Cyriacus (monk), 199
Cyrillic alphabet, 271
Cyrus the Great (king of Persia), 64–65, 68–69, 72, 111, 114, 115, 123
Czech Republic, *447*

Daedalus, 49
Damascus, as capital of Islam, 226
Damian, Saint, 307
Dante Alighieri, 339–42, 344, 364
Darius the Great (king of Persia), 65–66, *66*, 92–95, 122–23, *123*
dark ages, defined, 367
Dauphin (French royal title), 377
*David* (Bernini), *488*
*David* (Donatello), 402, *403*
David (king of Israel), 58, 436
*David* (Michelangelo), 402, *403*
Dead Sea Scrolls, 183
death, beliefs of ancient Egyptians about, 30–33, *32*
death mask (Mycenaean), *49*
*Death of Arthur, The* (Malory), 394–95
*Decameron, The* (Boccaccio), 364
Decius (Roman emperor), 192–93, 194
Declaration of Arbroath, 348–49
*Decretum* (Gratian), 314
deductive reasoning, 537
*Defense of Cadíz, The* (Zurbaran), *494*
De Fer, Nicolas, *475*
Delian League, 96–97, 101
democracy
    in archaic Greece, 84–85
    of archaic Greece, 51
    demos, defined, 85
    Peloponnesian War and failure of Athenian democracy, 102–5
    Pericles and, 96–97
    Plato and Aristotle on, 117, 119
    republic compared to, 153
Democritus (Greek philosopher), 133
Denmark
    European colonialism, 298
    High Middle Ages, 252
    Protestant as state religion (sixteenth century), 435
Descartes, René, 473, 536–40, *537*, *540*, *541*
*Descent from the Cross* (Michelangelo), 403, *403*
*Description of the World* (Polo), 325, 332–33
dialogue
    Aristotle and, 116–17
    Socrates and, 106
*Dialogue Concerning the Two Chief World Systems, The* (Galileo), 532–34
Dias, Bartolomeu, 413
diaspora, Jewish, 215
Diet of Worms, *432*, 432–33, *433*, 434
Digest (Roman law), 216
dioceses, defined, 193
Diocletian (Roman emperor), *193*, 193–95
Diomedes (*Iliad* character), 78
Dionysus (Greek god), 97, 134

*Discourse on Method* (Descartes), 537–39
*Discourses on Livy* (Machiavelli), 396
disease
    Black Death, 326, 333, 345
    bubonic plague, 356
    colonialism of seventeenth century and, 469–70
    "Columbia Exchange" and, 457–58, *458*
    Great Famine and Black Death, 350–56, *351*, *353*
    Justinianic Plague, 215, 356
    pandemics, 355–56
    plague (Roman Empire), 192
    pneumonic plague, 356
    septicemic plague, 356
    spread by European explorers, 419–22
*Divine Comedy* (Dante), 364
divorce
    ancient Egypt, 33
    ancient Rome, 160
    Hammurabi's code, 19
Djoser (pharaoh of Egypt), 28, 33
DNA, analysis from ancient Greece, 51
*Doctor Faustus* (Marlowe), 486–87
documentation
    "big book of fiefs" (King Alfonso II of Aragon), 205, 294, *295*, *295*
    capitularies, 240
    development of writing, 10, *10*
    Herodotus' histories, 98
    historical reality of Hellenistic period, 141–43
    library of Nineveh, 63
    printing press invention, 391–92, *393*, 394–95
    seals, *66*, *340*, 340–41
    Sparta and, 92
dogma, defined, 299–300
Dominican order, 308, *412*
Dominic of Osma, 308
Domitian (Roman emperor), 169
Donatello, 402, *403*
"Donation of Constantine," 371
*Don Quixote* (Cervantes), 483
double-entry bookkeeping, Late Middle Ages, 336
Dover, seal of, *340*
draconian punishment, 88
Drake, Sir Francis, 468
ducat (Spanish monetary unit), 464
du Châtelet, Emilie, 546
Duma (Russia), Peter the Great and, 517
Dutch East and West India Companies, 467, *469*
Dutch Reformed Church, 438
Dutch Republic
    absolutism, 506–7
    independence of (1609), 467
*Dying Gaul* (sculpture), 141, *142*

early civilizations, 2–37
    chronology, 2
    Egyptian civilization, 22–29, *23*, *24*, *26*, *27*, *28*, *29*

early civilizations, (*Continued*)
 Egyptian culture and society, 29–35, *30, 32, 33, 34*
 emergence of towns and villages, 7–8
 empire of Hammurabi, 18–21, *19, 21*
 Neolithic Revolution, 5, 6–7, *7, 8*
 overview, 3–4
 Sargon and Akkadian Realm, *16,* 16–17
 Stone Age societies, 4–5, *5*
 stories about great flood, 12–13
 Sumerian cities and early empires, 16
 Sumerian culture, 9–16, *10, 11, 14, 15*
 Ur and Amorites, *17,* 17–18
 urban development in Mesopotamia, 8–10, *9, 10*
Early Dynastic Period, 12–14
Early Iron Age
 evolution of alphabet, *56*
 Hebrews and scriptures, 56–58
 Hebrew unity during, 58, *59*
 King Solomon's reign, 58–59
 overview, 54
 Philistines, 55–56
 Phoenicians, 54–55, *55*
earth, debate about age of, 534–35
Eastern Europe
 absolutism, 509–13, *510, 511, 514*
 absolutism and, 509–14
 map, Holy Roman Empire, *291*
 medieval monarchies, 290–92, *291*
 medieval monarchies of, 290–92, *291*
 new kingdoms of (High Middle Ages), 251
Eastern Orthodox Christianity, 439
ecclesiastical prince, defined, 434
Eckhart, Master, 345
economic issues
 banking in Late Middle Ages, 336–37
 Carolingian Empire, 239–40
 of colonialism in sixteenth-seventeenth centuries, 463–65, *465*
 commerce and settlement, Late Middle Ages, 336–37
 Constantinople as economic center, 200
 downfall of poleis and crisis of, 115
 English monarchy and, 265
 of European exploration, 422
 feudalism concept and, 263
 during Hellenistic period, 131–32
 Italian wealth and Renaissance beginning, 369–70
 of Late Middle Ages, 336
 *Oikonomikos,* 119
 portable wealth (money and credit) in Middle Ages, 261
 poverty in sixteenth-seventeenth centuries, 465, *467*
 in Roman Republic, 159–61
 silver and gold from Spanish America (sixteenth century), 464
 of sugar trade, 459–62, *460*
 Vikings and, 258
Ecumenical Synods, 221
Edessa, as Crusader State, 296–97
Edict of Milan, 195

Edict of Nantes, 466, 501
education
 Byzantine Empire, 221
 elementary education, in High Middle Ages, *309,* 310–12
 High Middle Ages, *309,* 310–14, *313*
 *The Institutes* (Cassiodorus), 210
 monastic education, 208–9
 Renaissance in Italy, 368–69
 role of women, fourth and third/second centuries B.C.E., 138–39
 in tsarist Russia, 515
Edward I (king of England), 347–50
Edward II (king of England), 347, 349
Edward III (king of England), 349, 350, 375
Edward the Confessor (king of England), 263, 348
Edward VI (king of England), 443
Egypt
 Arab Spring, 135
 Mamluk Sultanate of Egypt, 329–30
 *see also individual names of leaders*
Egypt (ancient)
 Alexander the Great in, 123–24
 civilization of, 22–29, *23, 24, 26, 27, 28, 29*
 culture and society, 29–35, *30, 32, 33, 34*
 culture and society of, 29–35, *30, 32, 33, 34*
 Hebrews and, 57
 Imhotep and Step Pyramid, *27, 28,* 28–29
 irrigation by, *24*
 kingdoms and periods, defined, 22
 Narmer Palette, 25, *26*
 New Kingdom, 42–47, *43, 44, 45, 46*
 Old Kingdom, 25–29
 overview, 22, *23*
 power of pharaohs, 24–25
 Predynastic Egypt, 22–24
 Ptolemaic Egypt, 128–29, *129, 132*
 Sea Peoples and, 51–54
 urban planning of Alexandria, 176
 writing in, *27,* 27–28
Eiriksson, Leif, 335, 338–39
Eirik the Red, *335*
Eisenstein, Sergei, 293
*ekklesia,* 88
Ekron (Philistine citadel), 56
El ("god"), 69
Eleanor of Aquitaine, 287, *310,* 318, 319, 350
*Elements of Geometry* (Euclid), 137
El Greco, 487, *487*
Elisabetha (scientist), *541*
Elizabeth I (queen of England), 443, *445,* 445–46, 468, *469,* 477, 486
Elizabeth II (queen of England), *500*
England
 colonialism by, 298, 468–70, *470*
 crisis of kingship in England (sixteenth-seventeenth centuries), 477–83, *478, 479, 482*
 expansion of, Late Middle Ages, *347,* 347–50
 expulsion of Jews, 309, 347

Great Britain, naming of, 509
 Hundred Years' War, 349–50, 352, 375–79, *376*
 Hundred Years' War consequences, 409
 League of Augsburg, 508–9
 Magna Carta, 289
 medieval monarchies, 287, *287*–89
 monarchy established by, 263–65, *264*
 nobility in Late Middle Ages, 363
 Norman conquest of, 252
 Peasants' Revolt, 361, 362, 376, 387
 Protestant Reformation, 442–46, *443, 445*
 rebellion in 1381, 362
 religious conflict between Spain and (sixteenth century), 467–68, *469*
 unification of, under Alfred the Great, 244–45
 *see also individual names of leaders*
Enkidu (*Epic of Gilgamesh* character), 12–14
environmental issues
 Black Death and impact on, 360–61
 "Columbia Exchange" and effects on, 457–58, *458*
 environmental sciences during scientific revolution, 534, *534*–35, *535*
Epaminondas (Theban leader), 113–15
Ephesus, marble streets of, *141*
ephors, 90
*Epic of Gilgamesh,* 12–14, 63
Epicureanism, 133–34
Epicurus (Hellenistic philosopher), 133–34
Erasistratus (Hellenistic scientist), 137
Erasmus, Desiderius, *405,* 405–7, 432, 439
Eratosthenes of Alexandria, 137
Ermengarde of Carcassone, 318
Esarhaddon (Assyrian king), 68
Eschenbach, Wolfram von, 318
*Essays* (Montaigne), 484
Essenes, 184
Estates General (France), Louis XIV and, 500
ethics
 Aristotle on, 119
 Stoicism, 133–34
Ethiopia, 226
Etruria, 149
Etruscans, 148–49, *149*
Eucharist, 301, 344–45, 387
Euclid (Hellenistic mathematician), 137
Euphrates river, 8
Euripides (Greek playwright), 97, 121
Europe
 consolidation of (1100–1250), overview, 285–86
 expansion of (950–1100), 249–55, *251, 252, 253, 255*
 extension of commerce and settlement in Late Middle Ages, 334–42, *335, 336, 337, 340, 341, 342*
 impact of Crusades on western Europe, 278
 terminology for, 250
 *see also individual names of countries*
European-Atlantic world integration (sixteenth-seventeenth centuries)

arts, 483–91, *486, 487, 488, 489, 490*
  chronology, 454
  colonialism, 455–65, *458, 460, 462, 463, 464*
  crisis of kingship in England, 477–83, *478, 479, 482*
  religious wars in Europe, 465–70, *466, 467, 468, 469, 470*
  Thirty Years' War, 470–77, *472, 474, 475*
Evans, Sir Arthur, 49
Eve (biblical character), 70, 206
Exchequer, 287
excommunication, 270
*Execrabilis* (Council of Constance), 385
*Execution of the Streltsy, 515*
Exodus, 70
exploration (fifteenth-sixteenth centuries)
  America as goal of, 418
  by Columbus, 417–19
  consequences of, 422
  gold as goal of, 419–22
  map, *415*
  by Portugal, 412–17, 418–19
  scientific revolution and, 525
  slavery and, 416–17
  Spanish *consquitadores, 419,* 419–22, *420*
eyeglasses, invention of, 336, *336*
Ezekiel (Jewish prophet), 72
Ezra (Jewish prophet), 72

fables, inception of, 320
fairs, organized systems of, 258–59
Faith, doctrine of the, 308
Faith, Saint (Sainte Foy), 268, *268*
*faqirs,* 229
Fatimah (Muhammad's daughter), 227
Fatimids, 273, 278
female beauty, as ideal, 118, *118*
Ferdinand (Holy Roman emperor), 470–73
Ferdinand of Aragon, 294, 411–12, *412*
Ferrara, duke of, 397
Fertile Crescent, *11*
feudalism, 262
Ficino, Marsilio, 392
fief/fiefdom, 205, 263, 294, 295, *295*
Filmer, Robert, 499, *505*
Fioravanti, Aristotele, *411*
First Cataract (Nile River), 22
First Intermediate Period (ancient Egypt), 29, 42
First Punic War, 156–58, *158*
FitzStephen, William, 318
Five Good Emperors, 169, 189
Flanders
  expansion of England, Late Middle Ages, 350
  Middle Ages trade in, 258–59
  poverty in sixteenth-seventeenth centuries, 465
  sovereignty in Late Middle Ages, 345, 346
Fleury-Richard, François, *532*
Florence
  Medici family of (*see* Medici family)
  Renaissance in, 370–71, 392, 394, 396
*foederati,* 203

food, asceticism and, 198–200
football, gladiators compared to, *160*
Fourth Lateran Council of 1215, 299–300, 302–3, 308–9, 314
France
  Albigensian Crusade, 300
  Alsace-Lorraine, 243
  Black Death and impact on, 361
  Catholic League, 447
  Charles V (Holy Roman emperor) and, 439
  emergence, *288,* 289–90
  expulsion of Jews, 309
  Fronde, 477
  Hundred Years' War, 349–50, 352, 375–79, *376*
  Hundred Years' War consequences, 409
  Jacquerie Rebellion, 361–62
  Joan of Arc, *377,* 377–79
  Lascaux cave paintings, 5, *5*
  Louis XIV and absolutism, 493–502, *494, 496, 497, 500*
  nobility in Late Middle Ages, 363
  Normandy, 243
  Richelieu and, 476–77
  sovereignty in Late Middle Ages, 345–47, *346, 350*
  Thirty Years War and French power in Europe and North America, 473, *475,* 475–77
  Treaty of Utrecht, 508–9, *509*
  wars of religion in (sixteenth century), 465–66
  *see also individual names of leaders*
Francis (pope), *383*
Franciscan order, 308
Francis of Assisi, Saint, 306–7
Franks
  Abbasids and, 229
  legacy of, in Middle Ages, 255
  Louis VII, 287, 289
  overview, 203–4
  prosperity of, 232–35
Frederick I (Barbarossa; Holy Roman emperor), 290, 297
Frederick I (king of Prussia), 513
Frederick II (Holy Roman emperor), 300
Frederick III (elector of Saxony), 326
Frederick the Wise (elector of Saxony), 432–34
Frederick William (Great Elector of Prussia), 511–13, *514*
Frederick William I (the Great; king of Prussia), 513
"free-born Englishmen," 480
French Academy of Sciences, 541
French language, 250
French Revolution
  Cluny as target during, *266*
  overview, 290
French Wars of Religion, *266*
*Frequens* (Council of Constance), 384
fresco (Cella Septichora), *197*
fresco (Minoan), *50*
Fronde, 477
Gaius (Roman jurist), 177

Galen (second century scientist), 137, 207
Galerius (Roman emperor), 193, *193*, 195
Galilee, *182, 183*
Galileo Galilei
  birth of, 524
  Church challenge to, 526
  influence on Newton, 544
  Inquisition and, *532,* 532–34
  scientific theories of, 529–34, *531*
*Galileo Galilei Before the Inquisition* (Fleury-Richard), *532*
galleon model (Spanish), *414*
Gallican Catholics of France, 501, 503
garden design (Muslim, Middle Ages), *282*
Garden of Eden, 206
Gassendi, Pierre, 542–43
Gath (Philistine citadel), 56
Gaul, 208–9, 229, 232–35, 238–39
gender
  courts, chivalry, aristocracy of High Middle Ages, 315–21, *316, 317*
  patriarchal family and Protestant Reformation, 439, 441–42
  Roman cults and masculinity, 198–200
General Council (of Cromwell's army), 480
*General Scholium* (Newton), 545, 546
Genesis, 3, 12–13, 70, 535
genetics, DNA analysis from ancient Greece, 51
Geneva, Calvinism in, 438–39
Genghis Khan, 326–27, 331
Genoa, 333, 334–36
geology, scientific revolution and, *534,* 534–35, *535*
George I (king of England), 504
George III (king of England), 194
*Germania* (Tacitus), 173
Germany
  Anglo-Norman kings of England compared to kings of, 265
  German kingship and Holy Roman Empire, 290
  Late Middle Ages, 380
  Lotharingia, 243
  Protestant Reformation in, *426,* 426–34, *427, 428, 429, 430, 431, 432, 433, 434, 439, 440*
  *see also individual names of leaders; individual names of wars*
gerousia, 90
Gilgamesh (*Epic of Gilgamesh*), 12–14, 63
Giotto di Bondone, 338, *342*
Giza, pyramids at, 28, *29*
gladiators
  football compared to, *160*
  Roman Empire, *172,* 172–75, *173*
Glaucus of Lykia (*Iliad* character), 78
Globe Theatre (London), *486*
Glorious Revolution, 504–5
gold
  colonialism in sixteenth-seventeenth centuries, 463–65, *465*
  exploration (fifteenth-sixteenth centuries) and, 419–22

gold, (*Continued*)
  medieval demand for gold of Africa, 334
  Mongol robe, *328*
  Portugese pursuit of African gold, 413
  Vikings pursuit of, 258
Gold Coast (Africa), 413
Golden Age, of classical Greece, *94*, 96–101, *98, 99, 100, 101*
Golden Age, of painting, 488–90, *489, 490*
Golden Age, of Roman Empire, 172–73
Golden Horde, khanate of the, 333
Golden House, 172
Gospels, 183, 185, 188, 237
Gothic cathedrals, 320–21, *321*
Goths, 203, 208–9
Gracchi, 162–63
Gracchus, Gaius, 162
Gracchus, Tiberius, 162
*Grænlendinga Saga*, 338–39
Granada (Spain), 411
Grand Duchy of Muscovy, 327–28, 409, *410*
Gratian, 312, 314
gravity, theory of, 545–48
Great Britain
  battle of Hastings, 263–65, *264*
  name of, 509
  York Castle (England), *262*
  *see also individual names of leaders*
Great Famine, 350–56, *351*, 351–53, *353*
Great Khan, title of, 330
Great Northern War, 518–19
Great Pyramid of Khufu, 28, *29*
Great Schism, 381, *382*, 382–83, 426
Great Umayyad Mosque, 227
Great Wall, 326
Greece, 74–109, 110–45
  Athens, 87, 87–89, *88, 93*
  Attic peninsula, *79*
  chronology, 74
  culture of Archaic Greece, 80–87, *81, 82, 83, 84*
  downfall of Greek poleis, *112*, 112–15
  downfall of Greek poleis, artistic and intellectual response, 115–19, *116, 117, 118*
  emergence of Greek poleis, *76*, 76–80
  golden age of classical Greece, *94*, 96–101, *98, 99, 100, 101*
  Greek diaspora, *131*, 131–32
  Greek poleis transition to cosmopolis, 130–32
  Hellenistic kingdoms and, 126–30, *129, 131, 132*
  Hellenistic worldviews, 133–42, *137, 140, 141, 142*
  Hesiod (Greek poet), 39–40
  "Inland Expedition" and, 111, 113, *113*
  Islam and, 227
  literature of, rediscovered during Renaissance, 367
  Miletus, 92
  Minoan Crete and Mycenaean Greece, 48–54, *49, 50, 51, 52*
  overview, 75–76

Peloponnesian War ("greatest war in history"), 101–5, *103*
  Persian Empire and, 65
  Persian wars and, 92–96, *95, 96*
  poleis of, overview, 87
  Pythagoreans and Sophists, 105–6
  rise of Macedonia and, 111–12, *121, 121*–26, *122, 123, 124, 125, 126,* 127
  Socrates and, 104–5, *106,* 106–7, *107*
  Sparta, 89–92, *90, 91*
Greece, archaic
  aristocracy, tyranny, and democracy in, 84–85
  colonization and Panhellenism, 80–82, *81*
  culture of, overview, 80
  hoplite warfare, 83–84, *84*
  importance of horses to, 83, *83*
  male beauty as ideal, 82, *82*
  poetry of, 85–87
  Sappho of Lesbos and, 86
  Tyrtaeus of Sparta and, 85
Greece, classical
  art and architecture, 98–100, *99*
  Athenian literature and theater, 97–98, *98*
  daily life in Athens, 100–101, *101*
  Golden Age of, *94*, 96–101, *98, 99, 100, 101*
  Pericles, 96–97
  Roman expansion compared to, 150
  scientific revolution and, 525
Greece, Mycenaean, *49*, 50–51, *51, 52, 53,* 76
"Greek fire," 217, *217*
Greek Orthodox Church, 220
Gregorian chant, 236
Gregory I (the Great; pope), 236–37
Gregory of Tours, 230
Gregory VII (pope), 265, 269–70, 300–301
Gregory X (pope), *383*
Gregory XI (pope), 382
Gregory XIII (pope), 32, 164
Griffin Warrior (tomb), 50–51, *51*
Grimmelshausen, Hans Jakob Christoph von, 471
Gubla (Phoenician city), 54
guest friendship concept, 77, 78
guild system
  inception of, 320
  rebellion by guilds in 1378 (Italy), 362
gunpowder, invention of, 524
Gustavus Adolphus (king of Sweden), 473
Gutenberg, Johannes, 391–92

Habsburg dynasty
  absolutism and, 495, 509–14, *510*
  Thirty Years' War, 470–73
  war and balance of power (1661–1715), 508
Hadrian (Roman emperor), 169, 172, 189
Hadrian's Wall, *168*
*Haec Sancta Synodus* (Council of Constance), 384
Hagia Sophia (church), 221–22, *222*
Halley, Edmond, 544, *545*
*Hamlet* (Shakespeare), 487, 523
Hammurabi (king of Babylon)
  Code of Hammurabi, 18–19, *20*–21, *21*

  empire of, 18
  legacy of, 19–21
Hannibal (Carthaginian leader), 157
Hanseatic League, 361
haram, 229
*Harmonies of the World, The* (Kepler), 529
Harold Godwinson (king of England), 263–65, *264*
*Harvesters* (Bruegel the Elder), 488
Harvey, William, 540
Hasdrubal (Carthaginian leader), 157
Hastings, battle of, 263–65, *264*
Hatshepsut (queen of Egypt), *43*, 43–45, *45, 46*
Hattusilis III (king of Hittites), 42, 53
Hawkins, Sir John, 468
Hebrew Bible
  Book of Deuteronomy, 71–72
  Garden of Eden, 206
  Genesis, 3, 12–13, 70, 535
  on Maccabees, 135
  as "Old Testament," 183, 187
Hebrews
  development of Hebrew monotheism, 67–71, *70*
  early Judaism, *71*, 71–72
  Hebrew Bible, 56–58
  King Solomon's reign, 58–59
  monotheism of, 67–72, *70, 71*
  scriptures of, 56–58
  tribes of Judah and Israel, 58, *59,* 60–61
Hecataeus (Milesian philosopher), 92
heliocentric universe concept, 523–24
Heliogabalus (Roman emperor), 192
Hellenic League, formation of, 96
Hellenistic period
  architecture and sculpture, *140*, 140–41, *141, 142*
  Byzantine Empire and, 218
  Christianity in, 185–87, *186*
  Greek poleis transition to cosmopolis, 130–32
  kingdoms of, 126–30, *129, 131, 132*
  literature, 141–42
  religious variety during, 134–36
  Roman control following, *158,* 158–59
  science, 136–37, *137*
  skepticism, 134
  Stoicism and Epicureanism, 133–34
  worldviews, overview, 133
helots, 89
Henry I (king of England), 287
Henry II (king of England), 287–89, 319
Henry III (Holy Roman emperor), 269
Henry III (king of France), 466
Henry IV (German emperor), 269–70, 290
Henry IV (king of England), 377, 413
Henry IV (king of France), 465–66, *466,* 475
Henry IV (king of Germany), 265
Henry "the Navigator" (prince of Portugal), 413, 417
Henry V (king of England), 376–77
Henry VI (Holy Roman emperor), 290
Henry VI (king of England), 379
Henry VII (king of England), 379, 487

Henry VIII (king of England), 442–43, *443*
Hephaistion (Alexander the Great's lover), 126
heresy
    early Christianity and, 197–98
    Innocent III and, 300, 305–8
Hermann of Carinthia, 278–79
Herod Antipas, 183
Herodotus of Halicarnassus
    on Alexander the Great, 124
    on civilization of Greece, 75–76, 100
    on Great Pyramid, 28
    historic works of, 98
    Ionian Revolt and, 93
    on Persian Empire, 64
    on Phoenician colonies, 54
heroic tradition, Homer and, 77, 78
Herophilus of Chalcedon, 137
Hesiod (Greek poet), 39–40, 51, 77
Hevelius, Johannes, *541*
hierarchy, of Christian Church, 197
hieratic scripts, 27
hieroglyphs, 27, *27*–28
*Hijra,* 223
Hildegard of Bingen, *304,* 304–5, *305*
Hinduism, mathematics and, 280
Hipparchus, 137
*hippeis* (horsemen), 82
Hippo, Saint Augustine of, 206
Hispanioloa, 475
*History of the English Church and People, The*
    (Bede), 213
*History of the Goths* (Cassiodorus), 210
Hittites, 41–42, 48, 49–50, 51, 53
Hobbes, Thomas, 484, 541
Holbein, Hans (the Younger), *443*
holiness, pursuit of, 345
Holland
    League of Augsburg, 508–9
Holy Roman Empire
    defined, 242
    German kingship and Holy Roman Empire,
        290
    Habsburg dynasty and, 510–11
    Late Middle Ages and conflict in Italy,
        379–80
    Late Middle Ages conflict in Italy, 379–80
    Thirty Years' War, 470–73
holy war, doctrines of, 278
Homer (Greek poet), 49, 77, 78, 97
*Homme, L'* (Descartes), *537*
*Homo sapiens,* defined, 4
homosexuality
    male beauty as Greek ideal, 84
    Theban Sacred Band, *112,* 112–15, 122
Honorius (Roman emperor), 203
Hooke, Robert, 535, 540, *540,* 544
hoplite warfare, 83–84, *84,* 89
Horace (Quintus Horatius Flaccus), 173
*Consequences of War, The* (Rubens), 488, *489*
Horus (Egyptian god), 26, 30
Hospital of St. John at Jerusalem, 297
Host, 301–3
House of Wisdom, 331
Hugh Capet, 350

Huguenots, 465–66, 501
Hulagu Khan, *329,* 330
human body, asceticism and, 198–200
humanism
    Castiglione on, 397
    northern European Renaissance and, *405,*
        405–7
    Renaissance, 367–69, 371, 525
*humanitas,* 109
Hundred Years' War, 349–50, 352, 375, *376,*
    379
    cannons of fifteenth century, *375*
    Henry V, 376–77
    Joan of Arc and, 377–79
    legacy of, 379
    phases of, 375, *376*
Hungary
    Habsburg dynasty and, 511, 512–13
    High Middle Ages, 292
    Huns' conquest of, 251
    Mongol Empire and, 327
Huns, 203, 204
hunter-gatherer societies, 5, 6
Hus, Jan, *387*
Hussites, 387–88
Huygens, Christian, 540
Hvalsey (Greenland), church at, *335*
Hydaspes, battle of, 125
Hyksos, 42

ibn Munqidh, Usama, 277
Ibn Rushd, 314–14, *315*
Ice, battle on the, 293
Iconoclasm
    Byzantine Empire and Orthodox Christian-
        ity, 218–19, *219*
    legacy of, 219–21
iconography, of Egyptian pharaohs, 44
Ides of March, 165, *165*
Ignatius Loyola, 448–50
*Iliad* (Homer), 77, 78, 111
Ilkhanate, 328–30
Illinois Indians, 475
Imhoteph, pharaoh of Egypt, *27, 28,* 28–29
*Imitation of Christ* (Thomas à Kempis), *386*
imperialism
    consequences of Roman imperialism,
        159–62
Inanna (Akkadian goddess), 14, 17
Incas, roads of, 15
India, Portugese exploration and, 413
Indo-European languages/peoples, *41,* 41–42
Indo-European Medes, 63
Indonesia, 326
inductive method of reasoning, 536, 538
indulgences, doctrine of, 428–29, 447
infidels, Innocent III and, 300
Ingeborg Håkansdotter (duchess of Sweden),
    seal of, *341*
"Inland Expedition," 111, 113, *113*
Innocent III (pope), 298–300, 305–8
Innocent VIII (pope), 484
Inquisition, *532,* 532–34
*Inspiration of Saint Jerome* (Reni), *448*

*Institutes* (Roman law), 216
*Institutes, The* (Cassiodorus), 210
*Institutes of the Christian Religion* (Calvin), 437
*Instruction of Amenemhet* (ancient Egypt),
    34–35
*Instruction of Ptah-Hotep, The* (ancient Egypt),
    35
intellectualism
    Christianity's worldview, 205–7
    Crusades and, 286
    High Middle Ages, *309,* 309–15, *310, 313,*
        *315*
    leading to scientific revolution, 524–26
    philosophy of Plato and Aristotle, 116–19,
        *117*
    reform during fourth century B.C.E., 119
    reform during Late Middle Ages, *386,*
        386–88, *389*
    Renaissance humanism, 367–69
international law, of Roman Empire, 178
Investiture Conflict, 269–70, 300–301
Ionia, 79–80, *91, 92*
Ionian Revolt, 93–95
Iran (ancient), Indo-European Medes of, 63
Iraq, Ubaid culture, 8–9
Ireland
    Elizabeth I and Protestantism in, 446
    rebellion of 1565, 468
Irene (empress of Holy Roman Empire), 242
Iron Age, 38–73
    Aegean civilization, 48–54, *49, 50, 51, 52*
    Assyrian Empire, 41, *41,* 47, 54, 59–64,
        *62, 63, 64*
    chronology, 38
    Early Iron Age, 54–59, *55, 56, 57, 59*
    Hebrew monotheism, 67–72, *70, 71*
    Indo-European languages and peoples, *41,*
        41–42
    Late Bronze Age and transition to, 39–42,
        *41, 47*–48, *48*
    Neo-Assyrian smelting techniques, 63
    New Kingdom of Egypt, 42–47, *43, 44,*
        *45, 46*
    overview, 15
    Persian Empire, 64–67, *65, 66, 67*
    trade in, 40
"iron century," 495
Isabella (queen of Aragon and Castile), 294,
    411–12, *412, 413*
Isabella (queen of France), 349
Isaiah, 71
Ishtar (Akkadian goddess), 17
Ishtar gate, *71*
Isis (Egyptian goddess), 30, 134
Islam
    Abbasid dynasty, 227–28, 229, 245–46,
        270, 381
    ancient Egyptian pyramids and, 28
    Byzantine Empire and, 217, 225–27, *226*
    Canons of the Fourth Lateran Council on,
        303
    commerce and industry, 228
    conversion of Muslims to Christianity,
        Middle Ages, 308

Islam, (Continued)
  Crusades against, 277–78, 297
  end of golden age of, 331
  end of Muslim rule in Spain, 411–12
  High Middle Ages and culture of Muslim
    west, 278–83, 279, 281, 282
  intellectualism of High Middle Ages, 309,
    314–15
  mobility, opportunity, status, 229
  Mongol Empire and, 329–30, 371
  Muhammad and teachings of, 223–25
  neighbors of Byzantium, 229
  Order of Christ, 413
  papermaking and, 228, 228–29
  Pepin's defeat at Narbonne, 239
  Protestant Reformation and religious
    warfare, 439
  rise of Ottoman Empire and, 374
  Shi'ite-Sunni schism, 227
  Umayyad dynasty, 227, 227–28, 243
  Visigoths converted by, 215
Isocrates (Athenian orator), 119
Israel
  Jericho, 7–8
  tribes of Israel, 58
Israel, ancient
  kingdom of, 59
  tribe of Israel (Early Iron Age), 58, 59,
    60–61
Italy
  art, seventeenth century, 488–90
  Black Death and impact on, 361
  Constantine I in, 195
  Gregory the Great and, 236–37
  Holy Roman Empire and Late Middle Ages
    conflict in, 379–80
  Justinian's impact on western Roman
    Empire, 215
  Matilda of Tuscany, 265, 265–66
  medieval drama in, 366
  papal power, Late Middle Ages, 342
  rebellion by guilds in 1378, 362
  Renaissance beginning in, 366, 366–71,
    368
  Renaissance politics of, and philosophy of
    Machiavelli, 396, 396–97
  Renaissance politics of Christian Europe,
    409–12, 410, 411, 412
  revenge of Venice, 298
  Roman expansion in, 150–52, 151
  states of Italy (c. 1494), 396
  towns of eleventh century and citizenship,
    319–20
  women scientists of scientific revolution in,
    541–42
  see also individual names of leaders
"I think, therefore I am," 537
Ivan III (the Great; tsar of Russia), 409, 411
ivory pyxis, 281

Jacquerie Rebellion, 361–62
Jadwiga (female "king" of Poland), 380,
  380–81
Jagiello (grand duke of Lithuania), 380–81

Jagiellonian dynasty, 380, 380–81, 381
Jagiellonian University, 380, 386
Jamaica, 494
James, Saint, 186, 267
James I (king of England), 477, 536
James II (king of England), 503, 504
Jansen, Cornelius (bishop of Ypres), 484, 501
Jansenism, 484
Jason (High Priest), 135
Jeremiah (Jewish prophet), 70, 71
Jericho, 7–8
Jerome, Saint, 205, 207, 371, 448
Jerusalem
  Christian conquest of, 275–78
  as Crusader State, 297, 297
  Crusades and, 290
  first Temple, 64, 69
  Jesus in, 183
  King David and, 58
  second Temple, 64, 183–85, 184, 187, 225
  urban planning during Roman Empire, 176
Jesuit order, 448–50, 501
Jesus of Nazareth
  birth of, 168
  crucifixion, 347
  Eucharist, 302, 303, 344–45
  hierarchy of Church and, 197
  Investiture Conflict and, 300
  life and death of, 182, 182–85, 185
  orthodoxy, heresy, and imperial authority of
    Christianity, 197–98
  women's status in Christianity and,
    198–200
Joan of Arc, 230, 230, 377, 377–79, 386
Joan of Sicily, 297
João I (king of Portugal), 413
João II (king of Portugal), 413
John (king of England), 289–90, 299
John III Sobieski (king of Poland), 511,
    512–13
John of Damascus, 220
John of Leyden, 436–37
John the Baptist, 183, 186
Jones, Sir William, 41
Jonsen, Ben, 486, 487
Jordan, 7–8
Josiah (king of Judah), 71
journeymen, 320
Judah, kingdom of, 58, 59, 60–61, 63, 70–71
Judaism
  Babylonian Captivity and, 343
  Black Death blamed on Jews, 355, 356
  Byzantine Empire and, 217
  Canons of the Fourth Lateran Council on,
    303
  Christianity inception and, 184, 184–85,
    185–87
  conversion of Jews to Christianity, Middle
    Ages, 308–9
  Crusades against, 275–78, 296
  early Islam and, 223–24
  early monotheism and, 67–72, 70, 71
  expulsion from Europe, Late Middle Ages,
    309, 347

  expulsion from Spain, Renaissance, 411–12
  Hellenistic period and, 131, 135–36
  inception of, 40
  intellectualism of High Middle Ages, 315
  "Jewish badge," 300, 300
  Jews as money lenders in Middle Ages, 261
  literature and poetry, Middle Ages, 280, 281
  Persia and rise of Rabbinic Judaism, 215
  pogroms, 292
  Rabbinic Judaism, 315
  under Roman Empire, 187–89
  Roman rule and, 147–48, 170
  Sephardic Jews, defined, 412
  Torah, 72
Judea, 182, 183
Jugurtha of Numidia, 163
Julia Domna (Roman empress), 190–92, 191
Julia Maesa (Roman empress), 192
Julia Mamea (Roman empress), 192
Julian (the Apostate; Roman emperor), 200
Julian calendar, 32, 164
Julianne of Norwich, 386
Julius Caesar, 32, 479
Julius II (pope), 429–32
"junkers," 513
jurists, during Roman Empire, 177–78
"justification by faith" doctrine, of Luther, 427
Justinian (Roman emperor), 214, 214–17,
    216, 217
Justinianic Plague, 215, 356
Juvenal (Roman satirist), 173

ka, 28, 30–31, 33
Kaaba (shrine), 223, 224
Kadesh, battle of, 47
Karlsefni, Thorfin, 338–39
Kassites, 42
katharsis (catharsis), 97
Keftiu, 51
Kempe, Margery, 386
Kepler, Johannes, 528–29, 549
Keynes, John Maynard, 547–48
Khamerernebty II (queen of Egypt), 30, 33
khora, 80
Khufu (pharaoh of Egypt), 28, 29
Kiev
  High Middle Ages, 292
  Mongol Empire and, 327–28
"king in Parliament" (England), 504
King James Bible, 534
King Lear (Shakespeare), 487
"king's English," 392
kingship, Hammurabi's changes to, 21
King William's War, 508–9
Kirch, Gottfried, 543
Kircher, Athanasius, 535
Knights Hospitaller, 297
knights/knighthood, 262, 315–16, 316
Knights of the Garter, 363
Knights Templar, 297, 298, 347
Knossos (palace), 49, 50
"knowledge is power," 536
Knox, John, 438
Kochanowski, Jan, 486

Kochanowski, Ursula, 486
Korb, Johann Georg, 516
Kosovo, battle of (1389), 372
*kouros,* 82
Krak des Chevaliers, 297, *297*
Kraków (Poland), market square of, *260*
Kremlin, 409
Kublai Khan, 326, 328, 330, 332

Lancastrian dynasty, 379
language
    of Akkadians, 16–17
    Christianity and Constantine, 201–2
    Christianity inception and, 185
    cuneiform, 10, *10*
    education in Middle Ages, 310
    English usage in Church of England, 444
    Greek used in Roman Republic, 161
    hieroglyphs, *27,* 27–28
    Indo-European languages and peoples, *41,*
        41–42
    Islamic influence on western Europe,
        282–83
    Justinian and, 214–15
    "king's English," 392
    Latin used in Roman Empire, 172–73
    Linear A (Minoan script), 49–50
    Linear B (Minoan script), 49–50, *50,* 76
    Old Church Slavonic, 271
    papyrus of Gubla, 54
    of Philistines, 55–56
    Protestant Reformation on teaching of
        Bible, 441
    Rosetta Stone, *27,* 27–28
    of Sumerian cities, 11
    transition from Frankish to French, 250
*Laocoön* group (sculpture), 141, *142*
Lascaux, cave paintings of, *5, 5*
*Last Judgment* (Michelangelo), 401
*Last Supper, The* (Leonardo da Vinci), *399,*
    399–400
Late Bronze Age, 47–48, *48*
Latin alphabet, 251
Latin Church of Rome, 220
Latins, 149–50, 158
Law of the Twelve Tables, 153, 155
League of Augsburg, 508–9
legal issues
    "big book of fiefs" (King Alfonso II of
        Aragon), 205, 294, *295*
    Code of Hammurabi, 18–19, 20–21, *21*
    codification of Roman law, 216–17
    Law of Moses, 71–72
    Law of the Twelve Tables, 153, 155
    legal code of Ur, 17–18
    Neo-Assyriam, 61
    *Politics* (Aristotle), 120
    Roman Empire and reach of Roman law,
        177–78
    *see also individual names of acts*
Legnica, battle of, *328*
Leibniz, Gottfried, 543
Leo III (Byzantine emperor), 219
Leo III (pope), 242

Leo IX (pope), 269
Leo X (pope), 429, 432
Leonardo da Vinci, 398–400, *399, 400,* 402
Leonardo Fibonacci, 278
León-Castile, 294
Leopold I (Holy Roman emperor), 511,
    512–13
Lepidus, Marcus Aemilius, 166
*Letters on Sunspots* (Galileo), 530
Levant
    Early Iron Age, 54–59, *55*
    Hebrews of, 57, 58
*Leviathan* (Hobbes), 484
Leyster, Judith, *490, 491*
liberal arts concept, 310
library of Nineveh, 63
light, Newton on, 544–48, *545, 547*
Lindau Gospels, *237*
Lindisfarne Gospels, *237*
Linear A (Minoan script), 49–50
Linear B, 76
Linear B (Minoan script), 49–50, *50,* 76
Lingsberg Runestone, *251*
literature
    of classical Greece, 97–98, *98*
    classical learning and Christianity, 207–10,
        *210*
    emergence of prose, 116
    Golden Age, Roman Empire, 172–73
    Hellenistic period, 141–43
    of High Middle Ages, 318
    Late Middle Ages, 338–40
    Muslim, Middle Ages, 280–81
    of northern European Renaissance, 407–8
    reading ancient texts during Renaissance,
        366, 371, 526
    Renaissance, *393,* 394–97
    seventeenth century, 483
    Silver Age, Roman Empire, 173
    use of rhyme in High Middle Ages, 320
    writing following Black Death, 363–64, *364*
Lithuania
    Commonwealth of Poland and Lithuania
        (sixteenth-seventeenth centuries), 507,
        *507*
    Jagiello (grand duke), 380–81
    Poland-Lithuania and Great Northern War,
        519
    Polish-Lithuania Commonwealth, 474,
        507, *507,* 512–13
    Thirty Years War, 474
Livy (historian), *242,* 367
Loarre Castle, *294*
Locke, John, *505,* 505–6, 545
logic, Descartes on, 540
Lollards, 387, 388
Lombard, Peter, 314
Lombard League, 290
longboat (Viking), *245*
Longinus (legionnaire), 171–72
lordships, 261–63, 267–69
Lorenzo the Magnificent (Medici ruler), 396,
    398
Lothair I (Holy Roman emperor), 243

Louis, as name of French kings, 233
Louis IX (Saint Louis; king of France),
    346–47, 475
Louis the German, 243
Louis the Pious, 243
Louis VII (king of France), 287, 289
Louis XII (king of France), 409
Louis XIII (king of France), 476, 477
Louis XIV (king of France)
    absolutism, overview, 493–94, *494, 495*
    absolutism and patriarchy, 498
    administration and centralization by,
        499–500
    Charles II (king of England) and, 503–4
    Colbert and royal finance, 501
    colonialism under, 501–2
    invasion of Dutch Republic, 506
    League of Augsburg and War of Spanish
        Succession, 508–9
    religious policies of, 501
    Royal Academy of Sciences, *547, 548*
    staging of authority by, 495–99, *496, 497,*
        *500*
"love feasts," 187, *187*
Lower Egypt, 22, 42
Luanda, slave trade and, 462
Lucifer, 305
Lucius Junius Brutus, 150
Lucretia (Roman), 150, 152, 154, 156, 165
Lucretius (Roman writer), 161
lugals, 12–14
Luke, Book of, 185, 188
lunar calendar, 15
*Lusiads* (Portugese epic), 413
Luther, Martin
    biographical information, 426–27
    break with Rome, 429–32
    Calvinism and, 438, 439
    Charles V and condemnation at Worms,
        *432,* 432–33, *433, 434*
    effect of printing press invention and, *427,*
        429, *430,* 430–31, *431*
    German princes and Lutheran Church, 434
    "justification by faith" doctrine of, 427
    Ninety-Five Theses of, 425, 428–29
    overview, 425–26
    portrait, *426*
Lydia, kingdom of, 64–65, *65, 91, 92*

Ma'adi, 22
*ma'at,* 31, 34
*Macbeth* (Shakespeare), 487
Maccabees, 135
Macedonia
    Alexander's conquests, 122–26, *123, 124,*
        *125, 126*
    Antigonus, 130
    Islam and, 227
    Philip II, *121,* 121–22, *122*
    rise of, overview, 120
Machiavelli, Niccolò, 394, 395–97
Madeira, Portugese colonization of, 413, 417
Magellan, Ferdinand, 419
Magna Carta, 289

...ass, invention of, 524

...or, The (Velázquez), 488, 488
...s, Moses, 315
...us, 238
..., 413
...eauty, as Greek ideal, 82, 82, 84
...ry, Sir Thomas, 394–95
...mluk Sultanate of Egypt, 329–30
...andeville, John de, 325, 332
Mani (Persian prophet), 194
Manicheans, 194
Mannerism, 487
Mansur, al- (caliph), 227–28
Mantinea, battle of, 113–15
Marcion (second-century Christian scholar),
    187
Marcus Aurelius (Roman emperor), 169, 189
Marduk (Babylonian god), 18, 68
Marie de France, 318
Marie of Champagne, 318
marijuana, decriminalization of, 447
Marius, Gaius, 163
Mark Antony, 166, 167
Marlowe, Christopher, 486–87
marriage
    asceticism and, 199–200
    in Athens, 100
    Code of Hammurabi on, 19
    culture of High Middle Ages, 318
    Etruscans, 149
    founding of Rome and, 150
    Henry VIII and Protestant Reformation,
        442–43, 443
    mass marriage arranged by Alexander the
        Great, 125
    by priests, 300–301
    Protestant Reformation and Council of
        Trent on, 440
    Protestant Reformation and patriarchy, 439,
        441–42
    in Ptolemaic Egypt, 129
    reform of secular clergy (eleventh century),
        269
    in Roman Empire, 168
    Severan dynasty, 190
    in Sparta, 89
Mars (Roman god), 195
Martin V (pope), 383, 385
Marx, Karl, feudalism concept and, 263
Mary (Bloody Mary; queen of England),
    444–45, 468
Mary (Virgin), 303–5, 304
Mary Magdalene, 198
Mary of Modena, 503
Mary Stuart (queen of England), 503, 504,
    504–5
Mass
    doctrine of transubstantiation, 304
    inception of, 301–3
    Late Middle Ages, 344–45
Massachusetts Bay Colony, 468–70, 470, 483
Massacre of the Innocents, The (Bruegel the
    Elder), 488, 489

mastaba, 28
mathematics
    analytical geometry, 540
    education in Middle Ages, 310
    Galileo and, 529
    geometry, 106
    Hellenistic period, 136–37
    Kepler and, 529
    Muslim mathematicians, Middle Ages, 280
    Newton and, 544–48
Matilda of Tuscany, 265, 265–66
Matthew (Gospel), 197
Maximian (Roman emperor), 193, 193
Mazarin, Jules Raymond (cardinal), 477
measles, spread by European explorers,
    419–22
Mecca, 223, 224
mechanism view, 539, 540, 547
Medes, 124
Medici family
    Cardinal Giuliu de' Medici, 429
    Catherine de Medici, 465–66
    Cosimo de'Medici, 392, 533
    economic power, 336, 369, 379
    Galileo and, 531, 533
    Leo X (pope), 429, 432
    Lorenzo the Magnificent, 396, 398
    Piero de'Medici, 396
    The Prince (Machiavelli), 396
medicine
    Hellenistic period, 137, 137
    Muslim physicians, Middle Ages, 280
medievalism
    defined, 230, 230
    Medieval world (1250–1350), overview,
        325–26, 330
medieval monarchies
    Central and Eastern Europe, 290–92, 291
    emergence of France, 288, 289–90
    England, 287, 287–89, 288
    German kingship and Holy Roman Empire,
        290
    Magna Carta and, 289
    overview, 286
    "reconquest" of Spain, 293, 293–94, 294,
        309, 411–12
    Rus' and Novgorod Republic, 292–93
Medieval Warm Period, 255–57, 256
Medina, 223–24
Mediterranean world
    commerce and settlement, Late Middle
        Ages, 334–36
    European expansion (1000), 253, 253–54,
        257
    slave trade and fifteenth-century explora-
        tion, 413, 416–17
    see also individual names of countries
Meeting of Joachim and Anna, The (Giotto), 342
Mehmet II (the Conqueror; Ottoman sultan),
    372, 373
Menander (Greco-Bactrian king), 130
Menander (playwright), 116
Menkaure (pharaoh of Egypt), 30
Menshikov, Alexander, 517

Merian, Maria Sibylla, 543, 543–44
Merovech, 232
Merovingian dynasty, 232, 237, 238
Mesopotamia
    Fertile Crescent, 11
    Seleucids, 130
    urban development in, 8–9
    writing in, 9, 9–10, 10
Metamorphosis of the Insects of Surinam
    (Merian), 543, 544
metropolitans, 197
Mexico
    Aztec Empire of Mexico, 419, 419–22, 420,
        459
    Bartolomé de las Casas (bishop of Chiapas),
        421
Michael VIII Paleologus (Holy Roman
    emperor), 329
Michelangelo Buonarroti, 141, 400, 401, 402,
    403, 404
Micrographia (Hooke), 540
microscope, invention of, 524, 540
Middle Ages, Early, 212–47
    Carolingian Empire, 237–42, 238, 241, 242
    Carolingian Empire, collapse, 243–46, 244,
        245
    Christian conversion of Northwestern
        Europe, 230, 230–37, 235, 237
    chronology, 212
    defined, 213–14, 230, 230
    early Islam and, 223–29, 225, 226, 227, 228
    Justinian and, 214, 214–17, 216
    Roman Empire of Byzantium, 217, 217–23,
        219, 222, 232–33
    Rome's legacy and Christianity, 213–14
Middle Ages, High, 284–323
    agricultural revolution of Medieval Warm
        Period, 255–57, 256
    artistic renditions of, 299
    Central and Eastern Europe, 290–92, 291
    chronology, 248, 284
    consolidation of Europe (1100–1250),
        overview, 285–86, 286
    courts, cities, cathedrals, 315–21, 316, 317,
        321
    Crusades, 270–78, 271, 274, 275, 276,
        294–300, 296, 297, 300
    culture of Muslim west, 278–83, 279, 281,
        282
    East-Central Europe, 251, 252
    emergence of France, 288, 289–90
    England, 287, 287–89, 288
    European expansion (950–1100) and
        events leading to, 249–50, 253
    Frankish legacy, 255
    German kingship and Holy Roman Empire,
        290
    intellectualism, 309, 309–15, 310, 313,
        315
    Magna Carta, 289
    medieval monarchies, overview, 286
    Otto the Great, 254–55, 255
    "reconquest" of Spain, 293, 293–94, 294,
        309, 411–12

Roman Church religious reform and papal power, *266, 266–70, 268*
Rus', 251
Rus' and Novgorod Republic, 292–93
Scandinavian kingdoms and Cnut the Great, 252–53
unity and dissent in western Church, 300–309, *301, 304, 305*
urban growth and trade, 257–61, *258, 259, 260*
Viking initiatives, 250–51, *251*
violence, lordship, and monarchy of western Europe, 261–66, *262, 264, 265*
Middle Ages, Late, 324–57, 358–89
Black Death impact, *360,* 360–66, *363, 364*
chronology, *324, 358*
Council of Constance, 383–85
defined, 360
end of eastern Roman Empire, 371–74, *372, 373, 374*
extension of European commerce and settlement, 334–42, *335, 336, 337, 340, 341, 342*
Great Famine and Black Death, 350–56, *351, 353*
Great Schism, 381, *382,* 382–83
Henry V, 376–77
Holy Roman Empire and conflict in Italy, 379–80
Hundred Years' War, 349–50, 352, 375, *376, 379*
Jagiellonian dynasty in Poland, *380,* 380–81, *381*
Joan of Arc, *377,* 377–79
Medieval world (1250–1350), overview, 325–26, *330*
Mongol Empire and reorientation of west, 326–34, *327, 328, 329, 330, 331*
papal power and popular piety, 342–45, *343, 344*
rebirth and unrest (1350–1453), overview, 359–60
reformers, *386,* 386–88, *387*
Renaissance beginning in Italy, *366,* 366–71, *368*
spiritual challenges of, 385–86
struggles for sovereignty during, 345–50, *346, 347, 350*
warfare and nation building, overview, 374–75, *375*
Middle Kingdom (ancient Egypt), 25, 34–35
Middle Pasage, *462*
*migratio,* 150
Miletus, 92
military
Arab armies during Byzantine Empire, 217
asceticism and, 198–200
chivalry, 315–16, 319, 352
of early Romans, 150
exploration of fifteenth century and, 414–16, *415*
*foederati,* 203
hoplite warfare, 83–84, *84*

of Philip II and Alexander the Great, 121–26, *122*
Roman Republic, 162–63
of Sparta, 89–92
trireme warships, *93*
*see also individual names of wars*
millenarianism, 326
Miltiades (Athenian general), 94–95
Minoan Crete, 49–50, *50, 51*
Minos (king of Crete), 49
*missi,* 241
Mitanni, 42
Mithraism, 187, 195, 198–200
Moabites, 58
Modestinus (Roman jurist), 177
monasticism
asceticism and, 199
Benedictine order, 236, 252
Cistercian order, 301
Dominican order, 308
Franciscan order, 308
Luther on, 429
Mass and, 301–3
monastic education, 208–9
monastic reform movement, *266,* 266–67
Protestant Reformation and, 426
secular clergy and reform (eleventh century), 267–69
of seventh century, 234–36
Mongol Empire
bridging east and west, *331,* 331–34
expansion, 326–27, *327*
Grand Duchy of Muscovy, 327–28, 409, *410*
Mongol Ilkhanate, 328–30
Muscovy and Mongol Khanate, 327–28, *328*
overview, 326, *330*
*Pax Mongolica* and consequences, 330–31, *371, 372*
monolatry, 69–71, *70*
monotheism
of early Hebrews, 67–72, *70, 71*
Hebrew/Judaic, 67–71, *70, 71*
of Islam, 223, 279
*see also individual names of religions*
Montaigne, Michel de, 484, 485
Moore, R. I., 322
More, Sir Thomas, *406, 407,* 407, 443
*Morte d'Arthur, Le* (Malory), 394–95
mosaic (Roman Empire), *175*
mosaic (St. Peter's Basilica), *196*
Moscow
cathedral, *411*
Grand Duchy of Muscovy, 327–28, 409, *410*
Ivan the Great, 409
Moses (Jewish prophet), 56, 57, 71–72
*mos maiorum* (code of the elders), 153–54
Muhammad (Muslim prophet), 223–25
mummies, of ancient Egypt, 30–33
Münster (Germany), Anabaptists of, *436,* 436–37
music
education in Middle Ages, 310

Gregorian chant, 236
of northern European Renaissance, 408–9
use of rhyme in High Middle Ages, 320
Mussi, Gabriele de', 354
Mycenaean Greece, *49,* 50–51, *51, 52,* 53, 76
mystery cults (Roman), 161–62

Naples, Charles VII (king of France) in, 409
Naram-Sin of Akkad, 17
Narmer (king of Egypt), 24, 26
Narmer Palette, 25, 26
natives of Americas
colonialism of sixteenth-seventeenth centuries and, 456–57
English colonialism and, 468–70, *470*
European explorers' treatment of, 418
Illinois Indians, *475*
slaves at Potosi, 461
naturalism, 337
natural law, of Roman Empire, 178
naval technology/navigation, exploration of fifteenth century and, 414–16, *415*
Navarre, 294
navigation equipment, invention of, 336
Near East, early civilizations of, 4
Nebuchadnezzar (Chaldean king), 72, 126
Nefertiti (queen of Egypt), 46, 47
Neferty, prophecies of, 35
Neferure (queen of Egypt), 43
Nehemiah (governor of Judea), 72
Neo-Assyrian Empire, 60–61, *62, 63,* 63–64, 70–71, 226
Neolithic Era
defined, 4
Neolithic Revolution, 5, 6–7, *7, 8*
Neoplatonism, 194–95, 198, 525
Nero (Roman emperor), 169, 172, 189
Nerva (Roman emperor), 169, 189
Netherlands
Dutch Republic as exception to absolutist rule, 506–7
European poverty in sixteenth-seventeenth centuries and, 465, *467*
revolt of (sixteenth century), 466–67, *468*
Neustria, 239, 243
Nevsky, Alexander, 293
*New Atlantis* (Bacon), 536–37
New France, immigration to, 466
New Kingdom of Egypt
Akhenaten's reign in, *46,* 46–47
Hatshepsut's legacy, *43,* 43–45, *45*
Hyksos and, 42
pharaohs of eighteenth dynasty, 42–43
religious change and political change in, 45–46
Tutankhamun and, *46, 47*
New Model Army, 478
Newport, Christopher, 457
New Spain
slaves at Potosi, 461
social hierarchies in, 459
Thirty Years' War and, 473
Newton, Isaac, 524, 544–48, *545, 547*

New World
  Essays (Montaigne) on barbarism of, 485
  exploration/conquests, 417–22, 418, 419, 420
  Thirty Years War and French power in North America, 475, 475–77
Nicholas, Saint, 267
Nicholas II (pope), 269
Nile River, 22–24, 23
Niña (Columbus' ship), 414
Ninety-Five Theses (Luther), 425, 428–29
Nineveh
  library of, 63
  Neo-Assyrian Empire, 60–61, 62, 63, 63–64
  palace of, 63, 63
Nine Years' War, 508
nobility
  absolutism and, 495, 498–99
  defined, 316
  following Black Death, 362–63
  "junkers," 513
nominalism, 337
Normandy
  battle of Hastings, 263–65, 264
Norseman-land, 243
North America
  Columbus in, 417–19
  as exploration goal (fifteenth-sixteenth centuries), 418
  see also individual names of countries
northern European Renaissance
  architecture and art of, 408, 408
  Christian humanism and career of Erasmus, 405, 405–7
  literature of, 407–8
  music of, 408–9
  overview, 404
  Thomas More and, 406, 407, 407
Norway, 252, 435
Notre-Dame, Reims, 321
Notre-Dame-la-Grande, Poitiers, 321
Novels (Justinian legislation), 216
Novgorod Republic, 292–93
Novum Organum (Bacon), 536, 536–37, 538
Nubians, 29, 34, 42
nuclear family concept, 370, 371
nuns, Saint Teresa of Ávila and, 450, 451

obedience, Ignatius of Loyola on, 449
observation, scientific, 542–43
Octavian (Augustus Caesar), 165–69, 166, 170, 171
Odovacar (barbarian chieftain), 204
Ögedei Khan, 327
Oikonomikos, 119
oil paints, in Late Middle Ages, 365–66
"Old Believer," 517
Old Church Slavonic (language), 271
Old Kingdom (ancient Egypt), 25–29
Olga (Kievan princess), 271
oligarchy, defined, 89
Olympias (queen of Macedonia), 121
Olympic Games
  chariots used in, 83

inception of, 49
On Architecture (Vitruvius), 174, 403
"On Bubbles of Air That Escape from Fluids" (Bassi), 541
one-point perspective, of Renaissance art, 397–98, 398
On Painting (Alberti), 370
On the Art of Building (Alberti), 403
"On the Bubbles Observed in Freely Flowing Fluid" (Bassi), 541
"On the Compression of Air" (Bassi), 541
On the Duties of Ministers (Ambrose), 206
On the Family (Alberti), 370, 371
On the Nature of Things (Lucretius), 161
On the Revolutions of the Heavenly Spheres (Copernicus), 523, 528
On the War in Gaul (Julius Caesar), 163
oracle, at temple of Apollo at Delphi, 64, 81–82
Order of Christ, 413
Order of Preachers, 308
Order of the Friars Minor, 308
Order of the Star, 363
Oresteia (Aeschylus), 97
Orlando Furioso (Ariosto), 397
Orthodox Christianity
  Iconoclasm and, 218, 218–19
  imperial authority, 197–98
  reform of secular clergy (eleventh century), 267–69
Osiris (Egyptian god), 30, 32, 134
Osman Gazi, 371–72
ostracism, 87, 88
Otto I (the Great; Holy Roman emperor), 254–55, 255
Ottoman Empire
  exploration of fifteenth century and, 413, 416–17
  fall of Constantinople, 371, 372–73
  growth of, 374
  Habsburg dynasty and, 511, 512–13
  Mongols and, 371, 372
  Renaissance politics and increasing power of, 409
  rise of Ottoman Turks, 371–72
  slavery and social advancement in, 373–74
  Thirty Years' War, 470–73
Otto the Great, 254–55, 255
Ovid (Publius Ovidius Naso), 173

pagans, 200, 207
painting
  Golden Age, 488–90, 489, 490
  in Late Middle Ages, 337–38
  Mannerism, 487
  oil paints in Late Middle Ages, 365–66
  Renaissance painting techniques, 397–98, 401
palace bureaucracy, of ancient Egypt, 25
Paleolithic Era, 4
paleontology, 534
Palestine
  Alexander the Great and, 123
  Mongol Empire and, 329–30
  Roman rule in time of Jesus, 183

Palladio, Andrea, 404
Panhellenism, 80–82
papacy
  Avignon as capital of, 343, 343–44, 379
  challenges to Roman Church, Late Middle Ages, 381
  Council of Constance and failure of conciliar movement, 383–85
  Fourth Lateran Council of 1215, 299–300
  German emperors and, 290
  Late Middle Ages, papal power and popular piety, 342–45, 343, 344
  Luther's break with Rome, 429–32
  Papal States, 290, 300, 343, 396, 410–11, 429
  reform of (eleventh century), 269
  during Renaissance, 367
  Renaissance and growth of national churches, 409–11
  retirement of Benedict XVI, 383
  see also individual names of popes
paper
  early papermaking, 228, 228–29, 392
  printing press invention and, 302
Papinian (Aemelianus Papinianus; Roman jurist), 177
papyrus
  funerary, 32
  of Gubla, 54
Parliament (British)
  Civil War (England), 477–78, 478, 481
  establishment of, 289
  "king in Parliament," 504
  Restoration of Stuarts, 479, 502–4, 503
  William and Mary, 504
Parthenon, 76, 99, 100
Parzival (Wolfram), 318
Pascal, Blaise, 484, 540
Passion, relics of, 347
paternal supremacy, of Romans, 154
patria potestas, 154
patriarchy
  absolutism and, 498
  patriarchal family and Protestant Reformation, 439, 441–42
patricians, 152, 154
patriotism, during Renaissance, 394–95
patrons
  of arts, 398
  of science, 530–31
Paul, Saint (Paul of Tarsus), 183, 185, 185–86, 186, 195–96, 198, 371, 427
Paul III (pope), 446
Paul IV (pope), 446
Paulus (Roman jurist), 177
Pax Mongolica (Mongol Peace), 330–31, 371, 372
Pax Romana (Roman Peace), 165–69
Peace of Augsburg, 439, 470
Peace of Nystad, 519
Peace of Westphalia, 473–74, 474
Peasants' Revolt, 361, 362, 376, 387
Peasant Wedding (Bruegel the Elder), 488
Peasant Wedding Dance (Bruegel the Elder), 488

pedagogy, 109
Peisistratos (Greek aristocrat), 89
Peloponnesian War ("greatest war in history")
    downfall of Greek poleis and, 112–15
    failure of Athenian democracy and, 102–5
    inception of, 102
    map of colonies and alliances, 103
    Peloponnesian League, 101–2
Peloponnesus, 90
Pensées (Pascal), 484
Pentapolis (Philistine citadel), 56
Pepin (Austrasian nobleman), 238, 239–40
Pepy I (pharaoh of Egypt), 29
Perdiccas (Macedonian general), 126, 128
Pergamon, citadel of, 140
Pericles, 96–97, 101
Pernambuco Province (Brazil), 463
Perpetua, Vivia, 181, 198
Persepolis (Persian Empire), 65, 123
Persia, Abbasid caliphate in, 228
Persian Empire
    Alexander the Great's conquest of, 122–23,
        123, 126
    ancient Greece and, 91, 92
    coins, 65
    consolidation of Persian rule, 65–66
    Cyrus the Great, 64–65, 68–69, 72
    Mongol rule of, 329, 329
    overview, 64, 67
    seals, 66
    Seleucids, 129–30
    Zoroastrianism, 66–67
Persians (Aeschylus), 97
Persian wars
    Croesus (king of Lydia), 82
    Ionian Revolt, 93–95
    overview, 92–93, 95
    Xerxes' invasion, 95–96, 96
Peter, Saint, 185–86, 197
Peter I ("the Great": tsar of Russia), 495,
    514–19, 517, 544
Petition of Right, 478, 479
Petrarch (Italian poet), 366, 366–67, 370
phalanx, 83, 84, 150
pharaohs, power of, 24–25
Philip Augustus (king of France), 290, 297,
    299, 345, 346
Philip II (king of France), 289
Philip II (king of Spain), 445, 466, 468
Philip IV (king of France), 342, 345, 347,
    350
Philip IV (king of Spain), 473
Philippa of Lancaster, 413
Philip V of Macedonia, 158
Philistines, 55–56, 57, 58
Philosophical Transactions (Royal Society of
    London), 541, 544
philosophy
    classical learning and Christianity, 207–10,
        210
    inception of Greek philosophia, 92
    of Late Roman Republic, 161–62
    Milesian, 98
    Muslim philosophy and Christian theology,
        279, 279

Neoplatonism, 194–95, 198
Newton on purposes of experimental
    philosophy, 546
nominalism, 337
"philosopher-kings," 117
schools of Plato and Aristotle, 116–19
seventeenth century, 484–86
skepticism, 134
Socratic, 105, 106–7
Sophist, 106
Stoicism, 195
Stoicism and Epicureanism, 133–34
see also individual names of philosophers
Phintys (Hellenistic writer), 139
Phoenician alphabet, 56, 79
Phoenicians, 54–55, 79–80
phonemes, 10
Phryne (Athenian courtesan), 118
Physics (Aristotle), 314
Pico della Mirandola, Giovanni, 392
pictograms, 10, 10
Pilate, Pontius, 183, 347
Pilgrims, 468–70, 470
Piscopia, Elena Cornaro, 541
Pius V (pope), 446
Pizarro, Francisco, 422
Plataea, 94
Plato, 104, 116–19, 117, 138–39
"Platonic Academy," 392
Plautus (playwright), 161
plebians ("plebs"), 152–53
Pliny the Younger (Gaius Plinius Caecilius
    Secundus), 190–91
Plotinus (Hellenistic philosopher), 194–95
plows, for farming, 256, 256–57
Plutarch (Roman historian), 122
Plymouth (Massachusetts), Pilgrims of,
    468–70, 470
pneumonic plague, 356
Pnyx, 88, 88
poetry
    of Archaic Greece, 85–87
    Greek civilization and, 77, 78
    Muslim, Middle Ages, 280
    seventeenth century, 486–87
    use of rhyme in High Middle Ages, 320
pogroms, 292
Poland
    Benedictine Abbey of Tyniec, 252
    Cistercian Abbey, 301
    Commonwealth of Poland and Lithuania
        (sixteenth-seventeenth centuries), 507,
        507
    Great Northern War and, 519
    High Middle Ages, 292
    Jadwiga (female "king" of Poland), 380,
        380–81
    Jagiellonian dynasty, 380, 380–81, 381
    Kraków market square, 260
    Polish-Lithuania Commonwealth, 474,
        507, 507, 512–13
    reform movements, Late Middle Ages, 386
    Thirty Years War, 474
poleis (ancient Greece)
    defined, 80

downfall of, 112, 112–15
downfall of, and artistic/intellectual
    response, 115–19, 116, 117, 118
emergence of, 76, 76–80
transition to cosmopolis, 130–32
political theory
    absolutism, defined, 494
    aristocracy, tyranny, and democracy in
        Archaic Greece, 84–85
    autocracy of Peter the Great, 514–19
    consequences of Roman imperialism,
        159–62
    democracy, 51, 84–85, 96–97, 102–5, 117,
        119, 153
    Epicureanism and, 134
    Greek political satire, 94
    Magna Carta and establishment of British
        Parliament, 289
    oligarchy, 89
    philosophy of, in seventeenth century,
        484–86
    polis, defined, 80
    polity, 85
    Protestantism and government, 441–42
    res publica, 150, 250, 479
    thalassocracy, 49–50
Politics (Aristotle), 120
Polo, Marco, 325, 332–33
Poltava, battle of, 518–19
Polybius (Greek historian), 143, 147,
    150–51, 153, 155, 158
Pompey (Gnaeus Pompeius Magnus),
    163–64, 167
Poor Ladies, Order of (Poor Clares), 308
Poras (Indus Valley leader), 125
Portolan chart, 336, 337
portraits
    portraiture of Renaissance, 398
    self-portraiture of seventeenth century, 490,
        491
Portugal
    colonialism of sixteenth-seventeenth cen-
        turies, 456
    exploration (fifteenth-sixteenth centuries)
        by, 412–17, 418–19
    Luanda and slave trade, 462
    Treaty of Utrecht, 509
Potosi, slaves at, 461
pottery
    of early civilizations, 4, 7, 8
    Late Bronze Age, 47
    wheel invention and, 14, 15
Poullain de la Barre, François, 541
Powhatan tribe, 457
praetors, 177
Praise of Folly, The (Erasmus), 432
Praxiteles (sculptor), 116, 118
Predynastic Egypt, 22–24
Prester John (Description of the World charac-
    ter), 332–33, 413
"price revolution," 463
Prince, The (Machiavelli), 394, 395–97
Principate (Roman Empire), 177, 193
Principate of Augustus, 479
Principia (Newton), 524

*Principia Mathematica* (Newton), 544–45, 546
printing
 invention of printing press, 302, 391–92, 393, 394–95, 524
 Luther and, 427, 429, *430*, 430–31, *431*
Proba, Faltonia Betitia, 207
"Prophecies of Neferty," 35
prose
 emergence of, 116
 of Hellenistic period, 143
*proskynesis*, 125–26, *126*
prostitution, Protestant Reformation and, 442
Protestantism
 absolutism and, 495
 Huguenots, 465–66, 501
 Hungary and Habsburg dynasty, 511, 512–13
 Philip II (king of Spain) and, 466–67, *467*
Protestant Reformation, 424–53
 age of dissent and division (1500–1564), overview, 425–26
 chronology, 424
 Council of Constance and, 384
 domestication of reform, 439–42
 in England, 442–46, *443*, *445*
 events leading to, *386*, 386–88, *387*
 forms of Protestantism, *435*, 435–39, *436*, *437*
 Luther and reformation in Germany, *426*, 426–34, *427*, *428*, *429*, *430*, *431*, *432*, *433*, *434*, *438*, 439, 440
 overview, 305
 Protestant, defined, 435
 reformation, defined, 426
 Roman Catholic Church, rebirth, 446–51, *447*, *448*, *451*
Prussia
 Brandenburg-Prussia and absolutism, 509–14, *511*
 Great Northern War, 519
 "junkers," 513
Ptah-Hotep (official of ancient Egypt), 31
Ptolemaic Egypt, 128–29, 132, *132*
Ptolemaic system, *525*, 526–27, *530*
Ptolemy (Claudius Ptolemaeus), 136
Ptolemy II (Egyptian ruler), 128–29, *129*
Ptolemy of Alexandria, 122, 128–29, 132, *132*
Ptolemy XIII (Egyptian pharaoh), 164
Ptolemy XIV (consort to Cleopatra), 164
public works projects, of Roman Empire, 172, 174, *175*
Punic Wars
 First, 157
 overview, 156–57, *158*
 Second, 157, 158
 Third, 143, 157–58, 162
Puritans
 Calvinism and, 438
 Civil War (England) and, 478, 479, 480
Pylos (grave), *51*
Pythagoras, 105–6
pyxis, *281*

quadrants (instrument), 414
*quadrivium*, of learning, 310
Québec (Canada), exploration of/immigration to, 466, 475
*querelle des femmes*, 364
Qur'an, 224–25, *225*
Quraysh, 223

Ra (Egyptian god), 29, 42, 46
Rabbinic Judaism, 215, 315
rabbis, 215, 225
race/racial prejudice, racialization and slavery, 417
Raleigh, Walter, 456
Ramón de Caldes, 295
Ramses (pharaoh of Egypt), 47
Ramses III (pharaoh of Egypt), 52
Raphael (Raffaello Sanzio), *117*, 400, *401*, 429
Rashid, Harun al-, 242
Ravenna, Italy, 204
rebirth, defined, 367
"receiving tribute," 62–63
Reconquista of Spain, 293, 293–94, *294*, 309, 411–12
Reformed Church, 438
Regiomontanus, Johannes, 525
relics/reliquaries, 267, 268, *268*
religion
 absolutism and, 495
 of ancient Egypt, 23, 29, 30
 of ancient Greece, 81
 Assyrian religious ethos, 62–63
 Civil War (England) and, 477–83, *478*, *479*
 of early civilizations, 8, 9
 gods and religion of ancient Rome, 154–56
 great flood accounts, 12–14
 Greek civilization and, 77
 Hammurabi's use of, 18
 Hebrew monotheism, 67–72, *70*, *71*
 Hellenistic period, 134–36
 High Middle Ages, Roman Church religious reform and papal power, *266*, 266–70, *268*
 High Middle Ages and culture of Muslim west, 278–83, *279*, *281*, *282*
 in Late Middle Ages, 337–38
 of Late Roman Republic, 161–62
 myths and, 3
 New Kingdom of Egypt, religious change, 45–46
 Persian Empire and, 66–67
 policies of Louis XIV (king of France), 501
 pursuit of holiness, Late Middle Ages, 345
 scientific revolution and, 525, *526*, 534, 542
 scientific revolution and Galileo, 529–34, *532*
 spiritual challenges, in Late Middle Ages, 385–86
 Sumerian, 14
 wars of religion in sixteenth-century France, 465–66
 Xenophanes on images of god, 92
 *see also individual names of gods and deities; individual names of religions*
Rembrandt van Rijn, *490*, 491

Renaissance, 390–423
 architecture, 403–4, *404*
 art, 397–401, *398*, *399*, *400*, *401*, 402
 beginning of, in Italy, *366*, 366–71, *368*
 chronology, 390
 classicism, 367
 defined, 360, 367
 Europeans in New World, 417–22, *418*, *419*, *420*
 events of, in northern Europe, 404–9, *405*, *406*, *407*, *408*
 in Florence, 370–71
 humanism, 367–69, 371
 ideal of courtier, 397
 ideals of, overview, 392
 Leonardo da Vinci, 398–
 military conquests and overseas exploration during, 412–17, *414*, *415*
 overview, 391–92
 politics of Christian Europe during, 409–12, *410*, *411*, *412*
 politics of Italy and philosophy of Machiavelli, *396*, 396–97
 printing during, *393*, 394–95
 reading ancient texts during, 366, 371, 526
 "Renaissance man" ideal, 397
 scientific revolution and, 525
 sculpture, 401–4, *403*
Renaissance, Carolingian, 241–42
Reni, Guido, 448
*Republic* (Plato), 117
republic, defined, 153–54
*Republic, The* (Plato), 138–39
*res publica*, 150, 250, 479
Restoration of Stuarts (England), 479, 502–4, *503*
*rex*, 150
rhapsodes, 77, 78
Rhine Palatinate, League of Augsburg, 508–9
rhyme, in High Middle Ages, 320
Richard I (the Lionheart; king of England), 289, 290, 297, 318
Richard II (king of England), 362, 376–77, 379
Richelieu, duke of (cardinal of France), 476–77
Riga, bishopric of, 298
Rigaud, Hyacinthe, 496, *496*
roads, of Incas, 15
Robert of Ketton, 278–79
Rocroi, battle of, *474*
Rodin, Auguste, 141
Rollo the Viking, 262
Roman Catholic Church
 absolutism and, 495
 Catholic status, defined, 426, 432
 challenges of, Late Middle Ages, 381
 Council of Constance and failure of conciliar movement, 383–84
 Council of Trent, 302, 440, 447–48, *448*
 duke of Richelieu (cardinal of France), 476–77
 Great Schism, *382*, 382–84
 Louis XIV (king of France) and, 501
 on marriage as sacrament, 442

monastic reform movement, *266,* 266–67
popular and intellectual reformers, Late
    Middle Ages, 385–88, *386, 387*
Protestant Reformation and rebirth of,
    446–51, *447, 448, 451*
spiritual challenges, Late Middle Ages,
    384–85
Roman Empire, 146–79
    Alexander the Great and, 112, 122
    arts of, 116, 118, *118*
    Christianity and Rome's legacy, 213–14
    Christianity as minority religion in, *186,*
        *187,* 187–93, *191, 192, 193, 194*
    Christianity conversion in, 194–200, *196,*
        *197, 199, 200*
    chronology, 146
    consequences of imperialism, 159–62, *160,*
        *161*
    Constantine's rule and, 200–202, *202,*
        203–4
    Constantinople establishment and,
        200–205, *202, 204*
    constitution of early Roman Republic,
        152–53
    early triumphs of Roman Republic,
        150–52, *151, 152, 153*
    end of eastern Roman Empire, 371–74,
        *372, 373, 374*
    founding of Rome, 149–50
    Holy Roman Empire, defined, 242
    impact of fifth-century migrations by bar-
        barians, 204–5
    Islam and, 227
    Justinian's impact on western Roman
        Empire, 215
    map, 169
    overview, 147–48
    *Pax Romana* (Roman Peace), 165–69
    Polybius' written accounts of, 143
    Principate and Pax Romana, 165–69, *166,*
        *168*
    Principate of Augustus, 479
    reach of Roman Empire, *169,* 169–78, *172,*
        *173, 175, 176, 177*
    Renaissance art in, 400–401, *401*
    "restoring Republic" and struggle for
        power, 162–65, *164, 165*
    rise of Ottoman Empire and, 373
    Roman alphabet, 149
    Roman Empire of Byzantium, *217,* 217–23,
        *219, 222, 232–33*
    Roman foundation myths, 148–49, *149*
    Roman Republic and Roman identity,
        153–56, *154*
    Roman Republic transition to Roman
        Empire, 156–59, *157, 158*
    sacking of, 206–7
    as symbolic capital of Empire, under
        Diocletian, 193–95
    urban infrastructure issues of fifth-sixth
        centuries, 257
    urban planning of, during Roman Empire,
        *176*
Romanesque cathedrals, 320

Roman Forum, *184*
*Romeo and Juliet* (Shakespeare), 487
Romulus Augustulus (Roman emperor), 204
Rosetta Stone, *27,* 27–28
Roundheads, 478
Roxane (wife of Alexander the Great), 125
Royal Academy of Sciences, *547,* 548
*Royal Procession of Louix XIV, The* (van der
    Meulen), *497*
Royal Society of London, 540–41, 544, 548
royalty
    absolute monarchy, 494, 498
    Byzantine Empire lordship, 231
    Carolingian Empire, 238–39, 241
    Christianity and kingship, during Carolin-
        gian Empire, 241
    crisis of kingship in England (sixteenth-
        seventeenth centuries), 477–83, *478,*
        *479, 482*
    csar/tsar, 409
    Dauphin (French royal title), 377
    execution of Charles Stuart, 479, 482, *482*
    Great Khan title, 330
    growth of national monarchies, Late Middle
        Ages, 381
    Hammurabi's changes to kingship, 21
    Hundred Years' War and effect on British
        monarchy, 379
    Middle Ages monarchy of western Europe,
        261–66, *262, 264, 265*
    modern-day, *500*
    monarchy rejected by early Romans, 150
    Persian "king of kings," 66–67
    *pontifex maximus* (Roman emperors), 198
    queens of High Middle Ages, 318
    sovereignty, defined, 345
    *stadtholder,* 506
    *see also individual names of monarchs*
Rubens, Peter Paul, 488, *489*
Rubicon River, 164
Rudolph II (Holy Roman emperor), 529
*Rule of the Master, The* (Benedict), 209–10,
    237, 266, 301
Rumi (Persian poet), 331
Runic alphabets, *251*
Rus', 292–93, 327–28
Rus', 270
Russia
    absolutism and, 494, 514–19, *515, 517,*
        *518*
    Great Northern War, 518–19
    Moscow, 327–28, 409, *410, 411*
    Viking Rus', 251
    *see also individual names of leaders*
rutters/routiers (books), 414

sacraments, 344, 429, 442
Sadducees, 183–84
Saint Bartholomew's Day Massacre, 465–66,
    484
Sainte-Chapelle (Holy Chapel), *346, 347*
Saladin (Sala ah-Din), 277, 297
Samuel (Hebrew tribal judge), 58, 60–61
Samuel the Nagid, 281

sanitation
    in Middle Ages, 259–60
San Marco Basilica, 222–23
Sappho of Lesbos, 86, 87
Saracens, 303
Sarcophagus of the Muses, *107*
Sardis (Lydia), 65
Sargon, *16,* 16–17
Sargon II (king of Assyria), 59–60, 63
Sargon of Akkad, 16–17
Sargon the Great (king of Akkadians), 57
"Satire of the Trades, The (Middle Kingdom,
    ancient Egypt), 25
satyr plays, 94
Saul (king of Israel), 58, 60–61
Saxony, European colonialism, 298
Scandinavia
    Lingsberg Runestone, *251*
    Middle Ages and Cnut the Great, 252–53
    sovereignty in Late Middle Ages, 346
scholasticism
    development of, 312
    theology, 314–15
*School of Athens, The* (Raphael), *117,* 400, *401*
science
    of ancient Egypt, 32
    genetics, 51
    geography of Hellenistic period, 136–37
    Hellenistic period, 136–37, *137*
    innovation of Late Middle Ages, 336–37
    Muslim scientists, Middle Ages, 280
    naval technology/navigation and explora-
        tion of fifteenth century and, 414–16, *415*
    science, defined, 524
    Sumerian, 14–16
scientific revolution, 522–49
    Bacon and Descartes, *536,* 536–40, *537,*
        *540*
    chronology, 522
    Copernican revolution, 526–28, *527, 529,*
        *530*
    defined, 524
    Galileo and, *526,* 529–34, *531, 532*
    geology and environmental sciences, *534,*
        534–35, *535*
    historic context of, 524
    intellectual origins of, 523–26, *525*
    Newton, 544–49, *545*
    overview, 523–24
    Ptolemaic system, *525,* 526–27, *530*
    science, defined, 524
    scientific observation and human soul, 542
    state, scientific academies, and women
        scientists during, 540–44, *541, 543, 547*
    Tycho's observations and Kepler's laws, *528,*
        528–29, *531*
Scipio, Publius Cornelius, 157
Scone Abbey, 348
Scorpion (king of Egypt), 24
Scotland
    Abbey Church (Island of Iona), 235
    Black Death and impact on, 361
    Civil War (England) and, 477, 478
    Great Britain, naming of, 509

Scotland, (Continued)
    monasticism of seventh century, 235–36
    sovereignty in Late Middle Ages, 348–49
    "Whigs" name and, 503
sculpture
    fourth century B.C.E., 115–16, *116*
    of fourth century B.C.E., 115–16, *116*
    Hellenistic period, 140–41, *142*
    Renaissance, 401–4, *403*
seals, *66, 340,* 340–41
Sea Peoples, 51–54, 55
Second Punic War, 156–58, *158*
secular clergy, reform of (eleventh century),
    267–69
Sejm (Commonwealth of Poland and Lithu-
    ania), 507, *507*
Seleucids, 158–59
Seleucus (Persian ruler), 129–30
self-portraiture, of seventeenth century, *490,*
    *491*
Seljuk Turks, 272, 275, 294–96, 329, 371
Semitic peoples
    Akkadians, 16
    Amorites, 18
    Chaldeans, 63–64
    languages of, 41
Senate (Roman)
    Augustus' successors and, 168–69
    crucifixion used by, 162
    inception of, 150
    Julius Caesar's assassination, 164–65
    Law of the Twelve Tables, 153
    Punic Wars and, 157
    statutes written by, 178
    Sulla and, 163
Sennacherib (Neo-Assyrian king), *63, 63*
*Sentences* (Lombard), 314
Sephardic Jews, 412
septicemic plague, 356
serfs/serfdom, overview, 243, 257, 260–61
Sesostris III (pharaoh of Egypt), *34*
Seth (Egyptian god), 30
"seven-headed papal beast"/"seven-headed
    Martin Luther," *431*
Seven Years Famine, 351–53
Severan dynasty, empire of, 189–92, *191, 192*
Severus, Alexander (Roman emperor), 192
Severus, Septimus (Roman emperor),
    189–90, *192*
sex
    asceticism and, 198–200
    homosexuality, 84, *112,* 112–15, 122
    prostitution, 442
Seymour, Jane (queen of England), 443
Sforza dictators, of Milan, 398
Shakespeare, William, 483, 485, 523
Shalmeneser III (king of Assyria), 59
Shamash (Babylonian god), 18, *21*
Shi'ite Muslims
    Crusades and, 297
    Fatimids, 273, 278
Shi'ite-Sunni schism, 227
shipping
    naval technology/navigation and explora-
      tion of fifteenth century and, 414–16, *415*

slaves of Middle Passage, *462*
Shulgi (king of Ur), 17
*Sic et Non* (Abelard), 311, 312
Sicily
    as colony of Rome, 254
    expulsion of Jews, 309
Sidonius Apollinaris, 208–9
Siege of Vienna, 512–13
Silk Road, 326, 331
silver
    colonialism in sixteenth-seventeenth centu-
      ries, 463–65, *465*
    European exploration for, 422
    Silver Age (Roman Empire), 173
    Vikings and, 258
Simeon "the Stylite," Saint, 199, *200*
*Simplicissimus* (Grimmelshausen), 471
sin, Saint Augustine on, 206
Sisters of Charity, 450
Sistine Chapel, Vatican (palace), 400, *401*
Six Articles, Church of England, 443, 444
*Six Books of the Commonwealth* (Bodin), 484
Sixtus V (pope), 446
skepticism, 134
slavery
    in ancient Egypt, 33
    in ancient Greece, 89
    Aristotle on, 119, 120
    in Babylonian society, 19
    Caribans, 483
    of classical Greece, 100–101
    colonization of New World and, 457,
      458–63, *460*
    Dutch East and West India Companies, 467
    European exploration (fifteenth century)
      and, 413, 416–17, 422
    Goths and, 203
    human cost of slavery in New World,
      462–63
    Islam and, 229
    King Solomon and, 58
    Middle Pasage, *462*
    in Ottoman Empire, 373–74
    Portugese slave trade (fifteenth century),
      413
    Roman Empire, 178
    in Roman Republic, 157–58, 159, 161, 162
    of Sumerian culture, 11
Slavs, migration to Balkans, 270–71
smallpox, spread by European explorers,
    419–22
Smith, John, *457*
social pyramid, of ancient Egypt, 32–33
Society of Jesus, 448–50
Socrates
    *The Clouds* (Aristophanes), 104–5
    execution of, 92, 107, 134
    legacy of, 116, 119
    philosophy and, 105, 106–7
    *Republic* (Plato), 117
    Sarcophagus of the Muses, *107*
    sculpture of, *106*
solar calendar, of ancient Egypt, 32
Sol Invictus, 195, 196, 198–200
Solomon (king of Israel), 58–59, 69, 297

Solon (Greek poet, aristrocrat), 88–89
*Song of Roland,* 249–50, *275,* 397
Sophia, rebellion of Streltsy and, 516
Sophists, 105–6
Sophocles (Greek playwright), 97, 121
sovereignty
    defined, 345
    struggles for, during Late Middle Ages,
      345–50, *346, 347, 350*
    *see also individual names of rulers*
Spain
    absolutism and, *494*
    art, seventeenth century, *487, 488,* 488–90
    Columbus and, 325, 412, 417–19
    Julius Caesar and, 164–65
    Justinian's impact on western Roman
      Empire, 215
    League of Augsburg and War of Spanish
      Succession, 508–9
    literature and poetry, Middle Ages, 280,
      281
    Naples and Charles VII (king of France),
      409
    New Spain and social hierarchies, 459
    Reconquista of, *293,* 293–94, *294,* 309,
      411–12
    Renaissance and end of *convivencia,*
      411–12, *412*
    silver and gold from Spanish America
      (sixteenth century), 464
    slaves at Potosi, 461
    Spanish Armada and religious conflict with
      England, 467–68, *469*
    Spanish *consquitadores,* 419, 419–22, *420*
    Spanish galleon model, *414*
    Thirty Years' War and, 473–74, *474*
    Umayyad caliphate in, 228
    *see also individual names of leaders*
Sparta
    Agesilaus (Spartan king), 119
    downfall of Greek poleis and, 112–15
    Ionia, Lydia, Persian Empire and, *91*
    overview, 89–92
    Peloponnesian War ("greatest war in
      history"), 101–5, *103*
    Peloponnesus, *90*
    rise of poleis and, 80
Spartacus (Thracian slave), 162
Spice Islands, 326
spice trade, 413, 417, 467
Spinoza, Baruch, 540
*Spiritual Exercises* (Ignatius of Loyola), 450
*stadtholder,* 506
*Starry Messenger, The* (Galileo), 530, 531
Statute of Kalisz, 292
stele, of Babylon, 18
Stensen, Nils, 535
Step Pyramid, *27, 28,* 28–29
Stilicho, Flavius, 203
Stoicism, 133–34, 195
Stone Age societies, 4–5, *5*
Stone of Destiny, 348
St. Peter's Basilica, 196, *196,* 404, *404, 428*
St. Petersburg (Russia), building of, 514
Strasbourg, urban change to, *258*

Strasbourgh, Town Council of, 355
Strassburg, Gottfried von, 318
strategos, 97
Stratford-upon-Avon (England), Shakespeare
   and, 487
Streltsy, execution of, *515*, 516
Stuart dynasty, 477–83, 479, 502–4, *503*
stylus, development of, 10
Sufism, 229
sugar
   Civil War (England) and, 481–82
   French colonialism and, 475
   Louis XIV (king of France) and, 501–2
   slavery and, 417, 422, 459–62, *460*
Suger, Abbot, 310
Suleiman the Magnificent (sultan), 439
Sulla, Lucius Cornelius, 163
sultanate of Rûm, 329, 371
Sumer, 9–16, *10, 11, 14, 15*, 22
Sumerians, 226
*Summa contra gentiles* (Thomas Aquinas), 315
*Summa Theologiae* (Thomas Aquinas), 315,
   437
"Sun King," Louis XIV (king of France) as,
   495–98, *496*
Sunni Muslims
   Crusades and, 297
   rise of Ottoman Empire and, 374
   Seljuq Turks, 272, 275
sunspots, discovery of, 530, *531*
suras (Qur'an), 224
Susa (palace), 125
Sutton Hoo Ship Burial, *232*, 232–33, *233*
Sweden
   Cnut the Great, 252
   Great Northern War, 518–19
   League of Augsburg, 508–9
   Protestant as state religion (sixteenth cen-
      tury), 435
   Thirty Years' War, 473, 474
Switzerland
   Calvinism in Geneva, 438–39
   Protestantism in (sixteenth century),
      436–37
Syagrius, 209
Symmachus, Quintus Aurelius, 201
symposium (symposia), 84
*Syntagma Philosophicum* (Gassendi), 542–43
Syria
   Alexander the Great and, 123
   Christian traditions, 271
   Esarhaddon (Assyrian king) and, 68
   Late Bronze Age, 47–48
   Seleucids, 130
   Ugaritic alphabet, 47–48, 55

Table of Ranks (Russia), 515
Tabriz, 331, 333
Tacitus (Roman historian), 171, 173
Talmud, 215
*Tamburlaine* (Marlowe), 486
Tarquin the Arrogant, 150
taxes
   absolutism and Louis XIV (king of France),
      501

Civil War (England) and, 477, 478, 479
   Early Middle Ages, 231, 239, 245
   Glorious Revolution, 504
   under Louis XIV (king of France), 501
   Louis XIV (king of France) and, 501
   in tsarist Russia, 515
technology
   Middle Ages agricultural innovation, *256,*
      256–57
   Sumerian, 14–16
telescope, invention of, 524, 529, *531*, 544
*Tempest, The* (Shakespeare), 483
Templars, 277
Tenochtitlán, *419*, 420
Ten Thousand, *113*, 114, 119
Terence (playwright), 161
Terentius (wealthy Roman), 161
Teresa of Ávila, Saint, 450, *451*
tetrarchy, *193*, 193–95
Tetzel (Dominican friar), 428
Teutonic Knights, 293
textiles
   of classical Greece, *101*
   of early civilizations, 8, *19*
   Italy, Late Middle Ages, 362
   Mongol robe, *328*
   Phoenician, 54
thalassocracy, 49–50
theater
   of classical Greece, 97–98, *98*
   plays of Late Middle Ages, 366
   seventeenth century, 486–87
   *see also individual names of playwrights*
Thebes (New Kingdom Egypt), 45–46
   rebuilding of, 118
   Theban Hegemony, 121
   Theban Sacred Band, *112*, 112–15, 121–22
Themistocles (Athenian politician), 95–96,
   97
theocracy, defined, 438
Theodora (Roman empress), *216*
Theodoric the Ostrogoth (king of Goths),
   *204, 205*, 207–8, 210
Theodosius I (the Great; Roman emperor),
   200, 201, 203
Theseus (Greek hero), 50
thetes, 97
Third Dynasty (ancient Egypt), 25
Third Punic War, 143, 156–58, *158*, 162
Thirty-Nine Articles of Faith, 446
Thirty Tyrants, 103
Thirty Years' War
   devastation of, 471
   downfall of Bohemia, 470–73
   French power in Europe and North
      America, 475, 475–77
   overview, 470, *472*
   Peace of Westphalia and decline of Spain,
      473–74, *474*
   politics and consequences of, 473
   scientific revolution and, 533
   Sweden and invasion of Poland-Lithuania,
      474
"This Is My Body" (fresco), 344, *344*
Thomas à Kempis, 386

Thomas Aquinas, Saint, 308, 315, 437, 451
Thomas of Celano, 306–7
Thracians, 92
Thucydides, 49, 100
Thutmose I (pharaoh of Egypt), 43
Thutmose II (pharaoh of Egypt), 43
Thutmose III (pharaoh of Egypt), 43–44, *45*
Tiberius (Roman emperor), 169
Tiber River, 149
Tiglath-Pileser III (king of Assyria), 59
Tigris river, 8
time issues
   measurement of time, in Late Middle Ages,
      336–37
   Tycho's scientific theories about, 529
Timur the Lame (Tamburlane), 372, *372*, 486
Titian (Tiziano Vecellio), 400, *432*
tobacco plantations, 481
"toleration," 504
Torah, 72
Tories (Great Britain), 502–4
*To the Christian Nobility* (Luther), 429
Tower of Babel, 3, 41
"Town air makes you free" (German adage),
   259–60
towns, emergence in early civilizations,
   7–8
Trajan (Roman emperor), 169, 172, 189,
   190–91
transnational diplomacy
   Greek civilization and, 77
   during Late Bronze Age, 47, 57
transubstantiation, doctrine of, *304*
Transylvania, 292
*Treasure of the City of Ladies, The* (Christine de
   Pisan), 365
Treaty of Utrecht, 508–9, *509*
trees, of Neolithic Revolution, 7
triangular trade
   routes of, *460*
   slavery resulting from, 459–62
Tribonian (jurist), 216
tribunes, 152
"tribute," 62–63
Tripoli, as Crusader State, 297
trireme warships, *93*
*Tristan* (Gottfried), 318
triumvirate, 163
Trojan wars, 77, 78
*Trojan Women, The* (Euripides), 97
Tudor dynasty, 379
Turkey
   Anatolia, 4, 41–42, 49, 53, 123, 130, 217
   Çatalhöyük, Anatolia, 4, 7–8
Tutankhamun (pharaoh of Egypt), *46, 47*
*Two New Sciences* (Galileo), 534
*Two Treatises of Government* (Locke),
   505–6
Tycho Brahe, *528*, 528–29, *531*
Tyrrhenians, 148
Tyrtaeus of Sparta, 85

Ubaid culture, 8–9
Ugarit (Syria), 47–48, 54, 55
Ugaritic alphabet (Syria), 47–48, 55

Ukraine
  Black Death, 350
  Ivan the Great, 409
  Jagiellonian dynasty, 380
  Ottoman Empire (Late Middle Ages) and, 373
  Polish-Lithuanian Commonwealth, 474, 507
ulamas, 229
Ulpian (Domitius Ulpianus; Roman jurist), 177
Umar (caliph), 226, 227
Umayyad dynasty, 227, 227–28, 243
universities, inception of, 289, 312–14, 313
University of Bologna, 312–14, 541
University of Paris, 289, 312–14, 315, 378
un roi, une loi, une foi, doctrine of, 501
Upper Egypt, 22, 26
Ur, 16, 16, 17, 17–18
Urban II (pope), 272–73, 274–75, 294–96
Urban VI (pope), 382–83
Urban VIII (pope), 532–34
urbanization
  Black Death and impact on, 361
  cities of High Middle Ages, 315–21
  education in Middle Ages, 310
  emergence of towns and villages in early civilizations, 7–8
  Hellenistic period, 131–32
  metropolitans, 197
  Middle Ages urban growth and trade, 257–61, 258, 259, 260
  Protestant Reformation and, 441–42
  Roman urban planning, 176, 176–77, 177
  urban development in Mesopotamia, 8–10, 9, 10
Ur-Nammu (king of Ur), 17
Urraca (queen of Léon-Castile), 318
Ursulines, 450
Uruk, 9, 9, 11, 12–14, 17, 23
Ussher, James (archbishop of Armagh), 534–35
utopia concept, 117–19

Valerian (Roman emperor), 194
Valla, Lorenzo, 371
Valois dynasty, 350
Vandals, 203–4, 205
van der Meulen, Adam Franz, 497
van der Straet, Jan, 418
van der Weyden, Roger, 365–66, 368, 368
Vasco de Gama, 416
vassals, 263
Velázquez, Diego, 488, 488
Venice
  commerce and settlement, Late Middle Ages, 334–36
  oligarchy of (seventeenth-eighteenth centuries), 502
  Renaissance art in, 400–401, 401
  revenge of, 298
Venus pudica, 118
vernacular entertainment, in High Middle Ages, 320

Versailles
  absolutism and, 495–99, 497
  Peter the Great's emulation fo, 518–19
View of Toledo (El Greco), 487, 487
Vikings
  Greenland and, 335, 335–36
  invasions by, 243–45, 244, 245
  medieval monarchies, Rus' and Novgorod Republic, 292–93
  in North America, 338, 417, 419
  overview, 250–51, 251
  Rus', 251, 270, 292–93, 327–28
Villa of the Mysteries, 161
Vinland, 335
Virgil, 366
Virgil (Publius Virgilius Maro; Roman poet), 148, 173, 207
Virginia, colonization of, 456, 468
Virgin of the Rocks, The (Leonardo da Vinci), 399, 399
Visigoths, 215
Vitruvius Pollio, Marcus, 174, 403
Vladimir (prince of Kiev), 271
Vladimiri, Paulus, 386–87
Voltaire, 544, 546
von Bora, Katharina, 429
Vulgate, 205, 448

Wagner, Richard, 318
Waldensianism, 305–8
Waldo, Peter, 305–8
Wales, 347
Walid, al- (caliph), 227
Warm Period, Medieval, 255–57, 256
War of Spanish Succession, 508–9, 509
War of the Spanish Succession, 508–9
Wars of the Roses, 379
Wartburg (castle), 433, 434
weapons
  cannons, 375, 375, 414
  Leonardo da Vinci and, 399
wheel, invention of, 14, 15
Whig Party (Great Britain), 502–5
White Temple (Uruk), 9, 9
William of Orange (king of England), 467, 504, 504–5, 506, 508–9
William the Conqueror (king of England), 263–65, 264, 286–87
Winged Victory of Samothrace (sculpture), 141, 142
Winkelmann, Maria, 543
winter solstice, celebration of, 195
witchcraft, 483–84
Wittenberg, Luther at, 425, 427
Wladyslaw II Jagiello (king of Poland), 380–81, 381
Wlodkowic, Pawel, 386–87
women's roles/rights
  access to education in Middle Ages, 310–12
  of ancient Rome, 148–49, 150, 152, 154, 156, 165
  Byzantine Empire, 221
  Christianity and, 198–200

  Christianity inception and, 187
  of classical Greece, 97–98, 100–101, 101
  Code of Hammurabi and, 18
  court culture of High Middle Ages, 317
  early Islam and, 229
  education and role of women, fourth and third/second centuries B.C.E., 138–39
  English monarchy and succession, 350
  Eucharist and status of Mary, 303–5, 304
  European explorers' treatement of indigenous women, 418
  female beauty as ideal, 118, 118
  as gladiators, 172
  Greek poets, 87
  Jadwiga (female "king" of Poland), 380, 380–81
  medieval women with religious ambition, 386
  monasticism and, 236
  queens of High Middle Ages, 318
  queens regnant of England, 445
  querelle des femmes, 364
  reformed Catholic Church of seventeenth and eighteenth centuries, 450–51, 451
  Renaissance in Italy, 369, 370, 392, 397
  Roman Empire, 181–82
  of Roman Republic, 160–61
  status of, in ancient Egypt, 33–34
  in tsarist Russia, 514
  witchcraft accusations against women, 483–84
  women scientists during scientific revolution, 540–44, 541, 543
Worms, Diet of, 432–34
writing
  in ancient Egypt, 27, 27–28
  development of, 10, 10
  hieroglyphs, 27, 27–28
Wurm, Ole, 535
Wycliffe, John, 359, 386, 387

Xavier, Saint (Francis Xavier), 450
Xenophanes, 92
Xenophon (Athenian author), 111, 114, 119
Xerxes (king of Persia), 65, 95–96, 96

Yahweh (Hebrew/Judaic god), 67–71
Yersinia pestis, 355–56, 360–61
York (England), medieval drama in, 366
York Castle (England), 262
York dynasty, 379

Zagros Mountains (Ur), 17
Zara, Fourth Crusade and, 298
Zarathustra (Zoroaster), 66–67
Zealots, 183
Zeno of Citium, 133
Zeus (Greek god), 124, 140
Ziggurat of Ur, 17
Zoroastrianism, 40, 66–67, 134, 194
Zurbaran, Francisco, 494
Zwingli, Ulrich, 436
Zwinglianism, 436–37